MAD
★AS★
HELL

Also by Jack W. Germond and Jules Witcover

Blue Smoke and Mirrors: How Reagan Won and Why Carter
Lost the Election of 1980
Wake Us When It's Over: Presidential Politics of 1984
Whose Broad Stripes and Bright Stars?: The Trivial Pursuit
of the Presidency 1988

Also by Jules Witcover

85 Days: The Last Campaign of Robert Kennedy
The Resurrection of Richard Nixon
White Knight: The Rise of Spiro Agnew
A Heartbeat Away: The Investigation and Resignation of
Vice President Spiro T. Agnew (with Richard M. Cohen)
Marathon: The Pursuit of the Presidency, 1972–1976
The Main Chance (A Novel)
Sabotage at Black Tom: Imperial Germany's Secret War in America,
1914–1917
Crapshoot: Rolling the Dice on the Vice Presidency

JACK W. GERMOND AND JULES WITCOVER

MAD ★ AS ★ HELL

Revolt at the Ballot Box, 1992

WARNER BOOKS

A Time Warner Company

Copyright © 1993 by Politics Today, Inc.
All rights reserved.

Warner Books, Inc., 1271 Avenue of the Americas, New York, NY 10020

Ⓦ A Time Warner Company

Printed in the United States of America

First Printing: July 1993

10 9 8 7 6 5 4 3 2 1

Library of Congress Cataloging-in-Publication Data

Germond, Jack.
    Mad as hell : revolt at the ballot box, 1992 / Jack Germond, Jules
Witcover.
        p.   cm.
    Includes index.
    ISBN 0-446-51650-3
    1. Presidents—United States—Election—1992.   2. United States—
Politics and government—1989–1993.   I. Witcover, Jules.
II. Title.
E884.G47   1993
324.973'098—dc20   92-50533
                                                                          CIP

Book design by H. Roberts

In memory of Paul Tully

I hold it, that a little rebellion, now and then,
is a good thing, and as necessary in the political
world as storms in the physical.
—Thomas Jefferson; letter to James Madison
January 30, 1787

ACKNOWLEDGMENTS

If the presidential campaign of 1992 differed in any significant manner from others in recent years, it was in the hunger of voters for straight answers from the candidates and in the innovative ways that hunger was expressed, and was responded to by those candidates.

While campaigning in traditional ways through the primaries and then in the general election, the candidates also capitalized on the new enterprise and technologies in television to reach out more directly and personally to voters, often in contexts in which the voters could reach back to them. At the same time, thousands of voters labored in behalf of an independent candidate who shunned the traditional route. And behind these innovations and direct candidate contact, a small army of campaign professionals continued as in past years to shape the political tactics and strategies of the candidates.

In seeking here to provide a reliable account of the circumstances, events and voters' frame of mind that brought about the election of Bill Clinton, we have tried to meld all these elements through personal observation on the campaign trail and then in extensive post-election interviewing. Having witnessed the candidates' use of the new opportunities to communicate directly during the primaries and general election, and talking to voters as they did so, we then interviewed nearly a hundred of the key political figures who helped direct the various campaigns. Among those to whom we are indebted for their observations either during or after the campaign are:

President Clinton, for interviews along the way and in the Oval Office after his inauguration; also, Roger Ailes, former Representative John B. Anderson, Clifford Arnebeck, Paul Begala, Charles Black, Mark Bohannon, Gloria Borger, Janet Brown, Jerry Brown, Ron Brown, John Brummett, Patrick Buchanan, Iris Jacobson Burnett, Patrick Caddell, Dan Carol, James Carville, James Cicconi, Pat Clancy, Governor Mario Cuomo, Richard Darman, Don Devine, Tom Edsall, Mort Engelberg, Mike Foudy, Ed Fouhy, Jack Gargan, Mark Gearan, Bob Goodwin, Joe Grandmaison, Stan Greenberg, Frank Greer, Mandy Grunwald, Marisa Hall, Mark Halperin, Senator Tom Harkin, Sharon Holman, John Jay Hooker, Jesse Jackson, Ed Jesser, Hamilton Jordan, Dennis Kanin, Mickey Kantor, David Keene, Senator Bob Kerrey, Larry King, Tim Kraft, Marcia Kramer, Bill Kristol, Lionel Kunst; also, James Lake, Al LaPierre, Tom Luce, John Marino, John Mashek, Mary Matalin, Richard Moe, Clay Mulford, Dee Dee Myers, Tom Oliphant, Andy Paven, Ross Perot, Nancy Sanders Peterson, James Pinkerton, Victoria Radd, Tom Rath, Cokie Roberts, Senator Jay Rockefeller, Ed Rollins, Steve Rosenthal, Sal Russo, John Seigenthaler, Carole Simpson, John Solomon, James Squires, Fred Steeper, George Stephanopoulos, Orson Swindle, Bob Teeter, David Tell, Ginny Terzano, Alice Travis, former Senator Paul Tsongas, Paul Tully, Kimberly Usry, Denton Walthall, Paul West, Paul Weyrich, Governor L. Douglas Wilder, David Wilhelm, Carter Wilkie, Curtis Wilkie, Richard Winger, Senator Harris Wofford, James Wooten.

TABLE OF CONTENTS

BLOWING THE WHISTLE

In the early evening of October 18, the night before the three candidates for the presidency of the United States—George Bush, Bill Clinton and Ross Perot—were to hold their second debate of the 1992 campaign, the telephone rang in a farmhouse eighteen miles north of Richmond, Virginia. Kimberly Usry, a twenty-eight-year-old single woman who had only recently been laid off from her job as a marketing director for a traffic-control company, picked up the phone.

The caller was a representative of the famed Gallup polling organization. He started asking her questions about the approaching election, including whether she planned to vote for the reelection of President Bush.

"Not in hell!" she shot back, according to her recollection.

The caller then asked whether she had made up her mind between Clinton and Perot. She told him she had not, and so he put her down as "undecided" (!)—and invited her to the debate the following night at the University of Richmond.

Kim Usry accepted with enthusiasm, particularly because she was told she would be part of a small audience that would have the unprecedented opportunity to ask the candidates a question directly. Over the next twenty-four hours, she weighed the possibilities, appreciating that she might have the one-in-a-million chance to confront a present or future president with the one issue she most had on her mind.

The next afternoon, Kim Usry arrived at a holding room for invited guests at the university, and after a time she and the other 208 Richmond-area "undecideds" selected in the Gallup phone survey were marched into the auditorium of the Robbins Center. They were seated in a wide semicircle and Carole Simpson of ABC News, chosen to be the moderator, greeted them, going through a sort of warm-up. She asked them for sample questions—specifically not the ones they intended to ask the candidates if called upon—to get a sense of what subjects they would raise, and to impress on them the seriousness of their responsibility. When one woman attempted to show Simpson a question she had written, to ask her if she thought it was a good one, the moderator told her flatly that she didn't want to see or hear it.

The first presidential debate, at Washington University in St. Louis four nights earlier, had the customary format of a moderator and press panel, and the result had been a relatively traditional affair. Going in, the president was trailing the Arkansas governor by ten or more percentage points in most of the polls and his strategists were looking for him to close the gap with a strong and aggressive showing.

So George Bush went on the attack, criticizing Clinton for having protested against the Vietnam war twenty-three years earlier when he was a student in England, insisting "it's wrong to demonstrate against your own country or organize demonstrations against your own country on foreign soil." Several days earlier, when Bush first made the charge, Clinton had countercharged that the president was questioning his patriotism in the manner of Senator Joseph R. McCarthy of Wisconsin, the infamous communist witch-hunter of the 1950s. In the first debate, Clinton hit back in the same way again, noting that in the 1950s the president's own father, Senator Prescott Bush of Connecticut, "was right to stand up to Joe McCarthy. You were wrong to attack my patriotism. I was opposed to the war, but I love my country," he said, glaring at the president.

Kim Usry had watched that first debate and that exchange on television, and she hadn't liked what she saw and heard. So when the second debate started, she was primed to get something off her chest. After the first two questions and answers, concerning foreign trade and the federal deficit, she signaled to a young woman standing next to her on the aisle who was holding a microphone, then jumped up and was recognized by the moderator.

"I'd like to address all the candidates with this question," she said. "The amount of time the candidates have spent in this campaign trashing their opponents' character and the programs is depressingly large. Why can't your discussions and proposals reflect the genuine complexity and the difficulty of the issues, to try to build a consensus around the best aspects of all proposals?"

Simpson turned to the candidates. "Who wants to take that one?" then bluntly adding: "Mr. Perot, you have an answer for everything, don't you? Go right ahead, sir."

The Texas billionaire only recently had rejoined the fray after having pulled out of the presidential race in mid-July before he had properly gotten in. He brushed aside the moderator's put-down and agreed with the questioner. "And I have said again and again and again, let's get off the mud wrestling," he lectured, "let's get off personalities, and let's talk about jobs, health care, crime, the things that concern the American people. . . ."

Next, Simpson invited the president to respond. Instead, he went right back on the attack. "I believe that character is a part of being president. I think you have to look at it. . . . You know, nobody likes who shot John, but I think the first negative campaign [sic] run in this election was by Governor Clinton, and I'm not going to sit there and be a punching bag. I'm going to stand up and say, 'Hey, listen, here's my side of it.' "

The incumbent went on like that, raising the mention of his father by Clinton in the first debate and trailing off into a maudlin reminiscence of him: "I remember something my dad told me. I was eighteen years old going to Penn Station to go on into the navy, and he said, 'Write your mother,' which I faithfully did. He said, 'Serve your country.' My father was an honor, duty and country man. And he said, 'Tell the truth.' And I've tried to do that in public life, all through it. That says something about character."

In the next breath, though, he was attacking again: "My argument with Governor Clinton—you can call it mud wrestling, but I think it's fair to put it in focus—is I am deeply troubled by someone who demonstrates and organizes demonstrations in a foreign land when his country's at war. Probably a lot of kids here disagree with me. But that's what I feel. That's what I feel passionately about. I'm thinking about Ross Perot's running mate [retired Admiral James B. Stockdale, a former Vietnam prisoner of war] sitting in the jail. How would he feel about it? But maybe that's generational. I don't know."

Now it was Clinton's turn. Facing Kim Usry directly, he spoke to her as if they were the only two people in the room: "Let me say first of all to you that I believe so strongly in the question you asked that I suggested this format tonight. . . . I've been disturbed by the tone and the tenor of this campaign. . . . So I'm not going to take up your time tonight [defending himself against Bush's charges], but let me just say this. We'll have a debate in four days and we can talk about this character thing again. . . . Here's my point. I'm not interested in his [Bush's] character. I want to change the character of the presidency—"

Carole Simpson interjected that before the debate started she had asked the guests "how they felt about the tenor of the campaign." She turned to the audience: "Would you like to let them know what you thought about that when I said, 'Are you pleased with how the campaign's been going?' " The audience shouted back: "No!" Whereupon she invited someone else to talk about it.

Denton Walthall, a thirty-seven-year-old father of two with his dark hair tied in a ponytail, stepped up to the microphone. He too had been called by a Gallup representative, had declared himself to be undecided and was invited to attend the debate.

In advance, Walthall had dutifully prepared about a dozen issue-oriented questions. But driving to the university hours before the debate, he recalled later, he spotted a handmade sign held up along the road. It bore the international prohibition sign—a red circle with a red diagonal slash across it—and the words: NO UNEMPLOYMENT—NO CRIME—NO HOMELESSNESS. These were the basic issues, he said to himself, that the candidates should be addressing.

Driving on, Walthall remembered watching the televised debate ₂ the vice presidential candidates with his six-year-old son, Nicholas, two nights earlier. When Democratic nominee Albert Gore, Jr., made reference to a television report critical of the Bush administration, Vice President Dan Quayle had interrupted, observing: "Senator, don't always believe what you see on television." The boy turned to his father and asked: "Daddy, what can you believe on TV?" And with all the charges back and forth, Walthall thought, it was no wonder his son didn't know what to believe.

The handmade sign, Walthall said later, and his son's question got him to thinking as he approached the university. Why couldn't the politicians forget about the personal stuff and address real needs? He decided to ignore his prepared list of questions and ask one that really got to what was on his mind about the campaign. And when Kim Usry asked the candidates point-blank to stop "trashing" each other, he recalled, "I said, 'Amen, sister.' "

The answers they had given to Usry, especially Bush's, Walthall said later, really set him off. "I had heard the whole thing in 1988," he said. "Willie Horton, the pledge of allegiance, Boston harbor. It was the same thing all over again. I thought, 'Does this man have to stoop to all this to be reelected?' I said [to myself], 'The hell with it.' "

A bit nervous but determined, Walthall stood up and began:

"Forgive the notes here, but I'm shy on camera. The focus of my work as a domestic mediator is meeting the needs of the children that I work with, by way of their parents, not the wants of their parents. And I ask the three of you, how can we, as symbolically the children of the future president, expect the two of you, the three of you, to meet our needs, the needs in housing and in crime and you name it, as opposed to the wants of your political spin doctors and your political parties?"

Simpson tried to help him. "So your question is?" she asked. Walthall pressed on, and finally got to it. "Can we focus on the issues and not the personalities and the mud?" he asked earnestly. "I think there's a need. If we could take a poll here with the folks from Gallup perhaps, I think there's a real need here to focus at this point on the needs."

Clinton responded at once. "I agree with him," he said. Then Bush: "Let's do it. Let's talk about programs for children."

Walthall was getting more emotional. "Could we cross our hearts?" he inquired plaintively. "It sounds silly here, but could we make a commitment? You know, we're not under oath at this point, but could you make a commitment to the citizens of the United States to meet our needs, and we have many, and not yours again?''

Immediately Bush hedged. ''I think it depends how you define it,'' he said. ''I mean, I think in general let's talk about these issues, let's talk about the programs. But in the presidency a lot goes into it. Caring goes into it. That's not particularly specific. Strength goes into it. That's not specific. Standing up against aggression. That's not specific in terms of a program. This is what a president has to do. So in principle, though, I'll take your point and think we ought to discuss child care or whatever else it is.''

Perot jumped in. ''Just no hedges, no ifs, ands and buts,'' he snapped. ''I'll take the pledge because I know the American people want to talk about issues and not tabloid journalism. So I'll take the pledge and will stay on the issues.''

Clinton had the last word, and again he spoke it directly to the questioner: ''I worked twelve years very hard as a governor on the real problems of real people. I'm just as sick as you are by having to wake up and figure out how to defend myself every day. I never thought I'd ever be involved in anything like this.''

Anything like this. To the jobless woman from the rural Virginia farmhouse and the father with the ponytail, that was what the presidential campaign of 1992 had come down to: a sickening display of name-calling and personal attacks, all in the guise of the issue of ''character.'' In the end, Kim Usry voted for Perot, Denton Walthall for Clinton.

Shortly after the election, Roger Ailes, the media specialist for the Bush campaign in 1988 who saw only spot duty as a debate coach for Bush in 1992, told us he was convinced that Walthall had been a sort of ''plant,'' in the sense that his physical appearance alone gave away the likelihood that he would ask a hostile question, and so he was called upon. Commenting on Simpson's warming-up of the questioners by inquiring about their areas of interest, Ailes said: ''When you preinterview, you pretty well know what the question is going to be. That's a trick I've used with studio audiences for twenty-five years. You can pinpoint with ninety percent accuracy what they're gonna ask. If you find a forty-year-old guy with a ponytail who is working with kids, you know damn well [kin]d of question he's gonna ask.''

[Cha]rles Black, a chief Bush strategist, agreed. He recalled standing in the back of the hall while Simpson was warming up the audience and eliciting from the audience what kinds of questions were going to be asked, telling participants, he said, "what was or wasn't a good question." As far as he was concerned, Black said later, "Carole Simpson was screening questions [and] rehearsing the voters. She was doing a dry run, jumping in with follow-up questions, changing the subject." He became so concerned, Black said, that he phoned Bob Teeter, the Bush campaign chairman, in Bush's hotel suite and told him to prepare the president for anything—including hostile questions.

Black insisted later, to Simpson's firm denials, that "she was groomed on who to call on. . . . She knew that guy, I'm convinced, the guy with the ponytail who stood up and said we don't want any negative campaigning, we hope you folks will not say anything bad about each other. It had a chilling effect on everybody's going on the attack. . . . Bush got two good hits in on Clinton in the first ten minutes and then he never got any more. And he was right. The tone and the environment were such that he would have gotten booed, which is the worst thing that can happen to you in a TV setting like that."

Another Bush insider who played a key role in the debate negotiations and in preparing Bush, and was also present for the warm-up, was even stronger in his criticism of Simpson. She had voters read their questions, he said, and then told them whether they were too long or not sufficiently focused. "She said what were good subjects," he said. "She was not interested in patsies, she was trying to make good television." Beyond that, he said, "she built a group spirit. She started specifying that 'we don't want to be negative,' and built a group spirit around that."

None of this criticism, however, squared with the fact that Carole Simpson was not a free agent in choosing the questioners. Ed Fouhy, producer of the debates for the Commission on Presidential Debates, was in direct telephone communication with Simpson from the control booth throughout the debate. At the start he instructed her specifically which person to call on first, and thereafter either specified individuals or which sections of the audience to go to, so that the television cameras under his direction could be properly focused, assuring a seamless flow in the picture and sound that went out to the home audience.

With Simpson facing the candidates and her back to the audience most of the time, she was in no position to go hunting for specific people to call on, according to Janet Brown, director of the debates commission, who was sitting in the booth next to Fouhy and heard him instruct Simpson on who was to be recognized next. Simpson had her hands full allocating time fairly among the candidates and keeping the flow of the debate going, Brown said later.

Walthall flatly denied he was a plant or had been rehearsed. Reflecting on his question, he allowed that "it was really silly when I said 'cross our hearts,' but I was serious in what I meant." After the debate, he went home and turned on his television set to unwind. "The first thing I see," he recalled, "was one of Bush's anti-Clinton ads, the one with Clinton on the cover of *Time* [as a photo negative, the use of which prompted the magazine to sue the Bush campaign]. I thought, 'Here's this shit again. This guy hasn't made a commitment and we can pretty much expect this the rest of the way.' "

It was true enough. The president had made no explicit commitment to stop attacking Clinton on the "character" issue. But something happened that night in Richmond, and the back-to-back questions of Kim Usry and Denton Walthall had a lot to do with it. "It set him off his game," Jim Lake, the Bush campaign's communications director, said later. For the rest of the debate, Bush skipped direct references to Clinton's "character."

Ailes later acknowledged that the scolding on negative campaigning from Kim Usry and Denton Walthall had stopped the president in his tracks. "It moved him to go to his natural instincts, which was to be a nice guy," Ailes said. Teeter said later that Bush himself confided that the format "did not lend itself to a tough attack. . . . He couldn't do what we all had been telling him was the objective. . . . We wanted a debate that was more confrontational" between Bush and Clinton.

But that, David Wilhelm, the Clinton campaign manager, said later, was where the Bush campaign had made its greatest miscalculation, and why the Richmond debate was, as he put it, "the most dramatic crystallization of a mind-set that existed throughout the campaign, and it was something the Bush people never really understood.

"Bush kept trying to make the campaign about Clinton, and the American people wanted the campaign to be about them—their problems, their hopes, their dreams, their economy," Wilhelm said. "When we were at our best we kept talking about that, the things that mattered in the average voter's life. And when George Bush tried to make the campaign be about something other than that—Bill Clinton's draft record, or trip to the Soviet Union—people reacted very negatively. And when that fellow with the ponytail stood up and said essentially, 'Hey, make this about my problems,' it really crystallized the failure of the Bush strategy. If there was one moment that did it, that was it.''

In that same second debate in Richmond, another questioner perhaps underscored even more the gap between Bush and the average voter. Marisa Hall, a twenty-five-year-old single woman, was concerned that the candidates were out of touch with the trials that everyday people like herself were facing in the recession. There was a lot of talk from them about how the mushrooming national debt was undermining the nation's well-being, but she wasn't getting a sense of what it meant in terms of the individual.

"How has the national debt personally affected each of your lives?'' she asked. "And if it hasn't, how can you honestly find a cure for the economic problems of the common people if you have no experience in what's ailing them?''

Perot quickly responded that the national debt "caused me to disrupt my private life and my business to get involved in this activity. That's how much I care about it.'' He noted that "I came from a very modest background'' and that "as lucky as I've been,'' he owed it to the country's children and his own to try to do something about the sick economy.

Simpson then turned to the president.

"Well,'' he said, "I think the national debt affects everybody.''

"You personally,'' Simpson said, trying to nail him down in behalf of the questioner.

Bush seemed confused. "Obviously it has a lot to do with interest rates,'' he offered.

Simpson interjected again: "She's saying 'You personally. You on a personal basis. How has it affected you . . . personally?' ''

Bush: "I'm sure it has. I love my grandchildren. . . . I want to think that they're going to be able to afford an education. I think that that's an important part of being a parent. If the question—maybe I—get it wrong.''

Looking at Marisa Hall, the president asked her: "Are you suggesting that if somebody has means, that the national debt doesn't affect them? . . . I'm not sure I get—help me with the question and I'll try to answer it.''

"Well," the woman said, "I've had friends that have been laid off from jobs. . . . I know people who cannot afford to pay the mortgage on their homes, their car payment. I have personal problems with the national debt. But how has it affected you, and if you have no experience in it, how can you help us, if you don't know what we're feeling?''

Bush still seemed puzzled. Simpson stepped in again. "I think she means," she said, "more the recession—the economic problems today the country is facing, rather than the deficit.''

The president finally got the idea—in his fashion. "Well, listen," he said, "you ought to be in the White House for a day and hear what I hear and see what I see, and read the mail I read and touch the people that I touch from time to time.''

Bush went on to tell how he had gone to the Lomax AME church outside Washington, a black congregation, "and I read in the bulletin about teenage pregnancies, about the difficulties families are having to make ends meet. I talk to parents. I mean, you've got to care. Everybody cares if people aren't doing well.''

He was sounding very defensive now. "But I don't think it's fair to say, 'You haven't had cancer, therefore you don't know what it's like.' I don't think it's fair to say, you know, whatever it is, that if you haven't been hit by it personally—. But everybody's affected by the debt because of the tremendous interest that goes into paying on that debt, everything's more expensive. Everything comes out of your pocket and my pocket. So that's it. But I think in terms of the recession, of course you feel it when you're president of the United States. And that's why I'm trying to do something about it by stimulating the export . . . investing more, better education systems.''

Listening to Bush at such times was like listening to a phonograph record with the needle skipping. "Thank you," he said to Marisa Hall at last. "I'm glad you clarified it.'' In the Clinton holding room nearby where the Democratic nominee's chief strategists were watching, television adviser Mandy Grunwald recalled, "We all looked at each other. It was almost sad.''

Now it was Clinton's turn. He raised up off the stool against which he was leaning and strolled toward the woman. According to one aide who took part in Clinton's debate preparations, Clinton was told at the time that "the audience was his friend, he should go to the audience" if he was so moved, and he did. In the debate prep, Grunwald remembered, Clinton had asked: "How far can I go without losing the camera?" Now he walked as far as the previously calculated spot, then said to his questioner: "Tell me how it's affected you again. . . . You know people who've lost their jobs and lost their homes?"

"Well, yeah, uh-huh," she replied, somewhat taken aback by Clinton's direct approach. But he was just getting warmed up. Standing only a few feet from her, he didn't talk about learning about other people's troubles by reading about them on a church bulletin board.

"I've been governor of a small state for twelve years," he said. "I'll tell you how it's affected me. Every year Congress and the president sign laws that make us do more things and give us less money to do it with. I see people in my state, middle-class people—their taxes have gone up in Washington and their services have gone down, while the wealthy have gotten tax cuts.

"I've seen what's happened in the last four years when—in my state, when people lose their jobs there's a good chance I'll know them by their names. When a factory closes, I know the people who ran it. When the businesses go bankrupt, I know them.

"And I've been out here for thirteen months meeting in meetings just like this ever since October [1991], with people like you all over America—people that have lost their jobs, lost their livelihood, lost their health insurance. What I want you to understand is the national debt is not the only cause of that. It is because America has not invested in its people. It is because we have not grown. It is because we've had twelve years of trickle-down economics. We've gone from first to twelfth in the world in wages. We've had four years where we've produced no private sector jobs. Most people are working harder for less money than they were making ten years ago.

"It is because we are in the grip of a failed economic theory. And this decision you're about to make better be about what kind of economic theory you want. But just people saying I'm going to fix it [isn't enough] . . . what are we going to do? I think [what] we have to do is invest in American jobs, American education, control American health care costs and bring the American people together again."

Around this time, a television camera caught Bush looking at his wristwatch, and the shot was flashed to the millions and millions of Americans watching at home. The immediate impression to many was that he was getting impatient with the whole business and was wishing for the debate to be over. Later, aides insisted that the president was checking his watch because it seemed to him that his opponents were talking beyond the time allocated for each answer, as reached in the pre-debate negotiations.

If that was so, it was another example of the proper, rules-abiding George Bush being tripped up by his own rigid adherence to agreements made. Twelve years earlier in another famous presidential debate in Nashua, New Hampshire, Bush had agreed to a two-man debate with Ronald Reagan. When Reagan unexpectedly invited the other Republicans running for the nomination to join them, Bush sat stiffly and unyieldingly, enabling Reagan to make him look the poor sport. But Bush's position was that an agreement had been made, and gentlemen didn't break agreements. And here was another agreement being broken.

Later, Marisa Hall assessed the three responses. "Perot answered the question correctly," she said. "President Bush never answered it. It kind of upset me. He started talking about going to that black church, then he started talking about his grandchildren." As for Clinton, she said, "a lot of people were saying his answer had been rehearsed, but what he said made me feel good. And when he came toward me, I liked that." On election day, she voted for Clinton.

To point to a single question and answer in one debate as a revelation of Bush's political vulnerability would be unfair if it were not so typical of a seeming incomprehension of what average voters were feeling and saying all through the campaign year. Comparing the fears of a jobless worker unable to pay his house mortgage with the concern of a wealthy man about whether his grandchildren will be properly educated was ludicrous on its face.

In the Clinton holding room, the Democratic nominee's chief aides and strategists were whooping it up. When he walked over to Hall, who had just confused Bush with a simple question, and demonstrated at once that he understood, Clinton press secretary Dee Dee Myers said later, "that was probably the most memorable moment for the hundred million people who tuned in to the debates, because the contrast was so stark. Perot was having a good debate but no one was thinking about him as a real president. People out there were tuning in because Perot was good theater and because they were going to pick a president between the other two. That was the moment that most clearly distinguished them and I said, 'The campaign is over. George Bush is dead. He just killed himself.' We couldn't get to the press room fast enough [to start "spinning" reporters with that conclusion].''

Mickey Kantor, the campaign chairman, agreed. As soon as Bush said, ''in effect, 'I don't get it,' '' Kantor said later, ''we knew that was it, because we knew what Bill Clinton would do. . . . It was vintage Bill Clinton, and over his shoulder, that was when Bush looked at his watch. Now, did that win the whole campaign? No. But was it symbolic of everything the American people were concerned about? Absolutely. . . . First, somebody says, 'Quit throwing mud, and then Bill Clinton connects and George Bush doesn't. It gave us exactly what we wanted. I mean, I would have been happy then if we'd have shut off [the campaign], say, 'No more debates, that's the end. We're gonna stop campaigning,' and make that the end. That would have been the last image I would have wanted in the campaign.''

When Clinton came into the holding room afterward to an ''ecstatic'' welcome, one of those present said, it was clear he knew he had done well, but because he had not seen how Bush looked, and what the dynamic of the whole debate was coming over a television set, he didn't realize at first just how well. The staff did not keep him guessing.

Later, after the election, Clinton told us in an interview in the Oval Office: ''I'd like to tell you that I grasped the event, and the significance of it, at the time, but I didn't. But when I heard [President Bush] talking to that woman [Marisa Hall], I knew that she was asking him a different question than he was answering. I did know that.

''You know, it's not easy to listen to people anytime. It's a lot easier to be a good talker than a good listener. But in that format, with all that pressure, with one hundred million people watching, it's probably even harder to be a good listener. And one thing I thought about going into that debate was that these are real people; it doesn't matter whether they're for Bush or for Perot or for me, these are people who are out there living with the consequences of America today, and I have to listen to them. And I'm going to try to respond to them. I can give my speech, but respond to them.

"I really thought about it a lot, about the format, about how it was going to be different going in. . . . If we're having a debate and there's a press panel, and you ask me a question, one of your tough questions, it's a perilous question, I have to answer it. But if I have a minute and a half, I can answer it in thirty seconds then put my minute spin on it. With those people who were out there, I felt I had a lot less room to do that. . . . I saw the American people sort of screaming for me to pay attention to them and listen to them. So I knew I had done well with the questions because I listened to them and I watched them, and I had thought about them. But I had no idea it would have the impact on the voters that it apparently did."

For all the admonitions in Richmond against personal attacks, four nights later in the third presidential debate at Michigan State University in East Lansing, Bush was at it again. He began talking again about Clinton, about "this pattern that has plagued him . . . about trying to have it both ways on all these issues"—Bush on the campaign trail had been calling it "waffling." Clinton started coming back at him, then stopped. "I could run this string out a long time," he said, "but remember this, Jim [Lehrer, the moderator]. Those 209 Americans last Thursday night in Richmond told us they wanted us to stop talking about each other and start talking about Americans and their problems and their promise, and I think we ought to get back to that. I'll be glad to answer any question you have, but this election ought to be about the American people."

Several minutes later, though, Bush raised "this question about trust" again, repeating that "there's a pattern by Governor Clinton of saying one thing to please one group, and then trying to please another group," and that "that pattern is a dangerous thing to suggest would work for the Oval Office."

Clinton was right back with his friends from the Richmond debate. "I really can't believe Mr. Bush is still trying to make trust an issue," he said, "after 'read my lips' [his reneged-on no-new-taxes pledge in 1988] and [his promise of] 15 million new jobs and embracing what he called voodoo economics, and embracing an export enhancement program for farms he threatened to veto, and going all around the country giving out money in programs he once opposed.'' The president indeed had made those promises in the campaign and had been spreading government largesse of all sorts in states where he needed political help.

"But the main thing," Clinton intoned, "is he still didn't get it, from what he said the other night to that fine woman on our program, the 209 people in Richmond. They don't want us talking about each other. They want us to talk about the problems of this country."

In the remaining two weeks of the campaign, the governor of Arkansas never stopped reminding voters, as he dashed frenetically around the country by bus and jet plane, about the questions asked that night at the University of Richmond by the unemployed woman, the father with the ponytail and the voter concerned about how the "national debt" affected the candidates. Clinton deftly cast the three of them as the voice of America, crying out in protest against the demeaning of the nation's political process by an incumbent president who insisted on talking about personal matters instead of the serious problems facing the country, and didn't "get it" when asked how those problems touched him.

In a large sense, it was not a miscasting. Kim Usry, Denton Walthall and Marisa Hall did indeed express the public revulsion against negative campaigning, particularly when it was focused on matters of personal behavior and lifestyle, in a presidential election year in which millions of Americans were out of work or in fear of being so, or were without health care insurance or in fear of losing it.

Only four years earlier, American voters had looked on benignly or simply looked away as the same George Bush had resorted to the same sorts of negative campaign tactics to destroy the campaign of Democratic presidential nominee Michael S. Dukakis. Then, in 1988, it was Willie Horton, the furloughed murderer from Massachusetts—the black furloughed murderer—who raped a white woman in Maryland; the Dukakis veto of a state bill requiring teachers to lead the pledge of allegiance in their public school classrooms; the condemnation of pollution in Boston Harbor that Dukakis was attempting to clean up; the demonizing of the American Civil Liberties Union, to which Dukakis belonged.

This time around, however, the voters—given voice by the Kim Usrys, the Denton Walthalls and the Marisa Halls—had had a bellyful. They were, in one of the ever-whining George Bush's favorite phrases, "sick and tired" of the name-calling and the finger-pointing. They wanted the issues that had reduced the quality of their lives discussed and debated in the campaign. Like Howard Beale, the unbalanced television anchorman in the 1970s hit film *Network* and his aroused audience of fed-up Americans, they were proclaiming: "We're mad as hell and we're not going to take it anymore!"

They did not, as in the movie, throw open their windows, lean out and fill the night air with that declamation of their dismay. Instead, they trooped to the polls on Election Day, November 3, and voted in record numbers and in percentages not attained since John F. Kennedy narrowly defeated Richard M. Nixon for the presidency more than three decades earlier. And in place of the fictional Howard Beale, they had the real-life Ross Perot rallying them with basically the same message of discontent, impatience and resolve to take their country back.

In the movie, the character of the crazed television anchorman, played by British actor Peter Finch, met an untimely end, but in real life Perot managed to survive after bizarre behavior that made the comparison with the film character not entirely exaggerated.

The prime survivor of the whole fictionlike saga of the 1992 presidential campaign, however, was Bill Clinton, who correctly gauged the bubbling discontent with the tenor of the campaign process in the country and deftly nurtured it into the political weapon that drove George Bush from the White House.

There was, to be sure, much more involved than rebellion against negative campaigning in the defeat of a president who less than two years earlier had attained higher popularity ratings than any previous occupant of the White House in American history. In the ensuing period, a deep recession gripped the nation and held it fast, as the president first denied its severity, then denied its longevity, then prematurely proclaimed its end.

Bush, who had zestfully plunged into foreign policy challenges, capping them with a most impressive mobilization of world leaders behind his determined and successful effort to turn back Iraqi strongman Saddam Hussein's invasion of Kuwait, seemed strangely detached when he had to turn his attentions to the economic woes at home.

Part of it, his friends said, was the man's natural optimism—his sunny view that things would always get better, would always turn out for the best. It was an optimism born of the experience of a favored lifetime of family wealth and position, and sheltered from the experiences and hardships of all those who were not similarly favored. He always said he cared about others' problems, but the social and cultural gulf between himself—born into aristocracy, educated at the best and most prestigious schools and launched into business and politics by family money and connections—and the man in the street was immense. Never was that more apparent than in the stammering way he grappled with Marisa Hall's question about the "national debt."

The popular cliché about Bush throughout the campaign—embraced and spread at every opportunity by the Clinton campaign—was that "George Bush doesn't get it." Democrats never ceased telling voters that he didn't "get it" about the existence, depth and duration of the recession; about the hardships of daily life for people whose lifestyle was light years removed from his own.

When they scanned the newspapers while standing in unemployment lines or checking the want ads, they would see pictures of the president riding in a golf cart or on his boat at Kennebunkport, Maine. On the evening television news they would see him repeatedly at play when they were trying to find work, or fearful of losing the work they had. And when they read about how Bush had gone into a supermarket and didn't know what the price scanner at the checkout counter was all about, the incident only confirmed for millions that "George Bush just doesn't get it" when it came to the trials of their everyday lives.

On the other hand, Perot for all his wealth was a walking man-in-the-street, and every sentence and sound bite he uttered established that identity. (In explaining himself, he would tell his listeners "I can't sound-bite it for you"—and then do precisely that.)

As for Clinton, he knew what it took to persuade voters that he understood the condition of their lives. In a town-meeting exchange with voters one early morning in Winston-Salem, North Carolina, in the final days of the campaign—an event televised on the *CBS Morning News* show—a mother and part-time hospital worker named Debbie Gilbert tested Clinton on his knowledge of life at the level of the average American.

"Governor," she said, "I just have a hard time believing that many politicians today, who claim that they want to help ease the burden on the average American, can really do that, because I don't believe that politicians know what it's like to be in the shoes of the average American family. I want to know if you know how much it costs to buy a pound of hamburger, a pair of blue jeans, a tank of gas and visit the doctor's office.''

Clinton replied without hesitation. ''Well, gasoline is about $1.20, depending on what kind of gasoline it is,'' he said. ''Hamburger meat's a little over a dollar. A gallon of milk's two dollars. A loaf of bread's about a dollar now. . . . What it costs to go to the doctor depends on doctor visits. I know doctors that still do visits for fifteen dollars.'' When that one drew laughter, he added: ''I do, but not many.'' He continued: ''Blue jeans run anywhere from $18 to $50, depending on what kind you get.''

When the questioner rated Clinton's answers as ''pretty good,'' he explained why he was able to be so readily responsive. ''One of the virtues about being governor of a small state—both of my opponents have made fun of that,'' he said, ''is that the people know me and I know them. And every now and then my wife and I just get out and go to the grocery store and just talk to people in the grocery store, and walk up and down the aisles and listen.''

A few days later, in a speech in Southgate, Michigan, the president, commenting on Clinton's knowledge of prices, demonstrated that he too knew what one common household item cost. But in giving the price of milk at ''$2.70, say,'' he failed to indicate what quantity he was talking about—quart, half gallon or gallon, as if reciting a figure that had been handed to him by his staff.

To the end of the campaign, Bush pounded away at the idea that the ultimate issue on which voters should decide how to cast their ballots was personal trust. Did they have confidence that the individual they would vote for could be counted on to do what he said he would do? Clinton, he said repeatedly, was a ''waffler'' who first said one thing, then another. But didn't he himself say ''read my lips, no new taxes'' and then agree to impose them?

Still, Bush had established himself as a recognized world leader— even *the* world leader—in the preparations for and implementation of the Persian Gulf War. And the whole Communist bloc in Central and Eastern Europe had collapsed on his watch. In the aftermath of those triumphs,

Bush's popularity had reached or surpassed 90 percent in the most reputable public opinion polls.

How, in the course of less than two years, did George Bush fall so far that a reelection that had once seemed a certainty now appeared to be in such jeopardy? It had all begun so promisingly, so joyously, on that January day in 1989 when he took the oath of office at the Capitol and pledged to keep the Reagan Revolution on its path, and ''to make kinder the face of the nation and gentler the face of the world.''

CHAPTER 2

BETRAYING THE REVOLUTION

Well before George Bush became president of the United States, many conservatives in the Republican Party had held deep reservations about him as a true believer. He had, after all, once favored the position that abortion was a matter of a woman's choice. And who could forget his labeling of the sainted Ronald Reagan's plan for economic growth—tax cuts plus increased defense spending equals a balanced budget—as "voodoo economics" in the 1980 GOP primary campaign?

But once Reagan had—reluctantly—accepted him as his running mate that year, Bush had embraced Reaganomics and all other aspects of the Reagan Revolution as his own. That's the way it always was with George Bush; he might be wishy-washy in getting around to taking a position, but once he took it, he took it categorically. And he accepted as an article of political faith that when a presidential nominee chooses you as his vice presidential sidekick, you owe him total loyalty.

That complete commitment to the man who had given his political career a lease on life did not, however, satisfy some on the party's far right. "Bush never had one hundred percent confidence from ca rying conservatives because he did not come out of the conservative movement like Reagan did," recalled Charles Black, the key conservative Republican consultant who eventually served in Bush's campaign. "And having run against Reagan and having some policy differences with him back in the '80 campaign, he just never achieved their full trust."

Bush's fealty to Reagan not only failed to convince some conservatives of his trustworthiness but also often led to ridicule of him from their ranks. Conservative columnist George Will, who in 1980 demonstrated an interesting character trait of his own by secretly helping to coach Reagan for a debate with Jimmy Carter and then extravagantly praising his performance afterward on television, once called Bush a "lapdog."

But Bush also had important friends on the right, and none was more influential in winning conservative support for him than Lee Atwater, the young protégé of Senator Strom Thurmond of South Carolina who rose rapidly in party ranks by dint of his keen sense of Southern and conservative politics and an instinct for the political jugular. Tapped to be Bush's 1988 campaign manager (and stand-in for James A. Baker III, Bush's closest political friend, then hiding out as Reagan's secretary of the treasury), Atwater as early as 1985 deftly started reintroducing Bush to the conservative community as a totally dependable convert to the true faith.

Exhibit A was Bush's appearance as featured speaker at a dinner in memory of William Loeb, the late, vitriolic publisher of the ultraconservative *Manchester Union Leader* who in his time had called Bush a "hypocrite" and worse in print. In these and other transparent panderings to the right, Atwater was able to garner enough right-wing support for Bush to scuttle the hopes of then Representative Jack Kemp and other presidential hopefuls on the right, and establish him as the logical heir to the Reagan Revolution. Once Bush clinched the Republican nomination in 1988, the choice in the general election—Bush or liberal Democrat Michael S. Dukakis—was an easy one for conservatives.

It was especially so after Bush's acceptance speech in New Orleans, in which the presidential nominee addressed in the most categorical terms the one issue that was, for many conservatives, dearest to their hearts. Contrasting himself with Democratic presidential nominee Dukakis, Bush drew thunderous cheers and applause with these words:

"I'm the one who will not raise taxes. My opponent now says he'll raise them as a last resort, or a third resort. But when a politician talks like that, you know that's one resort he'll be checking into. My opponent won't rule out raising taxes. But I will. And the Congress will push me to raise taxes and I'll say, 'No.' And they'll push, and I'll say, 'No.' And they'll push again, and I'll say to them: 'Read my lips: no new taxes!' "

It was, by all odds, the most memorable line in the acceptance speech, and the one that, more than any other, helped sway wary conservatives. Ronald Reagan could not have delivered it better (and would have had little reason, having agreed by some counts to thirteen tax increases in his eight years in the Oval Office). At the time Bush delivered the lines, some campaign aides—especially his future budget director, Richard Darman—raised warning signals that it could come back to haunt him, considering the mushrooming federal deficit problem. But other political advisers like Atwater, media expert Roger Ailes and speechwriter Peggy Noonan insisted that he say something decisive and dramatic that would help bring him out of the shadow of eight years as Reagan's pliant vice president.

"It was the one issue that unified the right and didn't antagonize anybody else," according to James Pinkerton, a Reagan and Bush White House aide influential in policy matters. So Bush rehearsed the punch line, in the style of a Clint Eastwood tough-guy movie, and delivered it with the required bluster to banish lingering memories of the "wimp image" that had haunted him for so long.

The emphatic manner in which Bush made the no-new-taxes pledge was particularly effective among conservatives because he had always been considered somewhat shaky on the issue that to them was at the core of their philosophy of smaller and less intrusive government. Some of them remembered how, after Democratic presidential nominee Walter F. Mondale had stated flatly in his 1984 acceptance speech that he would raise taxes, Bush had muddled the Republican response with ambiguous answers that had to be contradicted by Reagan himself.

Reagan in a news conference after the 1984 Democratic convention said he had "no plans for a tax increase," but added that if, "after all our best efforts" at cutting costs the budget still was not balanced, "you would have to look at the tax structure" to meet government expenses.

Shortly afterward, in a radio talk from Santa Barbara, he said that as long as he was president there would be no increase in "individual income taxes." That remark raised questions about whether he would accept some other kind of tax.

When Bush, then his vice president, was asked about it, he repeated what Reagan had said, specifically that if "revenues don't add up and you're still in deficit" after cutting costs to the bone, "then he will consider revenue increases." His reply was just different enough to generate questions about whether there was a split between Reagan and his vice president on this critical issue of the campaign.

Bush at the time was scheduled to have lunch with Reagan at the president's ranch in Santa Barbara. When he got there the two men were bombarded with questions about tax policy. Going in for lunch, Reagan said flatly that "we have no plans for, nor will I allow any plans for, a tax increase." But afterward, Bush came out and in response to questions acknowledged that it was always possible that conditions might "change dramatically," and that accordingly "any president would keep his options open."

The resultant confusion irked Bush no end, and he dismissed inquiring reporters with one of his more famous and sillier Bushisms: "No more nit-picking. Zippity doo-dah! Now it's off to the races." It was left to Reagan to finally put the mini-controversy to rest. "My opponent," he said of Mondale, "has spent his political life supporting more taxes and more spending. For him, raising taxes is a first resort. For me, it is a last resort."

In 1986, as Bush was revving up for his own presidential bid, he caused more consternation among some conservatives when he declined to sign a no-new-taxes pledge being circulated by Grover Norquist, head of Americans for Tax Reform. At least two other candidates for the 1988 Republican presidential nomination, former Governor Pierre S. (Pete) du Pont of Delaware and Kemp, signed it along with about 140 members of Congress. Norquist kept pressing Bush, and a compromise was worked out in early 1987 whereby Bush agreed to sign a letter to a prominent Republican conservative, Representative Robert Dornan of California, that incorporated the exact language of the Norquist pledge. Norquist promptly had a million copies of the letter printed and circulated among conservatives.

In a fateful irony, it was this same pledge that du Pont handed to Senator Bob Dole in a debate among the GOP candidates in New Hampshire in the 1988 presidential primary. Dole declined to sign it, a refusal that later was credited with contributing to his pivotal loss there to Bush. Coupled with a stinging eleventh-hour Bush television ad accusing Dole of "straddling" the tax issue, the very pledge that Bush himself would not sign became a principal tool in his own nomination and election. Some wondered later what might have happened had du Pont turned to Bush instead of to Dole with his challenge to sign the pledge.

Still, ideologues whether on the right or the left have long memories, and many of those on the right remained suspicious of the Yankee-born transplant to Texas. When Bush in his 1988 acceptance speech promised a "kinder, gentler" nation, there was some griping on the right about it. Recalling the phrase later, Don Devine, a prominent right-wing consultant, asked: "Kinder, gentler than what? Obviously Reagan. It was a slap at Reagan from day one." Apparently overlooked was the fact that the new president pointedly began the speech by hailing his predecessor and political benefactor as "a man here who has earned a lasting place in our hearts and in our history." Bush went on, though, to promise "a new engagement in the lives of others—a new activism, hands-on and involved, that gets the job done." To those who chose to see this pledge too as a not-so-subtle slap at the notoriously hands-off Reagan in the day-to-day operations of government, hackles again were raised.

When Bush moved into the White House and not surprisingly began to put individuals of his own choosing into key administration positions, the griping continued. Old Reaganites growled that they were not being treated with proper sensitivity in the mechanics of transition, and they increasingly viewed Bush more as usurper than legitimate heir to the Reagan legacy.

"Almost from day one, there was a disenchantment with the manner in which the Bush team replaced Reagan people with Bush people," Jim Lake, the 1992 Bush campaign communications director, recalled after the 1992 election. "Not so much that they did it, but there was a sort of cavalier and arrogant, inconsiderate methodology that was not universal but frequent. A lot of people were handled with short shrift. It was sort of, 'Who am I, the enemy? I'm not the enemy, we've been here together.'

There was a disappointment at the us-and-them, enemy sort of approach.'' But, Lake added, ''that was inside-the-Beltway stuff. I don't think anybody outside knew, much less cared, about that.''

Bill Kristol, Vice President Quayle's chief of staff and an important conservative voice within the new administration, agreed about the snubs to the Reagan people. ''In the transition,'' he recalled, ''a lot of Bushies were saying, 'We're not going to be like Reagan,' which was foolish. . . . There were too many background comments like, 'Bush isn't like Reagan. He stays awake at meetings.' . . . A bad taste was left in a lot of Reaganites' mouths from the campaign through the transition that was unnecessary and unwise. On the other hand, that stuff could have been fixed with a little outreach and stroking.''

One complaint grew out of expectations that Bush would essentially be a caretaker over a continued Reagan administration, which obviously was what many conservatives hoped for. ''Republicans saw him in a historical context as the guy who would fill the Truman role,'' said David Keene, head of the American Conservative Union. ''He'd be the consolidator of the change. Roosevelt had Truman; Reagan would have Bush. In fact, Bush never saw himself that way. Immediately, he began to separate himself from the Reagan administration. He didn't see himself or project himself as sort of carrying on what had been done. It had to be something new, and if you were going to do something new, there had to be something wrong with what came before.''

Kristol viewed it all as a matter of poor communications. ''George Bush got a bum rap from conservatives,'' he said later, ''but on the other hand it was a failure of this administration to be unable to get credit from conservatives for the things we did that were continuing on the path Reagan laid out. We failed to explain on areas where we felt we had to diverge. Reagan was able to get away with all kinds of divergences from pure conservative principles. He somehow had a credibility and reserve of goodwill that George Bush didn't have.''

In an obvious effort to fill that void, as well as to reward a faithful lieutenant, Bush installed Atwater as Republican national chairman, from which post Atwater functioned not only as a fielder of complaints from the right wing but also as an interpreter of the right's political concerns to the president. ''The first year, 1989, was a good year for Bush,'' Paul

Weyrich, head of the Free Congress Foundation and one of the more influential voices on the Republican right, said later, "because Atwater stopped a lot of the nonsense" to which conservatives objected.

Nevertheless, Lake said, "there was a developing unease that there was no vision that Bush was trying to realize. . . . There were some people who felt that he needed to have some direction, rather than just coming in and attending to the day-to-day business that was going on, dealing with what came across your desk." And although Bush in the beginning was drawing such rave reviews from the public that his popularity in the polls was exceeding that of Reagan himself at his strongest, the conservatives missed few opportunities to snipe at him. This was especially so if anything occurred to raise suspicions about the sanctity of his no-new-taxes pledge.

Their confidence on the issue seemed at first to be reinforced even by the one Bush cabinet member the conservatives suspected most of being a closet tax-and-spender—Darman, just nominated to be director of the Office of Management and Budget. In his confirmation hearings, he informed the Senate Government Affairs Committee that neither he nor the new president had any intention of playing games with the no-new-taxes promise, such as asking for them under some euphemism such as "revenue enhancement." He himself would apply the old "duck test," Darman said: If it looks like a duck, walks like a duck and quacks like a duck, it's a duck. "If it looks like a tax, it's a tax," he testified, adding with a grin: "Ducks are off the table."

Less than two weeks after Bush was sworn in, however, word came from Secretary of the Treasury Nicholas Brady, an old Bush chum, that the new administration was considering requiring savings and loan and commercial bank depositors to pay a fee for the privilege of lending their money to said institutions. Congress, and conservatives especially, raised the roof. Bush quickly proclaimed that the notion was merely an "option" that hadn't even reached his desk. Many on the party's right who intended to take Bush up on his offer to read his lips, however, were wondering whether those lips were forming the word "maybe." By Darman's terms, this suggested S&L and bank "fee" sure looked and sounded like a duck to them.

Even before Bush was sworn in as president, however, he had demonstrated how firmly committed he intended to be to the no-new-taxes pledge. As candidate and president-elect, he rejected the work of a bipartisan National Economic Commission created specifically to give both parties political cover on any tax increases. Once he took office, he dodged the tax-increase bullet in his first year—fired at him, insiders said later, by Darman. Bush negotiated agreement with congressional leaders on a budget that specified savings that by all odds were unrealistic. It included $5.3 billion in new "revenues" that the administration optimistically said would result from its proposed lowering of the capital gains tax, which was not likely to happen (although, surprisingly, it did pass in the House as sixty-four Democrats knuckled under).

There was some sentiment in the White House that if the president got through one year without new taxes he could then get away with saying he had fulfilled his campaign pledge. Darman, according to one insider, pressed this case, arguing that if the president wanted to accomplish anything at all on the domestic front "you had to fix the budget deficit, and you couldn't do it without some kind of tax. You would be tied down to the deck."

Ed Rollins, the manager of the 1984 Reagan reelection campaign, recalled later a dinner early in the Bush administration at which Darman and Bob Teeter, the Detroit pollster who later was to become the Bush campaign chairman, discussed how long the Bush administration would have to hold to the no-tax pledge, and when it could be broken.

"I said, 'You guys are nuts, you can't break it,' " Rollins recalled. " 'You've got to basically try and make it through this term without breaking it, and certainly through the congressional elections.' " Rollins at the time was director of the National Republican Congressional Committee in charge of electing GOP House members. Most of his candidates, he said, had also taken the no-tax pledge and breaking it would be poison to their election chances.

Darman's apparent willingness to have Bush break the no-tax pledge did not prevail, however, against the political advice of most others, including Atwater, that going back on it would be political suicide. Meanwhile conservatives, while placated on the tax issue, found grounds to complain on other fronts.

In March, when the Senate rejected Bush's nomination of former Senator John Tower to be his secretary of defense, critics on the right charged that he had mismanaged the affair. And they griped when he agreed to a deal with Democrats on humanitarian aid only to the contras in Nicaragua.

In June, when the Beijing regime brutally suppressed pro-democracy forces demonstrating in Tiananmen Square, they scored Bush for failing to take stronger action. And when, after announcing there would be no high-level dialogue with China's leaders until they ended their repressive posture, he sent top aides Brent Scowcroft and Lawrence Eagleburger to Beijing to schmooze with them, the far right hit the roof.

In October, the conservatives groused about the administration's failure to seize on an attempted coup against Panamanian dictator Manuel Noriega to get rid of him. And when Bush held a very conciliatory summit meeting with Soviet President Mikhail Gorbachev at Malta, warnings were sounded on the party's right that the Cold War really wasn't over. Conservatives chided the president for accepting Gorbachev's word that the Soviet Union was no longer shipping arms to Nicaragua and leftist guerrillas in El Salvador.

In late December, however, the Bush-ordered invasion of Panama that ended in Noriega's surrender won the president favor on the right. And throughout that first year Atwater, from his post as party chairman, served effectively as the chief protector of Bush's political interests in dealing with the party's conservative base. He engineered such gestures to the right as a special presidential news conference at which Bush announced his support for a constitutional amendment banning flag-burning, and a visit to the memorial across the Potomac that depicts American troops raising the flag on Iwo Jima in World War II.

By the start of 1990, Bush's approval rating in the *Washington Post/ ABC News* poll had reached 79 percent, the highest figure attained by any first-year president since the end of that war. It topped the 77 percent achieved by John F. Kennedy after his first year in office. Remarkably, 74 percent of black voters and 66 percent of Democrats gave him favorable marks in the same survey. One Republican of presidential ambitions, Pete du Pont, who had been holding dinners with conservatives around the country with the thought of running against Bush in 1992, was so spooked by his numbers in the polls that he backed off.

Through all this, the problem of a rapidly increasing federal deficit born of the Reagan policies of borrow and spend hovered over the general sense of national well-being. In July of 1989, Alan Greenspan, chairman of the Federal Reserve Board, had warned that a slowing economy could slip into recession. But he added that with a careful monetary policy it was possible to avoid "an unnecessary and destructive recession." At the time, unemployment was at a politically acceptable 5.2 percent and steady.

Nevertheless, some of the political hands were worried. One night in August, Jim Lake, Charlie Black and Bob Teeter had dinner at the Jefferson Hotel in Washington and together they outlined a prospective speech to suggest to the president. It expressed his awareness of the economic condition, the need for adjustments in the changed world picture and what he intended to do about it. The next day Teeter presented it to Bush, informing him of the concerns expressed the night before that he needed to let the American people know he was on top of the situation. Bush agreed, but the speech never happened. Darman and White House chief of staff John Sununu, convinced that talk of recession was unwarranted, "talked him out of it," Lake said later.

But as the new year of 1990 began, more warning signs were flashing. Labor Department statistics showed that 98,000 manufacturing jobs had been lost in 1989, and producer prices had gone up 4.8 percent. Major banks began to drop their prime lending rates to counter what appeared to be an economic slowdown, reflected in a growth rate of only 0.5 percent in the gross national product for the final quarter of 1989 (later revised to 1.1). Bush's new budget of $1.23 trillion included many cuts previously proposed by Reagan and rejected by Congress, and was based on economic assumptions deemed far too optimistic by the Congressional Budget Office and numerous independent economists. Democrats who had swallowed the budgetary gimmicks in Bush's first year vowed not to go along a second time.

Conservatives complained about priorities in the Bush budget, but on key litmus-test issues he was in lockstep with them. When a civil rights bill aimed at strengthening laws against job discrimination was introduced, the Bush administration dismissed it as a "quota bill" and said it would introduce an alternative of its own that would not result in racial quotas in the workplace. And Bush continued to advocate a reduction in capital gains tax rates, a conservative favorite.

Atwater regularly reassured Republicans on the right that they had a good friend in George Bush—at the same time counseling the president on what he had to do to keep this important part of his political base happy. But in early March, the party chairman collapsed while giving a speech and was diagnosed as having a slow-growing tumor on his brain. His health quickly deteriorated and the president was denied his most astute hands-on political adviser, particularly in dealing with the most restive conservatives. Filling the void, eagerly, was Sununu, the former New Hampshire governor whose self-confidence in his own political skills, and arrogance in applying them, knew no bounds.

It was at this juncture, according to Weyrich, that Bush began to get into trouble with conservatives. Whenever issues had come up touching on their sensitivities including talk of a possible tax increase, Weyrich said later, Atwater was there to say to Bush: "Okay, you're the president. But do you really want to do this? Because if you do, you're gonna have problems with your base." With Atwater gone, Weyrich said, "I think the lack of that, arguing in political terms, really was the beginning of the problem. There was nobody over there who understood politics, including Sununu. He understood it, but he didn't argue it as effectively as Lee did."

As leading Democrats in Congress fretted over the growing deficit and pressed for action to reduce it, the right flank of the Republican Party remembered Bush's acceptance speech invitation of "Read my lips: no new taxes!" and reassured themselves that on this one most critical issue they had a man in the White House they could count on. Even though Bush was now faced with the prospect of brutal automatic budget cuts under the Gramm-Rudman "sequester" law, he had been so categorical in that pledge that it seemed inconceivable that he would go back on it.

Democratic congressional leaders, for their part, had vowed that while they recognized the need for new taxes to make a meaningful dent in the deficit, they were not going to take the rap for it politically. If there were to be new taxes, they wanted the president signed on with them. It seemed an impossible impasse, but when House Ways and Means Committee chairman Dan Rostenkowski, Mr. Taxes in the House, came up with a new plan in March to attack the deficit by freezing most spending and raising income tax rates, the White House was surprisingly, if tentatively, receptive. The no-new-taxes pledge continued to hang over Bush's head, but if it could be made to appear that he was forced into breaking it by the Democrats after drawn-out resistance, maybe . . .

Presidential press secretary Marlin Fitzwater called Rostenkowski's proposal "serious and thoughtful" and said it "gives us a basis for discussion." But at a news conference the next day, Bush said flatly that he would not support a tax increase, or for that matter a freeze on Social Security benefits. At the same time, he added, "I don't want to appear totally inflexible." House Speaker Thomas S. Foley was wary. No deal including a tax increase, he reiterated, was "politically and governmentally possible without the prior approval of the president." He called Bush's response "foggy" and "confusing."

When Congress in early May summarily dismissed Bush's budget proposal—the Republicans didn't even bother submitting it to a vote—and the House passed one of its own, the ball was in Bush's court. He responded by calling congressional leaders of both parties to the White House for negotiations on a deficit-reduction package that could win bipartisan support. After ninety minutes in the president's private quarters, Senate Majority Leader George Mitchell came out and told reporters that further budget discussions would be "without preconditions." And Foley added: "The presumption is that everything is on the table."

Did that mean taxes, too, in spite of "Read my lips"? Senate Minority Leader Dole said: "I don't know how you can have discussions otherwise." And House Minority Leader Robert Michel added: "I don't know how you make these figures match without doing some on revenues." But Bush had said categorically, "no new taxes." The next day Fitzwater reported that Bush had not discussed taxes "because his philosophy on this issue is quite well known."

Still, Republican conservatives began to get nervous. They knew that one of the president's principal economic advisers, budget director Darman, had been instrumental in 1982, when he was at the White House, in getting Reagan to sign on to the largest tax increase in history, and they suspected he was at it again, pressuring Bush to agree to new taxes. Three days after the White House meeting, nineteen House Republicans sent the president a letter reminding him of his no-new-taxes pledge, pressing him to keep it and urging him to step up efforts to gain a cut in the capital gains tax rate. Also, eight GOP candidates for the Senate wrote Bush and urged him to "reject any budget agreement which violates your pledge of no new taxes." They knew how much it meant to their own election chances.

Sununu, the conservatives' principal ally in the White House, or so they thought, sought to mollify them by saying in effect that the absence of preconditions meant only that the Democrats were free to propose tax increases, but they would be rejected. "We're allowing them to bring their good arguments for taxes to the table," he said. ". . . It is their prerogative to put them on the table and it's our prerogative to say no. And I emphasize the no." The Democratic leaders howled, and Fitzwater was sent out by Bush to reiterate that there would be "no preconditions to the talks." The conservatives became even more nervous, even though public opinion still opposed new taxes. An early May poll by NBC News and *The Wall Street Journal* found that 57 percent of those surveyed said Bush should stick to his read-my-lips pledge.

From the start of what soon came to be called the budget "summit" talks, it was clear that the Democratic congressional leaders were not going to let the president, having called them in to face the growing deficit crisis, simply pass the ball to them. They haggled over the true size of the deficit and insisted that Bush, at the height of his popularity, take the lead in coping with it.

For a time, the president tried to argue, on weak ground, that it was Congress's responsibility to lead the way. When, he said, some Democratic leaders told him, "You should go first," he replied: "Wait a minute. Who appropriates all the money, where's the revenue, who's got the obligation under the Constitution to raise the revenue? So let's not talk about who's going first." The problem with that argument was that the Constitution, under Article II, Section 3, stipulated that it was the president who was supposed to "go first" in laying out a legislative agenda, by providing "the Congress Information of the State of the Union, and recommend to their Consideration such Measures as he shall judge necessary and expedient. . . ."

House Majority Leader Richard Gephardt ridiculed Bush's contention. "It's the first time in this century we've seen a president want to give power to the Congress," he cracked. "The president is wrong if he thinks the budget is more our responsibility than his." When Darman produced a deficit-reduction plan limited essentially to spending cuts in domestic programs, the Democrats told the administration to get serious.

On the morning of June 26, George Bush finally did—to the shock of conservatives everywhere. In a two-hour breakfast meeting at the White

House, Speaker Foley informed the president that unless he was willing to agree that no effective deficit-reduction package could be hammered out without including some tax increases, the Democrats were going to walk away. Foley said he wanted something in writing so that the negotiations could go forward with the public clearly understanding that the effort was truly bipartisan. The Democrats were not about to go out on a limb and have Bush saw it off behind them. Bush, realizing he had come to the end of the line in his efforts to shunt the responsibility onto the Democratic-controlled Congress, finally agreed.

"Okay, well, let's do it," Bush said, according to Mitchell, in a manner that suggested to the Senate majority leader that the Republicans present—the president, Sununu, Darman and Brady—had already discussed the matter and were prepared to swallow the medicine. Bush asked Darman and Sununu to draft a statement and the two aides went into an adjoining room. They came out with a three-sentence joint statement for Bush and the congressional leaders written in the third person—an obvious dodge to give the president cover, and grounds to say later that he had been dragooned into the deal.

After reading the statement, Mitchell asked for an opportunity to caucus with Foley and Gephardt, and the three went into another room with the Darman-Sununu draft. They quickly agreed that Bush had to make the statement himself, and in the first-person singular. Mitchell jotted down the changes on the draft and the Democrats returned to the room. Bush looked at the changes, agreed to them and handed the draft to Darman to revise accordingly.

Instead of holding a news conference to disclose this critical development, however, Bush ordered the statement simply released, low key, to the press. Sununu came out of the meeting room and handed it to Jim Cicconi, an aide, as Fitzwater read it over his shoulder.

"You know what this means," the press secretary said to Sununu. "This means no more 'read my lips.' "

"No it doesn't," Sununu snapped. "Just put it out, word for word."

Fitzwater took the statement and tacked it up on the bulletin board in the White House press room—a sort of stealth missive delivered in the fashion of a hand grenade rolled under a door. This is what Bush's statement said:

"It is clear to me that both the size of the deficit problem and the need for a package that can be enacted require all of the following: entitlement and mandatory program reform, tax revenue increases, growth incentives, discretionary spending reductions, orderly reductions in defense expenditures and budget process reform, to assure that any bipartisan agreement is enforceable and that the deficit problem is brought under responsible control. The bipartisan leadership agrees with me on these points. The budget negotiations will resume promptly with a view toward reaching substantive agreement as quickly as possible.''

The statement was almost identical to the first draft except for putting it directly in Bush's mouth. The Democrats, according to Mitchell later, had considered balking at the phrase "tax revenue increases" instead of simply "tax increases" out of concern that the Republicans would contend that it really didn't mean what it clearly meant—that the president was breaking his Clint Eastwood–like pledge. But the Democrats decided that the Republicans would try to do that anyway, so they didn't insist on the change.

The Democrats were right. When word quickly got out, shocked conservatives on Capitol Hill squirmed and squealed. "He very explicitly didn't say 'raise taxes,' " House Minority Whip Newt Gingrich lamely observed. "He said 'seek new revenues.' " But Darman's duck had come waddling out of the White House press room, quacking the news unmistakably: if you read George Bush's lips now, he was saying, "New taxes after all." In short order, Republican Representative Robert S. Walker of Pennsylvania, a zealous witch doctor in the mysteries of voodoo economics, dashed off a letter to Bush and got eighty-nine House GOP colleagues to sign it, saying they were "stunned by your announcement" and informing him that a tax increase was "unacceptable."

Fitzwater at first tried to claim that the statement didn't say what it clearly did about "tax revenue increases." All the president was saying, he insisted, was that "everything is on the table" for discussion. Asked whether Bush was breaking his no-new-taxes pledge, Fitzwater dodged. Well, a reporter asked, did he think Bush would have been elected in 1988 had he not made the pledge, and instead had said new taxes would be needed (as 1984 Democratic nominee Mondale did to his later regret)? The president, Fitzwater offered, "said the right thing then and he's saying the right thing now."

Another reporter asked: Was this "the sound of concrete cracking" about Bush's feet? "This is the sound of a foundation being laid," the press secretary replied. Bush, nailed in the Rose Garden by reporters, said only that "I'll let the statement speak for itself." To conservatives, it did just that, and they were enraged at what they had just heard.

It was, Ed Rollins said later, "probably the most serious violation of any political pledge anybody has ever made." Jim Lake had foreseen the likely fallout. "I can remember having a conversation with Charlie Black in the period when they were talking about it," Lake recalled. "I said, 'Charlie, this is outrageous. If you're gonna go do this, you'd better lay a predicate out here. You'd better lay a foundation.' But nobody did it. From the very beginning of the administration . . . there seemed to be no real awareness that communications—about ideas, where you were going, what you were doing, why you were doing it—was important. . . . They never really understood the essential need, at the level of the presidency, that the president must convey to the American people his thoughts of where he's taking the country."

"There was a belief," Weyrich said later, "because the '88 election was really defined on that one issue, so clearly more than on any other issue, that Bush could never possibly go back on that, because it would be politically fatal. And so the assumption was that he would understand that, and that sort of thing wouldn't happen. There was genuine shock that the administration repudiated it, and repudiated it in the way that they did. There was no real explanation of this and there was no real apology—'I was forced into it' type of thing. There was no excuse."

The broken promise on taxes, political adviser Mary Matalin said later, had negative ramifications for Bush far beyond the tax issue. He had always had, she said, "a high honesty quotient" in the polls and this episode "really cut against his credibility, big time." From then on, she said, even when the administration scored achievements "nobody believed it. Or else they'd say something like, 'Why are you just doing it now? Why are you doing that in an election year?' "

That problem, Matalin said, preceded Bush's breaking of the no-tax pledge and went to "the minimal if not nonexistent political communications out of the White House" under Sununu, particularly after the death of Atwater, when Sununu seized all political decision-making for himself. That was why, she said, in her opinion, "John Sununu contributed more than any other single human being to the downfall of this presidency."

Bush himself, Black said later, "realized he was taking a big political risk, that he was putting a big chunk of his political capital on the table." If so, then why was the word put out in such a cavalier fashion? "It wasn't planned, it was just ad hoc," Black said. Well, he was asked, wasn't there a political person in the room? Black paused, then said: "Sununu." Another insider suggested that Darman, wanting the no-tax pledge abandoned all along, "snookered Sununu."

In a news conference three days after the posting of the Bush capitulation in the White House press room, the president was asked whether he could blame people for questioning whether he had really meant his no-new-taxes pledge. "I can understand people saying that," he replied. "I think it's wrong. I'm presented with new facts. I'm doing like Lincoln did, think anew" (a reference to Lincoln urging Congress in 1862 to "think anew" about the issue of slavery). Bush noted that Reagan before him had said he would not raise taxes but did so in 1982 when faced with new circumstances. "I've got to see the country go forward, and I've got to take the heat," he said. "And I think in the final analysis the American people will understand that."

The president would not, however, be drawn into a discussion about specific taxes, saying only that the negotiators were "free to discuss a wide array of options, including tax increases." And when Bob Dole in a television interview said Bush wasn't going to accept a budget deal that included increased taxes, the president authorized an aide to reiterate that "everything is up for discussion."

Meanwhile, Bush continued to take other actions favored by the conservatives, such as vetoing a bill requiring employers to grant unpaid leave to parents for births, adoptions and medical emergencies at home. But such issues were blocked from the radar screens of those on the party's right who had based their faith and support of George Bush on one position above all others: "Read my lips: no new taxes!" Black observed later: "Once they thought he had broken faith, it was easier to nit-pick things."

Had Bush not made the pledge so emphatically, so categorically, so defiantly, the faithful might not have been so jolted, and angry, about his cave-in. George Bush, though, had a way of going too far with tough-guy rhetoric, perhaps to make up for his personal courtliness and solicitousness that earlier had earned him the denigrating label of "wimp." In just one example, when he was clearly on his way to defeat for the 1980 Republican presidential nomination at the hands of Reagan, we asked him whether he was persevering in pursuit of the vice presidential nomination. His reply was: "Take Sherman and cube it." Translation: Even General William Tecumseh Sherman's famous statement that if nominated for president he would not run and if elected he would not serve was not strong enough to express Bush's rejection of the idea. Yet when Reagan asked him to be his running mate, he snapped up the offer in a split second—apparently without a thought that his earlier categorical statement would in retrospect seem utterly deceptive and dishonest.

The same, apparently, was so about his willingness to go back on his famously graphic invitation to the nation's voters to listen to what he was saying about taxes and take him at his word. With conservatives especially, "he put all his chips on the no-tax pledge," Bill Kristol said later. "It was not so much breaking it, but the way he broke it, the almost cavalier way he announced it; his clear failure, and the failure of those around him, to see what it meant in terms of his personal word, especially with the conservative Republicans. It seemed to reveal, perhaps somewhat unfairly, that there was no core of belief there.

"People understand that you can make pledges and you've got to break them, and there were ways to explain why he was doing what he was doing," Kristol said. "He didn't seem to acknowledge the extent to which he personally put his credibility on the line by breaking it. . . . It was a matter of, 'He doesn't stand for anything.' "

In all this, the guiding hand of Dick Darman was seen by conservatives long convinced that he was out to scuttle the no-new-taxes pledge. Convinced that the deficit problem had to be addressed in a more direct and forceful way, one critic on the right inside the White House suggested, Darman had created "a crisis atmosphere" that would force the president's hand. "Darman made a strong case that earlier budget estimates had been overtaken by events—the economy, the S&L bailout and so on—and the deficit would be significantly higher than expected," this critic recalled.

Also implied was the notion that Darman had struck a deal with the Democratic leaders on a tax increase in advance of the fateful White

House meeting. It was Darman's style, this insider said, to never take part in a meeting that he had not already stacked in his favor. In fact, he said, Darman would rebuke associates for failing to do likewise.

For his part, Darman had looked upon the read-my-lips bravado as a mistake from the start and, according to others in the speechwriting and review process, regularly knocked out any reference to it in speeches coming out of the White House. He liked to cite polls indicating that most voters thought taxes would have to go up to deal with the deficit, and relished the notion of negotiations with the Democratic congressional leaders or, as some of his critics were suggesting, collusion with them to strike a truly effective deficit-reduction deal including deeper spending cuts along with tax increases.

Darman also was known to believe that Bush in breaking the no-tax pledge did not suffer in the polls for that act in itself, but in his failure to explain why he had done it. Reagan (at the urging of Darman and James Baker) had accepted a tax package totaling substantially more than provided in the Bush budget deal and survived because, one veteran of the Reagan White House said, he "sold it as the greatest thing since sliced bread, and then changed the subject."

As the budget negotiations went forward, however, something was happening halfway around the world that would refocus Bush's attentions, and those of all Americans, from the perfidy of his broken pledge on taxes. On August 2, 1990, Iraqi forces invaded the tiny but oil-rich state of Kuwait. George Bush, whose whole experience in public life had groomed him to play on the international rather than the domestic stage, almost gratefully turned his eyes and his energies toward the Persian Gulf, with dramatic ramifications for the country, and for his own political fortunes.

MIRAGE IN
THE DESERT

When Saddam Hussein made his audacious plunge into neighboring Kuwait, he caught President Bush by complete surprise. For months, the president had been courting the Iraqi dictator, extending favorable conditions for the import of American heavy machinery of various sorts in the hope, as Bush put it later, of ''bringing him into the family of nations'' in a peaceful Middle East.

The president's ambassador in Baghdad, April Glaspie, had even told Saddam in an interview that later earned Bush intensive criticism that the Bush administration had ''no position'' on a longtime oil and border dispute between Iraq and Kuwait. That comment, the critics said, amounted to an invitation to Saddam to do whatever he wanted in the matter, and what he wanted—and did—was roll into Kuwait in force, seize the kingdom and drive the Kuwaiti royal family into exile.

Bush angrily called the action ''naked aggression'' but at first indicated that American military intervention was not being considered. Later the same day, however, his anger turned to determination to undo the deed when British Prime Minister Margaret Thatcher, one of his closest allies in the international community, pressed him at a meeting in Aspen, Colorado, to respond with force. "We're not ruling any options in," he said afterward, "but we're not ruling any options out." He quickly signed executive orders for a firm trade embargo against Iraq and the freezing of all Iraqi and Kuwaiti assets in the United States.

Only a few years earlier, such a move might have triggered a super-power confrontation with Iraq's strongest ally, the Soviet Union. But the erosion of Communism there and throughout Central and Eastern Europe—for which Bush unabashedly took much credit—had created a new world climate almost overnight. Now, Secretary of State James Baker and Soviet Foreign Minister Eduard A. Shevardnadze stood in the Moscow airport after a meeting and jointly condemned "the brutal and illegal invasion of Kuwait." Baker observed that "we might have been in earlier days viewing this very tragic action through an East-West prism." Instead, the two ranking diplomats announced "the unusual step of jointly calling upon the rest of the international community to join with us in an international cutoff of all arms supplies to Iraq."

Within days, the United Nations Security Council voted to impose a broad trade embargo against the invader. Saddam Hussein responded by annexing Kuwait. Oil prices shot up. Bush, who had immediately ordered an American aircraft carrier group to steam from the Indian Ocean to the Arabian Sea at the entrance to the Persian Gulf, now dispatched American troops to Saudi Arabia to let Saddam know he would encounter U.S. might if he attempted to subject that country, and its oil-rich fields vital to American interests, to a similar fate.

Thus began Operation Desert Shield, and what proved to be the diplomatic triumph of the Bush administration. Over the next five months, Bush in a most impressive display of international leadership persuaded most of the rest of the world, notably including the Soviet Union, to join in an unprecedented coalition through the United Nations to pressure Saddam to back off, or face military consequences. The American president demonstrated a toughness and resolve that astonished his political detractors at home and earned respect and support abroad, from London to Moscow and Tokyo.

From the start, Bush seemed almost eager for confrontation and a showdown. In informing Congress of his plans to impose severe sanctions against Iraq, he spoke categorically with the self-assurance of a Wild West gunslinger. "Iraq will not be permitted to annex Kuwait," he said. "That's not a threat or a boast. That's just the way it's going to be. . . . I cannot predict how long it will take to convince Iraq to withdraw from Kuwait. Sanctions will take time to have their full intended effect. We will continue to review all options with our allies. But let it be clear: we will not let this aggression stand."

This tough-talking, resolute George Bush struck a chord with the American people, so long frustrated by the years of Middle East hostage-taking and never-ending intrigues. Until now, his second year in the Oval Office had been marked by a slipping popularity at home, from a near-record 79 percent at the start of 1990 to 65 percent in July, according to *Washington Post*/ABC News polls. The conservative reaction to his broken pledge on taxes and discouraging economic statistics, including an unemployment rate of 5.5 percent in July, the highest monthly jobless climb in more than four years, had begun to take the bloom off his first-year acclaim.

But military crisis and the sending of American troops to danger zones almost always guarantee public approval for the national leader, and that was the case now. As he called up segments of the nation's military reserve forces, Bush's favorable ratings started to climb again. His political advisers were aware, however, that much depended on a swift resolution of the crisis. Ever since the sinkhole of the Vietnam War, Americans were wary of military adventures that might drag on indefinitely—the Vietnam Syndrome, some called the reluctance to use American forces to police trouble spots.

Among those skeptical about U.S. military involvement in the Middle East were many conservatives such as Patrick Buchanan, the controversial newspaper columnist and television commentator who had established himself after stints in the Nixon and Reagan administrations as one of the most popular voices on the Republican Party's far right. While smarting over Bush's broken no-new-taxes pledge, they took heart in his continued loyalty to another of their litmus-test issues—opposition to proposed civil rights legislation seeking to bar job discrimination. The conservatives viewed Democratic proposals as requiring racial quotas in hiring—although the legislation specified that quotas were not to be applied. When the Democratic bill passed Congress in early August, Bush made clear that he remained opposed, and eventually he vetoed it on grounds it would "introduce the destructive force of quotas" in the workplace. His veto was sustained by the margin of one vote in the Senate, and conservatives reserved final judgment on the president who they felt had betrayed them on taxes.

That sense of betrayal had endured throughout lengthy and contentious negotiations between the administration and the Democratic congressional leadership to forge an effective deficit reduction plan. With an eye on the Republican congressional critics of his broken pledge, Bush threatened to veto any spending bill passed by Congress that exceeded his own budget requests, although Congress continued to vote less money for most items than the president asked for. He berated congressional Democrats for endangering "the economic well-being of this country" by not achieving a budget deal.

At the end of September, a five-year deficit-reduction plan finally was agreed upon. At a Rose Garden ceremony, Bush accepted the result philosophically, and somewhat apologetically. "Sometimes you don't get it the way you want," he said, "and this is such a time for me. . . . But it's time we put the interests of the United States of America here and get this deficit under control." He then went on national television to build public support for the plan. "Tell your congressmen and senators you support this deficit-reduction agreement," he said. "If they are Republicans, urge them to stand with the president. If they are Democrats, urge them to stand with their congressional leaders."

Having thus put his prestige squarely on the line—and pointedly reminded conservatives once again of his broken pledge on taxes—Bush personally lobbied House Republicans in the White House and by telephone. He was stunned three days later when the House soundly rejected the plan, with right-wing Republicans noisily basking in I-told-you-sos. "The president gave away the crown jewel of his campaign promise to bring the Democrats to the table," said conservative California Representative Duncan Hunter. "That was 'no new taxes.' The president was extorted." At the same time, Democrats rebelled against new excise taxes that they said would fall unfairly on lower-and middle-income Americans.

Bush quickly raised the ante by himself rejecting a stopgap spending measure, technically closing the government's coffers and precipitating a shutdown of certain government functions. Because the action took place over a long Columbus Day weekend, tourists in Washington seeking to visit closed federal monuments and museums bore the brunt, but the image conveyed of a government at a standstill did not help the president's own image.

After new stopgap legislation was passed and accepted by Bush extending federal borrowing and spending authority, Congress went back to the task of writing an acceptable deficit-reduction bill. Bush, to the further chagrin of conservatives and others in his own party, told a news conference he would accept a boost in income tax rates on wealthier Americans—a demand by Democrats arguing for tax "fairness"—if they would accept the cut in capital gains tax rates that he wanted. But a delegation of Republican senators promptly called on him denouncing such a deal, and Bush backed off.

As the White House and congressional leaders continued to wrangle, the president found himself under attack from Republicans and Democrats alike. He added insult of his party's conservatives to the earlier injury of breaking his "read my lips" pledge when, while he was jogging in the rain in St. Petersburg, Florida, a reporter shouted to him: "Are you ready to throw in the towel on capital gains?" Bush disdainfully snapped back: "Read my hips!" and kept on jogging. The wiseacre remark resonated through the conservative community even more than his original Clint Eastwood takeoff itself.

Bill Kristol, Quayle's chief of staff, later called it "cavalier . . . a terrible sort of signal" to conservatives and voters generally. "It was a matter of, 'He doesn't stand for anything,' " Kristol said. And Paul Weyrich observed: "It suggested contempt for those of us who had taken him seriously. That was a serious mistake that was then masked over by the Gulf." He told the White House chief of staff and others in the administration, Weyrich said, "that as soon as the Gulf business wears off, Bush is going to be right back where he started to go right after the budget deal [in June], which was way, way down."

After much further maneuvering, agreement finally was struck on a plan that would provide $140 billion in taxes to reduce the federal deficit by $40 billion in the first year and just under $500 billion over five years. In the process, however, the political price to Bush became even more evident. Ed Rollins at the National Republican Congressional Committee wrote a memo advising GOP congressional candidates to distance themselves from Bush on the budget and deficit-reduction issue if they hoped to be elected.

Rollins, leading the Republican effort to elect more House members, had persuaded almost all the candidates to take the pledge against new taxes themselves, he said later, "because with Bush it was the one significant thing we still had to differentiate us from the Democrats, particularly in the post–Cold War period. So I yelled and screamed inside, and eventually outside, over how serious it was." When more than 100 members voted against the deficit-reduction package Bush had signed on to, Rollins said, "candidates became terribly confused, so I was advised by the Republican leadership [in the House] to give them some guidance." He drafted the memo and, as he routinely did, gave it to the congressional committee chairman, Representative Guy Vander Jagt of Michigan (defeated in 1992), to sign it. Vander Jagt, a close friend of the president, "knew what was going to happen," Rollins said later, and asked him: "Would you sign this one?" Rollins agreed.

In dispensing this advice, Rollins was doing no more than realistically assessing the political impact of Bush's broken pledge on taxes. "But the president just went batshit," Rollins recalled. "I became the focal point." But he was receiving polls from around the country that showed, three weeks before the midterm elections, "that twenty-five incumbents were going down. So what I basically had to do was dump all the challengers and just go save [incumbent] members."

Bush demanded privately that Rollins be fired. "Sununu accused me of leading the House Republicans in revolt against the president's tax plan, which was absurd," Rollins said later. "They [Bush's aides] kept saying, 'You're cooking your numbers, it's all false.' " But Rollins was acting on the basis of data from leading Republican pollsters. "I have great respect for this president," he said then, "but my job is to help House Republicans survive. I have to give the best political advice I can and, in this case, it's to run away from the budget package."

In the end, Rollins said, "I took the rap for the whole frustration of the House Republicans." But he refused to step aside under pressure and stayed on for several months thereafter. "In post-election polls in '90," he recalled, "the anger that Republicans had toward the president for breaking the tax pledge [resulted in] one of the lowest turnouts of Republicans in history in the congressional races in 1990.''

One Republican congressman seeking reelection, Peter Smith of Vermont, demonstrated the severity of Bush's troubles on the budget issue by noting to his own constituents in introducing the president at a Burlington rally that he had disagreed with him on the broken no-tax pledge. Later the same day, Bush went over to Manchester, New Hampshire, to speak in behalf of another Republican congressman, Robert C. Smith. When he got there he was greeted by the congressman's wife, who informed the president that her husband had to stay in Washington to vote—on a routine appropriations bill. Such was the presumed strength of George Bush's political coattails at this point.

A *Washington Post*/ABC News poll published on October 19 charted his slide. From the 79 percent job approval recorded at the start of the year, it was now down to 56 percent, after a brief boost resulting from his dispatch of American troops to the Middle East upon the Iraqi invasion of Kuwait. Those who said they disapproved of the way he was doing his job had doubled, from 20 percent to 40. Even support of his stationing of American troops in the Persian Gulf region until Iraq got out of Kuwait had dropped from 75 percent to 60. And most significant to political professionals, 79 percent in the same survey said they believed the country was "pretty seriously off on the wrong track," while only 19 percent said they thought it was going in the right direction. The figures marked the lowest confidence rating found in a major poll since 1974, during the Watergate affair. Still, there was little talk about the president's presumed bid for reelection in 1992 being in any jeopardy, and no Democrats were stepping forward to challenge him.

In the off-year congressional elections in November, the Republicans lost one Senate and eight House seats in what was widely seen as a rebuff to Bush for the whole tax and budget fiasco. Losing Republicans blamed his abandonment of his no-new-taxes pledge. Shortly afterward, Bush in effect told party conservatives that he had learned his lesson. Warning that the Democrats would seek further tax increases in the next Congress, he promised: "They're going to do it over my dead veto, or live veto, or something like that. . . . It ain't gonna happen, I'll guarantee you that."

Sununu, Bush's arrogant and contemptuous chief of staff, was even more pointed in describing what the attitude of the Bush White House was going to be from then on. Speaking to the Conservative Leadership Conference in Washington and boasting of how Bush had tamed Democratic spending proclivities in the budget deal, Sununu proclaimed: "There's not another single piece of legislation that needs to be passed in the next two years for this president. In fact, if Congress wants to come together, adjourn and leave, it's all right with us. We don't need them."

With the elections behind him, Bush was in fact able to give his full attention to the continuing crisis in the Middle East. In the months leading up to those elections, he had assured the American people that the military buildup was purely defensive. But now, with Saddam showing no signs of abandoning Kuwait, he authorized what was clearly a switch to establishing a powerful offensive capability in the Persian Gulf region. It called for nearly doubling the U.S. force commitment to 400,000 troops by early 1991 to make certain, Bush said, that the United Nations coalition against Iraq that he was skillfully building "has an adequate offensive military option."

The clear message was that if Saddam Hussein continued to defy the U.N. resolutions calling on him to withdraw from Kuwait, he would face expulsion. "I have not ruled out the use of force at all," Bush said, "and I think that's evident by what we're doing today." He expressed the hope that sanctions already in place would do the job "within a two-month period" but added that the United States had the authority to use force without further U.N. approval if it came to that.

Bush's hard-nosed attitude began to cause concern among many in Congress who either did not favor use of force against the Iraqi strongman or were fearful that once again an American president would lead the country into a shooting war without meeting the constitutional requirement that Congress, not the executive, shall declare war. Some called for a request from Bush to make such a declaration if he intended to go on the offensive, and the president promised to consult with Congress—unless unforeseen circumstances dictated otherwise.

It was reported, however, that in a bipartisan meeting with congressional leaders, Bush pulled a copy of the Constitution from his pocket, said he knew it said Congress had the power to declare war, then added: "It also says that I'm the commander in chief." Critics of the use of force, including such usually disparate figures as Pat Buchanan and Vietnam War critic George McGovern, took note.

Meanwhile, the Bush administration sought various rationales to justify the force buildup and the possible use of it. The president himself defended his actions on high moral grounds, saying the stakes were not the Gulf's rich oil supplies but traditional American opposition to aggression against small and helpless nations.

Jim Baker, however, usually the suavest of diplomats since laying aside the political hat he wore as Bush's 1988 campaign boss, put the matter in more political terms for Americans at home watching the unemployment rate steadily rise. Saying he wanted to bring the discussion "down to the level of the average American citizen," Baker observed that "if you want to sum it up in one word, it's jobs. Because an economic recession worldwide, caused by the control of one nation—one dictator, if you will—of the West's economic lifeline, will result in the loss of jobs for American citizens."

The validity of that concern was underlined by the Federal Reserve Board, which twice in three weeks lowered interest rates as a means to head off what many economists were now saying looked like a recession in the making. The Federal Reserve chairman, Alan Greenspan, danced around the use of that dread word, acknowledging that the economy had gone into a "meaningful downturn" in October but insisting it wasn't clear whether it was heading for a recession. He blamed rising oil prices as a result of the invasion of Kuwait, uncertainty in the Gulf situation and tighter credit by lending institutions. And, with limited optimism, he observed that "the world out there, when you look at the hard data, is not in as bad shape as it feels."

Soon after, however, the government's index of leading economic indicators was found to have fallen 1.2 percent in October, a drop for a fourth straight month. When the index fell for three months in a row, it was usually regarded as a sign that recession had set in. In October, the average factory workweek dropped, deliveries of goods from suppliers fell off, raw material prices, stock prices and new building permits all declined.

What was going on might have been only a "downturn" to Greenspan, but to workers getting pink slips, it was a lot more than that. And when the Labor Department's November unemployment figures were in—267,000 fewer payroll jobs and the jobless rate up to 5.9 percent, the highest in three years—the Federal Reserve lowered interest rates again to ease what Greenspan called a "credit crunch" resulting from anti-inflation policies by the Fed.

The next set of economic indicators out in late December showed a further drop, with manufacturers' orders for new consumer goods dipping sharply and new orders for durable goods nosediving 10.5 percent, tying a record slide. Nearly everybody was talking recession now—that is, everybody but the president and his administration. He was almost totally occupied now with the situation in the Middle East—and its ramifications in Congress.

With Saddam Hussein showing no signs of yielding in the face of the economic embargo imposed on him by members of the U.N. coalition crafted by Bush, the U.N. Security Council in late November, with American prodding, had specifically authorized the use of force against Iraq if its troops were not pulled out of Kuwait by January 15, 1991.

The action followed a Thanksgiving visit by Bush to American troops in Saudi Arabia during which he branded the Iraqi leader "a classic bully who thinks he can get away with kicking sand in the face of the world." Hinting at imminent action, he told the troops that "we are not here on some exercise. This is a real-world situation. And we are not walking away until the invader is out of Kuwait. That may be where you come in."

As tension mounted, Bush decided to send Baker to Baghdad to "go the extra mile for peace" and to try to convince Saddam Hussein that he meant business. After several delays, Baker met Iraqi Foreign Minister Tariq Aziz in Geneva only five days before the U.N. deadline and resolved nothing. Congress meanwhile was stirring over the prospect that the president seemed about to take the country into a shooting war without congressional authorization. Democratic Senators Tom Harkin of Iowa and Brock Adams of Washington demanded full debate on a resolution prohibiting Bush from using force in the Gulf without explicit authorization from Congress.

When Senate Majority Leader George Mitchell agreed to a debate, Bush dispatched his own request for an authorizing resolution—the first such request from an American president in seventeen years, since President Lyndon B. Johnson's bid for the Gulf of Tonkin resolution that gave him a free hand in Vietnam in 1974. For three days, heated debate ensued in the Senate and House, culminating in a largely partisan vote of support for Bush. The Senate approved by only five votes, the House by sixty-seven. Four days later, with the United Nations deadline passed, the United States was at war.

In the early morning of January 16, Operation Desert Shield became

Operation Desert Storm. American air power began a swift and unmerciful pounding of Baghdad and other targets in Iraq in a devastating display of state-of-the-art military technology. With satellite television bringing the sounds and views of war into millions of American homes, including displays of remarkably accurate air strikes and inflated initial claims of pinpoint destruction of enemy targets, a mood of national exhilaration swept the country.

Domestic woes for the time being were shunted aside, although the unemployment rate was now up to 6.1 percent, as the American people rallied behind their fighting men and women—and the bold and forceful commander in chief who had engineered this impressive response to the Iraqi tyrant he had compared in his more inflammatory moments with Adolf Hitler. A *Washington Post*/ABC News poll two days after the unleashing of American air power gave Bush a job approval rating of 79 percent.

By the time of his annual State of the Union address, thirteen days after the start of the air attacks, Bush was greeted on Capitol Hill in the manner of a conquering hero. He gave over a good portion of the speech to acclaiming the success of the war effort and the justice of the cause. "What is at stake is more than one small country," he said. "It is a big idea—a new world order where diverse nations are drawn together in common cause to achieve the universal aspirations of mankind: peace and security, freedom and the rule of law. Such is a world worthy of our struggle, and worthy of our children's future." Gone for the moment was Baker's justification for going to war in the oil-rich Middle East— protecting American jobs.

On the domestic front, Bush offered little more in the speech than his old recycled ideas spurned by the Democratic Congress in his first two years in office, including his tireless call for a cut in capital gains tax rates. But with Saddam Hussein to kick around, he could give short shrift to the developing economic slide at home and not worry much about approval ratings. Besides, in mid-February his Council of Economic Advisers in its annual report projected a swift recovery from the recession the Bush administration would not yet acknowledge was holding sway.

"This temporary interruption in America's economic growth," Bush told Congress in his economic report, "does not signal a decline in the basic long-term vitality of the U.S. economy." And with a war on, the Democrats felt obliged to mute their criticisms of problems at home while

Americans were risking their lives in a foreign land. Typical was the comment of Democratic Senator Paul Sarbanes of Maryland: "The difficulty I'm having is the almost sanguine attitude about the unemployment situation." The jobless rate had now reached 6.2 percent with 232,000 payroll jobs lost in January.

On the night of February 23, American and U.N. coalition ground troops were sent into Iraq, and a brilliant encircling movement masterminded by the American commander, General H. Norman Schwarzkopf, drove the Iraqi army to its knees in 100 hours. For the first time in a truly major military engagement since American armed forces were withdrawn from Vietnam in 1975 and American diplomats were driven from the besieged American embassy in Saigon, Americans found cause to exult over a military victory.

There had been, to be sure, Grenada under Reagan and Panama under Bush, but they were modest conquests compared to the hammering of the defiant Saddam Hussein and his huge Iraqi military machine, identified by U.S. intelligence to be "the world's fourth-largest fighting force."

Americans at home gave in first to relief and then to wild celebration, with the president rebounding even higher from the political doldrums that had beset him in his second White House year. In another *Washington Post*/ABC News poll, 90 percent of Americans surveyed approved of his handling of the war. A *New York Times*/CBS News poll put his job approval at 87 percent, the highest recorded since the June 1945 rating for Truman at the time of the German surrender in World War II. A *USA Today* survey was even better: 91 percent job approval.

On March 6, wild cheers and applause greeted Bush from both sides of the aisle when he reported to a joint session of Congress and the nation over network television that his New World Order—that unfortunate label used earlier by Hitler to describe his own vision—had passed its first test. American forces in the Gulf, Bush proclaimed, "set out to confront an enemy abroad, and in the process, they transformed a nation at home."

With the newfound domestic unity resulting from the success of the war, Bush said, "our first priority is to get this economy rolling again. The fear and uncertainty caused by the Gulf crisis were understandable. But now that the war is over, oil prices are down, interest rates are down and confidence is rightly coming back. Americans can move forward to lend, spend and invest in this, the strongest economy on earth." He told

MAD AS HELL / 51

Congress "we must bring the same sense of self-discipline, that same sense of urgency, to the way we meet challenges here at home."

When it came to specifics, however, Bush selected two areas of domestic legislation that hardly went to the heart of the economic situation—crime and transportation. "If our forces could win the ground war in 100 hours," he said, "then surely the Congress can pass this legislation in 100 days."

In the meantime, Bush invited the country to stage a prolonged celebration of the victory in the Gulf—a seemingly innocuous gesture that nevertheless would guarantee a continued spotlight on his great achievement in advance of his expected reelection bid in 1992. "Tonight," he told the nation, "I ask every community in this country to make this coming Fourth of July a day of special celebration for our returning troops. They may have missed Thanksgiving and Christmas, but I can tell you this: for them and for their families, we can make this a holiday they'll never forget."

Over the next four months, Americans took the president up on his proposal. As Iraqi forces withdrew from Kuwait and American troops began to come home, the scene on the homefront was like no other since the end of World War II. Welcoming parades blossomed in big cities and small towns across the nation, complete with yellow ribbons that had come to mark the long wait for American hostages held in Iran. And through it all, George Bush rode a wave of public approval that smothered any thought that he might encounter a serious threat to reelection the following year.

"The conservatives who were looking at it, like Pete du Pont, who came very close [to running]," Paul Weyrich recalled later, "got mesmerized by the polls. I told Pete, 'Don't be fooled by these polls. This is patriotism. We were in a war and people support the president during a war. It has nothing whatsoever to do with what the reality is going to be after we get out of this situation.' "

Du Pont had been holding private meetings with conservative leaders around the country for more than a year to sound out how much support a challenge to Bush would have among them. "He was very serious," Weyrich observed later. "He realized that as a former small-state governor who had been out of office for a number of years, that his real chance to do something was to take on Bush and beat him; that in all probability that come 1996, if Bush was reelected, you'd have all kinds of people like [Secretary of Defense Richard] Cheney and Quayle, and if Bush was defeated, then you would have other people from Dole to [Senator Phil] Gramm to [Reagan education secretary and Bush drug czar] Bill Bennett and other folks like that who would be in there. And measured up against them, he would have difficulty in terms of how long he had been out of office, and all that."

But while the country, and Bush, were reveling in the success of Desert Storm, the economy was still failing to respond. The index of leading economic indicators fell for a sixth straight month and the unemployment rate jumped from 6.2 percent to 6.5 percent, marking the greatest increase in a single month in five years, with another 290,000 salaried jobs lost. A month later, the jobless rate climbed again, to 6.8 percent.

Even so, Michael J. Boskin, chairman of Bush's Council of Economic Advisers, remained bullish. "Many of the preconditions for recovery are falling into place," he insisted. "Consumer confidence has rebounded, oil prices are back down to prewar levels, inventories are lean, the money supply has rebounded." None of this, though, was bringing much joy to men and women in the unemployment office lines. Neither did the report in May that the Big Three auto makers—General Motors, Ford and Chrysler—all reported major losses in the first quarter of 1991, totaling $1.86 billion.

Some of Bush's political advisers were getting nervous. "Inside the Beltway," Lake said later, "there was a developing unease that there was no vision that Bush was trying to realize, trying to move toward. The war, and the handling of the war, the breakdown of Communism and the whole East bloc failure caused people to forget about the economy. So it never really got full-blown, this unease."

In a short time, however, Bush's foreign policy luster was being smudged by Saddam Hussein's continued reign of terror in Iraq against Kurds and other persecuted dissident elements of the population, and by the decline of Soviet President Mikhail Gorbachev, in whom Bush had invested his support in that turbulent and disintegrating empire.

Also, second-guessing on the Bush administration's posture toward Iraq in advance of the invasion of Kuwait was intensifying. American Ambassador April Glaspie denied before a congressional committee that she had in effect given Saddam Hussein a green light by telling him in a

July meeting that "we have no opinion on the Arab-Arab conflicts, like your border disagreement with Kuwait," as she had been quoted in a transcript released thereafter by him.

Glaspie testified that the "so-called transcript" was an edited piece of "disinformation" and that she had told the Iraqi leader in no uncertain terms that the United States would not tolerate an invasion of Kuwait. Moreover, she said, Saddam "wanted me to inform President Bush that he would not solve his problems with Kuwait by violence—period." If there was an American mistake in the dealings with him, she said, it was in not realizing "he was stupid" in discounting her warning. But critics found that hard to swallow.

Added to all this was a developing mini-scandal within the Bush White House. Reports surfaced that the imperious Sununu had routinely been using military aircraft and other government transportation for personal and partisan political activities in violation of ethical standards. At first the White House defended him on grounds that he had to be in constant communication with the president, but as details of his trips became known, including ski vacations and trips to his dentist and a rare-stamp auction, pressures built for his removal.

Although Bush regarded Sununu as a valuable aide, his general boorishness and abrupt treatment of political friends and foes alike in Washington left him with few other defenders. One of the cardinal rules of life in the capital city is that he who fails to build goodwill in good times will have none in reserve to support him in times of trouble, and that rule applied in spades to Sununu.

On top of all this, Bush—and the country at large—experienced a scare in early May when the president suffered acute fatigue and shortness of breath while jogging at Camp David, the presidential retreat in the mountains of western Maryland. His doctor sent him off to the Bethesda Naval Hospital after detecting an irregular heartbeat in the sixty-six-year-old chief executive. At Bethesda, doctors found no heart damage but put him on drugs to slow his heartbeat—even as that of the collective nation quickened as the public considered the possible consequences: the ascendancy of Vice President Dan Quayle to the presidency.

That prospect had hung over the country ever since Quayle took his oath of office in January 1989. His own two years in the vice presidency had done little to assuage the concerns about his qualifications that had greeted his surprise choice by Bush to be his running mate on the 1988 Republican national ticket.

Quayle had, in fact, become America's national joke—the favorite butt of gags on the late-night television talk shows and the subject of endless ridicule not only from Democrats but among many members of his own party as well. His penchant for malapropisms, coupled with the look and recreational preferences of the young rich-kid stereotype, made him hard to take seriously by those who did not share his strong conservative views and almost worshipful attitude toward the man who had put him in constitutional line for the presidency.

Polls taken days after the president was stricken with what now was diagnosed as Graves' disease, a thyroid condition treatable with medication, were not reassuring about Quayle's ability to instill confidence in the public in a succession crisis. *Time* magazine found that 67 percent of those surveyed said they would not consider voting for Quayle for president in 1996, to only 19 percent who said they would. A *Washington Post*/ABC News poll found that 57 percent said they believed him not qualified to take over the presidency, and 54 percent said Bush should choose a different running mate for 1992.

Overshadowed by the president's illness and the speculation about Quayle were some modest signs of economic improvement at last. The nation's unemployment rate had dropped slightly in April, from 6.8 percent to 6.6, leading Boskin to declare the figures "good news" but cautioning at the same time that "you always want to see it confirmed over a span of time, not just for one month, particularly where there are some questions about the quality of the data over the past several months." The caution was well placed, in light of the fact that the economy lost 124,000 payroll jobs in the same month.

Economic indicators continued to improve slightly by June, leading Federal Reserve Board chairman Greenspan to declare that the economy appeared to have hit bottom in the second quarter just ending. But he hedged on how soon he thought the economy would start expanding.

On another front, conservatives took heart from Bush's negative response to passage again by the Democratic-controlled House of a revised civil rights bill aimed at discrimination in the workplace. Once again the president denounced it as a "quota bill" although this version, too, explicitly said quotas would be illegal. With his special elegance for language, he told a West Point commencement audience: "You can't put a sign on a pig and call it a horse."

Bush also regained some favor with his party's right wing when the Supreme Court's first and only black member, Associate Justice Thurgood Marshall, the eighty-two-year-old veteran of the nation's greatest civil rights battles, announced his retirement after twenty-four years on the bench. Bush quickly nominated another black jurist, forty-three-year-old Clarence Thomas of the U.S. Court of Appeals for the District of Columbia, to fill the vacancy. Thomas was regarded as one of the most conservative judges in the federal judiciary but not among the most scholarly. The move was seen widely as a further effort to move the Court rightward in keeping with a development conspicuously advanced by the appointments of Ronald Reagan.

The composition of the Court was of critical interest to all those on both sides of the running debate over national policy toward abortion. Opponents looked upon Thomas as insurance that the Court would overturn the landmark *Roe* v. *Wade* decision that had established the legality of abortion. Abortion rights activists saw Thomas's appointment as the likely death knell of that decision, and both sides threw themselves into the fight over his Senate confirmation.

Bush added fuel to the debate by insisting in introducing Thomas as his choice that he had "kept my word to the American people and to the Senate by picking the best man for the job on the merits," not on the fact that he was black. Critics scoffed at the notion that there was no better choice available and that race had nothing to do with the nomination. The American Bar Association gave Thomas a cool rating of "qualified" with not one member of the review committee rating him "well qualified." Bush also insisted he had never asked Thomas how he stood on *Roe* v. *Wade,* and Thomas in his confirmation hearings astonished his Senate interrogators by insisting that in all his years in law school and on the bench he had never discussed the historic and highly controversial decision with anyone!

A measure of Thomas's standing within the largely liberal black political community was the fact that most leading black organizations came out in opposition to his nomination or remained neutral. In the end, however, it was opposition from another major voting block—the women of America— that most indelibly marked the confirmation hearings of Thomas.

As the Senate Judiciary Committee was about to send the nomination to the full Senate without a recommendation on confirmation, a former aide to Thomas, Anita Hill, a tenured law professor at the University of Oklahoma, came forward and accused him of sexual harassment when she had worked for him at the Department of Education and later at the Equal Employment Opportunity Commission, from 1981 to 1983. Over one dramatic, widely viewed television weekend of Senate committee hearings, all hell broke loose in Washington.

Hill, who is black, faced extensive and at times abusive interrogation from the Judiciary Committee panel of eight white males who also heard flat denials from Thomas and his allegation that he himself was being victimized by the committee because of his race. Defenders of both Hill and Thomas testified, often emotionally, as character witnesses, and in the end Thomas was confirmed by a fifty-two to forty-eight vote, the closest confirmation of a Supreme Court justice in this century.

Women voters who supported abortion rights, already hostile to Bush, watched the proceeding with increasing bitterness toward the Judiciary Committee, Thomas and the man who had nominated him as the "best-qualified" person to fill the shoes of the almost deified Thurgood Marshall. *Roe* v. *Wade* certainly appeared to be down the drain. It was, abortion rights defenders feared, only a matter of time now when the challenge to it would come before this conservatively reinforced Supreme Court.

This intensifying concern, and deep resentment at the spectacle of the all-male Judiciary Committee in the virtually all-male (ninety-eight out of 100) Senate club treating Anita Hill as if she were a guilty party, had political ramifications beyond the Supreme Court or any of its rulings. Women's political groups rallied to start correcting the gender imbalance in Congress, fielding female candidates in record numbers for the House and Senate. Of 106 women who eventually ran for House seats in 1992, forty-eight won, as did six of eleven who had captured their party's Senate nominations in what was widely called "The Year of the Woman."

As the Clarence Thomas matter was developing over the summer, the bubble had burst on the brief period of economic optimism. The Labor Department's monthly reports on unemployment out in June and July found the figure had gone up again to 6.9 percent for May and then 7 percent for June, the highest of the Bush presidency. Democrats in Congress called on the president to extend the eligibility period for unemployment compensation beyond the twenty-six weeks then provided. Both Houses quickly passed enabling legislation over Republican opposition and sent it to the White House.

But while the Democrats watched the jobless figure, White House economists were looking elsewhere for signs of recovery. When the Commerce Department reported a modest 0.4 percent rise in the gross national product for the second quarter, Boskin insisted that the figure "further indicates that the recession appears to have ended in the spring and a recovery has begun."

Bush, recognizing the political impact of the jobless benefits extension, signed the legislation but then declined to make a fiscal emergency declaration required to release the funds. He had signed the bill, he explained, because doing so "at least demonstrates that I am concerned" about the high unemployment, but then added "I won't bust the budget" by spending the $5.8 billion involved. He again called for a capital gains tax cut, decried by the Democrats as another windfall for the rich, as the best way to "create jobs almost instantly." (Later in the session, Congress passed another jobless benefits bill requiring the spending of the necessary money, and Bush vetoed it. The Democratic Senate's bid to override the veto failed by two votes.)

It was now late August. The last of the Desert Storm victory parades was over and the bloom of that great Bush military success was fading. The president was being obliged to fight his battles on the domestic front that had not been nearly so hospitable to him. In a way, one Bush insider said later, "Desert Storm set a new standard of performance for Bush, and had a perverse effect. If he could do that, he could fix other problems if he applied himself."

On the foreign policy front, Bush watched in a detached fashion as the Communist bloc continued to crumble, culminating in a failed coup of party hard-liners to topple his old friend Gorbachev, the rise of Boris Yeltsin, president of the Russian Republic, and Gorbachev's resignation from the Soviet Communist Party, effectively ending its power after seventy-four years.

Within days, the Soviet Congress of People's Deputies, prodded by Gorbachev with Yeltsin in support, voted to cede major powers to the various republics. Bush, pressed at home to recognize the independence of the Baltic republics of Lithuania, Estonia and Latvia, did so only four days before the new Soviet provisional government under Gorbachev recognized them as independent states.

Bush's reaction to the collapse of Soviet Communism, and to the coup that attempted to oust Gorbachev, was remarkably cautious and even timid at first. His first impulse at the time of the attempted coup was to make the best of it. He limited himself to describing the move against Gorbachev as "disturbing" and "extra-constitutional," and said his "gut instinct" about the most visible coup leader, Soviet Vice President Gennady Yanayev, was that "he has a certain commitment to reform." Boris Yeltsin had to prod him into being more straightforwardly critical of the brief, renegade regime.

For all the turmoil in the Soviet Union and the nagging recession at home, Bush declined to be shaken from his routine. He continued to get away whenever possible to his summer home in Kennebunkport, where he played tennis and golf and sailed his favorite cigarette boat. Some political aides were concerned at the image projected by the nation's chief executive commenting on foreign and domestic matters of great moment from his golf cart, but Bush was not going to be denied his intensive recreational habits by such things.

At the insistence of his political advisers, he reluctantly agreed to a meeting with them at Camp David in August 1991 to discuss the outlook for his reelection campaign in 1992. Had Lee Atwater still been around, the political types were certain, the Bush reelection campaign would have been in shape long since. But Atwater's death in March after his long, debilitating illness left no one who was quite so persuasive with Bush on matters of political mechanics.

"We nagged him, and nagged and nagged, a whole bunch of us," Jim Lake, his eventual campaign communications director, said later. " 'When are you going to get started? When are you going to get started?' But he wouldn't budge." The Camp David meeting, Lake said, "was his way of throwing a bone to the guys who were nagging at him."

The meeting, Lake and others reported afterward, turned out to be more a social event than anything else, just to keep the politicos happy. With the presidential election year now only about five months off, they needed to start raising money and making plans for Bush's reelection, and they pressed him to start talking about what he intended to do to right the economy. "It was clear he didn't get it that day," Lake recalled. "He couldn't quite comprehend the urgency." He clearly wanted to put all that political stuff off for as long as he could, and focus on governing— and preferably in the foreign policy realm. He finally agreed to a start-up on fund-raising, but little else.

"His view was," said one of those at the meeting, "you govern. You shouldn't be whoring around doing something as sleazy as politics. But at the time he was riding high and didn't expect to have [a] primary [challenge]."

"George Bush," Lake said, "believes that the president of the United States, whoever he is, must be the leader of the free world; that only the United States and its leader has the moral authority, the economic base and the respect and admiration of enough of the world to really make a difference. And that is really where the president can really make a difference, and that's where it really counts—if our children don't have to fight wars, we don't have to spend our treasure, and if we're not constantly shedding blood someplace.

"I have no doubt," Lake said, "that he wanted to put off the campaign because he wanted to govern. Nothing happened in August— or in September or October or November, until December—because he really felt he wanted to be the president, and to govern. This politics stuff, that's not really what's important. Governing is important."

By the same token, Lake said, Bush was convinced, "coming from that generation of presidents," that his success in the Gulf War and other aspects of foreign policy would insulate him from serious opposition for a second term. "If you go off and end up with the kind of approval ratings he did out of an extraordinarily successful Mideast engagement, there's no possible way for any challenger to make any marks."

Others mentioned at the Camp David meeting, Mary Matalin re- called, that there was going to have to be a domestic agenda for the reelection campaign and that the president could not simply rely on his first-term foreign policy accomplishments. At the same time, she said, there was confidence that "if we could point to all the foreign policy accomplishments, we could not only accentuate the positives but focus on leadership" as an overriding issue to which the voters would respond.

Campaign chairman Bob Teeter told Bush around this time, Lake said, that because of the economy his reelection was not a sure thing, ''and that the president ought to go out and talk about the economy before the campaign began, and [present] a plan for the future on the economy.''

Teeter knew, and Darman shared the view, that there was a new aspect to the downturn, and that was business ''downsizing.'' Large numbers of white-collar workers were losing their jobs and, unlike blue-collar workers who were laid off in slack periods and hired back on when things got better, they were not going to get their jobs back. They were workers who were highly leveraged with house mortgages and kids in college or college loans still to pay off. Such factors, Teeter said later, generated ''tremendous apprehension about the future'' among them, many of whom were Republicans or Reagan Democrats, the blue-collar and middle-income suburban white voters lured away from their traditional party by the Great Communicator and retained by Bush in 1988.

Bush recognized, and said in many conversations with aides, that the economy was not coming back, but he didn't want any massive remedial program that would worsen the deficit morass. And internally Sununu and Darman were arguing that the best way to deal with the economy was to do nothing, because it was going to improve. The president's annual State of the Union message in January, they insisted, would be time enough to lay out what his economic plans were.

That view coincided with Bush's own preference to keep politics, and any aggressive domestic action, on the back burner in favor of playing on the grander foreign policy field. Many political insiders, frustrated by Bush's failure first to adequately explain his rationale for breaking the no-new-taxes pledge and then to talk about the slipping economy, feared trouble ahead. But administration economists kept insisting things were getting better. A rise of 2.4 percent in the gross national product in the third quarter, the Commerce Department subsequently reported in late October, indicated recovery, they said. ''Certainly the first few months of the recovery were stronger than the last couple of months,'' Boskin said, ''but the recovery is continuing.''

The campaign political group did meet regularly through the fall— Sununu, Teeter, Charlie Black, Craig Fuller [Bush's chief of staff as vice president], Bill Kristol and others—and the subject repeatedly came up about the need for the president to send an economic package to Congress before the State of the Union speech. But there was no agreement on what it ought to contain, or whether it made sense to send something up that would be slapped down by the Democrats. The so-called fairness issue haunted Bush political aides, knowing that any legislation approved by the Democrats was likely to contain higher taxes on the wealthy, which Bush was just as likely to veto.

"The problem was," one in attendance at those meetings said later: " 'What can we get passed?' " If the Democrats did tack on a "millionaires' surtax," this insider, a political adviser, recalled arguing, "I said, 'Screw it. If they put the thing on it, sign it.' Hell, it was political. I don't know about the economic side, but that wasn't my role. Nobody would disagree with the political urgency of doing something, but the debate would be, 'Well, maybe it's worse to send something up there that they won't pass, or they give us something we had to veto.' "

Among those pushing hardest in or out of the official Bush circle for an economic growth package were the old Reagan loyalists—Kristol, Bill Bennett, Jack Kemp, House Minority Whip Newt Gingrich and White House aide Jim Pinkerton—who met regularly in what one called "a floating crap game" to try to get the president to embrace their recommendations. There were discussions about having Bush keep Congress in session to act on a growth package, Kristol recalled, "so at least we could say, 'We're trying to fix it, but the Democrats won't let us' . . . but the bottom line was, it never happened. . . . Once the budget deal kicked in, that became the most effective argument internally against those economic growth measures. The budget deal ended up tying our own hands. Darman's response was that it also tied the hands of the Democratic Congress. They couldn't push through a lot of spending."

Kristol recalled later speaking at an annual meeting of Michigan Republicans at Mackinac Island at which he warned that a clear majority of Americans "think the country is on the wrong track. We Republicans have got to be on the right side of the wrong track." But spokesmen for the Bush campaign at the same meeting, he said, gave assurances that everything was proceeding satisfactorily.

On the political front in what the politicians called this off-off-year of 1991, there wasn't much action to occupy those on the Republican side. The only event of some passing interest was a special Senate election in Pennsylvania for a vacant Republican seat that seemed secure for the party. But by the time that election was over, it would send political reverberations reaching far beyond the borders of the Keystone State.

CHAPTER 4

WARNING ROCKET

When a small plane collided with a helicopter over Philadelphia in April of 1991, sending Senator H. John Heinz III of Pennsylvania to his death, the crash had major, unforeseen ramifications for the presidential politics of 1992. The immediate conventional wisdom was that his replacement in the Senate surely would be another Republican, Attorney General Dick Thornburgh. He had served as governor of the state from 1979 through 1986 and had left office with high approval ratings based on his success in reducing the state payroll and cutting taxes. Equally important, it was widely thought, he would have the blessing of his then exceedingly popular boss, the president of the United States, and Thornburgh's election would be seen in part as a confirmation of Bush's popularity as his own reelection campaign approached.

To be sure, the Democratic governor, Robert P. Casey, would choose an interim successor to Heinz to serve for six months or so until a special election could be held in November. But Democrats had not elected a senator from Pennsylvania since Joe Clark in 1962 and there was no obvious candidate with either statewide name recognition or political base. Casey seemed to confirm this speculation by casting around for a candidate, discussing the appointment with various elected officials and offering it to, among others, former Mayor William Green of Philadelphia and Lee A. Iacocca, the chairman of the Chrysler Corporation and a native of Allentown, Pennsylvania, both of whom turned him down. No one, it seemed, wanted the questionable honor of a Senate seat when the prospect was an uphill campaign against an opponent as formidable as Dick Thornburgh.

As a result, Governor Casey was obliged to turn to an old friend and political ally, Harris L. Wofford, the sixty-five-year-old secretary of labor and industry in Casey's cabinet and a man who had never run for anything since losing an election in junior high school.

Unsurprisingly, there was obvious hubris among the Republicans when Wofford was chosen. Ron Kaufman, the deputy director of the White House political office, told Paul West of *The Baltimore Sun* that the appointment "makes our job a ton easier now." The selection of Wofford, he added, "makes no sense politically. He's out of the political loop. He's not well known. He's from the east"—meaning the Philadelphia area rather than the Pittsburgh area, a supposed burden because the state's other senator, Republican Arlen Specter, was also a Philadelphian.

Thornburgh himself, presiding at the Justice Department, quickly signaled his intention to run, but also to delay as long as possible making an official entry into the campaign. There was no reason to allow some nobody the benefit of a long campaign in which to build his name recognition. Thornburgh would continue as attorney general through the late spring and most of the summer, at which point the Republican state central committee could be convened to ratify his nomination.

Thornburgh's optimism seemed justified. Wofford had been standing in the background shadows of the Democratic Party for thirty years, since the 1960 campaign of John F. Kennedy. Then, Wofford won his fifteen minutes of attention as the adviser who had urged JFK to make a supportive telephone call to Coretta Scott King when Martin Luther King, Jr., was arrested and jailed in Georgia. The gesture was credited with evoking a heavier and more monolithic turnout among black voters than expected.

Wofford had served as an assistant for civil rights to President Kennedy and as associate director of the Peace Corps. He left the federal government in 1966 to be president of the State University of New York College at Old Westbury and then later served as president of Bryn Mawr College for eight years. He practiced law in Philadelphia before returning to active politics as Democratic Party state chairman when Casey, with whom he had practiced in Washington during the 1950s, became the nominee for governor in 1986. When Casey went to Harrisburg, Wofford went along as secretary of labor and industry.

He was considered intelligent and personable, a man with a wide range of intellectual interests and experience but not the kind of person who would make a strong candidate himself. Perhaps because of his academic experience as a law professor as well as administrator, he was always being described as "tweedy," although corduroys were more his style. And his background and personality raised obvious questions about his suitability for the stump in a state with as much devotion to red-meat politics as Pennsylvania. He was, the consensus went, a 1960s liberal running in an era in which liberalism was very much out of fashion.

Thornburgh's history in politics was much more conventional. He had been a federal prosecutor in Pittsburgh, then had gone to Washington during the Gerald Ford administration to be assistant attorney general in charge of the Criminal Division of the Justice Department. Using that appointment as a springboard, he had returned to Pennsylvania to win the governorship in 1978 as a conventionally moderate Eastern Republican. Because he was opposed by a conservative Democrat, Peter Flaherty, he won a majority of the black vote and far more labor support than any Republican in the state except Specter had enjoyed.

Three months into his first term in Harrisburg, Thornburgh was confronted with the dangerous accident at the nuclear power plant at Three Mile Island, a crisis he handled with reassuring calm and competence. It won him widespread approbation from his constituents and, in the mysterious way American politics works, immediately placed him on the lists of those in the coming generation of Republicans with national potential. And that speculation was reinforced when, after the two terms the state constitution allowed a Pennsylvania governor, he returned to Washington to become attorney general as the replacement for the discredited Edwin Meese. Thornburgh was charged by then President Reagan with restoring the reputation of the Justice Department for competence and probity.

But Thornburgh's political persona had undergone some changes along the way. Although he originally was counted as a moderate Republican, he became increasingly conservative as a defender of Reagan and his economic and social policies in the early 1980s. He put his days as a supporter of the American Civil Liberties Union and as a member of Planned Parenthood behind him as he adopted strong positions against crime and against abortion rights. As attorney general he seemed to go out of his way to find conservative positions to espouse and to pick fights with the press that had always given him high marks. The prevalent view in Washington, one shared by some of his longtime political allies, was that Thornburgh was positioning himself for a place on some future Republican national ticket; he understood that it was essential to rid himself of any lingering identification as a linear descendant of that most infamous—in the eyes of the Reaganites—of Eastern Republicans, the late Nelson A. Rockefeller.

Even as governor, Thornburgh's move to the right had cost him something politically. Running for a second term in 1982, he was the odds-on favorite but defeated a throwaway Democratic opponent, an obscure congressman named Allen Ertel, by less than two percentage points, catching political professionals in both parties by surprise. Running against Thornburgh nine years later, Wofford recalled how Thornburgh had "squeaked through" in 1982, and the Democrat took some encouragement from that bit of history.

"I awakened the next morning after the election," Wofford said later, "and realized that if Allen Ertel, a rather colorless candidate with no money, had had some money, and if we all hadn't given up on him, he would have beaten Thornburgh then. It was that Thornburgh wasn't that well liked in the state. He had made a lot of enemies with labor, with blacks, with a whole range of people."

By the time Thornburgh left after that second term, however, his approval ratings had climbed above 70 percent on the strength of his success in reducing taxes and the state payroll, and leaving a substantial surplus in the state treasury. But Wofford remembered the Ertel race and drew comfort from what it suggested about Thornburgh's hold on the Pennsylvania electorate. Moreover, he convinced himself, as long-shot neophyte candidates are inclined to do in such circumstances, that his four and a half years as secretary of labor and industry had given him "more of a network than most people recognized" that would be helpful in a campaign. And, anyway, he conceded, he was "congenitally optimistic."

That optimism was quickly tested. Wofford's campaign took a benchmark poll and found him running 47 percent behind Thornburgh—a finding so discouraging that Wofford and his advisers could only hope that there would be no early public poll with similar figures. That hope dissolved within two weeks when a poll commissioned by a Pittsburgh newspaper found essentially the same gap—in this case, 44 points. But another survey by Michael Donilon, a Washington poll-taker, in July found some evidence that Wofford was not a totally hopeless case. Beyond that, not incidentally, it produced what may have been the first evidence that the electorate of 1991 and 1992 might be a different dish of tea.

The survey used a standard technique to measure potential. First it matched Thornburgh and Wofford and found that almost no one knew the first thing about this Democratic state cabinet official who had been appointed to the Senate two months earlier. Only 12 percent of the respondents had a "favorable" impression of Wofford and only 6 percent an "unfavorable" impression. Thornburgh's figures, by contrast, were 60 percent and 16 percent. Unsurprisingly, the matchup showed Thornburgh with 65 percent, Wofford with 21.

Then the poll-takers offered descriptions of the two candidates designed to elicit a more informed response. With any responsible professional, the goal in using this technique is to present the two candidates in language fair to both in terms of their assets as candidates. Some pollsters, however, have been known to tailor the descriptions to get the "right" answers to encourage a potential candidate.

In this case, Wofford was described this way:

"Harris Wofford says the rich get too many breaks in America, while working families keep falling farther behind. That's why Wofford supports a plan that would cut taxes on the average middle income family by more than six hundred dollars and would raise taxes on rich people who make over one hundred and thirty thousand dollars a year. Wofford also supports creating a national health insurance system because he says that's the only way that every working family will get affordable and available health care. Wofford has also introduced a bill that will make it easier for middle income families to get college loans for their children."

Republican Thornburgh was described this way:

"Dick Thornburgh says we need to fight for traditional American values again in this country. That's why, as governor, he cut taxes, removed thousands of people from the welfare rolls and left the state a two hundred million dollar budget surplus. And as attorney general he has been fighting alongside George Bush to get the nation's toughest crime law—one that will provide the death penalty for drug kingpins. Thornburgh has also been leading the fight against racial quotas—opposing the 1991 Civil Rights bill because he says it is a racial quota bill that forces employers to hire unqualified people based on the color of their skin."

Asked now how they would vote, the poll respondents turned things almost upside down: Wofford 45 percent, Thornburgh 42.

In itself, a survey such as this one is not enough to tell a campaign manager how his candidate is likely to fare. There are far too many imponderables—the way the two candidates perform, the issues that develop during the campaign, gaffes by one candidate or another and simply the visceral responses voters have to the cut of a candidate's jib. But this data did suggest to Wofford's managers that voters were far more focused on their own economic concerns than on social issues; that Thornburgh's successes as governor were not necessarily a free ticket to the Senate, and that his position as a close ally of President Bush was not necessarily a compelling asset, even though the same survey gave Bush an approval rating of 69 percent.

These managers were a pair of Southern boys named James Carville and Paul Begala, who soon would gain as much celebrity status as politics gives to noncandidates, by virtue of what they would do in Pennsylvania and shortly afterward on the national campaign scene. Carville, from Louisiana Cajun country, was a fast-talking, colorful, irreverent political pro with a knack for sighting and exploiting opponents' vulnerabilities and his own clients' strengths. He recruited Begala, his younger, feisty sidekick, from a Texas college campus and the two had run winning campaigns around the country, including those of Governor Casey and Democratic Senator Frank Lautenberg of New Jersey.

The poll findings buoyed Carville. "At that point," Carville said, "I think we knew then we had a live wire."

That information in the Democrats' hands also suggested that the

Republican candidate might be making serious strategic errors in behaving as a regal figure from Washington, delaying his decision on when he wanted the coronation to take place, and in relying on his connections to the president. Despite the lingering popularity Bush enjoyed from the war in the Persian Gulf, the poll respondents said, by 59 to 26 percent, that the country was "off on the wrong track" rather than "headed in the right direction." Political professionals hold that a "wrong track" number over 50 percent is always cause for concern for incumbents, and one close to 60 percent is an alarm bell.

Thornburgh added to the perception of himself as a latter-day Cincinnatus returning to his home as its savior. He stalled through the summer on making his candidacy official and continued to serve as the nation's chief law enforcement officer, brushing off editorialists' complaints against an attorney general raising money for a Senate campaign while still holding office. "His behavior and he himself hammered the nail in [the fact] that he was a high-powered Washington insider," Wofford recalled long afterward.

Thornburgh then handed Wofford an irresistible opening. In his August speech officially declaring his candidacy, he made a point of saying how he had "walked the corridors of power" in Washington. Somebody faxed the speech to Carville and Begala, and when Begala started reading it, Carville said later, "he said, 'I can't believe it! Look at what this guy's saying!' And he read it out [loud]. I said, 'Oh, no! He didn't say that!' Just about that time we were having this conversation about running against Washington. So immediately I tracked [Wofford] down."

"James got me on the radio phone two minutes after Thornburgh had said it," Wofford said. "He said, 'I think, Senator, you should go right out in front of City Hall [in Philadelphia] and give them your pitch that you want to turn Washington inside out, turn out the insiders.' " Wofford followed Carville's advice and, as he put it, "we got right in all the original stories . . . saying it's the people in the corridors of power who let us down. Let's turn them out."

The campaign did not turn around magically on the strength of that one Thornburgh gaffe and Wofford's quick exploitation of it. That may happen in the movies, but not in the real-world politics of a Senate campaign to which voters are not paying very close attention until the final weeks, if then. But it did define the structure of the campaign. On the one side, there was Thornburgh using his position, résumé and connections in high places as his prime credentials while attacking Wofford on his connections to Governor Casey, whose own fiscal problems had driven his approval rating down below 30 percent. On the other, there was Wofford defining Thornburgh as part of the establishment responsible for things being on the wrong track, and insisting the real issues were the availability of jobs, health insurance and educational opportunity.

Wofford focused narrowly on the middle class. On education, he would tell his audiences that the rich go to Princeton, the poor get Pell federal grants and the middle class gets nothing. On health care, the message was that the poor get Medicaid, the rich go to the Mayo Clinic and the middle class gets squeezed. One particularly memorable commercial on health insurance showed Wofford arguing: "If criminals have the right to a lawyer, I think working Americans should have the right to a doctor. That's why I'm fighting for national health insurance in the Senate."

Wofford had another serious problem to overcome—a lack of money such as any candidate suffers when he or she is forty points behind and portrayed in the press as a certain loser. Campaign manager Begala knew that the only solution lay in showing some movement that would counter that image, and that the only way to do that in this case was to throw the long bomb. Thus, around Labor Day, he decided to invest everything the campaign had on hand—about $250,000, a modest war chest in a state as large as Pennsylvania—in television advertising. "We spent every penny of it," he recalled. "We started moving right away"—and, not incidentally, attracting enough money to stay on the air for the rest of the campaign. "We never went dark after that," he said.

But the important thing about the signs of life in the Wofford campaign was that they gave Carville and Begala an argument to take to the Democratic Senatorial Campaign Committee in Washington in an appeal for its maximum funding, $980,000. Wofford's agents and some of his Senate allies began an intense campaign to get the money from the DSCC, by no means a certainty because the committee's chairman, Senator Charles H. Robb of Virginia, was opposed. The committee, Robb pointed out, had disbursed only $6 million to all Democratic Senate candidates in the 1990 election and now a single candidate in a special race was asking for one sixth as much just for himself. How could Robb explain that to those senators running in 1992 and in need of help from the DSCC?

Senate Majority Leader George Mitchell of Maine was sympathetic to Wofford but unwilling to pressure Robb. He had held the same job himself at one time, he said, and he wasn't about to "emasculate" the current chairman. There was, however, precedent for getting the committee to vote on the request rather than simply leaving the decision to the chairman, and the Wofford campaign pressed even harder for such a vote. "I probably threatened to douse myself in kerosene," consultant Carville recalled.

Begala was convinced the case was valid. "From June on," he said, "I was absolutely certain we could win the race. . . . We thought if the damned party doesn't stand with us now when we have a chance to change the whole dynamics of the political landscape, then fuck it, we don't deserve to have a party."

When the committee met to see the polling data and the commercials and hear the campaign plans, the key man proved to be Senator Lloyd Bentsen of Texas, the 1988 vice presidential nominee and one of the party's most influential elder statesmen. Making the case like a lawyer in court, Bentsen conceded that although the committee had "a fiduciary obligation" to other senators who would be running in 1992, "this is an investment we ought to make."

Bentsen had no sooner finished than Senator Tom Daschle of South Dakota, one of the Democrats in the 1992 group, took the floor. "I'm running in 1992," he told his colleagues, "and the best thing you can do to help me win in South Dakota is to help this man win in Pennsylvania because . . . right now there's a guy with some money thinking about running against me. But if Wofford wins, he goes away, and that will be happening all across the country."

The committee voted to give Wofford half the money as quickly as possible and deliver the rest later if the campaign continued to show promise. "The most unheralded event of the political season was when the DSCC went out and borrowed half a million dollars and gave it to Wofford," Carville said. From that point on, the trend line for Wofford rose steadily for the rest of the campaign, as Thornburgh's sank.

To the surprise of most, including Carville and Begala, Wofford proved to be a fast learner as a candidate and particularly adept at making thirty-second television commercials. Two leading Washington consultants, Robert Shrum and David Doak, portrayed him not first in terms of his connections to JFK or the Peace Corps, but instead as someone fighting on issues. The usual biographical commercials were delayed until the final days of the campaign at a time Thornburgh, his lead melting away, was floundering for a footing. Wofford, Carville recalled, "was a great candidate to camera."

Wofford also proved to be a candidate willing to accept the discipline of sticking to the central message of his candidacy despite a confessed tendency "to get off on one of my other long-term interests" and end up talking to a reporter from *The Washington Post* about Gandhi rather than health care. "James really helped me understand how you can only get through on a few things in a mass campaign and if you care about winning, you can only focus on those things," Wofford said. It was a lesson that Carville soon would bring to the 1992 presidential campaign with emphatic results—and media attention.

Wofford's candidacy seemed to pick up steam after a debate in mid-October in which he was widely judged as the winner. "I guess I really sensed a surge of support around the state," he recalled. But Wofford also knew that the response of campaign audiences can be deceiving. He had been in that John Kennedy campaign in 1960, after all, when huge crowds persuaded the Democrats and much of the press that Kennedy was on the way to a landslide but, in fact, won by a whisker.

So there was reason for caution, even if—as it appeared—Thornburgh's campaign was being compromised by one miscalculation after another. After weeks of attacking Wofford's demand for national health insurance, for example, the Republican candidate suddenly showed up to be photographed visiting patients in a hospital and offering his own plan for health care. It was a clear admission that the relentless Wofford focus on the economic issues and the middle class was paying a political dividend.

Wofford broke "the discipline of the message" only once, late in the campaign, when he suddenly made a public connection between his race and the presidential campaign to follow in the next twelve months. The campaign strategy had been to avoid mentioning the president at all. "Bush was not an issue," Carville said. "We never said Bush because

Bush was still popular.'' But, entering a labor rally in Washington, Pennsylvania, nine days before the election, Wofford was stopped by a man who told him: ''Senator, your election is going to mark the first day of the end of the Bush administration.''

Wofford liked the sound of it. ''I think I knew in my head, I'd been told a thousand times that Bush is very, very popular and you must never make this a referendum on Bush,'' he recalled, but when he began his speech to the union crowd he repeated what the man had told him, adding: ''Let me tell you, we can make that [come] true.'' The crowd loved it, and the press seized on the fresh story—Wofford making the election a referendum on Bush.

Back at campaign headquarters, Carville said, ''we went berserk.'' Wofford was subjected to a barrage of advice—from his campaign consultants, his sons, his staff, political allies like Representative John Murtha.

''All of them told me you can't ever say anything like that again,'' Wofford said—which, he added, gave him even more pleasure when he could say election night that his victory was indeed the end of the Bush administration. He defeated Thornburgh with 55 percent of the vote, a comfortable margin by any reckoning. ''The way it turned out, it was very smart,'' Carville said. ''[But] we were so hot with the health care thing and anti-Washington stuff we didn't want to step on our own story.''

After the election, the view grew that Wofford had won it largely by emphasizing the health care issue, and there is no question it played a major role in his success. Thornburgh played into that view with his belated attempt to build his own credentials on the health question, but it was clearly too late—and reinforced the notion that the Republican candidate was struggling for a way to neutralize the Democrat everyone had laughed away only six months earlier.

But the Wofford campaign was not just about health care by any means; the Democratic candidate never really offered a detailed plan of his own. The campaign was about the frustrations the voters felt at being so powerless in the face of the ineffectuality of the government in Washington. ''It was just about the middle class getting squeezed and government being unresponsive, and health care being illustrative to it,'' Carville said later.

Nor was it possible to sort out just how much of the triumph could be traced to the health care issue and how much to Thornburgh's failures as a candidate. "It's like when the crop comes, you say, 'How much is the rain and how much is the soil?' " said Carville, the Louisianian with a fondness for metaphor. "You can't have a crop without either one. We had fertile soil but Thornburgh gave us a good rain."

After the fact, at least, Begala could see a significant inference to be drawn from the campaign—that in this case "the mythology of the Dukakis lesson was wrong."

"The point is not to respond every time you're attacked," he said. "You know what Patton said—the purpose of war is not to die for your country, it's to make the other son of a bitch die for his country. The purpose of a campaign is not to respond to every attack, it's to make the other son of a bitch respond to your attacks. So that means finding the terrain that is more salient to your voters."

In Wofford's case, this meant ignoring almost all of the Republican attacks on social issues—gun control, pornography, abortion rights—to focus on the issues that the poll in July had identified. "We tried to make it all about the economy and all about Washington," Begala said. "You could tell that's where people's heads were." Again, the experience of the Wofford race on sticking to a winning message would have particular pertinence to what was about to follow on the national political scene, with George Bush seeking reelection.

The Republican response to the news from Pennsylvania was clouded by the conviction in party circles that Thornburgh had run such a wretched campaign. Charlie Black recalled seeing the results in terms of the argument the political people in the Bush camp were making to the White House. "It just reinforced what we were trying to say, that there was a great deal of unrest and disquiet out there and that we were on the wrong track politically because of the economy," he said later.

"It was important because, without the bad economic feeling and the unrest in the land, Wofford would have had no chance. Thornburgh still should have beat him, but the discontent among the voters aimed at Republicans gave Wofford the opening and Wofford went through it. Yeah, I saw some lessons in it but I didn't see a lesson that said, 'Oh, hell, this is the end of the world' or anything because Thornburgh still could have won if he'd done half the stuff he was advised to do."

The Republican strategists also questioned whether Pennsylvania was the kind of laboratory situation from which they could draw many conclusions. It was a state that was always closely contested and, more to the point, one they could afford to lose without any feeling that their base was in jeopardy. "We didn't take it lightly but we also didn't take it as directly analogous to the Bush political situation," said Black.

In the immediate aftermath of the election, Mary Matalin, then political director of the Republican National Committee, was blaming the outcome on the inadequacies of Thornburgh's campaign. But, she said later, "we knew it was bigger than Thornburgh not running a good race." Still, few if any Republican professionals were prepared to see the Wofford triumph as any genuine threat to a president who still had approval ratings in the 60 percent–plus area. "I don't remember anyone being cognizant of that, the harbinger of things to come," Matalin said.

But there were exceptions. Thomas Rath, a New Hampshire lawyer and Republican activist heavily involved in the Bush campaign for the presidential primary in his state, was clearly alarmed. "We have just seen the most enormous red flag in political history," he told *The Wall Street Journal*. "The 1992 presidential campaign has just turned from a cakewalk into a 12-month version of World Wide Wrestling."

The special election in Pennsylvania was not the only warning signal that the White House was receiving just then. Through the summer and fall, as the "wrong track" numbers inched up toward 70 percent, the president was coming under increasing criticism, and not only from Democrats, for not paying enough attention to business—especially domestic policy business. He always seemed to be playing golf or riding around in his cigarette boat at Kennebunkport when bad economic news surfaced. Or, if he wasn't there, he was off on another foreign trip, appearing on television with François Mitterand or John Major, talking about international affairs, rather than with Dan Rostenkowski or Bob Dole, doing business on the economy. Moreover, both Bush and his chief of staff, John Sununu, were showing signs of being rattled by the criticism.

The day before the special election—and also the day before Bush was to leave for Rome and The Hague for two international conferences—the Democratic National Committee pulled a political stunt that paid remarkable dividends. It unveiled a black T-shirt modeled on the ones rock music groups sell to fans to celebrate their world tours. The back carried the legend THE ANYWHERE BUT AMERICA TOUR and listed all the foreign ports of call the president had visited or was scheduled to visit. The message on the front read: GEORGE BUSH WENT TO ROME AND ALL I GOT WAS THIS LOUSY RECESSION.

The shirt was the brainchild of Dan Carol, the young director of research for the DNC, which had been coming up with similar gimmicks. Another was a "Hall of Shame" report purporting to list one hundred ethical lapses by Bush administration officials or Bush family members. It was compiled over the long months of trying to find a way to bring down to size a president with approval ratings that had reached unprecedented heights earlier the same year. "We wanted to do something to highlight all his trips abroad," Carol recalled. And after toying around with such ideas as organizing rallies in Rome, New York, or Rome, Georgia, to call attention to the president's neglect of the folks back home, the T-shirt became the weapon of choice. "What was his weak point and how could we exploit it?" said Carol.

The Democratic operative thought he was on the right track with the T-shirts when, before they were officially put on sale, he wore one to a barbecue restaurant in suburban Virginia called Red, Hot and Blue. The place had been partly owned by the late Lee Atwater when he was chairman of the Republican National Committee and was considered a gathering place for conservative yuppies. Several patrons, Carol said, stopped him to comment on the shirt and ask where he got it. He was sure he had a winner when California Representative Vic Fazio displayed one of the shirts on the floor of the House of Representatives and the story made the television network news programs.

But the man who sold the T-shirts for the Democrats was George Bush. He couldn't seem to let the gimmick go by unremarked, mentioning the "silly" shirts repeatedly over the next few weeks, beginning with his flight to Rome the morning after the election. Chatting with reporters aboard Air Force One en route to the NATO summit, the president was asked if he was "feeling the heat a little bit" because of the way the Democrats had been "pouring it on you for all this foreign travel."

"No, I see they are doing it, but I don't worry about that," Bush replied. "You know, I read the T-shirts and kind of the little gimmicks on the floor of the Congress. It's getting to be the silly season. . . . The only thing that worries me is being out of town when these people are doing crazy things.'' But a day or so later, with other international leaders standing at his side in Rome, he insisted his travel schedule was not going to be dictated by "people holding up a silly T-shirt."

Then, back home attending a Republican fund-raiser in St. Louis, he continued to display his preoccupation. "The liberals in Congress go and hold their press conferences, sell their funny little T-shirts and sabotage the initiatives that the American people want," he complained. "And I'm getting sick and tired of it."

Bush's inability to ignore the T-shirts was a business bonanza for Carol's office at the DNC, where interns were being pressed into service taking orders and dealing with suppliers. "This was like a Junior Achievement program," Carol recalled. In the end, the DNC sold some 15,000 shirts, first for $10 each and later for $15, and cleared $100,000 to be used in the campaign to prevent the reelection of George Bush.

But most intriguing about the episode of the T-shirts was evidence that the Democrats clearly had hit a nerve in the White House on the whole matter of Bush's travel abroad—and his consequent neglect of economic problems at home. On the night Harris Wofford defeated Dick Thornburgh, two things happened there.

Chief of staff Sununu, presiding over the weekly political meeting of White House and Republican National Committee staffs, provided them with facts and figures on presidential travel to refute the accusations—"Ron Brown's cheap shots," Sununu called them, referring to the Democratic national chairman—that the President was spending an inordinate amount of time abroad. That was to be the spin over the next few days.

But later that night when Mary Matalin was trying the spin on Ann Devroy, a White House reporter for *The Washington Post*, she learned that even while she was getting her marching orders, the White House was announcing that Bush's scheduled trip to Japan and the Far East had been postponed, ostensibly because the president didn't think it prudent to be out of the capital when Congress was winding down its session.

The confluence of events—Harris Wofford's triumph in Pennsylvania and a Bush White House obviously so shaken by the criticism of excessive travel abroad that a major overseas trip was being scrubbed— sent waves of hope through the Democratic Party. "You could see the country was moving Democratic,'' said Carville. ''You could just feel it underneath there.''

Others in the party may not have been as immediately optimistic. But they were buoyed by Wofford's self-effacing assessment of his own success: ''I was just lucky to be the messenger of a message that was there.'' That message, with significance for the presidential election just ahead, was clear: voters long accused of apathy were mad enough about unmet domestic needs and Washington's aloofness that they could be persuaded to take action at the ballot box.

For three years, even the notion that there might be any such message that could be used effectively against George Bush had seemed to be something no Democrat dared to accept. Now it was a notion that could not—and would not—be ignored.

CHAPTER 5

RUNNING FOR COVER

For the Democratic Party, the aftertaste of the 1988 presidential election was bitter and persistent. Losing an election is always disheartening under any circumstances but losing an election that may have been won—as Michael Dukakis may have won—was the foulest of political fates. At the very least, the Democrats were obliged to live with the divisions of their postmortems. Had Dukakis lost solely because of his own ineffectual campaign? Or was the loss the ultimate proof of a more fundamental reality—that conventional Democratic liberalism simply would not sell? Did anyone care about the future of a party that now had lost five out of the last six presidential elections?

Meanwhile, George Bush flourished in the White House, despite all the reservations about him on his own party's far right. He was not a politician held in awe by his rivals, as Ronald Reagan had been when he came to office in 1981, and he had little power to intimidate his opposition, even as demoralized as the Democrats were in 1989. But the unemployment rate was down to 4.9 percent, the lowest since 1973, and the press was gushing about the avuncular style of the new president who loved golf and horseshoes, cooked hamburgers, played with his grandchildren, held frequent press conferences and sometimes even jogged with reporters. His embarrassing defeat in the Senate's rejection of John Tower to be secretary of defense was offset by Democratic embarrassments of their own in 1989. The speaker of the House, Jim Wright, was forced out of Congress after an ethics investigation. Then the House majority leader, Tony Coelho, decided it would be prudent to follow suit after questions were raised about his business associations. They were succeeded by Thomas Foley as speaker and Richard Gephardt as majority leader, neither of whom offered a similar partisan edge.

Even before these troubles in Congress, the Democrats suffered through an unpleasant chapter in the choice of a new chairman of the Democratic National Committee. By any reckoning, Ronald H. Brown had credentials as good or better than any of his rivals for the chairmanship. But he had been associated with Senator Edward M. Kennedy, having served on his Senate and 1980 campaign staffs. Even worse, Brown had been the 1988 convention manager for Jesse Jackson. He was not just a liberal Washington insider but a black man, and Southern party leaders and others of a conservative bent resisted stubbornly. Then he began to enlist the support of the heaviest of the Democratic heavyweights and two of the winter book favorites for 1992, Senator Bill Bradley of New Jersey and Governor Mario Cuomo of New York. Brown was elected, but the contest had exposed an ugly fault line within the party.

All of this was fodder for those who had allied themselves with the Democratic Leadership Council, an organization that had been created in 1985 in response to the defeat suffered by the party behind another liberal, former Vice President Walter Mondale. The DLC originally was intended to be a direct counterweight to the Democratic National Committee, a place for Democrats to play on the national stage without being identified as "national Democrats"—a label that in the South and parts of the West meant "soft-headed liberals." The group originally had been denigrated as "a little white boys' club" because so few of its early members were either women or blacks. But by 1989 it had broadened its membership beyond such conservative Democrats as Senators Sam Nunn of Georgia and Charles Robb of Virginia to include more people like Gephardt and the youthful governor of Arkansas, Bill Clinton, who were considered determined moderates.

For the most devoutly liberal politicians like Cuomo and Jackson, the DLC was still a foreign body—Jackson derided the organization as "Democrats for the Leisure Class"—but at least some of the early stigma had been erased. And the DLC was solidifying its position as a permanent and respectable element of the Democratic Party, with serious studies of national problems and sometimes unconventional but interesting ideas about how to deal with them.

The first sign of political life for the Democrats in 1989 came in the elections of two governors that November, Jim Florio to succeed a popular Republican, Tom Kean, in New Jersey, and L. Douglas Wilder to succeed Gerald Baliles in Virginia, making him the first black to win a state governorship in an election since Reconstruction. But even these successes were somewhat tarnished by the fact that Florio and Wilder defeated Republican candidates, Representative James Courter in New Jersey and former state Attorney General Marshall Coleman in Virginia, whose campaigns were distinguished largely by their ineptitude.

In each case, the winning Democrats solidified their positions by taking early and strong stands for abortion rights in the wake of the Supreme Court's decision in the Missouri case that summer, which seemed to open the way to a full-scale attack in the near future on *Roe* v. *Wade*. When both Courter and Coleman tried to waffle on the issue, they paid the price of offending both sides and convincing no one. In Wilder's case in particular, it appeared that his aggressive action to control the agenda on the abortion rights question was responsible for causing enough defections among Republican women to provide his paper-thin margin of victory.

In any case, through much of 1989 domestic political maneuvering was obscured by events of far greater magnitude around the world. The transformation of the Soviet Union and Eastern Europe and the uprising at Tiananmen Square in China were clearly changes of far more interest to Americans than the tribulations of the defeated and dispirited Democratic Party. There were, nonetheless, signs of weaknesses in President Bush that might have given the Democrats reason to be encouraged about their future.

Bush appeared remarkably slow to grasp either the national excitement about the changes in Europe or the national anger directed at the Chinese government for its brutal repression of the demonstrators for democracy. At the very least, it seemed the president had a tin ear when it came to hearing his constituents. His willingness to kowtow to the Chinese, in particular, showed a national leader totally out of touch with the people he was leading.

But, as Ronald Reagan had done with the invasion of Grenada, Bush satisfied the most atavistic appetites of Americans with his invasion of Panama and seizure of Noriega to stand trial on drug charges. In January of 1990, with Bush's approval rating at 79 percent, if there was any ground for Democratic optimism about the prospects of defeating Bush in 1992, it was well disguised.

Even the Republican president's willingness to abandon his pledge of "no new taxes" later that spring was not seen as an undiluted benefit to the Democrats because, after all, many of them too had signed on to the tax package. And when Bush's approval rating slipped to 56 percent in mid-October, apparently in reaction to his broken promise on taxes, by this time he was involved in the confrontation with Saddam Hussein and ordering more troops into Saudi Arabia. It was hardly a propitious time for the Democrats to begin plotting their campaigns to unseat him.

There was, however, one bright spot for the Democrats in 1990. In the midterm elections, they captured the governorships of two of the largest and most critical states—Texas, where Ann Richards defeated Republican Clayton Williams, and Florida, where former Senator Lawton Chiles unseated Republican incumbent Bob Martinez. In both cases, though, close examination led to the conclusion that the Democratic success had as much to do with the weaknesses of the Republican candidates as with any change in national political directions. And, whatever their value as indicators of better things ahead, the glow of those successes was soon lost in the national preoccupation with the dramatic confrontation in the Persian Gulf, and the debate over whether Iraq should be attacked.

Ordinarily the potential candidates for 1992 would have begun to show themselves by now, first in the 1990 campaign itself, then immediately after the first of the year by "moving around"—showing themselves at party events, particularly in states with early primaries and caucuses, and by taking an increasingly prominent role on issues in Washington. Over the previous twenty years, the marathon campaign had become a staple for either party out of power, largely because of the way candidates get their money. Candidates without a national identification and following needed as much time as possible to build recognition worth a few points in a Gallup poll. That recognition in turn could be used as a credential to raise seed money to finance the kind of public activity that would drive those numbers up a little higher, and make it easier to raise more money.

Moreover, under the public financing system for presidential elections established in the 1974 federal election law, all contributions obtained during the year before the election year—in this case, 1991—were eligible for federal matching once a candidate qualified, by raising $5,000 or more in amounts of $250 or less in each of twenty states.

Since it was a rule of thumb that a candidate needed to raise $10 million or so to compete in the primaries, it was necessary to raise roughly half of that in the advance year. Not many candidates met that standard, and there were many examples of campaigns failing because they fell too far short and ran out of money too early in the primary season. That very thing had happened, for example, to Dick Gephardt in the contest for the Democratic nomination in 1988. So it was prudent to start as early as possible.

The long campaign served another purpose for the challengers and particularly those making their first entry into presidential politics. It gave them time to get the kinks out of their operations—and themselves—a few months before everyone was watching closely for gaffes. Those first-time candidates always seemed to underestimate the rigors of a presidential campaign and the hazards along the way and needed the time to get their sea legs. But when 1991 rolled around, President Bush had the country caught up in a war in the Persian Gulf and, the politicians reasoned quite sensibly, the last thing that would appeal to American voters would be the spectacle of partisan rivals trying to climb up his back. Once the fighting started in earnest in mid-January, there was a de facto moratorium on presidential politics that lasted for several months.

When the war ended as such an unqualified success in the eyes of most Americans, there seemed even less reason to believe the president could be challenged successfully. So the Democrats remained essentially cowed through the spring. There were, however, some stirrings on the fringes. Governor Wilder was testing the water, but few political professionals believed the country was ready for a black candidate. George McGovern also was talking about still another campaign, but the market for the 1972 nominee seemed even more limited.

Early in May the first announced candidate appeared. Former Senator Paul Tsongas of Massachusetts declared in his hometown of Lowell for the Democratic presidential nomination. But Tsongas seemed almost equally unlikely. In two terms in the House of Representatives and one in the Senate, Tsongas had won a reputation as a thoughtful and capable legislator. But he had been forced to retire in 1984 after his single senatorial term because he was suffering from cancer, an illness he now reported to have been cured. And his absence from the political scene had inhibited him in building the kind of political credentials prospective presidential candidates need. Finally, after Michael Dukakis, the demand for "another Greek from Massachusetts" was certainly limited.

There was no mystery about who ought to make up the Democratic field. There were at least three candidates from the 1988 campaign who might logically be expected to compete—Jesse Jackson, Senator Albert Gore, Jr., of Tennessee and House Majority Leader Gephardt. And there were five or six others who had signaled that they were interested in the presidency and were considered potentially serious players in the 1992 field: Bradley, Cuomo, Senate Majority Leader George Mitchell, Senator Sam Nunn of Georgia and perhaps Senator John D. (Jay) Rockefeller IV of West Virginia and Senator Lloyd Bentsen of Texas, the 1988 vice presidential nominee.

But most of them seemed to be telegraphing a preference to protect their political viability for 1996 rather than take the fall in 1992 against a candidate who seemed as unassailable as the George Bush of early 1991. They all had some other reason to offer. Gore was concerned about spending more time with his family in the aftermath of an accident in which his son was seriously injured. Bradley had experienced a close call in his own reelection campaign in New Jersey in 1990 and took it as a message to tend to business in the Senate for another term. Cuomo kept telling everyone that "I have no plans and no plans to make plans." But, in the pragmatic world of big-league politics, the rational inference was that the 1992 campaign looked like a loser.

There was some inspired speculation about several other Democrats—Clinton, Senator Tom Harkin of Iowa and Senator Bob Kerrey of Nebraska. But they were considered second-line candidates at best, and little apparent reason for party leaders to be bullish about their prospects for 1992. Ron Brown kept telling anyone who would listen that there eventually would be a strong field and that the president was more vulnerable than was generally realized. "I continue to believe," he said in March, "that the basic issues of the 1992 campaign are going to be bread-and-butter, domestic issues . . . and the president has no domestic policy whatsoever." But Brown's protestations were widely written off as the predictable and obligatory bravado of an out-of-power party chairman.

The first reason for any optimism came on May 7, 1991, when Rockefeller made a speech to a DLC meeting in Cleveland and then almost off-handedly told reporters who caught him backstage that he just might run after all. "The door is open," he said. "I'm looking."

The possibility of a Rockefeller candidacy was intriguing for several reasons. He was, in contrast to Tsongas or Wilder, a politician with some long-term capital to risk. At fifty-three, he could afford to wait for more auspicious circumstances, so the thought that he might not play it cozy like so many of his fellow Democrats obviously suggested he didn't consider Bush invulnerable. Beyond that, Rockefeller seemed to be a potential candidate who would not exacerbate the divisions between liberals and conservatives in the party. Although his record in two terms as governor of West Virginia and now seven years in the Senate had been conventionally liberal, he was seen first not as a "liberal" but as a "celebrity" and a rich one at that.

Rockefeller had never made any secret of his personal contempt for Bush, whom he saw as, like himself, a man who had been born to privilege, but who, unlike himself, had never been serious about using his opportunity to help those in less fortunate circumstances. "Early on I saw Bush as a phony," he said later. "I developed a true disdain for him. . . ." For Bush, he said, "the presidency was a trophy" rather than an opportunity. At the time he opened the door in Cleveland, Rockefeller's anger had been stoked by White House pressure exerted against Republicans on two commissions he was heading—one on medical care and one on children.

Rockefeller was nothing if not serious about the issues. In his first term in the Senate he had, as he put it, "buried myself" in issues primarily of concern to his constituents in West Virginia. He was conscious of the fact he was the first sitting governor of the state ever elected to the Senate and that he made it with only 51.8 percent of the vote despite a huge outlay of his personal fortune to finance his campaign. But in 1990, "blessed by a weak opponent," he had captured 69 percent of the vote. Now he felt liberated to lead commissions dealing with national problems and even to begin thinking about the presidency in a serious way.

Less than two weeks later Rockefeller was off to see what his potential might be in the New Hampshire primary still nine months in the future, and the reception he received and his own performance were at least mildly encouraging. At this embryonic stage of his campaign he was by no means a polished candidate with a practiced talent for delivering sound bites to the television cameras; on the contrary, he had a tendency to talk too long in too much detail about the issues—the problems of health care and children, for example—he considered most pressing. But he was, nonetheless, a man with an easy charm and a sometimes acerbic wit supporting the celebrity of simply being a Rockefeller.

His earnestness on issues was much like that his uncle Nelson Aldrich Rockefeller had displayed as a neophyte candidate for governor of New York way back in the 1950s. And, like his uncle, he found he enjoyed the campaigning. Riding around the back roads in New Hampshire, he told a reporter, "I've just become engrossed in this thing, in the intricacy of the process." Rockefeller also was finding the voters in New Hampshire more interested in the issues than he had expected. "People want to listen to people who are totally serious about what's going on in this country, which is not much," he said.

The signs of interest among New Hampshire Democrats, long accustomed to being courted over two or three years, were obvious. When the party's state chairman, Chris Spirou, held the annual Jefferson-Jackson Day dinner in May, it attracted a crowd of 450 to hear Tsongas and George Mitchell, compared to only sixty-eight people who had attended two years earlier. "It's happening," Spirou crowed, "it's happening."

The following morning about forty of the most active of the party activists crowded into the oceanfront home of Joe Grandmaison in Rye to meet Rockefeller and to give him a straightforward message: the economic situation is serious and we are sick and tired of the silence from Democratic leaders in Washington, when they should be fixing the blame on George Bush and the Republican Party. Grandmaison, a former party chairman and gubernatorial candidate with twenty years of activist history in the state, put it this way: "It's been more a sense of frustration that nobody [in Washington] has been saying anything." Joe Keefe, a lawyer and former congressional candidate, added: "It's got to the point where it's embarrassing."

There were, nonetheless, a few signs of life, in terms of both the mechanics and the message that would be important if the Democrats were to have any realistic chance of winning in 1992. For one thing, the relationship between the DNC and DLC had eased considerably. The so-called conservative group had come to include more Democrats almost all the way across the spectrum and to be viewed as more a forum for new ideas than a rival power center. And Brown had shown himself to be relentlessly optimistic in even the worst of times—"I always thought George Bush was a loser," he explained later—and an effective spokesman for the party, largely erasing the earlier reservations among Southern party leaders. Indeed, some state party chairmen from the South who had been most implacably opposed to his election had become close allies and even boosters.

Brown was determined to make the DNC a factor in the presidential campaign and he assigned the task to political director Paul Tully, a professional of prodigious appetites for food and drink and equally prodigious political insights. Under Tully's direction, the DNC had produced plans to lay the groundwork for the general election campaign no matter who was nominated—to have a strategic approach and some of the mechanics in place by the time a nominee was chosen, rather than beginning from scratch the day after the nominating convention. Tully's product included detailed plans for general election targeting that showed how the Democrats could win a national election despite all the recent history to the contrary.

In essence, it took as a base the states Dukakis had carried in 1988 and then identified the most closely contested states that Dukakis had lost in which the demographics also made it clear there were enough "persuadable" voters—essentially swing voters—to reverse the result in 1992. Tully also had a plan for extending the use of the "coordinated campaign"—plans under which Democrats in each state from the top of the ticket down would jointly do the things that it would be far more expensive to do separately, such as voter identification, registration and turnout programs. That kind of thing sounds so logical it should not have required a sales pitch, but candidates are often suspicious of even their party colleagues. So they had to be shown that the coordinated campaign could work in their states as it already had worked in many if not all of the thirty-three states that had adopted such an approach in 1990.

Tully developed a slide show he used to encourage groups of party workers, unions and potential contributors. When in the spring of 1991 Ron Brown convened a meeting of potential candidates and known fat cats at the Middleburg, Virginia, home of Pamela Harriman, widow of former Ambassador W. Averell Harriman and a very major Democratic contributor, Tully was there to make the case to the contributors that there was good use to be made of their money—and to the potential candidates that the 1992 campaign might not be as hopeless an exercise as they might think.

As Brown explained it later, "We were trying to get them to focus on the general election rather than the primaries"—and, not incidentally, to provide the funding for the plans. He told prospective candidates, he recalled, "We want you to designate us as your general election agents, so while you're fighting it out in the primaries, there's somebody focused on the general election period."

Mechanics aside, there also seemed to be a spreading awareness within the party that the ideological bickering of the past was a luxury Democrats could not afford when there were obvious issues of concern to voters. There was more talk about education and health care, less about the death penalty and who cast a vote for aid to the contras ten years earlier.

In June a speech by Governor Zell Miller of Georgia to a gathering of Southern Democrats in Raleigh, North Carolina, was given wide and generally approving circulation through the party—in large measure because Miller was a populist of impeccable liberal credentials who had carried one fifth or more of the black vote even against a black candidate, former Mayor Andrew Young of Atlanta, in winning the Democratic runoff for governor in 1990. In the key passage, Miller said:

"For too many presidential elections we have had things backward. We have chosen to fight on social issues rather than to run on the economic issues that shape the daily lives of American families. When the average American family stays up late into the night, they are not worrying about whether school prayer should be voluntary or mandatory, they are worrying about how to balance the checkbook and where they will find the money for junior's college tuition. Our party grew up around the economic issues that concern working Americans most deeply, and this is the common bond that unites us. But instead of rallying around those basic, unifying economic issues, we have allowed ourselves to be distracted by social issues that not only divide us but defeat us.''

Miller added this analysis of the 1988 fiasco: '' 'Dukakis liberal' became a code word for social values outside the mainstream of the middle class. Yet the basic error of the Dukakis campaign was not, as some suggested, its failure to answer the Bush assault on social issues. . . . Instead, the decisive, the devastating error of the Dukakis effort was its more profound failure to launch any assault of its own on economic issues, and because we failed to give people good reasons to vote for our nominee, the opposition was able to give them bad reasons to vote against him.''

The Georgia governor argued that each party had an ''elitist'' and a ''populist'' wing. Republican elitists, those most committed to protecting the wealth of the wealthy, were willing to campaign on the issues of the party's populists—social issues such as school prayer, the death penalty, abortion rights and gun control. In the Democratic Party, Miller argued, the elitists were the ones preoccupied with the social issues, while the populists centered on economic questions.

''The difference is that, unlike Republican elites, our elites demand that we run on their issues,'' he said. ''They are uncomfortable with economic populism and they historically tend to resist candidates who embody it. We also have a series of very active special interest groups, organized around liberal causes, that have imposed a filter through which only the purest of the politically correct can pass. To some, it is not enough to be pro-choice; it is demanded that the candidates favor taxpayer funding, even for abortion on demand. To others, it is not enough to endorse government support for the arts; it is demanded that candidates oppose any restrictions on the uses of arts funding, even if they are obscene. To still others, it is not enough to stand up for education; it is also demanded that candidates stand against every innovative idea that in any way infringes on the status quo—from teacher testing to merit pay.

"Don't get me wrong. I believe in a lot of the social issues which so many want our party to profess. But I also believe they cannot be the centerpiece of our presidential campaign. And to the extent that they are, we will not only continue to lose elections; ironically, we will also lose the very social goals that these Democratic elites regard as so important. . . . I did not become a Democrat to be a social liberal while ignoring fundamental economic choices. We must appeal to working families and the middle class. We have to again advance an economic agenda. We have to define it. We have to run on it. Because, my friends, that is the only way we will ever win."

One of those impressed by the speech was Bill Clinton, who spent the night in Atlanta with Miller and discussed it late into the evening. The speech, Miller told him, had been written with the help of three consultants—James Carville, Paul Begala and Bob Shrum. You should think about hiring them for your campaign, he told his colleague from Arkansas. As it turned out, however, those same consultants were very busy right then working for Harris Wofford in Pennsylvania and using the very same message Zell Miller had delivered at Raleigh.

Miller's line also was precisely the one being followed by the DLC—that the important thing was to focus on the middle class rather than wallow in the special concerns of Democratic constituencies. But by this point in 1991 it was a view not limited to the DLC. Attending the Democratic-dominated U.S. Conference of Mayors in San Diego that spring, Mayor Richard M. Daley of Chicago, for example, complained that the big-city executives were spending too much of their public attention on such high-visibility problems as AIDS and homelessness. "That's important," he said, "but we need to talk about the middle class. We need to focus more on education and things people are worried about."

Not all the tensions within the party had been resolved, of course. At the Cleveland meeting of the DLC in May, executive director Al From had deliberately excluded Jesse Jackson from the speakers' list with the full backing of Bill Clinton, thus assuring Jackson's appearance in the city for counterevents that week and his continued hostility toward the DLC. And the "delegates," many of them Washington lobbyists who had qualified by paying a registration fee, had passed a resolution that, among other things, objected to "quotas"—thus tacitly buying into President Bush's description of the Civil Rights Bill of 1991 then being debated in Washington as a "quota bill."

But by July there was at least the first stirring of an aggressive attitude toward Bush to replace the timidity that had been the rule since the 1988 election. Although the President's approval rating remained between 70 and 75 percent in public opinion polls, the most insightful professionals were pointing out that the "wrong track" number had crept up to 55 to 60 percent. And, based on studies of previous polls and election results, the evidence was that those who believe the country is off on the wrong track split two or three to one against incumbents. Such a split had occurred even in the Dukakis election, but the problem for the Democrats then was that a majority of the voters still thought the country was "heading in the right direction" rather than "off on the wrong track."

There was still, however, the problem of finding candidates. Bradley, Nunn and Mitchell were so adamant about not running that they were being written out of the equation. So was Lloyd Bentsen, although the Texas Democrat never shut the door entirely. In July, Gephardt announced that he would not be a candidate, and early the next month Gore followed suit. The stunner, however, was the August announcement by Rockefeller that he would not make the race because he did not feel prepared adequately for either a presidential campaign or the presidency.

Rockefeller's withdrawal was a particular jolt because it was clear that his candidacy was attracting enough interest across the party to have considerable potential for the nomination. And Democrats who knew him had relished the prospect of the patrician six-foot six-inch Rockefeller confronting a Republican president he held in such contempt. Moreover, Rockefeller had made it plain that he enjoyed the campaign and the prospect of running the country. "It's not just being president, not just the trophy," he said later. "You don't go there because it's there."

Rockefeller's explanation that he felt underprepared was a hard one for politicians to swallow; they are not often people afflicted with self-doubt and, on paper at least, the senator from West Virginia seemed as well equipped to make the race as anyone else in the field or even in the wings. The story that made the rounds was that his wife, Sharon Percy

Rockefeller, daughter of former Senator Charles H. Percy of Illinois, had opposed the campaign because it would force her to surrender the position she had just won as president of WETA, a leading public television station, in Washington, D.C. It was a job that would not permit her to campaign with her husband. Rockefeller himself called the conflict "another factor although not the major factor at all" in his decision. His wife, he pointed out, "had soldiered for me for twenty years" and he was reluctant to interfere with her career when she was enjoying particular success.

But the decisive element in the withdrawal, he said later, was his growing realization about how little he knew about national politics and what was involved in running for president. He recalled a trip to Texas where he had breakfast with Jack Martin, a street-smart operative in Austin who was Bentsen's principal political agent back home but whom Rockefeller had never met. Rockefeller was impressed by Martin, but when the breakfast was over, he said, "I didn't know if he was that smart or whether I just enjoyed the waffles."

When Lane Bailey, Rockefeller's closest adviser, presented him with a briefing book to study before he made his decision, he listed the names of nine professionals who might be considered for manager of the presidential campaign. "I had met three of them," Rockefeller said. The lesson he chose to draw was that if you are going to run for president, it takes some time to prepare.

Whatever the reason, Rockefeller's decision against running seemed to let some of the air out of the Democratic optimism. The inference again, inevitably, was that he had decided 1996 would be a better year—just as, incidentally, his Republican uncle Nelson had decided 1960 was not the right year to challenge Richard M. Nixon, a judgment he regretted for the balance of his political career.

With everyone running for cover, it now seemed that unless Mario Cuomo were to seek the nomination, the Democratic field would be a bunch of candidates who in other years would be on everyone's list—for vice president.

C H A P T E R 6

SECOND-STRING
SIX-PACK

The flight of the heavyweights from the 1992 Democratic field triggered the rush of second-line candidates. In the six weeks immediately after Labor Day, Doug Wilder, Tom Harkin, Bob Kerrey, Bill Clinton and, finally, Edmund G. (Jerry) Brown, Jr., the former governor of California, announced their candidacies. With Paul Tsongas already active for four months, the Democratic "six-pack" had been established as the successor to the "Seven Dwarfs" who had made up the party's field of candidates four years earlier—and was greeted with similar skepticism by the political community.

Although all six had impressive credentials in government service, at least on paper, none of them was then considered a truly national political leader. Wilder had gained some national prominence because of his precedent-setting success in Virginia; Brown had run for president twice before, but was distinctly in eclipse; Clinton was very highly regarded among his fellow governors, but not well known nationally.

The press and politicians quickly established a rough pecking order.

Kerrey, Harkin and Clinton were the candidates in "the first tier," if only because each held some statewide office. The others were consigned to "the second tier" for different reasons, with some conventional political logic. Tsongas's background was too unorthodox for him to be taken seriously. Few political professionals believed a black candidate could win, even if Wilder was serious about it. Jerry Brown was still viewed as "Governor Moonbeam" from his days in California and the two previous campaigns for Democratic presidential nominations in 1976 and 1980. He was the candidate best known to New Hampshire Democrats at the starting line but also the only one with negatives higher than his positives.

Only Ron Brown among prominent Democratic leaders seemed to find hidden virtues in the group. "I thought we had a lot better field than folks said," he recalled. "Part of it was just kind of getting some kind of perspective on the field." Some of the candidates whose absence was being bemoaned, such as Gore and Gephardt, were after all the same people derided as among the Seven Dwarfs four years earlier. Besides, Brown argued then and later, Bush's strength was being exaggerated. "There was no sense of direction," he said. "People were not enthusiastic about Bush, even those who said they would vote for him. There was a certain comfort level about him but . . . the country was sort of floating."

If any of the Washington-based candidates among the pack was particularly intriguing to Democratic professionals, it was probably Bob Kerrey. The political establishment in Washington and across the country always has some candidate it expects to do well because of how he looks on paper, without any real evidence that the voters are prepared to accept him. That was the case with then Senator Birch Bayh of Indiana in the crowded Democratic field in 1976, with then Senate Minority Leader Howard H. Baker, Jr., of Tennessee in the Republican competition in 1980 and with Senator John H. Glenn of Ohio in the Democratic campaign in 1984. Because they were formidable figures in Washington, it followed that they would be seen the same way elsewhere.

Kerrey raised similar expectations because in a single term as governor of Nebraska and three years in the Senate he had earned a reputation as an unorthodox but exciting political personality—the bachelor governor who had a relationship with Hollywood star Debra Winger while he lived in the governor's mansion in Lincoln—to the apparent delight of notoriously conservative Nebraskans. He was, in some particulars, a dream candidate for the Democratic Party at this particular juncture—a liberal largely immune from the usual Republican assaults on his patriotism because he had lost a leg and won the Congressional Medal of Honor as a Navy Seal during the war in Vietnam. When Kerrey opposed the attack on Iraq, no one dared accuse him of being faint of heart. And, beyond that, he was intelligent, articulate and engaging. He might have been the ideal candidate for vice president, to contrast with Dan Quayle and his credentials in the Indiana National Guard. If that would work, why not put him on the top of the ticket? It was a year in which Democrats were not being picky.

Kerrey himself had been thinking about making the race. "It had been on the radar screen in that I knew there were people asking me to run," he recalled. "Early in the year, I didn't seriously consider it. As the year wore on and there were fewer and fewer people in the race, I considered it more seriously." The prime factor, as it is with all candidates at one point or another, was simply deciding that he wanted to be president—"I had to cross a threshold," he said. But he also was clearly influenced, he said, by "the fact that Bradley didn't get in, that Rockefeller didn't get in, that Gore didn't get in, that Nunn didn't get in."

At the end of the war with Iraq, Kerrey felt more reason to run. "I thought it was desirable to beat Bush at the end of the Gulf War," he said. "I thought it was a mistake for Americans to get wildly enthusiastic over what was unquestionably a marvelous military effort but somehow struck to the heart of the citizenry in a frenetic way that I didn't like." Kerrey also had his own ideas of what he could do with the presidency. "I do have a vision," he said, "of what America could be like and what the world could be like if we did things differently today."

At the outset, it seemed clear that Kerrey had at least an identifiable market share available to him. In New Hampshire, many of the liberal activists who had been waiting for Rockefeller through the summer and had been left at the church or were now tiring of waiting for Cuomo rushed to support Kerrey. With Harkin in the field, it was clear that the Iowa precinct caucuses would be ceded to him and that the New Hampshire primary on February 18, eight days later than Iowa, would once again be the first testing ground.

This schedule was a reversion to the system that had dominated the presidential nominating process until a little-known one-term governor of Georgia, Jimmy Carter, won the Iowa caucuses in 1976 and made them what Howard Baker later called ''the functional equivalent of a primary.'' Up to that point, the New Hampshire primary had been the first step in sorting out the candidates and establishing a pecking order for the rest of the contest for party nominations. But once Iowa began to get so much attention—as it did increasingly in 1980, 1984 and 1988—New Hampshire became the equivalent of a semifinal, the test that would narrow the field in either party to two or at the most three survivors with any realistic chance of being nominated.

Now once again the primary would be the focus of political attention through the rest of 1991 and those first weeks of 1992. Tsongas, Kerrey, Clinton, Wilder and Brown all hinted at one time or another that they might take the risk of campaigning in Iowa in the hope of embarrassing Harkin and winning an attention-getting second place. But in the end, none was willing to spend the kind of money and time away from New Hampshire that would be required for such a questionable prize.

In the precinct caucuses, party members gather at schools, libraries, firehouses and people's homes and vote openly for their choices. Although Tom Harkin had some detractors back home, it would have been foolhardy to imagine a liberal home-state senator being upset or even seriously challenged in a vote of activist, and generally liberal, Democrats.

The importance accorded New Hampshire was subject to the familiar complaints of editorialists, political scientists and many big-state politicians. The state was too white, too small, too homogeneous in its population, culture and industry, the argument went, to provide a fair test of national candidates. The entire Democratic electorate, it was noted, could be lost in a corner of the Bronx. But there were other arguments for the primary. The state was small enough to enable candidates without much money to compete on even terms with their more affluent rivals. The campaign lasted long enough for the candidates to have time to make themselves relatively well known to the voters and, not incidentally, to smooth out the rough edges in their candidacies. And the voters there, like the caucus participants in Iowa, enjoyed the national attention, and as a result took their responsibilities seriously.

The argument for the validity of the New Hampshire primary as a testing ground carried added weight this time because the state was suffering through the worst of the recession. The unemployment rate was slightly under the national figure, but more than twice what it had been in 1988 or what New Hampshire voters had come to expect. The state had lost 50,000 nonfarm jobs over the previous three years, 10 percent of the total. The five largest banks had been folded into larger ones or into new entities combining their resources. The rate of increase in those qualifying for welfare and food stamps was among the highest in the nation, and the bankruptcy rate was close.

The concern with the economy in the electorate was so pervasive, a poll made for *The Boston Globe* found only 17 percent of voters approved of President Bush's handling of economic matters compared to a staggering 74 percent who disapproved. This was the state that had propelled George Bush to the Republican nomination in 1988, but now his overall approval rating was only 42 percent, his disapproval 47. The bottom line was that, whatever people elsewhere thought of the primary, New Hampshire voters were clearly going to have much to say about the direction of the 1992 presidential election campaign.

So Kerrey followed his declaration of candidacy with a week of the intensely personal campaigning that characterizes New Hampshire primary politics, meeting a hundred Democrats in Katie Wheeler's home in Durham for two hours, then another fifty in Patty Blanchette's living room in Portsmouth an hour later, traveling from diner to bowling alley, from luncheon to coffee hour. This was how it was done, and those early audiences were attentive and receptive to the handsome young senator from Nebraska as he talked earnestly about the failures of the health care system and answered questions about whether he would be, in contrast to Michael Dukakis, tough enough to fight back against George Bush, a concern obviously in the forefront of those Democrats' minds.

Near the end of that first week, eating clam chowder at the Oar House in Portsmouth, Kerrey was asked what had surprised him. ''It's a lot easier than I thought,'' he replied. It wasn't surprising that he felt that way. So far his contacts had been largely with the 3,000 or so New Hampshire Democrats most active in the party. The more important question of whether his appeal would translate to the 120,000 to 150,000 who might vote on primary day was still to be answered. And at this point all the candidates were so little known that opinion polls were essentially meaningless.

As November and December passed, the campaign in New Hampshire appeared to be taking shape. Tom Harkin had attracted a hard core of diehard liberals and labor leaders, many of the same people who had been behind Walter Mondale eight years earlier, and several figures from the political establishment, including former Senator John Durkin and a longtime legislative leader in Concord, Mary Chambers.

They liked it when Harkin argued that the Democrats had been "cheated out of our victory in 1988" by the failures of Michael Dukakis as a candidate rather than those of the Democratic Party. They liked it when he said, as he did repeatedly in the same words, "I think it's time for us to stand foursquare for the values of this party. It's time to say we weren't wrong, we were right." And they liked the way he tore into George Bush as he had when he declared his candidacy on an Iowa farm by saying, "I'm here to tell you that George Herbert Walker Bush has got feet of clay, and I intend to take a hammer to them." It was the old-time religion of the Democratic Party, the politics of absolution.

But as summer turned to fall and fall to winter, Harkin had not yet shown any sign that his support could be broadened beyond its liberal core. Kerrey had the "smart money"—the younger activists, many of whom had been with Gary Hart in 1984 and 1987 until the Donna Rice episode destroyed his candidacy.

Clinton's base lay with the few local Democrats who had formed a New Hampshire chapter of the DLC led by John Broderick, a Manchester lawyer, and a smattering of party activists including George Bruno, a former state party chairman who had been a friend of Hillary Clinton for almost twenty years. Tsongas was still being dismissed as a local phenomenon from across the border in Massachusetts with few supporters who were well known, although he did seem to have an interesting following of young people attracted to his economic message. If there was any significant support for either Wilder or Brown, it wasn't apparent to the naked eye.

But the tides of opinion in New Hampshire were not unaffected by what was happening elsewhere. On the contrary, it had become clear over the previous three or four primaries that a candidate needed some national credibility to score well in New Hampshire. That requirement was the reason that many candidates in both parties had been eliminated as serious factors in New Hampshire after flopping in Iowa.

In 1980, for instance, Howard Baker had given Iowa a secondary role in his campaign activity, planning to concentrate his time and money on New Hampshire. But after the Iowa caucus results came in with Baker a weak third behind George Bush and Ronald Reagan, Republicans in New Hampshire saw the contest as largely one between Bush and Reagan, and Baker never got off the ground. Similarly, in the Democratic campaign of 1984, John Glenn's campaign was fatally compromised by a fourth-place finish in Iowa while Gary Hart was given a strong push ahead by running a distant but still surprising second to Walter Mondale.

Even without Iowa as a factor in 1992, the New Hampshire primary was no longer an island. The voters followed the other preliminaries— the cattle shows and straw votes and debates—on their television screens. And, measured by the atmospherics that politicians use as a gauge when there is no hard data, Clinton was the candidate who seemed to be gaining the greatest momentum.

The governor of Arkansas had been a figure on the apron of the national stage for close to a decade. He was elected to the governorship in 1978, then defeated two years later when his constituents seemed to feel he had gone uptown on them too quickly, then resurrected with a comeback defeat of Republican Governor Frank White in 1982. He was prominent in the National Governors Conferences all through the 1980s and on everyone's list at one time or another for either national chairman of the party or vice president or—by 1988—even for the presidential nomination.

Clinton had a reputation as a strong personal campaigner, almost as effective as the recognized champion of Arkansas candidates, Senator Dale Bumpers. And he had enhanced his credentials as a national figure by becoming an active participant in the DLC, resigning his chairmanship of the group in 1991 only when he decided to make the presidential race. There were, however, rumors that he might have "a little problem with the ladies," as an Arkansas Republican once put it to a visiting reporter in Little Rock, but none had ever been established as he won repeatedly by growing margins in his home state.

Another problem for Clinton was the fact he had pledged in his previous reelection campaign that if kept in office he would serve out the full term. He was known to have considered making a bid for the presidency in 1988, and in his 1990 race his opponent charged in a debate that

Clinton was using the Arkansas governorship merely as a stepping-stone to the White House. The pledge was the result. It was a tough race in which Frank Greer, Clinton's media adviser, said the governor at one point told him: "I'm in serious trouble. If I lose, I'll never run for dogcatcher, let alone president."

Clinton survived that challenge but he was left with the pledge, which stood as a public declaration of unavailability for the presidency. On one occasion when Ron Brown was feuding with the DLC, he twitted the rival group—and its chairman, Clinton—by saying it was too bad the DLC didn't have a candidate, what with Clinton having pledged to finish his gubernatorial term, which ran through 1994.

Still hung up on the question in the summer of 1991, although a small group of aides was already laying the early groundwork for a candidacy, Clinton spent the Fourth of July speaking at about a dozen public events, asking voters whether he should seek the presidency in spite of his pledge. He told them he had already fulfilled most of his term's planned agenda, and soon—by political osmosis or design—signs proclaiming RUN, BILL, RUN began to appear at his speeches. So, in the manner of all good politicians, he finally bowed to the will of the people.

In Clinton's announcement speech delivered in front of the Old Statehouse in Little Rock, he had impressed other politicians and reporters with the way he defined himself as a different kind of Democrat. He paid homage to the traditional Democratic concern for the disadvantaged but put emphasis on the concerns of middle-class taxpayers. And he demanded personal "responsibility" on the part of welfare recipients as well as corporate executives who milked their companies while workers lost their jobs.

"Middle-class people are spending more hours on the job, spending less time with their children, bringing home a smaller paycheck to pay more for health care and housing and education," he told the friendly audience in Little Rock. "Our streets are meaner, our families are broke, our health care is the costliest in the world and we get less for it. The country is headed in the wrong direction fast, slipping behind, losing our way, and all we have out of Washington is status quo paralysis. No vision, no action. Just neglect, selfishness and division.

"For twelve years, Republicans have tried to divide us—race against race—so we get mad at each other and not at them. They want us to look at each other across a racial divide so we don't turn and look to the White House and ask, Why are all of our incomes going down? Why are all of us losing jobs? Why are we losing our future?''

A few minutes later he defined what he offered this way: "The change we must make isn't liberal or conservative. It's both and it's different. The small towns and main streets of America aren't like the corridors and back rooms of Washington. People out here don't care about the idle rhetoric of 'left' and 'right' and 'liberal' and 'conservative' and all the other words that have made our politics a substitute for action. These families are crying out desperately for someone who believes the promise of America is to help them with their struggle to get ahead, to offer them a green light instead of a pink slip. This must be a campaign of ideas, not slogans. We don't need another president who doesn't know what he wants to do for America. I'm going to tell you in plain language what I intend to do as president. How we can meet the challenges we face—that's the test for all the Democratic candidates in this campaign. Americans know what we're up against. Let's show them what we're for.''

In the fall of 1991, Clinton made a series of shrewd moves to meet unspoken questions about his candidacy. He gave a series of three speeches on issues, including foreign policy, at his alma mater, Georgetown University in Washington, that were clearly intended to resolve doubts about whether this small-state governor understood the nature of the problems confronting the next president. And he attracted network television coverage simply because he made those speeches within a few miles of the Washington bureaus of the networks, which were obviously reluctant when money was tight to go to the expense of covering unproven candidates on the road. But they were quite willing to send a correspondent and camera crew on a ten-minute drive.

In September, Clinton turned up to speak at the Democratic National Committee's executive committee meeting in Los Angeles, encouraging obvious stories about the leader of the DLC in the lion's den. He came away with higher marks than any of the other candidates who showed up—Tsongas, Harkin and Brown. The speech was toughly partisan in attacking Bush but, most importantly, it offered a coherent view of the kind of approach Democrats needed to take against the incumbent president over the next year. A few weeks later he made a similar speech to the Association of Democratic State Chairs in Chicago and won even more enthusiastic reviews from party regulars who had viewed him with varying degrees of suspicion up to that point. Standing in the back of the room, Paul Tully, one of the doubters a few weeks earlier, was exuberant, turning to a reporter and delivering his ultimate accolade with a broad grin: "Now that was a general election message. That was big-time politics."

Clinton's performance was particularly strong when compared to those of his two supposedly most serious rivals, Kerrey and Harkin, before the same group. The senator from Nebraska concentrated on a lecture on the ills of the health care system in a speech that could not be faulted for substance. But it did little to reassure the Democratic leaders gathered at the Palmer House that this charisma they had been hearing about really existed.

Harkin, on the night before Clinton spoke, had delivered his usual speech extolling Democratic dogma, and describing the need for a "real Democrat"—by implication himself—rather than "a warmed-over Republican." Clinton rose to the bait forcefully. "I'm a Democrat by heritage, instinct and conviction," he told the applauding state chairs. "My granddaddy thought when he died he was going to Roosevelt. . . . These people call me a Republican because I want to change and push this party into the future, not pull it to the right or left."

Filing out of the room after the session, a prominent labor leader wearing a Harkin button stopped a reporter. "Clinton was terrific," he said, "I could see him doing very well in Michigan."

"What about Harkin?" the reporter asked, nodding at the button.

"I like Tom," the labor leader replied, "but let me ask you, was that speech last night the only one Tom can give?"

The Chicago meeting, coming on the heels of Clinton's success at the earlier DNC meeting in Los Angeles and the Georgetown speeches, seemed to crystallize opinion in the political community that he was now the front-runner in the Democratic field. Supporters of his rivals complained that the press was "anointing" the Arkansas governor for some devious reason of its own. But the press depiction of Clinton as the leading candidate accurately reflected the consensus that had developed among the party activists who were paying the most attention, in New Hampshire and nationally.

Reflecting later on his sudden designation as the front-runner, Clinton saw it as a mixed blessing. "First of all, I was very apprehensive about it," he recalled. "I was afraid that rising too fast, before the American people got to know me and had any kind of base on which to evaluate me, made me vulnerable, made me a target, and might tend to obscure my message. Although I think it happened basically because I seemed to be somebody who had really thought about these things and had a coherent view of what I wanted to do as president, and why I was running."

Clinton's stature was reflected most clearly in the new support he was getting from liberals who had become increasingly pragmatic as the evidence mounted that George Bush might be vulnerable after all. Clinton might not be their dream candidate—he supported capital punishment, for one thing—but he was certainly acceptable on most other issues and more than acceptable on the stump.

Looking back much later, Harkin was convinced the Chicago meeting had been the turning point in favor of Clinton and against his own candidacy. The Iowa Democrat believed that, contrary to the press consensus, he had won the oratorical competition at the Los Angeles DNC meeting and had been doing well otherwise. He had been given surprisingly high marks after a meeting with IMPAC, a group of relatively conservative Democratic big contributors. A survey of big-city mayors had shown they considered him the candidate who would be best for the cities. And when he gave his speech in Chicago that night, he had been received with warmth and enthusiasm.

The new consensus for Clinton, Harkin was convinced, was a product of some clever maneuvering by David Wilhelm, the young professional from Chicago managing the Clinton campaign, to orchestrate who said what to the reporters covering the meeting. "Sunday I got all the press reports about [how] Clinton had just blown them out of the water— *The New York Times*, the *Chicago Tribune*, AP, UPI," Harkin said. "There I was reading all these quotes from different state chairs. Well, every quote I saw was from a state chair who was a supporter of Clinton's—[Bob] Slagle of Texas, a couple of others. . . . This was Wilhelm at work, I know this guy. . . . Wilhelm got into my knickers big."

In fact, however, whatever the level of orchestration Wilhelm managed that day, the response to Clinton went well beyond what he had going in—and unquestionably came at a cost to Harkin and the other candidates. "From that moment on," Harkin said, "Clinton got a two-week bounce out of that thing, and I mean he was riding high. . . . To me, it was really a turning point because he was able to overtake me in the eyes of Democrats, the party structure . . . as the logical candidate, someone who could win, that type of thing."

Clinton, too, thought the Chicago speech was important in establishing himself with the party, as the first step in giving the campaign credibility to reach out to the electorate in what he called "ever-widening circles" of Americans paying attention to the campaign. "Those people thought I had something to say and they liked the way I said it, and there was a lot of passion," he said. "I think they thought I'd fight the fight; if they went with me that I'd hang in there."

In mid-December, the perception of Clinton as the leader of the six-pack was reinforced at a Florida state Democratic convention in Lake Buena Vista. In a straw vote, he beat Harkin, who had the backing of organized labor, by 54 percent to 31. Although the vote was intrinsically meaningless, Clinton's campaign had made a serious effort, spending some $50,000 on an elaborate effort to assure his success, and to demonstrate organizational as well as rhetorical ability. But the victory was most striking because it included many liberal Democrats from south Florida who in other times might have been more inclined to Harkin or Kerrey.

In fact, Clinton's strength was so obvious before the convention that Kerrey's state coordinator, a veteran of Florida campaigns going back to Jimmy Carter in 1976, state representative Mike Abrams, recommended against making any effort in the straw vote to avoid the embarrassment of defeat. By this point, the notion that Clinton was on a roll was so widespread that the Arkansas Democrat was raising about $700,000 a week. "Clinton was definitely the winner of the 'pundit primary,' " Paul Begala said later, referring to the preliminaries on which the political community established an early pecking order.

But Kerrey's campaign enjoyed at least a temporary lift that weekend as well, despite his decision against competing in the straw poll. His speech to the Florida convention was widely judged the most effective he had delivered in the campaign up to that point, both in terms of his diagnosis of national issues and his use of his own special résumé. Recalling his months of hospitalization after being so seriously wounded as a

Navy Seal in Vietnam, he made the case that he was living proof of the essentiality of good government services. It was an approach that allowed him to talk about service without seeming to be exploiting his Medal of Honor.

The next night Kerrey also was generally rated as the winner of the first nationally televised debate of the campaign, broadcast by NBC and moderated by Tom Brokaw. He came off as the hero in the sound bite that was shown repeatedly over the next two days. Kerrey's opportunity came as Jerry Brown was dominating the debate with a persistent assault on the corruption of everyone in politics except himself—now that he was no longer a state party chairman squeezing lobbyists for money. The other candidates and Brokaw appeared clearly annoyed as Brown insisted on playing his one note about corruption whatever the ostensible topic— to the point that the debate was being badly distorted. He and Brokaw also had a dustup when Brown insisted on repeating his 800 telephone number to appeal for campaign contributions, which Brokaw said violated the rules of the debate.

Finally Kerrey turned directly to Brown and said: "I've got to tell you, I resent all this . . . special interest stuff that you are putting out because you seem to be saying that I'm somehow bought and paid for. Is that what you're saying?"

"I'm saying you are part of a system that is bought and paid for," Brown replied, only slightly chastened.

"Well, I disagree with you," Kerrey countered, icily.

As dramatic moments in television go, this one wasn't in the league with Lloyd Bentsen's 1988 rejoinder to Dan Quayle that "you're no Jack Kennedy." But it was the one moment of that debate that anyone would remember, particularly since front-runner Clinton had taken a very deliberate above-the-fray attitude that made him appear almost a bystander in the ninety-minute broadcast. And for Kerrey supporters in New Hampshire, it was—finally—some of the evidence they had been seeking that he was capable of better things.

Indeed, up to that point, the Kerrey campaign had seemed to be one mistake or misjudgment after another. Part of the problem was that the Nebraska Democrat simply wasn't ready for a presidential campaign when he plunged into it in October. "There's lots of areas where I wasn't prepared," he said later. "I was conscious, very conscious that I was making the decision very late, the decision that I want to be president, that perhaps there should be four or five years between the moment that you decide you want to be president and the day when you first start to run.''

In fact, just as Kerrey was entering the campaign, one of his closest political allies and friends, former Representative John Cavanaugh of Omaha, was warning him that he wasn't prepared. ''John Cavanaugh can justifiably say, 'I told you so,' '' Kerrey conceded much later. But when Cavanaugh made the argument at the time, he recalled, ''I would ask back to him, 'John, okay, so what? Now that you've reached that conclusion, do you want me not to run?' ''

''No,'' he said Cavanaugh replied. ''I want you to run.''

''Well, okay, so I've got a weak hand, that's all. I've got to walk in and make them think I've got a full house.''

Kerrey's principal problem was simply the lack of a consistent and focused economic message, particularly in contrast to the prescription for economic revival being offered by Tsongas or the appeal to the middle class being made by Clinton. At the outset his Kennedyesque message—''building for greatness''—was too much the rhetorical flourish for voters as preoccupied with the economy as those in New Hampshire. ''I still like the message that I had,'' Kerrey said later, ''but it didn't resonate with audiences concerned about losing their jobs. . . . We went into the teeth of an economic storm in New Hampshire.''

For a while Kerrey emphasized health care and his recommendation for a national health insurance program almost exclusively but, again, it was not direct enough. ''I failed to get it clearly inside a larger economic issue,'' he said. ''I didn't make it an economic issue.'' Speaking to a meeting of the unemployed in Concord one day, Kerrey wandered into discussing a proposal for cutting the number of cabinet departments from fourteen to seven—shades of Jimmy Carter—and describing health care reform as ''the most powerful economic engine,'' without ever getting to the obvious obsession of such an audience: jobs. Later in the campaign he began to talk about trade barriers and the Japanese, and their impact on the economy. One particularly striking commercial showed him on a hockey rink, an appropriate venue in New Hampshire, talking about how the United States left its net unprotected while the Japanese did not. But, again, it was one step removed from the immediate problem of those he was trying to reach. ''We had misread the audience with our television,''

he recalled. "It was a reflection of how I had misjudged the audience."
As for that particular commercial? "It says nothing about their life. Their
life isn't so much influenced by trade, though it is, [so] they're saying,
'We're out of work. So you run this fancy hockey ad, big deal. We're
out of work.' "

Kerrey also had trouble dealing with his military record, trying to
find a balance between being "naturally reticent" about talking about it
and appearing to be exploiting his Medal of Honor. In that first debate
on NBC, he made a conscious effort to deal with his personal history,
mentioning his military service several times, only to find it backfired.
"I'm aware that I've got to tell a story about who I am," he said later.
"I know I've got to get that out. But after the first debate, I was gun-shy
over referencing anything having to do with Vietnam, not just because
there were negative editorials, but even my son said to me, 'My God, do
you always [have to]? You mentioned it four or five times in the debate.'
Even he noticed it."

Whatever his troubles, Kerrey clearly appeared to be at least in the
ballgame in the final days of 1991. The same could not be said of Doug
Wilder, who had found no fertile ground in New Hampshire, a state in
which less than 1 percent of the population is black, and had made only
a token effort to do so in any case. Nor was there any evidence that Jerry
Brown's constant critique of the corruption of the political financing
system was being taken seriously by New Hampshire Democrats worried
about their jobs and businesses. Political reform was not high on their
agenda.

Wilder's campaign had been something of a puzzle from its inception. Indeed, a few months before he decided to run, he had told a group
of reporters over dinner in Washington that he probably wouldn't do it
because he doubted a governor of less than two years' seniority could
win the nomination. Nor was there any evidence to suggest either the
Democratic primary voters or the electorate in general were prepared to
accept a black nominee. He had defied that conventional wisdom in
winning two statewide elections in Virginia, for lieutenant governor in
1985 and governor in 1989. But in each case he had won against flawed
opponents by margins that should have been larger, and clearly would
have been had he been a white candidate.

Wilder and his chief political adviser, Paul Goldman, were not deterred. Early in 1991 they were convinced that the Persian Gulf War would be politically irrelevant in a few months and that the condition of the economy would dominate the politics of 1992. And they were equally convinced that there would be a market in the new Democratic Party and the country for "the new mainstream"—their phrase for the moderately conservative approach the black governor had taken on fiscal and some social issues.

There was also the question of whether Wilder might not have been driven to some degree by his rivalry, real or imagined, with Jesse Jackson to become the dominant black political leader in the country. Although they both protested to the contrary, Wilder and Jackson always had a tense relationship. Jackson saw Wilder as too conservative on the issues he considered most important. Wilder had come up through the political system, sixteen years in the state legislature and then the lieutenant governorship, rather than the civil rights movement, and seemed at least mildly contemptuous of Jackson for not having played earlier in the political arena.

In his two statewide campaigns in Virginia, Wilder had adopted a policy of not accepting help from surrogates from outside the state, thus effectively closing the door to Jackson—in much the same way Lyndon B. Johnson had eliminated Robert F. Kennedy from consideration for vice president in 1964 by ruling that no one in his cabinet would be chosen. Now with Jackson apparently having put his presidential ambitions aside for the moment, there was room for another black leader— and one who had won a state governorship, while Jackson had refused to run even for mayor of the District of Columbia.

Wilder was a particularly prickly politician with a long history of continuing public spats with other Democrats as often as with Republicans. He had become involved in rhubarbs with his immediate predecessor in Richmond, Gerald Baliles, and with former governor and now Senator Charles Robb. He often ascribed these disputes to the feisty Goldman, but Wilder himself wasn't shy. When, for example, Democratic National Chairman Ronald Brown issued a routine statement in 1990 commending the tax deal between President Bush and Democratic congressional leaders, the Virginia governor quickly gave to the press and then fired off an angry letter asking Brown where he got the authority to put the party behind higher taxes.

In testing the presidential waters, he was equally contentious. In July of 1991, for example, he used a speech to a convention of Young Democrats to take a shot at Governor Mario Cuomo of New York, chiding "those who travel to Washington and deliver blistering speeches on fiscal responsibility but then return to their home states where they have blistered their own citizens with deficit spending and other fiscal torture." He seemed to be following a time-honored technique for getting attention— picking a fight with someone better known and thus, by implication, putting himself at the same level. But Cuomo refused to be drawn into the game.

With Bill Clinton as the acknowledged front-runner, Wilder attracted attention with a trip to Arkansas to enlist the public endorsements of several black state legislators who might otherwise have been considered Clintonites. A couple of weeks later he complained that Jesse Jackson "had asked people not to support me"—a charge the civil rights leader, who had taken himself out of the picture, denied. But none of this political gamesmanship could erase Wilder's principal problem. He was running in a primary in which virtually no blacks would cast ballots. And he faced the prospect that in the first eleven states that would hold primaries blacks made up 25 percent of the population in only one, Maryland, unless, as subsequently happened, Georgia moved its date forward. His only hope rested in a respectable showing in New Hampshire that would keep his candidacy alive for the Southern primaries in March, in which their large black constituencies could make themselves felt.

But there was no sign of any progress in New Hampshire and Wilder's situation was becoming increasingly awkward. On the one hand, he could not spend the kind of time the primary voters seemed to expect— "It was a little surprising to me, the one-on-one that was necessary," he said later. On the other, he was getting increasing heat from voters, the press and political rivals back home for neglecting the state. A compilation by *The Richmond Times-Dispatch* in October found the governor already had spent 111 days out of the state in 1991, much of the time campaigning. "People felt I should have had more gratitude for being elected, the first elected African-American in the country," he said, "and before I could even settle into the job, I'm talking about running for another job."

By contrast with Wilder's apparently unseemly haste, Jerry Brown had entered the campaign carrying the heavy baggage of almost twenty years as a most unorthodox player on the national political stage. His career in California grew out of his position as the son of a popular regular Democrat, former Governor Edmund G. (Pat) Brown. The younger Brown won a term as secretary of state, an office he used effectively toward his election as governor in 1974 as the successor to Ronald Reagan. Once in Sacramento, his "small is beautiful" style attracted wide attention from the media. He chose to sleep on a mattress on the floor of a modest apartment rather than live in the state-owned governor's mansion, and to ride around in a blue Plymouth rather than a properly gubernatorial limousine.

But Brown won high marks for his willingness to make unconventional appointments to state boards and commissions and to address the thorny problems of the energy shortage, the environment and farm labor law. Even some of his most severe critics credited Brown with having been far ahead of other political leaders in understanding the need for a more aggressive government role in protecting the environment.

Brown also was determinedly ambitious, entering the campaign for the 1976 Democratic presidential nomination and winning several late primaries after Jimmy Carter had effectively locked up the nomination. But Brown also was gaining a reputation as a politician who flitted from one fad idea to the next and for making abrupt changes in course. In 1978 he campaigned vigorously against California's Proposition 13, which sought to apply rigid limits to local taxation. But once the measure was approved in the state's June primary, the governor embraced it enthusiastically in the general election campaign—in effect, leading by running to the head of the parade—in which he won a second term.

When Brown set off on still another run for the presidency, this time challenging incumbent President Jimmy Carter in 1980, his credibility was seriously undermined by an erratic performance and he never won a primary. When he made a run for the Senate in 1982, he was buried by his own history and Republican Pete Wilson, who later moved to the governorship himself.

Brown was, however, a very different politician with an interest in ideas and a knack for recognizing emerging issues before they were obvious to everyone in politics. And he had the interest in examining ideas of a onetime Jesuit seminarian, which in fact he had been before going to Yale Law School. Dinner with him at El Adobe, a favorite restaurant of his in Los Angeles, could go on for three or four hours of exchanging ideas and arguments.

Once, on a visit to Washington in 1978, he spent a long evening with editors and reporters from *The Washington Star* testing his thesis that politicians should not present their decisions to their constituents as morally correct. To do so, he argued, would put those constituents who disagreed with him in the position of being not just substantively and politically but morally wrong. His dinner companions tested the thesis with one hypothetical situation after another and Brown seemed completely engrossed. It was not the kind of conversation that you would have with many politicians.

Brown also had the remarkable memory so common in successful politicians. One of us had dinner with him in San Diego one night in the fall of 1978 in which the conversation centered on the politics of the growing, although not yet fully visible, concern about the safety of nuclear power plants. When we encountered him next on a Los Angeles street corner in May of 1979, shortly after the accident at the Three Mile Island nuclear plant in Pennsylvania, he greeted us by asking: ''Remember what I told you about those nuclear power plants?''

But Jerry Brown's uncanny ability to identify sore spots in the electorate was not matched by a talent for the laborious, painstaking work required to find solutions to those concerns. What he lacked in follow-through, however, he made up in chutzpah. He entered the 1992 campaign by somewhat grandly declaring his candidacy at Independence Hall in Philadelphia.

The inspiration for the setting and the lyrics came from veteran Democratic pollster and consultant Patrick Caddell, ostensibly out of politics and resettled in California. For several years, Caddell had been on the lookout for a candidate to test his theory of an electorate yearning for change, and to carry his message of political rebirth to it. He had tried with Gary Hart in 1984 and with Joe Biden in 1988, and now loaned that message to Brown, an old friend.

Brown said he was running against the ''incumbent party of Republicans and Democrats alike'' who had formed ''an unholy alliance of private greed and corrupt politics'' in Washington. It was a sentiment widely shared by the electorate of 1992 but exploiting this anger was one thing, finding a way to assuage it quite another.

Like George Corley Wallace of Alabama a generation earlier, Brown was demonstrating only that he could identify a significant vein of resentment against all politics as usual. There was no sign, however, that resentment alone would be enough to sustain Brown in New Hampshire or, for that matter, anywhere else.

Moreover, Brown was seriously compromised by the picture he had projected of himself over the years as a politician who kept reinventing himself. After his defeat for the Senate, he went into a de facto exile for several years, studying Buddhism in Japan and then working briefly for Mother Teresa at a refuge in India—before suddenly reappearing in California and running for, of all things, Democratic state chairman.

The notion of this man who had always disdained conventional political mechanics seeking such an office was mind-boggling, but now Brown insisted that he intended to do it and do it right. He got the job and at first that seemed to be the case. But his interest in nuts and bolts flagged after two years and he stepped down early in 1991 and began putting together a campaign for the U.S. Senate in 1992. The conventional wisdom held that he had a sufficient remaining core of support among California Democrats to be the favorite in the party primary for the nomination, but that he still carried too much baggage to win against a Republican in November.

At this point he heard from a former political adviser about how another Democrat, Lawton Chiles, had won a governorship in Florida by putting a $100 limit on campaign contributions. That gesture had proved to be an excellent metaphor for Chiles in presenting himself as a candidate free of the big-money special interests. But it also had produced about $5 million, enough to finance his campaign more than adequately.

Brown was fascinated by the idea. When one of us encountered him at a state party convention in Oakland early in 1991, Brown—still focused on a Senate campaign—inquired at length about how the Chiles strategy had played out. What he didn't seem to grasp was that Lawton Chiles had always limited contributions to his campaigns for the U.S. Senate and thus had built credibility as a reformist politician. Brown had just spent two years as a state chairman squeezing money out of big contributors. But the inconsistency didn't faze him. Who, he asked, knows the sin better than the sinner? He would use the $100 limit and an 800 telephone number to reach the broadest audience of voters who might be willing to risk that much in the name of clean politics. But as the New Hampshire primary campaign began in earnest, there was no sign this new reincarnation of Jerry Brown as a presidential rather than Senate candidate was proving persuasive.

Harkin's campaign also seemed stalled. As the candidates debated the differences among them on tax policy, the future of the economy and the complexity of the health care problem, the senator from Iowa still was being viewed largely in terms of his insistence on the old-time gospel of Democratic liberalism. His campaign manager, a veteran of New Hampshire campaigns named Kathi Rogers, continued to insist there was a market share there, and other longtime Democratic regulars agreed.

But there was also a growing suspicion that the electorate of 1992 was a different breed of cat. One reason was the growing evidence that Paul Tsongas, the most unlikely of candidates, was beginning to build a following among voters who agreed with his prescription of bitter medicine to revive the manufacturing sector of the economy.

As the year-end holidays approached, however, most voters in New Hampshire still had not begun to pay close attention. A poll for *The Boston Globe* found 40 percent of likely primary voters still undecided, a share large enough to put the entire poll into obvious question. But it did make clear that the contest was still to be shaped, let alone won or lost. And many of the political activists were still keeping their options open. They might be impressed by Bill Clinton or Bob Kerrey or even Paul Tsongas, but they still had not heard from the one Democrat many thought was the party's only possible savior—Mario Cuomo.

HAMLET ON
THE HUDSON

For more than seven years, ever since his keynote address to the 1984 Democratic national convention at San Francisco, Mario Cuomo had been a dominating figure in the party. In an era of bland politicians, he was vivid, complex, often vexing—always seeming to be larger than life, just as he appeared now to the six Democrats trying to be taken seriously in the early stages of the New Hampshire primary campaign.

In the preliminaries to the 1988 campaign, the widespread assumption in the political community was that the New York governor could win the nomination if he wanted it. Even as late as December of 1987, many Democrats believed he could have entered the competition and taken it away from Michael Dukakis or Richard Gephardt or any of the others of the Seven Dwarfs then in the field.

But Cuomo closed the door, or at least seemed to do so, with finality shortly before Christmas that year. Characteristically, he did so on a radio call-in show, thus delivering a small zinger to the reporters from Albany, New York City and Washington who had been pressing him for months on his intentions. It was something he clearly enjoyed doing every once in a while.

In the runup to 1992, the situation had changed somewhat. Liberals were still intrigued at the possibility of a Cuomo candidacy. In California many prominent party figures were convinced he was the one candidate most likely to assure the Democrats the prize they had to have in the general election—California's fifty-four electoral votes, one fifth of the total needed to be elected. But the defeat of another Northeastern liberal, and an ethnic candidate to boot, in 1988 had emboldened the more conservative Democrats of the South and West to give more public voice to their view that a Mario Cuomo simply wouldn't sell with their constituents. He might win the nomination, the theory went, but he could not win the general election. How many times did the Democrats have to make the same mistake?

But Cuomo was not a politician who could be taken lightly, whatever the context in which he was operating. His force of personality, combative style and graceful use of the language all made him a candidate who could not be ignored or, more to the point, judged solely by such conventional measures as whether he was too liberal on the issues.

Some Republicans liked to talk smugly about how he would be the dream opponent—another leftist governor whose record in state government could be shredded. But others were less certain. He was no Michael Dukakis, that was for sure. This was a candidate who would get right in George Bush's face, and they were far from confident Bush would perform well under that kind of pressure.

Moreover, in a somewhat perverse way, the fact that his party was facing an uphill fight against an apparently unassailable Republican incumbent might make the campaign more attractive to Cuomo. The odds might be ten to one against him, but George Bush was the kind of opponent—a preppy, white-shoe Republican who had gone to Andover and Yale—that a candidate from New York City's borough of Queens might relish as an opponent. And the growing evidence of economic distress, which Cuomo was quick to recognize, was creating the kind of playing field that could favor a Democratic nominee who could identify himself convincingly with Americans suffering that distress.

Cuomo would have none of it. He already had been fending off questions about his intentions for most of the last two years. When one of us joined him in Albany one morning for a day of travel as he campaigned for reelection in 1990, he suggested we were planning "another dumb story" speculating on his ambitions for the presidency. And, drinking coffee as he flew toward Buffalo later that morning, he angrily rejected the suggestion there might be something about the elitist Bush he would particularly enjoy challenging.

"That would be self-aggrandizing," he said, banging the table for emphasis. "It would be the height of egoism and the height of selfishness." The only reason he wasn't ruling himself out entirely was the dark inferences that such a statement would encourage. "They'd say, 'He must have colon cancer, he must have a Mafia uncle.' "

Cuomo had always angrily resented the perpetual speculation that because he was an Italian-American he had something to hide in his background. This ethnic stereotyping had always been a sore spot with a man who came out of his St. John's Law School class with the highest honors, but could not even win an interview from the big Manhattan and Wall Street law firms to which he applied. In fact, his personal life had been investigated inside out—by the Republicans in his first race for governor, among others—and there was not a shred of evidence that he or his family had anything to hide.

Through the spring and summer of 1991, Cuomo continued to brush off the presidential talk. And this time he had finally found the formulation that he enjoyed using and seemed to believe defied the attempts of the Kremlinologist reporters with whom he liked to joust to find hidden meanings in his rhetoric. "I have no plans and no plans to make plans," he kept saying.

At the same time, however, Cuomo continued to take the occasional initiative that he had to know would feed the speculation, while arguing vehemently and forcefully that the fact he had strong views on, for example, the failures of the Bush administration didn't necessarily mean he was obliged to run for president, or was even thinking about it. He had a responsibility as governor of New York, he would say huffily; the inferences you draw are your own problem. If you want to write another dumb column, be my guest.

But he did nourish the speculation even while insisting it had no basis in fact. In May he criticized the Democratic Leadership Council for what he called its "implicit position that we have something we have to apologize for and now we have to move to the middle.'' He thus positioned himself as one liberal who was not prepared to wear a hairshirt because of the failures of Walter Mondale or Michael Dukakis.

In July, Cuomo unloaded another attack on Bush's record on the economy, and in August he went to Hyannis, Massachusetts, at the invitation of the United States Conference of Mayors, many of whose leaders were outspoken in their support for him as a potential presidential candidate. He delivered another stinging critique of Bush and laid out in a dazzling monologue his own prescription for beating him in 1992. Basically, he said, the Democratic leaders in Congress should pass their own economic recovery plan, let Bush veto it, and then have the party's nominee run against him on it. Then Cuomo tantalizingly told the mayors: ''I'll do anything you ask me to do—as governor.''

Cuomo insisted the situation never met the criterion he had set for himself in considering whether to run for president—simply that he would be the best alternative available. Long after the fact, he recalled describing his view to Michael Dukakis in 1987 this way: ''The way it works for me, I would have to conclude there isn't anybody as good as I am. Now there may be a different test that others apply, and I don't care much. That's the one I apply and I can't say that to myself. I can't say I'm better than you and I can't say I'd have a better chance than you.''

In the fall of 1991, nonetheless, it became increasingly difficult for Cuomo to argue he never even thought about it, even if only while shaving. The public pressure was becoming too obvious. And when Cuomo made a trip to California in September, he found many party leaders there—including an old friend, Representative Nancy Pelosi— who clearly wanted him to make the race in 1992. And some of those close to Cuomo thought they detected a quickening of interest.

In October, with the field stripped of the other acknowledged heavyweights, Cuomo began to send a somewhat different signal. The turning point was a breakfast at the Regency Hotel in Manhattan with a small group of longtime supporters and campaign contributors—a de facto committee planning the annual fund-raiser to finance his state campaigns. It was a group Cuomo said was ''like family . . . people who had been with me for fifteen years.''

Cuomo described it this way: ''One guy stood up, Vincent Albanese, who I have had tremendous respect for for a long time, a good friend.

He said, 'Mario, let me ask you a question. What about the presidency? We never ask you, out of respect,' he says, 'none of us have ever said anything to you. We get teased once in a while . . . they say that you could win.'

"I said, 'Well, you know, it's possible.' He said, 'What do you say about the presidency?' I said, 'Vincent, Matilda [Cuomo's wife] is sitting here, we've grown up together,' I said. 'I'm telling you I've never had a discussion with Matilda.' And Matilda said, 'That's right.' I said, 'I've never reached the point where I believe that I could say to myself, "This country needs me." ' I said, 'I know what I'm good at, Vincent, I'm very good at some things, I'm not so hot at other things. I just have never reached the point when I could say my country needs me.'

"He said, 'Well, that's very interesting and we believe that and we understand what you're saying, but what about us? What if we thought the country needed you?'

"Now, as simple as that sounds, you have to understand the setting," Cuomo related. "I hate asking for money. I took money from these people. I lost three elections in one year in 1977 to Ed Koch [the Democratic primary and runoff and, as the Liberal Party nominee, the general election for mayor of New York City]. . . . They have given me money. They never get anything because we just don't do business that way, and here this guy is saying, in effect, that you didn't think about us. And I said, 'I'll tell you what I'll do'—this is on the spot—I said, 'I will think about it for the first time and I'll be honest about it.' "

He would ask his son, Andrew, and some of his other political advisers, Cuomo told them, to take a look at the potential. The process, he suggested, would take less than six weeks. But there was, he reminded his old friends, the one problem of having to settle on a state budget.

"So I left," Cuomo recalled. "Before I got out of that room the press had been told about the conversation, which I'll never understand but obviously someone in that room . . . dropped a dime, because as soon as I walked out the door, somebody said AP has a story, and it couldn't have been forty minutes later."

Confronted when he reached Albany later the same day, Cuomo brushed off his talk at breakfast as a courteous but essentially perfunctory response to his supporters. "They said, 'Will you think about it?' " he related. "I said, 'Sure, I'll think about it. I'm always thinking about it.'

I said I'd have to be mindless not to think about it. I don't talk about it, but I think about it. Of course I do.''

Cuomo was adamant in insisting nothing had changed. ''I said absolutely nothing,'' he said. ''You can't honestly say you have a big story. If you're asking me did you say anything new, the answer is no.''

But there was indeed something new and different in Cuomo's position—a tacit acknowledgment that he was giving active consideration to running, that he could no longer say he had ''no plans to make plans.'' In Chicago ten days after his Manhattan breakfast, he said he was ''looking at'' the possibility of running and would make a decision soon. ''There's still time left until sometime in November,'' he said. ''By then you have to either be in or not be in. There's only a few weeks to go and we'll see.''

Over those ''few weeks'' the Hamlet on the Hudson continued to ruminate in public about a candidacy. Appearing on a cable television program on Long Island, he framed the internal debate this way: ''What does my heart tell me? Go out and tell them, Mario. Take your best shot, whether you win, lose or draw.'' At the same time, he said, ''Your head tells you: how do you do that and do the right thing as governor? I'm working on my head at the moment.''

In an interview with the editorial board of *The New York Daily News*, Cuomo conceded that the question was being treated more seriously this time around. ''The pressure has been greater,'' he said. ''The issues are different now than they were in '88, in '84. The economy is much worse. The recognition of the economy being worse is clearer than it ever has been. . . . I'm at a different stage of my career.''

Meanwhile, pressure to make a decision one way or the other increased, much of it applied—although indirectly—by Democratic chairman Ron Brown, who had once been a law student in a class taught by Cuomo at St. John's. Brown had made no particular secret of the fact he had hoped Cuomo would run, but publicly his priority at this point was getting an early decision so the party could move ahead in settling on a nominee.

In conversations with John Marino, the New York Democratic Party chairman, and Michael Del Giudice, another longtime political intimate of Cuomo, Brown urged that the New York Democrat make a decision as early as possible so that the field would be established. The threat of a Cuomo candidacy was freezing Democratic activists and contributors who by this point might have been choosing another candidate to support.

Brown was being burdened by the fact that his old professor Cuomo refused to accept his telephone calls, insisting their only communication be done through Marino or some other intermediary. "I was not talking to Ron Brown," Cuomo said. "Close as I was, I refused to talk to Ron Brown. I sent him one message . . . the governor's not going to talk to you and the reason the governor's not going to talk to you is he doesn't want to compromise you."

"It was almost like he thought I was going to trap him," Brown said later, "or I was going to encourage him to do something he didn't want to do, or put him on the spot, to push him toward a decision. . . . [His indecision] was not helpful, and that's why I tried to step up and exert some leadership. There was a major natural force hovering and it kept people from focusing. . . . It was very distracting."

Some of the candidates already in the field, and particularly those groping for a foothold among liberals, were predictably anxious to see the Cuomo question resolved. "A lot of my supporters in a lot of places were just hanging back, waiting to see what Cuomo was going to do," Tom Harkin recalled. "I heard it constantly." Bob Kerrey was having the same experience. "We were all standing in his shadow for the first ten or twelve weeks," he said later.

The way the active candidates viewed the prospect of a Cuomo candidacy reflected their different positions in the field. The conventional wisdom was that Cuomo would do the most direct harm to his fellow liberal Harkin because of his appeal to the same old-line regulars and labor, as well as his connection with black voters that the Iowa Democrat could not hope to match. Some Kerrey supporters were more sanguine about a Cuomo presence in the race, reasoning, somewhat simplistically perhaps, that Cuomo juxtaposed against the DLC candidate, Bill Clinton, might polarize the campaign and cast Kerrey as the centrist alternative who could draw from both ends of the spectrum. Kerrey, unlike Harkin, was seen as a candidate with potential in the South because of the special credential of his military record.

The most intriguing possibility, however, was that Cuomo would offer an opportunity for one of the other candidates—and Clinton in particular—to establish his political bona fides by defeating the New

Yorker in New Hampshire. The candidate who did that, the theory went, would be the giant-killer who would instantly take on mythic proportions for the rest of the contest for the nomination, and into the general election against George Bush. What better way to demonstrate that the Democratic Party had turned a corner than by defeating the quintessential symbol of old-fashioned liberalism, Mario Cuomo?

Paul Tsongas, never lacking for self-assurance, was convinced that his best chance to catapult himself to the head of the list of ostensibly "serious" candidates would be to defeat Cuomo in the New Hampshire primary. Someone who beat Cuomo, Tsongas was certain, could not be written off as no more than a regional favorite.

But the Clinton campaign was not so sure they should welcome such an opportunity. As Paul Begala, one of the key advisers to the Arkansas governor, put it later, "There was a lot of whistling past the grave-yard. . . . A lot of that was us trying to pump ourselves up, get our juices flowing for the fight of a lifetime. Cuomo was not from Washington so it was not going to be very easy to make him the old politics. To do so would risk getting back on an ideological axis, where Clinton did not want to go. At the time, we were saying, 'Oh, yes, bring him on,' of course, because we have to. That's the kind of bravado, at least, that people in this business develop." But the truth, Begala conceded, was that "we were scared to death of him" because he was "such an 800-pound gorilla."

Meanwhile, the relationship between Cuomo and Clinton had become a touchy one. Cuomo was no admirer of the DLC and had been irked at the decision, which Clinton endorsed, to shut Jesse Jackson off the DLC speakers' program at the meeting in Cleveland earlier in the year. As the Democrats waited for Cuomo's decision, he gave an interview to *New York* magazine that made the relationship with Clinton even more tenuous. And, not incidentally, it raised some questions about whether Cuomo himself truly understood the special demands on the party to redefine itself for the 1992 electorate.

The magazine quoted Cuomo as disparaging Clinton's emphasis on welfare reform. "He says they shouldn't be on welfare forever," Cuomo said. "Maybe in his state they are. In my state, they're on for an average of two years." Questioned by *The Washington Post* about the remark, Cuomo explained it this way: "I don't want to make people on welfare a whipping boy—or lady, as is the case, since 80 percent of the people on welfare in my state and most states are women and children.''

It was the conventional liberal argument on welfare. Cuomo surely knew, as did Clinton, that the two-year average was beside the point. The goal in welfare reform was to find a way out for the substantial number of families who had been trapped in the system for one generation after another. And Cuomo surely knew that one of the prime concerns of the conservative Reagan Democrats—the critical target group for the party in 1992—was their conviction that welfare costs were too high and too perpetual.

Cuomo also derided another Clinton idea—making college education universally available under a plan in which students would repay the costs through payroll deductions or with public service work. It was a notion, opinion studies indicated, with enormous appeal to the middle-class voters Clinton was targeting. But Cuomo wasn't buying. ''Where do you get the money?'' he asked. ''Isn't this one of those big bureaucratic programs you're complaining about? Where are the details? . . . It's a lot of baloney.'' Asked about this comment, the New Yorker replied that he didn't want to get in a fight with Clinton, which was precisely what he had done.

For the Arkansas governor, the Cuomo attack was the ultimate political flattery, suggesting that he was the one, of all the party's dominant if still dormant potential presidential candidates, worth the attention. Indeed, at one point, some of Clinton's advisers urged him to go to Harlem and deliver a speech on crime that, implicitly at least, would be an attack on Cuomo. But Clinton himself scotched the idea. ''I don't want to pick a fight with someone who's not running against me,'' he said. ''If he's running, there's plenty of time for that.''

Ron Brown continued to send his message through Marino and Del Giudice, adjusting the ''deadline'' as time passed and Cuomo continued to debate with himself. Mario could help things along by making a decision in early October or late October. Or how about by Election Day, November 5? Or what about Thanksgiving? But Election Day passed and Cuomo continued to ruminate.

''It was not helpful,'' Ron Brown recalled. ''There was a major national force hovering when [political observers] were saying, 'This is a vice presidential field.' . . . I felt like we had to move the thing off dead [center]. We had to know what the field was and who the choices were. And as long as Mario and others were out there undecided, it kept people from focusing on what we had to do to get ready for a general election campaign. . . . People kept waiting for somebody else.''

On still another call-in program on public television the day after the election, Cuomo said: "I'll complete the process as quickly as I can and let you know as soon as I can." Asked on November 14 if he would announce his decision by Thanksgiving Day or New Year's Day or Valentine's Day or St. Patrick's Day, he replied: "All of those are possibilities." A few days later in Buffalo, he conceded feeling pressure to make up his mind. "That means you have to rush your decision," he said. "But if you have to rush your decision, and I don't have a [state] budget solution, then I would have to say no."

By this point, Cuomo was presenting the issue in terms of the complex negotiations in which he was involved with Republican leaders of the legislature over a new state budget. But again the signals were mixed. At one point, he suggested he would have to resign as governor if he were to run, apparently holding this out as a possibility. But then he went on to say that would be "a form of abandonment." In early December he told one interviewer that he "never said" he had to resolve all those state budget problems before reaching a decision to run. "What I said is that I have to be sure that my running for president won't make it more difficult, won't make it worse for the state."

Cuomo was also depicting himself, somewhat disingenuously, as lagging "way behind" the candidates already in the field. "The people out there don't know who I am," he said at a press conference on December 5. "Every time I meet somebody in Chicago, any group at all, maybe eighty percent of what the people say is, 'Gee, I didn't know you were that tall, I never heard you say that, Governor, I didn't know you had a sense of humor. Gee, I have this picture, I thought you were short, had baggy eyes and were very mean.' You've got to get to the people."

Cuomo was also growing impatient with the press preoccupation with his future. "You have all, every one of you without exception, commented on what a tiresome, repetitive process it is," he told reporters in Albany. "So I will save you all the dilly-dallying, the shilly-shallying and the vacillations. Let's just put aside these tawdry meanderings and let's concentrate on the budget."

A few days later, on December 16, Cuomo seemed to have developed a rationale for running even if the Republicans continued to thwart him on the budget. "If you made up your mind that they were doing this only to prevent you from running," he said, "then the solution would be to run. Then they would no longer have the motive to slow you up. And that would save the state, by running for president."

The issue of how a campaign would interfere with Cuomo's ability to perform as governor had always been one he cited to explain his recalcitrance. In the 1987–1988 cycle and again this time, he complained that a sitting governor couldn't take the time to run for national office. How could you spend weeks tramping through Iowa or New Hampshire when you were needed in Albany?

In fact, this was a straw man of impressive dimensions. Mario Cuomo was not some Bruce Babbitt forced to ride a bicycle across Iowa in 1987 trying to win a little press attention. He was not a Paul Tsongas required to stump day after day in New Hampshire trying to establish some credibility as a candidate. Cuomo was a national figure whose campaign from the start inevitably would draw heavy television network and newspaper coverage.

Perhaps most important, however, Cuomo seemed to have passed some invisible line, some indefinable point at which a politician becomes a celebrity and not just a political leader—a celebrity viewed with excitement and a certain amount of awe by ordinary people, essentially without regard to whether they agree with his politics. It is a rare status, bestowed in some mysterious way. Dwight D. Eisenhower had it when he returned from Europe to run for president in 1952. Nelson Rockefeller had it when he first ran for governor of New York in 1958. Robert Kennedy had it when he ran first for the Senate in 1964 and then for the Democratic presidential nomination in 1968. Ronald Reagan had it from the moment he announced his candidacy for governor of California in 1966. And now it was Mario Cuomo.

Whatever rationale he was using for staying out of the campaign, Cuomo was nonetheless positioning himself to make the race if he decided to do so. Marino gathered information on delegate rules and the primary and caucus process and drew up tentative lists of professionals for a campaign staff. Fund-raisers were alerted so that if he decided to enter the campaign he could raise the early money needed to qualify for federal matching funds. Cuomo himself met with Robert Shrum, a leading Washington consultant with campaign experience going back twenty years, to get his reading on how the campaign might be conducted. Cuomo agents scouted office space in Manhattan, Washington and New Hampshire.

The reports were encouraging. Money would not be a problem and, Marino reported, it would not be difficult to enlist the right people in the major states. "So all of it looked good except getting the [state] budget," Cuomo recalled. And by this time, the argument here centered on a gap of only about $200 million in a budget of $30 billion.

Cuomo blew hot and cold on whether there might be a deal, after all. At one point, he told the Republican leaders, he said, that he couldn't believe they would think it was in their interest to block his candidacy. "If I run for president and lose in the primaries, I'm dead meat," he said. "If I win, I'm gone and New York state has a president. How could that hurt any Democrat or any Republican? How can that hurt you?"

There was now a genuine deadline for his decision—December 20, the final day for filing to compete in the New Hampshire primary. Although it might have been possible for him to skip that test, he had already made it clear that he didn't intend to do it that way. If it was going to be a "go," it would start there.

Other Democrats and the press were growing impatient with the long public agonizing. At the Florida Democratic state convention, a write-in movement for Cuomo produced only 1 percent of the vote and there were choruses of booing and hooting every time his name was mentioned. Some professionals were suggesting that Cuomo already was playing "primary politics" by delaying his decision principally to rob his less-known rivals of time to compete.

On December 19, he told reporters in Albany that he wouldn't simply skip New Hampshire while leaving his options open for a final decision later, an option Ron Brown already had suggested would be damaging to the party. "The real deadline on New Hampshire is tomorrow," Cuomo said. "I wouldn't pocket veto the presidency."

On the contrary, those who talked to him early that evening were convinced he was up for the game. At one point, he asked Marino why, if he was going to run, "why wouldn't I go into Iowa?"—the Iowa precinct caucuses to be held eight days before New Hampshire. There were compelling reasons to focus for the moment on New Hampshire, but Marino liked what he was hearing.

Cuomo spent that night holed up in the executive mansion on Eagle Street in Albany, a sprawling Victorian house he had come to enjoy immensely once it had been improved with such refinements as a half-court basketball court. Talking at length with his son, Andrew, they speculated on the chances the Republicans would agree on a budget the next day, and Cuomo wrote two tentative statements—one a rationale for running without solving the budget stalemate, the other a statement explaining that he could not do it.

The morning of December 20, dozens of reporters and camera crews gathered outside his office on the second floor of the capitol, while others congregated at the gold-domed statehouse in Concord, where Cuomo's $1,000 filing fee and declaration of candidacy would have to be delivered by 5 P.M. Twenty-nine Democrats, nineteen Republicans and one Libertarian already had filed for places on the February 18 ballot, and during the day they would be joined by Harkin and Kerrey.

The declaration could not be filed with a fax or copy, but a signed original and check had been flown into Concord late Thursday and given to Joe Grandmaison, the New Hampshire political veteran who was acting as Cuomo's liaison, as a protection against the possibility of a snowstorm that would make it impossible for Cuomo to get from Albany to Concord in time.

Although it might have been legally acceptable for such a proxy filing to substitute for a personal appearance even without a blizzard, both Grandmaison and Marino recognized that would be seen as political arrogance in a state that likes to cut politicians down to size. "Joe desperately did not want that to happen," Marino said, "and I didn't want that to happen. I wouldn't do that in New York, let alone New Hampshire."

Grandmaison and Marino had become friends when Grandmaison also was serving as state party chairman a year or so earlier and, despite the differences in their bases and backgrounds, shared the most valuable asset for any political professional—street smarts. So it was not surprising that Marino had called Grandmaison in late October or early November to ask him if he might be willing to help if Cuomo decided to run.

Grandmaison had first come to national attention as the organizer of George McGovern's surprisingly strong showing in the 1972 New Hampshire primary, but he also had played key roles in several state and national campaigns thereafter—one of them as manager of Michael Dukakis's first campaign for governor of Massachusetts in 1974. So he replied that he was interested but only if he could be involved in more than New Hampshire. He wanted to be, he told Marino, "one of the five or six around the table" in a Cuomo campaign, to which Marino agreed.

On December 16, the Monday before the Friday deadline for filing, Marino called Grandmaison to ask, as the latter recalled, "what a schedule would look like" if Cuomo were flown into the state Friday to file the papers. The following day Grandmaison convened an instant committee to devise a schedule and then sent a fax to Marino's office in New York outlining a tentative plan and the steps that would have to be taken to prepare. By now the word was circulating through New Hampshire's small community of political activists and, Grandmaison said, "I started getting telephone calls from people who wanted to help."

Soon the list reached eighty or eighty-five people, including longtime liberal activists such as Sylvia Chaplain and prominent party figures such as former gubernatorial candidate Paul McEachern. The tentative schedule called for Cuomo to file his papers, hold a press conference in front of the statehouse, meet with sixty or seventy people who would make up the nucleus of his support and then meet with one of several networking groups of unemployed workers that had been formed in New Hampshire to talk about the economy. Grandmaison rented a bus and called Bob Molloy, another veteran state Democrat, and asked him to set up a sound system for the press conference. Marino dispatched a couple of advance men from New York to help with the mechanics.

At eight o'clock Friday morning Grandmaison positioned himself in the lobby of the Ramada Inn a block from the statehouse so he could keep in touch with Marino by using a pay telephone on the wall there. As the day wore on the crowd at the statehouse grew to 250 or so—the press, expectant supporters, the curious. People kept arriving and CNN kept showing a plane chartered for Cuomo poised on the tarmac at Albany. The candidate would be flown to Manchester and then driven the final eighteen miles to Concord. "Those of us from New Hampshire were getting somewhat giddy," Grandmaison said later.

But in New York, the optimistic enthusiasm Cuomo had displayed

Thursday night was missing. "Thursday night lifted my spirits immensely," Marino recalled. "By Friday morning I was talking to a different Mario Cuomo." The budget deal had not been made, after all.

Cuomo remained alone at the mansion on Eagle Street, making telephone calls and meditating. As the morning turned to noon to early afternoon, it was clear that time was running short. An alternative plan was developed to fly him directly to Concord if that were necessary. But it was also becoming clear that Cuomo wasn't going to do it. When Grandmaison placed his hourly call to Marino shortly after 3 P.M., the New Yorker told him: "Joe, he's going to announce at 3:30 that it's a no-go."

A few minutes later, just ninety minutes from the deadline, Cuomo broke the news to the reporters who had been spending hours guessing about his intentions. Citing the budget problem, Cuomo said: "It's my responsibility as governor to deal with this extraordinarily severe problem. Were it not, I would travel to New Hampshire today and file my name as a candidate in its presidential primary. That was my hope and I prepared for it. But it seems to me I cannot turn my attention to New Hampshire while this threat hangs over the head of the New Yorkers that I have sworn to put first."

Now that he had finally made the decision, Cuomo abandoned his coyness about whether he ever had wanted the prize. "I would be less than honest if I did not admit to you my regret at not having the opportunity to run for president," he said.

Cuomo conceded that it was possible to bypass New Hampshire and enter the race later but said he had no such intention. Instead, he said, he was meeting the "definitive deadline" set by Ron Brown. "You can't argue for that in logic or law," he said, "but I accept it and I understand the intelligence of it from his political point of view. Get Cuomo and everybody else out of the way and let's concentrate on the field we have."

At another point, he said: "I accept the judgment of the national chairman of our party that it would be in the best interest of the Democratic Party that I abandon any such effort now so as to avoid whatever inconvenience and disruption to the process is created by the uncertain possibility of another candidacy."

Whatever the reason, the Cuomo decision had cleared the air and defined the Democratic field. In the Clinton camp, it was obviously an important day. As Paul Begala recalled later, "We breathed a huge sigh of relief."

In Concord, Grandmaison walked from the Ramada to the statehouse and told the crowd Cuomo would not be coming after all. Before the sound system could be dismantled, however, Bob Kerrey arrived on the way to file his own papers with the secretary of state—and added a final bizarre touch to the day. "Kerrey walked up to the microphones," Grandmaison recalled, "and started, incredible though it may seem, started talking about the cost of energy"—at the moment the biggest political story in months had just broken.

With his television tuned to CNN in his office in Washington, Ron Brown was, as he said later, "incredulous watching his [Cuomo's] press conference." He had not spoken directly to Cuomo for months and had been forced to rely on messages sent through Marino, Del Giudice and the press. Now he felt he was being made the heavy who had forced poor Mario Cuomo to make this decision sooner than he might have liked. When Mike Royko of the *Chicago Tribune* wrote a column excoriating Brown for denying the Democrats their strongest candidate, Brown said, "I started getting the hate mail."

The notion that Cuomo had made the decision under pressure from Ron Brown was, on its face, laughable. Many of those close to the New York Democrat always had doubted that he would run, because he felt that obligation to his constituents and because he had always resisted the idea of having to go out and scramble for votes in unfamiliar territory.

Cuomo had always been extremely provincial, not just a New Yorker but a citizen of Queens who had never seemed at ease in Houston or Cleveland. Waiting for the decision that Friday in a television studio in Washington, Joe Klein, then a columnist for *New York* magazine and later with *Newsweek,* guessed an hour ahead of time that Cuomo wouldn't run. "He's probably saying to himself," Klein speculated, " 'St. John's is going to have a good [basketball] team this year and I won't be able to see the games.' "

Klein was being facetious, but in one sense he was not entirely off the mark. Although the budget deadlock was a serious problem for Cuomo, it didn't necessarily mean he couldn't run for the Democratic presidential nomination if—and this was the operative point—if he wanted the presidency badly enough. Most of those who run successfully for the White

House do indeed want the office with such a consuming passion that they will brush aside any obstacle, bend themselves into any configuration to get there.

Mario Cuomo was not one of them. Talking about it much later in his office in the World Trade Center in Manhattan, he put it this way: "I have difficulty with the notion of wanting it badly. I'm not sure what that means. I'm afraid some people want the office too much and I've always tried to guard against that. If you say, 'Did you have a great hunger for it?' I was always afraid of people who had too great a hunger for it. I thought they had the process backward. It shouldn't be that you desire the office and then you go out and get it. It should be that you are better than anybody else who's available. Otherwise, it's a very difficult thing to justify."

But if there were limits on Cuomo's ambition, there were others—in both parties—who were not so fettered.

CHALLENGE ON
THE RIGHT

Patrick J. Buchanan, the Republican right wing's angriest articulate voice on television and the nation's editorial pages, had always been dubious about George Bush. Sure, Bush supported supply-side economics—but only after Ronald Reagan put him on the national ticket in 1980; before then it was "voodoo economics." The same was true of his opposition to abortion; he was a politician whose views were a matter of convenience. Except on the Cold War, Bush seemed to lack the ideological moorings of a Ronald Reagan.

And now, after four years of Bush in the White House, the glories of Reaganism seemed increasingly distant. A few more years of this guy and old Dutch would be gone without a trace. Largely because of his doubts about Bush, Buchanan had thought seriously about running in 1987. But he feared his candidacy would serve only to dilute the potential base of support for another devout Reaganite, Jack Kemp. The idea never left Buchanan's mind, however, and he grew increasingly restive with

Bush's performance in the White House. If this was a committed conservative, the evidence was far from clear.

The notion of a television commentator and newspaper columnist running for president had been broached at other times. When Walter Cronkite was regarded by many as "the most trusted American," he was often touted as a potential presidential candidate. The same was true, to a lesser degree, of Bill Moyers, LBJ White House press secretary turned television sage. But Buchanan was different. Unlike Cronkite, he had a long identification with the Republican Party and had served in the White House under two Republican presidents, Nixon and Reagan. And, unlike both Cronkite and Moyers, he had a sharp ideological identification that had built him something of a cult following among like-minded conservatives who watched him regularly on such political talk shows as *The McLaughlin Group, Crossfire* and *The Capital Gang*—all with substantial audiences of political junkies.

In the fall of 1991, shortly after Buchanan had hinted he might run, a television colleague covering a David Duke rally at Evangeline Downs race track just outside Lafayette, Louisiana, found himself beset by white men in jeans and work caps all with the same message—as one put it: "When you go back home, tell old Pat to run."

In fact, Buchanan more than a year earlier had begun thinking actively about challenging the incumbent president, when Bush reneged on his promise not to raise taxes and joined the Democrats in the budget agreement. "Like a lot of conservatives," Buchanan said later, "I felt he'd broken the main commitment he'd made for us."

By January of 1991, Buchanan was putting his toe in the water, accepting an invitation from Governor Judd Gregg of New Hampshire to speak at a party dinner in Manchester. Buchanan realized that Gregg was trying to use him to send a message to President Bush that he had better give the state more of his attention. But symbiosis is what politics is all about, and the appearance also served Buchanan's purpose. It gave him a chance to test his message and cement an already close relationship with Nacky Loeb and Joseph McQuaid, the publisher and editor, respectively, of *The Union Leader*, the unfettered voice of conservative extremism in Manchester that still was a major influence in the state's politics.

But the context changed abruptly that night. "I got up to speak,"

Buchanan recalled, ''and when I got down, this guy put a camera in my face and said, 'There's explosions in Baghdad.' So I said we've all got to get behind our president.''

With Bush presiding over a popular war in the Persian Gulf, Buchanan told McQuaid, ''it would be ridiculous to have any kind of conservative challenge.'' As the war was playing out even more successfully than Bush might have dared to hope, such a challenge seemed even more ridiculous.

The war had caused a political problem for Buchanan in other ways because he had been one of the few conservatives to take a firm and characteristically outspoken position against military action, arguing vehemently that there was no national interest in the Gulf worth the risk of American lives. For his trouble, he noted later, the conservative *Washington Times*, which regularly ran his column, made him the first inductee in its Wall of Shame. His opposition to Bush on Gulf policy was a stance that put him in the company of, among others, George McGovern, and dismayed other rightists less devoted to what they called ''the new isolationism.''

Meanwhile, George Bush was enjoying the political fruits of vindication. Buchanan, a native Washingtonian, recalled being particularly impressed by the June 10 parade to celebrate the victory in the Persian Gulf—troops and tanks passing on Pennsylvania Avenue while Stealth bombers flew by overhead. ''You just said, 'This guy's invincible,' '' Buchanan remembered thinking. ''There hadn't been a parade like that in my hometown since Eisenhower. The whole country loved it.''

As Bush's postwar approval ratings began to fade, however, Buchanan's interest in running against him was revived. The ''triggering event'' for Buchanan was Bush's decision—''that cave-in,'' Buchanan called it—to accept the 1991 Civil Rights Act, which had become an issue of intense symbolic importance to liberals and conservatives alike. Bush had vetoed a similar measure in 1990 and fought the new version for months, insisting in the face of heavy conflicting evidence that it was a ''quota bill''—one that would require American employers to establish quotas for minority employees, or risk extended and expensive litigation.

The decision was more stunning to Buchanan because it came on the heels of what he saw as a great triumph for conservatives in general and

George Bush in particular, the Senate confirmation of Clarence Thomas for the Supreme Court. "Then he turned around and said, 'I'm going to sign the quota bill'—the quota civil rights bill—after he'd said, 'I'm not going to sign it, I'm not going to sign it, I'm not going to sign it.' " Buchanan wrote an angry newspaper column calling the Bush decision a betrayal following a long series of betrayals.

When his sister, Angela—known as Bay—read the column in California, she called and told him he should stop just writing angry columns and run for president.

The off-year election returns also began to suggest there was something different in the political water right now. Buchanan was impressed by Harris Wofford overturning a deficit of more than forty points in the opinion polls and winning that Senate election in Pennsylvania. And he noted that David Duke, although losing his race for governor of Louisiana to Edwin W. Edwards by a three-to-two margin, had captured a majority of the white vote and more than 60 percent of the non-Catholic white vote.

"What the elections told me," he said later, "was . . . there's really a movement out there, that if you could ignite it against the establishment of both parties, it might really go somewhere." Trying to measure his potential, sister Bay, who was to become his campaign manager, telephoned Nacky Loeb at the *Union Leader*, a call that produced a front-page editorial under the headline: RUN, PAT, RUN. For Buchanan, this was critical. "So then you knew," he recalled, "that if you went in there [the New Hampshire primary], you could pretty much count on strong support from the *Union Leader*, without which there's no sense going in there for a conservative against a sitting president."

From the outset, Buchanan's campaign was predicated on the notion that the New Hampshire primary offered his only real opportunity. His strategy would have to be, he said later, "score big in New Hampshire or come home." He knew economic conditions in the state were disastrous and thought he might be the vehicle for sending a message to the White House—that Bush had been too cavalier in his treatment of the state whose Republican primary had been so important to him four years earlier. He believed that Bush lacked the kind of hold on Republicans that Ronald Reagan had enjoyed; there were no Bushites as there were

Reaganites, no Bush Democrats as there were Reagan Democrats. And there was the history of the New Hampshire primary electorate defying the conventional wisdom and the establishment.

This was, after all, the state in which Eugene McCarthy had captured 42 percent of the Democratic vote in 1968 against President Johnson, a showing that ultimately forced Johnson out of the campaign. Buchanan remembered that phenomenon well. He was in New Hampshire at the time as a campaign aide to Richard Nixon, running in the state's Republican primary against Governor George Romney of Michigan. Nixon's one-sided victory there put him on the comeback trail to the White House—and Buchanan with him. New Hampshire was also the state in which Reagan came within a point of upsetting another incumbent president, Republican Gerald R. Ford, in 1976. "It wasn't a total lark up there," Buchanan said later. "You knew you could do something."

Buchanan also counted on the novelty of someone like him in the field. "What I knew I had going up there was a damned good story," he said. "Somebody coming off a talk show and challenging the president of the United States is good copy in a boring political season." His only concern, he said later, "was somebody else would get in there, [William] Bennett, [Pete] du Pont or even Duke," depriving him of "the clarity of coming off the talk show."

And with Bush still giving New Hampshire a cold shoulder, Buchanan figured he could use to good effect what he called "the old he-cared-enough-to-come" pitch to frustrated voters, a reference to the slogan Nelson Rockefeller used to upset the absent Barry Goldwater in the Oregon Republican primary of 1964.

So, on December 10, just ten weeks before the primary, Buchanan went to Concord and declared his candidacy. In his announcement speech at the state capitol, he urged "a new nationalism" and policies to "put America first." He touched the sore spots of resentment, particularly of foreign aid, and stressed generational change. "This race is not about personalities and it will not get into personalities," he told his supporters. "George Bush served bravely in America's great war. George Bush is a man of graciousness, honor and integrity who has given half a lifetime to his country's service. But the differences between us now are too deep. He is yesterday and we are tomorrow."

At another point, he defined it this way: "He is a globalist and we are nationalists. He believes in some pax universalis; we believe in the old republic. He would put America's wealth and power at the service of some vague new world order. We put America first.''

Despite his insistence that he would not ''get into personalities,'' Buchanan made a point of defining the ideological differences within his party in terms of Bush's actions. ''We Republicans can no longer say it is all the liberals' fault,'' he said. ''It was not some liberal Democrat who declared, 'Read my lips: no new taxes,' then broke his word to cut a seedy back-room deal with the big spenders on Capitol Hill. It was not Teddy Kennedy who railed against a quota bill, then embraced its twin. It was not Congress alone who set off the greatest spending spree in sixty years, running up the largest deficits in modern history. . . . No, that was done by the men in whom we placed our confidence and our trust and who turned their backs and walked away from us.''

Buchanan also was talking with increasing frequency about immigration, having deduced from what he heard that this, too, was a hot button with American workers worried about competition for their jobs. And, characteristically, he did it with the kind of extravagant and often inflammatory language that persuaded liberals he was racist and anti-Semitic. The latter was a particular problem for Buchanan, guaranteeing him clutches of Jewish demonstrators at many of his campaign appearances.

The question of whether Buchanan was an anti-Semite came to the fore when, during the debate over the wisdom of military action against Iraq, Buchanan buttressed his argument against it on a television program by pointing out, correctly, that Israel had a direct national interest in destroying the Iraqi military capacity. But, as usual, he voiced it in terms that invited a hot response: ''There are only two groups beating the drums for war in the Middle East—the Israeli defense ministry and its amen corner in the United States.''

The comment drew a wrathful column from A. M. Rosenthal of *The New York Times* accusing Buchanan of anti-Semitism. That column, in turn, set off a debate over Buchanan's history of controversial pronouncements and columns on issues having to do with Israel, including his long-running argument that the case against John Demjanjuk, accused of being a Nazi war criminal known as ''Ivan the Terrible,'' was flawed. Fellow conservative William F. Buckley wrote a long article in his magazine, *National Review*, in which he concluded that many of the things Buchanan had written or said about Jews "could not reasonably be interpreted as other than anti-semitic in tone and substance."

For those like ourselves who had known Buchanan for twenty-five years or more—back to the time Richard Nixon was running in New Hampshire in 1968—the question was vexing and complex. On the one hand, there was no question that Buchanan's prose and rhetoric was never run through a filter of sensitivity toward any group and, in cases involving Israel, could be seen as a reflection of anti-Semitism. On the other, if the definition of anti-Semitism requires an automatically hostile reaction to Jews and their interests, we believed from long personal exposure that Buchanan did not qualify. But whatever the truth of the matter, it was a label that had been firmly affixed to the conservative commentator and one that would stick to him in this campaign.

Although his declaration of candidacy centered more on foreign policy than domestic issues, Buchanan also touched some nerves when he included this passage: "When we say we will put America first, we mean also that our Judeo-Christian values are going to be preserved and our Western heritage is going to be handed down to future generations and not dumped into some landfill called multiculturism." When the statement caused a stir, Buchanan "explained" it this way on the David Brinkley program on ABC television: "I think God made all people good, but if we were to take a million immigrants in, say Zulus, next year, or Englishmen and put them in Virginia, what group would be easier to assimilate and would cause less problems for the people of Virginia?"

Interviewed on *The MacNeil/Lehrer Newshour*, Buchanan conceded that God created all men equal "in their basic natural rights" but added: "He did not create them all equally assimilable in an English-speaking society which . . . [has] British institutions and has basically a Euro-American culture. . . . I think when you decide on legal immigration, that matters of culture, of language or religion, of ethnicity have got to be taken into consideration. . . ."

This was the essential Buchanan. On the face of it, it might be impossible to deny that some groups are more easily assimilated into American society than others. That reality has played a part in immigration policy and law at times. But Pat Buchanan never used restrained language when it was possible to be colorful and provocative. And what could be more provocative than suggesting that some groups should be regarded as garbage being cast into that "landfill." It was the kind of language that made his columns and commentary so striking. But it was also the kind of language that seemed to appeal to the least noble attitudes of his followers. Although Buchanan looked down his nose at David Duke, his tactics sometimes were identical, and he made no bones of the fact he was appealing for the support of the Duke admirers.

In practical political terms, this perception of Buchanan imposed limits on his ability to reach beyond the most angry and reactionary of the extremists of the right, to enlist conservatives toward the center. He wasn't respectable enough for them. Thus, when one of us attended a Buchanan speech in a small New Hampshire town one snowy Sunday night, at least four or five couples who had been in the audience made it a point to say that although they were disappointed in George Bush and had attended this meeting, they would never—never—vote for Pat Buchanan. Maybe, one elderly woman said, she could bring herself to vote for a Democrat just this once, someone like that Paul Tsongas. "George Bush is a fool," she said, "but Mr. Buchanan is too scary."

Buchanan entered the primary campaign with few illusions about his potential. He acknowledged that it was "almost impossible" to take a nomination away from an incumbent president and that New Hampshire had many Republican loyalists who would stick with Bush in a primary even with their reservations about him. So Buchanan's hope was to expose the weakness of the president and force him to the sidelines as Gene McCarthy had done to Lyndon Johnson.

"If I get 45 percent," he told reporters in Concord that day, "they'll be writing their résumés in the Roosevelt Room the next morning." But there was also always that tantalizing possibility of defeating Bush and winning the nomination himself. "You might be ranked twenty-seventh but you got a title fight right up there in New Hampshire," he said later.

The reaction within the Bush campaign was more annoyance than concern. "We weren't entirely blindsided but we were a little surprised when Pat decided to get in," Charlie Black recalled. The conservative community in Washington is tightly knit and relatively small, and news passes rapidly through the grapevine. Ten days before his announcement, Black heard about a meeting at which Buchanan told his fellow right-wingers: "All right, I'm going to run, so now's the time, those of you who want to, now's the time to go call up Black and cut the best deal you can."

Bush himself was "offended" by Buchanan's decision, Black said. "Bush looks at things on the basis of personal relationships and he thought that he and Buchanan had always had a good personal relationship when they were around the White House together," Black recalled. "He didn't look at it in ideological terms like Pat does. 'Why would this guy want to run against me? We get along.' . . . He considered it another irritant but not an insurmountable problem."

The initial problem for the Bush campaign was that it still lacked either much structure or staff. The time set aside earlier for basic organizational work for the national campaign had to be used as well for preparing for an immediate test in New Hampshire. And the word that came back from Republicans there was consistently disturbing. Tom Rath, the Concord lawyer and Republican activist who had seen the threatening implications of Harris Wofford's success in Pennsylvania, was warning that Buchanan could get 30 to 35 percent of the vote against George Bush simply on the basis of the economic distress in the state.

Bob Teeter, the Bush campaign chairman, ordered a poll and the news wasn't good. "It showed," Black said later, "a great deal of Republican disaffection over the economy and a potential for a big protest vote against Bush." Few believed the threat of the Buchanan challenge had much to do with ideological divisions within the party. "I never heard anybody think it was ideology," Jim Lake said. "They all thought it was the economy."

But George Bush still resisted accepting that judgment, perhaps misled by economic statistics that understated the extent of the economic problem, particularly in New Hampshire. At one point, Teeter told his colleagues: "Boys, the president just doesn't get it. He sees the numbers and the numbers belie some of the suffering and personal experience out there." Even if he had accepted the idea that the economy was driving the electorate so completely, Bush appeared unable to do anything about it. When the White House finally realized in November that public concern about the economy had crystallized into a significant problem for the president, he stalled. Word went out that his plan for economic recovery would come in his next the State of the Union address to Congress—a full two months in the future.

This was the quintessential example of the Washington establishment response that baffles ordinary Americans elsewhere. In the capital, the State of the Union speech is one of the revered annual rituals: a joint session of Congress, members of the cabinet and the Supreme Court filing in to listen on the House floor, the galleries packed with the president's family and other Very Important People; the bright lights of national television, the president being led through the clutching senators and congressmen to the podium, the copy of the address being handed up to the Speaker of the House.

But to millions beyond the Beltway it is just another of those Washington ceremonies that interrupt the television schedule. The connection between the State of the Union address and whether you are going to have a job next week or meet your mortgage payment next month is tenuous. Bush may have thought he was reassuring his constituents with his promise to deal with the economy in late January, but it was hardly the kind of gesture likely to inspire their confidence. And, more than anything else, that reassurance was the political imperative of the moment, nationally and, more to the point, in New Hampshire.

"His credibility . . . on economic issues was so low that a lot of people wanted to vote against him to send a message," Black recalled. "Everybody who went up there [to New Hampshire] . . . [was] impressed with the fact that people were hurting and scared. They were just scared. It was different than anything I'd ever seen."

The result, Bob Teeter said later, was that the Bush advisers now knew that Buchanan could not be overlooked. "Obviously, it didn't take a great deal of genius to know that we had a hell of a problem," he said. The campaign's immediate goals at first, not expecting a primary challenge, were to establish Bush's credentials on the economy—that is, to impress on the electorate that he was concerned and had a plan to do something about it. And Teeter had thought there would be three months or more, while the Democrats were fighting with one another in the early primaries, to get that job done without distractions.

"In retrospect," Teeter said, "the Buchanan candidacy turned out to be incredibly damaging. . . . We thought we had one more window where we could get those things done . . . [but] we spent all that time fighting Pat Buchanan.''

Black noted that Buchanan had declared his candidacy at precisely the point the Bush campaign was just getting organized. ''All this time,'' he said, ''we should be gearing up, assembling a staff, building infrastructure, organizing the states, picking state leaders—we've got a big campaign on our hands in New Hampshire . . . we had to do it all at once and we never got ahead of the curve.''

Like the Democratic candidates who had been on the ground for weeks and in some cases even months, Buchanan now discovered just how preoccupied with—perhaps even obsessed by—the economy New Hampshire voters had become. After the initial flurry of major media attention, Buchanan enjoyed the new experience of campaigning, principally traveling with a small entourage—press secretary Greg Mueller and a handful of reporters—to drop in at diners, walk through stores along the main streets, visit the unemployment lines. ''It was great, I loved it,'' he said later. ''The most vivid impression you got was that they were really down. I was very moved by the whole thing.''

Retail campaigning in New Hampshire was hardly a new experience for Buchanan. But when he traipsed around the state with Dick Nixon in 1968, Nixon was the Republican establishment candidate, and here was Buchanan challenging the party establishment. Also, working New Hampshire as a candidate was quite different from tagging along behind somebody else, doing his errands.

Back then, Buchanan was the ever-uptight Nixon's buttress against an ever-inquisitive press, keeping us at bay as best he could. He played a key role in one of Nixon's most famous con jobs on reporters, on the first morning of his 1968 campaign in the state. The night before, Nixon had held a party for reporters at the old New Hampshire Highway Hotel in Concord at which he promised that relations would be different between him and his longtime tormentors. Then, as we slept, assured by Buchanan that nothing was scheduled early the next morning, he and Nixon slipped off to shoot television commercials with a stacked audience at a local town hall. Buchanan then and later managed to share Nixon's contempt for much of the news media (but not Nixon's paranoic fear) while getting rich as a member of it, and maintaining friendships in its ranks.

Now, twenty-four years later as a candidate himself, every day there seemed to be a new and striking case history from which to learn. An old woman breaking into tears while talking about her financial problems. A worker lined up outside a paper mill in Berlin waiting for his Christmas turkey and suddenly looking up at the Republican visitor and telling him: "Save our jobs." The owner of a submarine sandwich shop in Laconia relating how he ran a help-wanted advertisement for a part-time delivery-man offering pay just above the minimum wage and no health insurance, and received 250 applications from as far away as Nashua, more than an hour down the road.

Buchanan began to understand that Bush's perfidy on the tax bill was less important than these immediate concerns, and his own rhetoric began to change as he learned more. This phenomenon was common in the strange politics of 1992. Politicians usually set their own agenda, but this year the voters were determining what the topics would be.

Buchanan described it this way: "You go up there obviously with your own speech and your ideas and the more you talk to these people and the more you listen to them, the more what they say and what they think and what they're concerned about, the more that is worked through what you say, until what you say, you're speaking their language, their hurt and you're talking to their concerns, and I think it comes through."

Bush, meanwhile, was trapped in a political dilemma. On the one hand, it was risky for him to pay too much attention to New Hampshire and the challenge from some right-winger from a television talk show. That would suggest he was taking Buchanan too seriously and inflate the importance of the challenge. On the other hand, Tom Rath and Judd Gregg in New Hampshire and his advisers in Washington were telling him it was essential for the president to demonstrate that he remembered how important New Hampshirites had been to him four years earlier, that he recognized the dimensions of their problem, and that he was going to do something about it.

By December, while still delaying his official candidacy, Bush was beginning to show himself as a candidate by taking part in carefully staged media events elsewhere. In Chicago on the day Buchanan announced his candidacy, the president dropped in for a hamburger at the Billy Goat Tavern, a blue-collar lunchtime and after-work hangout for many workers from the Chicago newspapers nearby—but hardly a natural venue for the preppy president from Andover and Yale. Another day it was chicken-fried steak at Cafe 121 in Coppell, Texas. Still another was a visit to a Head Start center in Maryland. But like a celebrated earlier trip to a J.C. Penney's outside Washington to buy socks, none of these gestures rang true. And more to the point, none of them impressed the skeptical electorate of 1992. The time for media events had passed; it was time for some evidence George Bush understood these voters and their fears and was capable of doing something about it.

In New Hampshire, meanwhile, there were some small signs that Buchanan was hitting a nerve. By late December an opinion poll published by the *Concord Monitor* showed the president leading Buchanan among Republican primary voters, 58 percent to 30 percent. Those were the dimensions of a comfortable victory for anyone in most circumstances, but the figures also could be read as a warning signal to an incumbent president. If Buchanan was truly at 30 percent, the potential for serious embarrassment obviously was there. The White House began to react, dispatching more surrogates into the state, approving additional money for Medicaid costs, opening a passport office at the closed-down Pease Air Force Base near Portsmouth. "You got the sense," Buchanan said, "that something was happening or he [Bush] wouldn't be paying it all that much attention."

The expectations game was important, as it always is in presidential primaries. George Bush needed not only to win the February 18 primary but to do so with a vote impressive enough to put this upstart challenger in his place, to make Buchanan be seen as just some nut taking a flyer. Just what kind of showing would achieve that goal was far from clear, however. The conventional wisdom seemed to be that a 30 percent showing for Buchanan would not be entirely surprising; even the most popular politicians usually have a third of the electorate against them. But what if Buchanan got 35 percent? How would the press and political community interpret that? The goal in the Bush campaign, Charlie Black said, was to hold Buchanan under 40 percent and win by at least twenty points.

The campaign was never joined in the conventional sense—indeed, could not be. An incumbent president cannot spend weeks in New Hampshire attending coffees and visiting diners and bowling alleys or taking part in candidate forums sponsored by interest groups. Especially not against some television commentator. Bush already was universally known, and inevitably so was his record. His campaign would have to be his performance in the Oval Office and elsewhere. But once Buchanan declared himself, it was clear that the president's attention was focused on New Hampshire.

It was obvious, for example, why the rescheduled trip to the Far East had suddenly been converted from one designed to reassure the United States' allies into an economic pilgrimage. Leaving Andrews Air Force Base for Australia, Bush told reporters: "Let me make very clear the focus of this trip. My highest priority is jobs. . . . One way to get this economy growing again is to open up markets abroad for American jobs and services." Nor did many mistake the targets when Bush told the Farm Bureau Federation at Kansas City: "Do not listen to those prophets of doom, those frantic politicians who say we are a second-class power."

The Bush campaign operation, finally rid of the heavy hand of John Sununu running the show from the White House, began doing the mechanical things—sending in surrogates, organizing committees of supporters, setting up telephone banks, sending out mailings, planning and buying time for advertising—that these same Republicans had done so well in so many campaigns. At this point the Bush strategists also were insisting that the campaign would be about "family values" and the "stature gap" between Bush and his less-experienced rivals. Besides, they kept saying, when all is said and done, people "really like" George Bush. Once "the message gets out there" the problems will be solved. And Samuel K. Skinner, the new White House chief of staff, already was planning to shake up the communications office. In short, Bush's advisers were using the classic rationalization of the incumbent in trouble: it's not a failure of the candidate or policy, it's just a failure of communication.

In New Hampshire, Buchanan was finding his footing as a candidate and clearly feeling his oats as well after the first three weeks in his new career. "Mr. Bush, you recall, promised to create 30 million jobs," he delighted in telling one audience after another. "He didn't tell us he would be creating them in Guandong Province, Yokohama or Mexico." When Bush was scheduled to arrive in Tokyo, his challenger plastered a map of New Hampshire on a factory wall in Manchester and turned a giant searchlight into the heavens in an ostensible attempt to help the wandering president find the state. He told crowds that the voters of New Hampshire should "put a Denver boot on Air Force One" and maybe Bush would have time to come and see them then.

The next day Vice President Dan Quayle arrived to make Bush's case. "I understand you want to send a message," he said. "We've got the message. The president understands the problem and is going to do something about it. But please don't send us a message of protectionism. Please don't send us a message of isolationism." But the attempts to reassure New Hampshire Republicans that Bush was on top of their situation obviously were undermined by pictures on every television news broadcast of the president in Tokyo passing out and vomiting into the lap of Prime Minister Kiichi Miyazawa.

Finally, on January 15, just more than a month before the primary, the president himself arrived to campaign in person. But the day, built around a carefully choreographed meeting in the camera-friendly Exeter Town Hall, didn't quite work out as the Bush managers had hoped. Local Republican leaders were calling the visit a "mea culpa tour" designed to allow his followers to vent their anger at him, then get on with the business of reelecting a Republican president.

Unsurprisingly, it was the unevenness of Bush's own performance that thwarted the best-laid plans. He clearly had some trouble convincing himself this was the right approach. At the Exeter meeting, he seemed to hit the right note, telling the Republicans who had been given tickets: "I've known this economy is in a free-fall. Maybe I haven't conveyed it as well as I should have, but I do understand it." But he also continued to insist things might not be as bad as everyone imagined. "There are some fundamentals that are pretty darn good," he said at one point.

Nor could he resist a familiar complaint about his political opponents, saying: "I'm sick and tired of every night hearing one of these carping little liberal Democrats jumping over my you-know-what." He wasn't going to buy some "fancy quick-fix," by God. And, anyway, his political rivals are just "these people who just discovered New Hampshire on the road map." When someone tried to press Pat Buchanan's no-tax pledge on him, Bush reacted by turning away angrily. But—as was the case with that Democratic T-shirt—he could not leave it alone, telling his audience there was "talk about pledges and all that" when what was needed was a pledge to elect more Republicans.

The president also displayed his penchant for goofy non sequiturs, explaining to listeners in Dover that, whatever his burdens, he felt blessed: "Don't cry for me, Argentina." When he tried to refer to the Nitty Gritty

Dirt Band, it came out: "Nitty Ditty Nitty Gritty Great Bird." The most memorable moment, however, may have been when he appeared to read a stage direction from a card: "Message: I care." The president was supposed to summarize his message to the state by saying, "I'm here, I'm listening and I care" but, as Charlie Black observed later, "It got Bushized . . . he has this method of shorthanding everything." Or, as Jim Lake put it, "He was reading the words that had been put down there, because he didn't get it."

The bottom line was that the single day of campaigning was a mixed blessing, at best. Bush attracted substantial audiences and was received warmly on a bitter cold day. As the day progressed, the president seemed more at ease and his listeners more receptive. Rhona Charbonneau, the Republican state chairman, told traveling reporters at Portsmouth that Bush should win "at least 70 percent of the vote" against Buchanan, thus setting a standard that sent chills through his campaign operation. It was another case in which the cheering of the moment obscured the political realities.

By the end of the day, George Bush still had nothing to say that was persuasive about how he could help these frightened New Hampshire voters. And his advice to "stay tuned" for the State of the Union address still two weeks away was less than reassuring. A small-businessman and longtime Republican who had attended one event, a meeting in a hangar at Pease, told a visitor: "It was just some slogans and stuff. He's going to have to do better than that." In an editorial, *The Nashua Telegraph*, which had supported candidate Bush four years earlier, put it this way: "Bush did his best to appear his aggressive best, but unless he can match this attitude with specifics, his campaign forays will lack realism."

Bush didn't seem to grasp the seriousness of his situation. By now, polls were showing his approval rating consistently below 50 percent, and the "wrong track" number was running 75 percent or higher, a red-alert for an incumbent. But the president was making awkward little jokes about how he had soiled the prime minister's suit and trying to get by principally on a smile and a friendly wave from the steps of Air Force One. Even when, a week after his visit to New Hampshire, Bush dropped his opposition to an extension of unemployment benefits, he earned little political credit. Why in the world had he been fighting for weeks against an action that presidents of both parties routinely took in tough times?

By the time the State of the Union day arrived, expectations for the president's speech had been built to a level that he could not possibly fulfill. He tried determinedly, with a combination of bluster and blue smoke and mirrors. He evoked those fading memories of the triumph in the Persian Gulf, saying of the recession as he had of Saddam Hussein's invasion of Kuwait: "This will not stand. . . . We can bring the same courage and sense of common purpose to the economy that we brought to Desert Storm and we can defeat hard times together."

He challenged the Democrats in Congress to pass his economic plan by March 20 and threatened them with political retaliation if they did not do so. "From the day after that, if it must be, the battle is joined," he said. "And you know, when principle is at stake, I relish a good fair fight."

It was obviously an empty threat. Bush was in no position—and both sides knew it—to talk about joining any battle on the economy. Moreover, the specifics of the economic program on which he was staking so much were less than revolutionary—a reflection of the fact this was a president dealing with the prospect of another $400 billion deficit in the next fiscal year. Bush ordered a change in income tax withholding so that most taxpayers would enjoy an immediate increase in take-home pay— about a dollar a day—that would be made up in lower tax refunds in April 1993. He also recommended a temporary tax credit for first-time home buyers, a $500-a-year increase in the personal tax exemption for children, a reduction in the capital gains tax rate, an investment tax allowance, and more flexibility in the use of proceeds of Individual Retirement Accounts for home buyers and to pay medical and education expenses.

There was nothing intrinsically wrong with any of these proposals, and some of them—most notably the capital gains tax reduction—were things the president had been pushing all along. But, again, after all the weeks of building attention for the address, Bush had done nothing to suggest he understood the urgency of the concern in New Hampshire and elsewhere about economic distress.

The perception of his proposals as marginal was reinforced when Jack Kemp, his secretary of housing and urban development, described as "gimmicks" such things as the reduction of withholding to put more money into circulation. "I cannot sit here," Kemp said in a television interview, "and retain my credibility and say that allowing people another thirty dollars a month is going to spur economic recovery"—a judgment Kemp ruefully conceded was not "artful" when scolded by the White House a day later. But voters also had caught wise. A *Washington Post* poll quickly showed that 70 percent of the voters felt the plan did "not go far enough" on the economy and that half the voters were still saying the president does not "understand the economic problems people in this country are having."

Bush's managers were, nonetheless, encouraged. At least Bush now had something that could be called "the plan" on the table. And by setting that March 20 deadline for action, he appeared to have put the ball into the Democrats' court. This was conventional politics—control the agenda, force the other side to react to your initiative. But in the politics of 1992 there was already a growing body of evidence that playing the political game well by the old rules might not be relevant. And with his State of the Union address, the president had played his only real high card in the contest against Pat Buchanan in New Hampshire.

The president's campaign stepped up the attack on the conservative challenger, arguing that "a vote for Pat Buchanan is a vote for Ted Kennedy" and running a heavy concentration of television commercials trying once again to make the point that Bush "cared" about voters in the upcoming primary. "This state has gone through hell," the president said in one thirty-second spot. "It's gone through an extraordinarily difficult time and I am determined to turn this state around." With his official declaration of candidacy just a few days away, Bush granted "exclusive interviews" in the Oval Office with virtually every news outlet of any size in the state—urging voters, as he put it to *The Nashua Telegraph,* to "vote for me and send a message to the United States Congress."

After making his announcement of candidacy in Washington on February 12, six days before the primary, Bush flew to Concord and told the Republicans there: "I believe government is too big and it costs too much." Who could argue with that? But polls continued to show the rebellious attitude of those Republicans. One survey found, for example, that 93 percent of Bush supporters were backing him because they thought he would be the best president, while fully 53 percent of Buchanan supporters were intent on sending a message of their discontent with the president.

The president flew back into the state for a day and a half of campaigning over the final weekend before the vote, but he had little new to say about the central issue of the primary that Pat Buchanan and the five remaining Democratic candidates had been talking about now for several months. At Nashua, Bush told a rally of supporters, "I really honestly believe the people of New Hampshire are a little bit tired of the negative advertising and attack-dog tactics coming from the left and the right." It was a curious and unpersuasive statement coming from a man who just four years earlier had won the New Hampshire primary with a blast of negative advertising against Senate Minority Leader Bob Dole.

The president also was trying to remind Republicans of what was at stake. The central question, he told a pancake breakfast Sunday morning, was: "Who do you want to be president of the United States?" A late television commercial made the same argument, showing Bush as a towering success in foreign affairs and citing the special role of the primary. "In New Hampshire," the announcer's voice said, "we have a special responsibility. We don't just vote, we choose presidents."

Meanwhile, Buchanan had found another weak spot in Bush—his failure to follow up his State of the Union call for an added $500 a child tax exemption by omitting that specific item from legislation sent to Congress. A Buchanan television commercial showed Bush making the promise, with the voice-over saying: "Today he's abandoned your tax cut. Even his advisers admit it was just a speech for New Hampshire." Buchanan also was running, for the first time, commercials centered on his own plans and policy proposals, an obvious attempt to lift himself beyond the send-a-message rhetoric. And the challenger himself was as extravagant as ever, telling his volunteers that they would "cut through the hollow army of King George like a knife through butter."

Perhaps the most revealing thing about Bush's final campaign swing into the primary state was the fact that he brought movie star Arnold Schwarzenegger with him as what he told voters in Goffstown was a "special treat" for them. The audience loved it; reporters at the event thought the reaction was clearly more enthusiastic to "The Terminator" than to the Leader of the Free World. But whatever the reaction, this was the oldest of the old politics, the quintessential media event in a state whose citizens had been signaling frantically for six months now that they needed bread rather than circuses. The final opinion polls showed Bush with a comfortable lead—60 percent to 33 percent according to CNN, 54 to 26 according to *The Boston Globe*—but hardly a ringing testimonial to George Bush as either a president or candidate.

When primary day finally arrived, Buchanan profited politically by an anomaly, an error in the exit polls—the survey of voters leaving their polling places after they had cast their ballots. These polls generally have been quite reliable indicators of the actual returns. They cover a large sample of voters and because they are made outside the polling place, the poll-takers are assured they are dealing with actual voters, not just "likely" or "registered" voters. By the time of the 1992 election, there was only one exit poll of any moment, a survey conducted by an operation called Voter Research and Surveys. It was financed jointly by the television networks and leading news organizations that once sponsored their own separate surveys at great expense, usually producing basically identical results.

In theory, the polls are intended primarily to provide an understanding of how the vote broke down—which candidate won by how much among voters of different races, ages, economic circumstances, ethnic backgrounds and ideological identification. But on election days they become a running account of who's ahead and by how much, as the data accumulate in the computer systems of the sponsoring news organizations. Although the information is supposed to be closely held, the findings race through the political grapevine all day.

On February 18 the first exit polls had Buchanan running far behind with only 26 to 28 percent of the vote. But by early afternoon, they were finding a tight race in the Republican contest, each candidate with 49 percent of the projected vote. In midafternoon Buchanan went running and when he returned, he recalled, "Somebody said you and Bush are only about four points apart." The challenger and some of his friends drove over to a steakhouse in Nashua and on the way back began to hear the first actual returns, showing him ahead of the president in the raw vote in Manchester. "We were really sky-high," he said. More to the point, the final exit poll figures showing Bush with 48 percent of the vote and Buchanan with 42 created a mind-set in the press that the president was about to suffer a serious political embarrassment, a de facto defeat even as he was winning.

"I got an enormous benefit out of the fact that the exit polls were showing the race incredibly tight," Buchanan said later. "It looked like Bush was going to get the shock of his life. It looked like he was in real danger in New Hampshire and I think a lot of reporters started writing their leads and the talk around town . . . was that [there was] crisis management at the White House. All that crisis management and early returns [that] showed it closer than it was, was a tremendous benefit to me."

Buchanan had been hoping "to do what McCarthy did"—that is, run so far ahead of expectations—to be the "winner" even while losing. But he also had been nourishing "way in the back of your mind" the thought that there might be a political miracle in the making. And now the figures from the exit poll were suggesting that might be possible.

The same thoughts were running through the Bush campaign, particularly after Charlie Black and Jim Lake flew into Manchester and heard about the final exit poll numbers—and reports from Republican leaders that the turnout had been extraordinarily high. Black and Lake were supposed to be the spin doctors for the president on this occasion, charged with putting the best possible face on the results, as the hard returns continued to show Buchanan with more than 40 percent of the vote and Bush under 50. "That was scary there for a couple of hours," Black said, "because I never had it in mind that, hell, we could lose this, but I had it in mind if it was fifty-two to forty-eight we were in for a long primary season."

Mary Matalin, recalling that first primary night, said "you can't underestimate the shock value of that exit poll." The campaign staff, she said, was "in panic," so much so that a conference call was made from Washington to about 300 campaign operatives around the country to try to combat the impact. Teeter got on the line, she said, saying, "Don't worry; it's our low-water mark," but the damage to staff morale was done. "We'd won and everyone said we lost," Matalin recalled. "We were demoralized." And analysts on the air, she said, were asking "why we weren't doing better." By the time the official figures came in, she said, "the press couldn't pull back," continuing to report Buchanan's big surprise, "and that attitude was absorbed by field [the field staff]. . . . We never should have had that conference call."

Black and Lake met with Judd Gregg and Tom Rath at the Center of New Hampshire Holiday Inn in Manchester, then telephoned Teeter back in Washington. They recommended that the president quickly make a statement claiming victory but expressing generosity toward the Republicans who supported Buchanan, and repeating his understanding of their concern with the condition of the economy. But Bush was angry and refused to go to his victory celebration and make a statement. "The mood he's in right now," Teeter reported to his colleagues, "you wouldn't want him to do it anyway."

Finally, the president issued a statement that conceded the results were not all that he would have wanted. "This election was far closer than many had predicted," he said. "I understand the message of dissatisfaction." At the White House, press secretary Marlin Fitzwater underscored the recognition that Buchanan had become more than a minor annoyance, announcing that Bush would be campaigning virtually full-time from February 25 through March 10, the date of the Super Tuesday primaries, when voters in eleven states, seven of them in the South or border states, would go to the polls.

Back in Manchester, Black and Lake told television interviewers and reporters gathered at the Tara Sheraton Wayfarer that "a win is a win" and that they should remember poor George Bush had been under constant assault not only from Buchanan but also from all the Democratic candidates, while Buchanan had been enjoying a free ride.

Meanwhile, armed with what appeared to be more than 40 percent of the vote, Buchanan was exuberantly claiming victory. "Tonight we began as a little rebellion that has emerged into a full-fledged middle-American revolution," he told his cheering supporters. "We are going to take our party back from those who have walked away from us and forgotten about us." At another point he shouted: "Buchanan's brigades met King George's army . . . and I'm here to report they're retreating back into Massachusetts!"

The final official figures, however, were not as devastating to the president as either the exit poll that preconditioned the press and political community or the earlier returns that seemed to validate the exit poll.

Bush ended with 53 percent to 37 for Buchanan, with the other 10 percent representing votes for minor candidates and, more often, write-ins for Democrat Paul Tsongas. Just what skewed the exit poll was never entirely clear, but one theory was that more Bush supporters refused to respond to the poll-takers than did voters who had just cast their ballots for Buchanan.

But even given the inaccuracy of the head-to-head figures, the exit poll was full of warning signs for the president. Only 7 percent of the Republican primary voters, for example, listed the war in the Persian Gulf among the three issues they considered most important in making their decision. By contrast, half said it was the economy, one fourth cited taxes and one fifth the problems of the health care system. Almost 90 percent said the economy was "not very good" or "poor."

The question now was what Buchanan could do for an encore. "I knew damned well that George Bush was not going to step down from the presidency of the United States and give Pat Buchanan the Republican nomination by virtual default," he said later. And if Buchanan had been harboring such notions, they were quickly dispelled. Black found him having a celebratory drink with his friends at the Wayfarer election night, and told him: "Congratulations, Pat, get some sleep, because you've got thirteen primaries in the next three weeks."

Buchanan understood that moral victories, even those exaggerated by a faulty exit poll, were not going to do it. "You're going to have to beat him in a state and break it open," he recalled telling himself, "and Georgia was the one we picked."

C H A P T E R   9

SWIMMING AGAINST THE TIDE

One night in early November of 1991, Paul Tsongas was having dinner with two reporters at the Country Place in Merrimack, New Hampshire. Casually, he mentioned that he supported term limitations on officeholders. When the reporters seemed surprised, he said he didn't talk about it in the campaign because he feared it might be a distraction. "I've got to be a Johnny-one-note on the economy," he said. "I want people to say, 'This son of a bitch knows what he's talking about.' "

In his six months as a candidate for the Democratic presidential nomination, Tsongas had probably accomplished that purpose. Starting with his eighty-six-page tract, *A Call to Economic Arms*, the fifty-year-old former senator from Massachusetts had established himself as a political scold on what the Democratic Party needed to do to save itself, and the country as well. The party had to abandon its long tradition of bashing business and instead make common cause with it. There could be no true economic revival without a strong manufacturing base, and until there was a healthy economy, all the social goals of the Democrats would

153

remain beyond their reach. It was a thesis that was antithetical to traditional liberalism but not dissimilar to what was being heard from the more moderate voices in the party, and particularly the Democratic Leadership Council.

At that stage, Tsongas's views seemed essentially irrelevant. Although he had been out there as a declared candidate since April 30, he was still being lumped into the "second tier" of candidates, with Doug Wilder and Jerry Brown, a step below the supposedly more serious challengers, Bill Clinton, Bob Kerrey and Tom Harkin. There was no mystery about why. Tsongas had left the Senate in 1985 after a single term because of cancer, a non-Hodgkin's lymphoma, and had none of the conventional credentials for a candidate. Nor was he a compelling campaigner capable of electrifying an audience.

Tsongas himself was philosophical about all this, comforted by his certainty that he had the answers on the economy. "Nobody ever says to me, 'You're wrong on the issues,' " he said. "They say, 'You don't give a good speech,' or 'You're a Greek.' "

Tsongas was accustomed to being a lightly regarded underdog. He had come up through the political ranks in his native Lowell, Massachusetts, a mill town of 100,000 people forty miles from Boston that had been struggling for two generations, first to save and then to replace its old manufacturing base. Tsongas had served on the city council, then as a Middlesex County commissioner before being elected to the House of Representatives in 1974. After two terms he won a Democratic Senate primary in 1978 against two better-known rivals and then defeated an incumbent Republican, Senator Edward W. Brooke, who had been weakened by ethics charges.

Tsongas had won that Senate seat the same way he was now trying to win a presidential nomination—by relentlessly pressing his views on the electorate without benefit of either flashy advertising or a vivid public personality. When he entered the Senate primary, he ran some attention-getting commercials showing Massachusetts voters trying to pronounce his name—and failing spectacularly. The novel approach essentially solved that problem. From that point forward, however, the Paul Tsongas campaign was Paul Tsongas droning on the issues.

Before his cancer was diagnosed, Tsongas had been thinking about running for president in 1988—a piece of personal history that, in retrospect, he found ironic. If he had been well enough to run that year, the context would have been all wrong. "If I had been in New Hampshire in 1988," he said, "the discussion would have been about how much your condo appreciated the month before because those were boom times, and someone like me would have been irrelevant."

In any case, Tsongas put his ambitions on ice while he was undergoing treatment, until sometime in 1990. He was serving in those days on the boards of directors of several corporations, largely for high-technology firms, and was struck by his fellow directors' concern, he said later, about "the decline of the United States" and the frustration they felt "about our refusal to acknowledge the problem."

He was seeing evidence everywhere. "I remember driving down Route 93 from Lowell to Boston and passing people or being passed by people driving very expensive cars," he said, "and saying to myself, 'Don't they realize that there's a real capital problem in the United States, and if you spend $40,000 on a Japanese car . . . ?"

So Tsongas decided to write a book, and over a Thanksgiving vacation on Cape Cod began working on it. By the end of the year, he saw several options for himself—simply push the book, find some like-minded candidate to support—Senators Bob Kerrey of Nebraska and Bill Bradley of New Jersey were the two he had in mind—or run himself, either in a full-scale campaign or a symbolic candidacy in New Hampshire.

It soon became clear to him that running was the only alternative if he hoped to get any attention for his ideas about the economy and Democratic Party. He tried to arrange to speak about his ideas at a National Press Club luncheon in Washington, for example, but the press club turned him down. "It was obvious I had no forum to speak from," he said. So, with a clearance from his doctors, his wife and his three daughters, he and his longtime political intimate, Dennis Kanin, began to plan a campaign early in 1991.

Tsongas was not a naïf. He understood from the outset that he would be the object of ridicule, although he may not have fully appreciated the news media's fixation on the preposterous notion of "another Greek from Massachusetts." He enjoyed telling campaign audiences about breaking the news to an old friend that he was "thinking of running for president," to which the old friend replied: "President of what?"

"That was the basic reaction," Tsongas said later. "Everybody was very skeptical.'' And he had his own doubts as well. ''You lie in bed at 2 A.M. in Lowell, Massachusetts, and you think, 'You gotta be kidding, that you'd actually run for president.' '' But the tipping point came— ''the moment where I guess I decided in my own heart that something had to be done''—when he listened to President Bush deliver his State of the Union speech to the Congress after the Persian Gulf War, and be received with wild demonstrations of pride in the military success that had just been achieved.

''When he got to the domestic side,'' Tsongas recalled, ''he said we were the most productive nation on earth, and it was obvious he would not use his enormous political capital to deal with the realities that all of us saw out in the private sector. That was the moment where I was comfortable that even though there would be ridicule about running . . . there was a purpose to be served.'' It was something he could do, he decided, to meet ''the obligation of my survival'' of his cancer.

Over the next few months, Tsongas's sense of purpose was sorely tested. Money was hard to raise; the prosperous Greek-Americans who had contributed so heavily to Michael Dukakis in 1988 now felt betrayed and in no humor to help another candidate with superficially similar credentials. Where Dukakis had raised some $10 million in the year before his campaign, Tsongas raised less than one tenth as much. His operation was thin—his old friend Kanin as campaign manager once again; Andy Paven, an experienced advance man as his traveling companion; Ed Jesser, a street-smart Boston operative, as a consultant; a small handful of other pros; and his corps of volunteers in New Hampshire. Tubby Harrison, a Boston-based poll-taker who worked for both Dukakis and Tsongas, called it ''two or three people doing it on rubber bands.''

Said Tsongas: ''It was like a death march. No money. It was just slogging it out.''

The low point, Kanin said later, was the second half of 1991, when the campaign was being ignored and bringing in hardly any money. ''Nineteen thousand dollars a week for a presidential campaign—that's laughable,'' he said. When Kanin learned that a poll was to be taken by *The Boston Globe*, he borrowed against federal matching funds due to the campaign in January to finance a television commercial that might— and did—give Tsongas enough recognition to make a respectable showing.

The bad news was consistent. During the summer, Tsongas took his wife, Niki, and their daughters on a "vacation trip" to Iowa, where the first Democratic precinct caucuses would be extremely important if home-state Senator Tom Harkin didn't run. "It was like slogging through this sort of marsh of indifference," Tsongas said later.

Nearing the end of the year, Tsongas was desperate enough to consider folding his starving campaign. Instead, he violated a promise he had made to himself, exercised some stock options and sold $50,000 worth of stock he had always thought of as a college fund for his daughters. The news continued to be discouraging.

"In early January [of 1992] in Florida," he said, "there was a *New York Times* poll that showed I had two percent of the vote, a seven percent favorable, eleven unfavorable national rating. I remember I was sitting in the back seat of a car being interviewed when this reporter showed me that poll and said, 'What do you think about this?' I wanted to slit my wrists [but] I said, 'Oh, that doesn't mean very much.' "

In fact, the polls aside, the Tsongas campaign had begun to show some visibility in New Hampshire that some of the most astute political players recognized. With the Iowa precinct caucuses written off as a legitimate test of strength because of home boy Harkin, New Hampshire would be the first measuring stick of 1992. And Tsongas was approaching it as other long shots had done in the past—some successfully, some not—by grinding away at the consciousness of the electorate.

With the primary still more than three months ahead, he already had spent thirty days in the state and Niki was making less-heralded appearances two or three days a week. Tsongas had more than 150 volunteers in place, many of them young people who kept showing up outside other candidates' events, holding up signs proclaiming themselves: ANOTHER ECONOMIC PATRIOT FOR TSONGAS. If money was lacking, commitment was not.

There were indications that ubiquitousness might be paying dividends. An opinion poll in late fall showed most prospective primary voters didn't know much about any of the candidates but still placed Tsongas first, with 24 percent, with Harkin, the candidate who had spent the second-most time in the state, next with 12. Whatever progress Tsongas had made, however, was being dismissed by his rivals as a predictable reflection of support for a senator from a neighboring state. But Tsongas had not run for office in Massachusetts for thirteen years and had been out of office for seven, and a benchmark poll during the summer had shown him with only 7 percent of the vote, hardly a testament to a local favorite.

On the national political stage, Tsongas was essentially invisible, as *The New York Times* poll he had been shown in Florida demonstrated. But he had gone through many of the obligatory rituals of presidential year politics, speaking at state party dinners and meetings whenever possible, showing up at the relatively few cattle shows the Democrats were staging for their candidates this year and growing increasingly sophisticated about the way the game was played.

He had a lot to learn. Shortly after he had announced his candidacy, he attended a state party candidate forum with Harkin in Wisconsin and was stunned to hear the Iowa Democrat call for an end to the ''bullshit'' in politics. Eating dinner with a reporter in San Diego a few days later, Tsongas recounted the incident. ''He was so emotional,'' he said of Harkin, ''he actually said 'bullshit.' ''

Most everyone else in the political community already knew that this was a Harkin shtick—borrowed from another liberal candidate, then Senator Fred Harris of Oklahoma, who had tested the same shock technique in 1976. But Tsongas, at this stage of his campaign, was not much for gimmicks. The furthest he had gone—and he delighted in repeating the line over and over—was in accusing his rivals of offering ''Twinkie economics—tastes good but no nutritional value.''

But New Hampshire offered a different kind of opportunity for a grit-it-out, straight-ahead candidate with the self-assurance of a Paul Tsongas. Because it was such a small state, it was manageable even for a candidate having a far harder time raising money than his fellow Greek-American had found it four years earlier.

More to the point, because the economic conditions in New Hampshire were among the worst in the nation, there was a more receptive audience for a candidate so single-minded about creating jobs. And that receptive audience included a high proportion of white, middle-class, suburban and small-town voters who were not accustomed to living with direct threats to their livelihood. Furthermore, many of them were independents who could cast ballots in either party's primary if they had a reason to do so.

Many also were voters willing to read that eighty-six-page book. "The book was in demand," Tsongas said later. "Here we were with no money having to print more books because of the demand"—ultimately some 250,000 copies. There were, it appeared, serious voters abroad in 1992 who were determined to get answers. "People would say, 'On page forty-three, you said so and so,' and they would challenge me," he recalled. "What we gave them was something they could digest."

Tsongas was a more effective candidate with relatively small groups of people willing to listen to what he said rather than focusing on how he said it. His slight frame, sad-eyed, dour expression and the faint suggestion of a lisp seemed the antithesis of conventional charisma expected of presidential candidates grasping for attention. He was widely derided. When doctors put President Bush on a "bland diet" after his illness in Japan, David Letterman defined it as "dining with Paul Tsongas."

But he had a deadpan self-deprecating humor that often surprised his listeners and captured their attention. Handing out the lengthy booklet explaining his economic views, he would say with a slight smile, "Hang on to this, it's going to be valuable someday."

He enjoyed turning his political baggage against himself, telling audiences, as he told a group of self-important students at St. Paul's School: "When I got into this race, I went to the Swiss consul. I asked what would it take. We talked about falsifying of birth records. That wouldn't work. So I decided I'm Greek and I'm proud of it." Complaining about the reluctance of Greek-Americans to contribute to his campaign after their experience with Dukakis, he promised, "Next time I'm going to be Swedish." When the arrival of Sam Donaldson of ABC News diverted the attention of an audience in Nashua, Tsongas said: "Remember, I came here to see you. He came here to see me."

But he had an edge that surfaced at times. When one of those St. Paul's students kept pressing him to give the answer he wanted to hear to a question, Tsongas replied: "I'm not running a massage parlor. I'm not here to make you feel better. My job is to give you a better country." When a student at Dartmouth, Tsongas's alma mater, who opposed nuclear power plants chided him for serving on the board of a power company operating such facilities, and began explaining the health hazards from radiation, Tsongas fired back: "Don't ever lecture me about cancer. When you've had it and dealt with it, then we can have a discussion."

In the first debate among the Democratic candidates, he came through the television camera as diffident and preachy and perhaps a trifle smug— "Saint Paul," as he became known within the campaign. "It was just awful," he said. "It was an embarrassment to everybody in the campaign." Determined to do what needed to be done, Tsongas found a debate coach to advise him on how to dress and how to handle himself when the cameras were on him. His performances in subsequent debates were consistently improved, and he was able to add to his repertoire little jokes about his politically correct suits and ties.

Meanwhile, Tsongas's determined insistence on talking about the strengths and weaknesses of various economic proposals helped keep those issues at the center of the debate—and gave New Hampshire voters more insight into who the serious figures were in that debate. Clinton, it was obvious, was also a policy maven who could hold his own with Tsongas or anyone else in arguments about whether there should or should not be a tax cut for the middle class, investment tax credits or reductions in capital gains taxes. Although his views on health care were more fully developed, Kerrey also could talk with some apparent authority on economic issues, and Harkin finally produced a little booklet of his own about jobs, sketchy though it may have been. That left Jerry Brown, who was still framing every issue in terms of the way campaign money corrupted the political process.

The economic debate among the Democrats also served, inadvertently, to underline the failure of President Bush to confront the situation with a credible program of his own. Bush often complained about being "bashed" so much by the Democrats, but he gave them repeated openings with his own faltering campaign.

By the end of 1991, a rough pecking order had developed among the Democratic candidates in New Hampshire that did not necessarily reflect national opinion with precision, or the judgments of the political cognoscenti. With Mario Cuomo finally out of the way—for this cycle at least—Bill Clinton had become the leader of the pack in the primary campaign. He had become the acknowledged front-runner nationally with his series of attention-getting speeches and his success in the Florida straw vote.

Meanwhile, although not in the national picture, Tsongas had used quite a different route—through the back roads of the state—to establish himself as the principal rival to Clinton in terms of poll figures on the primary.

Neither Kerrey nor Harkin had found a significant footing in the state, and Brown and Wilder were not even in the picture. The conventional wisdom had it that either Kerrey or Harkin was likely to be the "real" competition for Clinton once they started spending money on television commercials—to which Tsongas replied, "They said that in September." Many professionals were convinced Tsongas would plunge like a stone once the voters realized they were nominating a president rather than applauding a local boy.

Tsongas was too different in too many ways. His description of himself as a "pro-business Democrat" was only the beginning of his apostasy. He was the only Democrat in the field who opposed the "strikebreaker replacement" legislation that was a first priority of organized labor. He supported nuclear power. He called the middle-class tax cut, which only Harkin joined him in opposing, "generationally irresponsible" because it would add to the federal deficit. He was the most outspoken free-trader in the field, joined only by Clinton in supporting the North American Free Trade Agreement that labor also opposed on grounds that American jobs would be lost to Mexico. Sure, he was liberal on social issues, including abortion and gay rights, but he was always harping on "old Democrats who are into giveaway, giveaway, giveaway, antibusiness corporate-bashing." If more of the liberals had known of his support for term limitations, they wouldn't have been surprised.

Then there was the question of Tsongas's health. He claimed the cancer had been cured and he had the statements of his physicians to support him. He competed with nationally ranked senior swimmers in national meets. And he had run an early commercial in which he appeared vigorously swimming the butterfly stroke in his Speedo suit. But, still, a man who had suffered from cancer? Paul Tsongas as the Democratic Party nominee for president of the United States was simply unthinkable.

None of this early handicapping of the candidates could be taken too seriously, however. At the same point in the 1984 campaign, the two leading candidates in New Hampshire were supposed to be former Vice President Walter Mondale and Senator John Glenn; the eventual winner, Senator Gary Hart, was no better known than either Kerrey or Harkin. The problem with the early judgments was that the only voters paying close attention were probably the 3,000 or 4,000 Democratic activists across the state, the ones whose names were on the state party's mailing lists. Their support was important to the candidates as a credential but, as Mondale had discovered eight years earlier, guaranteed nothing with the primary electorate at large.

Thus, the opinion polls being taken as the campaign year began in earnest and well into January were not being regarded too seriously by political professionals. They understood the polls were principally reporting unformed or only partially formed opinions based on the national press exposure of some of the candidates, especially Clinton, and the most assiduous personal campaigning within the state, especially that done by Tsongas.

But even if the polls were suspect, the perception of the New Hampshire campaign as an odd contest between Mr. Inside Tsongas and Mr. Outside Clinton was having an effect of its own, making it far more difficult for either Kerrey or Harkin to make himself a major element in the equation. Some of the liberals who might have been expected to sign on with one or the other of them—former gubernatorial candidate Paul McEachern, former state party chairman Larry Radway, former state party executive director Ricia McMahon—had chosen Clinton instead. By early January, it already was apparent that Jerry Brown, the best known of the candidates at the outset because of his previous campaigns in New Hampshire, was going nowhere. And Doug Wilder's campaign had hit such a dry hole that there was not even a ripple when he announced early in January that he was giving up the race to concentrate on affairs in Richmond.

There were also the usual also-rans trying to catch a political lightning bolt. Larry Agran, whose only credential was his brief service as mayor of Irvine, California, kept showing up at party functions and debates, demanding to be heard. To avoid embarrassing him in his home state, Democratic National Chairman Ron Brown had allowed Agran to speak at that Democratic National Committee meeting in Los Angeles in September, a gesture that Agran took as a certification of his bona fides. Lenora Fulani, candidate of the New Alliance Party, also kept protesting her exclusion from party events, sometimes backed by busloads of supporters from New York.

Eugene McCarthy, too, was campaigning in New Hampshire again, revisiting the scene of his glory twenty-four years earlier. But his campaign now seemed to consist largely of swapping old war stories with older reporters in the bar at the Wayfarer. Ralph Nader was running a write-in campaign as the symbol of "none of the above."

Two Chicago political consultants, Phil Krone and Don Rose, were conducting a write-in campaign for Mario Cuomo out of a second-floor office in Concord—and, to no one's surprise, Cuomo was being just ambivalent enough to make the possibility intriguing. Asked by *The Boston Globe* if he intended to repudiate the write-in campaign, he replied: "How can I not approve of people saying, 'You're so good, you should be president'?"

Just six days before the primary, Cuomo kept a long-standing date to speak at the Kennedy School of Government at Harvard and threw another log on the fire of speculation with a rollicking attack on Bush. Asked again why he wouldn't repudiate the draft, he countered: "In my own state, they're saying lousy things about me. If they're saying nice things about me in New Hampshire, I'm going to encourage them."

The Cuomo write-in campaign was being taken more seriously than others on the fringe because there was a long history of such campaigns succeeding in New Hampshire. In 1964, Ambassador Henry Cabot Lodge won the Republican primary entirely on write-in votes, defeating two candidates whose names were on the ballot, Barry Goldwater and Nelson Rockefeller. President Johnson also won the Democratic primary in 1968 on write-in votes; he had been unwilling to take the possibility of challenge seriously enough to qualify for a place on the ballot. (Johnson's victory, however, was widely interpreted as a setback when McCarthy won an embarrassing 42 percent of the vote against him, and it was shortly afterward that LBJ announced he would not seek another term.)

Krone and Rose were mailing postcards to 75,000 Democratic households, tailored for each locality, explaining how they could write in the New York governor's name. The question was simply whether the field of active Democrats was so unsatisfactory that a substantial number of voters would try to write a new "Mario scenario" before it was too late. Or was it more likely that the seriousness of the concern with the economy would make voters less likely to play around with might-have-beens and concentrate on the choices they were being offered?

By February, it was no longer possible for Tsongas's rivals or the press or anyone else to simply write him off as some local aberration. He was running even or ahead of Clinton in opinion polls whose validity increased with each passing day as more voters took an interest in the campaign. He was attracting large audiences of voters who, more to the point, now hung on every word. His lack of charisma had become a kind of charisma in itself, and he could depend on appreciative laughter when he greeted audiences with small jokes about the new and fashionable red ties he was wearing these days for the television cameras.

In short, the political atmospherics had changed through some mystical process hard to understand. "I think there is a smell to candidates," Tsongas said later, "and if the smell is he's going to lose, there's no interest . . . when I began to move in the polls, what seemed like a ludicrous campaign then began to smell like something that was possible."

Suddenly, Paul Tsongas had become the flavor of the month in the Democratic competition in New Hampshire. The candidate who could go unrecognized in a restaurant two months earlier now found a dozen cameras fighting for position to film him—swimming laps for exercise in an indoor pool. The case against him had been that he had no chance to win, and now that argument, Tsongas recalled, "began to break down."

On February 9, nine days before the primary, he arrived at a Sunday afternoon meeting at Daniel Webster College in Nashua and found more than 500 voters, nine television crews and perhaps fifty reporters from all over the world waiting for him. "What are you all doing here?" he asked in mock surprise and obvious delight as he walked onto the platform.

What they were doing there, they demonstrated, was trying to find out if this man had answers to their economic concerns. Tsongas talked for more than forty minutes, then remained on the podium for another two hours answering questions on every aspect of economic and domestic policy. No more than a dozen or two of his listeners drifted out as Tsongas mixed his earnest exposition with small dashes of the kind of humor that seemed appropriate for a Sunday afternoon meeting like this one.

It was a meeting strikingly similar to one Gary Hart had held in Nashua two days before he upset Fritz Mondale eight years earlier—an audience driven by interest in the candidate, people who arrived two or three at a time in their own cars, not a crowd bused in by an advance team. The message was plain: this was a year when slogans and sound bite politics weren't enough. Even a candidate prescribing bitter medicine could get a hearing if he was serious about what he was saying.

By the time the campaign reached its final weekend, Tsongas was clearly on a roll—a stature reflected in the final Democratic debate at St. Anselm's College in Goffstown. Led by Jerry Brown, the other candidates sniped at Tsongas on his support for nuclear power. The issue had once been a volatile one in New Hampshire although that was no longer true. But it gave Tsongas's rivals an avenue for attack. "Paul," said Bob Kerrey, "we're not trying to gang up on you. We're not saying you're wrong all the time, but this time you are."

In fact, they were trying to gang up on him, just as candidates always do on any front-runner. Unlikely as it might have seemed only six weeks earlier, Paul Tsongas had arrived. But as he did, attention had already been drawn away from the economic issues he was riding, toward something entirely different—the matter of Bill Clinton's personal life.

CHAPTER 10

TABLOIDMANIA

In early August of 1991, about two months before Bill Clinton's decision to seek the presidency, it was Hillary Clinton who raised within the Clinton political circle the specter of her husband's reputation as a womanizer. The rumors had hovered over him through his gubernatorial years, but the sources of them had such little credibility that not even *The Arkansas Gazette*, which editorially was a severe Clinton critic, had seen fit to publish them. Still, with speculation growing that Clinton would seek the White House in 1992 after all, his wife's antenna for political trouble was fine-tuned, and it was picking up plenty of signals.

Just weeks before, the conservative *Washington Times*, which did not take undue pains to be objective, had reported unverified rumors that Clinton had "extramarital affairs, illegitimate children and (had) used drugs," and *The New Republic* and right-wing columnist George Will had made references to similar rumors in pontificating about the proper role of the news media in dealing with them.

"These rumors are just flying around," Frank Greer, Clinton's media adviser, recalled the governor's wife saying at a meeting of political insiders at the mansion in Little Rock. "This is getting out of control. You may not have made a decision," she told her husband, "but if we want to move toward making a decision to run for president, we've got to deal with this." According to Chicago political sources, when Richard M. Daley, mayor of the city, was approached early to back Clinton, he expressed reservations because of the womanizing rumors. The prospective candidate's wife offered to talk to Daley about them, but the proper and staunch Irish Catholic Daley cringed from the notion of discussing such a subject with the man's wife.

Greer himself had been tracking down the rumors, going back to Clinton with each one. One that was getting particular currency was that Clinton had fathered a black child with a television newscaster from an Eastern city, which he flatly and heatedly denied. In fact, at one closed-door meeting with Democrats in Chicago at which he was running a gauntlet of questions about alleged philandering, he snapped: "Listen, I don't have a black baby!" The notion that Clinton would have a hidden child out of wedlock somewhere was certainly not in keeping with his strong policy position in favor of firm government action against deadbeat fathers—men who abandoned children and ducked out on paying child support.

Another old turkey that nobody in the inner circle was particularly worried about was a lawsuit against Clinton by a disgruntled former state employee named Larry Nichols. In it, he protested his firing and alleged that Clinton as governor had used state funds in the romantic pursuit of five separate women, one of whom Nichols identified as a Little Rock former television reporter and later nightclub singer named Gennifer Flowers. Nichols, who Greer said later "wanted to be a little Ollie North," had lost his job for using state phones to make more than 400 calls in behalf of the contras in Nicaragua.

During Clinton's 1990 reelection campaign, Nichols had held a press conference on the steps of the capitol in Little Rock to announce his lawsuit and the names of the women. But not one word was written in Arkansas at the time, Greer said, "because the press in Arkansas knew Larry Nichols, they knew it was off-the-wall, unsubstantiated, and it was completely untrue," as the local reporters concluded after further investigation.

The continuing rumors of other Clinton dalliances, however, led to a discussion within the Clinton inner circle about the matter, and whether they held the same potential for trouble of the sort that had driven Democrat Gary Hart from the 1988 presidential race. Clinton, Greer recalled, "agonized about this a lot—whether or not, since Gary Hart, the rules had changed; whether or not, in a hopeful sense . . . the press did feel they had to have substantiation from two sources or whatever, or whether or not somebody could just make something up, and say it and get it in print, and all of a sudden it's taken a life of its own. My naive sense was no, I had a lot of faith in the journalistic community."

Greer said he told his candidate: "Bill, it's not that bad. You know, people just can't make things up." To which Clinton would reply: "Frank, given these new rules, somebody *can* just make it up." Nor did Clinton and his advisers know, Greer said later, "that the tabloids would be paying them several thousand dollars to make it up."

Greer and other insiders advised the Clintons to seek some opportunity to reassure the voters about their marriage and commitment, as a means of coping with the rumors. Much earlier, after the Hart debacle, Clinton had told Arkansas reporters that he didn't think public officials had to answer what he called "have you ever" questions and he didn't intend to. The insiders argued that without doing so he could deflect the rumors by acknowledging that his marriage like many others had had its difficulties but was in good shape now.

The whole business grated on Clinton, Greer recalled. He would argue that the news media's attitude toward marital problems involving individuals in public life was itself potentially destructive. "What we're really doing with the standards that journalism and politics have set today," Greer recalled Clinton saying, "we're encouraging people to split up and divorce. If you're divorced, then nobody will ask any questions about you. But if you have some difficult times and work things out, you make a real effort to keep your marriage together, then you have to pay a price."

Also discussed at some of these meetings in August, Greer recalled, was the matter of Clinton's military record, or lack of it. "He always said, 'You know, I didn't serve in the military. I basically got a high lottery number. But Frank, I opposed the war in Vietnam. I didn't want to serve, and I was really thankful when I got a high lottery number. But it's never been an issue here because every time it's come up, the people involved, they all said that I did nothing wrong and that they'd back me up.' ''

Greer replied, he remembered later, that a lot of other people at the time opposed the Vietnam War and didn't serve, "and if you didn't do anything wrong in terms of avoiding the draft, it isn't going to be a problem." That judgment, Greer said later, "I felt in my core."

In any event, it was decided that the proper forum for flushing out the rumors of womanizing and other problems of Clinton's personal background was a popular breakfast meeting of Washington reporters organized by Godfrey Sperling of *The Christian Science Monitor*. Greer arranged for both of the Clintons to be guests in late September.

On the weekend before, many of Clinton's closest supporters from around the country were called into Washington to assess the political landscape and evaluate the pros and cons of a Clinton presidential candidacy. Attending at the Washington Court Hotel on Capitol Hill were representatives across the spectrum of Democratic political thought, and several openly expressed concern about the womanizing rumors. Clinton in effect rehearsed the "nobody's perfect" defense he was preparing for the Sperling breakfast.

The day before the breakfast, Greer had a conversation about Clinton with Gloria Borger of *U.S. News and World Report*, and he suggested that she ought to show up the next morning. About half an hour into the breakfast, the have-you-ever question hadn't come up yet so she popped it the most benign way she could. She reminded Clinton that he had talked about "a zone of privacy" regarding his personal life, and wondered whether he would talk about it.

Clinton, smiling, said: "I thought you would never ask." He then went on to say that his stated refusal to get into that area of questioning in the past stemmed from "all those rumors about me during my race for governor that were sparked by a disgruntled state employee [Nichols] who was working for my opponent. Those were false, and I said so at the time."

Clinton duly recited the preplanned response: "What you need to know about Hillary and me is that we've been together nearly twenty years. It has not been perfect or free from problems, but we're committed to our marriage and its obligations—to our child and to each other. We love each other very much.''

And that, Clinton and his political advisers hoped, would be that. That statement, Clinton said, ''ought to be enough'' to satisfy the have-you-ever question. Acknowledging that his marriage had ''problems'' was as far or farther than any previous presidential aspirant had gone publicly in alluding to marital infidelity.

What Clinton was counting on was an adherence by the news media to the time-honored journalistic code of reporting verifiable facts, not rumors of unproved allegations. At least the mainstream press, that is, as opposed to such embarrassments to the mainstream press as the supermarket gossip tabloids, to which nothing was sacrosanct. What he didn't figure on was that after the Gary Hart experience of the previous presidential election, important elements of the presumably more responsible news media had developed an itchier trigger finger on reports of personal misconduct by celebrated individuals in public life.

The standard of a generation earlier for deciding what and what not to report about a politician had been whether the alleged misconduct affected the performance of the duties to which he or she had been elected. That standard explained why it was possible for candidates for the highest public offices to entertain mistresses on the side or continue to be chronic drinkers without disclosure. If a senator showed up falling-down drunk on the Senate floor, that would be hard not to write about, but short of that, the code was to say or write nothing.

The subsequent disclosures, however, of President John F. Kennedy's dalliances, and then the Hart episode in which the Colorado senator seemed to be flaunting his extramarital escapades, made the news media collectively defensive about looking the other way when such activities were known about. Still, there remained within the mainstream news media generally a contemptuous attitude toward the sensationalist supermarket tabloids, which forever were reporting on such things as clandestine relationships between extraterrestrial beings and beautiful movie stars, and the like.

At first, it seemed that this contempt would continue to isolate the gossip and sex magazines and newspapers from the arena of responsible journalism, simply because mainstream practitioners would continue as they always had to treat them with disdain, in the manner of straight cops at the precinct station toward one bad apple on the take. When *Penthouse* shortly after Clinton's announcement of candidacy ran a raunchy, paid interview with a self-described rock star groupie from Arkansas named Connie Hamzy, in which she alleged merely that she had a near-encounter with Clinton in a North Little Rock hotel back in 1984, only CNN's *Headline News* of any national media mentioned it—and only once after swift damage control by the Clinton campaign of the sort for which it would soon became celebrated.

Prior to the CNN mention, a young and alert campaign press aide, Steve Cohen, had heard a local radio talk show host discussing the *Penthouse* article. He informed young, boyish-looking George Stephanopoulos, then Clinton's deputy campaign manager, who rounded up affidavits from several Clinton associates who saw the encounter. All swore that it was "Sweet Connie," as she called herself in the interview, who approached Clinton and that he had summarily rebuffed her. As soon as CNN mentioned the interview, Stephanopoulos showed the affidavits to the cable network and the story was dropped. Thereafter Cohen was known in the campaign as "Scoop," and the hopeful assumption was that the worst was over on the womanizing problem.

Clinton's very impressive performances in the early Democratic cattle shows, early fund-raising strength and notable endorsements by now had propelled him into the New Hampshire primary as the news media's consensus front-runner for the Democratic nomination. And with Mario Cuomo finally taking himself out of contention, he set his sights on victory there although Clinton pollster Stan Greenberg's internal polling had him in second place behind New Englander Tsongas, at about 20 percent.

Winning New Hampshire could in one swoop dispose of any charge that Clinton was a regional candidate, and at the same time set the stage for a decisive blow in the Super Tuesday tests, predominantly in his region of the South, shortly afterward. The campaign ran a sixty-second television spot in which Clinton simply faced the camera and talked about his plan for economic recovery. Almost at once he shot into the lead, with 37 percent in Greenberg's polling to only 25 for Tsongas.

"It's very interesting what people took away from that ad," Clinton recalled later. "What they really liked about it was its general emphasis on health care and jobs, and the fact that it seemed specific, and that there was a plan they could write for. . . . What gripped them was that I seemed to have a plan . . . and that it seemed to be a long-term plan, that I wasn't just promising to be in thirty or forty days and turn the world over." Like Tsongas's eighty-six-page booklet, he said, it was "counterintuitive . . . to what normally works in politics, which is the emotional thirty-second ad and all that."

"New Hampshire was the place," Clinton said, "but '92 was the year in which people really wanted to believe that they could be brought into the system [again]. They were properly skeptical of all the claims, and they thought at least if you were specific, even if you had to change or modify your position over time . . . that at least you had thought about the problems and you were moving beyond traditional politics."

New Hampshire was also proving to be an ideal place for the Clinton message. "People used to talk about how New Hampshire wasn't a good place to start [the presidential election process]," Clinton said later, "that it was not a good microcosm, it was more antigovernment. . . . This year it was a very good place to start, because while the economy objectively in some ways was no worse than several other states, the unemployment, food stamp and welfare rolls had tripled in three years. The average welfare recipient in New Hampshire was a middle-class person." A lot of them, he said, had their property taxes "folded in with their mortgage payments, so a lot of the welfare checks were coming in to unemployed white-collar people to keep their families in their homes. . . . So what you had was a state that was just riveted in its focus [on the state of the economy]. . . .

"It turned out in '92 that in all these town meetings people were really concerned with . . . mostly mainstream economic bread and butter issues. I think you couldn't get through there if you hadn't thought about and focused on what you believed and why, and what you would do. And nearly everybody who came out of there and went on to the other states was much improved [as a candidate] by the process.

"Because the state is so small, you couldn't leave New Hampshire without a human face on the problems of America. You couldn't campaign in New Hampshire without being able to call the name of somebody who had lost his job, or call the name of some child whose family had problems. You just couldn't do it. They were just there, staring you in the face all the time. It was an incredibly emotional experience."

Tsongas, however, was proving to be a formidable candidate in his own backyard. Like the tortoise in the fable, he had been assaulting the New Hampshire electorate inch by inch, tirelessly, and voters had a familiarity and a comfort level with him that neither Clinton nor any of the other three remaining Democratic contestants—Kerrey, Harkin or Brown—brought into the nation's kickoff primary. As Clinton's fortunes rose and fell over the next eventful weeks, Tsongas kept persevering like the determined swimmer he was, and his widely acclaimed aquatic television commercial showed him to be.

On January 16, all the trouble started for Clinton. It was a Thursday, which Clinton campaign strategists came to call "garbage day," because that was when the supermarket tabloids released the first copies of their new issues. The *Star*, a leading such tabloid, sent out an advance of its next issue that picked up on the dog-eared 1990 Larry Nichols lawsuit and ran with it.

Actually, the story had appeared a few days earlier in the *Daily Mail* of London but had drawn no attention in the United States. In any event, the Clinton campaign already had denials from the five women involved, including Gennifer Flowers, but that fact did not stop one so-called mainstream newspaper, the sensationalist tabloid *New York Post*, and then the rival *New York Daily News*, from latching on to the story in a big way. The *Post* headlined its story "Wild Bill" and the *Daily News* announced it as "I'm No Gary Hart." Another tabloid, the *Boston Herald*, and the Fox television network, also given to tabloid journalism, jumped aboard as well.

Clinton now got his first real taste of the news media of 1992 in full pursuit. As he entered the Sheraton-Tara Hotel in Nashua for a conference on health care issues, reporters, photographers, television cameramen, light and sound technicians flocked around him. Forewarned by his staff about the tabloid story, Clinton benignly dismissed it as "old news" already "thoroughly investigated, and it's not true." He noted that it "comes up as I start to do a little better" in the campaign, resurrected by a gossip sheet "that says Martians walk on earth and cows have human heads."

The candidate called the old lawsuit "totally bogus," brought by a man "fired for making illegal phone calls [who] tried to bribe me into giving him money, and I just wouldn't do it." Clinton moved along on the sea of shouting interrogators through the hotel lobby and onto an elevator, seemingly unruffled.

Frank Greer's "faith in the journalistic community" was being put to the test. *New York Post* editor Jerry Nachman defended picking up the supermarket tabloid story on the grounds that "there are filed court papers" and hence "absolutely public information," although the case had lain dormant for about two years, brushed aside by the Arkansas press as garbage. The managing editor of *The Arkansas Democrat-Gazette*, John Robert Starr, was reported by *The Washington Post*, in fact, as saying there was "no substance whatsoever to the charges," that Nichols was "not a credible fellow" and that "he had no evidence, nothing, except he heard the same rumors the rest of us have heard." Nachman, though, insisted that "it's become part of what we do in campaigns, going over the character thing."

That was true enough, especially since the Gary Hart self-destruction, helped along by an accommodating *Miami Herald* and others in 1987. There was a very major difference this time, though. These supposed members of the mainstream press, albeit with one foot firmly in the tabloid gossip business, did not go out, investigate and find the story themselves, establishing its truth prior to publication, as the *Herald* had done on the Hart liaison with Donna Rice five years earlier, at a considerable expenditure of time, effort and money. They simply picked up the *Star* yarn and ran with it on the technically valid but ethically questionable argument that it was in the public domain in the form of a lawsuit (soon dropped with abject apologies from Nichols, who disavowed his charges).

The managing editor of the *Daily News* at the time, Matthew Storin, made the case for his newspaper, in a tough circulation battle with the rival *Post*, that "a lot of people aren't going to run this story and they're going to end up running it a day later. So why not run it now?" He argued that Clinton "is running for president. Let's put it out there and have him react to it. If no one comes forward and backs him [Nichols] up, we'll all know it was a pig in a poke and go on to the question of capital gains."

That approach might have been valid had the Nichols lawsuit just been filed. But it had already been scrutinized by the Arkansas press, well aware of the womanizing rumors about Clinton, and judged not to be credible. The fact that it was picked up by a supermarket tabloid should have hung a handle-with-care label on the story in the eyes of mainstream editors, and indeed most of them either ignored the story altogether or gave it inside-page placement. *The Washington Post* had its media reporter, Howard Kurtz, write a story that featured the role of the news media as much as the stale allegations themselves—an approach that soon would be adopted by other news organizations as the story developed and they became ethically defensive about their own decisions on dealing with it.

The CNN shouting match, *Crossfire*, pitted Nachman against a Democratic television advertising consultant, Mandy Grunwald, who argued forcefully against devoting valuable television time to this kind of warmed-over rumor veneered by an old lawsuit and published in a supermarket tabloid. Grunwald was a business partner of Frank Greer but not then a part of the Clinton campaign, busy with other clients running for the Senate.

Had the whole matter died there, Clinton might have been out of the woods on the womanizing rap. But near the end of the next televised debate among the Democratic candidates, moderator Cokie Roberts of ABC News and National Public Radio, in what Greenberg later called "a fairly scurrilous form of journalism," injected the matter into the news media mainstream beyond argument. She asked Clinton to comment on "concern on the part of members of your party that these allegations of womanizing, that the Republicans will find somebody and that she will come forward late, and that you would lose the all-important Democrat women's vote."

Clinton replied that the allegations were "an example of what the Republicans have been trying to do to me for years," and he branded them as "a pack of lies" that his repeated elections in Arkansas proved were not a deterrent to his electability. He concluded by saying the Republicans should not be rewarded for "the kind of rumor-mongering negative and totally irrelevant stuff that they won on four years ago. I don't think the American people are going to fall for it again. And I know people who are bleeding and hurting in New Hampshire are not about to be sucker-punched by it." The reminder to voters of the Bush negative campaign of 1988 was one that would be heard repeatedly from Clinton, and with good effect, as the campaign progressed.

But it didn't stem the allegations. On the following Thursday, the next "garbage day," the *Star* outdid itself. Clinton had just returned to New Hampshire from Washington with his newly hired political consultant—James Carville, the more flamboyant member of the Carville and Begala team that had helped steer Harris Wofford to his upset Senate victory over Republican Dick Thornburgh in Pennsylvania in November. The team was a hot property after that surprise success and several presidential candidates had competed for its services, but Clinton had won out.

Carville hadn't planned to go to New Hampshire that day but he got a call from George Stephanopoulos at Washington National Airport. ''I think you ought to come up to New Hampshire with us,'' Stephanopoulos told him. ''You just had the sense, I don't know why,'' Carville recalled later, ''you knew something was going to happen that day.''

The governor was slated for another busy campaign day in the state, but he seemed his usual laid-back self as he came into the lobby of the Inn of New Hampshire, a top-grade Holiday Inn in downtown Manchester. He chatted amiably with several reporters and was pulled to the side by Mark Halperin, the ABC News producer in his traveling party. Halperin asked him a number of questions and Clinton responded, then went up to his room. Clinton was routinely late in starting his campaign day, so we thought nothing of it on this occasion.

In his private suite, however, Clinton discussed with aides what Halperin had questioned him about: the *Star* was prepared to unload on Clinton again. Stephanopoulos got hold of an advance copy sent by telephone facsimile to the hotel. It was an eye-popper, bearing the headline: ''They Made Love All Over Her Apartment.'' Gennifer Flowers provided a first-person account of how, by her testimony, Clinton over a period from 1977 to 1989 had often jogged from the state capitol to her apartment and turned it into a veritable playground of sexual athletics.

The tabloid also reported that Flowers had turned over some fifteen taped telephone calls with Clinton from December 1990 until recent days, and it quoted from one it said had taken place between Clinton and Flowers on the previous September 23, about a week before his formal declaration of presidential candidacy. Flowers had been expressing concern about the pressures she was encountering from the news media, and the tape had the voice identified by Flowers as Clinton's saying: ''If they ever hit you with it, just say no and go on. There's nothing they can do. I expected them to look into it and come interview you. But if everybody is on record denying it, no problem.''

The story did not come totally out of the blue to Clinton. He had indeed talked recently to Flowers, whom he acknowledged he knew and whom he had helped get a $16,000-a-year state job with an agency that handled appeals on rejected unemployment benefit claims. She had told him of the tabloid press pursuing her and offering her as much as $50,000 to say that she had had an affair with Clinton.

It was this pursuit, Clinton said later, to which he was referring in conversation with her—while declining to verify that it was his voice on any particular tape. This development, clearly, was much more serious than the first, but maybe—just maybe, some of the Clinton advisers hoped—most of the mainstream press would again lay off it, considering the very suspect source. In case that didn't happen, though, it was time to gear up for damage control, "to get out there as fast as we could with our side of the story," Carville said later.

When Clinton finally headed for Claremont, Carville stayed behind in Manchester and contacted Hillary Clinton, who knew all about the Nichols lawsuit and the Flowers rumors and indeed about the woman's phone calls to the governor. She was in Atlanta, and when she heard the news she said she was ready to fly wherever the strategists decided, to be with her husband to help throw water on the fire. It was tentatively decided that she should go to Washington, where Clinton would meet her to do some television show that night, possibly ABC News's *Nightline* if it could be arranged.

After that, Carville proceeded to confer by phone with campaign operatives in Little Rock and Washington on how best to cope. The Little Rock headquarters was put to work tracking down a year-old letter from Flowers's lawyer, Robert M. McHenry, to Little Rock radio station KBTS threatening to sue because a talk show host had "wrongfully and untruthfully alleged an affair between my client, Gennifer Flowers, and Bill Clinton."

Surely that letter would convince the mainstream press that a hard-pressed Flowers had made up the story for money—and indeed the *Star* subsequently acknowledged it had paid her an unspecified sum for the interview and tapes. As soon as the letter was located, copies were reproduced for inquiring reporters.

Without a sign that the day was in any fashion out of the ordinary from the routine on the campaign trail, Clinton, accompanied by Stephanopoulos and Begala, set off by van for a plant tour and talk in Claremont, on the western side of the state. The weather was miserable, wet and foggy, making it impossible to fly. But it was decided that the candidate had to maintain the appearance of normality in the face of this latest threat.

On top of that, Clinton knew he had to return to Little Rock that night to deal with eleventh-hour appeals for a stay in the scheduled execution of a man named Rickey Ray Rector, sentenced to death for the killing of a police officer. Holding the life of any person in one's hands is a huge responsibility under any circumstances, but this particular case presented Clinton with a dilemma quite beyond his immediate political travail.

The convicted forty-year-old man had, eleven years earlier, turned the gun on himself after having shot the policeman, destroying part of his own brain and turning himself into, in the word of his lawyer later, a ''zombie'' with severely impaired mental faculties. As a man unable to understand now what he had done or even to comprehend death, the lawyer argued, ''his execution would be remembered as a disgrace to the state.''

Clinton, however, was firmly on record as a presidential candidate in support of the death penalty, and his position on that issue drew a major distinction with the opposition of the old liberal Democratic leadership from which Clinton was so determined to separate himself in voters' eyes. The odds were strong that he would let the execution take place, but both decency and prudent politics required that he spend the day of the execution in his Little Rock office giving the matter of the requested executive clemency thorough consideration and reflection.

First, though, was the matter of getting through the campaign day in New Hampshire. As his van rolled through the bleak winter storm and across hazardous icy roads, Clinton kept his mind occupied by reading *Lincoln on Leadership*, a gift from Mario Cuomo. By the time he arrived at the American Brush Company in Claremont, a successful small business that made paint brushes, word of the *Star* story had reached the press corps traveling in other campaign vans—one of which bore Halperin, toting a copy.

He and ABC News correspondent Jim Wooten circulated it among the host of reporters whose vans had arrived in advance of Clinton's small motorcade. They read the Flowers account with a mixture of professional interest and titillation, and when Clinton came into the small foyer of the plant in a crush of television and still cameras, and tape recorders held over the crush to pick up his words, they bombarded him with questions.

Clinton was physically trapped in the small foyer. "The story is not accurate, the story is just not true," he said, obviously chagrined. "She's obviously taking money to change her story." Putting aside his precampaign vow not to discuss reports of marital infidelity, Clinton knew he had to respond. He acknowledged that he had received calls of distress from Flowers, but he said he had told Hillary about each one and that she had advised him to return the calls.

"I did call her back every time she called me," Clinton said. "She said she was frightened, she felt beleaguered, she felt pressure, she felt that her life was being ruined by people harassing her" and later "offering her bribes to change her story." He also said he had told Flowers "to just tell the truth," and when advised that the *Star* story had made no reference to that, Clinton responded: "Well, I'm sure they didn't put that in there. I told her that several times." He also noted that "the lady had a lawyer that threatened to sue people who were saying the very thing that she's saying, just a year ago."

Clinton went onto the work floor of the paint brush plant, mingling easily with the employees and finally standing up on a high platform and delivering his standard stump speech as if nothing untoward had happened to upset his campaign. When he was through, however, he disappeared up the front stairway to the plant's offices, where he was closeted with Stephanopoulos and Begala, conferring by phone with Carville in Manchester and his other political advisers in Washington and Little Rock.

"We were trying to figure out how deep the wound was," Stephanopoulos said later, "and whether we had to go for radical surgery right away, or if we had time to stabilize the patient and keep moving."

The weather outside was getting progressively worse, and it became clear that Clinton wasn't likely to make his next scheduled event at Plymouth State College to the northeast.

While we reporters pondered what to do with this developing story growing out of a questionable account of marital infidelity first aired by a supermarket tabloid of general disrepute in mainstream journalism, copies of the letter from Flowers's lawyer to the Little Rock radio station had been faxed to the Claremont factory and were distributed by Clinton aides. The letter made it easier for most of us to decide that the whole business had to be reported. Here, after all, was a presidential candidate who, by responding to reporters' questions and then going behind closed doors for a couple of hours to confer with his campaign strategists in what clearly was a crisis atmosphere, had altered his campaign day and advanced a story that had the potential of destroying his candidacy. Had those of us bird-dogging Clinton that day simply ignored what was going on, we would have left ourselves open by that point to allegations of cover-up and favoritism toward Clinton.

The question had become not whether to report what had been published and its aftermath, but how—in what context. It was, to be sure, the tail of American journalism wagging the dog, but reporting the consequences now seemed to most of us there unavoidable. So a line of reporters formed at the single pay phone in the American Brush Company cafeteria to dispatch the news of the latest womanizing scandal that had rocked the presidential hopes of Bill Clinton.

Some major newspapers, like *The New York Times*, handled the story gingerly the next day, the *Times* relegating it to eight inches over the headline, "Clinton Denounces New Report of Affair," on an inside page. But on its evening news show on the night of the Claremont scene, WMUR-TV in Manchester carried a vivid report showing Clinton bombarded with press questions, and shortly afterward the Associated Press moved a story from Claremont as well. The major television networks, however, did not report what was going on in this critical day in the Clinton campaign, except for a brief reference in a Clinton profile on NBC.

It was after 7:30 that night, after the network evening shows, when Clinton finally came down to the front office area of the plant amid much confusion about whether he was going on to Plymouth or back to Manchester. Several of us in the press entourage piled into a van that we thought would be following Clinton, but in short order realized that we had lost sight of the Clinton van. What we didn't know at the time was that Clinton had abandoned all notions of going on network television that night and instead had gone on to Manchester, where he boarded a plane back to Little Rock, flying much of the night in order to be at his desk to give full attention to the unhappy matter of the scheduled Rector execution. More than two hours after our press van left Claremont, with a Clinton volunteer from Florida at the wheel driving for the first time on icy New England roads, we returned to Manchester only fifty miles away, still in the dark about his whereabouts.

In the meantime, ABC News, which in its wisdom had decided after all its spadework not to report the *Star* story or Clinton's very public responses on its network evening news show, did decide to devote *Nightline* to an analysis of the ethics of running the story. Whether by intent or not, this approach amounted to bringing the supermarket tabloid report into so-called responsible journalism by the back door.

When the possibility of getting the Clintons on the show fell through, its producers began casting about for other guests. They settled on Larry Sabato, a University of Virginia political science professor who had recently written a book called *Feeding Frenzy* on the handling by the news media of campaign rumors and scandals, and Jonathan Alter, a young media critic for *Newsweek*, and were looking for a third participant. Someone had seen Mandy Grunwald on *Crossfire* a week earlier and decided she would fit the bill. As things turned out, *Nightline* and its host, the self-assured Ted Koppel, got more in her than they had bargained for.

Grunwald strolled into her firm's office at about eight o'clock that night, after it was clear the Clintons wouldn't be making the *Nightline* appearance and she had been confirmed for the show. Greer and Greenberg were still on the phone, as they had been all afternoon, talking to Carville in Manchester and campaign manager David Wilhelm and other Clinton strategists in Little Rock in what had turned out to be a floating conference call.

She told them she was going to do the show. "What do you want me to say?" she remembered later asking them. "Oh, don't worry about it. You'll be fine," was the reply, and they went back to their conference call. Here was what was potentially a critical moment in the campaign, and as the brainstormers were agonizing over how best to defuse the bomb, along came the perfect vehicle in which to do it, handed to them with a big bow around it—and they told Grunwald in effect, she said, to wing it!

Wing it, she did, with a vengeance. "I'm enough of a student of television, and I watch Koppel enough," she recalled later, "that I knew that he hadn't done anything on the primaries, and he hadn't done anything about the election in fact, and it was three weeks to go [until the New Hampshire primary].'' Grunwald went home and planned what she was going to say ''as I was washing my hair,'' she said, ''and I was actually a nervous wreck. I know enough about politics to know it was kind of a big moment. I didn't have such a sense of self-importance that I thought it was going to make or break the campaign, but I knew the heat of the day was intense.''

After years of prepping clients for television appearances, she was faced with having to prep herself, and she found being the one going before the cameras intimidating. Once she got there, however, she performed like a veteran defense lawyer. Koppel, after comments from the other guests, turned to Grunwald, asking whether it was possible to put that sort of story in proper ''perspective, or does it develop a sort of momentum of its own?''

GRUNWALD: Well, programs like this are not a help, Ted. This is the first program that *Nightline* has done on any topic relating to the Democratic presidential candidates. You haven't been talking about the middle class. You haven't talked about why Bill Clinton has captured people's imagination. Here you are—

KOPPEL: Oh, now, now wait a second. Wait a second. You're making a charge that's not accurate. We've done a number of programs on the middle class. We've done a number of programs on—

GRUNWALD: You have not.

KOPPEL: —the issues, unemployment. You're quite right. We haven't done a program on Bill Clinton.

GRUNWALD: But here we are just a couple of weeks before the New Hampshire primary. People are about to go out there and vote. . . . They have real concerns. And you're choosing with your editorial comment, by making this program about some unsubstantiated charges that . . . started with a trashy supermarket tabloid. You're telling people that something you think is important. That's not context. You're setting the agenda and you're letting the *Star* set it for you.

KOPPEL: All right, let me—

GRUNWALD: And I find that troubling.

Grunwald aggressively accused *Nightline* and Koppel of sleazy journalism—introducing the womanizing allegations in the guise of a serious discussion of journalistic ethics. The usually composed Koppel seemed taken aback and defensive. Grunwald's very public scolding of Koppel on his own show dominated it, shaking its pretense of being a responsible forum for discussion of the ethics of handling an attack on a public figure paid for by a sensationalist supermarket gossip and scandal sheet. For many viewers long irritated by Koppel's rather know-it-all treatment of guests, Grunwald became an overnight heroine, and not only in the Clinton campaign.

Her feisty performance did not, however, end the crisis atmosphere, or a debate within the Clinton camp about what to do about it. The Washington contingent, according to Greenberg later, did not want Clinton to go on the air at once, fearing he was not properly prepared, but "we hadn't quite realized how much he had already responded" to direct questions in Claremont.

"The idea was to get out front of the thing as soon as we could," Carville said later, "and get out our explanation. At that point, we knew the thing was going to be what we call in the campaign a cluster fuck— I mean, you know when you're gettin' it."

Once it was clear that Clinton could not do *Nightline* that night, the staff had begun casting about for another early opportunity. ABC's *Good Morning America* the next morning was one possibility, but the producers were unwilling to give Clinton what his aides felt was a sufficient amount of time to tell his side of the story. Instead, another ABC program on prime time Friday night, *20/20*, was offered, but Clinton declined, saying he did not wish to make what would clearly be a political appearance on the night Rector faced death. The situation gave Clinton and his aides time to gather their wits and decide what to do.

Clinton spent the next day as scheduled in seclusion in Little Rock, as he always did when pondering whether to grant a reprieve to someone on death row or let the execution go forward. Begala, to bolster his candidate's spirits, at one point sent the governor an adage favored by Georgia secretary of state Max Cleland, who had suffered the loss of three limbs in Vietnam: "Life breaks us all, but some of us emerge stronger in the broken places."

While Clinton reflected on this, on Rector's fate and on the events of the last days, his staff nailed down two weekend national television appearances for him, the first on the next day, Saturday, on the CNN *Newsmaker Saturday* show and the following morning, Sunday, on ABC's *This Week with David Brinkley*.

With those two appearances settled, however, another offer came from Steve Kroft, a correspondent on CBS's *60 Minutes*, the nation's most-watched news show. Kroft pointed out to Stephanopoulos that the show would go on Sunday night immediately after the Super Bowl. The offer was too good to refuse, considering the Clinton campaign strategy to get the Clintons before the largest possible audience.

On the condition that there would be no sensational promotion of the appearance, the Clinton strategists agreed to give CBS an exclusive interview, to be taped Sunday morning. The other appearances were canceled, with apologies. CNN was particularly rankled because its Saturday show had bumped Mario Cuomo to make room for Clinton.

"We broke the commitment, thereby starting a very rocky relationship with CNN for the rest of the campaign," Begala said. "We did the right thing strategically. I feel bad that we gave a commitment and had to break it, but when *60 Minutes* offers you a special edition after the Super Bowl with an audience of a hundred million viewers, you say yes. And when they say the condition is you cancel CNN, you say okay."

Clinton declined to stay Rector's execution, and it took place on schedule. The next day, Saturday, the Clintons returned to New Hampshire for an upbeat, morale-boosting rally in a Manchester high school gym, after which they headed for Boston, where their segment of *60 Minutes* was to be taped late the next morning. They were checked into the Ritz-Carlton hotel off Boston Common and tried to relax with some friends and key political advisers. Among them for the first time was Mandy Grunwald, who, after her performance on *Nightline* and her recognized expertise in television, had been asked to come to Boston to help prepare the Clintons for the taping.

It turned out, she said later, that they didn't need much prepping. It already was their instinct, she said, to do what she had done—"not to just sit there and be defensive, but to lash back at the press" and to express their "personal outrage at the process." Beyond that, Grunwald recalled, "nobody told them what to say about their marriage. They knew what they wanted to say. It was actually very emotional, both in the prep meetings and watching *60 Minutes*, to hear them talk about their marriage.'' According to others, when Hillary Clinton was asked at one point in the prep session how she felt about her family, she started weeping, expressing concern about how the show would affect their daughter, Chelsea, then eleven years old.

There was more prepping the next morning but the Clintons were ready. The taping took place in a private room with fireplace in the hotel, with the Clintons sitting side by side. According to a key Clinton adviser in the room, just as the interview was to start, *60 Minutes* senior producer Don Hewitt, who had been a producer of the famed first 1960 debate between John Kennedy and Richard Nixon, knelt down at Clinton's left elbow and said: "When he asks you if you committed adultery, say yes. It will be great television. I know. I know television. The last time I did something like this, Bill, it was the Kennedy-Nixon debates and it produced a president. This will produce a president, too."

The Clinton adviser said later: "I was dumbfounded. This guy was coaching my candidate to confess adultery on his show! Clinton listened impassively."

Kroft indeed tried repeatedly to get at the issue of infidelity in more than an hour of questioning. Each time Clinton would recite his standard reply—that he had not had an affair with Gennifer Flowers, but that he had been responsible in unspecified ways for "wrongdoing" and for "causing pain in my marriage."

While contending that he had "said things to you tonight and to the American people from the beginning that no American politician ever has," he balked at Kroft's specific question about committing adultery, saying that he was "not prepared tonight to say that any married couple should ever discuss that with anyone but themselves."

The closest he came to implying infidelity was when he said near the end of the interview: "I think most Americans who are watching this tonight, they'll know what we're saying, they'll get it, and they'll feel that we have been more candid. And I think what the press has to decide is, are we going to engage in a game of 'gotcha'?" Clinton recalled a time "when a divorced person couldn't run for president, and that time, thank goodness, has passed." Then he asked: "Are we going to take the reverse position now that if people have problems in their marriage and there are things in their past which they don't want to discuss which are painful to them, that they can't run?" And his wife weighed in: "I don't think being any more specific about what's happened in the privacy of our life together is relevant to anybody besides us.''

Perhaps Clinton's most effective moment came when Kroft, trying to characterize the Clintons' relationship, said he thought ''most Americans would agree that it's very admirable that you've stayed together—that you've worked your problems out and that you've seemed to reach some sort of understanding and arrangement—'' Clinton broke in: ''Wait a minute, wait a minute, wait a minute. You're looking at two people who love each other. This is not an arrangement or an understanding. This is a marriage. That's a very different thing.''

Hillary Clinton added: ''You know, I'm not sitting here, some little woman standing by my man like Tammy Wynette. I'm sitting here because I love him, and I respect him, and I honor what he's been through and what we've been through together. And you know, if that's not enough for people, then heck, don't vote for him.''

The sense of the campaign strategists watching the interview on closed-circuit monitors in a control room was that Clinton had taken some hits but had survived. Afterward, he had lunch with members of *The Boston Globe* editorial board and spoke of his dilemma on being less than explicit about the have-you-ever question. ''If I say no, you all will just go out and try to prove me wrong,'' he said at one point. ''And if I say yes, that will mean there is no end to it. I'm not complaining, though. I signed on for the whole ride. If I made any mistake, it was talking about all this at all.''

While Clinton was at the editorial board lunch, his wife was in another room in the hotel having sandwiches and beer with some old Boston friends, including Rick Stearns, a fellow Rhodes Scholar and McGovern campaign alumnus with Clinton. The candidate walked in while Begala was on the phone with his wife, like Begala a transplanted Texan, telling her how the taping had gone. Clinton took the phone. ''Well, Diane,'' he said, ''I think it went pretty well until they showed me that picture of the sheep. I told them it was Begala. I hope you don't mind. I gave him up for a good cause.''

When the show came on after the Super Bowl that night, to an estimated audience of 34 million viewers, the interview had been cut to about fifteen minutes, but it was packed with drama and unprecedentedly personal revelation by a presidential candidate and his wife about their marriage. Nevertheless, Begala said later, "we were very angry with the editing," and realized the campaign had made a mistake in not insisting that the interview be done "live to tape"—doing one run-through for the allotted air time and no more. If so, it might have caught another dramatic moment, when a television lamp tipped over and Clinton grabbed his wife off the sofa to safety.

But the one thing that the Clinton strategists regretted most about the cuts, one of them said later, was one observation by the candidate. "No one wants to be judged," he had said at one point, "on the worst moment of his life."

That moment, for Clinton, was not over. The next day at the Waldorf-Astoria in New York, the *Star* produced Flowers at a press conference. Dressed in a bright red jacket with her brassy blond hair flowing from conspicuously dark roots, she did not make the most compelling witness as she insisted Clinton was "absolutely lying" in saying they had never had an affair.

"I was Bill Clinton's lover for twelve years and for the past two years I have lied to the press to protect him," she said. "The truth is, I loved him. Now he wants me to deny it. Well, I am sick of all the deceit and I'm sick of all the lies."

Prior to the playing of selected portions of the tapes she said she had made of Clinton phone calls, Flowers insisted that "when people hear my tapes, I think they will realize that I am not a woman that he saw and spoke to infrequently. My tapes go far beyond what Bill described." But when excerpts were played, only twelve minutes out of an hour or more she said she had made available to the *Star,* nothing definitive was heard to establish an affair between them.

Much later, Carville argued that the very fact that the tapes were presented with segments omitted was the best evidence that if presented whole they would have vindicated Clinton. "Why would someone present the tape and take something out of it?" he asked. "The only reason they'd take something out of it is because there's something in there that they don't want you to hear." Carville noted that there were twelve separate edits in the tape, and he pointed out that in a court of law, "there's a good reason for the rule that unless something is whole, it's not evidence."

CNN, which Clinton had given short shrift in canceling its Saturday news show and preferring *60 Minutes,* carried the event live and all the other network news shows picked it up that night. Democratic National Chairman Ron Brown immediately condemned CNN for practicing "trash journalism and titillation television" but Tom Hannon, CNN's political director, defended the live coverage. "We think our viewers are entitled to a direct opportunity," he said of Flowers, "to evaluate her credibility in an adversarial context with reporters."

The whole womanizing story, which up to now had been treated as if it had fenders by *The New York Times* and with all the affection usually afforded a dead fish by other news organizations in the mainstream, had finally made the jump from the supermarket counters of America into the nation's living rooms. In the past, such stories had been enough to bury political candidates. But here was one who took this one head-on, and was surviving.

Although a *Boston Globe* poll in New Hampshire reported a sharp drop in Clinton's support, internal opinion samplings by Greenberg for the campaign found that Clinton's backing in the state, which had been going up rapidly, was stalled by the Flowers story but leveled off rather than plunging. "There was some shifting around in who was supporting us, as a result of the story," he said later. Clinton, he said, "lost ground with older women but gained ground with younger men, which is what you'd probably expect, given the issue."

But subsequent focus groups, Greenberg said, found that voters "hated Gennifer Flowers—men too, but women particularly. They knew she was paid. They didn't know whether she had an affair or not, but what they did know was the source of the story was Gennifer Flowers, which undermined her story. . . . They knew it was tabloid, they knew it was money. . . . The most important thing we learned was their comfort with the way Clinton was addressing the question."

At the same time, the Clinton campaign did its share to paint Flowers as the wicked witch in the piece, and in the process to make the mainstream news media feel uncomfortable about the way they were taking their lead from a gossip tabloid. In fact, Carville said later, "I think Gennifer Flowers [the story] had a positive impact on the coverage, because I think after everybody went through it, no one felt very good about it. It was my job, I was out there trying to make people feel bad about it."

Nationally, other polls were indicating public annoyance with the focus on Clinton's personal life. In an ABC News survey, 80 percent of those asked said they didn't think the issue of whether Clinton had had an extramarital affair should be an issue in the campaign.

The most politically embarrassing aspect of the whole business was turning out to be a remark the voice identified as Clinton's on one of Flowers's tapes had made about Mario Cuomo. The voice referred to Cuomo as a "mean son of a bitch," and when Flowers suggested that the New York governor might have "Mafioso" connections, the voice replied, "Well, he acts like one."

While still challenging the veracity of the tapes, Clinton told reporters he was trying to reach Cuomo to apologize. Cuomo in turn told reporters that Clinton "ought to save himself his quarter," deploring the taped remarks as "part of an ugly syndrome that strikes Italian-Americans, Jewish people, blacks, women, all the different ethnic groups." Clinton publicly apologized, saying that "if the remarks on the tape left anyone with the impression that I was disrespectful to either Governor Cuomo or Italian-Americans, then I deeply regret it. At the time that conversation was held, there had been some political give-and-take between myself and the governor, and I meant simply to imply that Governor Cuomo is a tough and worthy opponent." Cuomo was not pleased, but he eventually cooled down, although he told us later that Clinton never did reach him then to apologize personally.

If the Flowers affair did not severely damage Clinton in New Hampshire, it did generate concerns among Washington politicos about "electability" and speculation that other Democrats might enter the race, particularly an irate Cuomo. *The New York Post* did its bit to push that development along with this headline regarding Cuomo's response to the alleged Clinton remarks: "Cuomo Says Clinton Talks like Bigot."

Cuomo reiterated that he was not a candidate, but when self-starters from Chicago moved into New Hampshire and set up shop for a Cuomo write-in effort without his blessing, he ran true to form. "I wouldn't presume to interfere with the good people of New Hampshire," he said. "Who am I to tell the people of New Hampshire, 'You shouldn't do that'?"

Beyond the customary Cuomo tease, there were few other prospective new starters in view. House Majority Leader Richard Gephardt seemed to some to leave the door open a crack to a late presidential bid, but nothing came of it. The polls in New Hampshire, where righting the dismal economy held the voters' concentration, continued to indicate that Clinton had weathered the storm, for all the doubts about his "electability" flourishing among assorted reporters, columnists and political wise men in Washington.

The other Democratic candidates in the field began to complain, in fact, that the Flowers story had so dominated the news and kept the focus on Clinton that they were dropping off the political radar screen. A *USA Today*/CNN poll nationally found 42 percent of Democrats surveyed favoring him to only 16 percent for the runner-up, Jerry Brown. And although Paul Tsongas continued to be Clinton's strongest rival in New Hampshire in local polls, the fact that he trailed Brown nationally reflected how lightly regarded he remained as other than a regional candidate.

For Clinton, the fact that the Flowers story had originated in a supermarket tabloid, that she had been paid for it, and that she herself was therefore seen as less than credible, had enabled him to dodge the bullet. But just as he did, another was winging his way—also out of his past.

C H A P T E R   1 1

DODGING THE DRAFT

After a few days out of New Hampshire, Clinton returned on Wednesday, February 5, feeling terrible physically. He struggled through a speech at a school in Concord and then took to his bed with a fever at Days Hotel, where the Clinton campaign was headquartered. On top of his physical condition, Clinton was worried about a story he knew was about to break regarding his draft record—and not in some sleazy supermarket tabloid this time, but in *The Wall Street Journal*—a fortress of mainstream journalistic respectability.

Sure enough, the next morning—another Thursday, another ''garbage day'' in the Clinton campaign lexicon—the newspaper quoted a retired army recruiter in Arkansas, Colonel Eugene Holmes, as saying that Clinton in 1969, during the Vietnam War, had signed up for the Reserve Officers Training Corps (ROTC) program at the University of Arkansas Law School to avoid the draft, and then ''was able to manipulate things so that he didn't have to go in.''

Clinton was stunned, especially because Holmes was the source of the story—a man who repeatedly over the years had told inquiring reporters that Clinton had behaved correctly in the matter.

Clinton had been studying at Oxford on a Rhodes Scholarship at the time and as an ROTC enrollee he was given a further deferment and permitted to return to England to finish that program. He said then that he intended to enter the law school, and the ROTC program, in the fall of 1970 but in the fall of 1969 he decided not to go into ROTC upon finishing at Oxford and asked to be put back in the draft. He was reclassified 1-A on October 30 but in the first draft lottery on December 1 he drew a number too high for induction. In the fall of 1970, with no draft worries, he enrolled at the Yale Law School, not Arkansas.

Those at least were the facts known and acknowledged by Clinton at the time the story broke. Holmes had now told the *Journal*, however, that he was led to believe in 1969 that Clinton had planned to return to Arkansas and enter the law school there later that year, and would not have received the deferment otherwise.

Like the womanizing stories, this one also was an old turkey that had been chased around the political barnyard in Arkansas by reporters during Clinton's earliest gubernatorial campaigns and, after inquiries with Holmes and other military and draft officials, abandoned as unworthy of continued pursuit. But now the *Journal* also quoted Opal Ellis, the Republican executive secretary of the draft board in Clinton's hometown of Hot Springs, as saying the town was "proud to have a Hot Springs boy with a Rhodes Scholarship" and that Clinton pressured the draft board to defer him and accordingly the board "was very lenient with him" and "gave him more than he was entitled to."

The Clinton campaign was caught unprepared. For all these years, Clinton had relied on Holmes to verify that he had done no wrong regarding the draft, and his aides continued to do so. It was, Begala acknowledged later, "a mistake. What if Holmes got hit by a beer truck?" He and other aides immediately sat down with Clinton to review the whole story once again, prodding his memory.

Carville was on the shuttle en route from Washington to New York to make a speech when he picked up a copy of the *Journal* and glanced at the story. "I can remember just having a pit in my stomach all morning, giving the speech," he recalled. He phoned Stephanopoulos in New

Hampshire, telling him, "Man, this thing don't have the right kind of feel to it." The other political advisers in New Hampshire had already reached the same conclusion—that if they thought they had been through fire over Gennifer Flowers, the real inferno was just flaring.

Again it was damage-control time. All pertinent papers from Clinton's draft file were faxed from Little Rock to Manchester, digested and used as a base to subject the candidate, fever and all, to a dry-run press conference on his draft history.

The next morning, as Clinton walked into the lobby of the Sheraton-Tara in Nashua—the same place he was first confronted by a host of reporters and cameramen on the Larry Nichols lawsuit allegations barely three weeks earlier—he was mobbed again and bombarded with questions about the *Journal*'s draft story. "I was not seeking to avoid military service by this [signing up for the Arkansas ROTC]," he insisted. "I could not have known that this [high] lottery number would come about or that all the lottery people wouldn't be called."

As for suddenly deciding to decline the ROTC deferment and subject himself to the draft, Clinton insisted that because several of his friends from Arkansas had been killed in Vietnam, "I just didn't feel right about having a four-year deferment" through Oxford and then law school. "I put myself into the draft when I thought it was a one hundred percent certainty that I would be called." And regarding Opal Ellis's remarks that he had put pressure on the draft board, Clinton said he "had absolutely no conversations with her to that effect, ever," adding that "she's had twenty-three years to tell this story and has never done it before." He called the whole business "an unbelievable rewriting of history."

The Clinton press office in Little Rock, meanwhile, released a brief chronology of Clinton's draft record and called the allegations "recycled Republican charges . . . first raised when Clinton ran for governor in 1978 by a retired air force lieutenant colonel, who then was working for Clinton's Republican opponent. They were false then, and they are false now." And Stephanopoulos in New Hampshire handed out copies of an *Arkansas Democrat-Gazette* story of the previous October in which Holmes was quoted as saying he had dealt with Clinton on his draft status "just like I would have treated any other kid."

But what media critic Sabato had dubbed the "feeding frenzy" was on. At a town meeting in Exeter that night, Clinton was hit with the question again, and he insisted that "I did not do anything wrong, and I certainly didn't do anything illegal."

The new charges nevertheless dominated the political coverage the next day, but at another question-and-answer session at New Hampshire Technical College in Stratham, no voter raised the issue and the staff began to hope that the worst was over. Greenberg meantime had conducted a focus group—a roundtable discussion with selected voters to gauge public attitudes—and found little concern or ill-will toward Clinton over the latest development in the news.

At that point, however, came what Carville later called "one of the biggest mistakes I think I made. He [Clinton] was really sick and he wanted to come home, and I said, 'No, goddamn, what we found is, if you stay out of the news cycle you get clobbered up there.' " That, indeed, was what had happened to Ronald Reagan in the 1976 Republican primary in New Hampshire, when he left the state brimming with confidence on the final weekend, leaving the field to President Gerald Ford, and lost narrowly. And in 1980, George Bush spent the final weekend of the primary basking in sunny Texas while voters shivered in New Hampshire—and wound up voting for Reagan.

Now Carville argued: "What you need to do is get Hillary and Chelsea, bring them up to the Ritz-Carlton in Boston. Let's get room service there, let's just take him out one time a day and just go into New Hampshire, and get our side of the story." But he lost the argument. "I guess I just didn't hold my ground," he said later in discussing his "mistake." "We all went down to Arkansas that weekend and the whole thing just went to hell in a handbasket. You could see, Tsongas was coming up before that, there were some little signs for concern but nothing [concrete]. But that Sunday night poll was just awful, and you knew it was real."

At the governor's mansion that night, the key political strategists and Clinton held a stock-taking meeting. David Wilhelm recalled that "we did not feel the necessary urgency during that meeting because we had some evidence from focus groups that when people were presented with an explanation of the draft [story], they seemed to be satisfied. I guess what we forgot," he said, "was that you have to get that message out, you have to explain it. The fact that a focus group knew the explanation was not sufficient for the rest of the people who were not part of that focus group, who had not been given that explanation.''

Shortly before midnight, Greenberg called in with his latest polling numbers from New Hampshire, and the news was worse than anyone had thought. ''Meltdown,'' he told Carville, giving the rough numbers showing Clinton to be in a free-fall, from a high-water mark of 37 percent to 17 in only a few days, with Tsongas surging into the lead and campaigning now, remarkably to many, with the aura of a winner. ''This was not shades of gray,'' Greenberg said later. ''We had a whole new race.''

A new *Boston Globe* poll had Tsongas pulling essentially even with Clinton. ''We started ripping up the schedule,'' Wilhelm said, ''trying to see what we could do to get this back on schedule.'' A conference call involving Clinton, Carville, Begala, Wilhelm, Greer and Greenberg was patched together. One idea floated was to buy television time for Clinton to field questions from callers. Another was to have Clinton go on the attack, blaming the Republicans for slandering him. Still another, advocated by Greer, was to prepare television ads with Clinton attacking the tabloids and appealing to the voters for fair play.

''We decided we had to do everything possible to change the dynamic,'' Greer recalled. ''We had to get past the feeding frenzy [of the news media].''

The team, with the Clintons overseeing it all, set to work then and there. Begala and Stephanopoulos started on a short speech text for Clinton, a departure from his customary extemporaneous style. Hershel Gober, the Arkansas state director of veterans' affairs, was awakened and called on to tape a testimonial for his boss they had written and that Greer then rushed to New Hampshire radio stations. A still sick and weary Clinton finally turned in, understanding full well that the fate of his presidential bid was now hanging in the balance, and would likely depend on what happened over the remaining eight days before the New Hampshire primary.

Early the next morning, Monday, Bill and Hillary Clinton and aides flew back to New Hampshire, with the candidate working over Begala's speech text hitting hard at the notion that the latest questions about Clinton's veracity—about ''Slick Willie'' as his critics increasingly referred to him—was the work of a ''Republican attack machine'' honed in the

1988 presidential campaign. Clinton was slated to deliver the fighting speech at the Nashua airport but the authorities refused to grant clearance for a political use of the premises.

Another, much more significant factor, however, was about to alter the day's plans drastically. Mark Halperin, the same ABC News producer who had figured in the confrontation of the candidate regarding the Gennifer Flowers story earlier, met the plane and handed Stephanopoulos a copy of a letter that was to throw the campaign into a tailspin again.

The letter, long and anguished, had been written from Oxford in December 1969 by the twenty-three-year-old Clinton to Colonel Holmes, explaining, after thanking Holmes "for saving me from the draft," why he had decided to withdraw from the Arkansas ROTC program and submit himself to the draft after all. The letter was written only days after the lottery had given him such a high draft number—311—that he was safe from induction.

The young Clinton confessed his thorough opposition to the Vietnam War, saying he had earlier taken a minor job with the Senate Foreign Relations Committee so that in some small way he could work daily "against a war I opposed and despised with a depth of feeling I had reserved solely for racism in America before Vietnam." He wrote of having "written and spoken and marched against the war," going "to Washington to work in the national headquarters of the [anti–Vietnam War] Moratorium, then to England to organize the Americans here for demonstrations here. . . ."

Clinton went on that he had studied the legality of the draft when he was an undergraduate at Georgetown and "came to believe that the draft system itself is illegitimate." No government "really rooted in limited, parliamentary democracy should have the power," he argued, "to make its citizens fight and kill and die in a war they may oppose, a war which even possibly may be wrong, a war which, in any case, does not involve immediately the peace and freedom of the nation."

There was a basic difference, he wrote, between World War II and the wars in Korea and Vietnam on this latter score. He praised two Oxford friends who were conscientious objectors and said he himself had considered that option but "decided to accept the draft in spite of my beliefs for one reason: to maintain my political viability within the system." He had prepared himself for "a political life" and was determined to pursue it. In other words, he was saying, he understood that his political future risked being jeopardized by draft resistance and he wasn't willing to run the risk.

At the same time, Clinton wrote, after signing the ROTC letter of intent "I began to wonder whether the compromise I had made with myself was not more objectionable than the draft would have been" because he had no interest in ROTC "and all I seemed to have done was protect myself from physical harm," as well as deceiving Holmes "by failing to tell you all the things I'm writing now."

After Holmes had cleared his draft deferment, Clinton wrote, "the anguish and loss of my self-regard and self-confidence really set in." Before leaving for the fall term in Oxford, he said, he sat down and wrote a letter to the chairman of his draft board in Arkansas saying "I couldn't do the ROTC after all and would he please draft me as soon as possible." But he never mailed the letter, young Clinton went on, "because I didn't see, in the end, how my going in the army and maybe going to Vietnam would achieve anything except a feeling that I had punished myself and gotten what I deserved." So he went back to England.

Clinton closed the letter by saying he hoped that "my telling this one story will help you to understand more clearly how so many fine people have come to find themselves still loving their country but loathing the military, to which you and other good men have devoted years, lifetimes, of the best service you could give."

After Stephanopoulos read the letter, Begala recalled, "for the ten thousandth time in the campaign, he says, 'We're through.' He hands me the letter, and just like George, the first thing my eye sees is, 'thank you for saving me from the draft.' I gotta tell you, my knees buckled." It had the ring of a death knell to Clinton's presidential hopes. And the line about "political viability"—that he had acted to save his own political future—wouldn't help either, nor would the closing reference to "loathing the military." All in all, the letter had disaster written all over it, or so it seemed.

When Stephanopoulos handed the letter to his candidate as the Clintons along with Carville and Begala crowded into a small room in the airport, Clinton scanned it and seemed unperturbed. He turned to his wife and said: "This is mine. I remember writing this letter." Her response, Begala recalled, was, "This is terrific. This is exactly what you were

thinking at the time. This proves everything that you were saying, Bill''—
that he had indeed, as he had said all along, voluntarily made himself
available for the draft.

The youngest of those present, Stephanopoulos and Begala, did not
see it that way, but the man with the best political antenna on the staff,
Carville, agreed. ''When the letter hit,'' he recalled later, ''they said,
'Oh God, this is the end of whatever.' And I said, 'Get that sumbitch
and put it in the paper, man. Make this thing as public as we can get
anything.' ''

Begala recalled his partner declaring to Clinton, ''This letter is your
best friend.'' Here, Begala said, ''was the generation gap, because George
and I were looking at each other and saying, 'Are they reading the same
letter we are?' The younger set argued, Begala recalled, that ''what the
press is gonna do, they're not going to [read] it in its entirety,'' but instead
would pull out the most damaging phrases. ''Hillary and James said,
'We've got to make them read it in its entirety. That's why we've got to
take it to voters. . . . This letter will free us. It won't sink us.' ''

His reasoning, Carville said, was that ''this was a story people felt.
It showed that he was sort of tortured by the whole thing. People were
tortured by the war. If you were Bush's age (at sixty-seven a World War
II veteran) or George or Paul's age (both in their early thirties and post-
Vietnam), it looked like a bad deal. If you were my age (forty-five and
a Vietnam-era veteran), there was a real sort of anguish. The people I
served with, I can't tell you the people who said, 'Look, he just didn't
want to get his ass shot off. That's fine with me.' Who did?''

Carville said he recognized the political risks in Clinton's reference
to Holmes ''saving me from the draft'' and salvaging his own ''political
viability,'' but believed that the letter ''taken in its whole'' would be a
plus for Clinton. ''If we go out and get in front of it and make it public,
then people think you've got less to hide. There's very little doubt he
joined the ROTC not to be drafted.''

The question now was how to handle the letter to turn what at first
blush appeared to be a political suicide note into an affirmation of Clinton's credibility on the draft issue. At Halperin's request, Clinton agreed
to an interview with the ABC reporter on the story, Jim Wooten. First he
delivered his planned speech vowing to ''fight like hell'' against the same

"Republican attack machine" that had done in Michael Dukakis in 1988, attempting at the same time to get the campaign focus back on his economic agenda. "For too much of the past couple of weeks," he said, "this election has been about me, or rather some false and twisted tabloid version of me, when it should have been about the people of this state."

The references to the 1988 Bush campaign against Dukakis were more, however, than simply a smokescreen behind which a candidate under attack could hide. Well aware of the growing mood in the country against negative campaigning, generated in considerable part by revulsion to those 1988 tactics and best remembered in the Willie Horton prison furlough story, the Clinton campaign deftly hung Horton around the necks of the Republicans generally, and Bush in particular, especially later. "The divide-and-conquer strategy helped George Bush and Roger Ailes convince people," Clinton told his Nashua audience, "that the greatest threat to their jobs, schools, children and future in 1988 was a convict named Willie Horton and a governor named Michael Dukakis."

After the speech, Clinton toured a yogurt factory in nearby Londonderry and then went into a small room there for his interview with Wooten, arguing that the letter supported what he had said all along about his draft record. Then the candidate returned to Manchester and waited for the evening television news, and Wooten's public disclosure of the letter. But Wooten before the show informed Clinton that there were some aspects about its surfacing that he wanted to check out.

Wooten didn't know it at the time, but the source of the letter to ABC News was retired Lieutenant Colonel Clinton Jones, deputy to Holmes at the Arkansas ROTC in 1969. Jones, saying later that he was merely "trying to get some facts on the table," denied that he was involved in any "Republican plot" or that he had been paid by anybody to release the old letter.

It turned out that Jones was in Myrtle Beach, South Carolina, at this time and had asked a hotel clerk there to make some copies of the letter for him. The clerk spirited away a copy for himself and faxed it to a friend in Washington, who in turn sent one copy to Clinton's Washington office and another to, of all people, former Air Force Major General Richard Secord, a convicted player in the celebrated Iran-contra affair, who then sent it to ABC's *Nightline*. This string of events once again brought the show's host, Ted Koppel, into the Clinton campaign saga when he received the letter quite independent of Wooten, who didn't have any idea, either, that Koppel by now also had it.

Carville, as already noted, wanted Clinton to make the letter public post-haste, and to the widest audience possible. But Clinton, aides insisted later, felt honor-bound to Wooten to let him break the news in what would have been a major journalistic scoop. Campaign aides did, however, go about the mechanics of arranging for advertising space in the main New Hampshire newspapers. The sooner the better was the attitude, Greenberg said. The strategists didn't want the story to break in the final days of the primary, he said, or for that matter smack in the middle of Super Tuesday.

The Clintons flew off for a major fund-raising dinner in New York at which the candidate managed to mangle the famous Mark Twain quote about reports of his death being "greatly exaggerated," saying instead that reports of his own demise were "premature."

On the flight back to New Hampshire, the Clintons were in an unusually good mood. He was still physically in great distress from the cold or flu he could not seem to shake, and he astonished the few reporters flying with him by popping prescription pills with seeming abandon. He and his wife played pinochle with a couple of reporters and reminisced about their days in the Vietnam antiwar movement and Southern politics, including the bizarre case of another governor, Bill Allain of Mississippi, whose problems made Clinton's pale by comparison. It was Allain who in the last days of his 1983 campaign was confronted by accusations of liaisons from a group of alleged homosexual transvestites—and was elected anyway.

The plane landed in Keene after midnight, and Clinton insisted on searching out an open Dunkin' Donuts shop, where he devoured a bowl of soup and a couple of bagels with tuna salad. Then, as the others in the party watched, weary but bemused, the candidate settled into a long discussion on health care with a surprised late-night customer. If Clinton was worried about the latest bombshell that was about to fall on his campaign, he gave no indication of it.

All but lost in the intense focus on the approaching New Hampshire primary were the Iowa precinct caucuses held that night. With native son Tom Harkin in the presidential race, all the other candidates had prudently decided to save their time and money and leave the state to him. But not wanting to be embarrassed in his own backyard, Harkin had spent an inordinate amount of resources there in winning 76.5 percent of the vote. It was like kissing your sister, and at the price of a chance to make a stronger showing in New Hampshire, where he was going nowhere. Tsongas, sending a stealth representative into the state late, finished third with 4.1 percent behind "uncommitted," which had 11.9 percent.

The Iowa caucuses, critical in other presidential years, had been reduced to a footnote in the story of the 1992 campaign. Business was so slack in the bar at the Hotel Savery, the traditional wall-to-wall hangout of assorted political operatives, reporters and junkies, and in Guido's restaurant that Guido himself, who reveled every four years in greeting the Peter Jenningses, the Tom Brokaws and the John Chancellors of the television news firmament, went abroad during caucus week.

The action remained in New Hampshire, and on the next afternoon, Koppel got into the picture again. He called David Wilhelm, the campaign manager in Little Rock, telling him it was "important that the governor and I talk." The subject, naturally, was the Clinton letter. Here was ABC News once more bringing bad news to the campaign, making some in Little Rock wonder whether the network had become the channel for Republican antics. But Koppel, knowing Secord's history, was himself wary of the circumstances by which the letter had come to him, and the motivation of its sender. He told Wilhelm only that he was "under the impression that my source might have gotten it from someone in the Pentagon." Only when Wilhelm told him did Koppel find out that his own ABC colleague Wooten had a copy of the letter and had already interviewed Clinton about it.

Koppel knew that a critical aspect of the campaign had fallen into his lap and he invited Clinton onto *Nightline*. Stephanopoulos handled the negotiations, and when he asked Koppel where the letter had come from, Koppel pleaded ignorance again, once more saying it was his "impression" that it had come from the Pentagon.

"We went bananas [at Koppel's answer]," Begala said. "We decided we'd call a press conference, release the letter, and announce that the Pentagon had put this out, and that we were going to go on *Nightline* and talk about it." If it was true, here was a grand opportunity to really nail the Republicans not only for going negative against Clinton on the sneak but also possibly for breaking the law by circulating material protected by privacy laws.

The next day, Clinton himself called Koppel, telling him he wanted to release the letter but wanted to confirm that the source had been the Pentagon, as Koppel had indicated. "It was clear in our minds," said Mickey Kantor, the campaign chairman, who was listening in on the call, "that from Ted Koppel's perspective [the letter] came from the Pentagon," or Clinton never would have made such a public charge. So Clinton went out and held a news conference in a Manchester Airport hangar while aides handed out copies of the letter.

Clinton reported that Koppel had "confirmed to me that it is his understanding that ABC received a letter from two different sources, both of whom got it from the Pentagon. If this is true, the leak violates the Federal Privacy Act." He disclosed that he would be appearing on *Nightline* that night to discuss the whole matter.

Koppel later in the day called back, Kantor said, saying "he had talked to his lawyers" and backed off, saying he had learned that the letter had not, in fact, come from the Pentagon. That left Clinton with a bit of egg on his face—and without a very strong counterattack issue with which to divert attention from his own problems.

Later, on a flight to Claremont, Clinton seemed depressed to reporters aboard his small plane. As he walked up to his seat he said hello to Tom Edsall of *The Washington Post*, who with his wife, Mary, had just written an insightful book about how the Democratic Party, in the public perception that it pushed policies benefiting blacks, had contributed to the flight of conservative whites to the GOP in the Reagan-Bush era.

Another reporter, Curtis Wilkie of *The Boston Globe*, told Clinton he had recently written that he was the best-positioned Democratic candidate to address the problems of race raised by the Edsalls, to which Clinton lamely replied: "I was." Wilkie asked: "What do you mean, 'I was'?" Clinton caught himself. "Oh, hell, I am," he said. "It's just that I'm so busy fighting wars that are twenty-three years old. . . ."

Much later, Clinton told us that even in these most trying moments, he never thought about quitting the race. Had his wife asked him to, he might have, he said, "but she never did. I was glad [the allegations against him] happened in New Hampshire because I trusted those people

. . . I thought I got in the race for certain reasons, and nothing anybody said or did affected those reasons, or what I thought was my ability to do the job. I just figured I'd hired out for the whole race, and if the people wanted to take me out, they were free to do it at any point along the way, and I was going to stay until they made that judgment.

"It never occurred to me to quit, not a single time. To me, quitting would have been the worst thing. Getting beat in an election is not a dishonorable thing to have happen, and I certainly could have understood it if at any time along the way the voters had decided they just didn't want to take a chance. They didn't know me, they knew all this bad stuff about me. Why should they risk this thing? I figured the best thing for me was to plow ahead every day and demonstrate a commitment to the things and people who had gotten me into the race."

That same night in Dover, Clinton gave one of his most memorable speeches of the campaign before the local Elks Club, a deft mixture of emotion, defiance and counterattack. Playing off the popular ridicule of Bush's reference to "the vision thing" that critics said Bush lacked, Clinton said that public service in politics was "the work of my life" and that his dreams for the country were his "vision thing." He said he hoped parents in the audience "never raise a child without the vision thing. . . . Life would be bleak and empty without the vision thing."

Then Clinton began talking about gratitude in public life. He noted that Bush had been resurrected politically in 1988 by the voters in the New Hampshire primary after having run third in the Iowa caucuses, yet in the next three years as president had spent only three hours in the state, "mostly on his way to and from Kennebunkport, while you tripled your unemployment, welfare and food stamp rates."

He went on: "They say I'm on the ropes because other people have questioned my life, after years of public service. I'll tell you something— I'm going to give you this election back, and if you'll give it to me, I won't be like George Bush. I'll never forget who gave me a second chance, and I'll be there for you till the last dog dies."

After the speech, Clinton seemed emotionally drained, but still ahead was his appearance on *Nightline* to address the Holmes letter. Before airtime, Koppel asked Clinton to read the letter on the air, but Clinton declined. So Koppel by his own choice and with Clinton's assent, read the whole thing, consuming a major portion of the half-hour show, as

Clinton sat listening attentively and merely confirming by nods the sentiments expressed therein.

When Koppel was finished reading, Clinton told him that "the important thing is that the letter is consistent with everything I've been saying for the last eighteen years, since I was first asked about this in late 1978 [when he was running in Arkansas]. I was in the draft before the lottery came in. I gave up the deferment. I got a high lottery number and I wasn't called. That's what the records reflect. A Republican member of my draft board has given an affidavit in the last couple of days saying that I got no special treatment and nothing in the letter changes that, although it is a true reflection of the deep and conflicted feelings of a just-turned-twenty-three-year-old young man. I felt that at the time."

Koppel then asked Clinton for his views on the draft generally, and how he thought the issue would "play in your neck of the woods, down South, where indeed support of the army is a stronger issue than perhaps most other parts of the country." Clinton replied: "I was reelected five times to run things, in tough times, with no help, by good people who heard all this stuff. If you're looking for somebody that's already been tested, you ought to go with me."

The judgment of the campaign staff afterward was that once again the candidate had survived a major test. "I know that show got us out of the woods with the press," Begala said. Koppel, he said, treated the interview "the way it ought to be treated. It wasn't just a sort of ambush, gotcha, chickenshit journalism." Reporters, just as Begala and Stephanopoulos had done, had seized on the damaging phrases for their morning stories, but after they saw *Nightline*, began to see it as Carville and Hillary Clinton had. The polls did not show any immediate upturn, however, and the jury that counted would not be in until primary night, now six days away.

The draft story seemed to hang on in New Hampshire, more than had the womanizing rap against Clinton. "When people don't know you," he reflected in an interview much later, "even if they don't want to believe something bad about you, in the early going at least an election can be a process of elimination. So that if they hear two bad things about you instead of one, I think the question then is, should you be eliminated?"

The draft allegations, he said, "came to have legs partly because the press thought that there was still more to come out. The story just stayed alive, and there was this whole question whether everybody knew everything they needed to know and I had told them everything they needed to know, and if there was something they didn't understand. . . . It lingered in the news longer, and frankly, my opponents felt more comfortable raising questions about it [than about the womanizing allegations]."

This final stretch came in retrospect to be the finest hour of the Clinton campaign to many of its campaign warriors. After Cuomo had taken himself out of the picture in December and Clinton had moved ahead in the New Hampshire polls and had become the recognized frontrunner, the hope had been to win the state and then roll south into the Super Tuesday primaries to sew up the nomination then and there. "If we had won New Hampshire," Carville said later, "that would have shut the whole thing down." But the Flowers story had further fueled the issue of the trustworthiness of "Slick Willie" and softened him up somewhat, and the draft story had put him on the ropes.

Now the struggle was to get him back up to a respectable showing in the state, feeding the spin that Tsongas as a New Englander should have been the favorite there all along. "We came to believe," Greenberg said later, "that getting 25 percent and having as much space between Kerrey, Harkin and us as between Tsongas and us was the threshold we needed to pass" to come out of New Hampshire in credible shape.

To achieve that goal, Carville said, it was necessary to get Clinton maximum exposure in the final days, and he was more than willing to go all out. "We were answering everything, we were taking it as it came," Carville said of every opportunity offered to get the candidate on television and radio, and before large crowds.

At the same time, the Clinton campaign, part of which was in Little Rock, part in Washington, part in New Hampshire and part wherever the candidate happened to be, became centralized in New Hampshire for the do-or-die push. "The sense," Mandy Grunwald recalled later, "was all hands on deck. . . . My sense was it was the first of the war rooms" that subsequently were set up in each primary state along the road toward the nomination.

Mickey Kantor came to Manchester and functioned, in Carville's words, "like a trainmaster," presiding over early-morning meetings at which everyone got his two cents in on what the candidate needed to say and do to survive down to the wire. "Mickey was very impressive," Grunwald said. "There were a lot of disparate voices and he really got everybody organized. That was an incredible week in terms of each day there was a major television test that Clinton put himself through, any one of which, given how fragile the campaign was, could have blown up the campaign.''

After the *Nightline* show, there were two paid television appearances in which Clinton fielded questions from voters, one in a small town-meeting format and one a call-in, plus a debate on the final Saturday night and a spot on one of the network Sunday morning interview shows. Instead of opting for the most controlled environments in which risks of off-the-wall questions could be avoided, Grunwald said, ''his reaction was, 'Let me out there.' He was working twenty hours a day and he wanted as many forums as possible to connect with people.''

In advance of the two paid appearances, the campaign ran a statewide promotion ad for them with Clinton personally urging voters to watch, observing that he knew they had heard a lot *about* him and now he wanted them to hear *from* him. Greer set up a ''roadblock'' for the promotion—buying all available television for a specific time slot in the Boston area and New Hampshire—so that anyone watching television on any channel would see it. Successful fund-raising, in the midst of all the travail, brought in $1 million in February, enabling the Clinton campaign to take such aggressive actions.

A research firm was hired to round up a small group of undecided voters for the first paid Q-and-A session, and in neither that one nor the telephone call-in show did anyone ask about Gennifer Flowers. There was one question touching on Clinton's draft problems, but it was indirect and easily answered—would he, if elected, be able to perform the functions of commander in chief. The campaign strategists breathed a modest sigh of relief.

Tsongas, meanwhile, was enjoying his own rising fortunes, but not gloating, and declining to be drawn into the controversy over Clinton's draft record. ''This too will pass,'' he said at one point. ''I didn't get depressed over the hard times and I'm not going to get euphoric over the good times.''

As *The Boston Globe* poll finally showed Clinton making a modest recovery but still about eight percentage points behind Tsongas, he began to address directly the question of whether his scandal-ridden campaign could win. ''I'm electable,'' he told a voters' panel in Concord. He had always been able to overcome negative attacks in the past, he said, ''and

I will, if there is enough time. . . . If you say I'm electable, by definition I'm electable.''

Tsongas, holding to the high road, said that the draft issue was ''worthy of discussion but should not be the total focus of this campaign,'' adding that he considered Clinton a friend and that the frenzy over his record during Vietnam was ''irrational.'' Vietnam war hero Kerrey, while saying he was ''tremendously sympathetic to Governor Clinton's dilemma'' and that ''the Vietnam War is not an issue in 1992 and should not be,'' continued to run radio ads raising the question of Clinton's electability. In the final debate of the primary, however, none of the other candidates raised his personal problems—a critical factor for his man, Kantor said later, because ''they allowed Bill Clinton to get back on message.''

In the final days, the Clinton campaign bore down. In addition to the early-morning mass meetings, Kantor held smaller sessions with smaller circles of advisers at which specific problems or television events were thrashed out, after which he would assign one or two of the principals to boil down the conclusions and present them to Clinton, so that he would get the most important points of view without an accompanying Babel. In advance of that week's debate and later ones, the advisers would come up with questions, Grunwald recalled, much tougher than any that ever were asked. Carville especially, she said, reveled in ''scaring the hell out of his candidate for no reason at all.''

From all this, Greenberg said later, ''the solidarity of the campaign was first forged in New Hampshire,'' rather than descending to bickering in a crisis period as often happened in high-stakes campaigns. ''Everybody was in the same hotel, it was like a college dorm,'' Carville recalled. ''In some ways, it was the most fun part of the whole campaign. In the culture of the Clinton campaign, New Hampshire was not that much of a nightmare because it was fun. There was real camaraderie up there.''

Clinton and Tsongas campaigned energetically and effectively down to the wire. Clinton beat a steady path to the television stations in Manchester, riding next to the driver in a van with aides and occasional reporters. On one such trip as the primary approached, he told us he was certain there was nothing else in his past that could be thrown up at him, and that all he could do now was reach as many voters as he could and answer all questions tossed his way. He seemed neither optimistic nor pessimistic, just determined to pack as much voter contact as he could into the remaining hours. At the same time, aides distributed 20,000 videos of Clinton making his pitch, enabling voters to watch him in their own living rooms, at a time of their own choosing.

For all this effort, the Clinton campaign on primary eve was apprehensive. "The whole landscape had changed in a period of two weeks in New Hampshire," Greer said. "The day before the primary, the polls still had Clinton going down, and if you looked just at the numbers, we were on the precipice of coming in third, which would have been disastrous." But Clinton that night had a more optimistic feeling, born of his intensive exposure to the voters in the final, frenetic week.

Tsongas had benefited from Clinton's absence from the state on the weekend the draft story broke, and he too was driving to the finish before large and enthusiastic crowds that would not have seemed possible to any impartial observer who had seen him retailing rather forlornly across the state months and months earlier.

In the end, both men reached the goals they had sought down the homestretch—Tsongas an impressive winner with 33 percent of the Democratic vote and Clinton just managing the 25 percent that his strategists believed he needed to survive the state on an upbeat note and head toward presumably more favorable circumstances and political climate in the South.

For the other Democrats, New Hampshire seemed the beginning of the end: Kerrey 11 percent, Harkin 10 percent, Brown 8 percent, Cuomo 4 percent on write-ins, and consumer advocate Ralph Nader 2 percent, also on write-ins.

Tsongas had won but Clinton's survival forced him to share the spotlight on his big night, and doubts about his appeal outside New England remained strong. As for Clinton, he was prepared to make the most of the situation, to declare his second-place finish as a glass half full rather than half empty. As the exit polls came in that afternoon, Begala was the first to make the point within the campaign that Clinton had to cast the result not as a near-miss but as a comeback. There was some dispute later whether Begala or Grunwald actually came up with the expression "The Comeback Kid," but Clinton used it that night to describe himself—in a primary election he had been on the way to winning handily until two stories out of his past had risen up and nearly knocked him out of presidential contention.

At the suggestion of Joe Grandmaison, the former New Hampshire state party chairman who had been in Cuomo's corner until he finally folded his cards, Clinton went down early to his supporters, to accentuate the positive before his finish was cast by others as a defeat. He had taken a lot of hits, he told the voters of New Hampshire that night, but no more than the people of the Granite State had taken through the Reagan-Bush years. And if nothing else, he concluded, "at least I've proved one thing: I can take a punch."

In getting through the trial by fire in New Hampshire, the Clinton insiders believed they had learned important lessons about their candidate, about the news media and about the mind-set of the voters in the 1992 election year, and what they had to concentrate on as the Democratic nomination moved on to the next tests.

"It was clear just in the tracking of numbers," television consultant Grunwald said later, reflecting on the experience of New Hampshire, "that there had been no meltdown after Gennifer Flowers; there had been after a weekend of the draft story. We did not understand [at first] what the alchemy between the two issues was, what long-lasting question it raised about Clinton. . . .

"We also didn't realize how lucky we were to have an election [then]. If we had had that three-week period in December instead of in January, if there hadn't been a vote, so that you all knew and we all knew how people, real people, feel about all this, both those issues could have festered. And they certainly did from one point of view, but they could have festered in a different way, and maybe been lethal, I don't know. But it was very fortunate in retrospect that you had a moment when people could say, 'No, this doesn't matter. We're real people, We reject the notion that this is what's going to determine our president.' And I think that was crucial to the timing of it . . . the ability to have people ratify your point of view, and we obviously took advantage of that in terms of what he [Clinton] said on election night."

The long-lasting question to which Grunwald referred was the credibility, the trustworthiness of Bill Clinton, at the core of the womanizing and draft issues and inherent in the nickname "Slick Willie" first laid on him in Arkansas and emerging increasingly now. It was true, as Grunwald suggested, that New Hampshire curtailed the festering of those two issues with voters. But it was also true as she indicated that they continued to fester among a news media that had not yet picked up on what the voters were saying about those issues.

In permitting Clinton to survive with a respectable second place, they were saying that in themselves the allegations of womanizing and draft-dodging didn't matter, except as they might reflect on Bill Clinton's credibility to do what he was saying he would do to deal with the faltering economy being neglected, in their eyes, by the man who had been in the White House for the previous three years.

With the New Hampshire primaries for both parties concluded, the spotlight that had focused so relentlessly on that small state would now, in the next weeks, swing wildly from one state and region of the country to another. On the next Sunday, February 23, Democratic voters would caucus in Maine, and two days later both parties would conduct primaries in South Dakota. Then, in a rush, primaries or caucuses would be held by one or both parties on the following Tuesday, March 3, in seven states: Georgia, Maryland, Minnesota, Colorado, Idaho, Utah and Washington state; on March 7 in South Carolina, Wyoming and Arizona; and on March 8 in Nevada.

Then, on March 10—Super Tuesday—would come the preconvention season's single busiest day at the polls, with primaries in Texas, Florida, Louisiana, Mississippi, Tennessee, Oklahoma, Massachusetts and Rhode Island and caucuses in Missouri, Delaware and Hawaii. The candidates obviously could not compete with equal intensity in all of these state contests after New Hampshire, so targets had to be chosen. On the Republican side, as already noted, Buchanan chose to make his major stand against Bush in Georgia; among the Democrats, each candidate had his own priorities based on local support and hopes as the campaign plunged into this most frenetic travel period of the year.

In all these states, for Bill Clinton the same question remained a haunting roadblock to the Democratic nomination. Could, and would, the voters believe and trust this relative stranger from Arkansas who was asking to lead the country for the next four years?

Many who had soured on President Bush, or hadn't made up their minds about him and were uncertain about Clinton and Tsongas, yearned for another choice. Two nights after the New Hampshire primary, they suddenly had one.

BILLION-DOLLAR MESSIAH

At 4:16 P.M. on Saturday, June 1, 1991, at the Hilton Plaza Inn in Kansas City, a man named Jack Gargan stood before a regional meeting of an organization called the Coalition to End the Permanent Congress and announced that he was setting out to elect H. Ross Perot president of the United States. He knew the exact time, Gargan said later, because he checked his watch. "I knew I was making history so I wanted to get it right," he said.

"You heard it here first," he told the applauding audience of fellow critics of a Congress that had built up a huge federal deficit. Perot, the famed Texas self-made billionaire businessman, "is too modest to seek the office," said Gargan, "but I think he's too patriotic to refuse."

Afterward Gargan, who had been urging Perot to run, phoned his quarry in Dallas and told him: "Well, the fat's in the fire." But Perot, as he had repeatedly told Gargan, said it was out of the question. "Well," Gargan replied, "that's what a draft is." Recalling that conversation

211

later, Gargan added: "He never gave me any encouragement, but he never gave me any discouragement, either."

Gargan's idea of Perot running for national office did not hit the hard-charging Texan out of the blue. According to retiring Chrysler Corporation chairman Lee Iacocca in an interview on *Larry King Live* after the 1992 election, "Ross and I almost did it two years ago, but we decided a third party wouldn't cut it." He and Perot, Iacocca said, had done an "Alfonse and Gaston" act on which of them would be the presidential candidate and which his running mate, before abandoning the idea.

Gargan, a sixty-two-year-old semiretired financial planner from Tampa driven to political action by his outrage against the congressional pay raise and the savings-and-loan scandal, was the head of an organization known as THRO, for Throw the Hypocritical Rascals Out. He had met Perot for the first time only days before the Kansas City meeting, when he called on the Texas business tycoon in his office in Dallas. Gargan told Perot, he said later, that "you are the only person who can turn this country around, and my job is to see that you run for president."

Most men who had never run for even the lowliest public office might have been bowled over by the proposition. But according to Gargan Perot "was intrigued," and even engaged in Gargan's speculation about "possible vice presidential candidates [to run with him]. I left the meeting, with him saying that he was a businessman, not a politician, and that he was not interested. But I remember when I left, he said, 'You know, Jack, I'm a man of action. If I see a poisonous snake, I don't call a committee to kill it.' And I said, 'Well, Mr. Perot, I'm a man of action, too, and when I see a man who ought to be president, I go out to get him.' " It seemed a serendipitous meeting, and Gargan took it from there.

A few days later at a THRO town meeting in Seattle, he asked those in attendance: "What do you think of Ross Perot for president?" Again he got an enthusiastic response, as indeed he continued to get as he traveled the circuit of anti-Congress, anti-establishment citizens like himself.

Although Gargan had not met Perot before he visited him at his Dallas office, the two men had talked on the telephone. In 1990, when THRO began to get some national publicity, Perot had called its founder and offered his help. Gargan told him he didn't need any right then but wouldn't forget his offer. In April 1991, Gargan invited Perot to address a meeting of about sixty better-government groups in Tampa, but Perot begged off, pleading another engagement. Soon after, THRO's steering committee met and unanimously voted to ask Perot again. Gargan did so, promising him a big audience by throwing the meeting open to the public. Perot said he'd be there.

That was enough for Gargan, and after his first in-person meeting with Perot on May 30 he flew to Kansas City and made what he now calls his "historic" announcement of the Draft Perot movement. Then he began making plans for the Perot speech that he saw as the spark that would ignite the drive to put him in the White House.

On November 2, about 3,000 residents of the Tampa area packed into the Thomas Jefferson High School to hear the rags-to-riches Texas celebrity. Gargan had run a newspaper ad in *USA Today* announcing the meeting and forty-two state representatives of THRO showed up. When Perot arrived, he was greeted with signs held aloft throughout the audience, paid for by Gargan, that said: PEROT FOR PRESIDENT and ROSS FOR BOSS.

On hand to introduce him was 1980 independent candidate John B. Anderson, recruited by a friend to do so although Anderson had never met Perot. Anderson in his 1980 campaign had built on the work of former Governor George Wallace of Alabama in 1964 in opening state ballots to independent presidential candidates, becoming the first such candidate to qualify for ballot position in all fifty states. Anderson said later he was "mildly taken" with Perot at the time "because of his plainspoken ways," although he recalled that Perot was not overly enthused about being introduced to the crowd by him. "Ross wanted the band to play "the Star-Spangled Banner" rather than my introduction," Anderson remembered.

Perot's theme was "It's Your Country"—a slogan that voters all over America came to recognize as synonymous with the super-patriotic, feisty computer services magnate. As he spoke, eight or ten THRO members planted by Gargan in the front row began to chant: "Run, Ross, Run!"

When the speech was over, to ringing cheers and applause from the audience, Gargan got up and made the pitch again. "I don't know about you folks," he said, "but I think this is the man who ought to run for president." The place erupted in cheers again, as a smiling, noncommital

Perot stood there waving. At the airport, Gargan pushed him again. Perot told him: "I'm a businessman, not a politician." But when Gargan would not let up, Perot said, "We'll see," and boarded the plane.

"I just kept on his case," Gargan said later. In phone calls and letters over the next three months, he continued to urge Perot to run. "You have no idea what support you have out there," he would tell his target, but the answer was always the same: "Jack, I'm not a politician."

In THRO's newsletter to more than 100,000 members around the country in late January 1992, Gargan ran a box that said: "If you think Ross Perot should be a candidate for President of the United States, here's his address. Here's his phone number." In short order, Gargan said, "his secretary told me he was absolutely inundated with letters and phone calls."

Ross Perot was hardly the first nonpolitician to come down the pike and find himself the quarry of others who wanted him to run for president. But most of those who got anywhere at all were recruited by politicians, not a host of private citizens. That was so with Generals Dwight Eisenhower and Douglas MacArthur, and in both cases they made their entry into presidential politics through the Republican Party, not as independents. Members of THRO and others who wrote or phoned Perot were Republicans, Democrats, Libertarians and independents of several stripes, and they were motivated not simply by the inspirational Perot story and his no-nonsense, it's-that-simple approach to problem-solving.

An essential ingredient of their interest in him was their increasing disgust with politics-as-usual, with the whole political process and with the men and women who practiced it professionally. That was the reason most members of THRO were involved in that organization, and many, many others who were not members shared their frustration with the way things were in the politics of the country. Ever since the election of John F. Kennedy in 1960, voter turnout had dropped every four years, until by 1988 only about half of all eligible voters bothered to cast votes for president.

Anti-incumbency seemed to be sweeping the country and veteran members of Congress by the scores began announcing their intention to retire, either out of concern that they would be rejected at the polls or because they too were frustrated with the inability to get things done. Perot over the years had built a reputation in business—and in derring-do, as in the rescue by a Perot-hired team of his employees held hostage in Iran—as, he would put it, a can-do kind of guy. When he talked about "cleaning out the barn" or "looking under the hood," listeners understood what he was saying. Coming from a politician, it all might sound like hokum, but Ross Perot not only wasn't a politician but he clearly shared the contempt for them felt by millions of average Americans as another presidential election approached.

Gargan kept calling and writing Perot, urging him to become a candidate, to no avail—until Gargan got a phone call from Perot in late February telling him that he was going to be on the CNN's *Larry King Live* interview show. Unbeknownst to Gargan, another private citizen, lawyer-businessman John Jay Hooker of Nashville, had also been on Perot's trail, trying to persuade him to become a presidential candidate. The previous October, before Perot made his speech to THRO in Tampa, Hooker, a former Democratic gubernatorial and senatorial candidate in Tennessee, had telephoned him and made the same pitch as Gargan had, coming at Perot from a somewhat different angle.

"Let me ask you a question," Hooker began. "Do you think the country is governable, with the deficit we have, and the racism and the rest of it? What would you do?" The questions started Perot's motor, and he began to talk. "Twenty minutes later he stopped," Hooker recalled. "I never had heard a stronger voice. He rang a bell with me. All the talk, he said, was about dividing the pie, when the answer was you had to make the pie bigger." Perot made the argument that was to become familiar to television viewers and listeners in the next months, that the answer to economic recovery was rebuilding the nation's manufacturing base and then expanding American exports. It was exactly what Hooker wanted to hear.

Through November and December, Hooker had been calling Perot three or four times a week, he remembered, with Perot always saying he wasn't interested in becoming a candidate but nevertheless continuing the conversations. "On December 18 I bet him a dollar he would run. He bet he wouldn't," Hooker said.

In early February, Perot was in Nashville to do a radio interview. The night before, he met with Hooker and they talked for four hours in Perot's room at the Stouffer Hotel, during which time Hooker told him at one point he could be "another Eisenhower." Perot replied: "I'm no

Eisenhower,'' to which Hooker responded: ''You could be. Give people a chance to make you one.''

In advance of the meeting, Hooker had been doing research on how an independent candidate for president gets on the ballot in the various states. He had talked to Richard Winger, a California expert in the field, and Winger had sent him several memos, which Hooker had dispatched to Perot, writing across the top of the first one: ''Ross: We've got plenty of time. Let's go!''

The next morning, after the radio show, station WLAC had a small reception for Perot to which about fifty prominent citizens of Nashville were invited. Perot spoke and answered questions. To Nancy Sanders Peterson, a local businesswoman, Perot came off as another politician getting ready to be a candidate, although he hadn't said so, limiting himself to critical comments about President Bush and Congress. Finally, she raised her hand and, as she recalled later, said: ''You sound a lot like a Monday morning quarterback. . . . Are you going to run? If not, why? And if you won't be head coach, who would you recommend?''

Perot dodged, saying he would be a square peg in a round hole in the White House. But she pressed him: ''Well, under what conditions would it take for you to run?'' Perot pondered for a moment, then blurted: ''I really am not interested in being in public life, but if you feel so strongly about it, register me in fifty states. If it's forty-nine, forget it. If you want to do fifty states, you care that much, fine, then I don't belong to anybody but you. I would not want to run in any of the existing parties because you'd have to sell out.''

A reporter for *The Nashville Tennessean* wrote a short story about the reception under the headline ''President Perot?'' and so did *The Nashville Scene,* a local alternative weekly, but neither got much attention outside Nashville. Hooker, though, saw an opening and seized it, functioning in the next months as a sort of midwife to the birth of a Perot candidacy.

First he called an old friend, Bert Lance, the former budget director in the Jimmy Carter administration and later Democratic Party chairman in Georgia, for advice. Lance told him he had to get nationwide publicity for what he was doing, and he suggested interviews with prominent Washington correspondents or with Larry King.

Hooker was a frequent viewer of the Larry King show and liked that idea. He didn't know King but one of his good friends, John Seigenthaler, retired editor of *The Nashville Tennessean*, did. Hooker got him to call King and ask him to accept a phone call from Hooker. "Tell the guy to call me," King said. Hooker did, filling King in on his conversations with Perot, although he did not mention the business about running if voters put him on the ballot in all fifty states.

It so happened that Perot was already scheduled to be on King's show, but Hooker sparked King's interest in Perot's presidential musings. (Later, at a chance meeting with Seigenthaler, King told him: "If you hadn't called, I never would have taken that call. Now I'm making history.")

When Perot phoned Gargan and told him he was going to be on the show on February 20, that was the first Gargan knew about it, because he and Hooker were unaware of the Draft Perot activities of the other. "All this time," Gargan said later, "Ross never once told me about John J. Hooker and he never told John J. Hooker about me"—behavior that later became more understandable as Perot insisted that the whole draft business had developed strictly from spontaneous combustion among his "volunteers."

Subsequently, a producer for the Larry King show called Gargan to ask whether it would be a good time to ask Perot about a presidential candidacy. He wasn't in his office but his secretary, who was privy to the conversations her boss was having with Perot, said she was sure it was.

Hooker had also been urging Patrick Caddell, the longtime Democratic pollster now living in California and informally advising Jerry Brown in his own insurgent presidential campaign, to talk to Perot. Caddell had long believed that the country had grown so disillusioned with politics-as-usual that voters were ready to rebel through the ballot box, if only they could be persuaded they could make a difference, and if only there was someone on the scene who could so persuade them.

Caddell had done polling for Hooker in his unsuccessful runs for statewide office in Tennessee but had not heard from him in some time when Hooker called out of the blue and asked him what he thought about Perot as a presidential candidate. Caddell told him it was an intriguing idea and in fact, although he had never met Perot, had been thinking about calling him. Hooker, who had mentioned Caddell to Perot as someone with ideas about insurgent politics, encouraged him to do so.

Caddell called, telling Perot he knew he didn't want to run for president but wanted to talk to him about building a political movement. Caddell flew to Dallas, where Perot met him at the airport for a long lunch and talk, in which Perot continued to express no interest in running but listened intently as Caddell laid out his thoughts about the possibilities of an anti-establishment movement.

Caddell at that time was involved in a project dealing with interactive television that dovetailed with Perot's own interest in creating "electronic town-hall" meetings through which to cull public sentiment on major issues. The two hit it off. Among other things, Caddell told Perot that as a result of John Anderson's legal steps in winning ballot access in Ohio in 1988, he could not be kept off the ballot anywhere if he did decide to run. Later, back in California, Caddell sat down and wrote Perot a long personal letter laying out why he should do so.

On the day of the Larry King show, Perot and his wife, Margot, checked into the Hay-Adams Hotel just across Lafayette Park from the White House, had dinner, and Perot departed for the CNN studio while she returned to their room to watch the show on television. King, noting the mood of voters who "wished somebody else were running, and some undoubtedly have this guy in mind," began with the obvious question: "Are you going to run?"

Perot's response was unequivocal: "No."

"Flat no?" King asked. The answer wasn't what he had been led to believe it would be from his conversation with Hooker.

"Getting all caught up in a political process that doesn't work," Perot said, ". . . I wouldn't be temperamentally fit for it." King reminded him that Hooker "is strongly urging you to do it." Perot acknowledged that he was getting "a tremendous number of calls and letters," but he then changed the subject, giving King's audience a taste of prime Ross Perot as a national Mr. Fix-it.

The host began a long discussion of what was wrong with America by asking him to "give me something Ross Perot would do if he were king." Perot replied that if he had one wish "it would be to have a strong family unit in every home. It's the most efficient unit of government the world will ever know.'' Then he launched into a sermon that would soon be familiar to millions of Americans:

"The first thing I'd like for you to do, all of you, is look in the mirror. We're the owners of this country. We don't act like owners. We act like white rabbits that get programmed by messages coming out of Washington. We own this place. The guys in Washington work for us. They are our servants. . . . The second wish is that everybody in this country would start acting like an owner. . . . The third thing I'd ask for is the electronic town hall. . . . With interactive television every other week, say, we could take one major issue, go to the American people, cover it in great detail, have them respond and show by congressional district what the people want. Now don't you think that would kind of clear Congress's heads about whether or not to listen to folks back home or listen to their foreign lobbyists on an issue? Sure it would.''

Perot was just getting warmed up. Soon the Rossisms were flowing out like a swollen river:

On shaping up American business: "If we have a losing football coach, we know what to do—get a new coach, get a new quarterback, start with basics, clean it up. . . . Our primary problem in this country now is to create taxpayers. You create taxpayers by building strong growing companies. . . .''

On special interests in Washington: "Let's clean up the system first. . . . We pass a simple law. We, the owners of this country, tell the guys: pass a law that if you were elected or appointed or worked in Washington, you cannot be a lobbyist for a foreign government, foreign individual for ten years. You go to Washington to serve, not to get rich. . . .''

On trade with the Japanese: "When they do a negotiation for an industry the most experienced people in their industry put together a plan. We've got a bunch of young people that blew up balloons in the election. . . . My favorite story is when they brought trucks into the United States and got them declared cars, and cut the import tariffs from twenty-five percent to two and a half percent. That's like getting an elephant declared a horse at the dock.''

On dealing with the federal deficit: "We can't waste a year on stupid jump-starts. Novocain-in-the-knee shots, that sort of thing.''

King interrupted to get the conversation onto the crop of candidates who at this point were challenging President Bush. Perot said he respected them for running but added "there's some wonderful people in the country who ought to be running who are not. I wish they would run." It wouldn't, however, "be appropriate for me to name any," he said. But he did have kind words for Democrat Paul Tsongas when King asked about his eighty-six-page agenda for economic revival.

"He is thinking," Perot said. "It is orderly. It is logical. It involves pain. It involves sacrifice. That's another thing—not to aim it at any one candidate—look for a candidate that has the guts to look you in the eye and tell you, 'This won't be pretty.' [Just as Ross Perot was now doing.] You know, going to the dentist to get your teeth fixed has a little pain attached to it, but it has a long-term benefit. We cannot go from where we are to where we need to be on a pain-free trip."

As for President Bush, Perot said that "in all candor" he didn't believe he understood business; that in his overriding interest in international affairs he just "doesn't like to work on domestic issues [but] I think he realizes now he's got to get into it. My unsolicited advice, and I hope it doesn't offend him, is to get a bunch of people around him that understand this and go to work on it night and day." When King asked whether he would volunteer, Perot replied: "Only if they're serious. And I will not be used as a Hollywood prop . . . because they've used me before. . . ." He didn't elaborate—not right then.

It was not until a caller from Plattsburgh, New York, asked Perot what voters "as the owners of this country" could do to tell "the people in Washington and all the other bureaucrats to do what we want them to do" that he gave the listeners and viewers a hint of what specifically he had in mind.

"Well, it's this simple," he began. "You know, I go back to when people are always asking me to run and I explain to them that one of the reasons I don't want to run is I don't think any one person can do this job. . . . For example, whoever you decide to back, you're going to have to stay in the ring after Election Day. . . . Just that one person . . . has got to have your organized visible support to make this system work. . . . We can have a revolution in this country. I urge you to pick a leader that you're willing to climb in the ring with, stay with, stay the course."

For the moment, Perot let it go at that. After a few more callers, none of whom picked up on what Perot was suggesting, and with time running out for the show, King very casually made one more try at the obvious question:

KING: By the way, is there any scenario in which you would run for president? Can you give me a scenario in which you'd say, "Okay, I'm in"?

PEROT: Number one, I don't want to.

KING: I know, but is there a scenario?

PEROT: Number two, you know, nobody's been luckier than I have. And number three, I've got all these everyday folks that make the world go round writing me in longhand—

KING: Is there a scenario?

PEROT (riding right over King's question): —now that touches me. But I don't want to fail them. That would be the only thing that would interest me. And so I would simply say to them and to all these folks who are constantly calling and writing: if you feel so strongly about this, number one, I will not run as either a Democrat or a Republican, because I will not sell out to anybody but the American people—and I will sell out to them.

KING: So you'd run as an independent?

PEROT (as if King weren't there): Number two, if you're that serious—you, the people, are that serious—you register me in fifty states, and if you're not willing to organize and do that—

KING: Wait a minute. Are you saying—wait a minute.

PEROT: —then this is all just talk.

KING: Hold it, hold it, hold it, hold it—

PEROT: Now stay with me, Larry—

KING: Wait, wait, wait. Are you saying—

PEROT: I'm saying to the ordinary folks—now I don't want any machine—

KING: —this is a "Draft Ross Perot on an independent—"

PEROT: No, no, no. I'm not asking to be drafted.

KING: Okay.

PEROT: I'm saying to all these nice people that have written me—and the letters, you know, fill cases—if you're dead-serious—

KING: —start committees—

PEROT: —then I want to see some sweat—

KING: —in Florida, Georgia—

PEROT: —I want to see some sweat. Why do I want to see some sweat? I said it earlier. I want you in the ring. Why do I want you in the ring? Because I can't do the job, and nobody can do the job, unless you will go in the ring.

In the course of a few minutes, Perot had gone from unwilling citizen to reluctant candidate to the Man in the White House telling his supporters that he won't be able to get the job done unless they stick with him after the election. King seemed bowled over by the news scoop that appeared to have dropped smack in his lap.

"Well, wait a minute," he said to Perot, finally able to get a full sentence in. "Are you saying groups all across America, all across America, can now, in New York, Illinois, California, start forming independent groups to get you on the ballot as an independent, and you would then, if this occurred in fifty states with enough people, you'd throw the hat?"

PEROT: I'm not encouraging people to do this—

KING: If they did?

PEROT: —but the push has to come from them. So, as Lech Walesa said, "Words are plentiful, but deeds are precious." And this is my way of saying, "Will you get in the ring? Will you put the gloves on? And do you care enough about this country to stay the course?" Now I want your promise, also, that, if we [Perot laughs], you know, got lucky and climbed the cliff, you wouldn't climb out of the ring the day after election. You're going to have to stay there for the fight. Then all of these changes could be made.

Now he was wound up and ready to close the sale. "Now recognize," he said, "you're listening to a guy that doesn't want to do this. But if you, the people, will on your own—now I don't want some apparatus built. I don't want two or three guys with big money around trying to do this. Between now and the convention we'll get both parties' heads straight. Number two, I think I can promise you're going to see a world-class candidate on each side. And number three, by the convention, you might say, 'Cripes, you know, it's all taken care of.' "

In other words, Perot was suggesting, such a grass-roots effort would so scare the Democrats and Republicans that they would start listening to the average voter. "But on the other hand," he said, "we're set, and if you're not happy with what you see and you want me to do it, then I don't want any money from anybody but you, and I don't want anything but five bucks from you because I can certainly pay for my own campaign—no ifs, ands and buts—but I want you to have skin in the game. I want you to be in the ring. Now then, God bless you all who have written me and called me. The shoe is on the other foot.''

Having made his pitch, including the suggestion that volunteers kick in five dollars apiece just so they would feel they had a stake in the effort, Perot turned to King. ''I expect everybody to go very silent at this point, Larry,'' he said, like a kid saying to the American people, ''Put up or shut up,'' with the expectation that they would shut up. ''That puts it to bed,'' he concluded.

Or so Ross Perot thought, or said he thought. The moment the show was over, the CNN switchboard in Washington lit up and stayed lit up. And when Perot got back to his hotel room, his wife met him incredulously with ''I can't believe you did that!'' Perot assured her that ''it'll never happen,'' but moments later an envelope was shoved under the door. When Perot opened it he found a five-dollar bill—the first ''skin in the game'' from an anonymous supporter.

In Dallas, Perot's longtime lawyer and friend, Tom Luce, a 1990 Republican gubernatorial candidate importantly bankrolled by Perot in that losing effort, was working out on his treadmill at home and watching, unaware in advance of Perot's appearance. ''I almost fell off,'' he remembered. And in Los Angeles, Hooker was sitting in a hotel room watching the show with Caddell when Perot made his offer to ''the owners'' of the country. Hooker and Caddell were elated that he had taken that step, and Caddell thought the fifty-state ballot challenge a particularly brilliant if risky move.

King meanwhile had gone from the CNN studio to his radio studio in suburban Arlington, Virginia, for his late-night call-in show. On the air, he started getting calls from listeners who wanted to know how they could reach Perot. ''I told them I had no idea,'' King recalled. Perot had left no phone number to call, or address to write, at the end of the television show.

Early the next morning at Perot's office in Dallas, the switchboard was engulfed with calls. The volume was so great that Perot authorized the leasing of an 800 toll-free number, and in the next two weeks, more than a million individuals phoned asking what they could do in their own cities and towns to get Perot on the ballot. Employees of Perot Systems manned the phones, taking names, addresses and skills, without much idea of where to go from there.

Perot persuaded Luce, an unsuccessful Republican gubernatorial candidate in 1990 whose campaign debt of nearly a million dollars had been picked up by Perot, to organize the effort. He also asked Luce to call Caddell and solicit his advice on ballot access. Caddell flew to Dallas again and conferred with Luce, assuring him that Perot could not be blocked from any state ballot. (Much later, however, Luce pointedly told us that while Caddell had sent many memos to Perot, he had played no larger role than Hooker, Gargan "and thousands of other people who were calling Ross . . . and throwing their two cents in.")

Perot also told Luce, the lawyer remembers, that Gargan had researched the ballot access question thoroughly, and he asked Luce to meet with him and other informed Gargan associates. Perot was concerned, Luce said, that he not put people around the country to great effort if legal prohibitions would render their activities fruitless.

Gargan meanwhile, acting on his own, set up a coordinating committee in Washington, assuming his embryo efforts and experience in insurgent politics would be his ticket to a key role in the campaign. Gargan recruited Lionel Kunst, another veteran congressional critic and political maverick, ballot access expert Winger and others, telling Perot he was putting together a team that could be trusted and knew what to do to organize a successful petition drive.

Soon after, Luce called Gargan and asked him and his associates to come to Dallas. On March 7, they met with Luce at the Hyatt at the Dallas–Fort Worth Airport. Luce brought with him a platoon of lawyers from his own firm who, according to Winger, were "totally ignorant about ballot access," and apparently none too happy to be dealing with "outsiders." Luce said later the meeting was informative and "got us way down the road," but he still hadn't satisfied himself it was doable.

When Gargan reported on the coordinating committee he had set up in Washington, he recalled later, "they didn't like that at all. The shit really hit the fan. There was a very conscious effort of some of Luce's subordinates to dump me quick. They felt I was a threat to them. They branded me an opportunist. I told them all off."

Luce acknowledged later that "there was some friction early on" about the opening of the Washington office and "resistance to that in the sense that I didn't think that ought to be done with respect to people that Ross really didn't know, and they ought not to be out using his name in raising money under his name when Ross had said he didn't want people contributing money." (Perot had, however, talked on the Larry King show about people putting "skin in the game.")

In any event, shortly afterward, Gargan was ordered to shut down the Washington office. Perot was upset, he was told, because when the office phone was called, "somebody's answering it saying, 'Perot for President.' " Gargan was aghast. "That's what grass roots is all about," he replied. But the office was shut down. "My theory is that Ross wanted to maintain top-down control," Gargan said later. "That's his style." The incident was another signal of things to come.

At the Dallas airport meeting, Gargan and his group cautioned Luce and his associates to avoid problems with the Federal Election Commission, before which Perot had already filed as a candidate under the agency's strict watchdog stipulations on any presidential campaign activity. They also immediately raised questions about Perot financing his own campaign, as he had said he would do in giving his supporters "a world-class campaign."

"I thought it was a mistake for him to use his own money," Gargan said later. Another of the "outsiders," a Washington public relations man named Mike Foudy, agreed. "I felt that if he just financed it out of his hip pocket," he said, "he would run the risk of being tagged a dilettante." He and others thought it was a much better idea to accept the limit of $100 from any one person, as Jerry Brown was doing. But Perot had made up his mind.

Gargan and his associates wrote to Perot, telling him he was making a mistake, to no avail. As they feared, cartoonists began drawing Perot with bags of money as his ticket of admission to the presidential race. "Tom, this is just the beginning," Foudy recalls telling Luce at the time. "Perot wanted to be drafted," he said later, "but he wanted it to be a controlled draft."

The immediate question that had Luce and the lawyers anxious, Winger said later, was getting on the ballot in Texas, which had an early deadline for the filing of petitions. The law stipulated that no one could sign who had voted in that year's primaries, which were in March, so that left only two months to collect the 55,000 signatures required. Consideration was given to hiring a firm to get them but the "outsiders" argued that it would be bad public relations for a campaign that was supposed to be driven by volunteers—the folks Perot had dubbed "the owners" of the country—to buy "hired guns" of the sort Perot spoke so vehemently against to do the job. Luce's lawyers were skeptical that volunteers could pull off this relatively sophisticated distilling of prospective petitioners, but finally agreed that the task should be left to the grass roots, which were already stirring in Texas and around the country.

Quietly, there was one prominent former political professional traveling to Dallas during this early period giving advice to Luce and Perot's chief business associate, Mort Meyerson, without any compensation. Hamilton Jordan, the prime architect of Jimmy Carter's winning presidential bid in 1976 and later his White House chief of staff, shared Perot's view that the country was in decline and needed basic reform, and he volunteered his help.

Jordan had been out of active politics, except for a brief unsuccessful bid of his own for a Senate seat from Georgia, since Carter left the White House, and at the time was a key executive at Whittle Communications in Knoxville, Tennessee, in its ambitious program to improve classroom education. He had been supporting the candidacy of Paul Tsongas as, he said later, "the only person in either party telling the American people the truth" about what needed to be done. But intrigued by Perot, Jordan began spending his weekends in Dallas, counseling Luce and Meyerson in whatever ways he could, but never expecting to get involved any deeper.

Perot during this period started working the television news and talk shows with a vengeance. He did CBS's *60 Minutes* and the Phil Donahue show, after which MCI, which by now had installed 100 new lines into the mushrooming Perot operation, reported a jam of 18,000 calls in one thirty-second period—unprecedented in telephone history. The response was so immense that a computerized call-routing system was installed from Tampa.

In mid-March, Perot addressed the National Press Club in Washington. He went through his litany of what was wrong with the administration and Congress, including the lack of business sense in coping with the recession. Of the $4 billion deficit, he mused that "maybe it was voodoo economics. Whatever it was, we are now in deep voodoo, I'll tell you that.''

Although Perot repeatedly disdained sound bites, nobody was better at spinning them out than he was. In this one he managed in a few words to remind voters what George Bush originally had called Ronald Reagan's economic agenda, which Bush then embraced, and then to ridicule his famous characterization of trouble as "deep doo-doo." But he never mentioned his own political musings until the first questioner asked: "Will you run for president?" Only then did he repeat the fifty-state challenge that had triggered the avalanche of phone calls around the country. He said he had told Larry King that "it's too complicated," but "to my amazement, and I guess everybody's amazement, there are people at work in fifty states on their own initiative. Now, will it happen? I don't know. The ball is in the owners' court.''

Later the same day, Perot did a long interview on C-SPAN, the public affairs cable outlet, repeating that if the people who had been writing to him "on their own, as the owners of this country, want to go out in fifty states with nobody programming them, nobody telling them what to do, and put me on the ballot as an independent, I will run as their servant." In all that followed, Perot continued to insist "the owners" were doing all the petition-gathering and other organizational efforts on their own with "nobody programming them, nobody telling them what to do." But his own very strong insistence on maintaining tight control of everything said and done in his name or concerning him ran directly counter to that contention.

Perot also said in the C-SPAN interview that if the fifty-state stipulation was met he would be obliged to name a running mate to qualify for ballot access in certain states. "I will have to have a vice president who I feel is a more qualified person than I am," he said. "I will not just reach for an empty suit to play golf and go to funerals. This person will have to be totally qualified to replace me if anything should happen to me." He said that "the acid test is could that person be chief of staff"— a unique notion of how a vice president would serve, reminiscent of Reagan's toying with the idea of putting former President Ford on the ticket with him in 1980 in what came to be referred to as a "co-presidency."

Shortly afterward, citing the pressures of time, Perot selected a "provisional" running mate as a stand-in for his eventual choice, for the purposes of ballot qualification. He chose an old friend, former navy combat pilot and decorated Vietnam War hero, retired Vice Admiral James B. Stockdale, who had spent seven years as a prisoner of war in North Vietnam. From the start, it was clear that Stockdale did not meet Perot's own qualifications to serve as vice president, but he was, after all, only to be a seat-warmer for Perot's eventual choice.

All was not smooth sailing for Perot in these early public exposures, for all his talent in dominating an interview with his filibuster answers and it's-that-simple dismissals of tough questions. Appearing before a meeting of the American Society of Newspaper Editors, he bristled in the face of direct inquiries about his intentions and record, asking at one point: "Do we have to be rude and adversarial? Can't we just talk?" Once again, under pressure, Perot signaled things to come.

He was also learning the perils of speaking his mind, as when he threw out the idea on the NBC *Today* show that a fortune could be saved by eliminating Social Security benefits for wealthy individuals like himself. Attempts to get him to spell out in further detail how he planned to reduce and eventually eliminate the huge federal deficit were brushed aside with a promise to provide a comprehensive plan later.

Early on, also, came another warning signal—that Ross Perot was a man with light regard for the privacy of others and a penchant for sleuthing. In mid-April, *The Wall Street Journal* reported that two months earlier Perot had sent a lawyer and two airplane pilots in his employ to interrogate a prison inmate in Missouri about his claim that he had piloted an American Blackbird spy plane bringing George Bush from Madrid in 1980. The flight was alleged to have taken place after secret meetings with Iranian officials as part of the "October Surprise" to delay release of American hostages until after the Carter-Reagan election campaign, in which Bush was running for vice president.

The man, Gunther Russbacher, known as a veteran con artist with a record of falsely claiming associations with well-known people, was declared a fraud by the Perot aides after he was unable to answer questions about the Blackbird's operation. Perot acknowledged that he had sent his men to investigate after an appeal from Russbacher that he had been railroaded, but he dismissed the inquiry as "a simple surgical check on his credibility" and insisted he had no intention at all of trying to implicate

Bush in an October Surprise that could have rocked his hopes for reelection.

As Perot continued to work the television news and talk show circuit, Perot-for-president petition campaigns were springing up all over the country in a self-starting political operation unprecedented in its scope. The "owners" were picking up the ball that Perot had put "in their court" and running pell-mell with it. But their efforts were not entirely self-starting in many places. Perot's first financial filing with the Federal Election Commission showed he had spent more than $400,000 of his own money—still a far cry from his boast that he was ready to spend whatever it took—$100 million or more—to give the voters that "world-class campaign," but hardly peanuts either. And for all his expressed disdain for "hired guns" in politics, he started conferring with some of the best of them in Washington, a city he had derided in his National Press Club speech as one of "sound bites, shell games, handlers and media stuntmen who posture, create images and talk—shoot off Roman candles but don't ever accomplish anything."

As the Perot phenomenon grew, Perot also instructed a number of his key employees at Perot Systems, many of them former military officers, to oversee the development of the Perot petition efforts in the various states, dispatching them to give local volunteers guidance on how to qualify for the ballot in each state. In some states, more than one group sprang up, creating tensions and sometimes clashes. The Perot emissaries—later dubbed "the whiteshirts" by some of the "outsiders" because of their immaculate appearance and austere manner—reported the disorder back to Dallas, and Perot was not pleased.

But the petition drives were having such astonishing success all over, and the fledgling Dallas operation was having such trouble keeping up, that the grass-roots effort—the "prairie fire," some called it—just kept spreading of its own momentum, for all of Perot's penchant for control. Perot, with his talent for the pithy, told British interviewer David Frost that his volunteers were "moving like locusts across a wheat field."

The polls told the story: A *New York Times*/CBS News survey in late April had Bush ahead with 38 percent of those surveyed, to 28 for Clinton and 23 for the upstart Perot. A *Washington Post*/ABC News poll a couple of days later had it even tighter: Bush 36 percent, Clinton 31, Perot 30. Veteran political consultants began to sit up and take notice.

David Garth of New York, who had managed John Anderson's independent campaign in 1980 that got only 7 percent of the vote, drew this comparison: "We had no money. If Perot is in the twenties [in the polls] and can spend $100 million, and if he runs the right kind of campaign, he can get one third of the vote and win [in a three-way race]."

In Texas, where the petition drive was going gangbusters in spite of the stringent stipulations of the law, a poll by Texas A&M among 674 likely voters had native-born Texan Perot running first, with 35 percent, to 30 percent for Texas transplant Bush and 20 percent for Texas neighbor Clinton. "Put Perot against Bush and ask who is more the Texan," said veteran Republican pollster Richard Wirthlin, "and it won't take two seconds to answer that one."

The political implications were obvious: at a minimum, in a close race between Bush and Clinton, if Bush could be denied his "home" state and its thirty-two electoral votes, Perot could be the Bush spoiler. But although it was clear from the start that Perot had a special dislike for the president, he insisted that if he got into the race, it would be to win.

After what his volunteers had already achieved, Perot told David Frost, "Now it's my turn. I owe them a world-class campaign and they want a victory, not a 30 percent effort. . . . Let's go back into my life. I don't ever compete to be second or third. That is a characteristic, and I will admit it openly, and anybody that's ever been around me will say once you hunker down for the competition, whatever it is, you compete to win."

In the short span of two months—from Perot's appearance on *Larry King Live* to the end of April—the feisty Texas billionaire had moved from the status of oddity to potential political monkey wrench—or more. As the primary competition played out within the Democratic and Republican parties, the little big man with the crew cut and salesman's palaver was casting an increasingly long shadow over the presidential politics of 1992.

CHAPTER   1 3

NOT LISTENING

Two days after the votes were counted in the New Hampshire pri-
mary, President Bush—or, more precisely, White House chief of staff
Sam Skinner—made a decision that on its face seemed to have nothing
to do with the president's aspirations for reelection. A man named John
E. Frohnmayer was fired as chairman of the National Endowment for the
Arts. For those who knew who he was, however, the message was clear:
Pat Buchanan had torn a gaping hole in the Bush campaign's right flank
that required immediate repair.

In informed conservative Republican circles, the firing of Frohnmayer meant a recognition at the White House that Buchanan now constituted a serious political threat, not so much for the Republican nomination,
but to the party unity essential to Bush's reelection chances in the fall.
Bush simply could not afford defections among the right-wingers, so red
meat had to be tossed their way, and quickly. John Frohnmayer was that
red meat.

As chairman of the NEA, Frohnmayer for several months had borne the brunt of conservative rage for allowing federal funding of graphic and in some cases sexually explicit art. In October, Bush himself had suggested Frohnmayer should think about stepping aside. But like many presidents, this one found it difficult to do the face-to-face dirty work, and Frohnmayer hung on through weeks of continuing controversy and not-very-subtle hints that he had overstayed his welcome. "It was," one campaign insider said, "a comedy of errors."

It was no coincidence, however, that Frohnmayer, a lawyer from Oregon, was thrown overboard the same day Pat Buchanan attacked the NEA for "subsidizing both filthy and blasphemous art" and made it clear that he intended to make that record part of the debate in the March 3 Republican primary in Georgia. As Jim Lake put it later, "There was a real concern about the right, not just in Georgia. . . . [The firing of] Frohnmayer was a symbolic gesture to the right that needed to be done."

In a sense, Georgia was an ideal place for Buchanan to use the Frohnmayer issue in his campaign to force the president into retirement. Originally the conservative commentator-columnist had hoped to go from New Hampshire to the South Dakota primary on February 25, but he had been shut off the ballot there on a technicality. And when he appealed to Clayton Yeutter, the former secretary of agriculture who had taken over as chairman of the Republican National Committee, he was—to no one's surprise—brushed off.

But the Georgia primary a week later offered special opportunities. It had always been fertile ground for the most conservative Republicans. In 1976 Ronald Reagan defeated President Ford there by more than two to one, and in 1980 Reagan trashed George Bush, with 73 percent of the vote to 13. The hard-core Republicans in Georgia were white, suburban and conservative, but anyone could vote in either party's primary so there was also the possibility of a heavy turnout among "born-again" or evangelical Christians, who the poll-takers said had made up 60 percent of the Republican primary vote in 1988. It was not an electorate that would be happy with the federal government paying for dirty pictures.

Buchanan was well aware that he could not sustain his candidacy indefinitely simply by beating expectations as he had done with 37 percent of the vote in New Hampshire. "Somewhere you've got to beat the president in a primary," he said, "and then this firestorm we've talked about has got to ignite. There's no question that the daunting number of primaries in the next three weeks is an enormous hurdle to overcome, which is much higher than the first one.''

Just what Buchanan expected this "firestorm" to accomplish was never entirely clear. By the time the votes were counted in New Hampshire, the deadline for qualifying had already passed for more than thirty primaries. But Buchanan also suspected that if he could actually defeat the incumbent president, the doubts about Bush might force him to the sidelines and open the situation for someone, if not necessarily for Buchanan himself. On the other hand, he also recognized that Bush was a tenacious politician who unquestionably could amass the needed delegates if he simply slogged through the rest of the primaries, whatever his winning margins. In many states the Republicans, unlike the Democrats, awarded their delegates on a winner-take-all basis, which meant that victories in the expectations game—such as Buchanan's in New Hampshire—were worth nothing at the cashier's window, however gratifying they might be otherwise.

The one thing that was clearest to Buchanan was that the Georgia primary would be a great deal different from the test in New Hampshire. Although there was some obvious economic distress in parts of the state, the unemployment rate was only about 4 percent, well below the national average, and there was no single-minded preoccupation with economic issues as there had been in the earlier primary. The answer obviously was a strategy that relied most heavily on the social issues that would touch the nerves of those culturally conservative evangelicals who had become such an important element of the Republican Party.

Thus, it was no surprise when Buchanan unveiled a thirty-second television commercial playing on the NEA funding. It included a clip from a film called *Tongues Untied* that showed slow-motion pictures of gay black men in leather harness and chains dancing while the legend on the screen read: "This so-called art has glorified homosexuality. Bush used your tax $$$ for This." And the audio said: "In the last three years, the Bush administration has wasted our tax dollars on pornographic and blasphemous art too shocking to show. This so-called art has glorified homosexuality, exploited children and perverted the image of Jesus Christ. Even after good people protested, Bush continued to fund this kind of art. Send Bush a message. We need a leader who will fight for what we believe in.''

The accusation against Bush was obviously a bit of a stretch. The film-maker had received a $5,000 grant from the Rocky Mountain Film Institute, which had received the money from the American Film Institute, which in turn had received it from the NEA. And Bush supporters in Georgia howled that the ad was so tasteless it would backfire. "It just caused a firestorm down there," Buchanan recalled later, "and the Bush people went berserk." But the ad obviously struck a nerve with some voters.

And although Buchanan had been uneasy enough about the ad to have it test-viewed by his mother, the attack on the gays was a natural for a candidate who sometimes referred to them as "the pederast proletariat" and argued that AIDS was a divine retribution being visited on gays because of their sexual orientation. So Buchanan refused to back away from a commercial he insisted made a valid point. "The president has spoken about obscene and blasphemous art," he told reporters, "but he hasn't done anything about it. It's a pattern. He says one thing and does another."

The White House and Bush campaign strategists also understood the new realities of campaigning in Georgia rather than New Hampshire. The firing of Frohnmayer was not the only gesture made to the conservatives in the aftermath of New Hampshire and the recognition that Buchanan's showing there meant he was going to be a continuing problem. "It put him in good enough shape so we had to campaign at least through Super Tuesday," Lake said. So the White House also chose this time to put a hold on a proposed regulation that would have required churches to report any gifts over $500 to the Internal Revenue Service. The regulation was intended to give the tax collectors a cross-check on charitable deductions, but the churches feared it would have a chilling effect on their contributors, who would resist having their names included on government lists.

The Bush campaign also reacted sensitively to complaints from some evangelical leaders because its general chairman, former Secretary of Commerce Robert Mosbacher, had held a meeting with a gay rights organization—explaining that it had been held for the purely "personal reasons" of Mosbacher, who had a daughter who was openly gay. The White House also moved to stifle a plan by the Department of Veterans Affairs to open some veterans' hospitals to nonveterans as an experiment, an initiative that had evoked a hot response from the veterans' organizations that are so important as social centers in many smaller Southern communities.

The Bush campaign believed that the less intense focus on the economic issues in Georgia might allow the president to take approaches that might have been seen as irrelevant and even counterproductive when used on voters preoccupied with their jobs. One of those was Buchanan's vigorous opposition to the use of military force in the Persian Gulf a year earlier, a position that presumably would not sit well with Southern voters, who polling data indicated were more patriotic and supportive of the armed services than other Americans.

The campaign quickly produced a thirty-second television commercial featuring retired General P. X. Kelley, the former commandant of the Marine Corps. The spot described Buchanan as "Wrong on Desert Storm, Wrong for America" and depicted Kelley saying: "When Pat Buchanan opposed Desert Storm, it was a disappointment to all military people . . . and I took it personally. I served with many of the marines who fought in Desert Storm. The last thing we need in the White House is an isolationist like Pat Buchanan. If he doesn't think America should lead the world, how can we trust him to lead America?"

The commercial was noteworthy because it was such a direct attack on the challenger coming at a time when President Bush still was refusing to mention his name, thus observing a long outdated political myth that simply mentioning your opponent exalts his status. Bush was still talking about "those who didn't support us then and . . . those who second-guess us now" on the war, as if the voters didn't know about Pat Buchanan. In a speech to South Carolina Republicans in Charleston three days after New Hampshire, Bush said, "Let's not listen to the gloom and doom from all those intense talking heads"—his favorite phrase for those like Buchanan who appear on television talk shows—"who are happy only when they say something negative."

Although Buchanan may have been on the defensive on the Persian Gulf, he had issues of his own that seemed likely to have sting in the South. One of them was that Civil Rights Act of 1991 that was the last straw drawing him into the campaign in the first place. Speaking to the annual Conservative Political Action Conference in Washington, Buchanan made his case against the "quota bill" in terms of class warfare. "Now if you belong to the Exeter-Yale GOP club," he said, "that's not going to bother you greatly because, as we know, it is not their children who get bused out of South Boston into Roxbury, it is not their brothers who lose contracts because of minority set-asides, it is not the scions of Yale and Harvard who apply to become FBI agents and construction workers and civil servants and cops, who bear the onus of this reverse discrimination. It is the sons of middle America who pay the price of reverse discrimination advanced by the Walker's Point [Bush's Kennebunkport home] GOP to salve their social consciences at other people's expense. If I am elected, my friends, I will go through this administration, department by department and agency by agency, and root out the whole rotten infrastructure of reverse discrimination, root and branch.''

It was rhetoric worthy of George Wallace in his heyday twenty years earlier when the Alabama governor used to talk about the ''the average citizen—your steelworker and your beautician'' being wronged by the social manipulation of the liberals and ''pointy-headed bureaucrats who couldn't park a bicycle straight.'' More to the point in 1992, it was rhetoric aimed directly at the supporters of David Duke, the rabble-rouser from Louisiana who had failed to qualify for the Georgia ballot. Although the former Ku Klux Klan leader was still officially a challenger to Bush and Buchanan, his campaign had never lifted off the ground even enough for him to qualify for federal matching funds. And, although Buchanan had once considered Duke a potential rival—he threatened mockingly in December of 1991 to ''sue that dude for intellectual property theft''—he now knew that potential Duke voters could be reached with the right rhetoric.

Campaigning in small towns in the South, Buchanan was a master of innuendo and riposte in playing on their resentments. When he told an audience, for example, that his hometown of Washington had been a fine place ''before all that crowd came rolling into town and took it,'' no one imagined he was talking about the liberal bureaucrats. The same was true when he complained in an interview about walking down Connecticut Avenue and finding ''these guys playing bongo drums . . . in the town I grew up in.''

He was a master of derision, describing the vice president as ''Little Danny Quayle'' and establishment Republicans as ''kennel-fed conservatives'' and ''Exeter and Yale Skull and Bones Republicans.'' He drew hoots of appreciative laughter when, borrowing a line from a television comedian, he said, "You know, I have a lot of respect for Teddy Kennedy. What other fifty-nine-year-old do you know who still goes to Florida for spring break?"

Buchanan's campaign in the Georgia primary was not, however, a well-crafted exercise. Indeed, he spent the entire weekend after the New Hampshire primary stumping in Florida, a state in which he knew he had no chance of winning and one that awarded its delegates on a winner-take-all basis. And after a two-day bus trip through small Georgia communities like La Grange, Perry, Fitzgerald, Griffin and Fayetteville, he detoured off for two days in South Carolina, in whose primary four days after Georgia's he was no factor, before finally returning to the Atlanta suburbs where the votes were.

On another day he ducked over to Tupelo, Mississippi, to put flowers on the graves of two Buchanan ancestors who had served in the Confederate army. When asked about the rationale behind his scheduling, he shrugged and laughed.

Bush, meanwhile, was focusing narrowly on what he saw as his challenger's vulnerabilities as well as his own. But he was still a snakebit candidate. With the primary just a week away, the president flew to California for a campaign fund-raiser and, with Barbara Bush at his side, paid a call on Ronald and Nancy Reagan that was designed to produce a public embrace for the network news. Instead it was an embarrassment. Reporters and camera crews who accompanied the Bushes to the Reagan home in Bel Air were left behind a gate wrapped in plain brown paper. There was no photo opportunity, no comment—only an official White House still photo showing the two couples smiling awkwardly into the camera.

Nor did Reagan attend the fund-raiser at the Century Plaza, a short block from his office. There was, the press was told, a previous commitment. The incident was all the more embarrassing because it came on the heels of a story in *The Washington Post* about the problems Bush was facing in winning California's fifty-four electoral votes. The story said Reagan had told friends that one of Bush's troubles was that "he doesn't seem to stand for anything"—which was just what Pat Buchanan was telling other Republicans every day. In Washington the whole episode was written off as "Nancy's revenge." It was no secret that Nancy Reagan had never been a Bush enthusiast from the time he was chosen for the ticket in 1980 over her friend Paul Laxalt.

Bush's campaign in Georgia was largely a return to the so-called values issues and media events that he had employed with such success in the 1988 campaign. Speaking to a party rally in Atlanta, he drew cheers when he played off Buchanan's slogan, declaring "We put America first so long as we put family first" and repeated such bromides as "parents know better than some bureaucrat in Washington, D.C." and "yes, we believe there's a place for voluntary prayer in our children's classrooms."

There was nothing subtle about the Bush strategy. On the final Sunday before the primary, Episcopalian Bush had been scheduled to attend services at the Peachtree Presbyterian Church, one of whose parishioners was an old friend. But early that week the campaign, in a message to the born-agains, announced he would attend services, instead, at the First Baptist Church of Atlanta, a congregation of some 15,000 Southern Baptists whose services were regularly televised to a wide audience throughout the state.

The economic issues that had dominated the Republican campaign were largely overlooked in Georgia. But in an election eve interview published by *The Atlanta Journal* on primary day, the president took a further step to clean up his image, confessing that the 1990 budget agreement with Democratic leaders of Congress that raised taxes had been a "mistake" he would not repeat. "Listen," he said, "if I had it to do over, I wouldn't do what I did then for a lot of reasons, including political reasons." Bush said he thought the deal would result "in total control of domestic spending and now we see Congress talking about raising taxes again."

In a separate interview the same day with conservative columnist Cal Thomas, Bush also pointed to the tax increases Ronald Reagan had felt obliged to approve in 1982 but later was sorry he had accepted. "But he had to do it and he regretted it," the president said, "and I had to do it and I regret it." The strategy was obvious. Bush and his campaign advisers had recognized that reneging on "read my lips" had become such a continuing vulnerability that there was no choice but to try to put it behind him once and for all.

When the votes were counted election night, it was clear that Bush

had not yet solved his political problems. He won Georgia with a respectable 64 percent of the vote, an improvement of eleven points over his
New Hampshire total, to 36 for Buchanan, almost identical to his vote in
the earlier primary. "We've done it again," the ebullient Buchanan told
his followers without explaining how losing almost two to one qualified
as a success. Bush confined himself to another written statement designed
to placate the rebellious within his party. "To those who have been with
me in the past but did not vote for me today, I hear your concerns and
understand your frustration with Washington," he said, implying that
these were protest votes against some amorphous "they" rather than
George Bush personally.

The figures from exit polling and returns from other primaries on
March 3 sent warnings to both candidates. Bush won Maryland by 70 to
30 percent and Colorado by 68 to 30—with Buchanan achieving his 30
percent in each state without doing any significant campaigning in either.
That performance suggested that the conservative commentator's candidacy was almost irrelevant, because there were 30 percent of Republican
voters opposed to Bush anywhere. That point had already been demonstrated in South Dakota, where 31 percent of Republicans cast their votes
for "uncommitted" after Buchanan failed to win a place on the ballot.
Viewed in that light, Buchanan's strenuous campaigning in New Hampshire and Georgia was worth about 6 or 7 percent.

On the other hand, the evidence that this hard core was consistently
testing out at 30 percent was a menacing reality for the president. These
were, after all, Republican primaries, and defections of that scale from an
incumbent Republican president were more than he could accommodate in
the general election.

The exit polls in Georgia and Maryland also uncovered some bad
news for George Bush. In each state one Republican in seven said they
intended to vote for a Democrat against Bush in November and more than
one third said they disapproved of Bush's performance in office. And
despite the Bush campaign's attempts to exploit the Persian Gulf War
issue in Georgia, only 12 percent of voters there said it influenced their
votes. In short, although the president seemed to have a clear field toward
the nomination for a second term, he had done little or nothing in these
first primaries to alter the perceptions that made him a vulnerable incumbent. And his campaign was still being compromised by tensions and

poor communications between the White House staff under Sam Skinner and the political operation being run by Bob Teeter.

Criticized on the outside as being ruthlessly political, the Bush operation on the inside in 1992 was at times laughably scrupulous. According to Mary Matalin, who was chief of staff at the Republican National Committee before becoming the Bush-Quayle campaign's deputy manager, White House counsel C. Boyden Gray imposed a rule requiring strict separation of political and policy discussions, presumably to avoid running afoul of Federal Election Commission regulations. Yeutter and other party officials, Matalin recalled, "could not meet with any cabinet member unless there was a lawyer present and no policy discussions took place. One time Boyden found out that we were having a meeting with Lou Sullivan [secretary of health and human services] to talk about black turnout, black registration, and Boyden canceled the meeting." Matalin sighed: "See what I mean about the White House?"

When Skinner took over from the dictatorial Sununu, she said, the White House and the campaign committee moved on their own tracks. "There was no synergy," she said, "and if you don't have it, you're certainly not going to get it in the middle of the campaign." If she had to talk to somebody on the White House staff about a political matter, Matalin said, she had to notify Teeter, who would call Skinner, who would call Gray to get approval. "People at the White House were freaked out," she said. If she called someone there to convey or ask for information, she said, she was likely to be told: "I can't talk to you."

As a result, Matalin said, "an immediate impediment was put up between the two structures." In addition, she said, "we soon discovered that the English language was heard in two different ways. We heard it politically and they heard it governmentally." In other words, when the campaign was addressing a matter in terms of the reelection effort, the White House continued to look at it in policy terms. Something that might be considered helpful to advance the president's reelection would not be timed for optimum political impact because the White House did not think in those terms, and did not look to the campaign for political guidance.

Such problems, however, mattered more in the long term than in the short. Buchanan was effectively all through as a challenger, although he obviously threatened to be a continuing irritant to the president. The conservative commentator had used an appearance on the David Brinkley show on ABC to send what he called "a signal . . . that I was ready for a cease-fire in place" if he lost in Georgia. If Bush were the nominee, he said, he intended to support him in the general election.

But when Newt Gingrich, the Georgia congressman who served as Republican whip in the House, and longtime Bush political lieutenant Rich Bond, now chairman of the Republican National Committee, both lashed out at Buchanan because of the NEA commercial, and Gingrich on television compared him with David Duke, Buchanan got his back up. He said he would fight it out all the way to the end. "I said, 'California, here I come.' . . . and so you were sort of locked in to going to California"—to competing through the final primaries in early June. "Tell Little Richard [Bond] we'll see him in Orange County," Buchanan said, for emphasis. Bond had replaced Yeutter as party chairman in a move to bring more partisan political experience to the post. But in this instance Bond's aggressive style only seemed to exacerbate the situation.

In the days immediately after the Georgia vote, the president plunged into full-scale campaigning across the South while his advisers in the White House and campaign operation conducted a semipublic debate over whether he should be behaving politically or presidentially. Bush himself, off for appearances in Florida, South Carolina, Tennessee, Louisiana and Oklahoma, said he wanted to make it clear "we're not taking anybody for granted." But Mosbacher told an interviewer that the president had "a million things to do" in Washington and should be back there.

The testiness and tension in the Bush campaign was apparent when even the usually good-humored White House press secretary, Marlin Fitzwater, lost his cool at the persistent questioning of the president and what he was doing. When Bush was about to make a speech at Oklahoma Christian University, most of the White House reporters were gathered in a press center in a building nearby to listen to the speech piped in on closed-circuit television and to write their stories, a customary procedure on White House trips. But Fitzwater suddenly walked in, ordered the sound turned off and told the reporters if they wanted to hear the speech, they would have to go to the auditorium. "I'm sick of all you lazy bastards," he said. The incident was trivial and Fitzwater later apologized, but it added more fuel to the perception of a campaign under great stress.

Buchanan, meanwhile, was continuing to display what was clearly overweening self-confidence, given his record to this point. Visiting the Alamo in San Antonio, he declared: "They said he's beat me seven to nothing. He's going to have to beat us fifty nothing. We're going to find some state where we take the king down and after that we're going to win and win and win."

As a practical matter, however, Buchanan had little left in his arsenal. He was shut out in the Super Tuesday contests on March 10, losing all eight Republican primaries by huge margins. He had hoped to attract a heavy vote in Michigan from blue-collar culturally conservative voters who had rallied behind George Wallace a generation earlier. But when the votes were counted on March 17, he came away with only 25 percent of the vote in Michigan, 23 in Illinois. The Michigan result, he said later, "was a great disappointment." He still had federal matching money available, nonetheless, so he tried several other states because "we needed a place to go before we went to California." But even in North Carolina, the home ground of arch-conservative Republican Senator Jesse Helms, he was able to get only 22 percent of the vote. It was clear by now that Buchanan's grand dreams of scuttling the president somewhere on the road to California had gone up in smoke.

One old political and personal friend, however, counseled him against carrying the fight to the Golden State. He called Nixon, now an expatriate in New Jersey but still the self-styled world's greatest political expert, after his Michigan loss to report his progress. "Nineteen [defeats] for nineteen. Not bad, eh?" Buchanan informed him. Nixon replied: "Buchanan, you're the only extremist I know that has a sense of humor." But Nixon warned him about California: "Bush is going to lose [the state] and they'll blame you."

If George Bush had a problem, however, it was not Pat Buchanan; it was his own weaknesses as a candidate and national leader, and particularly the poverty of his understanding of, and interest in, domestic issues. His flaws were never more evident than they were in the wake of a jury verdict freeing four policemen who had been shown on a videotape beating a black man named Rodney King a year earlier. The riots that exploded in South Central Los Angeles were the most destructive in the history of the United States—fifty-three deaths, more than 2,000 injured, 5,000 fires that destroyed hundreds of small businesses, damage estimated to exceed $1 billion. Millions upon millions of Americans watched them unfold on their television screens as the first hours of racial rage evolved into days of epidemic and systematic looting and burning.

Nothing in Bush's public career, his service as president for more than three years or his own intellectual interests, had prepared him for this crisis. Rather than flying to Los Angeles to confront the situation, the president remained in the White House for nearly a week, groping for a way to deal with a challenge in which the politics was far more complex than in attacking Saddam Hussein.

His first response, at a state dinner, was as insensitive as it was baffling: "The court system has worked. What's needed now is calm respect for the law. Let the appeals process take place." The president of the United States apparently was unaware that an unsuccessful prose-cution has no right of appeal—that the Fifth Amendment in the Bill of Rights stipulates: ". . . nor shall any person be subject for the same offence to be twice put in jeopardy of life or limb. . . ."

Two days later Bush made a televised speech telling Americans that the turmoil in Los Angeles was "the brutality of a mob, pure and simple" rather than an emotional protest against either the verdict in the Rodney King case or conditions in the inner city. He also dispatched agents of the Justice Department and, later, a special team headed by David T. Kearns, the former Xerox executive serving as deputy secretary of educa-tion, to report on what the federal response should be.

Conspicuously out of the loop in those first days was the man who should have been most logically at the center of things, Jack Kemp, the former congressman from New York serving as secretary of housing and urban development. Kemp had won high marks for his aggressive promotion of a Republican urban agenda that included, among other things, a plan to allow public housing tenants to purchase their apartments, and the creation of urban enterprise zones in which tax incentives would encourage creation of jobs in the inner cities.

Because of that history, Kemp probably had more acceptability in the black community than any other Republican since Nelson Rockefeller twenty years earlier. But Bush had always considered Kemp a bore be-cause he was so focused on issues and had such complicated ideas for confronting problems. When Kemp was on the list of potential vice presidential nominees in 1988, a friend of Bush cautioned us that there was no chance Kemp would be chosen. "George has visions of Jack arriving for lunch carrying a bunch of manila folders under each arm,'' he said. Moreover, despite Kemp's credentials as a devout advocate of supply-side economics throughout the Reagan years in the White House, he was viewed with suspicion by some of the most extreme conservatives within the Republican Party because of his determined advocacy of efforts to broaden the party by attracting more black voters.

As criticism of Bush's languor increased, the White House—as well as campaign operatives—began to recognize the president was suffering new political damage. The first reaction predictably was blame-placing. Press secretary Fitzwater was trotted out to say: "We believe that many of the root problems that have resulted in inner-city difficulties were started in the sixties and seventies''—when the Democrats were promulgating all those social welfare programs that didn't work. The line was so preposterous it offered an easy target for the leading Democratic candidate, and Bill Clinton quickly seized it, saying: "It's just amazing. Republicans have had the White House for twenty of the last twenty-four years and they have to go all the way back to the sixties to find somebody to blame. I don't care who's to blame. I want to do something about the problems.''

Bush, who had been scheduled to travel to Los Angeles long before the rioting, finally arrived on the scene six days after it had erupted— with Jack Kemp now conspicuously at his side for window-dressing. Bush made the obligatory rounds and was photographed talking with schoolchildren, inspecting a burned-out shopping center, meeting with merchants in Koreatown and black church leaders. "We are embarrassed by interracial violence and prejudice,'' he said. "We're ashamed. We should take nothing but sorrow out of all that and do our level best to see that it's eliminated from the American dream. We will do what we can.''

The television film showed an empathetic president but, as was the case with the economy, Bush had built no credibility on the question of what to do about the condition of American cities. He was confronted repeatedly by pickets and hostile questioners. When one suggested he was spending too much of his time with the wealthy, Bush replied: "I don't want to sound defensive, but why do you assume I am only concerned about Beverly Hills?'' The answer, of course, was that he had never demonstrated any concern for South Central Los Angeles until it went up in flames.

By the end of the visit, Bush was touting what he called an "action agenda" that he intended to press back in Washington. Unsurprisingly, it was made up largely of proposals from Kemp that the president had shown little or no interest in pushing for three years. But, with the polls showing Bush having lost five percentage points in a week, presumably because of the riots and his failure to respond more forcefully, Kemp was now back on the first team in the photo ops and the policy discussions alike—George Bush's new best friend.

The president himself was suddenly very visible in demonstrating his concern for the disadvantaged, popping up one day at a prenatal care clinic in Baltimore, another day with some black children at a playground in the Anacostia section of the District of Columbia. As always, however, there were little misfires to remind everyone that George Bush had a tin ear. On the second day of his trip to Los Angeles, he visited Scott Miller, a firefighter hospitalized in critical condition after being shot during the riots. The president commended Miller on his courage but, apparently at a loss for small talk, added: "I'm sorry Barbara's not here. She's out repairing what's left of our house [at Kennebunkport]. Damned storm knocked down four or five walls. She says it's coming along." Bush obviously was not equating the storm damage at his fancy Walker's Point vacation retreat with the riot damage in Los Angeles. But it was characteristic of him to say something that would allow that inference to be drawn. Miller, flat on his back, no doubt felt real sorry for poor George.

As a practical matter, there may have been nothing Bush could do immediately about the politics of the riots in Los Angeles. "By definition," Charlie Black said later, "Republicans are on defense when you've got inner-city riots and problems at the top of the news. . . . It was very unfortunate timing politically because it came at a time when you already had economic unrest and a lot of people had this insecure feeling about where the country was and where it was going. To have the worst urban riots in our history and people killed and all that, and huge problems for rebuilding and everything in a major city, it just reinforced the bad feelings about the country and about the government."

But it was also true that the riots had presented an opportunity for the president to display on a critical domestic issue the kind of national leadership he had shown in the war in the Persian Gulf only fifteen months earlier. The hard truth, however, was that this president was as unable to present himself as credible on urban problems as he had been on the economy. The riots, like the primaries earlier, had exposed political weakness rather than uncovering political strength.

George Bush's problems by this time were transcending the storm damage at Kennebunkport and the riot aftermath in South Central Los Angeles. It was true that by early June the focus on the riots had blurred and Pat Buchanan was out of the campaign, at least temporarily, for heart valve surgery after losing to Bush in every primary along the way. But the time and resources it took to deal with him made the Buchanan challenge, Teeter acknowledged later, "incredibly damaging."

Original plans to spend the first three or so months of the year getting the president's economic message in shape and sold to the voters, he said, had to be postponed. "I thought we had one more window where we could get those things done," he said, "but the window closed. . . . We spent all that time fighting Buchanan. . . . We knew he was a threat on the right. You just had to look at New Hampshire." There never was, Teeter said, "a big pro-Buchanan vote, but he became a vehicle for everybody who was mad at Bush on the economy."

And now, in addition to the Democrats harping on the president's failure to cope with the stagnant economy, there was this fellow Ross Perot stirring the bushes with his increasingly disturbing petition drive to put his name on the presidential ballot in all fifty states. It was impossible to predict how that phenomenon would play out, but it was abundantly clear already that Perot had no love for George Bush and was daily poisoning the political well against him with his wisecracks about the country being in "deep voodoo."

And then there was the trouble within Bush's own political family. Sam Skinner at the White House was infinitely more likeable than the departed Sununu but the reelection campaign was finding that the White House operation under him simply was not politically attuned to the opportunities of incumbency, or geared to exploit them. And proposals submitted from the campaign seemed to be going down a black hole.

It wasn't like that at all in 1984, when Jim Baker was the White House chief of staff masterminding the Reagan reelection campaign, or in 1988, when he oversaw the early Bush campaign while serving as Reagan's secretary of treasury and finally took over as campaign manager.

Baker was a man who knew how to make decisions quickly and firmly and get them implemented effectively and without delay. But Jim Baker was now Secretary of State James Addison Baker III, perched loftily over at Foggy Bottom and trotting the globe in a huge government jet on missions of war and peace. The last thing he wanted was to descend once again into the trenches of unseemly campaign politics. But something had to be done.

Two key White House figures who had often been at odds on economic matters, budget director Dick Darman and Bill Kristol, Vice President Quayle's chief of staff, encountered each other one day in this spring of uneasiness in a corridor of the Executive Office Building adjacent to the White House where each had his office. They agreed that genuine efforts had been made to make the political operation in place work under Skinner, and that they would continue to try. But maybe, they agreed, the only alternative was to get Baker back, and sooner rather than later.

That sentiment was widely shared at the reelection committee as well. Jim Lake was telling Teeter around the same time: "If we don't make a change over there [at the White House], we can't win." And there was probably only one individual who could persuade Baker to return—the man who had made him secretary of state, the president of the United States. Some internal lobbying clearly was in order.

On the Democratic side, meanwhile, Bill Clinton also had survived his party's primary in New Hampshire and had headed south, leaving behind the wintry weather and, he hoped, the pesky allegations of personal misbehavior that had nearly derailed him there. He knew he could count on a warmer climate in his native region. But how warm the voters would be, in this mecca of true-blue patriotism, to a candidate with a shady draft record was a question that still needed answering.

C H A P T E R 1 4

SALVATION

On primary day in New Hampshire, hours before Bill Clinton proclaimed himself the Comeback Kid on the strength of his second-place finish, chief Clinton strategist Carville was on a plane headed for Atlanta and the Georgia primary two weeks later, on March 3.

An old hand in Southern politics who had run the successful gubernatorial campaign of Democrat Zell Miller, now strongly in Clinton's corner, Carville figured that the Georgia primary, standing by itself on the Southern political calendar a week before the Super Tuesday collection of presidential primaries and caucuses dominated by Texas, Florida and other Southern states, could be the early breakthrough for his candidate. Miller conveniently had persuaded his legislature to move the Georgia primary date forward, out of the clutter of Super Tuesday, a move that offered Clinton a golden opportunity. With luck—and hard campaigning—Georgia could restore Clinton's image as a winner after the scars inflicted on him in New Hampshire, and set him up to emerge as the clear front-runner after Super Tuesday.

In focusing on Georgia, the Clinton campaign was assigning a low priority to the next two state contests on the calendar—the Maine caucuses and the South Dakota primary—without quite conceding them to the other candidates; neither of them would mean much if Clinton could win Georgia and then do well on Super Tuesday.

Tsongas, counting on at least a regional boost from his New Hampshire victory, set his immediate sights on Maine but also staked claims in the Maryland and Colorado primaries and in caucuses in Washington state, all on the same day as the Georgia primary, in the hope of offsetting an expected Clinton victory there. A Tsongas sweep from coast to coast would go a long way toward demolishing his image as a regional candidate. Concerned about such a sweep and deciding that Tsongas would be too strong in Maryland, especially in the Washington, D.C., liberal suburbs, the Clinton campaign assigned a higher resource priority to Colorado than to Maryland, while still focusing mainly on Georgia.

Tsongas also made a flying trip to South Dakota where, at a cattle auction, he stood out like a fully clothed man in a nudist colony. Kerrey and Harkin also headed for South Dakota and its primary a week away in a fight for identity as the Midwest candidate and modest salvation from their weak showings in New Hampshire. That left Jerry Brown, who elected to concentrate on Maine, on the basis that his guerrilla-style campaigning might be more effective in the low-turnout caucus process.

Brown, playing on Tsongas's support for nuclear energy, mobilized Maine's environmental activists and embarrassed Tsongas by holding him to a virtual tie. The first official tally was Tsongas 30 percent, Brown 29, Clinton 15, Harkin 5 and Kerrey 3. Although Brown claimed an edge on the basis of the final results later, in the perceptions game that dominated the news media coverage at this stage of the race, Tsongas's appearance of victory, however close, was what mattered.

Just as Clinton had done in New Hampshire, Tsongas chose to emphasize the positive—his margin over Clinton, not Brown, saying of the Maine result, "I feel fine about it. My fight is with Bill Clinton at this point."

Tsongas's view that the race had already become a two-man affair between himself and Clinton escaped most observers that early, but not Clinton. "The whole sense of how to deal with Tsongas came from Clinton," Grunwald remembered. "Right after New Hampshire, the campaign lost its equilibrium because you went from being in a multi-candidate field where it wasn't clear who would emerge from the pack to being in a virtually two-person race. And instead of being in this intimate setting where you could drive to everything and all you focused on was WMUR [the Manchester television station], then you were all over the map. It was a very different kind of campaign, and it took everybody a while to both focus on the message point of view and a logistical point of view, how to make that transition.''

"There was a period of time," Greer agreed, "probably for about five days to a week, where through polls and focus groups in Georgia, Maryland and Colorado we were trying to assess how we should adjust the message of the campaign. More so than at any other point in the campaign, it was a point at which we were a bit adrift for a short period of time, probably because we had thrown everything into figuring how to come out of New Hampshire as the Comeback Kid. . . . And we were going into a territory like Georgia where we didn't know how the draft story was going to play.''

Grunwald remembered that "Clinton was the one who really pushed everyone and said, 'Look, we are not doing this right. This is a two-person race. We have got to compare my plan to his [Tsongas's] plan and focus people on the economy, and which economic approach is going to work.' He dragged the campaign into the right message.''

Kerrey and Harkin, however, were not ready to concede that the race had already shaken down to Clinton against Tsongas. Each reasoned that if he could post a victory over the other in South Dakota, he could gain a toehold in the campaign as the prime challenger to Clinton, on the assumption still widely shared that Tsongas would fade outside New England and the East. And so the senators from neighboring Nebraska and Iowa worked the cold and barren prairie state as if it were a main event.

The other three major candidates, plus the super-longshot former mayor of Irvine, California, Larry Agran, joined them for a debate on farm and rural issues in Sioux Falls the Sunday night before the primary, but the real contest in the state remained between Kerrey and Harkin for practical survival.

Kerrey, who had started earlier than Harkin in South Dakota and had campaigned in a notably lower key, scored an impressive victory over him on primary night, winning 40 percent of the vote to Harkin's 25. Clinton, who had made little effort in the state, managed 19 percent, ahead of Tsongas's 10 and Brown's 4. Kerrey told cheering supporters: "Tonight we struck gold in the Black Hills of South Dakota . . . and tonight we begin a rush for gold, a rush for delegates in the South, the West and throughout this country."

As already noted, the next week's voting schedule, dubbed "Junior Super Tuesday" by the phrase-makers, included in addition to Georgia, Maryland, Colorado and Washington state, a primary in Utah and caucuses in Minnesota and Idaho.

What Kerrey did, however, was go south first, with the idea of ambushing Clinton there, only to shift gears and head west—too late to claim that region for his own. "The whole calculus," he told us after the election, "was that having finished third in New Hampshire, it was essentially over." Had the 1992 process begun in South Dakota, where he had a base, Kerrey said, the whole year might have been different. But, he said, after his New Hampshire showing out of his home region "in order for me to get back in the race, I had to get up on the board in the Western caucus states, and failed to do it. . . . Tactically it was probably a mistake to go into the South right after [the South Dakota primary]. If I had been smart, right after South Dakota I would have driven all the way to the West."

But south Kerrey went—and immediately made, in his own view, another mistake. Speaking at Spelman College in Atlanta, he did what he had said he would not do. Clearly in the context of the furor over Clinton's draft record, Kerrey stated flatly that "Bill Clinton should not be the nominee of our party because he will not win in November." If Clinton was nominated, he said, he was "going to be opened up like a soft peanut" in November. Shortly afterward, in a news conference, Kerrey said it wasn't Clinton's draft history that bothered him, but rather his insistence on blaming others for his current political problems concerning that record.

"I don't object if anybody who in conscience said, 'The [Vietnam] war is wrong and I will not serve,' " Kerrey said. "But that is not what we have. There is an effort to say, 'Once again my draft board did this,' or 'This was an honest mistake,' or 'Republicans were trying to do this to me.' There is an evasion of responsibility. And that is the problem and difficulty I have.'' He also lamented the fact that ''it was the men and women who went to Vietnam who suffered when they came home, and all of a sudden all the sympathy in this campaign is flowing to somebody who didn't go.''

The remarks, in light of Kerrey's earlier reluctance to criticize Clinton's draft history, were immediately taken by the assembled reporters as political hardball from a candidate scrambling to elbow his way back into contention, and Clinton deftly treated them as such. In a written statement from Denver, where Clinton was doing spadework in advance of the Colorado primary, he said: ''I don't know which Bob Kerrey to respond to—the Bob Kerrey who repeatedly told the people of New Hampshire that he did not want this issue discussed, or the Bob Kerrey who's trying to tell the people of Georgia this is an issue today. . . . I hope that tomorrow he'll wake up as his old self, remind himself he came home as an opponent of the Vietnam War, remind himself of the facts of my case, that I did nothing dishonorable or wrong.''

Demonstrating his own instinct for the political jugular, Clinton went on: ''It appears that Bob Kerrey, like George Bush, would rather play politics with patriotism than address problems here at home. That's what George Bush will do in November when he points out that Bob Kerrey opposed Operation Desert Storm even after the conflict began.'' Working in a reference to Kerrey's opposition to the very popular Persian Gulf War effort was an old trick of Tricky Dick Nixon, and completely worthy of him.

''In retrospect,'' Kerrey told us after the election, ''I made a mistake going after Clinton on the draft. It was an unusual moment at Spelman College.'' He had just given a speech, he said, ''during which I ad-libbed a reflection about being in airborne school in Georgia.'' There, he said, he had been ''stunned'' that the enlisted men in his battalion ''were mostly black, mostly from poor families and they did not seem to be qualified to be in airborne. And I said at the time to this black audience, mostly black kids, 'I bet a lot of these kids died.' I remembered that, I remembered the nature of the privilege that I felt, to have been able to go to college and get into officer candidate school, and how college mattered. And that was the message.''

After the speech, Kerrey said, someone came up and told him he was one of Kerrey's drill instructors at the time and agreed. He told

Kerrey about a program that "lowered the standards of eligibility for the draft in 1968 and went out and got 100,000 poor kids who otherwise wouldn't have qualified, drafted them and sent them to Vietnam. So then I go into a press conference and I was asked about Bill Clinton's draft, and I just went high-order explosion.

"It was viewed as a calculated move. It was an emotional response to the moment, and a mistake. You don't get into a campaign and get all emotional, particularly on an issue like that, and drive something like that out. Because when I got to Colorado, that's all I heard about. So instead of going into Colorado as somebody who had won a Western state [South Dakota] in a primary, I went into Colorado as a guy who had just gone after Clinton on the draft in Georgia, which didn't help me much."

That one foray was the only one Kerrey made into the South in the week before the Georgia primary—a fact that fed the impression that he had gone down there directly from his South Dakota victory to hit Clinton between the eyes on the draft, to his own political benefit. In any event, he said later, his relations with Clinton, with whom he had served as a fellow governor, were "strained" thereafter.

With or without comments from Kerrey on Clinton's draft record, the issue was supposed to face its acid test in the South. The region's reputation as the most pro-military, patriotism-on-your-sleeve region in the country was well deserved. Dixie supplied an inordinate share of the nation's men and women in uniform and housed an overabundance of its military installations, thanks to the seniority of many of its members of Congress sitting on, and often chairing, strategic committees. But after the solitary Kerrey assault, little of a substantial nature was heard about Clinton and the draft thereafter. And in Zell Miller in Georgia, Clinton had one of his most outspoken and aggressive supporters and surrogates anywhere in the country. Miller, a decorated veteran, cast Clinton as a much-put-upon victim of scurrilous attack.

When Clinton came to Atlanta after his runner-up finish in New Hampshire, Miller told the cheering crowd that "maybe they'll stop treating him like the only fire hydrant at a dog show." He painted Tsongas as a pro-business Republican in Democrat's clothing and warned that he would lead the party "back down that well-worn path of defeat" that the Democrats knew so well, by being "on the side of the big CEOs and against the rights of shareholders."

Clinton himself, acting quickly on his view that he was now in a two-man race against Tsongas, took up the same theme in Colorado, where he hoped to prevent that feared Tsongas coast-to-coast sweep and at the same time establish himself as more than a Southern candidate. In a slashing, provocative press conference in Denver, he took after Tsongas as a "soulless economic mechanic" whose proposals to benefit business first at a time workers were in dire straits "smack of trickle-down economics." He ridiculed praise of Tsongas as having the courage to oppose middle-class tax cuts of the sort Clinton proposed, saying he was "tired of what is cold-blooded being passed off as courageous. . . . I fail to see," he went on, "what is courageous about telling people who have already been plundered in the 1980s" by the Reagan-Bush tax policies that benefited rich Americans "at the top of the totem pole who made a killing in the eighties" that there will be no tax cuts for them.

An indignant Tsongas replied: "Is Bill Clinton now our resident expert on courage? To suggest that saying yes to middle-class tax cuts is an example of profiles in courage is a phenomenally interesting definition of the term." Tsongas charged that Clinton's concern for the middle class was being driven by polling data indicating proposing tax cuts was good politics rather than good economics, and that if enacted they would drive up the federal deficit. This latter charge particularly angered Clinton, who had said repeatedly in talking of the tax cut for the middle class that he would make up for it by imposing higher taxes on the wealthy—the "fairness" theme that key Democrats in Congress also were pushing as a way of continuing to picture the Republicans as the party of the well-to-do.

In launching this attack on Tsongas, Clinton was revealing a developing resentment toward what he saw as a carping righteousness in the former senator. But Clinton was motivated in his verbal assault by more than passion. He was determined to focus the campaign now on his differences with the New Englander, and to underscore Tsongas's most glaring vulnerability—that he sounded like a Republican trying to win Democratic primary votes.

"I believe that the chief factor in the decline of America and our productivity is our failure to develop the capacity of our people and to organize our economy to compete and win," Clinton said in Denver. "Paul Tsongas believes the main factor is our failure to provide tax incentives to American business. . . . If you want somebody who talks tough but acts easy on the people at the top of the totem pole, you should vote for Senator Tsongas. If you thought the policies of the eighties were basically sound but need some good fine-tuning, you should vote for Senator Tsongas. . . . Franklin Roosevelt didn't get this country off its back by saying the only thing we have to fear is lack of venture capital.''

Clinton continued the attacks on Tsongas in television ads using a 1991 quote from *The Boston Globe* that had him saying if elected he would be ''the best friend Wall Street ever had''—a quote Tsongas said was taken out of context. Tsongas called party chairman Ron Brown urging him to get all the candidates to desist in negative campaigning, warning at the same time that ''if we continue like this for another three or four months, then we will have a very battered and bloody party'' going against Bush in the fall. He accused the Clintonites of having ''this kamikaze attitude that if they don't get [the nomination] they're going to take everybody else down with them.'' In the same breath, however, Tsongas said he had approved television ads of his own ''that demonstrate that we know how to fight back. We're now in a counterpunch mode.''

The next night in a debate in Denver, there was no smoking of any peace pipes. The battle was joined by Clinton in discussing energy policy in a state known for antinuclear environmental activists: ''We do not need to do what Senator Tsongas wants to do—to build hundreds of more nuclear plants to become energy independent.''

Tsongas broke in angrily: ''That is a lie. That is a lie. That is a lie.''

Clinton shot back: ''You don't want to build more nuclear power plants? Say you don't, then. Let's get you on record for the first time. Say it. Just say no. Just say no.''

Tsongas sidestepped the challenge, countercharging that Clinton had been running a ''misleading'' ad against him, and trying to pass the peace pipe. ''Take a pledge, let's all agree,'' he said. ''No ads. No attacking each other. No ads against each other.''

''What about your ad, Senator?'' Clinton asked, referring to Tsongas's latest ''counterpunch.''

''I started yesterday because you've been on my back for a long time,'' Tsongas said. He renewed his call for Clinton and the others to take a no-attacks pledge: ''Put your hand up. Put your hand up, Bill. No negative ad. Put your hand up.'' Clinton and the others ignored him.

Clinton, in going after Tsongas on the nuclear issue, was aware that it could benefit Jerry Brown, but his objective, again, was to keep Tsongas from winning both Maryland and Colorado and slaying his regional albatross. And he wasn't the only one to attack Tsongas. Kerrey and Harkin, both wanting to replace him as the alternative to Clinton, tried to undercut him with a Western audience to whom he was a stranger.

"I hate to keep reminding my friend Paul Tsongas that manufacturing is not the engine that drives our economy," Harkin said. "The engine is people." And Kerrey hit him as a Yankee out of his element. "Paul, you're from Lowell, Massachusetts, there's no question about that. You understand manufacturing in New Hampshire," he said. "What gives me pause is whether or not you understand agriculture and Western issues."

Tsongas shot back, reminding Kerrey he had run what was widely seen as a protectionist—and ineffective—ad in New Hampshire, and challenged him to air it in Colorado. "It was a lousy ad," Kerrey acknowledged. "Why would I want to put something on the air that didn't work?"

"The issue," Tsongas replied loftily, "is not whether it worked, but what you believe in." Saint Paul was in his pulpit again. At one point, Clinton remarked: "No one can argue with you, Paul, you're always perfect." Tsongas snapped back: "I'm not perfect, but I'm honest."

The Tsongas bashing continued, less heatedly, in two more debates over the weekend, one in Atlanta and the other at the University of Maryland. In the latter, Harkin charged that Tsongas had started the negative attacks against him as far back as the summer, and called for "no more of this self-righteousness." And Clinton defended his own ads on Tsongas's pro-business economic agenda, arguing that "the American people are entitled to know what the differences between our positions are, and if you won't tell them, somebody needs to."

Even as Tsongas was again pleading for his rivals to lay off negative ads, he was airing a new one on radio criticizing Clinton for an embarrassing gaffe relating to Jesse Jackson, in an obvious attempt to capitalize in Georgia, where blacks were expected to constitute as much as 40 percent of the primary vote.

Four days earlier, as Clinton was sitting in a television studio in Little Rock doing a series of interviews via satellite with out-of-state stations, an aide told him—erroneously—that Jackson had just endorsed Harkin in Jackson's native state of South Carolina. Unaware that there was a microphone open to a station in Phoenix, Clinton blurted out: "It's an outrage! It's a dirty, double-crossing, back-stabbing thing to do!" He then instructed an aide to call Jackson, according to a tape supplied by the Phoenix station, KTSP, and "say, 'Listen, I came to his house at midnight, I have called him, I have done everything I could for him.' . . . To hear this on a television program is an act of absolute dishonor. Everything he has bragged about, he has gushed to me about trust and trust and trust. It's a back-stabbing thing to do. . . . We'll see if I embrace him in public. . . . If he wants to talk to me about it, fine, but this is a terrible way to find out about it. . . ." (Media adviser Frank Greer observed later, laughing: "I warned him a thousand times about microphones.")

Now, in advance of the South Carolina March 7 primary, Tsongas's ad said of Clinton: "He didn't wait for the facts. No, Bill Clinton didn't wait to find out if it was true. He just attacked. The man he attacked, Jesse Jackson, the Reverend Jesse Jackson—Paul Tsongas doesn't go around attacking respected national leaders like Jesse Jackson."

Jackson, ever cool, had played down the incident, saying "the press would like to make this into an issue of controversy between the two of us, but we should not allow the campaign to be diverted onto these side issues." But the episode—and the fact that Jackson, while not formally endorsing Harkin, had campaigned with him in South Carolina—added one more page to the book of uneasy relations between Clinton and Jackson. It didn't help Clinton's image as the surefooted, controlled political robot, either.

Among black voters in Georgia, however, Clinton had more than enough other leadership support to weather the minor squall. Beyond Governor Miller, he also had an array of prestigious black leaders behind him, including Mayor Maynard Jackson of Atlanta and Congressman John Lewis, one of the authentic heroes of the civil rights movement of the 1960s. Such backing, along with Clinton's own established rapport with Southern blacks in an exceedingly low general turnout of only 9.2 percent, brought Clinton a sweeping victory in the state on March 3— despite last-minute jitters by Carville.

The success with the black vote in Georgia, Greenberg said, was "a learning experience" on how well a Southern white candidate with his own ties to other elements of the black political leadership and a connection of his own with black voters could do without Jackson prominently in his corner. It was a lesson that sustained Clinton in future dealings with him.

A severe case of nervousness nevertheless had gripped the Clinton strategists on the morning of Georgia and the other March 3 primaries. If their candidate didn't do extremely well in Georgia, beating expectations of his strength in a Southern state, and Tsongas ran a close second while winning Maryland, Colorado and Washington state, Clinton would be in trouble.

Clinton won a whopping 57 percent of the Georgia vote in the field of five against only 24 percent for Tsongas, with the other three candidates in single digits. Most significant, in polls taken as voters left their voting places, four of five Georgians interviewed said that Clinton's draft history had no effect on how they voted. If the draft issue was not buried, it certainly seemed to be in a comatose state now.

Tsongas, however, was not finished, nor was Jerry Brown. The former Massachusetts senator, showing strength outside of his home region, beat Clinton in Maryland, 40 percent to 34, won the Utah primary with 33 percent to 28 for Brown and only 18 for Clinton, and also Washington state's caucuses. Brown, a recipient of the fallout from Clinton's attacks on Tsongas on the nuclear issue, surprised again in Colorado by edging Clinton 29 percent to 27, with Tsongas at 26. Harkin salvaged the Idaho caucuses, with 30 percent to 28 for Tsongas and 11 for Clinton, and the straw poll at the Minnesota caucuses, with 27 percent to 19 for Tsongas and 10 for Clinton, but these latter two tests were insignificant and Harkin was on the ropes.

More so was Kerrey, who ran no better than fourth in any of these states and abandoned the race two days later, retracting his earlier observation that Clinton was unelectable. "With each passing day," he said, "it is clear that the only unelectable candidate is George Bush."

Clinton had won only one of the six tests on Junior Super Tuesday but it clearly had been the most important one, as a preview to the Southern-dominated Super Tuesday collection of primaries and caucuses a week later. Also significant, Stephanopoulos said later, was Brown's victory in Colorado, denying Tsongas grounds to claim he was a truly national candidate. "I think I could make the argument," he said, "that

Brown won Clinton the presidency when he won Colorado. I think if Tsongas wins Colorado, you're in a different ballgame.''

After the fact, Tsongas agreed that the Colorado defeat was the one that finally doomed his campaign. To try to counter the nuclear power issues, he and Dennis Kanin had decided to run a rebuttal commercial over the final weekend but they could not come up with the money to produce and air it in time. "So we went from an eight-point spread to third place," Tsongas said. "That was the moment the brass ring was lost."

Greenberg's polls found a 10 percent "bounce" for Clinton out of the Georgia victory—an increase in his standing in the polls—and it helped convince other Southerners, Greenberg said, that a Clinton vote was okay even after all his publicized troubles, especially concerning his draft record. Also, he said, no polls were taken in Florida after the Georgia result, so the message of Clinton's acceptability flowed in there from Georgia unfiltered.

On the next Saturday, Clinton topped his Georgia showing in the South Carolina primary, winning 63 percent of the vote, in spite of the flap over his outburst against Jackson, to only 19 for Tsongas.

Eight states were holding primaries on Super Tuesday, March 10—Florida, Louisiana, Mississippi, Oklahoma, Tennessee and Texas in the South and Southwest, plus Massachusetts and Rhode Island—and three were holding caucuses—Delaware, Hawaii and Missouri. Clinton concentrated on his home region, but Tsongas made a substantial effort in Florida to add another state to Maryland as evidence that he could win outside New England, and once again the sparks flew between Tsongas and Clinton.

Clinton homed in on Tsongas as an advocate of old-fashioned Republican trickle-down economics and an increased gas tax, and his campaign ran a television ad in Florida, which it had first used in Georgia, that took dead aim on the Sunshine State's high elderly population. It quoted Tsongas's campaign pamphlet as proposing "a cut in cost-of-living adjustments for older Americans," leaving the distinct impression that Tsongas was talking about all Social Security benefits, when in fact he was referring to Medicare only. "This made Tsongas go ballistic," Greer recalled, while straight-facedly defending the ad. Tsongas accused Clinton of lying about him.

Meanwhile, in a debate in Dallas, a relentless Jerry Brown, determined to elbow his way into the limelight, took after the front-running Clinton. He seized on a photograph taken with Senator Sam Nunn, a strong Clinton supporter, at a Georgia "boot camp" for predominantly black first-time offenders. Clinton and Nunn, he said, looked like "colonial masters" in what he said was "almost a Willie Horton" in attempting to play the race card—an allegation resented by Clinton. When Brown also noted that Arkansas had no state civil rights law—Clinton's state legislature had rebuffed his attempt to get one—Clinton snapped: "Jerry, chill out. . . . Nobody has a better civil rights record than I do."

In all this, Tsongas said very little, but later in a Dallas news conference Clinton inadvertently re-ignited his feud with Saint Paul when he said of Tsongas's favoring tax incentives for business rather than a middle-class tax cut: "We cannot put off fairness under the guise of promoting growth. It won't work. It's not America."

Tsongas, apparently under the impression Clinton had said "it's not American" and hence had questioned his patriotism, erupted the next night in Florida, charging that Clinton was using "code words" to foster division. Reporters checking tape recordings of the Clinton news conference confirmed that Tsongas had erred, but it was clear his onetime friendly attitude toward Clinton had turned to ashes. He insisted that Clinton was slurring his Greek ancestry and declared that "this is one Greek who fights back"—an allusion to fellow Massachusetts Democrat Michael Dukakis, widely criticized in 1988 for failing to respond to attacks by the Bush campaign.

Tsongas escalated the war of words in Fort Lauderdale by holding up a teddy bear and saying: "This is my opponent—pander bear." Clinton, he charged, "will say anything to get elected," referring to Clinton's call in Connecticut to save the Seawolf nuclear submarine that was to have been built at Groton but was now slated to be scrubbed. Clinton shot back: "You want to talk about pandering. It wasn't me that went to New York and said I'd be the best friend Wall Street ever had. That was Senator Tsongas."

And so it went over the final weekend before Super Tuesday as the candidates campaigned frenetically to cash in on the campaign's single richest day of delegate gathering yet. Tsongas's talk of Clinton pandering to older voters on Social Security and tax cuts, Kantor argued afterward, helped rather than hurt Clinton. And by now, Greenberg said, Clinton had found "clarity in our contrast with Tsongas—Bill Clinton for people, Tsongas for more trickle-down—and we decided that was all we'd talk about." On Saturday, Clinton won lightly contested caucuses in Wyoming and Tsongas did the same in Arizona, and on Sunday Brown ran first in Nevada, but all eyes were on the bigger prize on Tuesday.

All eyes, that is, except Harkin's. As voters went to the primary polls and caucuses in eleven states, he faced the reality of his shortage of funds and diminished appeal of his aggressively, even defiantly, old liberal message and quit the race. His withdrawal in advance of the Michigan primary a week later was somewhat surprising, inasmuch as Harkin's strong labor support might have been expected to make him a contender there. As it was, by pulling out, Harkin—who subsequently endorsed and campaigned for Clinton—gave Clinton the opportunity to play up his basic differences with Tsongas on key labor issues in the state.

Super Tuesday was a bonanza for Clinton. He won eight of the eleven contests decisively, including delegate-rich Texas and Florida, the latter one state in the South that Tsongas had hoped to salvage. Instead, it was not even close: Clinton 51 percent, Tsongas 35, Brown 12. Tsongas managed to win only his own state of Massachusetts, neighboring Rhode Island and the Delaware caucuses.

"The people of the South heard the worst about me," Clinton said, "but they saw the best." As for Tsongas, he remained defiant—and bitter. "Super Tuesday was meant to eliminate somebody like me," he said. "Well, I'm still here." And he added: "I'm going to tell you something, Bill Clinton. You're not going to pander your way into the White House as long as I'm around."

With a widening lead in delegates—728 by one count to 343 for Tsongas—Clinton now set about seeing that Tsongas would not be around much longer. From the beginning, the Clinton strategists had looked upon Illinois, which along with Michigan would hold its primary the next Tuesday, as the place where their candidate could nail down the Democratic nomination. Mayor Richard Daley of Chicago, eldest son of the legend, and his politically savvy brother Bill, a Chicago banker with strong union ties, did not publicly endorse Clinton but gave the nod for many of their supporters to help him.

In addition, Clinton's campaign manager in Little Rock, David Wilhelm, was a young but veteran political strategist from Chicago who had played a critical role in Rich Daley's mayoral campaign. His knowledge of the Illinois political terrain, coupled with the opening in Michigan afforded by Harkin's withdrawal, poised Clinton for a knockout blow against Tsongas, now seen as the remaining but severely weakened obstacle to the nomination. Brown, as from the beginning, was regarded more as an irritant than a threat. The day before Super Tuesday, the Clinton campaign started running negative ads against Tsongas in Illinois, charging that his economic plan was pro-business and antiworker.

In targeting Illinois as the key, Kantor said later, "we played off what happened, frankly, to Al Gore in 1988, when Gore should have been in fairly good shape after Super Tuesday but didn't have either the resources or the plan for Illinois or Michigan." The Clinton campaign had both, and as in New Hampshire the main campaign operation was shifted from Little Rock to Chicago to facilitate decision-making and implementing.

While Kerrey and Harkin remained in the race, Clinton had sought to claim the mantle as the Washington outsider in a year when Washington was taking its lumps. Their departure made it harder for Clinton to make the case, but the incentive continued to be great. Two days after Super Tuesday, the House of Representatives voted, 426–0, for full disclosure of all the bad checks written on the House's internal bank by 296 present and fifty-nine former members. The development was only the latest contributor to the antipolitics mood gripping the country, and Clinton was not hesitant to try to capitalize on it.

The notion, however, that Clinton could ever be regarded as an outsider anywhere politics was being played was laughable. He was the consummate politician, as comfortable in the back rooms as in voters' living rooms—a fact that served him well, especially in places of high-powered urban politics like Illinois and Michigan.

In Illinois, Carville said later, "the fact that Tsongas couldn't deal with the Chicago politicos hurt him. Because even non-Chicago people [would say], 'These guys are a fact of life, and the fact that you can't deal with these people is a sign of weakness.' In Michigan, I think the fact that he couldn't deal with labor problems was damaging, even among some nonunion voters, [who said,] 'Those are the facts of life in Michigan. Good politicians have to be able to deal with unions in Michigan.

Good politicians have to be able to deal with ward leaders in Chicago.'
. . . The most effective Republican politicians in those states don't beat
up on ward leaders and labor because voters see that as a sort of measure
of leadership. . . . Bethesda [an upscale Washington, D.C., suburb] was
the perfect place for Tsongas.''

Both states, however, provided good laboratories for measuring the
public appeal of contesting economic proposals, with unemployment at
8.5 percent in Illinois and 9 percent in Michigan, highest in the Midwest,
and both well above the national average. In Michigan particularly, Clinton made much of Tsongas's opposition to a key litmus-test issue for
organized labor—federal legislation that would bar hiring strikebreakers
as permanent replacements for striking employees.

Visiting an auto parts plant in Detroit, Tsongas patiently explained
his reasons to workers brought together to ask him questions, and they
clearly were not mollified. Tsongas, in a blue satin United Auto Workers
jacket, looked as out of place with these blue-collar workers as he had at
the cattle auction in South Dakota weeks before. Tubby Harrison, Tsongas's pollster, said later: ''The problem with our candidacy is that there
was no political message at all.'' That is, when Tsongas asked voters to
sacrifice, such as paying a higher tax on gasoline, they ''were never told
how they would get something back,'' he said.

Jerry Brown, seeking to fill the vacuum with labor after Harkin's
withdrawal, worked the union halls diligently, also always in one or
another UAW jacket presented to him along the way. He embraced organized labor's opposition to the North American Free Trade Act (NAFTA)
being pursued by Bush and given conditional approval by both Clinton
and Tsongas. Brown by now was establishing himself as the Zelig of the
1992 campaign, as in the Woody Allen movie character who, chame-
leonlike, took on the characteristics and appearance of whichever group
was at hand.

In a debate in Chicago on the weekend before the two primaries,
Brown said he would not ''give George Bush a blank check to go down
there and send his business buddies who will abandon workers in Illinois,
Michigan and this country to get two-dollar-an-hour cheap labor.'' It was
a message that played well with blue-collar workers in both states, and
Brown won the endorsement of the Michigan teamsters and a number of
other local unions.

Perhaps the most significant pair of campaign events during the hectic week, however, concerned the issue of racial harmony. Clinton first went to Macomb County, the nearly lily-white middle-class suburban enclave just north of heavily black Detroit famed as the "home of the Reagan Democrats," and made an emotional plea for an end to racial divisions and suspicions.

"I do not believe we have any hope of doing what we have to do in America unless we can come together across racial lines again," he said at Macomb County Community College before a sedate audience that was hardly the redneck stereotype of the Reagan Democrat. "This is a crisis of economics, of values," he said. "It has nothing to do with race. . . . The one thing that it's going to take to bring this country together is somebody's got to come back to the so-called Reagan Democratic area and say, 'Look, I'll give you your values back, I'll restore the economic leadership, I'll help you build the middle class back.' But you've got to say, 'Okay, let's do it with everybody in this country.' "

The next morning, Clinton went before a black congregation at the Pleasant Grove Baptist Church in Detroit and repeated essentially the same message. Telling his audience about his words to the Macomb audience the previous day, Clinton said: "I come here to challenge you to reach out your hand to them, for we have been divided for too long. . . . On Tuesday, tell the people of Macomb County, 'If you'll give up your race feelings, we'll say we want empowerment, not entitlement, we want opportunity, but we accept responsibility, we're going to help be a part of the change.' "

The two visits were an intentional effort to present Clinton as an unorthodox politician, a "different kind of Democrat." "We wanted to show," Wilhelm said later, "that Bill Clinton's message of linking economic opportunity to individual responsibility was a message that would sell among Reagan Democrats as well as African-American voters. . . . The critique of the Democratic Party in recent years has been that it is impossible to do that. If you are going to succeed in regaining the support of Reagan Democrats, or white ethnic middle-class voters, you have to do things that push off the base vote of the party.

"That twenty-four-hour period, maybe better than any other, demonstrated how Bill Clinton's message mattered," Wilhelm said, "and elicited support from wings of the party that people thought simply could not work together. . . . The message of individual responsibility, which so many felt was a message that was oriented toward those who had left the party because of the perceived permissiveness of the party, elicited just as much enthusiastic support from African-American voters as it did from any other group.''

All this was reminiscent of the posture of Robert Kennedy in his 1968 presidential primary campaign in Indiana, when he successfully ran as a tough law-and-order candidate while holding the overwhelming support of black voters. "We talked about it," Wilhelm recalled. "I wouldn't say that it was a model that we were trying to emulate, but we certainly knew enough about that race and understood he had a populist appeal on economic issues but also emphasized law and order and responsibility to one's community and family. And maybe somewhere in our subconscious, that race, and that month of his, was something that helped us.'' But rather than a positive model that drove the Clinton campaign, he said, "if anything, it was more a desire to learn from the mistakes of the most recent Democratic campaigns—an unmodel, if you will.''

Carville said later that the Clinton strategists "always wanted to have this kind of going-against-the-grain element in the campaign.'' Ironically, he said, there was discussion within the campaign earlier of having Clinton demonstrate his willingness to go against the grain by opposing the reelection of Congressman Gus Savage, a prominent, entrenched black Chicago Democrat accused of sexual harassment and other misconduct. But a good opportunity did not present itself at the time, and the gambit of showing Clinton bucking up against a traditional Democratic special interest group was held for another occasion—with considerably more political impact when it occurred. The idea, Carville said, was "if you took it on in one arena, you sort of had to take it on somewhere else. You couldn't just attack racism. You couldn't just go lecture [one side].''

Clinton himself called it "counter-scheduling.'' Later, he told us: "I thought the only way for a Democrat to build a coalition for change, that is, for me to get a mandate in the election to do something instead of just be against somebody else, [was] to try to show that I would say the same things to everybody everywhere. And you had to go into territory that wasn't particularly friendly to your message and say things that people didn't necessarily want to hear, because I think we've all got to do some things to change. And I thought that on race and on economics, that was very important to say. There were other issues too, on education, on crime. I thought those things had to be said, and I did. Really, as a deliberate strategy, no Democrat had tried to do it since Bob Kennedy, and I felt then . . . and I still feel that there is a kind of hunger for that out there."

One other, inadvertent case of going against the grain during this week caused the Clinton campaign considerable heartburn when Hillary Clinton, chatting with voters and reporters at the Busy Bee coffee shop in Chicago, defended her role as a professional woman pursuing her career at the same time she was the wife of a state governor.

In a debate the night before, Brown had charged, going beyond what had been reported in a newspaper story, that candidate Clinton was "funneling money to his wife's law firm . . . the kind of conflict of interest that is incompatible with the kind of public servant that we expect as president." Clinton denied it and strenuously defended Hillary. "I don't care what you say about me," he told Brown, "but you ought to be ashamed of yourself for jumping on my wife. You're not worth being on the same platform with my wife."

Now, when she was asked at the coffee shop whether there may have been an appearance of impropriety in her law firm's dealings with her husband's administration, she said: "I suppose I could have stayed home, baked cookies and had teas. But what I decided was to fulfill my profession, which I entered before my husband was in public life."

Professional women found no fault with that answer, particularly in this "Year of the Woman" when the nation's majority gender was reaching conspicuously for a greater share of political power. But from other quarters, chiefly among conservatives and religious fundamentalists, came the suggestion that she was denigrating women who played the homemaker role. Perhaps more than anything else Hillary Clinton said in the campaign, that offhand remark caused her grief down the road.

It did not, however, alter the outcome in the Illinois and Michigan primaries the next day, in which her husband won in each state with 51 percent of the vote. Tsongas was second in Illinois with 26 percent, but Brown, by virtue of his hard campaigning and pro-labor rhetoric, beat him out for second in Michigan, where Tsongas's pro-business views seriously hurt him with labor.

The nomination now appeared to be in hand for Clinton. Party chairman Ron Brown began to put the word out that he considered the nomination settled, and that the party ought to close down the competition and get on with planning for the fall campaign. But Jerry Brown insisted that the Arkansas governor would not "be given a coronation" and that he himself intended to challenge him all the way.

Tsongas, running a more conventional campaign than Brown and more dependent on contributions for television advertising, staff and travel, announced two days later that he was "suspending" his campaign because "we simply did not have the resources" to continue.

"The obligation of my survival has been met," he said, alluding to his recovery from cancer, which he said had been a factor in his decision to run. "It's been a helluva ride." One thing he would not be, he said, was a spoiler by staying in the race and attacking Clinton when it was clear he himself could not be nominated. "That is not what I'm about," he said. "I did not survive my ordeal [against cancer] to be the agent of George Bush's reelection."

Jerry Brown, though, had no such qualms. It was clear that he, like Jesse Jackson in 1984 and 1988, was shifting from a serious pursuit of the nomination to leadership of a cause on which he could build a longer-range movement of the politically disenchanted—and sustain this latest phase of an erratic personal career. Bill Clinton would have to press on, to another phase—and another hurdle—on the path to his lofty objective, this time back east to Connecticut and then New York, land of tabloids, talk shows and one of the most demanding electorates anywhere.

WINNING, BUT LOSING

Paul Tsongas's sudden "suspension" of his campaign caught the Clinton strategists by surprise. They thought the man from Lowell, Massachusetts, would be looking to his neighboring state of Connecticut, next on the primary calendar, to regroup for a final showdown in New York two weeks thereafter, but they were wrong. Tsongas said later that he thought he could win Connecticut but "you looked at New York and all you could see was [Clinton advertising] in Buffalo and Schenectady and no chance to respond."

Confident of winning both Illinois and Michigan, Carville and Greenberg on the eve of those primaries had pressed for Clinton to go into Connecticut to knock Tsongas out. Greenberg said later his polling showed Clinton to be within a couple of points of Tsongas and that victories in Illinois and Michigan would push him ahead. It was seen by them as a no-lose situation; if Tsongas were to win Connecticut it could be written off as a regional victory only, and the showdown would be in New York anyway.

Consequently, the Clinton campaign started running television ads against Tsongas in the Hartford area while low-balling Clinton's prospects in his backyard. But when Tsongas took himself out, the Clinton campaign—prodded by Hillary Clinton's friend and adviser, Susan Thomases—intensified its focus on New York, leaving an opening for Jerry Brown. As in Maine earlier, he worked Connecticut diligently. At the same time, many in the Tsongas operation refused to fold up shop, hoping a strong showing for their man would persuade him to stay in the race after all.

From Illinois, Clinton had returned to Little Rock and by the time he reacted to the Tsongas withdrawal and got to Connecticut he had missed the Thursday news cycle and was not into the campaign dialogue with Brown until the Friday before the primary.

The combination of Brown's guerrilla campaigning and the resurrection effort in Tsongas's behalf caught the high-riding Clinton in a squeeze. Brown hammered him as an establishment politician riding a corrupt process to the nomination who would lead the Democratic Party to another defeat in November. When it was disclosed that Clinton had just played a round of golf at the all-white Little Rock Country Club, Brown accused him of "an arrogance, a complacency, a smugness," and Clinton, acknowledging that playing there was "a mistake," vowed not to do so again until the club was integrated. Tsongas earlier had accused Clinton of pandering to Connecticut voters by endorsing continued work on the Seawolf nuclear submarine program at Groton slated for termination by Bush, and the allegation appeared to hurt him.

Clinton painted Brown as a spoiler who would say or do anything to win votes and "wouldn't mind reelecting George Bush" by so doing. To which Brown replied: "What is this, the Politburo? There is only the candidate picked by the power structure? I'm not the spoiler. Slick Willie is the spoiler. If he gets the nomination, he is going to ruin the whole Democratic Party."

Brown promised to give Clinton "a wake-up call" on primary day and he did just that, eking out a 37 to 36 percent upset over him in Connecticut, with Tsongas drawing 20 percent as a withdrawn candidate. Exit polls indicated that Brown had been the clear beneficiary of that withdrawal, with 35 percent of his voters saying they would have cast ballots for Tsongas had he remained in the race, to 23 percent who said they would have voted for Clinton. With Tsongas still running, these polls suggested, he would have won about 40 percent of the vote and Brown would have dropped to third. That result would have been less embarrassing to Clinton than losing, however narrowly, to Brown. Clinton consoled himself, aides said later, by attributing the setback to "buyer's remorse"—having just about made the purchase, having second thoughts before leaving the store.

A more serious cause for concern to Clinton came out of the same exit polls. When the voters were asked whether they thought he had "the honesty and integrity to serve effectively as president," 48 percent said no, to 46 who said yes. The result was ominous after all Clinton had been through, and as he headed into the New York primary with a revived Brown on his neck. It was one thing to win a string of primary victories and quite another to do so with the voters still believing you couldn't be trusted in the White House—a troublesome cloud looking toward the fall campaign against Bush.

Going into Connecticut, Greer said later, "everybody thought he was preordained. All of a sudden, people were saying, 'We don't think we want this guy,' and then we're going into the meat grinder of New York." Greenberg said his own polling immediately after the Connecticut loss showed the race even in New York. "We sat on it," he said of his poll, because the press perception was that Clinton remained comfortably ahead there, "but we knew we were potentially in trouble."

The problem was not simply in New York, Kantor said later, but nationally, and particularly in the political community in Washington, where Clinton already had been pronounced dead and buried a few times and had to be dug up each time. There was, he said, a "Bill Clinton Is Flawed Club" in Washington, so "we couldn't afford to lose a primary, because people were not ready to join the cause" and in fact some Democrats were poised "to look for somebody else to walk into this race." And with loose cannon Jerry Brown as the sole active opponent, the course of the next two weeks was not predictable.

The Clinton strategists approached New York—the city, not so much the state—as if it were a hornets' nest, and with good reason. Its television, radio and tabloid newspaper corps had a deserved reputation for sensationalism to the point of political cannibalism. They took pride in their image as the bully boys in the toughest neighborhood anywhere.

Jerry Nachman, editor of *The New York Post*, who seized the first *Star* story on the Larry Nichols lawsuit and bled it into the journalistic mainstream, was quoted in *The Washington Post* as observing: "This is New York. Everything else is an out-of-town tryout."

Local columnists, licking their chops to get their shots in at the frontrunner from Arkansas, charged the rest of the press corps with rolling over for him and vowed to make up for the kid-gloves handling. It seemed as if the New York news media felt they had to live up to their bad reputation—and many did.

For Clinton, there was also the question of the volatile Mario Cuomo. Prior to the Connecticut vote, Cuomo had observed that Clinton, with whom he had had some celebrated run-ins, was close to having their party's nomination "locked up." Now, however, when Brown made a pilgrimage to Albany as a resuscitated contender, Cuomo proclaimed that "the presumption of ascendancy for Clinton is now rebuttable." Brown rejoiced that "we've gone from a conclusive presumption to a rebuttable presumption." In a left-handed compliment, Cuomo said either Clinton or Brown would be better than Bush but that he wasn't going to endorse either one. "I don't think it would help them much," he said. "I'm not so popular myself right now."

Recognizing that he could no longer afford to ignore Brown and concentrate on the fall election against Bush, Clinton in New York stepped up his criticisms of a Brown proposal for a federal 13 percent flat tax across the board for all Americans. Clinton bashed the idea as regressive and a "war-on-New-York tax" because it would eliminate the income tax deduction for payment of state and local taxes that in high-tax New York would mean "a $4 billion bill" for taxpayers in the state.

Brown meanwhile turned up the heat on Clinton, describing him as the "scandal-of-the-week" candidate who was "taking the Democratic Party for a ride" to defeat. As Brown got more and more personal, party chairman Ron Brown stepped in, reprimanding him as having "crossed the line in terms of inappropriate attacks" against Clinton in a "scorched earth policy." Brown, campaigning in Wisconsin, which also had a primary on April 7, brushed the chairman's admonitions aside. "The trouble is, there's such a trail here that the media has to keep bringing stuff out. Our party chairman does a disservice to somehow cover it up and be quiet about it." To Ron Brown, he demanded: "If you can't be neutral, then step aside, because this insurgency doesn't stop."

Jerry Brown's tactics, and tenacity, were particularly disturbing to the party chairman because his prime objective all year had been for the party to have a brief, decisive and bloodless primary season in order to focus on the general election challenge to Bush as early as possible.

In the white-hot political atmosphere of New York, Clinton found himself fending off blows daily. At a fund-raiser in Manhattan, an AIDS activist accused him of "dying of ambition," producing one of the rare occasions on which Clinton lost his temper in public. "If I were dying of ambition," he said rather incongruously, "I wouldn't have stood up here and put up with all this crap I've put up with over the past six months. I understand you're hurting," he went on, but "you can't stop hurting by trying to hurt other people." And when the heckler continued to berate him, Clinton blurted: "I've had about enough of this. I have listened to all these attacks, attacks on me [for not caring about the victims of AIDS]. That's just a bunch of bull. Don't you understand that one of the problems in this country is we all devalue each other? We've got to go back to putting some value on the integrity of people's lives."

At a Harlem hospital center, New Alliance Party candidate Lenora Fulani interrupted a Clinton speech and demanded "democracy" in the form of opening debates to herself and long-shot Democratic candidate Larry Agran. After she had gone on for about fifteen minutes of heckling, Clinton finally walked out, shouting: "I want to thank those of you here who really want democracy. I think Harlem should fight for free speech. Free speech in Harlem! Fight for the First Amendment!"

The Clinton campaign decided that the best way to cope with Brown, and to get Clinton's message out amid the in-your-face news media frenzy that was New York, was to debate Brown directly and repeatedly. In one such debate, Clinton ran into another buzz saw when a local reporter asked him a question in a way that required a straight answer. He gave it, but his penchant for fudging and evasion won out in the end—to his further political discomfort. The question was about past drug use, and his standard answer when asked on all previous occasions had been the one that he had given only four days earlier before the editorial board of *The New York Daily News*, according to the Associated Press: "I have never broken the laws of my country."

That response, like all the previous ones, should have tipped off the press corps, especially in light of Clinton's history of dissembling on tough questions, of the cute evasion. For years, according to veteran Arkansas reporter John Brummett, he had been saying in his home state in response to questions on drug use that he had never broken any of its laws. Yet for some reason no reporter had gotten the picture, and had asked the obvious follow-on question—until now. One of the panelists at a candidates' forum over WABC-TV was Marcia Kramer, a WCBS-TV reporter who had been traveling with the Clinton entourage and was familiar with his talent for dodging verbal bullets. When she read the answer he had given to the newspaper, she said later, "it was like this alarm bell went off in my head."

So she pressed him. Reminding him that he often bristled when referred to as "Slick Willie," she observed that his answer on drug use seemed to have been carefully crafted. Okay, he hadn't broken the laws of his country. What about any state law or one of another country when, for instance, he was a student at Oxford?

"I've never broken any state laws," he answered, "and when I was in England, I experimented with marijuana a time or two." Then he added: "And I didn't like it, and I didn't inhale, and I didn't try it again."

The answer was vintage Clinton, and perhaps as revealing about him as any answer he had given all year concerning his political thought process. He had known perfectly well each time the general drug-use question had been asked over the years what the inquirer really wanted to know, but each time he had given a lawyer's response—answer only the specific question asked and don't volunteer anything beyond. Even now he threw up that defense for all his past dissembling. He told reporters after the debate: "I said I've never broken the laws of my country, and that is the absolute truth." Had the *Daily News* editors "asked me the same question," he said, "I would have given the same answer."

The next day, Clinton again defended his previous dissembling. In 1987, he said, when he was first asked in Arkansas about drug use, "I said what I believe in. I think there is a limit to what people ought to have to say. But I am running for president now. People finally asked me a direct question. I gave them a direct answer."

The afterthought—"and I didn't inhale"—was also revealing of Clinton's habit of trying to minimize something that might hurt him politically, as well as opening him to a ridicule that lasted throughout the campaign. It was always a mystery how someone with such sensitive political antennae about most things could fail to anticipate the political fallout of such a ludicrous and self-serving alibi.

The admission of brief marijuana experimentation twenty-three years earlier, in what was a typical act of his generation, was in itself no big deal. As Clinton himself observed, 1988 presidential candidates Bruce Babbitt and Al Gore had similarly acknowledged marijuana use during the Vietnam War era without apparent harm to their candidacies. But the incident fueled the sense among many voters that Clinton was a man who was someone other than he presented himself as being; there always was something that had to be pried out of him, and then he would always have some tortured explanation or alibi. He had ridiculed Paul Tsongas earlier as being "perfect" and had admitted that he himself wasn't, yet his imperfections seemed to surface only when someone else dug them out or when he was backed to a wall to acknowledge them. And even then, he seemed more often than not to dodge and weave.

The episode was equally embarrassing, or should have been, to the great army of reporters—ourselves included—who had followed Clinton's political career for a decade or more, were familiar with his standard response of not having "broken the laws of my country" on drug use, and had never followed up with the obvious question. But such lapses in the press corps were hardly new.

In 1959, for example, when President Dwight D. Eisenhower, asked at a White House news conference to provide a major decision in which then Vice President Richard M. Nixon, expected to seek the presidency in 1960, had been involved, Eisenhower replied that "if you give me a week, maybe I can think of one." The answer was read as a blow to Nixon's claim of high-level experience, yet at the next news conference a week later, nobody asked Eisenhower whether he had been able to "think of one." So perhaps Clinton knew what he was doing when he continued his dodge on past drug use well into the 1992 campaign.

On the other hand, two polls of nationwide sentiment, released at this time, one by a New York television station of New York voters and the other by *The New York Times* and CBS News, underscored the scope of continuing voter doubts about Clinton's trustworthiness. Asked again whether he had the "honesty and integrity" to be president, 57 percent of those in the New York poll said no, to only 29 who said yes, and in the national survey the responses were 54 percent no, 26 yes.

These figures understandably shook the Clinton camp. The New York tabloids were now having a field day with "I didn't inhale" as Clinton's advisers brainstormed on how they could get the dialogue back on their candidate's economic proposals and differences with Jerry Brown. Although the New York airwaves were now being choked with political news and candidate appearances and interviews, the Clinton campaign suddenly proposed a series of six more debates, a rate of one a day, until primary day. The gambit by Clinton's admission was an effort to get past the clutter of renewed reportage about his personal past in the press and go directly to the voters.

All that voters "have heard is bad stuff dumped on them about me," he said, and what with distortions in the news media about his positions, "at least the people who watch the debates will hear them." At a black church in Queens, Clinton lamented: "I have seen myself turned into a cartoon character of an old-time Southern deal-maker by tabloids and television ads—a total denial of all my life's work." Hank Morris, a New York Democratic consultant, translated for *The New York Times:* "They decided they'd rather debate Jerry Brown than the New York press."

The strategy in one sense worked, because Brown and the questions asked in the debates stuck essentially to substantive issues like taxes and welfare. But in Clinton's eagerness to go directly to the voters, he fell prey to yet another peril of the television era—the scandalmonger masquerading as journalist, in the presence of talk show host Phil Donahue. Donahue, whose bread and butter was sensationalism but who sought to lacquer it with a veneer of serious demeanor, single-handedly sought to bring the campaign dialogue back to where it was in New Hampshire by resurrecting the Gennifer Flowers story.

Donahue subjected Clinton to a rehash of all the old questions, starting with: "Now, Governor, may I just characterize what I think may be some of the suspicions or the concerns of some Americans?" He then launched into a general recitation of "suspicions fueled by allegations," to which Clinton responded with his standard comment that his marriage had had problems but was solid now. He and his wife had never separated, Clinton said, but "it was none of your business if we did."

Donahue went on: "Part of the 'Slick Willie' problem is caused by what some analysts see as your ability to deflect questions and to give answers which really don't speak—" Clinton broke in: "We need the ability in politics to deflect some questions," he said. "You folks would kill us if we didn't." The studio audience applauded in agreement.

Still, Donahue perservered, asking about marijuana smoking and inhaling. Clinton was exasperated: "What difference is it if I said I inhaled or not?" Donahue replied: "The difference is the appearance of dancing around these issues . . . the pattern of tap-dancing around direct answers to potentially embarrassing questions."

At one point Clinton told him: "I don't believe I or any other decent human being should have to put up with the kind of questioning you're putting me through." And when Donahue still pressed on, Clinton told him that if he kept up the same line of inquiry, "we're going to sit here a long time in silence, Phil." Again the audience applauded.

Clinton operatives later sought to make the best of the situation by saying the exchange had demonstrated once again their candidate's ability to stand up to hostile questioning, and had evoked sympathy for him in the face of Donahue's opportunistic sprint on the low road. That no doubt was so, as evidenced in the comment of one young woman when Donahue raced into the audience, microphone in hand, for reaction: "I think, really, given the pathetic state of most of the United States at this point— Medicare, education, everything else—I can't believe you spent half an hour of airtime attacking this man's character. I'm not even a Bill Clinton supporter, but I think this is ridiculous." The studio audience cheered and applauded.

Several days later, Clinton appeared again on the Donahue show, this time with Jerry Brown, and the host astonished both candidates by informing them minutes before airtime that he intended merely to introduce them and then step aside, letting them debate without interruption. Donahue's surprising abstinence—perhaps the product of the audience disfavor with his behavior in the first Clinton appearance—resulted in one of the best, most serious, issue-oriented exchanges of the whole campaign. Clinton, Frank Greer said later, had come to the studio with a tough game plan to deal with another expected verbal wrestling match with Donahue. Instead, he said, "we had about four minutes to game-plan" how to deal with Brown without the specter of Donahue hanging over the debate.

Getting in the ring with the electronic media bully boys had one other positive moment for Clinton. In an interview with one of New York's most obnoxious but popular drive-time radio hosts, Don Imus, who had regularly been referring to Clinton as "Bubba," the candidate informed him that where he came from, Bubba was a synonym for "mensch," Yiddish for somebody who was the salt of the earth. Thereafter, the Clinton operatives always referred to the Imus interview as one of the brightest spots of the days in "the meat grinder."

Clinton was also helped by a decision by Jerry Brown to proclaim, first in Connecticut but then more conspicuously in New York, that he wanted Jesse Jackson as his running mate. Jackson had remained anathema to many Jewish voters in New York City, where they often constituted as much as 40 percent of the Democratic primary vote, ever since his slur in the 1984 campaign about New York being "Hymietown." But in an apparent effort to cut into the black vote, Brown showed up at a Jackson voter registration rally in downtown Manhattan and latched on.

Jackson made clear he was not endorsing Brown, praising him faintly only as "a man who brought substance to the campaign," but Brown threw his arm on Jackson's shoulder and proclaimed: "Reverend Jackson has made himself available, and we're going to make him available as the next vice president of the United States." Jackson replied that he was "honored by his request" but said his objective was "to empower the people. If by chance the party's nominee [pointedly not specifying Brown] were to make such a request and the convention were to ratify it," Jackson said, "I would be honored to accept it."

The reaction in the Jewish community was not long in coming. As Brown was telling the Jewish Community Relations Council the next day that "the number one goal for survival of a free society is healing the division between black and white," Dov Hikind, a state assemblyman from Brooklyn, broke in. "You insult the Jewish community by picking Jesse Jackson," he shouted. Anyone who had accepted the support of Louis Farrakhan, the Nation of Islam leader who once called Judaism a "gutter religion," Hikind said, was unacceptable as a vice presidential nominee. Others in the room tried to quiet the heckler, and he was finally hustled out of the room.

When Brown tried to defend his decision, saying that as a longtime defender of Israel he would be making the decisions as president, someone else called out: "What happens if you die, Governor?" Others in the audience made a point of collaring reporters and telling us they had no problem with a black as vice president—but not Jackson. If Clinton had any worry about winning the Jewish vote in New York, it vanished with Brown's gesture to Jackson and black voters. "A vote for Jerry Brown is also a vote for Jesse Jackson," warned *The Jewish Press*, an influential weekly.

That night, Greenberg polled Jewish voters regarding the Jackson matter and found, he said, that Brown "had dropped into single digits. It was a massive and immediate collapse." When we asked Brown much later why he had indicated he would choose Jackson as his running mate if nominated, he said he was well aware "that Jackson had problems in New York [among the Jewish community] but he had strengths elsewhere. And I thought it was important to say something real in all the talk about change. I was trying to basically lay out a really different alternative."

A new peril for Clinton surfaced on the final weekend before the New York vote. Paul Begala was walking through the lobby of the Clinton headquarters hotel when John King of the Associated Press strolled over. "I'm going to ruin your night," he said. "Clinton got a draft notice."

Begala thought nothing of it, because he recalled that Clinton had mentioned earlier that he thought he had gotten something like that but it had never turned up. But now an old political opponent in Little Rock revealed a 1969 letter indicating that Clinton had indeed received a draft induction notice in April of that year, which did not square with the impression he had left when the first stories about his draft record had broken during the New Hampshire primary. Then he had said he signed up for the ROTC program at the University of Arkansas in anticipation of being drafted in the fall of 1969, making no mention that he had actually received an induction notice before applying for the ROTC slot.

Clinton insisted now that he had simply forgotten about the notice, that it had arrived in England after the induction date indicated had passed, that he had contacted his draft board in Hot Springs and was told to ignore it. "They said, 'Look, this is a routine deal. We will extend this. Don't worry about it. You will have to come home this summer and make some decision,' '' he recalled. Grilled about the latest development by reporters outside his midtown Manhattan hotel, Clinton sought to brush the matter off. ''I'm sorry if twenty-three years later it looks unusual,'' he said. ''But I can tell you at the time it never occurred to me as being anything unusual.''

The tabloids leaped on the latest wrinkle in Clinton's draft story, but *The New York Times* barely gave it a yawn. The campaign had long since moved on to other issues, although campaign strategists for President Bush, tracking the story diligently, were tucking it away for future use. It got barely more mention than an interview with Hillary Clinton in the new issue of *Vanity Fair* magazine in which she said it was ''apparently well known in Washington'' that President Bush had had an extramarital affair. The tabloids jumped all over that one, with such headlines as ''Hillary Goes Tabloid'' and ''Hillary's Revenge.'' The candidate's wife promptly said it was a ''mistake'' for her to respond to a question that way, ''but nobody knows better than I the pain that can be caused by ever discussing rumors in private conversation.''

More of a cloud hanging over Clinton on the eve of the New York primary was the ''suspended'' candidacy of Paul Tsongas, who had won 20 percent of the vote from the sidelines in Connecticut and in whose behalf a stealth campaign was being waged in New York. Tsongas sparked the hopes of supporters by saying on one of the Sunday network interview shows that he was considering reentering the race, based on his and Clinton's showings in the New York primary. Tsongas's vote in Connecticut had been a key factor in Clinton's loss to Brown there, and aides feared recent history could repeat itself in New York, with much more dire results.

Those concerns, however, were unwarranted. Clinton won New York decisively with 41 percent of the vote, and the vote for Tsongas— 29 percent, good enough for second place—proved to be a windfall for the Arkansas governor by pushing Brown, with 26 percent, into third place and out of serious contention once and for all. The Tsongas vote of about 279,000 without an active candidate was, however, notable as an indication that many Democrats nervous about Clinton and his past were still looking for some other option to him. In Wisconsin, where Brown had hoped to spring another upset, Clinton won over him, 38 percent to

35, with 22 for Tsongas, who said later that he would have reentered the race only if Clinton had lost to Brown in both New York and Wisconsin. When that didn't happen, he said, "the idea had no legitimacy."

Clinton also won lesser victories over Brown in Kansas and Minnesota that helped produce headlines the next day that he had scored a "sweep"—a psychologically important pronouncement, Kantor said later. "For all practical purposes," he said, "it ended the nomination process and quieted down all the naysayers and doomsayers in Washington."

Relieved, Clinton at a victory party in New York called the experience of the primary there "like a ride on the Coney Island Cyclone, with ups and downs and twists and turns. And now that I'm through it all, I admit, I've had a ball." He even had kind words for Jerry Brown, who graciously conceded defeat but still gave no sign of bowing out of the race—and the diminishing national spotlight on him. Tsongas, however, faced reality for a second time and announced he would not be reentering the contest for the nomination.

Clinton appeared home free for the nomination at last, although he vowed to press on, not wanting to leave the impression in Pennsylvania, the next major state on the primary calendar, or any of the others where Democrats had not yet voted that he was taking them for granted. It should have been a time of rejoicing and relaxing within the Clinton inner circle, but it was not—again because of the exit polls. As after the Connecticut primary, they showed that nearly half of all Democratic voters in the New York primary surveyed believed Clinton lacked the "honesty and integrity" to be president. Many Brown and Tsongas voters told the exit pollsters they preferred independent candidate Ross Perot, who was climbing rapidly in the polls, to the Democratic front-runner.

Another poll by *The Washington Post* taken a few days after the New York primary produced the same ominous result. To the "honesty and integrity" question, 55 percent expressed no confidence in Clinton, to only 34 percent who did, and when asked for their presidential preference, voters surveyed put Perot in a virtual tie with Clinton—Clinton 24 percent, Perot 23—behind Bush's 37 percent. Clinton was faring no better in this poll despite the fact 55 percent said they disapproved of the way the president was handling his job.

Reflecting later on the intensive, bare-knuckles scrutiny he underwent leading up to and through the New York primary, and on the clinging doubts about him, Clinton told us: "The only thing that bothered me about it was, I felt there for several months there was such a discord, a disconnect, between how the people I met and talked to and communicated with, the people who watched the town meetings on television, felt and how everybody else in the world felt. The cumulative impact of these repeated stories was that I couldn't be defined in any other way.

"But I finally realized that the only way I could ever change that was by hanging in there and doing what I was doing; that the voters would make a decision ultimately. . . . It was extremely frustrating, but what we finally did was to try to settle on a long-term strategy to try to deal with it. It was a very deliberate decision by me that I had to find a way to get people to define me in terms of the whole person I was."

"I kept saying, 'We're winning, but we're losing,' " Greer recalled. "The serious problem was winning the nomination and then being so wounded that you can't win the general. And we always ran the campaign [in a way] so that we could win in November. We had to stand back and figure how we win the war as opposed to fighting each battle tactically" in the primaries.

The key to doing so was finding out what it was exactly that was causing Clinton to "lose while winning"—to fail to overcome voters' doubts about his trustworthiness to sit in the Oval Office, even as they were expressing their preference for him over the available alternatives. It was, although the Clinton insiders did not put it quite this way, like the old Henny Youngman joke: "How's your wife?" "Compared to what?" As long as the "what" was Brown or Tsongas, Clinton was going to win among the growing number of Americans who were fed up with George Bush. But another "what" was coming along in Perot, and the jury was out on him.

One reason for Clinton's problem was obvious: he always seemed to be sliding off questions, giving evasive answers unless nailed down with specific questions, as in the go-around on smoking pot. Donahue, for all his deplorable excesses, was right about that. But beyond that, why weren't voters really buying into what was a genuine American success story: poor boy, broken home, hard worker, rising to be governor of his state at a remarkably early age, commended by his peers as the nation's best?

The Clinton strategists decided to find out the answer, and thus was born what came to be called inside the campaign "The Manhattan Project"—an intensive research undertaking to gauge voter attitudes and concerns about Bill Clinton to learn what they knew and didn't know about him. The name was used inside the campaign to connote an all-out research effort but not advertised because of the nature of the real Manhattan Project—the search for the unlocking of the atom and development of the atom bomb. What the researchers discovered was not going to assure victory, but the information culled from the project, they hoped, would help them get Clinton through the wall that was blocking him from becoming a competitive general election candidate.

The day of the New York primary, Kantor called in Carville, Greenberg, Grunwald and the other top strategists and told them, with New York apparently won, to break off and make the study, with an eye to the long-term problems of perception facing Clinton looking to the general election. Greenberg and his partner, Celinda Lake, Carville and Greer set out in a series of discussions with academics and politicians, polls and focus groups to crack the enigma of candidate Clinton.

What they learned over the next several weeks was that the Bill Clinton the voters were seeing bore little resemblance in most important ways to the Bill Clinton they knew. The details of his womanizing and draft problems were not the problem, Grunwald said later. Voters knew all they wanted to know about each, and in fact the focus on them, she said, "blocked out other information about him." They liked the toughness of him, she said, and were intrigued by his ability to survive, "but they had this sort of shorthand—Gennifer Flowers, draft, I didn't inhale—and they didn't know anything more."

One of the first focus groups, in Allentown, Pennsylvania, according to Greer, uncovered that the voters gathered together "had no idea where this guy had come from and what he stood for. They thought he had been born with a silver spoon in his mouth. They thought that he was a child of privilege, that he had gone to all these Ivy League schools, and wasn't that much different than George Bush. It was phenomenal, shocking to us, but it shouldn't have been because we hadn't done any biographical work since one spot in New Hampshire."

Voters, Grunwald said, figured, " 'How could a kid from Arkansas, which they of course thought chauvinistically was some two-bit state, wind up at Oxford and Yale and governor? Well, his daddy must have helped him.'. . . When they learned that not only did his daddy not do anything, but there was no daddy, and he had worked for everything he had in his life, and he had worked very hard against some pretty decent odds, it totally changed their view of who he was, what he had been through, what he was proposing for the country.''

At the same time, however, Greer recalled, the voters tested ''thought he was always political, he was always cutting the corners, rounding the edges, not shooting straight.'' One voter bowled over the focus group operatives by observing that if Clinton was asked what his favorite color was, ''he'd say, 'plaid.' ''

With Pennsylvania the next primary and Brown trying desperately to shoehorn himself back into the picture by working the labor vote, the Clinton strategists decided to address Clinton's revealed problem immediately. They rejected one idea for Clinton to give a kind of tell-all Richard Nixon ''Checkers'' speech and instead started running a lengthy biographical television spot that started: ''His father died just before he was born, and his mother and her family struggled to give him better opportunities, to preach that with hard work, faith and a good education, anything was possible.''

At the same time Clinton returned more forcefully and consistently to his economic message, and to the case that he understood out of his own humble middle-class experience in Hope and Hot Springs, Arkansas, what working people were going through in the clinging recession. A second television ad was aired showing a mother who had lost her health care and a man whose lifelong job had been snuffed out in a plant closing, with Clinton talking about his agenda for change and concluding with a line from his Comeback Kid speech in New Hampshire: ''Some people say I've taken some hits lately, but nothing like the hits the American people have taken.''

Clinton also did statewide television town meetings from Philadelphia and Pittsburgh with advance promotions in which Clinton himself urged voters to tune in, as was done in New Hampshire at the time the womanizing and draft stories had the campaign on the ropes. And he gave another of his ''against the grain'' speeches at the University of Pennsylvania's Wharton School. He told the students that their celebrated business school was ''a powerful symbol of where our country went wrong in the 1980s . . . where Michael Milken got the idea to use junk bonds to leverage corporate buyouts'' and where Donald Trump, "who glorified the art of the deal,'' learned his moves. Photographs of both hung on the school's "Wall of Fame,'' he noted, "until Trump went bankrupt and Milken was on his way to jail.'' He urged them to put morality back into business, and the students cheered and applauded the challenge.

In one sense, Clinton's running "against the grain'' was curious. It seemed to defy another characteristic of him as a politician—an inordinate desire to please everyone all the time. That inclination was never clearer than in another speech during the Pennsylvania primary—on Earth Day at Drexel University. Clinton dealt with virtually every environmental issue on the table, comparing his positions with Bush's. But what made it memorable was a single digression. He suddenly began talking about how as a small boy he had been surprised to discover after he moved "into town''—Hot Springs—that there were just as many snakes, spiders and tarantulas on the ground as there had been in Hope. Then he added: "We had to figure out how to make them our friends rather than our enemies.''

On the stump, Clinton's primary victories by now had given him the aura of a winner, if only in terms of the Democratic nomination. When he toured Philadelphia's famed Italian Market one morning, vendors and customers alike crowded around him reaching to shake his hand as he examined the wares with Mayor Ed Rendell at his side. But he was never completely out of the woods. From across the street at one point, a man called out to him, and when Clinton looked up, he heard this shouted question: "If you cheated on your wife, what would you do to the country?'' Clinton forced a weak smile, waved the man off and turned back to surveying the unmenacing carts of broccoli, corn and other less toxic subjects.

The presumptive Democratic nominee was hearing discordant notes from another quarter in Pennsylvania as well. Democratic Governor Robert Casey, skeptical of Clinton's ability to win in the fall and noting the low primary turnouts, said in an interview: "We've got a tiny minority of Democrats voting for Bill Clinton, and he is winning every race without generating any sparks, any enthusiasm, any momentum. . . . People have a tremendous unease about him.'' Clinton's strategists recognized the same thing, but were not happy to have the Democratic governor of the state saying so publicly. Casey, an outspoken foe of abortion, had long been arguing that the party was on the losing side of the abortion issue, and Clinton was pointedly for abortion rights.

None of this criticism made any difference when Pennsylvania Democrats went to the polls on April 28. Turnout again was low, with the outcome a foregone conclusion, and Clinton beat Brown by more than two to one, 57 percent to 25, with 13 for Tsongas. Much more significant for the Clinton inner circle was the fact that when the network exit pollsters again asked the "honesty and integrity" question, 62 percent answered that they thought Clinton had those qualifications, to 34 percent who said no. "Bill really felt we had turned the corner," Greer said.

Some minor headaches remained, including pressures from Jesse Jackson. After a meeting with Clinton in Kansas City three days before the Pennsylvania vote, Jackson left without endorsing him and was quoted in a New York tabloid interview as saying: "I see myself as a running mate for the Democratic Party. . . . If I am rejected this time, I am prepared to react." It seemed like the same old stuff Jackson had tried with Michael Dukakis in 1988, but he quickly backed off, saying "at no time did I threaten the candidate or the party over the vice presidency or anything else." In any event, Clinton was not ready to undertake the selection of a running mate yet and he wasn't about to let Jackson under the tent, as would soon become abundantly clear.

On May 12, however, Clinton did announce a three-person task force headed by Warren Christopher, deputy secretary of state under Jimmy Carter, and aided by Vernon Jordan, a prominent Washington lawyer and former head of the National Urban League, and former Governor Madeleine M. Kunin of Vermont. They began extensive conversations with party leaders about the choice and eventually started interviewing possible selections.

Clinton was sweeping through the remaining primaries routinely now and focusing his campaigning increasingly on President Bush. When America's worst race riots broke out in Los Angeles, Clinton was quick to criticize Bush's initial comment that "the jury system has worked." He expressed hope that the president "would at least acknowledge that the facts of the case as evidenced by the film lead a lot of Americans, and not just black Americans, to wonder about the accuracy of the verdict.'' Later he chastised Bush for waiting so long to embrace the proposals of his own housing secretary, Jack Kemp, for urban enterprise zones and other initiatives to address inner-city problems.

The final primary day, June 2, in California and five other states, which earlier had been expected to be decisive, was an anticlimax, with Clinton again winning everything in sight including Jerry Brown's home state, which the Arkansan won by 47 percent to 40. By now, most of the ''buyer's remorse'' appeared to have subsided, at least among Democratic primary voters.

Still, however, Clinton continued to trail Bush in the national polls and was in danger of falling into third place behind Perot, who was climbing fast and grabbing all the headlines. ''There was nothing we could do to break through,'' Stephanopoulos recalled. ''Even when we won we were judged by the exit polls.'' Large numbers of voters told the pollsters that they really preferred Perot—to the point, Stephanopoulos said, that the exit polls ''became more important than the actual results.''

To Begala, it was ''the worst time in the campaign'' because ''we were doing everything right, honing our message, and Clinton was hitting his stride, but we were being totally eclipsed by Ross Perot.'' Greer agreed. ''The low point emotionally was the night of the California primary,'' he said. ''We had won the nomination, and we turned around and coming down the track was this train, and written on the headlights was 'Ross Perot.' ''

Clinton also hit bottom emotionally on the night of his California victory because of the exit polls indicating voters would have voted for Perot had he been on the ballot. ''Nobody was laying a glove on him,'' Clinton told us later. That night, he said, ''was much more of a low point than what had happened in New Hampshire. Because when I was in New Hampshire, I felt I had really connected with those people. They had been coming in big numbers even when I was dropping in the polls, and I knew that if we could find a way to appeal to their innate sense of fairness, that they would in some sense decide that my campaign should go on.''

But after that, through the California primary, he said, ''every primary was a struggle. I thought if I could just get through and win the nomination and there were three people who wanted to be president, that in a way the whole primary trial would be a plus, and there would then have to be some balanced scrutiny of the record and positions, the complete character of each contestant, and that I would have an opportunity from June to July to carry out our strategy. . . . But a lot of people just shut it down. They weren't listening."

Through this period, Clinton displayed a frustration with the news media's continued focus on what he called "process questions." After having survived all the personal allegations and the challenges of all comers, the appearance of a page-one story in *The New York Times* on the prospects for a brokered convention was illustrative of his complaint. Although he himself was a political animal to the core, he felt there was too much political clutter going on for his policy message to get through. He wanted to talk about his economic and other proposals, not about polls, the "horse race" and such things as whether Perot helped or hurt him or Bush more. In a long interview with him as his car was stalled in a San Francisco traffic jam around this time, Clinton conveyed his coolness to such questions on sheer politics and process.

Much later, campaign press secretary Dee Dee Myers observed: "Bill Clinton is part policy wonk and part political strategist, and he's very good at both. He really enjoys the give-and-take of politics, he really enjoys the day-to-day demands of governing. What he found out was that every time he uttered a word about politics, he got tremendous coverage. When he talked about policy, nobody listened. And so as the campaign went on he learned to say less about politics, because when he did, that was what ended up being the lead of everybody's story." For this reason, Greer said later, "we counseled him not to talk process."

On the advice of Hollywood television situation comedy producers Harry Thomason and his wife, Linda Bloodworth-Thomason, and others on the staff, Clinton found that one way to get beyond the news media's focus on process questions was to work the television talk show circuit. Since the Manhattan Project had established clearly that voters still did not have a clear idea of who Bill Clinton was, the best and most cost-effective way to deal with the problem was television exposure, and then more television exposure, offbeat or otherwise, and hope voters would start paying attention. What's more, he couldn't seem to get enough of talking to them. During a break in one appearance on the Larry King show, King asked him whether he wasn't worn down by the pace. Clinton seemed surprised at the question. "I love this," he said.

The whole focus on the talk shows, especially of the pop culture variety in the period after the California primary, Grunwald said, was known inside the campaign as "the Arsenio strategy," after Clinton's appearance on the Arsenio Hall late-night show. There, he played "Heartbreak Hotel" on his saxophone, wearing dark shades and looking and sounding cool to that special audience not likely to be reached with a heavy speech on his economic agenda.

Grunwald said she had become particularly interested in the approach when a chambermaid at a hotel in Wisconsin during that state's primary told Clinton, "I saw you on Donahue. You were great!" The woman, Grunwald said, did not seem to be the type who read the newspaper every day or followed the campaign, but her reaction "was very much a personal one—'I know you. I have a sense of who you are.' " There was a whole audience of prospective voters out there that was not being reached on a personal level by traditional means, but could be reached. And, an important consideration to a campaign running low on money at the end of the primary trail, the talk show circuit was free.

Shortly after the Arsenio show, Clinton did a national town meeting on television and then another with young voters on the MTV cable outlet. To the surprise of many, the questions from the young audience revealed mostly the same concerns among the music video set that were on the minds of their square elders—jobs, the economy and fears about the future.

The Clinton campaign, in addition to being on the lookout for ways to reach untapped audiences, also continued to seek means to show the candidate "going against the grain," to demonstrate that he was indeed a different kind of candidate. An opportunity was about to present itself in this regard, handed unwittingly to Clinton by an irreverent member of the MTV generation—a young rap entertainer who called herself Sister Souljah.

C H A P T E R 1 6

JETTISONING JESSE

With Bill Clinton now on an apparently unimpeded course to the Democratic nomination, one question lingered within the party: what to do about Jesse Jackson. Ever since he had decided to get into elective politics as a candidate for the 1984 nomination, the civil rights leader had been a mixed blessing for the Democratic Party and its candidates.

Jackson's unprecedented candidacy had an enormous significance to black voters, who took great pride in his ability to compete effectively at the highest level of American politics. His most obvious appeal was to the young blacks he urged to stay in school, stay away from drugs and take part in the process. But beyond them, particularly in that first campaign in 1984, he reached effectively into all segments of black society. A few leaders such as Andrew Young, a close adviser to the Reverend Martin Luther King, Jr., and later a congressman and mayor of Atlanta, viewed him with a jaundiced eye because of their experience with his showboating style during the civil rights movement. But most blacks of all levels of educational and economic achievement admired his audacity and determination. Jackson held his own, or more than his own, in televised debates with white candidates, and "Run, Jesse, Run," was not just a chant from the young.

But it was equally true that Jackson was a red flag to more conservative white voters, in the South and the industrial Northeast and Midwest. They were intimidated by his in-your-face style and saw him as a political radical demanding special treatment for blacks at their expense. Jackson himself was not inclined to mute his demands in the interest of keeping these whites within the Democratic Party.

On the contrary, his position was that he represented the party's single most loyal voter bloc and the one whose fealty was absolutely essential to the success of any Democratic presidential candidate. As a result, in both 1984 and 1988 he had brought about public confrontations with the party's presidential nominees that had given many voters the impression—largely unjustified—that they had caved in to the civil rights leader to buy his endorsement and support.

In 1984, Jackson had finished third far behind Walter Mondale and Gary Hart in the contest for the Democratic nomination. Yet rather than throw in behind the ticket of Mondale and Geraldine A. Ferraro, he stood aside as the leader of a separate force, reconfiguring his candidacy as a movement and sailing through the convention in San Francisco, and the entire summer, without delivering an endorsement. Finally, he agreed to attend a meeting of prominent black Democrats in St. Paul on Labor Day weekend, although also insisting on a separate meeting of his own with Mondale at the nominee's home just outside the city.

After that session, Jackson and Mondale were driven to the parking lot of a school nearby for a press conference—where, with Mondale standing uncomfortably at his side, Jackson pointedly refused to use the word "endorse" to express his support for the ticket. Later that night, under pressure from other prominent blacks at a meeting in the St. Paul Hotel, Jackson finally delivered his endorsement. But the whole episode sent a picture through the television networks of the civil rights leader jerking around the Democratic nominee for president. It was an image that persisted throughout that campaign—and was clearly a contributing factor to Mondale's inability to win even 30 percent of the white vote in the Deep South states such as Alabama, Georgia, Louisiana and North Carolina with large black populations.

Four years later, Jackson finished second—but a distant second—to Michael Dukakis and, again, made the most of his opportunity, withholding his endorsement until a convention-eve session in an Atlanta hotel after another media circus of several days' duration. This one was set off by Jackson's learning from the press, rather than directly from Dukakis himself, that Senator Lloyd Bentsen of Texas had been chosen for the vice presidential nomination. The mistake had been purely mechanical, a case of a misplaced telephone call. But Jackson wasn't willing to let it go by, when a display of indignation and bruised feelings obviously could give him added leverage at the convention.

Once again the electorate was being given apparent reason to believe another Democratic nominee was caving in to Jesse Jackson. And, once again, a Democratic presidential nominee was beaten by embarrassing margins among white voters in the South and some working-class areas of the Northeast and Midwest. Although few would argue that Jackson was the prime factor in those defeats, there was little doubt, considering the role of race in American politics of the 1980s, that among many white voters he was a heavy piece of political baggage.

The pattern had become clear in presidential and, alarmingly for Southern Democratic leaders, many statewide contests, as well. In states with large black populations, white candidates with any identification as liberals needed only 30 to 35 percent of the white vote because they could count on winning 90 percent of the black vote. But, paradoxically, the states in which these candidates needed the fewest white votes were the ones where it was most difficult to enlist them. Their best opportunity lay in states such as Tennessee, Kentucky or Arkansas, where they needed 40 percent or more of the white vote because there were relatively fewer blacks—and the Democrats were not identified as ''the black party'' with which some white voters were so reluctant to identify themselves.

A racial pattern sending a similar message emerged in the Democatic primaries when Jackson was an active candidate, particularly in 1988. His share of the white vote was consistently largest in those states in which the black share of the population was smallest. It was easier for white liberals in Oregon, for example, to identify with Jackson and his boast of a ''rainbow'' than it was for white working-class voters in New Jersey or Michigan.

This time the situation was different. Jackson had not competed in the primaries, and his refusal to run for mayor of the District of Columbia in 1990 had diminished his validity as a serious political figure. But he was still an influential voice with black Americans, and his relationship with Bill Clinton and the Democratic Leadership Council had not been a comfortable one. He had not forgotten that Clinton was chairman of the DLC at the time he was barred from speaking at its Cleveland meeting in May of 1991. The situation had been further exacerbated, moreover, by the incident during the primary season when Clinton, mistakenly thinking he was sitting at a dead microphone, blew up angrily when misinformed that Jackson had endorsed Tom Harkin in South Carolina.

Jackson originally responded with an unusually mild statement, but on second thought decided to take offense. "I'm disappointed with his overreaction without verification," he said in an interview on CNN, which repeatedly ran the clip of the outraged Clinton. "I'm disturbed by the tone of the blast at my integrity, my character. I felt blindsided by what I finally saw and heard him say." As was the case with the Lloyd Bentsen episode four years earlier, Jackson wasn't going to miss an opportunity to react to any perceived slight.

Clinton had followed a policy of maintaining a distance from Jackson throughout the primary period, and his advisers were telling reporters privately that this was the way it was going to be. Jackson had no delegates, they argued, so he had no special claim on a place at the convention in New York or in the general election campaign. More to the point, by this stage of the campaign Clinton had enlisted valuable support from black officeholders such as Representatives John Lewis of Georgia and Mike Espy of Mississippi and Mayors Maynard Jackson of Atlanta and Kurt Schmoke of Baltimore. If the goal was to increase black turnout, which declined precipitously from Mondale to Dukakis, these officeholders could deliver just as well as Jesse Jackson. Or, at least, so the theory went.

Clinton's campaign through the primaries had appeared carefully staged to avoid the kind of identification with black leaders and causes that could thwart his more obvious appeal to the Southern whites and Reagan Democrats elsewhere, who were essential to his prospects of building a winning coalition in the general election. Clinton's appearances at black events often seemed timed so that they would be too late for the television network news that night or so that they would be overshadowed in newsworthiness by other events.

And, happily for Clinton, although there was muttering from a few black leaders, most of them were pragmatic enough to understand that the first imperative was to elect a Democratic president after twelve years of Ronald Reagan and George Bush. So they let his neglect slide in a way they might not otherwise have done. The prickly Jackson might be grumbling there in the background, the Clinton managers said, but he was no longer the only game in town.

There were, however, some prominent Clinton supporters, particularly in the South, who thought the Arkansas governor needed to do more to separate himself from Jackson and had advised him to find a way to emphasize that distance so it would be clear to white voters. None of Jackson's white competitors in 1984 and 1988 ever had confronted him in any seriously forceful way, even when, in 1984, there were the allegations of anti-Semitism after his reference to New York as "Hymietown."

The one candidate who ventured into open criticism of Jackson was Senator Joseph Biden of Delaware at an early stage of the preliminaries to the 1988 contest. And Jackson had come back at him so harshly that the lesson for other campaigns was to tread very softly. But this time Jackson seemed less insulated from criticism, and Bill Clinton was told on more than one occasion that he could help himself immensely by, as one longtime party activist and fund-raiser in Alabama put it, "telling old Jesse where to stuff it."

There was never any evidence that Clinton approved such a strategy explicitly, but late in the spring—whether inadvertently or not—he followed it.

En route to a June 13 appearance before a meeting of Jackson's Rainbow Coalition in Washington, Clinton learned that the previous night the group had heard from Lisa Williamson, a rap singer known as Sister Souljah who had caused a stir with some angry rhetoric in the aftermath of the Los Angeles riots. On May 13, *The Washington Post* had published a story about an interview in which Sister Souljah was asked if she thought the violence had been "wise."

She replied: "Yeah, it was wise. I mean if black people kill black people every day, why not have a week and kill white people? . . . In other words, white people, this government and the mayor were well aware of the fact that black people were dying every day in Los Angeles under gang violence. So if you're a gang member and you normally would be killing somebody, why not kill a white person?''

Clinton had decided he should address the Sister Souljah rhetoric before a black audience, just as he had been telling home truths to other audiences such as those in Detroit and Macomb County during the Michigan primary campaign and in his blast at business greed at the Wharton School during the primary in Pennsylvania.

So, with Jackson sitting at his left in a conference room of the Sheraton Washington Hotel, Clinton chastised the Rainbow Coalition for giving the rap singer their conference as a forum. Her remarks to the *Post*, he said, had been ''filled with a kind of hatred that you do not honor today and tonight.'' He added: ''If you took the words 'white' and 'black' and reversed them, you might think David Duke was giving that speech.''

Jackson, who had listened in silence while staring stonily ahead, was clearly nonplussed. ''I don't know what his intention was,'' he told reporters who quickly crowded around him afterward while a gospel singer sang in the background. ''I was totally surprised.''

Later, after meetings with Clinton and his own advisers, Jackson held a press conference at which he defended Sister Souljah, arguing that she had been ''misunderstood'' and suggesting she had been misquoted when, in fact, the interview had been tape-recorded by the *Post*'s reporter. Jackson's willingness to defend the rap singer quickly recalled his silence eight years earlier when one of his most militant supporters was Louis Farrakhan.

But now Jackson's focus was on the critic rather than the object of the criticism. Clinton, he said, had shown ''very bad judgment'' in assailing her at the Rainbow meeting. ''It was unnecessary, it was a diversion,'' Jackson said. ''I don't know why he used this platform to address those issues.''

Clinton had tried to couch his criticism by depicting the rap singer's rhetoric as foreign to the purposes of the Rainbow Coalition and by making a point of citing his own ''mistake'' earlier in the spring when he played golf at an all-white country club in Little Rock. ''We have an obligation, all of us, to call attention to prejudice wherever we see it,'' he said. But there was no question that he had confronted Jackson on his home turf in a way that was certain to attract heavy attention from the news media, a situation almost certain to evoke a response.

Jackson said later that he "really was stunned and amazed" by Clinton's remarks. The two men had met for about thirty minutes in a suite in the hotel before the conference session, and Clinton had given no hint of his intention to raise the question of Sister Souljah's remarks. Moreover, Jackson recalled, he thought he himself had shown restraint repeatedly in the months before the meeting, passing up more than one chance to take what he called "a clear shot" at the Arkansas governor.

During the height of the Gennifer Flowers controversy, Jackson said, he had telephoned Clinton "to express my sensitivity and concern" about the preoccupation of the press with the issue, at the expense of attention to more important concerns—just as he had done, he said, with Gary Hart during the Donna Rice episode in 1987.

A week or so later, Jackson said, he had called Clinton again to urge him to consider a reprieve for Rickey Ray Rector, the brain-damaged convicted killer scheduled to be executed in Arkansas. Clinton told him, Jackson said, that he was "praying about it" but that all legal options apparently had been exhausted. The day after the execution, Clinton flew to Washington to appear before a meeting sponsored by the Rainbow Coalition, whose members were not happy about Clinton's permitting it to go forward. But, Jackson said, they "chose to be restrained in their displeasure about what had happened the very night before.

"We did not make it a point by which to define him, which we could have done because our people were in that mood," Jackson said. "They were very angry about it. . . . We could have reacted to our displeasure by disinviting him." Instead, he said, Clinton was given "a fair hearing" and "left unscarred. . . . It was not a showdown moment because we chose not to make it a showdown moment."

The next dustup came when Clinton erupted in that television studio about Jackson campaigning with Harkin in South Carolina. This time, Jackson said, he thought they had reached an agreement to avoid such problems in the future. Clinton had called him at about two o'clock in the morning to apologize for the outburst, Jackson recalled, and the two agreed that henceforth they would communicate with each other privately when either had a complaint, before going public. The policy, said Jackson, would be "open lines before we have open mikes. . . . This was another time that we could have shot at him if that were our interest."

What Jackson called the "accumulation of signals" of ill will continued to build, he said, while he himself continued to show restraint. Next there was the visit of Clinton and Senator Sam Nunn to a Georgia prison camp the day before the March 3 Georgia primary—a ploy Jackson figured was designed to produce pictures and stories "calculated to be on the front page" that would depict Clinton as tough on crime. Jackson called the visit "a version of the Willie Horton situation," but again one on which he showed restraint. And then there was Clinton's "mistake" two weeks later in playing golf at an all-white country club in Little Rock, a breach that Jackson again allowed to pass with what he considered great restraint.

In Jackson's view, there was a pattern of consistent behavior on Clinton's part from the time he shut Jackson out of the DLC convention in Cleveland in 1991 clear through to his attack on the rap singer at the Rainbow conference. "There was a straight line from that meeting to Souljah," he said.

After Clinton had made his remarks and the conference session ended, Jackson and Clinton returned to the hotel suite. By this time, Jackson was seething. "I said, 'You violated us. Why did you do this?' " he said he told Clinton. The governor replied, Jackson said, that he was "offended" at the allegation, pointing out that he had praised the Rainbow Coalition highly and that his remarks on Sister Souljah had been just a fraction of what he had said. But Clinton, Jackson noted later, produced from his pocket a piece of paper containing the text of Sister Souljah's controversial observations—proof that Clinton had come primed to make an issue of them.

The meeting between the two men was sufficiently civil, however, that, as both said later, Jackson invited Clinton to come back to the meeting later and play his saxophone. "Even then," Jackson said, "we didn't realize the political ramifications and calculation of what had happened."

Clinton's remarks, nonetheless, had struck a nerve with the press and attendees at the conference, to which Sister Souljah had been invited as a participant to a youth workshop. "Afterwards," Jackson recalled, "people were enraged. They were prepared to go [outside the hotel] and confront him [Clinton] at his car, go to his hotel and other kinds of things,'' until dissuaded by Jackson.

Jackson's anger built when Frank Watkins, a longtime close adviser, informed him that he had been warned in advance that Clinton was going to say something newsworthy. ''I got word from one of the reporters that this was going down,'' Watkins said later. ''I didn't know exactly what it was, but that he was going to do or say something that would be offensive to the Rainbow, and this was part of their 'counter-scheduling' strategy.''

Much later, Clinton while acknowledging his campaign's use of a ''counter-scheduling'' strategy on other occasions, as in his Macomb County, Michigan, speech, insisted that it didn't apply to the Sister Souljah incident. ''There were some people, some folks in our group, who really thought I should go there as counter-scheduling and just take her on,'' he said, ''which was the way it got played, what I said. I made a deliberate decision that I didn't want to do that because I didn't know her, I had never had any contact with her, and also because even though Jesse and I had had differences, I was immensely impressed with his Rebuild America, his economic plan, and I was there in effect trying to compliment him for emphasizing some things that had not been emphasized before on his part. . . .

''So I read what she said and I decided that I should make a very different point, which I honestly tried to make . . . although because I was there on Jesse's doorstep and because I had done so much counter-scheduling before, it's not the way it came out. The point I was trying to make when I read about what she had said . . . was here was this obviously really articulate, really intelligent, really passionate young woman, clearly a role model, who was saying things that I strongly disapprove of. . . . But the importance of her to me was how urgent it was for us to take on these tasks and to take them on together, because we were in danger of losing a whole generation. You had all these kids that were out there in trouble and then you had young people like her who were doing well but were so alienated that they couldn't be reached.

''So the point I was trying to make was a very different one than the one that came out, which was that we didn't have a lot of time and here's somebody saying something that I strongly disapprove of who's obviously representative of a certain point of view, and we'd better move and move now to try to bring these folks back in the fold. That's the point I was trying to make. As it turned out, because I was there with Jesse and because of the past habits of counter-scheduling and maybe [because] there were some people in my crowd who wanted me to deliver a different message that I deliberately decided not to deliver because I didn't think it was the right thing. I wanted to reach out an olive branch to someone I strongly disagreed with as a way of symbolizing what I thought we had to do. So I kind of regretted the way it came out, actually.''

There was still another complicating element in the situation. Well before the meeting, Clinton and his strategists had decided they would "shut down" any speculation about Jackson as a possible vice presidential nominee by telling him early that he wouldn't be selected. To temporize as Dukakis had done in 1988, they feared, would set off another round of controversy and raise unrealistic expectations in the black community that would have to be disappointed.

Thus, during one of their private meetings that day—Jackson thought it was the first, others the second—Clinton told Jackson that he wouldn't be his running mate. As Jackson recalled it, Clinton said: "I've made a choice about my ticket, and given our calculations, I don't think that would work.''

Jackson said he replied that his advisers also had done some calculations on how his presence on the ticket could change the election arithmetic in a positive way. He said he offered to give Clinton an analysis that was "at least worth assessing and calculating.'' Clinton said he would read it. But after the blowup over Clinton's remarks about Sister Souljah, Jackson said, he decided not to provide the material to him.

Long after the fact, Clinton described to us in positive terms his decision to inform Jackson directly that he wasn't going to be on the Democratic ticket. "I told him that I was not going to select him,'' Clinton said. "I did it basically out of personal respect. I did it because . . . I thought he was a very important part of the Democratic coalition and a very important leader in America, because I wanted to have a good, honest, open relationship with him, and I just wanted to do it personally. It's not something I wanted to delegate, something I wanted to do on the phone, and it was coming on time for me to make a decision. I was getting close to a decision and I wanted to look him in the eye and tell him myself. I think it was something I should personally do.''

Asked what the reason was for not selecting Jackson, Clinton diplomatically observed that he was already moving toward another choice that would be an "utterly different, unconventional decision." He added, however, that "I just didn't think it was the right thing to do at this time . . . either substantively or politically." His uneasy history with Jackson went unmentioned, but certainly was a factor, along with the obvious question of whether any black candidate, and this one especially, would hurt rather than help the ticket "at this time."

Jackson said later that he knew the Clinton campaign would suggest—as it did—that he reacted heatedly to Clinton's remarks on Sister Souljah "because we were disappointed" about being shut off the ticket, "but that was not the case at all." If he was going to react angrily to that circumstance, Jackson argued, he would have been much more likely to do so four years earlier after he had received several million votes in the primaries. (He had, however, complained at length in 1988 about hearing the news from someone else that Dukakis had picked Lloyd Bentsen.)

"This had strictly to do with insulting our audience," Jackson said, a view he came to hold with greater force the more he thought about it. "He [Clinton] actually was talking to the TV audience," he said. "He was not talking to the people who were there. He was using the people who were there as a platform to spread his message."

This perceived slight was the issue on which Jackson's anger finally focused as his friends and advisers drove home the point to him. As Watkins told him the day after the conference: "The guy came into your house, kicked you in the balls, and turned around and walked out." Jackson, Watkins said, "still didn't want to believe it," but finally did.

If there was any doubt about Jackson's anger, he resolved it over the next few days. He complained bitterly and repeatedly that Clinton had abused his hospitality in an attempt to reach the white working-class voters who had deserted the Democratic Party in large numbers in the previous three campaigns. Jackson said the presumptive nominee had "again exposed a character flaw" by conducting what amounted to "a very well-planned sneak attack without the courage to confront but with a calculation to embarrass" Jackson himself. The Clinton strategy was designed, the civil rights leader told *The New York Times*, "purely to appeal to conservative whites by containing Jackson and isolating Jackson." It was an excellent piece of political analysis but not one designed to improve the relationship between the civil rights leader and the Arkansas governor.

Clinton and his advisers professed to be surprised by the intensity of Jackson's anger, but Clinton refused to back down. Talking to reporters at Little Rock, he said: "I bragged on the Rainbow Coalition and its programs. I criticized divisive language by Sister Souljah. If Jesse Jackson wants to align himself with that now and claim that's the way he felt, then that's his business."

Reached by *The New York Times*, Jackson replied with one of his typical formulations: "The attempt to align me with her is an attempt to malign me with her." Appearing on the CBS program *Face the Nation* a couple of days later, Jackson added: "As we reached out, Bill Clinton pushed off and so we don't want to interfere with the campaign, nor do we want to be a foil for any tricks."

Ten days after the original incident, Jackson was still beating the same horse. The night before he was to speak at the annual meeting of the U.S. Conference of Mayors in Houston, Jackson received a call from an old ally who had been one of the chairmen of his 1984 campaign, Mayor Maynard Jackson of Atlanta. Maynard Jackson's message was direct: it is time, he told Jesse Jackson, to cool down this feud with Clinton. When the press asks you about it in Houston, give them a "no comment." Otherwise, they won't pay any attention to your own proposal for an urban investment bank.

For his part, Maynard Jackson was fully behind Clinton. He had followed his own advice and turned aside questions about the Sister Souljah incident. And in a closed meeting of Democratic mayors, Maynard Jackson had taken the lead in making the case for what proved to be a strong declaration of support for the economic program Clinton had announced only two days earlier, and now was bringing before the conference. Nor was Maynard Jackson alone; other black mayors such as Sharpe James of Newark and Norman Rice of Seattle also were quick to praise the Clinton initiative.

But when Jesse Jackson arrived, it was clear he wasn't ready to take Maynard Jackson's advice and put the whole thing behind him. Although he used his speech to the mayors to call Clinton's economic program "a step in the right direction [that] shows an authentic concern for the urban crisis and the need to reinvest,'' he pointedly refused at a press conference to endorse Clinton.

And he was obviously unready to forget Sister Souljah. Clinton, he told reporters, was trying to "distance" himself from Jackson to seek white votes. The civil rights leader was derisive about Clinton's argument that he had been speaking out of anger at Sister Souljah's rhetoric. "When Bill Clinton said he's left the all-white country club," he reminded reporters, "he didn't say he left because of moral outrage. He just said he'd left.''

Clinton could have made his point about Sister Souljah, Jackson suggested, by simply not attending that Rainbow Coalition meeting. "If the issue was distancing,'' he said, "there was distance before he came.'' When a reporter pointed out to him that he had nice things to say about Clinton's economic program, he looked up with a thin smile and replied: "I have been consistently nice. I have good manners.''

When the press conference ended, Jackson took a reporter aside outside the conference room and explained he had no choice but to respond to Clinton's "distancing" strategy. "He used our meeting to do it,'' he said. The notion of Jackson complaining about a politician using someone else's forum was laughable on its face; he had made a career of transforming other leaders' events into forums for himself.

But the message was obvious that Jackson was in no hurry to heal the breach. On the contrary, he may have had visions of another "summit" meeting such as those Mondale and Dukakis had granted—the kind of media event that would be catnip for the press and television cameras soon to be gathered in huge numbers for the nominating convention at New York.

Press attention was meat and drink for Jesse Jackson. When he was campaigning for the party ticket in the general election campaign of 1988, he used to telephone the national editor of *The Washington Post* and others to brief them on his schedule for the day. But as a player on the fringe, that kind of attention wasn't being paid until the controversy over Sister Souljah. Now, as one longtime Jackson friend put it, "You'll notice he was back on the front page of *The New York Times* last week. It's been a long time since that happened.''

But Clinton and his managers were just as determined that there would be no such attempt at rapprochement. Jackson didn't have any delegates this time, they said, and he was not going to be given special treatment. "Why in hell do we have to deal with him at all?" a Clinton confidant asked in tones that answered the question.

After the fact, Clinton and his advisers insisted there had been no deliberate, carefully contrived plan to affront Jackson, that the whole episode had been a natural next step in the policy Clinton was following of "going against the grain"—telling audiences things they didn't necessarily prefer to hear. As Mickey Kantor, chairman of the Clinton campaign, described it, "We had a whole campaign . . . of going to Macomb County and going to a black church [in Detroit], going to Floyd Flake's church [in New York] and then going to an Orthodox Jewish dinner, to try to show symbolically, as well as in terms of what Clinton wanted to do programmatically, that he wanted to bring disparate communities together in this country. His immediate gut reaction was that [what] Sister Souljah had been saying, in effect, in her music was the antithesis of what Bill Clinton was trying to do."

Within the campaign, Kantor said, the discussion centered not on "Bill Clinton standing up to Jesse Jackson" but instead on the candidate being consistent in his approach. "We were so focused on what he had been doing, and what we had tried to project for months at that point became the issue—that if you go before the Rainbow Coalition, you don't just back off of that issue and tell them what they want to hear."

"Had we gone to Rainbow and not said something about it," George Stephanopoulos said later, "you think that every Republican . . . wouldn't have been on us for that? They'd have beaten the crap out of us."

So Clinton and his advisers discussed how Jackson might react, how angry he might be—but not whether to take the risk. "He couldn't go in front of this audience and not say something," Kantor said. "It would be impossible for Bill Clinton. . . . Not saying anything was a continuation of the same kind of politics which had led us to get our clocks cleaned in every election."

According to Paul Begala, Clinton originally intended to make public his criticism of Sister Souljah shortly after the riots in Los Angeles in a speech before the Show Coalition, a group of Hollywood celebrities that was active in raising money for the Democratic campaign. The plan was to make the point that people in the entertainment business had a moral responsibility to speak out when one of their own was advocating racism. But the event in Los Angeles, he said, proved to be "a philanthropic thing" at which such a scolding speech would have been out of place.

"So he put the speech on the shelf," Begala recalled. "It was not going to be a central thrust of the campaign but he just felt that he was going to be Bill Clinton and put appeals for racial unity in all of his speeches. . . . Then he felt something of a moral obligation if you see something like this, to speak out against it, to be against racism wherever you see it. Then time passes, two or three weeks, and Clinton's going to be at the Rainbow Coalition and Mandy Grunwald notices on the program the day before is Sister Souljah, so what do you do? It's pretty easy for Clinton. You have to be true to yourself. You have to be true to your views. So we dusted off the appropriate parts of the Sister Souljah speech and gave it there."

But, Begala insisted, "it was not, as some think, an overt attempt to find something to stick in Jesse Jackson's eye for the sake of doing it. . . . The purpose of the speech wasn't just to piss off Jesse."

All this sounded reasonable long after the fact. But it was also true at the time that some Clinton strategists were encouraging the idea that this was a candidate who would not be kowtowing to Jesse Jackson and just might find a way to prove it. Nor was it any secret that Clinton was getting advice from allies, particularly in the South, that he needed to make his independence from Jackson as clear as possible. And that, in turn, would involve a deliberate strategy that the timing in this case seemed to suggest. If Sister Souljah's rhetoric was so offensive, why did Clinton have to wait an entire month? Was there no other way to make his message heard? Was it necessary to drop the bomb on Jackson at a Rainbow Coalition conference without giving him any advance notice?

Longtime Jackson-watchers have come to realize, however, that Jackson's anger is sometimes more tactical than emotional, a display turned on and off as another way to achieve some specific purpose. In this case, the continuing attacks by Jackson right through the mayors' conference in Houston already had served to put him back in the Democratic equation as a force with whom Clinton apparently would have to reckon before the Democratic convention opened in New York in three weeks.

Within the Clinton campaign, however, there was no inclination to accord Jackson anything that looked like special treatment. The candidate and his advisers all were fully aware of the experiences of Mondale and Dukakis—and with the political price each had paid. Dealing with Jackson was notoriously difficult, as the Clinton managers were also aware.

"Somebody said [Mondale campaign manager] Bob Beckel met with him seventy-two times," Carville said. "I couldn't meet anybody on the face of this earth seventy-two times." The bottom line was a decision simply to ride out Jackson's rage and avoid any appearance of being too conciliatory. "Nobody ever said there'd be one of those big summit meetings," one Clinton adviser said.

This approach rested heavily on the confidence that Clinton could rely on those other black leaders. "Bill Clinton did not need an envoy to the African-American community," Mickey Kantor said later. "He did not need a visa." When John Lewis earlier said of Clinton, "He can walk the walk and he can talk the talk," Kantor said, "in the African-American community that was remembered." And Clinton, said his press secretary, Dee Dee Myers, "just wouldn't cede the turf to him [Jackson]."

In political terms, however, the issue was less whether Clinton could enlist heavy black support without Jesse Jackson than whether he could win more support from Southern whites and Reagan Democrats in the north by taking on Jackson so directly and visibly. As the campaign wore on, it became apparent that, premeditated or not, the Clinton posture toward Jackson resonated throughout the electorate. As Stephanopoulos put it later, "It stood for something larger than what it was"—dramatic evidence this was a "different kind of Democrat."

We heard about it repeatedly from Democrats in the South all through the general election campaign. As Al LaPierre, executive director of the party in Alabama, recalled: "People would come up to me and say, 'Dammit, we've finally done something right. . . . It was really amazing that one instance worked so well." And we heard it from blue-collar workers in the industrial states outside the South. Kevin Mullaney, an electrician in North Philadelphia, later told one of us, "The day he told off that fucking Jackson is the day he got my vote."

Just how much of a price Clinton might pay in terms of black support for affronting Jackson was impossible to determine. Clinton was winning heavily among blacks during the primaries. But, unsurprisingly, black turnout in the primaries was far lower than it had been when Jesse Jackson was a candidate.

The task in political arithmetic was simple enough—whether whatever losses in the black vote Clinton might suffer from a lower turnout in November would be offset by the message he had sent to white Democrats. At the moment, however, another problem was looming ever larger in Clinton's aspirations to collar white Democratic votes. His name was Ross Perot.

SEARCHLIGHT ON INSPECTOR PEROT

While President Bush was methodically if uninspiringly disposing of the challenge of Pat Buchanan, and Bill Clinton was surviving the pitfalls of the Democratic primaries and his own past, the phenomenon of Ross Perot and his bandwagon of volunteer ''owners'' of the country had continued to roll on. It was fueled up to now essentially by the high-octane energy of the glib, fast-talking Texas billionaire as he worked the television talk show circuit, assuring his admiring millions of supporters that if only they would ''stay in the ring'' with him, together they would crack the gridlock in Washington and change America.

He was, as he had promised, putting some of his own money into the drive to place his name on the ballot in all fifty states, but the $400,000 in his first filing with the Federal Election Commission was only small change by his reckoning. From Maine to California, voters were opening petition offices and manning petition tables in shopping malls at their own expense to advance the cause.

As the weeks flashed by, however, Perot found himself increasingly pressed on the talk show circuit to get beyond the clever one-liners and sound bites of the sort he continued to decry from "the politicians," and spell out exactly what he had in mind to end the recession and eliminate the nation's staggering deficit. When he did use hard figures and they were questioned, he would duck, or promise an explanation later.

One claim was that he could cut $180 billion by eliminating government waste, fraud and abuse; another was that he would save $100 billion a year by asking well-off older people like himself to decline monthly Social Security and Medicare checks to which they were entitled. When his figures were challenged on the NBC News show *Meet the Press*, he grew testy and insisted the numbers had been given to him by a government expert "whose name is a household word," but he declined to supply it.

In a speech before the American Newspaper Publishers Association in New York in early May, Perot announced that he was going to cut back on his whirlwind schedule of television appearances and interviews to focus on getting ready for a full-blown candidacy. He said he would "spend all my time building an organization, finalizing a strategy and developing carefully thought out positions on each of the major issues." These were all undertakings his effort badly needed, as he confessed to the publishers.

"Night and day," he said, "there is saturation bombing. There are Patriot missiles going down air shafts in my office from all your good reporters wanting to know my position on everything from mosquitoes to ants."

Lack of specificity was not Perot's only problem at this point. As the phenomenon continued to exceed expectations, threatening to make him a very serious factor in the fall outcome of the presidential campaign, news media scrutiny was intensifying proportionately. Even before Perot burst on the political scene, he had a reputation as a man with a short fuse and a suspicious nature. Now individuals who had been subjected to either, or said they had been, began to tell the world. And reporters began to probe for whatever they could find that would reveal who this man who would be president really was, and what made him tick.

The publisher of *The Fort Worth Star-Telegram*, Richard L. Connor, came forward with a story that Perot three years earlier had threatened to release compromising photographs of one of the newspaper's employees in retaliation for the publication of an unfavorable story about his son, Ross Jr. "I was just stunned by it," Connor said. "It was sort of seamy, extremely mean-spirited. . . . I remember how shocked I was that this guy would stoop to that level." Perot's response was that he had called to "complain about the accuracy of a story" but that he had made "no comments of a personal nature about anyone."

This and similar stories soon gave rise to the characterization "Inspector Perot"—a man with a fixation for investigating others, allegedly with the intent of digging up dirt that could be used as threats, or out of a suspicion or fear that someone else was acting out of suspect motives.

An Associated Press reporter in Washington, John Solomon, routinely checking on Perot's finances as he became a more formidable prospective candidate, dug out Nixon White House logs from the National Archives indicating that Perot, far from being the Washington outsider he claimed, with nothing but contempt for establishment politics, had been—as Solomon wrote—"the ultimate insider." Solomon quoted former Richard Nixon White House aide Peter Flanagan to that effect, and another Nixon White House hand, convicted Watergate figure Charles Colson, called Perot "an amazing operator," unmatched in his ability "to muscle himself in quicker [than others] into the president's own confidence."

The AP reporter found White House memos indicating that Perot in private meetings with Nixon had offered to spend $50 million in public relations efforts to boost Nixon's image, including purchase of the ABC television network and a major newspaper, and another $10 million to establish a pro-Nixon think tank. Colson said Perot "never put up a nickel" but "parlayed that offer" into Oval Office access. Perot denied it all, saying Nixon aides would try to get money from him for various "beautiful and strange ideas," but that he always turned them down.

The AP story also reported that the Nixon White House had intervened with the Internal Revenue Service after it had questioned Perot's deduction of a political contribution to the 1968 Nixon campaign on his corporate tax return and had interceded with other agencies to assist Perot in various financial disputes, indicating he knew the levers of Washington power to push, and pushed them.

Such stories only fed Perot's deep conviction that the Republican Party and the Bush White House were out to get him. At the time this story first appeared, one of us had an hour's interview with Perot in his Dallas office. When he was asked whether he believed the Bush campaign had planted the story with the AP reporter, Perot replied without hesitation: "Sure I do. Do you really think anybody could dig through all the files of the Nixon Library, with everything scattered all over the place? I think if you talk to that reporter, he'll tell you he found it all piled in one place. That's what he told me."

But Solomon, who found the papers in the National Archives, not the Nixon Library, told us it was Perot himself, when the reporter talked to him on another matter, who said some things that gave him the idea to check the Archives, and that he had never talked to anybody in the Bush administration or the Republican Party in advance of finding the Nixon logs and memos relating to Perot.

At first, the critical stories about Perot did not make a dent in the spread of his movement or the success of his volunteers around the country in collecting the petitions in the various states necessary to place his name on the November ballot. The first state where volunteers qualified him, without any appreciable effort by Perot or his Dallas associates, was Tennessee. But the first major test came in Texas, where state law required 53,000 signatures of Texans who had not voted in the state's March 10 primary to be collected in five weeks' time. The Texas volunteers produced more than 200,000 names, delivering them to Secretary of State John Hannum in an elaborate ceremony on the steps of the state capitol on deadline day.

Without the enlistment of professional politicians—Perot made a point of emphasizing that fact in our interview—the Texans for Perot staged a cheering, foot-stomping parade up Austin's broad Congress Avenue. It was complete with cowgirls on horseback and a banner stretched from one curb to the other reading AMERICA IS READY FOR YOU, ROSS PEROT, toted by about twenty supporters chanting, "Goodbye Bush, Hello Perot!"

At the capitol, volunteers carted nearly a hundred boxes of signed petitions and piled them before a platform where Perot addressed the crowd of several thousand under a wilting sun, giving them his standard speech about giving the country back to its "owners." Commending their efforts, he said that all the political experts had said "ordinary people couldn't get this done," but "you showed 'em." Still, he played it coy, saying only that he would announce whether he would be a candidate "whenever we're ready."

The stories about Perot's past were coming faster now, tarnishing his shining armor. *The Dallas Morning News* reported that Perot's father in 1955 wrote a letter to then Senator Lyndon B. Johnson of Texas asking his help in getting his son released from active duty in the navy after only two years of the four-year hitch required upon his graduation from the Naval Academy. Perot said he had no recollection of the matter.

Several days later, the Associated Press reported the existence of another letter, this from Perot himself to Representative Wright Patman of Texas, again asking help in winning early release from the navy because, Perot wrote, he found it to be "a fairly godless organization" marked by "drunken tales of moral emptiness" and promiscuity on the part of his fellow sailors.

There were also stories of a Wall Street fiasco in which he lost a fortune, of a broken pledge of $2.5 million to the Ronald Reagan presidential library, and of a complaint from Republican Senator Warren Rudman of New Hampshire, mentioned as a possible Perot running mate, that a private investigator claiming to be working for Perot was nosing around about him.

The Republicans, just as Perot had been saying, started what appeared to be an orchestrated assault on him. The day after the Rudman complaint, House Minority Leader Bob Michel called Perot "frightening" and a "demagogue" with a dangerous streak of "authoritarianism." The next day, White House press secretary Marlin Fitzwater labeled Perot "a pig in a poke and a dangerous and destructive personality," adding: "Being afraid of the unknown may soon make people ask, 'What kind of monster are we buying here?' "

These observations came on the heels of a most impressive showing for Perot in the Oregon primaries of both major parties. The networks' exit polls found that an astounding 45 percent of Democratic voters and 41 percent of Republicans said they were going to vote for Perot in November. In addition, he received 13 percent of the Democratic primary vote and 15 percent of the Republican on write-in ballots. Also, the *Los Angeles Times* poll had him surging ahead in California, with 39 percent of those surveyed to 26 percent for Clinton and 25 for Bush. The attacks on "Inspector Perot" didn't seem to be hurting him much as he continued to work the television and radio talk show circuit—in spite of his announcement that he would be laying off to concentrate on his much-awaited plan for cutting the deficit.

What was hurting, however, was the ability of the close Perot associates who were trying to run the quasi-campaign, lawyer Tom Luce and business lieutenant Mort Meyerson, to cope with the organizational challenges growing with every passing day. More and more states were undertaking and completing petition drives and calling on Dallas to produce Perot for celebrations just like the one in Austin that marked the filing of petitions for Texas ballot access.

A televised rally linking supporters in six states by satellite from Orlando, Florida, developed glitches and attendance at some sites was disappointing, indicating a lack of the sort of professional planning Perot had said he didn't want, but that Luce and Meyerson were coming to believe was essential.

The trick was finding the right political pros who could solve the organizational problems while accepting Perot's insistence that the campaign be an unconventional one, to match his unconventional style. His image as the anti-establishment nonpolitician was a central element in his appeal and could be tarnished by the arrival at the Dallas headquarters of a team of "hired guns" so recently and thoroughly criticized by Perot.

For several weeks now, as already noted, Luce had been conferring with Hamilton Jordan, who had volunteered his services on a part-time basis without pay. Jordan was a thoughtful and not entirely conventional political strategist who understood and appreciated Perot's unconventional approach to politics. "I read everything I could get my hands on about Perot," he said later, and was impressed with him.

On his own, Jordan began to work up charts laying out his ideas for a Perot campaign beyond the petition phase, presenting them to Luce and Meyerson for their consideration and, if they chose, for Perot's, whom he had never met. He made the basic case that voters were so hungering for reform that they would take some risks with a newcomer, but that, as he put it later, Perot could not be "scary or worrisome" and hope to keep their support. He noted that Perot in starting out as a newcomer had "the advantage of writing largely on a clean slate," but if the campaign "didn't define Perot, other people would define him."

Compared to other recent third-party or independent candidates,

Jordan noted, Perot had the advantages of financial resources, broad appeal and intensity of support without the limits of any narrow ideology. But in the end, he warned, Perot would have to answer satisfactorily one question: "Can he govern?"

Jordan argued that Perot as a newcomer to politics could not be expected to know everything and that he could finesse that shortcoming by sticking to the central problem of righting the economy, and a few other issues such as education and political reform about which he had definite ideas, and saying about other issues raised: "We'll argue about these after we fix the economy. Your government is broke and doesn't have the resources to fix these problems. . . . All these things are important, but we can't do anything about them until we deal with the core issues. All these emotional issues, if all you care about is how to settle these issues, go somewhere else. Don't vote for me."

He was trying, Jordan said later, "to come up with an honest way to deal with the fact that Perot wasn't well versed on a hundred issues, and that wasn't what people wanted from him anyway. They wanted to know where he stood on these kinds of gut issues." This approach would underscore his concentration on the issue most on voters' minds and would validate another concept of Jordan's—that Perot would be well served by campaigning unconventionally in what he called "a learning posture"—conspicuously on his own, without press coverage.

One week, he suggested, Perot would hold a town meeting somewhere off the beaten path, meet with workers, do a couple of interviews. The next week he would spend his time talking to people calling in on the Perot 800 number phone bank; the next, he would go for a briefing by AIDS researchers; then go to his home town of Texarkana and make a speech on who Ross Perot was. The next week, he would call on Sam Nunn, a Clinton backer, for a talk on defense issues and on Warren Rudman, a Bush backer, to discuss the budget deficit.

"My point was," Jordan said later, "without sacrificing your unconventional style, this was a way to go out and put yourself in a learning posture, show people you're concerned about all these things and, in fact, develop useful kinds of information." Perot, he said, was "a quick study. I thought he would in fact learn, and I thought it would look good to the American people."

Jordan also had ideas for putting the volunteers to work once the petition drives were completed, arguing that they constituted the campaign's "muscle" that would atrophy if not exercised. He suggested holding 20,000 "Perot parties" in private homes around the country to recruit more volunteers, and a "Project Greyhound" in which volunteers in Texas would be trained in political organization and sent out by bus through twenty or twenty-five smaller states, mostly in the West, to give direction to local Perot supporters.

Luce and Meyerson liked these ideas because they did seem to be within the framework of the unconventional campaign on which Perot was insisting. But the campaign nevertheless continued essentially on the petition-gathering track, along with Perot's seemingly tireless appearances on television news and talk shows. In late May, the two Perot lieutenants, overwhelmed by the mushrooming growth of the Perot phenomenon, broached the subject of Jordan coming aboard full-time, after first softening up Perot on the need for professional help—again within the framework of Perot's insistence on an unconventional campaign without "handlers." Jordan was reluctant, but intrigued.

Around the same time, Luce called Ed Rollins, the manager of Ronald Reagan's 1984 reelection landslide, who, after his somewhat stormy tenure as head of the Republican congressional campaign committee in which Bush had tried to force him out, was back in private consulting practice in Washington. Rollins recalled later that he had been watching the Perot grass-roots operation in his home state of California and was fascinated by it.

"The volunteer movement was really something unbelievable," he said. "I kept saying to Teeter and others in the Bush campaign, 'Don't underestimate this thing. This thing is very, very powerful.' There was discontent in the country, which obviously was something I had watched closely through the congressional committee, and I saw real dangers in Bush's reelection." Bush's broken tax pledge, Rollins recognized, had resulted in "an underbelly that was very soft" and a "wrong track" reading on the direction of the country that spelled real trouble.

At this time, Governor Pete Wilson of California, an old Rollins friend, asked him to go out to California and help him run the state for the whole Republican ticket, but when Bush got wind of it he blew the whistle on the idea. There was a minor furor in political circles as a result and Luce, hearing about it, phoned Rollins and invited him to talk in

Dallas. Patrick Caddell previously had also discussed the Perot campaign with Rollins, but he told both of them he couldn't get involved. One reason was that Rollins's wife, Sherrie, had just taken a high-profile political job in the White House, as head of the Office of Public Liaison, dealing with various public interest groups.

About a week later, Luce and Meyerson were in Washington and had dinner with Rollins. The best he could do, he said, was provide advice "from afar" and assist them in finding others who could help, but it had "to be totally stealth" in fairness to his wife.

Luce and Meyerson called again from Dallas a week later. "We've gone to Ross," Rollins was told. "This won't work, doing it behind the scenes. We want you out front, we want you public, and we want to get a Democrat." Rollins suggested Caddell, and when he was vetoed came up with Jordan. "Hamilton's out of politics, he understands the outsider campaign," he said.

The two Perot lieutenants, already working for weeks with Jordan, called him, he remembered, "and said, 'We've got a crazy idea and want to try it on you' "—pairing him with Rollins. "I told them that I was flattered, that I was interested, that I was surprised," Jordan said, "but that I didn't think they had thought it through, because I thought there would be a potential firestorm among their own supporters when they did this, because it seemed at variation with what Perot had been saying— no handlers, and all that."

But the two Perot aides wanted to pursue the idea, and the result was a meeting over Memorial Day weekend in Jordan's office in Knoxville among Luce, Meyerson, Jordan and Rollins. "We both were very reluctant and had significant reservations," Rollins recalled. Luce and Meyerson pressed them, asking what it would take to get them aboard. Rollins said Perot offered only to match what they were making in their current jobs and would require that they have no other clients—no problem for Jordan, who was out of politics. (Much later, Jordan showed one of us an uncanceled check from Perot for a month's pay—$75,000—that he hadn't decided to cash, sensitive to the "hired gun" label.)

Shortly afterward, Jordan and Rollins went to Dallas to meet Perot. Beforehand, they discussed the campaign again with Luce and Meyerson, and Rollins said later he made a point of warning what it would be like. "What Perot has to understand if you hire people like us, we're very visible," he told them. "Part of the campaign will be, I'll be on television talking about strategy and tactics, and if he's going to go batshit every time that occurs, how are we really going to be able to do the job?"

Jordan, however, was less inclined to see his role as a public spokesman, and more than Rollins he bought in to the Perot idea of an unconventional campaign that would be compatible with the notion that Perot was a different breed of cat. They agreed between themselves, however, Rollins said, "that there could be only one campaign manager," and that Rollins would have that day-to-day role and Jordan would focus on broader strategy and message.

Luce and Meyerson had reservations about whether Perot would buy the arrangement, but they said they would take it to him—the first of many missions of shuttle diplomacy required by the nature of Perot's modus operandi. "Hamilton and I walked out of there that night saying, 'Shit, he's not going to buy off on this,' Rollins recalled. 'He's got reservations. He hasn't a clue what's involved here.' We had bad vibrations."

The next day, however, when they met with Perot for about five hours, he appeared to buy in to everything that had been proposed. "He couldn't have been more charming," Rollins said. "He thought this was great, just what we needed, no reservations about anything."

Jordan came armed with more charts, having read Perot correctly as someone who liked to deal with visual aids rather than reading long-winded papers. He presented them, making such points as the importance of Perot staying on the message of his campaign regardless of the flak thrown up at him. Perot seemed to grasp readily the need for that kind of discipline. "I found him smart, shrewd, charming, quick on the uptake—and in some ways naive," Jordan recalled.

After the meeting sealing the deal, Jordan went off to a summer camp he runs for cancer-stricken children but in the next several days made trips to Perot petition operations in Tennessee, North and South Carolina and Georgia to appraise them for himself. "I was very impressed with what I saw," he said later, not only with how effectively they were being run but with the sincerity and commitment of the people attracted to the movement.

Rollins remembered later, "I walked out of there that night saying, 'I may have just met the next president of the United States.' " He called

Sherrie from the airport and said the same thing. "She was terribly upset, so I flew back and went to my cabin to think about it." By now the word was getting out—from Rollins himself, the Perot aides were convinced—and he was besieged with phone calls from fellow Republicans trying to talk him out of it. Jim Lake of the Bush campaign was dispatched to Rollins's hideaway in the Shenandoah Mountains to dissuade him, in vain. In the end, Rollins joined the Perot army as field general—to the continued chagrin of Sherrie Rollins, who decided she would have to resign her White House job, despite Bush's sympathetic understanding of her situation. She remained very publicly committed to his reelection.

"I had argued with her," Rollins said later, "that if they were smart, the president would say, 'Listen, this is what marriages are all about today. I've got the best Rollins, and if her idiot husband wants to go off and work for this nutcase, so be it.' He would have been a hero to every working woman in America."

The arrangement, announced at a press conference in Dallas but dribbled out first in the press and confirmed by Sherrie Rollins's resignation, was big political news. Here was Ross Perot, vehement foe of professional politicians as corrupters of the political process, hiring two of the biggest names in the business. Luce put the most positive spin on it he could. "It is very comforting to me," he said, "and I know it is very comforting to the volunteers, to know they'll have people who will be with us who have been through this before and can help us in terms of expertise."

Jordan, who had been skeptical about how it would go down with the volunteers, was pleasantly surprised. "It showed Perot had a sort of Reaganesque ability sometimes to have it both ways," he said after the campaign. "He said he was going to do it his own way, and he brings in two hacks, two hired guns, and everybody says, 'Boy, that was smart.' "

Indeed, the move brought new and instant credibility to the Perot campaign. Here were two high rollers taking a flyer with Perot, and Perot was being a realist in recognizing that his grass-roots movement had graduated to another level, requiring the help of professionals who had been down the road before. Rollins, it was true, had overseen the fairly easy reelection of an extremely popular president in a conventional campaign, but Jordan had ridden a little-known long shot into the White House, although he hadn't been able to keep him there for a second term.

The fact that Jordan was a Democrat and Rollins a Republican made the case, intentionally, that the Perot movement was a haven for the disaffected in both major parties.

At the same time, said Sal Russo, a California consultant and Rollins associate who also joined the operation in Dallas, the hiring of Jordan and Rollins brought closer press scrutiny to the campaign. "When Ed was hired and Hamilton was hired," he said, "I think the press thought, 'Well, shoot, amateur night in Dixie is getting pretty serious.' "

Bush made no immediate comment on the development, and in a subsequent news conference dodged questions on Perot. Clinton, however, said the hirings showed that Perot was "a politician like the others seeking the presidency," adding, "I'd like to know how much they were both paid to do it." Ron Brown, the Democratic party chairman, chimed in: "I think it makes a travesty of Ross Perot's claim that he's not seeking handlers and doesn't need handlers."

Perot put his new team in place one day after the publication of yet another major poll chronicling the remarkable climb of his political fortunes. The latest *Washington Post*/ABC News survey had him leading the field with 34 percent to 31 for Bush and 29 for Clinton. And the network exit polls in three major states on the final primary day of the season brought more good news for Perot: 46 percent of the Republicans surveyed in California and 33 percent of the Democrats said they would have voted for him had his name been on the primary ballots; in Ohio, 46 percent of the Democrats and 32 percent of the Republicans; in New Jersey, 35 percent of the Republicans and 29 percent of the Democrats. Jordan and Rollins appeared to be taking the reins of a runaway political horse.

Around the Perot headquarters, the atmosphere was heady and homey. Russo was taken with the innocently warm mood that prevailed. He first met Perot at a birthday party for him at the headquarters, where middle-aged "Perot girls" in patriotic costume sang a homemade Perot song and, Russo remembered, "did a dance routine right out of twenty-five years ago. It was hokey but kind of fun—Americana personified, and it controverted the idea that the era of the volunteer was over."

A story was told at the party of how a telephone worker was up in the ceiling installing a line when this little guy in a close-cropped haircut came along. "Hey, bud, would you mind passing up that wire?" the worker asked him, whereupon Ross Perot stood there and fed the line up to the worker, never identifying himself. "After the birthday party," Russo said, "I never saw that Ross Perot again."

The negative stories continued to roll off the nation's presses against the wealthy Texan. A comment on an ABC News talk show that he would not appoint homosexuals or adulterers to his cabinet got the gays upset, if not the adulterers. "I don't want anybody there that will be a point of controversy with the American people," he said, nor would it be "realistic" to lift the ban on homosexuals in the armed forces.

The Dallas Morning News reported that lawyers for Perot had gotten a Dallas judge to permit Perot security guards to search a Perot tenant's house without a warrant after the man was nine days late in paying his monthly rent of $7,500. *The Washington Post* reported Vietnamese officials claiming that Perot, a vehement critic of North Vietnam for allegedly holding American prisoners long after the Vietnam War, had later discussed the possibility of Perot investments there—a charge that particularly outraged Perot. There were stories recounting his onetime proposal for a police sweep on Dallas neighborhoods for illegal drugs, brushing aside constitutional guarantees of privacy and due process; about questionable business dealings; about hiring private eyes to sleuth on the extramarital and other activities of employees and business competitors, and even investigating his own children.

Vice President Quayle also got into the act, digging out a statement Perot had made on ABC News's *Good Morning America* about eight months earlier in which he said "Germany and Japan are winning" in world competition because "they got new constitutions" after their defeats in World War II. Addressing the conservative Federalist Society in Washington, Quayle in boosting Bush said "it would be a very bad idea to replace a genuine statesman with a temperamental tycoon who has contempt for the Constitution of the United States." And so it went.

The worst of it all came in a *Washington Post* story reporting that Perot had investigated George Bush and his sons in 1986 and informed Bush, "in what Perot portrayed as a friendly warning, that two of Bush's four sons were said to be involved in improper activities." Perot, the story said, informed Bush that "a Florida investigator told him that one son had visited a known gun smuggler." On Christmas Eve that year, it went on, "Bush sent Perot a short handwritten note defending his sons. 'They are all straight arrows,' he wrote, 'uninvolved in intrigue.' "

Bush, who up to now had restrained himself about Perot, finally lashed out. In an interview on ABC News's *20/20* show, yet another of the free airtime programs being worked by all the candidates to an unprecedented degree in this campaign, the president said of the *Post* story: "If he was having my children investigated, that is beyond the pale. . . . Leave my kids alone. . . . I am sick about it if it's true, and I think the American people will reject that kind of tactic." Quayle added: "Imagine Ross Perot having the IRS, the FBI and the CIA under his control."

Perot spokesman James Squires accused the White House of mounting "a series of hysterical attacks designed to mischaracterize Ross Perot in the public's mind," in a tactic that was "the staple of Republican presidential politics for more than a decade." Perot himself called the story "part of an election year fantasy carefully crafted by the Republicans . . . to destory my credibility." He added: "Do I run around the world hiring investigators? No . . . I'm not an investigative personality."

In any event, Jordan and Rollins were finding out that they had a candidate on their hands who may have walked the straight and narrow personally but carried a lot of baggage in his business past and in his present notions, and also was a loose cannon who went wherever he wanted whenever he wanted and said whatever he pleased to whomever he pleased. That was fine for an average citizen, but potentially disastrous for a presidential candidate whose every movement and utterance were held up for scrutiny and criticism. Perot's assurances when Jordan and Rollins signed on that he was going to listen to them and accept certain imperatives of major league campaigning were beginning to ring hollow in their ears.

"In fairness to Perot," Jordan said, contrasting his early campaigning with Jimmy Carter in advance of 1976, "we made our mistakes when nobody was watching. Carter had two years to learn the game, to be in Iowa. This guy was like he was just dropped out in a parachute in the middle of the Super Bowl and was supposed to know exactly what to say and do."

Perot would spend whole days calling reporters and editors complaining about stories that he said were unfair or untrue, frustrating Jordan and Rollins in their efforts to get decisions from him on broad operational and strategy questions vital to the effective development of the campaign. Jordan at one point told him, "Ross, you've got a powerful message. You're on a message track and you've launched it, and at the end of the campaign, if you've stayed on that message track, you'll be elected president. Every day when you get out you should think about nothing but staying on your message. Every day, when everybody else gets out, they're gonna try to drag you off of the message. The Republicans are going to do it, the press is going to. If you stay on it, you win. If you don't stay on it, you lose." Perot, Jordan said, "understood that in the abstract, but he was just incapable of doing it."

One problem was that Perot was enthralled with television. He would make his own appointments, then fly off without telling Jordan or Rollins where he was going or what he was doing. Sometimes they would flick on a television set and see him there in midinterview, generously sprinkling pithy one-liners on a variety of subjects over the airwaves, all the while insisting that he could not sound-bite an answer to this or that question of substance.

On one occasion, he showed up for the NBC News *Today* program for an interview with Katie Couric and stayed for the full two hours, getting himself twisted in knots over his notion of having affluent older Americans like himself give up their Social Security and Medicare benefits. He finally insisted he was only talking about asking them to do so voluntarily. He said he'd gladly do so himself, and also work without pay if elected president, to which a caller replied: "Well, you can afford to." This was hardly staying on the message that could win for him.

Through all this, Perot insisted that only he could speak for himself. He bristled whenever Rollins, a political games-player, would go on television and talk strategy. Perot would call Rollins, Russo said, and ask him: "How do you know what I think unless you ask me? How can you answer any questions?"

Perot got particularly exercised, Russo recalled, when Rollins went on television and effectively disinvited Jesse Jackson from any involvement in the Perot effort. Jackson at the time was talking to Perot on the phone in what Rollins saw as an effort to use a relationship with Perot as leverage on Clinton, who was largely cold-shouldering him. Rollins,

Russo said, "drove a stake in Jesse Jackson's heart, when he believed, I think correctly, Jackson was just using Perot as a stick to beat up Clinton, to get things." Rollins told Jackson, Russo said, that the Perot campaign "was not seeking his support. It completely chopped Jesse's legs off and completely wiped out his leverage with Clinton." All this, however, went over Perot's head and he blamed Rollins for driving away a helpful source of support.

Perot's idea of press relations, Rollins said, was to do all the talking himself and to have a bunch of what Perot called "sweet young things" dealing with reporters because reporters "wouldn't be mean to them."

Through all this, the public focus continued to remain on the petition drives, which were gaining ballot access for Perot in state after state. The progress provided a ready catalyst for moving Perot around the country, but always before wildly partisan crowds of volunteers emulating the Austin rally by personally presenting the requisite thousands of signatures, followed by an inspirational thank-you speech from the man himself. Over the course of a week in mid-June, he flew from Sacramento and Irvine, California, to Denver, then Boston and Annapolis, where a flotilla of private boats accompanied him to the site of a dockside speech. Reporters wanting to cover this odyssey were obliged to scramble on their own for commercial aircraft because the unconventional campaign of Ross Perot did not have provision for the conventional press plane.

Perot was greeted like a savior by his adoring followers, but behind all the cheering Jordan and Rollins began to note that the negative stories and other allegations against their candidate were beginning to take their toll. A *New York Times*/CBS News poll had ominous portents. While Perot remained in a virtual tie with Bush, 32 percent for the president, 30 for Perot and 24 for Clinton, the percentage of voters who had a negative opinion of the Texas billionaire had more than doubled in the last six weeks. The survey found specifically that Perot's suggestion that well-off older Americans give up Social Security and Medicare benefits to help cut the federal deficit had only 10 percent support, even among Perot backers.

"The numbers on top still looked pretty good but the internal numbers started to look terrible," Jordan said later. "Perot just looked at the top, but you'd look under it and you'd see that the negatives had tripled in three or four weeks. Underneath we were cruising toward a big drop."

One of Jordan's charts spelled it out. "Perot has dominated the political press for the last thirty days," it said. "The pressure to define Perot has increased proportionately." While "Perot has worn well," the chart said, "there will be a day of reckoning" if the campaign failed to shift gears.

"There was just an enormous question mark [about Perot] all through May and June," Jordan said later. "This guy had come like a comet out of the sky. We were in that bubble for about thirty or forty days and people were asking, 'Who in hell is this guy?' "

As the end of June approached, Jordan and Rollins understood that unless some steps were taken to stem Perot's slippage and particularly to define him in more definite and favorable terms, the criticism of him, which he and his loyalists were convinced was motivated by the Bush campaign, could destroy his chances to be elected. They worked up elaborate remedies for the decline. All they had to do was sell them to Perot. They would soon learn, however, that it would take a salesman of Perot's own talent to close the deal.

PICKING THE SOUTHERN LOCK

When President Bush in May 1991 was discovered to have an irregular heartbeat after a day of considerable physical exertion, and the public spotlight inevitably swung onto Vice President Quayle, Bill Clinton was among the first Democratic leaders to sound the alarm. "As the weeks and months go by," Clinton said, "he [Bush] will have to answer to the American people about this issue: does he believe, and does he believe again in 1992, that the vice president is the best person in America to succeed him if he's unable to continue?"

At the time, Clinton, as governor of Arkansas, had not yet disclosed that he would seek the presidency in 1992, but the issue of presidential succession was on his mind—unlike most Americans. Although lip service often was paid to the importance of having the person "a heartbeat away" from the presidency who was best qualified to assume that awesome responsibility, and presidential nominees always said it was a prime, or *the* prime consideration in their selection of a running mate, history suggested it was too often otherwise.

Voters certainly did not seem to take the matter seriously into their thinking on how they would vote in a presidential election, the best illustration being their support of Bush after his surprise choice of Dan Quayle. If they had, they would have punished Bush for selecting a running mate they told pollsters repeatedly and emphatically they did not believe was qualified to sit behind the great desk in the Oval Office.

When the time came for Clinton to choose the 1992 Democratic vice presidential nominee, he obviously had all the customary political factors in mind—characteristics that would help him get elected. But according to all those who dealt with him in his preparations and deliberations for making the choice, the matter of possible succession to the presidency was critical from the start. His campaign chairman, Mickey Kantor, said later that when Clinton in his presence privately charged Warren Christopher with the principal role in the search for a running mate, he instructed him to use "one criterion only—'If something happened to me, who would make the best president of the United States?'"

Clinton, Kantor recalled, told Christopher, "'You pick the best person. Give me the best people.' He was going to pick the person, [but] we started out with a fairly lengthy list and went through an extremely detailed process." Aware that five of the previous nine vice presidents—Truman, Johnson, Nixon, Ford and Bush—had gone on to become president, Kantor said, Clinton recognized that he could be selecting a future president and took that responsibility seriously.

One reason, Begala suggested later, was that Clinton was particularly mindful of the matter of mortality, his father having died at such a relatively young age—only twenty-nine when he perished in a car accident just months before the birth of his son Bill. "It sounds too much like psychobabble," another insider said later, "but when you lose your father like that, I would suspect that as a dimension to your approach to this kind of question, you think of your own mortality."

Clinton's press secretary, Dee Dee Myers, said the candidate also wanted someone "who had experience where he was weak," such as in foreign affairs and Washington, and who "shared his world view" as a new Democrat. But his "overriding concern," she said, "was, he was not going to be a nominee who picked Dan Quayle. He thought that that was just a crass political decision. He blamed Bush totally. Most people sort of thought, 'Oh, Quayle, what an idiot,' but Clinton looked at it and thought, 'Oh, Bush, what a dumb choice,' because he sees everything in the context of history—everything—about the presidency, and for him it was an irresponsible decision on Bush's part to choose this man who [in Clinton's mind] was clearly incapable of being president.''

Clinton himself, in an interview later, was more diplomatic in discussing Bush's choice of Quayle, but it all came down to the same thing. ''I thought he [Bush] seemed to have acted rather quickly and to have been motivated by political concerns—more about categories than substance, the kind of thing they always accuse the Democrats of,'' Clinton said. ''Quayle was from the Midwest, he [Bush] was from someplace else, and Quayle was from the conservative wing of the party, Quayle was part of the new generation. It was something that looked good but wasn't. . . . The president picked him because the categories seemed right, even if the first question [was he qualified to be president?] didn't get asked or answered.

''My determination was, let's ask the first question first. And I looked over dozens of names of people, dozens. When Christopher was managing this process for me, I always said, 'I've got to have somebody that if I drop dead, would be a good president. That is the first criterion.' Then I wanted somebody who really understood this time, and I wanted someone who was generally in harmony with the direction that I had staked out, not somebody who would agree with me on everything, but generally in harmony with the direction. And finally, if I could find him, I wanted someone who had some strengths or experience that was different from my own.''

Clinton's observation at the time of Bush's irregular heartbeat reflected that view and, according to Kantor, he also believed that the process used in selecting Quayle and too many other recent running mates, Democratic as well as Republican, had not been ''dignified'' in terms of the treatment of prospective choices. It was not that the choices themselves were not good ones—Carter's selection of Mondale and Dukakis's choice of Senator Lloyd Bentsen of Texas were considered particularly distinguished—but Clinton was not enthusiastic about the manner in which they were picked.

Early in the process, Kantor said, he, Clinton and Christopher all read up on the history of vice presidential selection and Clinton concluded that the process itself had to be ''done correctly,'' that it should be "dignified and should be confidential. . . . The whole experience of [picking] vice presidents affected him, and obviously Quayle was part of that process."

Ironically, the view that the procedure for selecting a running mate should be carried out in utmost privacy was also held by Bush in 1988 when he picked Quayle. Aides said he thought the very public selection processes used by such recent Democratic presidential nominees as Jimmy Carter in 1976, Walter Mondale in 1984 and even Michael Dukakis in 1988, wherein they summoned or met the persons under consideration in the glare of television lights, had been "demeaning." Consequently, Bush was determined not to put the Republicans he was considering as his running mate through anything like that. So he never personally interviewed any of them about the job, and the result was Dan Quayle.

Clinton by contrast always planned to interview personally the individuals whom he would most seriously consider, but insisted that the process of drawing up an initial long list and winnowing it down would be done in the greatest privacy, in deference to all those whose names were thrown into the pot. And when that list had been winnowed, he instructed that those on the short list be afforded special privacy and dignity in how they were treated.

About the only presidential nominee since World War II who openly acknowledged that he didn't apply the "best qualified" yardstick in making his choice of a running mate was Republican Barry Goldwater in 1964, who told reporters he had chosen a feisty, extremely partisan but pedestrian upstate New York congressman, William E. Miller, because "he drives Lyndon Johnson nuts." In the end, however, most nominees select the person calculated to provide the most help in winning the election, or risk the least harm.

The operative axiom, in fact, is that a running mate does not necessarily have to help the ticket, but he or she should not hurt it. In 1968, when Richard Nixon was casting about for a ticket mate, his pollsters found that all prominent Republicans tested would be a drag, and that Nixon ran strongest alone. The result was his choice of a relative nobody, Governor Spiro T. Agnew of Maryland (who didn't remain a nobody for long).

Clinton was not, obviously, blind to all the conventional factors of geography, age, ideology and the rest that traditionally went into the choice of a running mate. But a measure of how subordinate they were in his thinking was the fact that his political advisers, who ate, drank and slept such calculations, were given a minor role in the selection process. In fact, according to Greenberg, one of their specific recommendations was ignored—that Clinton not choose a fellow Southerner to run with him.

"The political team," Greenberg said later, "was asked for a general memorandum on the criteria that they would recommend on selection. Mandy had conversations around with the consultants on our thinking on it, and drafted a memo." But that memo, according to Greenberg, included "a specific provision that [the choice] not be a Southern candidate." He remembered, he said, "specifically putting [in] a footnote, because I dissented from [that provision] because I thought that Gore was the right choice."

Greenberg said he and his fellow consultants "never had a unified view of who the choice ought to be, nor were they an integral part of the decision-making process. There was a general memorandum that went to Clinton and went to Christopher, and Clinton individually conferred with us on our thinking about it." As a political junkie himself, Clinton would "sometimes run names by" the political types, Greenberg said, "but the campaign team was not part of the ongoing process of selecting the VP."

Assisting selection task force members Christopher, Kunin and Jordan was Mark Gearan, a 1988 Dukakis campaign aide who later became director of the National Governors Association, and who in that capacity had become a close aide to Clinton, then chairman of that association.

Although, Gearan said, "there certainly was a school of thought that you needed to broaden the age, geographic, ideological, religious element of the ticket," Clinton in his instructions "took those subjects off the table." As a result, the long list of about forty names that was put together by the task force was not limited to prominent elected officials. Some business leaders and academics were also on it, Gearan said.

When the process began in early June, Christopher personally solicited the views of about ten to fifteen senators and some House leaders, and Clinton talked to many of them and a number of governors by phone, Gearan said, always keeping his own counsel. "I think he asked everybody in sight, from pollsters to chambermaids, what they thought," Grunwald said, "but never saying, 'Well, here's what I'm thinking.' "

At the same time, another team of legal experts headed by Washington lawyers Richard Moe and Victoria Radd set about compiling research on every phase of the public records of the individuals on the long list, on a strictly confidential basis. Moe, who had been chief of staff to Walter Mondale when he was vice president and had become an expert in the vice presidential selection process, had written papers for the Democratic National Committee on the subject and was one of the first people with whom Christopher conferred. Summaries of the public records of those on the long list were written and given to Christopher, who reported on them to Clinton. This process had become standard practice in both parties at least since 1972, when Senator Thomas Eagleton of Missouri failed to inform party nominee George McGovern that he had undergone shock treatments for depression, and was dropped from the Democratic ticket.

By mid-June, the list had been reduced basically to five names— Senators Al Gore of Tennessee, Bob Graham of Florida, Bob Kerrey of Nebraska and Harris Wofford of Pennsylvania and Representative Lee Hamilton of Indiana, who had won national prominence as an even-handed chairman during the televised Iran-contra hearings.

Another set of lawyer teams was assigned to the vetting process, also an outgrowth of the Eagleton affair. One team was formed for each of those on the short list, who submitted answers to a questionnaire, after which the lawyers checked for anything in that prospective candidate's background that might be a disqualifying factor. Reports again went to Clinton by way of Christopher. No political operatives were involved in the vetting, one of the lead lawyers said later, and "the process was not driven by political considerations."

According to Greenberg, a sixth name was also in the mix for a time—Governor Cuomo—but he was never vetted by the lawyers. "I know a message was delivered to Clinton that Cuomo was interested," he said later. Traditional considerations were fed into the assessment, he said, such as "whether New York and New England would come across [for Clinton] in any case and what the cost would be elsewhere, particularly in the South, if he were on the ticket." Also, the pollster said, there was sentiment for a "nonpolitical" choice, and Cuomo's selection would have been seen widely as one of political ticket balancing—an Easterner, a liberal, a Catholic with a Southerner, a moderate, a Baptist.

Cuomo said in an interview later that although he had "a couple of conversations" with Christopher, he "never" indicated any interest in being on the ticket. He brushed aside reports at the time that he had hung up abruptly when Christopher began describing the thorough vetting process in terms Cuomo saw as reflecting on his ethnicity. "There never was any objection to any investigation," Cuomo said. "If that had been the question, my answer would have been, 'I'm certain you have done negative research [on potential rivals for the nomination]' because they did, 'and I'm certain you included me.' So, in my case, it would be easier, because you wouldn't have to go through that [vetting] process."

Gore was the first to be interviewed by Clinton, under circumstances worthy, Gearan said, of "a bad detective movie." In keeping with Clinton's insistence on total secrecy, Gearan engineered an elaborate scenario to avoid the news media and it worked. Clinton was in Washington for the National Education Association convention in mid-June and was staying at the Capitol Hilton downtown. Gearan rented a room two floors below Clinton's where no reporters or staff people were staying, under his wife's maiden name, Mary Herlihy.

Late that night, with Clinton in his suite and reporters and cameramen keeping watch in the hotel lobby, Gearan in a rented car with driver picked Gore up at the Senate. They drove to the hotel's service entrance, where a door was quickly opened and closed as Gore was whisked out of the car and taken by freight elevator to "the Herlihy Room." It was now about eleven o'clock, and Gore, a morning person, was getting weary while Clinton, a night person, was just getting warmed up. He walked down the vacant stairwell two flights for the meeting.

Gore had been told it would probably last about an hour, but it went on for two and a half hours in the living room, while Gearan and Bruce Lindsey, Clinton's longtime personal aide and friend from Arkansas, waited in an adjoining bedroom, watched television and periodically glanced at their watches. Clinton, Gearan said he learned later, was very impressed by a man he had not known well before. Gearan and the driver took the exhausted senator from Tennessee back to Capitol Hill.

About a week later, Clinton interviewed three more finalists, one at a time, in "the Herlihy Room" at the same hotel—Graham, Hamilton and Wofford, each for about an hour, with the same cloak-and-dagger scenario engineered by Gearan. The press stakeout had grown in size and frenzy and Hamilton compared the stealth entry to an underground meeting he once had with Libyan strongman Muammar Qaddafi.

At one point John King, the Associated Press reporter, checked Gearan's shoes, because he had spied a pair of shoes getting out of the car as the service entrance door was closing and hoped to make an identification of the mystery arrival. On another occasion, a camera crew in a van chased Gearan's car, tried to film the occupants through the closed window and reported later that it wasn't clear whether the person in the front seat was Christopher or a woman. Which caused Gearan, the occupant, to wonder: "Do I look like a woman, or Warren Christopher? I'm not sure."

The fifth finalist, Kerrey, went to Little Rock from Nebraska for a late-night interview with Clinton that lasted about an hour and a half. Contrary to some reports, Clinton aides said later, the presidential nominee gave serious consideration to Kerrey, and the defeated presidential candidate said he was satisfied that was so. He wasn't lusting after the job, he said after the election, but "I thought I could help him win. I still believe I could have, much in the way that Al did, and in the end, I don't think as much as Al did. He asked me in Little Rock who I'd recommend and I recommended Gore."

While he could have projected the same generational appeal on the ticket with Clinton, Kerrey, who is single, said, "it would have been Bill, Hillary and Bob, instead of Bill and Hillary and Bob and his wife." Clinton never told him that was a factor, he said, "but I'd be surprised if it wasn't," though not a major one.

It was now July and the nominee was close to making his decision. In the final week before he reached it, Greenberg said, he along with Carville and Stephanopoulos were called in by the nominee, but by that time the short list had been settled on without much influence from the political arm of the campaign. The virtue of an all-Southern ticket in Texas, where Perot was now threatening Bush in a state critical to the president's reelection chances, was obvious, although the campaign strategists insisted to the end that that consideration was not prominent in the selection.

Several days before the announcement, Clinton summoned Gearan from Washington to Little Rock to start preparations for it. Continuing to carry out Clinton's insistence that the whole matter of vice presidential selection be handled with dignity and style, Gearan pulled together a group of Democratic operatives who had been involved in it in the past— Eli Segal from the McGovern campaign, Dick Moe and Mike Berman from the Mondale campaign and John Sasso from the Dukakis campaign—to work out the details. Then Christopher at Clinton's direction flew to Gore's home in Carthage, Tennessee, for a final review.

It so happened that Graham, planning to seek reelection to the Senate in November if he wasn't picked by Clinton, had to file the next day, July 9, or forget it. So Clinton had to make up his mind that night. Christopher, Lindsey and Gearan had dinner at the Capitol Hotel in Little Rock and then drove to the executive mansion in Lindsey's red convertible, with the top down, causing another press frenzy as reporters and cameramen besieged the task force chief for some inkling as to the choice. Gearan said later he still didn't know who it was going to be, but he had a fair idea.

In a living room, Christopher again reviewed the bidding on the finalists before Bill and Hillary Clinton, Gearan and Lindsey. The conversation soon settled on Gore, and after some more talk, Clinton simply said, "Okay, that's it, let's give him a call." He got up and went over to a phone, whereupon Lindsey suggested that the historic moment ought to be captured on film. So Clinton waited while Lindsey got Chelsea's Instamatic or some other family camera and snapped the scene. Then Gearan took another picture as Clinton got through to Carthage, where he heard the senator's wife, Tipper, on the other end of the line. He said he hoped he hadn't awakened her, but he had to. Gore was on the phone in a flash in another room, where staff aides were taking another picture.

Clinton told him he had thought about it and, as Gearan remembered, said, "I think you'd be an excellent choice and I'd like you to run with me." There was a brief pause and then Clinton flashed a thumbs-up sign to the others in the room. Clinton told his new running mate that Gearan would be flying to Tennessee early the next morning to bring the Gores to Little Rock for a press conference the next day.

In the end, Greenberg said, one strong point in Gore's favor in his view was that because Clinton "did not come out of the primaries well defined, the Gore choice had the advantage of reinforcing the image as young, moderate, smart, Southern, and an antipolitical choice—a choice that would seem to be nonpolitical in its motivation, because it wasn't the typical balancing.''

Hamilton, for example, would have seemed "too conventional a choice," Greenberg said, "and we felt we had to do something unconventional. Given our relative inexperience, we couldn't do something that would make us look like we were jeopardizing national security, but we did need to do something that said, 'This ticket is different.' Hamilton would have been a good choice, but it would not have created excitement around the ticket. It wouldn't have sent the message that these were a new kind of leaders." Begala agreed. He called the selection of Gore "the defining decision of the campaign."

Grunwald argued later against the notion that Clinton was motivated by a "Southern strategy" to cut into Bush's base in Dixie, especially with Perot still in the picture at the time. "My sense is he did it because they [Clinton and Gore] share an attitude about public service that he felt comfortable with," she said. "And Gore is as serious about the issues he cares about [as Clinton is]." Dee Dee Myers said Clinton mused to her the day before the announcement that Gore would be a "risky" choice, and she gleaned from that comment that "he liked the risk factor about it, that it wasn't a political decision, that this was the person who met his criteria, and that people couldn't say this was the obvious, politically correct choice."

Clinton to the end, indeed, clung to his insistence that his overriding consideration was that the person chosen be the one best qualified to assume the presidency if anything were to cut short his own tenure, and that he was committed to meet his responsibility for assuring qualified presidential succession.

By all his stated criteria, Clinton said later, "I thought Gore was the best. Even though there was not the age difference that a lot of people thought I needed, or the regional difference that a lot of people thought I needed, or the ideological difference a lot of people thought I needed . . . it turned out to be a great choice."

Among the chores still to be completed was notification of the finalists who had not been selected. Clinton called each of them personally the next morning, avoiding the fiasco that Dukakis had suffered four years earlier when Jesse Jackson learned from a reporter in an airport that Bentsen, not himself, had been picked as the Democratic vice presidential nominee. "There are some things," Dukakis campaign alumnus Gearan said with a grin, "you learn from history."

The introduction of the youthful, joyous Bill and Hillary and Al and Tipper team the next day outside the governor's mansion in Little Rock was a smash hit. Clinton said of his choice: "The man standing beside me today has what it takes to lead this nation from the day we take office." That was something George Bush would be hard-pressed to say about his selection, if indeed he decided to keep Dan Quayle on the Republican ticket at the approaching Republican convention.

Clinton said later that his selection of Gore "had a lot to do with my election. I think in a funny way it was one of those decisions that was bigger than you might have thought. . . . I didn't sense it was going to be as electric as it was until we walked out the back of the governor's mansion at the announcement, and I looked at him and Tipper and their kids, and Hillary and Chelsea, and for the first time it just hit me like a bolt; this is going to be an awesomely popular thing. I didn't really know it until then, but somehow it made a statement to the American people about me. I took them seriously because I took the job [of vice president] seriously, and I really picked someone that was smart and accomplished and strong and even younger than I was.

"It worked and I don't know why it worked, but it was another one of those things. Maybe '92 was a year where all these counterintuitive decisions worked. Maybe it will never be that way again, but my gut feeling is that it always will work for a nominee for president to pick a person that he believes would be a superb president and in whom he has confidence, because the relationship becomes apparent to the American people. It sort of resonates, it has a harmony, it has a feeling. People get it."

From start to finish, the process of selecting the 1992 Democratic vice presidential nominee had been precisely what Clinton had ordered— orderly, dignified and confidential. The serendipity of the choice itself was not fully appreciated at the time, but that would come before long.

NEW YORK: SETTING A TONE

Although the choice of Al Gore had been politically invigorating, the thousands of Democrats who began to gather in New York for the party's national convention had valid reasons to be uneasy.

For a generation, conventions had not served their original purpose—making a decision on a nominee for president. That decision now was foreordained by the results of primaries, precinct caucuses and state conventions in all fifty states. But a convention was still a valuable ritual to the party, quite beyond the exposure the ticket would be given by four days of press coverage. It was an opportunity for Democrats from different regions and different backgrounds to find the political commonalities that bound them together and to agree to tolerate their differences.

A Democrat from Montana could learn from a delegate from New Jersey, for example, why it was important for their party to put itself on record for more jobs in the inner cities—and the Montanan could explain to his fellow Democrat why a gasoline tax is political poison in the Far West.

Quite beyond that, the conventions were revealing exercises in defining the differences between the two political parties. Anyone who watched both conventions inevitably would be struck by the contrast between the white middle-class homogeneity of the Republican delegates and the extraordinary diversity of those who called themselves Democrats. And anyone who listened would be similarly struck by the differences between the parties in the issues they chose to emphasize and the positions they adopted as part of their dogma.

Most important politically, the conventions were supposed to send the nominees for president and vice president into the general election campaign with the cheers of the delegates ringing in their ears, and the attention of the voters focused positively on what they had to say. The three major television networks—ABC, CBS and NBC—had decided against gavel-to-gavel coverage in favor of an hour or so of prime time each night, arguing that the news value of the conventions merited only that much attention, but raising the obvious suspicion they knew where the money was. The full conventions still would be available through CNN, PBS and C-SPAN, nonetheless, and the number of households with cable television now exceeded those that did not have that option. Most major newspapers also provided saturation coverage of even the most banal and predictable events.

For the Democrats, however, conventions seemed too often to be minefields—occasions on which the party compromised its nominees rather than helped them. The most chaotic had been the 1968 Democratic convention in Chicago that nominated Hubert Horatio Humphrey of Minnesota—but only after four days of fiercely angry protests in the streets by demonstrators against the war in Vietnam, tumult within the convention hall itself and ultimately a crackdown on the protesters that an investigating commission later described, accurately, as a "police riot."

Humphrey and his running mate, then Senator Edmund S. Muskie of Maine, eventually recovered to the point that Humphrey lost to Republican Richard Nixon by only a whisker. But it was impossible to believe that the ugly images from that convention had not made Humphrey's campaign far more difficult than it otherwise would have been. Indeed, that conventional wisdom had become so deeply ingrained in the Democratic Party that it had not held another national convention in Chicago despite all of the city's attractions as a site for any political celebration.

Four years later, in Miami Beach in 1972, the Democrats indulged their new fervor for small "d" democracy to the point that they projected a picture of a party totally lacking in discipline. The most convincing proof was the fact that the nominee, George McGovern, was not introduced to make his acceptance speech until well after 2 A.M. EDT, late enough to be past bedtime for most voters in all the mainland time zones. McGovern then compounded the political felony of the disorderly convention by choosing a vice presidential nominee, then Senator Thomas Eagleton of Missouri, whose electric shock therapy fell so far short of political correctness that Eagleton eventually had to be replaced on the ticket.

In 1980 the convention voted to nominate President Jimmy Carter for a second term over the challenge of Senator Edward Kennedy of Massachusetts, once again ratifying the results of the primaries. But the most memorable television images of the convention were those of the hapless Carter pursuing Kennedy around the podium on the final night trying to arrange the traditional tableau of victor and vanquished, hands clasped and held aloft in a show of political unity—what politicians call "the armpit shot."

Four years later the convention in San Francisco that ratified the nomination of Walter Mondale was electrified by his choice of then Representative Geraldine Ferraro of New York to be the first woman nominated for a place on a major party ticket. But the convention was marred repeatedly by internal bickering—one of the memorable images this time was of black delegates booing Andrew Young, one of the certifiably genuine heroes of the civil rights movement. And Mondale used his acceptance speech to indulge in some of the most politically destructive candor in the annals of American politics by telling the nation that, yes, if he was elected he would raise taxes.

This time the man responsible, Democratic National Chairman Ron Brown, was determined that this was going to be a different kind of convention. He had spent three years bringing the party apparatus from the depths of the defeat in 1988, plotting and cajoling to get an early de facto decision on a nominee for 1992 and preparing a campaign plan to give the nominee a quick start. And along the way he had built his own reputation to the point that no one thought of him as "Kennedy's man" or "Jesse's man" but as a political leader of rare skill and sophistication.

He wasn't going to fritter all that away with some disaster in Madison Square Garden.

What Brown understood from the party's twelve years out of power and from the way the 1992 primaries and caucuses had played out was that his fellow Democrats were energized by the possibility of recapturing the White House. And, given the condition of the economy, they were not in a humor to argue endlessly over how many ideological nuances could be stuffed on the head of a pin. Brown was prepared to tolerate dissent but he was not willing to allow it to spoil his convention.

Many of Brown's fellow Democrats—the activists and professionals and hangers-on as well as the delegates—were more tempered in their optimism. They had watched the opinion polls showing Bill Clinton running third behind George Bush and Ross Perot, with his support threatening to drop below 20 percent and his negatives still at a dangerous level. They were aware that the turnout in the primaries after New Hampshire had been consistently and conspicuously low, a potential warning signal for the general election, when any Democrat profits from a high level of voter participation. And, most of all, they were still wondering if there were not some ''other shoe'' about Clinton's personal life that might drop during the general election campaign and cost them the opportunity that seemed to be there. The young governor of Arkansas had shown himself to be a remarkably tenacious candidate, but he clearly had not resolved all the doubts about himself.

There was, however, another current running through the Democrats who gathered in New York that weekend—pragmatism. They, too, had understood, if perhaps dimly at first, the message of the primaries. They recognized that this was not a time to argue about ideological purity. They were, after all, about to nominate a candidate who favored the death penalty, had a mixed record at best on the environment and talked about the ''responsibility'' that welfare recipients must demonstrate. The weakness of George Bush, they understood, was his failure to come to grips with the serious concerns of the electorate on domestic problems. If they could get through this convention without making a hash of things, perhaps Clinton could prove he had the ability to provide a convincing alternative.

One clear measure of the difference in this Democratic convention was the fact there were so few sticky problems to be resolved. Even the protests in the streets were minor league. Militant blacks like Al Sharpton and Gus Savage marching outside might be worth a few paragraphs or a few seconds on the local news in New York and Chicago, but not on the networks.

The most pressing problem was what to do about Jesse Jackson, who may have lacked the delegates to be a factor on the convention floor but remained an important party leader whom Ron Brown was determined to enlist—under his own terms. And the basic rule was that no one who had not endorsed the ticket would be allowed to speak at the convention. "At that point, believe it or not, I thought I was in charge," Brown said later.

In the days leading up to the convention, Brown held several conversations with Jackson. They had been friends for years and often political allies. Four years earlier Brown had served as Jackson's convention manager, so he had the credentials to make the case. The message was plain: You've got to be inside and the only way to be inside is to endorse the candidate. It's the best thing for you and for the party. "He knew that I was real clear on how to be inside rather than outside," Brown recalled.

But the civil rights leader also knew that he held few high cards. "He didn't have 1,200 delegates [as in 1988]. . . . There were no options there. It wasn't that hard a sell," Brown said.

Hard sell or not, Brown was credited with defusing a potentially serious problem. As George Stephanopoulos put it later, "The single best decision we made, one of them was, 'you only speak if you endorse.' It was the best rule we ever had. . . . It was easy, it was a one-liner. . . . [Brown] was able to do that piece of business and it was a masterful job. It made sure it wasn't a traditional Democratic convention."

Jackson said later there never was any specific demand from Brown that he endorse Clinton as a price for a place on the convention schedule. "That was not the truth," Jackson said. "The opposite of that took place. There were no preconditions." He said Brown called on him at his Rainbow Coalition office in downtown Washington twice in the days leading up to the convention, on each occasion discussing possible times for his speech. Jackson said he "remained noncommittal" on whether he would endorse Clinton but that Brown understood that he, Jackson, had no intention of giving a convention speech that would damage the party. Whatever the details of those conversations, however, it was clear from

Brown's repeated public statements that Jackson was aware of the prime requirement for qualifying for the speaking program and chose to meet it.

Jackson made a point of endorsing the "ticket" rather than Clinton specifically, and of doing it on his own television show on the Saturday night before the convention opened. And appearing on NBC's *Meet the Press* the following morning, he was still complaining that Clinton was trying to distance himself from some elements of the Democratic coalition, obviously meaning blacks and himself. "I think at this stage that pushoff has insulted and infuriated a lot of people," he said. But whether Jackson acknowledged it or not, the critical requirement had been met. Jackson was more or less on board, and it had been accomplished without Clinton paying public obeisance to him.

Then there was the matter of handling Governor Robert Casey of Pennsylvania, an adamant opponent of abortion rights who had been preaching all year that the Democratic Party's commitment to choice was offensive to those Democrats who disagreed, and destructive politics as well. But Casey had irked Ron Brown during the platform hearings when he insisted on characterizing the party position as "abortion on demand"—thus adopting the inflammatory language of the most extreme conservative opponents of abortion rights. Now Casey was having daily press conferences pressing his demand that he be given a place on the speaking program to present his dissent.

But the Pennsylvania governor, although the head of his state's delegation, had not endorsed Bill Clinton so Brown simply shut him out on that basis. The Republicans quickly complained that Brown's "gag rule" was stifling dissent in his own party, but if many delegates were upset, it was never apparent. Even within the Pennsylvania delegation, there were leading Democrats impatient with Casey and anxious to get on with the business at hand.

At one point Brown tried to reach Casey over the telephone in his delegation on the floor, hoping to find some formula to end the impasse. But when that attempt failed, Brown never followed through, a lapse he said later was a "mistake." But the party chairman had a sense of proportion about Casey's complaint. "It was getting old, really," he said.

The controversy that received the most attention from the press was probably the most artificial—the demand from Jerry Brown and his rabid followers that the defeated candidate be allowed to address the convention. In fact, Brown was always entitled to speak because his name was going to be put into nomination, and the rules allowed him to use that time to be heard. What Ron Brown would not give him, however, was a formal place on the program with the other defeated competitors for the nomination—Paul Tsongas, Tom Harkin and Bob Kerrey. They had endorsed Clinton so they were entitled. So was Governor L. Douglas Wilder of Virginia, who had gone along after appearing to be flirting with a defection to Ross Perot. But Jerry Brown had not, so he would not be given the same opportunity. It was that simple.

The former California governor characteristically milked the situation for all it was worth, holding media events such as a brief visit to a soup kitchen in Spanish Harlem the day before the convention opened. He sneered at the demand for an endorsement as "enforced uniformity" and insisted it would be no more than a "verbal fig leaf." On the floor at the opening Monday night session, his supporters chanted "Let Jerry Speak!" and at one point rushed toward the podium as if to take it over. The disruption was so noisy that at one point the following night, Ron Brown turned over one of his functions, as presiding officer, to Representative Nancy Pelosi of California so that he would not be there to evoke more chants.

Jerry Brown also had produced what he modestly called a "humility agenda"—the idea of "Jerry Brown" and "humility" together was mind-boggling. He wanted the party to adopt, as part of the convention rules, calling on members of Congress to return their pay raises, surrender many of their perks and, presumably, solve the basic problem of money corrupting American politics. But Brown didn't have the votes to change either the platform or the rules, and Ron Brown had devised the floor schedule in a way that would minimize the exposure given to this lonely dissenter.

But the press abhors a news vacuum and, lacking any real story, reporters and camera crews pursued the Jerry Brown protest, forcing Ron Brown and some agents of the Clinton campaign to try to reach an agreement that would elicit the California Democrat's endorsement and give him a formal place on the program. In retrospect, some of them thought Jerry Brown would have liked to make such an agreement but was unable to control his own supporters enough to make a commitment that could stick.

Ron Brown, once again taking the lead in dealing with an imposing ego, held several conversations with Jerry Brown and some of the ostensible leaders of his campaign, but without success. "There was no decision-making process in that campaign," he said later. Others had a similar experience. "His supporters were so riled up, I think it was hard for him to pull back," James Carville recalled. At the same time, he said, Brown "didn't want the dance to end."

Moreover, the would-be negotiators were having a difficult time even determining just what Jerry Brown was seeking.

"We were a little bit like the press," Carville said. "We never knew exactly what they were thinking there because it was like the Oklahoma weather. Every fifteen minutes you talk to them it was somebody else and something different. But clearly the thing was that we weren't going to make any deals." Or, as Stephanopoulos put it, "Jerry couldn't figure out how to do it . . . he couldn't figure out the politics of his own people."

Brown told us later, however, that he had made specific requests directly to Clinton in a telephone conversation of what it would take to win his endorsement. He wanted the $100 limit on contributions and the prohibition of political action committee money included in the party platform, he said, which would have then given him "a rationale" for the endorsement. He said he understood as a practical matter that Congress probably would not enact such legislation, but Clinton "didn't even offer a carrot. They didn't want to give my candidacy any credibility."

When Brown did finally speak, as he was nominated early Wednesday evening, he offered his by now familiar attack on "the influence of power and money" without any endorsement of his party's ticket, although he did promise to "fight for this party." But now that the "controversy" was over and there was no "story" left, the speech was given the scant press attention the entire episode had deserved.

Jerry Brown had brought something new and entirely different to the 1992 campaign with his $100 limit on campaign contributions and his 800 telephone number. And he had attracted some support among those most alienated from the system, many of them young people who didn't know about his history of reinventing himself for every new situation.

But he had also left such a bad taste in so many Democratic mouths as to raise doubts that he would ever have substantial influence in his party again.

Meanwhile, the convention offered a program designed to send the clear message that the Democratic Party of 1992 was a different party from what it had been, and its nominee truly "a different kind of Democrat," independent of the constituency groups—the "special interests," according to the Republicans—and committed to middle-class Americans worried about their jobs and health care. There were all the usual Democratic touches of political correctness; one night the benediction was offered in English and then in Navajo. But the first priority clearly was projecting an image that would not repel independents and Reagan Democrats watching in their homes across the nation.

Of the three keynote speeches, only one seemed to rouse the audience. Former Representative Barbara Jordan was as impressive as always in terms of her rhetoric but she never mentioned Bill Clinton. And Senator Bill Bradley, back in the arena in which he had played ten years as a star of the New York Knicks, never managed to capture the full attention of the delegates.

The most compelling and intriguing keynote came from Governor Zell Miller of Georgia, written in concert with Clinton campaign advisers, including his old friend Paul Begala. Miller used conventionally partisan tough language about George Bush and the Republican Party: "For twelve years the Republicans have dealt in cynicism and skepticism. They have mastered the art of division and diversion. And they have robbed us of our hope." And he took the convention's first open shot at Ross Perot's claim to be an outsider: "If he's an outsider, folks, I'm from Brooklyn. Mr. Perot's giving us salesmanship, not leadership."

But the key passages were those designed to tell the vast television audience that Bill Clinton was not just a friend of the working class but a product of it:

"I'm for Bill Clinton because he is a Democrat who does not have to read a book or be briefed about the struggles of single-parent families, or what it means to work hard for everything he's received in life. There was no silver spoon in sight when he was born three months after his father died. No one ever gave Bill Clinton a free ride as he worked his way through college and law school."

The Miller speech also was designed to underline the positioning of Clinton as someone different from the liberals of the past. "Bill Clinton," said Miller, "is a Democrat who has the courage to tell some of those liberals who think welfare should continue forever and some of those conservatives who think there should be no welfare at all that they are both wrong. He's a Democrat who will move people off the welfare rolls and onto the job rolls."

The platform adopted the following night was similarly tailored to reflect the putative transformation of the party, on the off chance that voters might read it. Although the platform made the customary genuflection to liberal dogma on most social issues, it also included some planks that never would have survived the editing process in other recent conventions. One said: "We offer a new social contract based neither on callous, do-nothing Republican neglect nor on an outdated faith in programs as the solution to every problem."

Clinton and the convention program did not ignore the liberals, of course. On the same day the platform passed, Clinton's only public appearance was before the National Women's Political Caucus, where he made a point of reaffirming his support for abortion rights. And on the podium that night, the party's commitment on the issue was underlined even more clearly by the appearance of six Republican women who had decided to vote Democratic in 1992 because they supported choice on abortion.

The speakers that night also included two victims of AIDS who spoke movingly about the need for a more concentrated federal effort to deal with that scourge—Bob Hattoy, an environmentalist working in the Clinton campaign, and Elizabeth Glaser, who had contracted AIDS through a blood transfusion and unknowingly passed it on to two of her children, one of whom had died.

By Wednesday, the third day of the convention and the night on which Clinton was to be nominated, all of the potential problems seemed to have been resolved and the Democrats were reveling in their satisfaction. They were holding a convention without self-immolation, even sending positive messages. The notion that they might actually win the election began to seep into their thinking. The reservations about Clinton that had seemed so disturbing only a few weeks earlier had receded.

There was even some good news from other quarters. A new *Wash-*

ington Post/ABC News poll had Clinton leading Bush, 42 percent to 30, and the faltering Perot down to 20. A week earlier it had been Bush 35, Clinton and Perot 30 each. The electorate clearly was reacting to the choice of Gore and the early display of enthusiasm in Madison Square Garden.

Mario Cuomo was to deliver the speech nominating Clinton, although it had taken some persuading by Ron Brown in the weeks before the convention. On the face of it, the question of who delivered the nominating speech shouldn't have mattered much. But Cuomo held a special place as an icon of the liberals and his relationship with Clinton had been testy. Brown wanted to tie up still another political loose end, to send his nominee into the general election campaign under the most auspicious circumstances. And, predictably, the Cuomo speech couldn't be arranged without some contortions.

"Mario wasn't returning Clinton's calls [then], so I called Mario," Brown recalled, "and we had a terrific conversation, talked for maybe fifty-five minutes about everything, fifty-five minutes of him telling all the reasons he couldn't speak at the convention. He'd done that."

Finally Brown played his trump card, telling Cuomo: "This is my convention. I brought it to New York, you're my law school professor, you're the governor of the state. I'd look silly if you don't come and do something and make an appearance at the convention."

The next day, Brown said, Cuomo called back and, as Brown remembered it later, the conversation went about like this:

CUOMO: How long is that speech supposed to be?

BROWN: As long as you want it to be, Mario.

CUOMO: You really want me to do this, don't you?

BROWN: Yes, I really want you to do it.

CUOMO: Clinton really wants me?

BROWN: Yeah, Clinton really wants you to do this.

CUOMO: I think I have been much more persuasive on this issue, but I'm going to defer to your judgment.

So Cuomo wrote the speech over the following week and went to the Garden Wednesday afternoon to rehearse it for the Clinton advisers assigned to help him. "They hated it and I didn't like it either," Cuomo said. The speech didn't do enough, they decided, to "equate" Cuomo and Clinton, so the New York governor went back to his office, rewrote some of it, and this time everyone was satisfied once a few minor changes were made.

The result was a rhetorical tour de force—the Democratic Party's premier orator singing the praises of its presidential nominee, excoriating the opposition Republicans and—most importantly—making common cause with a governor of Arkansas in their definition of their party and their mission:

"Bill Clinton believes, as we all here do, in the first principle of our Democratic commitment: the politics of inclusion, the solemn obligation to create opportunity for all of our people, not just the fit and the fortunate—for the aging factory worker in Pittsburgh and the schoolchild in Atlanta, for the family farmer in Des Moines and the eager immigrants sweating to make their place alongside of us here in New York City and in San Francisco.

"For all the people . . . from wherever, no matter how recently, of whatever color, of whatever creed, of whatever sex, of whatever sexual orientation, all of them equal members of the American family, and the neediest of them, the neediest of them, deserving the most help from the rest of us. That is the fundamental Democratic predicate."

An hour later, the ritual of the roll call completed, Clinton was nominated on the first ballot with 3,372 votes to 596 for Jerry Brown, 209 for Paul Tsongas and 74 scattered among other candidates. When the vote from Ohio put Clinton over the top, the television networks showed him celebrating with Hillary at an Arkansas party at Macy's a long block from the Garden—a block he walked to claim his prize. Tradition dictated that the nominee would not go to the convention hall until he was ready to deliver his acceptance speech, but Bill Clinton was not a politician inclined to allow tradition to interfere with an opportunity for more positive television exposure. The walk was a carefully crafted bit of show business supervised by Clinton's Hollywood friends, Harry Thomason and Linda Bloodworth-Thomason, with television bringing the triumphant Clintons—Bill, Hillary and Chelsea—along the sidewalks of New York amid cheering crowds.

All that remained was the acceptance speech. Unsurprisingly, the nominee talked longer than might have been prudent, some fifty-four minutes, long enough for one network to cut away to show a child in the audience who had fallen asleep. But Clinton used the speech to spell out his basic message to the largest television audience he had ever enjoyed to that point.

There was nothing subtle about his appeal to the political center. "One sentence in the platform we built says it all," he said. "The most important family policy, urban policy, labor policy, minority policy and foreign policy America can have is an expanding entrepreneurial economy of high-wage, high-skilled jobs. And so, in the name of all those who do the work and pay the taxes, raise the kids and play by the rules, in the name of the hardworking Americans who make up our forgotten middle class, I proudly accept your nomination for president of the United States."

When the applause and cheering died down, Clinton added even more pointedly: "I am a product of the middle class and when I am president, you will be forgotten no more."

Like most acceptance speeches, Clinton's was largely a codification and compilation of all the things he had been saying during his long march toward the nomination. He defined the "New Covenant" he had been describing for months—with the obvious hope of persuading the press to seize on the phrase as a latter-day "New Deal" or "New Frontier"—this way: "The New Covenant is a solemn agreement between the people and their government based not simply on what each of us can take but what all of us must give to our nation. We offer opportunity. We demand responsibility. We will build an American community again."

The speech touched off the final demonstration of the convention—thousands of Democrats cheering and singing on the convention floor while their new champion, his family and his political allies danced to "Don't Stop Thinking About Tomorrow" and sang "Circle of Friends" on the podium. It was a moment of glory Bill Clinton clearly had been imagining for at least a decade now. But even at the height of his political success, he found himself sharing top billing with another story, and another severe critic of the status quo—Ross Perot.

CHAPTER 20

TEXAS HARA-KIRI

In the six weeks or so leading up to the Democratic National Convention, the volunteers for Ross Perot had continued to make impressive progress in their petition drives around the country. But behind the scenes in Dallas, where political professionals Jordan and Rollins were digging below the surface "horse race" numbers in the polls—who's ahead and who's behind—the campaign was going around in circles.

As state after state was falling in line toward the objective of ballot position in all fifty jurisdictions, Jordan and Rollins, and Luce and Meyerson, too, were aware that it was imperative to shift from the petition-gathering mode, which in large measure was self-generating at the local level, to a real campaign mode. One difficulty was that from the Dallas end, the field operation of about thirty-five people had been placed—by Perot himself—in the hands of the head of his personal security force, a former military officer named Mark Blahnik who had absolutely no political experience.

Blahnik by the professionals' judgment was a nice enough fellow, but hardly the man to take a civilian army of volunteers and whip it into an effective campaign organization. Asked later whether Blahnik was a problem, Jordan threw his head back, laughed, and said: "He was Perot's security guy running the field for us. Does that sound like a problem? That was the Perot way."

It was not just Blahnik, but the fact that most of the field operatives—individuals sent from Dallas out to the states to help on ballot access and, eventually, to sort out internal disputes among the volunteers—were also political neophytes recruited from the ranks of Perot Systems. "Perot took great pride in his field staff," Sal Russo remembered. "He talked to them at all levels." They were regarded by the professionals as "Perot's ears and eyes of what was going on in the fifty states," Russo said, and were dubbed "the whiteshirts"—a spit-and-polish bunch, mostly military veterans, with close-cropped hair and conservative suits and ties, right out of the Perot dress manual that he always insisted did not exist.

"As this thing started, Perot made Mark political director," Rollins said, "and Mark was scrambling, one of these guys working twenty hours a day trying to do all things for Perot. These were nice young guys, never been in a campaign, didn't have a clue, and they're out there with this grass-roots mob, spending money like wild with no concept about anything relating to politics. Once they got the petition drives done, they didn't know what to do next. But from day one, Perot made very clear we were not to have anything to do with his volunteers or his field staff. That was the first warning signal," Rollins said. "After the first day, if I'd had a gun I'd have blown my brains out." Instead, he stayed on and hoped for the best.

So did his old business partner, Russo, who had the same misgivings. "Perot was definitely a control freak," he said. "Nobody ever knew everything that was going on [but him]. He departmentalized things for security reasons," and that was one reason the security staff was so important to him.

Many of the volunteers in the various states, however, were very suspicious of the whiteshirts, coming in to what the volunteers had been led by Perot to believe would be their own show. Part of the problem, Russo said, was that the whiteshirts dispatched from Dallas "were used to the military command structure, [which was] 'good luck' with volunteers. And part of it was, because this was a self-starting volunteer army around the country, thousands of dedicated, loyal Americans who saw an opportunity to take their country back were well motivated. But you had in the mix a couple of charlatans, crooks, thieves and assorted bad people who saw this as some sort of gravy train. . . . I think 99.9 percent were the dedicated, hard workers, but there were rotten apples in the mix— embezzlers, I think there was a child molester. So there was a shakedown period where they tried to weed out the bad apples, or there were people who were just mentally unbalanced.''

One of Perot's earliest supporters, a man named Pat Clancy in Oklahoma, said he asked the whiteshirts who dropped in on him: ''What have you got to do with the Oklahoma grass-roots effort?'' He told them, he said later, ''to butt out and go back to Texas.'' But in the end, he said, he was forced aside.

There were also cases, Russo said, of competing Perot volunteer groups in one town, and the whiteshirts were sent in to referee and make a choice on the local leadership, leading the individual or faction who lost out to charge strong-arm methods from Dallas. Soon a string of negative stories of this nature filled local newspapers around the country, tarnishing the image of the movement as a bottom-up crusade. Finally, another veteran of the Jimmy Carter campaigns with outstanding credentials as a field organizer, Tim Kraft, was brought in to ''work with'' the Perot-anointed chief of the whiteshirts.

Kraft, a cool-headed operative who largely orchestrated Carter's 1976 breakthrough in the Iowa precinct caucuses, set himself to welding the Dallas operatives and the volunteers in the field and held a training session in Dallas. There were, he acknowledged later, ''the usual turf battles and resentments toward politicians'' among many volunteers, particularly within states, ''but it wasn't anything we hadn't seen before'' in other campaigns.

''We weren't going to change the fundamental fact that this was a volunteer-driven campaign,'' Russo said later. ''We wanted to utilize the volunteers in a way that could have caused Perot to win. We never lost sight of the volunteers' role, because it was the one unique advantage he had. We weren't organized to do that, but we could have been. We could have put on the most awesome grass-roots campaign ever assembled in America.''

Beyond the headache of revamping the volunteer effort from a petition-collecting to a campaign mode, the most important task for the professionals now was to define Ross Perot in terms that would make him the most formidable vote-getter possible, before the opposition was able to define him in ways that would cast doubts about him among undecided voters and strip away the considerable support he already had.

That effort to undermine Perot's image and reputation was already well under way. Shortly after the California primary in which the network exit polls found a remarkable groundswell for Perot among both Republican and Democratic voters, the Bush campaign held four sets of focus groups in Fresno and Riverside, California, Columbus, Ohio, and Paramus, New Jersey—the town where the celebrated Willie Horton story first was identified as a decisive issue for Bush in the 1988 campaign.

It was at the earlier Paramus focus group that the story of the black convicted murderer furloughed from prison in Massachusetts who committed rape and mayhem in Maryland caused Michael Dukakis's credibility to plummet, especially when paired with his vetoing of a state bill requiring public school teachers to lead their classes in daily recitation of the pledge of allegiance.

This time around, the focus groups produced nothing quite so dramatic as ammunition for a Bush campaign on the attack. But according to Fred Steeper, the Bush pollster, comments from the voters did confirm marked uneasiness about the modus operandi of Ross Perot—the stories about spying on employees and competitors and so on. The participants expressed a sense that there was something weird about the little man from Texas with the huge bankroll. The Bush campaign concluded that playing on that perception could cool off the red-hot Perot, as the Willie Horton and flag-pledge stories had started the front-running Dukakis on his downward slide in 1988.

The focus group reactions to Perot, Charlie Black said later, were "pretty damned favorable to Perot," but there were some negative observations, "like, 'He sounds like a dictator, has to have his own way, a one-man band.' And the stuff on spying was coming out, the beginnings of Inspector Perot—all that was surfacing, so it was clear that that was the way to pin him down."

One major problem for the Bush campaign created by Perot, Bob Teeter said later, was the fact that "he was forcing the country almost exclusively onto a message that was our worst"—dealing with the economy. And no matter what Perot said, it was perceived as anti-Bush, as well as being basically conservative, thus drawing conservative Republicans from Bush's base. At the same time, Teeter said, Perot was bringing Democrats into the process, "at least a significant number of whom would not have voted" at all had he not been in the picture.

That Perot was, indeed, anti-Bush, was beyond question. In our interview with him in May, he had talked again and again in critical terms about the Bush administration, never once commenting on Clinton until asked, and then he had little to say about him. Bush himself professed to be in the dark about why Perot was so hostile to him. During a break in an interview with Larry King later in the year, Bush asked King: "What's Ross Perot got against me? You know him better than I do."

Charlie Black had two theories. "Bush was always the kind of guy Perot looked down on because he never made real money," Black said. But more likely, he said, the hostility came from the fact that in 1986, Perot had asked Reagan to send him to Southeast Asia to look for Americans missing in action from the Vietnam War. "Guess who got to call Perot back," Black asked, "and say he couldn't go over there?"

The challenge of driving up Perot's negatives, Black said he realized from the positive comments, would be much harder than nailing Dukakis had been four years earlier. But in this case, he noted, the American news media was already engaged. "It was more like 80 percent the press, with us stoking the fire as we could," he said.

Bush himself, according to Mary Matalin later, never shared the view that his campaign should go after Perot. He thought that Perot would "implode" and that Clinton was always the primary foe, she said, but "there was not a major dispute [within the campaign] because the people who were arguing to attack him [Perot] were vehement about it and were making good sense. The president's attitude was, he was not enthusiastic about it because he had his own feelings about where the Perot candidacy was going. But he literally said, 'You guys get paid to worry about this, so do what you have to do'—something like that. It was not a concern to him." In other words, it was the same old George Bush, holding his nose while others did something he said was distasteful to him—but not distasteful enough for him to call off the dogs.

Later, Matalin said, some in the campaign "tried to take credit" for shooting Perot down with the attack strategy, "but the truth is, we were supposed to take a few surgical strikes [at Perot]. It was not even like an affirmative, signed-in-blood decision. But the discussion led toward the feeling that we couldn't get back to getting Bush's positives up" as long as Perot was riding high. "All summer our goal was to get Bush's positives up. Darman and some of the others were of the persuasion that you couldn't get near to getting Bush's positives up until you got Ross's negatives up. You would continue to be an uncredible messenger on the positive side if there was some other guy who was credible trashing him every day. Then it snowballed."

As first one administration source and then another, each on his own, she insisted, weighed in against Perot—Quayle, Fitzwater, party chairman Rich Bond, drug czar Bob Martinez, others—it became, she said, a "spontaneous eruption." With Bush resisting going into "the campaign mode" and everybody in his camp anxiously and nervously "waiting for the campaign to start," Matalin said, ". . . the Republican community inside the Beltway takes it as a signal and they start shooting away, and it just got out of control."

She and David Carney, the White House political director, "sat back there and laughed, and said, 'We love to see our campaign collapse into place.' We were not supposed to nuclear bomb the guy. It was supposed to be a little bit of Death by a Thousand Cuts."

Matalin and Carney, she said later, tried to make the argument that it was not wise to alienate the Perot supporters with overt attacks on their hero. "Just common sense will tell you," she argued, "we're gonna need these guys. He is not going to make it all the way through. People are not going to waste their vote. . . . We thought in the end these guys were going to largely come our way, and why make them crazy?"

In Dallas, though, Perot's closest associates like Luce and his son-in-law and campaign counsel, Clay Mulford, were convinced that they were witnessing Son of Willie Horton—the full-blown rebirth of the intentional, carefully orchestrated negativism of the 1988 Bush campaign hatched out of those original Paramus focus group soundings. They cited a column by Thomas Oliphant in *The Boston Globe* at the time laying out what had been culled by the Bush campaign from those focus groups as evidence of the Bush "dirty tricks" team at work again. In doing so, they were stretching the definition of dirty tricks quite a bit, but what they read was enough to convince them that it was 1988 all over again, but with independent Ross Perot, not Democrat Bill Clinton, cast by the Bush campaign as Michael Dukakis.

Luce later noted a sequence of events that followed swiftly after the focus group sessions. First Bush said of Perot to reporters that "it's too much of a gamble to put the country in his hands." Then Fitzwater said "it's shocking and frightening to see that kind of bizarre behavior on the part of a presidential candidate." Then Black said the next day that "the thing that gives people some hesitancy is Perot's MO. He's authoritarian, his use of investigators." Then Quayle raised the question of "having the IRS, the FBI and the CIA under his control. Who would be investigated next?" From June 21, the day Oliphant's column appeared, Luce said later, "starting for about the next ten days, almost on a daily basis, a new surrogate [was] trotted out to use words like 'bizarre,' 'frightening,' 'shocking,' 'investigator.' There was a concentrated attack, and polls showed it was causing his numbers to go down."

Clearly, Luce was never going to be convinced that all this occurred without careful orchestration, especially after the experience of 1988. Even press criticism, he insisted, had Republican origins, and he knew that was so because reporters would bring him fax copies bearing derogatory information about Perot on Republican Party letterheads. "All that stuff was being fed by the Republicans," said Luce, himself a former GOP gubernatorial candidate.

He was not suggesting, Luce said later, that there was some kind of conspiracy between the press and the Bush campaign to get Perot. Rather, he said, the press was by now investigating Perot independently and the Bush campaign contributed to a developing feeding frenzy, making "a conscious decision to take their guns off Bill Clinton, and let him get off the ground." That, he said, "was their fatal mistake. He was winded, he was down for a nine count and they let him go to a neutral corner and get well, because they turned all these guns off of Clinton onto Perot, and concentrated on Perot for three weeks. In doing so, they let Bill Clinton completely withdraw from the front pages of the papers, get out of the vortex of the negative press that Bill Clinton was in. In that time he redid his economic plan, people quit talking about Gennifer Flowers, and he came back with the Democratic convention and his economic plan. . . . It enabled him to sound substantive while Bush was throwing rocks at Perot."

The Clinton strategists agreed completely. The Manhattan Project had established that it no longer was the substance of the womanizing and draft issues that bothered voters, but what came off as his excessively "political" answers, summed up in "Slick Willie." In this period, Wilhelm said later, "we began, and he began, filling in the answers to some of those questions, first by introducing him biographically and [as] a human being" on the talk shows.

At the same time, Clinton was reworking his economic plan, which he felt needed updating in light of what had gone on in the campaign, and in the country's economic outlook. Although he continued to rail against such pet peeves as "deadbeat dads" who ducked out to avoid paying for their child care responsibilities, and to trumpet his "domestic peace corps" whereby America's youth would get college educations in return for community service, he knew the election would not turn on either issue. They were what Grunwald called "mirage issues," just as, the Clinton campaign was now convinced, were the issues the Bush campaign was pushing regarding Clinton's "character." So Clinton zeroed in on the economy, and as he did, as Greer said later, "fate shined on us."

It was just then, Wilhelm noted, that "Ross Perot and George Bush got into a shoving match, and at the time they were being political, we put out our [new] economic agenda. I think that was one of the key periods of the campaign," he said, "because we were teetering after the California primary, and I actually think that if George Bush had gone on the attack [against Clinton] during that period, we might have suffered nicks and cuts that we could never have recovered from.

"But instead, he and Perot tussled, giving us almost a free opportunity for people to give us a second look. They took that second look, so that by the time the Democratic convention rolled around, I think people were already starting to look at Bill Clinton differently. . . . The Bush people's failure to really hit us when we were down, providing us an opportunity to introduce Bill Clinton, and for Bill Clinton to introduce himself, was very, very critical."

"The Republicans made a fatal mistake turning their howitzers on Ross Perot," Stephanopouios said. "It gave us an opportunity to come up the middle."

Clinton told us later that the Bush-Perot squabbling helped him because "by then the whole country was where New Hampshire was. They were very worried about their economic circumstances. They were really worried about a government that didn't function; they were sick and tired about the politics of blame; they just wanted something done." The bad blood between Bush and Perot, for whatever reason, "was palpable," Clinton said, "and the American people basically wanted the president to worry about them and not about some other politician."

Perot, always suspicious about the involvement in his campaign of "hired guns," as he still called them, didn't quite blame Jordan and Rollins for the assault on his reputation in the news media that was going on all this time. But, according to Russo, Perot would observe that "there had never been an unfavorable newspaper story written about me until you guys came along"—a testimony, if nothing else, to Perot's limited reading habits. He also stepped up his charges that Bush was using dirty tricks against him, to the point that GOP chairman Bond called in to Perot on the Larry King show one night and challenged him to produce "one shred of evidence" to back up his bombast. The campaign, it began to seem, was becoming one big television talk show.

In the face of the attacks on Perot, and with the conviction of his associates that it was now open season for the Bush forces on Ross Perot as some kind of weirdo, the matter of defining him in positive terms, and without wasting any more time, became imperative. That was where the professionals, Jordan, Rollins and the troops brought in largely from GOP ranks by Rollins, came in. They knew how to do it and had proved so in the major leagues of politics. But there was always the question of whether what they knew how to do would square with Perot's own views of how to campaign, and whether they could convince him that they did know.

"The hiring of people doesn't have anything to do with whether you have an unconventional campaign or not," Luce said later. "I wanted to run a professional unconventional campaign, and I don't think that's an oxymoron. We went to great lengths to make sure that both Hamilton and Ed were signed on to running an unconventional campaign." They agreed, Luce said, but "there was disagreement with Ed subsequently as to how we defined, 'unconventional'. . . . I knew Hamilton had a good understanding and wanted to run the campaign in a very different way."

Perot was strong in emphasizing, Luce said, "that the way campaigns were run was part of what we were running against, part of what we were trying to change. And we were always trying to define as we went along how we could do it better. . . . In that early phase, we were clearly doing things differently and in an unconventional way. The rallies were planned by the volunteers; they were not planned by advance men.''

This approach, in what Luce called ''the petition phase,'' was continued after the arrival of Jordan and Rollins, ''and neither one proposed changing that phase of what we were doing. We couldn't ever reach agreement on what we were going to do going forward.'' Disagreements over novel ideas and the timing of carrying them out mounted, even as the arrows of criticism kept raining down on Perot. ''It frustrated Hamilton and Ed,'' Luce said, ''but you have to understand that what Ross thought was important was to talk about issues and communicate about issues. Ross was continuing to do that every time he appeared on television. As far as he was concerned, the campaign was doing just fine. Ross always felt that when he was appearing on television, talking directly to the American people, that was the way to campaign.''

As for professional politics and its way of doing business, Luce said with a wan smile, ''he looked at it as if it were a virus, and he was afraid to let the antibodies get into his bloodstream.''

As Jordan sought to strike a responsive chord with Perot with his charts on long-range thinking and planning, Rollins and others began peppering Luce and/or Perot with memos pressing for decisions on specific key matters that needed resolving at once. One of them was picking a real running mate to replace the stand-in, Admiral Stockdale. The first deadline for filing an official slate for the fall election was August 11 in South Dakota, and after that, one memo dated June 22 warned, ''the deadlines begin to cascade.'' The memo added that ''we should take at least one month to do a minimal background review of the potential candidate—unless we want to 'surprise' the nation as Bush did with Quayle. This means we need a name by the second week of July.'' The memo also suggested that the selection of the running mate might be made at the time of Perot's declaration of candidacy, the date of which also had not been nailed down.

A longer campaign plan dated July 1 said the choice of a vice presidential candidate ''may be the single most important decision Mr. Perot makes. Vice presidential candidates rarely add a great many votes to a ticket, but they can often do great damage. A careful strategy to orchestrate the buildup, announcement and aftermath must be devised. We cannot allow a 'Quayle unpreparedness' incident to strike the campaign.''

Perot, according to John Jay Hooker, the Nashville businessman/ politician who was one of the earliest Perot enthusiasts, had already discussed some names with him, some conventional like Paul Tsongas, Warren Rudman and General Colin Powell, and some quite unconventional. These included Bernadine Healy, director of the National Institutes of Health, Sharon Rockefeller, president of public television station WETA in Washington, D.C., and wife of Senator Jay Rockefeller of West Virginia, and Anne Armstrong of Texas, former Republican Party co-chair and ambassador to England under Reagan. James Squires, the former *Chicago Tribune* editor who was a Perot spokesman and adviser, said a New York federal circuit judge, Amalya Kearse, a black woman, was high in Perot's considerations.

Hooker also heard from other sources inside the campaign that radio and television reporter Cokie Roberts was on the list. Roberts, who heard the report and was as astonished as others who heard it, said the only explanation she could think of was that she had written an opposite-editorial-page piece in *The New York Times* that Perot may have seen as favorable to him although she certainly had not endorsed his candidacy. She said she asked Luce and he denied it. Also denied by the Perot campaign was another name floating about—former Reagan Attorney General William French Smith. Smith, however, was already automatically disqualified by virtue of the fact he was dead. In any event, at this point Perot kept dodging on a vice presidential choice.

The June 22 memo also pleaded for ''a tight schedule of focus groups and polls,'' both of which Perot was dead-set against. ''Why should I pay good money when I can pick up a newspaper,'' he would thunder, ''and read the polls there for free?'' The memo pleaded for data to help determine what was and wasn't working: ''This campaign is swinging at a fast pitch in a darkened stadium. We may be hitting, because we can hear the screams of the fans. But we have no idea where the ball is going.'' But Perot thought polls and focus groups were simply to find out what people wanted, and then to pander to them. ''I'm not a parrot,'' he would say, according to Russo. The professionals would tell him that he might be spending millions on a message people didn't understand, and it was prudent to find out. But he still wasn't buying. Money for polling, Russo said, finally was hidden in another budget item.

Still another memo pressed Perot on another key matter: "We have to make a final decision on the convention by next week or our options will be very limited. This could be another defining event in the campaign and must be carefully done. If we are doing fifty, five or one convention, we have to start now." Jordan was proposing state conventions in each of the fifty states together with one grand national affair over two days, held in some huge arena or park.

Also under consideration, Russo said, were five regional conventions at such sites as the Rose Bowl in Pasadena and Shea Stadium in New York, or even what he called "a Woodstock in someplace in Missouri or someplace in the middle of the country, have parades from all over the country assembling and have a million people. Actually we called Guinness [Book of Records] to find out what the record was for the most people ever assembled in America." The biggest free event, he was told, was a New York Philharmonic concert in Central Park, which drew nearly 900,000, and the largest paid event was a rock concert in San Bernardino, California, attracting more than a million.

"The idea would be to try to break that record," Russo said. "We had all that Hollywood entertainment support, and it would be just a week-long celebration of America." Joe Canzeri, one of the Republican Party's premier advance men who helped "handle" Quayle in the 1988 campaign, was aboard for Perot now and he was convinced it could be done. But again the planners couldn't get a decision from Perot.

A one-page, single-spaced memo dated June 30—with the narrowest of margins to satisfy Perot's limited patience with written presentations— repeated the same points about a running mate and his announcement of candidacy and told him pointedly: "We are starting to see erosion in our support because voters do not believe you are addressing issues. We need a comprehensive plan to release our issues papers in a way to put this issue to rest." But that to Perot was conventional politics and he wanted no part of it. Wasn't he out there on television telling voters where he stood?

Finally, there was the urgency to counter the attacks. "We must convince voters that Perot is not a jump into an unknown void," one internal paper said. "Attacks on Perot will continue centering on converting the driven, can-do, patriotic, successful businessman into a quirky, sick, obsessive, paranoid billionaire. The best thing we can do is recognize that there can be doubt sown in the mind of the electorate. That doubt can kill us because it will stop momentum and slowly erode our base vote.''

Another memo warned: ''Given the pummeling the campaign has taken in the past two weeks, it is more important than ever to have our media and advertising in place. The two lines of attack which seem to be taking hold are Perot's suspected 'authoritarian' tendencies and his lack of specificity. Paid advertising will go a long way to deflect both attacks.''

But Perot was cool to paid television as well. When Jordan proposed that a biographical film be produced to show on television or have Perot go on live in conjunction with the 20,000 ''Perot home parties'' he had recommended, to give the state volunteer organizations something tangible to do and expand the Perot base, he balked at the cost. ''Why don't we just do it on Larry King?'' he asked. ''I'll just get Larry to give me an hour. All you guys know how to do is come up with ideas on how to spend my money.'' What Perot could not or would not grasp was that it was essential for his campaign to control the message that went out, to convey specific information to counter reports and impressions that were hurting him.

Perot seemed to see no urgency in the matter, but the professional staff was now near desperation. Another memo dated July 3 pressed for a ''generic defense—a commercial designed to be put on the air quickly to defend against any number of attacks while a specific defense spot is being prepared.''

But money was always an issue with Perot—and whether he could trust those who were asking for large chunks of it for what he saw as conventional campaigning. When Rollins was unable to find a firm budget for the campaign, he went to Perot, he recalled later, and asked him: ''Are you for real on the $150 million figure? You've got to understand, I've been around a lot of rich people who keep saying 'Whatever it costs to get elected,' but I haven't seen many of them actually dip into their pocket. You've got to understand, it's gonna cost at least $150 million just to stay even with the two national committees in the presidential campaign, and you've got the added burden that you've got to be on television all summer defining yourself.''

Also, he said he told Perot, he couldn't pay the professional consultants who had broken ranks with their own parties "what you pay your security guys." But Perot, Rollins said, denigrated all of them as "hired guns," when "in his particular case we were there because we believed in change, or in him. It was sort of like the volunteers were honorable and we a bunch of whores because we took money."

On another occasion, Rollins said, he got the idea of putting up 5 million Perot yard signs all over the country on the Fourth of July. "There never had been 5 million yard signs," he said, "and my strategy was to make people think. 'Gee, I'm joining something, I'm not such a kook to be out here thinking I'd be, being for Perot.' You look out into the neighborhood and all of a sudden you see twenty or thirty signs, and they're on prominent Republicans' or Democrats' front yards.

"So I went in to Perot, and Perot goes, 'So what is this gonna cost?' And I said, 'Well, a buck or two apiece.' He goes, 'Ten million dollars for yard signs? Can't they make their own yard signs?' I said, 'Ross, they're not going to make their own yard signs. That's not the idea behind this. This is tremendous advertising.' But he wasn't having any of it."

Nor did Perot want to send a mail piece to the millions of individuals who had called the Perot phone bank in Dallas volunteering to help. Jordan said Perot's "computer nerds" had compiled lists of millions of names apparently just because they were there, with no plan or intention to do anything with them, other than sending some names out to state petition drives early in the game. The neglect was frustrating to the professionals, who saw, as Jordan put it, "an enormous army out there waiting to get orders." But Perot's attitude about direct mail, Rollins said, was "this is junk I get on my desk every day that I throw out. I'm not going to spend any money on junk mail."

Rollins despaired. "All the tools which you normally use in a political campaign weren't there." When Rollins worked up a campaign budget for submission to Perot, it came to $152 million. "I prepared it with all of his people," Rollins recalled. "What I tried to do was surround him with all of his people because I knew he wasn't comfortable with us—quote—political whores. I thought if I surrounded him with his own people, they get to realize we know what we're doing, we're professionals, we're not trying to rip him off and spend his money. Ironically, he was being ripped off," Rollins said. "Tom Luce didn't know from shit.

Every vendor would walk in the door, and say, 'Gee, I want to sell you this list of 7 million names of hot political activists.' What they'd sell to the [major party] national committees for one tenth of a penny per name, they'd sell to the Perot thing for a buck. Contracts that Luce had already entered into were absurd, because they just didn't know. It was every vendor's dream. The vault was open.''

Luce and Meyerson said they would submit the Rollins budget to Perot for him, because, they told him, "when you're dealing with money Perot is very, very sensitive and we don't want you to take the brunt of it.'' When Perot saw it, Rollins said, "he blew up, and cut the budget in half, arbitrarily. He eliminated the whole issues division,'' where budget expert John White was working up the plan for deficit reduction and economic recovery that Perot had promised to deliver to the voters. When White submitted the plan, Rollins said, Perot hardly looked at it.

"These guys keep sending me big thick books,'' Perot told Rollins. "I don't want big thick books.'' Perot set the base budget at about $72 million with the understanding separate big-ticket items like the expansive convention ideas, if agreed on, would be up for negotiation with him.

Luce and Meyerson told Rollins, he said later, "just please bear with us. He will spend whatever you need in the end. He just doesn't trust you or your guys. He thinks you're trying to rip him off.'' Rollins replied: "Well, that's a hell of a nice environment to be working in.'' Every time he came over to the campaign headquarters, where Rollins was moving new staff in, he'd erupt. "He'd say,'' Rollins recalled, 'What the hell's going on here? We're building a Pentagon here.' ''

Rollins argued that the Perot operation "was very bare bones'' compared to the Clinton and Bush campaigns. "He kept saying, 'You don't understand the way I do things. I want a little guerrilla squad. I want to get the job done, I don't want this big army, this big bureaucracy. That's why I've always been better than my competitors.' I said, 'Ross, you don't even understand what the mission is. You can't get by with guerrilla operations. Your candidacy has got to be different from any other candidacy, but I assume you want to win.' '' ("Maybe it was a false assumption,'' Rollins said much later.)

But the most serious problem about money was Perot's reluctance to spend it on the production of the television commercials the professionals insisted were absolutely essential, immediately, to define him in a positive light and "stop the hemorrhaging" caused by the negative stories and attacks on him. At one point, David Wolper, regarded by many as the best maker of documentary films in Hollywood, and Gerald Rafshoon, Jimmy Carter's media man in 1976 and 1980, were brought in to talk to Perot, but he found them too glitzy for his tastes.

Rollins, undeterred by Perot's unexpected penny-pinching, sought the services of Hal Riney, one of the most successful—and expensive—television advertising men in Los Angeles. Riney had produced the famous "Morning in America" ads for Ronald Reagan's 1984 reelection campaign, managed by Rollins, and he was known for his effective "feel-good" style demonstrated in those Reagan ads. His work tended to the emotional, and the thought was that he would be the ideal man to capture the high spirit of the Perot movement.

While Rollins was talking to Riney, Jordan, knowing Perot's attitude about "big-league guys who charge high prices," tried a parallel track. Luce told him about a young Dallas television ad man named Andrew Wilson and Jordan hired him to do a quick biographical commercial on Perot to hold the fort. With Perot's obstinacy in mind, Jordan told Luce: "I can sell this kid, because he's not costing a lot, and he's local."

In a mere thirty-six hours, young Wilson produced a superb if a bit ragged five-minute commercial, mostly from stock footage, that was cut into sixty-second spots. It captured the essence of Ross the Good and presented other people in the context of their own personal experience with him in a straightforward way, devoid of slickness. One sixty-second segment shown to Perot started with a woman talking about her husband, who had been taken prisoner in Vietnam in 1965. She told about receiving a phone call out of the blue in 1969 from Perot, whom she had never met, saying, "I'd like to know what I can do to help your family." He did help, she said, until her husband was released. The spot then showed him saying, "Ross Perot is a very unusual person. He looks for things that ought to be done because it's the right thing to do, and then he tries to figure a way to do them."

The spot then showed Perot's sister talking about him growing up in Texarkana and worshipping his father, then presented a Perot shipmate in the navy, then Mort Meyerson on Perot as a businessman, and finally Perot's wife, Margot, simply talking about how they had met and how he had always told their children, "It's not what you have, but what you are, that's important."

It was a terrific ad produced for only $12,000 under severe time pressure—and Perot hated it. When Jordan showed it to him, he went ballistic, berating Jordan in the most offensive language and calling it the worst he had ever seen. He complained that the spot—a first, rough cut—didn't have the POW story straight, that he didn't like something his sister had said, and that the lighting on his wife was terrible. Taken aback at the ferocity of Perot's assault on him, Jordan left shaken—and recognizing that this could be the beginning of the end for him in the Perot campaign.

"This young guy produced that in thirty-six hours, and if he had five more days, no telling what he would have come up with," Jordan said. "But I was trying to get something on the air. We were starting to fall apart. . . . When we showed this to people who knew Perot, they cried." And when he showed it to a meeting of Perot state coordinators gathered in Dallas, the reaction was immediate and positive. "They all said, 'Put it on right now,' " Jordan recalled.

Jordan was at the end of his rope, particularly in light of his treatment at Perot's hands and what seemed the futility of it all, given Perot's attitude. When Perot called him shortly afterward in what Jordan saw as the closest Perot could bring himself to an apology, he told him: "You know, Ross, I'm not accustomed to people talking to me like that. You talk about high-paid help and all of this. Why the hell did you bring us in, if you weren't ever going to listen to us?"

A couple of days later, in the first days of July, Jordan went over to Perot's office and told him he was leaving. "It was probably a mistake to hire us," he said. Perot answered, according to Jordan: "It probably *was* a mistake to hire you guys. The difference between you and Rollins is, I like you. I don't like Rollins and I don't trust him. He's got Washington disease. He talks to the media too much. This is just another business deal for him. These leaks have got to stop."

Rollins had been accused of leaking from the start, with stories about himself and Jordan going to work for the Perot campaign. He flatly denied that he leaked but at the same time said later that Perot and his unpolitical associates did not understand that "public people" like himself talked to the press as part of the job of communicating the views of the campaign. For that reason, he went on headline television interview shows, which drove Perot crazy. At the same time, however, Rollins said later that Perot would be critical of Jordan in conversations with him.

In any event, Jordan told Perot he was getting out as soon as he could find a gracious way to do so. "Where I got stuck was, I couldn't figure a way to get out. I didn't want to be seen jumping ship. I wanted to get out, but I really didn't want to harm him. I still believed in what he was trying to accomplish." But he told Luce, Meyerson and Rollins he intended to leave.

Meanwhile, Rollins had convinced Riney to try his hand. "He does great Americana-type stuff," Rollins recalled, "so I thought, 'Boy, this would be a natural—Perot with his stories of his famous charitable givings and all that stuff, his Norman Rockwell office and Remingtons. These two are a match made in heaven.' " They had one good meeting, Rollins said, with the soft-spoken Riney, who uses his own voice on many of his commercials, apparently making a good impression. But afterward Perot balked. "Someone had told Perot that Riney had once spent a hundred thousand dollars putting a goat on the top of a mountain," Rollins said, and he wasn't going to spend his money on any such stunt.

Rollins assured Perot that if it had happened—and Riney later told Rollins he couldn't recall any such incident—there would have been a sound advertising reason. The original plan was for Riney to do a television documentary on Perot, but Perot insisted on writing the script himself, Rollins said, and when Riney looked at it, he said it would take three and a half hours of airtime to do it.

Riney proposed instead, Rollins said, "that we talk conceptually about what we're gonna do," and tried to explain to Perot what the process was—first the approach, a script and storyboards before shooting anything. "Perot was, like, 'I want it tomorrow,' " Rollins said. "Riney would say, 'If you want something tomorrow I can do something tomorrow, but it's not going to be what I would be proud of, and what you would be proud of.' "

Perot's response, Rollins said, was "You don't understand, I get can-do people. When I wanted to move food to Vietnam, I got these can-do people. We had the planes loaded and there." Rollins told him he could do that, too, but moving food on a plane to Vietnam was "not what it takes creative talent to do.'' The real problem, Rollins said, was that a friend of Perot's in Dallas with a local background in radio and television, Murphy Martin, kept telling him ''he didn't need to hire Hollywood crews at fancy prices'' and he could get a couple of local cameramen and do the job for a song. ''That was sort of going in Ross's ear,'' Rollins said.

Rollins, however, pressed for using Riney, although Luce and Meyerson, knowing Perot, told him he was pushing his luck. ''I thought it was that important,'' Rollins said. ''If Hal Riney walked on us, it would be so hard to get somebody good, to get up and functioning, you'd lose another three or four weeks. So I pushed hard to get Riney.''

Riney went ahead and made a quick commercial in New York, using the man-in-the-street technique of testimonials for Perot interspersed with street scenes of voters being petitioned for their signatures on corners and in malls—heavily in the emotional, touchy-feely mode for which he was celebrated. Perot hated that one too and Riney was sent back to the drawing board.

Rollins had Russo get hold of Riney's ''Morning in America'' spots for Reagan in 1984 to show Perot, but he never said what he thought. ''There was a feel to Riney's stuff,'' Russo said later. ''That was the feel we wanted, but if Perot didn't like it, that was a clue we had a big problem. . . . Unfortunately, the first Riney spots didn't have a lot of facts in them, but that wasn't their purpose.'' It may have been, Russo said later, ''that Perot is an engineer, and engineers by their training are always looking for the facts, they have a slide rule, they're calculating, and they're always doing things in a sequential order. Suddenly you come in with a television spot that's supposed to connect with people's emotions. An engineer is not going to like that.''

Another conversation with Perot centered on money. ''Tell me what one of these things costs,'' he asked Riney. Riney replied, according to Rollins, ''Well, Ross, I can't give you a specific cost. It depends on how much it costs to shoot.'' Perot shot back: ''Hal, I've never dealt with anybody who couldn't tell me the price of what they're selling.''

Rollins told Perot that when he headed the Republican congressional committee and ''we absolutely were going to lose with twenty percent of the vote, we'd send out two guys with a video camera. It would cost $3,000 just to do that. It was just garbage, knowing they were going to lose. If you're going to spend $120,000 a minute to put an ad on the air—He goes, 'What?' And I said, 'Well, that's what a minute of prime time costs.' And he goes, 'No way. You guys are nuts if you think I'm going to spend that kind of money when I can get an hour free on Larry King.' "

Riney told him he could make a cheaper commercial, for $50,000 or $75,000, but he had to think about the quality and the fact that the commercial would be seen over and over again and had to have staying power. Perot told them to go back and talk to Luce, and as they left the office, Rollins said later, "Perot walks me down the hall, Riney goes ahead, he puts his arm around me and says, 'Everything's going to be okay, don't worry about this. We'll get this thing worked out.' Meanwhile, he calls Tom [Luce] over to his office and tells him, 'Tom, get rid of this guy [Riney]. How outrageous. His prices are absurd.' "

"The next day there was a story in *The Wall Street Journal*," Rollins said, and he was asked for a comment. "I said, 'It's unfortunate it didn't work out. Hal Riney's the best in the business. It just didn't work out.' Perot just went batshit. He thought I had taken Riney's side against him, and how could I do that?" I walked back and said to Riney, 'Hal, you just saw the end of this campaign. This guy obviously doesn't want to be president.' "

On Friday night, July 10, according to Rollins, he had dinner at the home of Tom Luce and his wife. "In the course of the dinner, Tom must have gotten up ten times to take a call from Perot," he said. "He was really worked up over [a report that] ABC was going to go with a story about one of his daughters [involving] a college professor. As Tom explained the story to me, it had been a serious relationship and Perot had had them under surveillance. The college professor had claimed Perot had confronted him and said, 'My daughter's never going to marry a Jew.' He was really worked up over the story."

Jim Squires said later that the story, which had been kicking around for months and had repeatedly been raised by reporters interviewing Perot, drove him crazy, not only because it painted him—erroneously, he said—as prejudiced but because it was an embarrassment to his daughter, now married and a mother.

On the next day, Perot, who had avoided set-piece political appearances before special interest groups, preferring to address friendly audiences of his volunteer supporters, agreed with grave reservations to speak to the National Association for the Advancement of Colored People in Nashville. Rollins and Squires had been telling Perot there were certain major forums in the summer he had to address. "These people aren't for me," Rollins said Perot told him, but he finally relented, but barred the usual advance work that was routine in a conventional campaign.

It was a disaster. Insisting on preparing his own remarks, Perot got himself into a rambling recollection of his childhood in Texarkana and how his parents had brought him up free of racial prejudice. Even in the hardest times, he said, his father always made sure to pay his black employees because, he would say, "they are people, too, and they have to live." During the Great Depression, he said, his mother would always feed hoboes who came to the door hungry, "many of them black."

In the course of discussing the sick economy, Perot observed that "it's going to be a long, hot summer. . . . Now I don't have to tell you who gets hurt first when this sort of thing happens, do I? You people do. Your people do. I know that. You know that."

A young listener called out: "Your people? Our people!" And somebody else demanded: "Correct it!" Perot didn't seem to hear what had been said, and he plunged ahead, seemingly unaware that his words had offended some in the audience as patronizing. Later, talking about crime in the cities, he said: "Now good, decent people all over this country, and particularly your folks, have got bars on the windows and bars on the doors, and they're sitting up at night with a shotgun across their knees. And we have abandoned their neighborhoods to crime."

As Perot spoke, his words drew frowns from NAACP leader Benjamin Hooks and other officials on the platform behind him. Flying back to Dallas, an aide tried to explain to Perot why his words had offended many in the audience. It happened that CNN had broadcast the speech live, and that night Perot telephoned the CNN bureau in New York, where the Democratic National Convention was about to open. In conversations with anchorman Bernard Shaw, CNN president Tom Johnson and Tamara Haddad, a producer for Larry King, Perot kept complaining about how the news media was out to destroy him, saying over and over, "This is the last straw!" He was offered airtime to defend himself but declined.

Later, Perot offered an apology—sort of. "It never occurred to me that they would be offended and if I offended anybody in any way I certainly apologize," he said. But the wolves were on him. What Perot said, observed Ron Brown, the Democratic national chairman, "shows a man who is out of touch with real people out there." And Brown's Republican counterpart, Rich Bond, said Perot's performance "underscores the fundamental tin ear that Ross Perot does have when it comes to national politics."

Rollins, learning what had happened, remembers thinking, "This thing is over. I'm getting out of here. . . . I was getting up every day, spending fifteen hours with my people, trying to win. And he clearly had decided that he didn't want to win."

Luce and Meyerson were talking to Perot all weekend, and on Monday, Rollins said, "they said, 'This thing is not working. He doesn't want to run the kind of campaign you want to run.' I said, 'Well, that's obvious. What he doesn't understand is that if he doesn't run a campaign, he can't win. I'm not trying to run Ronald Reagan's campaign all over again. But you've got to go on television, you've got to define yourself. There's certain elements in the campaign to get your message out. You're not willing to do any of them. If we continue to do what we're doing now, we've dropped nine points in a week. By the time the Democrats are finished with their convention we'll be down another five points and then the Republicans will batter the shit out of us for a week.' I said, 'We'll be sitting here at ten points at the end of the summer and we'll never be able to get back in this race again.'

"Meyerson said, 'Isn't there some in-between?' I said, 'There's no in-between. You either run a campaign or you don't run a campaign. We are not running a campaign. . . . We don't have a press operation, a field operation, we don't have any commercials, we don't have any goddamn thing. We have a candidate who on his whim gets on television and says whatever the hell he wants to say. He won't study the issues. I promise you, we're going to lose it all.' "

Luce and Meyerson went over to see Perot again and came back asking, Rollins said, "Okay, what will it take?" Rollins, exasperated because he had sent numerous plans on what decisions were needed with no response from Perot, agreed to give him one last plan.

On Tuesday, Rollins, Jordan and the other professionals sat around waiting to hear from the candidate. By this time, the word was circulating that Jordan was unhappy and wanted out. All fingers pointed at Rollins again, but he denied again he had leaked the story, arguing that reporters were calling from the Democratic convention. Jordan, trying to pick his own time and manner of leaving, denied the report.

On Wednesday morning, at a staff meeting, an irritable Luce began complaining again about leaks and blaming Rollins, telling him, Rollins remembered, "You're the only one who has a stake in getting rid of Hamilton." Rollins told him he would be the last one to want to see Jordan, another proven professional, leave. But Rollins's reputation for talking to reporters made it a hard sell.

That morning, Jordan remembered, the top staff people "had a great meeting" of two or three hours with Perot in which he indicated acceptance of all the recommendations made to him and "how to roll them out" in an orderly and effective way. Jordan was encouraged.

A few hours later, Luce, Meyerson and Rollins went to lunch where, depending on who tells the story, Rollins resigned or was fired. Perot, Luce told Rollins, "wants all of the professionals out of here." Rollins told him that if he and his people went, there would be nobody left "but the Perot Systems people," but Luce was adamant. Rollins later characterized his departure diplomatically as "a mutual decision" but added, "if I had said, 'No, I don't want to leave,' I'm sure they would have fired me." Luce said it was more direct than that.

That afternoon, in Luce's office, Jordan said, Perot "told me two things. He told me he was going to get rid of Ed because he said he didn't trust Ed, and that he hoped that I would stay. He said, 'If you're not going to stay, though, I'd rather that you leave now with Ed, and not have two big stories instead of one big story.'

"And I said, 'Well, Ross, will things continue as they have been?' And he said, 'Well, I don't know. Am I going to turn everything over to you and other people to make all my decisions? No. You also should know that I may just decide to pull the plug on this whole thing.' That was the first time I'd heard him say that, and I didn't believe him when he said it.

"He said, 'This thing is unbelievable. My family's privacy has been invaded.' He had asked me several times, 'What is it like if you make it to the White House?' I said, it just gets worse. It doesn't get any better. He said, 'I just can't stand for my kids to be public figures. . . . What was it like for Amy Carter?' I said, 'It was different. Amy Carter was a little girl. Your kids are, comparably speaking, grown-up.' It really weighed on him that what he did was going to have consequences for his children. He was very sincere about that.''

In fact, Jordan said, at one point he told Squires, the press spokesman, ''he was willing to give the press the number of his kids, but he wasn't going to give them their names!''

Shortly afterward, Rollins went into Jordan's office, told him he was leaving and asked whether he would be leaving with him. He was about to have a press conference to break the news. Jordan told him Perot had asked him to stay, and he felt after denying he was leaving earlier he could not do so now. Jordan said later, laughing: ''I damn sure didn't want to go out with Ed Rollins. I didn't want to go out under that same cloud.''

That night, Perot called Luce and Meyerson and asked them to come to his house. There, Luce said later, ''he told us he decided he was not going to run. He told us all the reasons that have now become known. He told us everything he said the next day plus what he later revealed about his daughter. He just said he saw no need to put his family through this.'' But he did not explicitly say, Luce said, what it was concerning his daughter that had driven him to his decision.

''He told me he wasn't going to get back into the race,'' Luce said. ''I've known Ross for over twenty years. I've been probably as close a friend as he had, and I don't think he would have lied to me about it. . . . I think if he intended to come back, he would have asked me to stick around.'' Instead, Luce went back to his law firm in Dallas, which still represents Perot.

Squires, who also talked with Perot the same night, said there actually were four stories concerning young people close to Perot—two of his daughters, Ross Jr. and David Meyerson, son of Mort Meyerson, who Perot thought of as another son—that drove him to abandon his candidacy. In addition to the one alleging surveillance of an old flame of one of his daughters and one concerning the second daughter's wedding, only later revealed, Perot was upset about public statements regarding the campaign that the two young men had made, convincing him that all four of his loved ones were being damaged by the campaign.

The next morning, Perot's announcement hit the country like a bombshell, and nowhere more so than at the Democratic National Convention in New York, where the delegates were looking forward to presidential nominee Clinton's acceptance speech that night. If Perot was aware that he was stepping on Clinton's big night, he showed no signs of it as he told assembled reporters and the live television cameras why he was not going to run after all.

His reasons were so farfetched that we were moved in our newspaper column to write from New York: "If Ross Perot were Pinocchio, his nose would be growing all the way from Dallas to here after the whopper he unleashed on the country to explain why he was leaving millions of dedicated volunteers in the lurch."

"Now that the Democratic Party has revitalized itself," he said, taking note for the first time of that alleged phenomenon, "I have concluded that we cannot win in November and that the election will be decided in the House of Representatives [if he remained a candidate and no one received the required majority in the electoral college]. Since the House of Representatives does not pick a president until January, the new president will be unable to use the months of November and December to assemble the new government." Continuing the campaign, he said, "would obviously put [the election] in the House of Representatives and be disruptive to the country . . . so therefore I will not become a candidate."

He did, however, urge Perot volunteers in New York state to complete their petition drive "so that everybody running for president will know the names and addresses of all the people who are unhappy with the way things are today." That request started speculation almost at once that Perot was playing some sort of game—speculation that began to grow in intensity not too much later in the year.

The immediate reaction was one of shock and, among Perot's millions of volunteer supporters, a mixture of deep disappointment and anger. Asked at the news conference how he would respond to the charge that he was a quitter, Perot said: "People can say anything they want to say. I'm trying to do what's right for my country. Now, that probably makes me odd in your eyes, but that's what I'm trying to do." After parrying some more questions, Perot turned and strode out of the room and the campaign headquarters, without so much as a thank-you to his staff and phone bank volunteers now faced with a new deluge of calls from bewildered and heartsick Perot loyalists.

It was left for Meyerson to say that Perot "knew he would hurt the volunteers and that he feels deep regret about that.'' Nothing probably hurt the volunteers more than the fact that he had not told them that personally.

In the end, Rollins said later, ''I think he realized the job of being president was a lot tougher than he thought. My sense was when he got into this thing he saw it as a little volunteerism in Washington—'I'll go there for a couple of years and straighten the mess out.' And then he realized it wasn't gonna be fun, but a very tough political environment. I said to him one time, 'You know, this thing is like war, Ross.' He said, 'No, this is not like war. People don't lose limbs. Those are people who are tough.' I said, 'I promise you, Ross, you may not lose limbs, but it's as close to war as you'll ever find. You're trying basically to dismantle the political system of America. There are so many people with vested interests in you failing. They're going to do everything possible [to beat you].' '' Perot apparently came to agree that Rollins was right.

Suddenly, the 1992 race for the presidency was turned upside down. The remaining contenders swooped down quickly on the remains. Speaking to the Perot volunteers from Wyoming, where he was vacationing, Bush said he shared ''many of their same principles . . . and we welcome them warmly into our campaign.'' And in New York, Clinton, who watched the Perot press conference on television with aides who didn't know what to make of it all, walked into another room to place a call to Perot. He also took time from preparations for his acceptance speech to invite the shocked Perot army ''to join us in our efforts to change our country and give our government back to the people.''

Some in their disappointment switched at once, including a Democratic delegate who had been prepared to cast her vote for Perot and came out for Clinton. But many others, refusing to believe that their dream of taking back their country from the politics-as-usual crowd behind the leadership of the feisty independent from Texas who had called on them repeatedly to ''stay in the ring'' with him, hoped against hope that they had not seen the last of Ross Perot.

CHAPTER 21

TWO FOR
THE ROAD

Ever since Michael Dukakis came out of the 1988 Democratic convention with a seventeen-point lead in the polls and quickly lost it, it had been remembered how, in the period before the Republican convention, he had gone back to Massachusetts and tended to state business—while the Bush campaign methodically chewed him up. The Clinton strategists were determined that there would be no repetition. Clinton and new running mate Al Gore were going to hit the ground running out of New York, and keep running until November 3. The question was how and where.

Well before the convention, the Clinton planners had settled on a cold electoral college strategy—in which states they were going to work hardest and deploy the most resources, in which states they would make some effort in hopes of winning or forcing Bush to spend his resources, and which states they would largely ignore either because they appeared to be safe for Bush or could be reasonably counted on as safe for Clinton.

In the four years leading up to the election year, party National

Chairman Ron Brown and his able and intense political director at the Democratic National Committee, Paul Tully, had already done the spade-work on a specific 1992 electoral college strategy. After a meeting in a Washington suburb in 1991 at which all the prospective Democratic presidential candidates were briefed, newspaper stories reported that the plan was so specific that certain states already were being written off, obliging Brown to say, with fingers crossed, that a fifty-state strategy was being planned. That was true enough, but tentative plans were for some of the fifty to get little more than a nod.

The plan also included tighter linkage than in recent years between the Democratic national ticket and state tickets in what was called a "coordinated campaign" strategy. In previous years, and particularly in 1988 with Michael Dukakis at the head of the ticket, many local and statewide candidates had run away from the national standard-bearer, especially in the South where the nominated liberal jeopardized their own chances of election. This time, the hope was that they would embrace the ticket enthusiastically.

Tully was a bear on making the coordinated-campaign idea a func-tioning reality in the Democratic Party as it had been for years in the Republican, and on electoral vote targeting. And in assigning priorities in allocation of campaign resources to the various states, he was a walk-ing, fast-talking encyclopedia of political facts and figures. He conveyed his treasury of information and analyses in a trademark patois of word abbreviations of Ds [for Democrats] and Rs [Republicans], generously seasoned with grunts and punctuated by raised eyebrows, wide grins and flailing arms. Understanding Tullyspeak was an essential prerequisite for fellow campaign workers and reporters alike who wanted to grasp what really was going on. Once Clinton had the nomination secured, Tully was dispatched to Little Rock to lend his general and specific political savvy to the campaign headquarters.

The party's electoral college strategy had as a central precept that the string of industrial states from New York and New Jersey, through Pennsylvania and Ohio, into Michigan and Illinois would be the key to victory. David Wilhelm, the Clinton campaign manager, who was overseeing the electoral vote strategy from Little Rock, emphatically shared this view. As a native of small-town Ohio who had cut his political eyeteeth in Illinois, running winning campaigns for Senator Paul Simon and Mayor Richard Daley in Chicago, Wilhelm knew the territory.

In mid-April, two memos blossomed from the Democratic camp that, taken together, were to have far-reaching ramifications for the Clinton campaign. On April 15, Steve Rosenthal of the Democratic National Committee political staff wrote one to his bosses, Ron Brown and Tully. Five days later, Carter Wilkie, a young campaign aide then working in Indianapolis in advance of the Indiana primary and unaware of Rosenthal's memo, wrote another and sent it to "Clinton strategists and staff" in Little Rock.

Rosenthal specifically proposed a pair of "nationwide voter-registration bus caravans" to set out immediately after the Democratic National Convention, one from New York bearing presidential nominee Clinton and the other from Los Angeles with the yet unselected vice presidential nominee in the lead bus. The scheme, Rosenthal wrote, would be "a way to keep the media focused on our 'momentum' and also as another way to avoid any lag (à la Dukakis) following the '88 convention."

Rosenthal proposed that the nominees ride the buses for a full three weeks, or at least drop in on them from time to time with celebrities and well-known elected officials filling in as surrogates. All "would take part in a series of rallies in large and small cities, suburban and rural areas— based on our targeting," the memo said, and the two bus caravans would meet in Houston for one final rally two weeks before the Republican National Convention there.

"The message that would come out of this," Rosenthal wrote, "is that the Democratic campaign has hit the ground running, is organized and is taking its message directly to the American people . . . as a takeoff on the old 'whistlestop' campaigns." The memo made clear that the caravans would be focused on voter registration that could "utilize the skills of the union organizers" available to the campaign and would work through "each state's coordinated campaign plan" to benefit all candidates on the Democratic ticket.

Wilkie's April 20 memo, which did not specify travel by bus although that was the logical means of transportation for the region he wanted covered, was pegged originally for three approaching primaries along the Ohio River. "The Indiana, Kentucky and Ohio contests," he wrote, "come at a time when Clinton must tell his life story, connect with ordinary Americans and begin to define himself as a Democrat in touch with traditional, middle American values. Both banks of the Ohio River are populated by Democrats who are mainly economic populists and social traditionalists. Rather than visit southern Ohio, Indiana and Kentucky at separate stages, the campaign should take advantage of the regional culture and local TV markets that transcend state boundaries and schedule an old-fashioned, three-state swing. . . ."

Wilkie suggested that such a tour "place a premium on visits in small settings in small towns, i.e., a speech to local Democrats from the front porch of a supporter's home, the steps of a county courthouse, or the pulpit of a Methodist church." This approach, he wrote, would "remind people of the forgotten Democratic Party roots in small-town, traditional middle-class American communities and the aspirations of the forgotten middle class."

Wilkie was intrigued by the cultural roots that had buried themselves into the soil of Appalachia through West Virginia, Ohio, Kentucky and Indiana—economic populism and social traditionalism—and thought he saw a kinship with Clinton's own roots and agenda. To take a sounding on his scheme, before writing the memo, he had phoned his friend Mort Engelberg, a Hollywood producer and political junkie who amused himself advancing campaign trips for Clinton and previous Democratic candidates. He asked Engelberg whether such a trip through this region, with stops at settings reflecting the culture of the region mentioned in his memo, was feasible. Engelberg said why not?

Wilkie bounced his idea off local reporters, and they reacted very positively toward it. Most of them, Wilkie said later, did not work for news organizations that could afford to send them on the very expensive jet plane trips the candidates made, and this was their shot "to be the boys on the bus" in their own bailiwicks.

So Wilkie put his thoughts on a single sheet of paper, made photocopies and sent the memo to Wilhelm and other members of the Clinton senior staff. That same day or the next, Wilkie said, Bob Boorstin of the Clinton staff called back and told him: "Great! We're going to do it—after the convention." No mention was made of Rosenthal's memo of five days earlier, which specifically called for his proposed bus caravans to set out at that time.

Wilkie remembered the letdown. "I was so depressed," he recalled. "I said, 'You guys don't understand. We've got these primaries.' " If the trip was done after the convention, he said, "nobody will be around. You'll be wasting your time." But that was the decision.

Several weeks before the Democratic convention, Engelberg was on the phone with Bev Lindsey, then Clinton's campaign scheduler. They talked about what was going to be done after the convention and Engelberg expressed weariness with the old, conventional routine of the nominees flying from one media-market airport to another and another, holding tarmac rallies with, as Engelberg put it later, "a bunch of white politicians in suits." What about, he suggested, a bus trip?

Around this time Rosenthal had sent another version of his original memo to Wilhelm, an indication that no action had been taken on the basis of that first one. Wilhelm as the Clinton electoral vote specialist felt strongly that in order to win the two states with which he was most familiar, Illinois and Ohio, it would be important to muster downstate support for Clinton—outside Chicago and Cook County in Illinois and outside Cleveland in Ohio. A good way to do so, he became convinced, was by sending Clinton through the southern parts of these battleground states—and others in the Rust Belt of the East and Midwest, an idea that coincided with Wilkie's scheme.

"We had Bush in the White House, we had Perot not leaving television studios, we had Bill Clinton—who was not very well known yet by the American people but was really extraordinary at person-to-person campaigning," Wilhelm said. "We knew we would be attacked as liberals who don't understand the values of middle-income America, and we had to leave New York, and had to go somewhere, and we'd already figured out what the showdown states were. Why not take a trip through [them], showcase Bill Clinton at his best, which is in a very grass-roots style of campaigning, which would put the lie to what certainly would be attacks on him as some sort of tax-and-spend liberal?"

Wilhelm saw the states bordering on the Ohio and Mississippi rivers as the key to the election, and what better way to reach them? Trains were out; they were too expensive and the atrophied rail system limited too severely the routes that could be taken.

Traveling by bus in the jet age seemed at first comical. After all, hadn't jet travel and television communications revolutionized presidential campaigning? Nearly a third of a century earlier, Richard Nixon, the victim of a foolish pledge to campaign in all fifty states before Election Day, had stretched himself so thin in 1960 going to places with insignificant numbers of voters and electoral votes that he crossed the finish line bedraggled, exhausted—and defeated. Over the next eight years, as he plotted his comeback in presidential politics, Nixon had learned his lesson. When he ran again in 1968, and won, he adopted the tarmac strategy that had become standard ever since—focus on major media markets, make quick hits in and out of them by jet for maximum television coverage, and leave the boondocks largely to the vice presidential nominee.

But Engelberg, who had produced the *Smokey and the Bandit* movies and understood the romance of the open road, saw the possibilities of taking the Clinton persona and message to the highways and byways. "Having been on the road with this guy in one way or another for the past year," he said later, "I found that the times I was with Clinton and he was in unstructured kinds of situations [were] real good, because he was good in one-on-one informal stuff. It also elevated him, because he seemed to respond to that kind of environment."

At the outset, Engelberg said, he found "no great enthusiasm" for the idea of a bus trip among the top campaign strategists in Little Rock—although many later claimed at least a portion of its paternity. Engelberg phoned fellow Californian Mickey Kantor, now chairing the campaign from Little Rock. Focused as nearly everyone in Little Rock was at the time in discussions on the vice presidential selection and convention plans, Engelberg said, Kantor seemed to him not to have heard about the idea. "Literally, Mort had to fight for it," Kantor said later. "A lot of people at first [said], 'Oh, God, you put two Southerners on a bus—what would it look like?' " But then a consensus started to build for it, he said.

Engelberg, Kantor said after the election, "was insistent and incessant, and so was Bev, in our doing it, and other people picked it up, and now, today, you will find many mothers and fathers to that idea". . . . In any event, he said, "it doesn't matter whose idea it was. It worked."

The one major figure in the campaign who admitted that he didn't think much of the idea at the time was Carville. He said later it started out "a sort of mediocre idea" but caught on and became "symbolic" of the Clinton style and campaign.

Engelberg recalled pitching Kantor that "if we did this, it should be issue-driven—every stop we made should not be a rally but a message kind of event, and we should stay out of the big cities, but hit the big-city media markets" along the way. Also, he made the case that having the presidential and vice presidential nominees together coming directly out of the convention would be an irresistible magnet for press coverage, on both the national and local levels. "I kept saying that if you keep these guys together we'll have a great hunk of the national press corps with us, plus the fact that a bus as opposed to a plane means we'll have a lot of local people, which if nothing else I guarantee you we'll own [for example] the Columbus media for the day before and the day we're there. I always felt we would dominate the media."

For one thing, Engelberg said, echoing Wilkie's view, a lot of local newspapers "cannot afford the twelve or fifteen hundred bucks that a seat on the plane costs today, but a hundred and fifty bucks for a seat on the bus meant, for example, we could get a lot of Philadelphia media on board in New York to make the trip with us and stay on an extra day [through Pennsylvania]."

After the idea had been weighed in Little Rock for several days, Engelberg recalled, Kantor called back and gave him the go-ahead. The first step was laying out a route. Engelberg knew the bus trip would be leaving from the convention in New York, and the original thought was to have it end in Little Rock. Considering where the major battlegrounds were, most of it as Wilhelm also noted easily fell in place—across New Jersey, into Pennsylvania, Ohio and on west. At this time, Clinton had not selected his running mate, but Engelberg deduced—without any inside information, he said later—that Gore and Hamilton were the finalists. So he planned two preliminary routes, one dipping down from Ohio into Tennessee in the event Gore was the choice and the other going up into Indiana if it was going to be Hamilton.

Next, Engelberg in conjunction with Bev Lindsey and then Susan Thomases, who had taken over scheduling, set out to find specific places to go within the framework of Wilhelm's battleground states strategy. Still well in advance of the convention, Engelberg flew to Philadelphia, the obvious first media market to exploit after leaving New York, rented a car and started driving west. Accompanying him was Bruce Garamella, a veteran advance man. First, though, they decided on Camden, New

Jersey, across the Delaware River from Philadelphia, as the initial stop outside New York, at a General Electric aerospace plant that had suffered sharp cutbacks but had a strong worker retraining program of the sort Clinton was advocating.

Engelberg and Garamella then worked their way across Pennsylvania, with guidance from Carville, who knew the state well after having run the Wofford campaign, and Celia Fischer, the Clinton state coordinator working out of Philadelphia. They drove up to Valley Forge and other likely places in eastern Pennsylvania looking for picturesque sites that also had activities that dovetailed with the Clinton message, finally settling on York for the first overnight. They also chose what was billed as "the world's largest truck stop" at Carlisle, "a good place to do infrastructure—talk about bridges and highways," Engelberg said. "And it just so happened that it was a very interesting kind of picture, because as far as the eye could see you've got these giant semi-trailer trucks, a very picturesque café there. . . . We knew it would be a good picture there, [the candidates] walking around with a bunch of truck drivers and hopefully sitting down and talking infrastructure."

As Engelberg and Garamella meandered their way through Pennsylvania and Ohio, it became clear that the tour was not likely to make it all the way to Little Rock in the time allotted, so it was decided to terminate it after a thousand miles in St. Louis, in another targeted state. The selection of Gore as Clinton's running mate turned out not to be a factor in the scheduling, and the first trip was routed through Indiana, not Tennessee, after all.

Some ranking members of the staff remained cool to the whole idea. One of them, encountering Engelberg at the convention, asked him what he was up to. When he told him, the reply was, "Oh, yes, you got your way. We're doing the bus trip." Engelberg said later, "I felt like Lee Harvey Oswald, like I was being set up as the single assassin; everything short of Fair Play for Cuba leaflets in my hotel room." And he told *The Boston Globe*'s Curtis Wilkie: "If you find some bones on the side of the road along the way, they'll be mine."

Engelberg as busmeister leased only eight buses for the trip, one assigned to each of the candidates and the rest for staff and about 150 newspeople of various descriptions, and a couple of vans for television and still cameramen. He had a small team of assistants led by twenty-year-old Jason Goldberg, who loaded twenty-five pounds of ice, sandwiches and a case of soft drinks on each bus for the first day—totally inadequate since there was no stop for lunch or dinner before arriving in York late that first night. The second day the order was increased to 800 pounds of ice and sixty cases of soft drinks.

There were other opening-day snafus. Planning in advance, Engelberg sent the vans on ahead, figuring "they could get this wonderful shot of the bus after we come out of the [Lincoln] Tunnel [to New Jersey], with the New York skyline in the background." But on the way to the tunnel, the motorcade passed the vans, stuck in traffic. And before the motorcade reached the toll booth for the New Jersey Turnpike that would take the entourage south to Camden, Secret Service agents reported the presence of a stowaway, a homeless woman, on one of the staff buses. The motorcade had to be halted at the toll booth to disembark the unwelcome interloper on the campaign that bragged it was "Putting People First." So much, Engelberg laughed later, for "the well-oiled machine."

Otherwise, the scheme of conveying the Clinton message along the route worked out well. At a turnpike rest stop about eight miles north of Camden, the motorcade stopped and took aboard six workers from the GE job retraining program who visited with Clinton and Gore and briefed them on what they would see at the plant. This approach was followed throughout this and subsequent bus trips.

But it was not logistics, good or bad, that became the trademark of what some signs along the way were soon calling "Bill and Al's Excellent Adventure." It was the men and their message of generational change, delivered in words and in their strikingly youthful and vigorous appearance, together with their young, blond and stylish wives.

"Change is the key to your security," Clinton told the workers at the Camden plant. "The other side is saying we've been in charge for twelve years and if you want change, vote for more of the same. That approach doesn't make sense. Their approach has failed."

Along the way, Clinton and Gore made a special pitch to the supporters of Ross Perot, now that he had withdrawn. At a New York rally kicking off the bus trip, two Perot organizers in New York state had announced their conversion to Clinton, and the Democratic nominee and his running mate pounded away at their message of change at every stop. The Perot pullout had helped give Clinton, *The New York Times* reported, the largest bounce recorded after a party convention in fifty years, putting him 24 percentage points ahead of Bush, 55 to 31, in the *Times*/CBS News poll.

The Republican opposition seemed stunned by the aftermath of the Perot decision, catapulting the Democratic ticket into such a lead. Appearing with Bush in Provo, Utah, on the second day of the Clinton-Gore bus trip, Republican Senator Jake Garn ridiculed the Democratic pair as "a team of pretty boys," but that flip dismissal failed to grasp a political phenomenon that was now being revealed on the open highways through Pennsylvania.

When the bus tour arrived in York near midnight, two hours behind schedule, for the first overnight stay, a crowd of several thousand people were waiting outside the candidates' hotel. "This happened for the next five days," Engelberg recalled. "It was what you would like to do if you're a good advance man, but it just happened. That was the first time I felt, 'Something's going on here.' " Mark Gearan, who was now assigned as Gore's chief aide, said: "We weren't competent enough to advance that kind of trip. Every advance kid we had was in New York. We just rolled out of there hoping for the best. Something else was happening."

The stop the next day at "the world's largest truck stop" in Carlisle was all that Engelberg had hoped for. Bill and Al, dressed casually in sport shirts and slacks, climbed into the cab of a semi—Bill behind the wheel, naturally. Both went into the diner and sat at the counter discussing things like speed limits and other trucker concerns with the customers, while Hillary and Tipper played some miniature golf outside.

At a rest stop along the Pennsylvania Turnpike, Bill and Al tossed a football around in the best Kennedy tradition, and the next day, at Weirton, West Virginia, they had an opportunity, not to be passed up, to tap the Kennedy legend again. Speaking beside a bust of Kennedy, who had visited the troubled steel town during his 1960 campaign as FDR had done in 1932, Clinton reminded the crowd of Kennedy's visit and his message then and his own message now, that "it's time for a change."

On into Ohio the bus tour rolled. After a stop for a discussion with farmers at the farm of Democratic state chairman Gene Branstool outside of Utica, a small town northwest of Columbus, the buses went on past a crossroads where Branstool had informed Engelberg he could produce a few hundred people. When they got there late that night, more than 3,000 were waiting. Clinton and Gore got out and spoke, as they were increasingly obliged to do as the bus trip itself began to take on the reputation of a happening.

But it was the appearance and the style of Clinton, Gore and their wives as much as the campaign rhetoric that seemed to capture the small-town crowds and the hundreds who gathered at crossroads and other truck stops along the way. Gore particularly, so stiff and earnest in his failed 1988 presidential bid that he became the brunt of robot jokes, became more relaxed and even playful in the role of second fiddle.

Running mates as a rule seldom campaign with the standard-bearer, and when they do it is almost always in a subordinate, even subservient role, but Clinton saw to it that Gore got nearly equal billing. He invited Gore to answer voters' questions addressed to himself, especially when the subject was one on which Gore had superior background, such as the environment. And Gore developed into a first-class crowd warm-up speaker, with a laugh-getting ritual that became standard on the tour.

After reciting a long list of Bush-Quayle failures, he would intone: "Bush and Quayle have run out of ideas. They've run out of energy. They've run out of gas, and with your help come November, they're going to be run out of office!" He would wind up his pitch by shouting: "It's time for Bush and Quayle to go!" Then he would ask the crowd: "What time is it?" And on cue the roar would come back: "It's time for them to go!"

Clinton, his head thrown back in boisterous laughter as if he were hearing the routine for the first time, would then step up to the micro-phones. Gesturing to Gore, he would say, as he did at one stop in Wilmington, Ohio: "I made a pretty good decision, didn't I? It would suit me for this election to be based on the first decision George Bush made [as a presidential nominee in 1988] and the first decision I made."

In a more serious vein, Clinton often would tell crowds that the one reason he had selected Gore was that he believed him to be the best person to assume the presidency if anything were to happen to him. And compared to the way Bush was keeping his stand-in, Dan Quayle, at arm's length, the embrace emphatically conveyed the sense that here was a genuine relationship of mutual respect and confidence.

By this time Al Gore was like a kid who couldn't be dragged off the

384 / Jack Germond and Jules Witcover

roller coaster at an amusement park. The Gores had been scheduled to drop off the tour when it reached Louisville and go home to Tennessee, but as the departure point approached, Gore turned to Gearan and asked: "Why are we leaving?" When Gearan told him briefing sessions were planned for him home in Carthage, he said they could be done on the bus, that he wanted to stay to the end.

The Clintons and the Gores took to riding for hours in the same van, visiting and, in the case of the two men, experiencing a bonding that became obvious to their fellow bus travelers. After the longest of days, they would sit on the bus talking, talking, talking, while the rest of the entourage groaned for them to get off and go to bed. Soon, when Gore would go into his warm-up and end with, "What time is it?" weary reporters would shout back: "It's time for us to go!" On one occasion later, when the two ticket mates sat in Clinton's bus, locked in a post-midnight gabfest at the end of the day's schedule, aides took to rocking the huge bus back and forth to get them out.

As the buses moved on, dipping into Kentucky and Indiana and on into Illinois, the crowds grew larger and more enthusiastic. Often there were protesters present, usually toting anti-abortion signs, but except for them the mood was cheerful and even celebratory. As the buses sped by more crossroads in the middle of nowhere, signs began to crop up saying: GIVE US EIGHT MINUTES AND WE'LL GIVE YOU EIGHT YEARS. The appeal proved irresistible to the two candidates, who would stop the motorcade, hop off, shake hands and say a few words, thus assuring further late arrivals down the road.

Gene Randall of CNN ribbed Engelberg, suggesting he had hired extras to move from crossroads to crossroads to give the illusion of Clinton's crowd appeal. (It would not have been the first time. During the 1988 Iowa caucuses, most of the cars in a motorcade across the state by televangelist Pat Robertson were packed with supporters, who piled out at each stop and quickly assembled to hear their man make the same speech he had made at all the stops before.)

On the final night of the trip, a crowd more than doubling the local population waited two hours beyond the scheduled arrival time in Vandalia, Illinois, site of the state's first capitol where Abraham Lincoln served in the legislature. It was just the kind of setting that Carter Wilkie had in mind when he wrote his memo back in April. Clinton told his listeners that Lincoln "is turned over in his grave tonight to think of what George Bush and Dan Quayle have done to the Republican Party and the United States of America." And the next day for the trip's windup, another crowd estimated at 30,000 jammed downtown St. Louis streets in a scene more typical of late October in a presidential election year. The bus trip had succeeded far beyond expectations, and the team of Bill and Al was cemented in a way that George and Dan never could, or would, be.

After the election, Charlie Black of the Bush-Quayle campaign credited his opponents with a master stroke in the bus trip coming directly out of the Democratic convention. The practical effect, he said, was "they turned a four-day story into a twelve-day story" by extending that very successful convention beyond its adjournment and maintaining the bounce derived from the convention itself against attempts even then by the Republicans to cut the Clinton-Gore team down to size.

Beyond that, Jim Lake said, the timely withdrawal of Ross Perot at the end of a successful convention, followed by the bus trip, was golden for Clinton. "The minute he [Perot] bails out in the middle of this halo [the convention], all these people who were anti-Bush become pro-Clinton," Lake said. "Clinton and Perot couldn't have sat down and planned it better. We didn't know it at once, but we soon saw it."

Before the final rally in St. Louis, Bruce Lindsey asked Engelberg to send him a memo with his thoughts on how another bus trip in some future time should be done, based on what he had learned from this one. On the plane back to Los Angeles, Engelberg wrote it out in longhand, advising at the outset, "Let's not kill the goose that laid the golden egg," but wait a month before trying it again. When he got home, he typed it out, intending to send it by fax to Little Rock the next morning. But when he got up, he found a message to him on his fax machine, informing him that there would be another bus trip in ten days.

The second trip picked up basically where the first had left off, in East St. Louis just across the Mississippi River in Illinois. This time, Engelberg recalled, "everybody wanted a piece of it"—staff and press alike. Fourteen buses were required to handle the increase, and special props were built, including what Engelberg called "a rally in a box." It was a small stage equipped with a sound system that could be folded up into the undercarriage of Clinton's bus. Before leaving, Engelberg's crew practiced setting it up until they could do it in seven minutes, while the candidates were working the ropeline, shaking hands with voters. (The aforementioned Pat Robertson motorcade across Iowa four years earlier also had such a contraption.)

The Secret Service also stepped in, armor-plating the front of Clinton's bus and installing bulletproof glass, with the idea that he would be able to stand up and wave to crossroads crowds as the bus went by—a notion that did not calculate Clinton's seeming inability to resist stopping. "They came to see me," he would tell aides, "I'm going to get out and talk to them." Television lights were installed inside the bus so that crews could come in and do their job without first having to set up all their cumbersome equipment.

The second bus trip was a much shorter affair, up the Mississippi for less than three days with stops in small riverfront towns in Missouri, Iowa and Wisconsin, then ending in Minneapolis. Many stops along the way were called "impromptu," but often local Democratic officials, notified of the bus route, would advise the campaign that they intended to have a crowd at this or that crossroads or truck stop. If the crowd materialized, the motorcade would then stop, and most times it did. As a result, the motorcade would roll up hours late to the entrance to the hotel or motel where the candidates would be staying overnight. As late as 2:30 A.M. in small towns on the route, hundreds or even thousands would be waiting to greet them. And of course Gore would have to ask them "What time is it?" and Clinton would have to give his own answer: "Time for a change."

The highlight of the first day was a visit to Hannibal, Missouri, Mark Twain's boyhood hometown, where Clinton quoted his observation that "petrified opinion and old ideas never did anything to break a chain or free a human soul." While Bill and Al weren't quite Tom Sawyer and Huck Finn, they did do a fair imitation of small-town boys who hadn't forgotten their roots. The notably articulate Clinton started talking about his "momma" and beginning his remarks with phrases like, "Well shoot, folks."

At Burlington, Iowa, before a massive crowd with the muddy Mississippi flowing slowly by, he talked about how "I've grown up loving the land that borders this river," and "all the troubles this river has seen." He would also make a point of telling the crowds that "Al still lives on a farm" in Carthage, Tennessee, although Gore had spent much of his time as a youth in Washington as the son of a United States senator and still put in most of his time there.

By now they were behaving like a couple of brothers, if not twins, with Clinton frequently telling crowds that "Al and I" would do this or that for them when they were elected, and with Gore referring to "the Clinton-Gore team." Clinton didn't seem to mind a bit, and continued laughing at Gore's introduction, which he was now laying on with voice rising and arms flailing.

At a forum in Davenport, Iowa, when Clinton was asked a foreign policy question and gave a short, unimpressive response, Gore took the microphone and recalled that President Bush in a recent speech had emphasized how important it was to have an experienced voice on the end of the line when a crisis call came into the White House in the middle of the night. When Bush's wealthy friends called, Gore said, he always answers at once, but "when the average American family calls up" to tell him how bad things are, "they're getting a disconnect." Clinton stood there wearing a slight grin that suggested he was wishing he'd have said that.

Pat Deluhery, an Iowa Democratic state senator watching the team at work at the Davenport forum, told us afterward concerning Clinton: "He's made two fabulous choices. First he's picked this guy [Gore] and then this bus thing. People love it. They have to come out and see these two young guys who look and act like they're ready to go."

At the final stop of the second trip, another large crowd waited in the rain for hours in downtown Minneapolis for Clinton's arrival. From his bus, he called the crowd over a cellular phone, with his words hooked up to a microphone, apologized for being so late and asked them not to leave. They stayed, and when he got there, Clinton stood before a statue of the venerated Hubert Humphrey, with another former vice president from Minnesota, Walter Mondale, standing by. As he started to brag on Gore, about to call him the best vice presidential selection ever, he stopped, grinned, and added: "who was not from Minnesota!"

The Republican convention was now only days away, so Bill and Al put their buses away for a while, but afterward resumed their Excellent Adventure. In all, they made seven full-fledged bus trips and two others for parts of a day before election day. The trips, Engelberg mused later, "became sort of a metaphor—symbolic of this campaign: this is for everybody. The difference in the bus as opposed to Harry Truman's train trips, if you wanted to see Harry Truman, you had to go down to the train station. The beauty of these bus trips was that we took the bus to a Head Start center, or we took the bus to a factory, and in a sense we were bringing the campaign to the electorate."

As Clinton and Gore thus rolled merrily along toward the fall campaign, the team of Bush and Quayle was stumbling toward the Republican convention in Houston. Bush was continuing to insist that he had no thought of discarding the man he had said in 1988 was qualified to be president. But others in their party, after four years of Dan Quayle remaining that celebrated heartbeat away from the presidency, still had their doubts. They wondered how firm George Bush really was on the point—and whether anything could be said or done to change his mind.

STILL NO
JACK KENNEDY

While the Bill and Al traveling road show was playing to smash audiences across small-town America, the Republican team of George and Dan—Bush and Quayle—was doing solo acts, as the two had all through the previous four years, intentionally keeping their distance. With Pat Buchanan disposed of as a threat to Bush's renomination, the president preferred to get back to governing and leave the campaign stumping to the vice president, who in spite of endless ridicule from the Democrats and in the news media had proved to be an effective drawing card and record-breaking fund-raiser for his party.

Ever since Bush had shocked and dismayed many fellow Republicans at the party's national convention in New Orleans four years earlier by selecting the young and gaffe-prone Hoosier senator as his running mate, political duets by the two were few and far between. The reason was understood by all who had witnessed or read about Quayle's disastrous run as the Republican vice presidential nominee in 1988 and his erratic performance as Bush's understudy in office thereafter.

Two episodes haunted him from the 1988 campaign. The first and best remembered by voters was his ambush at the hands of Democratic vice presidential nominee Lloyd Bentsen in their debate in Omaha. Much of that debate was focused on Quayle's youth—he was forty-one at the time but much younger-looking and immature—and hence on his qualifications to take over the presidency if fate were to so dictate.

Quayle was defensive. "It's not just age, it's accomplishments, it's experience," he said at one point. "I have far more experience than many others that sought the office of vice president of this country. I have as much experience in the Congress as Jack Kennedy did when he sought the presidency. . . ."

Bentsen stiffened, then glared at Quayle. "Senator," he said in a rejoinder from which Quayle would never recover, "I served with Jack Kennedy. I knew Jack Kennedy. Jack Kennedy was a friend of mine. Senator, you are no Jack Kennedy."

Quayle was stunned, as the audience erupted in applause and laughter. That one exchange became a political albatross around his neck thereafter, to the point that, once elected, the young vice president chose to turn it into a joke. At a book party on the occasion of our account of the 1988 campaign in which the debate exchange was reexamined, Quayle graciously came, stood up and said: "I knew Teddy White. Teddy White was a friend of mine. And believe me, you guys are no Teddy White."

But politically, Dan Quayle's reputation as an inexperienced naïf could not be laughed off. Neither could the second experience that left scars on him from the 1988 campaign. That was the Bush campaign's assigning of handlers to hold a tight rein on him as he stumped through the smaller towns and states, the customary fate of vice presidential nominees. They saved him from some but not all the political pitfalls he encountered, but he chafed at their close supervision and at news stories about it.

He began to blame the handlers, longtime professional consultants Stuart Spencer and Joe Canzeri, for not permitting him to be himself—which, when he was, sometimes had embarrassing results. Losing his temper at one point, he told reporters: "There is not going to be any more handler stories, because I'm the handler." He dubbed himself "Doctor Spin" and told reporters that if they had any questions to come to him, not to one of the handlers. But Spencer and Canzeri continued to watch over him, and he survived the campaign.

As vice president, Quayle insisted on having his own people around him, and he functioned politically on a much freer rein than during the campaign, but still under the general direction of the Bush administration's political operation, as was expected of any vice president. Bush continued to insist that he had made a good choice but did not go out of his way particularly to showcase that choice.

Quayle was given a few special assignments and met with the president weekly for a private lunch, in the pattern of Bush himself when he was Ronald Reagan's vice president. And like Bush under Reagan, Quayle was a fawning man-in-waiting, ever loyal and outspokenly supportive of Bush in every way. In inner counsels, however, he spoke up much more often than Bush ever did at political and policy staff meetings with Reagan. He was regarded as a strong voice for conservative viewpoints within the Bush administration, bolstered by his astute and politically attuned chief of staff, Bill Kristol, and others.

Outside the administration, however, Quayle continued to be regarded as the pratfall-plagued political mistake. Although he went for months at a time without saying or doing anything to reinforce that reputation, he slipped occasionally enough to keep it alive and the brunt of public ridicule. That fact governed his usefulness for the president. On the one hand there was a desire to put him in situations where he could combat the impression of being a dim bulb. On the other, there was always the realization that he could misstep, and an understanding that his role as emissary for the president did not always carry the force desired. Still, Dan Quayle was vice president of the United States, and that fact alone counted for a great deal, especially in the international diplomatic community.

After less than two weeks in office, Bush sent the new vice president to South and Central America to perform largely ceremonial duties, as a way of getting his feet wet. He performed adequately, except for an observation in El Salvador that the United States was committed to "work toward the elimination of human rights" in the region.

Shortly afterward, back home, when the Republican National Committee's executive committee censured former Ku Klux Klansman David

Duke upon his election to the Louisiana state legislature as a Republican, Quayle commended the party for its "censorship" of Duke.

On a trip to the Pacific, he treated the locals at a military base in Honolulu to a little geography lesson: "Hawaii has always been a very pivotal role in the Pacific. It is in the Pacific. It is a part of the United States that is an island that is right here." And in Pago Pago, American Samoa, pronounced "Pango Pango" but which Quayle called "Pogo Pogo" as in the old comic strip, he referred to the local children as "happy campers," which was taken as condescending. These slips were trivial, to be sure, but they got much press attention and froze the image of Dan Quayle as an empty suit.

His interest in golf, which he had played with considerable skill and dedication ever since college, also became a prominent trademark, and not always in a constructive manner. On the same Pacific trip, after a round on the local links in Singapore, he showed up late for dinner at the home of the fuming prime minister, who greeted him with "I hear you had some golf."

Back home again, Quayle rewarded what came to be known in the press corps as "the gaffe watch" with his twist on the slogan of the United Negro College Fund, that "A mind is a terrible thing to waste." Run through the Quayle language mangler, it came out "What a waste it is to lose one's mind, or not to have a mind, is being very wasteful. How true that is."

Dan Quayle, as vice president just as vice presidential candidate, was always good for a laugh. But for Republican politicians, especially those already looking ahead to the prospects for a second Bush term, "the Quayle problem" was no laughing matter. A *Washington Post*/ABC News poll in early August of 1989 found that 52 percent of 1,022 persons interviewed didn't think Quayle was fit for the presidency and 38 percent said Bush should get himself another running mate in 1992.

On and on it went. Visiting the site of the latest San Francisco earthquake, Quayle called it "a heart-rendering sight" and judged that "the loss of life will be irreplaceable." Voters continued to laugh and shake their heads. But a vice president has a constituency of one, and that one remained firm in his support. Bush in November told *The Dallas Morning News* that Quayle "absolutely" would be on the ticket with him in 1992 if he wanted to be.

Quayle's reputation, however, was inhibiting his ability to perform the traditional job of presidential emissary abroad. After the Bush administration's invasion of Panama in early 1990, he was sent to Latin America to smooth sensitivities and explain the American decision, but Venezuela and Mexico declined to receive him. It was on this same trip that he bought the infamous "anatomically correct" doll in Valparaiso, Chile, that added to his image as a sophomoric clown. A March 1990 Gallup poll found 54 percent said he wasn't qualified to be president and 49 percent thought Bush should dump him in 1992.

But Dan Quayle had his strengths, too. For the 1990 congressional campaign, he raised a record of more than $15 million for party candidates. And when Bush decided to go to war in the Persian Gulf to turn back the Iraqi invasion of Kuwait, Quayle was a visible, outspoken defender. Even then, though, Quayle seemed to do himself no good politically. Speculation began that one of the stars of the American military effort, General Colin Powell, chairman of the Joint Chiefs of Staff, might and ought to replace Quayle on the Bush ticket in 1992. A *New York Times*/CBS News poll of 1,252 adults found 56 percent viewed Powell favorably to a dismal 19 percent for Quayle.

In May, the hospitalization of Bush for an irregular heartbeat after a day of jogging and other strenuous physical exercise gave higher visibility than ever to "the Quayle problem." A *Time* headline asked: "Is He Really that Bad?" with a poll showing 52 percent of those surveyed thought Bush should bounce Quayle and 24 percent saying they would be less likely to vote for Bush if he didn't. The *Newsweek* cover, showing Quayle swinging a golf club, was no better: "The Quayle Handicap . . . Is He a Lightweight—Or Smarter than You Think?"

When Bush was asked whether he might reconsider keeping Quayle on the ticket, he shot back: "Do you want that by hand or do you want it by word?" He said he would prefer not emulating a former vice president, Nelson Rockefeller, who once conspicuously replied to a heckler's taunts by extending his middle finger into the air. Quayle, the president said, was getting "a bum rap in the press, pounding on him when he's doing a first-rate job. And I don't know how many times I have to say it, but I'm not about to change my mind when I see his performance and know what he does."

In the next weeks, Quayle traveled to Japan and India and shortly afterward to Eastern Europe on what were essentially gaffe-free trips, but few reporters went along and it didn't seem to matter anyway. A mind-set had taken hold with the American people that Dan Quayle was in over his head. Fortunately for him, it was a view that George Bush either didn't share or hoped wouldn't make any difference to voters in 1992 just as, apparently, it hadn't in 1988.

At home, Quayle took on his own legal profession, complaining there was entirely too much litigation going on, charging it was undercutting American competitiveness in the global market. It was a view that came out of the President's Council on Competitiveness headed by Quayle, which critics attacked as a pro-business vehicle for end-running government regulations.

Quayle had no shortage of critics, even in the funny papers. Garry Trudeau, author of the "Doonesbury" strip, resurrected the story of an Oklahoma prison inmate who was put into solitary confinement in the final days of the 1988 campaign when he was about to hold a news conference charging he had sold drugs to Quayle when Quayle was in law school. A strip character was portrayed as having been told the Drug Enforcement Administration had a file on Quayle. It turned out there was such a file but the DEA had found the accusations to be groundless. But it was a fact that the inmate, Brett Kimberlin, serving a fifty-one-year term for drug smuggling and a bombing, had been put in solitary on orders from the Bureau of Prisons days before the 1988 election.

Through all this, there continued much speculation about Quayle's political fate and much wishful thinking among his critics that Bush, out of his own political travail, would finally ditch his hapless vice president. But from the start of the planning for 1992, it was always identified as the Bush-Quayle campaign, with the president continuing to give Quayle his unqualified endorsement.

In the fall, as economic conditions failed to improve, Quayle was among those inside the administration who pressed for the president to speak out. At one point, according to Bob Teeter, the vice president called him in and said, "We've got to do something." Much more than Bush, Quayle had been out around the country, and he knew that the sense of drift was eroding the president's support. But the argument from Darman and others that recovery was around the corner was the one Bush wanted to hear, and it prevailed.

Early in January of the election year, Quayle was the beneficiary of a largely favorable series about his vice presidency in *The Washington Post* by two of its top reporters, David Broder and Bob Woodward, but even in that series his problem was identified, by Republican Senator Warren Rudman of New Hampshire. "Dan Quayle has a long way to go to be really qualified to be president in terms of leadership qualities," Rudman said, "for a very unfortunate reason not of his doing—and that is the perception with which he is held by the American people."

When the Pat Buchanan challenge emerged in New Hampshire and began to look serious, Quayle was dispatched there to bring the message that Bush cared, but it was the sort of message that could not be delivered effectively by a surrogate. Quayle's words could not counter the feeling of resentment, fed by Buchanan, among New Hampshire Republicans, who, after all, had bailed Bush out in their 1988 presidential primary after he had finished an embarrassing third to Bob Dole and Pat Robertson in the Iowa caucuses. Buchanan poked fun at Bush's decision to send "little Danny, the pit puppy," to do political battle for him.

Quayle's trip to the first primary state came only hours after word from Tokyo that Bush had gotten sick and collapsed at a state dinner, and that fact focused as much or more on the same old question of presidential succession as on Quayle's political mission. As soon as Air Force Two landed in Nashua and Quayle stepped off to field the press's questions, he was asked about his qualifications to take over if necessary. "I'm ready," he said, and ended the press conference.

But Bush's unhappy experience in Japan put Quayle and the possibility of succession in the limelight once more. *The Manchester Union Leader,* supporting Buchanan, ran a cartoon showing a beaming Quayle on a map of the United States, surrounded by the horrified faces of five citizens. The caption was "Home Alone," after the popular movie then playing about a wild youngster left at home by his parents.

Later, walking along a ropeline at a shopping mall outside Manchester, a woman stopped him as he shook her hand. Reporters were kept too far away by Quayle's Secret Service agents to hear the conversation, but the woman, a lawyer named Karen Heller, later recounted it to us.

"I don't have it in for Vice President Quayle," she said. "In the past I've been a Bush supporter. Right now I'm undecided and I told him that. I said I like him as a vice president and I like him as a man, but I like him as a vice president only if I know that he would never be president, which of course no one can guarantee. I said to him, if the polls showed that his being the vice president was a hindrance to President Bush's campaign, what would he advise President Bush to do?'' Quayle, she went on, ''sort of avoided the question'' and told her ''the polls were nothing . . . but manipulated by the media.'' Later, she said the conversation hadn't changed her mind, and she thought Bush should drop him from the ticket.

Quayle tried to put the best face on the Buchanan challenge. He said it was helpful because ''it's already energized the president's campaign. . . . We're starting the campaign earlier than we had anticipated.'' His enthusiasm was genuine, because in private he had been pressing for getting the campaign into high gear. He told voters: ''I understand you want to send a message. We've got the message.''

Nevertheless, New Hampshire voters gave Buchanan a surprising 37 percent of their votes against an incumbent president. Three days after the primary, Quayle took his case for Bush to the Conservative Political Action Conference in Washington. Without mentioning Buchanan by name, he lectured the audience that ''the only real question facing us today is whether our president will enter the general election campaign from a position of strength or from a position of weakness. Anyone has the right to wage a symbolic campaign,'' he said, ''but it would be irresponsible to endanger all that we have achieved.'' And he told his fellow conservatives that opposing Bush would ''risk being out of power for a generation.''

Quayle did not mention what a defeat in November would do to his own ambitions, but that went without saying. As Buchanan faded, Quayle was able to breathe easier, but there was always something to bring him unfavorable publicity. In April, a report of the General Accounting Office, Congress's investigative arm, disclosed that he had been using military planes to go on golfing junkets. He said in some cases political events were involved and he had partly reimbursed the government, but again tongues wagged from coast to coast.

On May 19, at the Commonwealth Club of California in San Francisco, Quayle finally carved out his own voice in the campaign as the defender of ''family values.'' He blamed the riots in Los Angeles on ''lawless social anarchy'' that was the result of a ''breakdown of family structure, personal responsibility and social order.'' And he called for "social sanctions" against women "irresponsibly" bearing children out of wedlock. He chose as his target one of the most popular television situation comedies in which the central character, unmarried, gave birth.

"It doesn't help matters,'' Quayle said, "when prime-time TV has Murphy Brown—a character who supposedly epitomizes today's intelligent, highly paid, professional woman—mocking the importance of fathers, by bearing a child alone, and calling it just another 'lifestyle choice.' ''

If Quayle wanted to set off a firestorm, and there were indications he intended to do just that, he could not have picked a better, higher-visibility target. Many viewers ridiculed the spectacle of Quayle taking on a fictitious television character, but others saw his remarks as a fusillade in the continuing battle over abortion. His right-wing constituents, who had come to look upon him as their chief advocate and protector within the Bush administration, applauded his initiative, while abortion rights activists condemned him.

The creator and executive producer of the television show, Diane English, one of the latter, said: "If the vice president thinks it's disgraceful for an unmarried woman to bear a child, and if he believes that a woman cannot raise a child without a father, then he'd better make sure abortion remains safe and legal.''

The White House at first backed up Quayle, though without much visible enthusiasm, and then Bush retreated by saying he was "not going to get into the details of a very popular television show.'' But Quayle had struck a sharp chord and was playing it for all it was worth. "It's a speech that had to be given, an important speech,'' he told reporters. "I know it's risky territory when someone like myself begins to talk about values. It can come across, perhaps, as preachy, as moralistic.'' But, he said, "the discussion will get beyond Murphy Brown and it will give me an opportunity to talk about values.''

The day after the Murphy Brown speech, Quayle took that opportunity outside a predominantly black school in South Central Los Angeles. "Hollywood thinks it's cute to glamorize illegitimacy,'' he said. "Hollywood doesn't get it.'' Before Quayle was through, he found himself in an exchange with actress Candice Bergen, the real-life Murphy Brown. And in the process he moved into the forefront of the whole focus on "family values" that the Bush-Quayle strategists hoped not only would reinforce their ticket's support among the party's right wing but also would provide a vehicle for getting at the "character" issue against Clinton.

From all indications, Quayle and his staff hit on the idea themselves and rode with it before the top campaign people realized he had done so. It never would have happened in the 1988 campaign, but Dan Quayle's days as putty in the hands of handlers were over, especially with the campaign working overtime this late in the year to shore up its conservative base and Quayle its most popular active figure on the party's right.

Soon after the Murphy Brown assault, Quayle followed up with an attack on the nation's "cultural elites," who, he told a Southern Baptists convention in Indianapolis, "respect neither tradition nor standards. They believe that moral truths are relative and all 'lifestyles' are equal. They seem to think . . . that fathers are dispensable and that parents need not be married or even of the opposite sexes. They are wrong." And as for the "scorn of the media elite" that he said had been rained down on him since his Murphy Brown speech, he said, "I wear their scorn as a badge of honor."

Clinton did not let this one go by without comment. "How dare Dan Quayle talk that way about anybody?" he said. "I'm tired of people with trust funds telling people on food stamps how to live." But Quayle was on a roll now. "Now that we have your attention," he told reporters in North Carolina, "tune in, stay tuned, because we're going to talk about values." And in New York, he castigated the distribution of condoms in the city's schools and blamed its many problems on "the entrenched government establishment and its liberal ideology."

Quayle began to sound like vice presidential predecessor Spiro Agnew, who in the Nixon administration had gone to war against what he called "radical liberals" and the "nattering nabobs of negativism" in the news media. And it was at this juncture too that Quayle joined the Republican onslaught against Ross Perot with his description of the Texas billionaire as a "temperamental tycoon."

But just when Quayle was hitting his stride, he put his foot in his mouth again. At a children's spelling bee being supervised by Quayle at the Luis Muñoz Rivera Elementary School in Trenton, New Jersey, twelve-year-old William Figueroa correctly spelled the word "potato" on a blackboard. Quayle, trying to be helpful, told him: "That's fine phonetically, but you're missing just a little bit." With coaxing from Quayle, the boy added an "e." Quayle had been given a yellow flash card with the word misspelled and simply passed on the misspelling.

In the local newspaper, *The Trentonian,* the boy was quoted as saying the incident "showed that the rumors about the vice president are true—that he's an idiot." Later, he told an Associated Press reporter that Quayle "is an okay guy, but he needs to study." So much for Dan Quayle being taken seriously. Signs began to appear in his speech crowds reading MR. POTATOE HEAD and other variations.

All these happenings stirred the concern that already existed within the Bush campaign about what Quayle on the ticket might do to what now appeared to be the president's very uncertain reelection chances. One Republican senator, James Jeffords of Vermont, was openly suggesting that dumping Quayle would help Bush in the fall. Quietly, campaign chairman Bob Teeter had a poll taken testing how Quayle and other possible running mates would affect the strength of the Republican ticket. Experienced pollsters like Teeter knew that the identity of the vice presidential nominee seldom had any appreciable impact on the outcome of an election, but bad numbers in the right hands could help make the case for deep-sixing the erratic young man from Indiana.

Teeter's poll, Kristol said later, "didn't make much difference. It didn't show as much as he hoped it would show. If it had showed a more dramatic result, it could have been used to bolster the dump-Quayle scenario." Still, according to others close to the campaign, some key figures did press for the vice president's removal, but rather halfheartedly in light of Bush's stated intentions and the lack of strong supportive polling data.

Those said to be interested to one degree or another in replacing Quayle included, in addition to Teeter, campaign director Fred Malek, Charlie Black, Rich Bond and Jim Baker, although in Baker's case and standard practice for him, he stayed in the background. The basic argument, one insider said later, was that Quayle was "baggage we don't need" in what already was becoming an uphill fight.

Among those being mentioned by the dump-Quayle insiders to replace him were Dick Cheney, first, and then Bob Dole because both had been under public scrutiny, Cheney in his confirmation hearings when he went to the Pentagon, and Dole as a former presidential and vice presidential candidate, and either one could stand a frisk.

Fortunately for Quayle, Kristol said later, "the people involved never had the nerve to really move beyond talk to conspiring. There were a couple of weeks there where I was worried, where we took a couple of acts to try to make sure to flush out the possible conspirers."

When a *Wall Street Journal* story appeared indicating some conservatives thought Quayle ought to step aside for his own sake, and other stories in the same vein followed, it was taken in the Quayle camp as a tipoff that the wolves were out. So were rumors about Bush's health, immediately squashed by Bush's doctor. The president called it "a crazy time on rumors" in which it was being suggested that not only he but his wife and Marilyn Quayle were ill. "I don't know what's going on," he said—perhaps forgetting how rumors about Dukakis's health had been spread by his own campaign in the summer of 1988 as part of the effort to reduce his lead in the polls.

Kristol, according to conservative stalwart Paul Weyrich, began calling "movement conservatives" like himself, warning that talk of dumping Quayle was "fairly serious." Kristol, Weyrich said, "urged those of us who had been favorable toward Quayle to make our views known, which we tried to do. The trial balloon was such that Bush understood that he would have a problem if he selected another nominee."

The argument he put forward, Weyrich said, "was not that this would be a betrayal of conservatives, because he could have picked somebody just as conservative." But the Democrats, he warned, would "make you reargue your initial judgment [on Quayle], and I don't see how that helps you. Even if you get somebody else, you're already stuck with that decision. If it was wrong, it was wrong four years ago. If you get somebody else, it's going to suggest that you didn't know what you were doing and you made a terrible mistake. Unless you want to say that, which presumably you don't, I think you'd be very hard-pressed to come up with somebody else."

Weyrich said he told this to Malek, Jim Pinkerton, one of the most conservative White House aides, and—importantly—to the president's son George W., known as "Junior" to the insiders, who he understood conveyed it to his father. "I continued to believe," Weyrich added, "that very few people vote on the basis of the vice presidential candidate. While

Quayle didn't help him any, I don't think he hurt him that much. If Quayle were the problem, then George Bush never would have been at ninety percent approval rating during the Gulf War, because Quayle was such a liability. That didn't affect anything. . . . He would have been fodder for nightclub jokes but he would not have been an issue.''

When a reporter asked Bush, ''Is the vice president's chair a little uncertain these days?'' he replied, ''No, it's very certain.'' But that didn't stop what he called a media feeding frenzy.

Two days later, Quayle went on the Larry King show and again got into the headlines when King asked him, following on the Murphy Brown flap, what he would do if his own young daughter became pregnant when she grew up. Quayle said he would ''counsel her and talk to her and support her on whatever decision she made'' but that he would ''hope that she wouldn't make that decision [to have an abortion].''

Somewhat lost in the resulting furor over a seeming contradiction with his firm anti-abortion position was another exchange on the show. Asked whether he might take himself off the ticket, Quayle said he had had ''a number of discussions'' with Bush, ''and believe me, if I thought that I was hurting the ticket, I'd be gone. I want George Bush reelected.''

That, one insider said later, ''opened the door a little to the pressure. But having opened the door, it was important to close the door.'' So Quayle went to see Bush, got from him firsthand that he did indeed want him to stay on, and ''then we put that word out,'' this insider said, ''and closed the door we had opened. It was surprising how well it worked.'' When a reporter asked Quayle flat out on July 24, after he had met with Bush, whether he would be staying on the ticket, Quayle replied: ''Yes,'' declining to provide details of his talks with the president. A couple of days later in Birmingham, Alabama, Quayle said the question of his seeking reelection as vice president was ''a closed issue,'' and that ''the president has never wavered on this issue, in public or in private. The only people who are bringing this up are my opponents and the media.''

Concerning the halfhearted dump-Quayle effort, Kristol said later: ''What was striking was their lack of resolution and boldness. I'm not sure that a strong and bold attempt to depose Quayle wouldn't have worked. I'm amazed that we were able to bluff them back as easily as we could. . . . They just didn't have the guts to force the issue.''

Of more concern inside the Bush campaign as the Republican National Convention approached was the chaos within the campaign itself, and the war that continued to go on between the campaign and the White House. More and more, talk was heard of the return of Jim Baker, ensconced in the prestigious and demanding position of secretary of state and resisting being pulled back into what he saw as the demeaning game of politics.

When Ross Perot bailed out on the final day of the Democratic National Convention, sending Clinton surging in the polls and Bush falling back, the president's appeal to Perot supporters came from Baker's ranch in Wyoming, where the two old friends were enjoying their annual fishing vacation. A few days later, the word was out: Baker would be back to take over the troubled campaign. Nothing was said about when and in what capacity, but Republican political workers everywhere were saying the sooner the better, and it didn't matter what the title. Wherever Jim Baker was, he was always in charge, and things got done.

It was with that expectation, or at least hope, that the ragged forces of the Bush-Quayle campaign and White House headed for Houston and the coronation of the same ticket that had brought the Republican Party victory four years before.

HOUSTON: CAVING IN TO THE RIGHT

The week before the Republican National Convention opened, its tone was set by the party's platform committee, gathered in Houston to write the document on which President Bush ostensibly would run for a second term. The Republicans routinely held their platform sessions in the days immediately before their conventions to assure the party another week of press and television attention. And the plan this time was to highlight a different topic each day—domestic policy, foreign policy, national defense, family values—and force the press to focus on them one by one.

As a practical matter, however, there was only one issue that was likely to get any attention. It was whether the platform would include the same tough provision against abortion rights that had been written into the documents of 1984 and 1988, calling for a constitutional amendment forbidding abortion even in cases of rape and incest. In fact, there was never any doubt about the intentions of the Bush campaign. When the platform committee held preliminary hearings in Salt Lake City in May,

Bob Teeter had passed the word to abortion rights supporters that the campaign would give "not one inch."

But the way the issue played out was important, nonetheless, because it would be a measure of the relative strength of moderate Republicans and the hard-line social issue conservatives, including the Christian Coalition led by evangelist Marion G. (Pat) Robertson and the followers of the redoubtable Phyllis Schlafly, leader of the Eagle Forum. If there was one issue likely to define their concepts of "family values," it was abortion.

Beyond that, the issue was intriguing because it was one on which George Bush had pushed himself into an extremist corner with a position potentially damaging in a close election.

The president's stance on abortion had changed radically over the years. As a candidate for the Republican presidential nomination in 1980, he had described himself in New Hampshire as opposing abortion and federal funding of abortions, but also opposed to a constitutional amendment that would overturn *Roe* v. *Wade*, the 1973 Supreme Court decision that legalized abortion. In an interview with *Rolling Stone* magazine early in 1980, Bush had conceded that his principal rival at the moment, Ronald Reagan, "opposes me for not wanting to amend the Supreme Court decision on abortion," and added: "I happen to think it was right." In short, he held what became known as the pro-choice position.

But once Bush joined Reagan's ticket, he became an echo on his opposition to abortion rights. His position had undergone some "evolution," he said in 1984. He now favored a "human life amendment" although he would add exceptions for rape and incest as well as for circumstances in which the life of the mother was threatened. By 1988, Bush was going a step further. "My position has evolved, and it's continuing to evolve in favor of life," he said in a debate with Democratic nominee Michael Dukakis at Winston-Salem. "I'm for the sanctity of life and once that illegality is established, then we can come to grips with the penalty side. And, of course, there's got to be some penalties . . . to enforce the law, whatever that may be."

When the press quickly raised the question of whether he now intended to prosecute women who had abortions as well as the physicians who performed them, campaign manager Jim Baker held a quick press conference to explain the candidate didn't mean that at all. And Dukakis was so inept a candidate he never fully exploited the opening he had been given. Shortly after taking office, Bush cleared up how far he would go: ''After years of serious and sober reflection on the issue, this is what I think: I think the Supreme Court's decision in *Roe* v. *Wade* was wrong and should be overturned. I think America needs a human life amendment.''

As president, moreover, Bush continued to harden his position. He vetoed District of Columbia appropriation bills that would permit local tax funds to be used for clinics that performed abortions. He opposed the use of fetal tissue in medical research. And, finally, he approved the so-called gag rule that prohibited personnel in federally funded abortion clinics from even discussing abortion with pregnant women.

But because Bush had made that ''evolution''—essentially a total turnaround—on the issue, he continued to be pressed on whether he might evolve even further. But five days before the platform committee was to meet, he made it clear that wouldn't happen. ''No matter the political price—and they tell me in this year that it's enormous—I am going to do what I think is right,'' he said. ''I will stand on my conscience and let my conscience be my guide when it comes to matters of life.''

The politics of the abortion issue were not as clear as Bush suggested. Opinion polls found few voters who would claim they planned to base their vote primarily on the abortion issue, and they were divided about evenly in most surveys. But Supreme Court decisions permitting states to impose restrictions on the right to an abortion had energized the pro-choice groups and given the issue new pertinence with voters not preoccupied with other questions. Studies of some election returns had found that a small percentage of Republican women, most often in the suburbs, would cross party lines to vote Democratic on the choice issue if the differences between the candidates were clear. The one thing all the political experience had shown, as Bush well knew, was that the politician who tried to straddle the issue got the worst of both worlds.

As the platform committee assembled in Houston, it was obvious that there would be no significant change in the abortion language, although there might also be included some other wording, perhaps in a preamble, that would recognize that other views could be acceptable within the party. This was the so-called big-tent approach advocated by the late Lee Atwater when he was the party's national chairman. Charles Black, the campaign adviser assigned to oversee the platform deliberations, said, "We won't change the substantive language" of previous planks, but added, "there might be some additional recognition of diversity."

But as far back as the May hearing in Salt Lake City, Schlafly had made it plain she would consider any softening language "a cave-in" on the part of George Bush, and it was soon apparent the religious right committee members were equally unyielding.

Nor were there any formidable voices urging change. One group, Republicans for Choice, was led by Ann Stone, a political consultant in Washington, and another, the National Republican Coalition for Choice, by Mary Dent Crisp, a moderate who had once been vice chairman of the party. But neither was made up of Republican heavyweights with any influence. The only other dissenters from the hard line were some office-holders facing campaigns for reelection, including then Senator John Seymour of California and Senator Arlen Specter of Pennsylvania, who were arguing for leaving the abortion issue out of the platform entirely.

There were also some Republican governors from states with heavy concentrations of Republican moderates who were pro-choice, including Pete Wilson of California, William Weld of Massachusetts and John McKernan of Maine. But whether they would be willing to challenge the president on the issue at the convention was unclear. Wilson, the most potentially influential, was heading the Bush campaign in his state and not inclined to defy his candidate in Houston.

The subcommittee voted seventeen to three to retain the language of previous platforms after a parliamentary ploy was used to prevent any substitute being brought directly to a vote. The debate was emotional and sometimes bizarre. One committee member, Virginia Phillips of Alaska, described how she had been obliged by a medical condition to have an abortion as a young woman. She reported that "it wasn't a Sunday afternoon stroll" but instead a traumatic experience. The subcommittee chairman, a lawyer from North Carolina named Mary Potter Summa, confided that she was four and a half months pregnant and very aware of "what is in me. It's not a rock. It's not a Coke bottle. It's a human life"—and, she added, one that was kicking her and pressing on her bladder at that very moment.

The following day the full committee ratified the subcommittee action, rejecting by eighty-four to sixteen an attempt to remove the plank entirely and shouting down by voice votes other attempts to amend it or add some softening language to the platform. The pro-choice Republicans never came close to enlisting the twenty-seven votes they needed on the 107-member committee to bring a minority report to the convention floor, or the majority of six state delegations that also would have allowed that procedure.

The issue would have been effectively throttled if, on the same day the platform committee voted, Bush himself had not taken what was essentially a pro-choice position in an interview on NBC. Asked what he would do if one of his granddaughters wanted to have an abortion, he replied, "Would I support my child? I'd put my arm around her and say, if she were trying to make that decision, encourage her not to do that. But of course I'd stand by my child, I'd love her and help her, lift her up, wipe the tears away and we'd get back in the game."

"So in the end the decision would be hers?" the interviewer asked.

"Well," Bush replied, "who else's could it be?"

That, of course, was precisely the point of the pro-choice movement—that the decision should rest with the woman involved—"who else?" But neither Bush nor Dan Quayle, who had given a similar answer to a similar question about his daughter a couple of days earlier, seemed to see any conflict between their private feelings of protectiveness toward their own families and their extreme positions on abortion as a public policy question.

The platform plank, like those in 1984 and 1988, finally read: "We believe the unborn child has a fundamental individual right to life which cannot be infringed. We therefore reaffirm our support for a human life amendment to the Constitution, and we endorse legislation to make clear that the Fourteenth Amendment's protections apply to unborn children. We oppose using public revenues for abortion and will not fund organizations which advocate abortion. We commend those who provide alternatives to abortions by meeting the needs of mothers and offering adoption services. We reaffirm our support for appointment of judges who respect traditional family values and the sanctity of innocent human life."

The abortion plank was not the only one on which the religious right showed its political muscle in the preliminaries to the Republican convention. The platform also specifically opposed "any legislation or law that recognizes same-sex marriages," supported "home-based schools," celebrated "our country's Judeo-Christian heritage and rich religious pluralism" and said "elements within the media, the entertainment industry, academics and the Democratic Party are waging a guerrilla war against American values."

The attention given to these questions was striking in the face of the whole year's experience with the electorate's concentrated focus on quite a different question—the condition of the economy. But here, too, there was a development that Bush didn't need. At the subcommittee level, a group of supply-side Republicans led by then Representative Vin Weber of Minnesota managed to insert language calling the 1990 tax increase Bush had approved "a mistake." Bush himself had used the term, but it was still jarring enough in the party's official platform that the White House ordered the word "recessionary" substituted in the final version.

The harsh and defiant Republican tone also was evident in a bitter attack by the party's national chairman, Rich Bond, on Hillary Clinton. In a speech to the Republican National Committee, he drew a picture of Clinton as president being advised by "that champion of the family, Hillary Clinton, who believes kids should be able to sue their parents rather than helping with the chores as they are asked to do. She has likened marriage and the family to slavery." The description was an outlandish interpretation of an essay Hillary Clinton had written for the *Harvard Education Review* in 1974 entitled "Children Under the Law."

The Bond attack was an indication that Republican strategists were now convinced—mistakenly, polls soon showed—that Hillary Clinton was so unpopular with the voting public that she was vulnerable to direct attack. It was a strategy no one could recall being employed against a candidate's wife so directly even in the days when Eleanor Roosevelt was a controversial figure. Clinton clearly didn't share that assessment. "That's pitiful, they're getting pitiful," he told reporters traveling with him in Pittsburgh. "This comment by Bond is pathetic. . . . It's going to be very difficult for the American people to take them seriously if they can't do any better than that."

Bond also joined with Dan Quayle in an attack on the news media that was fuel for the same social conservatives most caught up in the abortion question. Bond's complaints were the predictable ones about press favoring Clinton over Bush. But they conveniently ignored the press coverage of the Gennifer Flowers episode and Clinton's draft history, which had made the Democratic nominee, at least in Republican eyes at that moment, most vulnerable.

But Quayle had a better ground for his charge of "sleaze" in the news media. *The New York Post* had just front-paged a story about a book that quoted a deceased ambassador as having said he had arranged a place for an assignation between then Vice President Bush and his longtime assistant, Jennifer Fitzgerald, in Switzerland in 1984. The gossip about Bush and Fitzgerald had been making the rounds in Washington for years and had been investigated thoroughly by several news organizations without a shred of evidence uncovered to support it. The result was that most newspapers ignored the "story" until the New York tabloid put it into the public arena—and gave Quayle a legitimate beef.

The Bush campaign, however, had a bigger problem even before the convention formally opened. The political dialogue was depicting a party that was angry, defensive and—most important politically—preoccupied with issues such as abortion and homosexual rights that were not the ones of prime concern to the voters. Many of the mainstream Republicans and longtime Bush supporters already assembled in Houston were clearly upset about how the abortion issue and harsh rhetoric would play with like-minded Republicans and independents back home.

After listening to Bond, for example, Elsie Hillman, a national committee member from Pennsylvania and chairman of the Bush campaign there, told one of us: "Not all of us agree with all of that, you know." She added that it was necessary for the president to provide some positive reinforcement for regular Republicans with positions on issues important to them. "He's not there yet," she said. "He has to give them a reason, just a glimmer of a reason."

Instead, coming into the convention, the Republicans and their president continued to send conflicting signals about what their message would be. In interviews over the weekend before he was to go to Houston, Bush said he would be making some new proposals on the economy. He thus invited speculation that his acceptance speech would be still another attempt to seize control of that issue before it was too late—and none too soon, as polls showed the "wrong track" number approaching 75 percent.

In another interview over PBS after the convention opened, Bush inadvertently fanned that speculation by saying in response to a question about his second term that "you'll see plenty of new faces, plenty of changes." With demands from the party's right wing that Secretary of Treasury Nicholas Brady and budget director Richard Darman be dumped right then to demonstrate basic economic change, CNN took Bush's remark and ran with it. CNN reporters on the convention floor and elsewhere were assigned to seek out cabinet members and ask them whether they expected their heads to roll. Soon the convention was awash with rumor as one after the other the cabinet heads ducked and weaved—but none fell.

The rhetoric in Houston, however, was centered far more on "family values" and on the characters of Bill and Hillary Clinton than on cabinet changes, or on how to produce more jobs for the nine million Americans who were unemployed. And no speech was more stunning than the one Pat Buchanan, Bush's onetime rival for the nomination, delivered on the convention's opening night:

"The agenda Clinton and Clinton would impose on America—abortion on demand, a litmus test for the Supreme Court, homosexual rights, discrimination against religious schools, women in combat units—that's change, all right. That's not the kind of change America needs, it's not the kind of change America wants, and it is not the kind of change we can abide in a nation that we still call God's country."

Buchanan contrasted Bush as a young fighter pilot with Clinton: "I'll tell you where he was. When Bill Clinton's time came in Vietnam, he sat up in a dormitory in Oxford, England, and figured out how to dodge the draft. Let me ask the question of this convention: Which of these two men has won the moral authority to send young Americans into battle?"

But of all the passages in Buchanan's take-no-prisoners assault, none hit with as much force as this one: "My friends, this election is about more than who gets what. It is about who we are. It is about what we believe and what we stand for as Americans. There is a religious war going on in this country for the soul of America. It is a cultural war as critical to the kind of nation we shall be as the Cold War itself. And in that struggle for the soul of America, Clinton and Clinton are on the other side and George Bush is on our side."

Buchanan's prime-time appearance had been the product of extensive negotiations with the conservative commentator who had made such a harsh case against Bush during the early primaries. Bob Teeter originally believed there was too great a risk involved in letting Buchanan speak in prime time. He feared that Buchanan might use the occasion to endorse Bush with such faint praise that his tepid support would set off a new round of damaging stories about the president's problems with conservatives.

But the Bush campaign's polling numbers were telling them there was still work to be done to solidify the conservative base. So Jim Lake was dispatched to New York during the Democratic convention in July to negotiate with Bay Buchanan, Pat Buchanan's sister and campaign manager. At a meeting at the Star Delicatessen, Lake told her that Pat would have to agree to endorse Bush. She replied that he fully intended to do so. The key questions were when—Buchanan insisted on a prime-time appearance because "we had three million votes" in the primaries—and whether Buchanan would make the endorsement in the speech or beforehand.

In subsequent negotiations over the next three weeks, it became clear that Buchanan wanted to do it during the speech itself. He had consulted Richard Nixon, his old boss, who advised him that was the right time to get the maximum effect. But Teeter continued to be suspicious, fearing that the campaign was being set up for a damaging embarrassment. He agreed to go ahead only after Lake reported that Buchanan would show the speech to the Bush campaign managers forty-eight hours before it was to be delivered. Lake told Teeter he was confident the endorsement would be unstinting. "I trusted them [the Buchanans] to do what they promised. . . . [I told them], 'If you screw me, I'll be dead forever.' "

The result was a meeting in convention director Craig Fuller's trailer at the Astrodome on the Saturday night before the convention's opening on Monday, when Buchanan would speak. Bay Buchanan brought the text and while Fuller read it, Lake faxed a copy to Teeter, who was at the White House talking to Bush about Buchanan's convention appearance. The language was sufficiently enthusiastic for Teeter to reassure his candidate. None of the Bush insiders, however, saw the pitfalls in the harsh language Buchanan was planning to use to attack Bill and Hillary Clinton and make his case that a religious war was under way.

"I read the speech and it had a great endorsement," Lake recalled later. "I really paid no attention to anything else. I was totally concerned with, Is this going to be a strong endorsement of George Bush? Is it going to make our conservative base happy?"

Thus, the eventual backlash came as a surprise to the Bush strategists.

"Even that night at the convention," Lake said, "I didn't sense any of that . . . the offending stuff didn't really become an issue for forty-eight hours."

Buchanan himself insisted that he delivered the three things that the Bush campaign asked him to do in the speech: praise Reagan, who would follow him on the platform, endorse Bush and "take apart" Clinton. "I came home and wrote the speech in that order, to those specifications," he said later. And he insisted that his speech did no harm to Bush's chances. As he was delivering it, he said, "the Bush people were cheering their heads off." It was the "subsequent demonizing and trashing of the speech" by the news media that did the damage, he said.

Buchanan's speech was the distillation of the case the delegates of the religious right felt driven to make at Houston—that there was a moral high ground they occupied. Their political adversaries were not just wrong on the substance, they were morally wrong. As Pat Robertson put it to the cheering delegates, "When Bill and Hillary Clinton talk about family values, they are not talking about either families or values. They are talking about a radical plan to destroy the traditional family and transfer its functions to the federal government."

On the convention floor, the mood of the religious right delegates was heady at their influence—and hostile to those they saw as their enemies. A middle-aged man brimming with barely suppressed rage accosted one of us on the convention floor and said: "I watch you on television all the time and I hate everything you say." When it was suggested that was why television sets have off buttons, he was not mollified. He insisted he had "one thing I'm going to say to you whether you like it or not." The one thing: "You can't be a Christian and be a Democrat."

This moral element was something new at this level of American politics. In the past, extremists on both ends of the ideological spectrum had demonstrated hard edges of hostility and anger; no one who was there could forget the Barry Goldwater delegates shouting their rage at the press at the 1964 Republican convention in San Francisco. But the argument had always centered on who was "right" and "wrong" in their approach to government. It had usually been possible for conservatives and liberals to behave with civility and even good humor toward those with whom they totally disagreed; indeed that was still the case where they came together regularly—in Congress, for example. But the delegates of the religious right were a different breed of activists who believed those who disagreed with them were not just wrong, but evil.

The Bush campaign strategists later tried to dismiss the reaction to the tone of the convention as little or no factor in the general election campaign. "We went in at thirty percent and we had a hell of a base problem," Teeter said, "and we came out with about forty percent and we did get a lot of that base back." The argument that the images of the convention had cost Bush "a big chunk of votes," Teeter said, was never supported in the campaign's polling figures.

Teeter said Buchanan's speech was "not helpful" and conceded there were things the campaign might have done differently at Houston, that "in those famous words, mistakes were made. . . . But it was not as big a thing at the time and it was not a giant negative."

Charlie Black contended that "the convention itself wasn't bad" but that the campaign had not been effective in managing how it was interpreted. "The mistake we made in the convention, in my opinion, is we lost control of the spin," he said, particularly in the first few days. The imperative, he said, was always to get the conservative base energized, and the Houston meeting accomplished that.

Lake also was puzzled by the criticism the convention's tone evoked. "I had no idea it would cause as much backlash as it did," he said. "We still felt we had to, we still did have to, tie down the base. We hadn't done that yet and that was why we wanted Buchanan there."

But reporters at the convention were finding many mainstream conservatives alarmed and dismayed by the tone and religious content of the rhetoric, the pictures of Pat Robertson and Jerry Falwell perched in the VIP section of the Astrodome, the repeated attacks on abortion rights and homosexuals.

The morning after Buchanan's speech, one longtime Bush supporter from the Farm Belt, a middle-aged woman who worked as a vice president of a major corporation, telephoned one of us to talk about it. "It wasn't just the speech," she said, "it was the people all around me cheering while Buchanan was saying those things. What's happened to my party?" Then she burst into tears, sobbing and saying over and over, "I can't believe what's happening here."

But George Bush himself had given his supporters license by his own predilection for casting politics in moral terms. Speaking to the Knights of Columbus a few days before the convention, Bush said: "I stake my claim to a simple belief: the president should try to set a moral tone for this nation. I believe that a central issue of this election year should be: who do you trust to renew America's moral purpose, who do you trust to fight for the ideas that will help rebuild our families and restore our fundamental values?"

In one sense, that approach might have been chalked off to Bush recognizing that Clinton might be vulnerable on the trust question because of Gennifer Flowers and his waffling on the draft. But Bush had employed a very similar approach in 1988 when he used the controversy over the pledge of allegiance to the flag to suggest that Michael Dukakis might be less patriotic than a president should be. The fact was that Bush would do whatever it took, and if that involved firing up the religious right's sense of moral outrage, so be it.

The offensive on family values continued to dominate the convention through its third night and the official nomination of the president for another term. Bush himself appeared on the podium with his wife, Barbara, five children and twelve grandchildren to produce what were designed to be the ultimate family pictures for the television cameras. But the rhetoric that night was not equally benign. Marilyn Quayle, wife of the vice president, presented herself as a member of the baby boom generation quite different from Bill Clinton.

"We are all shaped by the times in which we live," she said. "I came of age in a time of turbulent social change. Some of it was good, such as civil rights. Much of it was questionable. But, remember, not everyone demonstrated, dropped out, took drugs, joined in the sexual revolution or dodged the draft," she said to wild cheers from fellow moralists in the hall. "Not everyone believed that the family was so oppressive that women could only thrive apart from it."

In his acceptance speech, Dan Quayle sounded the themes that were the message of the whole convention. "Like so many Americans, for me, family comes first," he said. "When family values are undermined, our country suffers. All too often, parents struggle to instill character in their sons and daughters only to see their values belittled and their beliefs mocked by those who look down on America. Americans try to raise their children to understand right and wrong, only to be told that every so-called lifestyle alternative is morally equivalent. That is wrong.

"The gap between us and our opponents is a cultural divide. It is not just a difference between conservative and liberal. It is a difference between fighting for what is right and refusing to see what is wrong."

Not all of the Houston rhetoric was red-hot. Ronald Reagan delivered what may have been the best speech of the convention using his usual mix of the partisan and the inspirational. Barbara Bush's speech following Marilyn Quayle's was a conspicuously low-key encomium to her husband. And, in the face of the convention's drumfire of criticism of homosexuals and homosexual rights, there was a striking emotional reaction to the speech of a forty-four-year-old woman who was HIV-positive, Mary Fisher, daughter of industrialist and Republican fund-raiser Max Fisher.

By the time Bush arrived to deliver his acceptance speech, expectations for the occasion had reached towering proportions. The conventional wisdom among politicians and press was that this was his single last best opportunity to regain control of the campaign agenda and present himself as a convincing voice on the economy. But the speech fell far short. Bush did advance some obvious attention-getting proposals—for an across-the-board tax cut, increases in the personal tax exemption, reductions in capital gains tax rates. But there were no specifics about how much and just when.

The one new proposal on the fiscal situation was a plan to allow taxpayers to specify that 10 percent of their taxes would have to be used for deficit reduction—an idea his own administration had pooh-poohed as unworkable in congressional testimony earlier. Indeed, the hollowness of the Bush economic program was clear the following morning when campaign chairman Teeter announced that the plan would be sent to Congress after the November election. The implication was that the voters would have to take it on trust—from a candidate whose lack of credibility on economic issues had put him on the defensive for the entire campaign.

Carville, the Clinton strategist, said later that Bush's failure to make himself credible on the economy was the real convention failure, not the extremist excesses. "I thought they were hurt more by what they didn't say than what they said," he observed. "They had a chance to draw some economic distinctions and talk about some things that were just left out on the table. If you use your convention to get your base back, that's not a very good way to use a convention. You've just got to take your base for granted.

"They just couldn't show enough, as far as I was concerned, of Falwell and Pat Robertson, who are much more visible to people than Buchanan is, or Marilyn Quayle. . . . People out there know who Falwell and Pat Robertson are. That hurt more. They could have been out there talking about the football scores. It isn't so much what you say but what you don't say. . . . The idea that some Republican strategists were saying they couldn't win by talking about the economy [was ridiculous]. They couldn't win without talking about it. Or health care, or something. Most people don't wake up in the morning thinking they're in a religious war. Most people don't wake up in the morning worrying about gays."

The week in the Astrodome nevertheless had given Bush a bounce in the numbers. *The Washington Post*/ABC News survey immediately after the convention showed Clinton leading, 49 percent to 40, compared to 60 percent to 34 before the convention. Other surveys found similar figures—leads for Clinton ranging up to 14 percent where they had been running consistently above 20 percent before Houston.

But the convention also had exposed significant fault lines in the Republican Party. There were clear gulfs between the Christian Coalition social conservatives, who made up perhaps one third to one fourth of the delegates, and the mainstream Republicans who had been the heart of George Bush's original base. But even if Bush suffered no serious defections from either group against Bill Clinton in November, they would not be enough together to elect him.

And the convention had offered essentially nothing to the independents and Reagan Democrats the Republican president needed to win a second term, or to those who had supported Ross Perot earlier in the year. The central issue was the economy and the central question whether George Bush could offer a coherent program to come to grips with that problem. But the answer from Houston had been that "family values" were the issue and "Can you trust Clinton?" was the question.

The stage was now set for the general election campaign, and the Republican Party still didn't have a handle on how to salvage the presidency of an incumbent who had yet to make an effective case for a second term. So, as in 1988, some other way would have to do.

GHOST OF
WILLIE HORTON

Well before the bashing of Bill Clinton at the Republican convention, the Bush campaign—which its candidate had vowed would leave the negative tactics of 1988 behind and take the high road in 1992—had been back on the attack again. The prime target had been Ross Perot until his withdrawal in mid-July, but once he seemed safely out of the way, the Bush strategy turned to the task of cutting Clinton down.

Four years earlier, the situation for Bush had been markedly the same. Then as now, he was running as much as seventeen percentage points behind the Democratic presidential nominee after the rival party's convention. And then as now, with his own support stagnant, his strategists decided that the route to victory would be not to make voters feel better about him, but worse about his opponent.

In 1988, the vehicles had been the Willie Horton prison furlough story, Dukakis's veto of a state bill mandating recital of the pledge of allegiance in Massachusetts schools, his membership in the American Civil Liberties Union, pollution in the Boston Harbor and other issues equally critical to the state of the nation. Their use had been widely credited with Dukakis's fall and defeat—and widely criticized as demeaning to the political process. Bush had vowed this time around that he would not tolerate such doings, but as with other categorical pledges, he didn't keep this one either when political necessity seemed to dictate the imperative of "going negative" against Clinton.

Just as in 1988, when focus groups by the Bush campaign had identified the Willie Horton and other stories as exploitable vulnerabilities of Dukakis, similar sessions, as already noted, found the soft spots in public attitudes about Perot that were then put to practical use. They also found that Clinton, in spite of his string of primary victories, remained the subject of considerable public doubt and mistrust. Other focus groups by the Clinton camp itself uncovered the same doubts, and the campaign labored diligently in the later primaries and thereafter to dispel them, by giving voters more information about Clinton's humble beginnings, storybook struggle and climb to political prominence.

The focus groups run by Stan Greenberg and associates found that while such matters as the allegations of womanizing and draft-dodging against Clinton remained in voters' minds, he was able to overcome them by focusing the campaign on the voters' economic worries and offering a plan to deal with them—while Bush spent his time taking shots at Perot. By the time the fall campaign came around, Grunwald said, "people had already factored in" the personal issues in making their judgments about Clinton.

But the Bush campaign continued to believe, on the basis of their own focus-group findings in April and June, that Clinton could be damaged with voters by raising such issues of "character and trust." Once Perot had stepped aside, pummeled by negative stories about him that the Perot campaign was convinced came directly from the Bush operatives, they were free to turn their fire on Clinton.

Only two days after Perot's pullout, during a Bush visit to Utah, Senator Garn reopened the issue of Clinton's draft record. Noting that Clinton had written that he chose not to go to Canada to avoid the draft because "at twenty-three he was thinking of his future political career," Garn told 15,000 listeners at Brigham Young University: "We don't need those kinds of politicians in either party, so let's vote for those candidates who have the courage of their convictions."

Two days after that, Quayle joined in, suggesting during a television satellite hookup to Ohio stations that Gore "was probably put on that [ticket] because he went to Vietnam. I am sure Bill Clinton does not want to talk about character and some of the other things, so I think Al Gore was put on the ticket to shore up Bill Clinton's inadequacies."

At the same time Bush, while claiming to be staying out of "the campaign mode" until the Republican convention, began criticizing Clinton's revamped economic plan, trotting out the standard Republican tax-and-spend indictment against Democratic liberals and charging that Clinton could not be trusted to guard the nation's security. Bush told some defense workers that the military budget, which Clinton was targeting for cuts modestly below Bush's own, was "more than a piggy bank for folks who want to get busy beating swords into pork barrels." These were, however, criticisms on policy positions and as such perfectly legitimate, if exaggerated.

Meanwhile, though, Bush's agents were at work, with a vengeance. Among the president's most loyal—and outspoken—defenders was the Bush-Quayle deputy campaign manager and political director, Mary Matalin, a savvy and saucy tough-talking operative with blue-collar, suburban Chicago roots. A veteran foot soldier in the Bush political ranks who was instrumental in his survival against Bob Dole and Pat Robertson in a drawn-out fight for delegates in Michigan in 1988, Matalin had carried much of the load as political director at the Republican National Committee during the illness of her close friend Lee Atwater. Having moved over to the reelection committee, she had spent much of the summer seething over the indecision and chaos between a politically rudderless White House and the campaign, and yearned for Bush to get into the fray with both feet.

Beyond all that, Matalin was particularly frustrated at what she saw as a pattern of distortion on issues by Clinton, and the failure of the news media to call him on it. In a speech in Houston, Clinton had charged that Bush if reelected was going to cut funds for local law enforcement, which, she said, "was a total lie." The campaign's opposition researcher, David Tell, by this time had compiled a substantial file of what Matalin called Clinton's "evasions and slickness," and it was decided to put out a "lie of the day" press release, subsequently toned down to "distortion of the day."

Up to this time, the communications division of the campaign was putting out erudite daily "talking points" in newsletter form for the campaign field offices and the press. But, Matalin recalled, "they were so boring we stopped reading them ourselves. I said we've got to do something different." The result, she confessed later, "was high wisenheimer." In the most slashing, bitter—and often sophomoric—language, Matalin, press aide Torie Clarke and the White House political operative Dave Carney began collaborating on a new, livelier version designed to grab attention. They succeeded, beyond their expectations and, eventually, their desires.

The press releases started going out in late July and caused no ripples at first. Matalin, however, in defending the offensive against Clinton, denied to a *New York Times* reporter that the campaign was repeating personal charges against him. "The larger issue is that he's evasive and slick," she said. "We've never said to the press that he's a philandering, pot-smoking draft dodger."

"The way you just did?" the reporter asked.

"The way I just did," Matalin replied. "But that's the first time I've done that. There is nothing nefarious or subliminal going on."

Putting negative remarks in circulation by denying having said them was an old Dick Nixon trick. Ron Brown immediately jumped on the exchange, and using another old political trick, "absolved" the perpetrator and blamed a higher-up. "Anyone who knows Mary Matalin," he said, "knows she is a true political professional. She would never have used such a vicious smear unless she was instructed to do so." He noted a news conference back in April at which Bush said he had "made specific instructions in writing to our people to stay out of the sleaze business." Brown asked: "Is this insubordination or obedience? Is his political director getting a public reprimand and a private pat on the back?"

That was just the start of it. On Sunday, August 3, Matalin issued the fourth of her "distortion of the day" press releases headlined: "Sniveling Hypocritical Democrats: Stand Up and Be Counted—On Second Thought, Shut Up and Sit Down!" Some twenty statements by or about Clinton were printed, together with sources, usually newspaper articles. One of them quoted Clinton aide Betsey Wright as saying she was in charge of dealing with "bimbo eruptions," an accurate quote and description of what Wright was doing in Little Rock—coping with new allegations or reported allegations of other womanizing episodes by Clinton floating around or being investigated by various news organizations.

The Clinton campaign immediately demanded that Matalin be fired for violating Bush's no-sleaze policy. It was an uneasy moment for James Carville, who was romantically involved with Matalin but still politically at war with her. He empathized with her, while recognizing that she had blundered, to the benefit of his own candidate. Clarke, traveling with the president, defended the press release, but shortly afterward White House deputy press secretary Judy Smith released a statement on Air Force One saying "the president is determined to keep this campaign out of the sleaze business."

White House chief of staff Skinner phoned Matalin and told her the president wanted her to apologize. Matalin, ever the political animal, thought that was a bad mistake. Her immediate attitude, she said, was " 'Do you really want me to apologize?' I thought that was a bad political thing. 'Fire me, don't make me apologize.' The pure, dispassionate political analysis was, 'Fire me or defend me,' but don't do like, 'She's sorry.' I knew we'd get crucified if we tried to have it both ways." Skinner backed off and Matalin put out a statement that only by a stretch of the imagination could be called an apology.

"With respect to our project to expose daily the negative campaign against the president and the hypocrisy of our opponents," she wrote, "it would appear to some that I might have violated, at least in spirit, the president's dictate to the campaign that we avoid references to Governor Clinton's personal life. I regret if the tone of my statement left the wrong impression in that regard." Then she added: "I stand by my criticism of the Clinton campaign and the Democratic Party for their unprecedented hypocrisy and for daily disparaging, in the most egregious and personal terms, the President of the United States."

Matalin said later her chief concern was that the incident had "stepped on the story" of a good campaign day for her boss. When he finally called her from the plane, she said, "I started crying. 'I'm sorry, I've ruined your day.' " Bush told her, she said, not to worry about it, that it was about time somebody hit back at all the attacks against him. "He understood the overarching objective of that memo," she said, and told her to keep it up, but not get carried away. And because it was a time when everybody else was standing back and letting the Clinton campaign hit at him, she said, he appeared to appreciate what she had tried to do.

In an interview in *The Washington Times* about a week later, Bush said of the incident that he "got cross-threaded with Mary Matalin, who I support strongly in her taking the attack to the enemy, but only because one characterization out of twenty [the "bimbo eruptions" reference] seemed to me to be doing that which I said I wouldn't do."

Matalin insisted later "it was never the campaign's strategy to personally attack Clinton. Even the woman's stuff. As the resident woman," she said, "I was the sounding board for this stuff. And I knew from the Sperling breakfast [the Washington reporters' group at which the Clintons had openly discussed their marital situation] that that was off the table, not because he was so good [in defending his marriage], which he was, but because she [Hillary Clinton] was so good. I remain convinced that one of the things that sealed Gary Hart's fate was the pitiful, painful pictures of Lee Hart standing behind him, looking like just what she was—the cheated-on wife. And I thought that the voter reaction was going to be, 'If Hillary can take it, we can take it, and it's nobody's business.'

"So that part of the character issue was never on the table," she said. "What was on the table and became perceived as a negative attack against him [Clinton] was the nature of his character . . . that you really gotta think about—do you want this man in the White House? This is what I was trying to tell that *New York Times* reporter. . . . You've got to know who your president is, somewhere and sometime. You've got to have some sense of who this guy is, and if he won't tell you the truth about his past, why should you believe what he's saying about your future?"

Beyond the personal reference to Clinton's earlier womanizing troubles, the Matalin press releases, which she continued daily after her "apology" but without a focus on his past personal problems, were embarrassingly amateurish in their wild swings at him. She took to referring to him as "Boy Clinton" and to his campaign bus as "the pandermobile," peppering her comments with pathetic efforts to be cutting and cute at the same time. She wrote, for example, that Clinton's bus had just "brie-zed through Wisconsin's Dairyland yesterday, trying to peddle a tax policy with more holes in it than a pound of Swiss cheese.'' Or this one: ''Slick Willie's tax-and-spend chickens come home to roost—with a few surprises still hiding in the henhouse.''

Matalin said afterward that for all the handouts' shortcomings, they were a tonic to Bush field workers as frustrated as she was at their candidate's and campaign's lack of sharp counterpunching. ''For as sophomoric as you all thought it was,'' she said, ''it was the first positive reaction [the campaign headquarters] got from the field. My two biggest phone days [with approving calls from the field] were Murphy Brown and 'bimbo eruptions.' . . . The field force—the county chairmen, the thousands of little workers, they loved them. They went crazy. They thought they were funny, they remembered the points because they were couched in these metaphors. . . . We had to give them something, so I gave them something. They loved it. It inspired them to fight.'' And in the process, she insisted, a lot of information on Clinton damaging to him got out to the public.

The trouble, though, was that also in the process, the whole exercise, which came off as exceedingly mean-spirited to those not among the Bush faithful, played directly into the hands of a prime Clinton strategy—to paint the 1992 Bush campaign as a carbon copy of 1988, as Son of Willie Horton. In the environment of an electorate up in arms against politics as usual, fanned by the complaints of Ross Perot, this strategy proved to be a critical ingredient in the election's outcome.

From the very start of the campaign, the Clinton strategists had made a point of reminding voters of the Willie Horton and other 1988 negative attacks on Dukakis. Every time Bush or a Bush surrogate said the slightest thing that could be taken as a disparaging word about Clinton, his operatives would immediately cry their version of the old Ronald Reagan line against Jimmy Carter in 1980: ''There he goes again.''

The fact was that there was very little in the 1992 Bush attacks on Clinton that came close to the 1988 allegation that Dukakis's irresponsibility had turned loose a convicted murderer who was black who then went out and raped a white woman. That blatant appeal to racial prejudice, wrapped up in the charge that Dukakis was soft on crime, hit a low in negative campaigning that even the 1992 Bush operatives—while publicly defending it as factual—recognized had to be avoided this time around.

Well before her ''distortions of the day'' backfired, Matalin noted, "they had been bashing us all year and calling us negative campaigners. That was irritating the president and was a very frustrating environment." Ron Brown as Democratic party chairman in fact had been calling Bush a dirty campaigner ever since 1988, "and had largely sucked you guys [the press] in," she said, and it was then conveyed to the public, conditioning voters to believe it. "But that notion that we were negative campaigners," she acknowledged, "did back us off of doing negative ads. Many discussions about advertising of the negative variety included how hard you guys were going to come down on us."

(In the October 1992 issue of *Harper's* magazine, *Harper's Index* reported that the name Willie Horton was mentioned sixty-nine times in *New York Times* articles from January through August of 1992, compared to only thirty-three times during the 1988 presidential campaign in which Horton was made a live issue by the Bush campaign.)

Matalin recalled that she and Teeter wanted to consider doing ads on Clinton's Arkansas record between the two conventions but "were dissuaded because of how you all would respond." There was, notably, nothing wrong with pointing up an opponent's record in office, provided it was not distorted. But so spooked had the Bush campaign become by the ghost of the Willie Horton that its 1988 predecessor had unleashed on the voting public that it pulled its punches—and still got hammered for "going negative."

The Bush strategists, Matalin said, thought if the voters didn't have a memory of Willie Horton, the press would remind them. "If it was branded negative campaigning, whether or not it was," she said, "people had this knee-jerk reaction to it. We did not think we could withstand the press assault, given this sort of article of faith that we were negative campaigners."

Teeter said later he thought more significant than the Clinton camp intimidating the Bush strategists directly against going negative was how the press was already conditioned to expect negative campaigning from the Bush campaign. "There was a disproportionate interest [among the press] in what was a negative commercial and what was a negative speech and when we were going to do it and if we were going to do it," Teeter said. "I think that probably in the broader sense the conditioning of the press and to some degree the public from '88 limited how you could attack and what you would do negative. . . .

"I don't think anybody ever had any views that you weren't going to attack Clinton or run any negative commercials because they said, 'There they go again.'" At the same time, he said, "you almost went into the campaign knowing that your degrees of freedom on negative spots because of '88 were less than they were in '88." At the same time, the public mind-set on Bush as a negative campaigner gave Clinton a freer hand to hit at him. "There was nothing we could do to make people think we were more negative than Bush," Stephanopoulos said. "There was just no way."

Within those limitations, though, Bush and his campaign did their best to undercut Clinton in the voters' eyes. Addressing the annual convention of the Catholic lay organization the Knights of Columbus in New York, the president immodestly asked: "If you're looking to restore America's moral fiber, why buy a synthetic when you can get real cotton?" He reiterated his unflinching opposition to abortion—unflinching, that is, since joining the Reagan Revolution—and took some glancing shots at Clinton without mentioning his name.

"Some think it's okay to hand out condoms in schools," he said, "but oppose amending our Constitution to allow our kids to put their hands together in prayer." And later: "I believe that a central issue of this election year should be, 'Who do you trust to renew America's moral purpose? Who do you trust to fight for the ideas that will help rebuild our families and restore our moral values?'" The words "trust" and "family" and "values" were becoming staples in his speeches, all obviously for comparison purposes with the scandal-scarred Clinton.

Others, meanwhile, were being much more direct. After Bush had said in an interview in *Time* that he would fire anyone henceforth who dealt in private innuendo, including "the issue of marital infidelity," he remained silent when his campaign general chairman, Robert Mosbacher, told reporters marital fidelity "should be one of the yardsticks" for measuring the candidates. A CNN reporter at a Kennebunkport news conference had asked Bush directly about recurring reports of infidelity involving himself and he had angrily denied them and castigated the reporter for raising the issue on nationwide television. Mosbacher said those reports were "totally uncorroborated" whereas Clinton lacked credibility "based on what he has denied and what he hasn't denied."

Bush took no action when U.S. Treasurer Catalina V. Villalpando, before the New Jersey delegation at the Republican convention in Houston, offered a more direct slur against Clinton. She linked him to former San Antonio Mayor Henry Cisneros, a Clinton supporter who three years earlier had withdrawn from public office after acknowledging an extramarital affair, by asking: "Can you imagine two skirt-chasers campaigning together?" Bush's response was, "Nobody is going to be able to control everything that everybody says." And he didn't seem to try as other Republicans used the Houston convention to attack his Democratic opponent, directly or by inference, on everything from draft-dodging to womanizing and drug use.

Immediately after the convention, Bush took up the call. The election, he told a large crowd in Woodstock, Georgia, standing in a driving rain, "is a choice about the character of the man you want to lead this nation for another four years," and "about families and leaving the world a better and more prosperous place." And with his customary tough-guy words that belied his easygoing, preppy manner, he told the crowd: "So you tell Governor Clinton and that Congress, 'If you can't run with the big dogs, stay under the porch.'"

Bush spoke after one of the GOP's meanest pit bulls had warmed up the crowd with a stinging attack on Democratic "weird values," referring to the hot story of the hour, a nasty child custody fight between movie actors Woody Allen and his former lover, Mia Farrow, in which Allen had declared his love for one of her adopted daughters. "I call this the Woody Allen plank," Gingrich oozed. "It's a weird situation, and it fits the Democratic Party platform perfectly. If a Democrat used the word 'family' to raise children in Madison Square Garden, half their party would have rebelled and the other half would not vote. . . . Woody Allen had nonincest with his nondaughter because they were a nonfamily." A Bush spokesman afterward said only that "the president does not want to make Woody Allen an issue."

On other occasions in other places, Bush hewed to legitimate criticisms of Clinton on issues ranging from auto fuel efficiency, in Michigan, to free trade agreements with Mexico, in Missouri, but always with an emphasis on "trust." Compared to 1988, to Willie Horton and flag pledges and Boston Harbor, he was on the high road, but that didn't stop the Clinton campaign from saying "there he goes again," especially when surrogates did the mud-slinging for him and he remained mute.

Wilhelm said later that while the Clinton campaign "certainly reminded people" of the Bush record on negative campaigning, "the best teacher of that was 1988."

After Labor Day, when the president appeared in ultraconservative Orange County, California, with former President Reagan and another of his party's hand grenade specialists, Representative Robert Dornan, he held his tongue as Reagan needled Clinton as a draft evader and Dornan called him "Chicken Little of Little Rock." Clinton, Dornan said, spent his time during the Vietnam War "eating compulsively to the point of exhaustion . . . throwing darts [and] drinking ale" in an Oxford pub while other Americans his age fought and died. To that, a Bush spokeswoman said Dornan was "entitled to his opinion—free speech."

Bush himself was careful, with the ghost of Willie Horton always hovering, to leave the personal shots at Clinton to such surrogates. Aides continued to press him to make the case for himself, for what he would do in a second term to right the economy and address the other demanding problems on the domestic front. Finally, in a carefully constructed speech before the friendly Economic Club of Detroit, among the nation's most prestigious forums for discussing the state of the economy, Bush on September 10 laid out an "Agenda for American Renewal" that essentially was a repackaging of his old conservative remedies, with a few new concepts.

The first was a proposal to downsize, or as he put it to "right-size," the federal government. He said he would cut the White House operating budget by one third if Congress would do the same with its own. Another was a broad pledge to extend to European and Pacific Rim countries the free trade approach proposed for Mexico. The rest was a retread of such ideas as the line-item veto, congressional term limits, capital gains tax rate cuts, urban enterprise zones, tuition vouchers for school choice, voluntary earmarking of income taxes for deficit reduction, a cap on product liability damage suits and a ban on political action committee contributions.

Although the speech was largely a rehash of Bush proposals rejected or ignored by the Democratic Congress, it was at last a coherent recitation of what Bush intended to do in his second term. Insiders credited Jim Baker and his team for pulling it together and orchestrating its airing and distribution to the electorate—a cohesion and decisiveness sadly lacking all year, until Baker's move from the State Department to the White House.

Bush repeated the highlights that night in a five-minute paid television appearance and the campaign prepared a slick twenty-nine-page brochure of the plan. "We had satellite links to everyplace," Jim Lake recalled, "and we spent a lot of money sending out those 'Agenda for American Renewal' magazines with the plan in it—and it lasted one day. We should have carried on with that for two weeks, a long period of time, driving that home. But something came up that caused us to get off of that."

That weekend, Lake said, as the campaign's communications director he tried to get Baker or his chief lieutenant, Bob Zoellick, to go on the major network interview shows to tout the plan, "but Baker wouldn't do it. It was a way in my opinion to send a signal that this is important, this is real, and to send a signal to the press corps that Baker had really put his reputation on the line here; this must be something good. But we weren't able to get that done." The signal that many in the press corps expecting a strong follow-up got, instead, was that once again Jim Baker, who never wanted to be pulled back into the dirty business of politics in the first place, was keeping his distance.

One thing that "came up" at this time was the potential for reopening the whole draft issue against Clinton. Quayle was scheduled to address the annual convention of the National Guard Association in Salt Lake City in mid-September, and the campaign decided that Bush should replace him. Learning of the switch and anticipating a broadside attack, the Clinton campaign got its candidate invited to speak right after the president and prepared a strong rebuttal. Reporters from around the country rushed to the convention to witness the bloodletting firsthand. Surely Bush would seize the opportunity to raise the issue of Clinton's failure, under still suspicious circumstances involving a flirtation with the Arkansas ROTC program, to serve in the military during the Vietnam War. The fact that Bush had decided to take over from Quayle, and that Clinton had changed his own schedule to appear on the same day, added to the anticipation of fireworks.

Instead, the guardsmen, the news media and the national audience watching on television were treated to an episode that well illustrated the manner in which the Bush camp's concern about being painted once again as an agent of negativism in politics affected the 1992 campaign dialogue. Bush, leading off, took pains to discount what he said was "a great deal of speculation . . . that I was going to come out here and use this forum to attack Governor Clinton.'' He went on: "I want to tell you, I do feel very strongly about certain aspects of the controversy swirling around Governor Clinton. But I didn't come here to attack him.''

Bush then launched into a defense of Quayle and his service in the Guard, an issue in the 1988 campaign, praising him for his "candor,'' lack of which Clinton had been accused regarding his own draft record. He worked his way around to raising the issue of "using influence to avoid the military,'' without pinning it explicitly to Clinton. And he argued that such questions "matter because, despite all our problems at home, we can never forget that we ask our presidents to lead the military, to bear the awful authority of deciding to send your sons and daughters in harm's way.''

Bush, telling of a letter sent to him by the mother of a helicopter pilot who had died in the Gulf War, stammered as his voice choked, noting that this was a responsibility that faced all presidents. "And does that mean that if you've never seen the awful horror of battle that you can never be commander in chief?'' asked this World War II combat pilot. "Of course not, not at all,'' he answered himself. "But it does mean that we must hold our presidents to the highest standard, because they might have to decide if our sons and daughters should knock early on death's door.''

The softness of the president's allusions to Clinton surprised the governor and his entourage. A strong defense of his draft record had been prepared but was scrapped when Clinton learned on his way to the convention that Bush had not attacked him directly. The Democratic nominee then spoke without notes about his support for a better-equipped National Guard and a better-educated work force to restore economic well-being at home.

Afterward both sides declared "victory,'' the Bush camp for keeping the Clinton draft record in the news without attacking him on it, the Clinton side for what its strategists said showed the draft issue was behind them. More notable was the fact that Bush had the ideal forum for taking the gloves off against Clinton on what his strategists said they believed was still a killer issue against him, and he fired what essentially was a blank cartridge. Once again the concern about being painted as too negative had intruded.

With less than seven weeks to go to the election, Bush still trailed Clinton badly, by 15 percentage points in the latest *Washington Post*/ABC News poll. The time had come for Bush to stop playing Mr. Nice Guy. Six days after the gentle encounter in Salt Lake City, he finally went bareknuckles on the draft issue. In a radio interview with ultra-right-wing talk show host Rush Limbaugh in New York, he attacked what he called Clinton's "total failure to come clean with the American people" on the matter. His opponent's "fundamental difficulty," he said, "is that he has not told the full truth, the whole truth, nothing but the truth."

Bush told his host that he wasn't "trying to make it a big issue" but that "it's not going to go away." Inaccurately charging that Clinton in his famous letter to Colonel Holmes had called the military "immoral," Bush said: "I have a very different concept of military service. I'm sure I would never call the military immoral." Clinton had said in the letter he considered drafting Americans for the Vietnam War "illegitimate" and wrote of the dilemma for young men like himself who loved their country but "loathed the military." But Bush went on: "I believe that the commander in chief should not have a mind-set to say the military is immoral. Now, maybe he's changed his view on that. . . . Let's find out. Let's let him level with the American people."

Clinton was asked about Bush's remarks as he campaigned in Chicago with Admiral William C. Crowe, the former chairman of the Joint Chiefs of Staff under Bush and Reagan who had recently endorsed him. He pointed to Crowe and said he "has more credibility on truth-telling than George Bush" and wouldn't have endorsed him had he shared Bush's views on the subject.

The specter of Willie Horton continued to intrude. Floyd Brown, a filmmaker who in 1988 under "independent expenditure" provisions guiding the Federal Election Commission had on his own produced and aired a television ad showing Horton, was at it again. This time he prepared ads providing a telephone number viewers could call to hear what he said were the taped conversations between Clinton and Gennifer Flowers. Bush campaign lawyers complained to the FEC demanding that Brown be required to inform contributors that his Presidential Victory Committee had nothing to do with the Bush-Quayle campaign. At the same time, White House press secretary Fitzwater called Brown's activities "despicable" and said they "have no place in the American political system."

Four years earlier, Bush professed to be equally appalled at Brown's Willie Horton ad, while conveying basically the same message from the stump. This time, with good reason to believe that the womanizing issue against Clinton had long since flamed out, he told reporters "we will do everything we can within the law to see that this man does not use my name in raising funds for these nefarious purposes."

Late in September, the Bush strategists decided that their best shot at Clinton might, after all, be his Arkansas record, which could reasonably be attacked without unleashing a torrent of criticism about going personally negative. They sent the president and Air Force One on a dizzying 2,500-mile encirclement of Arkansas, putting down in all six states bordering Clinton's home base—from Missouri to Oklahoma, Texas, Louisiana, Mississippi and Tennessee—and hitting at his stewardship as a five-term governor. Up to this point, he said, "I have resisted the urge to focus on Governor Clinton's record. But I must tell you, I am very tired of the distortions, tired of the half truths. And the stakes are too high to let America be deceived by a negative campaign. So today I have chosen to lay it on the line, talk about my opponent's record . . . in Arkansas. . . . And that means explaining the Grand Canyon that separates his rhetoric from the reality of his record."

Bush said Clinton's environmental record was so bad and "the rivers are so polluted, the fish glow in the dark." On crime, he said, his opponent was a "Doberman pinscher" as a candidate but a "Chihuahua" as governor. And in an allusion to the old draft issue he offered an observation of which Tricky Dick Nixon himself would have been proud. Asked about it at a rally of supporters at the airport in Shreveport, Louisiana, Bush said: "No, I am not going to talk about the draft today. I'll let the American people make up their own minds about that. All I will say is that I am proud I put on the uniform of my country."

In the end, it always seemed to come back to the draft issue, and by implication the question not only of Clinton's honesty in dealing with it but also his patriotism—another throwback to the Bush campaign of 1988. Then it was Dukakis's veto of the state bill requiring school teachers to lead their students in recitation of the pledge of allegiance to the flag, recommended to him by his legal advisers on grounds the bill was an abridgment of the First Amendment.

Clinton learned of Bush's attacks on his Arkansas record on the same day the governor was campaigning at Michigan State University, site of what would have been the first of a series of presidential debates had Bush not balked at participating. He challenged the president to make his charges face-to-face, but Bush preferred long-range firing at this point.

The Clinton team in Little Rock was now cautiously confident, but driving hard. All hands took to heart the blunt reminder of the campaign's overriding focus that Carville after the Democratic convention had posted in the "war room," where daily strategy and "rapid response" to Bush's attacks and revealed vulnerabilities were determined:

> Change vs. more of the same.
> The economy, stupid.
> Don't forget health care.

Campaign manager Wilhelm remembered later that on the next night, September 24, Paul Tully, whose state-by-state targeting was now the heart of the campaign's strategy, said: "We still have work to do, but we're ninety percent of the way there." It was a goal toward which Tully had worked heroically despite many disappointments through all his adult years, and he was relishing the prospect. After another of the prodigious dinners of good food and good talk for which he was known, Tully retired for the night a happy man, and died in his sleep.

The loss hit the campaign hard, personally and politically. Clinton broke off campaigning and attended a memorial service at the Washington Cathedral at which he was only one of hundreds of Democrats, famous and unknown, who paid homage to a man who had brought zest and wisdom to the party's quests for the presidency over the years. Many young men and women who had learned campaign organizing—and the joy of playing hard, dedicated politics for causes beyond themselves—under Tully's guiding hand, came from around the country to say goodbye to him.

The campaign moved on, and in spite of the Bush campaign's awareness of the perils of being seen as more negative, Clinton's patriotism, like Dukakis's in 1988, was coming to the fore as a late-campaign issue. Congressman Dornan on the House floor began to raise questions about a trip Clinton had made to Moscow as a tourist while he was a student at Oxford in 1969, during a school break (one of as many as 60,000 Americans to visit the Soviet Union that year). Clinton had said he didn't remember much about it other than walking around looking at the sights, or who he may have seen there. He did remember, he had said, meeting a Georgetown professor and peace activist at a train station in Norway.

The question of Clinton's activities while he was a student abroad took on a sinister wrinkle when *Newsweek* reported that several pages appeared to be missing from the State Department's passport file on him. The discovery came, the newsmagazine said, as the department was attempting to respond to requests from several news organizations under the Freedom of Information Act investigating a rumor that Clinton had considered applying for foreign citizenship as a means of escaping the draft. But the FBI, which was ordered to investigate the allegation of the missing pages, reported a few days later that the file appeared to be intact. The very disclosure that the State Department had been searching through Clinton's passport files, however, triggered suspicions of Republican dirty tricks that soon would surface, and be exploited by the Clinton campaign.

Dornan kept pressing the case, even winning an audience with Bush and Jim Baker in the Oval Office to urge that the Moscow trip be made a major issue in the final, critical month of the campaign. The blatantly pro-Bush *Washington Times* ran a banner headline on the trip, but the story seemed to be going nowhere until Bush appeared on CNN's *Larry King Live* on the night of October 7, from San Antonio.

When King asked Bush about the Clinton trip, he replied: "I don't want to tell you what I really think because I don't have the facts. But to go to Moscow, one year after Russia crushed Czechoslovakia, not remember who you saw there. . . . You can remember who you saw in an airport in Oslo but you can't remember who you saw in Moscow?" He criticized Clinton's previously disclosed participation in demonstrations against the Vietnam War in England and demanded that Clinton tell the American people "how many demonstrations he led against his own country from a foreign soil. . . . I cannot for the life of me," he said, "understand mobilizing demonstrations and demonstrating against your own country, no matter how strongly you feel, when you're in a foreign land."

Once again, the Bush strategy was tied to events of the past, in a country and at a time voters were hurting economically and fed up with harping on personal questions about the candidates. Clinton's spokesman, George Stephanopoulos, called Bush's performance a "sad and pathetic ploy by a desperate politican. If he worried as much about what most Americans are going through in 1992 as he does about what Bill Clinton did in 1969," he said, "we'd all be in much better shape. He sees the handwriting on the wall."

Once more the Clinton operatives were saying "there he goes again" on negative personal attacks. Two days later, Bush appeared to be backing off, responding to a question about Clinton's trip on ABC News's *Good Morning America*. "Clearly, if he's told all there is to tell on Moscow, fine," he said. "I'm not suggesting there is anything unpatriotic about that. A lot of people went to Moscow. And so that's the end of that as far as I'm concerned." One reason may have been that mention of Moscow, according to Greenberg, sent Clinton's poll numbers climbing.

Later that very same day in Cincinnati, however, Bush said he would continue to criticize Clinton for "demonstrating against your country in a foreign land when soldiers . . . are dying in Vietnam. . . . It is wrong to demonstrate against your country when your country's at war," he repeated, "and I'm not going to back away from that one single bit."

The more Bush went on the personal attack, the more he was inflicting wounds on himself. *The Washington Post* reported a survey by Brown University that found 52 percent of those polled in Boston—admittedly a heavily Democratic city—believed the president was responsible for keeping the campaign on the low road, to only 15 percent who blamed Clinton. A Brown professor, Darrell West, was quoted as saying: "Bush is losing the blame game. In 1988, Bush was much more negative than Michael Dukakis but wasn't blamed for it. . . . A lot of the press coverage has accentuated the idea of Bush attacking."

The ghost of Willie Horton had indeed come back to haunt the man who had made him famous four years earlier. Bush had other specters chasing him now as well. They were face masks and head masks of chickens that were appearing at campaign rallies for both Bush and Clinton around the country, together with signs that read CHICKEN GEORGE— manifestations of voter dissatisfaction with Bush's foot-dragging on long-proposed televised debates with his Democratic opponent. Time was getting short, and the odds were still long against him. George Bush could not afford to be called "chicken" much longer.

SMART BOMBS VS. BUCKSHOT

Even before Labor Day, the conventional opening date for presidential general election campaigns, the Clinton strategists had already fired the first shots in what had come to be called "the air war"—the competition for votes through paid television and radio commercials.

The Clinton ads began running in August, a week after the Republican National Convention, and where they were run was just as significant as when. Eschewing the traditional general election practice of advertising nationwide on incredibly expensive network television, the Clinton planners targeted specific battleground states and began assaulting them with unprecedentedly heavy buys in cheaper local markets. In the process, they left many states uncovered by paid commercials and abdicated the broad national television audience to the Bush campaign—at least in the realm of purchased time.

The Clinton strategists' unconventional timing and targeting sent a distinct message: they were determined not only to define their candidate in their own terms before the Bush campaign did it for them, but to do so intensively in the key states that could win the election for them. From the outset, it was clear that their first priority was controlling the agenda, and delineating the critical zones of combat, for the air war of 1992.

"We wanted to define Clinton in those battleground states before they defined us," Mandy Grunwald, the campaign's advertising expert, said later. From August through the election, she said, the Clinton campaign ran about twice as much paid television in the selected battleground states as the Bush campaign, which hewed largely to the traditional approach of buying mostly network time. "We had two weeks on the air when they didn't have a single spot on the air, which was unbelievable," she said. "It was just stupid of them, and for another three or four weeks we were outspending them at higher point levels [intensity of airtime] in those states."

The goal, Grunwald said, was to have two tracks running simultaneously in the target states—one defining Clinton in the most positive terms, one criticizing Bush and keeping him on the defensive. There was a desirable third track as well, she said, which was responding to Bush's attacks. "You can live in a world where you have to pick two out of three," she said. "You can't live in a world where you have to pick one out of three. . . . We didn't want to be in a situation in a battleground state where we could only run one track, and a lot of this walking away from the network[s] was born of the desire [to run two tracks]."

The targeting strategy grew out of the experience of a Clinton team whose strength was running statewide rather than presidential campaigns. "We all come from running Senate and gubernatorial campaigns," Grunwald said, "and knowing what it takes in a . . . [particular] state to win a campaign. And a lot of our focus was, we were going to treat Michigan and Colorado and Georgia as we would treat [them in state races]."

The conventional wisdom among politicians holds that paid advertising is less important in presidential elections than in campaigns for lesser offices, because candidates for president get so much news coverage— "free media," in the lexicon of political operatives—that the commercials have less impact.

There is obvious validity in that view, at least to the extent that in presidential campaigns it is far more difficult to build or alter a perception of a candidate with advertising alone. For example, in Jimmy Carter's 1980 campaign against challenger Ronald Reagan, the president's strategists made television commercials designed to depict him as a strong leader. But when run they were juxtaposed against news stories on the television networks showing him being jerked around by the Ayatollah Khomeini in the Iran hostage situation.

Television and, to a lesser degree, radio commercials can have an effect on voters, however, when by endless repetition they are a prime source of the "information" the voters receive about a candidate. And, more importantly, they can have an effect when used to reinforce perceptions of a candidate already in the voters' minds.

In the 1992 contest, the Bill Clinton strategists scheduled their television spots onto the tracks Grunwald talked about. First, they pressed their own case with saturation coverage in the key states—"smart bombs" zeroing in on specific targets with pinpoint precision. Second, they underlined reservations about President Bush that already had been identified by the opinion polls all through the primary season and summer. And when necessary and when they had the resources, they responded to Bush's attacks. But more often Clinton did so himself, and quickly, through the ample free media that the heavy general election coverage brought him.

The first sixty-second spot, run in ten states targeted by the campaign as critical to Clinton's election prospects, used footage of the candidate reaching into crowds to shake hands on the post-convention bus tour, at his desk as governor and delivering his acceptance speech in Madison Square Garden. The accompanying text emphasized his promise to raise taxes on those who earned more than $200,000 a year and invited voters to write for a copy of his economic plan.

As read by the announcer, it was a distillation of the message Clinton had been sending all year and would continue to send—that Clinton was the candidate of change and economic progress. At the same time, the commercial was an attempt to inoculate him against the attacks on his record as governor of Arkansas that the campaign expected from President Bush:

"Something's happening. People are ready, because they've had enough. Enough of seeing their incomes fall behind and their jobs on the line, enough of a government that just doesn't work. They're ready for change. And changing people's lives—that's the work of his life. Twelve years of battling the odds in one of our nation's poorest states. Arkansas now leads the nation in job growth. Incomes are rising at twice the national rate. Seventeen thousand people moved from welfare to work. That's progress, and that's what we need now. Change, real solutions. Bill Clinton has an economic plan to rebuild America that invests in our own people. Education. Training. Eight million jobs in the next four years. Those making over $200,000 have to pay more. The rest of us get a break. It's a plan to put people first again. And six Nobel Prize economists say it will work. For people, for a change, Bill Clinton for President.''

In targeting more than 80 percent of the $35 million to $37 million available for advertising in battleground states, and even in particular markets within those states, the Democrats enjoyed a luxury resulting from the fact that they entered the general election campaign with such huge leads in so many states. They could safely count the electoral votes in these states as assured, or at least as assured as anything ever is in a presidential election campaign. "We never bought network television time until the last two weeks," Grunwald said. "That's never been done."

Using the targeting profile that had been developed early in the year by Paul Tully, the campaign held weekly meetings in Little Rock to make the decisions about where to spend how much in the days ahead. Such flexibility was permitted by the fact that as many as fifty media buyers were standing by to put in the orders when those decisions were made. The decision-makers, in addition to Tully himself before his death, regularly included David Wilhelm, Stan Greenberg, field director Craig Smith and Grunwald. Also, the others in the campaign with extensive political experience in statewide races in the battleground states knew the media markets and what it took to win in them.

The strategists decided to ignore two groups of states in placing their commercials. One was made up of those clearly beyond reach because they were so congenitally Republican—such hopeless cases as Virginia, Kansas and Nebraska. These states were, in effect, written off even though at the time there were polls showing Clinton running even or ahead of Bush in most of them. Indeed, at the outset, the earliest polls showed Clinton clearly trailing only in one of the fifty states—Utah.

Some of these were difficult calls. Early in the campaign, polls were showing Clinton leading by eight to ten points in Alabama, and Democrats there had been in Clinton's corner early. But the Clinton strategists realized it was likely to be difficult ground in the long run—possible but not likely. In some cases, the key consideration was simply figuring the cost-benefit ratio. Florida, for instance, looked susceptible to Clinton throughout the campaign but a full-scale media assault on the state would have cost several million dollars—too much to pay for the potential benefit. As Wilhelm put it one day during the campaign: "We don't need to win them all. We don't need 450 electoral votes."

The toughest decision may have been one against an intense effort in Texas. Here again early polls were encouraging, and the Clinton managers were intrigued by the possibility of defeating George Bush in his home state or, at the least, forcing him into spending much of his treasure to protect his base there. Moreover, the campaign in Texas was headed by Gary Mauro, the state land commissioner and one of its two or three most skilled political operatives, and he was arguing, perhaps predictably, that Texas was within range for Clinton.

In this case, the brain trust in Little Rock temporized, spending a small amount of the "soft money" available through the Democratic National Committee to buy some test commercials while postponing a final decision into October, when Texas finally was effectively written off. As Grunwald put it later, "We walked away from a lot of states where we held leads . . . there were a lot of temptations out there."

The most politically significant, and risky, decisions were those to withhold advertising in states in which Clinton seemed to be in an unassailable position, including not just such traditionally Democratic bastions as Massachusetts, West Virginia and Rhode Island, but some of the major states whose electoral votes were crucial—California, New York and Illinois. "Our gamble was," said Grunwald, "that [we] would not need advertising to win these states."

This strategy required a certain amount of nerve on Wilhelm's part. When what had been a lead of close to thirty points in California narrowed to under fifteen late in the campaign, he and his California campaign director, Los Angeles lawyer John Emerson, had to decide whether the state's fifty-four electoral votes were still safe or needed to be reinforced with advertising, financed from an emergency contingent fund. They decided the Clinton margin would hold in this case, but there were several such questions raised in other states during the course of the campaign.

The key factor in all these decisions was Greenberg's polling data. Some of the runaway states might be getting tighter but, the polling expert kept saying, there was no reason to panic. This approach, Grunwald said later, "meant that California watched seven weeks of negative ads about Bill Clinton and never heard an answer." But by not buying advertising in the nation's most populous state, Grunwald estimated, the campaign saved between $5 million and $7 million of a total advertising budget of $35 million, or enough to allow saturation commercial coverage in the most closely contested major states.

In Ohio, for instance, the Clinton campaign was spending more on television than the candidates in the leading statewide races, buying as much as a thousand rating points a week—meaning the average viewer would see the Clinton spots ten times during that period. "Our premise was," Grunwald said, "if we're going to contest, we're going to run a full campaign. . . . If we're there, we're going to own the airwaves. And if we can't do that, let's not be there."

By contrast, the Bush campaign never enjoyed that same luxury. As Bob Teeter said later, the first priority for the Republican operation was to lift Bush's numbers in the national opinion polls, so that he would appear competitive and voters would begin to focus on the choice between the two men. In short, the incumbent president still had to establish his credibility. Until that happened, there was no point in spending money to try to pick off the electoral votes of particular states. The only course available was to spend most of the Bush money on network television—spraying buckshot everywhere—and that was what was done through most of the campaign, at least until the final two weeks.

(Through September, the air war was waged between the Clinton and Bush camps. But in the end, the Ross Perot campaign spent more than either of the major party campaigns on television advertising—about $45 million. As in the Bush campaign, most of it went for network television, with a large proportion on longer programs rather than spots. But Perot was never a direct combatant in the air war because he never became fully engaged in the charges and countercharges that the Republican and Democratic candidates directed at each other. Instead, the Perot spots late in the campaign were aimed largely at undercutting the press, to counter its contention that the independent candidate had no realistic chance of winning the White House. In one commercial, Perot was shown saying: "You got to stop letting these people tell you who to vote for.

You got to stop letting these folks in the press tell you you're throwing your vote away. You got to start using your own head.'')

The reliance on the networks obviously meant that the Bush campaign was spending relatively as much money in states the president already was assured of winning as in those where he needed a breakthrough. But given the goal of improving his national position, it didn't matter much whether whatever new support could be elicited came from states that were closely contested or not.

The Bush strategy, even if dictated by circumstances, did mean that in many states seven weeks or more passed in which Bush campaign attacks on Clinton did indeed go unchallenged by Clinton commercials. But Clinton was able to answer personally on the free media, or through his surrogates and state campaign operations. That was one of the reasons for the weekly meetings in Little Rock—to keep the campaign "always vigilant," as one adviser put it, against the possibility of any nasty surprises.

If there was a clear difference in the advertising strategy of the two campaigns in deciding when and where to run their commercials, there was an equally stark contrast between the content of their commercials. And that contrast spoke volumes about the shape of the campaign.

Once Clinton strategists had managed a certain amount of inoculation against attacks from the Bush campaign, they followed the first two tracks mentioned by Grunwald more or less simultaneously. One was intended to define the governor of Arkansas as a "different kind of Democrat"—not another traditional liberal in the mold of Walter Mondale or Michael Dukakis—who represented change and, for the electorate, hope of a serious attack on the fundamental problems of the economy. The other was a strategy of keeping the voters' attention focused on George Bush and on the economic issues that, all the polling data continued to tell the Clinton campaign, were still the prime concern, even preoccupation, of most of the voters of 1992.

In this regard, Grunwald said, the model for her was the 1980 Reagan television strategy against Carter—another "incumbent president in a weak situation and people very worried about the economy." Although Reagan campaigned on the stump to "get the government off the backs of the American people" and "stand tall in the world," she said, "neither of those phrases ever appeared in his advertising . . . ninety percent of his spots were about the economy. . . . It amazed me how single-minded and focused the advertising was.''

One of the early positive Clinton commercials announced ''The Clinton Plan'' and showed the Democratic nominee leaning on his desk talking into the camera: ''Government just isn't working for the hardworking families of America. We need fundamental change, not more of the same. That's why I've offered a comprehensive plan, a real plan to rebuild America, create 8 million new jobs, invest in education and job training, insure quality, affordable health care for all. We're going to ask the rich to pay their fair share so the rest of America can finally get a break. A plan to put government back on your side. Read it yourself. Together we can make America work again.''

Another thirty-second commercial also focused on the economy and economic fear in particular. It bore the legend ''The Republican Record,'' and under those words showed a kind of political odometer tracking the number of unemployed as the figure moved up past 9.5 million Americans out of work. As the figure grew, the announcer said: ''You're looking at the results of years of Republican neglect. The highest unemployment in eight years. The Republicans actually stalled the extension of unemployment benefits, blocked a middle-class tax cut that would help the economy, cut Medicare for senior citizens and tried to reduce college loans. . . . The worst economic record since the Great Depression. Aren't you ready to say enough is enough?''

The commercials designed to depict Clinton as a ''different kind of Democrat'' showed the presidential nominee and his running mate, with this voice-over description: ''They're a new generation of Democrats, Bill Clinton and Al Gore. And they don't think the way the old Democratic Party did. They've called for an end to welfare as we know it, so welfare can be a second chance, not a way of life. They've sent a strong signal to criminals by supporting the death penalty. And they've rejected the old tax-and-spend politics. Clinton's balanced twelve budgets and they've proposed a new plan investing in people, detailing $140 billion in spending cuts they'd make right now. Clinton-Gore. For people, for a change.''

Clinton had used the welfare issue to help define himself as different throughout the campaign, particularly in the South and, perhaps to a lesser extent, with audiences of blue-collar Reagan Democrats in the Northeast and Midwest. One thirty-second spot showed Clinton speaking from the governor's mansion in Little Rock and saying: "For so long government has failed us, and one of its worst failures has been welfare. I have a plan to end welfare as we know it—to break the cycle of welfare dependency. We'll provide education, job training and child care, but then those who are able must go to work, either in the private sector or in public service. I know it can work. In my state we've moved 17,000 people from welfare rolls to payrolls. It's time to make welfare what it should be—a second chance, not a way of life."

The Bush campaign also ran positive spots that attempted to combine, at least by implication, his stature as a world leader and military hero. But what was missing was any coherent message to answer the central question of the campaign—whether he now could be relied upon to confront and deal with the economic distress. His first sixty-second commercial attempted to create a dramatic atmosphere with film of war planes taking off, a computer printing out his message and music building in the background while he was shown, in an excerpt from his acceptance speech, saying: "The world is in transition. The defining challenge of the nineties is to win the economic competition. To win the peace, we must be a military superpower, an economic superpower and an expert superpower. In this election, you'll hear two versions of how to do this. Theirs is to look inward, ours is to look forward, prepare our people to compete, to save and invest so we can win. Here's what I'm fighting for: open markets for American products, lower government spending, tax-relief opportunities for small business, legal and health reform, job training and new schools built on competition ready for the twenty-first century."

Another Bush commercial run later attempted to use his role in the Persian Gulf War and on the world stage. It showed pictures of Scud missiles and fighter planes, hostages and President Boris Yeltsin of Russia interspersed with labels such as "Persian Gulf Crisis—1991" and "The Coup against Gorbachev—1991" and, more to the point, "Today's Unknown Threat." At the end the camera zoomed in on the leather chair behind the president's desk in the Oval Office and the legend that appeared on the screen read: "President Bush. Commander in Chief."

The sound track had President Bush announcing: "Just two hours ago allied air forces began the attack on military targets" and simulated the voices of news broadcasters saying such things as "if revolutionaries and terrorists are armed with nuclear and chemical weapons, it may pose new challenges to the President.'' Finally an announcer was heard saying: ''In a world where we're just one unknown dictator away from the next major crisis, who do you trust to be sitting in this chair?''

This approach was the heart of the Bush campaign's case—that Bill Clinton lacked the experience and character to be trusted in the White House, while George Bush already had demonstrated his ability to function in a crisis. But the problem for the Republicans was that this pitch was simply irrelevant in terms of the 1992 electorate. The voters already knew what Bush had done in the Persian Gulf and had factored it into their tentative decisions.

They also knew the Cold War was a thing of the past. The Bush campaign appeared to have forgotten, perhaps out of necessity, that the first question of politics is, ''What have you done for me lately?'' And what it lacked in its arsenal of commercials was even one that could make a convincing case for Bush on domestic issues. The Republican strategists tried once, with a five-minute commercial derived from his speech to the Economic Club of Detroit, but it fell so flat they dropped it within days.

Lacking a positive case that voters would see as pertinent, the Bush strategists relied heavily on negative commercials—again aimed at raising questions about Clinton they hoped would lead voters into making comparisons. Clinton's record as governor of Arkansas was a target off and on as the campaign progressed. One early—and funny—spot showed fast-forward film of state legislators applauding while Clinton signed bills in Little Rock, a clip of Clinton himself playing the saxophone, with bluegrass music in the background. Said the announcer:

''To pay for his increased spending in Arkansas, Bill Clinton raised state taxes. And not just on the rich. He increased the sales tax by thirty-three percent, imposed a mobile-home tax, increased the beer tax. He assessed a tourism tax, created a cable TV tax, supported a tax on groceries. And now, if elected president, Bill Clinton has promised to increase government spending 220 billion dollars. Guess where he'll get the money.''

Such ads were mild stuff compared to what the Bush campaign of 1988 had run against Dukakis. But two others, perhaps the most vivid and memorable commercials of the campaign, struck at Clinton in the same sinister way that marked the Bush ads of four years earlier.

The most controversial was a thirty-second spot that used a *Time* magazine cover from the heart of the primary season in April showing a photo-negative image of Clinton with the headline: "Why Voters Don't Trust Clinton." The ad seemed to imply that the magazine was currently raising the question. The voice-over announcer said: "He said he was never drafted. Then he said he forgot being drafted. He said he was never deferred from the draft. Then he said he was. He said he never received special treatment. But he did receive special treatment. The question then was avoiding the draft. Now, for Bill Clinton, it's a question of avoiding the truth."

The commercial backfired, however, when legal action by protesting *Time* officials persuaded the Bush campaign to take it off the air—thus reinforcing the constant needling from the Clinton campaign that the Bush campaign was playing old-fashioned "dirty-trick" politics. As a practical matter, the spot probably fell short in another way by, once again, stressing an issue voters already had taken into account. Those who were going to vote against Clinton on the draft didn't need to be reminded; those who were not were not likely to be persuaded at this point. Grunwald later called the ad "a colossal mistake . . . we found it made people angry . . . to keep harping on the draft issue."

The single most evocative commercial of the year was a thirty-second spot showing black-and-white images of storm clouds gathering, with thunder in the background, and dissolving to a barren landscape on which a single buzzard was perched on a leafless branch of a dead tree. The legend across the screen read: "America Can't Take That Risk."

Although the pictures seemed to suggest the aftermath of nuclear war, the message dealt with Clinton's record in Arkansas: "In his twelve years as governor Bill Clinton has doubled his state's debt, doubled government spending and signed the largest tax increase in his state's history. Yet his state remains the forty-fifth worst in which to work, the forty-fifth worst for children. It has the worst environmental policy, and the FBI says Arkansas has the biggest increase in the rate of serious crime. And now Bill Clinton wants to do for America what he has done for Arkansas. America can't take that risk."

The repeated attacks on Clinton's record as, to use one Bush phrase, "the failed governor of a small Southern state" was a throwback to the attacks on Michael Dukakis's service as governor of Massachusetts that were so successful for Bush in 1988. But the differences in the situation were too clear to have the same effect. Dukakis had never controlled the 1988 agenda so was kept on the defensive; Clinton had been on the offensive since July. More to the point, Bush was no longer a candidate with a clean slate; he was now a president with a record to defend.

The Clinton campaign had recognized from the outset, nonetheless, that many voters would feel they didn't know much about the challenger and that many others might have erroneous ideas about him. One, as noted earlier, was that Clinton had come from a privileged background because he had attended Georgetown University and Yale Law School. So, in addition to spots trying to put his Arkansas record in a more positive light, the Clinton campaign ran one early sixty-second commercial confronting the trust issue with excerpts from a biographical film used at the Democratic National Convention.

It included black-and-white still pictures from Clinton's youth, including his meeting with President Kennedy, mixed with color film of the candidate reminiscing about his life. "I was born in a little town called Hope, Arkansas, three months after my father died," Clinton said on the film. "I remember that old two-story house where I lived with my grandparents. They had very limited incomes. It was in 1963 that I went to Washington and met President Kennedy at the Boys Nation program. And I remember just, uh, thinking what an incredible country this was, that someone like me, you know, had no money or anything, would be given the opportunity to meet the president. That's when I decided that I really could do public service because I cared so much about people. I worked my way through law school with part-time jobs, anything I could find. After I graduated, I really didn't care about making a lot of money. I just wanted to go home and see if I could make a difference. We've worked in education and health care, to create jobs, and we've made real progress. Now it's exhilarating to me to think that as president, I can help change all our people's lives for the better and bring hope back to the American dream."

The Clinton campaign also was quick to respond—using the third track—to that most graphic ad showing the barren landscape. Less than twenty-four hours after it aired, the Clinton strategists countered with a thirty-second commercial in battleground states carrying such legends as "Bush ads are misleading and wrong" and "Arkansas leads the nation in job growth." The ad cited such sources as CBS and the Bureau of Labor Statistics and had an announcer say: "No wonder *The Washington Post* says George Bush is lying about Bill Clinton's record, and why *The Oregonian* concluded, 'Frankly, we no longer trust George Bush.' "

But if there was a critical moment in the air war, it had far less to do with what voters thought about Bill Clinton than what they thought about George Bush. Despite all the efforts of the Republican strategists to prevent the campaign from becoming a referendum on Bush, both sides discovered that it was just that.

Beginning with the first negative commercial against the president, the Clinton managers found that their single most effective way to undermine him was to show Bush himself on the screen. That spot and several others depicted Bush making a statement, then flashed on the screen a legend refuting his claims—thus reminding the electorate of his failures.

The spots were often tricky. In the first one, the president was shown saying, "The economy is strengthening," while the legend cited unemployment at a six-year high. Not mentioned was that Bush had made the statement in October of 1991, and the jobless rate peaked in March of 1992. In another, Bush was shown in 1988 saying, "We will be able to produce 30 million jobs in the next eight years," followed immediately by the voice of an announcer saying, "Under George Bush, more private sector jobs have been lost than have been created."

Bush was also shown saying, "And I am an environmentalist," to which the announcer retorted: "The Sierra Club says Bush allowed this administration to, quote, 'gut clean air rules.' " Then Bush: "I want a kinder and gentler—" and the announcer: "Uh, uh. We can't afford four more years."

Some of the claims in the Clinton and Bush negative ads were subject to dispute on the facts and the sometimes misleading juxtaposition of information. And both campaigns were aware that in 1992 every news organization of any seriousness had "ad police" on the job—reporters examining the factual claims in the spots and refuting them when they didn't hold up, thus offering ammunition to the opposition that a revival of Willie Horton was taking place.

Mandy Grunwald said the Clinton campaign tried to reinforce the credibility of spots by citing official or quasi-official sources—the Bureau of Labor Statistics, the census bureau or perhaps some newspaper or magazine. "Almost every major charge we used came through a third-party citation," she said. But the key was using Bush himself.

"With Bush we, as often as possible, had him use his own words and what we found in our research was . . . it was more credible [and] people thought it was more fair: 'It's true. He said it himself. It's his own words. I remember when he said that.' " In short, it was "more devastating" to be fair—or at least to appear to be fair.

In key battleground states like Ohio and New Jersey, the Clinton strategists found, Bush's approval ratings that began at 32 or 33 percent when the general election campaign opened could be driven down to 26 to 27 percent with heavy use of commercials in which he appeared speaking for himself.

"The ads kept it focused and kept his job performance [ratings] down," Grunwald said. Indeed, every time the president's approval rating would creep up to 29 or 30 percent, she recalled, "we would pump up the focus on Bush."

The Bush managers would not concede that using their candidate out front was a negative. But two opinion surveys made at midcampaign indicated that voters found Clinton commercials more believable and they blamed Bush more than Clinton for the negative aspects of the campaign.

As the campaign went on, it became clear from the design of the Bush commercials that the president's strategists were getting a similar message from their own research. That was why they were using commercials like the barren landscape with the buzzard in the tree, instead of showing Bush himself. And it was clearly the reason they began running spots showing not Bush but supposedly ordinary citizens talking about him or Clinton, taped in a shaky, amateurish fashion that was supposed to suggest sincerity or, at least, an absence of slickness.

One showed eight people sitting in booths eating breakfast at an International House of Pancakes restaurant in St. Louis. The "conversation" included these remarks: "I still have a lot of confidence in my president." . . . "I feel we need Bush to keep us from a big-spending Congress." . . . "I don't trust Clinton." . . . "The man says one thing and does another." . . . "First he denies it and then he says, well maybe it happened. You can't trust him." . . . "Clinton gets in, what we're going to see are more taxes." . . . "One thing that's got me definitely for Bush is I remember what happened the last time we did things the way Bill Clinton wants to do them."

A similar commercial shot at a union rally in New Jersey was clearly aimed at stopping the erosion from the Republican president on the part of blue-collar Democrats who had voted for Reagan and Bush in the past.

It had voters saying about Clinton: "I don't believe him. I don't believe him one bit." . . . "I don't know much about Clinton except promises." . . . "He tells everybody what they want to hear." . . . "Well, he wants to spend more money, and the only place he can get it is from the taxpayers." . . . "Higher taxes." . . . "Less food on the table." . . . "Broken promises." . . . "Less clothes on the kids' back." . . . "I don't know how we can take any more taxes." . . . "Less money to go to the doctor." . . . "He's raised taxes in Arkansas. He'll raise taxes here." . . . "Just less of everything."

The commercials sought in capsule form to make the case Bush had to make for a second term—that Clinton could not be trusted and that Bush was the safe choice. And because voters always feel there is some risk in voting for a challenger, the spots had some effect, at times raising Clinton's negatives a few points.

But as was the case with the entire Bush campaign, the spots were missing the point. The voters were looking for evidence that the president had a plan for dealing with the economic situation, and there was no such evidence in the commercials. On the contrary, they reinforced the suspicion that Bush was playing the old-fashioned negative politics-as-usual that the voters had shown repeatedly all year they would not accept.

(At the very end of the campaign, the Bush strategists tried one final negative ploy. They ran a heavy schedule of radio commercials that were tailored for specific states with claims that, for example, a Clinton administration would shut down off-shore drilling and take away hundreds of thousands of jobs in Louisiana, or that he would impose energy taxes that would raise utility bills "over $350" in Maine, Michigan and Maryland. The radio spots ran too late to get much press attention, but the Clinton campaign quickly responded with radio rebuttal ads of its own, with an announcer saying: "It's the same old story. George Bush will say anything to get elected. He said so himself. . . . So the next time you hear a George Bush ad, ask yourself, isn't it time for a President who will fight for American jobs?")

Through all this, Bill Clinton stayed "on message" about the economy. He knew the key to winning was pounding Bush relentlessly on the issue, and in that effort he was soon to have considerable help, from a familiar source.

C H A P T E R   2 6

HE'S BACK!

Almost from the moment old sailor Ross Perot threw himself over the side in a Dallas news conference on the final day of the Democratic National Convention, he had regretted the political drowning attempt. He had not gauged the depth of anger and sense of abandonment that the act would create among the millions of volunteers who had put themselves on the line for him and his "movement." And his departure without a special word of explanation or apology to them was particularly grating. Meyerson conveyed those sentiments to him as Perot contemplated in seclusion what he had done and how he had done it.

At 4:45 A.M. Hawaii time on July 16, the ringing of a telephone had broken the predawn hush in the home of a former Vietnam prisoner of war and Perot friend named Orson Swindle. Sleepy-eyed, Swindle roused himself and heard the voice of Darcy Anderson from the Perot headquarters in Dallas.

"I've got some bad news," Anderson told him. "Ross is pulling out."

"What?"

Swindle, appointed the Hawaii coordinator and manager for the campaign by Dallas only two weeks earlier, was dumbfounded. Anderson told him to turn on his television set because Perot would be going on live shortly. Swindle slipped into his clothes and drove at once to the Perot petition drive headquarters in downtown Honolulu. By this time, CNN was reporting that Perot was about to quit, and volunteers began streaming into the office—a scene being repeated in cities and towns across the mainland as word leaked out.

The mood was a mixture of bewilderment and disbelief. "These were just average people," Swindle said later, recalling the scene. "They had no particular sophistication about politics. That's the last thing they had. They came from diverse backgrounds. Some were out of work, some were housewives, some were hardworking people fortunate enough to have a job. We sat around and started talking, and they said, 'Orson, you know him. You've got to go back and talk him into staying in this damn thing.' So everybody just immediately committed to [the idea that] we're going to get him back into the race. We started laughing, and the mood shifted from one of sadness to one of challenge."

Swindle and Bob Hayden, the campaign's self-starting state coordinator in California, were of the same mind. They talked and Hayden initiated a "fax network" to other state coordinators urging them to meet in Dallas that weekend at their own expense to take stock and "talk to Ross." Perot was alerted and he passed the word for them to come ahead. It was, after all, their movement and their country, and they were "the owners."

On Friday night, one day after his pullout, Perot appeared again on *Larry King Live*, from New York, and in the course of the interview talked about mobilizing his shocked troops into an army of patriots to keep the heat on Bush, Clinton and congressional candidates. At one point he described his own chance of election as a "very, very, very long shot," but that thinnest of reeds was seized by some Perot stalwarts to hope that he could be made to change his mind about an active candidacy. "I have not gone away," he said. "I will stay with them right through the end. I will help and support them any way I can, and play any role they want me to."

On Saturday, July 18, about forty people gathered at the campaign headquarters in north Dallas to press their case on Perot. Swindle was not among them, his plane to the mainland having been repeatedly delayed. In advance, they had met and worked out with Hayden the questions they wanted to ask Perot and who would ask them. Then they were taken by bus to the headquarters, presumably to keep the press at bay. Reporters were barred as the man himself walked into the old campaign press room, his old jauntiness having never left him.

According to Cliff Arnebeck of Columbus, Ohio, one of those present, Hayden had prepared a statement on behalf of the others to read to Perot, but Perot brushed it aside and launched into a monologue of his own. "I know you wouldn't be here if you didn't want me to be your candidate," Arnebeck remembered Perot saying. But there might be a better way, he went on, to accomplish the goals that the movement had set to reform the politics of the country. That was to put out a platform for change and maintain an organization behind it, which he would support financially.

Then, as Arnebeck remembered, Perot told the volunteers that "if neither party steps up to the plate and addresses our issues, we can get back into this," adding, "If anybody thinks I've quit, they may be in for an October surprise. The ads are in the can." He had referred to them the night before on the Larry King show, calling them "killas from Manila."

In the course of his remarks, Perot spotted someone operating a video camera, and he ordered it turned off. His paranoia about the press had not been diminished by his withdrawal, although reporters had been kept outside.

Perot, according to Arnebeck, went on to discuss conversations he had had with Mikhail Gorbachev and Boris Yeltsin about helping their country's terrible economic state, in return for information about American POWs and MIAs. Then the state coordinators were invited to ask Perot questions. One by one, Arnebeck said, "they were all saying there was one thing he could do to keep the movement alive, and that was to come back into the race."

Perot heard them out but gave them no reply. Afterward, Arnebeck remembered, some Perot staff people—the whiteshirts—circulated among the volunteer leaders telling them that Perot had not been happy about the meeting, and that the visitors had not been forceful enough in pressing him to become a candidate again.

The next morning, on Sunday, the state coordinators met again, this time at the Sheraton Park Central hotel not far from the campaign headquarters, and again Perot staffers, according to Arnebeck, were telling them that they hadn't leaned on Perot hard enough to get back in. It so happened that attending another meeting at a nearby hotel was John Anderson, the 1980 independent presidential candidate. A delegation including Arnebeck was sent to talk to him about the wisdom of forming a third party.

When Anderson was told of the previous day's discussions and Perot's allusions about returning to the fray, he expressed the opinion, Arnebeck recalled, that Perot was just having second thoughts and regrets about his precipitous retreat. He had created a major credibility gap for himself, Anderson said, and if he entertained any thoughts about coming back he ought to do so at once. He could justify his action by saying the volunteers would not buy his plan of reform without him at the head of it, and therefore he was obliged to bow to their wishes and stay in the race. The longer he waited, Arnebeck recalled Anderson saying, the wider his credibility gap.

Arnebeck and the others returned to the Sheraton Park Central where the second day's meeting was under way and conveyed to others the advice Anderson had given. Together with the urgings from the whiteshirts, the idea of pressing Perot to come back into the race had a rebirth. Among those in the forefront in addition to Arnebeck were the Texas coordinator, Jim Surer, and Donna Gilbert of Alaska.

Swindle had arrived by now and he walked into the meeting "not knowing a single person in the room," he said. "I looked around and I was exposed to my first example of some rather bizarre people who had tagged along to this movement. I sat there in utter amazement, picking out the personalities—that one's got a political agenda of his own, this is a real freako that wants to find a big train he can jump on to ride. Everybody there was emotional. There was movement on the part of several of these people—'We're just going to draft Perot.'

"When they started talking about how they were going to force Perot, I got up and said, 'Hey, guys, I'm Orson Swindle. I don't know any of you and I certainly respect your enthusiasm for what you want Mr. Perot to do. But I do know him and have known him for some time, and the one thing you are not going to do is force him to do anything. The man will go in the other direction.' ''

Swindle in effect took over the meeting for what he later called ''a grieving session'' about Perot's withdrawal and what to do next, and he was not happy about the efforts of Arnebeck, Gilbert and the others to lean on Perot. But they persevered anyway, urging the group to agree to a statement calling on him to stay in the race, ''not to force him to do something he didn't want to do,'' Arnebeck said later, but in line with Anderson's counsel ''to give him a credible basis on which to reenter the campaign after saying he had dropped out.''

Swindle was presiding when Arnebeck suddenly got up, went to a blackboard behind him, Swindle said, and started writing something to the effect of ''We hereby reaffirm our support of Ross Perot for president of the United States.'' Swindle tried to intervene. ''I said, 'What in the hell are you doing?' He said, 'We're gonna draft Perot.' I said, 'Go sit down, please. We've got a lot of things to talk about.' ''

One by one, however, the state coordinators walked up and signed their names to the draft resolution on the blackboard. That afternoon, the blackboard was moved to another location, where Donna Gilbert asked for a vote on it. Swindle, informed that Perot was on his way over, balked but ''they finally pressed on with this so-called draft statement,'' he recalled. ''Everybody was on it but me.'' When Perot walked in and saw the blackboard, Swindle said, ''he just bristled.'' Hayden, according to Arnebeck, said to Perot: ''Ross, this isn't a setup. I didn't know about it.''

Perot sat in a chair and invited the others to sit around him in a semicircle so they could talk. Some pulled up chairs and others sat on the floor. They started to give vent to their feelings of disappointment. A woman from Colorado, Arnebeck said, told Perot she had sacrificed a great deal to join him and he had let her down. Another coordinator read a letter from a Vietnam veteran, Arnebeck recalled, that said: ''I didn't want to go to Vietnam but I had to. I was drafted. Now you're being drafted.'' Perot, according to Swindle, replied, ''You just don't understand.'' In addition to the reasons he had given publicly for withdrawing, he said, ''I have some personal reasons.''

When somebody asked him whether he had failed to anticipate the flak he was going to get from the press, Arnebeck said, Perot said that as far as he was concerned, it was nothing compared to what prisoners of war had to go through, but he didn't realize what an ordeal it would be for his family. "If this goes out of the room, I'm out," he quickly added, implying that if his enemies knew they could reach him through his loved ones they would subject his family to even more abuse. But he was no more specific than that.

Some of the coordinators told Perot what Anderson had said about the need for him to move quickly, to close his new credibility gap, if he were to get back in the race. He seemed to some to be wavering. At one point he observed that if the other candidates didn't shape up to their satisfaction "I suppose we could be the 800-pound gorilla and come back in." At another point he suggested that the coordinators go back to their states and find out how their volunteers felt, but they told him it wasn't necessary—they all wanted him back in the race. (They meant, to be sure, those who hadn't already left the Perot movement in scorn at his betrayal.)

"I think I should talk to my family," Perot told the coordinators. He went out of the room with some of the whiteshirts. Some of the coordinators began to feel they were pressing him too hard and if crowded too much he would indeed balk. So they sent a representative in to tell him they weren't demanding an immediate answer. But shortly afterward, as Swindle recalls it, Perot came out and told the coordinators: "My decision is, if you want to know right away, I'm not going to do it." He told them to go home, think about it, and come back in a couple of weeks, when they would then talk about the future of the movement.

At the end of July, the coordinators gathered in Dallas again, but this time without the "troublemakers" who had tried to force a draft on Perot, who were not invited. By this time, Arnebeck and others in the draft effort had concluded that Perot had not wanted to be drafted then for the simple reason that he had already decided on a grand strategy: he would lie low for the next two months and, as he had said at the first meeting, come back and spring an "October surprise." If he had returned as an active candidate right then, obviously, he would have opened himself to a resumption of the investigations of his business practices, his penchant for investigating others, and all the rest of what was summed up under the label Inspector Perot.

Much earlier, Perot had argued to his political advisers that the smartest—and most frugal—thing for him to do was to stretch out the petition drives until September. "Perot used to say," Hamilton Jordan recalled, " 'y'all always want to spend my money. We need to keep our powder dry.' " With the Democratic and Republican nominees not shifting into high gear until after Labor Day, he thought, he could easily wait until then himself. Perot's campaign counsel and son-in-law, Clay Mulford, also said Perot often talked of waiting until September, before going all out.

Jordan produced charts that showed that it was a myth that voters waited until after the World Series to make up their minds on how they would vote. In fact, Jordan told Perot, 90 percent had pretty much decided by Labor Day. Therefore, he argued, mindful of Perot's constant interest in getting the most for his buck, resources spent early would be directed at a much larger universe of undecided voters than money spent late in the campaign. But Perot clung to the idea that he could hold off—an idea that dovetailed with the scenario of withdrawing in July to avoid the intense press scrutiny and getting back in late in the game, when he could bring his immense wealth to bear in television advertising.

Those who came to the late July meeting, however, did not harbor thoughts that Perot was anything but sincere in his statements that he did not intend to get back into the race unless the failure of the two major parties to straighten up forced his hand. Without the folks who wanted to draft Perot, Swindle said, "it was a far more calm meeting. The emotion was there, but it was far more controlled emotion. Some people had fallen by the wayside. We obviously saw in that first meeting that some of those people did not have his best interests at heart, did not have the movement's best interests at heart. So some changes were made. We relied greatly on Perot's field staff [the whiteshirts] to select who would come down there."

Having weeded out Rollins, Jordan and the other professionals, the purge of undesirable elements among the volunteer forces was now under way, leading to numerous stories of heavy-handed incursions by the whiteshirts at the grass-roots level and reinforcing the image of Perot as a control freak. Swindle later chalked up most of the complaints to local leadership squabbles among factions, but there was no doubt that Dallas had made its authority felt.

"The charlatans came out of the woodwork for this thing," Swindle said. "All the fringe elements, people who wanted to make a fast buck on T-shirts, it was just everywhere." There were also problems of meeting Federal Election Commission requirements, and all of this taken together "got to Perot," Swindle said, because "Perot is a man who likes to be in control." And the trouble with grass-roots politics, Swindle said, was it resisted control. "The minute you'd try to invoke any control, they'd say, 'This is grass roots, we don't want any top-down.' Then they'd say, 'By the way, will you send us some money?' "

In any event, the second phase of the Perot operation was not going to tolerate such goings-on. "We came back decidedly more orderly, more focused," Swindle said. "The group consensus was we definitely wanted to get Ross back in, but we knew we had to get him on the ballot in all fifty states so we decided we would form an organization." Thus was born United We Stand America.

On August 6, Swindle sent out a memo to the state Perot offices justifying the choice of people invited to the latest Dallas meeting: "They were essentially those with whom the field coordinators and Ross Perot were most knowledgeable and with whose leadership and organizational skills they were most comfortable." Swindle concluded: "Please, folks, let's cut out the internal positioning and get on with the really important issues at hand—insuring the election of Ross Perot as the next president. ACCEPT THE APPOINTED LEADERSHIP! We have work to do."

Decisions were made to reduce the operations in California and other states that had already placed Perot on the ballot—about twenty-five at this stage, and Perot agreed to continue to fund the petition drives in the other states. That willingness fed the theory that Perot was intending all along to get back into the campaign later. "It was open," Swindle conceded. "Why else would we want to put him on the ballot if it wasn't open?" It was Swindle's notion, in wanting to see Perot back in eventually, that if he could be qualified for ballot position in all fifty states, it would then be hard for him to refuse to run, especially when his own credibility was at stake.

The one place where a major financial burden was involved in achieving ballot position was New York state. Perot committed to bankroll that effort and also to give each of the fifty states a minimum of $7,500 a month for operating expenses, with more for the larger states. The rationale, Swindle said, was to keep the volunteers together until United We

Stand America could be put on its feet after the election. But outside the Perot operation, the suspicion remained among some that he was holding his troops in readiness for that threatened "October surprise." Swindle discounted that as too farfetched. "If it was a scheme," he said later, "my God, surely we could have come up with something better than this. We never recovered from the July 16 withdrawal."

So the petition drives continued, with Perot pumping about $6 million into his movement in July, bringing his total to $12 million with more to come. Meanwhile, he stayed in the news with the publication of his long-awaited plan to deal with the federal deficit, a bit of bad-tasting medicine that called for cutting spending by about $416 billion and increasing taxes by $302 billion, including a high-profile boost in gasoline taxes reaching fifty cents a gallon in five years. He brought out his overall plan in a paperback book called *United We Stand: How We Can Take Back Our Country* that with the help of self-purchases hit the best-seller lists and climbed rapidly.

At the Republican National Convention in Houston in mid-August, departed campaign manager Ed Rollins predicted that Perot would be back in the race before November, a notion fed by a Perot response on NBC's *Today* show when asked whether he'd consider doing so if either of the two parties failed to come up with a satisfactory agenda. "I wouldn't have a choice," he said, if that's what his volunteers said they wanted—which after all was what they had said explicitly to him only a month earlier in Dallas. "I do belong to them," he said, "and it would be their decision, whatever they feel is appropriate."

By this time, Perot had been qualified for ballot position in thirty-six states, with another six on the verge, with petitions filed but not yet verified. Swindle's notion of forcing Perot's hand by reaching the fifty-state goal seemed well within reach now.

Perot himself, however, continued to play guessing games. On September 11 he paid an undetected call on White House chief of staff and de facto Bush-Quayle campaign chief Jim Baker at his home, for an undisclosed reason. In a C-SPAN program the next day, asked again about running, he said: "If the volunteers said, 'It's a dirty job but you've got to do it,' I belong to them. . . . Let's try to get the two parties to step up to the plate. If they don't we'll do what we have to do." But then he added: "But there's no plan for an October surprise or a September surprise. There is nothing planned."

By September 15, Perot was on the ballot in forty-seven states and the District of Columbia, and a *Washington Post*/ABC News poll found that 16 percent of likely voters were saying they intended to cast their ballots for him whether he was running or not. On September 18, Perot said on the *Today* show that he might be "trapped" into running because he wanted to buy television time to talk about his economic plan but the networks "won't sell it to me unless I declare as a candidate. So I may be the first guy in history that had to declare he was a candidate so he could buy TV time." Jim Squires later vouched for the accuracy of this rationale for Perot getting back in.

On September 19, the target of fifty states was reached with qualification in Arizona, which was overseen by Swindle himself. From Phoenix, he flew to Dallas and applied the heat on Perot directly. By this time, Swindle said, Perot "was now thinking, 'We're gonna do this thing.' I said, 'Ross, you've got to do it now. You don't have a choice. They're not doing what you said they had to do. They're not changing. . . . Bush cannot win this election. It looks like Clinton is going to win it and damn it, let's go beat Clinton. You've got to keep your word now.' We started talking about how to do it."

Swindle wasn't the only one over the summer who had been nagging Perot about getting back in the race. John Jay Hooker from Nashville, who in a sense assisted at the birth of the Perot presidential adventure from near the very start, had continued his telephone courtship of the Texan. In frequent conversations, Hooker appealed to Perot's sense of personal pride and integrity, telling him repeatedly that his reputation—his place in history—would always be tarnished if he didn't make up for the July withdrawal that had shattered his credibility. In his melodramatic but persuasive fashion, Hooker told Perot he owed it to his country, to his family, even to his mother in heaven to put things right by getting back into the race.

On September 22, Perot threw out another tantalizer. He said on CBS's *This Morning* show that he had "made a mistake" in dropping out and giving the two parties a chance to address the important issues on their own. On the way out of the studio, he ran into Democratic

National Chairman Ron Brown, who was just going in for an appearance. Perot at Brown's request waited until Brown was off the air and the two went into a makeup room to talk.

"Neither you nor I want to see George Bush reelected," Brown told him. "We should spend all our waking hours to see that that doesn't happen." Perot replied, according to Brown: "You don't understand. I have to talk to my volunteers."

BROWN: Come on.

PEROT: No, you don't understand. My volunteers decide.

Brown tried to persuade Perot that Clinton shared a lot of his positions on the issues and said he'd like to talk to him further about it. Whereupon Perot invited him, and other Clinton campaign leaders, or even Clinton himself, to go down to Dallas to talk to the volunteer leaders themselves.

The two parted, and when Brown got down to the lobby he spied Perot on a pay phone. He learned that Perot was calling Baker to extend the same invitation to the Bush campaign. Perot got on a plane and flew to Washington to meet Baker that afternoon, and that was how it came to pass that the Clinton and Bush campaigns found themselves, in effect, paying homage to Perot in the vain hope of keeping him out of springing an October surprise after all.

Squires said later that all this time Perot really was pressing to get Clinton to accept three principles regarding the budget deficit that would have persuaded him not to get back into the race: acknowledging publicly that the price to voters would be painful, that new revenues would have to be raised and that entitlement programs would have to be cut. Talks were held with Clinton campaign chairman Kantor, Squires said, to no avail.

On September 28, high-level teams from the Bush and Clinton campaigns dutifully trooped to Dallas to genuflect before the Texas billionaire and assembled state coordinators and make pitches designed, with little hope by now, to deter him from reentering the race. The Bush team included campaign chairman Teeter, White House National Security Adviser Brent Scowcroft, Secretary of Housing Jack Kemp and Senators Phil Gramm of Texas and Pete Domenici of New Mexico, ranking Republican on the Senate Budget Committee. Included at a separate session for the Clinton team were campaign chairman Mickey Kantor, former

Chairman of the Joint Chiefs of Staff Admiral William Crowe, Senator David L. Boren of Oklahoma, New York economist Felix Rohatyn and Washington lawyer Vernon Jordan.

The meetings, in which each team tried to make the case that its candidate was closer than the opposition's to Perot on key issues, convinced no one of anything beyond the willingness of both major party campaigns to kowtow to Perot to avoid any appearance of snubbing him or his supporters. Neither the Bush nor the Clinton campaign felt it could chance telling Perot to go to hell, although that distinctly would have been the preference in both camps. Kemp, in fact, appeared miffed at the indignity of it all and walked off early. It was abundantly clear now that Perot was going to reenter the race.

Even before he did, however, negative stories were resuming. CBS News reported and the Perot petition committee confirmed that it had hired a San Francisco law firm specializing in investigations to check into the backgrounds of certain Perot state coordinators and volunteers who did or might handle money for the campaign. Among those checked out was Arnebeck, the ''troublemaker'' who had been so aggressive in trying to draft Perot right after his July withdrawal.

Perot disclosed that he was having the Perot volunteers polled on whether he should run again, and Swindle subsequently reported that of 150,000 of them contacted, 93 percent wanted him to run. Also, Perot installed an 800 telephone number for the same purpose, but individuals who called got a recording thanking them for registering their desire for him to become a candidate again—whether they wanted him to or not.

By October 1, when Perot announced his reentry, it was hardly an October surprise. In another Dallas news conference, he confessed again that he had ''made a mistake'' and regretted having hurt his supporters back in July, but said he was now ready ''to give it everything I have'' in an unconventional one-month sprint for the presidency. Perot insisted that he would not ''spend one minute answering questions that are not directly relevant to the issues that concern the people'' and walked out, only to come back as reporters demanded that he field their inquiries.

The scene turned raucous, as he complained of news media bias against him. ''Everything here is the usual, hostile negative yelling and screaming,'' he complained before finally walking out—and into the 1992 campaign again.

At this point, he was registering only 14 percent support in the latest *Washington Post*/ABC News poll, compared to 38 percent in early June. A *USA Today*/CNN survey was even more discouraging: Clinton 52 percent, Bush 35, Perot 7.

Perot said his running mate would continue to be Admiral Stockdale, it being too late and politically unlikely that at this juncture he could get anyone of greater public recognition or stature. As for the strategy in the month ahead, Swindle summed it up. "We're going to let Perot be Perot," he said.

By now, it was clear that Perot would not permit it to be otherwise. He revved up another round of television talk show appearances and paid $380,000 for thirty minutes of prime time on the CBS television network to discuss personally, with the use of color charts and a metal pointer, the major problems facing the American economy and how they came to be. He promised solutions in subsequent telecasts.

The presentation was straightforward without frills—the kind of thing the professionals would have scoffed at—and it drew a remarkable audience of 16.5 million viewers, more than watched most regularly scheduled entertainment shows or the National League baseball playoff game.

Maybe Ross Perot knew what he was doing after all with his unconventional methods. He could no longer, however, avoid the conventional. Even before he had reentered the race, Bush and Clinton in agreeing to a series of three presidential debates and one vice presidential debate starting on October 11 had invited him to participate if he became a candidate. Obviously they didn't want his intrusion, but their strategists realized there was no choice, with all those potential millions of Perot voters up for grabs again. And so the stage was set for the debates: George Bush, Bill Clinton and the self-styled 800-pound gorilla.

CHAPTER 27

SQUARING OFF

In an age in which it often seemed the only important things took place before the television cameras, the debate over debates had become one of the familiar rituals of American presidential campaigns. And, like most rituals, this one had become almost totally predictable. The candidate who held the whip hand—that is, the one leading at the time— controlled the terms of the debates.

When the Commission on Presidential Debates was established in 1987, largely on financing from foundations and a few individuals, the hope was that the debates would become institutionalized and routine. That was because so many voters—perhaps too many—had come to depend on them as a prime source of information in deciding which candidate to support. The commission was totally bipartisan; its chairmen were Frank J. Fahrenkopf, a former chairman of the Republican National Committee, and Paul G. Kirk, a former chairman of the Democratic National Committee. So presumably neither campaign had anything to fear from operating under its auspices. Moreover, the political professionals in both parties were delighted with the thought that the commission would free them of the necessity of dealing with the League of Women Voters, whose sponsorship of some debates in earlier years had been contentious, and with whose officials the parties often had little common purpose or cultural affinity.

But in both the 1988 and 1992 campaigns, the George Bush managers were no happier with the commission than with the organization the pols called "the lady voters." James Baker, running the 1988 Bush campaign, insisted the debates could only be negotiated directly with the Michael Dukakis campaign—and confirmed the wisdom of his position by successfully insisting on just two debates, each with a panel of reporters to get in the way of anything that might resemble a genuine exchange between the candidates. There was also that single vice presidential debate between Republican Dan Quayle and Democrat Lloyd Bentsen, friend of Jack Kennedy.

Baker was a firm believer in the idea that the debates, if they were to be held at all, were the "property" of the candidates and of such political significance that the conditions under which they would take place had to be in the hands of the campaign managers, who would be guided by their candidates' best interests. Also, Baker did not want the debates to become "institutionalized"—that is, have them reach the stature that a candidate would be obliged to participate, and under rigid conditions not agreed to by him, when it might not be to his political advantage to do so.

Four years later, the Bush campaign now once again rejected the commission plan, which Clinton had accepted as soon as it was advanced during the summer. It called for three presidential debates and one vice presidential debate, each with a single moderator rather than a panel of reporters. The Democratic debates during the primary season had demonstrated, if further proof were needed, that a single-moderator format produced far more coherent expositions of the differences among candidates than an examining board of posturing reporters.

Under the commission plan, the presidential debates were to be held on September 22 in East Lansing, Michigan, October 4 in San Diego and October 15 in Richmond. The vice presidential debate would be held September 29 in Louisville. Each would last ninety minutes. But on

September 3, with time running out for making the debate arrangements in East Lansing, Bob Teeter told reporters: "I would expect that there would be debates, but we will not accept the commission's proposal as it's outlined now." Campaign officials passed the word that Jim Baker— pulling the strings from behind the curtain—wanted only two presidential debates, each with the panel-of-reporters format. It was good enough last time, the Bush campaign argued, so they were just following that precedent.

"We thought we might could do a little better," Charlie Black said later. With Bush running behind there was the chance the campaign might want "to roll the dice" with more debates or late debates.

But this time the situation was quite different from what it had been in 1988. If one candidate was holding the high cards, it was Bill Clinton, still leading by ten to fifteen percentage points after all the dust from the conventions had settled, and far enough ahead in so many big states— California, New York, Illinois and Pennsylvania—to be in a commanding position. Even with that dominant position, however, Clinton needed the debates to "close the sale" with voters who experienced some feeling of risk in choosing a challenger over an incumbent president.

Mickey Kantor, Clinton's campaign chairman, put it this way: "We were not going to debate under any circumstances, but we wanted debates. We thought debates were important. In a sense, we had a Ronald Reagan 1980 problem; the final sale had to be made that Bill Clinton was credible, so we wanted debates. We knew from the very first that we needed them."

The Bush strategists also understood they needed the debates. They had reached the point that it was essential to change the dynamics of the campaign. "You got to the position," Teeter said later, "where it was clear we weren't moving. From the beginning of the fall until we got to the debates, we didn't move at all." The imperative for the Bush campaign, he said, was "to get people to focus on the choice between Bush and Clinton, not just a referendum on the last three years."

The strategists in each camp also were fully aware of the thinking in the other. "Both sides knew there were going to be debates," Teeter said. "They clearly were in a position where they made enough public statements and were in bed enough with the commission, and I think their natural ideology is they wanted to be pro-debate." Similarly, Kantor said he thought the Republicans "had a sort of theological position" against the commission running the debates but were certain to agree anyway. "They had to have debates, almost regardless," he said.

There were, nonetheless, strategic and tactical considerations for both campaigns. One issue was format. The Bush managers wanted that panel of reporters because it reduced the risk of the kind of freewheeling confrontation in which the president was not at his best. The Clinton managers were equally convinced the less-structured format of a single moderator would allow him to show himself to best advantage.

Bush himself tried to put the most positive face on his resistance to the single moderator. When Bernard Shaw, a CNN anchor who had been one of the panelists in a 1988 debate, asked the president if he would agree to the change, Bush replied: "I don't like that format particularly. I thought when you and others asked tough questions at the 1988 debates, it livened things up. So I don't know. I'm not inclined to say I think that's a brilliant idea. I saw nothing wrong with the former format." Among other things, Bush obviously remembered Bernie Shaw's killer question to Dukakis in 1988 about how he would respond if someone killed his wife, Kitty.

Another question, a more significant one, was the timing of the debates. The Bush camp wanted one as late as possible in the campaign, when voters were paying the closest attention and might be more prepared to see the election more as a choice than the straight referendum on Bush that Teeter feared. The Clinton campaign was adamant that it would agree to no debate later than October 19, two weeks before the election. The key factor here, Kantor said, was the fear that the Bush campaign would inject some late attack to which Clinton, as the lesser-known quantity in the equation, could not react adequately in the last few days before voters made their final decisions.

"We were sure they would," he said later. Even as the debate particulars were being negotiated, he said, "they're out there in Suitland [Maryland] going through boxes." The reference was to the search by Bush administration officials of Bill Clinton's passport files at the National Archives' National Record Center outside Washington, looking for politically damaging information.

But whatever the competing strategies and reasons for Bush to stall, the Bush campaign appeared to underestimate a different element in the political context of 1992. Voters were demanding that the candidates make themselves and their intentions crystal-clear. This was not a year in which the political professionals were going to be able to get away with cute games that denied the electorate full access to the process. On the contrary, the debate-over-debates ritual was entirely too characteristic of politics as usual.

Nonetheless, a letter over Teeter's name finally went to Kantor on September 14 formally rejecting the plan advanced by the commission and adding: "President Bush would welcome an opportunity to debate with Governor Clinton under the same terms and conditions that were agreed upon for the 1988 presidential debates."

Kantor would have none of it. "We plan to sit down with the commission," he said. "We welcome their participation. We've had the same position for ninety-five days"—when the commission first issued its invitation.

Clinton and his strategists clearly understood they held the political high ground. With the whole question of the debates hanging in abeyance, the Democratic nominee pressed his advantage, deriding Bush on the stump for his refusal to participate. Speaking to students at the University of New Mexico in Albuquerque, Clinton said: "I've listened to all their macho talk, but when it comes time to go man to man, plan to plan, where is he? One of the greatest boxers that ever lived, Joe Louis, said, 'You can run but you can't hide.' It's not from me that George Bush is hiding. He's hiding from an honest discussion with follow-ups on a record he wants to hide from, a record that has given this country its worst economic performance in fifty years, the first decline in industrial produc- tion in our history, a decline of $1,600 a year in the average family income, 2 million more people in poverty since he's been president."

Bush tried to fight back. Appearing on a radio talk show in New York with Rush Limbaugh, the president protested that he was not "a professional Oxford debater"—unlike Clinton, who was a Rhodes Scholar at Oxford—but was quite prepared to debate. "If people . . . don't think we've got an economic program, I've got a chance for them to compare it eyeball to eyeball with Governor Clinton. If people think that service to country is important, we can talk about that one. If people think that world peace doesn't matter anymore, I'd like to talk about that one with him standing there."

On the other hand, Bush went on, "I'm not going to let this new man dictate the terms" and change a format that had been used regularly since 1976. "Why would I change as the president?" Bush asked. "I'm not going to do it."

But Bush was holding a weak hand. Opinion surveys began showing that voters—63 percent of them in a poll conducted for *The New York Times*—knew it was Bush ducking the debates.

As noted earlier, Clinton turned up in East Lansing on September 22, the day the debate would have been held under the schedule proposed by the commission and rejected by Bush. "I showed up here to debate today," he told several thousand students from Michigan State University, standing before a sign that read BILL CLINTON. THERE'S NO DEBATE ABOUT IT. Bush was not "ducking this debate" because he was a weak debater, Clinton added, but because he couldn't defend his record.

It was an obvious ploy, a version of the empty-chair routine candidates at lower levels of politics had used for years to dramatize their own willingness to debate and their opponents' refusal to do so. Ordinarily, such political stunts don't have any measurable political impact, but this time the situation was quite different. For one thing, there were those hecklers dressed in chicken costumes or holding signs calling him "Chicken George"—a gimmick with irresistible appeal for the television cameras.

The first chicken was a young volunteer who appeared on his own at East Lansing. But the Clinton campaign had a "special projects" or "counterevents" unit working out of an office in the Washington suburb of Arlington, Virginia, that encouraged more chickens to appear at Bush events over the next several days. In Michigan, a critical state for Bush, the damage was particularly telling. "We took a beating up there for a week," Black said, "and even after that there was hangover, all the restaurants with 'Chicken George' on the menu and all." *The Lansing State Journal* gave over its full editorial page the next day to a scathing criticism of Bush as a no-show, accompanied by a large photograph of the empty hall where the debate would have taken place. Editorial comment throughout the state was comparable.

But the Bush strategists were unyielding. When the commission tried to find a way out of the impasse by offering to meet with the two campaigns to discuss a new debate schedule, Kantor quickly accepted but

Teeter continued to insist that the negotiations should be conducted only between the two campaigns, with no intermediaries.

Meanwhile, the pressure continued to build on the president. Although Teeter said there was never any evidence they lost any votes in the end because of the debate strategy, "Bush was beginning to take a hit. We were not losing any votes because of it, [but] our problem was we weren't gaining any votes and we were behind and we needed more people to begin to take a look at it. . . . Hell, we were down to our base at that point."

The Clinton managers were convinced Bush was being hurt by the delay. "The American people wanted engagement," Kantor said later. "They wanted connection to the process, they wanted people to speak directly to them. That's why it hurt. I was surprised it hurt them as much as it did and I think they were surprised it hurt them as much as it did."

The president was also obviously being thrown off his stride by the "Chicken Georges" who showed up in increasing numbers everywhere he went, just as a year earlier he had been spooked by the Democratic National Committee T-shirts poking fun at his foreign travel schedule. Standing on the rear platform of a whistlestop campaign train through the Midwest, Bush spotted one protester in costume holding up a sign that read: CHICKEN GEORGE WON'T DEBATE.

"You talking about the draft-record chicken or are you talking about the chicken in the Arkansas River?" he asked the "Chicken," who remained silent. Bush apparently was referring to reports of extreme pollution in the river resulting from Arkansas's major chicken-processing industry. "Which ones are you talking about? Which one? Get out of here. Maybe it's the draft? Is that what's bothering you?" It was not the kind of serious discussion of the nation's economic problems that the voters of 1992 were seeking.

The Clinton campaign was delighted by Bush's dialogue with the chicken. "He legitimized the chicken," Iris Jacobson Burnett, who worked in the special projects office, said later. "Then everybody wanted to be a chicken."

Bush, far from seeing the political damage the chicken hecklers were inflicting on him, relished the exchanges with them. At campaign stops, Mary Matalin said, "he would ask, 'Where's the chicken?' He would yell at the chicken. He loved it. 'Where's that chicken chicken?' And

30,000 people loved it. I'm supposed to be saying to him, 'Quit talking to the chicken,' and I'm saying, 'That was hilarious!' '' When she and others tried to convince the president that not debating was hurting him, he would reply: "You have no data. Get data." So Matalin got it from campaign pollster Fred Steeper and Bush started to listen.

Clinton, meanwhile, continued to pound him on debating. In Louisville, Kentucky, on the day the second debate was to be held there but also had been canceled, Clinton told a midday rally: "Here in Louisville it occurs to me that you can't be a Louisville slugger if you don't stand up to the plate." Around the same time, however, after more than a week of being besieged by chickens, the Bush campaign finally reacted.

Speaking to a rally at Austin Peay State College in Clarksville, Tennessee, where costumed chickens waved signs saying READ MY BEAK: DON'T BE CHICKEN. DEBATE, Bush departed from his text and challenged Clinton to four televised debates on the four Sundays remaining before election day, two with the single-moderator format Clinton preferred and two with a panel of reporters. Bush also called for two vice presidential debates and said Ross Perot, now threatening to reenter the campaign, would be welcome to participate if he reactivated his candidacy.

"Let's get it on," George Bush, hipster, shouted to the Austin Peay students.

The Bush initiative—or, more accurately, strategic retreat—broke the impasse, and the following night negotiators for the two campaigns met in the Washington office of Kantor's law firm to begin ironing out the particulars. The Clinton team included, in addition to Kantor, Democratic National Chairman Ron Brown, television producer and Clinton friend Harry Thomason, Washington lawyer Tom Donilon and Clinton staff aide Bev Lindsey. The Bush negotiators included Teeter, Fred Malek, Dick Darman, campaign counsel Bobby Burchfield, and Robert Goodwin, a veteran of debate negotiations and arrangements in several previous campaigns.

What was most intriguing was the absence of Jim Baker, who had built a reputation of epic proportions for his hard-edged skill in debate negotiations. Stories about him bluffing and bamboozling the Dukakis negotiators four years earlier had become part of political legend. But Baker was a man who understood when he was holding a small pair, and he had a long history of distancing himself from unsuccessful political enterprises. He was, the smart guys in Washington said, "always sick that day" when something went wrong.

Baker was also still stiffly resisting being characterized as a political apparatchik; it was enough of a comedown to leave the portfolio as secretary of state to be White House chief of staff once again. So he maintained the fiction that Teeter was running the campaign. That September 14 letter from Teeter to Kantor, for example, had been drafted in Baker's office by Goodwin for Baker's signature. But when Baker read it, he told Goodwin: "This looks fine, but put Teeter's name in place of mine. I'm not the campaign manager this time." It was done—unknown to Teeter at the time, Goodwin said.

But in the negotiations that opened the night of September 30 and resumed the following day, it soon became apparent that Baker was very much a presence if physically absent. Frequently, the Bush team asked for a recess and left the room to caucus and make telephone calls. "It was clear every time," Kantor said, "that they had to go out and call Baker . . . or call somebody." At one point he needled Teeter, saying: "Do you have authority to make decisions? Because I do."

Goodwin later said that in internal Bush campaign meetings on debate negotiations, Baker was "tolerant" of Teeter's plans, listening to them but then turning them around and redirecting them. Darman was also a kibitzer, sometimes questioning why Bush should debate at all. On those occasions, Teeter would remind him of the reality of the polls showing the president well behind. Baker at one meeting observed, Goodwin said, that "our numbers are at rock-bottom. We can't continue to throw buttonhooks"—in football, a pass thrown to a receiver who goes only a short distance upfield and turns to catch it.

The tone of the debate negotiations with Baker as an invisible hand, several of the participants said, was never rancorous, perhaps because both sides understood from the outset that it was just a question of agreeing on mechanics. The Clinton campaign held the iron side—a CNN poll released during the second day of the bargaining showed him leading by seventeen percentage points. And on more than one occasion, Kantor made a show of throwing his pencil down on the table and saying his candidate was the one who didn't need the debates. Goodwin recalled him telling Teeter at one point: "We've got 330 electoral votes locked up. I don't understand why you're being so obstinate. . . . Don't you realize we're eighteen percent [sic] ahead?'' And Teeter said later it seemed that "three quarters of the time" the Clinton negotiators were threatening to walk out. But there never was any serious danger of a breakdown.

When it was all over, it was clear that Kantor and the Clinton campaign had gotten the best of it. "Bush was behind the eight-ball on the debates," Goodwin said. The one nonnegotiable demand from the Clinton side had been that there would be no debate later than October 19, and that was precisely what the final schedule showed. There would be ninety-minute presidential debates on October 11 in St. Louis, October 15 in Richmond and October 19 in East Lansing, with a vice presidential debate on October 13 in Atlanta.

The Clinton campaign, realizing how low the expectations would be for Quayle, and thus easy to surpass, offered at one point to drop the vice presidential debate. But Quayle, hoping to recover from his disastrous 1988 debate showing, wanted to do it. His negotiators proposed that the candidates be permitted to bring notes and props, but the Democrats refused. What Quayle wanted, Goodwin said later, was to bring Gore's new book on the environment onto the set and quote from it.

As matters turned out, the critical debate decision had more to do with format than schedule. From the outset, Teeter had made it plain that the Bush campaign's one nonnegotiable demand was having a three-reporter panel for the first debate. And the implication was that this would be a trade-off for a single-moderator debate and perhaps another divided half and half.

But when Kantor telephoned Clinton during one break in the talks, Clinton suggested his negotiator should, as Kantor recalled it, "see if they will agree to one of these to be a town meeting. Let real people ask questions." Clinton had done many of these during the primaries and had mastered the direct talking to voters.

Kantor was not optimistic that Teeter would accept but promised to give it a try. Bush after all had been doing his "Ask George Bush" sessions for years. "In some ways I think it piqued their interest because they had this incredible anger toward the press," Kantor said, and this would be another way to show contempt. Nonetheless, he said, "My view was they'd never accept this, they'd never give Bill Clinton a chance to deal with real people in an open forum." Kantor's fellow negotiators—

Ron Brown, Tom Donilon and Jack Quinn, another Washington lawyer with long political experience—also were dubious. "They all said," Kantor recalled, " 'They'll never agree to that, they'd be crazy to do that.' "

But after another caucus and presumably another telephone call to Jim Baker, the Bush campaign agreed, and the die was cast for that very different—and even pivotal—Richmond debate on October 15.

In the end, all of the alarums and excursions of the debate over debates may have had little direct effect on the election. Teeter was convinced that the back-and-forth thrusts and parries were trivial. "You can add them all up together and put them next to the economy and they're small," he said. "Our objective was to get people to focus on the choice."

Charlie Black, however, was not so sure. He recalled going to dinner in Lansing the night after the final debate there, almost a month since it had originally been scheduled, and opening his menu to find "Chicken George" still among the entrées. He was convinced, he said, that the campaign "waited a little bit too long to roll the proposal [from Bush for four debates] out there. We always knew we would have a proposal, we would go on offense on the issue . . . and we probably should have pulled the trigger a little earlier on the proposal."

The significant thing politically was that the Bush campaign had allowed almost the entire month of September to be frittered away in trying to get off the defensive on the debates issue. It had desperately needed to use that time to build the president's image as a man who could and would deal with the economy more effectively than he had managed in his first four years in the White House.

Beyond that, the final schedule for the four debates over nine days had the effect of freezing the campaign in place for that period. The press focus now was on preparations in both campaigns—both candidates were doing mock debates with stand-ins for their opponents—and on the speculation about what would constitute political success or failure. The consensus among the professionals was obvious: because he was behind, the president needed to make some kind of breakthrough in terms of being convincing on the economy.

Because Clinton was a challenger from Arkansas and still carried relatively heavy negatives, his imperative was to establish himself as properly "presidential." "People were ready to vote against Bush,"

David Wilhelm said later. "They needed to see that Clinton was okay." As for Ross Perot, who by now was back in the race, he would be free once again to play himself, to the hilt, because he was not considered an equally serious competitor. (The Bush and Clinton campaigns, Goodwin said later, held out the option of dropping Perot from further debates if he fizzled in the polls after the first or second one.)

But everyone in the Bush and Clinton campaigns realized that the debates had the potential, even if it seemed remote, for changing the nature and direction of the contest. There was always the possibility of some gaffe that would brand the governor from the baby boom generation as unprepared for the office. There was always the possibility of some dramatic exchange leaving a vivid perception of one candidate or another ascendant. Few in the political community could forget the moment in 1980 when Ronald Reagan, shaking his head more in sorrow than in anger, said to President Jimmy Carter: "There you go again." Nor was it likely anyone would forget Michael Dukakis's dry, legalistic response to Bernie Shaw's "killer question" in 1988.

In the first 1992 confrontation in St. Louis, however, nothing that dramatic happened. Roger Ailes, the hard-nosed and irreverent media consultant who had advised Bush in the 1988 debates, flew in on Air Force One with the president. His assignment was to relax him and get him to focus on the key elements of the debate strategy, one of which obviously was to throw Clinton on the defensive. He loosened Bush up with such things as referring to Perot as "Shrimpo" and describing him as "a hand grenade with a bad haircut."

The most contentious moment of the debate came when, responding to a question about "issues of character," Bush condemned Clinton for participating in demonstrations against the war in Vietnam while he was a Rhodes Scholar in England.

"I think it's wrong to demonstrate against your country or to organize demonstrations against your country on foreign soil," Bush said. "Maybe, they say, well, it was a youthful indiscretion. I was nineteen or twenty flying off an aircraft carrier and that shaped me to be commander in chief of the armed forces. And I'm sorry, but demonstrating—it's not a question of patriotism, it's a question of character and judgment."

Clinton, obviously well prepared for the issue, countered: "You *have* questioned my patriotism. When Joe McCarthy went around this country attacking people's patriotism, he was wrong, and a senator from Connecticut stood up to him named Prescott Bush. Your father was right to stand up to Joe McCarthy. You were wrong to attack my patriotism. I was opposed to the war, but I love my country.'' (The record on Bush's father had been dug up and printed in a column in *The Boston Globe* that very morning and quickly made its way into Clinton's awareness in St. Louis.)

Bush rather lamely insisted that ''I didn't question the man's patriotism. I questioned his judgment and his character. If what he did in Moscow, that's fine. Let him explain it. He did. I accept that.'' Bush didn't elaborate as to what Clinton ''did in Moscow.''

Clinton made it clear from the outset that he intended to deal with the stature question—a governor from a small state taking on the president—in the most direct way. Responding to the first question about differences among the candidates, he turned toward Bush and said: ''Tonight, I say to the president, Mr. Bush, for twelve years you've had it your way. You've had your chance and it didn't work. It's time for a change.''

To which Bush replied: ''Change for change's sake isn't enough. We saw that message in the late seventies. We heard a lot about change. And what happened? The misery index [inflation rate plus interest rate] went right through the roof.''

But Bush never made a persuasive case on the economy, and seemed to fly in the face of the national consensus of concern by trying to minimize the problem, as he had done all year. ''Now I know that the only way he can win,'' he said of Clinton, ''is to make everybody believe the economy is worse than it is, but this country's not coming apart at the seams, for heaven's sake. We're the United States of America.''

In what was an attempt to demonstrate he meant business in trying to right the economy, Bush said at one point: ''What I'm going to do is say to Jim Baker when this campaign is over, 'All right, let's sit down now. You do in domestic affairs what you've done in foreign affairs, be the kind of economic coordinator of all the domestic side of the house . . . that includes all the economic side, all the training side, and bring this program together.' '' In other words, after having called Baker in to save his reelection campaign, he would turn over the domestic challenge to him—an incredible acknowledgment that his chief of staff had more credibility with the American people than he had himself.

For Perot's part, he drew frequent laughter from the studio audience with small jabs at his opponents and the political establishment. Responding to questions about his experience for the presidency, for example, he replied, "Well, they've got a point. I don't have any experience in running up a $4 trillion debt. I don't have any experience in gridlock government. I have experience in not taking ten years in solving a ten-minute problem." And he got the biggest laugh of the night when, defending his call for higher gasoline taxes to cut the deficit, he observed that "if there's a fairer way, I'm all ears."

The instant polls after the debate disagreed narrowly on whether Clinton or Perot was the winner, but they did agree that Bush was the loser. And the same was true of the talking heads on television. Walking back to the president's holding room from her seat in the audience, Barbara Bush told a staff member, "I thought he did really well. I'm really pleased." But after a few minutes of watching the television commentary, she emerged saying: "I can't stand to listen to them." Walking to the presidential limousine, Jim Baker told Bush: "Now we've got to flush him [Clinton] out."

Whatever the validity of the verdicts of polls and pundits, the one thing that was clear was that Bush still "didn't get it" with his continuing attempts to center the debate on character or the "trust issue," as it was usually defined by the Bush campaign. Indeed, the campaign's own focus groups on the night of the first debate found Bush evoked far more doubts about Clinton when he depicted him as another tax-and-spend liberal Democrat than when he talked about trust and character.

Once again, it was a case of a campaign that did not grasp the difference in the electorate of 1992. These voters already had factored into their consideration the history of Bill Clinton dodging the draft and had decided it was not disqualifying. So they were ready to move on to the issues that affected their own lives much more than whether Bill Clinton organized a demonstration in London twenty-three years earlier.

Two nights after that first presidential debate, the confrontation between the three vice presidential nominees gave the Bush campaign an unexpected lift. Vice President Dan Quayle, the goat of the corresponding debate with Lloyd Bentsen four years earlier, came out of his corner attacking Clinton relentlessly on his economic program and personal history, charging that the Democratic nominee "does not have the strength of character to be president." Although Al Gore held his own, repeatedly attacking the Bush administration's record on the economy, the major "story" of the debate was that Dan Quayle had shown Bush the kind of aggressiveness he needed to display to be effective in the two remaining presidential debates.

The clear loser of the night was Ross Perot's running mate, retired Admiral James Stockdale, who demonstrated beyond any doubt that experience counts in big-league politics. Stockdale began by asking rhetorically, "Who am I? Why am I here?" It was a line he had rehearsed in advance, and according to Ed Fouhy, the debate's producer, Stockdale that afternoon had been arresting in practice. But over the ninety minutes of the real thing, he answered the questions with a performance that made it clear he shouldn't have been there, whatever his much-admired qualities of intellect and character. At one point, for example, he cut short his answer on a question about health care by confessing, "I'm out of ammunition." At another, after standing mute as Quayle and Gore argued heatedly, Stockdale confessed, "I feel like I'm a spectator at a Ping-Pong game."

But no one in either the Bush or Clinton campaign expected the vice presidential debate to have any significant effect on the presidential campaign. Even Quayle's weak performance as the nominee in 1988 never showed up in opinion surveys as a factor in the decisions of voters choosing between George Bush and Michael Dukakis.

So the most that could be said was that Quayle had taken at least a small step toward building his own credibility and, more to the point, provided a good example for Bush to follow in the second presidential debate in Richmond two nights later. Unhappily for Bush, however, the "town-meeting" format of that debate and the role of people like Marisa Hall, Kim Usry and Denton Walthall who deplored the spectacle of candidates trashing each other, made it impossible for the president to take that kind of approach.

According to Ed Fouhy, Bush seemed uncomfortable in that setting from the start. For one thing, the Richmond debate started two hours later than first scheduled as a result of a conflict with the baseball playoffs caused when the Oakland Athletics failed to end its series with the Toronto Blue Jays the night before. "That damned Oakland," the president muttered several times. And when Fouhy told him, "Mr. President, you're going to get a much bigger audience," Bush flashed him a disdainful look.

Furthermore, Bush's campaign aides had alerted him by this time to what they saw as the pitfalls of audience participation under Carole Simpson as moderator. In addition, the candidates were fitted with wireless microphones to enable them to move away from the stools on which they would be perched—a gimmick that Clinton duly put to his advantage in the town-meeting format he himself had proposed. When Bush said he was "not sure I get" the gist of Marisa Hall's question about how the "national debt" personally affected him, and Clinton then strode over to her and demonstrated that he did get it, it was what the late Lee Atwater would have called "the defining moment" of the campaign.

Thus, the stakes were sharply raised for the third and final debate in East Lansing four nights later. Bush had been counted as the loser of the first two meetings, and there was no sign in either public or private polling data that he was gaining on Clinton. Nor had he managed to establish his credibility on the economy even with such initiatives as his speech to the Economic Club of Detroit and publication of his new "agenda" for a second-term approach to the economy. "The later and later you got in the campaign," Bob Teeter said, "the more it was perceived as campaign rhetoric."

The importance both campaigns had attached to the final debate was evident in one bizarre episode. Two nights before, Bev Lindsey and Brady Williamson, the Clinton aides overseeing on-site debate preparation, collared Bob Goodwin, their opposite number in the Bush campaign. They needed, they told him, to check out a report—that Gennifer Flowers would be in the audience for the debate and seated with Barbara Bush! The notion was preposterous, as Goodwin quickly assured the Clinton operatives, but the fact the rumor was circulating at all was an indicator of the high stakes in the debate. (A similar rumor had made its way into the Dukakis inner circle before the last presidential debate in 1988—that the Maryland victims of Willie Horton would be planted in the audience by the Bush campaign. That one also was unfounded.)

In the end, the final debate confrontation proved anticlimactic. By virtually all estimates, Bush performed far better than in either of the earlier debates and probably as well as he had all through the campaign, making his points with more visible force than usual and sticking to the story line his campaign had crafted.

Yet for all the admonitions in the Richmond debate against negative campaigning, Bush took a tar brush to Clinton's record in Arkansas, frankly acknowledging he had to, to win. "You haven't heard me mention this before," he said, "but we're getting close now, and I think it's about time I start putting things in perspective. And I'm going to do that. It's not dirty campaigning because he's been talking about my record for a half a year here, eleven months here. So we've got to do that. I gotta get it in perspective." It was as if he were repeating the coaching he had received from his strategists before the debate started.

Clinton, after reminding the audience that "Mr. Bush's Bureau of Labor Statistics says that Arkansas ranks first in the country in the growth of new jobs this year," a few minutes later in a rejoinder to Bush on trickle-down economics recalled that "those 209 Americans last Thursday night in Richmond told us they wanted us to stop talking about each other and start talking about Americans and their problems. . . ."

And when Bush started to talk about "trust" again, Clinton reminded him of "read my lips" and repeated that "the main thing is he still didn't get it, from what he said the other night to that fine woman on our program, the 209 people in Richmond." And at the close of the debate, he told of how he was "especially moved in Richmond a few days ago when 209 of our fellow citizens got to ask us questions. They went a long way," he said, "toward reclaiming this election for the American people and taking their country back." Bill Clinton was not about to let the voters forget that previous debate, and what he was convinced it revealed about George Bush.

Nevertheless, Black said later, "Bush did a good job in that last debate. I don't give a damn what the numbers and the polls said, he got our message out there and got done exactly what he needed to get done, and that helped jump-start us. We were on a pretty good run there for a while."

None of the candidates could complain about not having an ample opportunity to make his case to the widest possible cross-section of the electorate. Contrary to the usual pattern of declining interest in debates, the audience grew over the three debates—just as Clinton adviser Harry Thomason had predicted. The first one attracted more than 80 million viewers despite the competition of a major-league baseball playoff game on CBS; the second more than 84 million and the third 88 million—and those numbers did not include the millions watching CNN and C-SPAN on cable systems or PBS. Indeed, it appeared likely that the audience for the final debate exceeded 90 million viewers.

Taken together, however, the three debates had not accomplished what the Bush campaign needed—a significant change in the dynamics of the entire campaign. The election was now two weeks away and Bill Clinton was still holding a lead in the double digits. And the president was being further compromised by the political stupidity of some of his own supporters at the State Department who had rooted through Clinton's passport files on the same days, as Mickey Kantor noted, that the debates were being negotiated.

The context was that dark suggestion promoted by right-wing Republicans in the House of Representatives, particularly Bob Dornan of California, and later encouraged by Bush himself, that there was something fishy in the trip to Moscow Clinton made while a student at Oxford. At the same time, an implausible rumor began to circulate that when Clinton was at Oxford he also had written letters trying to find out if he could avoid the draft by renouncing his U.S. citizenship or seeking dual citizenship of some other nation. It was an illogical speculation in light of his stated insistence in those days, in the letter to Colonel Holmes, that he wanted to preserve the viability of a future political career.

The State Department acknowledged, however, that the assistant secretary of state for consular affairs, Elizabeth M. Tamposi, a longtime Republican activist from New Hampshire who had been placed in the job by John Sununu, had ordered subordinates to search Clinton's passport files at Suitland after the close of business on September 30 and October 1. The justification was said to be requests from news organizations under the Freedom of Information Act. When the after-hours search was disclosed by *Newsweek* and *The Washington Post*, the department conceded that it was "clearly a mistake" and pointed the finger at Tamposi.

But the notion that she would have ordered such a search on her own was hard to accept. And subsequent departmental investigations established that during this period she had conversations about the matter with Janet Mullins, an aide to Jim Baker who had served in the White House political office, and had tried unsuccessfully to telephone Margaret Tutwiler, Baker's closest White House aide, to report on what was happening. The operative question—never answered during the campaign—obviously was whether Jim Baker had been just a little too clever this time.

For Clinton, the disclosure was a political bonanza, particularly after it was learned that the search had also covered the files of his mother, Virginia Kelley, although no Freedom of Information request had asked that this be done. The Democratic candidate began using in every speech an attack on "political hacks rifling through my mother's files trying to find dirt"—a thrust that invariably evoked boos and hisses from his listeners. And Clinton consistently evoked laughter when he would say, as he did repeatedly, that the Bush administration "was not only rifling through my files but actually investigating my mother, a well-known subversive. It would be funny if it weren't so pathetic."

Bush tried to put some distance between himself and the story, saying that the search into Mrs. Kelley's files was "most reprehensible," while adding that it would be "a stretch" to connect it to his campaign.

The challenger's mother joined the chorus of condemnation. "I'm insulted, I'm indignant," she said. "You know I'm at the age that I lived through Hitler and his Gestapo. I lived through the police state. I do not want this to happen to my country."

Here was another example of the snakebit campaign of George Bush, appearing to be playing the "dirty tricks" politics of the past when the voters were seeking answers to questions about their future that had nothing to do with Bill Clinton's passport. And, with the opportunity of the presidential debates come and gone, time was running out on the beleaguered president.

SHORT-CIRCUITING
A SURGE

With the last of the televised debates behind them, the three candidates had two weeks to make their final pitches to the voters. All the major public opinion surveys continued to show Clinton ahead by various margins in samplings after the third presidential debate. His lead ranged from nineteen percentage points in the *Wall Street Journal*/NBC News poll (47 percent to 28 for Bush and 19 for Perot) down to five in the *New York Times*/CBS News poll, with most of the others somewhere in the middle.

Clinton's pollster, Stan Greenberg, was not worried by the latter survey or any of the others. His own poll had leveled off at a seven-point lead and was staying there. More significant, Greenberg knew that much more important than the national polling numbers were those taken in each of the states, and Clinton was comfortably ahead in more than enough for an electoral college victory. His leads in such large and critical states as California, New York and Illinois were so big that the campaign was able to divert resources and candidate time from them and focus on closer targets, or states where Bush led but would be forced to spend heavy resources of his own if they were contested by Clinton.

Two questions in the *Wall Street Journal*/NBC News poll offered particular comfort for Clinton. In response to one, 54 percent said they were satisfied with his explanation on the draft issue to 38 percent who said they still had doubts. In reply to another, 51 percent said they bought his explanation on the Moscow trip, to 31 percent who said they had doubts. Neither was exactly a ringing exoneraton, but at least he was now getting the benefit of the doubt.

The debates to which Bush had looked forward as a means of closing the gap between himself and Clinton had not achieved that end, and instead had helped propel Perot back into the picture. With his message of better economic times around the corner not credible to most voters, the president was left with the same imperative that confronted him in 1988, in his race against Dukakis. He had to find a way to make the public think less of the opposition. Those questioners in the Richmond debate had let him know they would not look kindly on further personal attacks, but it was too late now to worry about a backlash from going negative.

Complicating the task was the pesky matter of the search for Clinton's passport files. It continued to be an embarrassment to Bush that Clinton exploited on the stump, telling Northern audiences that the Bush administration had sent bureaucrats on an after-hours search through an old, musty file room and even looked into "my mother's" files, which before Southern audiences became "my momma's."

(A week after the election, Bush fired Tamposi after *The Washington Post* reported that the passport files of Ross Perot also had been searched. Tamposi told *Newsweek* that she had acted under indirect orders from the White House; that the assistant secretary for legislative affairs, Steven K. Berry, had told her the search had been requested by Janet Mullins, and that Margaret Tutwiler had known about the search. Berry was demoted and eventually left the department for a job on Capitol Hill.

(A report by the State Department's inspector general, Sherman Funk, held that "there was indeed an attempt to use the Department of State," its records and employees "to influence the outcome of a presidential election," but that there was no evidence of White House involvement. The report was widely criticized as inadequate and Acting Secretary of State Lawrence S. Eagleburger eventually ordered the investigation to be continued. At the same time, the Justice Department and the General Accounting Office both stepped in to investigate as well, the GAO requesting the records not only of Mullins and Tutwiler but of Baker, who had acknowledged he had learned of the search when it was going on. Finally, Bush's attorney general, William P. Barr, appointed an independent prosecutor, Joseph E. diGenova, a former U.S. Attorney, to determine whether crimes had been committed, and if so, by whom.)

Bush undertook a two-day whistlestop train trip through the South coming out of the last debate, and he threw himself with some newfound zest into his task. He seemed never happier than when he was on the attack and playing the underdog, whether it was against Clinton, the pollsters whose numbers showed him facing a severe uphill climb, or the members of the news media, who, he was convinced, never tired of gleefully reporting that fact.

At a rally in Spartanburg, South Carolina, the night after the last debate, he roared: "Don't listen to these pundits telling you how to think. And don't listen to these nutty pollsters. Remember, things are decided in the last couple of weeks in this campaign. And now people are going to decide: who do you trust to be president of the United States?"

It all came down, in this final push, to the issue of trust. All along the route through the Carolinas, Bush hammered at what he called "a pattern of deception" in Clinton's statements, whether about his personal history or his record as governor of Arkansas. In Kannapolis, North Carolina, he reminded the crowd that Clinton had said in the final debate that he wanted "to do for the country what I've done for Arkansas." Bush added: "We cannot let him do that."

In a part of the country dotted with Waffle House restaurants, Bush visited one and made the obvious linkage with what he said was Clinton's manner of slipping off hard questions. Thereafter he took to labeling fuzzy Clinton statements, such as his equivocation on support of Bush in the Persian Gulf, as "a waffle house."

Almost giddy at times with enthusiasm for the fight, he took to ridiculing Al Gore as "the ozone man," eventually shortened to a title, "Ozone Man," and finally simply "Ozone" in allusion to the Democratic vice presidential nominee's expressed concern about the diminishing ozone layer and other environmental fears. If the president of the United States to some ears sounded somewhat silly in this exercise, many in the pro-Bush crowd loved it. At the least, it lent a certain lightness to a campaign that too often had bogged down in whining and bitterness.

Another light touch was added along the way when an unidentified couple and their three children standing along the tracks on signal dropped their trousers and, as Bush's train rolled by, ''mooned'' the leader of the free world!

In a day or two, the Bush attack on Clinton had settled in to the two words he would pound relentlessly through election day—''character and trust.'' In Vineland, New Jersey, he said: ''My argument with Bill Clinton is he tries to be all things to all people. In the Oval Office you cannot do that. . . . You cannot lie and you can't be all things to all people.'' But the Clinton campaign, determined never to fall into the turn-the-other-cheek mode that crippled Dukakis in 1988, had its expert rapid-response operation in Little Rock at full throttle. In selected target states, the campaign was running a thirty-second television commercial showing Bush making his now-infamous ''read my lips'' invitation to voters during the Republican National Convention. The message clearly was, Who is George Bush to be talking about lying?

As the campaign headed into its final full week, and most polls began to indicate that Clinton's lead was shrinking, the Bush campaign began to take heart. Most of the surveys still had the Arkansas governor comfortably ahead, but one, by *The New York Times* and CBS News, had him leading Bush by only five percentage points, 42 to 37, with Perot at 17. And a *Time*/CNN poll, which had Clinton leading by seven among all registered voters surveyed, said the lead shrunk to only three when the sample was confined to ''likely voters.''

Slowly, cautiously, the Bush operatives began to talk of a late ''surge'' for the president. Such talk was particularly suspect after the 1988 election, when the strategists for Dukakis excitedly reported a similar phenomenon, but Bush in the end had been elected by a comfortable margin of nearly eight percentage points, winning 426 electoral votes in forty states. In the final stages of that campaign, Dukakis had struck the theme to voters that he was ''on your side,'' a message geared to bring blue-collar Democrats back to the fold, and in the excitement of the final days it seemed to crowd-counters to be working. But large and even enthusiastic crowds were always an unreliable barometer of voting patterns, as Walter Mondale had found out four years earlier.

In the closing days of the 1988 campaign, too, Dukakis had finally stopped turning the other cheek and had generated notable crowd excitement by at last responding to Bush's negative tactics. He took to citing brochures picturing Willie Horton that were being distributed by an allegedly independent group in Illinois, demanding that Bush stop their circulation. "When you throw garbage in the street," he would say, "you've got a responsibility to go out there and clean it up."

But four years later, Bush had no similar wretched excess on the part of the Clinton campaign to cite as a way of rallying wavering Republicans and independents to his side, or to keep the Reagan Democrats aboard. Still, there were signs that Republicans, having had their fling with Perot or loyalty to their party winning out at the end, were coming home.

One who professed to see them was Republican Governor John Engler of Michigan. He was ushered into the press room in Detroit after a Bush speech to report about polls he claimed were showing that Perot was cutting into Clinton's lead and that, when narrowed to "likely" voters, were indicating a surge for the president. Reminded of the Dukakis claim of a surge in 1988, Engler replied: "This is real. His wasn't."

For all that, the dimensions of the task that Bush faced were demonstrated by his campaign schedule. From Michigan he spent most of one day on the next-to-last weekend in the sparsely populated states of South Dakota and Montana, with three electoral votes each, that he should have had in his pocket by now. In poker terms, Bush had to draw to an inside straight in the electoral college to be reelected, and he could not afford to let even these few electoral chips slip away. A few days earlier, a confident Clinton had made a brief raid into Montana as part of a four-state Western swing into what should have been safe country for the heir to the Reagan Revolution.

Another sign that Bush was going all out was the appearance of the heretofore Invisible Campaign Manager, Jim Baker, on Air Force One. Baker not only had been keeping out of the public eye now that he was getting his fingernails dirty in politics again; when he was identified on one occasion as the campaign manager, he corrected the statement, saying he was the White House chief of staff. According to *The New York Times*, although Baker had now surfaced, he "remained camera shy, turning his back and hiding his face this evening to get out of the camera shot" as Bush received a gift from a Montana supporter. Earlier, however, in Sioux Falls, he told reporters that the election was "absolutely doable, and we're going to win."

In all this, both Bush and Clinton competed for the most part in the final days as they did before Ross Perot reentered the race—against each other. Aware that Perot would siphon off a certain number of popular votes, each side was confident that in the real race, for electoral votes, Perot would not make much of a dent, if any. More than any national poll, where the two major candidates were going now was telling the story of the campaign. Both were concentrating on the industrial belt from New Jersey west through eastern Wisconsin, the acknowledged battleground states, in all of which Clinton was running ahead or at worst even. But beyond that, Bush was still occupied shoring up his base in the South and the West, while Clinton was forcing him to defend that base by courting it in selected states where the polls said he was running close.

Much earlier, Clinton campaign manager David Wilhelm in Little Rock had crafted a very specific battle plan that set aside what he called "top end" states—thirteen of them plus the District of Columbia— where, based on polls, past performances, strengths of state tickets and other factors, it was judged Clinton could win without expending major resources. The states were Democratic standbys Massachusetts, Rhode Island, Minnesota, Hawaii and West Virginia (although the latter began to look tougher than expected); plus Arkansas, California, New York, Illinois, Washington, Oregon, Vermont and Connecticut. They were largely bypassed the last week (and he won them all).

The second Wilhelm category was what he called "play hard" states—eighteen that were deemed winnable with an all-out campaign: Maine, New Jersey, Pennsylvania, Delaware and Maryland in the New England and Middle Atlantic regions; North Carolina, Georgia, Louisiana, Kentucky, Tennessee and Missouri among the Southern and border states; Ohio, Michigan, Wisconsin and Iowa in the Midwest; Colorado, Montana and New Mexico in the West. By the last week, Clinton was focusing on the largest of these (and in fact won all but North Carolina, losing there by a single percentage point).

The third category Wilhelm called "big challenge" states, a diplomatic way of saying Clinton's chances were not good in them and would be largely written off. There were ten considered almost sure losers: Alaska, Virginia, Mississippi, Indiana, North Dakota, Nebraska, Oklahoma, Wyoming, Idaho and Utah; and nine more that merited watching only, with a modest effort where warranted: Alabama, Arizona, Florida, Kansas, New Hampshire, Nevada, South Carolina, South Dakota and Texas. (Clinton lost all the "sure losers" and narrowly won two of the nine others—New Hampshire and Nevada.)

Mickey Kantor, the Clinton campaign chairman, told us in an interview in Little Rock shortly after the Republican convention that, for the first time in years, it was going to be the Republican candidate rather than the Democratic who would have to "thread the needle" in the electoral college to eke out a victory, and as November 3 approached, his words, and Wilhelm's calculations, were holding up.

While Clinton and Bush concentrated on each other, Ross Perot at last decided to hit the campaign trail. Since his disastrous appearance before the NAACP in Nashville in July, and his return as an active candidate on October 1, he had confined his political appearances almost exclusively to the television and radio talk shows that had first provided him an entrée onto the national political stage and, along with his healthy bankroll, kept him there. The NAACP experience, however, apparently cured him of venturing into potentially hostile waters, and he chose on Sunday, October 25, to address two crowds of supporters, one in Flemington, New Jersey, and the other in Pittsburgh.

Earlier, Perot had taped an interview for CBS's *60 Minutes*, and he urged his audiences in both places to be sure to watch it. In fact, he gave the faithful a preview—that the real reason he had dropped out of the race in July was that the Bush campaign had threatened to sabotage his daughter's wedding the next month! Offering no proof, he proclaimed that "I could not allow my daughter's happiest day of her life . . . to be ruined because of people who will do anything to win." He said he "realized this was a risk I did not have to take" if he were not a candidate "and I stepped back." Later, he acknowledged that "I cannot prove any of that happened. I just got these reports. But it was a risk I could not take."

This explanation seemed to soothe many in the crowd and it sent reporters scurrying to telephones, and many others to television sets when *60 Minutes* went on the air that night. On the show, Perot said that one of his sources was a former California police officer, Scott Barnes, known to government investigators as a publicity hound given to soliciting news organizations with tales of secret intelligence work involving famous people.

"I received multiple reports that there was a plan to embarrass her [daughter Caroline] before her wedding, and to actually have people in the church at the wedding to disrupt her wedding," Perot said. "I finally concluded that I, as a father who adores his children, could not take that risk. And, since the wedding was on a finite date [August 23], I made the decision that I would step aside." He said two unidentified Republican sources had told him in June that certain Republicans were going to "smear" his daughter by producing a fake photo concocted by computer.

In an interview with the *Boston Herald*, Perot said that while he didn't know how the wedding would be sabotaged, "watch how they disrupt rallies; watch how they tried to disrupt the Democratic convention. . . . They got a bunch of neo-Nazis there that do this kind of stuff." "They" was not specified.

Perot also reported that after he had quit the race in July, he was given a videotape of a park-bench meeting in Dallas between a "very senior person in the Bush campaign" and a contract employee of the CIA at which plans were discussed to wiretap his office. Perot said he had sent the tape to the FBI, which in August had investigated allegations that phones in Perot's Dallas office had been bugged and the tapes had been offered to James Oberwetter, the Texas chairman of the Bush-Quayle campaign.

Barnes had claimed that the Bush campaign had hired him to bug Perot's phones, and CBS reported that the FBI, to check out the claim, had asked Perot to make a recording of his voice, which was then taken by an FBI undercover agent to Oberwetter in a sting operation. The agent, CBS said, told Oberwetter he was working with Barnes and had a Perot tape he could have, but that Oberwetter turned down the offer.

By chance, one of us had lunch with Oberwetter, a business executive, in Dallas after the approach was made. He described how he had refused to allow the contact man who had phoned him to come to his office. Instead, he said, he met him outside the building, quickly realized something was fishy and refused to accept the material. At the time, Oberwetter said, he had no idea who was involved, but he suspected he was being set up, and probably filmed.

All this apparently was what Perot had alluded to in the final presidential debate when he accused "the Republican dirty tricks group" of going to "extraordinary sick lengths" to destroy his family's reputation. In our interview with him in his Dallas office back on May 12, well before the two Republican sources were alleged by him to have told him of the wedding sabotage plans, Perot said:

"I marvel at the stuff they get into, because the first rule of war is don't shoot yourself, right? Remember I said that. . . . Let's assume you bring up an issue that is going to totally embarrass you. That's not too smart, right? Then, if you see me not responding to it, it's probably an issue I would never have brought up, never discussed. They have brought it up. I'll discuss it in October, and they're going to be so sick they brought it up."

Perot declined to be more specific, but added that the Republicans were "down to childhood pranks now. I don't know what else they'll bring up. They're just goofy." Perot observed that when two gorillas fight they throw dust in each other's faces, suggesting this was what the Bush campaign was doing to obscure other issues that might be brought against the president.

"If I had been in charge of deregulation in the eighties," he said in the interview, "and oversaw the savings and loan and banking mess— and the vice president [Bush] had that job, which the press scrupulously never talks about—and if I had been involved in any terrorism all through the eighties, and if my fingerprints were all over Noriega and Saddam Hussein in terms of creating them and supporting them, and if I had been squarely in the middle of letting the national debt go from one trillion [dollars] to four trillion, I would probably spend all my time throwing gorilla dust in the air."

Perot mentioned nothing about his daughter's wedding at the time, but he said he would have more to say "at a time that's appropriate, and they'll be wandering around, whining for mother, because it's the same old story. They can dish it but they can't take it. . . . They think that this is going to cause me to stop doing this. That's their objective. . . . Once that starts, I'm in to the end of the fight."

Yet two months later, he was out of the race, saying nothing about plots against his family. In interviews after the election, Tom Luce, who ran the Perot campaign until his July pullout, and Orson Swindle, who ran it afterward, both said Perot the night before withdrawing had referred to concern over his family's privacy, but without the specifics he was now letting the nation in on through his stump speeches and the *60 Minutes* interview.

The reaction was electric, and if it was Perot's intention to turn the country against Bush, it had another immediate effect—to rekindle all the talk about his own "weirdness," "Inspector Perot" and all the rest. White House press secretary Fitzwater told reporters: "There's simply nothing to it. It never happened. There haven't been any dirty tricks against Ross Perot. This business about his daughter is just crazy, and he's been told that, and he knows that."

(Later that week, in an interview with David Frost, Perot acknowledged that after the third presidential debate Barbara Bush "came up to me and said, 'We didn't investigate your children.' And my reaction was, 'Certainly, I am sure she thinks that. But how does she know what the Republican dirty tricks crowd is doing?' "

(In the same interview, when Frost asked him whether it was true that he had told his supporters back in July, the weekend after getting out of the race, that he had threatened an "October surprise" reentry, Perot replied that "I may have said [it] in that meeting, but never publicly, because they wanted me to stay in the race." He said he told them that if [Bush and Clinton] "don't respond to you, and we're on the ballot in all fifty states, we can come back in." The remark lent credence to the existing speculation that he had dropped out of the campaign in July to avoid further press scrutiny, intending all along to reenter in October when it would be too late for the press to pursue that scrutiny effectively.)

The next day in Dallas, an irate Perot stalked into a press briefing by his son, took the microphone and repeated the charges—but admitted again that he had no proof. He said the Bush campaign and White House never told him that they weren't involved until he went on *60 Minutes*, and did so then "at a time when they were trying to get millions of people who supported me to join them." But, he added, "I accept their word. . . . Let's put it behind us."

At the same time, Perot unloaded on the press as unfair to him, assailing "your bizarre stories and your twisted, slanted stories" and adding: "I am sick and tired of you all questioning my integrity without a basis for it. I am sick and tired of you ignoring the people who can confirm the articles when you run your stories." And he stormed out. Why, if Perot was now so willing to drop the issue, did he choose to air it in the first place over such a high-visibility outlet as the top-rated Sunday television show? The "weird" factor was emerging again. Fitzwater was quick to call on the news media to continue its investigations of him "and prevent us from electing a paranoid person who has delusions."

Perot immediately raised the stakes with an unprecedented paid television blitz, filling the airwaves with a host of new commercials of thirty and sixty seconds' length—full of the sound bites he professed to despise from a narrator—to go with half-hour "infomercials" he was now serving up personally. By now, according to *The Washington Post*, Perot had spent $57.5 million since his initial talk of running, more than half of it—$37 million—in the twenty-six days since his reentry into the race, far more than either Bush or Clinton. Included was a full hour on the ABC network at a cost of $940,000. Back in the early summer, Perot had been a penny-pincher when it came to the expensive television ads his "hired guns" wanted him to buy. But now he was doing it his way, and money seemed to be no object.

Perot's television format was simple and straightforward—the candidate himself on camera with charts and a pointer, explaining, for example, how the federal deficit got to the size it was. He taped a half-hour discussion of his plan to reduce the deficit by raising gasoline and other taxes and ran it twice, both times to surprisingly large audiences.

But buying huge blocks of television time did not seem to make as much sense this time as it might have in the past, what with all the television talk shows and morning and evening news shows all but installing revolving doors in their studios for the candidates to drop by and peddle their political wares. Even Bush, who had denigrated them earlier and vowed he would not demean himself by joining the parade, was now working them as diligently as the others.

On three succeeding nights in the final week, Clinton, Perot and Bush dutifully trooped into television studios to chat with Larry King and his coast-to-coast callers. But the most memorable moment for King, the talk show host said later, was one that demonstrated why Ross Perot had such a hold on so many people in this year of voters who were fed up with politics-as-usual, and the politicians who practiced it.

During his interview with Perot in his Washington studio, King said, a bomb threat had brought about forty police to sweep the building. Afterward, downstairs where Perot's car and driver awaited with no Secret Service or other security, the captain of the detail said, "Mr. Perot, we're going to escort you back to the airport and we're going to see that you get safely on your plane."

Perot balked. As King recalled the conversation, Perot told the officer: "No, I don't want any of that. Listen, I'm a citizen. I'm on the ballot but I'm a citizen." The officer informed him that he had the authority to declare someone a public personality who required police protection, "and I'm not leaving you." But Perot still balked. Turning to the assembled police in uniform, King recalled, "Perot makes a speech. He says, 'I don't want any of you to die for me. You're young men, you have children. I've lived a full life. I don't want anybody here risking himself for me.' "

King continued: "And these guys are staring, like, 'We'll walk through the wall for you, Ross.' One of the cops says [to King], 'I've never had an experience like this.' I thought they were going to applaud. Now they negotiate. Perot says, 'Okay, you've gotta do what you've gotta do. No sirens. If you blare sirens you bring attention to yourself, you get in accidents with sirens.' One cop looks at me and says, 'Yeah, you know, we do have accidents.' "

After further negotiations, King said, Perot finally agreed to having one car in front, other cars in back, but no sirens. "Then when they're leaving," King remembered, "Perot says, 'I want to go to the Vietnam Memorial.' The captain says, 'I don't think that would be wise, Mr. Perot.' Perot says, 'No, I haven't been there in a while, I don't want any fanfare, I just want to go.' So he went off to the memorial and then the airport."

If voters were fed up with politics, they were certainly getting an overdose of bad medicine in these closing days of the campaign. Or was it possible that this forced feeding, with increased opportunity for voters themselves to talk to and question the candidates, was igniting a spark of greater interest in the whole business?

Whatever the voter reaction, it was the strange story about the sabotage of his daughter's wedding as the real reason for his July withdrawal that was providing fodder for the talk show circuit now, not Ross Perot's primer on deficit reduction. Bush on NBC's *Today* called Perot's charges "crazy," adding: "I mean an allegation that we would wittingly or in any other way try to break up a man's daughter's wedding, particularly [when he was] not even in the presidential race at that time—what in the world would be the reason for that?"

Clinton gleefully declared a plague on both opposition houses. "So now we've got this bizarre situation where Bush and Perot have accused each other of investigating each other's children," he told a rally in Saginaw, Michigan. "I want to tell you something, folks. I want to investigate your children—their problems, their promise, their future," and that was what Bush and Perot ought to be talking about.

In a final concentrated swing across the South, Clinton and Gore led the largest bus tour of their campaign through North Carolina on a marathon day that ran from early morning in Winston-Salem eastward across the state until the wee hours of the following day. By now the bus trip phenomenon had become a magnet in itself for curious voters, and the two candidates performed according to the well-established script.

Gore went through his melodramatic warm-up painting Clinton as a log-cabin country boy who rose to be the governor of his state and ending with his question, "What time is it?" Everywhere, the crowds seemed to know the answer as they shouted back: "It's time for them [Bush and Quayle] to go!" Then Clinton would take over, making certain this time to remind his listeners how Bush and Perot were scrapping between themselves while he continued to address the concerns of the middle-class voter.

From North Carolina, Clinton's campaign plane hopscotched into Georgia, Florida, Louisiana, Texas, Mississippi and Kentucky over the next three days, with Clinton insisting he was not merely trying to force the Bush campaign to expend resources there, but was out to win in those states. Along the way, he repeatedly reminded voters of the passport flap, narrating how political agents from the Bush State Department "in $600 suits" had gone rummaging through an old warehouse after-hours looking for dirt in his files.

Clinton also took note of an article in *The New Yorker* magazine quoting former Soviet President Gorbachev as saying Bush once told him "not to pay any attention to what he would say in the presidential campaign" about taking credit for the end of the Cold War. "He's telling foreign leaders the truth," Clinton said, "but he won't tell you the truth." Bush had his nerve, he suggested, making character and trust the centerpieces of his campaign against him.

Bush meanwhile was campaigning through Iowa, Kentucky and Ohio armed with some long-awaited good economic news. He reported that the gross domestic product for the third quarter of 1992 had gone up 2.7 percent, the most encouraging indication that the long recession really was over and the country was on its way to economic recovery. He paired the news with a warning that a Democratic victory would bring a return to "the failed policies that brought us a misery index going right through Gore's ozone layer."

But statistics, the Bush strategists knew, were nothing you could put on the dinner table, and that good economic indicators that came so close to the election were not going to translate into meat and potatoes for average Americans in time to affect many votes.

One statistic did give them hope, however, that things were turning their way. On the next day, October 27, exactly a week before voters would be going to the polls, a new *USA Today*/CNN poll by the Gallup organization proclaimed that the race had become virtually a dead heat, with Clinton leading Bush by a bare percentage point among "likely" voters—41 percent for Clinton, 40 for Bush, 14 for Perot.

The figures were astonishing in their contrast with most other public polls showing the Clinton lead narrowing somewhat but certainly not that much. Talk of a surge rippled anew through the Bush campaign—and from the lips of its designated spin doctors to reporters in the Bush traveling entourage. They insisted that their own polling, by veteran Fred Steeper of Detroit, was confirming the surge. And everywhere Bush hammered at "this pattern of deception" he saw in Clinton—dodging the draft was not the question, but that he was lying about it.

As Bush's adrenaline began to pump, his speech became zanier. At a rally at Macomb County [Michigan] Community College, he said of Gore: "You know why I call him Ozone Man? This guy is so far off in the environmental extreme, we'll be up to our neck in owls and out of work for every American. This guy's crazy. He is way out, far out. Far out, man!" Once again, he was George Bush, hipster. He also took to referring to Clinton and Gore as a couple of "bozos," causing chagrined aides to suggest to him privately that the expression hardly enhanced his "presidential" image.

The next day, in Columbus, Ohio, Bush did some spinning of his own, telling a rally that Clinton supporters "feel it slipping away from them" and continuing his zany patter. "Governor Clinton and Ozone, all they do is talk about change," he said. "If I want foreign policy advice, I'd go to Millie [his dog] before I'd go to Ozone and Governor Clinton." Then he would break into his trademark lopsided grin, to the crowd's cheers. As for Clinton's "waffling" on issues, he said, "You cannot have a lot of buts sitting there in the Oval Office." That one got a lot of howls, too, from some in the audience, if not from his consternated aides.

Clinton down the homestretch sought to keep Bush in his sights, attempting to turn the trust issue back on him, even when asked about Perot's latest charges. "He can't prove what he said and that bothers people," Clinton said on the *Today* show, "but . . . don't forget that Mr. Bush has said himself he would do anything to get reelected. I mean, Mr. Perot may not be able to prove those charges but the Bush campaign has been the most reckless campaign with the truth of any campaign that I've seen in modern American history."

Even when he was asked by a caller about the old Gennifer Flowers charges, after saying that he had told her "to tell the truth," he added: "But if you're concerned about the truth, let's talk about the truth," and he repeated the Gorbachev quotation about what he said Bush had told him concerning what he might say in the campaign.

The Bush entourage was still riding the wave of the perceived surge on the afternoon of Friday, October 30, going into the final weekend of the long campaign, when it hit the shoals. The president had addressed a convention of Kentucky Fried Chicken franchise owners in Nashville and Air Force One had brought him into St. Louis, where he received a surprise eleventh-hour endorsement from a Democratic governor, William Donald Schaefer of Maryland.

Schaefer was at war with his own Democratic Party at home at the time and while he didn't say so, the betting in the press corps was that he was rolling the dice in hopes there would be a place for him in a second Bush administration, if there was one. Maryland by now was rated a shoo-in for Clinton and Schaefer himself could not have delivered it under any circumstances anyway. It was reminiscent of the endorsement in 1972 of presidential candidate Edmund Muskie by an Indiana senator after Muskie had finished fourth in the Florida primary, prompting Democratic veteran Frank Mankiewicz to deem it "the first case in recorded history of a rat jumping aboard a sinking ship."

Bush, however, was taking support from whatever quarter he could get it. He had just joined Schaefer in addressing a relatively modest crowd outside a suburban St. Louis industrial park on the gray, blustery afternoon, and was heading for Milwaukee and yet another talk show appearance that night with Larry King, when word came that the Iran-contra affair and his alleged role in it had suddenly raised its head again.

A federal grand jury had delivered a new indictment against Reagan Secretary of Defense Caspar W. Weinberger, sought by Iran-contra independent counsel Lawrence E. Walsh. It alleged that Weinberger had falsely told the House committee investigating the affair in 1987 that he had not made notes of related meetings in 1985 and 1986, when he had made voluminous notes. A previous indictment had been dismissed by the court as lacking in specificity.

Among the papers released with the indictment was a Weinberger note dated January 7, 1986, describing a White House meeting among Reagan, Bush and senior aides at which a plan was discussed to sell TOW antitank missiles to Iran in return for five American hostages held in Lebanon. The note read: "President [Reagan] decided to go with Israeli-Iranian offer to release our 5 hostages in return for sale of 4000 TOWs to Iran by Israel. . . . George Shultz [the secretary of state] + I opposed. . . . Bill Casey [director of the CIA], Ed Meese [the attorney general] + VP [Bush] favored as did [National Security Adviser John M.] Poindexter."

All through the long investigation of the affair, Bush had said he never realized the deal was a swap of arms for hostages, in contradiction of stated policy, until he learned the findings of a Senate intelligence committee investigation in December 1986 from Republican Senator David Durenberger of Minnesota, the committee chairman. Whenever the issue had come up in his 1988 presidential campaign, Bush insisted that he had answered the question of what he knew and when he knew it many times over. The issue was the subject of his celebrated confrontation with CBS News anchorman Dan Rather during the 1988 Iowa caucuses campaign, in which Bush aggressively stonewalled Rather and in the process did much to counter the so-called wimp image that critics had plastered on him.

Now, however, there appeared to be strong evidence that he knew what was going on long before he said he knew. In an appearance on the *Today* show earlier in the month, he had appeared to backtrack, saying he had known about the arms-for-hostages deal "and I've said so all along, given speeches on it." But when the new indictment came out, including the Weinberger note, White House counsel C. Boyden Gray reverted to Bush's original position, that he left the 1986 meeting considering the missile sales not an arms-for-hostages swap but a scheme for "creating an opening to Iran."

Both Clinton and Gore quickly jumped on the story as evidence that it was Bush, not Clinton, who had a "trust" problem. At an impromptu press conference in Pittsburgh, Clinton charged that the new evidence "not only directly contradicts the president's claims but also diminishes the credibility of the presidency." And Gore, in Bangor, Maine, not hesitant to draw a Watergate parallel, called Weinberger's note a "true smoking gun."

Back at the Bush headquarters, somebody handed Charlie Black the Associated Press story dated 2:34 P.M. about the new indictment. "I guess I didn't verbalize, 'Well, this race is over,' but I knew that was about it," he said later. "I took it home and laid it on my dresser . . . one memento of the campaign." He believed that Steeper's numbers were right and that there had, indeed, been a surge—until then.

Bush, on *Larry King Live* from Racine, Wisconsin, that night, insisted there was "nothing new" to the whole matter, and he used the same circumlocution that had served him well throughout the 1988 campaign—that he did not believe that Reagan ever regarded the arrangement as an arms-for-hostages swap. But that was not the question. The question was what Bush believed and knew, and on that he continued to evade.

Callers pummeled the president with questions, including one from Clinton spokesman Stephanopoulos, which Bush again brushed aside as old stuff, charging the Clinton campaign with "desperation last-minute politics when you feel something slipping away." This campaigning by talk show was getting ridiculous when the mouthpiece for one candidate could call in and grill the opposition candidate—especially when he was the president of the United States. But it made for great show biz.

If there was a feeling of something slipping away now, however, it was within the Bush camp, where others shared Black's reaction that the surge, which they were convinced was real, would be nipped by the resurrection of the old bothersome business of Iran-contra. Steeper had reported just the night before, Black said, that Bush was drawing even nationally, picking up a point or two nightly, and closing Clinton's lead to a few points in such key states as Ohio, Michigan and New Jersey. If the trend line continued at the same rate, Steeper projected, Bush would nudge ahead of him by Election Day.

Stan Greenberg, Clinton's pollster, sharply disagreed, however, that there ever was a surge in this last week of the sort Steeper claimed. On the Tuesday before the election, he said, his own polling saw a temporary drop to five percentage points as the Republican base began to come home to Bush, but nothing like the CNN/*USA Today* survey that suggested that the race was dead even. When Bush spent a full day in Ohio in the final week and seemed in the polling to turn the state around, ''we were scared to death,'' Stephanopoulos recalled. But the nervousness in Little Rock was relieved, he said, as Greenberg's polling shortly found Clinton back up at seven points and steady, where it basically remained, he said, through Election Day. ''Stan was like a great family doctor,'' Stephanopoulos said, telling the often pessimistic young aide and the excitable Carville about the talk of a Bush surge: ''You can say what you want. It's not moving.''

While the fat leads in major states like California and Illinois inevitably came down, reducing the national figures, Greenberg said, there was no danger of losing those states and the electoral vote picture stayed secure. Also, he noted, the Bush campaign was running unanswered television advertising in base Republican states, bringing some of that base home in the last week in states the Clinton campaign never counted on winning.

Steeper's projection of Bush's closing trend, Greenberg argued later, was fine as far as it went, but you couldn't assume that it would continue right through the election absent a negative development like the Weinberger indictment. A true surge, he said, would be the switching of voters from the opposition candidate or the movement of undecided voters, not merely the return of a base the candidate needed to be competitive. Steeper later acknowledged that "you can't assume that a trend will continue" indefinitely, but said his evidence was statistically solid that Bush had been reducing Clinton's lead "by a point a day," until the Weinberger indictment, hard on the heels of Perot's bizarre charges of Bush agents threatening wedding sabotage, killed off the surge.

The problem with the return of the Iran-contra issue, the Bush strategists realized, was not simply or even primarily that Bush would be disbelieved by voters. Rather, the injecting of the story was going to divert public attention from his message—the charge that Clinton could not be trusted with the presidency—and require spending precious time in the closing days on damage control.

"The last four nights," Black said, "two of them, instead of Clinton on defense, Bush on offense, [you had] Bush on defense, and reminding people of something, it wasn't new, but it reminded them of something they didn't like about Bush. It was all the news."

Carville, for his part, shrugged off the Weinberger indictment as a critical factor. " 'Bozos' and that crack about his dog Millie hurt more," he said. And Greenberg said that whatever took Bush off the message voters wanted to hear from him—how he would fix the economy—hurt him, even when he talked about Clinton and the draft or his trip to Moscow. "Once Bush was advancing the story rather than the press advancing the story, it made it political. Bush was not a credible presenter of that argument. Then once Bush took it over the line to the Moscow trip, [going too far by raising] the question of patriotism, he lost the press and lost the public. It just looked whacko."

It was now Saturday, October 31—Halloween—and the Bush campaign had hoped to chase the hobgoblins away with a day-long train trip on an old freight line from southeast to north-central Wisconsin, with all the trappings of an old-fashioned political whistletop. The scheduling was surprising to many in the press corps because Wisconsin, although clearly a state still up for grabs, had only eleven electoral votes and there were many larger states with more that might have commanded a full day of the president's fast-diminishing campaign time.

But Bush strategists reasoned that since their candidate could not afford to lose any battleground states, Wisconsin was as good a place to go as any, especially by train. The planners knew that there are few political events that are better magnets for news and television coverage than a whistlestop train ride, and they scheduled a stream of radio and television interviews by local stations with Bush along the 279-mile route.

"What we were finding this year more than usual," Black said later, "was that stops in the states weren't having that much impact. The half life on them was about two days only; it used to be about a week. So you're really gearing most of it to the news. And because of the change in the way everybody was handling their news, doing a lot of local TV interviews and Larry King and stuff like that, it was more important than doing an extra stop. The best press we got in the whole campaign was those train trips, so we made a calculated decision to do a train trip that Saturday, and there were only a certain number of places you could do them."

Furthermore, the Bush planners understood that an essential ingredient for an effective campaign day was an enthusiastic, upbeat candidate, and they knew that Bush drew strength and optimism from such events, to which big crowds were easy to attract. Even in the television era, small-town America still thrilled at the visit of a president, and the opportunity to bring children down to the depot for a piece of family history that would be long remembered.

The day dawned gray, overcast and windy at the flag-bedecked train station in Burlington, "Chocolate City, U.S.A.," named after a large plant there. A huge crowd packed in around the depot and the glistening Wisconsin Central engine, spit-polished to pull nineteen passenger cars including "The Baltimore," a custom private car at the end, along the long route to the last stop at Chippewa Falls. The mood was cheerful and expectant, despite the intrusion of a single-propeller plane overhead hauling a special message for Bush: IRAN-CONTRA HAUNTS YOU.

The president, suffering from a head cold but clearly buoyed by the turnout, started out using the holiday to accuse Clinton of a campaign of fear-mongering. "Today is Halloween, our opponents' favorite holiday," he said. "They're trying to scare America," he said, by trying to convince voters that the country was "a nation in decline," but the 2.7 percent gross domestic product increase proved otherwise. If Clinton was elected, he warned, "every day is going to be Halloween. Fright and terror!"

As the dark day wore on, Bush seemed to get progressively giddier, until, at Oshkosh, making the same reference, he shouted: "Fright and terror! Witches and devils everywhere!" At the same stop, he finally responded to the latest Iran-contra story, casting it as a desperate Clinton gambit. A "panicked" Clinton, he said, had begun "a series of personal attacks on my character, and he has basically called me a liar" regarding what Bush knew and when he knew it about the arms-for-hostages swap. Clinton, he said, "has now latched on to these silly little charges, accusations, in a desperate attempt to stop his free-fall in the polls," adding that "being attacked on character by Clinton is like being called ugly by a frog."

At Stevens Point, Bush said the latest charges were "part of a Democratic witch hunt," and that the only way Clinton could win was by finding "a last-minute smoking gun" where there was none. It happened that a member of the prosecutorial team that had pressed for the new Weinberger indictment was a Democrat and onetime Clinton contributor, leading some in the Bush entourage to conclude that the whole business was a partisan plot. But the fact remained that Walsh, who approved the seeking of the second indictment, was a Republican.

Nevertheless, inside the Bush campaign, a story circulated of a warning from a Democratic source that a bombshell was about to be dropped on Bush, fueling suspicions of foul play. David Tell, a young Republican in charge of opposition research for the Bush campaign, had become friends with his counterpart at the Democratic National Committee, Dan Carol, who incidentally had produced the T-shirts of Bush's travels that were such a success in 1991. In fact, on occasion the two opponents, Tell said later, swapped information they had on Ross Perot. They would call to tease each other about how the campaign was going, Tell said, and on the day before the Weinberger indictment broke, Carol told him he "had one last bomb to drop," without specifying what it was.

(After the election, Tell said, he phoned Carol to congratulate him on the outcome and asked him directly if the Weinberger indictment was the bomb to which he had referred and, Tell said later, "he did not say no." Carol said he remembered talking to Tell on Tuesday or Wednesday of the final week and being irritated by Tell's needling him about the purported surge. So, Carol said, he told Tell: "Listen, David, we're going to drop a bomb on you Friday, a big bomb." But, Carol insisted in the retelling, "I was completely bluffing." And when Tell called him about the election, Carol said, "I played cute. I said nothing to lead him otherwise." In fact, he told us, he had encountered resistance anytime he had tried to get even information from Walsh's office that was already on the public record.

("I know this," Black said later. "Lawyers and prosecutors in this town [Washington], and especially people who are high-profile like special prosecutors, are very politically sensitive, and very politically smart. I further know that everybody over there [in Walsh's office] is a liberal Democrat, and there were plenty of legal ways not to do that on the Friday before the election. I further believe that some Democrats around town knew on Thursday something big was coming. At least they were bragging about it. It was a hell of a coincidence."

(Black said he had heard about the Carol-Tell conversations. "It's not proof of anything," he said, "but I'd damn sure like to have some investigator put that guy [Carol] under oath and see what he has to say, and where he got it. I'm not accusing anybody of anything, except it's not possible that those Democratic prosecutors didn't fully calculate what they were doing politically. I'm not saying the Clinton people or the DNC were in on it. I don't know. And I'm not saying that alone cost us the race. The momentum might have been tailing off for some other reason or something, but we had a real good race going there.")

In responding to the Weinberger note and the Clinton comments during the Wisconsin whistlestop, the president sought to deflect the issue, but at the same time he was guaranteeing by his remarks that the story would have another day's life in the national news cycle. Fitzwater, standing next to the tracks at one stop in the late afternoon, was peppered with reporters' questions about the impact of the charges. The whole story, he replied, was "only" costing the campaign a day's time—one of the three remaining before election day.

For all that, Mary Matalin said later, the president "was having a whale of a time," as he always did on the train trips. He often sounded mean-spirited, again calling Clinton and Gore "bozos" but quickly apologizing as he remembered the caution from his aides. Then he would flash that somewhat sappy grin and start rambling in choppy Bushspeak—sentences starting with verbs that often went off into the ether.

But above all as a campaigner he understood what it meant to average

Americans to see a president of the United States—not just George Bush—in person, Matalin said, and he reveled in the shouted greetings, waves and other signs of affection along the way. At times he would stand on the rear platform, waving back as the train rolled by, and at others he would send greetings of his own over a public-address system, microphone in hand. When a radio reporter who had been shuttled into his car for a brief interview on the Wisconsin run commented to him about the crowds and asked how he felt about the turnout, Bush beamed and said: "Great! I've only been mooned once!"

The next day, the final Sunday, worse things happened to him. He endured a long CNN interview on which the Iran-contra matter came up again, and although he had said he didn't want to hear any more about polls and state-by-state electoral calculations, he was informed that he had dropped about five percentage points in his own polls in the wake of the Weinberger indictment. "He was cranky, doubly cranky," recalled Matalin.

At one point, when she gave him a sheet of paper with some numbers on it, he threw it across the table, saying, "I don't want to see them anymore." But he snapped out of it, she said, because "he really thought the polls were whacky." So did she, she said, because the election was coming down to a referendum on two men, "and we believed that when people went into the polling booth they would vote on that choice, and we had the superior candidate."

In these final days, Teeter said later, "he knew we were behind . . . we were moving, but we were never at a point where we were close to being ahead, but you didn't know what Perot would do, you had that wild card in there. We knew where we could get our most likely 270 [electoral votes], but we were behind in all of the key states. Our chances of making it were slim. . . . The problem was, we had to have an electoral miracle—we were in the worst of the inside-straight strategies. Not only you had to hit it, you even had to have some breaks. There was never a time where you really felt you ever got a break or a series of breaks that gave you an upper hand for a while."

Still, he said, Bush "was a guy who was working as hard as he could. He was smart enough to know that when you're behind there's only one thing to do—get yourself geared up and go out and campaign as hard as you can and hope it works, hope you get enough breaks or make some to get you going.''

Bush therefore doggedly pressed on, again trying to milk the draft issue against Clinton, this time with a charge that friends of the governor in Arkansas had destroyed his ROTC records, which the Clinton campaign promptly denied.

As a parting shot, Representative Guy Vander Jagt, defeated for reelection in an earlier Republican primary but finishing out his term as chairman of the National Republican Congressional Committee, held an election-eve news conference in Salt Lake City and charged that Clinton was having an affair with a wire-service reporter assigned to his campaign. The charge, also quickly denied, then was faxed to newspaper offices, one of the faxes arriving at the Washington Bureau of *The Baltimore Sun* around 10:30 that night, only shortly before voters in Dixville Notch, New Hampshire, were about to cast the nation's first presidential ballots in the village's quadrennial tradition.

Perot, back on the stump for one last swing that took him to Denver and Long Beach, California, finally turned his sights on Clinton. The target was somewhat surprising after Perot's almost single-minded focus on Bush, but the polls—which he vowed he never bothered with—were indicating that Clinton was the man to beat. Perot lit into him and Gore for acknowledging they had once smoked marijuana. ''Do you think the president of the United States and his wife should be good role models for your children?'' he asked his cheering supporters. ''Do you think it's appropriate to have senior government officials who have used drugs?'' The crowd shouted back: ''No!''

On a later half-hour paid television appearance, Perot used his charts and pointer to attack Clinton's record as governor in Arkansas. He charged that one in five jobs created in the state during Clinton's nearly twelve-year tenure had been in the poultry industry, adding that ''if we decide to take this level of business-creating capability nationwide, we'll all be plucking chickens for a living.'' Ever ready with the sound bites he disdained, Perot concluded: ''So I guess you can just sum it up: the chickens keep on clucking and the people keep on plucking after twelve years of Governor Clinton's leadership.''

Meanwhile, Clinton was sprinting to the finish through the industrial belt yet again, his voice so raspy that he winced as he croaked out a few words and then turned the microphone over to his wife. The man well remembered for the speech that never seemed to end at the 1988 Democratic convention spoke for only twenty-one seconds at a stop at a tailgate party outside Riverfront Stadium in Cincinnati, but he told the crowd: "We've fought for a year. We've got two days to go. Fight on!" Although the poll numbers were holding up, there was plenty of nervousness on the Clinton plane about what might yet happen, and it didn't escape the candidate. Paul Begala, as the end approached, told Dee Dee Myers: "I feel like a porcupine in a balloon factory."

The final day was a blur, as both Bush and Clinton raced frenetically by jet around the country, Clinton touching down in nine states in a thirty-hour nonstop marathon, Bush in six and Perot returning to Dallas for one final rally at which he danced with his youngest daughter, Katherine, to Patsy Cline's favorite—"Crazy." It was a fitting theme not simply for his off-again, on-again flirtation with the presidency and the American people, but also for the whole year of ups and downs, of scandalmongering and fearmongering. And it was played out before an electorate that had made clear its distaste for politics as usual, yet engaged itself in the dialogue through the phenomenon of talk-back television as never before.

On Election Day, this involvement manifested itself, after a thirty-two-year trend of steady decline in voter participation in the election of presidents, in an upturn at the polls—55.24 percent of the eligible voting age population, compared to 50.1 in 1988. The decision came early and was unambiguous, if not the blowout that had seemed in the making. Americans gave Bill Clinton 43 percent of their votes and 370 electoral votes in thirty-two states in every region of the country and the District of Columbia, to 38 percent and 168 electoral votes in the remaining eighteen states for Bush and a surprising 19 percent but no electoral votes for Perot.

A survey of 15,490 voters leaving their polling places, conducted by Voter Research and Surveys, a joint operation of the television networks, found a formidable coalition for Clinton. The Democratic nominee reversed the pattern of a generation and won among independent voters, garnering 38 percent of them to 32 for Bush and an impressive 30 for Perot. Clinton won among young voters ages eighteen to twenty-four—46 percent to 33 for Bush and 21 for Perot—who had flocked to Reagan and Bush in the three previous elections, as well as voters in all other age groups. And he won by two to one over Bush among Reagan Democrats, who had been a prime Clinton target for a year. Among first-time voters, it was Clinton 42 percent, Bush 32, Perot 22.

At the same time, the basic constituencies of Clinton's party held fast. Although the black turnout declined, Clinton captured 83 percent of the black vote to 10 for Bush and 7 for Perot. Among Jewish voters, he won 80 percent to 11 for Bush and 9 for Perot. And in the three-way race his 61 percent among Hispanics to 25 for Bush and 14 for Perot matched Dukakis's share of the same vote in a two-man contest four years earlier.

Bush's best showing was 53 percent among Southern white Protestants, who included many of the religious-right voters who had been so entranced by the emphasis on "family values" at the Republican convention. He was held to a virtual tie by Clinton among all white voters (Bush 40 percent, Clinton 39, Perot 20) and trailed him among men and women alike.

For all that, many said it was not much of a mandate for Clinton, only a plurality winner. Still, the overall message was clear enough: 62 percent of the voting American public wanted change from what George Bush had given them the previous four years. And this time they did not say so through the sort of apathy that had marked their turning away from the process since at least 1960. In larger numbers than ever before— 104,423,000—they stood up and were counted. The natural population growth could take part of the credit. But the bottom line was that something happened in 1992 that stirred more Americans to stop running from the political process, and start taking part in it.

CHAPTER 29

VOX POPULI

Why, after more than three decades of steadily increasing apathy and hostility toward the electoral process, did Americans in electing Bill Clinton and denying George Bush a second term post the largest percentage turnout since the election of John F. Kennedy?

Was it in large part simply because they became fed up with politics as usual and punished its most conspicuous practitioner? It was clear that they had had enough of gridlock in Washington, and Clinton as a Democrat offered the hope of working with the Democratic-controlled Congress. Voters wanted no more, either, of the kind of name-calling, personal slander, and negative radio and television advertising that by 1992 had threatened to smother all constructive political dialogue, yet continued to be employed by the Bush campaign. And for all the talk of shared responsibility between the executive and legislative branches in Washington, they continued to believe that the buck stopped where Harry Truman said it did—on the president's desk in the Oval Office, where Bush sat, his critics charged, idly.

Over those three decades since Kennedy's election, the public response to politics as usual had been quite the opposite of the increased turnout of 1992. More and more in those years, voters had shunned both of the great political parties and had opted out of the process, declining to make a choice that with each passing election was labeled the lesser of two evils. Wags reversed it. The evil of two lessers, they called the system that offered them what they saw either as inferior, inadequate choices or tweedledum and tweedledee.

That this disgruntled attitude was not by any means abandoned by the American public in 1992 can be seen in the fact that even the 55.24 percent turnout of the voting age population calculated by the Committee for the Study of the American Electorate for the presidential election paled in comparison with voter turnout in nearly all other Western democracies. The figure in its rawest terms meant that for every eligible voter who went to the polls, roughly one still stayed home. Nevertheless, the trend of recent elections *was* turned around, fueling hope that Americans as a whole saw something in the process or in the candidates that gave them reason for optimism.

Or was it more that their frustration had plunged so low by 1992 and their anger had grown so hot that, like people unable any longer to endure living under an oppressive yoke, they decided they had to take matters in their own hands? This motivation seemed much the more likely one. All of the nine more or less major candidates in the field had identifiable flaws or shortcomings in voters' eyes. Five Democrats—Wilder, Kerrey, Harkin, Tsongas and Brown—and one Republican—Buchanan—fell quickly by the wayside in the primary process, and the major party nominees—Clinton and Bush—survived bearing politically debilitating scars of the battle. The one major independent who did not face the primary voters—Perot—self-immolated at midcourse, only to resurrect himself in similarly scarred condition in the final month of the campaign.

If it was true that American voters were already "mad as hell" for several election cycles, what was it about 1992 that made so many of them decide that they were "not going to take it anymore," to the point of involving themselves in a political process they had shunned in those earlier election cycles?

For one thing, the world had changed in a dramatic fashion since the presidential election of 1988. The Cold War had ended, lifting the international climate of superpower confrontation and easing the threat of nuclear war in a truly significant way for the first time since the end of World War II. Americans were able to focus more of their attention on conditions at home and what their government in Washington was or wasn't doing to improve those conditions.

What they saw was economic decline that hit them not simply at the bottom rungs, with the poor and undereducated bearing the brunt as so often in past recessions. This time the blow was to the nation's solar plexus—the immense middle class that was the legacy of Franklin D. Roosevelt's New Deal, more recently wooed and won by Ronald Reagan—and in a more frightening manner.

Bob Teeter, in analyzing Bush's defeat, called it "a unique recession." Many white-collar, middle-income workers were being laid off or facing layoffs for the first time, Teeter noted, unlike blue-collar workers in the auto and other manufacturing industries who were accustomed to periodic layoffs and rehirings as the cycle of their businesses changed. "In most recessions where you have blue-collar guys laid off," he said, "almost everybody knew they were going to get called back in a couple of months, or six months, or sometime like that. And something like fifteen percent of the people in some worse recessions ended up losing their job and not getting their job back. In this one it was like forty percent who didn't, who were not going to get back to where they were.

"At the same time," he said, "you had real estate deflation, and people with a house that was worth less, and you had people with families who were educating their first generation. . . . So you had a family, the wife had worked, the husband had worked two jobs or something, they had sacrificed for twenty, twenty-five years . . . and the one way you were going to protect your kids from going through the stress and strain that you did was to get them a college education. Then the kids graduated from college and couldn't find a job." With the stories of "huge permanent layoffs" by General Motors, IBM and other giant corporations, Teeter said, "the apprehension and fear that spread way beyond the people who were actually looking for jobs" was what damaged Bush so severely.

Part of the problem was that the whole concept of restructuring of industries that came with the end of the Cold War threatened middle-aged workers with the prospect that the job they were doing would not be there much longer, or that if they were laid off, the job wouldn't be there when there was rehiring. Longer life expectancy confronted these middle-aged workers with greater need for health care insurance and no way to get it through continued employment, and no way to pay the high premiums on their own. And with this apprehension and fear came frustration at a stand-pat president and, in due course, anger.

Bush thought the whole matter of convincing voters that he understood and cared about how people were hurting economically, Jim Lake said afterward, "was election year rhetoric, so he couldn't make the sale. . . . It never was a part of him. He never got it." Teeter said Bush "did get it," but there was too much "disunity" among his economic team to decide on a clear and coherent path to follow.

It was in the context of this inability to address the nation's domestic ills effectively that another Bush insider observed that Bush's success in mobilizing the alliance that drove Saddam Hussein out of Kuwait proved in the end to hurt him politically, by setting "a new standard of performance" for him—"if he could do that, he could fix other problems if he applied himself." And by election time, it was all too clear to these potential voters that Bush was not fixing such problems at home, and couldn't be counted on to do so in a second term. Had the Cold War still been on, Bush White House aide Jim Pinkerton said, the president still would have been able to run on his foreign policy experience. But its end, and then the end of the Gulf War, moved the nation's focus, and inevitably the campaign debate, homeward.

Among staunch old Reaganites, there was a sense that the Reagan Revolution in Bush's hands was already over, with no sense of what would replace it, even if Bush were reelected. By contrast, Clinton offered a clear concept of basic change. As campaign manager David Wilhelm put it after the election, "it was the end of trickle-down economics, it was an economic agenda of putting people first, as we called it. That was a big idea, and unlike 1988 where at the conclusion of the campaign people woke up and said, 'Hey, what was *that* all about?' In 1992, people woke up and said, 'Well, I think I know what that was about.' The Reagan era was over, to the extent that Bush represented the third term of the Reagan era. A new economic philosophy had replaced it, and the election capsulized that, and that was understood . . . by the voter."

In attempting to finesse the economy as the central cause of voter apprehension, frustration, fear and anger by diverting attention to the question of Clinton's character and trustworthiness, the Bush campaign badly miscalculated. The sorts of scare issues that had worked for Bush against Michael Dukakis in 1988, in much better economic times, did not have the same effect against Clinton among voters more concerned about jobs than about such things as pollution in Boston Harbor or some new Willie Horton—or Gennifer Flowers.

Mandy Grunwald put it this way: "There was something unusual about this year that made it possible not to have Gennifer Flowers kill Clinton's candidacy, not to have the draft kill Clinton's candidacy. And that was just how scared people were about the fate of the country. People were engaged in the election in a completely different way than they were in '88 or '84, because the issues were so big and so prescient. It's an odd way to think about it, but there are a lot of issues that I consider 'luxury issues.' I think Boston Harbor and Willie Horton are 'luxury issues.' I think Gennifer Flowers is a 'luxury issue.'

"I mean 'luxury' in the sense that if you can put food on your table and pay your health care bills, and you [aren't] worried about whether you have a job, then you have the luxury to think about whether or not Michael Dukakis furloughed some guy and you can think about whether this guy [Clinton] dodged the draft twenty-three years ago. What was so unusual about this year was that people didn't have that luxury. And they had a very clear sense of how big the problems were, and they were really single-minded about keeping focus on those problems, because it mattered deeply to their lives what the state of the election was. I think that fundamental fact influenced everything, from the viewership of debates . . . to the dismissing of issues like the draft or his [Clinton's] trip to Moscow or any of that."

Charlie Black acknowledged after the election that the Bush campaign in going after Clinton on character and trust had counted on the voters to respond as they had in 1988 to the negative information on the Democratic nominee used against him. "The thing that surprised me about Clinton," he said, "was that he had more Teflon on those things— the lying, flip-flopping, the draft. The guy carried veterans [on Election Day]. I would have been shocked if you told me back in August, 'Hey, this all sounds good [about the Bush attack strategy on the draft issue], but Clinton's going to carry a plurality of veterans.' I would have said,

'Shit, I've got to rethink this whole race,' because I knew we'd play the draft thing.''

The Bush campaign, Black said, tested voter reaction to Clinton's use of the phrase "loathing the military" in his letter to Colonel Holmes, "all kinds of different things. Part of it was public opinion [about the Vietnam War], part of it was he did a pretty good job of spinning it around to, 'Hey, the issue was whether I was for or against the war.' The real issue about the draft was lying. We got that out through the *Time* ad and the other things we did, did get a bunch of people believing he was lying about it. But in the end that didn't matter much to them. We couldn't make it as salient as the economy. That's what it came down to.''

In this context, the Clinton campaign's constant reminder to the country that Bush was again "going negative" as he did against Dukakis in 1988—a reminder reinforced by the news media—instead of talking about the economic plight of people reinforced the notion that the voters didn't have the luxury to dwell on political mud-slinging.

"But you have to understand," Grunwald said. "They reminded *us*. You couldn't go to focus groups much without people using Willie Horton as a frame of reference. And one of the hangovers that I think all of us who've worked in Democratic statewide campaigns since '88 have seen— ask any pollster or media consultant—is that the topic of negative advertising has been a big topic for people. They felt manipulated by Willie Horton—burned by that experience—and they vowed it wasn't going to happen again. They weren't going to be fooled again. They were going to keep their eye on the prize.''

There were other "luxury issues" not mentioned by Grunwald that voters wouldn't or couldn't afford to buy that the Bush campaign tried unsuccessfully to peddle—"family values" and abortion, as best illustrated in Dan Quayle's jab at Murphy Brown and later the whole Hollywood "cultural elite." In better economic times—through most of the Reagan years and Bush's first two—these issues were or would have been golden, nurtured as they were by the Republican right wing.

In one of the great ironies of the 1992 campaign, Bush was obliged to invoke these and other "values" issues repeatedly in his long effort to appease his party's right wing after he had "betrayed" it in breaking his no-new-taxes pledge. That effort not only failed to stem conservative disillusionment with him but also led to a Republican national convention that showcased the party in its least attractive posture—a captive of narrowness, bitterness and exclusivity. Bush needed at that convention to tell voters what he would do to help them. Instead, they heard repackaged old ideas from him and encouragements to division from others, and the voters didn't have the luxury of casting their presidential ballots on the basis of either of them.

Added to this mix was the combustible Ross Perot—a match on dry tinder. He was in a real sense the embodiment of the American voter who was fed up with politics as usual and who felt he did not have the luxury of keeping his mouth shut any longer, or of paying attention to all the personal mud-slinging and diversions from the central issue. That issue, Perot said over and over again, was digging the country out of its economic mess, by taking national power from those who were abusing or squandering it, and giving it back to the people—"the owners" of the country.

Perot sought to mobilize all the apprehension, frustration, fear and anger in the country through the force of his own rather quirky personality and immense wealth, and fashion it into an effective political tool. His effort, though failed, was remarkable considering his inexperience in politics and the dismal history of third-party politics in America. There is no doubt it contributed greatly to shaking the political lethargy and apathy that had captured the country for so long, and to bringing about the demise of the Bush presidency, which he obviously so despised.

In Perot's undertaking, and in Clinton's ability to keep his own focus on the economy in the face of the assault on his character and trustworthiness, another new dimension in presidential politics played a key role. Talk show television to an unprecedented degree enabled the candidates, eventually including Bush as well, to tap directly in to the voters' frustration over having lost an effective voice in the political decisions that affected their lives, and to give it an outlet.

Perot, Clinton and Bush were asked by average voters on the air, and they answered, hundreds of questions, only a handful of which were of a personal nature, or of the "horse race" variety favored by political reporters and hated by most candidates. While a great many were softballs the candidates had heard many times and could knock out of the park with ease, many also went to the heart of the voters' deep concerns about the state of the country, and their own futures in it. Oftentimes the questions were not as smooth as they might have been coming from a professional interviewer or interrogator, but they often were more directly and personally tied to a voter's feelings, and sought to elicit the same kind of response from the candidates. The second presidential debate in Richmond, in the town-meeting or talk show format, was appropriately typical of what such linking of candidate with voter could reveal. When Marisa Hall asked Bush how the "national debt" affected him personally, and he replied that he was "not sure I get" the gist of the question, he left the impression that he simply did not comprehend how public policy affected the lives of average Americans. Clinton stepped forward and did, with his response about the problems of people in Arkansas he knew personally.

After the election, Clinton talked about the impact of greater direct voter involvement in the process. In pressing for the town-meeting format in which voters expressed their displeasure with politics as usual, he said, "I just had this instinctive feeling that this was an election that was terribly important to people and they wanted to lift it up, and sure enough that's what they did. There was a huge turnout, and I think all the stuff we did [to involve voters more directly], I hope we can keep it going."

Larry King, whose CNN call-in show became a regular stopping place on the campaign trail for all three candidates, naturally reveled in the phenomenon, but also underscored its significance to the process. "I think we've never had a year when we knew the candidates better than this year," he said after the election. "I don't think there could have been anybody saying, 'I don't know Bill Clinton' or 'I don't know George Bush' or 'I don't know Ross Perot' by the time they went to vote.

"What showed me the success of it was the audience that the debates had. I think this became a human-interest saga in which these three people and the vice presidential candidates were more than just an election. They were a television series about to end, on November third. It was like the last night of *Cheers*. These guys were going to go away . . . and the public had gotten so absorbed with them that by the time of the debates everyone was watching for something to happen . . . to see the energy."

Also, King noted, it is not so easy for a candidate to slough off a voter who calls in as it is to put aside or put down a celebrity interviewer. "When someone says [on the air], 'I'm out of work, what are you gonna do for me?' it gives a totally different perspective," King said, "than

Larry King or Dan Rather saying, 'What about the people out of work?' You are now hearing a human being out of work talking to a man who can affect his getting work. You can't beat that.''

King predicted that most of the best-known talk shows before long will be taking phone calls as a result of what happened in the 1992 campaign. "The public has become part of the story [of the campaign], and that can't change. It's like showing freedom in the Soviet Union. . . . It is vox populi. It doesn't matter that only twelve calls get in. What does matter is, is you feel, 'I could call this guy.' '' (In fact, King's show became a direct line of communication between the campaigns. Republican Party chairman Rich Bond called in to ask Perot to come up with evidence to back his charges of Republican smears; George Stephanopoulos called Bush to tweak him about Iran-contra at the time of the second Weinberger indictment.)

It seemed at times that the whole campaign was taking place on the nation's television screens, but there was nothing new in that. What was new, was the voice of the people speaking out loud and clear, calling directly for answers, over the news medium that had come to dominate presidential campaigns as it had come to dominate the social and cultural life of the country.

As a practical matter, only a handful of Americans actually were able to talk directly to the candidates. But the significant difference to the voters was, as King pointed out, that people just like themselves were questioning the candidates—were in effect surrogates for the average voter. Watching Clinton, Bush and Perot in that Richmond debate, anyone could imagine being the one asking the questions and influencing the process directly. It was no longer the sole province of journalists, whom they saw as part of the distant establishment rather than as their agents.

All these voices, for the first time since the end of World War II and the start of the Cold War, were talking almost exclusively in 1992 about the condition of life on Main Street, U.S.A. They had been quiet long enough. They had turned their backs on the political process long enough. They demanded to be heard—through Ross Perot's ballot petition drive, through Bill Clinton's town meetings, even through the "Ask George Bush" sessions, and through whatever electronic means were available to them. They demanded change, and on November 3, 1992, they forced it—from winter, in Clinton's Inaugural Address words, they "forced the spring."

In many ways, the election of 1992 was a confirmation of the findings of a study in June 1991 for the Kettering Foundation called *Citizens and Politics: A View from Main Street America*. It concluded that Americans, far from being apathetic to the political process, "do care about politics, but they no longer believe they can have an effect." They think, the study went on, "many of the avenues for expressing their views are window dressings, not serious attempts to hear the public," and they "want to know their concerns are understood." These conclusions provide clues to why, with the reach-out candidacies of Clinton and Perot, voter turnout increased in 1992, and why Bush's failure to connect with voter concerns was at the core of his defeat.

The Kettering Foundation study also concluded that Americans "want an ongoing relationship, especially in between elections, in which there is 'straight talk' and give-and-take between public officials and citizens." Almost from the moment William Jefferson Clinton took the oath as the forty-second president of the United States on the West Front steps of the Capitol, he set out to give them that relationship. He resumed the conversation with the American voters that had been a major factor in his election, and in the immediate weeks thereafter, he continued it as he strove aggressively to rally them behind the agenda for change that he had promised them during the campaign.

That agenda was, to be sure, considerably curtailed once Clinton faced the budgetary realities that were waiting for him when he entered the Oval Office. But as he went on television and in person around the country to enlist the people's support, he seemed to treat the presidency he had just assumed as a sort of extension of his successful campaign of going directly to the voters.

Before he held a single formal news conference as president to field questions from the experienced White House press corps, Clinton went to Detroit for a nationally televised "town meeting" with callers from Atlanta, Miami and Seattle linked up by satellite. A few days later, he met with a select group of children, carefully chosen, to take their questions for more than ninety minutes—again on television. And in between he climbed aboard Air Force One for trips to the Midwest and the West

Coast, playing the role of chief salesman for his economic proposals, going right to America's doorstep.

In doing all this, notably, he adopted not only the deficit-cutting emphasis of that other super-salesman, Ross Perot, in his homespun 1992 romance with the "owners" of the country, but his jargon as well. In his Inaugural Address, Clinton cautioned his fellow public servants not to forget "those people whose toil and sweat sends us here and pays our way," and in his enthusiasm he told the voters: "You have raised your voices in an unmistakable chorus, you have cast your votes in historic numbers, and you have changed the face of Congress, the presidency and the political process itself."

In his State of the Union speech, too, Clinton reminded the members of Congress assembled before him that they were the taxpayers' "hired hands" and that "every penny we draw" was "their money." Republicans talked about corraling the Perot voters in advance of 1996; Clinton set out from day one of his White House tenure to do so.

The jury was still out, however, on the new president's contention that the political process had truly been changed. Yet to be determined was whether this bear-hug embrace of the electorate—this new talk show presidency—could be sustained by its creator. Beyond that, the question was whether it could win over not only those mad-as-hell voters who gave the political process one more chance in 1992, but also the millions of Americans still turned away from it. After more than three decades of growing voter alienation, it was now in Bill Clinton's hands to convince them that the great American experiment was still worth the candle.

INDEX

DATE DUE

FEB 13 1998	

GAYLORD   PRINTED IN U.S.A.

Tables and figures

Contributors

Monica Briscoe, Lecturer, General Practice Research Unit, Institute of Psychiatry, London

William Bynum, Assistant Director, Wellcome Institute for the History of Medicine, London

Tai-Ann Cheng, Associate Professor of Psychiatry, National Taiwan University Hospital, Taipei

Anthony Clare, Professor of Psychological Medicine, St Bartholomew's Hospital Medical College, London

Brian Cooper, Professor of Epidemiological Psychiatry, Zentralinstitut für Zeelischegesundheit, Mannheim

Roslyn Corney, Senior Lecturer, General Practice Research Unit, Institute of Psychiatry, London

Graham Dunn, Senior Lecturer, Biometrics Unit, Institute of Psychiatry, London

Robin Eastwood, Professor of Psychiatry, Departments of Psychiatry, Preventive Medicine & Biostatistics, University of Toronto, Clark Institute of Psychiatry, Toronto

Leon Eisenberg, Presley Professor of Social Medicine & Professor of Psychiatry, Harvard Medical School, Boston

Ian Falloon, Consultant Physician (Mental Health), Buckingham Mental Health Service, Buckingham

Jonathan Gabe, Lecturer in Sociology, General Practice Research Unit, Institute of Psychiatry, London

Eric Glover, Senior Programmer/Analyst, Biometrics Unit, Institute of Psychiatry, London

David Goldberg, Professor of Psychiatry, The University Hospital of South Manchester, Manchester

David Hand, Professor of Statistics, The Open University, Milton Keynes

Assen Jablensky, Director, WHO Collaborating Centre for Mental Health, Medical Academy, Sofia

Rachel Jenkins, Principal Medical Officer, Mental Health Division, Department of Health & Social Security, London

Michael King, Senior Lecturer, General Practice Research Unit, Institute of Psychiatry, London

Gerald Klerman, Professor of Psychiatry, Department of Psychiatry, Cornell University Medical College, Westchester Division, White Plains, New York

Morton Kramer, Professor Emeritus, School of Hygiene & Public Health, Department of Mental Hygiene, The Johns Hopkins University, Baltimore

xii

Malcolm Lader, Professor of Psychopharmacology, Institute of Psychiatry, London

Annette Lawson, Institute of Human Development, University of California, Berkeley, Berkeley

Glyn Lewis, Research Worker, General Practice Research Unit, Institute of Psychiatry, London

Michael MacDonald, Professor of History, Department of History, University of Michigan, Ann Arbor

Anthony Mann, Professor of Psychiatry, Royal Free Hospital School of Medicine, London

Jair Mari, Associate Professor, Department of Social Medicine, Santa Casa de Sao Paulo, Sao Paulo

David Morrell, Professor of General Practice, Division of General Practice, United Medical & Dental Schools of Guy's & St. Thomas's Hospitals, London

Joanna Murray, Research Worker, General Practice Research Unit, Institute of Psychiatry, London

Anthony Pelosi, Research Worker, General Practice Research Unit, Institute of Psychiatry, London

Kenneth Rawnsley, Past President, Royal College of Psychiatrists, Emeritus Professor of Psychological Medicine, University of Wales College of Medicine, Cardiff

Darrel Regier, Director, Division of Clinical Research, National Institute for Mental Health, Alcohol, Drug Abuse, and Mental Health Administration, Rockville

Geoffrey Rose, Professor of Epidemiology, London School of Hygiene and Tropical Medicine, London

Gerald Russell, Professor of Psychiatry, Institute of Psychiatry, London

Norman Sartorius, Director, Division of Mental Health, World Health Organization, Switzerland

Biswajit Sen, Girindrasekhar Clinic, Calcutta

Deborah Sharp, Lecturer, Division of General Practice, United Medical & Dental Schools of Guy's & St. Thomas's Hospitals, London

David Skuse, Wellcome Trust Senior Lecturer, Department of Child Psychiatry, Institute of Child Health, London

Nigel Smeeton, Lecturer, General Practice Research Unit, Institute of Psychiatry, London

Jean Starobinski, Professor of the History of Ideas, Faculté des Lettres, University of Geneva, Geneva

Geraldine Strathdee, Research Worker, General Practice Research Unit, Institute of Psychiatry, London

Erik Strömgren, Professor of Psychiatry, Institute of Psychiatric Demography, Psychiatric Hospital, Risskov

Michele Tansella, Professor of Psychological Medicine, Cattedra di Psicologia Medica, Istituto di Psichiatria, Policlinico Borgo Roma, Verona

David Watt, Honorary Consultant Psychiatrist, Department of Medical Genetics, The Churchill Hospital, Oxford

Myrna Weissman, Professor of Epidemiology in Psychiatry, College of Physicians and Surgeons of Columbia University, New York

Greg Wilkinson, Senior Lecturer, General Practice Research Unit, Institute of Psychiatry, London

Paul Williams, Honorary Senior Lecturer, General Practice Research Unit, Institute of Psychiatry, London

John Wing, Professor of Social Psychiatry, M.R.C. Social Psychiatry Unit, Institute of Psychiatry, London

Foreword 1

The production of a Festschrift to signal the retirement of Professor Michael Shepherd is a felicitous way of honouring a renowned teacher. Close colleagues and students have come forward to describe their personal researches, selecting topics which reflect Michael Shepherd's influence on their work and thinking. Most of the contributors have been associated closely with him in the Institute of Psychiatry; they are drawn from a conspicuously wide range of scientific disciplines, medical and non-medical, which bear on the far-reaching applications of epidemiological methods to mental health problems. Other contributors have also collaborated fruitfully with Michael Shepherd and share his predilection for epidemiological studies. For a few the association has been more transient; their contributions are all the more significant as they reflect distinctive and independent viewpoints and ideas which nevertheless show striking consistencies with Michael Shepherd's scientific approach to psychiatry.

This book reminds me of another Festschrift, written some twenty years ago by grateful students and colleagues of Sir Aubrey Lewis on his retirement, in recognition of the unique way he had shaped British psychiatry.[1] The editors were Michael Shepherd and David L. Davies, both ardent admirers of Aubrey Lewis. We shall indeed appreciate better Michael Shepherd's view of psychiatry and psychiatrists if we recall the very high affection and regard in which he held Aubrey Lewis. It was quite natural that he should model himself on his mentor, even though they differed so much in their temperaments and backgrounds. Michael Shepherd has honoured Lewis's memory in several addresses and publications,[2] notably in his 1976 Adolf Meyer Lecture[3] and the paper he read, also in 1976, at the Aubrey Lewis Memorial Meeting of the Royal College of Psychiatrists.[4] There we have recorded Michael Shepherd's analysis of the personal and intellectual qualities of Aubrey Lewis, which made him the principal architect of British psychiatry at a time when it was first developing into a scientifically credible discipline. A comparison of the attributes of these two teachers is inescapable. Both were gifted with qualities of erudition and creative scepticism, often displayed with brilliance. Professionally they shared an eclectic approach tied to a multidimensional view of the causation of mental illness. In consequence, it was hardly surprising that the discipline of social psychiatry received a new impetus which was to set the scene for vigorous growth and expansion. As teachers they both exploited the Socratic method of conducting an argument as an effective device for imparting information and, beyond this, setting the limits of knowledge. Their scepticism – always rigorous but more a stimulant than a destructive force – led them to question the claims of uncritical enthusiasts, whether in the field of psychotherapy or

1

in treatment with drugs. For them questioning was not a clogging weakness, and they seldom failed 'to pick up and examine the little hedgehogs of doubt that sit by the therapist's path'.[5]

Michael Shepherd obtained his medical training at Oxford University Medical School and the Radcliffe Infirmary. In 1952, after house appointments and national service in the RAF, he joined the staff of the Maudsley Hospital. He has remained there ever since, apart from a one-year attachment to the School of Public Health at Johns Hopkins University, Baltimore, from where he completed a wide-ranging survey of American psychiatry. From reading the Festschrift to Aubrey Lewis it may indeed be argued that during the 1950s and 1960s the Maudsley was unrivalled in providing the best stimulation and environment for a psychiatrist eager to advance his subject, and there was little point in going elsewhere. In 1967 Michael Shepherd was appointed Professor of Epidemiological Psychiatry, the subject which he had done so much to establish at the Institute and which would alter, expand, and extend at the hands of increasing numbers of research students so that his imprint is now clearly visible in several departments of psychiatry in Britain and abroad. He holds a very broad view of the subject matter of epidemiology. In addition to the older recognized spheres of concern – the search for causal factors and the completion of the spectrum of disease – it embraces the establishment of outcome and the evaluation of the efficacy of treatment, including applications of the controlled clinical trial.[6,7] The last are usually viewed as the preserves of the clinical psychiatrists. But for Michael Shepherd such lines of division are artificial: he has argued convincingly that the store of knowledge on which clinical practice relies can be enlarged and given precision by contributions from the whole field of epidemiology. The signs of this breadth of outlook were evident in his earlier researches,[8] including his personal contributions to the clarification of morbid jealousy and clinical trials of neuroleptics. They were followed by a seminal international study of observer variations in psychiatric diagnosis. His awareness of the pitfalls of hospital-based studies led him to question cogently the value of psychiatric classifications based on hospital cases. In recent years he discovered the value of psychiatric research in the more representative population of patients who consult their general practitioners. This approach culminated in his establishing the General Practice Research Unit within the Department of Psychiatry in the Institute. This Festschrift happily reflects Michael Shepherd's breadth of outlook through its wide-ranging contributions. It also supports his dictum that 'In no branch of Medicine is epidemiology needed more than in psychiatry'.[6]

The appearance of this Festschrift also provides an apt illustration of Michael Shepherd's personal influence on the numerous contributors who, irrespective of their current professional seniority, began their research careers as trainees under his supervision. His standing as a teacher is indelibly established. He excels in the set-piece lecture, when he presents carefully honed ideas in an entertaining style: hence the frequency with which he is invited to deliver named lectures and keynote addresses. To colleagues within the Institute of Psychiatry and the Maudsley Hospital, his reputation as an outstanding teacher is based on a number of assessments. Foremost is his ability to attract within his fold young men and women eager to benefit from the intellectual stimulation obtained from contact with a man of ideas who will set them on a secure path of research. Generations of registrars at the Maudsley, attached to his clinical unit, have learned from him the complexities inherent in the assessment of psychiatric patients, the avoidance of glib diagnostic labels, and the moulding effects of personality and social background in determining not only the content but also, at times, the form of psychiatric illness.

Any appreciation of Michael Shepherd's achievements as an educator would be incomplete without acknowledging his success as foundation editor of *Psychological Medicine*, a journal internationally recognized for its high scientific standards and the quality of its articles. In more recent years this journal has further increased its impact through the linked publication of a series of monographs and the ambitious *Handbook of Psychiatry* in five volumes.

The epidemiological method tends to emphasize the study of groups of patients rather than the individual. I have called attention to Michael Shepherd's impressive gifts in assessing the individual patient and his qualities as a clinician. Lest anyone should believe these are overshadowed by his scientific excellence, I wish to quote from an autobiography of a gifted author who recounted her experiences as a patient at the Maudsley. She used a pseudonym, not hard to decipher in the light of her liking for French poetry. She describes her first meeting with her psychiatrist:

> Dr Berger, a tall dark pale man, with a chillingly superior glance and quellingly English voice, made another appointment to see me. Feelings of past unpleasantness and fear had been aroused in me by this visit to a psychiatrist: attracting his attention and observing his serious face had reduced my store of confidence. I knew, however, that if anyone could discover the 'truth' it would be he, alone or with his colleagues.[9]

On behalf of all his colleagues at the Institute and the Maudsley, I wish Michael a prosperous retirement and many years of creative activity. I am confident that he will continue to enrich psychiatry.

Gerald Russell

NOTES

1. Shepherd, M. and Davies, D.L. (eds) (1968) *Studies in Psychiatry*, London: Oxford University Press.

2. Shepherd, M. (1975) 'In Memoriam: Aubrey Lewis (1900–1975)', *American Journal of Psychiatry* 132 (8): 872.

3. Shepherd, M. (1977) 'A representative psychiatrist: the career and contributions of Sir Aubrey Lewis', *American Journal of Psychiatry* 134 (1): 7–13.

4. Shepherd, M. (1977) 'Aubrey Lewis: the makings of a psychiatrist', *British Journal of Psychiatry* 131: 238–42.

5. Lewis, A.J. (1958) 'Between guesswork and certainty in psychiatry', *Lancet* i: 171–5 and 227–30.

6. Shepherd, M. (1978) 'Epidemiology and clinical psychiatry', *British Journal of Psychiatry* 133: 289–98.

7. Shepherd, M. (1984) 'Editorial: the contribution of epidemiology to clinical psychiatry', *American Journal of Psychiatry* 141 (12): 1574–5.

8. Shepherd, M. (1969) 'Research in the field of psychiatry', *British Medical Journal* 4: 161–3.

9. Frame, J. (1985) *The Envoy from Mirror City: Autobiography 3*, London: The Women's Press, p. 99.

Foreword 2

For many a foreigner, Michael Shepherd is the perfect example of an Englishman. On the other hand, some of my English friends disagree and even see him as faintly foreign in his manner and speech. He is at home in many lands: when he first came to Yugoslavia he introduced me to artists I had never met before, although they were in and from the town in which I grew up and lived. Not only are his students spread all over the globe, but the remarkable width of his interests has brought him to places and people whom others of our profession rarely meet.

But even in places which he has not visited, his work has left indelible traces. They are particularly visible in three of his areas of interest, all essential to the development of psychiatry and of health care in general. These are: the area of mental disorder in general practice; the improvement of psychiatric diagnosis and classification; and the publication of matters of interest to psychiatry. In the first of these his work has helped to transform the education of general practitioners and to give priority to mental health programmes in many parts of the world; in the second it has helped to make psychiatry a more respectable discipline; and in the third (in particular with the appearance – now seventeen years ago – of *Psychological Medicine*, which he edits with so much brio and rigorous scientific attention), it has set a new standard in writing about psychiatric issues.

There are many things which could be admired in Professor Shepherd – his erudition, scientific acumen, and sense of humour, for example. Yet, if I was to search for the one which had most impact on his students, I would select his keen critical sense. It is not a tool which he has to apply with effort: its use comes easily. He has an ear for disharmony in science, clinical work, and health policy. The many foreign students who came to work under his supervision were not only trained in psychiatry – they were also offered an opportunity to learn how to think critically, with sound scepsis and reasoned caution. Years later, when most other knowledge gained in the course has become obsolete or forgotten, the Shepherdian stamp of critical and salutary scepticism is still present in all his old students, immediately recognizable and infinitely useful.

Contemporaries, students, and present-day younger collaborators have been invited to contribute to this volume. Most of them are British, a few are American, and a few are from other countries. There is no doubt that the papers assembled are as good as anyone in this field of endeavour could hope for. Other books may follow: however important this Festschrift may be, it is only one event in the stream of publications which have been, in one way or another, stimulated by Professor Shepherd and which will be appearing in different languages and different lands for many years to come.

Norman Sartorius

5

General introduction

Professor Michael Shepherd retired from the chair of Epidemiological Psychiatry at the Institute of Psychiatry (University of London) in September 1988. The impact of his work has led to a wide recognition of his enormous contribution to, and influence on, psychiatry. We thought it appropriate, therefore, to mark the occasion of his retirement by a work of academic scholarship.

While Michael Shepherd's work has spanned many areas of psychiatry, it is perhaps in the field of epidemiological and social psychiatry that his contribution has been greatest. The study of mental illness requires a wide variety of approaches, and the epidemiological approach is one of the most important. While it is concerned with definition, classification, aetiology, natural history, as well as the treatment and outcome of disease, the essential attribute of epidemiology is that it addresses the problem of disease in the context of the community as a whole. Thus, at a time when the trend in psychiatry is away from hospital treatment and towards care in the community, the epidemiological investigation of mental illness is increasingly important. We have, therefore, attempted to bring together theoretical considerations, scientific studies, and service evaluations.

The book is divided into five sections. The first is concerned with the scientific principles which underpin, and are a necessary 'tool-kit' for, investigations in epidemiological and social psychiatry, while the second is divided into three subsections, each of which is concerned with a particular area of enquiry within the general field. These areas of enquiry are taken from the 'Uses of Epidemiology' described by Jeremy Morris, and serve to emphasize the link between epidemiological psychiatry and medical epidemiology, while the content of each of the sections exemplifies the close relationship between scientific enquiry and clinical psychiatry.

The third section is concerned with the evaluation of psychiatric intervention, and is divided into subsections which focus respectively on the organization of services and the evaluation of specific treatments.

Although the contributors to the first three sections are drawn from many countries, the fourth section is specifically concerned with epidemiological and social psychiatric perspectives from an international point of view, while the fifth and final section is an overview which assesses the contribution of Michael Shepherd to the subjects under discussion.

The authors can be regarded as falling into three groups. First, there is a group of eminent investigators who, while perhaps not having worked directly with Michael Shepherd at the Institute of Psychiatry, have been closely associated with him in other ways. Second, there is a group who have worked under his supervision in the past and who have now themselves

6

attained positions of seniority, while the third group consists of younger workers who are currently members of, or are closely associated with, the General Practice Research Unit at the Institute of Psychiatry.

In structuring this book and commissioning the authors, we kept very much in mind the idea that this Festschrift should be a substantial addition to the literature in its own right, rather than a collection of reminiscences or personal statements. We believe we have achieved this: we hope that Michael Shepherd would agree, and that he would regard the contributions as fine examples of the scientific approach to psychiatry that he has striven to develop, to advocate, and to teach.

Paul Williams
Greg Wilkinson
Kenneth Rawnsley

Section One

The Scientific Principles of Epidemiological and Social Enquiry in Psychiatry

Introduction

We have categorized the scientific principles which underpin epidemiological and social psychiatry into three groups. The first subsection deals with historical origins. While case definition is of considerable current concern to psychiatric epidemiologists, Jean Starobinski describes how the definition of 'madness' was a source of debate well over 2,000 years ago. He also demonstrates the emphasis given by Hippocrates to 'arithmetic' in medicine. In the subsequent chapter, William Bynum describes the Victorian origins of psychiatric epidemiology.

The second subsection consists of three papers on the social sciences. As early as 1879, Henry Maudsley acknowledged that it was 'proper to emphasise the fact that insanity is really a social phenomenon, and to insist that it cannot be investigated satisfactorily and apprehended rightly except it be studied from a social point of view' (Maudsley 1879: vi).

One of the most influential figures in establishing the social scientific basis of psychiatry was Sir Aubrey Lewis (Shepherd 1980). Lewis's first research project was an anthropological study of the aborigines of South Australia: it is not inappropriate, therefore, that Annette Lawson discusses sociology and socio-anthropology in the first chapter in this subsection.

In contrast to the collectivist nature of these disciplines, psychology is essentially individualistic. It is perhaps for this reason that its contribution to social and epidemiological psychiatry has been relatively neglected, an omission which is remedied by Monica Briscoe in the subsequent chapter.

The increasing awareness that resources are not limitless has given rise to heightened interest in the economic evaluation of mental health care. Thus, Greg Wilkinson and Anthony Pelosi provide an overview of the principles and techniques of economic appraisal.

Sir Francis Galton observed that 'until the phenomena of any branch of knowledge have been submitted to measurement and number, it cannot assume the status and dignity of science'. Quantitative methods form the basis of virtually all investigations in epidemiological psychiatry: these are the topic of the third subsection. Geoffrey Rose discusses the need to adopt a population-based strategy, while Morton Kramer draws on administrative mental health statistics to illustrate the biostatistical approach. The value of fully utilizing such data in psychiatry was emphasized by Sir Aubrey Lewis over forty years ago, when he observed that 'so far as psychiatry is conceived as a branch of social medicine and public health, it must rely for its advancement upon methods which require accurate statistics such as it is the business of official intelligence to supply' (Lewis 1945: 492).

As Shepherd has noted, administrative statistics have been utilized in psychiatry since the nineteenth century. He commented further that 'the use of modern survey methods to study the nature and distribution of extramural psychiatric morbidity with more sensitive instruments represents the logical extension of this work' (Shepherd 1983: 20).

Thus, a host of techniques have been developed for identifying and estimating the extent of untreated psychiatric morbidity. These, broadly referred to as 'screening', are dealt with by David Goldberg.

Investigations using such techniques almost invariably involve computer analysis. Latterly, computers have also been used to collect such data – for example, there now exist several systems whereby respondents are assessed by means of direct interaction with a computer. These and other relevant aspects of information technology are dealt with by David Hand and Eric Glover in the last chapter of this section.

REFERENCES

Lewis, A. (1945) 'Psychiatric investigation in Britain', *American Journal of Psychiatry* 101: 486–93.

Maudsley, H. (1879) *The Pathology of Mind*, London: Macmillan.

Shepherd, M. (1980) 'From social medicine to social psychiatry: the achievement of Sir Aubrey Lewis', *Psychological Medicine*, 10: 211–18.

Shepherd, M. (1983) *The Psychosocial Matrix of Psychiatry: Collected Papers*, London: Tavistock.

Historical Origins

1

Who Is Mad? The Exchange Between Hippocrates and Democritus

Jean Starobinski*

As is known, the pseudo-hippocratic letters relating to Hippocrates' interview at Abdera with Democritus exercised considerable influence in the sixteenth and seventeenth centuries. Burton, in particular, makes the interview the central account in his 'satyricall preface' at the beginning of the *Anatomy of Melancholy*. The text, in spite of being a sort of historical novel – the work of a 'forger' said the philologists – rather than an authentic document, has had a deserved success. It is vouched for in a fable by La Fontaine, *Démocrite et les Abdéritains* (Democritus and the Abderites, viii, 26), and by a satirical novel by Wieland (*Die Abderiter*, 1774).

Who is mad? Who knows how to recognize madness? What authority permits a decision? That is what is at issue in the letters.[1] The first letter is addressed to Hippocrates by the Council and people of Abdera. It is an appeal for help and the admission of general distress. An important man is ill, and his illness imperils the entire city, which had placed in him its hope of 'eternal glory'. The city fears that it will be abandoned, so much does its own existence depend on that of the superior man in whom they had hitherto recognized a superior wisdom. Now Democritus is sick, says the letter 'because of the excess of wisdom that possesses him' (p. 320).

The alleged cause is not discreditable. In the eyes of the Abderites, predisposed to moderation, all excess, even of a virtue, is pernicious. This conviction, in the circumstances, gives rise to an imputation of illness, of delirium (*paracopè*), of paralysis of discernment (*apoplexia dianoias*). The Abderites believe that they already know the cause of the malady. They have pronounced judgement ('he is ill') before describing the symptoms. But they do not forget to go on to the description, in which figure, correctly placed, some of the ideas which doxographic tradition ascribes to Democritus. The 'clinical picture' indistinctly reveals the behaviour, the words, and the convictions of the alleged patient. 'He is oblivious of everything, even of himself, he stays awake by night as by day, laughing at everything, however

* Translated from the French by E.S. Hague

important or trivial.' He thinks that 'the whole of life is nothing', he says that 'the air is full of shadowy likenesses' (*eidolon*):

He listens to the sound of the birds, and, rising frequently at night, when alone he seems to be singing softly; at other times he says that he is travelling through infinite space and that there are innumerable Democrituses that resemble him. And his colour is as much changed as his mode of thought.

The disturbing signs, beginning with oblivion, can essentially be defined as the ignoring of normally accepted limits. Public opinion is alarmed at seeing them ignored: the boundaries between night and day, serious and comic, happy and unhappy events, earth and the subterranean world, human speech and bird song, singular and plural.

In the face of all these alarming signs, the only recourse for the Abderites is the physician, that is, the man who possesses the power to cure. They count on him to save 'the body of wisdom', and to become in this way the new founder (*Ktistes*) of the whole city. To make up Hippocrates' mind, they promise a substantial reward.

In Hippocrates' letter in reply, he promises to come but refuses payment. Democritus is a work of nature; in the circumstances, the physician considers himself summoned by nature. And he also calls in question the opinion reached by the Abderites. The physician wishes to retain complete freedom to arbitrate on the situation, to recognize the presence or absence of a morbid state: it may be that the Abderites are mistaken (*apatei*) in considering Democritus to be ill.

In another letter, addressed privately to Philopoemen, his host and friend in Abdera, Hippocrates says how difficult it is to distinguish the signs of 'excessive wisdom' from those of maladies produced by the black bile. He inclines to the first hypothesis, which does not prevent him from providing himself with hellebore, that is, the medicament regarded as efficacious in driving out melancholy. Those who seclude themselves, those who are silent, those who flee human society may be now contemplative, now raving sick men.

Addressing another correspondent (Dionysios of Halicarnassus), whom he asks to come to look after his house and his wife in his absence, Hippocrates once again expresses his doubts and criticizes popular opinion; when men talk of excess they always speak from the standpoint of what they lack; 'Thus the coward will see excess in courage, the miser will see excess in open-handedness' (letter 13, p. 335). Hippocrates puts clearly in doubt the norm which individuals cite as an authority when they make an accusation of deviation or aberration. He himself will formulate his opinion and his *prognosis* only after he has seen and listened to Democritus. The principle of the personal and direct examination is formulated clearly here.

In a letter to another recipient named Damagetes (letter 14), Hippocrates nevertheless expresses uneasiness about a symptom described by the Abderites: an undifferentiated laugh at every event in life. This means a lack of the sense of proportion that men must always retain. In advance, Hippocrates admonishes Democritus and imputes to him, as do the Abderites, a melancholic 'immoderacy':

> You laugh when someone is ill, you are delighted when someone dies . . .
> What an unpleasant man you are, O Democritus, and how far from wisdom, if you think that such things are not evils. Most certainly you are tormented by the black bile (*melancholais*).

Hippocrates could have been the sole arbiter. The author of the letters does not restrict himself to that. He gives Hippocrates assistance and Asclepios appears in a dream, escorted appropriately by enormous serpents and accompanied by the allegorical figures of Truth and Opinion.[2] The god declares that, as far as Democritus is concerned, his help will be of no use, for Democritus is utterly sound in mind. The dream is perfectly clear, but, when Hippocrates wakes, he still feels in need of an explanation. The author of the letters does not flinch from any effect: he reveals in his physician hero a perfect oneirocritic. Hippocrates declares to his correspondent: 'I do not reject dreams, above all those that keep an order. Medicine and divination are close cousins, for Apollo is the common father of the two arts' (letter 15, p. 343).

The introduction of the term divination (*mantikè*) is disturbing. For the terms *mantis* (diviner) and *mantikè* have been associated since antiquity with *mania* (madness) and *mainesthai* (to be a prey to fury, passion). Thus, the art of divination, considered as closely related to medicine, and which permits the declaration that Democritus is not mad, itself maintains a special semantic relationship with frenzy.

A letter on the best way to gather hellebore gives an idea of Hippocrates' technical knowledge (letter 16). We learn even more about the same subject in a later letter (letter 21). The author means to give us the highest idea of the pharmacological competence of the great physician, in the field that particularly relates to mental disturbances. But the question of diagnosis and of the indications for such treatment is still not touched upon. What can decide this is the interview with the patient.

This interview is described at length in the letter that is the culmination of the collection. This letter to Damagetes (letter 17) is the one most often quoted, imitated, translated, by writers from Sebastian Frank to Robert Burton. It deserves a painstaking commentary, for it relates a kind of drama, with many details of the staging, each of which is highly significant.

While, far off, the Abderites lament or try to make the alleged sick man laugh, the physician and the philosopher engage in conversation: this will

17

take the form of a philosophical disputation, by means of question and answer. Reading the letter we learn from the start the conclusions which Hippocrates has reached: 'It is as we thought, Damagetes: Democritus was not raving, but he scorned everything, and he taught us, and, through us, all men' (p. 349).

Hippocrates will give a perfect demonstration of his method: he brushes aside the bystanders. He wants to see and hear the man he is examining, 'to be near his words and his body' (p. 353). We see that the physical examination and the interview with the patient are closely linked. From a distance Hippocrates had already observed the individual's general appearance, the place of his activities, the things that interest him. The signs before they engage in conversation had still been ambiguous: they could lend themselves to an unfavourable interpretation. Democritus, seated under a very low plane-tree, is a man 'in a coarse tunic, alone, his body neglected, on a stone seat, his colour very yellow, emaciated, with a long beard'. So, later, did the famous painting and engraving by Salvator Rosa depict him. But this unusual man receives Hippocrates with perfect courtesy, asks his name, invites him to sit near him. He asks him whether he has come to see him about a public or private matter (*idion oud è epidemion*).

Hippocrates introduces himself as an ambassador, and, with an astute question, satisfies himself that his patient has no disturbance of memory or orientation: he knows who Philopoemen is and in what part of the town he lives. When interrogated about the book open in front of him and which he is engaged in writing, Democritus answers that it is a book on madness. The animals that he dissects in search of 'the nature and seat of bile' (p. 355) will enable him to gain a better understanding of the 'cause of madness'.

Democritus is trying to resolve a 'physiological' problem: bile 'exists in all naturally, but varies in degree in each one: if it is in excess, illnesses will occur, and it is a substance now good, now bad'. Most certainly, it is a question of rudimentary quantitative reasoning in the framework of a humoral postulate without real proof. No more is needed, however, for Hippocrates to admire the wisdom and profound tranquillity of the person with whom he is talking – tranquillity, he confesses immediately, that he does not himself enjoy. That is the turning point of the conversation, from which he will acknowledge the superiority of the philosopher, free of all ties, over the physician, still a captive to the cares of practical living: his thought is still engrossed in 'fields, house, children, debts, maladies, the dead, servants, marriages, and everything else.'

The philosopher's superiority, as can be clearly seen, is that of the *vita contemplativa* (*bioas theoretikos*) over the active life. From this, Democritus has no difficulty in exposing the innumerable vanities of human ambition, the folly of the quest for power, riches, pleasures. Hippocrates tries to plead the cause of practical life: 'to act is imposed by necessity.' Democritus replies that men are ridiculous through their lack of foresight, through their inability to face the consequences of their actions. His laughter, at all that happens to men, is therefore perfectly appropriate. But in thus exculpating himself from the accusation of madness, he throws the accusation back to everyone else: 'the whole world is ill without knowing it', says Hippocrates, coming to the logical conclusion. And in such a case, what can we hope for? Where is one to send 'a delegation' to find the remedy?

Such a complete generalization of illness (from which the contemplative philosopher alone excepts himself) leaves no room for any health in the world. There is 'an infinity of worlds' declares Democritus, a poor consolation. From this text, which dates from the beginning of the Christian era, one can infer how Christ, God incarnate, but whose kingdom is not of this world, would answer to this radical condemnation of the world's madness. It is to him that prayer could 'send a delegation'. The man in search of salvation should repudiate the alleged wisdom of the world, which is madness, and opt for 'the madness of the Cross'.

Democritus has found tranquillity in retreat and in the investigation of physical causes. His complaint against men becomes all the more implacable. The vehemence of the accusation leads to the avowed desire to harm mankind. The tranquil philosopher becomes a misanthrope: he would find pleasure in aggravating the evil in order to inflict the deserved punishment:

> As for me, I do not think that I even laugh enough, and I should like to be able to find something that would afflict them, something that was neither medicine to cure them nor a Peon to prepare remedies for them. (p. 373).

The justifications found for Democritus' vengeful argument are analogous to those formulated very much later by the Marquis de Sade: 'Don't you see that the world (*Kosmos*) is full of hostility to man (*misanthropos*) and has marshalled against him infinite evils' (p. 375).

How is it possible to orientate oneself in the world when all boundaries between good and evil are thus obliterated? The moral rule will be that of indifference to all that may happen to us and of knowing how to draw in ourselves 'the limits of calm and agitation' (p. 367).

Did Democritus, in the general purpose of his diatribe against the madness of the world, keep entirely calm? Hippocrates does not express the doubts that we might have. He is persuaded that he has found in Democritus a man who surpasses him: 'He smiled at my speaking thus and he appeared to me, Damagetes, as a divine being, and I forgot that he was a man.'

Instead of applying the treatment, Hippocrates received it: it was the physician who at the end of the interview went away provided with a beneficial remedy. He humbly declares to the man he was questioning: 'I have received from you the remedy that will increase my own understanding' (p. 379). Are we to believe that the author of the pseudo-hippocratic letters intended to demonstrate the superiority of philosophy, 'medicine of the intellect' over the art of medicine, the medicine of the 'body'?

The fact is that the author of the letters is bent on attributing to Democritus a twofold competence: he makes him a master of wisdom, and he attributes to him a medical work on madness (composed, it must be added, of long extracts from well-known hippocratical writings), a short treatise 'on the nature of man', as well as a letter lavishing advice on Hippocrates as if the latter needed a course in improvement.

The physician must judge maladies not only by sight but from the facts themselves, he must examine the rhythms of the malady in general, whether it is in its initial stage, its middle stage, or its wane, and, having observed the differences, the season, age, as well as the body as a whole, must then apply the treatment. (p. 383).

The anonymous author has obviously tried to show that the philosopher 'physiologist', starting from his knowledge of the world and the whole of nature can be a complete physician, as qualified as the specialist who has descended from Asclepios; but, in addition, philosophy possesses the knowledge of the rules of behaviour, that is, wisdom, which puts at a disadvantage those who possess only the medical art. In the preamble to his short letter on 'the nature of man' (letter 23), Democritus demonstrates the link between the two disciplines:

All men ought to know the art of medicine, O Hippocrates, and especially those who have acquired learning and are versed in its doctrines, for it is both beautiful and advantageous to life. I think that knowledge of philosophy is sister to medicine and lives under the same roof; indeed, philosophy frees the soul from passions and medicine rids the body of maladies. (p. 395)

One can see it, the miniature novel in the form of letters, which contains some very remarkable things formulated rather daringly, has managed to turn upside down the initial situation. The populace of Abdera, who demanded treatment for Democritus' madness, appears as the real patient in need of hellebore; it is the collective opinion that is unhealthy. The physician, who at first delivered his advice with perfect assurance, accepts the role of pupil. The philosopher, whose behaviour at first seemed abnormal, is revealed as the custodian of truth. The deceptive appearances have been dissipated.

Even in antiquity, the Abderites did not enjoy a reputation for intelligence. They have nevertheless found a defender, in the person of the French philosopher Pierre Bayle. In the article 'Abdera' in his famous *Dictionary*, he writes, apropos of the suspicion of madness held against Democritus: 'People would do the same today about a philosopher who made fun of everything.' (*Dictionary*: note K).

As usually happens in a pleasant fable, the pseudo-hippocratic novel makes use of the principle of all or nothing. If Democritus is mad, the council and citizens of Abdera are justified in being alarmed by his behaviour. If, on the other hand, Democritus is not mad, the whole community, in allowing itself to be deceived by appearances, must accept the accusation of madness. Such sweeping reversals of a situation have characterized present-day 'radical' thought whenever it has let itself be carried away by the temptation to mythify. 'Radical' thought, of course, no longer shares the elitist interpretation that long characterized the lesson drawn from the story of Hippocrates and Democritus. La Fontaine, in telling it, declares that he 'always hated general opinion'. Such a story shows that 'the people are an untrustworthy judge' (Book VIII, 26). In its rhetoric, 'radical' thought usually indicts 'society' while approving of the *vox populi*.

The present reader's attention may reasonably dwell on a detail in the last of Hippocrates' letters (letter 22). It is written to his son Thessalus, and contains recommendations on the basic knowledge necessary for medicine: geometry and arithmetic. Geometry 'will be useful in the location of bones, their displacement, and the whole arrangement of the limbs.' As for the 'order of arithmetic', it will be applicable enough to the periods, to the regular changes of fevers, to patients' crises, and to preventive measures (p. 393). Here, no doubt, it is a matter of a rudimentary arithmetic applied to forecasting the course of illnesses.

Hippocrates' counsel is sufficiently general to include half of the medieval *quadrivium* as well as the astrological calculations practised by the iatro-mathematicians of the Renaissance. The whole range of the possible application of mathematics to medicine (for us who know what happened in history) appears in embryo in the initial exhortation.

> Occupy yourself, my son, with the study of geometry and arithmetic, for it will not only make your life glorious and most useful in human affairs, but it will also make your mind more penetrating and more perceptive to profit from all that is useful in medicine.

The physicians who, towards the end of the eighteenth century, at the time of the 'return to Hippocrates', devoted themselves to the statistics of illnesses in correlation with the winds, rain, temperature, have certainly illustrated in yet another way this paternal injunction.

Hippocrates, whose example has so often been invoked in favour of 'clinical' observation, can certainly not be regarded as the inspiration for quantification in physiology. His interest, as has so often been repeated, is focused on qualitative phenomena that can be directly evaluated by sensory contact. But the text (certainly apocryphal) which we just read opens the path to everything from eighteenth-century calculation of probabilities to contemporary epidemiology. It points to the need to bring medicine, in its own domain, to the 'degree of certainty' – to use Cabanis's expression – that it can obtain through the legitimate use of epidemiology. To the words in which the imaginary Hippocrates of the novel exhorts his son, one is tempted to add these: 'Medicine and philosophy most certainly live under the same roof, and if the philosopher can give the physician a lesson in serenity, he will have performed a worthy deed, but if the physician deliberately uses the science of numbers he will be able to talk on equal terms with those who use this same science of numbers to decipher the laws of the cosmos. He will even be able, among the Abderites, to discern those who are less mad than others. And when the philosopher declares that "man is illness entire", he will be able to answer him by saying that such a generalization removes every chance of calmness which the philosopher, in his capacity as a man, wishes to attain. The humoral doctrine, and the very one that Democritus professes, sees illness as disproportion. That is why my dear Thessalus, I have bound you to have recourse to arithmetic. It will enable you to recognize relationships, proportions, and not to scorn any of the Abderites.'

NOTES

1. They are numbered 10 to 23 in the series '*Lettres, décrets et harangues*' in E. Littré (ed.) (1861) *Oeuvres Complêtes: volume IX*, Paris, 321–99.

2. The apparition of Asclepios in a dream generally manifests itself to patients who have come to consult him by *incubation* in his temple. I am unaware of any other example of Asclepios appearing to a physician, cf. Edelstein, L. and Edelstein, E. (1945) *Asclepius: A Collection and Interpretation of the Testimonies*, volume 2, Baltimore: Johns Hopkins University Press.

N.B. A good analysis, together with bibliographical references, can be found in Pigeaud, J. (1981) *La maladie de l'âme* (The Malady of the Soul), Paris: Les Belles-Lettres, 452–77.

2

Victorian Origins of
Epidemiological Psychiatry

William Bynum

In the nineteenth century, had there been chairs in psychiatry, the Professor of Epidemiological Psychiatry would have been called something like 'Professor of the Statistics of Insanity'. The *Oxford English Dictionary* is only moderately helpful in explaining why someone should now occupy a chair in Epidemiological Psychiatry. 'Epidemiological' ('of or pertaining to epidemiology') is given a first English usage of 1881; 'epidemiology' ('that branch of medical science which treats of epidemics') is first dated 1873, in the title of J.P. Parkin's book *Epidemiology, or the Remoter Causes of Epidemic Diseases*. 'Epidemic', both as noun and adjective, goes back much further, of course, and in its plural form, was the title of Hippocratic treatises. The editors of the *Oxford English Dictionary* failed to notice that there was established, in 1850, the London Epidemiological Society, which published transactions and did much to stimulate interest in the subject. Epidemiology itself, however, did not routinely deal with mental disorder. The first paper in the Society's *Transactions* of any psychiatric relevance did not appear until the 1901–2 session, when (Sir) Frederick Mott published his study on 'Dysentery in Asylums'. Unsurprisingly, the first rather than the second noun of the title was the operative word.

'Psychiatry' was even slower than 'epidemics' and its derivatives in establishing itself in the English language. Although the OED cites an 1846 usage, and both 'psychiatric' and 'psychiatrics' date from the 1847 English translation of Ernst von Feuchtersleben's *Lehrbuch der ärztlichen Seelenkunde*, as late as 1892, Daniel Hack Tuke's monumental *Dictionary of Psychological Medicine* gives only 'Psychiatrie (Ger.), Psychological Medicine'. The sparse entry in Hack Tuke's *Dictionary* reminds us that, whatever the Victorians did, they did not call it epidemiological psychiatry.

Tuke's *Dictionary* does, however, contain clues to the antecedents of the modern discipline. Three articles in particular are relevant to the history of epidemiological psychiatry: 'Epidemic insanity', 'Statistics of insanity', and 'Suicide'. Between them, they raise what strike me as the major preoccupations of those a century ago who sought to come to grips with the complex relationships between mental disorder, society, and populations.

Of epidemic insanity I shall say little, merely referring those interested to some passages in Shepherd's work (e.g. Shepherd 1978: 289), to the writings of the late George Rosen (Rosen 1968), and to the monograph of Robert Nye (Nye 1975). The article in the *Dictionary* on 'Epidemic insanity' leaned heavily on Hecker's great *Epidemics of the Middle Ages* in discussing what Gustave Le Bon would call the crowd psychology associated with such phenomena as the Flagellants, Dancing Mania, Tarantism, and the Convulsionnaires. That Hecker himself included his chapters on medieval episodes of 'psychic contagion' within a work primarily devoted to more conventional epidemic disorders reinforces the primary point of this essay, namely, that the historical roots of epidemiological psychiatry cannot be divorced from the scientific, medical, and social concerns of the last century.

I shall use the entries on 'Statistics of insanity' and on 'Suicide' to examine briefly the uses to which psychiatric statistics were put by those who collected them and the extent to which epidemiological concerns have enlivened some recent historical writings. The statistically-minded editor of the *Dictionary*, Daniel Hack Tuke, wrote both of the entries.

THE STATISTICS OF INSANITY

For the most part, what we may anachronistically call Victorian epidemiological psychiatry confined itself to the asylum. The only notable exception was suicide, only a fraction of which occurred within a psychiatric institution or was committed by patients recently released from one. Suicide apart, however, statistical concern was primarily directed towards patients already formally identified as suffering from mental disorder. The use of epidemiological techniques to elucidate disorders such as pellagra and kuru belongs to the present century (Roe 1973; Gajdusek 1975).

The scientific fascination with the security of numbers goes back to the Scientific Revolution of the sixteenth and seventeenth centuries. In the physical sciences, mathematics reigned supreme, with Newton's reputation extending far beyond the range of individuals able to fathom the nuances of his thought. Demographic and social studies by men such as John Graunt (1620–74) and Sir William Petty (1623–87) possessed a distinct quantitative flavour (Laslett, 1971), and in medicine, the 'iatromathematicians' visualized the human body as a machine understandable through physics and mathematics (Shryock 1948). Iatromathematics had fallen from grace by the middle of the eighteenth century, although the beginnings of multiple case reporting, from about that time, initiated another tradition of numbers in medicine most famously represented by the *method numérique* of Pierre Louis (1787–1872) (Tröhler 1978).

Despite these and similar developments within science and medicine, it is no exaggeration to speak of a 'statistical movement' in early Victorian Britain which went far beyond the realizations of earlier individuals. The decennial censuses, first conducted in 1801, became more accurate by the third or fourth headcount, and the civil registration of births, marriages and deaths, from 1837, brought some coherence to mortality patterns (Nissel 1987). Government departments, such as the General Register Office and the Board of Trade, possessed their quota of numerate civil servants, and government commissions and enquiries, such as that which looked into the operation of the Old Poor Law (1832), began to want more systematic information (MacDonagh 1977). Edwin Chadwick (1800–90) on the Poor Law Commission and William Farr (1807–83) at the GRO are merely two outstanding examples of the passion for numbers which characterizes the period. They were active both within and outside government circles, especially in the statistical societies which sprang up in London, Manchester, Glasgow, and elsewhere (Cullen 1975). Chadwick was particularly under the influence of utilitarianism, a reforming force which Hervey detects in the Metropolitan Commissioners of Lunacy, the body established in 1828 to oversee the asylums and madhouses of the metropolis. Both inspection and statistics came within the Commission's ken, supplemented in the provinces by local magistrates (Hervey 1987). The impetus towards centralization and standardization was consolidated by the 1845 Acts, which extended the Lunacy Commissioners' purview to the provinces, gave them greater powers, and required counties to build, from the rates, asylums for the care, cure, and custody of pauper lunatics.

The compulsion to provide specialized care for pauper lunatics led (at least initially) to the rapid expansion of the asylum system, since a number of counties had declined to act on earlier, permissive, legislation, and, at the time of the 1845 Act, certified pauper lunatics were almost as commonly housed in work- or poor-houses as in asylums (Scull 1979). The sheer number of asylums was bound to increase, but the increase in the average size of each asylum (from under 300 patients in 1850 to over 800 in 1890), or the fact that some counties, such as Middlesex, found it necessary to build more than one asylum, point to the principal epidemiological issues worrying Victorian alienists and statisticians: was insanity increasing, and, if so, why? That there were more individuals certified as insane was beyond dispute, but there were several reasons why this might have happened. Better diagnostic techniques, a greater public awareness of the indications of insanity, and a more efficient machinery to place pauper lunatics within the asylums (where they came under the Commissioners' view) could all have contributed to a larger number of identified lunatics. Better sanitary and environmental conditions and nursing care within the asylums could prolong the average lifespan of the insane, so that at any given time, there would be more of them.

The importance of these factors was agreed by the commentators at the time, and has been accepted more recently by Hare, Scull, and others who

25

have reopened the question (Hare 1983; Scull 1979; Scull 1984; Torrey 1980). The rate of insanity (number of insane divided by total population) was clearly rising during the second half of the nineteenth century; but the incidence of new cases was another issue. Hack Tuke was aware of this basic distinction, although his own terms were *existing* and *occurring* insanity, respectively. Indeed, I think he would have understood perfectly the Scull-Hare debate, and certainly appreciated the flaws in the statistics of insanity available to him. He discounted as totally unreliable any figures before 1859, because readmissions and transfers too often got lumped together with new cases, as each asylum reported its annual statistics. Early in the century, cure rates often suffered from a similar problem, since if the same patient were admitted and discharged 'cured' several times in a single year, he could count as multiple cures. (A helpful analysis of this issue may be found in the article on 'Curability of the insane' by Pliny Earle in Hack Tuke's *Dictionary*.)

In essence, Tuke insisted, the only squarely relevant figure for deciding whether the alleged increase in insanity was real or not was the rate of new cases, a figure continuously available only from 1878. No long-term trend was consequently available to Tuke in 1892, but the modest rise of new cases from 3.29 to 3.46 per 10,000 living (average for 1881–5 and 1886–90, respectively) was not, in his opinion, especially significant. My own assessment of the 'alleged increase in insanity' debate suggests that psychiatrists like Tuke, who denied a major increase in its real incidence, had much the better of the argument, although, as Hare has noted, there were those who felt that a great wave of insanity was spreading across Britain during Victoria's reign (Hare 1983). Hare himself is one of the 'realists', of course, suggesting that the disorder we now call schizophrenia was uncommon before the nineteenth century, and common by the time Bleuler actually gave it its modern name. (Incidentally, *dementia praecox* does not rate a mention in Tuke's *Dictionary*, although *hebephrenia* is given a brief definition.)

Whether the national statistics collected by the Lunacy Commissioners and others will bear the weight of Hare's interpretation is a matter of debate, but, as Tuke pointed out, the raw figures from mid-century until its last decade, while they do show a continuing increase in the number of lunatics, point to a diminishing rate of increase after about 1880. This strikes me as significant, given the fact that this ran counter to the dominant alarmist paradigm of the time, the concept of progressive hereditary degeneration as first comprehensively formulated by Morel (Morel 1857; Dowbiggin 1985).

Tuke recognized two further parameters which bore on the 'increase' question, although he was not sanguine that either one could be used very productively in the 1890s to answer it. The first concerned the relationships between the British experience and those of other countries. Scattered through the *Dictionary* were articles on the provision of psychiatric services for most European countries, the United States, Canada, Australia, etc. The difficulties in using different national statistics in any comparative analysis were insurmountable, since, as Tuke pointed out, different criteria were used in collecting them. American statistics, for example, contained many cases of acute alcoholism which in Britain would not have been admitted to any asylum and would, therefore, be absent from official figures. Accordingly, Tuke refused to speculate on the varying rates of insanity in different countries, even if reliable and comparable figures might have borne on the nagging subtext of the 'increase' question, viz., did insanity and civilization go hand in hand? His summary comment on the issue reflects his own healthy scepticism:

> It may be stated, without danger of contradiction, that the proportion of idiots and lunatics to the population in uncivilized nations is less than in those who are civilized. At the same time there are many reasons why the actual number accumulated in the latter should be vastly greater than in the former without a corresponding difference in the liability to mental disorders. If we consider only this liability we should recommend savages to remain uncivilized, but on the other hand we should decidedly recommend the class corresponding to savages (city-arabs, &c.) in a civilized community to enter the ranks of the educated and well-fed classes.
>
> (Tuke 1892: 1206)

Tuke was also aware that, beyond the visible cases of certified insanity, there existed what he called a 'considerable mass of borderland cases', and that these 'nervous disorders' were also alleged to be on the increase. While not denying that the incidence of nervous disorders might be rising, Tuke recognized that that aspect of the debate was informed only by 'impressions' and 'general observations', and, hence, no definite conclusions could be drawn. He would have appreciated both the problems and the importance of more recent comparative and cross-cultural epidemiological studies (e.g. Hoch and Zubin 1961; Hare and Wing 1970), and of research looking at the incidence of psychiatric morbidity within general practice (e.g. Shepherd *et al.* 1966) and the community (e.g. Srole *et al.* 1962; Plunkett and Gordon 1960).

Tuke's article on the 'statistics of insanity' was not simply about the alleged increase in insanity, however. It also dealt with a whole series of parameters – considered in the mass – about the influence of such factors as age, sex, marital status, and treatment, on the course and outcome of mental disease. Its causation, too, came under his statistical purview, as did the relative frequency of different forms of mental disorder. Causes were broken down into the typical Victorian categories of *moral* and *physical*, and almost 90 per cent of the forms could be accounted for by the broad diagnostic labels of mania, melancholia, or dementia. For virtually all of his statistics Tuke relied on the figures collected by the Lunacy Commissioners, but, when local medical superintendents had attempted to go further than was required by the statutory machinery, Tuke was ready to report more refined statistical findings. Thus, Dr Boyd of the Somerset County Asylum had broken down diagnostic categories (adding monomania, general paralysis, moral insanity, epilepsy, and delirium tremens to the grouping); and Dr Major of the West Riding Asylum had examined the role of alcoholic excess in the life histories of patients admitted to his care. Other studies which Tuke could refer to included the pioneering work of William Farr (1841) on the mortality of insanity; the classic monograph of John Thurnam (1845) on the statistics of insanity; the researches of Sir Arthur Mitchell (1877) on the Scottish scene; and the sensitive and numerate survey of Noel Humphreys (1890) on the 'increase' debate.

In the end, Tuke was aware that his statistics did not permit him to answer many questions, and that they represented the cumulative experience of many asylums and many medical superintendents. They were collected by many hands, albeit along guidelines laid down by the Lunacy Commissioners, and related primarily to patients just before, during, and just after psychiatric hospitalization. Even though the 1871 census had attempted to measure the extent of 'insanity and idiocy' in the general population, Tuke's statistics were essentially those of the asylum and its psychiatry. In only one significant area did he and his colleagues turn their numerical gaze on a phenomenon occurring largely outside the asylum. This was the question of suicide.

SUICIDE

Suicide occupies a special place within the history of the social sciences, principally because of Durkheim's classic monograph, which was first published five years after Tuke's *Dictionary* (Durkheim 1952). Tuke could consequently make no use of it, but he did have access to the man who was also Durkheim's most frequently cited authority, Enrico Morselli, the Italian psychiatrist whose own study of suicide had been translated into English in 1881 (Morselli 1881; Guarnieri 1988). In fact, except for the historical sections detailing attitudes towards, and legislation relating to, suicide from antiquity to the nineteenth century, most of Tuke's entry was derived from Morselli's monograph. He was also able to refer his readers to some English work, notably in the monographs of Forbes Winslow (1840), the mid-century psychiatric entrepreneur (Smith 1981; Shepherd 1986), and of W.W. Westcott (1885), the deputy coroner for Central Middlesex, as well as the article of William Ogle (1886), one of Farr's successors at the General Register Office.

Reflecting the broad concerns of Tuke's principal authorities, his article was permeated with a social, comparative, and statistical orientation. His first table summarized the incidence of suicide in nineteen countries or areas,

28

and included the fact that suicide was more than twenty-nine times more common in Saxony than Portugal. These crude figures were subsequently analysed, for many of the geographical areas, in terms of sex and age ratios, and variations in suicide in terms of seasonality, time of day, religion, political life, race, trade cycles, marital state, occupation, urbanization, population density, social condition, and alcohol consumption. The mode by which men and women chose to take their own lives was also subjected to numerical analysis.

Throughout Europe and North America – indeed, wherever statistics were being compiled – there was evidence that suicide was on the increase. The only exceptions reported by Tuke were Holland, where it had been stationary between 1870 and 1880, and Russia, Finland, and Norway, where its frequency had diminished during the 1870s. Morselli's own conclusion, quoted by Tuke, was that 'madness and suicide are met with the more frequently in proportion as civilization progresses' (Morselli 1881: 117; as quoted by Tuke 1892: 1224). Tuke was prepared to accept that significant geographical, occupational, ethnological, sexual, and religious variations existed in the incidence of suicide, but at the same time he fought shy of some of Morselli's sweeping conclusions for the simple fact that the figures themselves were subject to too many sources of error: under-reporting, doubtful circumstances, subterfuge, as well as the inadequate bureaucratic machinery for collecting statistics in many countries. 'All that we are justified in concluding is the apparent greater liability [to suicide] of the more cultured races of mankind', Tuke commented.

Victorian and Edwardian suicide has recently been brilliantly examined by Olive Anderson (1987), who has amply substantiated Tuke's suspicions about the quality of the statistics, even as they relate to Tuke's own country, let alone to other parts of Europe. Nevertheless, Anderson has been able to make creative historical use of the statistical legacy bequeathed to us by our Victorian forebears and has gone beyond what was available to Tuke in analysing some particularly full sets of surviving coroners' returns (one in Southwark, one in Sussex) from coroners especially concerned with the incidence and the individual circumstances of suicide. Incidentally, Anderson's shrewd examination of national patterns and regional variations of Victorian and Edwardian suicide shows the inadequacy of Durkheim's notion of anomie in explaining suicide as a social phenomenon, at least for England and Wales. Rates were higher in the wealthy, established, and rural southeast than they were in the turbulent areas of England's industrial north.

Anderson's study also demonstrates how historians can with good effect use earlier epidemiological data as well as subject historical collections of materials to their own analyses. MacDonald's investigations of suicide in the seventeenth and eighteenth centuries (described in more detail by him later in this book) confirm the second point (MacDonald 1977; MacDonald 1986; MacDonald 1988), and his dissection of the case notes of Richard Napier

(1559–1634) in essence presents a psychiatric epidemiology of an early-seventeenth-century general practice (MacDonald 1981). Neither Anderson nor MacDonald view suicide as a subject within the exclusive ken of psychiatry. Nor did Tuke: his article was broad in its terms of reference, suggesting that perhaps no more than 20 per cent of suicide cases could be attributed to insanity. Kushner (1986) has recently suggested that American psychiatrists failed to see the relevance of social studies such as Durkheim's, turning instead to psychoanalysis in their attempt to understand the psychodynamics of the desire to destroy oneself. The history of most of British psychiatry in the present century remains to be written, and the study of suicide is no exception. Nevertheless, Tuke's article suggests that, at the close of the last century, psychiatrists were cognizant of the importance of both social and psychopathological factors in the phenomenon.

CONCLUSION

This brief essay has done no more than point to some of the themes and literature relating to epidemiological psychiatry before the subject was actually called that. For the Victorians, epidemiology was concerned almost exclusively with infectious diseases. In the present century, the methods of the discipline have been refined and the objects of its analysis revealingly extended to many other kinds of disorders, such as neoplasms and diseases of the cardio-vascular system. Within British psychiatry, much of the impetus has come from the Institute of Psychiatry and the Maudsley Hospital, where Shepherd, Wing, Hare, and many others have continued traditions which were well established during the Aubrey Lewis era (Shepherd 1977; Shepherd and Davies 1968). But the fundamental importance of the subject was appreciated by Thurnam, Hack Tuke, and others a century and more ago. Despite shifts in vocabulary, Victorian psychiatrists may be said to have pioneered the epidemiological investigation of non-infectious disorders.

REFERENCES

Anderson, O. (1987) *Suicide in Victorian and Edwardian Britain*, Oxford: Clarendon Press.

Cullen, M.J. (1975) *The Statistical Movement in Early Victorian Britain*, Hassocks: Harvester Press.

Dowbiggin, I. (1985) 'Degeneration and hereditarianism in French mental medicine 1840–90', in W.F. Bynum, R. Porter and M. Shepherd (eds) *The Anatomy of Madness*, London: Tavistock, vol. I, 188–232.

Durkheim, E. (1952) *Suicide: A Study in Sociology*, translated by J.A. Spaulding and G. Simpson, London: Routledge & Kegan Paul.

Gajdusek, D.C. (ed.) (1975) *Correspondence on the Discovery and Original Investigations on Kuru: Smadel-Gajdusek Correspondence, 1955–1958*, Bethesda,

Maryland: National Institutes of Health.

Guarnieri, P. (1988) 'Between soma and psyche: Morselli and psychiatry in late-nineteenth-century Italy', in W.F. Bynum, R. Porter and M. Shepherd (eds) *The Anatomy of Madness*, London: Tavistock, vol. III, 102–24.

Hare, E.H. (1983) 'Was insanity on the increase?', *British Journal of Psychiatry* 142: 439–55.

Hare, E.H. and Wing, J.K. (eds) (1970) *Psychiatric Epidemiology*, London: Oxford University Press.

Hecker, J.F.K. (1859) *The Epidemics of the Middle Ages* (trans. B.G. Babington), London: Trübner.

Hervey, N. (1987) 'The Lunacy Commission 1845–60, with special reference to the implementation of policy in Kent and Surrey', two vols, PhD thesis, University of Bristol.

Hoch, P.H. and Zubin, J. (eds) (1961) *Comparative Epidemiology of the Mental Disorders*, New York: Grune and Stratton.

Humphreys, N. (1890) 'Statistics of Insanity in England, with special reference to its alleged increasing prevalence', *Journal of the Royal Statistical Society* 53: 201–45.

Kushner, H. (1986) 'American psychiatry and the cause of suicide, 1844–1917', *Bulletin of the History of Medicine* 60: 36–57.

Laslett, P. (1971) *The World We Have Lost*, London: Methuen.

MacDonagh, O. (1977) *Early Victorian Government 1830–1870*, London: Weidenfeld & Nicolson.

MacDonald, M. (1977) 'The inner side of wisdom: suicide in early modern England', *Psychological Medicine* 7: 562–82.

MacDonald, M. (1981) *Mystical Bedlam: Madness, Anxiety and Healing in Seventeenth-Century England*, Cambridge and New York: Cambridge University Press.

MacDonald, M. (1986) 'The secularization of suicide in England 1660–1800', *Past and Present* 111: 50–100.

MacDonald, M. (1988) 'Introduction' to facsimile reprint of John Sym (1637) *Lifes Preservative Against Self-killing*, London: Routledge.

Mitchell, A. (1877) 'Contributions to the statistics of insanity', *Journal of Mental Science* 22: 507–15.

Morel, B.A. (1857) *Traité des dégénérescences physiques, intellectuelles, et morales de l'espèce humaine*, Paris: Baillière.

Morselli, E. (1881) *Suicide: An Essay on Comparative Moral Statistics*, London: Kegan Paul.

Nissel, M. (1987) *People Count: A History of the General Register Office*, London: Her Majesty's Stationery Office.

Nye, R.A. (1975) *The Origins of Crowd Psychology: Gustave Le Bon and the Crisis of Mass Democracy in the Third Republic*, London and Beverly Hills: Sage.

Ogle, W.H. (1886) 'Suicides in England and Wales in relation to age, sex, season and occupation', *Journal of the [Royal] Statistical Society* 49: 101–35.

Plunkett, J. and Gordon, J.E. (1960) *Epidemiology and Mental Illness*, New York: Basic Books.

Roe, D. (1973) *A Plague of Corn: The Social History of Pellagra*, Ithaca: Cornell University Press.

Rosen, G. (1968) *Madness in Society: Chapters in the Historical Sociology of Mental Illness*, London: Routledge & Kegan Paul.

Scull, A. (1979) *Museums of Madness: The Social Organization of Insanity in Nineteenth-Century England*, London: Allen Lane.

Scull, A. (1984) 'Was insanity increasing? A response to Edward Hare', *British Journal of Psychiatry* 144: 432–6.

Shepherd, M. (1957) *A Study of the Major Psychoses in an English County* (Maudsley Monograph No. 3), London: Chapman and Hall.

Shepherd, M. (1977) *The Career and Contributions of Sir Aubrey Lewis*, London: Bethlem Royal and Maudsley Hospitals.

Shepherd, M. (1978) 'Epidemiology and clinical psychiatry', *British Journal of Psychiatry* 133: 289–98. (Reprinted in Shepherd (1983).)

Shepherd, M. (1983) *The Psychosocial Matrix of Psychiatry: Collected Papers*, London: Tavistock.

Shepherd, M. (1986) 'Psychological medicine *redivivus*: concept and communication', *Journal of the Royal Society of Medicine* 79: 639–45.

Shepherd, M. and Davies, D.L. (eds) (1968) *Studies in Psychiatry*, London: Oxford University Press.

Shepherd, M., Cooper, B., Brown, A.C., and Kalton, G.W. (1966) *Psychiatric Illness in General Practice*, London: Oxford University Press.

Shryock, R. (1948) *The Development of Modern Medicine: An Interpretation of the Social and Scientific Factors Involved*, London: Victor Gollancz.

Smith, R. (1981) *Trial by Medicine: Insanity and Responsibility in Victorian Trials*, Edinburgh: Edinburgh University Press.

Srole, L., Langner, T.S., Michael, S.T., Opler, M.K., and Rennie, T.A.C. (1962) *Mental Health in the Metropolis: The Midtown Manhattan Study*, New York: McGraw-Hill.

Thurnam, J. (1845) *Observations and Essays on the Statistics of Insanity*, London: Simpkin, Marshall & Co.

Torrey, E.F. (1980) *Schizophrenia and Civilization*, New York: Jason Aronson.

Tröhler, U. (1978) 'Quantification in British medicine and surgery 1750–1830, with special reference to its introduction into therapeutics', PhD thesis, University of London.

Tuke, D.H. (ed.) (1892) *A Dictionary of Psychological Medicine*, two vols, London: J. & A. Churchill.

Wescott, W.W. (1885) *Suicide: Its History, Literature, Jurisprudence, Causation and Prevention*, London: H.K. Lewis.

Winslow, F. (1840) *The Anatomy of Suicide*, London: Henry Renshaw.

The Social Sciences

3

A Sociological and Socio-anthropological Perspective

Annette Lawson

'. . . epidemiology represents a corpus of methods rather than a theory of science'   Felton Earls[1]

In 1958 I began work on my doctoral dissertation in the field known then as social psychiatry.[2] It was a time of great optimism. Mental illness, we believed ('we' – both social scientists and psychiatrists), could be unravelled. We could discover what it was about the social world (we spoke of social 'factors') that made people ill, that brought them into the mental hospital, that influenced the course of their illness, that enabled them to recover.[3] We also believed that much mental illness went undiscovered – it was out there in the community. Shepherd (1966: 173) wrote: 'The proportion of cases referred to psychiatrists is not more than one tenth of the total iden- tified.'[4] We needed to discover the rates, persuading those with the means to provide the skilled and expert help that would make the sick better.

This may be an exaggeration. Certainly there were conflicts within psychiatry, especially about the aetiology of mental illness and, hence, about the best and most appropriate forms of treatment. Psychiatry was also battling with other medical disciplines for recognition and a higher place in the hierarchy. And I am assuming a homogeneity to sociology that has never been achieved. That is, several strands, including social research, armchair theorizing, and social anthropology, have divided the camp in a society that, until late in this century, failed to offer institutional means for establishing the discipline, partly because so many alternative routes to government and influence were available.[5] None the less, sociology was at its height of respectability; there was a rapid growth in the discipline and Britain, it was said by Prime Minister Harold Macmillan, had 'never had it so good'. Money was made available to do research.

Hence, in the 1950s and 1960s, as much in the United States as in the United Kingdom, the classic sociological/epidemiological studies of mental illness in populations by Faris and Dunham (1967), Alexander Leighton (1959), D.C. Leighton et al. (1963), Hollingshead and Redlich (1958), and the Midtown Manhattan Studies (1962) by Srole and colleagues included both social scientists and psychiatrists as principal investigators. Although there has been a continuing struggle between the relativity of the cultural anthropologist and the universality of the medical epidemiologist, in Britain both leading psychiatrists like Aubrey Lewis and Morris Carstairs and anthropologists like C.G. Seligman and W.H. Rivers thought major new advances in understanding mental illness would be achieved by collaboration between social science and psychiatry.[6] It was a time of partnership with shared ideas about the nature of mental illness – a 'medical' model of a disease entity to be defined and diagnosed by expert psychiatrists and investigated by expert social scientists who understood about population studies and the importance of scientific methods of investigation, especially of quantitative methods. It is fair to say that neither Lewis nor Carstairs could have predicted the enormous theoretical shift that would occur to throw social science into rethinking its premises and hence its methodologies.

In this chapter, I sketch the developments in both epidemiology and sociology (the former concentrating on methods, the latter on theory) that have led to a certain dissolution of the partnership, exacerbated, perhaps, by the increasing importance of a medical background for the epidemiologist and the lack of psychiatrists working with or as anthropologists or sociologists.[7]

These developments lead me to make paradoxical and related claims: first, that epidemiological psychiatry is both well founded in sociological and social anthropological scientific features *and* that it fails adequately to answer problems by not employing the best of sociological and social anthropological theories and methods; second, that epidemiology largely contributes to advancing knowledge in a progressive way *and* that by failing to pay attention to the meaning and context of social action[8] it may function retrogressively.

A PARTNERSHIP BETWEEN EPIDEMIOLOGY AND SOCIAL SCIENCE

In the beginning, that is, in 1951 in Britain but more than fifty years earlier in France, Durkheim's *Suicide* was published.[9] One of the most famous of sociological texts, it is also a forerunner of epidemiological psychiatry. Well-known as it is to readers of this collection, it is important to recall what Durkheim did. Following in the footsteps of the great nineteenth-century 'moral statisticians' such as Quetelet in Belgium, Durkheim took published rates of suicide and showed that individuals undertaking the most deeply psychological and philosophically important action of ending their own lives did so in non-random ways. Protestants more often than Catholics,[10] married men less often than the unmarried,[11] intellectuals and the well-educated more than the less-well-educated, the divorced – that is, those without families – more often than would have been expected by mere chance. Durkheim, of course, did not stop there.[12] He set out to explain the variation in the rates that he had mapped. Suicide, he argued, was, in the sense he had shown, not merely an individual act, to be understood in terms only of each unique person's history and current position, or of their particular psychopathology, but also deeply social. It was an act undertaken in particular social conditions that had the effect of undermining the individual's sense of purpose and of meaning. The conditions were typified by 'anomie',[13] a state of normlessness, a state where clear moral goals, where social cohesion and social connectedness were lacking. In other words, a single theoretical construct – anomie – explained the relative lack of clear moral goals, and of relatedness to others that would be found in greater measure among Catholics than Protestants, the married than the unmarried.

Using this technique, Durkheim demonstrated the task of the sociologist; it is, as Merton later put it, 'to explain the rates'. It is not the purpose of the sociologist to explain the action of any given and particular individual. Indeed, Durkheim recognized that it was this that should be done by psychologists. Thus, he mapped also the terrain of these two disciplines.

Of course, the rates must first be discovered. Durkheim employed published figures, or those collected by governmental agencies. But the social survey and the discrete study of specially selected populations became the hallmark of sociological work, for it was recognized early that data collected for one purpose (administration, for example) were by no means complete or satisfactory for quite other goals. None the less, official data or specially chosen samples both rested on the assumption of the concrete reality of the social fact. There was a real rate out there in the real world to be discovered if only the correct tools and methods for investigation were employed. Having determined what this accurate rate was, the sociologist should explain it. Of course, it was not only the methods of the survey that might be at fault and thus produce untrue rates, but the analysis could also be erroneous. Durkheim has been criticized on both counts. In addition, the explanation might usefully indicate social measures for combating or lowering the rate, since the problem to be investigated was, usually, already identified as a social problem – something undesirable that was pathological for the body politic. Thus, Durkheim thought that new groupings, such as the syndicate, would develop to enable the modern person to be integrated when disintegration threatened, thus lowering the suicide rate. In other words, the whole endeavour was not only scientific but also deeply political. This, too, has been the focus of more recent attention.[14]

Following in Durkheim's footsteps, both epidemiologists and social scientists, at least of that group conducting empirical work, identified suffering, knew that it should be scientifically investigated and believed that knowledge would in and of itself lead to the better society, for the more information, the greater the tolerance that would be exercised. The good that was truth was both a means and an end. W.H. Sprott (1962)[15] thought the central message of British sociology up to that time had been that, through the best evidence one could accumulate about the social world, increased rationality and widened sympathy would be achieved.

The partnership between epidemiologist and sociologist was also healthy for another reason: there was a certain division of labour based on an acceptance of the different expertise each discipline brought to the enquiry. Thus, social scientists were not competent to define mental illness – that was for the expert psychiatrist. Just as the criminologist accepted the expert definition of lawyers as to what constituted crime, and of the executive arm of the state as to which criminal problems would benefit from sociological investigation, so social scientists as socio-technicians[16] worked in the service of psychiatry. The psychiatrist, on the other hand, accepted that the social scientist had particular methodological expertise – a knowledge of how to *do* the necessary science. Indeed, psychiatry accepted that, as its disease categories were so tenuous and not generally marked by physical signs, the sociologist's concepts of impairment or disability marked by social dysfunction could be the key to unravelling the rates of mental illness.[17] It was in this sense that sociology was a 'positive' science: it was an objective, value-free endeavour that could study social problems and produce knowledge enabling governments to make what *evidently* would be the right decisions. To use a distinction employed by Morris Janowitz (1970: 243–59)[18] and developed by Philip Abrams (1985: 182–3),[19] this was social science as 'engineering' that would, it was intended, lead to 'enlightenment'.

EPIDEMIOLOGY: EMBEDDED IN MEDICINE, FOCUSING ON MEASUREMENT

As long as these attitudes were shared, the goals and, hence, the methods of social science and epidemiology were also shared. But, as epidemiology has become increasingly embedded in medicine, the stress has been to develop harder and more rigorously bounded *medical* categories of disease that seek for universality and hence ignore the specificity and particularity of social context and historical moment.

This is how Eaton describes these assumptions:

> Epidemiology is a branch of medicine, and, thus, the assumptions of the medical model of disease are implicit. The most important assumption is that the disease under study actually exists – or, to put it another way . . . it is useful to engage in study involving the given disease category. In psychiatry this assumption is assuredly more tenuous than in other areas of medicine, because psychiatric diseases tend to be defined by failure to locate a physical cause, and validation of a given category of disease is therefore more subtle and complex. Eaton (1986)[20]

In fact, it is by no means only the psychiatric categories that are so intract-able. The NMR scanner throws the idea of multiple sclerosis as a disease constituted by its symptoms into disarray when it makes visible not one but many and old lesions existing at the time of the first symptoms. The new technique is taken to demonstrate an underlying pathology but symptoms and signs appear ever more disassociated. The HIV antibodies are found in people who have no symptoms and may never develop any symptoms of AIDS. Concepts such as carrier, potential patient, non-malignant or pre-cancerous growth, and sub-clinical illness are not, it seems to me, more robust than, say, schizoid personality, and some have social consequences as or more alarming.

None the less, epidemiological psychiatry does maintain a concept, especially with schizophrenia, of a single and universal entity, and that there *is* a physical cause to be located at some future date through clinical and experimental work in biochemistry or physiology. Indeed, Wing says that an 'essential element in any disease theory is the hypothesis that the cluster of traits is "symptomatic" of some underlying biological disturbance' (Wing 1978: 22). The less there is a social component, the better.[21] It is, thus, of critical importance that most effort is expended on constructing measures that most accurately reflect this specific disease entity. Given its model of the hard sciences, epidemiology, like sociology in its earlier manifestations, has concentrated on quantitative techniques, not on the kinds of interpretative, descriptive, narrative, or historical analyses that are more typical of anthropology and of qualitative sociology.

Hence, and because of somewhat gross differences in the rates of various clinically judged mental illnesses around the world in earlier studies that were explained by variations in diagnostic practice and inadequate case-finding,[22] psychiatric epidemiologists have developed such important diagnostic community-based tools as CATEGO, SADS, SADD, and the PSE including Wing's ID modification, as well as measures that can be applied by relatively unskilled people such as the GHQ.

The finest examples of studies using and developing such sophisticated instruments are, perhaps, the collaborative WHO[23] and the US–UK diagnostic projects, attempting to establish rates of mental illness in different societies.[24] The use of these standardized instruments, of case-registers,[25] of techniques of case-finding through local healers, alternative sources of care, and community leaders, as well as of statistical techniques for analysing data that deal more adequately with the problems of when illness events occur and how the course of illness can best be mapped, has resulted in diminished overall differences between study centres in the rates of the various diagnostic groups. There remain, however, wider variations in the affective or mood change and neurotic categories than in the psychotic,[26] suggesting more strongly than before that distress is manifested as somatic complaints as often as it is in emotional disturbance around the world, but that there may

39

be a 'core' illness called schizophrenia by western psychiatrists.[27] Early reports from the WHO collaborative study indicate, however, that its course varies substantially in urban and industrialized societies where it seems to take longer, the recovery rate is worse and disability greater than in rural and developing societies.[28]

The fact that it is now the affective disorders and the course of mental illness generally that vary most across cultures is best understood within a theory that explains mood disturbance and illness recognition, treatment, and outcome as the consequence of social events and social context, for it is these that vary most across cultures, not biology. When psychiatry insists on the discovery of biochemical or other individual and organic phenomena as *causing* illness, it misses the possibility of much more plausible, parsimonious, and, to my mind, scientific reasoning. To insist, in a word, on one possible type of cause is to scientize rather than to do good science.

Given the goals of epidemiology set out by Morris (1957)[29] and described in detail later by Shepherd (1982),[30] it makes sense that the questions asked are directed not only towards the fundamental issues of the nature of the disease, clues as to its aetiology, and the boundaries of the normal and the pathological[31] but also to more practical questions of treatment, provision of services, and the evaluation of various therapeutic interventions.

DIVERGENT QUESTIONS, GOALS, THEORIES, AND METHODS

Epidemiologists want to know 'how many? where? when? what happens? why? what is needed there to prevent and treat the illness?' Social scientists, however, not being medically trained, have a different agenda. They want to know 'how does this become recognized and classified as an illness? what does the person in whom the illness is said to reside and who believes himself or herself sick feel and think? what do those who consider that person sick feel and think? what actions are taken by each? what meaning do such actions have? how do the illness and its pattern of social interaction and treatment vary with other features of the social structure and cultural beliefs of that society, class or gender group? what is the structure and nature of the relationship between providers and receivers of therapeutic care?' Thus the differences between the epidemiological and the sociological or social anthropological approach and the methodologies most recently employed lie in the purposes for which each undertakes research and the uses to which it is hoped the work will be put. These goals are both affected by and affect a general theory (usually not spelt out or attended to by the epidemiologist) of the nature of illness; indeed, of human nature. Because this underlying general theory, and the purposes and outcome of epidemiological and sociological research, varies, the actual techniques employed in any given study have also, since Durkheim's *Suicide*, become increasingly divergent.

While epidemiologists have continued to map the distribution of mental illness with a special interest in schizophrenia, indicating that it is, for example, more common among young people, among lower socio-economic groups, among men rather than women, and in the central hotel and boarding house districts near the great railway terminals of cities,[32] sociologists have gone inside the mental institution unravelling its own madness,[33] have attached much importance to the societal reaction in the development of a 'career' that is stigmatized,[34] have shown how women's madness is stereotypically along lines permitted females and men's madness along stereotypically male lines,[35] that diagnostic and treatment patterns for black and other ethnic minority groups vary from those of the 'normal' (and more powerful) white groups with similar symptoms and the same diagnosis,[36] and have concentrated on the defining process itself,[37] and on paths to medical care.[38]

At the same time, there have been critiques of science that showed its activity as necessarily political. The very questions that are asked and left unexamined indicate this; thus, the over-representation of women among the depressed population is well reported in the literature, but the fact that unmarried men are over-represented, and the possible origins of this in the male psyche or environment, are not widely discussed in epidemiological research. Duster, in another context, uses the example of IQ studies to demonstrate that while correlational studies have been used to show the superiority of whites over blacks, the available evidence showing that Jews do better in schools than Gentiles has not been used to show the intellectual superiority of the Jews over Gentiles (Duster 1984).[39] Furthermore, since race is not a genetically homogeneous category, and since intelligence is not an objective phenomenon, such correlational studies depend for their validation on socio-political considerations. Littlewood (1986)[40] argues that not only should psychiatry apply social anthropology, but apply it to itself. If this were done, it would be seen that 'much of the endeavour of academic psychology and psychiatry is the reification and amplification of what is basically European folk psychology'.

Why did these two disciplines diverge in this way? Two answers are needed. First, the work of ancestors other than Durkheim became increasingly important and was developed during the 1960s and 1970s. Second, the upheaval in political and economic life that included the rapid growth of sociology in British universities was particularly favourable to the pursuit of these directions.

SOCIOLOGY: THE PURSUIT OF MEANING AND THE GROWTH OF QUALITATIVE METHODS

I have already pointed to the underlying model of disease and of human nature that underpins epidemiological work. It was this model that came under increasing attack as the work of ancestors other than Durkheim became increasingly important. Alfred Schutz[41] drew on Weber – particularly on his

41

concepts of *verstehen* (or empathetic understanding) and of the social actor's subjectivity, as well as on the work of Husserl, to produce a sociological phenomenology.[42] In this approach, it is the meaning of social action that is central and must be examined.[43] At the same time, the influence of George Herbert Mead became widely diffused. The 'I' of Mead's social actor is fundamentally constructed as the 'me' acts and reflects in relation always to the social world. It was, thus, not possible to accept uncritically the observer's truth; there had to be a detailed mapping of social *inter*action in order to build a meaningful picture of social *action*. Such an approach was particularly fruitful in deviancy studies where the concept of 'societal re-action' became central to understanding and explaining criminalization[44] or, indeed, the process of becoming and being a mental patient.[45]

The concepts that were developed by this school included 'career' and 'stigma'. These arose in conditions of secondary deviance. First, someone becomes disturbed or commits some law infraction. This is primary deviance. Various processes occur that might include that person coming before a psychiatrist or a judge. These people, occupying significant and powerful roles in the social structure, label the patient/offender. Now the possibility of secondary deviance occurs. The person may, in conditions where the behaviour that is labelled is stigmatized, take on the status of patient or criminal as their master-status. The label is sticky; it is not thrown off. New ways of behaving that confirm rather than deny the label are engaged in. The person enters a patient or criminal career. Such concepts led to a severely critical approach to the acceptance of expert definitions of the problem. It was the law-*makers* as much as the law-*breakers* who had to be studied, the labelling process as much as the characteristics of those labelled.

Work on mental illness in the late 1960s was also heavily influenced by the 'anti-psychiatry' of many psychiatrists such as Thomas Szasz in America and Ronald Laing in the UK. Their approaches were by no means unitary but Laing (among others) stressed the meaningfulness and centrality of the patient's own experience. At the same time in Britain, too, the new deviancy theorists[46] and critical criminologists,[47] putting a neo-Marxist view forward, were creating an entirely new climate in which to think about and investigate mental illness and the lives of mentally ill people.

Of course, none of these perspectives was without critics[48] and none is a complete explanation for the phenomenon of mental illness, but they have much to offer and they led to very different research agendas that stressed ethnographic and participant observer techniques, derived more from social anthropology than from survey research and the analysis of large-scale data sets. In Britain, there was a decisive move away from statistics and numeracy (also criticized on theoretical grounds)[49] in favour of qualitative work, perhaps, as I explore below, the result of the influx of not particularly numerate students, and faculty who were very much leaders of the new schools of thought.[50] In addition, there was a further, even more radical attack on traditional methods of sociological enquiry.

Originally an offspring of the phenomenology and interactionist schools, ethnomethodology[51] made the construction of the rate itself into the *topic* of research. A rate was no longer a resource, a step necessary as a spring-board for analysis and explanation. Indeed, when, in 1967, Douglas[52] returned to *Suicide*, intending not to undermine but to re-examine Durkheim's thesis, he ended by focusing on the social process of negotiation whereby the dead person becomes a suicide statistic – a process ignored by Durkheim. It was the detailed examination of this process (not of the relationship of the dead person to their families and social worlds) that laid bare the structure and culture, the norms of the society. In his examination he unravelled the 'everyday' and 'common-sense' decisions of family and friends, of clerks, coroners, and registrars. It was the rules according to which their judgements were made that illuminated social life.[53]

Such an approach directly contradicts that of trans- or cross-cultural psychiatry that now holds, for example, that schizophrenia, although it might be called by other names and have somewhat different cultural content and different outcomes, is found in roughly similar rates everywhere and that this fact will not be altered by the tools employed in its discovery.[54] Rather, the tools must be perfected *in order to* discover it. Yet it is clear that the tools employed do, quite fundamentally, alter what is discovered. At its most obvious, if a diagnostic interview schedule did not ask about drinking habits, there would be no alcoholism rate. DIS, the Diagnostic Interview Schedule,[55] used in the large-scale American Epidemiologic Catchment Area studies, is linked to DSM-III, and this manual changes each time it is issued by the American Psychiatric Association. Had the newly proposed diagnoses making women who remained in abusive relationships and men who committed rape but who fantasized about it beforehand[56] into mentally sick people been adopted in DSM III-R, the overall rates of mental illness for women and men would have increased overall. Perhaps there would be more sick than well people in each of the Epidemiologic Catchment Areas currently using DIS. As it is, Huffine has suggested that the equalization in the ratio of mental illness as between women and men appearing in these studies results from the fact that DIS, unlike other tools such as the Cornell Medical Index, emphasizes patterns of drug and alcohol use as mental illnesses and hence increases the male rate, thus reducing the female:male ratio.[57]

With ethnomethodology, sociology had seemingly come full circle, for we were no longer debunking or establishing common sense but investigating it. Sociology itself became just another way of accounting for life, no more and no less interesting. There were simply many ways of constructing meaning.

Given that literary scholars were busy analysing texts divorced from the social or psychological world and meanings within which they had been constructed, it is perhaps scarcely surprising that sociology, too, should have been required to examine different kinds of 'facts' and to face what it had hitherto taken for granted. Both activities were perhaps the product of an era at the end of optimism, in economic crisis and forced back on itself, an era which began to demonstrate impatience with the social and increasing dependence on and faith in the technological and the scientific.

This was all right if what you wanted from your work was to construct meaning, or, rather, to analyse how, in everyday life, it was done. But most sociologists still had other goals in mind, other questions they wished to pose. For these, among whom I number myself, ethnomethodology has been influential – it has meant that, even after a rate has been empirically questioned, it can never be uncritically accepted – but it has not led us to despair of posing the grander questions that Durkheim or Weber wished to pose. Wanting to pose such questions brings us back to the goals also of the epidemiologist, because, as I have pointed out, the very decision to pose certain and not other questions is political.

POLITICAL AND SOCIAL CHANGE

So, too, must the politics of the times enter as having both enabled and constrained the divergence of epidemiology and sociology, for their agendas arose within markedly different institutional settings. Epidemiology, to be taken at all seriously and to obtain resources and maintain precarious funding, had, like medicine itself (and especially those branches to which epidemiology was most closely allied – community and preventive medicine and, in our case, psychiatry) to turn away from its humanistic past and follow a model of 'hard science'. Technology (ushered in by the Wilson government in 1964) was the way of the future, whether translated as sophisticated computerized statistical packages, more standardized forms of measurement, or in hardware proper. That social science was also perceived as part of the technological revolution and given space and resources in the new technological universities founded at that time ignored the fact that the mass of students attracted to this field came from the humanities, had their eyes on the helping professions, journalism, or administration, were not particularly numerate, and were not budding scientists. Furthermore, top-ranking sociologists were part of the critique of society, including the critique of medicine and psychiatry explored here, that was also anti-'positivist' – a term that became merely abusive. This critique was allied to other broad, important socio-political changes elsewhere.

The Vietnamese conflict fundamentally altered the American political scene and it was accompanied and followed by sexual permissiveness and the cry for civil rights, particularly for black people but also for women, homosexuals, and people of various ethnic minorities. All these liberation movements stressed the importance of the history and experience of the people themselves. Women could not be spoken for; they had a voice of their own. This was no less true for black people who had been silenced for so long. Homosexuality was a

44

political choice and a particular, valid way of living in the world; it was not a mental illness or a condition that needed expert diagnosis and treatment. Hence its eventual disappearance from the American DSM in 1973 as a psychiatric diagnosis. These movements did not have the same powerful impact in Britain that they had in the United States, but London was the 'swinging city' and married women began to re-enter the market places of the world in increasing numbers.[58]

In addition, as the social climate changed, for example towards homosexuals, so there was, in fact, less distress among them of the kind that might lead to the psychiatric consulting room, because there was reduced stigma and greater opportunity for self-expression if not much greater opportunity in the social structure. (AIDS, of course, may swing opinion against gay men again.) Feminist scholars began to develop new theories about the psychology and development of women[59] that lend support to the newer feminist therapies that, instead of simply noticing women seemed to blame themselves for domestic strife and reported to professionals more often than men about relational problems,[60] offered both an explanation and strategies of treatment to address rather than suppress the problem.[61] Most recently, the idea that lay people – that is, *non-experts* in any particular social or medical problem – and those who actually suffer from such problems have to speak for themselves, are entitled to speak for themselves, and can affect their own destinies has resulted in powerful self-help groups, some still closely bound to the medical experts through advisory panels, others deliberately refusing such association because it gives less freedom for self-determination.[62]

In other words, there is no going back, though, in times of economic strain, regression is likely. Since the development of epidemiology has continued alongside that of sociology within these changing times, does it matter that the disciplines have followed rather different paths in their exploration of mental illness? What consequences in the sum of human happiness flow from that? There are, I think, both scientific and therapeutic consequences. Taking account of these consequences permits us to recognize the best areas in which the partnership might be revived.

REVIVING THE PARTNERSHIP

Littlewood has pointed out that the approaches that allocate to the culture a surrounding or content role – that is, that permit an acknowledgement, for example, that a certain diagnosis might be difficult to make when dealing with a person from a different ethnic background, or that a person's delusions may be culture specific – but not a generative one, have considerable difficulties in accounting not only for culture-bound syndromes such as *latah*,[63] but also for the appearance and disappearance of psychopathologies: 'such as agoraphobia, Briquet's syndrome, anorexia nervosa, exhibitionism, self-poisoning or,

45

perhaps, the chronic pain syndromes.'[64] Or, we might add, homosexuality. Who is to say how much misery was created by the recognition of homosexuality as a psychiatric disease? If these are scientific difficulties, the therapies that follow are likely, at the least, to be inappropriate and, at worst, to be iatrogenic. Fernando[65] challenges the very concept of depression among black people in Britain but also, given the high rates identified, moves to express this dilemma with respect to treatment. He suggests that racism acts as a 'poison'. Therefore:

> In dealing with a depressed person one should try to identify the blows to self esteem in recent events that arise from racism. An awareness of what happens is important because the patient has to develop strategies to safeguard self-esteem; finding alternative sources of self-pride may mean identifying with (for example) black movements, seeking ethnic therapists, or finding models (to identify with) that do not represent the dominant racial groups . . . Avoiding the issue by advising patients to 'accept' and lower expectations without understanding the situation is not helpful. Treatment within a model of depression caused by learned helplessness is to encourage strategies for self-assertion and control over events – not a 'coming to terms' or changing cognitive sets.   (Fernando 1986: 130–1)

Fernando, together with others interested in the concept of 'stress', employs epidemiological knowledge and strategies but grounds them in culture and in the specific meaning experiences have for the patient. This, it seems, is one area where the partnership between psychiatry and sociology and social anthropology proper (not merely as servicers of psychiatry) can flourish.

What the social conditions are that make for either particularly high or low rates of an illness *within* one culture or its more rapid or slower recovery rates remains an urgent topic of both epidemiological and sociological investigation. The sophistication of the concepts employed here has developed from straightforward 'stress', usually translated as 'life events' or 'social class' or 'marital status', to a multifactorial examination of particular stressors for particular gender and class and ethnic groups in given situations of 'vulnerability' that have powerful effects on self-esteem (Brown and Harris 1978)[66] and of complex interrelationships with psychological meaning, such as mastery and control over events and of one's own life (Thoits 1987).[67]

Of course, simple measurement of life events and outcomes does not *explain* the rates so obtained, any more than simply collecting data about diagnostic categories explains any differences found. It is this explanatory level that brings us back to our ancestors – both Durkheim and Weber. For Brown and Harris, for example, it is not simply that women, in the face of a severe life difficulty, are more vulnerable to depression if they lack a confiding relationship, a job outside the home, and have three children or more under 14 living at home; rather, it is the meaning of this that has to be understood. What is it about being a woman, about the relationship between women and men, about the place of paid employment, about roles (this is explored by Thoits) that is important? And, further, what are the psychological mechanisms (that might, of course, have organic concomitants) that are invoked in such situations? In a word, data-driven research – research that is done because there is a technique of measurement or analysis waiting to be employed – may add nothing to understanding.

Second, although the epidemiologist, working with a disease model, will expect to explain the incidence of any particular illness discovered by ignoring differences in meaning and reducing the possibilities to the smallest factor unravelled in *micro-analysis* of the genetics, biology, physiology, or chemistry undertaken in detailed laboratory studies of the blood groups, diets, viral exposure, hormone imbalance, brain chemistry, and so forth of the populations found to be most at risk compared with those least at risk, there is another direction to pursue.

The investigator can accept the definition as given of the disturbance but move to a broad *macro-analysis* that places the rate in the particular context in which it has been located and where it was generated, and is directed to taking account of particular meanings. Socio-anthropologist Nancy Scheper-Hughes's study of schizophrenia in rural Ireland furnishes an excellent example of the kind of work I have in mind (Scheper-Hughes 1979).[66]

Scheper-Hughes analyses the published figures that repeatedly show the highest rates of schizophrenia among Irish people, not only in Ireland but also in the United States after emigration. She stresses, too, another epidemiological finding: that the huge excess of schizophrenics in Ireland is among *single* people and men. This is not an illness of women or married people. Nor does it appear as early as it does elsewhere – rather it occurs first in young, bachelor men in their thirties. Nor do those who become sick marry and have children; they are outcasts from the pairing and child-bearing system. So a genetic disposition seems unlikely to provide an adequate explanation. Scheper-Hughes wants to understand and explain this differential, without denying a biological basis to the illness, but in terms of the cultural and structural worlds within which the Irish person is nurtured and in which they must survive. Using Thematic Apperception Tests and lengthy interviews, together with her own skills in participant observation, as she lived with her husband and two small children among the people of 'Ballybran', she identifies the heightened risk in terms of a whole complex of cultural and economic conditions. Patterns of farming, of emigration, of Catholicism and repressed sexuality, the specific position of individuals based on their gender and birth-order combine to drive the youngest sons mad and to exclude them from marriage and a satisfying maturity. She turns also to labelling theory for help in understanding why certain kinds of mental aberration are not identified as requiring hospital admission – the 'Saints' of her title – where others are.

Perhaps there is no answer in rural Ireland other than the massive hospitalization and drug therapies currently pursued, for the economic life of those areas is, she thinks, doomed; they are dying. On the other hand, perhaps profound socio-political change would reduce the rates of schizophrenia faster than any other treatment currently available.

In sum, the epidemiologist who can incorporate the best of sociological theorizing about the nature of the relationship between a particular set of structural and cultural conditions and the individual becoming disturbed, breaching social norms, being identified as mentally ill and requiring treatment, and the sociologist or social anthropologist who maintains always a critical and sceptical eye to any observation but who can join in the rigorous and, usually, numerically skilled work of the epidemiologist, have as much to offer one another in 1988 as they did in in 1958.

Acknowledgement: I am grateful to Colin Samson and Scott Pimley for help in the preparation of this chapter and to John Clausen for his comments on an earlier draft.

NOTES

1. Earls, F. (1987) 'Epidemiology of psychiatric disorders in children and adolescents', in G. Klerman, M. Weissman, P. Appelbaum, and L. Roth (eds) *Social, Epidemiologic and Legal Psychiatry*, vol. 5 of *Psychiatry*, New York: Basic Books, 133.

2. Lawson, A. (1966) *The Recognition of Mental Illness in London* (Maudsley Monograph No. 15), London: Oxford University Press. See pp. 1–2 for a definition of social psychiatry.

3. John Clausen summarizes social psychiatry now as embracing 'all those aspects of diagnosis, the aetiology, course and treatment of mental illness that are influenced by socio-cultural context in which each person develops', in 'Social psychiatry revisited', address to the Conference on Social Psychiatry, Tunghai University, Taiwan, 6 June 1987.

4. Shepherd, M., Cooper, B., Brown, A.C., and Kalton, G.W. (1966) *Psychiatric Illness in General Practice*, London: Oxford University Press.

5. See Martin Blumer's edited collection in honour of Philip Abrams (1985) *Essays on the History of Sociological Research*, Cambridge: Cambridge University Press, especially Halsey, A.H. 'Provincials and professionals: the British post-war sociologists', 151–64.

6. Using psychoanalysis, similar hopes were shared by members of the 'Culture and Personality' school represented particularly by Clyde Kluckhohn (1949), Margaret Mead (1928), Ruth Benedict (1934) and Abraham Kardiner, Ralph Linton, and C. DuBois (1945).

7. See Littlewood, R. (1986) 'Russian dolls and Chinese boxes: an anthropological approach to the implicit models of comparative psychiatry', in J. Cox (ed.) *Transcultural Psychiatry*, Bromley: Croom Helm. He points to increasing specialization, particularly in Britain: 'The syllabus for the examination for Membership to the Royal College of Psychiatrists in Britain includes social anthropology but no essay question has ever been set' (p. 38). In the United States, by contrast, chairs are held jointly in psychiatry and anthropology and Arthur Kleinman edits *Culture, Medicine and Psychiatry* from Harvard.

8. I use the term 'social action' in the Weberian sense: behaviour is the knees bent, the arms flexed, and the palms of the hands joined, the head bent and the eyes shut,

lips moving. Social action is praying. The praying might be considered a symptom of illness if the person does it in the middle of a busy street or continuously. It has a whole range of possible meanings depending on the particular individuals involved, their unique circumstances, desires, and beliefs.

9. First published in 1897 following an article that appeared in 1888 on suicide and the birth rate, which was falling as the suicide rate was rising, and a course of lectures in 1889–90.

10. In fact, Durkheim did not have the data to permit him to identify the person who had committed suicide with their actual religious affiliation; the measure was only one of the preponderance of one religion over another within a geographical area. Clearly, it is possible, if improbable, that all suicides were actually of Catholics in a predominantly Protestant area and vice versa. For a recent critique of Durkheim using similar contemporary data to those available to Durkheim, see Day, L.H. (1987) 'Durkheim on religion and suicide – a demographic critique', *Sociology* 21: 449–61.

11. Married women did not show this difference and the rates were not greatly different for men.

12. Durkheim did not actually begin there either. He had fairly well developed ideas about his theory before he used the empirical data. In other words, this was both deductive and inductive work.

13. He also described 'egoistic', 'altruistic', and 'fatalistic' forms of suicide but it is anomic suicide and anomie that has entered everyday sociology and captured the imagination as surely as has Marx's concept of 'alienation'. Steven Lukes, in his classic work on Durkheim (first published by Allen Lane in 1973), points out that 'anomie differs from egoism and altruism in that it depends not on how individuals are attached to society but on how it regulates them' (Lukes, Penguin edition, 1977: 207). (Fatalism occurs in over-regulation where the individual becomes powerless.) Thus, anomie is most clearly sociological; it is the result of social forces, of the 'social fact', as concrete as any material stick or stone, external to the individual and constraining (or enabling) action.

14. See Townsend, P. (1985) 'Surveys of poverty to promote democracy', and Baric, L.F. (1985) 'Reading the palm of the invisible hand: indicators, progress and prediction', both in M. Bulmer (ed.) *Essays on the History of Sociological Research*, Cambridge: Cambridge University Press.

15. Sprott, W.H. (1962) *Sociology at the Seven Dials*, London: Athlone Press.

16. Abrams, P. (1985) 'The uses of British sociology', in M. Bulmer (ed.), op. cit.

17. Srole *et al.* used impairment measures in the Midtown studies. See Srole, L., Langner, T.S., Michael, S.T., Opler, M.K., and Rennie, T.A.C. (1962) *Mental Health in the Metropolis: The Midtown Manhattan Study*, New York: McGraw-Hill.

18. Janowitz, M. (1970) *Political Conflict*, Chicago: Quadrangle.

19. Abrams, P. (1985) 'The uses of British sociology', in M. Bulmer (ed.), op. cit.

20. Eaton, W. (1986) *The Sociology of Mental Disorders*, New York: Praeger, p. 42.

21. Wing, J.K. (1978) *Reasoning About Madness*, London: Oxford University Press.

22. Richard Neugebauer, Bruce Dohrenwend, and Barbara Snell Dohrenwend, reviewing the prevalence of disorders in the American adult population, state that 'different concepts and methods have led to very different estimates of amounts of disorder in these studies'. From 'Formulation of hypotheses about the true prevalence of functional psychiatric disorders among adults in the United States', in B. Dohrenwend, B.S. Dohrenwend, M.S. Gould, B. Link, R. Neugebauer, and R. Wunsch-Hitzig (eds) (1980) *Mental Illness in the United States: Epidemiological Estimates*, New York: Praeger, pp. 45–94.

23. World Health Organization (1973) *International Pilot Study of Schizophrenia*, Geneva: WHO; also the current WHO *Collaborative Study*.

24. For the US–UK Diagnostic Project, see Cooper, J.E., Kendell, R., Gurland, B.J., Sharpe, L., Copeland, J.R.M., and Simon, R. (1972) *Psychiatric Diagnosis in New York and London* (Maudsley Monograph No. 20), London: Oxford University Press; WHO (1979) *Schizophrenia: International Follow-Up Study*, Chichester: Wiley.

25. Julian Leff has pointed out that the difference in mania found between Aarhus, Denmark, and Camberwell, London, in the IPSS (16 per cent: 5 per cent) disappeared when case registers were established in both centres, suggesting the first difference 'was an artefact attributable to differences in referral and admission practices'. Leff, J. (1986) 'The epidemiology of mental illness across cultures', in J. Cox (ed.), op. cit., 23–36.

26. Leff, in the work quoted above, summarizes these difficulties in cross-cultural work, pointing out that many societies have no words to express western concepts such as anxiety or depression and that even when local scales are devised, translation to produce universal categories remains fraught with difficulty.

27. Thus studies within urban areas using standardized measures have produced rates of schizophrenia that are comparable with other similar areas. See Hodiamont, P., Peer, N., and Syben, N. (1987) 'Epidemiological aspects of psychiatric disorder in a Dutch health area', *Psychological Medicine* 17: 495–505.

28. Sartorius, N., Jablensky, A., Korten, A., Ernberg, G., Anker, M., Cooper, J.E., and Day, R. (1986) *Psychological Medicine* 16 (4): 909–28.

29. Morris, J.N. (1957) *Uses of Epidemiology*, Edinburgh: Churchill Livingstone.

30. Shepherd, M. (1982) 'The application of the epidemiological method in psychiatry', in T.A. Baasher, *et al.* (eds) *Epidemiology and Mental Health Services: Principle and Applications for Developing Countries* (*Acta Psychiatrica Scandinavia* Supplement 296, vol. 65).

31. Shepherd, M., Oppenheim, A.N., and Mitchell, S. (1971) *Childhood Behaviour and Mental Health*, London: University of London Press. Listing the prevalence of so-called symptoms of childhood disturbance such as bed-wetting in boys made it possible to see that what was common at four was relatively uncommon at fourteen. Such findings have clear implications for the construction of a medical problem and for treatment. 'With these data,' Shepherd noted later, 'it has proved possible to construct a picture of behavioural *norms*' (Baasher, op. cit., p. 11).

32. Eaton, W. (1986) *The Sociology of Mental Disorders*, New York: Praeger, and Cockerham, W. .(1981) *The Sociology of Mental Disorder*, Englewood Cliffs, NJ: Prentice Hall, summarize these major and consistent findings.

33. Goffman, E. (1961) *Asylums: Essays on the Social Situation of Mental Patients and Other Inmates*, New York: Doubleday; Rosenhan, D. (1973) 'On being sane in insane places', *Science* 179: 250–8.

34. Lemert, E. (1967) *Human Deviance, Social Problems and Social Control*, Englewood Cliffs, NJ: Prentice Hall; Goffman, E. (1968) *Stigma: Notes on the Management of Spoiled Identity*, Harmondsworth: Penguin.

35. Chesler, P. (1973) *Women and Madness*, New York: Avon Books; Showalter, E. (1986) *The Female Malady: Women, Madness and English Culture, 1830–1980*, New York: Pantheon; Penfold, S. and Walker, G. (1984) *Women and the Psychiatric Paradox*, Milton Keynes: Open University Press; Joan Busfield argues that the typical excess of affective disorder in women and of schizophrenia in men may be the result of 'differential involvement of the psychiatric profession with women' (Busfield, J. 'Gender, mental illness and psychiatry', in M. Evans and C. Ungerson (eds) (1983) *Sexual Divisions: Patterns and Processes*, London: Tavistock, 106–35).

36. See Littlewood, R. and Lipsedge, M. (1982) *Aliens and Alienists: Ethnic Minorities and Psychiatry*, Harmondsworth: Penguin; Fernando, S. (1986) 'Depression in ethnic minorities', in J. Cox (ed.), op. cit., pp. 107–38; Schwab, J., Bell, R., Warheit, E., and Schwab, R. (1979) *Social Order and Mental Health: The Florida Health Study*, New York: Brunner/Mazel; Littlewood, R. and Cross, S. (1980) 'Ethnic

minorities and psychiatric services', *Sociology of Health and Illness* 2 (2): 194–201.

37. Smith, D.K. (1978) 'K is mentally ill', *Sociology* 12 (1).

38. Lawson, A. (op cit., 1966); Gurin, G., Veroff, J., and Feld, S.C. (1960) *Americans View Their Mental Health*, New York: Basic Books; Douvan, E. and Kulka, R. (1981) *Mental Health in America*, New York: Basic Books.

39. Duster, T. (1984) 'Biological knowledge', in T. Duster and K. Garret (eds) *Cultural Perspectives on Biological Knowledge*, Norwood, NJ: Ablex.

40. Littlewood, R. (1986) 'Russian dolls and Chinese boxes', in J. Cox (ed.), op. cit., 43.

41. Schutz, A. (1945) 'On multiple realities', *Philosophy and Phenomenological Research* 5: 533–76.

42. See Giddens, A. (1976) *New Rules of Sociological Method*, London: Hutchinson, pp. 23–33, for an account and critique of phenomenology.

43. See Brown, G. and Harris, T. (1978) *The Social Origins of Depression*, London: Tavistock, chapter five on 'meaning', for a discussion of this approach.

44. Leading scholars are: Schur, E. (1969) 'Reactions to deviance: a critical assessment', *American Journal of Sociology* 49: 499–507; Becker, H. (ed.) (1963) *Outsiders: Studies in the Sociology of Deviance*, Glencoe, Ill.: Free Press; Erikson, K. (1962) 'Notes on the sociology of deviance', in Becker (op. cit., 1963), and (1966) *Wayward Puritans*, New York: Wiley; Kitsuse, J. (1962) 'Societal reaction to deviant behaviour', in Becker (op. cit. 1963); and Lemert, E. (1951) *Social Pathology*, New York: McGraw-Hill. The last-named was the originator of the idea of primary and secondary deviance but his ideas were not really taken up until after they were further developed in 1967 in *Human Deviance, Social Problems and Social Control*, Englewood Cliffs, NJ: Prentice-Hall.

45. Scheff, T. (1966) *Being Mentally Ill*, Chicago: Aldine.

46. Cohen, S. (1971) *Images of Deviance*, Harmondsworth: Penguin (for the National Deviancy Conference).

47. Taylor, I., Walton, P., and Young, J. (1973) *The New Criminology*, London: Routledge & Kegan Paul; Taylor, I., Walton, P., and Young, J. (1975) *Critical Criminology*, London: Routledge & Kegan Paul.

48. Especially Walter Gove who conducted careful studies of various aspects of the labelling process, demonstrating its inadequacy to account, for example, for the difference in female and male rates of mental illness: Gove, W. (ed.) (1974) *The Labelling of Deviance: Evaluating a Perspective*, London and Beverly Hills: Sage; Gove, W. (ed.) (1982) *Deviance and Mental Illness*, London and Beverly Hills: Sage.

49. Hindess, B. (1973) *The Use of Official Statistics in Sociology*, London: Macmillan. And see also Box, S. (1971) *Deviance, Reality and Society*, New York: Holt, Rinehart and Winston, chapter five.

50. The paradox that British sociology is considered among the best in the world at the same time as its numeracy and sophistication in quantitative research are less advanced is set out in the ESRC report, *Horizons and Opportunities in the Social Science* (1987), chaired by Griffith Edwards.

51. Garfinkel, H. (1968) *Studies in Ethnomethodology*, Englewood Cliffs, NJ: Prentice-Hall; Cicourel, A. (1964) *Method and Measurement in Sociology*, Glencoe, Ill.: Free Press; Cicourel, A. (1968) *The Social Organization of Juvenile Justice*, New York: Wiley; Turner, R. (ed.) (1974) *Ethno-methodology*, Harmondsworth: Penguin.

52. Douglas, J. (1967) *The Social Meanings of Suicide*, Princeton: Princeton University Press. See also Atkinson, J.M. (1978) *Discovering Suicide: Studies in the Social Organisation of Sudden Death*, London: Macmillan.

53. Coulter, J. (1973) *Approaches to Insanity*, Chichester: Wiley, employs the ethnomethodological perspective in relation to other categories of mental illness.

54. Murphy, J.M. (1986) 'Cross-cultural psychiatry', in G. Klerman, M. Weissman,

P. Appelbaum, and L. Roth (eds) *Social, Epidemiological and Legal Psychiatry*, vol. 5 of *Psychiatry*, New York: Basic Books, chapter two.

55. Robins, L., Helzer, J., Croughan, J., and Ratcliff, K. (1981) 'National Institute of Mental Health Diagnostic Interview Schedule', *Archives of General Psychiatry* 38: 381–9.

56. 'Self-defeating disorder aka masochism' and 'paraphilic coercive disorder aka rapism'. The former remains in Appendix A. The latter has not been incorporated although sadism (excluding sexual sadism) is also in Appendix A. Various other paraphilic disorders that can include the commission of rape remain.

57. Huffine, C. (1987), personal communication.

58. Hakim, C. 'Social monitors: population censuses as social surveys', in M. Bulmer (ed.) op. cit., 43–44, notes that women were as involved in the labour force in mid-nineteenth-century England as they are now.

59. Miller, J.B. (1976) *Towards a New Psychology of Women*, Boston: Beacon (Harmondsworth: Penguin, 1978); Chodorow, N. (1978) *The Reproduction of Mothering: Psychoanalysis and the Sociology of Gender*, Berkeley: University of California Press; Gilligan, C. (1982) *In a Different Voice*, Harvard: Harvard University Press.

60. Lehtiner, V. and Konkama, M. (1987) 'Mental disorders in a sample representative of the whole adult Finnish population', in B. Cooper (ed) *Psychiatric Epidemiology: Progress and Prospects*, Bromley: Croom Helm.

61. Penfold, S. and Walker, G. (1984) *Women and the Psychiatric Paradox*, Milton Keynes: Open University Press.

62. The MS Society is an example of the former kind of self-help patient group, ARMS (Action for Research in Multiple Sclerosis) an example of the latter. In practice, members of both groups (and some join both) who have MS have become considerable experts in their illness, and both groups provide advice and support and raise funds for research. ARMS decides independently of medical advice which projects to pursue.

63. Although Kenny, cited by Littlewood, has suggested '*latah* in its cross-cultural distribution is no more of a paradox than is the fact that all people have hands, but only some cultures have exploited the fact in requiring them to be shaken in formal greeting'. Littlewood, R. (1985), in *Psychiatric Medicine* 17 (1), reviewing Simons, R.C. and Hughes, C.C. (eds) (1985) *The Culture Bound Syndromes: Folk Illnesses of Psychiatric and Anthropological Interest*, Dordrecht, Boston: Reidel.

64. Littlewood, R. (1986) 'Russian dolls and Chinese boxes', in J. Cox (ed.), op. cit., p. 50.

65. Fernando, S. (1986) 'Depression in Ethnic Minorities', in J. Cox (ed.), op. cit., 107–38.

66. Brown, G. and Harris, T., op. cit.

67. Thoits, P. (1987) 'Gender and marital status differences in control and distress: common stress versus unique stress explanations', *Journal of Health and Social Behavior*, 28: 17–22, argues that life events are not, in and of themselves, damaging to people of certain status groups (women, the unmarried, lower social class, etc.). Rather, the relationship with psychological disturbance is mediated by such factors as whether or not the events in question are controllable and whether or not the person has mastery over situations. For example, both depression and anxiety are positively correlated to a sense of mastery. Among married males there is a negative relationship with anxiety and depression but a positive relationship with mastery. Thus, it is particular roles that individuals hold that account for much of the stress (p. 18).

68. Scheper-Hughes, N. (1979) *Saints, Scholars and Schizophrenics: Mental Illness in Rural Ireland*, Berkeley: University of California Press.

4

The Contribution of Psychology

Monica Briscoe

'Many of the facts, and even some of the principles, that psychologists have discovered when they may have thought they were discovering something else are useful.'   (Skinner 1987: 782)

Definitions of a science are often misleading. In no case is this more true than that of psychology, for much confusion exists as to what should be its proper subject matter. The roots of this are largely historical. During the heyday of behaviourism, it was fashionable to define psychology narrowly as the science of behaviour. For a long time scientific psychologists ignored questions that were of central importance to the understanding of mind, while their activities were almost restricted to the study of learning in the rat. More recently, subjective factors have been readmitted so that psychology is now commonly regarded as the science of behaviour and experience (Pritchard 1986). However, within the discipline there are inevitably many different areas using different levels of explanation. This variety has prompted Beloff (1973) to propose that there is no single science of psychology but rather a number of sciences, each asking different questions, using different methods, and making different assumptions. Certainly, discipline boundaries are somewhat arbitrary and artificial, especially in the human sciences, and the essential core of psychology is particularly difficult to identify. However, Radford (1987: 283) has specified its particular focus of interest as being 'the individual as an emergent product of physiology and society'.

Not only is the essence of psychology difficult to define, but its relationship with the world to which it might be expected to relate is also particularly problematic. This is partly because the topics of theoretical interest tend to be very specific, seeking to explain only a tiny portion of behaviour as it occurs in a carefully defined and restricted situation. Thus it has been said, with some truth, that academic psychology 'consists in knowing more and more about less and less' (Watson 1963: 487). As a result, psychologists are not taken very seriously as experts, especially because the everyday experience of relating to other people necessitates everyone being his or her own psychologist. A scientific approach stresses certainty and lawfulness but most people do not view human behaviour as either comprehensible or predictable. It might be expected that a world full of essentially human problems and a science devoted to the analysis of (human) behaviour would be addressing each other constantly and productively. Yet, in practice, students of the subject tend to find that psychology is interesting but not particularly useful (Radford 1985). Because its subject matter lies within common experience, it is not only dismissed as nothing more than common sense but also compared unfavourably with other sciences. Ironically, a further degree of prejudice actually arises from the confusion of psychology with psychiatry, so that the former is tainted with the stigma of mental illness in the lay mind.

Psychiatrists are no more immune to such misconceptions than any other section of the population. And yet psychiatry is as much a branch of psychology as of medicine. A basic premise in psychology is that an appreciation of the wide variation in 'normality' is fundamental to the understanding of abnormal functioning. Major branches are concerned with the assessment of individual differences in personality and intelligence. This philosophy also underlies the procedures for post-graduate training in applied psychology. For example, as a prerequisite of their specialization, those wishing to become educational psychologists are required to undertake several years' teaching of normal children on top of their basic studies in general psychology. Medical education, on the other hand, concentrates on the diagnosis and treatment of pathological conditions; the study of normal functioning is abandoned at a relatively early stage. Nevertheless, some of the most successful examples of applied psychology are to be found in the clinical sphere. Psychologists have developed a wide range of behaviour and cognitive therapies, originally derived from learning theory but more recently incorporating a cognitive perspective also (Eysenck 1975). Other examples include the application of intelligence testing to the diagnostic process in neuropsychiatry. Thus, despite its comparative youth, psychology has established itself as a basic science of psychiatry, in a relationship paralleling that between physiology and somatic disease (Lewis 1967).

Farrell (1985: 14) has observed that it is its psychological subject matter which makes psychiatry important and distinctive in medicine, even though, 'as a psychological enquiry, psychiatry is still in a very primitive stage'. In view of this, it is hardly surprising that a number of ideological positions have evolved, including the biological, the dynamic, the behavioural, and the social, each of which places a different emphasis on the respective contributions of man, culture, and nature to the phenomenon of mental illness (Clare 1976). Interest in social psychiatry stems from the belief that mental illness is a product of civilization, a viewpoint which has been traced back to Democritus in the fifth century BC (Schwab and Schwab 1978). It seeks to discover the social causes of disorder in the hope that this will lead to the rational development of social methods of prevention, and that increased understanding of social influences on course and outcome will suggest appropriate techniques of treatment and rehabilitation. The topics of interest include all aspects of the social causes, concomitants and consequences of psychiatric disorder, together with social techniques for dealing with them. Social psychiatrists are also concerned with planning and evaluating social and medical services as well as the assessment of the psychiatric implications of public policy in such areas as employment, education, and housing.

There are three major causal hypotheses which have received a great deal of attention in this field. The first is that the loss of one's mother in childhood predisposes the individual to depressive illness in later life (Tennant, Bebbington and Hurry 1980), an approach with its roots in the psychoanalytic tradition (Bowlby 1958). The second is that recent exposure to adverse experiences or events leads to an increased incidence of psychiatric disorder. This model postulates that a vulnerable individual will develop an episode of disease only if it is triggered by a life-event stressor. However, findings from a number of studies indicate that less than ten per cent of the variance in the occurrence of episodes is linked to such adverse experiences (Rabkin and Struening 1976). Since there seem to be many individuals who do not develop disorders after such exposure, it seems that there must also be some quite powerful modifying influences. Third, there has been considerable interest in investigating the importance of social networks as just such a moderating variable for absorbing the impact of stress. Thus, it has been suggested that a deficiency in social relationships might be a causal factor in the onset of neurosis, although the evidence for this is limited (Henderson, Byrne and Duncan-Jones 1981).

These three views as to aetiology are in no way mutually exclusive (Brown and Harris 1978). It is, however, clear from them that social psychiatrists rely on no single underlying theory. Indeed, they draw on diverse disciplines, including biology, psychology, and sociology. The relation to sociology is particularly close because there is a common concern with the various social phenomena reflected in the relationship of society to mental illness and its sufferers. Hence, there are instances of considerable overlap in both topic and method, as, for example, in Durkheim's (1897) classic study of suicide. This involved the empirical exploration of the social correlates of suicide as well as theorizing about the influence of collective processes on the individual's tendency towards self-destruction. The distinction between sociology and social psychology is by no means clear-cut, but central to the former is the view that explanations at the societal level of analysis are satisfactory and not reducible to psychological or biological concepts. Important contributions to the ideas used in social psychiatry have also come from sociological approaches to deviance, stratification, collective behaviour, and institutions, as well as studies of the family, small groups, and social networks.

The main tool of the social psychiatrist is, however, the epidemiological method, which is essentially the study of human populations based on rates of illness. Epidemiology differs from clinical medicine in that its focus is not primarily on the characteristics of patients but on 'the patterns of disease occurrence in human populations and of the factors that influence these patterns' (Lilienfeld and Lilienfeld 1980: 3). The clinical approach cannot answer epidemiological questions since the information available is restricted to patients under medical care. Hence, clinical findings cannot be contrasted with those in other members of the same population who are free from the condition under consideration. Barker and Rose (1984) have pointed out that in order to conduct standardized examinations of large numbers of (mostly healthy) people, epidemiologists have to accept lower standards of diagnostic accuracy than clinicians. Conversely, 'problems of case definition and quality control of measurements must be considered more rigorously in population than in clinical studies' (Barker and Rose 1984: 30). The underlying philosophy of epidemiology is actually closely akin to that of the *nomothetic* approach within psychology. This seeks to build up an objective and quantitative picture of the parameters of a population. The aim of nomothetic research is the establishment of universal laws, generally through the use of the quantitative (mostly multivariate) and experimental methods of psychology. Such a strategy stands in contrast to the *idiographic* approach, in which the focus of concern is on the description of unique events and specific individuals, a position closely analogous to that of the clinician. Within psychology, researchers favouring the idiographic position tend to prefer a subjective approach and stress the need for intuitive understanding of each individual. It is, however, important to appreciate that the size of the population studied is not necessarily a criterion to be used in differentiating the nomothetic from the idiographic. This applies even when the population under consideration is restricted to a single individual. Thus, Freud (1900) was endeavouring to discover the general principles underlying dreaming on the basis of data derived primarily from himself. Moreover, among experimental psychologists, we find the example of Ebbinghaus (1885), who used just one subject in his search for general laws of memory. Although no absolute distinctions can be drawn, this may be contrasted with the essentially idiographic work of Luria (1969), who spent over thirty years studying a single case involving an unusual capacity for remembering.

What then does psychology have to offer epidemiological psychiatry? The primary contribution is methodological. A large body of knowledge has been developed both in the field and under laboratory conditions about observational methods, including interviewing techniques, questionnaire design, and attitude measurement (Davies 1972). Sadly, the psychological literature in these areas remains largely unknown to psychiatrists, resulting, at best, in unnecessary duplication of effort (e.g. at the pilot stage of a questionnaire) or, at worst, in the use of clumsy and badly constructed instruments. A specific example of the lack of communication between psychologists and psychiatrists interested in epidemiology concerns the failure of the latter to make use of standard psychometric tests for case identification. Thus, for example, it would seem that some of the tests of cognitive function developed by clinical psychologists might have considerable potential for exploring the epidemiology of dementia. In practice, however, these validated tests are often ignored and assessments attempted through the use of psychiatrists' own instruments.

The clinical interview is the major psychiatric tool for arriving at a diagnosis. Diagnosis is an application of both psychology and psychiatry. However, the categorization of mental disorder and the phenomenological investigations on which diagnoses are based arise largely from psychiatry, whereas the development of systematic interviews and the determination of their reliability and validity stem primarily from psychology (Oppenheim 1966). In itself the interview is a form of natural conversation and its special characteristics have only recently been appreciated. Psychology's successes in providing psychometric methods for assessing intelligence and personality by the use of systematic tests and inventories served to challenge the somewhat haphazard way in which interviews had been carried out by psychiatrists. The development of psychometric methods has also served to encourage the construction of self-rating inventories to be completed by patients as well as checklists for interviewers. Self-report instruments, such as the General Health Questionnaire (Goldberg 1972), have the advantage of eliminating interview bias and interpretation. The emphasis is on the individual's response rather than on the response of the interviewer to the patient's behaviour. Inevitably, however, such measures are useful principally for surveys of psychiatric morbidity in the general population, rather than being suitable for the classification of inpatients.

A major area of research in social psychology deals with the way people interpret the causality of events, and such research has great importance for psychiatry (Nisbett and Valins 1971). Attribution theory is concerned with meaning in social action and the motives and traits attributed to oneself and others under various conditions (Heider 1958). An attribution approach examines the way people appraise their inner states and behaviour and explain changes in feelings and experience (Harvey and Weary 1985). It is also concerned with the effects of such definitions on subsequent feelings and behaviour. The way symptoms and behaviour are conceptualized may have an important influence on the course of disorder, help-seeking, and rehabilitation. Thus, changes in assumptions about the capacity of the mentally ill to remain in the community are as much a product of changing attributions as of new knowledge. Historically, many attributions made to the helplessness, irresponsibility, and dangerousness of the mentally ill actually served to exacerbate such reactions by isolating and stigmatizing patients. Conversely, it is now clear that normalization of symptoms and an emphasis on positive aspects of behaviour and experience may do a lot to maintain and enhance social functioning. Thus, for example, it is increasingly recognized that the improvement of the mental health services depends on the strengthening of the family doctor in his therapeutic role rather than on a large proliferation and expansion of specialist psychiatric services (Shepherd 1987).

It is also clear that the difficulties faced by any individual may be determined as much by social structure as by personal traits. Increasingly, the problems characteristically experienced by members of particular groups are being examined in terms of the ways in which social attributions and environmental organization limit the opportunities for such individuals to adjust to their circumstances. Such a trend can be made out in the literature concerning sex differences in psychiatric disorder. Numerous studies report a higher prevalence of psychological distress in women (Weissman and Klerman 1977). This is particularly true of the neuroses and manic depressive psychoses (i.e., disorders which involve personal discomfort). By contrast, the sex difference is either reversed or non-existent when personality disorders and schizophrenia are under consideration (Dohrenwend and Dohrenwend 1976). It has been argued that these differences reflect the general strains in the social role of women in contemporary society, which include the stresses and frustrated expectations of the housewife role and the discrepancies between education and preparation of women for adult roles and the realities of their daily lives. Thus, it has been suggested that marriage is much more protective for men than for women, and there are also indications that single women fare better than single men (Briscoe 1982). Certainly, attitudes to women are still more negative than those towards men, while inequality between the sexes is often attributed to women's primary role of housewife rather than worker, which itself has disastrous consequences for their self-image. Women's disadvantaged status has been perceived as contributing to a low level of psychological well-being both directly, in that women find their situation inherently depressing, and indirectly through the socially conditioned mechanism of *learned helplessness* (Seligman 1975) whereby young girls are socialized to value the stereotype of femininity and develop a cognitive set against assertiveness and independence.

Apart from general approaches, methodological issues, and measurement techniques, psychology also has substantive contributions to make to epidemiological and social psychiatry. Among the most fundamental come from the study of psycholinguistics. It is known that people all share identical types of processing capacities and, on the whole, have similar personal and social needs. Thus, for example, groups of speakers need to refer to objects and actions in their environment, and hence certain kinds of linguistic units reflect the basic human need to communicate experience. Specific languages may differ considerably in their precise form, but *all* languages share the common requirement to refer to objects. This reflection of common human desires, aspirations, and anxieties among all languages has been termed *linguistic universality*. Naturally, particular cultures differ in their needs according to environmental factors, so that the kinds of things for which people have words may differ from one linguistic community to another. The existence of such linguistic differences, which directly reflect cultural differences, has led to the concept of *linguistic relativity*. Thus, for example, distinguishing various forms of rice is relatively unimportant in western technological cultures but much more important where rice is a staple diet. The Hanunoo of the Philippine Islands have names for ninety-two varieties of rice, but all ninety-two varieties are, for the English speaker, simply *rice* (Brown 1965). In this context, it has been observed that the English language is extremely rich in words to describe mood states. Thus, 'in addition to "depressed" one can be despondent, despairing, disconsolate, dispirited, disillusioned, gloomy, melancholy, miserable, morbid, morose, unhappy, sad, and so on' (Rack 1982: 106). In many non-European languages, however, the emotional vocabulary is far more restricted. In Yoruba, for example, one word suffices for both 'angry' and 'sad', two emotions which most Europeans would consider to be quite distinct. In Ghana, just three words cover all shades of unpleasant emotion, their meaning perhaps being conveyed by the somewhat ambiguous English term, 'upset'. In contrast to its rich vocabulary of introspective words, English is very vague with regard to family relationships. Terms such as 'cousin' and 'brother-in-law' cover a variety of different relationships and role obligations, which would merit different words in most family-oriented cultures. Hence, the concept of linguistic relativity shows that, rather than some languages being primitive, each culture develops a rich vocabulary around the issues which seem particularly important to these people at that time.

The essential question in this field is, therefore, whether the experience of emotional distress is the same even if the vocabulary is different? If language serves to chart an experience introspectively, then it is at least possible that the internal experiences concerned are modified by the words available. As Rack has put it, 'if the only available word is "upset", is the experience equally non specific? Does the Pakistani not know whether he is anxious or miserable? . . . Two depressed patients (English and Pakistani) may be having similar emotional experiences, but we cannot be sure they are identical' (Rack 1982: 107–8). Rather than words merely reflecting patterns of thought and interest within a given society (as common sense might suggest), in its extreme form the notion of linguistic relativity implies that patterns of thought are actually shaped by the words a society has agreed to use. Thus, language serves not only to report experience but also to define it (Whorf 1956). As a result of this there will obviously be difficulties in translation. Rack (1982) has observed that it might actually be quite pointless to ask an Urdu speaker (for instance) whether his feelings are mainly those of 'anxiety' or of 'sadness', although a great deal of psychiatric diagnosis depends heavily on just such a question. Similar problems arise even among different sections within English society; inarticulate groups are less able to translate their knowledge into thoughts so that much emotional and introspective knowledge remains unnamed for them (Bernstein 1971). The notion of linguistic relativity suggests that thought and language are not independent processes, with the latter being the overt manifestation of the former. Rather, it appears that our thinking about the world is only possible through the ways in which we reflect it in language. Such findings are of major importance in many applied fields, including education and general medicine, but perhaps nowhere more than in psychiatry because of the central role of language in its diagnostic process.

Mechanic (1985) has argued that psychiatry is primarily an applied social science and therefore its concerns cannot be differentiated from those of the social and behavioural sciences more generally. Psychology is both a social and a behavioural science and hence basic to both epidemiology and social medicine. There is still much truth, however, in Ebbinghaus' (1908) famous dictum that psychology has a long past but only a short history. Its long past lies in the philosophical tradition, its short history is that of the experimental method. Inevitably, therefore, its contribution to social and epidemiological psychiatry is found less in the direct application of psychological findings than in the lending and exchanging of methods for joint investigation.

REFERENCES

Barker, D.J.P. and Rose, G. (1984) *Epidemiology in Medical Practice*, third edition, Edinburgh: Churchill Livingstone.

Beloff, J. (1973) *Psychological Sciences: A Review of Modern Psychology*, London: Crosby Lockwood Staples.

Bernstein, B.B. (1971) *Class, Codes and Control*, St Albans: Paladin.

Bowlby, J. (1958) 'The nature of the child's tie to his mother', *International Journal of Psychoanalysis* 39: 1–34.

Briscoe, M.E. (1982) *Sex Differences in Psychological Well-Being*, (Psychological Medicine Monograph Supplement 1).

Brown, G.W. and Harris, T. (1978) *Social Origins of Depression: A Study of Psychiatric Disorder in Women*, London: Tavistock.

Brown, R. (1965) *Social Psychology*, New York and London: Collier-Macmillan.

Clare, A.W. (1976) *Psychiatry in Dissent: Controversial Issues in Thought and Practice*, London: Tavistock.

Davies, R.M. (1972) *Fundamentals of Attitude Measurement*, New York: Wiley.

Dohrenwend, B.P. and Dohrenwend, B.S. (1976) 'Sex differences and psychiatric disorders', *American Journal of Sociology* 81: 1447–54.

Durkheim, E. (1897) *Le suicide: étude de sociologie*, Paris: Alcan, translated by J.A. Spaulding and G. Simpson (1951) *Suicide*, Glencoe, Ill.: Free Press.

Ebbinghaus, H. (1885) *Uber das Gedachtnis: Untersuchungen zur experimentallen Psychologie*, Leipzig: Duncker & Humblot, translated by H.A. Ruger and C.E. Bussenius (1964) *Memory: A Contribution to Experimental Psychology*, New York: Dover.

Ebbinghaus, H. (1908) *Abriss der Psychologie*, Leipzig: Veit & Co., translated by M. Miller (1908) *Psychology: An Elementary Textbook*, Boston: Heath.

Eysenck, H.J. (1975) 'Psychological theories and behaviour therapy', *Psychological Medicine* 5: 219–21.

Farrell, B.A. (1985) 'Philosophy and psychiatry: some reflections on the nature of psychiatry', in M. Shepherd (ed.) *Handbook of Psychiatry Volume 5: The Scientific Foundations of Psychiatry*, Cambridge: Cambridge University Press, pp. 3–15.

Freud, S. (1900) *The Interpretation of Dreams*, translated by J. Strachey (1953), London: Hogarth.

Goldberg, D. (1972) *The Detection of Psychiatric Illness by Questionnaire* (Maudsley Monograph No. 21), London: Oxford University Press.

Harvey, J.H. and Weary, G. (1985) *Attribution, Basic Issues and Applications*, London: Academic Press.

Heider, F. (1958) *The Psychology of Interpersonal Relations*, New York: Wiley.

Henderson, S., Byrne, D.G., and Duncan-Jones, P. (1981) *Neurosis and the Social Environment*, Sydney: Academic Press.

Lewis, A. (1967) 'Empirical or rational? The nature and basis of psychiatry', *Lancet* ii: 1–9.

Lilienfeld, A.M. and Lilienfeld, D.E. (1980) *Foundations of Epidemiology*, second edition, Oxford: Oxford University Press.

Luria, A.R. (1969) *The Mind of a Mnemonist*, translated from the Russian by L. Solitariff, London: Jonathan Cape.

Mechanic, D. (1985) 'Social science in relation to psychiatry', in M. Shepherd (ed.) *Handbook of Psychiatry Volume 5: The Scientific Foundations of Psychiatry*, Cambridge: Cambridge University Press, pp. 69–79.

Nisbett, R.E. and Valins, S. (1971) 'Perceiving the causes of one's own behavior', in E.E. Jones, D.E. Kanouse, H.H. Kelley, R.E. Nisbett, S. Valins, and B. Weiner (eds) *Attribution: Perceiving the Causes of Behavior*, Morristown, NJ: General Learning Press, pp. 63–78.

Oppenheim, A.N. (1966) *Questionnaire-Design and Attitude Measurement*, London: Heinemann.

Pritchard, M.J. (1986) *Medicine and the Behavioural Sciences*, London: Edward Arnold.

Rabkin, J.G. and Struening, E.L. (1976) 'Life events, stress and illness', *Science* 194: 1013–20.

Rack, P. (1982) *Race, Culture and Mental Disorder*, London: Tavistock.

Radford, J. (1985) 'Is the customer right? Views and expectations of psychology', *Psychology Teaching*, special edition, 15–27.

Radford, J. (1987) 'An education in psychology', *Bulletin of the British Psychological Society* 40: 282–9.

Schwab, J.J. and Schwab, M.E. (1978) *Sociocultural Roots of Mental Illness: An Epidemiologic Survey*, New York: Plenum.

Seligman, M.E.P. (1975) *Helplessness: On Depression, Development and Death*, San Francisco: W.H. Freeman & Co.

Shepherd, M. (1987) 'Mental illness and primary care', *American Journal of Public Health* 77 (1): 12–13.

Skinner, B.F. (1987) 'Whatever happened to psychology as the science of behavior?' *American Psychologist* 42 (8): 780–6.

Tennant, C., Bebbington, P., and Hurry, J. (1980) 'Parental death in childhood and risk of adult depressive disorders: a review', *Psychological Medicine* 10: 289–99.

Watson, R.I. (1963) *The Great Psychologists*, Philadelphia: Lippincott.

Weissman, M.M. and Klerman, G.L. (1977) 'Sex differences and the epidemiology of depression', *Archives of General Psychiatry* 34: 98–111.

Whorf, B.L. (1956) *Language, Thought and Reality: Selected Writings of Benjamin Lee Whorf*, edited by J.B. Carroll, New York: MIT Press.

5

Economic Appraisal

Greg Wilkinson and Anthony Pelosi

Economic appraisal consists of methods for formulating problems of choice, and for identifying and organizing the data required to aid decision-making. In health care it is concerned with the explicit specification and examination of different options with a view to assisting choice; with the systematic analysis of the costs and consequences of the different ways of achieving competing objectives; and with judgements about how to allocate scarce resources among competing ends.

Although well known, the principles and techniques of economic appraisal have been insufficiently employed in the field of mental health (May 1970; Regional Office for Europe, World Health Organization 1976; Frank 1981; National Institute of Mental Health 1981), and there are a variety of reasons for this. Economic considerations may conflict with the traditional medical approach: some doctors object to being involved in economic appraisal, believing that their overriding concern is clinical care, though it is being increasingly recognized within the profession that it is irresponsible to be unconcerned about the cost of clinical activities (Jennett 1984). In addition, the scope of economic evaluation in mental health programmes is limited by a lack of accepted medical and epidemiological measures of process and outcome, as well as of the economic impact of identification and treatment (Wilkinson and Pelosi 1987). As a result, the most effective and efficient ways of delivering mental health care are not clear.

CONCEPTUAL FRAMEWORK FOR ECONOMIC APPRAISAL

General framework

Land, labour, and capital resources are consumed by health care in order to produce improvements in health. Health care may be conceptualized as a commodity, albeit with some unusual and interesting characteristics, and its consequences may be categorized and measured as: *health effects* – in natural units; *benefits* – associated economic benefits; and *utilities* – satisfaction with health effects.

63

Table 5.1 Health care as a commodity

* Resources devoted to it are substantial and appear to be growing
* Governments are the principal source of financial support for the industry
* Private and voluntary organizations are major providers of the commodity
* The effectiveness of the commodity is uncertain
* New producers of the commodity are entering the industry in large numbers
* Each claims to provide a different effective version of the generic commodity
* Supply of the commodity has shifted from large institutional bases to small dispersed settings
* The commodity is so important to certain individuals that access cannot be legally denied because of inability to pay
* Most consumers purchase the commodity at zero price
* Government agencies are under pressure to restrict the access of consumers and to facilitate competition among suppliers, aiming to contain expenditure
* Government and non-profit suppliers have been slow to adopt thorough economic appraisal

Adapted from National Institute of Mental Health (1981)

Scarcity and choice

Economics concerns the relationship between diverse ends and scarce means which have alternative uses. This starting point implies that choices have to be made between various courses of action, and that decisions about the types and the extent of health care provided should be guided by explicit economic consideration of the options available. Discussion then centres on the social and political principles governing choice, especially the issues: 'whose choice?' (individual, institutional, recipient group, governmental); the related problem of the differing valuation of utilities; and on considerations of equity and distributive justice.

It follows from the above that cost is mostly usefully understood in terms of '*opportunity cost*'. This is the benefit that would be derived from a unit of resource in its best alternative use: it is axiomatic that choice results in an opportunity cost equal to the value of the alternative forgone.

Effectiveness and economic efficiency

To obtain the most effective use from the scarce resources expended on health, it is necessary to express effects in the form of costs and conse-quences *to the population* of a particular type of activity, and the improvements that could be obtained if more resources were to be made available (Cochrane 1972). From this perspective, the rational assessment of effectiveness in mental health care is best based on epidemiological methods. The role of health economics is to complement medical and epidemiological evaluation and to provide an estimate of efficiency. Economic efficiency requires the minimization of costs and the maximization of beneficial

Table 5.2 Measuring the costs and consequences of health care

Costs	Consequences

Costs – for organization and operation of service
  – professional time
  – supplies, equipment, power
  – capital costs
Costs – borne by patients and families
  – expenses
  – put into treatment
  – time off work*
  – psychic costs*
Other costs
  – changes in resource use outside
    health sector
	(1) *Effects*
	  – changes in physical, psychological,
	    and social functioning
	
	(2) *Benefits* – for organization and
	    operation of service
	  – for original condition
	  – for unrelated condition
	  Benefits – for patients and families
	  – savings in expenditure or leisure
	    time
	  – savings in lost work time*
	
	(3) *Utility*
	  – changes in the quality of life of
	    patients and families

Adapted from Drummond *et al.* (1987)
* Indirect costs or benefits

consequences, with the implication that choices in health care should be made so as to derive the maximum possible benefit from the resources at disposal. It follows that inefficiency denotes waste of scarce resources.

Measuring costs and consequences of health care

In health care it is often possible to measure direct and indirect costs and consequences in monetary units, but many difficulties arising in the valuation of less tangible items remain to be resolved.

The margin

It is necessary to introduce the concept of the margin, which is the increment added to costs or consequences by a unit increase in provision. For example, the marginal cost of one additional person using an under-used CT scanner is lower than the average cost since the resources have already been committed to the facility: average cost is higher than marginal cost because the overheads have been spread over a relatively small number of users (Glass and Goldberg 1977).

The significance of this is that investment of resources should be increased when marginal benefit exceeds marginal cost. The most efficient level of provision is attained when marginal cost is equal to marginal benefit.

Table 5.3 A model for cost accounting

Income and expenses of patient and family	Costs to the rest of the community
Patients' earnings after tax	Hospital costs
Family's earnings after tax	Other health service costs
Social security receipts	Local authority costs
Charges for local authority services	Social security payments
Travel costs	Less taxation received
Total	Total

Adapted from Glass and Goldberg (1977)
Costs are indicated as −ve and benefits as +ve

A model accounting system

A model accounting system for each patient studied, which can be extended for each year of the investigation and for each form of treatment under consideration has been developed by Glass and Goldberg (1977) (see Table 5.3).

Costs

The range of costs measured in a given study depends on the viewpoint of the analysis. For example, an item may be a cost to the patient but not to the providing agency; costs common to specified programmes need not be considered; and some categories of costs may be excluded because they will not substantially affect decision-making.

In economic appraisal, costs refer to resources consumed and are not restricted to expenditure. For example, they include resource use not easily reflected in market price, such as use of leisure time and voluntary activity. The appropriate concept is that of opportunity cost, though this may be difficult to estimate. Similarly, marginal or incremental costs are more relevant than average costs (see above).

Although the costing of most resource use is straightforward, more difficult problems are raised by the derivation of values for non-market items, capital outlays, average/marginal cost distinctions, overhead costs, the estimation of indirect costs, and, importantly, allowance for the differential timing of costs (discounting). These topics are covered by Williams and Anderson (1975) and Drummond *et al.* (1987).

Effects

The measurement of health care effects is principally a matter of medical and epidemiological concern. In the framework of economic appraisal, an effect should, whenever possible, apply to a final health output (e.g. life years gained) or, less satisfactorily, to a closely related intermediate output (e.g. cases detected or patients treated).

In mental health care this usually requires valid and reliable measures of the patient's psychological, social, and physical functioning, and the burden of care on the patient's family. Since the ideal assessment is unattainable, it is important that explicit consideration should be given to the theoretical assumptions underlying the research instruments and other measures employed.

Benefits

The economic benefits of health care may be measured according to market valuations, clients' willingness-to-pay estimates, policy-makers' views, and professional opinion. The principles underlying the differing methods are described by Sugden and Williams (1979).

Market valuations exist or can be derived or estimated for most resource items. Nevertheless, a number of difficulties remain: for example, it may prove difficult to allow for the effects of health care on subsequent earnings and income (Glass and Goldberg 1977). If one form of treatment permits the patient to return to work earlier, the patient is better off by the difference between his after-tax income and his previous social security receipts and the community is better off in relation to the extent of his taxation and the reduced social security bill. In practice, to make an accurate assessment, it may be necessary to record earnings and social receipts annually for patients and their families. For these purposes social security benefits may be regarded as a cost to the 'rest of the community', since they are a transfer payment between the community as a whole and a particular patient and family.

A further question arises: how far should the valuation of intangible items be pursued (Drummond *et al.* 1987)? This depends on the amount of resources available to seek the relevant information, the extent to which that information is likely to alter the results of the study, and the likelihood that more informed decision-making will result. The extent to which quantification of intangible benefits is superior to qualitative assessment is not clearly established.

Even more difficult to value is the change in health status (including satisfaction in relationships, leisure, and occupation) of individuals receiving health care. Much attention has centred on the lack of an agreed measure of health benefits, particularly when different patient groups are compared, and the development of health status measurement as an empirical and explicit contribution to the resolution of some of these disagreements (Hurst 1983; Rosser 1983).

Utility

The perfect global measure of health would reflect the quality of life expectancy as well as its quantity, and would result in the derivation of a cardinal index based on a comparison of the relative valuations attached to different health states (Williams 1983).

Such utility values for health states may be obtained by judgement, from the literature, or by empirical measures (Weinstein and Fineberg 1980). Utilities sought depend on the approach of the study – the majority of utility analyses concern public policy decisions and so require a societal perspective. At the same time, it has to be stressed that the reliability and validity of measures of utility are uncertain: their main current justification is that they require explicit and objective specification (Drummond *et al.* 1987).

Techniques of economic appraisal

Five related techniques of economic appraisal are shown in table 5.4. These methods illustrate how the nature of health care consequences affects their measurement, valuation, and comparison to costs. Although economic appraisal of mental health services is discussed primarily in relation to cost-effectiveness and cost-benefit analysis, the evaluation of mental health programmes is rarely amenable to either of these techniques in their idealized form. There is seldom a single objective, and the different objectives cannot easily be combined or measured directly in monetary terms. Table 5.5 details a number of recent examples of economic appraisal in mental health.

Combining monetary and non-monetary costs and consequences

Full economic appraisal in mental health care would involve estimation of the

Table 5.4 Techniques of economic appraisal

---

* *Cost-analysis* – refers only to costs.
* *Cost-minimization analysis* refers to the identification of the least cost alternative of equally effective programmes with identical consequences.
* *Cost-effectiveness analysis* refers to the identification of comparative costs per unit effect of interest, where dissimilar programme costs are related to a single common effect, which differs in extent between alternative programmes. Cost-effectiveness compares the cost of achieving a goal by alternative means.
* *Cost-benefit analysis* refers to the identification of monetary costs and consequences of alternative programmes with disparate consequences, in order to express results in relation to a common (monetary) denominator: the ratio of monetary costs/benefits or the net benefit (or loss). To simplify, if benefits exceed costs, a cost-benefit analysis implies that the programme should be carried out.
* *Cost-utility analysis* refers to the identification of the utility or value of a specified level of health status, allowing for 'quality of life' adjustments to diverse treatment consequences and providing a common denominator (e.g. *QALYs*) for comparison of unlike consequences in different programmes.

Table 5.5 Recent examples of economic appraisal in mental health

Authors	Effectiveness and efficiency comparison
	Institutional care
Endicott *et al.* (1976)	Brief hospital care* with or without day care versus standard hospital care for newly admitted patients
	Community care
Weisbrod *et al.* (1980)	Community based* versus mental hospital treatment for chronically disabled patients
Fenton *et al.* (1982)	Home based* versus hospital psychiatric treatment for patients designated to receive hospital care
Hoult *et al.* (1983)	Comprehensive community treatment* versus hospital care for patients presenting for admission to hospital
(i) Schizophrenia	*Diagnosis related*
Jones *et al.* (1980)[1]	Two different services treating patients with schizophrenia: one, a psychiatric unit attached to a teaching district hospital*; the other, an area mental hospital with modern rehabilitation facilities
Falloon *et al.* (1985)	Behavioural family therapy* versus individual supportive psychotherapy as adjunct treatments in the aftercare management of schizophrenia in patients who continue to live in stressful family environments after treatment of the florid episode of schizophrenia
(ii) Neuroses	
Mangen *et al.* (1983)	Treatment by community psychiatric nurses* versus routine outpatient psychiatrist follow-up for patients with chronic neuroses
Ginsberg *et al.* (1984)	Behavioural therapy from a nurse therapist* versus routine general practitioner care for patients with neuroses (mainly phobics and obsessive-compulsives) in primary care
Dick *et al.* (1985)	Day hospital* versus hospital care for patients admitted as emergencies with neuroses, personality disorder or adjustment reaction

* Superior alternative in economic appraisal
[1] Not a randomised trial

costs of all services provided to achieve a specific aim and estimating the monetary value of all direct benefits (such as reduced use of hospital beds) and indirect benefits (such as reduced family burden). All these values should be corrected for inflation and interest discounted on funds saved or spent on future costs and benefits (Cardin *et al.* 1985). This objective has proved infeasible even in the most thorough analyses (Weisbrod *et al.* 1980).

As a practical solution, Glass and Goldberg (1977) characterize a method for interpreting the results of a study of alternative mental health services in which a conventional (monetary) economic appraisal is carried out, but non-monetary costs and consequences are measured separately. Following their scheme, two outcomes are possible. First, one service may be preferable – with monetary and non-monetary effects pointing in the same direction, or with no significant difference in one of the effects. In this case, one service dominates the other and should be preferred. Second, one service may be less expensive, but may provide a lower quality of service. An explicit judgement is then required about whether the extra quality that may be gained from the alternative service is worth the extra price – with worth being considered in relation to whether there are more valuable services which could be provided with the extra funds. These considerations may generate ideas for new services which combine the advantages of the previously specified services and are more cost-effective.

LIMITATIONS OF ECONOMIC APPRAISAL

The techniques of economic appraisal assume but do not establish the effectiveness of health services. Their value is clearly dependent upon the methodological criteria adopted in a particular investigation. Thus, economic appraisal can produce misleading findings if the range of costs and consequences relevant to a given study is not viewed comprehensively, if those not easily measured in monetary terms are omitted, and if there is no explicit presentation of variables for which quantitative measures are unavailable.

Moreover, the assumption is made in economic appraisal that resources freed or saved by preferred services are not wasted but are used in alternative beneficial ways. If these resources are squandered on ineffective programmes, overall health costs will increase without any improvement in the health status of the recipient group.

There are two further considerations. Although economic appraisal may help choice between services, it is less helpful in deciding whether to have a service at all. Also, the techniques of economic appraisal consume resources and should themselves be similarly appraised. They are likely to be of most benefit when programme objectives require clarification, options are significantly different, or large resource commitments are under consideration (Drummond *et al*. 1987).

Equity

The identity of recipient groups may be an important factor in assessing the social desirability of health policy, and the equitable distribution of costs and benefits across particular recipient groups thus becomes one of the competing dimensions upon which policy decisions are made. It is apparent that there may be a conflict between the pursuit of equity and of efficiency.

Clearly the pursuit of equity requires political definition as a goal of health care. Broad objectives of equitable health care provision may include equality of expenditure per capita; equality of input per capita; equality of input for equal need; equality of access for equal need; equality of use for equal need; equality of marginal met need; and equality of health (Culyer 1976). Equal treatment of equals (e.g. two groups of patients from the same area and with the same condition) may promote efficiency; unequal treatment of unequals (a group of patients with chronic schizophrenia versus a group with chronic renal failure) may mean that equity is exchanged for efficiency.

In addition, it is important to recognize that other areas of economics are relevant to mental health. For example, Segall and Vienonen (1987) have drawn attention to the development of an epidemiology of inequalities: the study of inequalities in income, wealth, and access to resources.

Ethics

Medical ethics is usually thought of in terms of individual virtue and duty, while economics embraces a broader concept of social ethics (Tancredi 1974). Economic appraisal may, therefore, appear to conflict with clinical judgement when medical values are challenged as not being conducive to the goal of maximizing health with the resources available. But as Mooney has argued in a related context:

> It is not a question of ethics *or* economics. Without a wider use of economics in health care inefficiencies will abound and decisions will be made less explicitly and hence less rationally than is desirable: we will go on spending large sums to save life in one way when similar lives but in greater numbers could be saved in another way. The price of inefficiency, inexplicitness and irrationality in health care is paid in death and sickness. Is *that* ethical? (Mooney 1980: 179)

Acknowledgement: Dr Wilkinson is supported by the Department of Health and Social Security. Dr Pelosi is a Wellcome Research Fellow.

REFERENCES

Cochrane, A.L. (1972) *Effectiveness and Efficiency: Random Reflections on Health Services*, London: The Nuffield Provincial Hospitals Trust.
Cardin, V.A., McGill, C.W., and Falloon, I.R.H. (1985) 'An economic analysis: costs, benefits, and effectiveness', in I.R.H. Falloon (ed.) *Family Management of Schizophrenia: A Study of Clinical, Social, Family, and Economic Benefits*, Baltimore: Johns Hopkins University Press.
Culyer, A.J. (1976) *Need and the National Health Service*, London: Martin Robertson.
Dick, P., Cameron, L., Cohen, D., Barlow, M., and Ince, A. (1985) 'Day and full-time treatment: a controlled comparison', *British Journal of Psychiatry* 147: 246–9.

Drummond, M.F. (1981) *Studies in Economic Appraisal in Health Care*, Oxford: Oxford University Press.

Drummond, M.F., Ludbrook, A., Lowson, K., and Steele, A. (1986) *Studies in Economic Appraisal in Health Care*, Oxford: Oxford University Press.

Drummond, M.F., Stoddart, G.L., and Torrance, G.W. (1987) *Methods for the Economic Evaluation of Health Care Programmes*, Oxford: Oxford University Press.

Endicott, J., Herz, M.I., and Gibbon, M. (1976) 'Brief versus standard hospitalisation: the differential costs', *American Journal of Psychiatry* 133: 518–21.

Falloon, I.R.H. (ed.) (1985) *Family Management of Schizophrenia: A Study of Clinical, Social, Family, and Economic Benefits*, Baltimore: Johns Hopkins University Press.

Fenton, F.R., Tessier, L., Contandriopoulos, A., Nguyen, H., and Struening, E.L. (1982) 'A comparative trial of home and hospital psychiatric treatment: financial costs', *Canadian Journal of Psychiatry* 27: 177–87.

Frank, F. (1981) 'Cost-benefit analysis in mental health services: a review of the literature', *Administration in Mental Health* 8: 161–76.

Ginsberg, G., Marks, I., and Waters, H. (1984) 'Cost-benefit analysis of a controlled trial of nurse therapy for neuroses in primary care', *Psychological Medicine* 14: 683–90.'

Glass, N.J. and Goldberg, D. (1977) 'Cost-benefit analysis and the evaluation of psychiatric services', *Psychological Medicine* 7: 701–7.

Hoult, J., Reynolds, I., Charbonneau-Powis, M., Weekes, P., and Briggs, J. (1983) 'Psychiatric hospital versus community treatment: the results of a randomised trial', *Australian and New Zealand Journal of Medicine* 17: 160–7.

Hurst, J. (1983) 'A government economist's attitude to the new measures', in G.T. Smith (ed.) *Measuring the Social Benefits of Medicine*, London: Office of Health Economics.

Jennett, B. (1984) 'Economic appraisal', *British Medical Journal* 288: 1781–2.

Jones, R., Goldberg, D., and Hughes, B. (1980) 'A comparison of two different services treating schizophrenia: a cost-benefit approach', *Psychological Medicine* 10: 493–505.

Mangen, S.P., Paykel, E.S., Griffith, J.H., Burcell, A., and Mancini, P. (1983) 'Cost-effectiveness of community psychiatric nurse or out-patient psychiatric care of neurotic patients', *Psychological Medicine* 13: 407–16.

May, P.R.A. (1970) 'Cost-efficiency of mental health delivery systems: 1. A review of the literature on hospital care', *American Journal of Public Health* 60: 2060–7.

Mooney, G.H. (1980) 'Cost-benefit analysis and medical ethics', *Journal of Medical Ethics* 6: 177–9.

National Institute of Mental Health, Series EN No. 1 (1981) *Economics and Mental Health* (DHHS Publication No. (ADM) 81–1114), Washington, DC: Superintendent of Documents, US Government Printing Office.

Regional Office for Europe, World Health Organization (1976) *Cost/Benefit Analysis in Mental Health Services: Report of a Working Group*, Copenhagen: Regional Office for Europe, World Health Organization.

Rosser, R. (1983) 'A history of the development of health indicators', in G.T. Smith (ed.) *Measuring the Social Benefits of Medicine*, London: Office of Health Economics.

Segall, M. and Vienonen, M. (rapporteurs) (1987) 'Haikko Declaration on actions for primary health care', *Health Policy and Planning* 2: 258–65.

Sugden, R. and Williams, A.H. (1979) *The Principles of Practical Cost-Benefit Analysis*, Oxford: Oxford University Press.

Tancredi, L.E. (ed.) (1974) *Ethics in Health Care*, Washington: National Academy of Sciences.

Weinstein, M.C. and Fineberg, H.V (1980) *Clinical Decision Analysis*, Philadelphia: W.B. Saunders Company.

Weisbrod, B.A. (1982) 'A guide to benefit-cost analysis, as seen through a controlled experiment in treating the mentally ill', *Journal of Health Politics, Policy & Law* 7: 808–45.

Weisbrod, B.A., Test, M.A., and Stein, L.I. (1980) 'Alternative to mental hospital treatment: II. Economic benefit-cost analysis', *Archives of General Psychiatry* 37: 400–5.

Wilkinson, G. and Pelosi, A.J. (1987) 'The economics of mental health services', *British Medical Journal* 294: 139–40.

Williams, A. and Anderson, R. (1975) *Efficiency in the Social Services*, Oxford: Basil Blackwell.

Quantitative Methods

6

The Mental Health of Populations

Geoffrey Rose

Epidemiology is the basic science of public health. Its origin in the mid-nineteenth century came about through the merging of three streams of thought: the concern of clinicians, who could not cure common diseases and therefore looked to their prevention; the new-found application of statistics to medical research, which offered some scientific rigour to the study of rather poor data; and the concern of social reformers and environmentalists, which provided the possibility of preventive action. The subject continues to need the collaboration of these three groups – clinicians, statisticians, and public health activists.

Epidemiology required the development of new research methods, appropriate to the study of groups or populations rather than individual patients; more importantly, it required a capacity to stand back and consider a population as the unit of study. Clinicians find this hard, because for them the natural unit of concern is the individual. It has proved particularly hard for psychiatrists, because their thinking is inevitably and properly more individualistic than that of the other clinical specialities. Psychiatry has, nevertheless, shown more interest in epidemiology than most other branches of medicine; but it has approached it largely from the standpoint of its particular concern for sick individuals.

Many urgent epidemiological questions confront a clinical psychiatrist. For example, in regard to depression, 'How many unrecognized and untreated cases are there in the community? How can they be identified? What sort of individuals get depression, and why? What is the condition's natural history, and can it be altered?' To answer such questions requires epidemiological methods such as surveys, the development and evaluation of screening instruments, case-control and cohort studies, clinical follow-up studies, and intervention trials. Thanks to such methods, now widely used by clinical researchers, the prevalence and natural history of psychiatric disorders are understood far better than 20 years ago; and one can hope that this extension of understanding has improved their recognition and clinical care. It has not, however, contributed much to their prevention: though it may have benefited sick individuals, it has done little for the mental health of populations. The purpose of this essay is to consider this wider field.

AIMS AND METHODS

The most commonly used methods of epidemiological enquiry are the cross-sectional (prevalence) survey and the case-control study. Each of these is concerned primarily with disease in individuals: the survey describes the frequency and distribution of cases, and the case-control study seeks to identify their distinguishing characteristics as clues to causation. Neither approach yields any direct evidence on the underlying factors which determine the incidence rate; study of these first causes calls for comparisons between whole populations with differing rates.

Such comparisons may be across countries (international), across sectors of populations (such as social classes or regions), or across time. Fortunately for epidemiology, most diseases seem to have incidence rates which vary widely across place or time, reflecting the socio-economic heterogeneity which is generally the underlying reason for the environmental exposures or patterns of behaviour which are the proximal causes of illness. This heterogeneity of incidence rates is the necessary condition for discovering the underlying causes; for a cause which is uniformly distributed does not influence the distribution of disease, and hence it is unrecognizable (even though if it were recognized it might be controlled).

Unfortunately, in cross-population studies the problem of confounding is much greater than in studies at the level of individuals: matching is difficult, and the true explanation of a correlation may be unsuspected. One can hope that the findings of cross-population and individual studies will reinforce one another, but this will happen only if there is a similar inequality of exposure to the cause both between and within populations. This is often not the case, and so there is a broad tendency for personal susceptibility factors to dominate the occurrence of individual cases but to explain little of the population differences in incidence, the latter being more under the control of socio-cultural and environmental influences.

CASES AND DISTRIBUTIONS

Clinical diagnosis splits the world into two: with regard to each disease there are those who have it and those who do not. This dichotomy serves well enough in clinical practice, both because treatment decisions are dichotomous and because selective referral brings to the doctor only the more severe examples of a condition. Thus, the distribution of a rating scale for depression in a hospital ward is likely to have two modes, corresponding to patients admitted for severe depression and the others (whose problems are different).

In population studies the situation is not like this, and rating scales for mental illness show continuous, unimodal distributions. 'It follows that to ask what fraction of a population is psychiatrically disturbed is a meaningless question' (Goldberg 1972: 3). This is, nevertheless, exactly what most surveys have attempted to do, because the investigators were determined to force on to the population those descriptive labels with which they were clinically familiar. 'The term "case" can be used in any way that the purposes of a clinician (*sic*) require' (Wing *et al.* 1978: 203), with the aim of identifying 'what proportion of a population would be thought to have a clinically significant psychiatric disturbance if they were interviewed by a psychiatrist' (Goldberg 1972: 3).

In this way the population reality has been constrained to fit the clinical preconception. In fact, it will not fit it, simply because disease in the population is nearly always a quantitative and not a qualitative phenomenon, the question being not 'Has he got it?' but 'How much of it has he got?' An individual's status should thus be described by numbers not labels, for 'in the community the epidemiologist is faced with large numbers of respondents who present with fewer, minor, and non-specific symptoms' (Williams *et al.* 1980: 101).

To anyone familiar with the field of blood pressure research, the story sounds familiar. Hypertension was once considered to be a distinct entity, and Pickering's suggestion that it was only the high tail of a distribution was at first very unpopular. 'Essential hypertension', he wrote 'is a type of disease not hitherto recognised in medicine in which the defect is quantitative not qualitative. It is difficult for doctors to understand because it is a departure from the ordinary process of binary thought to which they are brought up. Medicine in its present state can count up to two but not beyond' (Pickering 1968: 4). Since the Pickering revolution, however, the blood pressure of populations has increasingly been described in terms of its distributions (means and standard deviations) rather than by prevalence rates.

There are two reasons to plead for a similar development in epidemiological psychiatry. The first is statistical: when the Present State Examination, for example, is used in a survey it is a gross waste of information to report only the numbers of persons above and below a certain cutting point, for this fails to use the available grading of individuals within each of these broad categories. Case definition may be necessary for operational decisions (as in screening), but it is too inefficient to earn priority in research: a distribution should always be analysed first by statistics which describe its central tendency and its dispersion.

A second and far more important reason for describing mental illness quantitatively is conceptual rather than technical. So long as attention is confined to the conspicuous cases, the underlying causes of incidence and the means of controlling them will continue to evade attention. Partly this may

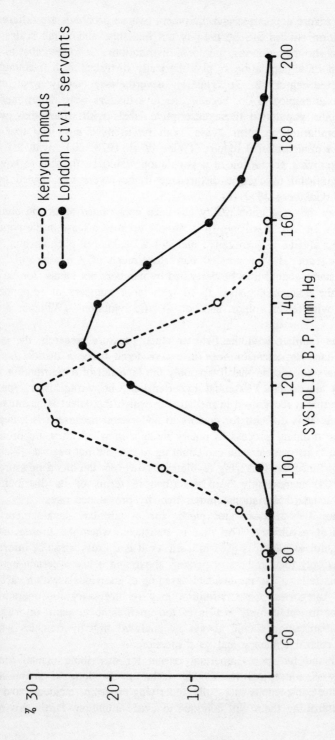

Figure 6.1 Distributions of systolic blood pressure in middle-aged men: (a) Kenyan nomads, (b) London civil servants.

be a willed defensive reaction: concentrating on sick and treatable patients diverts attention from the baffling problems of widespread minor neurosis and depression (which may be society's problem rather than the psychiatrist's).

A favourable shift in the whole distribution of risk may, nevertheless, be the only way to help those many individuals with a problem too small to qualify them for treatment as 'cases'. Even a small shift of this kind may produce an unexpectedly large reduction in the population burden, even though it offers little to each participating individual (the *prevention paradox*, Rose 1981). It also offers a powerful means to reduce the prevalence of 'cases'; in a normal distribution, half of those in the top decile will move to below that level if the population mean falls by as little as one-third of a standard deviation.

SPECIFIC EXAMPLES

The blood pressure analogy

Figure 6.1 shows the distribution of systolic blood pressure among Kenyan nomads and London civil servants. Nearly all research into the causes of hypertension has concentrated on the effort to explain why it is that within one population some individuals have much higher blood pressure than others. This question could be asked as well in Kenya as in London, since inter-individual variation is wide in both places; and the answers might well be similar. But even if the determinants of individual blood pressure could be fully understood, we should be no nearer explaining why hypertension is common in London but virtually absent in the Kenyan nomads; for the answer to this question must be sought in characteristics of the population as a whole, as a result of which the whole distribution is shifted up or down. The coefficient of variation is often a rather robust statistic, implying that the prevalence of high values ('cases') is determined by the value of the population mean.

The question, 'What determines the overall level of disease in a population?' is thus quite different from the question, 'What determines individual cases?' It is studied by different methods, it may yield a different answer, and the implications for prevention are quite different (Rose 1985).

Suicide and depression

In the nineteenth century medical interest in public health was stronger than nowadays. A century ago Durkheim (1951) found that suicide rates were stable and distinctive characteristics of populations. He, therefore, saw suicide as a collective phenomenon, in which personal factors were less important. More recent research has concentrated on the personal factors, with less interest than one would wish in the population experience. As with blood pressure, it is population factors which determine incidence rates.

81

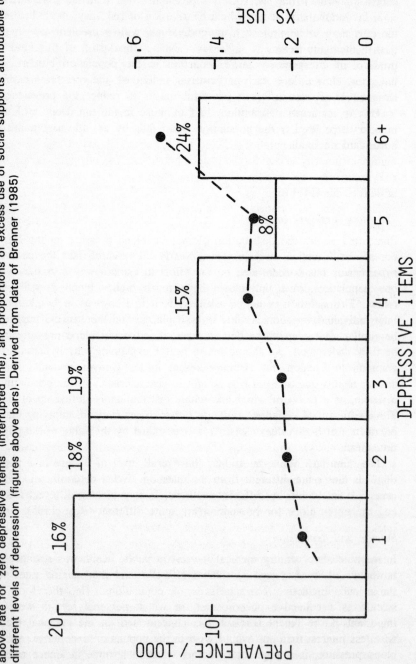

Figure 6.2 Prevalence of various numbers of positive depressive items (bars), frequency of excess use of social supports, above rate for 'zero depressive items' (interrupted line), and proportions of excess use of social supports attributable to different levels of depression (figures above bars). Derived from data of Brenner (1985)

Brenner (1985) applied a depression inventory in an American population and related the score (number of positive items) to the probability of using social supports. From his data it is possible to derive the results shown in figure 6.2. Of the total excess use of social supports associated with having more than zero depressive items, only a quarter arises among those individuals likely to be recognized as 'cases of depression' (6+ items). Two-thirds of the excess population burden of disability arises in individuals who have only between one and four positive items; they would not be recognized as cases of depression.

This is yet another example of a common phenomenon whereby a large number of people exposed to a small risk may generate a greater population burden than a small number exposed to a conspicuous risk (Rose 1981). The high-risk minority certainly need help; but to confine attention to this high-risk group may be to miss most of the problem.

The example of depression and its relation to use of social supports emphasizes the importance of widespread though slight individual disability. A possible 'collective disability' needs also to be considered. For any population there is *a mean depression score*, which not only determines the prevalence of clinical cases of depression and the total burden of depression-related individual disability, but which must also be some measure of 'population morale'; for presumably a more depressed community will collectively function less well than a community where spirits are higher. For all these reasons we need to know more about the determinants of this mean depression score, and its relation to collective societal functioning.

Alcohol

The alcohol intake of most populations follows a positively-skewed unimodal distribution. The mean intake varies, and these variations determine the prevalence of heavy drinking. To concentrate aetiological research and control efforts on the heavy drinkers is to fail to confront the real issue, for no country has yet achieved the truncated distribution of alcohol intake which such an approach impliedly seeks. Kreitman (1986) has reviewed the benefits of such an (unachievable) truncation, whereby no one would exceed the accepted 'safe limits' of intake; and he concludes that these benefits would be matched by an across-the-board reduction of 30 per cent of current alcohol intake – which is an achievable target, if society willed it.

For obvious reasons, society prefers to concentrate its attention on the minority of heavy drinkers, thereby exonerating the 'moderate drinkers'. This is doubly mistaken. First, the tail belongs to the distribution, however much the distribution may prefer to disown it! The alcohol intake and drinking attitudes of Mr and Mrs Average determine just how many problem drinkers there will be in that population. Secondly, as was seen for depression and social malfunction (figure 6.2), so it may well also be that the large number of moderate drinkers collectively generate more health and social problems than the small but conspicuous group of problem drinkers. If only the world really were divided into those with problems, and the rest of us – but the evidence does not support that view.

In regard to alcohol and road traffic accidents, society castigates and punishes the small minority of drivers with high blood alcohol levels, thereby exonerating the far larger number who drink and drive, but with levels inside the legal limit. The assumption – quite unproven – is that within this limit there is no important relation between blood alcohol and proneness to accidents. Data are needed on the distribution of blood alcohol levels in drivers who have accidents and in a representative sample of other drivers, and it would then be possible to calculate a dose-risk curve, linking exposure with outcome. Such data are not available, illustrating the currently blinkered approach which sees the alcohol problem only as the problem of heavy drinkers. In the absence of information on that crucial dose-response curve, one cannot know the limitations of current control policy. There is a similar need for research into the relation of moderate drinking to other behavioural problems.

It has become clear that heavy drinking destroys neurones and that alcoholics often have shrunken brains. But what is the shape of the dose-response curve linking alcohol intake and neuronal loss? Do moderate drinkers suffer moderate brain damage? Does every drink kill a few more brain cells? And if so, does it matter? If the effect were identifiable in individuals, one feels that it would be important; but if, say, a 10 per cent increase in average alcohol intake of a population led to a 1 per cent decline in average cognitive capacity, that effect – which might be statistically present in the population – would be inapparent in individuals. In discussing the mean depression score of a population, it was thought that this might well be important for collective functioning. Does the same apply to a small shift in the population distribution of cognitive functioning?

Aggression and violence

Like depression scores and alcohol intakes, the distribution of aggression is probably unimodally distributed; and if different societies were compared, it would probably be found that this distribution shifted up and down as a whole, for within one society there is a limited toleration of behavioural variations. For aggression, as for blood pressure, the coefficient of variation is probably a rather robust statistic.

This line of reasoning has major implications for research. It implies that we need to study not only the characteristics of 'psychopathic individuals', who are just the tail end of the distribution; more importantly, we need to study the determinants of the average tolerance of aggression in a society, for this determines the occurrence of 'psychopathy' and extreme violence. Football hooliganism (and wars) may diminish only when the whole population distribution of aggression can be changed.

CONCLUSION

The epidemiology of the mental health of populations could lay the basis, in a way that it has not so far done, for understanding and hence perhaps controlling the mass determinants of population means, prevalence rates, and incidence rates. What determines the population's mean level of depression, alcohol intake, or tolerance of violence? What is the relation between these average levels of exposure and the associated ill health or social malfunction? What is the psychiatric counterpart of the identification and control of water pollution, which so impressively reduced the incidence of cholera?

At this point psychiatric epidemiology and psychiatric preventive action merge into social research and social policy. The two cannot exist apart.

REFERENCES

Brenner, B. (1985) 'Continuity between the presence and absence of the depressive syndrome', paper presented at the 113th Annual Meeting of the American Public Health Association, Washington DC, November 1985.

Durkheim, E. (1951) *Suicide: A Study in Sociology*, translated by J.A. Spaulding and G. Simpson, Glencoe, Ill.: Free Press.

Goldberg, D. (1972) *The Detection of Psychiatric Illness by Questionnaire*, London: Oxford University Press.

Kreitman, N. (1986) 'Alcohol consumption and the preventive paradox', *British Journal of Addiction* 81: 353–63.

Pickering, G.W. (1968) *High Blood Pressure*, Edinburgh: Churchill Livingstone.

Rose, G. (1981) 'Strategy of prevention: lessons from cardiovascular disease', *British Medical Journal* 282: 1847–51.

Rose, G. (1985) 'Sick individuals and sick populations', *International Journal of Epidemiology* 14: 32–8.

Williams, P., Tarnopolsky, A., and Hand, D. (1980) 'Case definition and case identification in psychiatric epidemiology: review and assessment', *Psychological Medicine* 10: 101–14.

Wing, J.K., Mann, S.A., Leff, J.P., and Nixon, J.M. (1978) 'The concept of a "case" in psychiatric population surveys', *Psychological Medicine* 8: 203–17.

7

The Biostatistical Approach

Morton Kramer

The report of the Milbank Memorial Fund Commission on *Higher Education in Public Health* describes the many applications of biostatistics to investigations of problems in the health field:

> Biostatistics use statistical methodology to investigate problems in public health and medical care. In addition to collecting, analyzing, and retrieving data, designing experiments, and developing appropriate comparisons among population groups, biostatistics applies the techniques of inference and probability to the examination of biologic data. While interacting most continuously and closely with epidemiology, biostatistic interests extend into the congruent areas of vital statistics and demography, computer programming, computer systems and analysis, and program planning and evaluation. Through the continuing collaboration of epidemiologists and biostatisticians, the science and skill of designing experiments, analytic surveys, and data analysis have progressed to an advanced level. The actual work of these two types of specialists mesh so closely at times that it may be difficult for the outsider to distinguish between them. Through a fruitful working relationship, each in fact has come to learn a great deal about the other's methods and activities. Both as an arm of epidemiology and as a separate science, biostatistics serves as the major method of quantifying and analyzing health information specifically for application within public health.   (Milbank Memorial Fund Commission 1976: 62)

This statement makes it quite clear that biostatistics plays an essential role both in quantifying and evaluating community-wide health problems and in the design and implementation of basic, clinical, laboratory, and field research. This chapter will provide selected examples of one application of biostatistics: the collection and analysis of data on the utilization of mental hospitals and other psychiatric facilities (e.g. outpatient, inpatient, and transitional services). Other chapters of this volume will illustrate the uses of biostatistical and other quantitative methods in clinical, laboratory, and field research on mental disorders.

USES OF ADMINISTRATIVE STATISTICS ABOUT THE MENTAL HEALTH SERVICES

Statistics that describe the characteristics of mental health facilities and of the persons who use them provide the basis for an administrative epidemiology of mental disorders (Kramer 1975). They serve purposes similar to those described by Morris in his text on *Uses of Epidemiology* (1975).

Administrative statistics can be used for the following purposes:

1. to study historical changes in patterns of use of specific types of services; their staffing and financing, and to make projections for the future;
2. to assess the availability of specific types of services and the extent of their use, populations served, staffing, location, accessibility, costs, manpower, and quality, effectiveness, and efficiency of services rendered;
3. to study the working of health services with a view to their improvement;
4. to estimate chances of persons being admitted to a specific type of facility and their chances of being released alive from or dying in the facility;
5. to investigate the causes of institutionalization (for example, factors that determine pathways to care; behaviours and attitudes of consumers and providers of services; availability of community supports; and socio-economic factors).

In addition, the medical records of patients admitted to various types of facilities may be used in clinical, laboratory, and field research to carry out such other uses of epidemiology as:

6. to complete the clinical picture;
7. to identify syndromes;
8. to search for causes of health and disease.

Further elaboration and examples of specific uses may be found in various publications (World Health Organization 1963, 1969, 1971; Brooke 1963; Kramer 1969, 1977; Kramer *et al.* 1973; Kramer *et al.* 1973; Gruenberg 1968, 1986; National Institute of Mental Health 1983, 1985, 1987).

USES OF CENSUSES OF POPULATION AND VITAL STATISTICS

Population censuses provide basic statistics of a country and its geographical subdivisions by age, sex, race, socio-economic, marital status, household composition, educational level, and other characteristics of target populations. Such data are essential for computation of utilization rates of residents of a defined geographic area by specific demographic variables. Some national censuses provide basic data on the characteristics of their institutional population. Such data make it possible to compare characteristics of residents of mental institutions with those of residents of other institutions of interest to the mental health field. Vital statistics are also needed to provide birth, death, and migration rates of a target population and other indicators of the health situation of a population.

SELECTED ILLUSTRATIONS OF USES OF TREND DATA

The illustrations to be given in the following sections are derived from US Census Bureau publications on persons in institutions and from published analyses of data collected annually by the NIMH through its national reporting programme on the characteristics of the mental health services of the fifty states of the US and the characteristics of the persons using them (Redick *et al*. 1983). These data will illustrate only one of the uses of administrative statistics described earlier, namely, historical study of changes that have occurred in the utilization of mental hospitals and other types of institutions and of changes that have occurred in the use of specialty mental health services. Limitations of space do not permit other examples of applications of utilization statistics. The interested reader may find them in the references cited on p. 87.

These examples will be followed by three others to illustrate the potential effect on the prevalence of mental disorders of several important changes projected to occur in the US population by the year 2,000: (1) the increases in the numbers of persons 65–74, 75–84, 85+; (2) the increases in the Spanish-speaking population; and (3) the changes in the household composition and living arrangements of the population.

TRENDS OF THE INSTITUTIONAL POPULATION

At each decennial census the US Bureau of the Census enumerates inmates of the following institutions: correctional institutions; mental hospitals; residential treatment centres; tuberculosis hospitals; chronic disease hospitals; homes for the aged and dependent; homes and schools for the mentally handicapped; homes and schools for the physically handicapped; homes for dependent and neglected children; homes for unwed mothers; training schools for juvenile delinquents and detention homes (US Bureau of the Census 1953, 1973, 1984).

It is instructive to review the trends of number of persons resident in the

Table 7.1 Number, percentage distribution, and rate per 100,000 population of persons in mental institutions (mental hospitals and residential treatment centres), homes for aged and dependent, and correctional institutions: US 1950, 1960, 1970, and 1980.

Type of institution and total population of the US	1950	1960	1970	1980
	Number (000s)			
Total	1,566.8	1,887.0	2,126.7	2,492.1
Mental institutions	613.6	630.0	433.9	255.3
Homes for aged and dependent	296.8	469.7	927.5	1,426.4
Correctional institutions	264.6	346.0	328.0	466.4
All other	391.8	441.3	437.3	344.0
	Percentage of population in all institutions			
Total	100.0	100.	100.0	100.0
Mental institutions	39.2	33.4	20.4	10.2
Homes for aged and dependent	18.9	24.8	43.6	57.2
Correctional institutions	16.9	18.3	15.4	18.7
All other	25.0	23.5	20.6	13.9
	Number per 100,000 population of US			
Total	1,035.4	1,052.3	1,046.6	1,100.3
Mental institutions	405.5	351.3	213.5	112.7
Homes for aged and dependent	196.1	261.9	456.4	629.7
Correctional institutions	174.8	193.0	161.4	205.9
All other	259.0	246.1	215.3	152.0
Total resident population of US (000s)	151,326	179,323	203,302	226,546

Sources: US Bureau of the Census, 1953, 1973, 1984

total institutional population and their component parts for several reasons. First, factors that affect the use of any one type of institution, for example mental hospitals, can have both a direct and/or halo effect on the use of other institutions, such as nursing homes, and, in some instances, correctional institutions. Second, these trends reflect temporal changes in the many factors that determine the way a society uses the various institutions it has created. They have been created to serve various purposes. One type – the correctional institution – is for the incarceration of persons who have committed crimes against society. Other types provide a variety of services for persons who are mentally ill, mentally retarded, chronically ill or disabled, or have succumbed to problems that beset the aged. Still others provide services to persons who have manifested other kinds of behavioural and psychosocial problems – such as homes for unwed mothers and training schools for juvenile delinquents.

Table 7.1 provides the number and percentage of persons in all institutions

Figure 7.1 Distribution of persons in institutions per 100,000 population by type of institution, both sexes US, 1950, 1970 and 1980

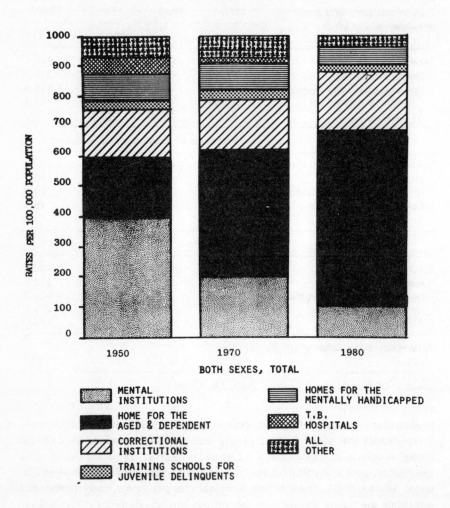

Sources: US Bureau of the Census, 1953, 1973, 1983

and the corresponding resident rates per 100,000 population for three major types of institutions for the years 1950, 1970, and 1980: mental institutions, homes for the aged and dependent, and correctional institutions. Figure 7.1 shows the changes in resident rates per 1,000 population.

Collectively, these three types of institutions have accounted for 75 per cent or more of the institutional population. However, striking changes occurred in the rank order of the number of persons resident in these institutions during this thirty-year period. In 1950 the mental institutions, which include mental hospitals and residential treatment centres, accounted for the largest number and percentage of all persons in institutions (613,600 or 39 per cent of the total), followed in order by homes for aged and dependent (296,800 or 19 per cent of the total), and correctional institutions (264,600 or 17 per cent of the total). All the other institutions accounted for 391,800 persons or 25 per cent of the total. By 1980 homes for the aged and dependent accounted for the largest number (1,426,400 or 57 per cent of the total), followed by the correctional institutions (466,400 or 19 per cent of the total) and mental institutions (255,300 or 10 per cent of the total). All other institutions accounted for 344,000 or 14 per cent of the total.

The percentage change in the numbers of persons in these three major categories of institutions as compared to that of the total population of the US is quite dramatic. Between 1950 and 1980 the total population of the US increased by 50 per cent (from 151.3 million to 226.5 million). The institutional population as a whole increased somewhat more rapidly, by 59 per cent. However, the population in homes for aged and dependent *increased* by 381 per cent and that in correctional institutions *increased* by 76 per cent, while that in the mental institutions *decreased* by 58 per cent.

Biostatisticians must not be content merely to collect data and to publish numbers. They must provide some insight into the factors operating in society that generate the data published in the statistical tables of a census volume or annual reports. The following is a conceptualization of several factors responsible for the trends just demonstrated.

The population trends for a specific type of the institution are governed by factors that determine the rate at which persons are admitted to the institution and other factors that determine their lengths of stay and the rates at which they are returned to the community or die in the institution. The following are broad classes of factors that have affected the size of the separate components of the institutional population: (1) social legislation that encourages and/or mandates programmes that affect the flow of people into and out of a specific type of institution; (2) discoveries of treatment for diseases that reduce or eliminate the need for institutional care or make possible shorter durations of stay in the institution; (3) demographic changes, particularly those that result in the creation of groups at high risk for institutional care; (4) skyrocketing costs of general hospital and domiciliary care for persons with chronic diseases that make it financially impossible to maintain

91

a subject in the community; (5) societal conditions and problems that are associated with high risk for mental disorders, crime, delinquency, and other types of psychosocial problems; (6) racist and other discriminatory practices that determine who gets institutionalized in a specific type of facility; (7) insufficient and inadequate community programmes for preventing admission to an institution or for facilititating release of inmates to the community; and (8) inappropriate living arrangements in the community for persons with chronic and disabling conditions. These factors are discussed at some length in a paper by this author (Kramer 1977).

The next section provides a specific illustration of factors that accounted for the large, rapid decrease in the number of residents of mental hospitals.

CHANGES IN LOCUS OF CARE OF PERSONS WITH MENTAL DISORDER

The striking decrease in the number of persons in mental hospitals was the result of a series of actions that changed the primary locus of care of persons with mental disorders from the large state hospitals to community-based services (Kramer 1977; Regier and Taube 1981). These included:

- federal and state legislation that mandated the development of community-based programmes for diagnosis, treatment, and rehabilitation of persons with mental disorders;
- expansion of out-patient psychiatric services, psychiatric units in general hospitals, and community mental health centres;
- development and use of psychoactive drugs;
- development of procedures to prevent inappropriate placements of persons in state mental hospitals and other procedures to reduce length of stay of persons admitted to these hospitals;
- expansion of nursing homes and other facilities for the aged as a result of Title 19 of the Social Security Act in 1965 (Medicaid) and the 1965 amendments to the Act (Medicare).

As a result of these and other actions, the resident population of the state mental hospitals dropped from its maximum of 559,000 in 1955 to 140,355 in 1979, a decrease of 75 per cent (figure 7.2) (NIMH, 1983). While the mental hospital population was decreasing, the use of other mental health facilities was increasing. During the period 1955–77 the total number of patient care episodes in all facilities increased from 1.7 million to 6.9 million, an increase of 306 per cent; the number of episodes per 100,000 population increased from 1,028 to 2,964 or by 188 per cent. The shift from in-patient to out-patient care during this period is shown in figure 7.3 which demonstrates the changes that occurred in the percentage distribution of the patient-care episodes specific for type of facility (Witkin 1980).

Figure 7.2 Number of resident patients, total admissions, net releases[1] and deaths[1] in state and county mental hospitals, United States, 1950–1980

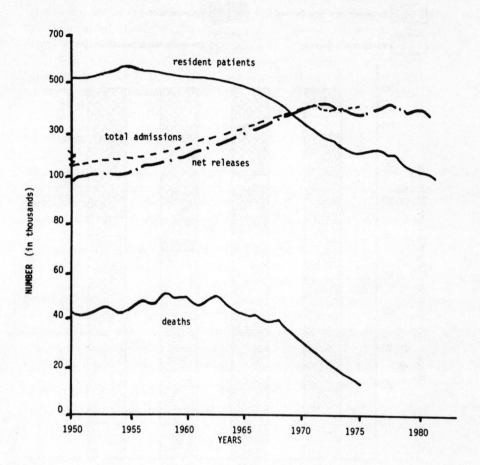

[1] Data available for the years 1950–1975.
Sources: Kramer, M. (1977); National Institute of Mental Health (1983)

93

Figure 7.3 Per cent distribution of inpatient and outpatient care episodes[1] in mental health facilities by type of facility: US, 1955, 1971, 1975, 1977

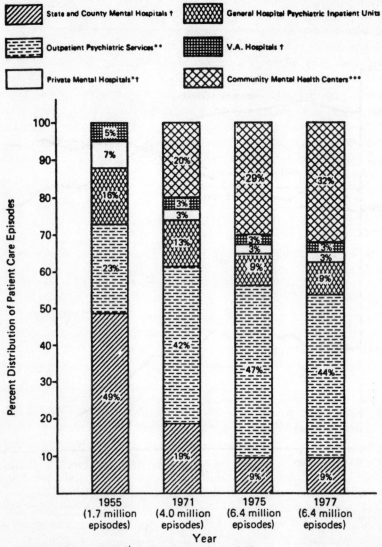

- State and County Mental Hospitals †
- General Hospital Psychiatric Inpatient Units
- Outpatient Psychiatric Services**
- V.A. Hospitals †
- Private Mental Hospitals*†
- Community Mental Health Centers***

*Includes residential treatment centers for emotionally disturbed children.
†Inpatient services only.
**Includes freestanding outpatient services as well as those affiliated with psychiatric and general hospitals.
***Includes inpatient and outpatient services of federally funded CMHCs.
1/Excludes day treatment episodes and V.A. psychiatric outpatient services.

Source: Witkin, M.J. (1980)

TRENDS IN PATTERNS OF CARE FOR THE AGED

Mental hospitals

Of particular interest are changes that have occurred in the use of state mental hospitals for aged persons with mental disorders. Figure 7.4 shows the marked change in the age-specific first admission rates to these hospitals. In 1946 and 1955 these rates reached their maximum of about 240 per 100,000 in the age group 65+. By 1972, the rate for this age group dropped to about 75 per 100,000, 69 per cent lower than in 1955 and to 40 per 100,000 in 1975, 83 per cent lower than in 1955. Indeed the shape of the first admission rate curve for 1975 was similar to that of the curve for 1885. However, the characteristics of the communities, living arrangements, family composition, and related phenomena of the population of the US in 1885 were quite different from those that existed in 1975.

Between 1965 and 1979 the resident patient rate in state mental hospitals for person 65 years and over dropped from 773 per 100,000 to 164 per 100,000, a decrease of 79 per cent (Kramer 1977; NIMH 1983). The decrease was the result both of reductions in first admissions and of placement of aged residents in nursing homes and release of others to the community.

Nursing homes

The National Center for Health Statistics (NCHS) provides data which demonstrate the striking increase in the number of nursing homes and their residents (NCHS 1979, 1981, 1983). The number of these homes increased from about 13,000 in 1963 to about 18,900 in 1977, a 45 per cent increase. During the same period, the number of residents increased from 491,000 to 1,303,000, an increase of 165 per cent (NCHS 1981; US Bureau of the Census 1984). More recently, the NCHS (1983) reported that in 1980 there were 23,065 nursing homes in the US with 1,396,132 residents. These numbers represent a 22 per cent increase in the number of such homes and a 7 per cent increase in the number of residents since 1977.

Figure 7.5 shows the trend of the number of persons per 1,000 population in nursing home beds on a given day, specific for age for the years 1963, 1969, 1973–4, and 1977 (NCHS 1981).

For all persons 65 years of age and over, the rate increased from 25.4 per 1,000 population in the year 1963 to 47.9, an increase of 89 per cent (figure 7.5). However, the relatively low rate for this total group masks the dramatic increases that have occurred in the rates among persons in the age group 65–74, 75–84, and 85 and over, i.e., among the separate age groups that constitute the 65 years and over group. Increases have occurred steadily in these age specific rates. As of 1977, the rates of all races combined increased with advancing age from 14.5 per 1,000 persons 65–74 to 215.4 per 1,000 for persons 85 and over, a 15-fold increase. For the whites the

Figure 7.4 First admission rates per 100,000 population by age, state and county mental hospitals, US, 1946, 1955, and 1975 and Massachusetts, 1885

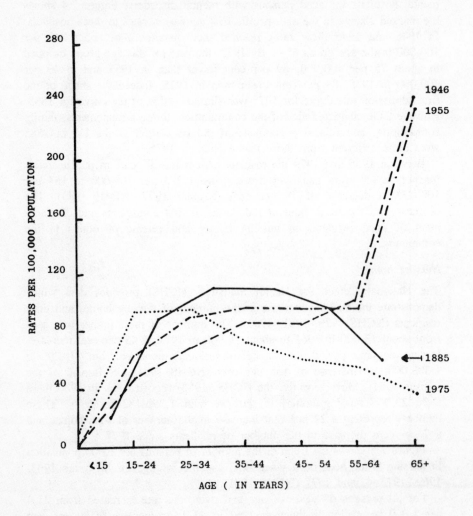

Sources: Kramer, M. (1977); Gruenberg, E.M. (1986)

Figure 7.5 Number of nursing home residents per 1,000 population by age for the years 1963, 1969, 1973–4 and 1977

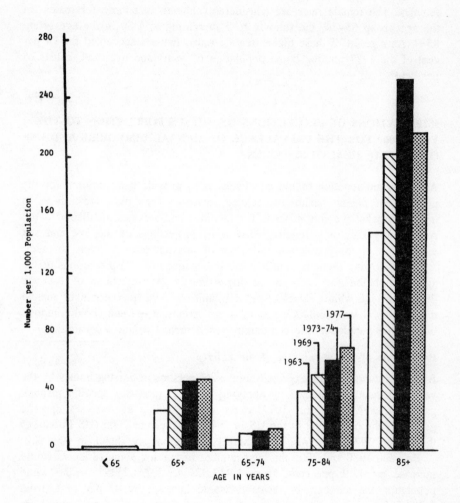

Source: National Center for Health Statistics (1981)

rates increased from 14.2 per 1,000 for persons 65–74 to 229.0 for persons 85 and over, a 16-fold increase. For the non-whites the corresponding rates increased from 16.8 per 1,000 to 102.0 per 1,000 (six-fold increase).

There are also considerable differences between the rates for males and females. The female rates are considerably higher than those for males. In the age group 65–74, the ratio is 1.25 increasing to 1.80 in the age group 85+. As a result of these higher female rates, females accounted for 74 per cent of the 1977 nursing home population 65 years and over and males, 26 per cent.

IMPLICATIONS OF PROJECTIONS OF THE US POPULATION TO THE YEAR 2000 FOR THE PREVALENCE OF MENTAL DISORDERS AND USE OF MENTAL HEALTH SERVICES

An important function of biostatisticians is to provide data required for the planning of mental health and related services. They must look ahead to determine what the future needs for facilities and services are likely to be. Accordingly they will require, *inter alia*, projections of the age and sex distribution of the population and a set of relevant rates to apply to them.

The following sections highlight the implications of: (1) projections of the aged population for beds in nursing homes; (2) projections of the age distribution of whites, blacks, and Hispanics for the prevalence of mental disorders in these populations; and (3) projections of the household composition of the population for community-based mental health programmes.

Projections of the population of the elderly

A crude estimate of the expected number of persons in nursing homes by the year 2005 can be obtained by applying the age, race, sex specific resident patient rates for the year 1977 to the corresponding age-race-sex specific groups of the population of the US in 1980 and the year 2005 (US Bureau of the Census 1979). The results of these computations are shown in table 7.2.

Between 1980 and 2005 the total number of nursing home residents would increase by 47.9 per cent, from 1,413,331 to 2,090,253. For the white population the numbers of residents would increase by 48 per cent, from 1,308,583 to 1,936,144 and for the black and others by 47.1 per cent, from 104,748 to 154,109.

These projections underscore the potential effect of the change in age composition of the population of the US between 1980 and 2005 on the need for additional nursing home beds. They also underscore the need for other data to assist administrators and planners to deal more effectively with problems currently encountered in providing adequate care for the elderly who require admission to these facilities and to develop alternate programmes of care.

Table 7.2 Illustration of the effect of population changes in the US between 1980 and 2005 on the number of residents of nursing homes, assuming 1977 resident patient rates applied to the projected population for 2005

Year	Total	White	Black/other
1980	1,413,331	1,308,583	104,748
2005	2,090,253	1,936,144	154,109
Increase	676,922	627,561	49,361
% increase	47.9	48.0	47.1

Projections of the white, black and Hispanic population

The Bureau of the Census publishes projections of the white, black, and Hispanic population of the US to the year 2080 (US Bureau of the Census 1986d). Table 7.3 shows the expected changes in these populations between 1985 and 2000 specific for age. The expected rate of growth of the Hispanic population exceeds by a considerable amount that of the white and black populations. The total white population is projected to increase by 9.6 per cent (from 203.1 to 222.6 millions) and the black by 23.0 per cent (from 29.1 to 35.8 millions). The Hispanic population is projected to increase by 45.9 per cent (from 17.3 to 25.2 millions). The expected increases in the numbers of persons in each of the age groups of the Hispanic population are quite extraordinary. Thus, the percentage increases specific for age are: under 18, 37 per cent; 18–24, 18 per cent; 25–44, 41 per cent; 45–64, 85 per cent; and 65 and over, 94 per cent.

Such changes will have a profound effect on the number of cases of mental disorder that will exist in this population group. The following computations, based on prevalence estimates from the Epidemiology Catchment Area Surveys, illustrate this effect (Regier *et al.* 1984).

The Epidemiologic Catchment Area Surveys, recently carried out in five catchment areas of the US, provide estimates of age specific one-month prevalence rates of mental disorders among whites, blacks, and Hispanics (Regier *et al.* in press). These estimates are based on computer analysis of responses to the Diagnostic Interview Schedule administered to a probability sample of respondents 18 years of age and over in each catchment area. Table 7.4 shows the results of the application of the age specific one-month prevalence rates in the age groups 18–24, 25–44, 45–64, and 65+ to the corresponding age groups of the populations of the whites, blacks, and Hispanics in 1985 and 2000. The expected number of cases among the whites would increase by 8.6 per cent (from 19.5 to 21.2 millions); among the blacks by 24.8 per cent (from 3.7 to 4.6 millions); and among the Hispanics by 48.0 per cent (from 1.6 to 2.4 millions). These projected increases in number of cases for the Hispanics plus those expected in the white and black

Table 7.3 Estimated population (in 000s) for whites, blacks, and Hispanics, US, 1985 to 2000

Age (years)	Year 1985	2000	Change in no. persons 1985–2000	Percentage change
White				
Total	203,111	222,654	19,543	9.62
< 15	42,123	44,314	2,191	5.20
15–24	32,883	29,002	− 3,881	− 11.80
25–34	35,323	29,590	− 5,733	− 16.25
35–44	27,620	36,335	8,735	31.63
45–54	19,529	31,662	12,133	62.13
55–64	19,759	20,605	846	4.28
65–74	15,188	15,589	401	2.63
75+	10,686	15,537	4,851	45.40
Black				
Total	29,078	35,754	6,676	22.97
< 15	8,061	9,500	1,439	17.85
15–24	5,732	5,672	− 60	− 1.05
25–34	5,212	5,316	104	2.00
35–44	3,404	5,811	2,407	70.71
45–54	2,336	4,124	1,788	76.54
55–64	2,003	2,355	352	17.57
65–74	1,410	1,589	179	12.70
75+	920	1,387	467	50.76
Spanish origin				
Total	17,287	25,224	7,937	45.91
< 15	5,317	7,344	2,027	38.12
15–24	3,311	4,124	813	24.55
25–34	3,254	3,804	550	16.90
35–44	2,129	3,803	1,674	78.63
45–54	1,376	2,811	1,435	104.29
55–64	1,015	1,619	604	59.51
65–74	553	1,041	488	88.25
75+	332	678	346	104.22

Source: US Bureau of the Census, 1979, 1986d

Table 7.4 Estimated number of cases of any dis-disorder for whites, blacks, and Hispanics, US, 1985–2000

	1-month prevalence Rate (%)[1]	Population Number (000s) 1985	Population 2000	Percentage Change	Actual number 1985	Expected cases 2000	Percentage change
			White				
18–24	15.14	23,817	19,816	−16.80	3,605,894	3,000,142	−16.80
25–44	14.73	62,943	65,945	4.77	9,271,503	9,713,699	4.77
45–64	9.96	39,288	52,267	33.03	3,913,084	5,205,793	33.03
65+	10.56	25,874	31,126	20.30	2,732,274	3,286,905	20.30
Total 18+		151,922	169,154	11.34	19,522,775	21,206,539	8.62
			Black				
18–24	20.10	4,128	3,772	−8.62	829,728	758,172	−8.62
25–44	17.84	8,616	11,127	29.14	1,537,094	1,985,056	29.14
45–64	18.23	4,339	6,479	49.32	791,000	1,181,121	49.32
65+	23.50	2,330	2,976	27.73	547,550	699,360	27.73
Total 18+		19,413	24,354	25.45	3,705,372	4,623,709	24.78
			Hispanic				
18–24	17.20	2,349	2,766	17.75	404,028	475,752	17.75
25–44	14.11	5,383	7,607	41.32	759,541	1,073,347	41.32
45–64	13.72	2,391	4,430	85.28	328,045	607,796	85.28
65+	12.50	885	1,719	94.24	110,625	214,875	94.24
Total 18+		11,008	16,522	50.09	1,602,239	2,371,770	48.03

[1] Based on weighted age specific rates for the five ECA areas specific for white, blacks, and Hispanics. (Regier *et al.* in press)

populations provide some indication of the increases in mental health, social, and related services that will be required to meet the needs of the diverse population groups in the US for mental health services.

Projections of household composition and living arrangements

Another demographic trend that will exacerbate the mental health problem in the US is that which is occurring in the family and household composition of its population (US Bureau of the Census 1985, 1986b). Between 1950, and 1985 married couple families increased by 48 per cent; families headed by a male without spouse (male householder families) by 91 per cent; families headed by a female without spouse (female householder families) by 182 per cent; and non-family households by 411 per cent. About 85 per cent of the non-family households consists of persons living alone (one-person households). The number of one-person households increased by 421 per cent during this period.

Projections between 1985 and 2000 of the number of households and their ratio per 1,000 population by type, shown in table 7.5, highlight the gradual decline in the number of married couple families per 1,000 population and accentuate the striking increases expected by 2000 in the numbers and ratios of the other types of family and non-family households (Kramer *et al.* 1987; US Bureau of the Census 1985, 1986c).

Several factors have brought about these changes in household and family structure: the increase in divorce rates; the increase in the number of widows and widowers; migration of workers to areas of the country with opportunities for employment; and trends in behaviour, life style, value systems, and aspirations of the members of the various social class strata of our society.

It is well known that persons who are separated, divorced, widowed, or never married, persons living alone or in non-family households and children living with one parent are at relatively high risk for developing a mental disorder. The US Census Bureau has recently published data on the changes in the living arrangements of several of these groups that have occurred between 1970 and 1985 (US Bureau of the Census 1986a). During this period the number of children who live in single-parent families increased by 78 per cent (from 8.2 millions to 14.6 millions); the number of divorced persons who live alone increased by 193 per cent (from 1.5 millions in 1970 to 4.4 millions); and the number of persons 65 and over who live alone increased by 59 per cent (from 5.1 millions in 1970 to 8.1 millions). Another characteristic of the female householder family with children is that a very large proportion of these families (about 35 per cent) live below the poverty level, a variable known to be a risk factor for mental disorder.

As a result of the continuing emphasis on community care, it is important to learn more about the living arrangements of persons in these high risk groups – who among them has a mental disorder; the role of this person in

Table 7.5 Type of households and family units, US, 1985–2000[1]

Type of household and family	1985	2000	Percentage change
	Number in 000s		
Total	86,789	105,933	22.1
Family households	62,706	72,277	15.3
Married couple	50,350	56,294	11.8
Other, male householder	2,228	3,282	47.3
Other, female householder	10,129	12,701	25.4
Non-family households	24,082	33,656	39.8
Male householder	10,114	15,452	52.8
Female householder	13,968	18,204	30.3
Living alone	20,602	28,944	40.5
Two or more persons	3,480	4,712	35.4
	Percentage of total		
Total	100.0	100.0	
Family households	72.3	68.2	− 5.7
Married couple	58.0	53.1	− 8.5
Other, male householder	2.6	3.1	19.2
Other, female householder	11.7	12.0	2.6
Non-family households	27.7	31.8	14.8
Male householder	11.7	14.6	24.8
Female householder	16.1	17.2	6.8
Living alone	23.7	27.3	15.2
Two or more persons	4.0	4.5	12.5
	No. of households per 1,000 population		
Total	363.7	395.3	8.7
Family households	262.8	269.7	2.6
Married couple	211.0	210.1	− 0.4
Other, male householder	9.3	12.2	31.2
Other, female householder	42.4	47.4	11.8
Non-family households	100.9	125.6	24.5
Male householder	42.4	57.7	36.1
Female householder	58.5	67.9	16.1
Living alone	86.3	108.0	25.1
Two or more persons	14.6	17.6	20.5
Population US (000s)	238,631	267,956	12.3

Source: US Bureau of the Census, 1987

103

the household (i.e., head of household, spouse of head, child, or other relative); the impact of the persons with a disorder on other persons in the household and vice versa – and to gather additional information about the familial aggregation of mental disorders and other disorders and disabling conditions (Downes and Simon 1954; Kellam and Ensminger 1980; Kellam *et al.* 1982; Rutter and Quinton 1984; WHO 1976). Indeed, more knowledge is needed about the family-household aggregation of mental and physical disorders in an era when the importance of primary health care and family-based preventive care is being increasingly emphasized.

The Eastern Baltimore Mental Health Survey provided a unique opportunity to collect data in a way that made it possible to allocate persons with a DIS disorder to the type of household in which they lived and to determine prevalence rates of specific DIS/DSM–III disorders among persons living in different types of households. Analyses of these data demonstrated that prevalence rates of mental disorders in male and female householder families, and non-family households are significantly higher than those found in married couple families (Kramer *et al.* 1987).

As a result of changes in the household composition of the nation during the past thirty years, results similar to those reported for Eastern Baltimore are likely to be quite general throughout the US and, probably, in other developed countries. This follows from the fact that female and male householder families and non-family households are heavily weighted with persons at high risk for mental disorder. As a result of the expected increases in the number of such households between 1985 and 2000, shown in table 7.5, and the high prevalence of mental disorders in these households, a marked increase can be expected in the number of US households in which one or more members will have a mental disorder.

CONCLUSIONS

Biostatistics plays an essential role in quantifying and evaluating community-wide mental health problems and in the design and implementation of clinical, laboratory, and field research on the mental disorders. This paper has illustrated only one of the many uses of biostatistics in the mental health field; namely, its use in the collection and analysis of data on utilization of mental health services. In particular, it has demonstrated how statistical data generated by the National Reporting Program for Mental Health Statistics in the US have been used to develop an administrative epidemiology of mental disorders based on systematically collected data on the characteristics of the mental health services and of persons who utilize these services. Illustrations have been given of how these data have been used to demonstrate changes in the locus of care of persons with mental disorders during the past twenty-five to thirty years. Other illustrations have been given of how demographic projections of a population, utilization rates of mental health services, and prevalence rates of mental disorder, derived from population-based epidemiologic surveys, can be used to provide quantitative estimates of future size of mental health problems and needs for mental health services.

Trends in use of mental health services similar to those in the US have occurred in many other countries (Freeman *et al.* 1985; International Journal of Mental Health 1983; World Health Organization 1980). As a result of population increases projected between 1985 and 2000 for age groups at high risk for mental disorder in all countries of the developed and developing regions of the world, it can be expected that there will be a large increase world-wide in the numbers of persons with mental disorder (Kramer and Anthony 1983; United Nations 1985). Administrators of mental health programmes will require statistical data on patterns of use of mental health services, epidemiologic data on the prevalence and incidence of mental disorders in their countries, projections of the age, sex, and other demographic features of their populations, to plan programmes to meet their needs for services. All of this emphasizes that the biostatistical approach will play an increasingly important role in planning, monitoring, and evaluating programmes for the prevention and control of mental disorders and their associated disabling conditions.

REFERENCES

Brooke, E.M. (1963) *A Longitudinal Study of Patients First Admitted to Mental Hospitals in 1954 and 1955* (Studies on Medical and Population Subjects No. 18), London: HM.

Downes, J. and Simon, S. (1954) 'Characteristics of psychoneurotic patients and their families as revealed in a general morbidity study', *Milbank Memorial Fund Quarterly* 32: 42–64.

Freeman, H.L., Fryers, T., and Henderson, J.H. (1985) *Mental Health Services in Europe: 10 Years On* (Public Health in Europe 25), Copenhagen: WHO, Regional Office for Europe.

Gruenberg, E.M. (1968) 'Epidemiology and medical care statistics', in M.M. Katz, J.O. Cole, and W.E. Barton (eds) *The Role and Methodology of Classification in Psychiatry and Psychopathology*, Washington, DC: US Government Printing Office.

Gruenberg, E.M. (1986) 'Mental disorders', in J.M. Last (ed.) *Maxey-Rosenau Public Health and Preventive Medicine*, 12th edn, Norwalk, Conn.: Appleton-Century-Crofts.

International Journal of Mental Health (1983) *International Perspectives on Deinstitutionalization* (guest editor, H. Goldman), Armonk, New York: M.E. Sharpe.

Kellam, S.G. and Ensminger, M.E. (1980) 'Theory and method in child psychiatric epidemiology studies in children', in F. Earls (ed.) *Monographs in Psychological Epidemiology*, New York: Prodist.

Kellam, S.G., Adams, R.G., Brown, C.H., and Ensminger, M.E. (1982) 'Long term evolution of the family structure of teen-age and older mothers', *Journal of Marriage and the Family*, August, 539–4.

Kramer, M. (1969) *Applications of Mental Health Statistics: Uses in Mental Health Programmes of Statistics Derived from Psychiatric Services and Selected Vital and Morbidity Records*, Geneva: World Health Organization.

Kramer, M. (1975) 'Diagnoses and classification in epidemiological and health services research', pp. 64–6, In N. Hobbs (ed) *Issues in the Classification of Children*, San Francisco: Jossey-Bass Publishers.

Kramer, M. (1977) *Psychiatric Services and the Changing Institutional Scene 1950–1985* (DHEW Publication No. (ADM) 77–433), Washington, DC: US Government Printing Office.

Kramer, M. and Anthony, J. (1983) 'Review of differences in mental health indicators used in national publications: recommendations for their standardization', *World Health Statistics Quarterly* 36: 256–338.

Kramer, M., Brown, H., Skinner, E.A., Anthony, J.C., and German, P. (1987) 'Changing living arrangements in the population and their potential effect on the prevalence of mental disorders: findings of the Eastern Baltimore Mental Health Survey', in B. Cooper (ed) *Psychiatric Epidemiology*, Bromley: Croom Helm.

Kramer, M., Rosen, B., and Willis, E.M. (1973) 'Definitions and distributions of mental disorders in a racist society', in C.V. Willie, B. Kramer, and B.S. Brown (eds) *Racism and Mental Health Essays*, Pittsburgh: University Pittsburgh Press.

Kramer, M., Taube, C.A., and Redick, R.W. (1973) 'Patterns of use of psychiatric facilities by the aged: past, present and future', in C. Eisdorfer and M. P. Lawson (eds) *The Psychology of Adult Development and Aging*, Washington, DC: American Psychological Association.

Milbank Memorial Fund Commission (1972) *Higher Education in Public Health*, New York: Prodist, p. 62.

Morris, J.N. (1975) *Uses of Epidemiology*, third edition, Edinburgh: Churchill Livingstone.

National Center for Health Statistics (1979) *The National Nursing Home Survey: Vital and Health Statistics* (Series 13, No. 43), Washington, DC: US Government Printing Office.

National Center for Health Statistics (1981) *Characteristics of Nursing Home Residents, Health Status and Care Received* (Vital and Health Statistics, Series 13, No. 27), Washington DC: US Government Printing Office.

National Center for Health Statistics (1983) 'An overview of the 1980 master facility inventory of nursing and related care homes', *Advance Data* 91.

National Institute of Mental Health (1983) *Mental Health: United States 1983*, edited by C.A. Taube and S.A. Barrett, (DHSS Pub. No. (ADM–83–1275)), Rockville, MD.

National Institute of Mental Health (1985) *Mental Health: United States 1985*, edited by C.A. Taube and S.A. Barrett, (DHSS Pub. No. (ADM–85–1378)), Washington, DC: Superintendent of Documents, US Government Printing Office.

National Institute of Mental Health (1987) *Mental Health: United States 1987*, edited by R.W. Manderscheid and S.A. Barrett, (DHSS Pub. No. (ADM–87–1518)), Washington, DC: Superintendent of Documents, US Government Printing Office.

Redick, R.W., Manderscheid, R.W., Witkin, M.J., and Rosenstein, M.J. 61983) *A History of the U.S. National Reporting Program for Mental Health Statistics, 1840–1983* (DHSS Pub. No. (ADM) 83–1296), Washington, DC: US Government Printing Office.

Regier, D. and Taube, C.A. (1981) 'The delivery of mental health services', in S. Arieti and H.R.K. Brodie (eds) *American Handbook of Psychiatry*, (2nd edn), New York: Basic Books Inc.

Regier, D.A., Meyers, J.K., Kramer, M., Robins, L.N., Blazer, D.G., Hough, R.L., Eaton, W.W., and Locke, B.Z. (1984) 'The NIMH Epidemiological Catchment Area

Program: historical context, major objectives and study population characteristics', *Archives of General Psychiatry* 44: 934–41.

Regier, D.A., Boyd, J.H., Burke, J.D., Rae, D.S., Meyers, J.K., Kramer, M., Robins, L.N. Gengl. L.K., Karno, M., and Locke, B.Z. (in press) 'One month prevalence of mental disorders in the U.S. – Based on five Epidemiological Catchment Area Sites', *Archives of General Psychiatry*.

Rutter, M. and Quinton, D. (1984) 'Parental psychiatric disorder: effects on children', *Psychological Medicine* 41: 853–80.

United Nations (1985) *World Population Prospects: Estimates and Projections as Assessed in 1982* (Department of International and Social Affairs, Population Studies No. 86 ST/FSA/SER a/86), New York: United Nations.

US Bureau of the Census (1953) *Census of Population 1950: Institutional Population* vol. IV, Special Reports part 2, Chapter C., Washington, DC: US Government Printing Office.

US Bureau of the Census (1973) *Census of Population 1970: Persons in Institutions and Other Group Quarters* (Final report PC (2) – 4E), Washington, DC: US Government Printing Office.

US Bureau of the Census (1979) *Projections of the Populations of the United States by Age, Sex and Race, 1983–2080* (Current Population Reports, Series P–25 No. 952), Washington, DC: US Government Printing Office.

US Bureau of the Census (1984) *Census of Population 1980: Persons in Institutions and Other Group Quarters* (Final Report PC–80–2–4D), Washington, DC: US Government Printing Office.

US Bureau of the Census (1985) *Households, Families, Marital Status and Living Arrangements* (March 1985, advance report, Series P–20 No. 402), Washington, DC: US Government Printing Office.

US Bureau of the Census (1986a) *Marital Status and Living Arrangements* (March 1985, Series P–20 No. 410), Washington, DC: US Government Printing Office.

US Bureau of the Census (1986b) *Households Families, Marital Status and Living Arrangements* (March 1986, Advance Report, Series P–20 No. 412), Washington, DC: US Government Printing Office.

US Bureau of the Census (1986c) *Projections of the Number of Households and Families, 1986–2000* (Series P–25 No. 986), Washington, DC: US Government Printing Office.

US Bureau of the Census; Gregory Spencer (1986d) *Projections of the Hispanic Population, 1983–2080* (Current Population Reports, Series P–25, No. 995), Washington, DC: US Government Printing Office.

Witkin, M.J. (1980). *Trends in Patient Care Episodes in Mental Health Facilities, 1955–1977* (Mental Health Statistical Note No. 154, DHSS Pub. No. (ADM–80–158) Sept. 1980), Rockville, MD: National Institute of Mental Health.

World Health Organization Expert Committee on Health Statistics (1963) *Hospital Statistics and Other Matters* (Eighth Report, Technical Report Series No. 261), Geneva: WHO.

World Health Organization, Expert Committee on Health Statistics (1969) *Statistics of Health Services and Their Activities* (Technical Report Series No. 429), Geneva: WHO.

World Health Organization, Expert Committee on Health Statistics (1971) *Statistical Indicators for the Planning and Evaluation of Public Health Programmes* (Fourteenth Report, Technical Report Series No. 172), Geneva: WHO.

World Health Organization (1976) *Statistical Indices of Family Health* (Report of a WHO Study Group, Technical Report Series No. 587), Geneva: WHO.

World Health Organization (1980) *The Work of WHO 1973–77* (Biennal Report of the Director General, chapter 4: 153–167), Geneva: WHO.

8

Screening for Psychiatric Disorder

David Goldberg

SCREENING VERSUS CASE FINDING

Many authors use the concept of a 'screening test' to mean no more than the use of an inexpensive test as the first part of a two-stage strategy of case identification, where the purpose of the first-stage is to enable those engaged in the more time-consuming task of administering the second-stage case-finding procedure to spend a greater proportion of their time interviewing subjects who will turn out to be cases. This procedure is properly referred to as *case finding*, and refers to 'the testing of patients who have sought health care for disorders which may be unrelated to their chief complaints . . . the execution of case-finding does not carry an implied guarantee that the patient will benefit, only that they will receive the highest standard of care available at that time and place' (Sackett and Holland 1975).

By contrast, *screening* is the testing of apparently healthy volunteers from the general population and separating them into groups with high and low probabilities of a given disorder. The objective of screening is the early detection of diseases whose treatment is either easier or more effective when undertaken at an earlier point in time, so that there is an implicit promise that those who volunteer to be screened will benefit. The requirement that application of the screening procedure will improve the prognosis is implicit in Wilson and Jungner's (1968) ten principles of screening and explicit in Grant's (1982) three conditions for screening.

Other requirements for screening tests are that the natural history of the condition should be understood and that there should be a latent or early symptomatic stage of the illness. We still know relatively little about the untreated course of minor illness, and the latter requirement cannot possibly be met by common mental disorders. However, Wilson (1986) has indicated that 'unreported illness' would be equally acceptable, and numerous surveys have shown that this requirement is easily satisfied.

Evidence that detection of psychiatric disturbance by screening test actually benefits the patient is hard to come by. An early study by Johnstone and Goldberg (1976) showed that detection of psychiatric disorder using the GHQ-60 caused patients to experience symptoms for an average of 2.1 months less than those in the undetected group, and presented suggestive evidence that this effect was especially marked for those with very high scores on their initial consultation. However, Hoeper *et al.* (1984) were unable to replicate this result, although there were a number of unsatisfactory features in the latter study (Goldberg 1984; Williams 1986; Burns 1986).

Before one could recommend that screening for mental illness should become health policy there would need to be uncontested evidence that patients benefit, so that previous reviewers of the field (Eastwood 1971; Goldberg 1974; Williams 1986) have all concluded that the time had not yet arrived. Until such evidence becomes available it should be clear that psychiatrists are in the business of case finding rather than screening, so that strictly speaking we should refer to 'case-finding tests' or 'putative screening tests'. However, both terms are clumsy, and in the remainder of the chapter we will follow common usage and call any inexpensive test or procedure that is applied to a sample in order to select probable cases for further examination a 'screening test'. All of them have been designed to form the first part of what is typically a two-stage research project.

It is still desirable to investigate possible benefits that may accrue to patients as a result of case-finding procedures, preferably using techniques of cost-benefit analysis described by Williams (1986). In addition to the kinds of mixed affective disorders detected by questionnaires such as the General Health Questionnaire (Goldberg 1978) or the Symptom Rating Questionnaire (Harding *et al.* 1980), it would be sensible to consider the costs and benefits of case finding for specific conditions such as alcohol dependence (King 1985; Saunders and Ausland 1987) or severe depressive illness. In the case of alcohol dependence, Kristenson *et al.* (1982) randomly assigned those with positive screening results to an intervention group and a no-treatment control: the former group were shown to have less disability and lower gamma-glutamyl transaminase relative to the latter at four-year follow-up.

In the remainder of chapter various aspects of two-stage survey designs will be considered, starting with the effects of refusals and going on to consider each stage in turn. Factors which affect the validity coefficients of a screening test will be reviewed with emphasis on data concerned with the GHQ, and the chapter will conclude with a short section on survey design.

THE EFFECTS OF REFUSALS

Condon (1986) has drawn attention to the variety of literary devices to which authors resort in order to give the impression that the sample reported upon is representative of the larger population at risk, and suggests that those who refuse are likely to be 'more paranoid, alienated and less compliant with treatment in general'. He points out that journals are likely to reject papers in which the non-representative nature of the sample is highlighted.

Williams and MacDonald (1986) have produced equations to model the effects of two kinds of bias that may arise in two-stage surveys due to refusal to participate: that due to illness and that due to defensiveness. Illness bias refers to the likelihood that psychiatrically ill individuals may be less likely to participate in case-finding surveys, and will, therefore, cause the sample studied to have rather too great a proportion of true normals. The authors show that this bias will have only a rather small effect on the estimated validity coefficients of the screening procedure, but will cause the investigators to underestimate prevalence of disorder.

Defensiveness bias refers to the tendency of those who wish to conceal their illness to refuse to co-operate with the survey. Such a bias will, of course, produce an underestimate of false negatives relative to true negatives, and thus sensitivity will be overestimated. The effect on specificity is negligible, and prevalence will be slightly underestimated.

If we assume that both types of bias are operating, the authors estimate that at a true prevalence of 25 per cent sensitivity will be overestimated and prevalence will be underestimated by between 5 and 6 per cent, while the effect on specificity is negligible. (These figures are derived by making the assumption that each type of bias reduces collaboration by 15 per cent at each stage of the case-finding procedure.)

CHARACTERISTICS OF THE SCREENING TEST

Type of screening procedure

Most screening procedures are pencil-and-paper tests, but other procedures include key informants, short structured interviews, and computer-administered tests. It is not known whether one kind of procedure is better than another, since it is unusual for researchers to compare different procedures during the same study. It has been usual for the type of procedure to be governed by available resources and the needs of a particular study: thus, computer-administered procedures are still relatively rare, while illiterate subjects must have a short structured interview by a research assistant.

Goldberg and Bridges (1987) compared the characteristics of screening by *key informant* (the family doctor) with screening by a *pencil-and-paper-test* (the GHQ-28). The criterion of illness was independent research interview by a psychiatrist using the DSM-III system. The family doctor was shown to be more specific than the GHQ (86 per cent vs. 75 per cent) but very much less sensitive (48 per cent vs. 87 per cent). Of those found to have psychiatric illnesses 41 per cent were detected by both screening procedures, a further 46 per cent by GHQ only, 7 per cent by family doctor only, while 5 per cent

Table 8.1 Validity indices for the DIS interview against research assessments by psychiatrists (diagnoses with < 20 patients omitted)

	Number in sample	Sensitivity	PPV	Specificity	NPV
Major depressive episode	22	40%	0.20	98%	99%
Phobias	184	27%	0.52	93%	82%
Alcohol-use disorders	62	30%	0.55	98%	95%
Drug-use disorders	27	7%	0.21	99%	97%

were missed by both screening procedures. A broadly similar study by von Korff *et al.* (1987) showed that the GHQ identified 39 per cent of the DSM-III illnesses, the family doctor 33 per cent. In this study, a substantial proportion of patients were identified as cases by both GHQ and family doctor, but not confirmed by the DIS interview.

Anthony *et al.* (1987) have considered the characteristics of the Diagnostic Interview Schedule (DIS) administered by lay interviewers as a screening test, when assessed against second-stage assessments by psychiatrists using a research assessment capable of generating DSM-III diagnoses. Although specificity and NPV were generally satisfactory, sensitivity and positive predictive values were not (see table 8.1).

It can be seen that negative predictive values are generally high in conditions of low prevalence, but that the DIS interview is generally insensitive for major diagnoses, and that the positive predictive value only exceeds 0.5 for alcohol-use disorder and phobias. The low sensitivity shown by the DIS interview may account for findings in von Korff *et al.*'s paper referred to earlier.

Computer-generated screening procedures have been described for both Briquet's disorder (Woodruff *et al.* 1973; Reveley *et al.* 1977) and alcoholism (Reich *et al.* 1975; Costello and Baillargeon 1978; Robins and Marcus 1987). They have two advantages over other screening procedures. The computer is able to incorporate precise decision trees for questions, and it is able to adapt the questions asked to an individual's earlier responses. This achieves great time savings without forfeiting accuracy. For example, for alcohol-use disorder, the computer-generated interview asks on average 50 per cent fewer questions than are contained in the DIS, yet achieves a sensitivity of 98 per cent and a positive predictive value (at an unstated prevalence) of 93 per cent. Figures for other diagnoses are equally impressive (Robins and Marcus 1987). It should be stressed that these coefficients are not comparable with those quoted in other work, since there is no independent clinical assessment as a criterion: the screening procedure is merely being compared with results of the whole interview.

A computer-administered version of the Clinical Interview Schedule has been shown to correlate highly with the same interview administered by a clinician (Lewis *et al.* 1988). There is no reason why such computer-administered screening procedures should not be targeted on specific disorders. These matters are discussed further by Hand and Glover in the next chapter.

Choice of screening test

There are now innumerable screening tests, some aimed at detecting a range of psychiatric disorders (for example, the Symptom Rating Questionnaire, the General Health Questionnaire or the Cornell Medical Inventory) while others purport to be diagnosis-specific (for example, the Zung Depression Inventory). Murphy (1981) covers six American screening tests and the GHQ in some detail, and shows that the similarities between them outweigh the differences. Langner's twenty-two-item screening instrument and the Center for Epidemiological Studies' Depression Scale (CES-D) both have unsatisfactory sensitivities, and the Hopkins SCL has somewhat lower specificity.

Those studies that have directly compared screening tests confirm this view. Thus Goldberg *et al.* (1974) compared the GHQ-30 with the Hopkins SCL-36, Maris and Williams (1985) compared the GHQ-12 with the WHO's SRQ, and Stefansson and Kristjansson (1985) compared the GHQ-30 with the CMI: all studies showed that the overall misclassification rates were within a few percentage points of one another. Choice of a particular instrument should, therefore, be determined by the availability of validity data for a comparable population, as well as the needs of a particular survey. Most information is available for the GHQ, and the factors which affect its validity will be considered later in this chapter.

It remains to ask whether it is reasonable to expect the design of screening tests to improve still further, or whether there is not some natural limit to what can be expected from a simple screening procedure. It is clear that any screening procedure which is merely a scaled-down version of the second-stage interview will produce optimal validity coefficients: this merely celebrates a tautology. However, there are indeed limits to what is likely to be achieved, for two reasons. The validity of any procedure cannot be higher than its own reliability, and in the present example both first- and second-stage assessments fall well short of perfect reliability even if the best examples of each are selected. The second reason is that screening procedures erect dichotomies on what are essentially continuously distributed dimensions: there are, therefore, natural limits to the validity coefficients that can be achieved.

Acceptability and ease of administration

Choice of a screening procedure will usually be determined by the available resources and the needs of the population being screened. Screening procedures which have been designed for patients attending general medical clinics (for example, the GHQ and the SRQ) may be more acceptable to respondents who do not see themselves as mentally ill than those whose items are entirely concerned with severe psychological malfunction.

When it is necessary to administer a screening procedure by research assistant (because of illiteracy or blindness), it is obviously desirable that the interview should be as short as possible. In this connection it is of interest that the validity coefficients for the GHQ-12 are almost as good as those for the GHQ-60; the main advantage of the longer questionnaire being that its positive predictive value is somewhat better (see p. 115).

Reliability

The form of reliability that is most relevant to screening procedures is their internal consistency, usually measured by Cronbach's *alpha* coefficient or by split-half reliability. Shrout and Fleiss (1981) have shown that, provided a test has moderate reliability, sensitivity and specificity are little affected. There is, however, a strong relationship between positive predictive value (PPV) and reliability, which is especially marked for conditions of low prevalence. If, for example, we consider a disorder with a prevalence of 3 per cent which can be measured with a PPV of 72 per cent with a perfectly reliable instrument – then an instrument with a reliability of 0.9 would reduce the PPV to 67 per cent, while an instrument with a reliability of 0.5 would only achieve a PPV of 36 per cent.

The more carefully constructed scales have been shown to have high reliability: alpha for the Beck Depression Inventory is 0.87 (range 0.76 to 0.95), while median values for the GHQ are 0.92, 0.88 and 0.82 for the 60, 30 and 12 item versions respectively. Many screening questionnaires give no information about their reliability, and these should be avoided.

Three types of validity

The *specificity* of a screening test is the proportion of correctly identified normals, or the true negatives expressed as a percentage of the non-cases. The *sensitivity* of a test is the proportion of correctly identified cases, or the true positives expressed as a percentage of the cases. Both of these coefficients are independent of prevalence, and they are, therefore, the most usually quoted coefficients.

A third type of validity coefficient measures the ability of the screening test to respond to severity of disorder rather than merely to the presence or absence of disorder: this is usually measured by a rank-order *correlation coefficient* between scores on the instrument and total severity scores on some standardized research interview. It is thus a measure of concurrent validity.

There have now been over seventy validity studies conducted with the General Health Questionnaire in various parts of the world, of which forty-five give sufficiently detailed accounts of sampling procedures to allow direct

Table 8.2 Variance-weighted mean (VWM) validity coefficients from 43 validity studies of the GHQ

	Sensitivity	Specificity
GHQ-12	89% (85%, 92%)*	80% (77%, 83%)*
GHQ-28	84% (77%, 89%)	82% (78%, 85%)
GHQ-30	74% (70%, 77%)	82% (80%, 83%)
GHQ-60	78% (75%, 82%)	87% (86%, 89%)
All	76% (74%, 78%)*	85% (84%, 86%)*

Source: Goldberg and Williams 1988
* 95% confidence limits

comparisons to be made between them. Williams, Goldberg and Mari (1988) have carried out a meta-analysis of these studies, in which each estimate of validity is weighted by its own variance: so that studies which have used superior sampling strategies are given more weight, and large studies will inevitably count more than small studies. When this is done it is possible to compare estimates of sensitivity and specificity which are *variance weighted means* (VWMs) for each version of the GHQ, and these are shown as table 8.2.

It can be seen that, surprisingly, the best sensitivity has been obtained by the GHQ-12, partly because these studies have tended to use large samples and thus have more precise estimates. It is also noteworthy that the GHQ-28 out-performs the GHQ-30 as regards sensitivity. However, it can be seen that all versions of the questionnaire have very similar specificities.

Prevalence dependent measures of validity

Three other measures of the performance of a screening procedure are often quoted, but are in fact highly dependent upon the prevalence of disorder in a particular sample. The *positive predictive value* (PPV) is the probability that an individual with a high score on the test will be found to be a case at subsequent examination; the *negative predictive value* (NPV) is the probability that a low scorer will be found to be a non-case; while the *overall misclassification rate* (OMR) refers to the percentage of misclassified respondents.

To the working clinician, the PPV is the most important thing about a screening test. However, it is important to grasp that the PPV of any test is highly dependent upon prevalence: as prevalence becomes lower, the PPV must necessarily fall as well. All three measures can be readily calculated for any screening test at a stated prevalence, providing that the sensitivity and specificity are known. Positive predictive value is the number of true positives divided by the proportion with high scores. So:

$$\text{Positive Predictive Value} = \frac{\text{Prevalence} \times \text{sensitivity}}{\text{Percentage with high scores}}$$

Similarly, negative predictive value is the number of true negatives divided by the proportion with low scores. So:

$$\text{Negative Predictive Value} = \frac{\text{Prevalence of non-cases} \times \text{specificity}}{\text{Percentage with low scores}}$$

Similar arguments apply to the overall misclassification rate (OMR) as those described above for the predictive values. It is meaningless to quote an OMR for a particular screening test, since it varies directly with prevalence. However, the variation is not nearly so dramatic as that for the PPV, as it depends upon the difference between the sensitivity and specificity coefficients.

$$\text{OMR} = (1 - P) \cdot \text{fp} + P \cdot \text{fn}$$

Where

OMR	=	Overall misclassification rate
P	=	Prevalence
fp	=	false positive rate ($= 1 - \text{specificity}$)
fn	=	false negative rate ($= 1 - \text{sensitivity}$)

It is possible to calculate the PPVs for different versions of the GHQ scaled to a prevalence of 30 per cent (i.e., a level appropriate to attenders in general practice settings), using either median and variance-weighted mean validity coefficients obtained from public validity studies:

PPV_{30}:

	Using variance-weighted mean coefficients	Using median validity coefficients
GHQ-12	0.65	0.65
GHQ-28	0.67	0.67
GHQ-30	0.63	0.63
GHQ-60	0.73	0.72

Whichever set of coefficients is used, the GHQ-60 has the best performance as a screening instrument, while there is no appreciable difference between the other versions.

115

CHARACTERISTICS OF THE CRITERION INTERVIEW

Reliability

In general, the correlation between any two measures is attenuated by their unreliability, since the validity of a measure cannot be higher than the reliability of the measure. Lord and Novick (1968) showed the general relationship to be as follows:

$$R_T = \frac{R_0}{\sqrt{(r_1, r_2)}}$$

Where:

R_T = True relationship
R_0 = Observed relationship
r_1 = reliability of 1st stage assessment
r_2 = reliability of 2nd stage assessment

If the second-stage interview is assumed to be error-free, then validity coefficients for a screening test such as the GHQ can be calculated by taking the median values for correlations between the GHQ and research interviews for each version of the GHQ, taking Cronbach's alpha as a measure of 'r_1', and assuming 'r_2' to be unity. These are shown in the first column, and can be seen to be greater than the observed relationships.

However, it is unreasonable to assume that the criterion is free from error. If we use the value of +0.92 for the reliability of the CIS (see Goldberg *et al.* 1970) the the 'true correlation' between the GHQ and the criterion interview rises still further, as shown in the second column:

Version of GHQ:	Obtained median correlation	Assume perfect criterion	Assume criterion interview = +0.92
GHQ-12	0.70	0.77	0.81
GHQ-30	0.59	0.63	0.72
GHQ-60	0.72	0.75	0.78

What effects does unreliability of the criterion have on the conventional validity coefficients, sensitivity and specificity? Consider two raters, A and B, who are conducting a validity study of a screening test in a population whose 'true prevalence' is 20 per cent. Assume that rater A obtains values of 75 per cent and 85 per cent for the sensitivity and specificity of the test.

Suppose that the two raters now carry out an inter-rater reliability study, and are found to disagree about 'case/non-case' in a proportion of the cases. We can now examine the effects that this will have on validity coefficients between the GHQ and rater B's assessments – assuming that disagreement between the raters is randomly distributed.

Percentage disagreement	Sensitivity	Specificity
0%	75%	85%
1%	73.6%	84.7%
5%	68.1%	83.3%
10%	60%	81.3%
15%	52.4%	79.4%

It can be seen that unreliability of the criterion has a pronounced effect upon sensitivity, but a much smaller effect upon specificity. Now it is likely that clinical judgements made by investigators carrying out validity studies are indeed imperfect, and that the error in their estimates of sensitivity coefficients is greater than their error in estimating specificity.

Since most investigators are unaware of the asymmetry, they calculate a cut-off score by doing the best trade-off between sensitivity and specificity. In their efforts to increase sensitivity at the expense of specificity they, therefore, lower the threshold score, and will in general tend to produce cut-off scores that are too low. Thus, the less competent the investigator, the lower the threshold.

Validity

It might be supposed that different research interviews generate rather different validity coefficients for a particular screening test, since each incorporates somewhat different concepts of psychiatric 'caseness'. Curiously enough, this seems not to be the case.

The most commonly used structured psychiatric interview employed in validity studies of the GHQ is the Clinical Interview Schedule (CIS) of Goldberg *et al.* (1970). The Present State Examination (PSE) has been used in twelve of the validity studies, and in four others other standardized psychiatric interviews provided the criterion assessment. *The VWM sensitivities for these three groups are within 1 per cent of each other.* Similarly, the VWM specificities for the three groups are within 3 per cent of each other.

Duncan-Jones *et al.* (1986) provide a clue as to how this might come about. These workers used techniques of latent trait analysis to analyse a set

117

of over 6,000 responses to the GHQ-12, and demonstrated that the test can be shown to be providing maximum information over a fairly broad range of values on the underlying dimension of severity of disturbance, although the information provided tails off markedly at each extreme. Put another way, this means that the test will discriminate rather poorly between individuals in groups of respondents who are psychologically very healthy or between individuals within groups who are psychiatrically very ill; but that it provides maximum discrimination over the whole intermediate range of severities (Duncan-Jones *et al.* 1986: 399 figure 3).

Grayson *et al.* (1987) showed that three commonly used research criteria for psychiatric illness are all included within this range. Thus, even if, for example, a 'DSM-III case' is slightly less severe a concept than an 'ID-Catego 5+' case, both are within the optimal range of measurement of the screening test. Similar validity coefficients are thus obtained by finding the optimal trade-off for sensitivity against specificity for each 'criterion' of psychiatric illness. It can be seen that the obtained values are indeed likely to be similar providing that the criterion comes within the maximal range of information provided by the test on the underlying dimension of disturbance.

FACTORS WHICH AFFECT THE VALIDITY OF A SCREENING TEST

The General Health Questionnaire will be used as the example of a screening test in this section, since it has been possible to perform meta-analyses of the validity coefficients reported in studies conducted in a wide variety of settings. It has thus been possible to address possible influences on the validity of a well-known screening procedure in an objective way (described more fully in Goldberg and Williams 1988).

We have seen that the length of the screening test and the nature of the validating interview make rather small effects on validity coefficients, but that sensitivity is affected by non-response bias and by reliability of the criterion interview. In general terms, we have seen that the former tends to cause overestimates of sensitivity, while the latter may cause it to be severely underestimated. We shall now consider the effect of five further possible influences.

Socio-demographic characteristics of respondents

Goldberg *et al.* (1974) examined overall misclassification rates with respect to a variety of socio-demographic variables. They noted that GHQ performed better with men than with women and with whites than with blacks, but that the differences were small and not statistically significant. They found no effect of social class or age on misclassification.

Tarnopolsky *et al.* (1979) found that the positive predictive value of the GHQ was higher in women than in men. However, a direct comparison of

Table 8.3 The relationship between sex and the validity of the GHQ

	Sensitivity		Specificity	
	Male	*Female*	*Male*	*Female*
Hobbs *et al.* (1983, 1984)	72	90	87	84
Jenkins (1985)	61	79	83	85
Vazquez-Barquero (1986)	48	67	86	86

the validity coefficients in men and women can be obtained from the studies of Jenkins (1985), Hobbs and his colleagues (1983, 1984) and Vazquez-Barquero *et al.* (1986). In each of the studies, the sensitivity was lower in the men than in the women, whereas this was not the case for the specificity (see table 8.3).

The finding is extended by the results of Williams *et al.*'s (1988) meta-analysis. The VWM sensitivity for the male data in table 8.3 is 64 per cent, the corresponding figure obtained from ten validity studies of female respondents was 80 per cent. As might be expected, the VWM sensitivity for thirty-one studies giving data for both sexes combined was exactly intermediate at 76 per cent! The table also shows that there was no substantial association between sex and specificity: a finding confirmed by the meta-analytic investigation.

Mari and Williams (1986) used ROC analysis to investigate the effects of five socio-demographic variables on misclassification by the GHQ-12 in their study in primary care in Brazil. While the pattern of results was complex, they found that, in general, men were more likely than women to be classified as false negative, while poorly educated respondents were more likely to be classified as false positive.

Language and culture

The GHQ has been translated into a wide variety of European, Asian, and other languages. Similarly, structured interviews such as the CIS and PSE have been translated and used in a wide variety of cultural settings. Many conceptual and practical problems arise when instruments designed and constructed in one culture are translated for use in another. Despite these problems, the GHQ appears to perform well in a variety of cultural settings, and has been translated into at least thirty-six languages.

Indeed, the VWM specificities for the English and the non-English studies in the meta-analysis were 85 per cent and 86 per cent respectively. The VWM sensitivity of the non-English studies was slightly higher than that for the English studies (78 per cent compared with 74 per cent), although the difference did not reach statistical significance ($Z = 1.68$). Cheng and Williams (1986) have shown that the addition of thirty specially designed

'Chinese' items to the GHQ-30 add a little to the validity of the GHQ: the overall misclassification rate with the GHQ-30 was 11.6 per cent, but this dropped to 9.6 per cent with the new 60-item 'Chinese GHQ'. This had the effect of improving the sensitivity of the revised instrument, and shows that taking local symptom patterns into account can slightly improve the overall discrimination obtainable.

However, in general it would appear that cultural factors make a rather small contribution to the identification of minor psychiatric illness, although it must be stressed that the research interviews used in these studies have all been designed in English-speaking countries. With this caveat, the item content of the GHQ identifies psychologically disordered people in a wide variety of cultures and languages.

Delay between stages

In a two-stage study it is desirable for the interview to take place as soon as possible after the questionnaire has been completed. Otherwise changes in the clinical state of respondents might be expected to result in lower validity coefficients than would otherwise be the case. Since the GHQ is designed to detect relatively acute changes in state, many of which are short-lived, the expected effect of delay is that a greater proportion of high-scoring respondents will be rated as non-cases on subsequent interview, i.e., will be regarded as false positives. A similar, but smaller, effect is to be expected from people becoming ill between questionnaire and interview.

The delay between stages is clearly stated in twenty-nine of the validity studies of the GHQ, and was one week or less in fourteen, and one month or less in a further ten. An effect in the predicted direction can be found for the sensitivity: the median values for the two groups of studies being 80 per cent and 70 per cent respectively. This was confirmed in Williams *et al.*'s meta-analysis, where the VWM sensitivities of the two groups of studies were 81 per cent for a delay between stages of up to one week, and 57 per cent for a delay of up to one month (Williams *et al.* 1988).

A similar effect was found for specificity, with VWM values of 86 per cent 62 per cent for the short and long delay respectively.

Interestingly, the values for the VWM sensitivity and specificity of twenty-four studies in which the interview was given at the same time as the questionnaire were 79 per cent and 83 per cent respectively – that is to say, no different from the values for a delay of up to one week. Even so, the implication for study design is clear: keep the delay between stages as short as possible.

Consulting setting

The validity of the GHQ has been investigated in a wide variety of settings, which can conveniently be considered in three categories according to their position on 'the pathway to specialist care' (Goldberg and Huxley 1980).

First are nineteen studies which have been conducted in a non-consulting setting, including community surveys and surveys of special groups such as students. Second are fourteen validity studies which have been located in the setting of primary medical care. Third are fourteen studies which have been conducted in the setting of secondary medical care. The VWM sensitivities and specificities are shown below:

Setting	VWM sensitivity	VWM specificity
Community	64%	85%
Primary care	83%	84%
Secondary care	81%	85%

Thus, it can be seen that the sensitivity is lower in studies in the community than in consulting settings, whereas the specificity appears not to differ between the settings.

Effects of physical ill-health

Since physically ill people score highly on screening tests it is not surprising that they are over-represented among those respondents classified as false positives. For example, Bridges and Goldberg (1986) had to raise the threshold score on the GHQ-28 as high as 11/12 in order to obtain optimal discrimination between cases and normals among neurological in-patients because of the very high levels of physical symptoms experienced by these patients.

If the GHQ is to be used with patients with severe physical illness, it may be necessary to raise the threshold in order to obtain an optimal trade-off between sensitivity and specificity.

Summary

It would appear that – when allowance is made for the size of the various samples – the sensitivities and specificities of the GHQ are fairly predictable, as shown by the fairly narrow confidence limits shown in table 8.2. The main reasons for carrying out further validity studies would be to establish the *optimal threshold* to be used in some new cultural or consulting situations, since the coefficients themselves appear to be relatively stable.

Table 8.4 gives a summary of the various factors which have been shown to have effects on screening procedures. It will be recalled that the nature of the second-stage case-finding interview, whether or not the study takes place in primary care or in a hospital setting, and factors relating to language and culture, all seem to have rather small effects.

Table 8.4 Summary of principal factors that affect the performance of screening procedures

	Sensitivity	Specificity	Correlation	PPV	Prevalence
for any screening procedure					
Illness bias	Little effect	Little effect			ca 6% under-estimated
Defensiveness bias	ca 6% over-estimated	Little effect			Slight under est.
Unreliability of screen	Little effect	Little effect	Attenuates	Attenuates at low prev.	
Unreliablity of criterion	Markedly depressed	Slightly depressed	Attenuates		
for GHQ:					
Length of screen	Little effect	Little effect		Increases steadily	
Delay between stages 1 week	Slightly depressed	No effect			
Delay between stages 1 month	Markedly depressed	Markedly depressed			
Sex	Males lower	No effect			
Community vs. consulting	Community lower	No effect			

SURVEY DESIGN

The main use of a case-finding test is to identify respondents who should be interviewed at greater length in order to identify true positives. Thus, an investigator may adopt a stratified sampling strategy in which as many as possible of those scoring above some arbitrary threshold are selected for interview, together with a probability sample of those with low scores. This is a perfectly legitimate use of a screening test, but it must be appreciated that it is not the optimal design for estimating validity coefficients.

To calculate the most precise validity coefficients in a new setting

If an investigator does not wish to rely on already published validity studies – either because none are available for the particular class of respondent, or because a new screening test is being studied – then the advice must depend on the estimated prevalence of disorder in the population to be examined.

If the estimated prevalence is between 25 and 35 per cent, it is best to select a random sample of respondents for the second-stage interview, since this will both allow the investigator to calculate a Relative Operating Characteristic (ROC) curve and provide the most precise estimates of validity coefficients.

An ROC curve is obtained by plotting sensitivity against false-positive rate (the complement of specificity) for all possible cut-off points of the screening procedure. ROC analysis was first developed in psychophysics to assess the ability of an observer to identify a signal against a background of noise (Swets 1964), and has been used in medical decision analysis by Weinstein and Feinberg 1980. Several investigators have applied ROC analysis to study the characteristics of screening procedures in psychiatry (Mari and Williams 1985, 1986; Bridges and Goldberg 1986; Bellantuono 1987; Surtees 1987; and Newman 1988). ROC analysis provides the best estimate of threshold score, and allows one screening procedure to be compared with another.

If, however, the estimated prevalence of disorder is low, then the use of a random sample of first-stage respondents for second-stage interview will result in the investigators spending most of their time interviewing non-cases. In such cases they may prefer to take either a truncated random sample (see p. 124) or a stratified sample.

Stratified sampling procedures have three disadvantages: it is essential to weight the data back to the original first-stage characteristics before calculating the validity cofficients; two strata models assume that the best threshold is known – whereas this is actually a most variable characteristic; and they produce less precise (in the sense of having larger variances) estimates of the validity coefficients (Williams *et al*. 1988).

Predicting prevalence from results of a screening test

This can readily be done by using known validity coefficients and substituting them in the formula shown below:

$$\frac{pHS + Specificity - 1}{Sensitivity + Specificity - 1}$$

Alternatively, it can be expressed as the sum of the true positives and the false negatives (both expressed as a proportion of the total sample), i.e.,

$$(PPV \cdot pHS) + (1 - NPV) \cdot pLS.$$

Where pHS, pLS denotes the proportion with high and low scores; PPV and NPV are the positive and negative predictive values.

To estimate the best threshold

The best threshold score is that which gives the best trade-off between sensitivity and specificity, and this is most easily calculated with an ROC curve. Sometimes researchers do not wish to take a random sample, since they do not wish to spend most of their time interviewing non-cases. An alternative strategy would be to take a *truncated random sample* in which all respondents with a score of zero are not selected for interview, but are assumed to be non-cases. A random sample of those with a score of one or more would be selected for interview. This strategy is considered in more detail by Goldberg and Williams (1988).

REFERENCES

Anthony, J., Folstein, M., Romanowski, A.J., von Korff, M., Nestadt, G., Chahal, R., Merchant, A., Brown, C., Shapiro, S., Kramer, M., and Gruenberg, E. (1987) 'Comparison of lay DIS and a standardised psychiatric diagnosis', *Archives of General Psychiatry*, in press.

Beck, T.A., Rial, W.Y., and Rickels, K. (1974) 'Short form of the Beck Depression Inventory: cross validation', *Psychological Reports* 34: 1184–6.

Bellantuono, C., Fiorio, R., Zanotelli, R., and Tansella, N. (1987) 'Psychiatric screening in general practice in Italy: a validity study of the GHQ', *Social Psychiatry* 22: 113–17.

Bridges, K.W. and Goldberg, D.P. (1986) 'The validation of the GHQ-28 and the use of the M.M.S.E. in neurological inpatients', *British Journal of Psychiatry* 148: 548–53.

Burns, B. (1986) 'General discussion: screening', in M. Shepherd, G. Wilkinson, and P. Williams (eds) *Mental Illness in Primary Care Settings*, London: Tavistock, 83.

Cheng, T.A. and Williams, P. (1986) 'The design and development of a screening questionnaire (GHQ) for use in community studies of marital disorders in Taiwan', *Psychological Medicine* 16: 415–22.

Condon, J.T. (1986) 'The unresearched: those who decline to participate', *Australian and New Zealand Journal of Psychiatry* 20: 87–9.

Costello, R.M. and Baillargeon, J.G. (1978) 'Alcoholism screening inventory: replication of Reich and extension', *British Journal of Addiction* 73: 399–405.

Duncan-Jones, P., Grayson, D., and Moran, P.A.P. (1986) 'The utility of latent trait models in psychiatric epidemiology', *Psychological Medicine* 16: 391–405.

Duncan-Jones, P. and Henderson, S. (1978) 'The use of a two-phase design in a prevalence survey', *Social Psychiatry* 13: 231–7.

Eastwood, M.R. (1971) 'Screening for psychiatric disorder', *Psychological Medicine* 1: 197–208.

Finlay-Jones, R.A. and Murphy, E. (1979) 'Severity of psychiatric disorder and the 30-item General Health Questionnaire', *British Journal of Psychiatry* 134: 609–16.

Gask, L., McGrath, G., Goldberg, D., and Millar, T. (1987) 'Improving the psychiatric skills of established general practitioners: evaluation of group teaching', *Medical Education*, in press.

Goldberg, D. (1974) 'Screening for disease – psychiatric disorders', *Lancet* ii: 1245–8.

Goldberg, D.P. (1978) *Manual of the General Health Questionnaire* Windsor: NFER/Nelson.

Goldberg, D. (1984) 'Screening for mental illness', letter, *Lancet* i: 224.

Goldberg, D. (1986) 'Use of the General Health Questionnaire in clinical work', *British Medical Journal* 293: 1188–9.

Goldberg, D. and Bridges, K. (1987) 'Screening for psychiatric illness in general practice: the general practitioner versus the screening questionnaire', *Journal of the Royal College of General Practitioners* 37: 15–18.

Goldberg, D.P., Cooper, A.B., Eastwood, M.R., Kedward, H.B., and Shepherd, M. (1970) 'A psychiatric interview suitable for use in community surveys', *British Journal of Social and Preventive Medicine* 24: 18–26.

Goldberg, D. and Huxley, P. (1980) *Mental Illness in the Community: The Pathway to Psychiatric Care*, London: Tavistock.

Goldberg, D.P., Rickels, K., Downing, R., and Hesbacher, P. (1974) 'A comparison of two psychiatric screening tests', *British Journal of Psychiatry* 129: 61–7.

Goldberg, D. and Williams, P. (1988) *The User's Guide to the General Health Questionnaire*, London: NFER/Nelson.

Goodchild, M.E. and Duncan-Jones, P. (1985) 'Chronicity and the General Health Questionnaire', *British Journal of Psychiatry* 146: 55–61.

Grant, I.W. (1982) 'Screening for lung cancer', *British Medical Journal* 284: 1209–10.

Grayson, D., Bridges, K., Duncan-Jones, P. and Goldberg, D.P. (1987) 'The relationship between symptoms and diagnoses of minor psychiatric disorder in general practice', *Psychological Medicine* 17, in press.

Harding, T.W., Arnago, M.V., Balthazar, J., Climent, C.E., Ibrahim, H.H.A., Ladrigo-Ignacio, L., Srivinatha Murthy, R., and Wig, N.N. (1980) 'Mental disorders in primary care: a study of their frequency and diagnosis in four developing countries', *Psychological Medicine* 10: 231–42.

Hobbs, P., Ballinger, C.B., and Smith, D.M.W. (1983) 'Factor analysis and validation of the General Health Questionnaire in women: and general practice surveys', *British Journal of Psychiatry* 142: 257–64.

Hobbs, P., Ballinger, C.V., Greenwood, C., Martin, B., and McClure, A. (1984) 'Factor analysis and validation of the General Health Questionnaire in men: a general practice survey', *British Journal of Psychiatry* 144: 270–5.

Hodiamont, P., Peer, N., and Syben, N. (1987) 'Epidemiological aspects of psychiatric disorder in a Dutch health area', *Psychological Medicine* 17: 495–505.

Hoeper, E., Nycz, G., Kessler, L., Burke, J., and Pierce, W. (1984) 'The usefulness of screening for mental health', *Lancet* i: 33–5.

Jenkins, R. (1985) 'Sex differences in minor psychiatric morbidity', *Psychological Medicine*, Supplement 7.

Johnstone, A. and Goldberg, D. (1976) 'Psychiatric screening in general practice', *Lancet* i: 605–8.

Johnstone, A. and Shepley, M. (1986) 'The outcome of hidden neurotic illness treated in general practice', *Journal of the Royal College of General Practitioners* 36: 413–15.

King, M. (1985) 'At risk drinking among general practice attenders: validation of the CAGE questionnaire', *Psychological Medicine* 16: 213–16.

Kristenson, H., Ohlin, H., Hulten-Nosslin, M., Trell, E., and Wood, B. (1983) 'Identification and intervention of heavy drinking in middle aged men: results and follow-up of 24–60 months of long term study with randomised controls', *Alcoholism: Clinical & Experimental Research* 7: 203–9.

Lewis, G., Pelosi, A.J., Glover, E., Wilkinson, G., Stansfeld, S.A., Williams, P., and Shepherd, M. (1988) 'The development of a computerised assessment for minor psychiatric disorder', *Psychological Medicine*, in press.

Lord, F.M. and Novick, M.R. (1968) *Statistical Theories of Mental Test Scores*, Reading, Mass.: Addison-Wesley.

Mari, J.J. and Williams, P. (1986) 'Misclassification by psychiatric screening questionnaires', *Journal of Chronic Diseases* 39: 371–8.

Mari, J.J. and Williams, P. (1985) 'Comparison of the validity of two psychiatric screening questionnaires using ROC analysis', *Psychological Medicine* 15: 651–9.

Murphy, J.M. (1981) 'Psychiatric instrument development for primary care research: patient self-report questionnaire' (report to Division of Biometry and Epidemiology of the NIMH, Washington, on Contract No. SOMO14280101D), unpublished.

Newman, S.C., Bland, R., and Orn, H. 'General Health Questionnaire as a screening instrument in a community survey', *Psychological Medicine*, (submitted for publication).

Reich, T., Robins, L.N., Woodruff, R.A., Taibleson, M., Rich, C., and Cunningham, L. (1975) 'Computer-assisted derivation of a screening interview for alcoholism', *Archives of General Psychiatry* 32: 847–52.

Reveley, M.A., Woodruff, R.A., Robins, L.N., Taibleson, M., Reich, T., and Helzer, J. (1977) 'Evaluation of a screening programme for Briquet's syndrome', *Archives of General Psychiatry* 34: 145–50.

Robins, L.N. and Marcus, S.C. 'The diagnostic screening procedure writer', in press.

Sackett, D. and Holland, W. (1975) 'Controversy in the detection of disease', *Lancet* ii: 357–9.

Saunders, J.B. and Ausland, O.G. (1987) *WHO Collaborative Project on Identification and Treatment of Persons with Harmful Alcohol Consumption*, Geneva: WHO.

Shrout, P.E. and Fleiss, J.L. (1981) 'Reliability and case detection', in J.K. Wing, P. Bebbington, and L. Robins (eds) *What is a Case?*, London: Grant, McIntyre.

Stefansson, J.G. and Kristjansson, I. (1985) 'Comparison of the GHQ and the CMI', *Acta Psychiatrica Scandinavica* 72: 482–7.

Surtees, P.G. (1987) 'Psychiatric disorder in the community and the General Health Questionnaire', submitted to the *British Journal of Psychiatry* 150: 828–35.

Swets, J.A. (1964) *Signal Detection and Recognition by Human Observers*, New York: Wiley.

Tarnopolsky, A., Hand, D.J., McLean, E.K., Roberts, H., and Wiggins, R.D. (1979) 'Validity of uses of a screening questionnaire (GHQ) in the community', *British Journal of Psychiatry* 134: 508–15.

Vazquez-Barquero, J.L., Diez-Manrique, J.F., Pena, C., Quintanal, R.G., and Labrador Lopez, M. (1986) 'Two stage design in a community survey', *British Journal of Psychiatry* 149: 88–97.

von Korff, M., Shapiro, S., Burke, J., Teitlebaum, M., Skinner, E.A., German, P., Klein, L., and Burns, B.J. (1987) 'Mental disorders in primary care: assessment by the DIS, GHQ and practitioner', *Archives of General Psychiatry*, in press.

Weinstein, M.C. and Fineberg, H.V. (1980) *Clinical Decision Analysis*, Philadelphia: W.B. Saunders.

Williams, P. (1986) 'Mental illness and primary care: screening', in M. Shepherd, G. Wilkinson and P. Williams (eds) *Mental Illness in Primary Care Settings*, London: Tavistock.

Williams, P. and MacDonald, A. (1986) 'The effect of non-response bias on the results of two-stage screening surveys of psychiatric disorder', *Social Psychiatry* 21: 1–5.

Williams, P., Goldberg, D., and Mari, J.J. (1988) 'A method for comparing validity coefficients in two-stage screening studies', Institute of Psychiatry, unpublished.

Wilson, J.M. and Jungner, G. (1968) *The principles and practice of screening for disease* (WHO Public Health Papers No. 34), Geneva: World Health Organization.

Wilson, J.M. (1986) 'Screening: general discussion', in M. Shepherd, G. Wilkinson and P. Williams (eds) *Mental Illness in Primary Care Settings*, London, Tavistock, p. 79.

Woodruff, R.A., Robins, L.B., Taibleson, N., Reich, T., and Helzer, J. (1973) 'Evaluation of a screening interview for hysteria', *Archives of General Psychiatry* 29: 450–55.

9

The Impact of Information Technology

David Hand and Eric Glover

The nature of the effects that computers and information technology have upon everyday life can be classified according to a position on a continuum. At one extreme of this continuum lies the striking effect – the new development which makes one sit up and take notice. And at the other extreme lies the subtle effect – the development occurring in the background which serves to make everyday life easier in some way. In between these two extremes lies a range of developments with intermediate impact.

Precisely the same is true of the impact of computers and information technology on psychiatry. There are the novel and exciting breakthroughs and there are the subtle but nevertheless very influential background changes. In this article we shall look at this range, presenting examples from various points to demonstrate how computers are already beginning to influence the development and practice of epidemiological and social psychiatry. The four topics we have chosen to illustrate the effects are statistics, computerized interviewing, computerized diagnosis, and artificial intelligence. These range from developments extending the work of pre-computer days to developments which were completely infeasible prior to the computer.

Perhaps we should also remark that our four examples by no means exhaust the ways in which computers and information technology are changing psychiatry. Other examples include the different kinds of brain scanners, simulation models for teaching purposes, sophisticated graphics tools for exploring neurochemical phenomena, and so on.

STATISTICS

Statistical techniques are the fundamental tools of epidemiological research, and statistical techniques are experiencing an extraordinary era of development, driven in part by the computer. Anybody with a passing familiarity with epidemiological psychiatry will have encountered concepts such as that of relative risk, but a cursory glance at the literature now reveals that reports of psychiatric research are liberally littered with the names of sophisticated new techniques. For example, in explicit recognition of the fact that it is not possible to characterize adequately the complexity of the human mind with just one or two scores, one sees increasing reference to multivariate techniques. Most readers will have seen accounts of cluster analysis (Everitt 1972, 1980) being used in attempts to clarify the typology of depression; accounts of factor analysis (Harman 1967; Tabachnik and Fidell 1983) being used in attempts to define personality more precisely (Eysenck 1981); and, more recently, accounts of multivariate analysis of variance (Hand and Taylor, 1987) being used to characterize the differences between groups of subjects. Other multivariate techniques which are beginning to appear in the psychiatric literature include correspondence analysis (Greenacre 1984; Dunn 1986) and linear structural relationship modelling (Everitt 1984).

The techniques listed above represent examples of methods which had their genesis in pre-computer days. For most of them it was possible to conduct such analysis by hand (or, at least, by mechanical calculator) although months rather than seconds would have been required. The fact that computers can perform the calculations very rapidly has had two effects. There is the obvious one that researchers now perform the analyses as a matter of course (a point to which we return below). Also there is the less obvious one that such computational facility has stimulated dramatic theoretical development of these techniques. Perhaps the prime example of this is the generalized linear model (McCullagh and Nelder 1983). This is a general structure, of which regression analysis and analysis of variance are special cases. Another very important special case is the log-linear model (Bishop, Fienberg and Holland 1975). This is particularly important in psychiatry because of the nature of psychiatric data (see below). A recent example of the use of this class of techniques in psychiatric research is given in Dunn (1986).

If the above represent theoretical and practical developments driven by the computer but having their origins in pre-computer-age methodology, then there are other developments which would have been inconceivable without modern computational power. Here, a perfect illustration is the bootstrap technique (Efron 1982). This permits one to assess the variation one would expect in an estimate, no matter how complex the estimator, by recalculating the estimate again and again using subsamples of the original data. The bootstrap idea is revolutionary – and very much a child of the computer age.

We referred above to the 'nature of psychiatric data'. Loosely, one might characterize it as involving mixed variable types, often ordinal and probably categorical. This poses particular challenges and, though it is by no means unique to psychiatry, it has led to a unique flavour to the class of statistical methods used in psychiatry. Similarly, the acknowledged difficulty of clearly defining many of the concepts has led to emphasis on exploring questions of reliability. Precise operational definitions have, therefore, been painstakingly constructed and in many cases the results, involving carefully structured interviews and the like, have greater reliability than in other areas of medicine. Again, the computer, using statistical methods such as factor analysis, principal components analysis, discriminant analysis, and item analysis, has played a key role. Of course, many questions remain open, and it is a rich and exciting area for statisticians who wish to develop some practically relevant methodological theory.

Recent discussions of the relevance of statistics to psychiatry include Hand (1985a) and Everitt (1987).

All that we have said so far about the impact of computers on statistics in epidemiological psychiatry is to the good, but there is also a dark side. Statistical packages are designed to be easy to use, but they are also easy to misuse. The computer will do the calculations on whatever numbers are fed to it – regardless of their validity or meaningfulness. And, of course, the very sophistication of modern statistical packages makes things far worse. In many cases the user may have a weak grasp of the theory underlying a technique he is attempting to apply. He may not even understand the output. Several recent papers have drawn attention to the extent of misuse of statistical methods in medical and psychiatric research (e.g. White 1979; Gore *et al.* 1977). The ideal answer of more statistical education – both of researchers in psychiatry and of statistical consultants – is perhaps a forlorn hope. However, a more recent development, which makes the future look brighter, makes full use of the ideas of information technology. This is the advent of the statistical expert system – computer programs which help a user to apply statistical methods correctly without making errors. They will guide, monitor, and advise the researcher. Hand (1986) gives a recent review of this rapidly developing field.

COMPUTERIZED INTERVIEWING

Computers have been used sporadically in psychiatry for interviewing patients over the past twenty years. The term 'computerized interviewing' now seems to be common, although it must be borne in mind that in the systems currently being used it is really only multiple choice questionnaires which are being talked about. No system, yet, is capable of understanding and replying to a patient's typed or spoken utterance, nor will it be for the foreseeable future.

Typically, in current systems, a series of questions is presented to the patient on the visual display screen of a computer. To each question a series of answers is proposed by the computer and the patient has to choose the answer he or she feels is most appropriate for them by touching a certain key on the keyboard.

Among the many papers which report these systems in use we mention the following as a representative sample. Psychiatric case histories: Slack and Van

Cura (1968), Coddington and King (1972), Dove *et al.* (1977), Carr *et al.* (1983); depression and suicide: Greist *et al.* (1973), Carr *et al.* (1981); phobia: Carr and Ghosh (1983); general screening and assessment: Krynicki and Gould (1984), Comings (1984), Lewis *et al.* (1988).

These researchers (and others not mentioned) have established the viability of using computers in this way. On the whole, patients did not object to using them and the results obtained were satisfactory to the people involved. Most of the computerized interviewing projects have been confined to hospital settings (with both in-patients and out-patients) and the patients involved have sometimes been psychotic. A typical 'consultation' with a computer usually lasts between fifteen and thirty minutes, although one group (Dove *et al.* 1977) used a very long interview which took nearly two hours to complete. Unusually, this took place in a general practice health centre and the researchers claim that the easy-going nature of the computer-patient interview had a definite therapeutic effect.

A project to computerize the Clinical Interview Schedule is being undertaken at the General Practice Research Unit, Institute of Psychiatry. For this purpose, the existing CIS, which was not a questionnaire, has been transformed into one by expanding some questions and deleting others. The initial computer program has grown into a general purpose one enabling any questionnaire to be set up. The current system, called PROQSY (PROgrammable Questionnaire SYstem), which is still under development, has been used in a general practice setting with some degree of success (Lewis *et al* 1988). In addition to the CIS, it enables many different sorts of interview to be designed and then administered by psychiatrists.

A script of the desired questionnaire is prepared on a word processor and is then submitted to the PROQSY driver program for execution. This takes place according to the branching and scoring commands which the psychiatrist has specified within the script. The driver program automatically scores the patient as the interview proceeds and outputs a data file suitable for statistical analysis at the end. Alternatively, a brief clinical report of the interview can be prepared. A typical question, answer, and command set (called a frame) looks like

IRRIT__CHILDREN

Have you felt like hitting one of your children recently?

1 No
2 Yes, but I didn't hit out
3 Yes, and I did hit out

if IRRIT < answer then IRRIT: = answer − 1;

if IRRIT == 0 then goto IRRIT__SPOUSE;

The answer is selected by typing the appropriate number key. Only the question and answer are displayed on the screen, but the Frame Label (first line) and the Frame Commands (last two lines) enable the psychiatrist to control the flow of the interview and to collect scores in a number of nominated variables (in this case IRRIT) according to the answers received. At the end of the interview the values of all the variables can be dumped to a file ready for inclusion as a record in a database or for clinical analysis.

From the experience gained in the GPRU and that reported by others, we can state that computerized interviews have the following advantages over human administered ones:

A1) Reliability is maximal. There is only one rater, the computer, and it is completely consistent. It never gets bored with patients and it never prejudges them. Patients can set their own pace and take as much time as they want.

A2) Interview structure can be more complex than is feasible for either self-report questionnaires or human administered interviews. Thus, complex branches may be set up to handle a large range of answering possibilities which a human interviewer would find difficult to cope with. Furthermore, questions can be tailored to suit specific social groupings.

A3) There is some evidence to suggest that people are more truthful to a computer than they are to other people in regard to certain areas of their lives (e.g. alcohol consumption, suicidal tendencies) which might concern deviant behaviour. This topic requires further research, however.

A4) Administering an interview by computer is cheap and easy (given the right facilities) when compared with the human method. Furthermore, most patients like it and some report beneficial effects.

A5) The computer method is thorough, and the multiple choice technique ensures that answers can't be fudged or skipped.

Against these must be set the disadvantages:

D1) The only communication between patient and interviewer is verbal and mostly one way, from computer to patient. Thus, possibly important auditory or visual clues emanating from the patient as to his or her mental state will be missed.

D2) The use of multiple choice questions makes the semantic range of answers discrete instead of continuous and thus suppresses any possible variation in meaning. Also, the interview designer may omit an important possibility from the answer set and the patient may be forced into giving a false answer. Moreover, the patient is not able to expand on the answer or to correct a misleading impression.

D3) Some patients cannot be interviewed by computer for a variety of reasons, such as timidity, illiteracy, poor eyesight, obesity, etc.

The chief uses of this form of interviewing for the psychiatrist would appear to be for epidemiological research and clinical screening, i.e., as an information gatherer, rather than for any therapeutic purpose. The assessment of psychiatric disorder by the various computer programs usually takes two forms. One is a numerical classification along one or more axes and the other is a brief verbal report based on the numerical score and possibly incorporating phrases excerpted from appropriate questions or answers. Mostly, the numerical scales, like the questionnaires themselves, are taken with minimal modification from existing questionnaires which have achieved some degree of acceptability among psychiatrists.

The prognosis for computerized interviews in general practice psychiatry is unclear at the moment. On the theoretical side, they will need to evolve away from the existing instruments if the advantages of computers are to be properly exploited, but in doing so they will become less acceptable for many researchers. On the practical side, it seems likely that, as computer hardware continues to fall in price and more and more general practices possess computers, greater use will be made of them by researchers in epidemiological psychiatry. However, practical difficulties and medical conservatism may delay or even prevent their widespread use in any clinical role.

COMPUTER-AIDED DIAGNOSIS

The possibility of using computers to assist in the diagnostic process is a very exciting one, and one which has attracted much interest in recent decades. For epidemiological and social psychiatry, the particular importance lies in the promise of replicable and reliable diagnoses as well as the potential for effective screening.

There are four basic types of approach, although naturally they overlap to some extent.

The *actuarial* approach begins with a large body of data describing patients with known diagnoses. From this, statistical methods are used to extract relevant information so that, when presented with a profile of symptoms for a new patient, one can calculate the probability that he belongs to each of the diagnostic categories.

A great many such schemes have been developed, many of them based on the ideas of statistical pattern recognition common to automatic EEG analysis and speech recognition. Hand (1981) describes such methods.

The second class of approaches is the *decision tree* approach. Here one progressively narrows down the diagnostic possibilities by answering a sequence of questions. The idea is an old one, but one which has grown with

133

the computer so that nowadays large decision trees require implementation on a computer.

The third kind of approach is illustrated by the CATEGO program. This is a hierarchical program which takes 500 items describing the patient and successively condenses them through a series of stages to arrive at a conclusion in terms of twenty-nine clinical categories. Sharp (1987) contains a brief description of the program.

The fourth approach to computer-assisted diagnosis is via *expert systems* technology. Basically such systems consist of a collection of 'rules' summarizing knowledge about (in this case) psychiatric illness. Each rule has the form 'IF (conditions) THEN (actions), where the 'conditions' describe some aspect of the patient and the 'actions' either represent some deduction about the patient or represent a diagnosis. (Sharp (1987) and Hand (1985b) give descriptions of rule-based systems.) More sophisticated expert systems contain complex causal models of the underlying disease process (e.g. Szolovits 1982).

ARTIFICIAL INTELLIGENCE

Artificial intelligence research impinges upon psychiatry in several ways. One is via expert systems for diagnosis and therapy, as outlined above. A second is via the recent revival in interest in neural networks. And the third is through attempts to model cognitive processes. We shall look at an example of the third here, one which has stimulated a considerable amount of controversy.

The basic idea underlying this use of artificial intelligence ideas is that the most effective way to test a theory of cognitive psychology is to attempt to build a working model. The supposition is that any gap in the theory will reflect itself in an inadequate performance for the model.

The most famous effort in this direction is undoubtedly that of the team led by K.M. Colby, a psychiatrist with an interest in paranoia. Over a period of years Colby and his co-workers created PARRY, a simulated twenty-eight-year-old paranoid man which, via a computer terminal, converses with interviewers in ordinary English. The theory under test was Colby's theory of paranoia – and the basic test method was to see if the simulation could be distinguished from a real paranoid patient. PARRY has internal representations of fear, anger, shame, and other affects and the strengths of these change during the course of the interview. The later versions of PARRY are intended to 'respond to treatment' by behaving in a less paranoid way if suitable therapeutic approaches are adopted by the interviewer. The challenge implicit in this is clear since normal behaviour is much less restricted than paranoid behaviour.

PARRY has attracted considerable interest – over 50,000 interviews have been conducted with various versions of it. However, it should be stated that PARRY has not yielded a definitive conclusion about Colby's paranoia theory. (But how much research in the behavioural sciences does yield a definitive conclusion?) What it has done is stimulate a tremendous amount of debate about the nature of scientific testing in behavioural research. Judging by this, PARRY is an important piece of work.

Colby (1981) provides a compact summary of the PARRY project, and the debate itself is encapsulated in the discussion following Colby (1981).

CONCLUSION

In an article as brief as this it is, of course, impossible to do more than scratch the surface of the way in which information technology is beginning to influence psychiatry. We mentioned a few 'striking' topics at the end of the first section which space would prevent us from discussing. There is also a whole host of subtle background topics which, likewise, we have been unable to discuss. These include such things as databases, word processors, and instrumentation. Schwartz (1984) discussed topics throughout the entire continuum of applications.

REFERENCES

Bishop, Y.M.M., Fienberg, S.E., and Holland, P.W. (1975) *Discrete Multivariate Analysis*, Cambridge, Mass.: MIT Press.

Carr, A.C., Ancill, R.J., Ghosh, A., and Margo, A. (1981) 'Direct assessment of depression by microcomputer', *Acta Psychiatrica Scandinavica* 64: 415–22.

Carr, A.C., and Ghosh, A. (1983) 'Response of phobic patients to direct computer assessment', *British Journal of Psychiatry* 142: 60–5.

Carr, A.C., Ghosh, A., and Ancill, R.J. (1983) 'Can a computer take a psychiatric history?', *Psychological Medicine* 13: 151–8.

Coddington, R.D., and King, T.L. (1972) 'Automated history taking in child psychiatry', *American Journal of Psychiatry* 129 (3): 52–8.

Colby, K.M. (1981) 'Modelling a paranoid mind,' *The Behavioural and Brain Sciences* 4: 515–60.

Comings, D.E. (1984) 'A computerized interview schedule (DIS) for psychiatric disorders', in M.D. Schwartz *Using Computers in Clinical Practice*, New York: The Hayworth Press, 195–203.

DeDombal, F.T., Leaper, D.J., Staniland, J.R., McCann, A.P., and Horrocks, J.C. (1972) 'Computer-aided diagnosis of acute abdominal pain', *British Medical Journal* ii: 9–13.

Dove, G.A.W., Wigg, P., Clarke, J.H.C., Constantinidou, M., Royapa, B.A., Evans, C.R., Milne, J., Goss, C., Gordon, M. and de Wardener, H.E. (1977) 'The therapeutic effect of taking a patient's history by computer', *Journal of the Royal College of General Practitioners*, 477–81.

Dunn, G. (1986) 'Patterns of psychiatric diagnosis in general practice: the second national morbidity survey', *Psychological Medicine* 16: 573–81.

Efron, B. (1982) *The Jackknife, The Bootstrap, and Other Resampling Plans*, Philadelphia: Society for Industrial and Applied Mathematics.

Everitt, B.S. (1972) 'Cluster analysis: a brief discussion of some of the problems', *British Journal of Psychiatry* 120: 143–5.

Everitt, B.S. (1980) *Cluster Analysis*, London: Heinemann.

Everitt, B.S. (1984) *An Introduction to Latent Variable Models*, London: Chapman and Hall.

Everitt, B.S. (1987) 'Statistics in psychiatry', *Statistical Science*, May.

Eysenck, H.J. (1981) *A Model for Personality*, New York: Springer.

Gore, S.M., Jones, I.G., and Rytter, E.C. (1977) 'Misuse of statistical methods: critical assessment of articles in *BMJ* from January to March 1976'. *British Medical Journal* i: 85–7.

Greenacre, M.J. (1984) *Theory and Applications of Correspondence Analysis*, London: Academic Press.

Greist, J.H., Gustafson, D.H., and Strauss, F. (1973) 'A computer interview for suicide risk prediction', *American Journal of Psychiatry* 130: 1327–32.

Hand, D.J. (1981) *Discrimination and Classification*, Chichester: Wiley.

Hand, D.J. (1985a) 'The role of statistics in psychiatry', *Psychological Medicine* 15: 471–6.

Hand, D.J. (1985b) *Artificial Intelligence and Psychiatry*, Cambridge, Cambridge University Press.

Hand, D.J. (1986) 'Expert systems in statistics', *The Knowledge Engineering Review* 1: 2–10

Hand, D.J. and Taylor, C.C. (1987) *Multivariate Analysis of Variance and Repeated Measures*, London: Chapman and Hall.

Harman, H.H. (1967) *Modern Factor Analysis*, Chicago: University of Chicago Press.

Krynicki, V. and Gould, R.C. (1984) 'A microcomputer program for scoring the SCL-90', in M.D. Schwartz *Using Computers in Clinical Practice*, New York: The Hayworth Press, 209–12.

Lewis, G., Pelosi, A.J., Glover, E., Wilkinson, G., Stansfeld, S., Williams, P., and Shepherd, M. (1988) 'The development of a computerized assessment for minor psychiatric disorder', *'Psychological Medicine*, in press.

McCullagh, P. and Nelder, J.A. (1983) *Generalized Linear Models*, London: Chapman and Hall.

Schwartz, M.D. (1984) *Using Computers in Clinical Practice: Psychotherapy and Mental Health Applications*, New York: The Hayworth Press.

Sharp, C.H. (1987) 'Expert systems and structured psychiatric assessment', MSc dissertation, Brunel University.

Slack, W.V, and Van Cura, L.J. (1968) 'Computer-based patient interviewing', *Postgraduate Medicine* 43: 68–74 and 115–20.

Szolovits, P. (1982) *Artificial Intelligence in Medicine*, Boulder, Colarado: Westview Press.

Tabachnik, B.G. and Fidell, L.S. (1983) *Using Multivariate Statistics*, New York: Harper & Row.

White, S.J. (1979) 'Statistical errors in papers in the British Journal of Psychiatry', *British Journal of Psychiatry* 135: 336–42.

Wing, J.K., Cooper, J.E., and Sartorious, N. (1974) *The Measurement and Classification of Psychiatric Syndromes*, Cambridge: Cambridge University Press.

Section Two

Epidemiological Studies of Mental Disorder

Introduction

This section, concerned with epidemiological studies of mental disorder, is divided into three subsections based on the *Uses of Epidemiology* as described by Jeremy Morris (1975). The structure serves to emphasize the link between epidemiological psychiatry and medical epidemiology.

The importance of the historical context for social and epidemiological psychiatry was discussed in section one. It is appropriate, therefore, that the first subsection here deals with the study of historical trends. As Morris points out, statements about such trends in medicine should be epidemiologically based, since they relate to the frequency of events among populations or samples at different points in time. The first paper, by Michael MacDonald, is based partly on work carried out while a Visiting Professor at the Institute of Psychiatry: it illustrates Bynum's (1983) conclusion that 'psychiatry must be, and must continue to be, a broadly based social enterprise with much to learn from its own past'.

The other two papers in this subsection are historical in a different sense. In them, history is taken to mean 'a course of events: a life story', rather than 'knowledge of past events' (*Chambers Twentieth Century Dictionary*, revised edition, 1972). Erik Strömgren's contribution illustrates the extensive Scandinavian tradition of longitudinal enquiry in psychiatry; then, Graham Dunn and Nigel Smeeton give an account of their studies of episodes of psychiatric disorder recorded by a sample of British general practitioners in the course of the Second National Morbidity Study. The contribution of longitudinal studies in psychiatry is well recognised and is difficult to overestimate (Leighton 1979).

The second subsection is essentially concerned with the intimate relationship between epidemiological enquiry and clinical psychiatry, which has been a consistent theme in Michael Shepherd's writings (e.g. Shepherd and Cooper 1964, Shepherd 1973, 1978, 1984, 1985). Morris's (1975) notion of epidemiology as being important in completing the clinical picture and the delineation of new syndromes is closely linked with this. This use of epidemiology was summarized by Morris as follows:

> The clinicians' experience of chronic disease is likely to be incomplete . . . numbers may be too few, with attendant troubles of chance variation. But even when numbers are large his experience may be peculiar and his patients unrepresentative, i.e. the picture may be biased. Such limitations apply also to the work of a hospital or any other clinical facility.
>
> The epidemiologist, who is concerned with the total of defined cases in a defined population and not merely with patients who present in particular hospitals, clinics or practices, can help to provide a fuller picture than is

obtainable in any or all of these. This fuller picture may prove to be a different one.

In psychiatry, Michael Shepherd's own enquiries have radically modified earlier views of the nature and distribution of mental illness in the population. For example, it is now generally accepted that psychiatric illness in the community is composed largely of minor affective disorders (Shepherd *et al.* 1966). From a large clinical perspective, it is apparent that this large pool of affective illness not only extends the spectrum of the concept of such disorders, but also bears pointedly on the aetiology of these illnesses and on the sterility of much work on their classification based on hospital cases (Shepherd 1978).

The use of epidemiological methods in the clarification of clinical psychiatric phenomena is addressed in the three chapters in this subsection. Gerald Klerman and Myrna Weissman concern themselves with anxiety disorders, Anthony Mann and Glyn Lewis deal with this theme in relation to personality disorders while Robin Eastwood explores the boundaries and relationships between physical and psychological morbidity.

Aetiology is the topic of the third and final subsection. John Wing examines causal factors and risks for schizophrenic psychoses; David Skuse considers influences on child development; Brian Cooper reviews the causes of psychiatric disorder in the elderly while Rachel Jenkins and Anthony Clare discuss mental health in women.

It is now generally accepted that the great majority of psychiatric disorders are multifactorial in origin: there is, in MacMahon and Pugh's (1970) words, a 'web of causality'. The problems associated with drawing causal inferences from epidemiological data have been discussed many times (e.g. Susser 1973). The best way to determine whether or not a statistical association is also a causal association is by means of experiment, a method not often available to epidemiologists. Despite a great deal of enquiry in recent years, the demonstration by Goldberger in 1914 of the aetiology of pellagra arguably 'remains the most elegant demonstration of the way in which the epidemiological method can be applied to elucidate the causes of a neuropsychiatric disorder' (Shepherd 1978).

REFERENCES

Bynum, W.F. (1983) 'Psychiatry in its historical context', in M. Shepherd and O.L. Zangwill (eds) *Handbook of Psychiatry; Volume 1: General Psychopathology*, Cambridge: Cambridge University Press, 11–38.

Goldberger, J. (1914) 'The etiology of pellagra: the significance of certain epidemiological observations with respect thereto', *Public Health Reports* 29: 1683–5.

Leighton, A.H. (1979) 'Research directions in psychiatric epidemiology', *Psychological Medicine* 9: 235–47.

MacMahon, B. and Pugh, T.F. (1970) *Epidemiology: Principles and Methods*, Boston: Little & Brown.

Morris, J.N. (1975) *The Uses of Epidemiology*, third edition, Edinburgh: Churchill Livingstone.

Shepherd, M. (1973) 'Research report: the General Practice Research Unit at the Institute of Psychiatry', *Psychological Medicine* 3: 525–9.

Shepherd, M. (1978) 'Epidemiology and clinical psychiatry', *British Journal of Psychiatry* 133: 289–98.

Shepherd, M. (1984) 'The contribution of epidemiology to clinical psychiatry', *American Journal of Psychiatry* 141: 1574–6.

Shepherd, M. (1985) 'Psychiatric epidemiology and epidemiological psychiatry', *American Journal of Public Health* 75: 275–6.

Shepherd, M. and Cooper, B. (1964) 'Epidemiology and mental disorder: a review', *Journal of Neurology, Neurosurgery and Psychiatry* 27: 277–90.

Shepherd, M., Cooper, B., Brown, A.C. and Kalton, G. (1966) *Psychiatric Ilness in General Practice*, Oxford: Oxford Univesity Press.

Susser, M. (1973) *Causal Thinking in the Health Sciences*, New York: Oxford University Press.

Charting Historical Trends

10

Psychiatric Disorders in Early Modern England

Michael MacDonald

The two central questions in the history of mental illness before 1800 are almost certainly insoluble. What we really want to know is whether the kinds of mental disorders and their prevalence have changed over time. No matter how full our sources or rigorous our methodology, we shall never discover answers to these problems that are conclusive. We are utterly dependent on the observations of contemporaries for information about mentally ill people in the past. And since the records that normal people kept about the men and women they judged to be abnormal reflected the values of their own time, they cannot simply be translated into present-day language and analysed statistically. To psychiatrists with historical interests this may seem an unduly pessimistic assertion. It is, after all, not difficult to find descriptions of patients in the past who complained of symptoms that closely matched categories of illness described in current systems of classification. But, in fact, notions about the types of mental illnesses and their relative seriousness have varied quite markedly in succeeding ages in western history. There is, as Stanley G. Jackson recently remarked in an authoritative survey of the history of melancholia and depression, both a remarkable consistency in the core symptoms attributed to some disorders and an equally remarkable variation in others (Jackson 1986).

The aim of this brief paper is to explore some of the issues that are raised by the historical study of classifications of mental disorder. I shall focus mainly on sixteenth- and seventeenth-century England, the field I have studied most extensively. Thanks to the survival of a remarkable source, the practice notes of the astrological physician Richard Napier (1559–1637), it is possible to reconstruct on the basis of descriptions of actual patients the main stereotypes of mental illness that were recognized during the period. I shall, therefore, begin with a brief description of psychiatric ailments in Napier's practice. I shall turn then to assessing the typicality of the observations that he recorded, and discussing some of the ways that cultural and social factors influenced the classification of various signs of mental and spiritual disorders. And finally I shall return, in the conclusion, to some broader reflections on the methodology of psychiatric history. I hope to show that, although we cannot create a psychiatric epidemiology of the past that meets the scientific standards set by Michael Shepherd and by other contributors to this volume, we can pose new questions that are both significant and answerable.

MENTAL ILLNESS IN A GENERAL PRACTICE

Richard Napier was an astonishing man, whose manifold interests and activities make him look exotic to modern eyes. The rector of Great Linford in Buckinghamshire, Napier was trained in theology at Oxford. He developed strong interests in science and magic, especially alchemy, conjuring, and astrology, and after 1597 he built up a huge astrological practice, which was devoted chiefly to the diagnosis and treatment of disease. Astrological medicine was not unusual in seventeenth-century England, nor did it differ much in practice from orthodox medicine – at least not on the very high level of competence at which Napier worked. Napier was not a charlatan or a quack; he was no less scientific than his colleagues with medical degrees in his methods of diagnosis and treatments. His practice notes are atypical only in that they are remarkably specific and uniquely numerous. He summarized the complaints of every patient he saw (or heard about), often merely abbreviating their own words. And he saw a lot of patients, at least 60,000 of them between 1597 and 1634, drawn from every social class and complaining of almost every kind of mental and physical affliction (Sawyer 1986). Napier's medical practice and the reliability of his case notes as a historical source have been discussed by myself (MacDonald 1981) and more fully by Ronald C. Sawyer (Sawyer 1986).

Among the patients who consulted Napier, about 5 per cent suffered from symptoms that he and his contemporaries regarded as the signs of a psychiatric affliction of one kind or another (MacDonald 1981; Sawyer 1986). An examination of the entire corpus of his practice notes yielded descriptions of the symptons of 2,039 clients whose complaints were primarily psychological and whose cases were recorded in ways that could be studied more or less systematically. Since the same patient sometimes returned for more than one consultation, the total number of separate case notes on mental disorders was larger, 2,483. The words and phrases that Napier and his clients used to describe abnormal mental conditions were very numerous, there were over 150 of them, and after 300 years their meanings have become elusive. The most common ones he recorded were 'troubled in mind' (33 per cent of consultations), 'melancholy' (19.9 per cent), 'mopish' (15.2 per cent) and 'light-headed' (15.0 per cent). The words 'mad' and 'lunatic' appeared in 5.5 per cent of consultations and 'distracted' in 5.4 per cent. All of these words might appear together with one or more of the others, although the overlap between 'troubled in mind', 'melancholy', and 'mopish' on the one hand and 'mad' and 'lunatic' on the other was relatively slight. 'Light-headed' and 'distracted' were somewhat more elastic concepts.

Some of these words and phrases, notably 'troubled in mind', 'melancholy', 'mopish', 'mad', 'lunatic', and 'distracted', were both symptoms and names for disorders. (It would be overly precise to call them disease entities.) Linking these common complaints with the symptoms that were typically associated with them is the first step to identifying the types of mental disorder Napier and his clients implicitly recognized. The methods I have used to identify significant links are unashamedly unscientific although they are as systematic and as rigorous as the source itself permits. I have explained some of the obstacles to analysing Napier's records using rigorous statistical techniques elsewhere (MacDonald 1987). They are, above all, neither more nor less than the words thousands spoke and one man thought important enough to write down, sometimes verbatim but often in his own summary, not a research instrument designed for statistical analysis. They therefore employ language that is elusive and allusive, inconsistent and inexplicit. Different words were used to describe the same symptom; the same word connoted different symptoms in different contexts. Much was implied that was not explicitly stated. Key complaints were sometimes made in different consultations spaced days or weeks apart, for nothing required Napier to write down what he had already recorded and well remembered. I have, therefore, followed a two-stage procedure to discover what symptoms were characteristically associated with one another. First, I performed a series of simple cross-tabulations, counting the symptoms recorded together with the common words and phrases listed above, and compared the results with the frequency distribution of symptoms among consultations by all disturbed patients. (The results, which cannot be reproduced here for reasons of space, are given in MacDonald 1981.) Second, I then reviewed all of the case notes again, looking for instances in which symptoms that were found together relatively frequently in the cross-tabulations were linked by implication in a single consultation or appeared in a sequence of separate consultations.

This procedure revealed that Napier recognized two distinctive forms of severe disorder and two distinctive kinds of milder disturbance. He also recorded other maladies that were identified by their causes, namely supernatural powers, including the devil and evil spirits, witches and God himself. Many signs of mental abnormality were not associated more frequently with any particular kind of disorder, natural or supernatural, than with any other. Stark insanity was usually indicated by one of four words and phrases – 'mad', 'lunatic', 'light-headed', and 'distracted' – which actually described two distinct but overlapping categories. The patients who were called 'mad' and 'lunatic' were particularly prone to violence and rage. They were physically uncontrollable and very threatening. Napier described Thomas Bassington as a lunatic, noting that he 'rageth and talketh and will strive with three that hold him down' (Ashmole MS 224: 228). The violence and threats of mad and lunatic people had a special quality, too – they were frequently directed at family members and neighbours. People who were 'light-headed' or 'distracted' were more given to idle talk – raving, incoherent speech – and less to violent rage. Both terms were a bit ambiguous. 'Distracted' sometimes indicated something very like violent madness; 'light-headed' shaded over into its modern meaning of mere vertigo. Significantly, the characteristics of the condition they usually described were virtually indistinguisable from the delirium caused by fevers and other life-threatening illnesses. 'Extreme sick', Napier wrote that Thomas Page was, 'like a distracted man. Calleth out on devils, raging, catching and pulling . . . Mind very much troubled; speaketh a little' (Ashmole MS 200: 237). The most severe kinds of mental illnesses were, as the listing above suggests, comparatively rare, comprising less than 15–20 per cent of all the consultations by disturbed patients. The precise figure is difficult to calculate because of the ambiguity of the phrase 'light-headed'.

An initial analysis was performed of the words denoting less severe kinds of mental disorder. 'Troubled in mind' was a generic phrase that could describe almost any psychological complaint short of madness, lunacy, and distraction. Except for the symptoms associated with those maladies, the distribution of symptoms in cases labelled 'troubled in mind' was much the same as it was in the general population of mentally disturbed patients. 'Melancholy' and 'mopish', in contrast, did exhibit some distinctive traits. The symptoms most conspicuously associated with patients Napier labelled as 'melancholy' were sadness, fearfulness, and 'fancies' and 'conceits'. Sadness and fear were the chief signs of melancholy. Here is how Napier described the condition of one Agnes Stiff:

> Troubled with melancholy, how to live for the death of her mother that died a quarter of a year since. Will weep and cry and wander abroad, she knoweth not whither, to her friends. Can follow no business. Yet can sensibly relate all things touching her infirmity as one that were wonderfully well.   (Ashmole MS 238: 42)

The 'fancies' and 'conceits' that Napier linked with melancholy included the sorts of delusions of worthlessness that severely depressed patients display today, but they also embraced bizarre delusions and hallucinations. Of Michael Adams Napier wrote: 'Mind much troubled with false conceits and illusions. Melancholy false fears touching Satan's illusions. Fearfulness of sin . . . fearful dreams . . . . Supposeth that he seeth many things which he seeth not' (Ashmole MS 224: 231). Patients whom Napier described as 'mopish' were especially likely to have some sort of disturbance of the senses, but they were less likely to complain of 'fancies' and 'conceits' than melancholy folk or the mentally disturbed generally. Mopish folk were inactive and particularly liable to display conditions that Napier and his informants identified as 'senseless' or 'disturbed in his senses'. In most instances this seems merely to have indicated a passive, withdrawn state, disengaged from normal conversation and activities. 'Not mopish but of good senses and understanding', he wrote of one patient, 'not mopish but sensible and healthy' (Ashmole MS 233: 5–6). Melancholy and mopishness were very common, together accounting for 32 per cent of all consultations for mental disorder. (In seventy-five instances both words appeared in the same case history.)

Napier and his patients thought that other afflictions were caused by supernatural powers. The astrologer treated hundreds of disturbed people who attributed their mental distress to witches, the devil and evil spirits or to religious doubt. The symptoms they complained of were less distinctive than one might have expected. A great many such patients were described simply as 'troubled in mind'. The profiles of possessed, bewitched, or spiritually troubled patients differed from those of the disturbed generally in two respects only. First, persons who said they were vexed by the devil or by witches were far more likely to have been tempted to suicide than other troubled souls. Many of Napier's patients who said they were 'tempted' described actual encounters with Satan or some evil spirit who enticed them to commit suicide. The anguished Richard Lea, for example, told Napier that a malevolent spirit 'will speak often to him and appear in the likeness of a man, enticing him to kill himself (Ashmole MS 215: 298). Second, people who thought they were possessed or haunted were much more likely to report strange visions, sounds, and even sensations than others. One patient simply felt the presence of an evil spirit. 'She is haunted, as she thinketh, with an ill spirit, and feeleth some living thing roll up and down in her' (Ashmole MS 416: 329). Supernatural powers, in other words, might provoke any sort of mental illness, but they were especially likely to be blamed for suicidal impulses and hallucinations or delusions.

THE WIDER PICTURE

All four of the main types of mental illness that Napier recognized – violent madness, delirious insanity, melancholy and mopishness – may be found in contemporary medical works, popular literature, and other sources. The division of mental afflictions into two main types – stark madness and emotional disorders – had become a medical tradition by Napier's day. In fact analogues to all four of the kinds of disorder noticed by Napier can be found in the works of the ancients. In England the thirteenth-century encyclopedist Bartholomaeus Anglicus followed their lead in dividing mental illnesses into 'madness' or 'mania' (violent insanity), 'frensie' (delirium without an accompanying fever), 'melancholy' and 'gaurynge [staring] and forgetfulness' (dementia and stupor) (Hunter and Macalpine 1963). There are obvious parallels between his categories and the ones Napier used. This was partly due to the influence of Bartholomaeus himself. His work was hugely popular for centuries: it had been translated from Latin to English and reprinted twenty times by 1500, and it continued to be reissued for decades after then. Medical writers, reviving and elaborating classical texts, simply reinforced the basic scheme. This fourfold set of stereotypes of mental illness did not exhaust all the symptoms of psychiatric abnormality – far from it. Nor was it simply the residue of a learned tradition. Analogues to the main types of disorder Napier recorded may be found in a wide variety of popular literature as well. And it can never be emphasized too much that Napier was to a unique extent the amanuensis of the men and women whom he treated. He certainly edited and altered what they said to him, but he had neither the time nor the inclination to recast what they told him in terms of an elite scheme alien to their own way of thinking. There was, in other words, a strong congruence between this basic set of stereotypes and lay conceptions of mental illnesses and their signs. It could hardly have been otherwise. There were no specialized agencies, such as the police and psychiatric profession, to identify the insane. People who were diagnosed as mentally ill were singled out for treatment by their families or neighbours or they sought help for themselves.

Napier's notion of what symptoms might be attributed to various supernatural agencies was broader than that expounded by many medical authorities. Here, too, he was more sensitive to the beliefs of the common people than many doctors. Among physicians, who were by no means sceptics, there was a strong tendency to associate supernatural maladies with intractable cases, particularly when patients displayed very unusual symptoms. Medical tracts and judicial handbooks stressed the significance of highly uncharacteristic actions, convulsions, swooning, and behaviour that seemed impossible to account for naturally, speaking learned languages one had never been taught, for example (Thomas 1971; Kocher 1953; Walker 1981). Napier's clients certainly regarded such actions as evidence of possible possession, haunting, or bewitchment, but they also invoked those causes to explain a very wide range of mental abnormalities and physical disorders (Sawyer 1986). His notebooks embody the popular conception of supernatural afflictions that his patients conveyed to him – his fidelity as a recorder and his interest in the supernatural prevented him from dismissing their fears. Although he often subsequently dismissed their suspicions as groundless, he wrote down what his patient told him.

Both the elite and demotic conceptions of supernatural maladies, however, agreed that suicide was caused by the devil and that strange sights, sounds, and sensations might well be the work of Satan or some other evil spirit. Suicide had been condemned for centuries as a diabolical crime, and the posthumous persecution of people who killed themselves in England was more intense in the sixteenth and seventeenth centuries than ever before or afterwards. Almost everyone believed that suicides were murderers who killed themselves at the instigation of the devil. John Sym, the author of the first English treatise on the subject of suicide, claimed that 'strong impulse, powerful motions, and command of the Devil' was a chief cause of self-murder (Sym 1637: 246–7). There was a close chronological correspondence between the rise and fall of witchcraft trials and the rise and fall of the punishment of suicide. The Elizabethan and Jacobean age was perhaps more preoccupied with satanic powers than any other era (Thomas 1971). Few were prepared to dismiss reports of remarkable visions or sounds out of hand, for they might well be evidence of unseen forces. Even the most incredulous physicians granted that possibility. In fact, in the late seventeenth century, when the almost universal faith in the ubiquitous presence of supernatural powers began to wane among the upper classes, prominent authors gathered together tales of apparitions and strange cases of diseases that they offered as empirical proof of the existence of such forces (Thomas 1971; McKeon 1987).

The mix of natural and supernatural disorders in Napier's practice was somewhat unusual. He was less specialized than many practitioners. But it was not at odds with contemporary conceptions of the causes of and remedies for the maladies of the mind. The centuries prior to about 1700 were characterized by a profound conviction that events in this world might have natural or supernatural causes. The content of the ideas that explained how the two kinds of forces at work in the world might cause diseases varied, of course, but the faith in their existence never waned. As a consequence, there was a profusion of possible explanations for mental and physical maladies and a corresponding profusion of treatments available for them. It is often said that people in medieval or early modern England could not explain or understand illness. Nothing could be further from the truth. They possessed, if anything, too many explanations for illness, all of them logically coherent, none of them leading to therapies that were markedly superior or inferior to their alternatives. The sixteenth and seventeenth centuries were thus a period of medical eclecticism, during which most diseases, including mental illnesses, might be attributed to secular causes or supernatural ones or to both. Patients consulted healers who were experts in physical remedies or spiritual healing or, like Napier, both. The characteristics of the illness, the circumstances under which it first appeared, the religious convictions of the patient and his family and past experience with a particular affliction or healer all played a part in deciding how to respond to an illness. The perception of the important signs of alienation or sickness cannot be disentangled from this matrix of ideas and therapeutic traditions.

The influence of beliefs about the supernatural and existence of spiritual remedies for such maladies is perhaps most noticeable in the way suicidal despair and hallucinations and delusions were interpreted. Some medical authors attributed suicide to melancholy, but in spite of the fact that melancholy became the most fashionable diagnosis of the period, self-destructive urges were regarded as primarily a spiritual affliction. They might *also* have natural causes, for melancholy was, as a contemporary cliché put it, the devil's bath, but these were secondary. The force of this conviction may be seen in the pattern of the natural maladies Napier and his clients associated with suicidal feelings. They were never attributed to madness or lunacy and only once to distraction. None of other leading symptoms of mental illness was strongly associated with suicidal feelings – they were a little more common than usual among the 'troubled in mind' but they were a little less common among 'melancholy' patients. Suicide, in other words, was not associated with depression as strongly as it is today, for it had an alternative explanation. And although the link between suicide and melancholy was made more often in printed tracts, it is plain that religious convictions about the meaning of self-destruction shaped contemporary conceptions of its medical significance. They also reinforced legal interpretations of suicide, which treated it as a premeditated act of homicide rather than as the outcome of mental illness (MacDonald 1977).

Religious beliefs similarly influenced contemporary interpretations of the meaning and seriousness of hallucinations and delusions. These were characteristically attributed to melancholy or to maladies with a supernatural cause, as we have seen. To us it is striking that they were so seldom linked with madness, lunacy, or distraction. And this was not because the familiar delusions of extreme depression – convictions of worthlessness, guilt and helplessness – predominated. For the sort of experiences that were regarded as melancholy delusions and hallucinations included flagrant distortions of thought or perception. Medical authorities and popular lore blamed melancholy for the most spectacular delusions of identity, and in fact stories about melancholics who thought they were something other than themselves were commonly repeated. The attribution of hallucinations and delusions to melancholy and to supernatural forces were expressions of the same general notion, I think. Since everyone knew that supernatural foces could create illusions, introject unwelcome ideas into people's minds and even assume the palpable shape of human beings, there was always the possibility that even the most bizarre tale might be true – that is to say, a devilish illusion rather than a manifestation of mental illness. By the same token, while some stories might seem for various reasons doubtful, it was unreasonable to regard them as irrefutable evidence of severe insanity. When they were attributed to natural causes, they were instead linked with melancholy, an affliction that was supposed to have a paradoxical effect of heightening the imagination as it lowered the spirits. Melancholics thus might be either the victims of delusions or they might be clairvoyant, capable of grasping truths denied to men and women of less imagination (Babb 1951). The classification of delusions and hallucinations, in other words, expressed a profound cultural ambivalence about the ontological status of abnormal perceptions and convictions.

Both potential suicides and people suffering from visions or delusions might be treated with medical remedies or with religious and magical therapies. In fact many authorities, particularly churchmen, recommended both. But these maladies figured large in contemporary accounts of spiritual healing by religious counsel, prayer, and fasting, exorcism and magic. They were first and foremost spiritual afflictions. Ancient taboos in the case of suicide and metaphysical traditions in the case of hallucinations and delusions imbued those disorders with profound symbolic significance. And healers used a variety of rituals and objects, equally symbolic, to restore the victims of suicidal despair or people apparently possessed or bewitched to health. They were often strikingly successful, and spiritual healing became a matter of fierce political controversy among contending religious groups in the sixteenth and seventeeth centuries (Thomas 1971; MacDonald 1982; Walker 1981).

The emphasis that contemporaries placed on violence and delirium in their descriptions of people who were utterly insane was influenced by considerations that were (literally) more down to earth. Prior to the appearance of growing numbers of asylums, workhouses, and prisons in the eighteenth century, people possessed very few resources for managing aggressive madmen. Houses were not equipped to confine violent lunatics, and families could not for long devote themselves to the exhausting and frightening task of caring for such people. The stress that contemporaries placed on the violence and energy of madmen and lunatics reflected a quite understandable fear that they might not be able to protect themselves. Court records are full of examples of neighbours who were terrified by the insane. The Lancashire quarter sessions, for instance, learned in 1641 of a lunatic who had 'fallen by God's judgement and visitation into a lunatic frenzy and distraction of his wits and senses – he lying bound in chains and feathers [sic] – every [one] of the neighbours fearful to come near unto him' (Fessler 1956: 903). And such fears were justified often enough by acts of brutality to lend them credence. Small wonder that so many sources agree that madfolk were dangerous. 'Take heed of mad folks in a narrow place', warned a seventeenth-century proverb (Smith and Heseltine 1966: 396).

The other stereotype of severe insanity was reinforced by both cultural factors and social conditions. Raving insanity (insane light-headedness or distraction) was, we have seen, very similar to the delirium that was frequently the prelude to death. Everyone who fell ill in early modern England rightly worried that he might die. The most common killers were infectious diseases for which there were no effective remedies. Moreover, when a patient was not patently feverish, there were few means to discover whether delirium had organic causes or was a manifestation of insanity. Oliver Heywood, a nonconformist divine, described in his diary three young people in his neighbourhood who 'fell into a kind of frenzy', two of whom quickly died. Joshua Bates was under deliration. At last it grew to a perfect distraction [so] that four men had much ado to hold him. He was bound, raved, raged, in a formidable manner, made rhymes, yea (which was sad) Satan used his tongue to swear many dreadful oaths, which he never did in all his life. In the morning I went to see him; he was a sad object. . . . That evening at ten o'clock he died.   (Heywood 1885: 31–2)

People were especially terrified by the prospect of sudden death, for it forestalled the rituals in which dying persons and their families and neighbours normally participated. These rites were deemed essential both for the soul of the deceased and the consolation of his survivors, who were liable to feel especially distressed if they could not be performed. Thus, both contemporary patterns of mortality and the customs that enabled survivors to deal with ordinary deaths heightened the uncertainty and fear that assailed people who observed a delirious person. It is easy to see why stereotypes of mental illness emphasized the similarities between raving insanity and the symptoms of mortal illnesses.

Contemporary attitudes also reflected the way in which the various kinds of mental illness were diagnosed among different social groups. Reverence for rank was one of the fundamental social values of the age. And some maladies were thought to be more suitable for the genteel than for the rude masses. Melancholy was the badge of breeding, an intellectual's affliction to which men and women of fashion aspired. When a lowly barber in Lyly's *Midas* complains that he is 'melancholy as a cat', he is chided for his pretensions: 'Melancholy? Marry, gup, is melancholy a word for a barber's mouth? Thou shouldst say heavy, dull and doltish: melancholy is the crest of courtiers' arms, and now every base companion, being in his muble fubles, says he is melancholy' (Bamborough 1951: 108–9). When Napier saw base folk who were heavy, dull and doltish he called them 'mopish'. The contrast in the social statuses of those diagnosed as 'melancholy' and 'mopish' was striking. Almost half of his melancholy patients were members of the aristocracy or gentry; less than 15 per cent of his mopish patients were. The affiliation of melancholy and gentility was almost certainly more in the eye of the beholder than in the actual distribution of fear and sorrow in the population as a whole. And it was not just in Napier's eye, either. Many of his patients who were aristocrats or gentlemen diagnosed *themselves* as melancholy.

CONCLUSION

Even in this very compressed discussion, it should be evident that the recognition and classification of psychiatric disorders was strongly influenced by contemporary beliefs, customs, and social conditions. This should come as no surprise. Any system for classifying diseases is made for a purpose, and that purpose is not usually simply the objective study of illness – although it may be for that, too. In the sixteenth and seventeenth centuries people formed coherent stereotypes of mental illnesss that reflected their conceptions of the causes of psychiatric disorders and their recognition of the resources available for managing and treating them. The system that they devised deserves considerable respect. Its basic elements had lasted for several hundred years before it began to break down in the eighteenth century. Laymen and experts alike found it adequate to identify mentally ill people, and many suffering men and women were successfully treated with medical, religious, or magical remedies. For that reason alone we ought to study it in its own terms: simply to see how and why it seemed to contemporaries to provide a perfectly adequate account of mental disorder and a satisfactory array of responses to it.

It would not do, however, to adopt a kind of uncritical cultural relativism. Decoding the system of classifying mental disorders in the past is only the first step to understanding their nature and their prevalence. It is apparent that many of the disorders described in early modern sources are apparently identical to those that are recognized today. Indeed, Jackson has made the more sweeping claim that the core symptoms of depression can be identified in medical sources from ancient times until the present (Jackson 1986). It is possible to discover case histories in Napier's notebooks that satisfy all of DMS–III–R's criteria for major depressive episodes, schizophrenia, dementia, obsessive compulsive disorder, anorexia nervosa, delusional (paranoid) disorder, various phobias, and all kinds of anxiety disorders. Michael Shepherd has, in fact, annotated several hundred of my notes on Napier's case histories with such diagnoses. This is an important finding, for it confirms that there are many similarities between mental illnesses in the past and in the present. And it is a challenge as well, for it points up the need to explain why some maladies are evidently perdurable in western society.

But the very exercise that demonstrates the adamantine durability of some symptom clusters also raises some insurmountable limitations on the historical study of psychiatric epidemiology using modern categories. For, as Arthur Kleinman has pointed out in several forceful discussions of cross-cultural psychiatry, the translation of indigenous perceptions of mental illness into modern western terms may lead to a massive misunderstanding of the kinds and distribution of mental illnesses in the past (Kleinman 1977, 1986, 1987). The principal pitfall is what Kleinman calls a 'category fallacy', the mistake of presuming that symptom clusters that are identical to syndromes recognized in western psychiatric classifications have a superior ontological status to those that resist reclassification. The danger here is that by ignoring instances in which behaviours are identified in other cultures as mentally abnormal, one may overlook variations in the ways that maladies are manifested in different cultural contexts and misconstrue the significance of afflictions that seem peculiar to particular cultures. For, as Kleinman argues, 'biological and cultural factors dialectically interact', to produce the patterns of symptoms that sufferers display and the frequencies with which various illnesses occur (Kleinman 1987: 450).

The perils that historians of mental illness in the west confront are somewhat less daunting than those facing psychiatric anthropologists. But they still place sharp limits on the conclusions we may legitimately draw. The prevalence of melancholy in Napier's practice and Shepherd's reclassification of a sample of his cases suggests that depression was very common. Evidence from other practice books and the relative frequency of suicide during the period reinforce the impression that depressive disorders were widespread in early modern England (Zell 1987). But the facts that melancholy was a fashionable affliction and that suicide was often not attributed to depression by contemporaries make it impossible to estimate with accuracy its prevalence among any practice or population. The same may be said for all of the other DSM–III–R categories I have mentioned. Every one of the clusters of symptoms associated with them was understood and explained differently three hundred years ago than it is now. All of them were liable to be recorded more or less often and in different contexts because of contemporary beliefs, customs, and institutions.

But if the study of the perception of mental illness in early modern England suggests that we need to moderate our aspirations, it also suggests a couple of new hypotheses that historians of psychiatry might consider. First, although the classification of various signs of mental abnormality has changed over time, there has been a very high degree of continuity in the *symptoms* themselves. Most of the actions and moods that seventeenth-century people regarded as evidence of insanity are still viewed as the tokens of mental illness today. The level at which cultural factors seem to have exerted their greatest influence therefore seems to have been at the stage of diagnosis – the point at which sufferers themselves, family members, and healers of various sorts recognized that someone was mentally ill and determined on a course of management and treatment. Second, the little that we know about how classifications of mental illnesses evolved indicates that changes occurred quite slowly prior to about 1750. This suggests that institutional changes in psychiatry in the eighteenth and nineteenth centuries affected the organization of mental abnormalities into stereotypes of disorder profoundly. Some promising beginnings have been made in the study of mental illness in this crucial period (Porter 1987), but a great deal more detailed work is necessary. Some crucial problems are the degree to which new nosologies were based on clinical observations, precisely how they altered older classifications and how well they matched popular conceptions of mental illness. By focusing on the units of analysis that seem most stable and tracing how and why they were combined to form more elaborate stereotypes, we may be able to see the dialectic between biology and culture at work over time.

REFERENCES

Ashmole MSS, Bodleian Library, Oxford (1597–1634) *Medical Practice of Richard Napier*, 60 vols.

Babb, L. (1951) *The Elizabethan Malady*, East Lansing, Mich.: Michigan State University Press.

Bamborough J.B. (1951) *Little World of Man*, London: Longmans, Green.

Fessler, A. (1956) 'The Management of Lunacy in Seventeenth Century England', *Proceedings of the Royal Society of Medicine* 49: 901–7

Heywood, O. (1885) *Oliver Heywood: His Autobiography, Diaries, Anecdote and Event Books*, vol. four, edited by J.H. Turner, Bingley: privately printed.

Hunter, R. and Macalpine, I. (1963) *Three Hundred Years of Psychiatry*, London: Oxford University Press.

Jackson, S.G. (1986) *Melancholia and Depression: From Hippocratic Times to Modern Times*, New Haven: Yale University Press.

Kleinman, A. (1977) *Patients and Healers in the Context of Culture*, Berkeley: University of California Press.

Kleinman, A. (1986) *Social Origins of Distress and Disease: Depression, Neurasthenia and Pain in Modern China*, New Haven: Yale University Press.

Kleinman, A. (1987) 'Anthropology and psychiatry: the role of culture in cross-cultural research on illness', *British Journal of Psychiatry* 151: 447–54.

Kocher, P.H. (1953) *Science and Religion in Elizabethan England*, San Marino, Calif.: Huntington Library Press.

McDonald, M. (1977) 'The inner side of wisdom: suicide in early modern England', *Psychological Medicine* 7: 565–82.

MacDonald, M. (1981) *Mystical Bedlam: Madness, Anxiety and Healing in Seventeenth-Century England*, Cambridge: Cambridge University Press.

MacDonald, M. (1982) 'Religion, social change and psychological healing in England, 1600–1800', in W.J. Sheils (ed.) *The Church and Healing* (Studies in Church History, 19), Oxford: Basil Blackwell.

MacDonald, M. (1987) 'Madness, suicide and the computer', in R. Porter and A. Wear (eds) *Problems and Methods in the History of Medicine*, London: Croom Helm.

McKeon, M. (1987) *The Origins of the English Novel, 1600–1740*, Baltimore: Johns Hopkins University Press.

Porter, R.S. (1987) *Mind Forg'd Manacles: A History of Madness in England from the Restoration to the Regency*, London: Athlone Press.

Sawyer, R.C. (1986) 'Patients, healers and disease in the Southeast Midlands, 1597–1634', unpublished Ph.D. thesis, University of Wisconsin-Madison.

Smith, W.G. and Heseltine J.G. (1966) *The Oxford Dictionary of English Proverbs*, second edition, edited by Paul Harvey.

Sym, J. (1637) *Lifes Preservative Against Self-Killing*, London.

Thomas, K. (1971) *Religion and the Decline of Magic*, New York: Scribner.

Walker, D.P. (1971) *Unclean Spirits: Possession and Exorcism in France and England in the Late Sixteenth and Early Seventeenth Centuries*, Philadelphia: University of Pennsylvania Press.

Zell, M. (1987) 'Suicide in pre-industrial England', *Social History* 11: 303–17.

11

Longitudinal Investigations in Psychiatric Epidemiology

Erik Strömgren

The goals of longitudinal studies can be of different kinds:

1) The purpose may be to study what happens to probands who can be characterized as belonging to a specific disease group, with the aim of describing the so-called 'natural history' of that disease.

2) The purpose may be to see if knowledge of the course and outcome of a disease can contribute to its delimitation.

3) If the course and outcome of a disease seem to be very variable, distinctions between cases with a favourable course and those with an unfavourable course may be studied separately with regard to initial symptomatology, premorbid characteristics, and environmental factors, with the aim of identifying traits which can make it possible to predict course and outcome at an early stage.

4) The main interest may be to see what happens to persons who are subjected to a certain kind of treatment. In such studies the establishment of comparison groups which receive no treatment, or some other treatment, is essential.

5) A number of studies have the aim of determining the incidence rates and life time expectancies, within certain population groups, for disorders and deviations of different kinds. Comparisons of the expectancies in the general population and among relatives of sick probands, respectively, are of basic importance for genetic studies.

Longitudinal studies can be performed either prospectively or retrospectively. Each of these methods has its merits and defects, as described with great clarity and realism by Robins (1979). It is often regarded as obvious that prospective studies are more trustworthy than retrospective studies, the probands being selected with a special purpose and described by well-defined criteria and then followed up continuously with regard to these criteria, whereas retrospective studies are supposed to suffer from insufficient accuracy and reliability of ascertainment of relevant criteria. Such drawbacks are of course of very different importance for different kinds of criteria. In retrospective studies it is usually clear which criteria to go for, whereas in prospective studies often a great number of criteria are registered which later on turn out to be irrelevant. The most serious drawback of prospective studies is the fact that it is often very difficult to keep them going on with unchanging intensity, not least because young researchers usually do not feel enthusiastic about investing too much of their time and energy in projects the results of which will be visible only decades later. The necessary patience is more likely to be provided by older researchers who are quite happy to leave the harvest to later generations. A realistic compromise is, therefore, a prospective study which, although the final results are far away, yields interesting results in a stepwise fashion during the whole period of investigation.

The population groups selected for longitudinal studies may be of two kinds: either cohorts or geographically determined population groups. One of the few studies which combined these approaches was the Lundby study, initiated by Essen-Möller (1956). All inhabitants in a Swedish community living there in 1947 have served as a cohort which has been followed up several times since, regardless of whether they are still in the community or have left it; in addition, all new inhabitants of the community have been investigated and followed up (Hagnell 1966, 1981; Hagnell et al. 1982, 1983).

Pure cohorts should preferably be birth cohorts, since all other kinds of cohorts constitute a selection of survivors. Birth cohorts investigated for psychiatric purposes were those of Klemperer (1933) and Fremming (1951), differing with regard to yield, Klemperer being able to identify only about 50 per cent of his probands, as compared to Fremming's 92 per cent. An even greater success was obtained by Helgason (1964) who retraced 99 per cent of his sample, all persons born in Iceland in the years 1895–7; this was not a true birth cohort since only those alive in 1910 were followed; excess mortality of mentally retarded children would make the sample less representative with regard to mental retardation, whereas it was unlikely that representativeness with regard to other mental disorders could be affected. A start with 12- to 15-year-old probands would reduce the amount of work to a considerable degree without loss of psychiatric information of any importance.

Cohort effects, in the sense that cohorts starting in different periods of time may differ as a consequence of environmental changes over time, can be useful for the distinction between genetic and environmental causes of mental disorders. It is, therefore, of great significance that the Helgason group is now engaged in a study of the spouses and children of the original probands. The results of this investigation will be a good opportunity to evaluate cohort effects.

It is not the purpose of the present chapter to give a comprehensive survey

159

of methods and results within longitudinal studies. Excellent surveys in this respect are available, e.g. the book edited by Mednick and Baert (1981), and, especially with regard to young probands, the review by Robins (1979). Instead, it seems appropriate to mention briefly some older studies which have played a great role in psychiatry and can serve as illustrations of the fact that longitudinal studies can contribute decisively to the understanding of psychiatric nosology. An outstanding example is the huge follow-up study performed by Mattauschek and Pilcz (1912, 1913) on syphilitics. The probands were 4,000 officers in the Austrian army who had acquired syphilis during the 1880s and 1890s. The follow-up was continued until 1911. The special conditions in the army made it possible to make a complete follow-up. At that time it was already well known that there was a connection between syphilis and General Paresis of the Insane (GPI); it had become increasingly clear that syphilis was a condition for the origin of GPI. It was an amazing result of the follow-up that only 5 per cent of the syphilitics acquired GPI. Mattauschek and Pilcz therefore studied what differences there were in the life histories of those who became paralytic and those who did not, and they found that all those who escaped GPI had had severe fevers during the first years after the syphilitic infection whereas those who did get the disease had not had similar infections. In this connection they mentioned the fact that in many tropical countries syphilis is practically endemic, but nevertheless GPI seems not to exist there. They stated expressly that these connections seemed to indicate new kinds of therapy in GPI. Peculiarly enough, there is no sign in the paper that they had any knowledge of what Wagner von Jauregg was doing in the same city, Vienna, at the same time – and had already been doing for several years – in the form of experiments with fever therapy in GPI.

The study of Mattauschek and Pilcz was a combined prospective and retrospective investigation carried out so systematically that important results must emerge. In contrast, some equally important findings might be mentioned which were obtained some fifty years earlier by pure serendipity (see Steenberg 1884) at a time when the aetiology of GPI was still the subject of great disagreement; syphilis was mentioned as one of the possible causes, but many other causes were seriously contemplated, and very few believed syphilis to be the *conditio sine qua non*. Already during the 1850s Esmarch and Jessen (1857) in Kiel had put forward the idea that GPI was caused by syphilis. The material on which they based this viewpoint was, however, very slight and not convincing. A few years later the following events occurred. A young doctor in Copenhagen, Valdemar Steenberg, who had worked for several years in a special hospital in Copenhagen which received all cases of venereal disease, paid a visit to one of his friends who worked in the mental hospital of Copenhagen, the Sct. Hans Hospital in Roskilde. His friend took him on ward rounds, and it turned out that Steenberg recognized a considerable number of the patients in the wards, because he had met them earlier in the department for venereal diseases in Copenhagen. It was obvious that all Steenberg's acquaintances among the psychiatric patients suffered from GPI as well. Immediately it became clear to him and his friend that the aetiology of GPI must be syphilitic. Starting with this observation, Steenberg continued to study the connection between the two diseases and wrote a thesis on it (1860) in which for the first time the connection between them was demonstrated quite convincingly. A few years later Steenberg started to work in the mental hospital in Schleswig. There he observed that cases of GPI were not nearly as frequent as among psychiatric patients in Copenhagen, and it turned out that all those in Schleswig who suffered from this disease had spent some time in Copenhagen, which was at that time within the Nordic countries the centre for culture, amusement, and venereal diseases.

GPI was the most frequent of those psychiatric disorders which, during the second half of the nineteenth century, was regarded as having an organic origin. A great number of severe mental disorders which could not be demonstrated to have an organic basis were still left, the functional psychoses. The epoch-making advance in the study of these psychoses was represented by the longitudinal studies of Kraepelin (1899) who demonstrated a high correlation between symptomatology and cause, thus contrasting dementia praecox and manic-depressive disorder. The correlation was, however, not complete; 13 per cent of dementia praecox cases turned out to recover completely. Manfred Bleuler's (1972) even more meticulous, indeed quite unique, longitudinal studies of schizophrenic probands, investigated by himself, showed a complete recovery of 20 per cent of the probands. Comparisons with older materials did not disclose any remarkable changes in the prognosis although advances with regard to therapy had of course modified symptomatology to a high degree in most cases.

Longitudinal follow-up studies of psychotic probands usually start with probands for whom the diagnosis has already been made. The search for possible causative factors must, therefore, be retrospective, and adequate control materials are very difficult to obtain. It is, therefore, difficult to say whether factors which are supposed to have a causative effect in the development of psychoses are indeed specific to the psychoses; in principle they may be more or less ubiquitous factors which are only noxious in persons who have a certain vulnerability. On the other hand, if cohorts, representative of the general population, are chosen for longitudinal studies, the number of psychoses arising in such samples will be so small that even if differences in their premorbid life histories are found, generalizations can usually not be made with any certainty. It is, therefore, an obvious advantage if for longitudinal studies a sample is selected which can be supposed to have an especially high risk of developing the disorder studied. No wonder that 'high risk' studies have become increasingly popular. One of the earliest and most well known is the Danish/American study on offspring of schizophrenic mothers, probands who can be supposed to have a risk of 10–15 per cent of developing schizophrenia. In such studies comparisons can be made between those probands who develop schizophrenia and those who do not, as well as with matched probands of 'neutral' origin. Such studies will have to be continued for several decades before the majority of questions raised can be answered. A follow-up of the probands of the Danish/American study when they were on average 23 years old (Parnas 1986) gave rise to the conclusion that a proportion of them had been subjected to early brain damage. The incidence of birth complications was significantly higher in those who suffered from schizophrenia or suspected schizophrenia than in those who did not. The results of CT scanning supported this distinction. Occurrence of schizophrenia-related abnormalities in the fathers increased the risk of developing schizophrenia in the children, a risk which was also connected with unstable home conditions during the first five years.

A special longitudinal study of schizophrenics was initiated by some observations made during the 1970s which seemed to indicate that cancer should be less frequent in schizophrenics than in the general population. A multinational study was organized by WHO with the aim of elucidating this problem. Studies were started in countries which had psychiatric registers as well as cancer registers. In Denmark the population studied consisted of 6,168 patients who had been diagnosed as schizophrenics during a nationwide census of hospitalized psychiatric patients in Denmark in September 1957. This population was linked with the Danish cancer registry. The patients were followed up until 1980. The follow-up was close to complete since only one patient could not be identified (Dupont et al. 1986). Among the males the incidence of malignant tumours was significantly lower than in the general population, due to a low incidence of lung and bladder cancer. In females the overall incidence of malignant tumours was lower than in the general population, but not significantly so, whereas the incidence of uterine cervical cancer was significantly lower. Mortensen (1987) tried to identify environmental factors modifying the cancer risk in schizophrenic patients. Whereas risk factors well known in other populations, such as occupation, sexual activity, and cigarette smoking, could also be demonstrated in the schizophrenic material, some factors special to the environment of schizophrenic patients, above all neuroleptic treatment, could be demonstrated to be of importance. Treatment with reserpine increased the risk of developing cancer whereas a number of neuroleptics, such as chlorprothixene, chlorpromazine and haloperidol, decreased the risk.

The cohort of schizophrenics which served as a basis for the cancer-schizophrenia study was, as mentioned, derived from a nationwide census in 1957 of hospitalized psychiatric patients in Denmark. Such census studies have been performed regularly with five-year intervals since 1957 (Weeke et al. 1986, Munk-Jørgensen et al. 1986), thus constituting a longitudinal study of hospital populations. The main feature was that the number of admissions remained nearly unchanged, while the total prevalence of in-patients and day-

162

Table 11.1 Census of patients in Danish psychiatric institutions in the years 1957, 1962, 1967, 1972, 1977, and 1982. Schizophrenia. Rates per 100,000

Age	1957	1962	1967	1972	1977	1982
			Males			
–14	0	0	0	0	0	0
15–24	18	28	34	50	41	31
25–34	96	76	67	85	91	106
35–44	167	129	102	98	89	107
45–54	253	203	156	121	96	91
55–64	363	300	225	186	132	95
65+	297	300	301	275	220	171
15+	132	118	101	97	83	78
			Females			
–14	0	0	0	0	0	0
15–24	12	11	14	22	12	11
25–34	51	41	33	36	42	41
45–54	134	75	57	57	54	51
55–64	378	290	207	167	106	70
65+	416	387	347	297	226	175
15+	140	117	96	86	69	66

patients showed only a slight decrease until 1982 (the increase of day-patients compensating for the decrease in in-patients), after which year changing policies caused a substantial and continuing decrease. The changes within the schizophrenia group are of special interest (table 11.1). During the period 1957–82 the prevalence (per 100,000) of schizophrenia had dropped from 132 to 78 in males and from 140 to 66 in females. This implies that whereas all other main diagnostic groups have showed increasing prevalences, the decreasing prevalence of schizophrenia has been able to compensate for this increase, thus leaving the total prevalence unchanged (until 1982). The changes within the schizophrenia group are, however, distributed very unevenly over the age groups. Within the age group 15–24 years there has been an unexpected increase during the years 1957–72, and since then a moderate drop. In female schizophrenics there have not been such remarkable changes, although, as in the males, the 1972 census showed a peak. It has been suggested that the increase in the prevalence of schizophrenic males in this age group could be due to misdiagnoses of drug psychoses which were mistaken for schizophrenia. The increase in drug abuse came, however, not until 1968, and in the males the increase in schizophrenia started long before that time.

163

Another striking feature is the conspicuous decrease of schizophrenia in females aged 45–64, much more expressed than in males of the same age group. A very probable explanation is the better response of female schizophrenics to combined drug and rehabilitation therapy which enables the greater proportion of these women to be discharged and stay in society.

More intriguing is the decrease in first admissions for schizophrenia which has taken place over the last fifteen years. In Denmark Munk-Jørgensen (1985, 1987) performed a longitudinal register study of all persons who had been admitted to psychiatric institutions in Denmark in 1972 and who during that year, or in connection with later admissions in the following decade, had received the diagnosis of schizophrenia. The annual statistics showed a conspicuous decrease in the rate of first admissions for schizophrenia, this diagnosis obviously being substituted to a considerable degree by diagnoses like borderline psychosis, reactive psychosis, etc. Many of those who ended up with a schizophrenia diagnosis did not receive it until the third or fourth admission or even later, sometimes several years after the first admission. Such sequences are of course well known, but they seem, at least in Denmark, to have acquired rapidly increasing importance in recent years. Different factors seem to contribute to this development. First there is, especially among younger psychiatrists, an increasing fear of 'labelling' patients with the diagnosis of schizophrenia, second, and partly as a consequence of this fear, the diagnosis of 'borderline state' has gained immense popularity.

These mechanisms seem to affect women more than men. It is, therefore, not only in the prevalence, but also in the incidence of hospitalized patients that the sex difference is conspicuous. In addition, there are some factors which may augment the difference which can be illustrated by findings made during a recent repeated survey study comprising the 'true' prevalence of schizophrenia on the Danish island of Bornholm in 1983, as compared with the prevalence in the year 1935 (Strömgren 1987, Bøjholm and Strömgren, to be published). The prevalence of schizophrenia was unchanged in males, but had decreased significantly in females. A tentative explanation for this difference between sexes is the following: Schizophrenia starts, on average later in females who have, therefore, more often obtained a more sheltered family and social position; in addition, the symptomatology is often more uncharacteristic initially in schizophrenic women. The mental health service on the island of Bornholm is well developed, so that a considerable number of females who would, if untreated, later develop definite schizophrenia are now taken on for efficient treatment with the result that clear-cut schizophrenic symptoms do not develop, and the diagnosis is never made.

It is obvious that similar mechanisms may be active also in male schizophrenics, but probably less frequently. The explanation for the fact that nevertheless the prevalence of schizophrenia has not decreased is no doubt that during the half century which has passed since the first census in 1937, the mortality of schizophrenics has decreased significantly.

Among the observations concerning (true or apparent) changes over time in the incidence of mental disorders, those of Hagnell *et al.* (1982, 1983) from the Lundby study deserve special attention, both from a theoretical and from a practical viewpoint: over a period of twenty-five years significant changes have occurred, an increase in the incidence of depressive disorders and a decrease in the incidence of organic brain disorders.

The small number of examples of longitudinal studies which have been mentioned in the preceding cannot, of course, allow any general conclusions, but they can serve as illustrations of some features characteristic of such studies. It is clear that prospective and retrospective studies each have their advantages and defects, that both of them can give rise to important conclusions, and that sometimes combinations of them are the best solutions. It is also clear that it is much easier to perform longitudinal studies in stable populations of moderate size which are well registered. Furthermore, the existence of special registers comprising individuals with diseases or other aberrations is particularly useful. This cannot be stressed too emphatically in a time when ill-founded aversion against all kinds of registers has become popular and even fashionable among influential politicians.

Some of the examples mentioned illustrate also that the dangers threatening the success of longitudinal studies do not all come from outside psychiatry. The increasing speed with which psychiatric concepts and terms are changing threaten to invalidate much serious and useful research.

REFERENCES

Bleuler, M. (1972) *Die schizophrenen Geistesstörungen im Lichte langjähriger Kranken- und Familiengeschichten*, Stuttgart: George Thieme Verlag.

Bøjholm, S. and Strömgren, E. 'Prevalence of schizophrenia on the island of Bornholm', to be published.

Dupont A., Jensen, O.M., Strömgren, E. and Jablensky, A. (1986) 'Incidence of cancer in patients diagnosed as schizophrenic in Denmark', in G.H.M.M. Ten Horn, R. Giel, W.H. Gulbinat and J.H. Henderson (eds) *Psychiatric Case Registers in Public Health*, Amsterdam: Elsevier Science Publishers.

Esmarch, F.R. and Jensen, W. (1857) 'Syphilis und Geistesstörung' *Allgemeine Zeitschrift für Psychiatrie und psychischgerichtliche Medicin* 14: 20–36.

Essen-Möller, E. (1956) *Individual Traits and Morbidity in a Swedish Rural Population*, Copenhagen: Ejnar Munksgaard.

Fremming, K.H. (1951) 'The expectation of mental infirmity in a sample of the Danish population (based on a biographical investigation of 5,500 persons born in the years 1883–1887)', *Occasional Papers on Eugenics, No. 7*, London: The Eugenics Society and Cassell.

Hagnell, O. (1966) *A Prospective Study of the Incidence of Mental Disorder* (Scandinavian University Books), Stockholm: Svenska Bokförlaget Norstedts-Bonniers.

Hagnell, O. (1981) 'The Lundby Study on psychiatric morbidity (Sweden)', in S.A. Mednick and A. Baert (eds) *Prospective Longitudinal Research: An Empirical*

Basis for the Primary Prevention of Psychosocial Disorders, Oxford, New York, Toronto, Melbourne: Oxford University Press.

Hagnell, O., Lanke, J., Rorsman, B., and Öjesjö, L. (1983) 'Current trends in the incidence of senile and multi-infarct dementia: a prospective study of a total population followed over 25 years; the Lundby Study', *Archiv für Psychiatrie und Nervenkrankheiten* 233: 423–38.

Helgason, T. (1964) *Epidemiology of Mental Disorders in Iceland: A Psychiatric and Demographic Investigation of 5,395 Icelanders* (*Acta Psychiatrica Scandinavica*, Supplement 173), Copenhagen: Munksgaard.

Klemperer, J. (1933) 'Zur Belastungsstatistik der Durchschnittsbevölkerung: Psychosenhäufigkeit unter 1000 stichprobenmässig aus den Geburtsregistern der Stadt München (Jahrgang 1881–1890) ausgelesenen probanden', *Zeitschrift für die gesamte Neurologie und Psychiatrie* 146: 277–316.

Kraepelin, E. (1899) 'Zur Diagnose und Prognose der Dementia praecox', *Allgemeine Zeitschrift für Psychiatrie und psychisch-gerichtliche Medicin* 56: 254–9.

Mattauschek, E. and Pilcz, A. (1912) 'Beitrag zur Lues-Paralyse-Frage (erste Mitteilung über 4,134 katamnestisch verfolgte Fälle von luetischer Infektion)', *Zeitschrift für die gesamte Neurologie und Psychiatrie* 8: 133–52.

Mattauschek, E. Pilcz, A. (1913) 'Zweite Mitteilung über 4,134 katamnestisch verfolgte Fälle von luetischer Infektion', *Zeitschrift für die gesamte Neurologie und Psychiatrie* 15: 608–30.

Mednick, S.A. and Baert, A.E. (eds) (1981) *Prospective Longitudinal Research: An Empirical Basis for the Primary Prevention of Psychosocial Disorders*, Oxford, New York, Toronto, Melbourne: Oxford University Press.

Mortensen, P.B. (1987) 'Neuroleptic treatment and other factors modifying cancer risk in schizophrenic patients', *Acta Psychiatrica Scandinavica* 75: 585–90.

Munk-Jørgensen, P. (1985) 'The schizophrenia diagnosis in Denmark: a register-based investigation', *Acta Psychiatrica Scandinavica* 72: 266–73.

Munk-Jørgensen, P. (1987) 'Why has the incidence of schizophrenia in Danish psychiatric institutions decreased since 1970?' *Acta Psychiatrica Scandinavica* 75: 62–8.

Munk-Jørgensen, P., Weeke A., Bach Jensen, E., Dupont, A., and Strömgren, E. (1986) 'Changes in utilization of Danish psychiatric institutions: II: census studies 1977 and 1982', *Comprehensive Psychiatry* 27: 416–29.

Parnas, J. (1986) *Risk Factors in the Development of Schizophrenia: Contributions from a Study of Children of Schizophrenic Mothers*, Copenhagen: Laegeforeningens Forlag.

Robins, L.N. (1979) 'Longitudinal methods in the study of normal and pathological development', in K.P. Kisker, J.E. Meyer, C. Müller and E. Strömgren (eds) *Forschung und Praxis: Grundlagen und Methoden der Psychiatrie*, Band I, 2, Auflage, Berlin, Heidelberg, New York: Springer-Verlag.

Steenberg, V. (1860) *Den syphilitiske Hjernelidelse*, København: Bianco Luno.

Steenberg, V. (1884) 'The role played by syphilis in the genesis of general paralysis: discussion' Congrés international des Sciences médicales, 8me Session, Copenhague 1884, X, Section de Psychiatrie et de Neurologie, 80–92.

Strömgren, E. (1987) 'Changes in the incidence of schizophrenia?' (The fifty-ninth Maudsley Lecture delivered before the Royal College of Psychiatrists, November 15, 1985), *British Journal of Psychiatry* 150: 1–7.

Weeke, A., Munk-Jørgensen, P., Strömgren, E., and Dupont, A. (1986) 'Changes in utilization of Danish psychiatric institutions: I: an outline of the period 1957–1982', *Comprehensive Psychiatry* 27: 407–15.

12

The Study of Episodes of Psychiatric Morbidity

Graham Dunn and Nigel Smeeton

It is well known that general practitioners (GPs) in Great Britain come into contact with, and are responsible for treating, the majority of patients with psychiatric disorders (Shepherd *et al.* 1966). It is not surprising, therefore, that one should look to records provided by GPs for important information about consultations and episodes of a wide variety of psychological problems. In particular, GPs are in a position to provide information on the natural history of these problems, on their patterns of incidence and recurrence, and on patterns of referral to other services. This information is rarely, if ever, available from other sources but the uncritical use of data provided by GPs, however, might be potentially misleading.

Unlike a psychiatrist, a GP cannot assume that a patient is consulting him because of psychological problems. Whether or not a psychiatric or psychological problem is detected is, of course, dependent on the state of the patient and what the patient is willing to reveal about this state. It is also dependent on the GP's background and beliefs as well as on the outcome of previous contacts that the patient has had with the GP. There is also the possibility that many people who suffer from various forms of psychological distress would never seek help from a GP. Those who do will have different 'thresholds'; many seeking help for relatively minor problems such as tension headaches or sleep loss, while others with psychotic symptoms such as paranoia or with dependencies on alcohol or other drugs might refuse to acknowledge that they need help.

Clearly, it is vital that the natural history of psychiatric disorders as seen in general practice be studied in depth. Small-scale, intensive, longitudinal studies (Kedward and Cooper 1966; Cooper *et al.* 1969; Mann *et al.* 1981; Dunn and Skuse 1981) are essential but, however detailed, they run the risk of being unrepresentative. Increasing their size and scope, however, would be a difficult and costly undertaking. Large-scale morbidity surveys, on the other hand, are comprehensive but the data obtained are, by necessity, relatively rather crude. The GPs taking part in the three UK National Morbidity Surveys (Logan and Cushion 1958; Logan 1960; GRO 1962;

HMSO 1974, 1979, 1986), for example, may not be representative of GPs in Britain as a whole; their diagnostic and case-finding criteria differ widely and have not been validated, and, when episodes rather than consultations are being recorded, there appears to be no clear-cut definition of what constitutes an episode of psychiatric disorder. Despite these criticisms, however, these morbidity surveys should provide some useful information, but much more work needs to be done on attempts to provide effective and valid ways of analysing and presenting the data (Dunn 1985).

It is the purpose of this chapter to review some of the problems encountered in these National Morbidity Surveys, with particular reference to the analysis of data provided by the longitudinal file of the Second Survey (HMSO 1979; RCGP 1980) and suggest some possibilities for solving them.

GENERAL PROBLEMS IN THE INTERPRETATION OF DATA FROM THE NATIONAL MORBIDITY SURVEYS

Case detection

The first problem in making any inferences concerning psychiatric morbidity from records provided by the Surveys is that they do not provide records of illness *per se*, but of consultations at which a psychiatric problem has been recognized. Many individuals suffer from various forms of psychological distress without ever seeking help from a GP. Others may not realize that there might be a psychological component to their physical ailments even though they do consult their GP for the latter problems. GPs, too, quite often fail to recognize the signs and symptoms of psychological distress in patients presenting with physical complaints (see Goldberg and Blackwell 1970, for example). For whatever reason, it must be acknowledged that surveys of this kind cannot, from their very nature, provide unbiased estimates of the incidence or prevalence of different types of disorder; they simply provide information on GPs' reported activities and may, in fact, be telling us more about the GPs than the patients themselves (Shepherd *et al*. 1966; Marks *et al*. 1979; RCGP 1980).

Episode definition

A serious flaw in the design of the Second National Morbidity Survey is its reliance on records of episodes of disorder in the absence of any clear operational definition of what constitutes an episode. It was simply left to the individual doctor to decide which consultations belonged to which episodes. In the second three years of the Survey only episodes were recorded, making it impossible to base any statistical analyses of the data on the consultations for which the episode patterns were inferred. Part of the problem has been summarized by Ashford:

Often the episode pattern of patient contacts can be recognised only by a study of the medical history over a long period and it is not possible for the doctor to determine at the time whether a particular contact properly forms the beginning of a new episode or part of an existing episode.

(Ashford 1972: 269)

Episode patterns can only be inferred from the data and decisions concerning the constitution of an episode should not be made at the time of data collection, particularly if the evidence used in making this inference is not itself summarized and recorded.

Another part of this problem is caused by apparent confusion concerning the concept of an episode. The National Morbidity Surveys fail to distinguish between episodes of *illness* and episodes of *care* (Ellis 1985; Hornbook *et al.* 1985; Keeler *et al.* 1986). Hornbook *et al.* (1985: 170) define an episode of illness as 'a single unbroken interval of time during which the patient suffers from a continuous spell of signs and/or symptoms that are perceived as sickness or ill-health'. They define an episode of care as 'a series of temporally contiguous health care services related to treatment of a given spell of illness or provided in reponse to a specific request by the patient or other relevant entity'. (Hornbrook *et al.* 1985: 171). Clearly, patterns of contact between a patient and a GP can be used to make inferences about both episodes of illness and episodes of care. It is not clear, however, which type of episode is being recorded by the GPs in the National Morbidity Surveys. Episodes of care are often easier to observe from medical records, but the possibility of multiple psychiatric diagnoses at a given consultation (see below) might imply that the GPs are attempting to record episodes of illness. Problems of case detection and diagnosis are relevant to inferences concerning episodes of illness. They are not, on the other hand, of paramount importance when considering episodes of care.

Diagnostic Practices

Another source of trouble, which is clearly related to the general problem of case detection, arises from the way in which GPs diagnose psychiatric disorders. Many GPs might not be interested in the use of formal diagnostic labels, but for the purposes of the National Morbidity Surveys they are required to use them. On the whole they appear to use labels for psychiatric disorders in a different way from psychiatrists. They have, for example, a tendency to miss many cases of depression and, instead, appear to give far too many patients a diagnosis of anxiety (Meyer-Gross 1954; Watts 1962; Clare 1982). The planners of the National Morbidity Surveys are aware of the difficulties of validating GPs' diagnostic practices but do not appear to be concerned by them. Logan and Cushion, for example, claim that a completely accurate identification is sometimes unnecessary and unwise, and they go on to state that 'To lay down standard diagnostic criteria is impossible and, in any event, the improvement in the records would probably be slight, particularly in large-scale enquiries, such as the present survey, where differences will to tend to cancel each other out' (Logan and Cushion 1958: 19). It is difficult to believe how anyone could possibly accept that this statement is true or that problems caused by confusion over the use of formal psychiatric diagnoses would not threaten the validity of the resulting 'morbidity' statistics.

To see why the lack of validation of diagnostic practices leads to serious difficulties in interpretation of the published statistics all one needs is to compare the First and Second National Morbidity Surveys. Consider, for example, the prevalence of 'depression'. There was a dramatic increase in the reported prevalence of depression between the First and Second Surveys. But does this represent a real increase in the prevalence of depression or does it reflect a change in the ways that GPs detect psychiatric disorders in general or, in particular, how they diagnose depression? In the absence of validation studies one cannot tell.

Immigration and Emigration

Clearly when one is calculating prevalence and incidence rates for any form of illness it is vital that one has a reasonably accurate knowledge of the number of people in the population at risk. Most people in Great Britain are registered with a GP but there are problems due to immigration and emigration. Many people, for example, will not register with a new GP when they move to a new area nor will they inform their former GP that they have moved from the area covered by his practice. A change in registration will often only occur when the patient falls ill and requires medical services.

In making inferences from longitudinal records (see below) one also has problems caused by incomplete data. Patients might leave the area or die before the study is completed. In addition, there are new patients entering the study population throughout the duration of the survey. If one chooses to study the psychiatric problems of the patients with complete records this might bias the results. Migrants, for example, might have different psychological problems from those who do not move.

THE SECOND NATIONAL MORBIDITY SURVEY

A general description of the Survey

The Second National Morbidity Survey was undertaken jointly by the Royal College of General Practitioners (RCGP), the Office of Population Censuses and Surveys (OPCS), and the Department of Health and Social Security (DHSS) (RCGP 1980). It was designed to yield information on episode and consultation patterns in a representative sample of general practices over a period of up to six years (1970–6). Sixty practices (115 GPs) took part in

1970–1, but only twenty-two contributed data for the whole of the six years of the Survey. The latter data comprise the longitudinal file of the Second National Morbidity Survey (RCGP 1980). The file contains complete six-year records of about 60,000 individuals, 43,000 of them providing details of psychiatric problems.

The work of the present authors has been based on patterns of episodes recorded in the longitudinal file of the Survey. This information was provided by the Medical Statistics Division of OPCS. The data file contains records of the number of episodes of psychiatric disorders (distinguished by a diagnostic code) for each of the six consecutive years. In each episode there is at least one consultation with the GP at which a relevant diagnosis has been made. The file also contains the numbers of consultations at which a psychiatric diagnosis was made for each of the first three years of the Survey. Details of some of the work done on analysing these data can be found in Dunn (1983, 1986) and in Smeeton (1986a, 1986b, 1987).

Since the Second Survey, a Third National Morbidity Survey has been undertaken, again jointly by the RCGP, OPCS, and DHSS (HMSO 1986). Its design was virtually identical to that of the Second Survey and most of the remarks made regarding the Second Survey apply to the Third. Conducted for one year from 1 July 1981, it involved forty-eight practices, 143 GPs, and 332,270 patients, including 282,253 with complete records for the twelve months. Diagnoses were additionally labelled as being serious, intermediate, or trivial. The main report (HMSO 1986) gives the episode distribution of all illness subdivided by age-group and sex but, as yet, no detailed analysis of the psychiatric data has been undertaken.

Variation Between Practices: Psychiatric Records

The results discussed here are based on preliminary investigations described by Dunn (1986). For the purpose of these analyses the data were simplified in the following way. For each of the patients, for the whole of the six years of the Survey, it was asked whether they had experienced one or more episodes (equivalent to one or more consultations with a GP) of, say, depression. If the answer was 'yes' the patient was coded as having a record of depression, but not otherwise. Similar codings were made for each of the other psychiatric disorders. These disorders are those defined by the College of General Practitioners' disease index (1963).

To summarize, each patient contributes a single record of a particular disorder if, and only if, he or she has received a diagnosis of that disorder at least once during the six years of the Survey. Taking all of the possible psychiatric problems, some patients will contribute no records at all, and others will contribute one, two, or even more records. Note that this simplification of the data avoids problems of episode definition but not those of case detection or diagnostic practices. Finally, only patients who were registered with the practices throughout the whole of the six-year Survey are

171

considered here. Those who joined or left the Survey population during the course of the study are ignored.

The practice sizes (indicated by the number of patients registered with the practice throughout the whole of the six years of the Survey) ranged from about 1,500 to approximately 6,500. The proportion of the registered patients having at least one psychiatric record ranged from 0.21 to 0.47, with a median value of 0.30. It is impossible to tell whether this variation in 'morbidity' is due to real differences in levels of psychiatric distress or to variation in the way in which GPs detect and diagnose psychiatric disorders.

Between-practice variation is much more marked if one considers individual diagnostic categories. Table 12.1 gives the proportions of those patients with at least one record of a psychiatric disorder who were given each of the eight most common diagnoses at least once during the Survey. There is great variability in these proportions, as summarized by the ratio of the highest to the lowest proportion, given at the foot of each column. The highest ratios relate to unclassified symptoms (code 150), physical disorders of psychogenic origin (code 135), affective psychosis (code 126), and neurasthenia (code 136).

Most GPs appear not to use the diagnostic category 'affective psychosis' (code 126). The GP or GPs in practice I, on the other hand, gave 20 per cent of the patients with at least one record of psychiatric illness this diagnostic label. As this is the practice in which 47 per cent of the registered patients received at least one record of psychiatric illness this finding implies that almost 10 per cent of the registered patients were thought to be suffering from psychotic symptoms at least once during the six years of the Survey! This is a particularly dramatic example of the problems to be faced in the interpretation of GPs' records. One is inclined to conclude that the records are revealing more about the GPs than they are about their patients.

Variation between practices: modelling episodes

This work, details of which are found in Smeeton (1986b), set out to investigate whether some individuals are more prone to episodes of mental illness than others. An analysis of the distribution of the number of episodes experienced by each individual with complete six-year records from the Second National Morbidity Survey was carried out. Only affective or possibly affective disorders were considered (affective psychoses, anxiety neuroses, phobic neurosis, depressive neurosis, physical disorders of presumably psychogenic origin, neurasthenia, insomnia, and tension headache), chronic disorders, such as mental retardation, with a single life-long episode not being deemed appropriate for study.

The psychiatric data file was subdivided by practice and sex, and theoretical statistical models were fitted to the forty-four subgroups. Under equality of proneness, the Poisson Distribution should provide a reasonable fit (Greenwood and Yule 1920). A flexible variable proneness model is the

Table 12.1 Proportion of psychiatric patients with each of the eight most common record types (× 100)

Practice	Record type*							
	130	134	150	135	146	147	126	136
A	41	13	15	20	13	7	11	0
B	63	41	2	1	16	4	0	0
C	38	33	18	9	17	10	0	4
D	39	50	3	33	13	9	0	0
E	15	51	35	32	5	8	1	6
F	68	25	2	3	20	16	0	0
G	49	32	9	19	4	7	14	8
H	35	68	8	2	2	6	1	0
I	32	22	41	13	9	4	20	18
J	35	48	12	6	7	4	2	0
K	10	21	60	17	8	17	0	0
L	52	28	11	16	7	9	0	1
M	56	48	1	1	9	7	0	0
N	57	40	8	10	23	7	2	2
O	43	31	11	16	21	12	2	2
P	25	21	36	22	19	8	5	10
Q	36	35	19	18	11	12	14	1
R	37	21	38	24	7	10	5	1
S	47	37	22	25	13	8	2	2
T	39	30	20	52	9	10	1	3
U	32	38	22	19	18	17	3	7
V	39	34	22	25	14	14	2	1
Mean	40	35	19	17	12	9	4	3
Ratio of highest to lowest	6.80	5.23	60.0	52.0	11.5	4.25	>50	>45

From Dunn 1986.
* Royal College Codes (in order of overall prevalence): 130, anxiety neurosis; 134, depressive neurosis; 150, unclassified symptoms; 135, physical disorders of presumably psychogenic origin; 146, insomnia; 147, tension headache; 126, affective psychosis; 136, neurasthenia.

Negative Binomial Distribution (NBD) (Greenwood and Yule 1920; Adelstein 1952). This model may also arise from formulations not dependent upon variable proneness (Irwin 1941). It is therefore necessary to check that individuals have consistent episode rates over time, by calculating the correlation between the numbers of episodes in the two halves of the six-year period.

The Poisson model turned out to be inadequate for all forty-four subgroups, suggesting some form of variable proneness model as an alternative. The NBD model provided a good fit in nearly all of the subgroups.

With correlations between the two halves of the six-year period ranging from 0.15 to 0.3 (statistically significant) there was some suggestion of a consistent pattern even though the correlation values were not impressive. Thus the variable proneness model explains the data observed reasonably well.

Looking at the forty-four subgroups, the variation across practices was considerable. The average number of episodes ranged from 0.134 to 0.555 for males and 0.327 to 1.125 for females. Thus, subdividing by sex, three to fourfold ratios between practices with the highest and lowest rates were observed.

The problems of collecting data from a number of practices have been highlighted once more. The question of episode definition is responsible for much of the between-practice variation. In addition, some practices used multiple diagnoses much more readily than others. In certain practices some individuals were given five or even six psychiatric labels over the six years. Even allowing for unrelated periods of illness, some of these patients must have been given several diagnoses at single consultations. With one episode recorded for each diagnosis at a consultation, practices which used multiple diagnoses frequently had far more individuals with large numbers of episodes (say ten or more). Thus, practices varied widely not only in *average* numbers of episodes but also in the *range* of values observed as seen in Smeeton (1986b).

Is it possible to salvage any results from this apparent mess? Although strongly influenced by the variation between the GPs, some clear findings about the patients nevertheless emerged. The females experienced about twice as many episodes as the males, on average, this being a consistent finding across all the practices. This sex difference was also found by Dunn (1983) in the stochastic modelling of anxiety and depression.

A consistent pattern related to age group and stability in the practice was also found (Smeeton 1987). Additional information on the numbers of entrants and leavers during each year of the Survey was provided by OPCS. Thus, entrants, leavers, and stayers were compared in the final year of the study, subdivided by age-group and sex, i.e., those with five years of records at the start of the final year and who stayed throughout that year were compared with those who joined or left during the final year. Transient individuals had, on average, six months' exposure. It was found that the average number of episodes experienced was highest among those aged 25 to 44 years. Entrants had a higher episode rate than stayers, above 15 years of age. Leavers tended to have similar episode rates to stayers.

The increased rate observed with the entrants could be due, in part, to a tendency for individuals to delay transfer to a local GP until one is needed. As leavers had similar rates to stayers, rather than reduced rates, it does seem that there may be some genuine increase among less stable individuals.

Thus, despite problems over between-practice variation, it is still possible to demonstrate the plausibility of the variable proneness theory, and indicate that females, the middle aged, and transient individuals are at increased risk of episodes of mental illness.

CONCLUSIONS

The results of these analyses have given us a broad overall picture of how GPs record the occurrence of episodes of mental illness in the community. How does this help the GP interested in local patterns of psychiatric morbidity? These findings are certainly not totally useless. The NBD model appears to act as an appropriate model independent of practice. However, due to the large between-practice variation, the exact results observed in one practice cannot be applied directly to another. Only general, rather than specific, statements can be made, such as about the apparent increase in risk among females, the middle aged, and individuals moving in and out of practices.

A more detailed understanding of episode patterns will only be gained by tackling the problem of between-practice variation. One approach would be to standardize the diagnoses of all GPs in the UK. This would be an extremely daunting task. Almost certainly, some GPs would see this as an attack on their independent judgement and would resist the implementation of any such attempt. Despite this, such an effort would be necessary in order to ensure that all morbidity statistics are reliable and meaningful.

A less ambitious approach would be the encouragement of studies in single practices. A GP seriously interested in looking at local patterns of psychiatric morbidity would certainly gain much from conducting a study of this type. Given the maintained interest of the GP, data can be collected over long periods of time (Dunn and Skuse 1981) and complex statistical models can be tailored to the experience of the individual practice. As a note of caution, such a model would clearly not be appropriate in other settings. Even in the practice for which it was designed it would need to be constantly checked, as changes in the staff at the practice might invalidate the model eventually. Indeed, the attitudes of the remaining staff might also change.

Finally, the National Morbidity Surveys themselves could provide a way of looking at individual practices over long periods of time. Sixteen practices were involved in both the Second and Third Surveys with records stretching from 1970 to 1982 (HMSO 1986). A comparison of data from the two surveys within these practices would be a useful first step. Further data collection from these practices would be far more useful than the future involvement of many more new practices. The problem of between-practice variation need not then make the results obtained totally meaningless.

What of the future? Training in the use of psychiatric labels needs to start at medical school and will take many years to implement. A medium-term solution might be the involvement of a modest number of GPs in the ongoing recording of episodes of psychiatric illness. An attempt to standardize the recording practices of these GPs would then be a more realistic possibility and the idea of obtaining meaningful statistics on episodes of psychiatric illness at some stage in the future may then be more than just an idle dream.

Acknowledgement: Nigel Smeeton is supported by the Department of Health and Social Security. Mrs P. Dixon of the Office of Population, Censuses and Surveys supplied the data on the new entrants and leavers.

REFERENCES

Adelstein, A.M. (1952) 'Accident proneness: a criticism of the concept based upon an analysis of shunters' accidents' (with discussion), *Journal of the Royal Statistical Society A* 115: 354–410.

Ashford, J.R. (1972) 'Patient contacts in general practice in the National Health Service', *The Statistician* 21: 265–89.

Clare, A.W. (1982) 'Problems of psychiatric classification in general practice', in A.W. Clare and M. Lader (eds) *Psychiatry and General Practice*, London: Academic Press, 15–25.

College of General Pracitioners Research Committee of Council (1963) 'A classification of disease: amended version', *Journal of the College of General Practitioners*, 6: 207–16.

Cooper, B., Fry, J., and Kalton, G. (1969) 'A longitudinal study of psychiatric morbidity in a general practice population', *British Journal of Preventive and Social Medicine* 23: 210–17.

Dunn, G. (1983) 'Longitudinal records of anxiety and depression in general practice: the Second National Morbidity Survey', *Psychological Medicine* 13: 987–906.

Dunn, G. (1985) 'Records of psychiatric morbidity in general practice: the National Morbidity Surveys', *Psychological Medicine* 15: 223–6.

Dunn, G. (1986) 'Patterns of psychiatric diagnosis in general pratice: the Second National Morbidity Survey', *Psychological Medicine* 16: 573–81.

Dunn, G., and Skuse, D. (1981) 'The natural history of depression in general practice: stochastic models', *Psychological Medicine* 11: 755–64.

Ellis, R.P. (1985) *Episodes in Mental Health: Issues and Literature Review*, Health Policy Center, Manuscript MH4, Hiller Graduate School, Brandeis University, Waltham, MA, USA.

General Register Office *Morbidity Statistics from General Practice, Volume III (Disease in General Practice)*, (Studies on Medical and Population Subjects No. 14), London: HMSO.

Goldberg, D. and Blackwell, B. (1970) 'Psychiatric illness in general practice: a detailed study using a new method of case identification', *British Medical Journal* ii: 439–43.

Greenwood, M., and Yule, G.U. (1920) 'An inquiry into the nature of frequency distributions representative of multiple happenings with special reference to the occurrence of multiple attacks of disease or repeated accidents', *Journal of the Royal Statistical Society* 83: 255–79.

Her Majesty's Stationery Office (1974) *Morbidity Statistics from General Practice, Second National Study 1970–1* (Studies on Medical and Population Subjects No. 26), London: HMSO.

Her Majesty's Stationery Office (1979) *Morbidity Statistics from General Practice 1971–2: Second National Study* (Studies on Medical and Population Subjects No. 36), London: HMSO.

Her Majesty's Stationery Office (1986) *Morbidity Statistics from General Practice, Third National Study 1981–82* (Series MB5, No. 1), London: HMSO.

Hornbrook, M.C., Hurtado, A.V., and Johnson, R.C. (1985), 'Health care episodes: definition, measurement and use', *Medical Care Review* 42: 163–218.

Irwin, J.O. (1941) 'Comments on the paper "Theory and observation in the investigation of accident causation" by Chambers, E.G. and Yule, G.U.', *Journal of the Royal Statistical Society (Supplement)* 7: 89–109.

Kedward, H.B., and Cooper, B. (1966) 'Neurotic disorders in urban practice: a three-year follow-up', *Journal of the Royal College of General Practitioners* 12: 148–63.

Keeler, E.B., Wells, K.B., Manning, W.G., Rumpel, J.D., and Hanley, J.M. (1986) *The Demand for Episodes of Mental Health Services*, The Rand Corporation, R–3432–NIMH, Santa Monica, California, USA.

Logan, W.P.D. (1960) *Morbidity Statistics from General Practice, Volume II (Occupation)* (General Register Office Studies on Medical and Population Subjects No. 14), London: HMSO.

Logan, W.P.D., and Cushion, A.A. (1958) *Morbidity Statistics from General Practice, Volume I (General)* (General Register Office Studies on Medical and Population Subjects No. 14), London, HMSO.

Mann, A.H., Jenkins, R., and Belsey, E. (1981) 'The twelve-month outcome of patients with neurotic illness in general practice', *Psychological Medicine* 11: 535–50.

Marks, J.N., Goldberg, D.P., and Hillier, V.F. (1979) 'Determinants of the ability of general practitioners to detect psychiatric illness', *Psychological Medicine* 9: 337–53.

Meyer-Gross, W. (1954) 'The diagnosis of depression', *British Medical Journal* II: 948–54.

Royal College of General Practitioners (1980) 'Second National Morbidity Survey', *Journal of the Royal College of General Practitioners* 30: 547–50.

Shepherd, M., Cooper, B., Brown, A.C., and Kalton, G.W. (1966) *Psychiatric Illness in General Practice*, London: Oxford University Press.

Smeeton, N.C. (1986a) 'Distribution of episodes of mental illness in general practice: results from the Second National Morbidity Survey', *Journal of Epidemiology and Community Health* 40: 130–3.

Smeeton, N.C. (1986b) 'Modelling episodes of mental illness: some results from the Second UK National Morbidity Survey', *The Statistician* 35: 55–63.

Smeeton, N.C. (1987) 'Surveys of mental illness in general practice', *The Professional Statistician* 6: 8–9.

Watts, C.A.H. (1962) 'Psychiatric disorders', in General Register Office *Morbidity Statistics from General Practice, Volume III (Disease in General Practice)*, London: HMSO, 35–52.

Completing the Clinical Picture of Disease and the Delineation of New Syndromes

13

Continuities and Discontinuities in Anxiety Disorders

Gerald Klerman and Myrna Weissman

The role that epidemiology can play in helping to define a clinical disorder lies at the heart of the interface between epidemiology and clinical psychiatry. Historically, physicians have described and defined disorders based upon their experience with patients receiving medical attention. Subsequently, epidemiologists seek to determine the rates of these disorders in community samples independent of treatment-seeking and to quantify the risk factors associated with their incidence, prevalence, morbidity, disability, and mortality. Thus, clinical medicine and epidemiology are in a continuing dialogue, dependent upon each other, while, at the same time, engaged in a dynamic tension. In few areas of medical science is this tension as strong as between clinical and epidemiologic psychiatry. Shepherd has made this interchange a major focus of his efforts. He has emphasized the need for a dialogue between the psychiatric epidemiologist and the clinical psychiatrist and a public health perspective to clinical psychiatry (Shepherd 1978: 289–98).

In this essay, we apply these concepts to a particular clinical condition in psychiatry – anxiety – and reconstruct recent developments which illustrate the important interchange between clinical and epidemiological psychiatry.

Specifically, we will focus on the controversies concerning continuities and discontinuities in the anxiety disorders. Those who hold a continuity view emphasize the similarities between the normal emotional states, including fear and anxious response to stress, and regard clinical conditions as an intensification and quantitative exaggeration of otherwise normal responses. In contrast, clinicians and epidemiologists who hold discontinuous views, emphasize the uniqueness of certain diagnostic categories, particularly panic disorder, agoraphobia, and obsessive-compulsive disorder. They point to the qualitative differences between serious anxiety conditions and the milder and more 'normal' conditions seen in general practice and detected in community surveys.

UNDERSTANDING ANXIETY STATES THROUGH THE SECOND WORLD WAR

While concern for emotional states (called 'passions', 'moods', 'affects' at different times) has permeated the history of psychiatry, interest in anxiety and in anxiety disorders only emerged in the latter half of the nineteenth century. This interest was part of the growing attention to conditions which came to be called neuroses, and represented a convergence of interests within the profession and within the larger society, particularly in North America, the British Isles, and western Europe.

Psychiatry, as a medical speciality, had its origins in the late eighteenth century with growing concern for the insane. Special institutions for the insane were developed in North America, the British Isles, and western Europe. As Foucault pointed out, mental illness was an 'invention' of the Enlightenment. It is not that lunatics and the insane did not exist before Pinel and Tuke, but rather, that they were considered under the jurisdiction of the law and the Church rather than medical practitioners and public health authorities.

Medical physicians first became involved in the care of the insane in institutions, usually called asylums, or retreats. Thus, the founding of the American Psychiatric Association in 1844 was as the American Association of Medical Superintendents of Asylums for the Insane. The name was not changed until the beginning of the twentieth century.

Psychiatric writings through the nineteenth century were focused on conditions which today we would consider psychoses. At the end of the nineteenth century the focus began to change. A small but increasing number of psychiatric practitioners began to practise outside the mental institutions. A few served in the military in the First World War, and many more later became involved in general hospitals, out-patient services, and private consulting practice. In these settings they increasingly saw non-psychotic individuals, whose mental problems manifested themselves in conditions designated today as phobias, obsessions, compulsions, and disturbances of emotional state and bodily functions.

In the second half of the nineteenth century, a large medical literature developed in an attempt to understand the problems of an increasing number of patients, often female patients of middle- and upper-class background, seeking help from medical practitioners. Various terms were coined: 'neurasthenia' by Baird in 1871, 'psychasthenia' by Janet in France. The concept of hysteria was revived, particularly in the writings of Charcot. The term 'anxiety' did not appear prominently until 1895, when Freud wrote his paper 'Distinguishing anxiety neuroses from neurasthenia' (Freud 1894, 1957). The work of Kraepelin and his school focused mainly on psychoses, particularly on manic-depressive insanity, now called bipolar affective disorder, and on dementia praecox, now called schizophrenia (Kraepelin 1921).

182

Freud and others, practising outside mental hospitals or university clinics, were devoting increasing attention to conditions which came to be called neuroses. Prominent among them were anxiety states. States of fearfulness and nervousness were described throughout the medical literature, but the term 'anxiety' captured not only the psychiatric world, particularly up to the writings of Freud and the growing influence of psychoanalysis, but also the world of the philosopher and the existentialist.

The experience of psychiatrists in the military in the First World War focused attention on various kinds of war neuroses, or traumatic neuroses. Conditions of shell shock and neurocirculatory asthenia were given prominence. A large number of neuropsychiatrists who had served in the military, gained experience with the affects of trauma and the resulting non-psychotic conditions. They saw changes in bodily function and symptoms of cardiac and gastrointestinal nature without the impairments of higher mental functions usually seen by psychiatrists in the classic psychotic states in mental institutions.

By the end of the First World War, there was growing acceptance of a concept of a continuum of anxiety states (Klerman 1986: 3). Influenced by Darwinian concepts of evolution, anxiety was seen as the clinical equivalent of normal fear (Darwin 1872). Neurotic conditions were arrayed on a continuum of increasing severity, including obsessions and compulsions, phobias, and anxiety states. Gradually the classification of agoraphobia as the most disabling form of phobia was developed, particularly by English psychiatrists, including Roth and associates in Newcastle (Meyer-Gross *et al*. 1954), and by Marks and Gelder (Marks 1969).

In this respect, it is interesting that three divergent theories – biological, psychodynamic, and behavioural – emerged in the period between the First World War and the Second World War, all of which accepted the descriptive nature of anxiety and anxiety states and the continuum between normal fears and anxieties and severe clinical states, particularly phobias and anxiety neuroses.

Biological theories

The basis for biological theories for anxiety and anxiety neurosis is to be found in the theories of Darwin, particularly his volume on the expression of emotions in animals and humans (Darwin 1872). In his writing, Darwin laid down the premise that emotional expressions, like anatomical structures, changed with biological evolution and played an adaptive function in the relation between species and their environment. Darwin also postulated the universality of certain basic emotions and their expession through motor and postural changes, linking human emotional experience with animals.

Cannon identified the role of the adrenal medulla and epinephrine as involved in alleviating the 'flight-fight' response and the important function of the endocrine system in adaptation (Cannon 1936). Cannon's views were expanded by the work of Selye in the decade immediately preceding the First World War. Selye (Selye 1956) identified the important function of adrenal cortical substances, particularly cortisol, and the regulation of adrenal cortical function through the pituitary organ. In animal research, he investigated the role of stress in precipitating the general adaptation syndrome. During the First World War, the older concept of psychic trauma was generalized into the new concept of stress. Selye's work expanded the endocrine system to involve not only the adrenal medulla, but also the adrenal cortex and the important connections between CNS centres, particularly the hypothalamus, pituitary, and peripheral endocrine organs. This endocrine work paralleled the important work on neuropharmacotherapy of the autonomic nervous system – its role in regulating cardiovascular, gastrointestinal, and motor responses – and the sensitivity of the autonomic nervous system, particularly the sympathetic system, to environmental changes, including emotional states. All these biological investigations accepted the continuity between normal states of fear and the clinical disorders. It was assumed that the clinical states of anxiety, neurosis and phobias, were quantitative intensifications of normal physiologic and emotional processes.

The psychodynamic view

The psychodynamic view has its origins in the writings of Freud (Freud 1926). Freud was the first to describe anxiety neurosis as a separate nosologic condition in his 1894 paper (Freud 1894, 1957). He regarded anxiety neurosis as an 'actual' neurosis, based on biological causes. Later, he modified his theory, developing his concept of anxiety as 'signal anxiety' in 1923. Sigmund Freud postulated that anxiety was an unconscious signal of the threatened emergence into consciousness of ego-threatening material, mostly instinctual. In this theory, anxiety was the intra-psychic emotion parallel to fear, the threat of an external danger. All neurotic symptoms were explained by a unified theory of pathogenesis whereby symptoms were attempts to defend against and manage anxiety. Unconscious anxiety and its defences were postulated as the central pathogenic mechanisms for all neurotic symptom formation, including hysterical symptoms, obsessive-compulsive, neurotic depressions, and phobias. This point of view was increasingly accepted in US psychiatric centres during and after the Second World War and found its official expression in the APA DSM-III classification of disorders (APA DSM-III 1980).

Although most of psychiatry in the United Kingdom and western Europe did not accept the Freudian theory of the pathogenic role of unconscious anxiety and defenses, the psychotic-neurotic distinction was widely accepted. Neurotic conditions were characterized: (1) descriptively by the absence of impairment of higher mental functions and (2) aetiologically by a presumed non-constitutional environmental and psychosocial causation, which might involve personality maladaptations as well as responses to immediate or long-standing environmental changes.

184

Behavioural theories

The basic theoretical foundation of behavioural theories was found in the work of Pavlov and his theory of conditioned reflexes. The full expression of a behavioural theory was to follow the important work of B.F. Skinner on the role of instrumental conditioning. Skinner's theoretical work found expression in therapeutic endeavours, particularly for the treatment of phobias, using techniques, such as desensitization, relaxation, and, most notably, exposure (Marks 1969). Recently, the repertoire of behavioural techniques has been expanded to other neurotic conditions – particularly panic anxiety – and obsessive-compulsive states, as well as sexual dysfunctions.

Currently, the behavioural theories of anxiety are in a period of great research and therapeutic vigour. The development of behavioural observational scales and the application of psychophysiologic methods to clinical research have given increasing scientific validity to behavioural interpretations of anxiety. Moreover, these research investigations have been complemented by growing evidence for the therapeutic efficacy of behavioural techniques for the treatment of anxiety, phobias, obsessions, compulsions, and depressive states.

DEVELOPMENT SINCE THE SECOND WORLD WAR: CHALLENGES TO CONTINUITY THEORIES OF ANXIETY

By the end of the Second World War, the continuum theories of anxiety state were widely held. Categorical psychiatric diagnosis as the basis for clinical epidemiologic research was in disfavour. Critics called attention to the low reliability of diagnostic assessments and to the wide number of mixed and transient anxiety states, which occurred in individuals faced with external danger, as in combat, or during wartime air raids.

The 'Golden Era' of social epidemiology

The period after the Second World War ushered in a 'golden era' of social epidemiologic research (Weissman and Klerman 1977: 98; Robins 1978: 697). Selye's concept of stress proved useful to military psychiatry during the Second World War and the combat experience provided a paradigmatic basis for understanding medical disorders in civilian life. Psychiatrists in the military saw large numbers of men who had presumably been screened prior to induction and in whom the role of vulnerability and predisposition had been minimized.

A large number of community surveys were undertaken after the Second World War and they had a number of features in common. These features included: (1) careful attention to sampling methodology; (2) extensive use of questionnaires and scales for interviewing; (3) rejection of an explicit

185

psychiatric diagnosis, e.g. a mental health/mental illness continuum; (4) focus on social factors as equivalent to military stress, e.g. poverty, low social class, migration, racial inequities, urbanization.

In these studies anxiety was conceived of as an important, if not the major, emotional reaction, mediating between the external environment (the stressor) and the internal reaction, whether it be mental illness or bodily change or physical illness. The writings of Sullivan and the interpersonal theorists had pointed out that in modern life the major threats to personal security were not external dangers – as had been true earlier in the history of the species, but were ongoing interpersonal events having to do with social status, personal role, and aspirations and frustrations in intimate and close relations.

Epidemiologic studies in general medical practice

In parallel with community samples, a number of investigators began intensive studies of psychiatric morbidity among patients seen in general medical settings, particularly in general practitioners' offices. The pioneering work in this endeavour was by Shepherd and his associates in their studies of London (Shepherd *et al.* 1966), out of which came the work of Goldberg (Goldberg 1978) in his various studies of psychiatric problems in general practice patients in Manchester. These studies demonstrated a high prevalence of psychiatric symptoms and morbidity in patients seeking medical assistance from general practitioners. As part of the methodologic advances in these investigations, Goldberg developed the General Health Questionnaire (GHQ) (Goldberg 1978). Previous work, mainly during the Second World War in the military, had made use of similar instruments, such as the Cornell Medical Index and the Health Opinion Surveys (HOS). These were extensively studied for reliability and discriminant validity using psychometric techniques; however, the Goldberg GHQ became the most widely used mode of assessing psychiatric morbidity in medical settings. Investigations using the GHQ and similar techniques documented high rates of psychiatric morbidity, often associated with symptoms of anxiety and depression. These symptoms were usually unrecognized and untreated by the general physician, who tended to see patients' complaints in terms of traditional medical disease categories. Theoretically, these studies, showing high degrees of association between symptoms of anxiety and depression, questioned the clinical value, as well as the epidemiologic validity, of traditional diagnostic efforts at identifying discrete syndromes.

Clinical research emphasizing discontinuities

A number of developments in the 1960s in clinical research came to challenge the continuity view. Some of this research made use of the availability of computers or multivariate statistical analyses. Other research began from clinical observations of the role of the new psychopharmacologic agents, particularly the MAO inhibitors or the tricyclic antidepressants and the benzodiazepines.

The development of multivariate statistical techniques and the availability of high-speed electronic computers made possible the application of these techniques to psychopathology in large samples. In the United Kingdom extensive controversy followed the use of multivariate techniques, particularly discriminate function and analysis, to identify subtypes within depression. In this work there was a controversy between the Newcastle group led by Roth and his associates (Meyer-Gross *et al*. 1954) and the London group, led by Lewis and his students (Shepherd 1986), notably Kendell (Kendell 1977: 3). Efforts were made to distinguish between anxiety states and depressive states. Factor analytic studies had identified separate anxiety and depression factors on many scales, particularly the Hopkins Symptom Checklist. Although these scales showed factorial independence, in clinical practice the anxiety and depression scales were almost highly correlated. Research in this area appeared to be unable to resolve the issues of the continuity or discontinuity between anxiety and depression.

More successful efforts were made with regard to the phobias. A combination of clinical research and factor analytic studies (Marks 1969) led to the proposal to separate phobias into three types – agoraphobia, social phobia, and simple phobia.

An important, and somewhat different line of investigation was under way in the 1960s and 1970s in the United States and the United Kingdom. Following the observations in the United Kingdom of the efficacy of MAO inhibitors for atypical depressions and many anxiety states, studies were undertaken to determine the possible efficacy of tricyclic antidepressants. Donald Klein noted the occurrence of panic attacks in the symptom picture of patients with severe agoraphobia who were often diagnosed pseudo-neurotic or borderline schizophrenic (Klein 1981). As part of a double blind randomized trial comparing imipramine to chlorpromazine, Klein observed the unexpected effect of imipramine in reducing panic attacks. Based upon this clinical observation, he pursued a number of studies refining the clinical syndrome of panic attacks and testing the therapeutic value of imipramine and other tricyclic antidepressants in their treatment.

Based on these findings, in the 1970s, anxiety neuroses were separated into two forms, generalized anxiety and panic anxiety. This separation was codified in the Research Diagnostic Criteria (RDC) and from the research in the NIMH Collaborative Programe in the Psychobiology of Depression, which used the SADS-RDC. The availability of standardized diagnostic criteria for distinguishing panic anxiety from generalized anxiety and linking panic anxiety to agoraphobia resulted in an increasing number of clinical studies on the validity of this distinction. Therapeutic studies indicated that two classes of antidepressant compounds, the tricyclic antidepressants and the MAO inhibitors, were useful in this condition (Klerman 1983: 3; Klerman *et al*. 1984: 539).

Thus, by the middle of the 1970s, an important line of investigation had challenged the continuity theory and emphasized the qualitative differences between panic anxiety and generalized anxiety and the differential efficacy of classes of psychopharmacologic agents in treating these disorders. Many of these nosologic and diagnostic concepts were embodied in the DSM-III, published by the American Psychiatric Association in 1980, embodying many of the features of the discontinuity point of view, but, at the same time, initiating many controversies and providing an important stimulus to empirical research.

CLINICAL AND EPIDEMIOLOGIC ASPECTS OF CURRENT CONTROVERSIES

The APA DSM-III, published in 1980, contained a number of important changes in the approach to anxiety and anxiety disorders. The previous continuity theory was abandoned, as well as the category of neurosis as a unifying and diagnostic classification. The previous category of neurotic conditions was broken down into a number of separate categories, in particular, affective disorders and anxiety disorders. Within the anxiety disorders two features were of note: the separation of panic anxiety from generalized anxiety and the linking of panic disorder and agoraphobia (APA DSM-III 1980).

These diagnostic distinctions were the focus of controversy among clinical and therapeutic researchers. Just at the time that the first large-scale epidemiologic studies of communities using clinical diagnostic approaches became possible, the integration of clinical and epidemiological research, described by Shepherd, became a real possibility in the US in the 1970s and 1980s (Shepherd 1978).

Recent epidemiologic research on anxiety disorders

In these new epidemiologic studies, structural interviews and diagnostic algorithms developed in the 1960s and 1970s were to be applied to probability samples of the communities in the United States. The diagnostic algorithms were initially developed in clinical settings by the group at Washington University in St Louis, led by Robins and Guze (Robins and Guze 1972), and were codified by Feighner. Similar developments were under way in the United Kingdom, where Wing developed the Present State Examination (PSE), which has been widely used in epidemiologic studies, e.g. the World Health Organization International Pilot Study on Schizophrenia (Wing et al. 1974).

Many of the features of these algorithms were incorporated in the SADS-RDC, developed by Spitzer, Endicott, and Robins in the NIMH Collaborative Program for the Psychobiology of Depression (Spitzer et al. 1978: 773). The

SADS-RDC came to be the most widely used diagnostic system in clinical, therapeutic, and family research in the United States (Endicott and Spitzer 1978: 837).

Since the 1980s, when the first multi-site community-based survey of psychiatric disorders in the United States was initiated by the National Institute of Mental Health, epidemiologic topics have been of increasing interest in psychiatry (Regier *et al.* 1984: 934; Klerman 1986b: 159). The data emerging from this survey have challenged the conventional view of the nature, frequency, risks, course, and co-morbidity of many psychiatric disorders, especially panic and agoraphobia.

There are four community surveys of treated and untreated persons which have incorporated the division of anxiety states into subtypes and used either RDC or DSM-III criteria.

(1) The New Haven Survey was the first application of the new structured diagnostic interview techniques (SADS-L and RDC) in a community sample of persons. The study was conducted in the New Haven, Connecticut, area in 1975, and included a sample of 511 probands (a follow-up of a probability community study) who were interviewed by clinically trained persons using the SADS-L which generated Research Diagnostic Criteria (RDC) (Weissman and Myers 1978: 1304).

(2) The National Survey of Psychotherapeutic Drug Use, conducted in 1979, was a survey of a probability sample of 3,161 adults living throughout the United States in which a symptom checklist, the SCL-90, was administered by survey interviewers. The primary interest was in drug use. However, based on an algorithm of symptoms, diagnostic counterparts of some DSM-III anxiety disorders, including panic and agoraphobia, were identified (Uhlenhuth *et al.* 1983: 1167).

(3) The Zurich Study, conducted by Angst and Dobler-Mikola (1984: 30), was a population study of 3,902 19-year-old men and 2,391 20-year-old women. Approximately 50 per cent of the population in this age group completed the SCL-90. Ten per cent of the total sample was selected to participate in a prospective interview study by having either high or low scores on the psychiatric self-rating instrument. Within one year of screening, about 500 persons were directly interviewed using a structured interview. DSM-III diagnoses were derived both from the checklist and the interview.

(4) The NIMH Epidemiologic Catchment Area Survey (ECA) (Klerman 1986b), by far the largest study, was conducted between 1980–4 and included a probability sample of over 18,000 adults using the Diagnostic Interview Schedule (DIS) which generated DSM-III diagnoses. The study was independently conducted at five United States sites: New Haven, Connecticut (Yale University); Baltimore, Maryland (Johns Hopkins University); St Louis, Missouri (Washington

University); Piedmont Area, North Carolina (Duke University); and Los Angeles, California (UCLA). This study provides the most comprehensive epidemiologic data available on panic and agoraphobia in large samples of adults (Myers *et al.* 1984: 959) (Regier *et al.* 1984: 934). This review will focus on the findings from the ECA data.

Panic symptoms

There is agreement that symptoms of panic are extremely common and that they occur in many psychiatric disorders. In an examination of panic attacks and panic disorder in the three ECA sites, von Korff *et al.* (1987: 152) found an increase in the onset of panic attacks in the 15–19-year-old group and rare onset in panic attacks after age 40. There was no clear demarcation between simple, severe, or recurrent panic attacks and DSM-III panic disorder in terms of autonomic systems, age of onset, and distribution of demographic factors. Panic attacks were quite common, with a six-month prevalence rate of 3/100. However, only 10 per cent of the population reported any history of panic attacks.

In a separate examination of the ECA five-site data, it was found that about 10 per cent of the sample (range 7.6 per cent to 11.6 per cent) answered positively to the question 'Have you ever had a spell when all of a sudden you felt frightened, anxious, very uneasy in situations, when most people wouldn't be afraid?'

The close association between current and lifetime rates of panic attacks noted by von Korff *et al.* (1985: 970) may be an artefact of reporting, or may suggest that a significant minority of individual persons have sporadic panic attacks, and that these are recurrent. Boyd and associates (1986: 983), in a separate examination of ECA data, also found a high prevalence of panic attacks in persons with other psychiatric disorders. The investigators recommend a flexible approach to classifying panic attacks until there is evidence from longitudinal studies or other data that indicates a clear separation of disorder from attacks.

Panic disorder

There is a convergence of findings concerning the epidemiology of panic disorder. The range of prevalence rates (one month to one year) was 0.4–1.6/100. The ECA study showed considerable consistency in six-month prevalence rates of panic disorder across the five sites: the rates were higher in women, in persons aged 25–44, and in the separated and the divorced. The increased risk in women as compared to men also has been found in family studies. The rates were lowest in persons over age 64. There was no consistent relationship to race or education. The mean age of onset was mid-to-late-thirties.

The relationship of panic disorder and agoraphobia

Of particular interest has been the relationship between panic disorder and agoraphobia. According to Klein's theory (Klein 1981), agoraphobia is a conditioned, learned reaction to unexplained panic attacks – a view that has been adopted by many clinicians and researchers who state that agoraphobia does not occur without panic disorder. At least two epidemiologic studies, however, have found cases of agoraphobia in the absence of current or past history of panic disorder. In a longitudinal study of young adults in Zurich, Angst and Dobler-Mikola (1984: 30) found that the one-year prevalence rate of agoraphobia without panic disorder was 1.6/100, while the rate for agoraphobia with panic disorder was 0.7/100. In the New Haven ECA site, the rate of agoraphobia with no history of panic disorder was 2.9/100, whereas the rate of agoraphobia plus panic was only 0.3/100 (Weissman, in press).

A more intensive investigation of the New Haven ECA findings revealed that of the 144 subjects with agoraphobia and no history of panic disorder, sixty-seven had experienced some panic symptoms. These attacks were often of insufficient number or magnitude to meet the criteria for the DSM-III. Furthermore, among the seventy-seven subjects with agoraphobia and no symptoms of panic, twenty-nine (38 per cent) had at least one other psychiatric disorder. Affective disorders were the most common diagnoses (Weissman, in press).

Although many subjects in the New Haven survey were identified by diagnostic criteria as having only agoraphobia and no panic disorder, one half did have panic symptoms. Of the other half with no symptoms of panic anxiety, more than one-third had another psychiatric disorder, usually major depression. Thus, only 33 per cent of the group diagnosed as having agoraphobia without panic disorder had neither panic anxiety nor other psychiatric disorders. If we consider only these forty-eight subjects as the cases of 'true' agoraphobia without panic, then the rate (1.0/100) is close to the rate 1.6/100 reported by Angst and Dobler-Mikola (1984: 30).

Co-morbidity

There is good evidence from epidemiologic studies for co-morbidity between disorders. Individuals who experience anxiety disorder tend to have other psychiatric disorders, including other anxiety disorders, over their lifetime. For example, in the 1975 survey, over 80 per cent of persons with generalized anxiety disorder had at least one other anxiety disorder; 30 per cent of persons with phobias had had panic disorder at some time. There was also an overlap between the anxiety disorders and major depression: over 7 per cent of persons with GAD, 2 per cent of persons with panic disorder, and 4 per cent with phobia had experienced major depression.

Similarly, on the basis of data from three ECA sites, Boyd et al. (1984: 983) found high co-morbidity between disorders. There was an 18.8-fold increased risk of panic disorder and a 15.3-fold increased risk of agoraphobia, given a major depression. There was 4.3-fold increased risk of alcohol abuse, given a panic disorder, and an 18-fold increased risk of panic disorder, given agoraphobia. The risk of major depression, given panic disorder, could not be calculated, due to the exclusion criteria of DSM-III.

CONCLUSIONS: THE ONGOING DIALOGUE BETWEEN CLINICAL AND EPIDEMIOLOGICAL PSYCHIATRY

This review of current controversies in the investigation of anxiety and anxiety disorders points out the dynamic interplay and mutual dependence between clinical and epidemiologic psychiatry. The recent proposals for the separation of panic anxiety from generalized anxiety and the discontinuity of agoraphobia and panic disorder from other anxiety disorders which originated in clinical research and which were embodied in the DSM-III classification have provided the basis for controversy, not only among clinicians and therapists who are sceptical of these formulations, but also among epidemiologic investigators.

The development of structured interviews and diagnostic algorithms embody these descriptions. The PSE, DIS, SADS-RDC, and the DSN criteria have been applied in large-scale community and family surveys. The epidemiologic data give partial, but not complete, support to some of these revisionist ideas. Using structured interviews and diagnostic algorithms, it is possible to make distinctions between generalized anxiety and panic anxiety, and to assess agoraphobia. Although the diagnostic inquiries for agoraphobia, particularly at the DIS, do not fullly mirror the clinical criteria, they, nevertheless, have provided a stimulus for investigation.

The new epidemiologic studies have clarified our thinking about the anxiety disorders.

(1) There is empirical basis for the separation of the anxiety disorders. These disorders have different epidemiologies; they have different rates and risk factors.

(2) The separation is best established for panic and agoraphobia.

(3) The high co-morbidity between the anxiety disorders and depression is *not* merely an artefact of sampling; i.e., persons with two disorders are more apt to seek health care. Community surveys, including both treated and untreated samples, also show high co-morbidity.

(4) There is a challenge to the concept that agoraphobia only occurs in the context of a history of panic disorder. There seem to be several diagnostic pathways to agoraphobia.

The discontinuity theorists have gained partial support from these recent epidemiologic studies. The epidemiologic research has confirmed the existence of a large number of adults, approximately 10–20 per cent, who experience sporadic or intermittent panic attacks, but who do not meet the full criteria of DSM-III panic disorder. Using techniques of genetic epidemiology, twin and adoption studies seem to lend partial support to evidence for familial aggregation of panic disorder and, to some extent, agoraphobia – but not for generalized anxiety disorder – supporting the discontinuity viewpoint.

In contrast, epidemiologic studies conducted in general practice and community health settings indicate a large reservoir of patients with symptoms of anxiety, often combined with symptoms of depression, many of whom do not meet criteria for major mental disorders. Many of their conditions are associated with recent stress and appear to be attempts of the individual to cope with life events, difficult circumstances, and stress. Anxiety and related symptoms serve as a stimulus to seeking health care. Thus, the health care system increasingly has become part of the means by which individuals in society cope with change, particularly those changes which impact on the individuals' and family members' emotional situation. At this end of the spectrum, continuity theories are highly useful and valid. Clinicians working in general health care settings, such as consultants to health maintenance organizations or family practice groups, are more impressed with the lack of differentiation of clinical syndromes and the essential continuity between normal adaptive functioning and psychopathology.

Looking to the future, it is likely that these trends will continue and that the continued interchange and dialogue between clinical and epidemiologic research in psychiatry will further clarify many issues. These issues involve a dynamic interplay, at times tense, conflictual, and disputatious, among groups of clinicians and between clinicians and epidemiologists. Neither group is of a single mind on these diagnostic or theoretical issues. As Shepherd has pointed out (Shepherd 1979: 191), these issues are of more than scientific and academic interest. Psychiatry has a uniquely social responsibility. The high prevalence and social disability associated with psychiatric disorders bring them into the centre of social concern.

REFERENCES

American Psychiatric Association (1980) *Diagnostic and Statistical Manual of Mental Disorders*, third edition (DSM-III), Washington, DC: AMA.

Angst, J. and Dobler-Mikola, A. (1984) 'The Zurich story: diagnosis of depression', *European Archives of Psychiatric Neurological Sciences* 234: 30–7.

Boyd, J.H., Burke, J.D., Gruenberg, E., Holzer, C.E., Rae, D.S., George, L.K., Karno, M., Stolzman, R., McEvoy, L. and Nestadt, G. (1984) 'Exclusion criteria of DSM-III: a study of co-occurrence of hierarchy-free syndromes', *Archives of General Psychiatry* 41: 983–9.

Cannon, W.B. (1936) *The Wisdom of the Body*, New York: W.W. Norton.

Darwin, C. (1872) *The Expression of the Emotions in Man and Animals*, London: John Murray.

Endicott, J. and Spitzer, R. (1978) 'A diagnostic interview: the schedule for affective disorder and schizophrenia', *Archives of General Psychiatry* 35: 837–44.

Freud, S. (1894, 1957) 'On the grounds for detaching a particular syndrome from neurasthenia under the description of "anxiety neurosis"', in J. Strachey (ed.) *The Complete Psychological Works of Sigmund Freud (Standard Edition) Volume III*, London: Hogarth Press.

Freud, S. (1926) 'Inhibitions, symptoms and anxiety', in J. Strachey (ed.) *The Complete Psychological Works of Sigmund Freud (Standard Edition) Volume XX*, London: Hogarth Press.

Goldberg, D.P. (1978) *Manual of the General Health Questionnaire*, Windsor: NFER/Nelson.

Kendell, R.E. (1977) 'The classification of depression: a review of contemporary confusion', in G.D. Burrows (ed.) *Handbook of Studies of Depression*, New York: Excerpta Medica, 3–19.

Klein, D.F. (1981) 'Anxiety reconceptualized', in D.F. Klein and J.G. Rabkin (eds) *Anxiety: New Research and Challenging Concepts*, New York: Raven Press.

Klerman, G.L. (1983) 'Significance of DSM-III in American psychiatry', in R.L. Spitzer, J.B.W. Wiliams, and A.E. Skodal (eds) *International Perspectives in DSM-III*, Washington, DC: American Psychiatric Press, 3–25.

Klerman, G.L. (1986a) 'Introduction', *The Journal of Clinical Psychiatry* (supplement) 47: 3.

Klerman, G.L. (1986b) 'The National Institute of Mental Health Environment Catchment Areas (NIMH-ECA) Program', *Social Psychiatry* 21: 159–66.

Klerman, G.L., Spitzer, R., Vaillant, G., and Michels, R. (1984) 'A debate on DSM-III', *American Journal of Psychiatry* 141: 53.

Kraepelin, E. (1921) *Manic-depressive Insanity and Paranoia*, translated by M. Barclay, Edinburgh: Livingstone.

Marks, I. (1969) *Fears and Phobias*, London: Heinemann.

Meyer-Gross, W., Slater, E., and Roth, M. (eds) (1954) *Clinical Psychiatry*, Baltimore, MD: Williams and Wilkins.

Myers, J.K., Weissman, M.M., Tischler, G.L., Holzer, C.E., Leaf, P.J., Orvaschel, H., Anthony, J.C., Boyd, J.H., Burke, J.D., Kramer, M. and Stoltzman, R. (1984) 'The prevalence of psychiatric disorders in three communities, 1980–1982', *Archives of General Psychiatry* 41: 959–67.

Regier, D.A., Myers, J.K., Kramer, M., Robins, L.N., Blazer, D.G., Hough, R.L., Eaton, W.W. and Locke, B.Z. (1984) 'The NIMH Epidemiological Catchment Area (ECA) Program: historical context, major objectives and study population characteristics', *Archives of General Psychiatry* 41: 934–41.

Robins, E. and Guze, S.B. (1972) *Classification of Affective Disorders: The Primary-Secondary Endogenous-Reactive and Neurotic-Psychotic Concepts in Psychobiology of Depressive Illness* (DEHW Publication (HSM) 79-9053), edited by T.A. Williams, M.M. Katz, and J.A. Shield Jr., Washington, DC: US Government Printing Office.

Robins, L. (1978) 'Psychiatric epidemiology', *Archives of General Psychiatry* 35: 697–702.

Selye, H. (1956) *The Stress of Life*, New York: McGraw-Hill.

Shepherd, M. (1978) 'Epidemiology and clinical psychiatry', *British Journal of Psychiatry* 133: 289–98.

Shepherd, M. (1979) 'From social medicine to social psychiatry: the achievement of

Sir Aubrey Lewis', in E.C. Rosenberg (ed.) *Healing and History Essays for George Rosen*, Folkestone: Dawson.

Shepherd, M. (1986) *A Representative Psychiatrist: The Career, Contributions and Legacies of Sir Aubrey Lewis* (A Psychological Medicine Monograph Supplement 10), Cambridge: Cambridge University Press.

Shepherd, M., Cooper, B., Brown, A.C., and Kalton, G.W. (1966) *Psychiatric Illness in General Practice*, London: Oxford University Press.

Spitzer, R.L., Endicott, J., and Robins, E. (1978) 'Research diagnostic criteria: rationale and reliability', *Archives of General Psychiatry* 35: 773–82.

Uhlenhuth, E.H., Balter, M.B., Mellinger, G.D., Cissin, I.H. and Clinthorne, J. (1983) 'Symptom checklist syndromes in the general population: correlation with psychotherapeutic drug use', *Archives of General Psychiatry* 40: 1167–73.

von Korff, M., Eaton, W., and Reyl, P. (1985) 'The epidemiology of panic attacks and disorder: results from three community surveys', *American Journal of Epidemiology* 122: 970–81.

von Korff, M., Shapiro, S., Burke, J.D., Teitelbaum, M., Skinner, E.A., German, P., Turner, R.W., Klein, L. and Burns, B. (1987) 'Anxiety and depression in a primary health care clinic: comparison of Diagnostic Interview Schedule, General Health Questionnaire, and practitioner assessments', *Archives of General Psychiatry* 44: 152–6.

Weissman, M.M. (in press) 'The epidemiology of panic disorders and agoraphobia', for Section 1, *Panic Disorders*, M.K. Shear and D. Barlow (section eds), *APA Annual Review of Psychiatry, Volume 7*, edited by A.J. Frances and R.E. Hales, Washington, DC: American Psychiatric Press.

Weissman, M.M. and Klerman, G.L. (1977) 'Sex differences and the epidemiology of depression', *Archives of General Psychiatry* 34: 98–111.

Weissman, M.M. and Myers, J.K. (1978) 'Affective disorders in a U.S. urban community: the use of research diagnostic criteria in a community survey', *Archives of General Psychiatry* 35: 1304–11.

Wing, J., Cooper, J., and Sartorius, N. (1974) *The Measurement and Classification of Psychiatric Symptoms*, Cambridge: Cambridge University Press.

14

Personality Disorder

Anthony Mann and Glyn Lewis

Despite diagnostic imprecision and terminological confusion, the concept of personality disorder remains indispensable to clinical practice.

Shepherd and Sartorius (1974: 141).

So begins a brief review of the discussion concerning personality disorder that preceded the publication of the ninth edition of the International Classification of Diseases (ICD–9). It is timely to reconsider the position as ICD–10 is being prepared. The intervening years have seen tentative efforts in research and some standardization of the assessment of personality disorder. However, personality remains one the most controversial and least studied areas of psychiatry, and the quantity of work has been minuscule compared to that on the symptomatology of psychiatric illness. The new section on personality disorder in ICD–10 has been assembled by dint of well-intentioned discussion rather than from research data. Comprehensive epidemiological data, to complete the clinical picture on personality disorder, is still some way away.

One reason for the lack of research must be the persisting doubts about the validity of the diagnosis of personality disorder. To what extent is the clinician using this term in a slipshod fashion to cover inadequate psychiatric assessment, to convey a value judgement, or to justify therapeutic failure? Behind such questions lie the doubts of those who believe that the concept of personality inherent in ICD definitions is flawed.

In this chapter both points of view will be presented: firstly, the arguments of those who aim to clarify 'the diagnostic imprecision and terminological confusion' while working within the traditional concept of personality disorder; and secondly, the point of view which criticizes the existing concepts, so advocating alternative research strategies. The concepts of personality will be discussed before recent research developments. The first author holds the former viewpoint, while the second maintains the latter, and this chapter has been written accordingly.

196

THE CONCEPT OF PERSONALITY AND PERSONALITY DISORDER

The traditional view

Personality is conceived by both ICD and DSM–III as a relatively fixed long-term collection of attitudes and behaviours by which one individual might be identified by another and into which the individual may have full or partial insight. These attributes are thought to become recognizable by adolescence, are generally stable throughout adult life, though they may modify with old age. Head injury is one of the few events that may alter this pattern. Against this background of personality, certain individuals may in clinical parlance be deemed as having a personality abnormality or personality disorder. To enter these categories the individual must posses certain types of attributes and behaviours without exclusion criteria that make them congruent with a particular description in ICD–9 or DSM–III.

The distinction between abnormal premorbid personality and personality disorder has never been defined formally. In practice, the first term is seen as a less marked variation and carries less suffering of handicap for the individual than the latter. Further, the former term is likely to be used if a diagnostic symptom state is also present as well as evidence of a personality abnormality. The latter is likely to be used if the personality attributes alone are the basis of diagnosis.

Clinical diagnosis of personality thus seems to require many arbitrary decisions based upon imprecise information. Where does the clinician derive data about personality attributes? How fixed through life do they have to be? How near a fit is necessary for a particular category to be chosen? How discrete and comprehensive are these taxonomic categories? Can stable personality traits be distinguished in a clinical setting from long-term neurotic symptoms? How much suffering and how much handicap is necessary for diagnosis of personality disorder? None of these questions is answered, yet the concept seems to remain 'indispensable to clinical practice'. Indeed, in 1974, 42 per cent of a consecutive series of Maudsley Hospital in-patient notes contained statements testifying to the significance of personality attributes to the understanding of the clinical picture (Mann et al. 1981a). However, clinicians still seem to use the concept of background personality for their practice despite its imprecision and operational difficulty.

Since 1974 the newer taxonomies have attempted to tackle some of the operational difficulties. DSM–III provides much more stringent inclusion and exclusion criteria for its diagnostic categories of personality; while ICD–10 has created parallel lists, one of personality accentuation, the other of personality disorder. Abnormal premorbid personality now can be classified, along with other diagnoses, rather than being omitted or subsumed under the more forbidding term of personality disorder. Both new systems have increased the range of personality types to try and make the total list more exhaustive. However, the fundamental questions about the clinician's concept

197

of personality, attitudes, behaviours, or self-concepts are not answered. Nor is the question of the persistence of such attributes. The justification for continuing with this imprecise term seems to have several roots. First, its history, for the concept of personality has been in use under one name or another for nearly 130 years. Second, there is the diagnostic imperative, for patients still present with complaints that seem similar to those with symptom states yet who have never developed symptoms. How are these to be labelled? Finally, much research into psychiatric illnesses, particularly into genetic linkage, uses the concept of spectrum which includes personality traits and is often necessary to provide an adequate model for the variable rates of expression of many psychiatric illnesses. It seems unlikely that personality abnormality will vanish from psychiatric parlance and, therefore, it seems relevant to pursue research in this area.

PROBLEMS WITH THE CONCEPT OF PERSONALITY AND PERSONALITY DISORDER

The nature of personality

The difficulty of defining personality and its use as a lay term have complicated discussion and added unnecessarily to the arguments over the nature of personality.

Personality can, therefore, mean different things to different people and can be defined in different ways. A very general definition might be: any psychological attribute of a person which varies between individuals. In the recent controversies over the nature of personality, no one doubts that people differ from one another in their psychological attributes. However, personality is also used in a much more specific way: personal attributes, as above (e.g. honesty), which are related to other attributes (e.g. conscientiousness) and endure over someone's whole lifetime. Within experimental psychology, this more specific view of personality is associated with those who conceptualize personality as 'traits' (e.g. Eysenck 1952; Cattell 1957) but a similar view of personality underlies psychodynamic personality theories (e.g. Storr 1979) and the categorical classification of personality disorders used in psychiatry.

Criticisms of trait theory have come from those experimental psychologists who emphasize the rational, cognitive determinants of social behaviour, who include both social learning theorists (Mischel 1968; Bandura 1977) and cognitive psychologists (Anderson 1980). Mischel (1968) in particular has argued that the trait theory of personality needs empirical support. One cannot begin to study personality if it is defined in a way which implies an unproven theory of personality.

Another point should be made before continuing. Personality can only be a description; it cannot explain or cause behaviour, though it is sometimes

198

used as though it could. Gilbert Ryle (1949) has lucidly argued against this sort of 'explanatory' statement as creating a 'ghost in the machine'. Furthermore, personality traits are usually defined using behavioural measures so it is tautologous to say that a trait caused the behaviour which was used to define the trait in the first place. Wootton (1959) had made a similar point about the use of the terms psychopathic or antisocial personality disorder to explain criminal behaviour, when the criminal behaviour has been used as grounds for the diagnosis.

Lay personality theories

It is a truism to say that ordinary people have their own concept of personality. Allport (1937) found over 11,000 trait terms in English (e.g. outgoing, shy, nervous, intelligent, etc.), and in ordinary social interaction we often ask 'What sort of person is this?: a question that is often answered with a trait term. Allport's list, rooted in lay psychology, formed the basis of Cattell's (1957) and other trait theorists' way of measuring personality. Subjects were asked to rate themselves or others on a variety of trait terms and the results subjected to factor analysis. Cattell, Eysenck, and others interpreted such findings as revealing the underlying dimensions of personality but one can also interpret the results as reflecting the theory of personality used by ordinary people.

This interpretation is supported by the key experiment of Passini and Norman (1966). In the late 1950s and 1960s one group had shown that factor analysis of trait ratings from a variety of different studies all produced a similar five-factor result (Norman 1963). But Passini and Norman (1966) found an almost identical five-factor solution when raters who had only seen people for less than fifteen minutes and had not spoken to each other were asked to rate the subjects as they imagined they would be. This 'five-factor personality structure' therefore appeared to reflect the way ordinary people characterize each other, rather than representing the underlying structure of personality. Tyrer and Alexander (1979), though, argue that the similarity of the factor structure in those with and without personality disorders supports the idea that personality disorder is an extreme variant of normal, but it could merely reflect the 'personality theories' used by the informants and interviewers.

Situations

One of the key issues in the personality literature has been the assertion that behaviour is influenced by the situation as well as by personal factors. Trait-rating scales already imply cross-situational consistency and to examine whether people really do behave similarly in different situations needs direct behavioural measurement.

A number of such studies has been done and Mischel (1968), among others, has pointed out that the correlation coefficients in these studies (with the exception of that for intelligence) are usually very modest, less than 0.3 and account for less than 10 per cent of the variance. For instance, Hartshorne and May's (1928) study of school children found that the average correlations between cheating on four different tests was only 0.26, though the correlation between cheating on the same test on different occasions was 0.66. Mischel and Peake (1982) conducted two 'delay of reinforcement' studies on the same group of children which only differed in a single respect – in one group the experimenter remained in the room. The correlation coefficient between the two was only 0.22.

Mischel's conclusions have been challenged (e.g. Epstein 1979) but the data against substantial cross-situational consistency seem overwhelming. Broad behavioural consistencies must exist (a correlation coefficient of 0.3 is significant if the sample is large enough) but are too small to be of any use in predicting the behaviour of individual poeple.

When a thinking and reasoning person enters a situation it would be unlikely, indeed maladaptive, for broad personality traits to have a strong influence on behaviour. Perhaps cross-situational consistency should be regarded as a sign of an 'abnormal personality'? Indeed, Tyrer *et al.* (1979) have suggested that cross-situational consistency is more apparent in those classified as personality disordered.

The medical concept of personality disorder therefore rests on the rather shaky foundations of traditional personality theory.

State vs. Trait: can neurosis be distinguished from personality disorder?

Social learning theory does not need to make the distinction between state and trait. All behaviour, whether exhibited over a great length of time or only covering a short period, would have the same basis in beliefs and attitudes and their interaction with the environment (Mischel 1968; Beck 1976).

Many authors have shown that those with personality disorder experience neurotic symptoms (e.g. Lazare and Klerman 1968; Slavney and McHugh 1974; Gunn and Robertson 1976; Thompson and Goldberg 1987). Furthermore, some personality inventories, particularly the scales measuring 'neuroticism', appear to correlate markedly with measures of mental illness, and change with recovery from depression (Coppen and Metcalfe 1965; Kendell and DiScipio 1968; Hirschfeld *et al.* 1983). The distinction between trait and state may be an attractive simplification but there is still no way of distinguishing a neurotic trait from a neurotic state, nor a personality disorder from a chronic neurosis. Shepherd *et al.* (1968), in their international study of diagnostic habits, noted that personality disorder in one culture was neurosis in another.

Replacing the concept of personality disorder with the simpler and more comprehensive idea of chronic neurosis would fit the available evidence, but some features of personality disorder are not neurotic symptoms. For instance, the concept of antisocial personality disorder, at least in DSM–III, includes committing crimes. But many critics have pointed out the legal and philosophical difficulties of psychiatric explanations of crime (e.g. Wootton 1959). There are, therefore, definite advantages if psychiatrists abandon the impulse to explain all deviant behaviour.

Personality disorder and mental illness

Among all the controversy there is, surprisingly, one area of relative agreement: that personality disorder is not a mental illness (Lewis 1974). Though Henderson (1939) and Cleckley (1941) disagree, more recently personality disorder has increasingly been distinguished from illness.

Whatever mental illness means (Lewis 1953; Farrell 1979), it implies among other things a lack of control over behaviour and a lack of responsibility for action. The inference that an action is not under control has been linked with sympathy and willingness to help (Weiner 1980). In the contexts of a psychological abnormality, mental illness can be seen as a label conferring reduced responsibility for behaviour, legitimizing medical care, and encouraging sympathy.

Lewis and Appleby (1987) have thus argued that the assertion that personality disorder is used as a derogatory moral judgement (Gunn and Robertson 1976) results from the exclusion of personality disorder from the category of mental illness. Their study provided some evidence for this, based on questionnaire responses to case vignettes given the diagnosis of personality disorder. Compared with control vignettes, cases with personality disorder were seen as manipulative, attention-seeking, less sympathetic, not deserving NHS resources, and not being mentally ill. Someone who has a personality disorder is seen neither as normal nor as mentally ill; the worst of all possible worlds.

The claim that personality disorder is a derogatory moral judgement seriously questions the place of personality disorder in a scientific classification of mental disorder. Classifying these individuals as suffering from chronic neuroses would rely less on precarious theories of personality, would not be attempting to explain all deviant behaviour, and hopefully would eliminate a pejorative term from the psychiatric taxonomy.

CLINICAL RESEARCH INTO PERSONALITY DISORDER

The traditional view

Assuming the concept of personality disorder as reflected in ICD–9 or DSM–III can be tolerated, several basic research steps have to be taken before embarking on studies of prevalence and associations.

These general principles will be discussed before three published assessment schedules are described: the Standard Assessment of Personality (SAP, Mann *et al.* 1981a), the Personality Assessment Schedule (PAS, Tyrer and

Alexander 1979) and the Personality Disorder Examination (PDE) (Loranger *et al.* 1987).

a) *Standardizing data collection:* In clinical psychiatric practice it is usual to interview an informant for data on personality because most patients' abnormal mental states distort self concepts. However, self-report of habitual traits is possible in patients with a primary diagnosis of personality disorder. The difference between self-report and informant ratings was demonstrated in a study that assessed DSM–III personality disorder (Stangl *et al* 1985). Cases for whom there was an informant were almost twice as likely to be given a diagnosis of personality disorder. Thus, informants seem to provide more diagnostic information though they may not be available and they may be biased. This last point has been addressed to some extent in attempts to establish inter-informant agreement. This was poor, both when staff members were informants and when self and informant ratings were compared (Tyrer and Alexander 1979). However, in a study of obsessional patients, there was better agreement when both informants were relatives (McKeon *et al*, 1984). The best source of reliable personality information has not yet been resolved.

b) *Definition of the boundary:* The severity of personality abnormality necessary for inclusion in a diagnosis of personality disorder needs to be established. The ICD–9 definition, although imprecise, implies that for a disorder to be present the individual will be suffering, or others will, on account of personality. The DSM–III definition indicates inflexibility of trait, subjective distress, or social impairment. These definitions are intended to separate personality disorder from an intermediate state where a trait is present but there is no personal suffering. Frances (1982) argued for a dimensional approach to personality disorder, obviating the need for such arbitary boundaries.

The three diagnostic schedules contain different criteria for severity. The PAS emphasizes the need for impaired social adjustment for a diagnosis of personality disorder. Using the PDE, the clinicians can make a judgement on the basis of the responses to the standard questions in the schedule or can use a predetermined value of the total score. In the SAP the personality abnormality is called marked (Grade 2) and is equivalent to personality disorder if the informant reports the personality attribute either as extreme ('the most houseproud person I know') or handicapping social functioning. However, the SAP differs from the other two schedules as it recognizes an intermediate (Grade 1) category, similar to the concepts of Personality Accentuation defined by Leonhard (1968) and of abnormal premorbid personality used clinically and now recognized in ICD–10.

c) *Development of the taxonomy:* A descriptive typology of personality has evolved, based upon detailed clinical vignettes such as the sensitive personality disorder (Kretschmer 1918) and the psychopathic disorders described by Schneider (1950). Some personality types are similar in clinical features to a psychiatric symptom state, others have putative aetiological relationships to a psychiatric syndrome.

Even the existing typologies, however, are unable to categorize those personality abnormalities relevant to psychiatric practice. For example, only nineteen of a consecutive series of forty-two abnormal personalities among neurotic patients and twenty-nine of fifty-seven abnormal personalities discovered among psychotic patients could be matched to an ICD–9 category (Mann et al. 1981a, Cutting et al. 1986). The more recently derived DSM–III typography overlaps with that of ICD–9 but contains some categories that have roots in psychoanalytic theory (borderline, narcissistic, and passive aggressive personalities) which have not yet met universal acceptance.

The PAS and SAP have dealt with the inadequacy of ICD–9 in two separate ways. The SAP incorporates two new categories, not found in ICD–9, derived from case-note accounts of abnormal personalities. For the PAS, personality data were collected from a range of subjects with and without abnormal personality, and subjected to a factor analysis which defined four main categories: socio-pathic, passive-dependent, anhankastic and schizoid, with nine sub-groups. It is claimed to provide a better fit for clinical personality data than the historical derived descriptions (Tyrer and Ferguson 1987). The PDE, in contrast to these two, has been designed to fit the DSM–III typology without modifications.

d) *Achievement of reliability:* As with any standard measure for research, personality assessments must be capable of generating good inter-rater reliability among users. To this end, well-designed questionnaires with clear directions and definitions combined with preliminary training are needed. The three schedules have now published evidence of adequate inter-rater reliability for some of the personality categories, a considerable improvement on the more dismal reports based upon clinical assessment rather than standardized assessment schedules (Walton and Presley 1973, Mellsop et al. 1982).

e) *Evidence of validity:* Two further forms of reliability need consideration, inter-temporal reliability and, for the schedules that derive data from informants, inter-informant reliability. Adequate reliability of these forms will, in part, confirm the validity of the assessment. Demonstrable stability of personality categorization over time, preferably despite fluctuations of symptoms, conforms with the ICD–9 concept of 'persistently deeply ingrained traits' while satisfactory inter-informant reliability would help to overcome anxiety about informants' bias and show that the attribute is not confined to one relationship or setting. However, external validity must in time be demonstrated, for example by concurrent validity with other forms of personality assessment and predictive validity between a personality category and specific physiological, behavioural, or illness variables.

The three schedules

The Standard Assessment of Personality. This is a brief interview of an informant along clinical lines in which informant data are used to classify the

Table 14.1 Reliability of SAP: Weighted Kappa Values

	Inter-rater	Inter-temporal	Inter-informant
Self conscious	0.67, 0.47	0.41, 0.96	0.88
Schizoid			
Paranoid		0.41	
Cyclothymic	0.85, 0.78	0.13	
Anhankastic	0.60, 1.00	0.74, 0.76	0.93
Anxious	0.61	0.42, 0.96	0.96
Asthenic			
Sociopathic	1.00		
Explosive	0.90		
Hysterical	0.91		

patient's personality as normal or into one of ten abnormal categories. The severity of the abnormal personality can be graded as a result of the interview. This schedule has now been used to assess patients' personalities in various settings: general practice (Mann *et al*. 1981a), hospital admission unit (Cutting *et al*. 1986), mental handicap hospital (Ballinger and Reid 1987), and for research (McKeon *et al*. 1984). Each of these research groups examined some aspects of inter-rater, inter-temporal, or inter-informant reliability of the assessment of the SAP categories. The results from these papers are grouped together in table 14.1.

Some categories of personality have been so rare in the populations studied, that reliability calculations were not possible. For the remainder, the weighted Kappa (KW) value is always greater than 0.4, considered adequate agreement at a level just statistically significant. The failure of the cyclothymic category to reach a satisfactory level of inter-temporal reliability suggests that this label might not be appropriately placed in a section on personality.

Some data on the distribution of the abnormal personality categories are available from the published studies. Thirty-three per cent of general practice patients with neuroses were classed as having abnormal personality compared with 44 per cent of the hospital admission cohort (Mann *et al*. 1981b, Cutting *et al*. 1986). In contrast, 75 per cent of the mental handicap sample were so graded (Ballinger and Reid 1987).

The general practice study showed some predictive ability of the SAP personality categories (Mann *et al*. 1981b). Patients assessed as having marked personality abnormality at the outset of a twelve-month follow-up period were discovered to be over-represented among the frequent attenders. They were also more likely than the others to present with symptoms such as headache and dizziness, and personality classification predicted receipt of psychotropic medication more accurately than did the initial symptom state.

The Personality Assessment Schedule. Data for this schedule can be derived from an interview with the subject, with an informant, or by personal observation of the patient by the interviewer. While an interview with an informant should always be sought, the subject's mental state may preclude self-report information. Twenty-four personality variables are rated on a nine-point scale, the highest scores indicating increasing social dysfunction as well as possession of personality characteristics to a márked degree. There is satisfactory reliability between two interviewers (KW more than 0.5 for all twenty-four variables). Inter-temporal reliability however varied for the twenty-four variables, the KW ranging from 0 to +0.59. However, once these personality data had been grouped into the four major diagnostic categories, agreement between the two occasions was much higher (KW 0.64) (Tyrer *et al.* 1982).

Personality Disorder Examination. Designed systematically to survey the phenomenology and life experiences relevant to the diagnosis of personality disorder in DSM–III, this schedule is administered by an interviewer (Loranger *et al.* 1987). The personality disorder can be categorized either by using a computer algorithm or by the clinician interviewer making a clinical diagnosis. Good inter-rater reliability was reported both for individual items of the schedule and also for the diagnostic classification (KW 0.7–0.96) for the five DSM–III categories that were sufficiently common for statistical calculations to be made. Surprisingly, borderline personality was included in these categories despite being reported elsewhere as hard to distinguish from other DSM–III categories (Pope *et al.* 1983) and in need of improved definition. Such contradiction implies that the PDE may need further evaluation.

Conclusion

In conclusion, the proponent can claim modest advances by the creation of standardized schedules that psychiatrists can use reliably to assess the current clinical concept of personality. However, the data generated so far are limited and few of them specifically derived for the purpose of exploring the distribution and relationships of personality categories.

ALTERNATIVE APPROACHES TO STUDYING PERSONALITY DISORDER

Reliability

Trait ratings require global judgements based on ambiguous data. This vagueness must contribute towards the unreliability of personality assessment, and the trait ratings themselves can be very unreliable even in research settings (Gunn and Robertson 1976). There is now a striking contrast between the mental illness section of DSM–III or ICD–10, with its exactly specified operational criteria, and the section on personality disorder, with its rather vague trait descriptions. Antisocial personality disorder continues to be the most reliable of all the categories (Mellsop *et al*. 1982), possibly because the criteria include behavioural items (mostly about infringements of the law) as well as trait terms. It is ironic that the most reliable of all the personality disorder categories has also attracted the most controversy about its validity (Wootton 1959; Frances 1980).

Validity

Pre-existing beliefs or schemata can influence perception, memory, and social inferences (Anderson 1980) and in general the bias acts in order to confirm such beliefs (Nisbett and Ross 1980). Trait ratings are particularly suscept-ible, and such a confirmatory bias challenges the validity of trait ratings in assessing personality and in part explains why personality continues to make intuitive sense despite evidence to the contrary.

Cantor and Mischel (1979) illustrated a bias in recalling trait terms. They asked subjects (Ss) to remember a set of trait terms that applied to an imaginary person (e.g. that together described an extravert). When Ss were asked later to recognize these items they also recognized items that were related to the original trait (e.g. extravert) but which had not been originally presented. Once impressions are formed, they can have a powerful influence on memory. As Mischel (1968) has asserted, trait rating scales lead to infor-mation about what is in the mind of the rater, as well as, or even instead of, the behaviour of the rated.

These biases may also influence clinical assessment. For instance, suicidal thoughts in someone with a personality disorder could be seen as manipulative or histrionic, and therefore attract less sympathy and importance than the same complaints in someone regarded as 'ill'.

Alternative approaches to studying personality

What are the alternative strategies in attempting to study this difficult area? Personal attributes are probably important in determining vulnerability to mental illness; how can these attributes be assessed and studied?

Social learning theorists think of personality as a collection of personal attitudes and beliefs. Warr and his colleagues have developed a scale measur-ing commitment to work (including, for example, 'Even if I was given £1m I would still want to work') and have shown that those with a higher commit-ment to work have better mental health when in work and worse mental health when unemployed. Furthermore, they could demonstrate some predic-tive value for the scale, both when adolescents became unemployed (Jackson *et al*. 1983) and in predicting worsening of mental health in middle-aged men as unemployment continues (Warr and Jackson 1985).

This series of studies provides a model for studying personal attributes and their relationship with mental illness and shows an interaction between attitudes and the impact of a life event; a different approach to the personal meaning of life events (cf Brown and Harris 1978). It also illustrates the link between an individual's attitudes and societal norms, in this instance the social and economic importance of the 'work ethic' (Weber 1930).

This discussion may seem unrelated to the traditional preoccupations of personality disorder research. However, attitudes to work vary between people and are in all senses part of someone's personality, and part of the clinical assessment, particularly of the unemployed. The social learning approach to personality has many advantages; it does not use trait terms as a means of assessment nor imply a pre-existing theory of personality. It looks at the particular attitudes and beliefs of interest rather than trying to give a comprehensive description of the whole person, a Herculean task. Finally, the causes of mental as well as physical disorders must ultimately require social and economic explanations. Describing personality as a collection of attitudes may clarify the links between these socio-economic forces and the more proximate causes of mental illness.

This approach is more precise, less 'terminologically confused' than traditional approaches to personality and in time may become more indispensable to clinical practice than that unhappy ragbag of diagnosis, the personality disorders.

Acknowledgement: Glyn Lewis is supported by the Health Promotion Research Trust.

REFERENCES

Allport, G.W. (1937) *Personality: A Psychological Interpretation*, New York: Holt.

Anderson, J.R. (1980) *Cognitive Psychology and its Implications*, San Francisco. Freeman.

Ballinger, B.R. and Reid, A.H. (1987) 'A standardized assessment of personality in mental handicap', *British Journal of Psychiatry* 150: 108–9.

Bandura, A. (1977) *Social Learning Theory*, Englewood Cliffs, NJ: Prentice-Hall.

Beck, A.T. (1976) *Cognitive Therapy and the Emotional Disorders*, International University Press: New York.

Cantor, N. and Mischel, W. (1979) 'Traits as Prototypes: Effects on Recognition Memory', *Journal of Personality and Social Psychology* 35: 38–48.

Cattell, R.B. (1957) *Personality and Motivation: Structure & Measurement*, Yonkers-on-Hudson: World Books.

Chodoff, P. and Lyons, H (1958) 'Hysteria, the Hysterical Personality and "Hysterical" Conversion', *American Journal of Psychiatry* 114: 734–40.

Coppen, A. and Metcalfe, M. (1965) 'Effect of a depressive illness on MPI scores', *British Journal of Psychiatry* 111: 236–9.

Cutting, J., Cowan, P.J., Mann, A.H., and Jenkins, R. (1986) 'Personality and psychosis: use of the standard assessment', *Acta Psychiatrica Scandinavica* 73: 87–92.

Epstein, S. (1979) 'The stability of behaviour: 1: on predicting most of the people much of the time', *Journal of Personality and Social Psychology* 37: 1097–125.

Eysenck, J.J. (1952) *The Scientific Study of Personality*, London: Routledge & Kegan Paul.

Farrell, B.A. (1979) 'Mental illness: a conceptual analysis', *Psychological Medicine* 9: 21–35.

Frances, A. (1980) 'The DSM–III personality disorders: a commentary', *American Journal of Psychiatry* 137: 1050–4.

Frances, A. (1982) 'Categorial and dimensional systems of personality disorder', *Comprehensive Psychiatry* 23: 516–27.

Gunn, J. and Robertson, G. (1976) 'Psychopathic personality: a conceptual problem', *Psychological Medicine* 6: 631–34.

Hartshorne, H. and May, M.A. (1928) *Studies in the Nature of Character: Volume 1: Studies in Deceit*, New York: Macmillan.

Henderson, D.K. (1939) *Psychopathic States*, London.

Hirschfield, R.M.A., Klerman, G.L., Clayton, P.J., Keller, M.B., McDonald-Scott, P., and Larkin, B.H. (1983) 'Assessing personality: effects of the depressive state on trait measurement', *American Journal of Psychiatry* 140: 695–9.

Jackson, P.R., Stafford, E.M., Banks, M.H., and Warr, P.B. (1983) 'Unemployment and psychological distress in young people: the moderating role of employment commitment', *Journal of Applied Psychology* 68: 525–35.

Kendell, R.E. and DiScipio, W.J. (1968) 'Eysenck Personality Inventory Scores of patients with depressive illness', *British Journal of Psychiatry* 114: 767–70.

Kretschmer, E. (1918) *Die Sensitive Beziehungswan*, Berlin: Springer.

Lazare, A. and Klerman, G.L. (1968) 'Hysteria and depression: the frequency and significance of hysterical personality features in hospitalised depressed women', *American Journal of Psychiatry* 124: Supplement 48–56.

Leonard, K. (1967) *Kinder-neurosen und Kinder-persönlichkeiten* (3 Auflage), Berlin: Veb Verlag Volk und Gesundheit.

Lewis, A. (1953) 'Health as a social concept', *British Journal of Sociology* 4: 109–24.

Lewis, A. (1974) 'Psychopathic personality: a most elusive category', *Psychological Medicine* 4: 133–40.

Lewis, G.H. and Appleby, L.A. (in press) 'Personality disorder: the patients psychiatrists dislike', *British Journal of Psychiatry*.

Loranger, A.W., Susman, V.L., Oldham, J.M., and Russikoff, L.M. (1987) 'The personality disorder examination: a preliminary report', *Journal of Personality Disorders* 1(1).

McKeon, J., Roa, B., and Mann, A.H. (1984) 'Life events and personality traits in obsessive compulsive neurosis', *British Journal of Psychiatry* 144: 185–9.

Mann, A.H., Jenkins, R., Cutting, J.C., and Cowen, P.J. (1981a) 'The development and use of a standardised assessment of abnormal personality', *Psychological Medicine* 11: 839–47.

Mann, A.H., Jenkins, R., and Belsey, E. (1981b) 'The 12-month outcome of patients with neurotic illness in general practice', *Psychological Medicine* 11: 535–60.

Mellsop, G., Varghese, F., Joshua, A.S., and Hicks, A. (1982) 'Reliability of axis II of DSM–III', *American Journal of Psychiatry* 139: 1360–1.

Mischel, W. (1968) *Personality and Assessment*, New York: Wiley.

Mischel, W. and Peake, P.K. (1982) 'Some facets of consistency: replies to Epstein, Funder & Bem', *Psychological Reviews* 90: 394–402.

Nisbett, R. and Ross, L. (1980) *Human Inferences: Strategies and Shortcomings of Social Judgement*, Englewood Cliffs, NJ: Prentice-Hall.

Norman, W.T. (1963) 'Toward an adequate taxonomy of personality attributes: replicated factor structure in peer nomination personality ratings', *Journal of Abnormal and Social Psychology* 66: 574–83.

Passini, F.T. and Norman, W.T. (1966) 'A universal conception of personality structure?', *Journal of Personality and Social Psychology* 4: 44–9.

Pope, H.G., Jones, J.M., Hudson, J.I., Cohen, B.M., Gunderson, J.G. (1983) 'The validity of DSM–III personality disorders', *Archives of General Psychiatry* 40: 23–30.

Ryle, G. (1949) *The Concept of Mind* London, Hutchinson.

Schneider, K. (1950) *Psychopathic Personalities*, translated by M. Hamilton, London: Cassel.

Slavney, P.R. and McHugh, P.R. (1974) 'The hysterical personality: a controlled study', *Archives of General Psychiatry* 30: 325–9.

Shepherd, M., Brooke, E.M., Cooper, J.E., and Lin, T. (1968) 'An experimental approach to psychiatric diagnosis', *Acta Psychiatrica Scandinavica* Supplementum 201.

Shepherd, M. and Sartorius, N. (1974) 'Personality disorder and the classification of diseases', *Psychological Medicine* 4: 141–6.

Stangl, D., Pfohl, B., Zimmerman, M., Bowers, W., and Corenthal, C. (1985) 'A standardized interview for DSM–III personality disorders', *Archives of General Psychiatry* 42: 597–601.

Storr, A. (1979) *The Art of Psychotherapy*, London: Secker & Warburg.

Tyrer, P and Alexander, J. (1979) 'Classification of personality disorder', *British Journal of Psychiatry* 135: 163–7.

Tyrer, P., Alexander, M.S., Cicchetti, D., Cohen, M.S., and Remington, M. (1979) 'Reliability of a schedule for rating personality disorders', *British Journal of Psychiatry* 135: 168–74.

Tyrer, P. and Ferguson, B. (1987) 'Problems in the classification of personality disorders', *Psychological Medicine* 17: 15–20.

Tyrer, P., Strauss, J., and Cicchetti, D. (1982) 'Temporal reliability of a schedule for rating personality disorders', *Psychological Medicine* 13: 393–8.

Thompson, D.J. and Goldberg, D. (1987) 'Hysterical personality disorder: the process of diagnosis in clinical & experimental settings', *British Journal of Psychiatry* 150: 241–5.

Walton, H.J. and Presley, A.S. (1973) 'Use of a categoric system in diagnosis of abnormal personality', *British Journal of Psychiatry* 122: 259–68.

Warr, P.B. and Jackson, P.R. (1985) 'Factors influencing the psychological impact of prolonged unemployment and of re-employment', *Psychological Medicine* 15: 795–807.

Weber, M. (1930) *The Protestant Ethic and the Spirit of Capitalism* London: Allen and Unwin.

Weiner, B. (1980) 'A cognitive (attribution) – emotion – action model of motivated behaviour: an analysis of judgements of help giving', *Journal of Personality and Social Psychology* 39: 186–200

Wootton, B. (1959) *Social Science and Social Pathology* London: George Allen.

15

The Relationship Between Physical and Psychological Morbidity

Robin Eastwood

The work done at the General Practice Research Unit at the Institute of Psychiatry has led to a better understanding of the role of the general practitioner in treating mental illness. The gain in knowledge has been significant in several areas, including the prevalence of mental illness in the community, the chronicity of this illness, the difficulties of diagnosis, and the realization of the important associations with physical illness and social factors. The early findings were summarized by Shepherd *et al.* (1966: 169). They made the following points:

> Emotional disorder in the survey sample was found to be related to a high demand for medical care. Those patients identified as suffering from psychiatric illness attended more frequently and exhibited higher rates of general morbidity and more categories of illness per head than the remainder of the patients consulting their doctors. Furthermore, patients with chronic psychiatric illness were particularly frequent attenders and appeared to constitute a highly vulnerable group from the point of view of loss of work and permanent incapacity.

Sub-studies further supported these main findings and enabled the group to take the view that 'chronic psychiatric disturbance is positively associated with other forms of chronic ill-health' (Shepherd *et al.* 1966: 170); and that the high illness-expectation could be seen as 'illness-proneness' (Hinkle and Wolff 1957) which might be further examined by longitudinal studies.

The stage was then set for the group to elaborate the findings by enhancing the methodology and further testing the relationships. The General Health Questionnaire was developed as a screening instrument (Goldberg 1972) and the Clinical Interview Schedule (Goldberg *et al.* 1970) as a diagnostic instrument. Mental illness appeared to have associations with both social factors (Kedward and Sylph 1974; Cooper 1972) and physical illness and I had the task of confirming the latter. The initial design and method problems were:

(1) To obtain a random sample of the general population;
(2) To screen and further examine for mental illness;
(3) To screen and further examine for physical disorder;
(4) To test the association between psychiatric and physical disorder.

SAMPLING

The need for a random sample of the general population was obvious and critical. Psychosocial factors influence illness presentation. Thus, clinicians presume that a biological component determines a consultation, but 'illness behaviour' is important, being a composite of the way in which an individual perceives, evaluates, and acts upon his symptoms in his particular social setting (Mechanic 1966).

There are those who are ill and fail to consult and, conversely, those who make a habit of consulting, whatever their state of health. Genuine illness has to be teased out from other factors in a medical consultation. This problem has been elegantly discussed by Goldberg and Huxley (1980). In their extensive review they particularly mention the work of Mechanic and his considerable contributions to our understanding of the determinants of perceived health status.

SCREENING

Screening for disease was in vogue in the 1950s and 1960s. Multiple screening surveys started in the United States and the proposed definition of the Commission on Chronic Illness (1957) was that screening was 'the presumptive identification of unrecognized disease or defect by the application of the tests, examination or other procedures which can be applied rapidly.' The World Health Organization monograph by Wilson and Jungner (1968) said that the purpose was to discover and cure disease in its early stages before medical help was sought and to make the best economic use of the available medical manpower. Screening for psychiatric disorder, in my study, has been discussed at length (Eastwood 1971, Eastwood 1975) and the utility of psychiatric screening has been dealt with elsewhere (Goldberg 1974; Goldberg and Huxley 1980; Goldberg 1986; Williams 1986). Suffice to make three brief points in regard to screening: first, apart from phenylketonuria, hardly any diseases have satisfied general screening criteria; second, psychiatric disorder has not been approved generally for screening; and third, this fortunately has not stopped psychiatric case finding for research purposes with a variety of screening instruments and clinical interview schedules. In the St Paul's Cray Study screening was done with the modified version of the Cornell Medical Index and the second stage with the Clinical Interview

211

Schedule. Today, the General Health Questionnaire would replace the Cornell Medical Index and the choice for the second stage would be between such instruments as the Clinical Interview Schedule, the Present State Examination (Wing *et al.* 1967) and the Schedule for Affective Disorders and Schizophrenia (Endicott and Spitzer 1978).

Screening for physical disease was the main intention of the St Paul's Cray study. Early assessments of screening (McKeown 1968) suggested that the evidence was deficient for most chronic disorders, particularly cost-effectiveness and natural history. Although screening for disease has not been found generally acceptable (South-East London Screening Study Group 1977), the St Paul's Cray screening protocol (Eastwood 1975) was adequate for testing the relationship between physical and psychiatric disorder.

RESULTS

Results of the St Paul's Cray study were as follows:

(1) A 71 per cent response rate was obtained with a fairly homogeneous population made up of persons between the ages of 40 and 64, largely married and of the skilled artisan class.

(2) From 369 clinical interviews, 124 matched pairs, consisting of a psychiatric patient and a normal control, were derived.

(3) The psychiatric cases were largely the minor, neurotic cases seen in general practice, although some were of moderate severity, with the men having more personality disorders and the women more hypochrondiacal neuroses. A substantial number of the cases, the less severe variety, had not been recognized by the general practitioners prior to the survey. Thus, 19 per cent of the men and 27.5 per cent of the women had a psychiatric disturbance unknown to the general practitioner and a further 21.6 per cent of the men and 25.2 per cent of the women were similarly unknown but had had a recognized psychiatric illness in the past. The more serious disorders were known to the general practitioners.

(4) Both male and female psychiatric cases had more major physical and major psychosomatic conditions than normal controls, and the males more minor physical conditions and minor psychosomatic conditions.

(5) Multiple physical disorders occurred more among the psychiatric cases and these increased with the severity of psychiatric disorder, especially major physical conditions.

(6) The findings confirmed a positive association between physical and psychiatric disorder with a tendency for clustering of illnesses to occur in some individuals (Eastwood 1975).

SUBSEQUENT WORK IN THE NEXT TWO DECADES

Since this study was mounted there has been a variety of investigations and commentaries. A literature search showed these to be legion and it would be impossible and invidious to attempt to include them all. What is done here is to describe several studies which have been seminal or accounts which have collated contemporary wisdom in this area (other publications are frequently cited in these works).

In the ensuing years several studies have fleshed out the findings. Goldberg and Blackwell (1970) undertook a unique study. Both were psychiatrists, with a common training, but it so happened that Goldberg was working, at that time, as a research psychiatrist and Blackwell as a general practitioner.

Some 200 attenders at the general practice survey were interviewed by both, with complete agreement upon diagnosis for two-thirds of the patients. Presenting symptoms were classified along a spectrum between entirely physical complaints and those entirely psychiatric. Least agreement occurred with physical illness in a neurotic personality, physical illness with associated psychiatric disturbance, psychiatric disturbance with somatic symptoms and unrelated physical and psychiatric disorder. 'Conspicuous psychiatric morbidity' was found in two-thirds and 'hidden psychiatric morbidity' in one-third, with the latter differing in both attitude toward illness and presenting physical symptoms.

What is unique about this study is that both physicians were trained psychiatrists from the same post-graduate school but functioning in different roles at that time. Their failure to agree in one-third of psychiatric cases, given their level of training, must indicate the inchoate nature of much morbidity at the general practice level. If difficult for these newly trained and enthusiastic specialists, then a most complicated clinical mosaic for the average generalist.

Goldberg *et al.* (1976) repeated the study in Philadelphia with similar findings. In *Mental Illness in the Community* (Goldberg and Huxley 1980), Goldberg points out how common it is for psychiatric patients, in all sorts of settings, to present with nonspecific physical symptoms. Later Bridges and Goldberg (1985) spelt out this somatic manifestation of psychiatric disorder, 'somatization', in general practice in DSM-III terms. In this study patients had to satisfy certain criteria: these were seeking help for somatic manifestations of psychiatric illness (these had to be considered by the patient to be caused by a physical problem when seeing their general practitioner); having a psychiatric diagnosis when seen by the research psychiatrist and a condition assumed to be treatable by a psychiatric means producing symptom relief. Some 417 inceptions were classified and in a subsequent analysis the following information emerged. The initial analysis showed that of patients presenting to their general practitioner 54 per cent had a physical disease, 13 per cent an adjustment disorder, and 33 per cent a psychiatric disorder. Subsequent analyses showed the relationship of these three presentations to each other and to somatization. Finally, the types of psychiatric presentation were presented. Thirty-two per cent had pure somatization disorder, 27 per cent a psychiatric disorder with co-existing physical illness, 17 per cent with a purely psychological presentation, and 24 per cent with facultative somatization. (Although these patients somatized to the general practitioner, they did not do so to the research psychiatrist.) Thus over 50 per cent of cases consulting general practitioners with a psychiatric disorder had a somatic presentation. Finally, while the general practitioners were good at recognizing purely psychiatric disorder, they tended to be misled by somatization. The rest of the undetected cases had a physical illness. In this important paper the authors discuss the implications of psychiatric illness in primary care presenting so frequently with somatic symptoms. They point out that the failure to detect and treat will be a burden to the patient, it may affect an accompanying physical illness, and could lead to a great deal of extra subsequent consulting behaviour. The authors wondered why the majority of patients with diagnosable psychiatric disorders only present somatically to their family doctor.

In a recent review of depression in primary care, Blacker and Clare (1987) argue for a reciprocal connection between mental and physical illness, but question any direct aetiology because of such factors as skewed consulting patterns and threshold effects by patients in primary care, possible age effects and physical illness delaying recovery from mental illness.

Corresponding work has been undertaken in Australia and the United States. Andrews *et al.* (1977, 1978) confirmed the relationship between physical and mental illness in a random sample in Sydney, and also looked at social factors. All illness was assessed by questionnaire. Twenty-four per cent had psychiatric and 46 per cent one or more physical conditions, with 15 per cent having an overlap. Psychiatric illness was independent of age and more common among females; physical illness was also more common, but to a lesser extent, among females and increased with age. All illness was predicted by life events, poor upbringing and poor social support, and, separately, low occupational status to physical illness and poor coping style to mental illness. Social factors accounted for some variance in physical illness (20 per cent) and mental illness (37 per cent).

The US findings come from the Epidemiologic Catchment Area studies (ECA). Shepherd (1987), in an editorial in the *American Journal of Public Health*, pointed out that his 1960s British study, identifying a 14 per cent period prevalence for psychiatric disorder in the community and largely treated by primary care physicians, had been subsequently confirmed and supported in Europe and the US. The ECA studies were set up in the late 1970s and have been described in detail (Eaton and Kessler 1985). The programme was set up to collect incidence and prevalence data for mental illness in several cities across the United States; and to assess the need for and utilization by both health and mental health services per person in community samples. The most recent paper by Kessler *et al.* (1987) from five of these cities found medical users to have a prevalence rate of 21.7 per cent, compared with 16.7 per cent for non-users, for DIS disorders. This confirms significant rates of psychiatric disorder among medical service users and reiterates that much psychiatric disorder is seen and treated by those in primary care.

Several authors cited in this paper have suggested that age has a bearing upon the connection between physical and mental illness. However, Eastwood and Corbin (1986) have pointed out that, based on empirical evidence, few conclusions regarding a generalized relationship between physical illness and depression in old age can be drawn. For a start, physical illness increases in old age and depression does not. Associations appear to be nonspecific, heterogeneous, likely multiple and require multi-variate analysis. In other words, 'the heterogeneity of evidence appears to support the concept of multiple etiology in chronic disease, both physical and psychological, and multiple responses by aged individuals to health-threatening agents across variable situations.' (Eastwood and Corbin 1986: 184)

LONGITUDINAL STUDIES

Another way of looking at the relationship between physical and mental disorder is the longitudinal method, which may be prospective or case control. This approach has been adopted many times in past decades with, perhaps, the most recent publication being from the Stirling County Group under the directorship of Professor Alexander Leighton. The authors point out that the gist of the previous findings has been a definite association between psychiatric disorder and premature death, with the trend being for death to be increasingly due to unnatural causes, suicide and accident, rather than natural ones. Some recent studies failed to show any excess of natural deaths in psychiatric patients, including such community surveys as the Midtown Manhattan.

The Stirling County study paper (Murphy *et al.* 1987) examined the association between affective disorders and mortality in a sixteen-year follow-up, 1952–68, from a general population in Nova Scotia. In 1952 there were 456 men and 547 women in the survey; 5 per cent of the men and 10 per cent of the women had co-existing affective and physical disorder. By 1968, 24 per cent of the subjects were dead. Depression, not age or anxiety, was significantly associated with excess mortality. (The Standardized Mortality Ratio (SMR) was 2.1 for men and 1.2 for women.) The association was striking in such groups as both sexes under 50 years of age, both with circulatory diseases and cancer in women. Most of the depressive illnesses and about half the anxiety states had a poor outcome. Physical disorders by themselves were at the outset not associated with excess mortality. The authors point out the familiar finding that women have more physical ailments than men but live longer and quote the Almeda County study to the effect that it is not physical health problems that bear on mortality but rather health practices such as diet, fitness, and alcohol consumption. The Stirling County Study suggests that psychiatric rather than physical problems predicate mortality. This means depression, rather than anxiety, with the paradox that men have higher mortality rates and less depression. The Stirling County Study differs from other studies in finding similar rates of depression for the sexes, which the authors think may be due to 'sexually neutral' questionnaires. Nevertheless, they suggest that, if the usual finding of an excess of depressed females is true, this may be because males die from depression while women survive disabled. They go on to say that, conversely, anxiety may make people vigilant and health conscious and thus make the women, who had more of this disorder, protected and, thereby, live longer. Finally, the study was undertaken when antidepressants were in their infancy and so it is unlikely that much of the depression was treated. It remains to be seen, therefore, whether chronically depressed people can avoid premature death through adequate treatment; and whether depression is aetiological to premature death by directly affecting the circulatory and immunological systems, or acts indirectly by producing dependency syndromes, slothful habits, and unfitness.

Vaillant (1979) examined the effects of mental health on physical health. An educationally homogeneous sample of white males from Harvard University, born around 1921, was followed for over thirty years and given serial examinations. Some 188 men were included in the sample. Poor adult adjustment was strongly associated with deterioration of physical health. Curiously, obesity, alcohol use, and cigarette smoking had a relatively weak association with health deterioration. Psychosocial factors explained 23 per cent of the health deterioration while longevity of ancestors, capacity to work hard, and freedom from physical disease explained 2 per cent of the remaining variance. Thus in the sample 'chronic anxiety, depression, and emotional maladjustment, measured in a variety of ways, predicted early aging, defined by irreversible deterioration of health' and 'positive mental health significantly retards irreversible midlife decline in physical health' (Vaillant 1979: 1253). The author says that, although previous research has attempted to link stressful life events and poor social supports in the development of chronic illness, it has ignored alcoholism, psychopathology, and maladaptive coping mechanisms. Finally, Vaillant speculates that 'stress does not kill us so much as ingenious adaptation to stress (call it good mental health or mature coping mechanisms) facilitates our survival' (Vaillant 1979: 1253).

PSYCHIATRIC MORBIDITY IN THE GENERAL HOSPITAL

Proceeding through what Goldberg and Huxley (1980) have termed a 'series of filters', it is possible to see the relationship between physical and mental illness at different levels of care. In a detailed review, Mayou and Hawton (1986) looked at psychiatric disorder in the general hospital. They point out that surveys of general hospitals, compared with those described for general practice by Goldberg and Huxley, have been of poor quality and that the research instruments have been found wanting. Nevertheless, they take the view that there is considerable psychiatric morbidity at all levels in general hospitals, much of it unknown to the hospital doctors.

Lipowski has written extensively in the areas of psychosomatic medicine and consultation-liaison psychiatry. Some selected papers were collated in a volume entitled *Psychosomatic Medicine and Liaison Psychiatry* (Lipowski 1985). In a paper entitled 'Physical illness and mental disorder – epidemiology' he sees four reasons for the increased attention to the relationship between physical and mental illness. First, consultation-liaison developments have brought psychiatrists in contact with physical illness on a considerable scale, second, the aging population brings with it increased risk of both mental and physical illness; third, chronic diseases have a high prevalence and may cause much psychiatric disorder although this needs documenting; and, finally, new medications and procedures have psychiatric sequelae.

He sees psychiatric disorders, judged to be causally related to physical illness, as being of three major classes: organic brain syndromes, reactive functional disorders, and deviant illness behaviour. Organic brain syndromes occur as a result of demonstrable or presumed cerebral pathology; 'reactive' functional disorders, mainly affective disorders, occur as a consequence of the meaning for a patient of a physical illness or injury. The term 'deviant illness behaviour' refers to a physically ill patient's behaviour that militates against recovery or optimal attainable health.

Lipowski, like Mayou and Hawton, underscores the poor hospital epidemiological information due to unreliable terms and methods. He indicates that existing epidemiological data indicate only concurrence and not a causal relationship between physical and psychiatric disorder. He accepts that such a concurrence has been reasonably well documented by community studies but concludes that hospital data are less satisfactory. While it is widely accepted that organic brain syndromes and affective disorders make up much of psychiatric morbidity in the medical population, Cavanaugh and Wettstein (1984: 203) assert that the 'medical inpatient studies to date permit few inferences about the prevalence of psychiatric distress, symptoms, or diagnoses.'

In a further paper entitled 'Physical illness and psychiatric disorder-pathogenesis', Lipowski indicates that specific agent models of causality do not apply and the concept of vulnerability is better. Obviously, physical illness may be independent, causal, or caused by psychiatric disorder. Lipowski makes an attempt to spell out multifactorial psychopathogenesis and suggests that the following psychosocial and psychobiological factors can influence a patient's response to physical illness in the direction of psychopathology:

(1) frustration of drives and needs;
(2) increased intensity of intra-psychic conflicts;
(3) failure of defence mechanisms;
(4) loss of self-esteem;
(5) alteration of body image;
(6) disruption of normal sleep-wake cycle;
(7) social isolation and alienation.

Elsewhere, Lipowski discusses somatization in 'Somatization: a borderline between medicine and psychiatry' (Lipowski 1986). He defines somatization as 'a tendency to experience and communicate psychologic distress in the form of physical symptoms and to seek medical help, [which] constitutes a very common and often exasperating problem' (Lipowski 1986: 609). He points out that more than half of the patients in primary care, given one of these diagnoses, present primarily with somatic symptoms, and somatization constitutes a major medical and economic problem.

DISCUSSION

It is quite clear that the epidemiological work in primary care carried out by Michael Shepherd and his group was seminal and heralded important work in that sphere. It pinpointed that the prevalence of psychiatric disorder in the community was considerable, that such disorders were largely managed by the general practitioner, and that they tended to be associated with physical illness and social difficulties. In the St Paul's Cray study, when every effort was made to exclude diagnostic, method, and sampling problems, physical and mental disorder were significantly related. Later work by Goldberg and his group showed how complex the presentations of psychiatric disorder are in primary care and how difficult it is for the general practitioners to treat the total person. Elsewhere, in Australia and the United States, the community findings were corroborated. (Epidemiology in the community now seems to have a primacy over that in general hospitals, since the research in the latter has been described as being inadequate.)

Subsequent work has shown that psychiatric patients frequently present with somatic complaints and are excessive attenders of medical facilities. So the conundrum is that psychiatric patients both appear to be physically ill often when psychiatrically disturbed and yet bear excessive risk of physical illness. They present mainly to general practitioners and, by dint of their symptoms, also to medical specialists. As a result they are often investigated for sundry medical conditions with exposure to medical hazards, such as radiation and drug toxicity, and their *actual* psychiatric conditions may be ignored. If they are bracketed as 'psychiatric', the patience of their medical attendants may wear thin and their *actual* physical conditions may be overlooked. Thus, 'illness behaviour', 'illness proneness', and 'clustering' of physical and psychiatric disorder may well not be incompatible and it behoves the generalist to take due note.

Nevertheless, according to MacMahon's criteria (1960), the relationship between physical and mental illness is still largely descriptive and correlational rather than causal. Putative causal mechanisms are discussed in psychosomatic journals but tend to be speculative. Epidemiology, however, deals with the mass aspects of disease. Hypotheses should be tested as to whether affective disorders, particularly depression, in a longitudinal sense, cause physical illness and premature death directly or indirectly via bad habits such as dependency syndromes and general unfitness.

Behavioural science and epidemiology, so often Cinderella topics in the medical school curriculum, will, in all likelihood, provide a part of the understanding of chronic morbidity and mortality rates.

REFERENCES

Andrews, G., Schonell, M., and Tennant, C. (1977) 'The relationship between physical, psychological and social morbidity in a suburban community', *American Journal of Epidemiology* 106: 324–9.

Andrews, G., Tennant, C., Hewson, D., and Schonell, M. (1978) 'The relation of social factors to physical and psychiatric illness', *American Journal of Epidemiology* 108: 27–35.

Blacker, C.V.R. and Clare, A.W. (1987) 'Depressive disorders in primary care', *British Journal of Psychiatry* 150: 737–51.

Bridges, K.W. and Goldberg, D.P. (1985) 'Somatic presentation of DSM III psychiatric disorders in primary care', *Journal of Psychosomatic Research* 29: 563–9.

Cavanaugh, S. and Wettstein, R.M. (1984) 'Prevalence of psychiatric morbidity in medical populations', in L. Grinspoon (ed.) *Psychiatry Update: The American Psychiatric Association Annual Review, Volume III*, Washington, DC: American Psychiatric Press.

Commission on Chronic Illness (1957) *Chronic Illness in the US: Volume 1: Prevention of Chronic Illness*, Cambridge, Mass.: Harvard University Press.

Cooper, B. (1972) 'Social correlates of psychiatric illness in the community', in G. McLachlan (ed.) *Approaches to Action: A Symposium on Services for the Mentally Ill and Handicapped*, London: Oxford University Press.

Eastwood, M.R. (1971) 'Screening for psychiatric disorder', *Psychological Medicine* 1: 197–208.

Eastwood, M.R. (1975) *The Relation Between Physical and Mental Illness*, Toronto: University of Toronto Press.

Eastwood, M.R. and Corbin, S.L. (1986) 'The relationship between physical illness and depression in old age', in E. Murphy (ed.) *Affective Disorders in the Elderly*, Edinburgh: Churchill Livingstone.

Eaton, W.W. and Kessler, L.G. (eds) (1985) *Epidemiologic Field Methods in Psychiatry: The NIMH Epidemiologic Catchment Area Program*, New York: Academic Press.

Endicott, J. and Spitzer, R.C. (1978) 'A diagnostic interview: the schedule for affective disorders and schizophrenia', *Archives of General Psychiatry* 35: 837–44.

Goldberg, D.P. (1972) *The Detection of Psychiatric Illness by Questionnaire* (Maudsley Monograph No. 21), London: Oxford University Press.

Goldberg, D.P. (1974) 'Psychiatric disorders', *Lancet* 2: 1245–7.

Goldberg, D.P. (1986) 'Discussant on screening, part 2,', in M. Shepherd, G. Wilkinson, and P. Williams (eds) *Mental Illness in Primary Care Settings*, London: Tavistock.

Goldberg, D.P. and Blackwell, B. (1970) 'Psychiatric illness in general practice: a detailed study using a new method of case identification', *British Medical Journal* 2: 439–43.

Goldberg, D.P., Cooper, B., Eastwood, M.R., Kedward, H., and Shepherd, M. (1970) 'Psychiatric interview suitable for using in community surveys', *British Journal of the Society of Preventive Medicine* 24: 18–26.

Goldberg, D.P. and Huxley, P. (1980) *Mental Illness in the Community: The Pathway to Psychiatric Care*, London: Tavistock Publications.

Goldberg, D.P., Rickels, K., Downing, R., and Hesbacher, P. (1976) 'A comparison of two psychiatric screening tests', *British Journal of Psychiatry* 129: 61–7.

Hinkle, L.E. and Wolff, H.G. (1957) 'The nature of man's adaptation to his total environment and the relation of this to illness', *Archives of Internal Medicine* 99: 442–60.

Kedward, H.B. and Sylph, J. (1974) 'The social correlates of chronic neurotic disorder', *Social Psychiatry* 9: 91–8.

Kessler, L.G., Burns, B.J., Shapiro, S., Tischler, G.L., George, L.K., Hough, R.L., Bodison, D., and Miller, R.H. (1987) 'Psychiatric diagnosis of medical service users: evidence from the Epidemiologic Catchment Area Program', *American Journal of Public Health* 77: 18–24.

Lipowski, Z. (1985) *Psychosomatic Medicine and Liaison Psychiatry: Selected Papers*, New York: Plenum Medical Book Co.

Lipowski, Z. (1986) 'Somatization: a borderland between medicine and psychiatry', *Canadian Medical Association Journal* 135: 609–14.

McKeown, T. (1968) 'Validation of screening procedures', in *Screening for Medical Care* (Nuffield Provincial Hospitals Trust), London: Oxford University Press.

MacMahon, B., Pugh, T.F., and Ipsen, J. (1960) *Epidemiologic Methods*, Boston: Little, Brown.

Mayou, R. and Hawton, K. (1986) 'Psychiatric disorder in the general hospital', *British Journal of Psychiatry* 149: 172–90.

Mechanic, D. (1966) 'Response factors in illness: the study of illness behaviour', *Social Psychiatry* 1: 11–20.

Murphy, J.M., Monson, R.R., Olivier, D., Sobol, A., and Leighton, A.H. (1987) 'Affective disorders and mortality', *Archives of General Psychiatry* 44: 473–9.

Shepherd, M. (1987) 'Mental illness and primary care', *American Journal of Public Health* 77: 12–13.

Shepherd, M., Cooper, B., Brown, A.C., and Kalton, G. (1966) *Psychiatric*

Illness in General Practice, London: Oxford University Press.

South-East London Screening Study Group (1977) 'A controlled trial of multiphasic screening: results of the South-East London screening study', *International Journal of Epidemiology* 6: 257–63.

Vaillant, G.E. (1979) 'Natural history of male psychologic health: effects of mental health on physical health', *New England Journal of Medicine* 301: 1249–54.

Williams, P. (1986) 'Mental illness and primary care: screening', in M. Shepherd, G. Wilkinson, and P. Williams (eds) *Mental Illness in Primary Care Settings*, London: Tavistock.

Wilson, J.M.G. and Jungner, G. (1968) 'Principles and practice of screening for disease' (WHO Public Health Papers, No. 34), Geneva: WHO.

Wing, J.K., Birley, J.L.T., Cooper, J.E., Graham, P., and Isaacs, A.D. (1967) 'Reliability of a procedure for measuring and classifying "Present Psychiatric State"', *British Journal of Psychiatry* 113: 499–515.

Identification of Causal Factors and the Computation of Individual Morbid Risks

16

Schizophrenic Psychoses: Causal Factors and Risks

John Wing

The scientific literature on causal and risk factors in schizophrenia is now so immense that even a summary based only on studies whose design and methods are adequate by the standards of their time would run into volumes. Michael Shepherd (1987) has recommended Warner's schema (1985), modified from that of Strauss and Carpenter (1981), which lists risk factors under four headings, depending on the period during which they first operate: pre- and peri-natal, infancy and childhood, immediate pre-onset, and long-term 'career'. Each item in the four lists has its own substantial literature and, as soon as one tries to use the schema, it becomes clear that theories of pathology, causation, precipitation, and exacerbation tend to interact without respect for its categories. Nevertheless, with further modification, it is convenient for exposition.

Since much of the relevant research uses the epidemiological method, it is appropriate to begin with the two principal terms in the calculation of the rate of incidence of schizophrenia. In the numerator is placed the number of cases of schizophrenia or of some specified subgroup of it, with an onset in a given period, usually a year. In the denominator is placed the number of people in the population at risk, subdivided according to the risk factor under investigation. If proper epidemiological principles are followed, the relative risk associated with each factor can be calculated by comparing the resulting incidence (or in some cases, with great caution, the prevalence) rates. Since schizophrenia can rarely be confidently diagnosed until adolescence or adult life, estimating the effect of potential risk factors occurring in childhood requires a longitudinal design. Relative risks can also be assessed by using less demanding research designs, for example, case-control studies.

One of the chief sources of difficulty in comparing the results of research into risk factors is variation in the criteria used for diagnosis, a problem compounded by the fact that diagnostic concepts are often tied to theories of aetiology. The US-UK Diagnostic Project (Cooper *et al.* 1972) and the International Pilot Study of Schizophrenia (WHO 1973) demonstrated the problem and indicated one way to tackle it by using standardized techniques of data collection and applying standard classifying rules (Wing *et al*. 1974). Since then, the American Psychiatric Association has accepted the need to specify the criteria for diagnosis and the third and revised third editions of its *Diagnostic and Statistical Manual*, DSM–III (1980) and DSM–IIIR (1987), have provided explicit criteria. The tenth edition of the *International Classification of Diseases* will adopt a similar approach (WHO 1987).

These rule-based systems are 'top-down', in the sense that they begin with the need to specify the criteria for each diagnosis. After prolonged negotiation between parties representing various conceptual approaches, a compromise set of rules is published that both achieves a degree of consensus and imposes a degree of uniformity on those who use it. A 'bottom-up' system begins with the phenomena, ideally with a glossary of differential definitions of symptoms and signs (Wing 1983). The item-pool can be sufficiently broadly based to allow the application of rules from a variety of classifications. If agreement on the phenomena can be obtained, diagnostic disagreement is reduced even without the application of standard rules (Cooper *et al*. 1972; Shepherd *et al*. 1968).

The 'bottom-up' approach also allows an examination of the contribution of specified symptoms or syndromes to any variation found in incidence rates. In the case of schizophrenia several such syndromes are evident, each having some claim to a partially independent status. These include: the positive syndrome, chiefly composed of symptoms regarded by Kurt Schneider as 'of the first rank', which is almost always accompanied by other psychotic phenomena; the paranoid syndrome, comprising other delusions not congruent with affect; the 'negative' syndrome of slowness, underactivity, flattening of affect, lack of motivation, poverty of quantity or content of speech and poor use of non-verbal means of communication; and thought disorder, manifested in various degrees of incoherence of speech and neologisms. It is only recently that such syndromes have been examined in their own right, as distinct from their contribution to an overall diagnosis. Other syndromes of relevance are those of the autistic spectrum (Wing, L. 1982) and motor syndromes of various kinds. Manic and severe depressive syndromes may also modify the diagnosis. Most studies exclude schizophrenia that appears in a context of recognizable cerebral disease.

Problems in comparing incidence rates arising from variations between the denominators are most clearly demonstrated in studies involving countries whose population statistics are of doubtful reliability, and where estimates of the population size and indices such as birth and death rates may be seriously inaccurate. Even in countries with well-developed population censuses, the numbers and characteristics of recently arrived migrants and of people who are not part of a well-recognized household must be estimated with caution. Prevalence rates are even more susceptible to errors in estimating the denominator since the number of active cases during any recent period of time will have accumulated over a much longer period, during which population criteria might have changed (Der and Wooff 1986).

All studies of schizophrenia that use rates must, therefore, be scrutinized carefully before use is made of the figures for comparative purposes. Rates of first admission to hospital, for example, long provided a mainstay for epidemiological research, on the fairly reasonable assumption (Ødegaard 1952) that most of those afflicted are eventually admitted. The life-time expectancy rate was regarded as stable at about one per cent. Recent trends in first admission rates, however, have shown a decrease in England (Annual Reports of Mental Health Statistics), Scotland (Eagles and Whalley 1985) and Denmark (Munk-Jørgensen 1987). Against this must be set the fact that 'first contact' rates, which cover contacts with services other than hospital wards, have shown no such decline. In Camberwell, they remained steady at about 12–15 per 100,000 population per year between 1964 and 1984 (Wing and Der 1984). In Nottingham, the rate is similar when ICD–9 criteria are used (Cooper et al. 1987). A multinational study of the incidence of schizophrenia found similar first contact rates in all the centres involved, whether in developed or developing countries (WHO 1986).

Two decades of studies, principally in Scandinavia, suggested that the lifetime risk of schizophrenia was remarkably similar at just under one per cent. Shields (1978), using Camberwell Register data, estimated it at 0.90 per cent to age 65. Nevertheless, the question of whether the rate has fluctuated over time has received far from unanimous answers and still remains unresolved (Cooper and Sartorius 1977; Goldhamer and Marshall 1953; Hare 1983; Scull 1979, 1984; Torrey 1980; Warner 1985). In former times, rates tended to be higher in the USA than in the UK (Kramer 1961), and high rates were reported in Eire, Finland, Iceland, and the Federal Republic of Germany. A consensus on lower rates may be due, in part, to the use of standardized methods of data collection and classification but the requirement, in DSM–III, for the course to be taken into account, means that even lower rates must be expected, as a recent study in Nottingham has suggested (Cooper et al. 1987). A report on schizophrenia research commissioned by the Neurosciences and Mental Health Board of the Medical Research Council suggests that a standard data base should always be collected and the rules at least of ICD–10 and DSM–IIIR applied, in addition to any local diagnostic system (MRC 1987). In the longer term, robust research results will, in turn, refine the diagnostic criteria.

In spite of these introductory reservations, a few risk factors have emerged with a degree of solidity and stability that encourages confidence and several others deserve, at the least, substantial further attention.

PRE- AND POST-NATAL RISK FACTORS

The risk factor most securely associated with schizophrenia is genetic. The disorder, whether broadly or narrowly defined, occurs more commonly among the first degree relatives of those afflicted than in control groups or the general population. It is more frequent in the adopted-away children of schizophrenic mothers than in other adoptees. And in twins, if one member of a pair has schizophrenia the other is two or three times more likely to be similarly affected when the twins are monozygotic than when they are dizygotic. (For a review of the complexities associated with these simple facts, see Part III of the volume edited by Häfner, Gattaz and Janzarik, published in 1987, and the MRC report referred to above.)

Increased risks of this order do not suggest straightforward mechanisms of inheritance. Only about a fifth of sufferers have a close relative with the disorder and the concordance in identical twins falls well short of the total agreement needed for full genetic determination. There have been many attempts, both in purely genetic and in a combination of genetic and environmental terms, to unravel the mystery. (For the moment, *purely* environmental theories are in disorderly retreat.) The most prominent of the competing theories are: (a) that there are inherited and non-inherited forms of schizophrenia, (b) that the genetic contribution (or contributions, since more than one gene may be involved) determines a predisposition which can become manifest following environmental insults of various kinds, and (c) that some or all of the various schizophrenia syndromes have their own particular risk factors. These ideas are not mutually exclusive.

A second pre-natally determined risk factor is sex, which is most conveniently discussed in terms of age of onset. While the lifetime risk has been shown to be approximately equal in most studies, it has long been observed that the onset is earlier in men than in women (Noreik and Ødegaard 1967; Lindelius 1970; Watt, Katz and Shepherd 1983; Wing and Fryers 1976). It is well known that communication disorders of many varieties, including aphasia, dyslexia, and disorders in the autistic spectrum, are commoner at birth in boys than girls. With rare exceptions, however, schizophrenia is not manifested frankly until after puberty. Nevertheless, the possibility that it is also a developmental disorder, with possible 'premorbid' or subclinical manifestations, must be considered. This would be true whether risk factors that were not genetic in nature had or had not contributed during the pre-natal period. In fact there is evidence that what Pasamanick called 'the continuum of reproductive casualty' includes, as one of its possible consequences, schizophrenia developing later in life.

The most consistent part of the evidence concerns season of birth. The excess of winter births in both hemispheres of the world, though small, can hardly be a matter of chance. A critical review of more than twenty studies, carried out in fourteen countries, suggested that the results were not artefacts of methodology or design but could best be explained as due to brain damage by a seasonal risk factor such as viral infection, nutritional deficiency, or perinatal complication. Moreover, affected individuals were likely to have an early onset, less genetic loading, and better prognoses (Boyd *et al*. 1986). Mednick and colleagues (1987) refer to a follow-up study of young adults who had been at the second trimester of foetal development during the serious A2 influenza virus epidemic in Copenhagen in October/November 1957. They had a higher rate of admission with a diagnosis of schizophrenia compared with controls.

The recent reporting of high rates of schizophrenia in patients admitted to hospital for the first time, or making first-ever contact with psychiatric services, among Afro-Caribbean residents in the UK, raises a further question as to whether environmental risk factors are responsible. Not only is the incidence three or more times greater in those born in the West Indies than in native-born residents (Dean *et al*. 1981; Harrison *et al*. 1988), but it appears to be substantially higher still among the second generation, who were born in the UK (Harrison *et al*. 1987). Studies of early childhood autism in immigrant populations suggest that viral infection during an immigrant mother's pregnancy, while she has not developed antibodies, or some other environmental insult, might explain the excess in immigrant groups (Akinsola and Fryers 1986; Gillberg *et al*. 1987; Wing, L. 1979).

Genetic studies of schizophrenia have not been carried out as thoroughly, or to the same extent, in Third World compared with developed countries. The similar incidence across countries reported in the latest WHO report, mentioned earlier, does not eliminate genetic variations because there could be a differential incidence of subtypes. However, there is little evidence of variation due to 'ethnicity'. The apparently better course in developing countries (see below) could be interpreted as due to a higher proportion of environmentally precipitated acute schizophrenias, appearing without long-term 'personality' precursors, although there is little systematic evidence one way or the other. The very high risk in children of first-generation immigrants would then require explanation; consideration being given to the risk factors, including infection, occuring perinatally, as well as during later life.

McNeil and Kaij (1978), in a thorough review of the risks of obstetric complications, investigated using a variety of designs and methods, concluded that they 'are a risk-increasing factor to be taken seriously in the etiology of schizophrenia'. Murray and colleagues have linked this conclusion to the fact that nearly all studies that have collected data on the presence or absence of peri-natal abnormalities in those who subsequently developed schizophrenia and had CT scans performed showed that early hazards were significantly associated with increased ventricular size in adulthood. Moreover, the relationship was particularly noticeable in those without a family history of schizophrenia (Murray *et al*. 1987).

RISK FACTORS DURING CHILDHOOD

Genetic, intra-uterine, and perinatal risk factors, if present, combine to form a predisposition to schizophrenia that may or may not be sufficient for its later manifestation. Other risk factors may operate during childhood to increase this vulnerability. For example, a substantial literature has accumulated around the subject of parental rearing patterns. Empirical tests of hypotheses derived from such theories have been more than usually plagued by poor design and methodology and have rarely, in fact, been concerned directly with parent-infant interaction and its subsequent effects in adulthood. Such evidence as exists, derived mainly from studies of communication patterns in the parents of adult offspring diagnosed schizophrenic (Singer *et al.* 1978), is unconvincing. One of the most obvious problems, diagnosis (Rutter 1978; Hirsch and Leff 1975), is illustrated by data from a current longitudinal study (Wynne *et al.* 1987) in which, of sixty-three index parents diagnosed as schizophrenic according to DSM–II (much used in earlier research), only eighteeen were so diagnosed according to DSM–III. At the moment, there is little evidence to suggest that the parents of those who later develop schizophrenia have any specific characteristics, other than genetic, that constitute additional risk factors.

More general factors in child-rearing must also be considered. If relevant, they should show up in studies of adopted-away children of mothers afflicted by schizophrenia. A research project with this design, not yet completed, is being carried out by Tienari and colleagues (1987), who have examined all such offspring born in Finland in the years 1928 to 1979, together with matched controls. Preliminary results suggest an interaction between genetic and environmental factors, in that schizophrenia appears more frequently in children with a genetic loading but is also concentrated and more severe in the most disturbed adoptive families. The latest results from the Copenhagen high-risk project (Mednick *et al.* 1987), which began with a cohort of adolescents, one or both of whose parents had suffered from schizophrenia, also point to an interaction between genetic, perinatal, and environmental factors in probands compared to controls.

Since criteria for schizotypal personality disorder were laid down in DSM–III, several studies have been undertaken to determine their relationship to schizophrenia. Kendler (1981, 1987) has argued that the criteria can be divided into two groups: one closer to the negative symptoms of schizophrenia (social isolation, odd speech, aloofness, and suspicion), one closer to the positive (magical thinking, ideas of reference and recurrent illusions). Whether the DSM–III items are well chosen, and whether Kendler's division of them makes clinical sense, is not here the point. The 'negative' items are said to be commoner among the biological relatives of people with schizophrenia, but so (Kendler and Gruenberg 1982) is paranoid personality disorder. Whether any of the three predict the later manifestation of schizophrenia is a moot point.

Schizophrenic and paranoid psychoses can begin during childhood, usually in the immediately pre-pubertal years. The symptoms are typical except for the obvious pathoplastic effects of age. There should be no confusion with psychoses having an onset in early childhood, usually on the basis of a global language disorder (Ricks and Wing 1975), since the symptoms of the latter are quite distinct, the children do not develop schizophrenic psychoses in later life, and there is no increase in the frequency of schizophrenia in first-degree relatives (Kolvin 1971; Wing, L. 1982). One other possible confusing condition (in fact, a variant of early childhood autism) is Asperger's syndrome (Asperger 1944, 1968; Wing, L. 1981). Like Kanner's syndrome, it has often been misdiagnosed as schizophrenia, and may account for a proportion of the cases labelled as 'simple schizophrenia' or schizoid personality.

Retrospective studies of the childhood years of those who have already developed schizophrenia tend to show a higher frequency of disturbed or withdrawn behaviour compared with controls (Robins 1970; Bower *et al* 1960; Watt 1978). As part of any predisposition manifested in personality disorder such as 'schizotypy' (DSM–III). or schizoid personality (ICD–10), the clinical observation that people presenting with frank schizophrenia for the first time have often become withdrawn and odd over quite long periods, sometimes reaching back into childhood, suggests that cognitive abnormalities may already have been present. Such results as are available indicate a global intellectual deficit (though verbal skills are better preserved than non-verbal) before clinical onset in a proportion of cases, usually correlated with a poor prognosis (Lane and Albee 1965; Offord 1974; Watt and Lubensky 1976). The IPSS two-year follow-up (WHO 1979) indicated that socially isolated or underperforming patients had the worst outcome. In general, negative impairments manifested before clinical onset are the best predictors of later outcome (Wing 1987 and in press).

Such considerations suggest that a proportion of those who later become frankly schizophrenic are likely to show a range of other characteristics: single status, poor employment record, domicile in a socially isolated area, recent migration, and relative poverty. This will particularly be true of males. These results of classical epidemiology are well known and properly attributed mainly to 'drift' rather than to causal factors (Cooper 1978). (The study by Dunham in Detroit, published in 1965, is a useful reference, since he had earlier been associated with a causal hypothesis.) There is, however, a further consideration. A high intelligence, a helpful and supportive family and educational background, occupational skills that are in demand, an economic environment that provides plenty of opportunities for employment, a society that is not highly competitive – these and other factors may protect against the development of schizophrenia even in someone who is already at higher than average risk (Warner 1985). On the other hand, as Cooper (1961) pointed out, someone who is deprived of such benefits is likely to become more vulnerable: an example of disability amplification operating long before clinical presentation.

THE IMMEDIATE PRECURSORS OF ACUTE 'POSITIVE' EPISODES

The positive syndrome of schizophrenia is more dramatic and publicly visible than the negative, or than any pre-clinical manifestations of eccentricity or social withdrawal. In a proportion of cases the clinical onset is, or appears to be, relatively sudden. Putative precipitating factors are more likely to have been present in such cases. (They are nearly always determined retrospectively.) An acute schizophrenic syndrome can follow the misuse of amphetamine, and 'alcoholic hallucinosis' is a well-known diagnosis, although not represented as such in ICD–10. The account of Evelyn Waugh's own experience, in *The Ordeal of Gilbert Pinfold*, puts it down to over-indulgence in port and potassium bromide, the tranquillisers of the time, in addition to family, religious, and occupational problems. Such disorders may be accompanied by disorientation in minor degree. They usually clear up fairly quickly and rarely follow a chronic course with a negative impairment. Schizophrenic symptoms accompanying cerebral disease such as temporal lobe epilepsy are also well documented.

Such cases account for only a small proportion of acute onsets. Commoner environmental precipitants are psychosocial in nature. One of the first to be demonstrated was iatrogenic, relapse after years without positive symptoms of long-stay patients suddenly exposed to unrealistic expectations of social performance during a course of rehabilitation, followed by recovery (to the previous level of functioning) when sheltered conditions were reinstated (Stone and Eldred 1959; Goldberg *et al.* 1977; Wing *et al.* 1964: Wing, L *et al.*, 1972).

Since then, attention has focused chiefly on other 'life events', usually adverse and stressful, that put stress upon an individual (Brown and Birley 1968; Steinberg and Durrell 1968). There is no suggestion that such events are in any way specific in their effect; they operate through an existing vulnerability. The most recent replication of such a result was in six of seven centres taking part in a WHO collaborative study (Leff 1987). However, Dohrenwend and colleagues (1987) and Tennant (1985) are cautious in their assessment of the significance of the effects. Certainly, there is a paucity of properly conducted studies and a failure to distinguish clearly between precipitation of first florid onset and precipitation of florid relapse as part of a chronic course. The problem of the course criterion indroduced into DSM–III also complicates intepretation of the many studies carried out using its rules and exacerbates the difficulty of defining 'onset'. The status of 'stress' as a risk factor for the onset of schizophrenia remains uncertain. Much of the evidence so far concerns course rather than first onset (Wing 1986).

A third non-specific factor that has attracted considerable attention has become reified under the label 'emotional expression' (EE), although the concept is wider than that (Brown *et al.* 1962; Brown *et al.* 1972; Vaughn and Leff 1976). High EE does not occur in all relatives and it does occur in the relatives of people with many other (including physical) diseases. Leff (1987) has recently discussed the interactions between life events, EE, and prophylactic medication as they affect the course of schizophrenia. The first evidence that intervention based on such theories can improve the course has been provided by Leff and colleagues (1985). All three environmental factors, unrealistic expectations, life events, and EE, can be summed up as environmental intrusions on people whose capacities for social communication are impaired, whether by 'premorbid' factors or as part of the clinical condition. It is somewhat artificial to theorize about them in isolation from each other. Each has a supportive as well as a toxic aspect. Low EE relatives, for example, seem to exert a beneficial influence.

FACTORS INFLUENCING THE COURSE AND OUTCOME OF SCHIZOPHRENIA

Manfred Bleuler (1978) has suggested that about 25 per cent of patients in a first episode of schizophrenia are likely to have a good outcome after about five years. About 10 per cent never improve. These two proportions have not, he thinks, changed much during his long lifetime. Between the two extremes, the outcome depends quite substantially, in his view, on the influence for good or ill of environmental factors. Some of these, for example the precipitants of acute episodes, and the protective effects of medication and social support, have been considered earlier. Others, such as factors that influence the severity of the negative impairment, are usually considered in the context of the long-term course, although there is no obvious reason why they should not operate at any time, including before clinical onset, if an underlying vulnerability is present.

The environmental factors likely to increase negative impairment are social under-stimulation (Wing and Brown 1970; Wing and Freudenberg 1961) and over-medication. It has been argued, therefore, that people with chronic schizophrenia have to walk a tightrope, balanced between twin dangers; unrealistic expectation on one side and a strong temptation to withdraw from efforts at social adjustment on the other. These dangers arise from a common source. A reduced ability to communicate freely with others, which is 'intrinsic' in the sense of being based in biological impairments, depends (if it is not so severe as to be incapacitating), as much on his or her lifestyle and self-attitudes, and on the toxicity or benevolence of the environment, as it does on the intrinsic deficits (Wing, 1975, 1977, 1987b).

These arguments suggest that the more favourable course of schizophrenia found in developing countries (Murphy and Raman 1971; WHO 1979), if not due to the predominance of a relatively benign subtype, differential mortality, etc., may be found to be associated with a less 'stressful' environment. Some preliminary evidence concerning the family environment already suggests this (Leff *et al*. 1987).

CONCLUDING COMMENT

This very broad and brief summary of risk factors in schizophrenia began with a discussion of the daunting methodological problems that must be overcome if the results of risk research are to be taken as seriously as those of genetics. One or more of these problems, notably diagnosis, the calculation of rates, the selection of case controls, and the conduct of longitudinal surveys, is likely to prove a substantial obstacle so far as comparison between the results of different studies is concerned.

The classification of risks as though they operate in a cumulative hierarchy, from conception to death in old age, is misleading. Most factors, apart from those operating at conception or during the period of maturation of the nervous system, could exert their effects at any period. Theories of interactive causation need not recognize such artificial boundaries. Although it is sometimes dispiriting, when trying to review the enormous literature on risk factors, to note how frequently theories come into favour, then disfavour, with possible repetitions of the cycle, often in association with the advocacy of different 'product champions', several lines of real progress are discernible.

The idea that a few interlinked pathologies underlie the phenomena of schizophrenia, leading to vulnerability to a variety of environmental risk factors, remains highly plausible and eminently suited to the opportunities for interactive host-and-environment research presented by the new non-invasive methods of investigating brain structure and function. It is important to remember, however, that the eventual end-point of such investigations is to develop better theories of how such physical mechanisms can produce symptoms that take the form both of abnormal subjective experiences and of abnormalities of behaviour, each of which can be modified through environmental action. The relationship between the positive and the negative syndromes remains at the heart of the mystery.

REFERENCES

Akinsola, H.A. and Fryers, T. (1986) 'A comparison of patterns of disability in severely mental handicapped children of different ethnic origins', *Psychological Medicine* 16: 127–33.

American Psychiatric Association (1980) *Diagnostic and Statistical Manual of Mental Disorders*, third edition, Washington, DC: APA.

American Psychiatric Association (1987) *Diagnostic and Statistical Manual of Mental Disorders*, third edition, revised, Washington, DC: APA.

Asperger, H. (1944) 'Die autistischen Psychopathen im Kindesalter', *Archiv für Psychiatrie und Nervenkrankheiten*. 117: 76–137.

Asperger, H. (1968) 'Zur Differentialdiagnose des kindlichen Autismus', *Acta Paedopsychiatrica* 35: 136–45.

Bleuler, M. (1978) *The Schizophrenic Disorders: Long-term Patient and Family Studies*, translated by S.M. Clemens, New Haven: Yale University Press.

Bower, E., Shellhamer, T., and Daily, J. (1960) 'School characteristics of male adolescents who later became schizophrenic', *American Journal of Orthopsychiatry* 30: 712–29.

Boyd, J.H., Pulver, A.E., and Steward, W. (1986) 'Season of birth: schizophrenia and bipolar disorder', *Schizophrenia Bulletin* 12: 173–86.

Brown, G.W. and Birley, J.L.T. (1968) 'Crisis and life changes and the onset of schizophrenia', *Health and Social Behaviour* 9: 203–14.

Brown, G.W., Birley, J.L.T., and Wing, J.K. (1972) 'Influence of family life on the course of schizophrenic disorders: a replication', *British Journal of Psychiatry* 121: 241–58.

Brown, G.W., Monck. E., Carstairs, G.M., and Wing, J.K. (1962) 'Influence of family life on the course of schizophrenic disorders', *British Journal of Preventive and Social Medicine* 16: 55–68.

Cooper, B. (1961) 'Social class and prognosis in schizophrenia', *British Journal of Preventive and Social Medicine* 15: 17–41.

Cooper, B. (1978) 'Epidemiology' in J.K. Wing (ed.) *Schizophrenia: Towards a New Synthesis*, London, Academic Press.

Cooper, J.E., Goodhead, D., Craig, T., Harris, M., Howat, J., and Korer, J. (1987) 'The incidence of schizophrenia in Nottingham', *British Journal of Psychiatry* 151: 619–26.

Cooper, J.E., Kendell R.E., Gurland, B.J., Sharpe, L., Copeland, J.R.M., and Simon, R. (1972) *Psychiatric Diagnosis in New York and London. A comprehensive study of mental hospital admissions. Maudsley Monograph No. 20*, London: Oxford University Press.

Cooper, J.E. and Sartorius, N. (1977) 'Cultural and temporal variations in schizophrenia: a speculation on the importance of industrialisation', *British Journal of Psychiatry* 130: 50–5.

Crow, T.J. (1985) 'The two syndrome concept: origins and current status', *Schizophrenia Bulletin* 11: 471–86.

Dean, G., Walsh, D., Downing, H., and Shelley, E. (1981) 'First admissions of native-born and immigrants to psychiatric hospitals in south-east England, 1971', *British Journal of Psychiatry* 139: 506–12.

Der, G. (1987) 'The effect of population changes on long-stay in-patient rates', in J.K. Wing (eds.) *Contributions to Health Service Planning and Research*, London; DHSS.

Der, G. and Wooff, K. (1986) in G.H. ten Horn, R. Giel, W.H. Gulbinat, and J.H. Henderson (eds) *Psychiatric Case Registers in Public Health*, Amsterdam: Elsevire, pp. 338–42.

Dohrenwend, B.P., Shrout, O.E., Link, B.G., and Skodoe, A.E. (1987) 'Social and psychological risk factors for episodes of schizophrenia', in H. Häfner, W.F. Gattaz, and W. Janzarik (eds) *Search for the Causes of Schizophrenia*, Heidelberg: Springer-Verlag, pp. 275–96.

Dunham, W.H. (1965) *Community and Schizophrenia: An Epidemiological Analysis*, Detroit: Wayne State University Press.

Eagles, J.M. and Whalley, L.J. (1985) 'Decline in the diagnosis of schizophrenia among first admissions to Scottish mental hospitals from 1969–78' *British Journal of Psychiatry* 146: 151–4.

Frith, C.D. (1987) 'The positive and negative symptoms of schizophrenia reflect impairments in the perception and initiation of action', *Psychological Medicine* 17: 631–8.

Gillberg, C., Steffenburg, S., Börjesson, B., and Anderson, L. (1987) 'Infantile autism in children of immigrant parents: a population based study from Göteborg', *British Journal of Psychiatry* 150: 856–8.

Goldberg, S.C., Schooler, N.R., Hogarty, G.E., and Roper, M. (1977) 'Prediction of relapse in schizophrenic patients treated by drug and sociotherapy', *Archives of General Psychiatry* 34: 171–84.

Goldhamer, H. and Marshall, A. (1953) *Psychosis and Civilisation*, Glencoe Ill.: Free Press.

Häfner, H., Gattaz, W.F. and Janzarik, W. (eds) (1987) *Search for the Causes of Schizophrenia*, Heidelberg: Springer-Verlag.

Hare, E.H. (1983) 'Was insanity on the increase?' *British Journal of Psychiatry* 142: 439–55.

Harrison, G., Owens, D., Holton, A., Neilson, D., and Best, D. (1988) 'A prospective study of severe mental disorder in Afro-Caribbean patients', to be published.

Hirsch, S.R. and Leff, J.P. (1975) *Abnormalities in Parents of Schizophrenics: A Review of the Literature and an Investigation of Communication Defects and Deviances*, London: Oxford University Press.

Kendler, K.S. (1987) 'Diagnostic approaches to schizotypal personality disorder: an historical perspective', *Schizophrenia Bulletin* 11: 538–53.

Kendler, K.S. and Gruenberg, E.M. (1982) 'Genetic relationship between paranoid personality and the ''schizophrenic spectrum'' disorders', *American Journal of Psychiatry* 139: 1185–6..

Kendler, K.S., Gruenberg, E.M., and Strauss, J.J. (1981) 'An independent analysis of the Copenhagen sample of the Danish Adoption Study of Schizophrenia: II: the relationship between schizotypal personality disorder and schizophrenia', *Archives of General Pscyhiatry* 38: 982–4.

Kolvin, I. (1971) 'Studies in the childhood psychoses: I: Diagnostic criteria and classification', *British Journal of Psychiatry* 118: 381–4.

Kramer, M. (1961) 'Some problems for international research suggested by observations on differences in first admission rates to the mental hospitals of England and Wales and of the United States', in *Proceedings of the Third World Congress of Psychiatry*, volume three, 153–60.

Lane, E. and Albee, G. (1965) 'Childhood intellectual differences between schizophrenic adults and their siblings', *American Journal of Orthopsychiatry* 35: 747–53.

Leff, J. (1987) 'A model of schizophrenic vulnerability to environmental factors', in H. Häfner, W.F. Gattaz, and W. Janarik (eds) *Search for the Causes of Schizophrenia*, Heidelberg: Springer-Verlag, 317–30.

Leff, J., Wig, N., Ghosh, A., Bedi, H., Menon, D.K., Kuipers, L., Korten, A., Ernberg, G., Day, R., Sartorius, N., and Jablensky, A. (1987) 'Influence of relatives' expressed emotion on the course of schizophrenia in Chandigarh', no. 3, *British Journal of Psychiatry* 151: 166–73.

Leff, J., Kuipers, L., Berkowitz, R., and Sturgeon, D. (1985) 'A controlled trial of social intervention in the families of schizophrenic patients: two-year follow-up', *British Journal of Psychiatry* 146: 594–600.

Lindelius, R. (1970) 'A study of schizophrenia', *Acta Psychiatria Scandinavia*, Supplement 216.

McNeil, T.F. and Kaij, L. (1978) 'Obstetric factors in the development of schizophrenia', in L.C. Wynne, R.L. Cromwell, and S. Matthysse (eds) *The Nature of Schizophrenia*, New York: Wiley, 401–29.

Medical Research Council (1987) *Research into Schizophrenia* (Report of the Schizophrenia and Allied Conditions Committee), London: MRC.

Mednick, S.A., Parnas, J., and Schulsinger, F. (1987) 'The Copenhagen High-Risk Project, 1962–86', *Schizophrenic Bulletin* 13: 485–95.

Munk-Jørgensen, P. (1987) 'Why has the incidence of schizophrenia in Danish psychiatric institutions decreased since 1970?' *Acta Psychiatrica Scandinavia* 75: 62–8.

Murphy, H.B.M. and Raman, A.C. (1971) 'The chronicity of schizophrenia in indigenous tropical peoples', *British Journal of Psychiatry* 117: 489–97.

Murray, R.M., Lewis, S.W., Owen, M.J., and Forster, A. (in press) 'The neurodevelopmental origins of dementia praecox', in P. McGuffin and P. Bebbington (eds) *Schizophrenia: The Major Issues*, London: Heinemann.

Noreik, K. and Ødegaard, Ø. (1967) 'Age of onset of schizophrenia in relation to socio-economic factors', *British Journal of Psychiatry* 1: 243–9.

Offord, D. (1974) 'School performance of adult schizophrenics, their siblings and age mates', *British Journal of Psychiatry* 125: 12–19.

Ricks, D.M. and Wing, L. (1975) 'Language, communication and the use of symbols in normal and autistic children' *Journal of Autism and Childhood Schizophrenia* 5: 191–221.

Robins, L.N. (1970) 'Follow-up studies investigating childhood disorders', in E.H. Hare and J.K. Wing (eds) *Psychiatric Epidemiology*, London: Oxford University Press.

Rutter, M. (1978) 'Communication deviance and diagnostic differences', in L.C. Wynne, R.L. Cromwell, and S. Matthysse (eds) *The Nature of Schizophrenia*, New York: Wiley.

Scull, A. (1979) *Museums of Madness: The Social Organization of Insanity in Nineteenth Century England*, London: Allen Lane.

Scull, A. (1984) 'Was insanity increasing? a response to Edward Hare', *British Journal of Psychiatry* 144: 432–6.

Shepherd, M. (1987) 'Formulation of new research strategies on schizophrenia', in H. Häfner, W.F. Gattaz, and W. Janzarik (eds) *Search for the Causes of Schizophrenia*, Heidelberg: Springer-Verlag.

Shepherd, M., Brooke, E.M., Cooper, J.E., and Lin, T.Y. (1968) 'An experimental approach to psychiatric diagnosis', *Acta Psychiatrica Scandinavica*, Supplement 201, Copenhagen: Munksgaard.

Shields, J. (1978) 'Genetics of schizophrenia', in J.K. Wing (ed.) *Schizophrenia: Towards a New Synthesis*, London: Academic Press, 56.

Singer, M.T., Wynne, L.C., and Toohey, M.L. (1978) 'Communication disorders and the families of schizophrenics', in L.C. Wynne, R.L. Cromwell, and S. Matthhysse (eds) *The Nature of Schizophrenia*, New York: Wiley.

Steinberg, H.R. and Durell, J. (1968) 'A stressful social situation as a precipitant of schizophrenic symptoms: an epidemiological study', *British Journal of Psychiatry* 114: 1097–105.

Stone, A.A. and Eldred, S.H. (1959) 'Delusion formation during the activation of chronic schizophrenic patients', *Archives of General Psychiatry* 1: 177–9.

Strauss, J.S. and Carpenter, W.T. (1981) *Schizophrenia*, New York: Plenum, chapter 2.

Tennant, C.C. (1985) 'Stress and schizophrenia: a review', *Integrative Psychiatry* 3: 248–61.

Tienarie, P., Sorri, A, Lahti, I., Naerala, M., Wahlberg, K., Moring, J., Pohjola, J., and Wynne, L.C. (1987) 'Genetic and psychosocial factors in schizophrenia: the Finnish Adoptive Family Study', *Schizophrenia Bulletin* 13: 477–95.

Torrey, E.F. (1980) *Schizophrenia and Civilisation*, New York: Aronson.

Vaughn, C. and Leff, J.P. (1976) 'The influence of family and social factors on the course of psychiatric illness', *British Journal of Psychiatry* 129: 125–37.

Watt, D.C., Katz, K., and Shepherd, M. (1983) 'The natural history of schizophrenia: a five-year prospective follow-up of a representative sample of schizophrenics by means of a standardized clinical and social assessment', *Psychological Medicine* 13: 663–70.

Watt, N.F. (1978) 'Patterns of childhood social development in adult schizophrenics', *Archives of General Psychiatry* 35: 160–5.

Watt, N. and Lubensky, A. (1976) 'Childhood roots of schizophrenia', *Journal of Consulting and Clinical Psychology* 44: 363–75.

Warner, R. (1985) *Recovery from Schizophrenia: Psychiatry and Political Economy*, London: Routledge & Kegan Paul, 24.

Wig, N., Menon, D.K., Bedi, H., Ghosh, A., Kuipers, L., Leff, J.P., Korten, A., Day, R., Sartorius, N., Eernberg, G., and Jablensky, A. (1987) 'Expressed emotion and schizophrenia in North India: I: the cross-cultural transfer of ratings and relatives' expressed emotion', *British Journal of Psychiatry* 151: 156–73.

Wing, J.K. (1975) 'Impairments in schizophrenia: a rational basis for social treatment', in R.D. Wirt, G. Winokur, and M. Roff (eds) *Life History Research in Psychopathology, Volume 4*, Minneapolis: University of Minnesota Press.

Wing, J.K. (1977) 'The management of schizophrenia in the community', in G. Usdin (ed.) *Psychiatric Medicine*, New York: Brunner Mazel.

Wing, J.K. (1983) 'Use and misuse of the PSE', *British Journal of Psychiatry* 143: 111–17.

Wing, J.K. (1986) 'Commentary on "Stress and Schizophrenia" by C.C. Tennant', *Integrative Psychiatry* 4: 57–8.

Wing, J.K. (1987) 'Has the outcome of schizophrenia changed?' in T.J. Crow (ed.) 'Recurrent and Chronic Psychoses', *British Medical Bulletin* 43: 741–53.

Wing, J.K. (1987) 'Long-term adaptation in schizophrenia', in N.E. Miller, and G.D. Cohen (eds) *Schizophrenia and Aging*, New York: Guilford Press, 183–6.

Wing, J.K. (in press) 'The nature of negative symptoms', in T. Barnes (ed.) *Negative Symptoms in Schizophrenia*, London: Gaskell Press.

Wing, J.K., Bennett, D.H., and Denham, J. (1964) *The Industrial Rehabilitation of Long-Stay Schizophrenic Patients* (Medical Research Council Memorandum No. 42), London: HMSO.

Wing, J.K., and Brown, G.W. (1970) *Institutionalism and Schizophrenia*, London: Cambridge University Press.

Wing, J.K., Cooper, J.E., and Sartorius, N. (1974) *The Description and Classification of Psychiatric Symptoms: An Instruction Manual for the PSE and CATEGO System*, London: Cambridge University Press.

Wing, J.K., and Der. G. (1984) 'Report of the Camberwell Psychiatric Register, 1964–1984', Medical Research Council Social Psychiatry Unit, mimeo.

Wing, J.K., and Freudenberg, R.K. (1961) 'The response of severely ill chronic schizophrenic patients to social stimulation', *American Journal of Psychiatry* 118: 311.

Wing, J.K., and Fryers, T. (1976) *Psychiatric Services in Camberwell and Salford, 1964–1975*, London: MRC Social Psychiatry Unit.

Wing, L. (1979) 'Mentally retarded children in Camberwell', in H. Häfner (ed.) *Estimating Needs for Mental Health Care*, Heidelberg: Springer-Verlag.

Wing, L. (1981) 'Asperger's syndrome', *Psychological Medicine* 11: 115–29.

Wing, L. (1982), chapters 29, 30, and 34, in J.K. Wing and L. Wing (eds) *Psychoses of Uncertain Aetiology*, Cambridge: Cambridge University Press.

Wing, L., Wing, J.K., Griffiths, D., and Stevens, B. (1972) 'An epidemiological and experimental evaluation of industrial rehabilitation of chronic psychotic patients in the community', in J.K. Wing and A.M. Hailey (eds) *Evaluating a Community Psychiatric Service*, London: Oxford University Press, 283–308.

World Health Organization (1973) *The International Pilot Study of Schizophrenia*, Geneva: WHO.

World Health Organization (1979) *Schizophrenia: An International Follow-up Study*, New York: Wiley.

World Health Organization (1986) 'Early manifestations and first-contact incidence of schizophrenia in different cultures: a preliminary report', *Psychological Medicine*, 16: 909–28.

World Health Organization (1987), chapter five on 'Mental, behavioural and development disorders, FOO–99', in *ICD–10 Research Diagnostic Criteria*, Geneva: WHO.

Wynne, L.C., Cole, R.E., and Perkins, P. (1987) 'University of Rochester Child and Family Study: risk research in progress', *Schizophrenia Bulletin*, 13: 463–76.

Psychosocial Adversity and Impaired Growth in Children: In Search of Causal Mechanisms

David Skuse

In 1976 the Committee on Child Health Services, chaired by Professor Donald Court, reported to the Secretaries of State (DHSS 1976). Three years of 'unremitting enquiry' had led, *inter alia*, to the conclusion that a significant correlation between social class and the prevalence of ill-health and disability among children persisted in our society. The effect of the environment could also be seen in growth. The Committee commented (p. 50) 'short stature can be normal; it can also be a disease of the social environment and an important pointer to a group of socially deprived children'. These comments are echoed in the recent report *Investing in the Future*, produced by the Policy and Practice Review Group at the National Children's Bureau (NCB 1987).

The key phrase 'an adverse family and social environment can retard physical . . . growth' (p. 50) begs the question 'How?' What are the mechanisms by which social disadvantage results in stunted children in a relatively prosperous, developed society such as our own? If there is to be provision of assistance to those in the community whose children are at risk, what form of intervention is most likely to be effective in ameliorating the consequences of that social deprivation?

The aim of this contribution is, first, to discuss the evidence that there is an undoubted association between certain indices of social deprivation and the impaired growth of many children raised in those conditions; second, to review critically the evidence for some of the mechanisms that have been proposed, emphasizing the often contradictory nature of that evidence; third, to propose a unifying hypothesis about the mechanisms by which 'psychosocial adversity' may affect growth and development, drawing upon findings from work of myself and colleagues with deprived families living in conditions of socio-economic disadvantage in the inner city. Emphasis will be placed upon the use of epidemiological research designs to generate hypotheses about causal mechanisms, which may then be tested in complementary case-control studies.

I propose to examine the association between 'poor home conditions' or 'psychosocial adversity' and short stature by discussing briefly genetic influences on growth, then certain broad environmental variables, such as social class, which are known to differentiate children with retarded growth from those who are fulfilling their genetic potential. Finally, I shall consider a number of specific mechanisms by which these broad environmental variables may exert their effect.

GENETIC INFLUENCES ON GROWTH

The correlation between parent and child heights increases during the first two years of the child's life, and then changes little until puberty. During adolescence the correlation decreases, corresponding to differences between children in the timing of the adolescent growth spurt – but eventually the correlation reaches levels slightly above the prepubertal values. Values of 0.5 to 0.6 are usually found for sample sizes above 500 pairs. The question arises, to what extent do such correlations result from genetic influences, and to what extent do they reflect a common environment or assortative mating?

This is a complex issue, and one which is not answered by an observation such as the fact that parent-child correlations (mother's, father's, and mid-parental height correlated with child's height at 5–11 years) are on the whole very similar across all social classes in England and Scotland (Rona 1981). The interesting question here remains unanswered; viz, are the correlations higher when the two generations remain in the same social class, and are they lower when there has been upward or downward movement between generations?

A normal curve of distribution of a quantitative character in a population may be generated entirely by its genetic determination. Normally, however, the total phenotypic variance is divided into a) additive polygenic effects; b) environmental effects; c) other sources (Roberts 1985). The additive genetic contribution expressed as a proportion of the total variance is the hereditability: a variable that may be estimated in a number of different ways. Genetic analyses of adult height are complicated because, besides being subject to environmental variation, stature changes with age and differs between the sexes. Furthermore, in European populations parent-child correlations may reflect an appreciable degree of assortative mating, which in a recent British survey (Mascie-Taylor 1987) was found to be largely *independent* of age or social and regional background, being related more closely to stature. That is rather a surprising finding, for there is certainly a tendency for people to marry those similar to themselves in terms of educational and social background, a major part also being played by geographical propinquity.

Both environmental and genetic hypotheses have been advanced to explain secular trends (Martorell 1985). For example, that they reflect an improved standard of living, especially in nutrition and sanitation. Also, that a potential contributory factor is genetic heterosis, or hybrid vigour, resulting from the breakdown of breeding isolation brought about by increased social and geographical mobility. Whatever the explanation, ultimately, secular changes in growth must depend upon systematic phenotypic deviation in the stature of offspring from their parents, and trends towards greater adult height in new generations must result from the fact that children outgrow their like-sexed parent (Bielicki 1986).

ENVIRONMENTAL INFLUENCES

Social class

Since the Second World War there have been numerous large-scale epidemiological surveys on the effect of the socio-cultural environment in England and Scotland upon child development (e.g. the National Study of Health and Growth, Rona *et al.* 1978; and the Preschool Child Survey, Fox *et al.* 1981). The NSHG was set up to provide surveillance of primary schoolchildren, concentrating on height as the main measure of nutritional status.

Analysis of data on the 1946 birth cohort (comprising children born in the UK during one week, see Douglas and Simpson 1964) revealed that the difference in the height of infants between the two extremes of the social-class distribution was 2 cm by the age of 2 years. This finding was confirmed by the later NSHG survey and various other surveys, both national and regional, have reported similar values (e.g. Fox *et al.* 1981). There has been almost no change in the last thirty years in terms of the relative differences between the most and least advantaged (top and bottom) social groups in the United Kingdom. However, the proportion of the population in the lowest social class (V – unskilled manual workers) is decreasing.

In both the 1946 and 1958 national birth cohorts (the latter also known as the National Child Development Study, Goldstein 1971) there was a tendency for a gradient of stature within the non-manual classes (i.e., from social class I–IIIa), but this was not observed in the NSHG, whose first cohort was born in 1976. At present, differences in height in children of primary school age are mainly due to the short stature of those in social class V. The absolute differences in mean height between social class increase with age. At age 2 the difference between the two extremes of the social class spectrum is about 0.33 standard deviation units, but this increases to 0.5 standard deviation units by age 4. Eventually, the difference reaches 0.6–0.7 standard deviation units by the time children enter primary school. Rona *et al.* (1978) report a study of 9–11 year-old English boys and girls measured in 1972. When the groups were classified according to their father's occupation it was found, as in previous surveys, that the children of fathers in non-manual occupations were taller than those of manual workers at most ages.

It is important to note that no association was found by the NSHG between the rate of growth in a year and father's social class in school-age children, once dependency of height gain on initial height was accounted for. In other words, the gap between the two extreme social class groups increases with age, but most of the increase (about 90 per cent) occurs before the child enters school. Thereafter, the child enters a stable trajectory of growth velocity.

There is an interaction between the effects of social class and the number of siblings in the family (Rona *et al.* 1978). Expressed as standard deviation scores from the median, there is little evidence of any effect of sibship size upon the height of English children in the non-manual groups, unless that figure is greater than five. However, there is a marked reduction in the height of children of manual workers for sibship groups of two or more. Of course, a distinction ought really to be made between sibship size and ordinal position. For example, it is unlikely the adversity of being in a large sibship group (e.g. of five) will be as marked on the first as on the fifth-born child. 'Number of younger siblings' is a wise modification to ordinal position status (Goldstein 1971), when undertaking data analysis of this nature.

Profile of social distribution of stature

A very important observation has been made about the *profile* of the distribution of stature among the children of manual workers. As has already been discussed, this is usually approximately normally distributed. At any particular age 50 per cent of the population will be above or below the 50th centile (median) of what is an approximately Normal or Gaussian distribution, although the absolute position of the median (the 50th centile) will vary between populations of children from different countries, or between relatively homogeneous sub-populations within countries (defined, for example, in socio-economic terms). In their recent survey of English schoolchildren Rona *et al.* (1978) found that the distribution of heights is not merely shifted downwards, but is 'spaced out' at the lower extremes of social class. The difference in stature between the children of manual and non-manual workers, of primary school age, is about 2 cm at the 50th centile, but is nearly 4 cm at the 3rd centile. This finding suggests that there is an excess of very small children of manual workers, which ties in with the reports from epidemiological surveys by both Lacey and Parkin (1974a, 1974b) and Vimpani *et al.* (1981).

Stability of growth patterns and secular trends

When one considers the growth rates of different social groups the absolute differences (measured in, for example, centimetres) in actual height gains are not a very satisfactory indicator of the period when the maximal effect of the social environment is operative. Taller children grow faster than shorter children, therefore the variance about the median increases with age. There

243

is also a strong tendency for individual children to remain in the approximately same centile of the height distribution after the first year or so of life (Smith *et al.* 1976; Smith *et al.* 1980; Elwood *et al.* 1987; Moar and Ounsted 1982).

As I have already emphasized, in the UK, social-class differences in height begin to emerge around two years of age. From this age onwards there is a consistent tendency for children from social class I to outgrow those from the lower social classes (Elwood *et al.* 1987). There is also some tendency for the head circumference of children from social classes I and II to grow more rapidly than those from social class V – although this difference achieves statistical significance only after 3 years of age (Elwood *et al.* 1987). The distribution of reduced stature is related more closely to social factors than to geographical differentiation (Mascie-Taylor and Boldsen 1985), although in England Caucasian children living in poor inner-city areas are approximately 1 cm shorter than the national average at 5–11 years of age (Rona and Chinn 1986). There was a tendency for the height of children studied by the NSHG (Rona *et al.* 1978) to be *less* in more densely populated areas than in less densely populated areas.

Secular trends in stature might be expected to *diminish* the differences between the growth of children from upper and lower social classes. One example that is often quoted is that of Sweden where obliteration of social-class gradient in stature was demonstrated by Lindgren (1976). Subsequently, a similar picture was found in Norway (Brundtland *et al.* 1980; see Bielicki 1986). It is, however, important to note that this finding should not be taken to mean that *social class* differences no longer exist in Scandinavian society. The lower classes have to some extent caught up with the upper ones but there are *still* significant differences in economic control, political influence, incomes, education, and social prestige (Bielicki 1986). Lindgren (1976) followed the course of growth of a large urban epidemiological sample of schoolchildren from 1964 to 1973. She concluded that differences in height had been eradicated by a relatively larger gain in the lower social groups than the higher.

The Dunedin birth cohort study, in New Zealand, has reported statistically significant but relatively small correlations between socio-economic status and stature (0.11 and 0.12 for boys and girls respectively) (Silva *et al.* 1985). However, the difference in mean stature between those at the top and bottom of the socio-economic scale is just two-thirds the magnitude of the corresponding British values as reported by Goldstein (1971).

Compared with other European and North American growth statistics, British 7 year olds are among the smallest, the median stature of boys of this age being nearly 0.7 s.d. below that of the tallest North American groups (Waterlow 1985). There has been a great deal of debate about the significance of such international comparisons (see, for example, Graitcer and Gentry 1981; Goldstein and Tanner 1980) but the weight of current opinion seems to be that mean sizes of children from different populations are, on the whole, due more to environmental factors than to genetic ones, at least up until puberty, excepting for certain races in the Far East (Martorell 1985; Martorell and Habicht 1986).

But even in the Far East there have been marked secular trends in the direction of increased stature over the past thirty years. Between 1957 and 1977 almost all the secular change in the height of young adults has been due to change in leg length. Final sitting height has changed little, if at all (Martorell and Habicht 1986). Incidentally, the *tempo* of change has affected both sitting height and leg length, both body segments reaching their pubertal growth spurt nearly a year earlier in 1977 than in 1957.

The relevance of this observation, an aspect of differential growth rarely commented on in reports of secular trends, is that there is evidence that 'psychosocial adversity' exerts its main effect upon leg length (Meredith 1984). It might be thought that under-nutrition would be a prime candidate as an explanatory variable, but Tanner (1978) believes under-nutrition in man does not alter body shape significantly; a malnourished European child 'by no means acquires the short legs of the Asiatic'. One is nevertheless tempted to draw an analogy between the chronically undernourished short-legged Asiatics and the clinical findings of western doctors, faced with children who have been subject to severe emotional deprivation and neglect, who report subischial lengths (stature minus sitting height) to be less than 70 per cent of the population mean (McCarthy 1981).

The best explanation for secular trends of this nature is thought to be an improvement in some aspect of the social and material conditions for the population concerned (Rona 1981). In the *most* advantaged strata of society the trend is *least* marked, a point neatly made by an observation by Bakwin and McLaughlin (1964) who found the height of students from modest social backgrounds entering Harvard university had increased nearly 4 cm between 1930 and 1958, whereas entrants from wealthy backgrounds did not change at all in height over that period. There is no evidence that the secular trend of growth has persisted since the mid-1950s in the United States but it *has* done so in Britain (Chinn and Rona 1984).

Unemployment

There has been much dispute over the interpretation of the findings that there are significant differences in stature between the children of employed and unemployed fathers, even within the same social class. For instance, Tanner (1987) has commented that there is unlikely to be any causal connection through a process of sub-optimal nutrition that might accompany a brief period of unemployment.

Unfortunately, most studies of the association between unemployment and children's growth have failed to take account of the differences between short- and long-term unemployment, asking only (for example) if the head of household has been out of work in the previous four weeks (Rona and Chinn 1984). Differences in height between children of the employed and unemployed have been found *within* each social class but the effect is largest in social class V where it is reported to be as large as 0.6 s.d. at school age (Rona and Chinn 1984). Nevertheless, the evidence points to the fact that such differences in stature are associated with long-term cultural and material hardships, rather than single brief episodes of unemployment.

Psychosocial adversity

In a small proportion of the population, maybe 5 to 10 per cent, many adverse social circumstances are linked (Rona 1981). It seems to be especially among that subgroup that socio-economic factors are in some way associated with a threat to the normal growth of children. These effects can be detected very early in a child's life. A recent Swedish study, longitudinal in design, examined the social circumstances of a group of thirty-four infants with abnormally low rates of weight gain in the first eighteen months of life (Kristiansson and Fallstrom 1981). An excess of 'psychosocial' risk factors was found more commonly in the families of these infants than in a comparison group. Such factors included unemployment, paternal ill health, dependence on social welfare, abuse of alcohol and drugs, single parenthood, and a history of criminal offences. Kristiansson concluded that 'psychosocial stress' was in some way a causal factor. However, he made no attempt to ascertain by direct observation how such stress might be affecting the *parenting* of the infants concerned.

A somewhat similar conclusion was reached by Lacey and Parkin (1974a, 1974b) who conducted a well-known epidemiological study of the growth of a cohort of children born in 1960 in Newcastle-upon-Tyne. The children were examined at 10 years of age. Their stature at that age was compared with standards for height at successive ages in UK children (Tanner 1978).

The study is often quoted as being of 'all' children born in 1960 (of Newcastle-upon-Tyne mothers), who were below the 3rd height centile at 10 years of age. In fact, only approximately 45 per cent of the original cohort were examined. Of those actually measured, 3.63 per cent were considered 'short normal' and 0.71 per cent had an organic disease or disorder to account for their short stature. An additional 0.58 per cent of children under the 3rd centile for height (total 4.92 per cent) were not investigated because of parental refusal. Social-class distribution of the sample was skew in comparison with the 1961 and 1962 cohorts of the Newcastle Survey of Child Development, with nearly twice as many parents of short normal children in social classes IV and V. Parents of short children were smaller than adults in the general population, an average about 1 standard deviation below the median.

The authors rated the care of their short normal sample from observations made at home visits, in terms of 'good, average or poor'. No details are given about how those ratings were derived, nor indeed about how a similar 'social score' was arrived at. Nevertheless, the important conclusion was reached that an adverse score on both variables was found far more frequently among the families of short normal children than among even the most disadvantaged in the general population (viz. social class V). They state 'poor home conditions have been of importance in causing the short stature of at least 30 per cent of the children under the 3rd height centile in Newcastle-upon-Tyne'.

Maternal care

This has rarely been assessed directly, but is usually discussed in the context of proxy measures such as maternal age or single parenthood. Children whose mothers were less than 25 years of age when they gave birth are on average 0.6 cm smaller than those whose mothers were older than 25 years (Goldstein 1971). Maternal age does not seem to affect birthweight, but this small but significant difference in their children's stature seems to persist even after allowance is made for other relevant biological factors (such as parity). Goldstein concludes, 'This effect [may represent] residual social factors associated with the mother's age, for example, illegitimacy'. Certainly the NSHG (Garman *et al.* 1982) reported that children from two-parent families are usually taller than those from one-parent families, but the difference is very small. When adjustments have been made for birthweight, number of sibs, mother's and father's stature, and mother's educational background, *statistically significant* differences were found only in respect of girls from Scotland. Interestingly, persons in one-parent families are on average shorter than those in two-parent families, and their children have on average lower birthweights.

Apart from the survey of Lacey and Parkin (1974a, 1974b) and the recent work conducted by myself and colleagues (*vide infra*), direct measures of maternal care and growth have not been done, except in a study of thirty years ago by Douglas and Blomfield (1958). They found a very small association between standard of maternal care, as reported by health visitors, and children's height at 4.25 years. Only in children from intermediate social classes was there a tendency towards shorter stature in those children whose mothers were given the poorest ratings.

The inconclusive findings of former studies should not be taken to imply that caretaking quality is not a relevant variable. As Rona (1981) emphasizes, all the operational variables that have been used to measure the standard of maternal care have been unsatisfactory.

Thus, we may conclude, with regard to broad environmental influences on children's growth:

1. There is *no* inevitable difference between the stature of children in the upper and lower social classes – even though many inequalities in the

distribution of resources to those classes continue to exist.

2. Since the Second World War in the UK the absolute difference in stature between upper and lower classes persists but the proportion of the population in the lower range of the social-class distribution is decreasing. The finding is largely accounted for by an *excess* of very small children, mainly from social class V. The magnitude of the statural difference is exacerbated when there is associated unemployment.

3. By far the greater part of the growth retardation in disadvantaged groups, relative to national norms, is evident by the time the child enters primary school at age 5 years. Substantial differences are initially seen within the first year or two of life.

SPECIFIC INFLUENCES

I shall now consider some of the relatively specific factors that are known to be intervening variables between general environmental influences and rates of physical development.

Birthweight

During infancy a reassortment of relative sizes among children comes about, those who are larger at birth tending to grow more slowly and those who are smaller often growing more quickly. The correlation between length at birth and adult height is low – about 0.3. By six months it has risen to 0.5 and by one year to 0.7. By two years a stable pre-pubertal level of 0.8 is reached (Tanner 1986). Nevertheless, small-for-dates babies often stay small (Smith *et al.* 1976). There is now good evidence that those who are born relatively long, but of low weight (type II) will tend to catch up in weight, length, and head circumference by the age of one year. But those who are of low birthweight for their statistical age and who are also short (type I) will tend to stay small (Holmes *et al.* 1977). In view of the difference in prognosis of the two conditions, it is obviously crucial to distinguish between them in epidemiological research, especially in view of the fact that some intra-uterine insults – such as chronic maternal under-nutrition associated with socio-economic deprivation (Lin and Evans 1984), alcohol abuse (Smithells and Smith 1984) or smoking (D'Souza *et al.* 1981) – may be associated with type I rather than type II intra-uterine growth. Unfortunately, such data are rarely reported.

For many years a difference in the birthweight of infants born to mothers from different social classes has been recognized, both in developing as well as more socio-economically advantaged countries (e.g. Rosa and Turshen 1970). However, the broad association between social class and birthweight conceals a complex web of other associated variables. Recent evidence suggests that the finding may be accounted for entirely by specific factors such as poor weight gain during pregnancy, smoking, inadequate ante-natal care, use of alcohol, etc.

A large epidemiological survey at the University of Kansas Medical Center (e.g. Miller *et al.* 1976), on more than 2,700 white women and their single-ton infants, found *no* differences in the incidence of low birthweight babies (defined as weighing < 2500g but over thirty-seven weeks gestation) across four socio-economic groups, once indices such as cigarette smoking during pregnancy, alcohol or drug abuse, and maternal malnutrition were taken into account. These data accord with smaller-scale surveys in this country (e.g. Ounsted and Scott 1982). In a recent careful investigation of 483 women living in the city of Oxford, Stein *et al.* (1987) found no association between social class and birthweight (once factors such as smoking were controlled for) but he did discover low income to be an independent predictor of birthweight, over and above unemployment. He also measured the expectant mother's psychiatric state using the Present State Examination (Wing *et al.* 1974) but found *no* evidence of an association between psychiatric morbidity, adverse life events, or long-term social difficulties and birthweight.

Smoking

There is substantial evidence that smoking during pregnancy results in newborn infants who are both lighter and shorter than those born to women who do not smoke, even after gestational age differences are taken into account (Meredith 1975). Smoking is significantly more common among parents from a poor social environment or limited educational background (59 per cent of social class V mothers, 15 per cent of social class I) (Rona *et al.* 1985).

Analyses of data from the National Study of Health and Growth (NSHG) in England and Scotland have shown that the number of cigarettes smoked by parents at home is significantly associated with the attained height of their children aged 5 to 11 years. This relationship is statistically significant, *even after* allowing for parental height, child's birthweight, mother's smoking during pregnancy, overcrowding, and number of siblings (Rona *et al.* 1985). Passive smoking therefore seems to have an effect on the linear growth of the child, *independent* of genetic factors, the social environment, and mother's smoking in pregnancy.

The mechanisms by which parental smoking and the linear growth of their children are linked have not been clarified. There are a number of potential aetiological processes. One possibility is that the infants of such parents have an excess of respiratory illnesses in infancy (e.g. Chen *et al.* 1986). Accordingly, it may be these recurrent illnesses that lead to a diminution of linear growth. However, there does not in general seem to be any close correlation between the number of *minor* respiratory illnesses during this period and an infant's rate of growth (Elwood *et al.* 1987).

An alternative hypothesis is that the food intake of children from families who smoke is diminished, perhaps because there is direct suppression of their appetite. Alternatively, families of smokers may provide smaller portions (Bergen 1981). This may be due either to the parents' own diminished appetite or, perhaps, the lower allocation of the families' resources for food purchase (Rona et al. 1985).

Third, cigarette smoke may contain components that have a directly harmful effect upon growth outside the uterus (e.g. Richardson et al. 1975). If that is the case, it has been postulated that the aetiological factor is likely to be the level of carbon monoxide in the child's environment. Perhaps an intermittent moderate increase in carbon monoxide, resulting in carboxyhaemoglobin formation, leads to a significant decrease in the amount of oxygen released at tissue level and a lowering of the efficiency of the cytochrome chain (Hamosh et al. 1979).

Fourth, passive cigarette smoking may be associated with an excess of digestive disorders in infants, including post-prandial colic (Said et al. 1984). A dose-response relationship between the number of cigarettes smoked by parents and the frequency of post-prandial colic has been reported. This association has also been investigated by an epidemiological survey of infants born in Tayside during 1980 (Ogston et al. 1987). Parental smoking was found to be associated with a higher frequency of reported alimentary disorders (as well as respiratory illnesses) in the first year of the child's life. It was hypothesized that there might be a link between parental smoking and reflex intestinal activity. The component of cigarette smoke responsible has not yet been identified.

Finally, a longitudinal study of children between 6 and 11 years of age demonstrated a dose-response relationship between the amount of current maternal cigarette smoking and attained height (Berkey et al. 1984). Analyses indicated that the observed association at that age was almost certainly due either to *former* exposure in utero and/or during *early* infancy. In light of Rona et al.'s (1981) conclusion that the association between the number of smokers in the home and their children's height could not be explained by maternal smoking during *pregnancy*, the authors hypothesize that it was sustained exposure to the products of smoking during the *first year of life* that produced an effect still observable in 6 year olds.

Illnesses

It has been known for many years that illness in childhood can have a significant effect upon the rate of growth, although a slowing of that rate is more likely to be found as a result of a relatively severe illness or in children who have a chronic condition such as recurrent respiratory illness or asthma (Elwood et al. 1987).

Recent evidence (Rogers 1984; Tanner 1986) has shown that during periods of acute illness children of school age grow more slowly than during corresponding periods without illness, but that on recovery from that illness they grow more rapidly, demonstrating 'catch-up' growth provided their nutrition at this time is good. There is no evidence that recurrent minor illnesses are associated with lower eventual heights nor even with reduced velocities over a period of one year or more (Elwood *et al.* 1987; Tanner 1986).

Nutrition

Children have higher requirements for energy, per unit body weight, than adults. This is due partly to a need to cover their higher metabolic rate per unit weight, which is twice that of an adult during infancy, but also to provide energy for the purposes of growth (Widdowson 1985). The energy cost of growth is highest in the first few months after birth. It then falls rapidly throughout the first year, from 30 per cent of normal energy intake at 1–2 months to 3 per cent at 9–12 months and only 1 per cent by 18–24 months (Bergmann and Bergmann 1986). Per unit body weight, energy intake has been reported to be greatest in normal healthy infants during the interval fourteen through twenty-seven days of age, decreasing thereafter. The correlation between weight gain and caloric intake is statistically significant (between 0.4 and 0.7) for both sexes during the first ten months of life. The ratio of dietary energy contributed by carbohydrates and fat does not seem to affect growth rates (Fomon *et al.* 1976). In the developed world, protein intake is rarely a limiting factor in determining rates of linear growth (Tanner 1978).

When energy availability is deficient, growth and maintenance become competitive, and growth disorders, as well as reduced activity levels, may ensue. Infants eat mainly for energy (Bergmann and Bergmann 1986).

Many studies have attempted to demonstrate an association between deficient nutritional intake, social deprivation, and retarded physical growth of children in the developed world. Most of these investigations have been of children of school age. For example, Hackett *et al.* (1984) conducted a two-year longitudinal survey of dietary intake and growth in height and weight of 11- and 12-year-old English schoolchildren. The expected differences in height and weight were found between the social classes, but there was no significant correlation between energy or protein intake and height and weight increments during the period of the study, even within social classes.

A careful prospective survey of ninety-one families with children under 4 years of age found that the energy intake of children from families headed by a manual worker was higher than those from children of non-manual workers (Black *et al.* 1976). This finding not only replicated the results of earlier investigations (e.g. Widdowson 1947) but also anticipated the results of later epidemiological surveys in other settings. For example, Jones *et al.* (1985) in the USA examined associations between various measures of child growth, dietary variables, and an index of poverty status in a sample of 13,750 black and white children aged 1–17 years. Differences in growth were not consistently associated with differences in the dietary intake of energy between poverty groups. and in the 1–5 year age range poor children seemed to have a higher energy intake than comparisons from families above the poverty level. Differences *did* however exist in child growth variables, in the expected direction.

Nevertheless, we know from innumerable studies in the developing world that, when children are faced with chronic but moderate deficiencies of nutrients, they will grow less in weight and height, but will manage to main-tain *normal proportions* of weight to height so long as the severity of nutritional deficiency does not increase dramatically (e.g. Martorell 1985; Martorell and Habicht 1986). They will, therefore, be stunted. Stunting refers to retardation in linear growth, as measured by total body length or height. Wasting, in contrast, has to do with the relationship of body weight to length, and is usually seen when either severe food shortages or infections impair the body's ability to regulate growth and sustain adaptation to adverse circumstances (Waterlow 1985). It is important to note that, when faced with chronic but moderate deficiency of nutrients, the child will grow less in height and weight, but will manage to maintain fairly normal proportions of weight to height (i.e. will not be extraordinarily skinny) (Alvear *et al.* 1986).

In the developing world, the mean length of infants at birth is usually near the 50th centile of growth charts applicable to relatively affluent societies. Then, in societies where chronic under-nourishment is endemic, between the second and sixth months (when energy needs for growth are relatively high) supine length begins to fall precipitously relative to western standards as rates of linear growth begin to be affected (see Martorell and Habicht 1986).

A similar profile of growth trajectories has been reported in clinical populations of infants aged 2 to 28 months who were failing to thrive in a western society. The important observation was made that in those who were *proportionately small* for their age, or stunted (i.e. > 80 per cent ideal body weight for length), there was no significant correlation between caloric intake and weight gain in hospital (Schaffer Bell and Woolston 1985). Even high intakes of energy were often associated with little percentage weight change. There was, however, a slight tendency for the highest percentage change to occur in the youngest subjects (i.e. under 9 months). In contrast, those who were relatively underweight for their length gained weight in proportion to their ingestion of energy-rich nutrition.

Catch-up growth

In favourable environmental conditions the trajectory of growth in height of children is so constant that it may be represented by a relatively simple mathematical curve (Preece and Baines 1978). Should adverse circumstances supervene, the rate of growth starts temporarily to slow down, whether because of acute malnutrition, or in association with organic disorders such as growth hormone deficiency or coeliac disease. After rectifying the disorder a phase of more rapid or accelerated growth is seen which persists until the child's growth is back on the pre-existing trajectory (Tanner 1986). Some children will catch up very quickly, but others may take relatively longer, yet eventually end up on the predicted trajectory. In general, the more severe the growth-retarding influence, the longer it acts, and the earlier in life it occurs, the worse the ultimate outcome.

The completeness and speed of catch-up may depend upon the nature of the growth-retarding influence (e.g. growth hormone deficiency seems to be more devastating than hypothyroidism). Somehow, the growth-retarded child recognizes that it is small, but it also recognizes when it is restored to normal size – since, when approaching the normal curve, the rate of growth slows down and settles back on to it, no overshoot occurring in stature.

There is no general agreement about whether growth retardation caused by malnutrition in early infancy is a reversible or an irreversible phenomenon (Alvear *et al.* 1986). However, there is evidence that the possibilities for catch-up growth are very limited once the child reaches 3–5 years of age. If he or she is already small the probability is that they will remain small throughout the growing years, eventually becoming a small adult (Martorell 1985).

First year as sensitive period

There is a long-established view, based upon work both with animals (e.g. McCance and Widdowson 1962) and with humans (e.g. Eid 1971) that early infancy represents in some way a sensitive period with regard to growth. There are relatively few studies that have specifically examined this issue. One such investigation by Eid (1971) examined 132 infants who were failing to thrive during the first year, 88.5 per cent of whom had a physical disease or disorder to account for the pattern of growth. Subjects were followed up to 5 years of age, by which time 16 per cent of those who had received active treatment were still significantly growth retarded (height and weight < 3rd centile) as were 37 per cent of those who had not received active treatment. The authors concluded that, if the failure to thrive had not been corrected during the first year, there was a significantly greater retardation in subsequent height, weight, and head circumference. Unfortunately, there is little discussion of the fact that half of the children in the treatment group were small-for-dates babies, as were all of those in the untreated group, i.e. this was an example of poor study design because the small-for-dates babies might have had a limited capacity for catch-up growth. Both groups had birthweights significantly lower than a comparison group. Waterlow *et al.* (1980), among others, have reported that the rate of weight gain in infants in the developing world begins to fall off sharply, when compared to a reference population, as early as 3–4 months. The pattern of growth thenceforth is very similar to that seen in Eid's sample (Eid 1971).

Additional data on these questions are provided by an intriguing case comparison study of the Bedouin in the Negev desert (Dagan *et al.* 1983). The growth and feeding practices of 353 Bedouin infants were studied; they were fed irregularly whenever they expressed hunger, but as soon as the baby stopped eating mother would stop feeding. Breast feeding was prolonged (63 per cent at 12 months) and there was little supplementary nutrition with animal products. Fruit and vegetables were introduced later (to only 50 per cent of infants by the seventh month of life) than for the comparison group of Jewish children living in the same area. Rice, the most important supplementary food, was introduced only after six months. During the first half of the first year the mean weight of Bedouin infants progressively approached the 3rd centile of the NCHS curves (WHO 1983), and there was also progressive stunting of supine length. The infants did seem to be malnourished relative to the comparison population, because of poor feeding practices. Yet, weight for length remained approximately normally distributed about the median (50th) NCHS percentile, and triceps skinfold thickness was only slightly diminished. Catch-up growth did not subsequently occur to any great extent, the adult height of Bedouin men and women being between the 10th and 15th centiles for a western population (Groen *et al.* 1964).

In a totally different setting, Pollitt and Leibel (1980) studied a sample of nineteen children between 12–59 months of age from one out-patient department in the urban United States whose heights and weights were below the 3rd centile. These children had failed to thrive without organic disease or disorder, yet had not been premature or small for dates. No significant differences between the degrees of thinness or obesity were found between the groups, although there had been a downward drift in weight-gain rates since birth. Although the children in a comparison group, growing well, had a statistically higher intake of calories, in both groups the value for virtually all nutrients was very close to or above the recommended dietary allowance (NAS 1974). The index children had a history of poor feeding *within the first year of life*, and the pattern of growth exhibited by several of the cases was very similar to that seen in malnourished infants and pre-schoolers in developing countries (Waterlow *et al.* 1980). The authors conclude that *current* malnutrition seemed an unlikely explanation for the poor growth rates of their case sample, although the measures of intake were crude. The implicit corollary is that malnutrition occurred at an *earlier* age and the children had not 'caught up', but continued growing at a steady low average velocity.

Thus we may conclude:

1. Although the lower social classes tend to have children who are of lower birthweight, due either to shorter periods of gestation or because they are lighter for dates, these differences alone are *not* sufficient to account for persisting growth retardation. Comparable light birthweight children from the upper social classes show catch-up growth to

trajectories within the normal range within two years.

2. Growth trajectories are largely established within the first year or so of life. This is a time when the developing organism is especially vulnerable to environmental insults, because a small diminution in rate of growth for relatively briefer times will have a more devastating effect. If the growth trajectory diverges drastically from the ideal population median during this period there is probably a *limited opportunity* for full catch-up growth, even if circumstances later improve.

3. When all the specific postulated aetiological factors are considered the final common denominator seems likely to be nutritional deficiencies. Given the evidence that a close correlation between energy intake and growth has been demonstrated in western infants only within the first year and given the findings on the timing of growth delays in disadvantaged populations, it seems a reasonable working hypothesis that growth delay attributed to so-called 'psychosocial deprivation' may ultimately be due to under-nourishment at a *very early stage* in an infant's life. Such under-nourishment is likely to be linked to inadequate parenting, exemplified by poor feeding practices. It may be exacerbated by an infant's persistent exposure to cigarette smoke and associated relatively high carbon monoxide levels.

PARENTING STYLES AND GROWTH DELAY AMONG INNER-CITY INFANTS

Research by myself and colleagues over the past five years has sought to provide some answers to the questions raised by a consideration of the nature of social adversity and its relation to children's growth. An epidemiological approach has been taken, and all assessments of parenting have been done blind to the children's case/comparison status. The population under investigation has comprised the inhabitants of a geographically delimited, racially heterogeneous inner-city area (population 140,000) in which there are approximately 2,500 births each year. In socio-economic terms the district is relatively homogeneous and quite severely disadvantaged (South East Thames Regional Health Authority 1984). Two whole population surveys have been conducted. The first centred on a cohort of 1980 births (the 1980 birth cohort) for whom limited longitudinal data were available between birth and four years of age. At one year of age, nearly 5 per cent of full-term Caucasian singletons were found to have weights below the 3rd population centile on national charts (Skuse 1987). Their profile of growth since birth, at near normal birthweights, was virtually identical to undernourished infants from less developed countries (Waterlow *et al.* 1980).

The great majority had no organic disease or disorder that could account for their condition. Few (28 per cent) had received hospital referral,

255

investigation, or treatment; of these who had been seen, most cases of growth retardation did not recover.

The 1980 birth cohort survey aimed to examine, at four years of age, those children in the community with the *poorest* rates of growth, in terms of weight gain, since infancy. A case-comparison design was used, full details of which are given in Dowdney *et al.* (1987). The case group were stunted, with heights and weights in proportion but on average below the 3rd population centile on national charts, even when their parents' stature was taken into account.

In view of the strong evidence that, although the origins of such growth problems seem to lie in a complex interaction between child and family variables, the proximal cause is inadequate nutrition for the infant's needs (Skuse 1985), a particular emphasis was placed on nutritional assessment. Direct observations were made of family interactions during meal-times when the children were four years of age. Detailed dietary information was obtained, and a history of feeding practices and problems was taken from the mother (Heptinstall *et al.* 1987). Findings indicated that neither quantity of food intake (calorie/protein) nor gross environmental variables distinguished the case and comparison groups. However, the meal-time observations revealed considerably more disorganization and negative attitudes in case-group families, the number of instructions and negative comments to the index child being significantly higher than in comparison families. Interview data revealed that the observed pattern of lack of supervision, coupled with a somewhat arbitrary and insensitive approach to control of feeding, seemed to have characterized the case mothers' parenting style from the earliest days. For example, 35 per cent of the case group had frequently been fed as infants by bottles propped in their mouths, nearly four times as many in the comparison group. Incidentally, one in every three mothers of growth-retarded 4-year-olds reported that their children stole food, whereas only one comparison mother made this complaint.

When the data on feeding practices had been analysed, there was compelling evidence that a period of chronic and severe under-nourishment was likely to have occurred in early infancy. All case children had begun to fail to thrive *within the first year of life*. The design of the 1980 birth cohort 'catch-up' prospective study generated challenging hypotheses on the factors associated with a poor prognosis, but it was not possible adequately to test them.

A second, truly prospective, epidemiological study was therefore designed, with the intention of examining postulated causal mechanisms, derived from analysis of the original data. Again a whole population survey technique was used, in exactly the same geographical area as before. The sampling frame comprised all 1986 births in the district (the '1986' birth cohort). Cohort infants have been monitored since birth, cases and comparisons being examined at approximately 12 to 15 months of age. Data collection on this investigation is still in progress but a substantial pilot survey, using a case-comparison design, has been completed. Semi-structured interview and direct observation techniques within subject's homes were employed. The research design anticipated the hypothesis that growth delay among inner-city infants is usually the outcome of a subtle interaction between the individual biological and psychological characteristics of the child and features of the caretaking environment which fail to meet that child's specific and particular needs (Skuse 1985). Inappropriate management can exacerbate pre-existing delays or disorders in age-dependent processes (such as the acquisition of oral-motor skills). Disruption in normal processes of adaptation and change may result in poorly regulated and unpredictable children who fail to signal their needs clearly and unambiguously.

The results of the pilot survey showed case infants possessed characteristics of behavioural style, communication skills, oral-motor behaviour, and attentional processes in line with the above hypotheses. Such features were found in association with mothers who expressed more negative emotion, showed less reciprocity, and were poorer managers of their infant's behaviour (Wolke *et al.* 1987). No significant differences were found between the groups in terms of the quantities of nutrition *presented* to the infants by their mothers, but case infants did possess characteristics that rendered them more difficult to feed successfully, therefore their actual *intake* was probably deficient due to food loss, refusal, etc. (Subsequent data collected on the 1986 birth cohort, using multi-method assessments of nutritional status, have confirmed this impression.) Their behavioural style was either irritable and fussy *or* apathetic and undemanding. The latter picture characterized infants who were most seriously underweight and was reminiscent of the 'reductive adaptation' described by Jackson and Golden (1987) in which energy resources are conserved during conditions of severe shortage, by a reduction in energy expenditure. Case mothers' style of feeding and associated contextual features (such as positioning and ambient noise) accentuated the problem (Mathisen *et al.* 1987). None of the case subjects in the pilot survey had an organic aetiology of their failure to thrive. Little indication was found of overt child abuse, rejection, or deliberate neglect of case infants.

In conclusion, there is substantial evidence that the small size of children from developing countries is not due, on the whole, to ethnic variations but rather to the effects of environmental factors. Among these, poor nutrition seems to be the most important. Growth patterns of a significant minority of infants from deprived inner-city areas in western countries seem to be very similar to those of their stunted brethren overseas. A parsimonious hypothesis about mechanisms states that the proximal aetiological factors are also similar, and evidence has been adduced which supports that view. Following failure to thrive in early infancy, affected children do *not* completely catch-up in their growth rates, at least so long as they continue to live in the same family unit. Early poor rates of weight gain probably precede a similar pattern of retardation in the development of stature.

One further test of the proposed causal chain would be a trial to alter feeding practices among mothers of infants believed to be at risk. Such studies have already been undertaken in poor, under-privileged communities in South and Central America, and elsewhere (see Martorell and Habicht 1986).

Of course, those interventions aimed to provide additional nutrients to impoverished communities. There is no suggestion from our work that poverty among inner-city families is the determining factor leading to under-nourishment of case infants. Adequate food *is* available, in quantity if not in quality. The essential problem seems to be that some mothers do not recognize, or adapt to, the special qualities of 'at risk' infants, especially the characteristics of their neuromotor development and behavioural style. Such mothers may, in contrast, have coped perfectly well with other children, who lack such characteristics and whose growth has been correspondingly unremarkable.

Further pilot work has demonstrated that it is possible and indeed relatively easy to alert many such mothers to the problem. Video-feedback techniques are used, based upon the thesis that an intervention aimed at changing *maternal* responsivity and emotional expression is likely to be followed by a rapid change in child behaviour, leading to greater reinforcement for the mother (Crittenden 1985). Interactions are videotaped in the home and immediately played back, with a commentary by the observer. Dramatic results have been documented after a relatively few sessions with this technique.

A parent health education study along these lines is now planned, using a novel case-comparison factorial design to assess the impact of such an intervention upon *all* families containing a growth- retarded infant, who live within the geographical boundaries of an inner-city health district.

REFERENCES

Alvear, J., Arjaza, C., Vial, M., Guerrero, S., and Muzzo, S. (1986) 'Physical growth and bone age of survivors of protein energy malnutrition', *Archives of Disease in Childhood* 61: 257–62.

Bakwin, H. and McLaughlin, S.M. (1964) 'Secular increase in height: is the end in sight?' *Lancet* 2: 1195–6.

Bergen, S. (1981) 'Parental smoking at home and height of children (correspondence)', *British Medical Journal* 282: 1612.

Bergmann, R.L. and Bergmann, K.E. (1986) 'Nutrition and growth in infancy', in F. Falkner and J.M. Tanner (eds) *Human Growth: A Comprehensive Treatise: Volume 3: Methodology: Ecological, Genetic, and Nutritional Effects on Growth*, London: Plenum Press, 389–413.

Berkey, C.S., Ware, J.H., Speizer, F.E., and Ferris, B.G. (1984) 'Passive smoking and height growth of preadolescent children', *International Journal of Epidemiology* 13 (4): 454–8.

Bielicki, T. (1986) 'Physical growth as a measure of the economic well-being of populations: the twentieth century', in F. Falkner and J.M. Tanner (eds) *Human Growth: A Comprehensive Treatise: Volume 3: Methodology: Ecological, Genetic, and Nutritional Effects on Growth*, London: Plenum Press, 283–305.

Black, A.E., Billewicz, W.Z., and Thomson, A.M. (1976) 'The diets of preschool children in Newcastle upon Tyne, 1968–71', *British Journal of Nutrition* 35: 105–13.

Brundtland, G.H., Liestøl, K., and Walløe, L. (1980 'Height weight and menarcheal age of Oslo schoolchildren during the last 60 years', *Annals of Human Biology* 7: 307–22.

Chen, Y., Li, W., and Yu, S. (1986) 'Influence of passive smoking on admissions for respiratory illness in early childhood', *British Medical Journal* 293: 303–6.

Chinn, S. and Rona, R.J. (1984) 'The secular trend in the height of primary school children in England and Scotland from 1972–1980', *Annals of Human Biology* 11(1): 1–16.

Crittenden, P.M. (1985) 'Maltreated infants: vulnerability and resilience', *Journal of Child Psychology & Psychiatry* 26: 85–96.

Dagan, R., Sofer, S., Klish, W.J., Hundet, G., Saltz, H., and Moses, S.W. (1983) 'Growth & nutritional status of Bedouin infants in the Negev desert Israel: evidence for marked stunting in the presence of only mild malnutrition', *American Journal of Clinical Nutrition* 38: 747–56.

Department of Health & Social Security, Department of Education & Science, & Welsh Office (1976) *Fit for the Future* (Report of the Committee on Child Health Services, Chairman Professor S.D.M. Court), London: HMSO.

Douglas, J.W.B. and Blomfield J.M. (1958) *Children Under Five*, London: Allen & Unwin.

Douglas, J.W.B. and Simpson, H. (1964) 'Height in relation to puberty family size and social class', *Millbank Memorial Fund Quarterly* 42: 20–35.

Dowdney, L., Skuse, D., Heptinstall, E., Puckering, C., and Zur-Szpiro, S. (1987) 'Growth retardation and developmental delay among inner city children'. *Journal of Child Psychology & Psychiatry* 28(4): 529–41.

D'Souza, K., Black, P., and Richards, B. (1981) 'Smoking in pregnancy: associations with skinfold thickness, maternal weight gain, and fetal size at birth', *British Medical Journal* 282: 1661–3.

Eid, E.E. (1971) 'A follow-up study of physical growth following failure to thrive with special reference to a critical period in the first year of life', *Acta Paediatrica Scandinavica* 60: 39–48.

Elwood, P.C., Sweetman, P.M., Gray, O.P., Davies, D.F., and Wood, P.D.Q. (1987) 'Growth of children from 0–5 years: with special reference to mother's smoking in pregnancy', *Annals of Human Biology* 14(6): 543–57.

Fomon, S.J., Thomas, L.N., Filer, L.J.Jr., Anderson, T.A., and Nelson, S.E. (1976) 'Influence of fat and carbohydrate content of diet on food intake and growth of male infants', *Acta Paediatrica Scandinavica* 65: 136.

Fox, P.T., Elston, M.E., and Waterlow, J.C. (1981) *Preschool Child Survey* (DHSS Report of Health & Social Subjects no. 21), London: HMSO, 64–84.

Garman, A.R., Chinn, S., and Rona, R.J. (1982) 'Comparative growth of primary schoolchildren from one and two parent families', *Archives of Disease in Childhood* 57: 453–8.

Goldstein, H. (1971) 'Factors influencing the height of seven year old children – results from the national child development study', *Human Biology* 43: 92–111.

Goldstein, H. and Tanner, J.M. (1980) 'Ecological considerations in the creation and use of child growth standards', *Lancet* i: 582–5.

Graitcer, P.L. and Gentry, E.M. (1981) 'Measuring children: one reference for all', *Lancet* ii: 297–9.

Groen, J.J., Balogh, M., Levy, M., and Yaron, E. (1964) 'Nutrition of the Bedouins in the Negev Desert', *American Journal of Clinical Nutrition* 74: 33–46.

Hackett, A.F., Rugg-Gunn, A.J., Appleton, D.R., Parkin, J.M., and Eastoe, J.E. (1984) 'Two-year longitudinal study of dietary intake in relation to the growth of 405 English children initially aged 11–12 years', *Annals of Human Biology* 11(6): 545–53.

Hamosh, M., Simon, M.R., and Hamosh, T. (1979) 'Effect of nicotine on the development of fetal and suckling rats', *Biology of the Neonate* 35: 290–7.

Heptinstall, E., Puckering, C., Skuse, D., Dowdney, L., and Zur-Szpiro, S. (1987) 'Nutrition and mealtime behaviour in families of growth retarded children', *Human Nutrition: Applied Nutrition* 41a(6): 390–402.

Holmes, G.E., Miller, H.C., Hassanein, K., Lansky, S.B., and Goggin, J.E. (1977) 'Postnatal somatic growth in infants with atypical fetal growth patterns', *American Journal of Diseases of Children* 131: 1078–83.

Jackson, A.A. and Golden, H.M.W. (1987) 'Severe malnutrition', in D.J. Weatherall, J.G.G. Ledingham, and D.A. Warrell, (eds) *Oxford Textbook of Medicine*, second edition, Oxford: Oxford Univerisity Press, pp. 812–28.

Jones, D.Y., Nesheim, M.C., and Habicht, J.P. (1985) 'Influences in child growth associated with poverty in the 1970s', *American Journal of Clinical Nutrition* 42: 714–24.

Kristiansson, B. and Fallstrom, S.P. (1981) 'Infants with low rates of weight gain: II: a study of environmental factors', *Acta Paediatrica Scandinavica* 70: 663–68.

Lacey, K.A. and Parkin, J.M. (1974a) 'Causes of short stature: a community study of children in Newcastle-upon-Tyne', *Lancet* 1: 42–5.

Lacey, K.A. and Parkin, J.M. (1974b) 'The normal short child: a community study of children in Newcastle-upon-Tyne', *Archives of Disease in Childhood* 49: 417–24.

Lin, C.C. and Evans, M.I. (1984) *Intrauterine Growth Retardation: Pathophysiology and Clinical Management*, New York: McGraw-Hill.

Lindgren, G. (1976) 'Height weight and menarche in Swedish urban school children in relation to socioeconomic and regional factors', *Annals of Human Biology* 3: 501–28.

McCance, R.A. and Widdowson, E.M. (1962) 'Nutrition and growth', *Proceedings of the Royal Society B* 156: 326–37.

McCarthy, D. (1981) 'The effects of emotional disturbance and deprivation on somatic growth', in J.A. Davis and J. Dobbing (eds) *Scientific Foundations of Paediatrics*, London: Heinemann.

Martorell, R. (1985) 'Child growth retardation: a discussion of its causes and its relationship to health', in K. Blaxter and J.C. Waterlow (eds) *Nutritional Adaptation in Man*, London and Paris: John Libbey, 13–29.

Martorell, R. and Habicht, J.P. (1986) 'Growth in early childhood in developing countries', in F. Falkner and J.M. Tanner (eds) *Human Growth: A Comprehensive Treatise: Volume 3: Methodology Ecological Genetic and Nutritional Effects on Growth*, London: Plenum Press, 241–62.

Martorell, R., Yarborough, C., Klein, R.E., and Lechtig, A. (1979) 'Malnutrition body size and skeletal maturation: interrelationships and implications for catch-up growth', *Human Biology* 51(3): 371–89.

Mascie-Taylor, C.G.N. (1987) 'Assortative mating in a contemporary British population', *Annals of Human Biology* 14(1): 59–68.

Mascie-Taylor, C.G.N. and Boldsen, J.L. (1985) 'Regional and social analysis of height variations in a contemporary British sample', *Annals of Human Biology* 12(4): 315–24.

Mathisen, B., Skuse, D., and Wolke, D. (1987) 'Oral-motor dysfunction and growth retardation amongst inner-city children', *Developmental Medicine & Child Neurology* (in press).

Meredith, H.V. (1975) 'Relation between tobacco smoking of pregnant women and body size of their progeny: a compilation of published studies', *Human Biology* 47: 451–72.

Meredith, H.V. (1984) 'Body size of infants and children around the world in relation to socioeconomic status', *Advances in Child Development and Behaviour* 18: 81–146.

Miller, H.C., Hassanein, K., Chin, T.D.Y., and Hensleigh, P. (1976) 'Socioeconomic factors in relation to fetal growth in white infants', *Journal of Pediatrics* 89: 638.

Moar, V.A. and Ounsted, M.K. (1982) 'Growth in the first year of life: how early can one predict size at twelve months among small-for-dates & large-for-dates babies?' *Early Human Development* 6: 65–9.

National Academy of Sciences, National Research Council (1980) *Recommended Dietary Allowances* 9th edition, Washington, DC: National Academy of Sciences.

National Children's Bureau (1987) *Investing in the Future: Child Health Ten Years after the Court Report* (A report of the Policy and Practice Review Group National Children's Bureau), London: NCB.

Ogston, S.A., Du V. Florey, C., and Walker, C.H.M. (1987) 'Association of infant alimentary and respiratory illness with parental smoking and other environmental factors, *Journal of Epidemiological Community Health* 41: 21–5.

Ounsted, M. and Scott, A. (1982) 'Social class and birthweight: a new look', *Early Human Development* 6: 83–7.

Pollitt, E. and Leibel, R.L. (1980) 'Biological and social correlates of failure to thrive', in L. Green and F.S. Johnston (eds) *Social and Biological Predictors of Nutritional Status, Physical Growth, and Neurological Development*, New York: Academic Press.

Preece, M.A. and Baines, M.J. (1978) 'A new family of mathematical models describing the human growth curve', *Annals of Human Biology* 5: 1.

Richardson, D., Coates, F., and Morton, R. (1975) 'Early effects of tobacco smoke exposure on vascular dynamics in the microcirculation', *Journal of Applied Physiology* 39: 119–23.

Roberts, D.F. (1985) 'Genetics and nutritional adaptation', in K. Blaxter and J.C. Waterlow (eds) *Nutritional Adaptation in Man*, London and Paris: John Libbey, 45–59.

Rogers, A. (1984) *The Effects of Illness on Growth During Childhood and Adolescence*, M.Phil. thesis, Oxford: Oxford University Press.

Rona, R.J. (1981) 'Genetic and environmental factors in the control of growth in childhood', *British Medical Bulletin* 37(3): 265–72.

Rona, R.J. and Chinn, S. (1984) 'The National Study of Health and Growth: nutritional surveillance of primary school children from 1976–1981 with special reference to unemployment and social class', *Annals of Human Biology* 11(1): 17–28.

Rona, R.J. and Chinn, S. (1986) 'The National Study of Health and Growth: social and biological factors associated with height of children from ethnic groups living in England', *Annals of Human Biology* 13(5): 453–71.

Rona, R.J., Chinn, S. and Du V. Florey, C. (1985) 'Exposure to cigarette smoking and children's growth', *International Journal of Epidemiology* 14(3): 402–9.

Rona, R.J., Du V. Florey, C., Clarke, G.C., and Chinn, S. (1981) 'Parental smoking at home and height of children', *British Medical Journal* 283: 1363.

Rona, R.J., Swan, A.V., and Altman, D.G. (1978) 'Social factors and height of primary schoolchildren in England and Scotland', *Journal of Epidemiological & Community Health* 32: 147–54.

Rosa, F.W. and Turshen, M. (1970) 'Fetal nutrition', *WHO Bulletin* 43: 785–95, Geneva: WHO.

Said, G., Patois, E., and Lellouch, J. (1984) 'Infantile colic and parental smoking', *British Medical Journal* 289: 658–60.

Schaffer Bell, L. and Woolston, J.L. (1985) 'The relationship of weight gain and caloric intake in infants with organic and nonorganic failure to thrive syndrome', *Journal of the American Academy of Child Psychiatry* 24(4): 447–52.

Silva, P.A., Birkbeck, J., and Williams, S. (1985) 'Some factors influencing the stature of Dunedin 7 year old children', *Australian Paediatric Journal* 21: 27–30.

Skuse, D. (1985) 'Non-organic failure to thrive: a reappraisal', *Archives of Disease in Childhood* 60(2): 173–8.

Skuse, D. (1987) 'Social deprivation and early intervention: research to practice', in G. Hosking and G. Murphy (eds) *Prevention of Mental Handicap: A World View*. (Proceedings of the RSM Forum on Mental Retardation), London: RSM.

Smith, A.M., Chinn, A., and Rona, R.J. (1980) 'Social factors and height gain of primary schoolchildren in England and Scotland', *Annals of Human Biology* 7: 115–24.

Smith, D.W., Truog, W., Rogers, J.E., Greitzer, L.J., Skinner, A.L., McCann, J.J., and Harvey, M.A.S. (1976) 'Shifting linear growth during infancy: illustration of genetic factors in growth from fetal life through infancy', *Journal of Pediatrics* 89(2): 225–30.

Smithells, R.W. and Smith, I.J. (1984) 'Alcohol and the fetus', *Archives of Disease in Childhood* 59: 1113–4.

South East Thames Regional Health Authority (1984) *Statistics and Operational Research Department* (District Health Authority A.C.O.R.N. populations), unpublished..

Stein, A., Campbell, E.A., Day, A., McPherson, K., and Cooper, P.J. (1987) 'Social adversity, low birthweight and preterm delivery', *British Medical Journal* 295(ii): 291–93.

Tanner, J.M. (1978) *Foetus into Man: Physical Growth from Conception to Maturity*, London: Open Books.

Tanner, J.M. (1986) 'Growth as a target-seeking function: catch-up and catch-down growth in man', in F. Falkner and J.M. Tanner (eds) *Human Growth: A Comprehensive Treatise: Volume 1: Developmental Biology Prenatal Growth*, London: Plenum Press, 167–79.

Tanner, J.M. (1987) 'Growth as a mirror of the condition of society: secular trends and class distinction', *Acta Paediatrica Japonica* 29: 96–103.

Vimpani, C.N., Vimpani, A.F., Pocock, S.J., and Farquhar, J.W. (1981) 'Differences in physical characteristics, perinatal histories, and social backgrounds between children with growth hormone deficiency and constitutional short stature', *Archives of Disease in Childhood* 56: 922–8.

Waterlow, J.C. (1985) 'What do we mean by adaptation?' in K. Blaxter and J.C. Waterlow (eds) *Nutritional Adaptation in Man*, London and Paris: John Libbey, 1–11.

Waterlow, J.C., Ashworth, A., and Griffiths, M. (1980) 'Faltering in infant growth in less-developed countries', *Lancet* ii: 1176–8.

Widdowson, E.M. (1947) *A Study of individual children's diets* (Medical Research Council Special Report Series 257), London: HMSO.

Widdowson, E.M. (1985) 'Responses to deficits of dietary energy', in K. Blaxter and J.C. Waterlow (eds) *Nutritional Adaptation in Man*, London and Paris: John Libbey, 97–104.

Wing, J.K., Cooper, J.E., and Sartorius, N. (1974) *The Measurement and Classification of Psychiatric Symptoms*, London: Cambridge University Press.

Wolke, D., Skuse, D., and Mathisen, B. (1987) 'Behavioural style in failure to thrive infants: a preliminary communication', *Journal of Pediatric Psychology* (in press).

World Health Organization (1983) *Measuring Change in Nutritional Status*, Geneva: WHO.

18

The Epidemiological Contribution to Research on Late-life Dementia

Brian Cooper

Epidemiological research on dementia is currently in a highly frustrating phase. Hardly a month goes by without reports of new, challenging findings in neuro-pathology, biochemistry, or molecular biology, which seem to offer the promise of scientific advance in this field. Yet the epidemiologist remains uncomfortably aware that primary degenerative dementia is essentially a diagnosis of exclusion, which cannot be definitely confirmed during life and, indeed, not always *post mortem*; that no biological marker is available for use in case identification and, finally, that neither for dementia of Alzheimer type (DAT) nor for multi-infarct dementia (MID) is it yet clear whether we are dealing with a single disease entity or with the final common pathway of a number of different morbid processes. Until these issues have been resolved, the pace of epidemiological progress is unlikely to accelerate.

While brain-imaging and electrophysiological techniques play an increasing role in hospital-based investigation (McGreer 1986; Fenton 1986) each has so far found only limited application in field studies, for obvious practical reasons. Here the most pressing need is for the establishment of differential-diagnostic criteria, based on the phenomena of disease and validated against autopsy findings. Diagnostic guidelines for dementing illness are incorporated in the manuals both for the standard American psychiatric classification DSM–III (APA 1980) and for the current draft form of the International Classification of Diseases, Tenth Revision – ICD–10 (WHO 1987); in addition, more detailed criteria have been proposed by a multi-disciplinary work group in the USA (McKhann *et al.* 1984). These various systems of classification, which are said to be mutually compatible, can undoubtedly help clinicians to arrive at a more accurate diagnosis; so far, however, they have not been made fully operational for research purposes.

Reports on the accuracy of differential diagnosis by clinical methods have varied a good deal in their conclusions. In the more careful of recent studies, the efficiency of clinical diagnosis, judged as a screening procedure, has been of the order of 70 per cent, while its positive predictive value – i.e. the probability that it will be confirmed at autopsy – has ranged from 55 per cent to 80 per cent (Rocca *et al.* 1986). These results pose a question as to whether the diagnostic accuracy in field studies is yet high enough to permit the testing of aetiological hypotheses in relation to specific disease entities (Liston and La Rue 1983).

DESCRIPTIVE EPIDEMIOLOGY

Prevalence and incidence studies

A recent meta-analytical study (Jorm *et al.* 1987) examined data on the prevalence of late-life dementia from forty-seven field studies, carried out during the forty-year period 1945–85. The estimates were found to vary widely both between countries and between individual studies, largely as a function of the research methods employed. Nevertheless, two general trends could be discerned. To begin with, there was a relative excess of DAT among women and of MID among men. Second, there was a consistent relationship between the estimates for successive five-year age-groups above 60, the age-specific prevalence ratio doubling on average for each additional 5.1 years of age.

In figure 18.1 the smooth age-curve is based on pooled data from the twenty-two field studies analysed by Jorm *et al.* (1987) which give age-specific prevalence estimates for dementia or closely related diagnoses (senile psychoses, organic psychoses, or chronic brain syndromes). Since not all these studies achieved full population coverage, the pooled estimates are somewhat lower than those derived from the individual field studies also represented in figure 18.1, each of which was fairly comprehensive in coverage. Nonetheless, the age-related curves appear to be similar in all the studies, once allowance is made for random fluctuation, This degree of uniformity suggests that the different investigators were studying the same phenomenon. Any more far-reaching interpretation of the data can only be speculative, since prevalence ratios are a function of the course and outcome of a disease, as well as of its incidence in a population, and in the case of dementia too little is known about the range of variation around each of these axes.

For the same reason, prevalence estimates make an unsatisfactory basis for aetiological research. In this context incidence rates – i.e., rates of occurrence of new cases in defined populations – must be established, and any variation compared with the distribution of suspected risk factors. The basic practical difficulty resides in monitoring the onset of new cases and making a reliable diagnostic assessment. Psychiatric first-admission rates are sometimes used to estimate the so-called 'treated incidence', but in respect of dementia this index tells more about the utilization of treatment agencies than it does about the frequency of occurrence in the elderly population. Most cases of late-life dementia are not referred to psychiatrists, and those

265

Figure 18.1 Age-specific prevalence of late-life dementia (findings of field studies)

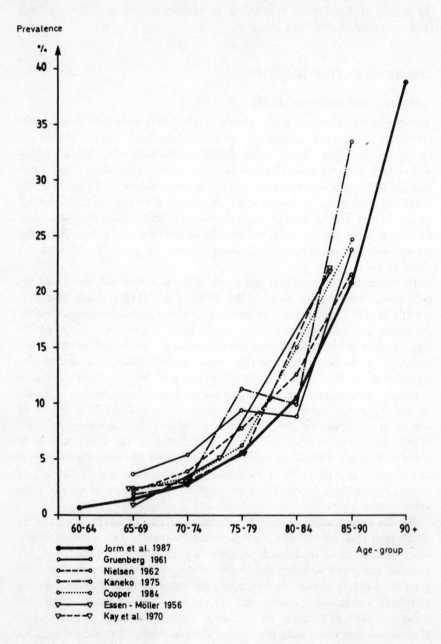

Prevalence

%

Jorm et al. 1987
Gruenberg 1961
Nielsen 1962
Kaneko 1975
Cooper 1984
Essen – Möller 1956
Kay et al. 1970

Age - group

Table 18.1a Treated incidence of organic mental disorder in the elderly population, reported from hospital-census and case-register studies. Annual age-specific rates per 1,000 population

Author(s)	Survey area & period	Sample size	Age-group			
			60–69	70–79	80+	Total (60+)
Adelstein *et al.* 1968	Salford, UK, 1959–63	M 9,228 F 15,581	1.1 0.8	2.4 2.8	6.9 6.7	1.9 2.1
Akesson 1969	Swedish islands, 1964–7	M 2,071 F 2,127	0.3 1.2	4.8 3.6	8.6 13.7	2.6 3.5
Helgason 1977	Iceland, 1966–7	M 22,206 F 25,130	0.8 0.7	2.6 2.8	9.4 8.3	2.3 2.5
Mölsä *et al.* 1982[1,2]	Turku, Finland, 1966–76	M 6,378 F 13,104	0.8 1.4	4.0 7.7	15.6 21.0	1.9 4.1

[1] Age-groups 65–74; 75–84; 85+
[2] Nursing home and community nursing cases included

Table 18.1b Incidence of organic mental disorder (severe or moderately severe) in the elderly population, reported from area field surveys. Annual age-specific rates per 1,000 population

Author(s)	Survey area & period	Sample size[1] (persons aged over 60)	Age-group			
			60–69	70–79	80+	Total (60+)
Bergmann *et al.* 1971	Newcastle, UK (a) 1960–4; (b) 1964–7	760 (2,000)	–	–	–	15.0
Hagnell *et al.* 1981	'Lundby', Sweden, 1947–57	655 (4,224)	5.1	18.8	57.3	16.3
	dto. 1957–72	696 (7,959)	2.9	14.8	33.7	10.7
Nielsen *et al.* 1982	Samsø Island, Denmark 1972–7	1,564 (6,580)	2.8	22.7	34.6	12.0
Nilsson 1984	Gothenburg, Sweden 1971–81	364 (2,665)	–	16.2	–	–
Bickel and Cooper 1988	Mannheim, F.R.G. 1978–86[2]	314 (1,912)	4.8	12.2	34.1	17.8[3]

[1] Figures in brackets refer to numbers of 'person-years' at risk
[2] Age-groups 65–69; 70–79; 80+
[3] Total for age-group 65+

admitted to institutional care tend to be at a relatively advanced stage of the disease.

In tables 18.1a and 18.1b estimates of the incidence of dementia derived from hospital and case-register studies are juxtaposed to others reported from a number of area field surveys; all the studies were carried out in European countries. The rates for 'treated incidence' vary between 1.9 and 2.6 per 1,000 for men and between 2.1 and 4.1 per 1,000 for women, based on the age-range above 60 years. The true incidence on the other hand, as indicated by field-survey findings, is of the order of 10 to 16 per 1,000 for both sexes combined, or about four times as high as the treated rates. It need scarcely be added that analogous studies of populations which have fewer hospital facilities, e.g. in developing Third World countries, would reveal much bigger disparities. Both for aetiological research and in the estimation of service needs, therefore, community-based surveys must be regarded as indispensable.

Studies of incidence may help to throw light on the nature of the relationship between pre-senile and senile dementia. If these categories indeed represent different nosological entities, one would expect the corresponding age-specific incidence rates to show evidence of bimodality; whereas, if they are sub-groups of a single disease, separated only by an artificial age limit, a unimodal distribution could be anticipated. Incidence rates for pre-senile dementia are difficult to estimate with any accuracy, because cases are rare in the general population. Data from the Israeli National Register of Neurological Disease (Treves *et al.* 1986) permit treated incidence rates to be computed for the age-range 40–60 years, using this age group of the national population as the denominator. The rate for both sexes combined increases steeply with age, from 0.3 per 100,000 at 40–44 years to 5.8 per 100,000 at 55–59 years. If the age-related curve, which corresponds to a doubling in incidence rate with each three to four additional years of age, is extrapolated beyond 60 years, it conforms quite well to the estimates derived from hospital census and case-register studies in a number of other countries (Rocca *et al.* 1986). To this extent the empirical data provide support for the view that DAT is a single pathological process, and that age alone is unsatisfactory as a basis for division into specific sub-categories. The findings are, however, far from being definitive, because of the qualifications surrounding treated-case data.

Prediction of individual risk

Can descriptive surveys help towards achieving a better prediction of individual risk? The evidence for some degree of familial aggregation suggests that dementia does not strike randomly, but this in itself is not of much help in prediction. Prospectively designed cytogenetic and immunologic studies, which may eventually throw light on the question, are so far wanting. More immediate promise is offered by evidence that the cognitive performance of 'young-old' persons may be useful as a pointer in identifying those of them who, given survival into later old age, will become clinically demented. La Rue and Jarvik (1986) were able to examine this issue in their longitudinal study of elderly twins. Those subjects who developed the clinical features of dementia were found to have had lower mean scores than other persons on tests of cognition administered some twenty years earlier. The authors did not, however, calculate the positive predictive value of these tests.

More recently, a preliminary report from a community-based study has suggested independently that premorbid cognitive performance may be an important indicator of risk for dementia. Bickel and Cooper (1988), in an eight-year follow-up of a representative sample of old people in Mannheim, noted a raised incidence of dementing illness among those who, at the first interview, had manifested mild memory defects, though without functional disability at that time. Once the influence of subclinical deficits was partialled out by statistical analysis, age ceased to be of predictive significance: in other words, the risk appeared to be no greater for the aged than for the young-old, given the same standard of cognitive performance. Of thirty-four new cases of dementia developing in the follow-up period, fourteen had been rated initially as subclinically impaired in cognitive performance.

If this tentative finding is confirmed, the way may be open to an earlier identification of persons at high risk for dementia, and hence for secondary preventive measures. Whether the cognitive deficits should be regarded as early signs of an incipient dementing illness, or as premorbid attributes of the individual which increase his susceptibility to the disease, must remain for the present an open question.

ANALYTICAL EPIDEMIOLOGY: COMPARATIVE AND CONTROL STUDIES

Analytical epidemiology is a logical extension and development of the descriptive population survey. It proceeds by exploring differences in the occurrence of disease by person, time, and place, and relating these to the strength of exposure to suspected risk factors. Because of a dearth of suitable research, little is known as yet about differences in the incidence of dementia by time and place. The repeated field studies in 'Lundby' have suggested a possible decline in the frequency of senile dementia (Hagnell et al. 1983), while a direct comparison of samples of old people in London and New York, based on a standard interview technique, has indicated large disparities in this respect, which are unlikely to have a genetic explanation (Copeland and Gurland 1985); but these are both isolated findings, which await replication.

Leaving aside the possible significance of exotic neuropsychiatric disorders, such as kuru (Gajdusek 1977) and the Guam-Parkinsonism syndrome (Hirano et al. 1966), such epidemiological clues as we have to the aetiology of DAT have been derived from case-control studies, in which

269

samples of clinically diagnosed cases have been matched with control groups drawn either from among other hospital patients, or from the local community, or both. Only a handful of such studies have been reported (Bharucha *et al.* 1983; Heyman *et al.* 1984; French *et al.* 1985; English and Cohen 1985; Amaducci *et al.* 1986), although others are currently in progress. This research strategy, while currently the most favoured by epidemiologists, presents formidable difficulties. Quite apart from the problems of differential diagnosis, already referred to, the degree of exposure to individual risk factors cannot as a rule be ascertained accurately. All the studies so far have had to employ a retrospective design, which is notoriously weak for aetiological inquiry, and especially so when the affected persons tend to be unreliable as informants about their own medical history and life course. While the research findings have pointed tentatively to a number of possible causal links, the nature and strength of associations vary from one study to another and, indeed, within a single study according to the type of control group used as a standard of comparison. Since the evidence has been ably reviewed by others (Rocca *et al.* 1986; Henderson 1987), only a brief resumé of the more promising causal hypotheses will be given here.

Genetic determinants

Though it is now generally accepted that genetic factors play some part in determining the incidence of DAT, their precise role and importance remain matters for debate. The earlier population-genetic studies reporting familial aggregation displayed serious faults of method and tended to exaggerate the excess of risk in affected families, in that they underestimated the frequency of dementing illness in the elderly population as a whole. The kind of large-scale twin study required to assess the strength of genetic determination poses great practical difficulties in the field of geriatric research. Hence the contribution of population-based studies to this question has been a modest one (Bergmann and Cooper 1986).

In view of recent progress in molecular biology, which has again thrown up the possibility of a major gene locus for DAT (Kang *et al.* 1987), there has been a recent renewal of interest in this field, and studies are now being undertaken which avoid at least some of the earlier methodological weaknesses.

A recent multi-centred case-control study in Italy (Amaducci *et al.* 1986) reported a significant increase in the frequency of dementing illness among the first- and second-degree relatives of patients with diagnosed DAT. The results are summarized in table 18.2. But this, like most genetically oriented inquiries, was focused primarily on pre-senile or early-onset dementing illness; i.e., on cases becoming manifest before the age of 70. That the age of onset may be of critical importance in this context is suggested by the widely cited findings of Heston and his co-workers (Heston *et al.* 1981).

Heston's study, based on a sample of cases confirmed at autopsy,

Table 18.2 Associations between DAT in probands and a family history of dementing illness: case-control comparisons

Affected family members	Relative risk (odds ratio)	
	Hospital-patient control-group	Community control-group
Mother	2.20	3.33*
Father	3.50	1.00
Siblings	11.00**	5.50*
First-degree relatives	5.00**	2.56*
First- or second-degree relatives	6.67***	3.44***

Source: Amaducci *et al.* (1986)
* significant at 5% level
** significant at 1% level
*** significant at 0.1% level

demonstrated a familial predisposition among the siblings of early-onset dementia patients, who revealed an increased risk for dementing illness, especially when one or both parents had also manifested the condition. In cases of clinical dementia first apparent after the age of 70, no increase in morbid risk was detected among other family members. It appears that cases of early-onset dementia tend to cluster in certain families, possibly because the influence of a genetic or other risk factor to which they are exposed advances the age at which cognitive decline commences and accelerates its progress. Even of the early-onset cases in this study, however, three-fifths showed no evidence of familial aggregation. To what extent deviation from a Mendelian pattern of inheritance can be explained in terms of mortality (Folstein and Powell 1984) is not yet established.

The role of environmental toxins

A number of research findings have pointed to possible associations between DAT and exposure to a range of chemical products, including metallic salts, organic solvents, pesticides, and pharmaceutical products. For some time aluminium seemed a promising candidate, because of its implication in secondary dementia among patients on long-term haemodialytic treatment (Dunea *et al.* 1978). The neuropathology of this condition is, however, quite distinct from that of DAT and, moreover, after some fifteen years of research no firm evidence of a causal link has yet been identified. Although in case-control studies it has not been possible to measure directly the strength of exposure to aluminium, such indirect methods as assessment of the intake of aluminium-containing antacid preparations, as a palliative for peptic ulcer or chronic indigestion, have been employed without confirming the association.

The most challenging evidence to date for a possible toxic factor has

271

Figure 18.2 Cumulative risk of DAT among siblings of DAT patients

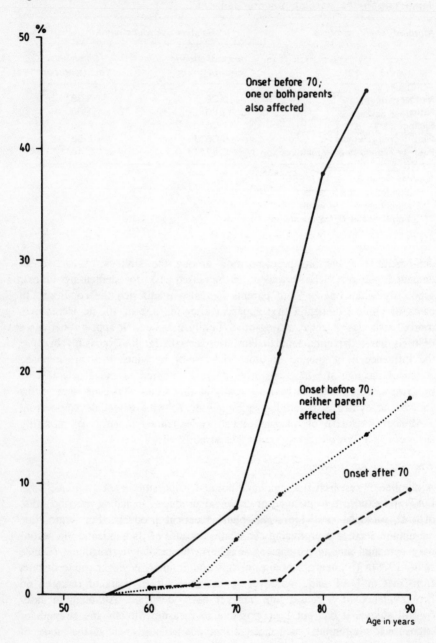

Source Heston *et al.* (1981)

Table 18.3 Associations between DAT and earlier viral infections: case-control studies

Authors	Relative risk (odds ratio)	Significance level
Heyman *et al.* 1984		
– Influenza		
(1918 pandemic)	3.65	NS
– Herpes zoster	3.33	NS
Amaducci *et al.* 1986		
– Encephalitis	1.00	NS
– Herpes zoster	0.62	NS

Table 18.4 Associations between DAT and reported contacts with animals: case-control comparisons

Type of animal	Relative risk (odds ratio)	
	Hospital-patient control-group	Community control-group
Dogs	2.83*	0.67
Cats	1.75	1.29
Cagebirds	0.87	0.68
Any kind of domestic animal	2.36**	0.95
Cattle	1.63	1.22
Game	1.00	1.25

Source: Amaducci *et al.* (1986)
 * significant at 5% level
 ** significant at 1% level

come, not from case-control studies but from investigation of the exotic neuropsychiatric syndromes which have been found in local endemic pockets. The Guam-Parkinsonism syndrome, in which some features of an Alzheimer-type pathological process are found, has long been suspected of having a dietary cause because of the steady fall in incidence which was observed as more and more foodstuffs were imported into Guam and other affected areas, replacing the traditional diet. Earlier causal hypotheses focused on an excess or deficiency of trace elements, but recently suspicion has also lighted on neuro-excitatory amino-acids found in a local plant from which formerly sago flour was extracted in large quantities (*Lancet* 1987). The relevance for dementia research of neurotoxic amino-acids found in various plant species seems destined to be a subject of increasing epidemiological scrutiny in the next decade.

The relevance of earlier viral infections

Demonstration of the transmissibility of kuru and Creutzfeld-Jakob disease sparked off a train of investigations of DAT, all of which have yielded negative findings (Corsellis 1986). Case-control studies have been used to test for a possible viral aetiology by estimating the relative frequency of earlier viral infections affecting the central nervous system. Apart from enquiries about meningitis, encephalitis, and Herpes zoster infection, such indirect evidence as a history of skin grafting, ingestion of animal brains, contact with animals, and travel in endemic areas has also been examined, but so far with no consistently positive results. The study by Amaducci and others (1986) reported some suggestive evidence of an association with exposure to domestic animals, especially dogs, which would seem to merit further inquiry, but this finding has yet to be replicated by other workers.

Dementia as an auto-immune disease

To place DAT in the broad category of auto-immune diseases postulates a pathogenetic process rather than an aetiology, and relegates empirical causal inquiry one stage further. Nevertheless, findings from the laboratory suggesting a source of immunoglobulins in the central nervous system (Williams *et al.* 1980) have stimulated epidemiologists to examine associations within families between DAT and diseases believed to be mediated by auto-immune reactions. Interest in this possibility was reinforced when an increase in myelo-proliferative disorders (lymphoma, lymphosarcoma, and Hodgkin's disease), and more generally of diseases considered to be 'related to the immune system' were reported to have a raised incidence among first-degree relatives of probands with DAT (Heston *et al.* 1981). However sound the underlying theoretical assumptions, this finding has not been confirmed by other workers and, moreover, no relative excess of allergies, asthma, or rheumatoid arthritis has been detected in the medical records of old people with DAT, as compared with controls (Heyman *et al.* 1984; French *et al.* 1985; Amaducci *et al.* 1986). The increased incidence of thyroid disease – a disorder also linked to the auto-immune system – noted by Heyman *et al.* (1984) in the medical records of DAT patients, also lacks confirmation from other studies. Once again we are confronted by intriguing but isolated findings, whose significance it is not yet possible to assess.

Head injury as a predisposing factor

Because of individual case reports, head injury has long been suspected as one possible risk factor of DAT. Studies of former professional boxers have confirmed the presence of Alzheimer-type changes, notably formation of neuro-fibrillary tangles, in persons with Dementia pugilistica whose mental deterioration may have begun many years after retirement from the ring (Corsellis *et al.* 1973). Inquiry after a history of earlier head injury, severe enough to cause loss of consciousness, has therefore been included in a

274

Table 18.5 Associations between DAT and a history of earlier head injury: case-control comparisons

Authors	Relative risk (odds ratio)	Significance level
Heyman *et al.* 1984	5.31	0.05
Mortimer *et al.* 1985		
– Patient control group	4.50	0.05
– Community control group	2.80	NS
Amaducci *et al.* 1986		
– Patient control group	3.50	NS
– Community control group	2.00	NS

number of case-control studies, but with no consistent findings. In the light of present evidence it seems improbable that a single episode of cerebral contusion in earlier life is often of aetiological significance, though severe or repeated trauma may be so. Few people are subjected to repeated head injury to an extent comparable to professional boxers, so that this particular risk factor is intrinsically implausible as a major determinant of the incidence of DAT in elderly populations.

Towards an integrated model: shared and cumulative effects

Attempts have not been wanting to combine the various hypotheses in a single aetiological and pathogenetic model. It has been postulated that a number of different risk factors may share some mediating pathogenetic effect in common. Thus, different noxae could pick out a *locus minoris resistentiae* in hippocampus or basal nuclei, leading to diffuse secondary degenerative changes in the neocortex (Ball *et al.* 1985). A biochemical abnormality, such as abnormal peroxidation with production of free oxygen radicals, could be the missing pathogenetic link if, as is suspected, this abnormality is present in the brain following a number of different kinds of insult (Henderson 1987). Such models must, however, be tested in the laboratory and have as yet no direct significance for epidemiological research.

More immediately relevant in this context is the notion of a clinical 'threshold' for dementia (Roth 1982), according to which the effect of earlier brain insults combines with age-related degenerative changes to overstep the line at which functional decompensation occurs and mental impairment becomes manifest. Earlier head injury, viral encephalitis, or exposure to one or more neurotoxins can all serve, according to this concept, to advance the point in time at which decompensation occurs. The dementing disorder then represents the end result, not of a single specific aetiology, but rather of a variety or combination of types of brain insult to which individuals are exposed over the life span. This of course does not preclude the possibility that in any given society one form of insult may predominate and act as the main determinant of incidence over prolonged periods of time, much as alcohol abuse has done with respect to hepatic cirrhosis.

Such a general model would help to explain the prolonged latent period that often elapses between exposure to a risk factor and the onset of clinical dementia, as well as the positive association between Alzheimer-type and cerebrovascular dementia, which is suggested by the relative frequency of mixed forms in the elderly population (Tomlinson *et al.* 1970). It has obvious implications for the methodology of case-control studies and for analytical epidemiology more generally.

STUDIES OF THE COURSE AND OUTCOME OF DEMENTING ILLNESS

Hospital-based studies

Our knowledge of the course and outcome of late-life mental disorders is remarkably limited, the firmest information being still that derived from the study of psychiatric hospital patients. This has consistently revealed a large excess of mortality in association with organic mental disorders (Bickel 1987). In particular, mortality among patients with a diagnosis of senile dementia is of the order of four times that for the elderly population as a whole. The recorded causes of death suggest a general tendency towards multi-morbidity, rather than specific associations with somatic disease.

Up to the 1960s, patients suffering from dementia had a mortality rate of around 50 per cent in the first six months following hospital admission. More recently the rate has fallen to around 30 per cent, while at the same time the proportion of patients discharged from hospital has increased. The trend towards an improved prognosis is, however, much less pronounced after two years, at which point in time the mortality rate is still above 60 per cent. The research findings summarized in figure 18.4 provide little indication of a significant increase in survival rates at this stage.

It must also be remembered that most hospital-based studies give no information concerning the fate of patients once they have been discharged from hospital care. Probably in a high proportion of cases no more than a change of institution, from hospital to geriatric home, is involved. In some countries a large-scale shift in the locus of care for mentally impaired old people has occurred within the past two or three decades, from clinical to non-clinical residential care (Jaeger 1987), a transition more readily explained in socio-political terms than by any real improvement in the outcome of illness.

Community-based studies of course and outcome

Anamnestic data suggest that dementing conditions have as a rule been clinically apparent for some years by the time the affected persons are

Figure 18.3 Outcome after six months, elderly psychiatric patients with organic mental disorders

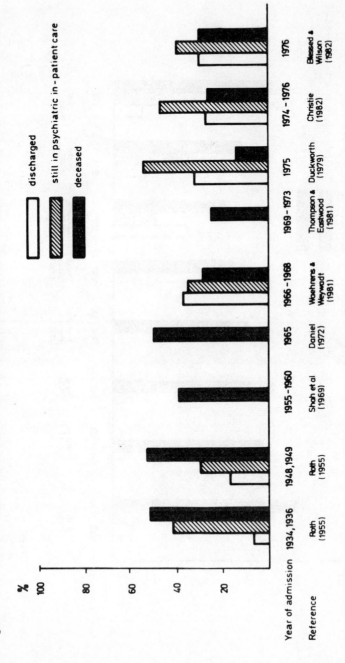

Source Bickel (1988)

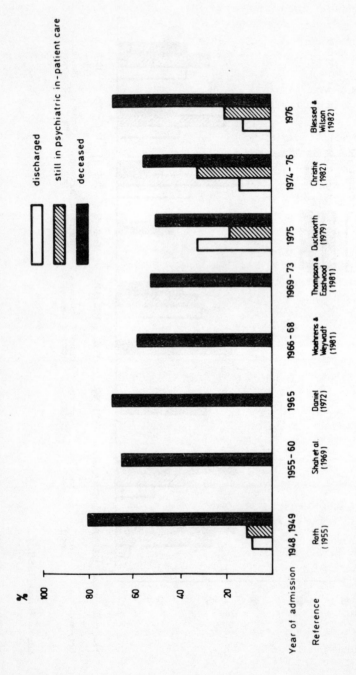

Figure 18.4 Outcome after two years, elderly psychiatric patients with organic mental disorders

Source Bickel (1988)

admitted to hospital care (Wang and Whanger 1971). Furthermore, it can be inferred from field-survey findings that most old people with dementia never enter psychiatric institutions (Bergmann and Cooper 1986). One would expect cases identified in the community to be on average clinically milder, or at an earlier stage of deterioration, than those studied in hospital. The few community-based longitudinal studies so far undertaken confirm that this is broadly the case, and lend some support to the view that there has been a limited improvement in medical prognosis in recent decades. Nevertheless, a diagnosis of organic mental disorder continues to have serious implications, in terms of mortality risk, admission to institutional care, and dependency on others.

These issues were examined in some detail in the recently completed longitudinal study of old people in Mannheim. After four years, the mortality rate among those with organic mental impairments was 46 per cent, compared with 20 per cent in the cohort as a whole (Bickel 1987). By means of an events-analytical technique, it was possible to estimate the influence of psychiatric status on the survival time, while holding constant other factors such as sex, age, and degree of physical impairment. The presence of an organic mental disorder was found to predict a reduction of 54 per cent in survival time, and that of functional mental illness a reduction of 47 per cent, once these other factors had been partialled out.

When the status of the elderly cohort was again reviewed after eight years, differences between the diagnostic groups emerged more clearly. By this time mortality among those with organic mental disorders was 81 per cent, compared with 42 per cent in the remainder of the sample. The findings of a survival analysis using the Kaplan-Meier method of estimation (Chase *et al.* 1983) are shown in figure 18.5. Persons initially diagnosed as having a 'functional' mental illness and those categorized as cases of 'mild dementia' shared a similar mortality curve in the earlier follow-up years, but the survival curves then diverged. The risk for the 'mild dementia' group began to approach that for the clinically demented, whereas that for the group with functional mental disorders approximated increasingly to the level of risk for the mentally normal group. Over the follow-up period as a whole, the mortality curves for organic and functional mental disorders differed markedly, underlining the importance of this basic diagnostic distinction in community surveys of the elderly.

Longitudinal studies of old people have shown a greatly increased frequency of long-stay institutional care among those with organic mental impairment (Bergmann 1977; Teresi *et al.* 1984; Campbell *et al.* 1985). While the findings in Mannheim were at first inspection broadly consistent with those of earlier studies, detailed analysis revealed a more complex picture. In order to control for the effects of age, physical health status, and differing survival times, a regression analysis was undertaken, which permitted simultaneous assessment of a number of independent variables in the

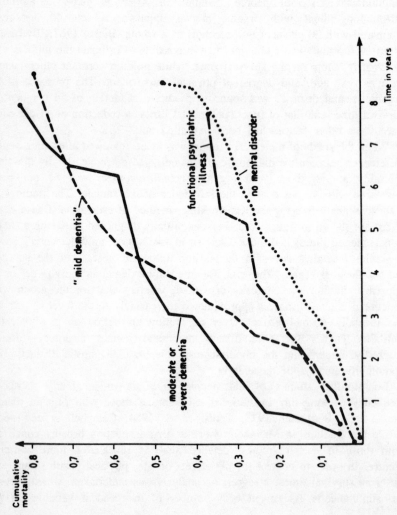

Figure 18.5 Cumulative mortality according to initial mental status (Kaplan-Meier estimation)

presence of 'censored' data (Allgulander and Fisher 1986). Against expectation, the initial diagnostic category was found to have no influence on the interval from first interview to geriatric home admission: this despite the fact that dementing disorders are found frequently among geriatric home residents and, indeed, are often the immediate reason for admission. A possible explanation is that old people with clinically manifest dementia are more likely to remain in the community if they have good family support. Provision of care by other members of the family, once commenced, tends to be continued for long periods. Hence the decision for or against institutional admission is often taken relatively early in the course of the illness. Cases of dementia identified in community surveys therefore tend to be found disproportionately among those old people who enjoy some measure of family support. This is a selective factor which should be borne in mind when interpreting the findings of cross-sectional surveys.

Table 18.6 Influence of selected predictor variables on the probability of geriatric home admission

Predictor variable	Coefficient[1]	Effect on rate of geriatric-home admission[2]
Each additional year of age	0.083** (0.029)	+8.6%
Onset of clinical dementia	1.825*** (0.345)	+520.0%
Admission to any hospital	1.322* (0.541)	+275.0%

[1] Standard errors shown in brackets
[2] Percentage increase or decrease for a unit change in each variable
   * significant at 5% level
  ** significant at 1% level
 *** significant at 0.1% level

In keeping with this hypothesis is the finding that occurrence of a new case of dementing illness increased the probability of admission to a geriatric home more than fivefold and appeared, indeed, to be the single most important determinant of the demand for institutional care (cf. table 18.6).

CONCLUSION

These research findings underline the need for a more systematic and intensive approach to the epidemiological aspects of late-life dementia, on two

281

main grounds. First, it seems improbable that laboratory investigation alone can elucidate the nature of the causal nexus for a group of disorders which, on present evidence, must be to some extent environmentally determined. The causal research of recent years has been largely concentrated, as the above review indicates, on Alzheimer-type dementia. There are, however, no rational grounds for neglecting the cerebrovascular group of dementias, which in the short term may well afford greater opportunities for preventive action. The search for causes of both these broad disease-categories will call for prospectively planned longitudinal and case-control studies, and for an increasing emphasis on international collaborative projects.

Second, even if a major scientific breakthrough in neurobiological research can be anticipated within the next one or two decades – and this must still be regarded as an optimistic assumption (Besson 1986) – translation of the aetiological findings into large-scale therapeutic or preventive programmes, calling in all probability for a massive and sustained investment, could not be expected to yield rapid returns. World demographic projections leave no room for doubt that, over the next generation, the absolute numbers of cases of late-life dementia will continue to increase rapidly, or that the additional burden of disability and dependency will fall disproportionately on those poor developing countries of the Third World whose care facilities are least adequate to meet the growth in demand (Jablensky 1979; Kramer 1980). It is, therefore, vital to start planning ahead now for the next half-century, and epidemiological research can help to provide the necessary rational basis for doing so.

Acknowledgement: I am grateful to Dr Horst Bickel for much valuable assistance with the preparation of this review.

REFERENCES

Adelstein, A.M., Downham, D.Y., Stein, Z., and Susser, M. (1968) 'The epidemiology of mental illness in an English city', *Social Psychiatry* 3: 47–59.

Akesson, H.O. (1969) 'A population study of senile and arteriosclerotic psychosis', *Human Heredity* 19: 546–66.

Allgulander, C., and Fisher, L.B. (1986) 'Survival analysis (or time to an event analysis) and the Cox regression model: methods for longitudinal psychiatric research', *Acta Psychiatrica Scandinavica* 74: 529–35.

Amaducci, L.A., Fratiglioni, L., Rocca, W.A., *et al.* (1986) 'Risk factors for clinically diagnosed Alzheimer's disease: a case-control study of an Italian population', *Neurology* 36: 922–31.

American Psychiatric Association (1986) *Diagnostic and Statistical Manual of Mental Disorders*, third edition, Washington, DC: APA.

Ball, M.J., Hachinski, V., Fox, A., *et al.* (1986) 'A new definition of Alzheimer's disease: a hippocampal dementia', *Lancet* i: 14–16.

Bergmann, K. (1977) 'Prognosis in chronic brain failure', *Age and Ageing* 6 (supplement): 61–6.

Bergmann, K. and Cooper, B. (1986) 'Epidemiological and public health aspects of senile dementia', in A.B. Sørensen, F.E. Weinert, and L.R. Sherrod (eds) *Human Development and the Life Course: Multi-Disciplinary Perspectives*, Hillsdale, NJ: Erlbaum, 71–97.

Bergmann, K., Kay, D.W.K., Foster, E.M., *et al.* (1971) 'A follow-up study of randomly selected community residents to assess the effects of chronic brain syndrome and cerebrovascular disease', *Psychiatry II: Proceedings of the 5th World Congress of Psychiatry, Mexico*, Amsterdam: Excerpta Medica, 856–65.

Besson, J. (1983) 'Dementia: biological solution still a long way off', *British Medical Journal* 287: 926–7.

Bharucha, N.E., Schoenberg, B.S., and Kokmen, E. (1983) 'Dementia of Alzheimer's type (DAT): a case-control study of associations with medical conditions and surgical procedures', *Neurology* (NY, supplement 2) 33: 85.

Bickel, H. (1987) 'Psychiatric illness and mortality among the elderly: findings of an epidemiological study', in B. Cooper (ed.) *Psychiatric Epidemiology: Progress and Prospects*, London: Croom Helm, pp. 192–211.

Bickel, H. (1988) 'Verlauf und Ausgang psychischer Storungen im Alter', in R.K. Olbrich (ed.) *Prospektive Verlaufsforschung in der Psychiatrie*, Berlin: Springer, pp. 83–98.

Bickel, H. and Cooper, B. (1988, in press) 'Incidence of dementing disorders in an elderly population cohort', in B. Cooper and T. Helgason (eds) *Epidemiology and Prevention of Mental Disorders*, London: Routledge.

Blessed, G. and Wilson, I.D. (1982) 'The contemporary natural history of mental disorder in old age', *British Journal of Psychiatry* 141: 59–67.

Campbell, A.J., McCosh, L.M., Reinken, J., and Allan, B.C. (1983) 'Dementia in old age and the need for services', *Age and Ageing* 12: 11–16.

Chase, G.A., Folstein, M.F., Breitner, J.C.S., *et al.* (1983) 'The use of life-tables and survival analysis in testing genetic hypotheses, with an application to Alzheimer's disease', *American Journal of Epidemiology* 117: 590–7.

Christie, A.B. (1982) 'Changing patterns in mental illness in the elderly', *British Journal of Psychiatry* 140: 154–9.

Cooper, B (1984) 'Home and away; the disposition of mentally ill old people in an urban population', *Social Psychiatry* 19: 187–96.

Copeland, J.R.M. and Gurland, B.J. (1985) 'International comparative studies', in T Arie (ed.) *Recent Advances in Psychogeriatrics*, Edinburgh: Churchill Livingstone, pp. 175–95.

Corsellis, J.A.N. (1986) 'The transmissibility of dementia', *British Medical Bulletin* 42: 111–14.

Corsellis, J.A.N., Bruton, C.J., and Freeman-Browne, D. (1973) 'The aftermath of boxing', *Psychological Medicine* 3: 270–303.

Daniel, R. (1972) 'A 5-year study of 693 psychogeriatric admissions in Queensland', *Geriatrics* 27: 132–58.

Duckworth, G.S., Kedward, H.B., and Bailey, W.F. (1979) 'Prognosis of mental illness in old age: a four-year follow-up study', *Canadian Journal of Psychiatry* 24: 674–82.

Dunea, G., Mahurka, S.D., Mamdani, B., and Smith, E.C. (1978) 'Role of aluminium in dialysis dementia', *Annals of International Medicine* 88: 502–4.

English, D. and Cohen, D. (1985) 'A case-control study of maternal age in Alzheimer's disease', *Journal of the American Geriatric Society* 33: 167–9.

283

Essen-Möller, E. (1956) 'Individual traits and morbidity in Swedish rural population', *Acta Psychiatrica Scandinavica*, supplement 100.

Fenton, G.W. (1986) 'Electrophysiology of Alzheimer's disease', *British Medical Bulletin* 42 (1): 29–33.

Folstein, M.F. and Powell, D. (1984) 'Is Alzheimer's disease inherited? a methodological review', *Integrative Psychiatry* (September-October), Amsterdam: Elsevier, 163–70.

French, L.R., Schuman, L.M., Mortimer, J.A., *et al.* (1985) 'A case-control study of dementia of the Alzheimer type', *American Journal of Epidemiology* 121: 414–21.

Gajdusek, D.C. (1977) 'Unconventional viruses and the origin and disappearance of kuru', *Science* 197: 943–60.

Gruenberg, E.M. (1961) 'A mental health survey of older persons', in P.H. Hoch and J. Zubin (eds) *Comparative Epidemiology of the Mental disorders*, New York: Grune & Stratton, pp. 13–23.

Hagnell, P., Lanke, J., Rorsman, B., and Ojesjo, L. (1981) 'Does the incidence of age psychosis decrease? a prospective longitudinal study of a complete population investigated during the 25-year period 1947–1972: the Lundby study', *Neuropsychobiology* 7: 201–11.

Hagnell, O., Lanke, J., Rorsman, B., *et al.* (1983) 'Current trends in the incidence of senile and multi-infarct dementia', *Acta Psychiatrica Nervenkr* 233: 423–38.

Helgason, T. (1977) 'Psychiatric services and mental illness in Iceland', *Acta Psychiatrica Scandinavica*, supplement 268.

Henderson, A.S. (1988, in press) 'The aetiology of Alzheimer's disease: can epidemiology contribute?', in B. Cooper and T. Helgason (eds) *Epidemiology and Prevention of Mental Disorder*, London: Routledge.

Heston L.L., Mastri, A.R., Anderson, E., and White, J. (1981) 'Dementia of the Alzheimer type: clinical genetics, natural history and associated conditions', *Archives of General Psychiatry* 38: 1085–90.

Heyman, A., Wilkinson, W.E., Stafford, J.A., *et al.* (1984) 'Alzheimer's disease: a study of epidemiological aspects', *Annals of Neurology* 15: 335–41.

Hirano, A., Malamud, N., Elizan, T.S., Kurland, L.T. (1966) 'Amyotrophic lateral sclerosis and parkinsonism-dementia complex on Guam: further pathologic studies', *Arch. Neurol.* 15: 35–51.

Jablensky, A. (1979) 'Priorities for cross-cultural mental health research in old age', in World Health Organization *Psychogeriatric Care in the Community* (Public Health in Europe, 10), Copenhagen: WHO Regional Office for Europe, pp. 103–12.

Jaeger, J. (1986) 'Trends in der stationaren gerontopsychiatrischen Versorgung in der Bundesrepublik Deutschland', *Z. Gerontol.* 20: 187–94.

Jorm, A.F., Korten, A.E., and Henderson, A.S. (1987) 'The prevalence of dementia: a quantitative integration of the literature', submitted for publication.

Kaneko, Z. (1975) 'Care in Japan', in J.G. Howells (ed.) *Modern Perspectives in the Psychiatry of Old Age*, New York: Brunner Mazel, 519–39.

Kang, J., Lemaire, H.G., Unterbeck, A., *et al.* 'The precursor of Alzheimer's disease, amyloid A4 protein, resembles a cell-surface receptor', *Nature* 325: 733–6.

Kay, D.W.K., Bergmann, K., Foster, E.M., *et al.* (1970) 'Mental illness and hospital usage in the elderly: a random sample followed up', *Comprehensive Psychiatry* 11: 26–35.

Kramer, M. (1980) 'The rising pandemic of mental disorders and associated chronic diseases and disabilities', in E. Strömgren, A. Dupont, and J.A. Nielsen (eds) 'Epidemiological research as a basis for the organisation of extramural psychiatry', *Acta Psychiatrica Scandinavica*, supplement 285, 62: 382–97.

Lancet (1987) 'A poison tree', editorial, *Lancet* ii: 947–8.

La Rue, A. and Jarvik, L.F. (1986) 'Towards the prediction of dementias arising in the senium', in L. Erlenmeyer-Kimling and N.E. Miller (eds) *Life-Span Research on the Prediction of Psychopathology*, Hillsdale, NJ: Erlbaum, 261–74.

Liston, E.H. and La Rue, A. (1983) 'Clinical differentiation of primary degenerative and multi-infarct dementia: a critical review of the evidence: Part I: clinical studies', *Biological Psychiatry* 18: 1451–65.

McGreer, P.L. (1986) 'Brain imaging in Alzheimer's disease', in M. Roth and L.L. Iversen (eds) 'Alzheimer's disease and related disorders', *British Medical Bulletin* 42 (1): 24–28.

McKhann, G., Drachman, D., Folstein, M., *et al.* (1984) 'Clinical diagnosis of Alzheimer's disease: report of the NINCDS-ADRDA Work Group', *Neurology* 34: 939–44.

Mölsä, P.K., Marttila, R.J., and Rinne, U.K. (1982) 'Epidemiology of dementia in a Finnish population', *Acta Neurologica Scandinavica* 65: 541–52.

Mortimer, J.A., French, L.R., Hutton, J.T., and Schuman, L.M. (1985) 'Head injury as a risk factor for Alzheimer's disease', *Neurology* (Cleveland) 35: 264–7.

Nielsen, J. (1962) 'Gerontopsychiatric period-prevalence investigation in a geographically delimited population', *Acta Psychiatrica Scandinavica* 38: 307–30.

Nielsen, J.A., Biörn-Henriksen, T., and Bork, B.R. (1982) 'Incidence and disease expectancy for senile and arteriosclerotic dementia in a geographically delimited Danish rural population', in G. Magnussen, J. Nielsen, and J. Buch (eds) *Epidemiology and Prevention of Mental Illness in Old Age*, Hellerup, Denmark: EGV.

Nilsson, L.V. (1984) 'Incidence of severe dementia in an urban sample followed up from 70 to 79 years of age', *Acta Psychiatrica Scandinavica* 70: 478–86.

Rocca, W.A., Amaducci, L.A., and Schoenberg, B.S. (1986) 'Epidemiology of clinically diagnosed Alzheimer's disease' *Annals of Neurology* 19: 415–24.

Roth, M. (1955) 'The natural history of mental disorder in old age', *Journal of Mental Sciences* 102: 281–301.

Roth, M. (1982) 'Some strategies for tackling the problems of senile dementia and related disorders within the next decade', WHO Working Paper IRP/ADR 117 (01)/6, unpublished.

Shah, K.V., Banks, G.D., and Merskey, H. (1969) 'Survival in atherosclerotic and senile dementia', *British Journal of Psychiatry* 115: 1283–6.

Teresi, J.A., Golden, R.R., and Gurland, B.J. (1984) 'Concurrent and predictive validity of indicator scales developed for the Comprehensive Assessment and Referral Evaluation Interview Schedule', *Journal of Geronotology* 39: 158–65.

Thompson, E.G. and Eastwood, M.R. (1981) 'Survival rates and causes of death in geriatric psychiatric patients', *Canadian Psychiatric Association Journal* 17: 17–22.

Tomlinson, B.E., Blessed, G., and Roth, M. (1970) 'Observations on the brains of demented old people', *Journal of Neurological Science* 11: 205–42.

Treves, T., Korczyn, A., Zilber, N., *et al.* (1986) 'Presenile dementia in Israel', *Arch. Neurologica* 43: 26–9..

Waehrens, J. and Weywadt, B. (1982) 'Prognosen for förstegangsindlagte gerontopsykiatriske patienter', in G. Magnussen, J. Nielsen, and J. Buch (eds) *Epidemiology and Prevention of Mental Illness in Old Age*, Hellerup, Denmark: EGV, 81–3.

Wang, J.A. and Whanger, A. (1971) 'Brain impairment and longevity', in E. Palmore and F.L. Jeffers (eds) *Prediction of Life Span*, Lexington, Mass.: Heath, 95–101.

Williams, A., Papadopoulos, N., and Chase, T.N. (1980) 'Demonstration of CSF gamma-globulin banding in senile dementia', *Neurology* 30: 882–4.

World Health Organization (1987) Chapter V (F) on mental, behavioural and developmental disorders, in *Tenth Revision of the International Classification of Diseases*, draft for field trials, Geneva: WHO.

19

Women and Mental Illness

Rachel Jenkins and Anthony Clare

One of the more consistent findings of epidemiological research is that women report symptoms of both physical and mental illness and utilize physicians and hospital services at higher rates than men. This chapter sets out to explore this phenomenon, in relation to mental illness, from a detailed examination of the current epidemiological evidence in the light of potential explanations of the sex differences.

Sex differences in morbidity and mortality have attracted considerable attention for several centuries. In the seventeenth century, John Graunt, the founder of demography, noted that, while women attend doctors more frequently than do men, their life expectancy is no less than that of men. Graunt took the view that either women were generally cured by their physicians or that the men suffered from untreated morbidity (Graunt 1667). This paradox between apparent morbidity and actual mortality still exists today, and is illustrated in table 19.1 with figures from current UK sources.

Is the apparent excess of women's mental illness more artefactual rather than real? Is it due to social and environmental pressures or is it inherent in biology? If biological, is it hormonal and as closely linked to women's reproductive systems as has so long been assumed? It behoves us to examine the evidence carefully.

EVIDENCE FOR SEX DIFFERENCES IN AFFECTIVE DISORDERS

Sex differences in hospital admissions

Among the statistics reviewed by Weissman and Klerman (1979) for treated cases of depression, western countries such as the United States and England report higher rates of treated depression in women than in men. This accords with the figures in table 19.2 for episodes of psychoneuroses and affective psychoses treated in England in 1982.

However, Weissman and Klerman note exceptions in studies arising from several developing countries such as India, Iraq, New Guinea, and Rhodesia,

287

Table 19.1 A comparison of life expectancy, certified sickness absence and use of health services for all disorders (physical and mental)

	Males	Females
Life expectancy[1] (years at age 0) England and Wales 1983–5	71.8	77.6
Hospital discharges[2] (rates per 1,000) England and Wales 1985	101	110
Persons making use of out-patient[3] facilities (rates per 1,000) GB 1984 in 3 months reference period	130	130
Persons making physician[4] visits in a 14-day reference period (rates per 1,000) GB 1984	110	150
% of persons consulting a doctor[5] in last 14 days who obtained a prescription from the doctor GB 1984	74%	74%
% of persons absent from work[6] because of sickness in a 7 day reference period GB 1984	4.5%	5.1%

[1] *Health and Personal Social Services Statistics for England 1987*, p. 14
[2] *Health and Personal Social Services Statistics for England 1987*, p. 74
[3] *General Household Survey*, p. 135
[4] *General Household Survey*, p. 139
[5] *General Household Survey*, p. 140
[6] Central Statistical Office (1988) *Social Trends 18*, London: HMSO: 74.

where rates are either equal in men and women, or higher in men. Two further exceptions have been reported by Haavio Manilla (1976) and Ananth (1978) for Finland and India respectively. Thus, it seems that the sex ratio of treatment indices for depression and the psychoneuroses is not an invariable finding but one that varies from culture to culture. A female excess of treated cases is usually although not always found in western countries, but not always found in studies of developing countries.

Sex differences in general practice consultations

The evidence from both national and primary care surveys in the US supports the view that women seek help from doctors at a greater rate than men (Gurin, *et al.* 1960: Dohrenwend and Dohrenwend 1976; Horowitz 1977; Veroff 1981). Data for the UK may be obtained from the Third National Morbidity Survey of General Practice (see table 19.3 OPCS 1987).

It can be seen that general practitioners, taken as a whole, record more consultations in women than in men for 'all diseases and conditions', 'all mental disorders', and for the psychoneuroses. General practitioners also record more episodes of these conditions in women than in men but this does not account for the excess consultation rate in women for the psychoneuroses,

Table 19.2 Comparison of recorded episode rates of psychiatric illness in general practice and admission rates to psychiatric hospitals for the year 1982 in men and women (rates quoted per 100,000 population England and Wales)

ICD category	Episode rate recorded in general practice		All psychiatric admissions	
	M	F	M	F
All mental disorders 290–319	5,540	11,270	330	451
Senile and presenile dementia 290	10	30	27	46
Organic psychosis 291	10	10	2	1
Schizophrenia, schizoaffective and paranoid states 295–297	170	210	60	58
Affective psychosis 296	140	280	32	67
Other, and unspecified psychoses 292–4, 298, 299	60	100	24	35
Psychoneuroses 300	3,210	8,390	25	51
Personality disorders and sexual deviation 301–2, 307–9, 312–5	260	250	29	33
Alcoholism and drug dependency 303–4	260	140	17	41
Other psychiatric conditions 306, 310, 316	1,750	3,450	1	1
Mental retardation 317–9	40	40	1	1

where women consult, on average, 4.3 times per illness episode, compared with a rate of 2.5 times per illness episode for men. There is no particular sex difference in the average number of consultations per episode for 'all diseases and conditions' or for 'all mental disorders'.

Sex differences in prescriptions

Examining data from the General Household Survey (OPCS 1985), more women than men report taking prescribed medication, but there is no sex difference in the percentage of persons consulting a doctor who obtained a prescription from the doctor (see table 19.1).

Where psychotropic drugs are considered, women are higher users than

Table 19.3 A comparison of certified sickness absence and use of health services for mental disorders in men and women

		Males	Females
Hospital admissions per[1] 100,000 background population England and Wales		364	482
General practice episode rates[2] per 100,000 population England and Wales 1981–2		3,540	11,270
Certified incapacity[3] for mental disorder 1985	days	292,000	198,000
	spells	4,512	3,877

[1] *Health and Personal Social Services Statistics, 1987*, p. 130
[2] *Morbidity Statistics from General Practice – Third National Morbidity Survey 1987*, p. 196
[3] Personal communication, Robert Chew, OHE, 1987
Not all employed women are contributing to national insurance and hence included in the DHSS incapacity figures

men (Parrish 1971) and this holds across all age groups (Murray *et al.* 1981). This topic is dealt with in the chapter by Williams and Gabe elsewhere in this book.

Sex differences in community surveys

Rates of treated illness are underestimates of rates of illness in the general population since they are affected by individuals' readiness to recognize illness in themselves and to seek medical care for their symptoms, by the availability of medical services, by the primary care physician's ability to diagnose illness and treat it, and to refer on to the specialist service if necessary (Goldberg and Huxley 1980). In order to further our research into sex differences in depression it is important to look at community studies where it is hoped that the sex-biasing effects of the different filters into medical care should cease to influence reported rates of illness. However, close examination of the methodology of reported community studies shows that this is not always the case. For example, some 'community' studies actually ascertain prevalence rates from counts of individuals reported by all the primary care physicians in a given area (Sorenson and Strömgren 1961), or by the case reports of individuals in a given area (Weeke *et al.* 1975). It is readily apparent that such rates are affected by the readiness to acknowledge symptomatology in oneself and to seek medical care, and the readiness of the physician to recognize illness and act upon it by referral to specialist institutions, and the ease with which the individual may be admitted to in-patient care.

Jenkins (1983, 1985) has reviewed community surveys for the US, UK, Australia, and the developing countries from a methodological standpoint, in relation to sex differences, and found that those studies with adequate sampling, appropriate case-finding techniques, adequate data on the characteristics of respondents and the reasons for non-response do not provide nearly such a clear picture of excessive depression in women. Comstock and Helsing (1976) found a sex difference in whites but not in blacks; Linn et al. (1979) in a survey of elderly whites found no sex differences at all. Finlay-Jones and Burvill (1977) found no sex differences in adults aged from 30 to 39, persons born in Britain and emigrated to Australia, and in married persons in social class V. Bash and Bash-Liechti (1969, 1974) found a sex difference in urban areas but not among the rural population in Iraq; Dube and Kumar (1973) found that mental illness was more frequent in females in rural areas, but predominated in males in urban areas. In the rural areas, the female excess was almost entirely due to the category of hysteria, found largely among the uneducated. Orley and Wing (1979) found no sex differences in overall psychiatric morbidity nor in depression among Ugandan villagers. Bebbington et al. (1981) did find a sex difference in Camberwell.

Sex differences in surveys of homogeneous populations

Parker (1979) and Jenkins (1983, 1985) have pointed out the methodological significance of choosing a homogeneous sample of men and women to examine sex differences in prevalence of depression. If social variables are controlled or reduced and no sex difference is found in a homogeneous sample then one must consider the possibility that those social factors account for the sex differences found by other workers in non-homogeneous samples.

Parker (1979) reported a study of 242 students undertaking the one-year postgraduate Diploma of Education at Sydney Teachers' College. The sexes were equally represented and the response rate was high. No sex difference was found on the measures of trait depression, self-esteem, duration of episodes, or frequency of depressive episodes. This study provides support for the findings of two other comparable groups. Golin and Hartz (1977) gave the Beck Depressive Inventory to 446 college students and found that 25 per cent of the males and 25 per cent of the females scored as depressed. Hammen and Padesky (1977) also gave the Beck Depression Inventory to 2,272 male and female college students enrolled in introductory psychology courses. No sex differences were found in the degree of depression experienced by students.

It is important to assess how far groups of university students form homogeneous groups suitable for examining sex differences in prevalence. First, homogeneity is probably not achieved within some specialities, such as medicine where, until recently, fewer women were accepted into training than men. Second, the age range found amongst university students is predominantly 18–21, which is not the age group where sex differences are usually reported, but rather in the age group 25–44. Thus, there is still a need to seek and study homogeneous groups older than university students.

291

Third, there is evidence that students are exposed to special risk in that their suicide rate is many times that for the equivalent age group in the general population (Carpenter 1959). The risk of being exposed to the competitive and demanding world of higher education may differ between the two sexes (Horner 1972).

It is interesting at this stage to look briefly at sex differences in psychiatric illness in children. The Isle of Wight studies formed a useful source of data for this purpose (Rutter *et al.* 1976). In the age group of 10 to 12-year-olds, the researchers found that emotional disorders were slightly more common in girls, while conduct disorders were very much commoner in boys. No sex difference in outcome existed. In the age group of 14 to 15, emotional disorders were equally common in the two sexes, while males exhibited a much higher risk of conduct disorders, resulting in the overall prevalence of psychiatric disorder being twice as common in boys as in girls (Graham and Rutter 1973).

Unfortunately, many so-called surveys of homogeneous populations are, in fact, surveys of primary care attenders. Therefore, they are not suitable for prevalence estimates since they are affected by readiness to consult doctors, which differs between the two sexes (Hinkle *et al.* 1960; Kidd *et al.* 1966; O'Mahoney and O'Brien 1980). In addition, close scrutiny reveals that some are not in fact homogeneous for occupation or marital status (e.g. Hinkle's (1960) study of female telephone operators and male craftsmen). In others, the two sexes occur in differing proportions and, therefore, perhaps under different environmental constraints (e.g. Farmer and Harvey's (1975) survey of medical students). Here it is interesting to note that Lloyd and Gartrell (1981) found no initial sex difference in adjustment in first-year medical students, but sex differences were found by mid-year and at the end of the first year. Those surveys which come closer to satisfying the criterion of homogeneity and which survey the base population rather than those who consult medical services are not able to demonstrate any sex difference in the prevalence of depression (Golin and Hartz 1977; Hammen and Padesky 1977; Parker 1979). Studies of schoolchildren provide further evidence of no overall sex differences in the prevalence of psychiatric disorder (Rutter *et al.* 1976). There is a notable shortage of adequate surveys of homogeneous populations in the age groups over 25, probably at least partly due to the lack of occupations in western countries without some degree of sexual differentiation by task, grade, or pay.

It was in order to fill this gap that Jenkins carried out a study of a homogeneous population, selected to minimise occupational, social and role differences between the sexes (Jenkins, 1983, 1985). This study, of executive officers aged 20–35 in the Civil Service, found no significant sex difference in the prevalence of minor psychiatric morbidity, its symptom profile, or its outcome after twelve months, in a relatively homogeneous group of men and women of similar age, education, and occupation, and subject to similar levels of social stress and support. These findings are of interest because they suggest that there can be little or no overall contribution from biological factors or from sex differences in upbringing to the commonly reported excess of depression in women, since, if there were such a contribution, an excess of depression in women would be visible even in homogeneous populations. Therefore, there is a need for studies of the homogeneous populations, both in older age groups, and in different social settings to see if these findings are replicated. Any such study should measure the degree of heterogeneity remaining in relevant environmental and personal variables, so that it is possible to make comparisons between studies.

EXPLANATIONS OF REPORTED SEX DIFFERENCES

Constitutional

Genetic theories. While there is little doubt that there is a significant genetic contribution to the aetiology of major affective disorders (Price 1968; Gershon *et al.* 1971; Rosenthal 1971), the evidence concerning the genetic contribution to neurotic affective disorders is conflicting. Here, twin studies reveal divergent results which may in part be due to differences in selection procedures applied to twin pairs. Early studies were often based on samples drawn from a single hospital or consisting of twins detected in an uncontrolled way. Shields and Slater (1971) found a concordance rate which was almost three times higher in monozygotic (MZ) than in dizygotic (DZ) twin pairs (40 per cent v. 15 per cent). Schepank (1973) summed the results of thirteen studies, finding a concordance rate in MZ twins more than double that of DZ twins (59 per cent v. 28 per cent). Torgersen (1983), recognizing the importance of using a complete nationwide sample of neurotic twin patients, examined all twins admitted to any in-patient or out-patient psychiatric institution in Norway for a diagnosis of neurosis, and their co-twins.

He analysed his data separately for anxiety and depressive neuroses, and found a proband concordance rate for neurotic depression of 21 per cent in MZ twins and 27 per cent in DZ twins, indicating no genetic contribution to depressive neurosis.

Despite these persuasive findings that heredity does not contribute to non-hospitalized depressive neurosis, it has nonetheless been suggested that either X-linkage or autosomal inheritance with sex-related liability thresholds accounts for the female preponderance of depressive illness in general. For X-linkage to explain the usual male-female differences in community studies one would have to postulate a dominant X-linkage gene which produced liability to non-psychotic depression and which played a role in the majority of minor depressions affecting women (i.e. it would be a common gene). The evidence is against this because even in bipolar affective illness, X-linkage,

293

if it exists, is responsible for only a small proportion of genetic depressions (Gershon and Bunney 1976), and there is no evidence of X-linkage in unipolar mild depressions. The hypothesis of autosomal linkage with sex-related liability thresholds receives no support from the reported data for bipolar illness or unipolar illness. Autosomal linkage remains the most likely hypothesis for depressive psychosis, but not with sex-related thresholds. Again, there is no evidence for autosomal linkage in unipolar mild depression. Indeed, there is no evidence that heredity has a major effect on depression in non-psychotic female psychiatric patients. Since non-patient samples are less severe, there is even less chance of heredity playing a major role here.

The evidence from genetic studies indicates that the influence of sex on liability to affective disorders is therefore likely to be environmental rather than genetic.

Hormone theories. Sex differences in hormones have been invoked to explain behavioural and psychological differences between men and women. Frankenhauser and her colleagues have examined the physiological and psychological response to stress in men and women (Frankenhauser *et al.* 1976, 1978). They demonstrated that females are less prone than males to respond with increased adrenaline release and with increased cortisol release when exposed to various challenging and demanding influences in the psychological and social environment such as a matriculation examination. Despite both sexes performing equally well in the examination, the females reported more intense negative feelings than did the males and none of the sense of success and satisfaction that was a rather common feeling among the males. These results suggest an interesting potential mechanism whereby, under stress, women may perform as well as men, yet nonetheless experience worse self-esteem.

While these studies have succeeded in correlating catecholamine metabolite levels with a measure of self-esteem under stress conditions in men and women, no studies have yet succeeded in definitely correlating clinical state in men and women with levels of gonadal hormones (Weissman and Klerman 1979). The evidence that mood changes may be caused by cyclical changes in female hormones therefore remains circumstantial, from observations that depression tends to occur in association with events in the female reproductive cycle, including menstruation, use of contraceptive drugs, childbirth, and the menopause.

There is strong evidence of an increase in depression in the post-partum period, although the evidence that the hormonal and other metabolic changes taking place during and after childbirth in women who develop either mild mood disturbances or fully fledged psychoses are any different from those of normal women is weak and inconclusive (Nott *et al.* 1976; Ballinger *et al.* 1979; Handley *et al.* 1980). However, there remain a number of potent circumstantial arguments that hormonal and other metabolic changes may be important in puerperal illness, which were recently summarized by Kendall *et al.* (1981).

The menopause is not associated with an increased risk of depression (Green and Cook 1980) and the balance of evidence at the present time suggests that where depression does occur at the time of the menopause, environmental factors are still more important in its aetiology than the menopause itself (Slater and Roth, 1969; Ballinger 1975, 1976; Green and Cook 1980). There is evidence that premenstrual tension is associated with depression, but the evidence relating this association to specific hormonal changes remains conflicting (Clare 1980).

Environmental explanations of the reported sex differences in minor psychiatric morbidity. Research on mental illness in the community has provided evidence that life events, such as the death of a spouse or job loss, and chronic social stresses, such as financial hardship, social isolation, migration, and low social class, are implicated in the aetiology of depression (Dohrenwend and Dohrenwend 1974; Liem and Liem 1978). Furthermore, social supports may ameliorate or buffer the effect of social stresses (Cobb 1976; Gore 1978) on health and reduce the liability to depression. It has been argued that women, by virtue of the roles they occupy, experience more life events and chronic social stresses, and less social support than men, and that this differential exposure to risk factors explains women's greater vulnerability to depression.

Social stress. The empirical data available so far suggest that there is no difference in the rates at which men and women experience acute life events or adversity (Myers *et al.* 1971; Dekker and Webb 1974; Newman 1975; Henderson *et al.* 1980). However, the possibility remains to be tested that women in general may experience more undesirable life events by virtue of their lower socio-economic status overall (Myers *et al.* 1975), since there is much evidence that women still have less overall status than men, both at home and at work, and frequently earn less even when in comparable jobs (General Household Survey 1987). There is no evidence that life events have more impact on women than men (Paykel *et al.* 1971: Personn 1980). However, there is evidence that women experience more chronic social stress than men. Radloff and Rae (1979) reported that women were more exposed than men to low education, low income, low occupational status, fewer leisure activities, and more current and recent physical illness.

Social supports. There are few studies which specifically address the question of whether women experience less social support than men. Miller and Ingham (1976) found that casual, less intimate friends as well as intimates afforded protection from developing illness, and that 'Psychological symptom

295

levels probably vary with social support even when there is no serious life event present'. It is, therefore, apparent that contacts with colleagues at work may also be supportive to the individual, and it may be that the housewife experiences relative isolation in the home, having less frequent daily verbal exchanges with other individuals than does her counterpart in the office.

Henderson *et al.* (1979) found that males reported more availability of social integration than females, while females scored higher on the quality or adequacy of the social integration. Females scored more availability of attachment than males, but there was no sex difference on the quality or adequacy of the attachment. It was the authors' view that special attention should be paid to those social bonds which promote self-esteem – both the esteem of self in terms of appearance, abilities, competence, and position in a dominance hierarchy, as well as the degree to which one believes one is lovable by others. The question is, therefore, whether such self-esteem is more likely to be derived from a close intimate attachment or the more loose social integration within a group. The esteem of self in terms of appearance, abilities, competence, and position are probably more likely to be derived from social integration within a group, while the extent to which one believes one is lovable by others may be obtained from both kinds of social bond. If the important attributes of self-esteem are more likely to be derived from social integration, then Henderson's finding, that males reported quantitatively more availability of social integration than females, may be of crucial significance to the question of whether women experience less social support than men. While females report a better quality of social integration, in terms of self-esteem thus engendered, quality may not make up for quantity. Henderson found that for minor psychiatric morbidity social integration has a stronger association with symptom level than does attachment for women. For men, the strength of the association of symptom level with social integration and with attachment was the same. Henderson concluded that 'social bonds appear to be related to morbidity in a manner independent of the challenge of adversity'. While these primary questions afford some hope of elucidating the nature of the sex difference in prevalence of minor psychiatric morbidity, it is clear that as yet little research attention has focused on them and further work is required. In the meantime, the evidence suggests that women in general do experience more chronic social stresses – such as lower occupational status and lower income – than men, and women also experience less availability of social integration – a factor with a strong negative association with minor psychiatric morbidity.

Sex roles. Some considerable attention has been paid in the literature to the elaboration of complex hypotheses, based upon interpretations of western sex roles, which are intended to provide explanations for women's greater prevalence of reported mental illness. Sex role hypotheses have proved difficult to test convincingly and this may be attributed partly to their inadequate specification and partly to the lack of directly measurable social indicators which might be used to assess their explanatory power.

Interaction with constitution. It has been suggested that sex differences in the early upbringing and social environment of males and females place a permanent stamp on the phenotype of the individual, thus affecting constitutional vulnerability to psychiatric illness in adult life (Chesler 1971, 1972; Chodorow 1974). The learned helplessness model proposes that helplessness is the salient characteristic of depression and that it results from learning that one's actions do not produce predictable responses (Seligman 1975). Cochrane and Stopes-Roe (1980) argue that girls are traditionally more sheltered than boys, women have less initiative in selecting their spouses than do men, their life styles face more disruption with the advent of children, and they have to follow their husbands geographically and socially. This relatively low ability to influence their environment may make females more prone to 'learned helplessness' than males.

Evidence certainly exists to support the notion of sex stereotypic belief about male and female abilities (Williams and Best 1982), and also supports the view that such stereotypes are influential in the development of male and female abilities (Rheingold and Cook 1975). There is some evidence that stereotypic female abilities encourage low self-esteem, but how far this phenomenon accounts for the reported sex differences in illness rate has yet to be assessed.

Interaction with environment. Regardless of the influence of early environment, it has been suggested that sex differences in adult sex roles lead to men and women being differentially exposed to environmental risk factors. Gove (1972) argues that if women are biologically more susceptible to mental illness than men, we would expect women to have higher rates of mental illness in each marital category. His literature review concluded that married women do indeed have higher rates than married men, but single women, the divorced, and the widowed do not have higher rates than their male counterparts – indeed the reverse is true. Gove asserts that a role explanation accounts for these discrepancies. Being married is presumed to be a less stressful and more satisfying experience for men than for women in western society where traditionally the women works for the husband, and does the housework, and looks after the children for him, while the man goes out to work, associates with colleagues, and earns money. Even if the married woman does work it is often in an intrinsically unsatisfying job. More recent workers have recognized that the experience of marriage may differ among groups of different educational attainments and social expectations, and have investigated the effects of such factors as social isolation, poverty, and the presence of children. These more searching studies have established that the relationship of marital status to psychiatric illness is complex, and differs among groups of different educational attainments and social expectations, with social isolation, poverty, and the presence of children being important complicating factors (Meile *et al.* 1976; Pearlin and Johnson 1977; Cochrane and Stopes-Roe 1980).

Two opposing views are to be found in the literature. The first is that employment in women increases their role obligations (since they usually still retain their home-making tasks in addition to their paid employment), and that this may cause overload which predisposes the women to more ill-health than housewives. The other view is that employment increases affiliation and this extra social support is protective against morbidity. In addition, the extra role obligations make it less likely that such employed women will adopt a sick role.

Thus, while some studies find clear health advantages in employed women versus unemployed women (Cumming *et al.* 1975; Mostow and Newberry 1975; Nathanson 1980), such studies find that the relationship of employment status with psychiatric disorder is complicated by other factors such as duration of employment (Waldron 1976; Welch and Booth 1977), and the presence or absence of a confidante (Brown and Harris 1978).

Effect on reporting behaviour and diagnostic habits. This section examines the extent to which sex roles and sex stereotypes influence the illness behaviour of men and women, and the diagnostic habits of physicians. Four major hypotheses are examined. First, it has been suggested that women's traditional sex role as home-maker is more compatible with adoption of the sick role (visiting a doctor, taking medication, spending time in bed) than is men's traditional sex role as bread-winner (Mechanic 1965; Glaser 1970). There is vigorous opposition to this view. Parsons and Fox (1952) suggest that the nature of a woman's household and family responsibility make her illness more disturbing to family equilibrium than illness in her husband. Marcus and Seeman (1981) examined data from the Los Angeles Health Survey and demonstrated that role obligations do explain male/female differences in illness behaviour but not in illness *per se*.

Second, it has been suggested that differences in sex stereotypes result in men and women being socialized into different patterns of perception of illness and help-seeking behaviour based on those stereotypes (Mechanic 1964). There is speculation that women more readily translate diffuse feelings of psychological distress into conscious recognition of themselves as having emotional problems (Verbrugge 1979).

Several studies have suggested that it is culturally acceptable for women to be expressive about their difficulties while men are expected to bear their problems with greater self-control and to be reluctant to admit symptoms of distress (Komarovsky 1946; Phillip and Segal 1969; Cooperstock 1971). Psychological studies have indicated that women are more likely than men to disclose intimate information about themselves, especially unpleasant feelings such as anxieties and worries (Horowitz 1977; Briscoe 1982).

Jenkins, exploring several different aspects of illness behaviour in relation to minor psychiatric morbidity, reported that women without minor psychiatric morbidity have higher self-assessment of ill-health scores, a higher frequency of general practitioner consultations in the preceding twelve months, and take more sickness absence than do men without minor psychiatric morbidity (Jenkins 1985). There was no particular sex difference in prescribed medication or in 'over the counter' drug consumption in individuals without minor psychiatric morbidity. Increasing severity of psychiatric clinical state is associated with a greater increase in self-assessment of ill-health score, frequency of GP consultations, consumption of prescribed medication, and frequency and duration of sickness absence in men than in women. Thus it appears that women's illness behaviour may be less closely linked to the severity of their symptoms than is men's illness behaviour. It is as if men's illness behaviour is more 'realistic' than that of women. This may relate to the different socialization patterns of men and women and to their different tendencies to express their emotional difficulties (Briscoe 1982).

Third, it has been suggested that, because sex stereotypes exist, the social consequences of expression of symptoms differs between the sexes. Phillips (1964) presented subjects with descriptions of behaviour in which the disturbed individual was described as either a male or female. He found that men were rejected more than women for descriptions of the same behaviour. Phillips argues on the basis of his study that illness is stigmatizing for men but not so for women, and that, therefore, women are more willing to report symptoms in interview and are more likely to seek professional help for them. Unfortunately, although the majority of doctors are male, Phillips used only women as raters. These findings have received support from the studies of Broverman *et al.* (1970), Coie *et al.* (1974) and Hammen and Peters (1977), although Yamamoto and Disney (1967), using the same methods as Phillips (1964), failed to find differences in the rejection of disturbed individuals on the basis of their reported sex.

Fourth, it has been suggested that sex stereotypes affect the diagnostic habits of physicians. Broverman *et al.* (1970) have provided an empirical demonstration of a double standard of mental health among clinicians.

However, there is no evidence from recent studies that judges of either sex are partisan towards their own kind (Kosherak and Masling 1972; Lewittes *et al.* 1973; Schlosberg and Pietrofesa 1973; Werner and Block 1975; Zeldow 1975).

It may be concluded that, while evidence for the discrimination against women in the mental health field exists, the conditions for its occurrence are rather circumscribed and may be declining. There is some evidence that at least a part of the observed sex difference in the prevalence of depression in men and women may be attributed to women being more likely to recognize problems in themselves and to seek help for them. It does, indeed, appear that illness is less stigmatizing for women than for men. The evidence that women are more likely to be diagnosed as ill than men remains conflicting. The fixed role obligations hypothesis explains sex differences in illness behaviour rather than in illness *per se*. However, the existence of these 'artefactual' mechanisms does not exclude the possibility that some of the observed sex difference is real, due to either inherited or acquired risks.

SUMMARY

Thus, a female excess in the prevalence of minor psychiatric morbidity is found in most of the treatment statistics, although not all, and in some community studies, with important and notable exceptions. Surveys of homogeneous populations, where care is taken to minimize occupational, social, and role differences between the sexes, do not reveal a female excess in the prevalence of minor psychiatric morbidity in schoolchildren, students, or young working adults aged 20–35. Any coherent theory of sex differences must, therefore, take these findings into account.

In view of the substantial genetic evidence that the excess of depression in women is environmental in origin rather than genetic; in view of the paucity of any direct endocrinological evidence linking mood change in men and women with gonadal hormones; in view of the evidence from homogeneous surveys that, when social variables are controlled and reduced, the sex difference disappears; and in the light of the nineteenth-century experience, all claims that the excess of depression in women is explained by their reproductive biology – or indeed by their constitution in general – should be treated with grave caution.

REFERENCES

Ananth, J. (1978) 'Psychopathology in Indian females', *Social Science and Medicine* 12: 177–8.

Ballinger, C.B. (1975) 'Psychiatric morbidity and the menopause: screening of a general population sample' *British Medical Journal* iii: 344–6.

Ballinger, C.B. (1976) 'Psychiatric morbidity and the menopause: clinical features', *British Medical Journal* i: 1183–5.

Ballinger, C.B., Buckley, D.E., Naylor, G.J.A., and Stansfield, DA. (1979) 'Emotional disturbance following childbirth: clinical findings and urinary excretion of cyclic AMP', *Psychological Medicine* 9: 293–300.

Bash, K.W. and Bash-Liechti, J. (1969) 'Studies of the epidemiology of neuro-psychiatric disorders among the rural population of the province of Khazestran, Iran', *Social Psychiatry* 4: 137–43.

Bash, K.W. and Bash-Liechti, J. (1974) 'Studies of the epidemiology of neuro-psychiatric disorders among the population of the city of Shiraz, Iran', *Social Psychiatry* 9: 163–71.

Bebbington, P., Hurry, J., Tennant, C., Sturt, E., and Wing, J.K. (1981) 'Epidemiology of mental disorders in Camberwell', *Psychological Medicine* 11: 561–79.

Briscoe, M. (1982) *Sex Differences in Psychological Well-Being* (Psychological Medicine Monograph Supplement 1), Cambridge: Cambridge University Press.

Broverman, L., Broverman, D., Clarkson, F., Rosenkranz, P., and Vogel, S. (1970) 'Sex role stereotype and clinical judgements of mental health', *Journal of Consulting and Clinical Psychology* 34: 1–7.

Brown, G.W. and Harris, T. (1978) *Social Origins of Depression: A Study of Psychiatric Disorder in Women*, London: Tavistock.

Carpenter, R.G. (1959) 'Statistical analysis of suicide and other mortality rates of students', *British Journal of Preventive and Social Medicine* 13: 163.

Chesler, P. (1971) 'Patient and patriarch: women in the psychotherapeutic relationship', in V. Gornick and B.K. Moran (eds) *Women in Sexist Society*, New York: Basic Books.

Chesler, P. (1972) *Women and Madness*, London: Allen Lane.

Chodorow, N. (1974) 'Family structure and feminine personality' in M.Z. Rosaldo and L. Larnphere (eds) *Woman, Culture and Society*, Stanford: Stanford University Press.

Clare, A.W. (1980) 'Psychological and social aspects of premenstrual complaint', MD thesis, National University of Ireland.

Cobb, S. (1976) 'Social support as a moderator of life stress', *Psychosomatic Medicine* 38: 300–14.

Cochrane, R. and Stopes-Roe, M. (1980) 'Factors affecting the distribution of psychological symptoms in urban areas of England', *Acta Psychiatrica Scandinavica* 61: 445–60.

Coie, J.D., Pennington, B.F., and Buckley, H.H. (1974) 'Effects of situational stress and sex roles on the attribution of psychological disorder', *Journal of Consulting and Clinical Psychology* 42: 559–68.

Comstock, G.W. and Helsing, K.J. (1976) 'Symptoms of depression in two communities', *Psychological Medicine* 6: 551–63.

Cooperstock, R. (1971) 'Sex differences in the use of mood modifying drugs: an explanatory model', *Journal of Health and Social Behaviour* 12: 238–344.

Cumming, E., Lazer, C., and Chisholm, L. (1975) 'Suicide as an index of role strain among employed and not employed married women in British Columbia', *Canadian Review of Sociology and Anthropology* 12 (4): 462–70.

Dekker, D.J. and Webb, J.T. (1974) 'Relationships of the social readjustment rating scale to psychiatric patient status, anxiety and social desirability', *Journal of Psychosomatic Research* 18: 125–30.

Dohrenwend, B.S. and Dohrenwend, B.P. (1974) *Stressful Life Events: Their Nature and Effects*, New York: Wiley.

Dohrenwend, B.P. and Dohrenwend, B.S. (1976) 'Sex differences and psychiatric disorders', *American Sociological review* 81: 1447–54.

Dube, K.C. and Kumar, N. (1973) 'An epidemiological study of manic depressive psychosis', *Acta Psychiatrica Scandinavica* 49: 691–7.

Farmer, R.D.J. and Harvey, P.G. (1975) 'Minor psychiatric disturbance in young adults', *Social Science and Medicine* 9: 461–74.

Finlay-Jones, R.A. and Burvill, P.W. (1977) 'The prevalence of minor psychiatric morbidity in the community', *Psychological Medicine* 7: 474–89.

Frankenhauser, M., Dunne, E., and Lundberg, U. (1976) 'Sex differences in sympathetic-adrenal medullary reactions induced by different stresses', *Psychopharmacology* 47: 1–5.

Frankenhauser, M., Rauste Von Wright, M., Collins, A., Van Wright, J., Sedvall, G., and Swahn, C.J. (1978) 'Sex differences in psychoneuroendocrine reactions to examination stress', *Psychosomatic Medicine* 40 (4): 334–43.

Gershon, E.S. and Bunney, W.E. (1976) 'The question of X-linkage in biopolar manic depressive illness', *Journal of Psychiatric Research* 13: 99–117.

Gershon, E.S., Bunney, D.L., and Goodwin, F.K. (1971) 'Towards a biology of affective disorders', *Archives of General Psychiatry* 25: 1–15.

Glaser, W.A. (1970) *Social Settings and Medical Organisation*, New York: Atherton Press.

Goldberg, D.P. and Huxley, P. (1980) *Mental Illness in the Community: The Pathway to Psychiatric Care*, London: Tavistock.

Golin, S. and Hartz, M.A. (1977) 'A factor analysis of the Beck Depression Inventory in a mildly depressed population', unpublished typescript from the University of Pittsburgh, quoted in Parker (1979).

Gore, S. (1978) 'The effect of social support in moderating the health consequences of unemployment', *Journal of Health and Social Behaviour* 19: 157–65.

Gove, W.R. (1972) 'The relationship between sex roles, mental illness and marital status', *Social Forces* 51: 34–44.

Graham, P. and Rutter, M. (1973) 'Psychiatric disorder in the young adolescent', *Proceedings of the Royal Society of Medicine* 66: 1226–9.

Graunt, J. (1667) *Natural and political observations mentioned in a following index, and made upon the bills of mortality*, quoted in Glass, D.V. (1963) 'John Graunt and His Natural and Political Observations', *Proceedings of the Royal Society* B159: 1–32.

Green, J.G. and Cook, D.J. (1980) 'Life stress and symptoms at the climacteric', *British Journal of Psychiatry* 136: 486–91.

Gurin, G., Veroff, J., and Feld, S. (1960) *Americans View Their Mental Health*, New York: Basic Books.

Haavio-Manilla, E. (1976) 'Ecological and sex differences in the hospitalisation of mental illness in Finland and Sweden', *Social Science and Medicine* 10: 77–82.

Hammen, C.L. and Padesky, C.A. (1977) 'Sex differences in the expression of depressive responses on the Beck Depression Inventory', *Journal of Abnormal Psychology* 86 (6): 609–14.

Hammen, C.L. and Peters, S.D. (1977) 'Differential response to male and female depressive reactions', *Journal of Consulting and Clinical Psychology* 45 (6): 974–1001.

Handley, S.L., Dunn, T.L., Waldron, G. and Baker, J.M. (1980) 'Tryptophan, cortisol and puerperal mood', *British Journal of Psychiatry* 136: 498–508.

Henderson, S., Duncan-Jones, P., Byrne, D.G., Adcock, S., and Scott, R. (1979) 'Neurosis and social bands in an urban population', *Australian and New Zealand Journal of Psychiatry* 13: 121–5.

Henderson, S., Byrne, D.G., Duncan-Jones, P., Scott, R.A., and Adcock, S. (1980) 'Social relationships, adversity and neurosis: a study of associations in a general population sample', *British Journal of Psychiatry* 136: 574–83.

Hinkle, L.E., Redmont, R., Plummer, N., and Wolff, H.G. (1960) 'An examination of the relationship between symptoms, disability and serious illness, in two homogeneous groups of men and women', *American Journal of Public Health* 50 (9): 1327–36.

Horner, M.S. (1972) 'Toward an understanding of achievement related conflicts in women', *Journal of Social Issues* 28: 157–75.

Horowitz, A. (1977) 'The pathways into psychiatric treatment: some differences between men and women', *Journal of Health and Social Behaviour* 18: 169–75.

Jenkins, R. (1983) 'Some epidemiological observations of minor psychiatric morbidity', MD thesis for Cambridge University.

Jenkins, R. (1985) 'Sex differences in minor psychiatric morbidity', *Psychological Medicine* (Monograph Supplement 7) Cambridge University Press.

Kendell, R.E., Rennie, D., Clarke, J.A., and Dean, C. (1981) 'The social and obstetric correlates of psychiatric admission in the puerperium', *Psychological Medicine* 11: 341–50.

Kidd, C.B., Caldbeck, J., and Meenan, J. (1966) 'A comparative study of psychiatric morbidity among students at two different universities', *British Journal of Psychiatry* 112: 57–64.

Komarovsky, M. (1946) 'Cultural contradictions and sex roles', *American Journal of Sociology* 52: 184–9.

Kosherak, S. and Masling, J. (1972) 'Noblesse oblige effect: the interpretation of Rorschach responses as a function of ascribed social class', *Journal of Consulting and Clinical Psychology* 39: 415–19.

Lewittes, D.J., Mosell, J.A., and Simmons, W.L. (1973) 'Sex role bias in clinical judgements based on Rorschach interpretations', in *Proceedings of the 81st Annual Convention of the American Psychological Association* 8: 495–6 referred to in Zelcher, P.B. (1978) 'Sex differences in psychiatric evaluation and treatment', *Archives of General Psychiatry* 35: 89–93.

Liem, R. and Liem, J. (1978) 'Social class and mental illness reconsidered: the role of economic stress and social support', *Journal of Health and Social Behaviour* 19: 139–56.

Linn, N.W., Hunter, K.L., and Perry, P.R. (1979) 'Differences by sex and ethnicity in the psychosocial adjustment of the elderly', *Journal of Health and Social Behaviour* 20: 273–81.

Lloyd, C. and Gartrell, N.K. (1981) 'Sex differences in medical student mental health', *American Journal of Psychiatry* 138 (10): 1346–51.

Marcus, A.C. and Seeman, T.E. (1981) 'Sex differences in health status: a re-examination of the nurturant role hypothesis', *American Sociological Review* 46: 119–23.

Mechanic, D. (1964) 'The influence of mothers on their children's health attitudes and behaviour', *Paediatrics* 33: 444–53.

Mechanic, D. (1965) 'Perceptions of parental responses to illness: a research note', *Journal of Health and Human Behaviour* 6: 253.

Meile, R.L., Johnson, D.R., and Peter, L. (1976) 'Marital role, education, and mental disorder among women: test of an interaction hypothesis', *Journal of Health and Social Behaviour* 17: 295–301.

Miller, P. Mc. and Ingham, J.G. (1976) 'Friends, confidantes and symptoms', *Social Psychiatry* 11: 51–8.

Mostow, E. and Newberry, P. (1975) 'Work role and depression in women: a comparison of workers and housewives in treatment', *American Journal of Ortho-psychiatry* 45: 538–48.

Murray, J., Dunn, G., Williams, P., and Tarnopolsky, A. (1981) 'Factors affecting the consumption of psychotropic drugs', *Psychological Medicine* 11: 551–60.

Myers, J.K., Lindenthal, J.J., and Pepper, M.P. (1971) 'Life events and psychiatric impairment', *Journal of Nervous and Mental Disease* 152: 149–57.

Myers, J.K., Lindenthal, J.J., and Pepper, M.P. (1975) 'Life stress, social integration and psychiatric symptomatology', *Journal of Health and Social Behaviour* 16: 421–7.

Nathanson, C.A. (1980) 'Social roles and health status among women: the significance of employment', *Social Science and Medicine* 14A: 463–71.

Newman, J.P. (1975) 'Sex differences in life problems and psychological distress', Master's Thesis, University of Wisconsin, Madison.

Nott, P.M., Franklin, M., Armitage, C., and Gelder, M.G. (1976) 'Hormonal changes and mood in the puerperium', *British Journal of Psychiatry* 128: 379–83.

Office of Population Censuses and Surveys (1980) *General Household Survey 1978* (Series GHS, No. 8) London: HMSO.

Office of Population Censuses and Surveys (1987) *General Household Survey (OPCS) 1985* (Series GHS, No. 14), London: HMSO.

O'Mahoney, P. and O'Brien, S. (1980) 'Demographic and social characteristics of university students attending a psychiatrist', *British Journal of Psychiatry* 137: 547–50.

Orley, J. and Wing, J.K. (1979) 'Psychiatric disorder in two African villages', *Archives of General Psychiatry* 36: 513–20.

Parker, G. (1979) 'Sex differences in non-clinical depression: review and assessment of previous studies', *Australian and New Zealand Journal of Psychiatry* 13: 127–32.

Parrish, P.A. (1971) 'The prescribing of psychotropic drugs in general practice', *Journal of the Royal College of General Practitioners* 21 (supplement 4): 1–71.

Parsons, R. and Fox, R. (1952) 'Illness, therapy and the modern urban American family', *Journal of Social Issues* 8 (4): 31–44.

Paykel, E.S., Prusoff, B.A., and Ulenluth, E.H. (1971) 'Scaling of life events', *Archives of General Psychiatry* 25: 340–7.

Pearlin, L.I. and Johnson, J.S. (1977) 'Marital status, life strains and depression', *American Sociological Review* 42: 704–15.

Personn, G. (1980) 'Life event ratings in relation to sex and marital status in a 70 year old urban population', *Acta Psychiatrica Scandinavica* 62: 112–18.

Phillips, D.L. (1964) 'Rejection of the mentally ill: the influence of behaviour and sex', *American Sociological Review* 29: 679–87.

Phillip, D.L. and Segal, B.E. (1969) 'Sexual status and psychiatric symptoms', *American Sociological Review* 34: 58–72.

Price, J. (1968) 'The genetics of depressive behaviour', in A. Coppen and A. Walk (eds) *Recent Developments in Affective Disorders* (British Journal of Psychiatry Special Publication No. 2) Ashford, Kent: Headley Brothers, 37–54.

Radloff, L.S., and Rae, D.S. (1979) 'Susceptibility and precipitating factors in depression: sex differences and similarities', *Journal of Abnormal Psychology* 88: 174–86.

Rheingold, H.L. and Cook, K.V. (1975) 'The contents of boys' and girls' rooms as an index of parents behaviour', *Child Development* 46: 459–63.

Rosenthal, D. (1971) *Genetics of Psychopathology*, New York: McGraw-Hill.

Rutter, M., Tizard, J., Yule, W., Graham, P., and Whitmore, K. (1976) 'Research report: Isle of Wight Studies 1964-1974', *Psychological Medicine* 6: 313–32.

Schepank, H. (1973) 'Erb-und Unweltfaktoren bei neurosen Ergebnisse der Zwilling Forschung und andere Methoden', *Nervenarzt* 44: 449–59, quoted in Katschnig, H. and Shepherd, M. (1976) 'Neurosis, the epidemiological perspective', in H.M. Van Praag (ed.) *Research in Neurosis*, Utrecht: Bohn, Schelerna and Holkena, pp. 5–21.

Schlosberg, N.K. and Pietrofesa, J.J. (1973) 'Perspectives on counselling bias: implications for counsellor education', *Counselling Psychology* 4: 44–54.

Seligman, M.E.P. (1975) *Helplessness: On Depression, Development and Death*, San Francisco: W.H. Freeman.

Shields, J. and Slater, E. (1971) 'Diagnostic similarity in twins with neuroses and personality disorders', in J. Shields and I.I. Gottesman (eds) *Man, Mind and Heredity: Selected Papers of Eliot Slater on Psychiatry and Genetics*, Baltimore: Johns Hopkins Press.

Slater, E. and Roth, M. (1969) *Clinical Psychiatry*, London: Balliere, Tindall & Cassell.

Sorenson, A. and Strömgren, E. (1961) 'Frequency of depressive states within geographically delineated population groups', *Acta Psychiatrica Scandinavica* supplement 162: 62–8.

Torgersen, S. (1983) 'Genetics of neuroses: the effects of sampling variation upon the twin concordance ratio', *British Journal of Psychiatry* 142: 126–32.

Verbrugge, L.M. (1979) 'Female illness rates and illness behaviour: testing hypotheses about sex differences in health', *Women and Health* 4: 61–79.

Veroff, J.B. (1981) 'The dynamics of help-seeking in men and women: a national survey study', *Psychiatry* 44: 189–200.

Waldron, I. (1976) 'Why do women live longer than men? Part I', *Journal of Human Stress* 2: 2–13.

Weeke, A.B., Videbeck, T.H., and Dupont, A. (1975) 'The incidence of depressive syndromes in a Danish county', *Acta Psychiatrica Scandinavica* 51: 28–41.

Weissman, M.M. and Klerman, G.L. (1979) 'Sex differences and the epidemiology of depression', in E.S. Gomberg and V. Franks (eds) *Gender and Disordered Behaviour: Sex Differences in Psychopathology*, New York: Brunner/Mazel.

Welch, S. and Booth, A. (1977) 'Employment and health among married women with children', *Sex Roles* 3: 385–97.

Werner, P.D. and Block, J. (1975) 'Sex differences in the eyes of expert personality assessor: unwarranted conclusions', *Journal of Personal Assessment* 39: 110–13.

Williams, J.E. and Best, D.L. (1982) *Measuring Sex Stereotypes: A Thirty Nation Study* London: Sage.

Yamamoto, K. and Disney, H. (1967) 'Rejection of the mentally ill: a study of attitudes of student teachers', *Journal of Counselling Psychology* 14: 254–68.

Zeldow, P.B. (1975) 'Clinical judgements: a search for sex differences', *Psychology Reports* 37: 1135–42.

Section Three

The Evaluation of Psychiatric Intervention

Introduction

Current resource constraints are increasingly focusing attention on the need to evaluate treatment modalities (Wilkinson and Williams 1985). This activity has not always been a priority in psychiatry, as Shepherd has noted:

> The relatively short history of modern psychiatry has witnessed the rise and fall of many different forms of treatment. At the present time few branches of medicine stand more in need of reliable methods for the assessment of their therapeutic claims. If this unsatisfactory state of affairs springs in some measure from an uncertainty about the causes and nature of most psychiatric illness it also reflects a failure on the part of many workers to have applied to psychiatry well recognised principles of clinical investigation.   (Shepherd 1981: 99)

The three major treatment modalities in psychiatry are physical, psycho-social, and behavioural: chapters in the first subsection deal with each of the three. In the first, Malcolm Lader provides a 'state of the art' review of the methodology of clinical trials of psychotropic drugs. One of the most important of these was the trial of the treatment of depressive illness organized by a special subcommittee of the Medical Research Council (MRC 1965), of which Michael Shepherd was the secretary.

However, the conditions of a controlled clinical trial, in which drugs are prescribed for a carefully selected group of patients and their effects rigorously monitored, are clearly different from those that apply in routine clinical practice. Thus, in the comprehensive evaluation of psychotropic drugs, it is necessary to complement clinical trials with studies of utilization in a social context. This is the topic of the following chapter by Paul Williams and Jonathan Gabe.

While the introduction and development of psychotropic drugs is generally agreed to be a major advance, it is at the same time also acknowledged that social factors are a profound determinant of mental disorder and that psychosocial approaches constitute a necessary component of the management of psychiatric and emotional disturbance. The evaluation of such techniques are dealt with by Roslyn Corney and Joanna Murray. Their chapter and the one which follows, in which Ian Falloon describes behavioural approaches in the family management of schizophrenia, emphasize the importance of the multi-disciplinary team in this context. The concept of the multi-disciplinary team, and the nature and responsibilities of its members, are especially important at a time when, as at present, services are undergoing rapid change.

The second subsection is concerned with the evaluation of service provision. Traditionally, the focus of the psychiatric services has been the mental hospital, and David Watt appraises their current role. However, in many countries the provision of services is shifting from an institutional to a primary care and community base. Arguably the most radical change has taken place in Italy: it is appropriate, therefore, that the subsequent chapter, on the evaluation of community psychiatric services, is written by Michele Tansella. As he points out, the development of such services has provided plentiful opportunities for service evaluation; these have, regrettably, not been fully exploited.

It is now widely accepted that the primary care services play a pivotal role in providing mental health care to the community. This is exemplified in the conclusions of the WHO working party on psychiatry and primary medical care:

> the crucial question is not how the general practitioner can fit into the mental health services, but rather how the psychiatrist can collaborate most effectively with primary health services, and reinforce the effectiveness of the primary physician as a member of the mental health team.(WHO 1973: 27)

Here, the contribution of the general practitioner is discussed by Deborah Sharp and David Morrell, while Geraldine Strathdee and Michael King consider the interface between general and specialist psychiatric services.

Ultimately, the responsibility for the planning and provision of mental health services for populations rests with politicians, and hence policies and priorities are politically determined (even so, policy is often made *post hoc*: for example, Gronfein (1985) noted that in the USA closing mental hospital beds preceded the policy of deinstitutionalization by several years). The relationship between psychiatric research and public policy is ill-defined: Leon Eisenberg casts light on this topic in the final chapter in this section.

REFERENCES

Gronfein, W. (1985) 'Psychotropic drugs and the origins of deinstitutionalization', *Social Problems* 32: 437–54.

Medical Research Council (1965) 'Report by its clinical committee: clinical trial of the treatment of depressive illness', *British Medical Journal* i: 881–6.

Shepherd, M. (1981) *Psychotropic Drugs in Psychiatry*, New York: Jason Aaronson.

Wilkinson, G. and Williams, P. (1985) 'Priorities for research on mental health in primary care settings', *Psychological Medicine* 15: 515–20.

World Health Organization (1973) *Psychiatry and Primary Medical Care*, Copenhagen: WHO Regional Office for Europe.

Specific Treatment Approaches

20

Clinical Trials in Psychiatry

Malcolm Lader

Our inability upon all occasions to appreciate the efforts of Nature in the cure of disease, must always render our notions, with respect to the power of art, liable to numerous errors and multiplied deceptions.(Paris 1833:50)

Psychiatric disorders cover a range of conditions with a wide assortment of natural histories. Most are characterized by a fluctuating or relapsing/remitting course. Therefore, it is particularly important to assess the efficacy, and for that matter the apparent unwanted effects of psychiatric remedies in a manner which minimizes the influence of natural variations in severity and other biasses. This requirement applies to non-pharmacological as well as to drug treatments. For a variety of non-scientific reasons, such as the claimed difficulties in defining 'efficacy' in treatments involving dynamic psychotherapy, the assessment of treatments in psychiatry has been most systematic with respect to pharmacological agents (Johnson 1983).

But there are problems. Almost all psychotropic drugs used in psychiatry were discovered by accident, usually in the search for another class of drugs, sometimes after following a line of reasoning which turned out to be based on false premises (Ayd and Blackwell 1970). These remedies are established empirically not rationally and their efficacy has to be carefully established and not taken for granted because of an appealing theoretical rationale.

A second consequence of the serendipitous origins of many psychotropic agents relates to unwanted side effects. Because the drugs were stumbled on by chance, no prior attempts could be made to confine the range of activity of the compounds to wanted effects only. Both the antipsychotic and the antidepressant groups are notorious for their wide range and severity of side effects, often to the point of jeopardizing compliance. Thus, clinical trials must carefully assess the whole range of drug effects. Furthermore, practical field trials, such as post-marketing surveillance, are appropriate to assess the effectiveness in practice of any new drug and to complement the more formal clinical trials.

The area of psychopharmacology has not escaped the problem of serious

313

adverse effects. The removal of zimeldine and nomifensine testifies to the powerful effects which psychotropic drugs can have outside the CNS. Because of the first such disaster, with thalidomide, regulatory agencies were set up to control the development and marketing of new compounds. These controls have been tightened inexorably with both commercial and scientific consequences. The former is that it now costs between fifty and a hundred million dollars to develop a new chemical entity to its launch on its market. The latter is that drug companies must design drug evaluation studies to accord with the requirements of the regulatory authorities whenever possible and appropriate.

In this article, I shall attempt to address some of the issues relating to the evaluation of psychiatric drugs. I shall sketch in the outlines rather than going into compendious detail and I shall concentrate on the principles rather than the practical minutiae. Some topics such as adverse effects and risk/benefit assessments are hardly touched upon (Walker and Asscher 1987).

AIMS OF TREATMENT

The aim of therapy is to restore 'health' or to prevent its breakdown. Doctors, including psychiatrists, seldom question this goal to which, indeed, most dedicate their working life. The WHO definition seems worthy but sententious: 'Health means more than freedom from disease, freedom from pain, freedom from untimely death. It means optimum physical, mental and social efficiency and well-being.' However, mental health is a complex concept which has been the subject of some fascinating essays (e.g. Lewis 1953). Perhaps more than with physical health, there is a positive aspect to mental health, the sense of well-being. This can, of course, become pathologically intense, as in mania.

By and large, drug treatments in psychiatry aim to rectify some behavioural or symptomatic abnormality. The behavioural abnormality may be phobic avoidance or a compulsive ritual or it may be a specific act such as suicide in the context of severe depression. Symptoms in psychiatry are psychological but physical symptoms may also be prominent, especially in anxiety and depression. In some instances the aims may appear quite modest and directed at the social consequences of a psychiatric disorder. For example, a patient suffering from chronic schizophrenia who is inert and unsociable may be 'activated' to the point where he is able to attend work punctually; this may seem a modest aim but may have immense consequences such as keeping the patient gainfully employed in the community.

Sometimes, the aims of treatment are difficult to define or different health professionals have different aims which may even be incompatible. For example, 'activating' a chronic schizophrenic in-patient may make him easier to rehabilitate but it may also make him truculent and aggressive. The social workers and nurses involved in his care would have very different views on the 'success' of the drug intervention. Drawing up a balance-sheet of the effectiveness of a drug requires input from several sources.

As well as different practical outcomes, there are ideological differences. The medically-trained psychiatrist is often primarily concerned with symptom reduction or the normalization of 'abnormal' or 'deviant' behaviour. The psychologically-trained behaviour therapist is concerned that drugs will facilitate rather than hinder his behaviour modification programmes. But the analytically-trained psychotherapist might eschew drugs altogether in the belief that any symptom reduction is more than outweighed by drug-induced interference with development of the personality and interpersonal relationships.

Finally, financial considerations obtrude. The costs of health care in all western countries continue to escalate, partly as a result of the changing demography, partly because medical technology has become much more sophisticated and expensive, and partly because health expectations have been raised. Psychiatry has taken part in these changes to a fairly modest extent. Nevertheless, the cost of drug treatments may become an important factor in the choice of therapy. For example, the discharge of a chronically institutionalized patient to the community may necessitate substitution of an expensive depot preparation for a cheap oral one. It is important to know the relative usefulness of the two forms of therapy, not just in terms of efficacies in a comparable clinical trial but also in day-to-day practice.

NATURE OF CLINICAL TRIALS

Pious platitudes abound concerning the usefulness of non-systematic clinical observations. Thus, it might appear that giving a drug to a patient and observing his or her response provides information concerning the efficacy of that drug in the treatment of the patient's disorder. Unfortunately, some inferences drawn from unsystematic observations may not merely be weak or unsubstantiated but actually wrong. The persistent use of venesection over a century or two despite the careful observations of thousands of practitioners testifies to the gullibility of the medical profession. Nor is our record since the mid-nineteenth century – the dawn of 'rational medicine' – unsullied by similar fads and fancies. In psychiatry this century, schizophrenic patients have undergone mutilating bowel excisions or dental extractions to expunge presumed foci of infection. The vigour with which these campaigns were conducted can only raise questions as to whether beliefs of delusional intensity were solely the prerogative of the patient. In psychopharmacology, a host of drug treatments was tried on no discernible rational basis and, worse, persisted in despite not one jot of evidence of any efficacy, but only of toxicity. The LSD episode provides a vivid example, Even now, some

315

schizophrenic patients are exposed to exceedingly high doses of neuroleptic medication despite the lack of any evidence that such doses are needed routinely (Aubree and Lader 1980).

How has this come about? The roots of the problem lie in the difficulties of defining psychiatric syndromes, the chronicity and severity of many of these conditions, and the understandable wish on the part of the therapist to help his patient. The formal clinical trial is constituted in such a way as to minimize the biasses which bedevil apparently simple clinical observations.

The elements of the clinical trial have been thoroughly debated. The test treatment should be tested against a dummy treatment, the placebo, which contains all the attributes of the test treatment except for the active pharmacological principle, Patients meeting pre-set diagnostic and perhaps other criteria (e.g. demographic) should be allocated randomly to one or other of the treatments. Assessments of psychiatric state and symptom severity during treatment should be carried out 'double-blind', neither patient nor physician knowing which treatment has been given. Finally, appropriate statistics should be used to attempt to disprove the null hypothesis that the test and dummy treatments do not differ in efficacy.

Such an ideal trial is never attained in practice and each of the steps outlined above has its particular difficulties in clinical trials in psychiatry.

DEFINITION OF SAMPLES

The conclusions of a scientific experiment, clinical trials included, must be communicable to other scientists, otherwise the study is not worth doing. (Indeed, an unpublished study may raise ethical problems – a topic touched on later.) Essential to such communication is a well-defined clinical system of diagnoses. Unfortunately, psychiatric diagnosis is neither sufficiently standardized nor sufficiently reliable to provide more than an approximation to such precise definition of syndromes or disorders.

The clinician's solution to this problem is to use as his working standard, not a formal diagnosis, but an informal formulation. In this way he can communicate fairly succinctly the nub of a case without necessarily squeezing it into an ill-fitting diagnostic category. But this stratagem is too cumbersome for a research study. Furthermore, definitions and nosologies developed for the clinician or epidemiologist may not be entirely appropriate for the clinical researcher. For example, International Classification of Diseases (ICD–9) (1980) uses different types of criteria for different diagnostic categories and the DSM–III of the American Psychiatric Association (1980) also contains many inconsistencies although its operational definitions are often very useful. Perhaps the best categorical instrument for research purposes is the Research Diagnostic Criteria which is constructed in such a way as to ensure as few false positive inclusions as possible at the cost of some false negative exclusions (Spitzer *et al.* 1978).

Of course, one can argue that such highly formalized criteria for patient definition run the risk of the trial ending up with such a spuriously homogeneous group as to be unrepresentative of the wider population in which the drug will actually be used. But this argument may lead to a worse outcome, namely that the indications for a medicine become so ill-defined as to be worthless scientifically and dangerous clinically. The widespread use of the benzodiazepines beyond definable anxiety disorders to any condition with any perceptible psychological component is a reminder of the dangers of this laissez-faire diagnostic policy. What is needed is a careful definition of a core group and establishment of the efficacy of a drug in that group. Then, other groups nosologically contiguous with the initial group are studied to provide a penumbra of indications.

But there is one other factor which is generally glossed over. This refers to the way in which patients come into the trial. In the UK, most patients are seen initially by a general practitioner who usually tries one or more treatments before admitting failure and referring the patient for specialist advice. If a patient is referred on without such trials-of-therapy, it generally means that he is untypical in terms of severity, chronicity, social or personality problems. The patient referred after treatments have failed is untypical by being refractory to those treatments. Thus, many out-patient trials of antidepressants are carried out on patients who have failed to respond to standard antidepressants such as prothiaden and amitriptyline favoured by UK general practitioners. Trials on depressed in-patients are subject to many other biasses, e.g. towards suicidal ideation and behaviour and social isolation. Sometimes, hospital-based doctors running clinical trials attempt to accelerate their recruitment rate by canvassing local general practitioners and asking them to send up newly-presenting patients of appropriate type, untreated, for prompt assessment and inception into the trial. This is perfectly legitimate provided this strategem is clearly explained in the ensuing publication.

Differences between countries may be quite major. For example, in the USA many patients present directly to a psychiatrist who consequently sees a very different sample from his counterpart in the UK where general practitioner screening is the norm. Furthermore, some sick people in the USA may not seek help because of financial constraints. Some clinical trials recruit patients by publicity campaigns in the local media. Indeed, one enterprising researcher is supposed to have advertised for depressives on local radio at 5 a.m., thereby obtaining a sample characterized by early morning awakening. A further factor is that such subjects are motivated to enter and remain in the trial by the prospect of free treatment. For all these reasons, it is important to establish and document the provenance of patients studied in a clinical trial.

THE TYPE OF COMPARISON

Although the standard comparison should be between test medication and placebo, this is not always practicable, usually for ethical reasons. For example, it is generally accepted in the UK that tricyclic antidepressants are sufficiently effective in moderate-to-severe depressives to preclude the use of dummy medication. In the USA, placebo-controlled antidepressant trials are accepted, probably because the typical patient is mildly rather than moderately ill. However, because tranquillizers are viewed as only partially effective with appreciable side effects and are used in less important indications, placebos are generally accepted as comparators.

The solution to the antidepressant problem is to use a standard such as imipramine or amitriptyline. It is necessary, however, to establish the efficacy of the standard medication in the context in which it will be used. It cannot be taken for granted that, because an extensive literature attests to the efficacy, albeit not complete, of the standard, it will prove effective in that clinic in the particular type of patient seen. But this in itself poses a further problem in that the efficacy of the standard cannot be established against placebo because that study is regarded as unethical. The answer is to assess a cohort of patients in a manner as closely akin to that of a controlled trial as possible. For example, ratings are made, side effects sought, and compliance encouraged as if the patients were participating in a formal double-blind evaluation. The ratings are averaged and should follow those published in the literature. Without such a ploy, it is impossible to decide from the double-blind controlled comparison of test versus standard, which fails to refute the null hypothesis, whether the two drugs are equally effective or ineffective.

DESIGN CONSIDERATIONS

Clinical trials should be designed to answer one prime question, such as 'does this treatment lessen symptoms in this type of patient?' Other questions concerning onset of action, type of effect, side-effects, and so on must remain subordinate. Later, a fuller profile of the drug can be constructed. The experimental design must isolate and attempt to answer that main question.

The usual design is the parallel-groups design where patients are randomly allocated to one of two or more treatments. Cogent reasons are needed not to use this standard approach. The usual alternative is the cross-over design but this makes statistical assumptions that may be difficult to sustain. In particular, the cross-over design assumes that the state of the patient is the same at the start of each successive treatment, i.e., that the disorder is chronic and is not irreversibly affected in some way by any of the treatments.

Although many psychiatric disorders are distressingly chronic, most fluctuate and are influenced in subtle ways by treatments. Restoration of the status ante quo cannot be assumed. In favour of cross-over trials is the substantial reduction in the number of patients needed to show an effect when they are used as their own controls.

There are many other design strategies such as the sequential trial, incomplete block design, factorials, and so on, any of which may be appropriate for a specialized application. Expert statistical advice is needed to clarify the assumptions made.

BLINDEDNESS

Much ritual obeisance is paid to the principle of the double-blind procedure as the way to minimize bias in a comparative trial. The medications look, smell, and taste the same and neither the patient nor the rater know which treatment is being given. Such untainted assessments are especially needed in psychiatry where subjective evaluations are frequent and observational measures prone to error. Unfortunately, because of the fortuitous discovery of most psychotropic drugs, selectivity of action was not a property of the earlier compounds in each class – those which tend to be used as the standard. If a newer compound is more selective, with fewer side effects (and there is not much point introducing a less selective compound with more side effects), it may be quite apparent to the patient and in turn to the rater that major differences obtain between the two compounds. The rater inevitably becomes unblinded knowing, for example, that a complaint of dry mouth is attributable to amitriptyline rather than to a selective 5-HT uptake inhibitor or of restlessness to haloperidol rather than to a selective neuroleptic.

The extent of this problem can be assessed by asking the rater to guess which of the treatments the patient is receiving and seeing whether his accuracy is significantly greater than chance. It is also worth asking him why he made that guess. But this strategy cannot salvage a trial in which the blindedness has been significantly jeopardized. It is better to try and minimize bias by separating the rating of efficacy from that of side effects. This requires two raters, the first enquiring about general progress and side effects, and adjusting dosage if the regimen is a flexible one. The second rater confines his questioning to that needed for the formal assessments.

DOSAGE SCHEDULES

Too frequently, the dosage of psychotropic drugs is arrived at by a protracted sequence of trial-and-error and not by establishing a dose-effect curve. Regulatory authorities are becoming stricter in this respect and some such as the Food and Drugs Administration in the USA recommend a four-group study: a) placebo; b) presumed subtherapeutic dose; c) presumed therapeutic dose; and d) presumed supratherapeutic dose. The risk-benefit ratio should be optimal with (c).

This can only establish the approximate mean effective dose. Biological variation will mean that the optimal dose will vary from patient to patient. Carrying out an efficacy trial at one single fixed dose, usually (c) above, may underestimate true efficacy and overestimate side effects. It is generally preferable to use a flexible dose regimen with pre-set decision points concerning raising or lowering the dose, which are adhered to closely. It may take a little time to establish the optimal dose for each patient but it is time well-spent. It also reflects clinical practice.

THE POWER OF THE TRIAL

Most trials are too small to yield worthwhile results (Freiman *et al.* 1978). Because of the modest improvements generally attained, expected differences between treatments are also narrow. For example, 70–80 per cent of depressed patients respond to a typical tricyclic antidepressant and about half that percentage to placebo. Consequently, it is difficult to show lesser effectiveness than the standard for a newer drug but also difficult to show differences from placebo. Even more of a problem would be posed by a test compound which helped 90 per cent of patients.

Power calculations result in some very high figures per group. For example, let us suppose that, in the case of a new antidepressant with a low incidence and severity of side effects, it is decided that it is only worth the expense of full development if it can be demonstrated with 95 per cent confidence (i.e, only a one in twenty chance of being wrong) that it is at worst 10 per cent less effective than amitriptyline. Let us assume the latter helps 70 per cent of patients, i.e., produces an adequate clinical response as measured by a standard rating scale. Even if we accept a 20 per cent risk that even if the drug is really equally effective one will fail to show it (a 20 per cent false negative risk), 332 patients are needed in each group. The typical study with thirty in each group will detect a standard response rate of 70 per cent and a test drug response rate of 40 per cent with the same degrees of confidence and error.

ORGANIZATION OF TRIALS

Increasing appreciation by regulatory authorities of the need for trials with large numbers of patients has led to major exercises involving several centres. Such multi-centre trials have been commonplace in, say, the area of cancer chemotherapy but are the exception in psychiatry. Those that have been conducted have generally been organized by official organizations such as the Medical Research Council or the National Institute of Medical Health. Recently, however, two large-scale studies have been mounted evaluating alprazolam in the control of panic attacks. The first trial involved hundreds of patients in several centres in the USA and Canada and compared alprazolam with placebo (Klerman *et al.* 1986). The second involved centres throughout the world, over a thousand patients, and compared alprazolam, imipramine, and placebo. Both required a great deal of preparation, organization, logistic support, quality control, and data handling. The major resources, human and financial, that were devoted to the task were beyond the bounds of most non-commercial funding agencies.

On a more modest scale are the co-ordinated general practitioner studies. These provide risk-benefit assessments in the milieu in which most psychotropic drugs are prescribed. The problem is that general practitioners do not accrue sufficient numbers of any but the most common psychiatric disorders. Multi-centre studies can too often threaten to degenerate into quasi-marketing exercises with each GP contributing less than ten patients. It is essential that the raters are properly trained and that they are 'calibrated' against more experienced researchers.

Epidemiological techniques can be used to evaluate the effectiveness of a medicine. for example, if lithium had had a major effect in preventing manic and hypomanic episodes, the rate of admission for these conditions should have fallen since the widespread introduction of lithium over the past two decades. A survey by Dickson and Kendall (1986) failed to show such an effect.

EXCLUSIONS AND DROP-OUTS

Clinical trial protocols include a section on inclusion and exclusion criteria. Some of the exclusion criteria relate to toxicological concerns, for example excluding pregnant women, others are more arbitrary and may reflect some pre-conceptions about the type of patient who should respond. Ethical considerations may be important: for example, severely disordered patients may be excluded from treatment with an untried remedy. It is, however, often illuminating to follow up patients excluded from a trial and presumably given standard treatment. For example, Leff and Wing (1971) attempted to follow up patients not included in a trial of maintenance therapy in schizophrenia and achieved a success rate of 95 per cent. Non-trial patients comprised those more ill and those less ill than trial patients.

The question of drop-outs is always a vexing one (May *et al.* 1981). But it is important to divide patients who fail to complete the study into those who terminate early because they recover, those whose treatment is changed because of failure to respond, and those whose side effects are too severe for them to continue. In addition, some patients drop out for administrative and operational reasons, e.g, moving away from the district. Analysing outcome data in terms of completers only may give a misleading estimate of the risk/benefit ratio of a compound (Sackett 1980). Including all patients who are entered into the trial – the 'intention-to-treat' approach – is better practice and is now usually required by regulatory authorities. In this strategy, the scores at the point of drop-out are carried forward to the end-point of analysis. Similarly, if the 'disposal' of the patient is being recorded, e.g, back to the GP or to continuing support, drop-outs should be included to render more valid comparisons between treatments.

Another instance where patients may be lost to a trial concerns placebo 'run-in' periods. Some trials incorporate a week or two of placebo treatment before allocation to the treatments proper. Spontaneous or placebo-related improvement may take place, lowering the patient's psychopathology score below that for inclusion. Placebo run-in periods may, however, distort the trial itself. Thus, if one group of patients is to receive placebo, the drug-placebo comparison will be vitiated because placebo responders have already been excluded and the active drug will appear more effective than it really is.

ASSESSMENT OF PSYCHOPATHOLOGY

Assessment in psychiatry usually refers to two features, the symptoms of the illness, if any, and behavioural abnormalities, if any. It has traditionally taken place in the course of an interview with the patient, together with interviews with friends, relatives, and nurses. Special observation of the patient's behaviour is instituted usually by nurse, doctor, or clinical psychologist (Burdock 1982). This informal approach has changed over the years with increasing sophistication and an emphasis on structured or semi-structured interviews, the results of which are recorded on specially constructed scales (Hamilton 1986).

The simplest form of assessment is an overall so-called Global Rating of Severity. Despite its apparent crudity, it is capable of yielding quite reliable data, sensitive to drug effects. Next, a simple check list of symptoms can be used, predicated on the principle that patients with a severe form of disorder will have more symptoms than those with a mild disorder. As long as the check list contains more than twelve or fifteen items, this holds good. However, no account is taken of the severity of each symptom.

On a more complex level, the development of item gradings is quite a sophisticated process. It is important that one dimension only is rated at a time; for example, frequency, severity, or subsequent handicap should not be mixed in one item. The next process, giving numbers to grades of frequency or severity, is recognized by psychometricians as a very arbitrary undertaking. It implies that the grades are equal in intervals when they are usually no more than ordinal. Nevertheless, the sum of items is generally regarded as a measure to which parametric statistics can be applied. By and large, no gross violations of statistical purity are perpetrated.

The types of scale available relate mostly to the user, the patient himself, or require an observer. The observer can be a psychiatrist, psychologist, nurse, or relative. Informal observations can be made or a structured or semi-structured interview undertaken.

It is most important to distinguish between instruments designed to measure change and those meant to establish a diagnostic or sometimes prognostic profile. The former contain items which are sensitive to change but which may not be pathognomonic of the condition. For example, the Hamilton Rating Scale for Anxiety contains items concerning depression, the Scale for Depression, anxiety items. This is justified as anxious patients are often depressed as well, and vice versa, and the symptoms resolve with treatment. It is important to recognize this 'cross-talk' in the evaluation of a therapeutic agent. Thus, an anxiolytic may show limited 'efficacy' in the treatment of depressed patients because the anxiety items such as initial insomnia alter, although true depressive ones do not.

The diagnostic profile instruments can be used as entry criteria to a study but not usually as measures of change. However, different instruments have different criteria and some may affect the responsiveness of a selected group to a particular medication.

Whatever scales are used, proper training in their use is essential. Raters should be skilled in the necessary assessments, especially when attempting to elicit psychotic phenomena. They should be 'calibrated' against experienced raters to avoid errors such as leniency, when they are reluctant to use an extreme score, and proximity, when similar scores are given to adjacent items.

Patients need careful instruction about self-rating. The purpose of the scale should be explained, together with the mechanics of rating. In particular, the time focus should be specified, i.e., whether the rating is here-and-now, for the past few days, or whatever. The first use of a scale by the patient should be carefully supervised and the patient corrected if all the ratings are extreme or absent. Computer-based assessments have become popular but, again, the patient must be familiarized with both the computer and the questions.

OBJECTIVE TESTING

The vagaries of rating scales are such, or at least are perceived as such, that many investigators have sought the Holy Grail of the objective test of the diagnosis of depression, or failing that the severity of depression. A host of measures from many disciplines have been tested, regarded as full of initial promise, intensively investigated, and then found to be insensitive, unreliable, nonspecific, or cumbersome, or any combination of these. Examples include the Sedation Threshold (Shagass 1954) and salivary flow rate (Palmai *et al.* 1967). Most recently, the Dexamethasone Suppression Test has been thoroughly studied on thousands of patients; little of clinical use has emerged (Gitlin and Gerner 1986). Nor do the biochemical tests of amine and neuroendocrine status seem any more promising.

More limited objectives are achieved by psychological tests. These include perceptual and cognitive tests such as the Cancellation and Digit Symbol Substitution Tests, memory tests, and psychomotor tests such as simple key-tapping speed. Many such functions are impaired in depressives and clinical recovery is attended by improvement (Lader *et al.* 1987).

Physiological, biochemical and psychological tests can all be used more effectively to quantify the side effects of psychotropic drugs. For example, antidepressants with anticholinergic properties lessen salivary flow and anti-psychotic drugs increase plasma prolactin concentrations. The elec-troencephalogram (EEG), usually quantified mathematically, provides a sensitive albeit empirical measure of dose-and time-effects as well as some qualitative impression of the type of psychotropic drug effect (Fink 1981).

All in all, however, such objective tests are of limited validity. Despite their high reliability, they remain research tools and have yet to establish themselves in the routine evaluation of new psychotropic chemical entities.

THE TYPE OF RESPONDER

In most comparative trials, attempts are made to identify the type of responder. First, the type of patient who responds to any treatment is sought. Some patients do well however they are treated. Others may respond to one but not another treatment and vice versa.

A good example of the former is provided by the multi-centre studies carried out by Rickels and his collaborators on responsiveness to antianxiety drugs. They found that older rather than younger, female rather than male, and higher than lower social classes responded better (Rickels *et al.* 1978). Patients who recognized that their symptoms were related to psychological problems and were prepared to try drug therapy did well. The closer the patient approximated to the text book description of Generalized Anxiety Disorder, the better the response, especially when more ill. Physicians could detect who would respond well, a finding with obvious implications for the design and conduct of clinical trials where doctors can exercise major influences on the selection of patients.

Differential responsivity has been sought repeatedly with respect to the two main groups of antidepressants, the tricyclic compounds and the monoamine oxidase inhibitors. Surprisingly few indicators have been found, the most robust being that depressed patients with phobic anxiety do well with MAOIs (Paykel *et al.* 1979).

COST-BENEFIT ANALYSIS

Escalating health costs have forced caring agencies, private and governmental, to evaluate treatments in economic terms (Hurst 1984). A large number of factors must be considered, especially as much psychiatric illness is chronic and results in social and occupational handicap (Rosser and Kind 1978). But non-economic values are also important. The benefits of relieving suffering are inestimable. And, family and friends also suffer seeing a loved one in anguished depression or in a truculent or inert phase of schizophrenia.

Thus, effective treatment for major mental disorders would have profound economic and humanitarian benefits. Drug therapy is relatively cheap compared, for example, with the total costs of an in-patient admission. But lesser conditions are common and mild symptomatic relief not to be undervalued. Against this, side effects are often frequent, severe, or chronic and must be entered into the equation.

ETHICS

This is a large topic which has been reviewed by doctors, moral philosophers, and theologians (e.g. Burkhardt and Kienzle 1978; Schafer 1982; Helmchen 1983). Particular problems relate to clinical trials in psychiatry, mainly with respect to informed consent and forcible detention of disturbed patients. Also, the doctor-patient relationship may be jeopardized.

However, provided the usual ethical guidelines are adhered to, psychiatric trials present the same dilemmas as psychiatric practice in general. As the treatment steps are detailed in the clinical trial protocol, the ethical problems are thrown into sharper relief. Flexibility is needed during the conduct of the trial, with the researcher remaining sensitive to the ethical issues involved. It is always helpful for the researcher's colleagues to be kept informed of the progress of the trial to constitute a sort of informal ethical peer review.

Then the study must be completed, analysed, written up, and published. It is unethical to expose patients to the hazards of research, however apparently minimal, and not to communicate the results of that research to the scientific community. Unfortunately, the bias in the traditional way of doing this – the refereed journal – is against publishing negative trials, those where the compound proves ineffective. It is to be hoped that the advent of the 'Information Revolution' will allow such data to be kept on file, but easily accessible by interested clinicians. Finally, the data must be communicated to clinicians in such a way as to influence their prescribing

(Avorn and Soumerai 1983). But that is another issue.

The clinician is compelled to hold the balance between the scales of laboratory data on the one hand and stochastic theory on the other. Though his experience and judgement are essential it will be necessary for him to adopt a more experimental role in the future if he is to cooperate fully with the pharmacologist and the statistician, whose techniques he should understand if full weight is to be given to observations made in the clinical setting. Shepherd (1959:S125)

REFERENCES

American Psychiatric Association (1980) *Diagnostic and Statistical Manual of Mental Disorders*: third edition, Washington, DC.

Aubrée, J.C. and Lader, M.H. (1980) 'High and very high dosage antipsychotics: a critical review', *Journal of Clinical Psychiatry* 41: 341–50.

Avorn, J. and Soumerai, S.B. (1983) 'Improving drug-therapy decisions through educational outreach: a randomized controlled trial of academically based "detailing"', *New England Journal of Medicine* 308: 1457–63.

Ayd, F.J. and Blackwell, B. (eds) (1970) *Discoveries in Biological Psychiatry*, Philadelphia: Lippincott.

Burdock, E.I. (1982) 'Problems and profits in quantitative evaluation', in E.I. Burdock, A. Sudilovsky and S. Gershon (eds) *The Behaviour of Psychiatric Patients*, New York: Marcel Dekker, 3–7.

Burkhardt, R. and Kienzle, G. (1978) 'Controlled clinical trials and medical ethics', *Lancet* 2: 1356–9.

Dickson, W.E. and Kendell, R.E. (1986) 'Does maintenance lithium therapy prevent recurrences of mania under ordinary clinical conditions?', *Psychological Medicine* 16: 521–30.

Fink, M. (1981) 'Classification of psychoactive drugs: quantitative EEG analysis of man' in H.M. van Praag *et al.* (eds) *Handbook of Biological Psychiatry, Part VI*, New York: Marcel Dekker, pp. 309–26.

Freiman, J.A., Chalmers, T.C., Smith, H., *et al.* (1978) 'The importance of beta, the type II error and sample size in the design and interpretation of the randomized control trial: survey of 71 "negative" trials', *New England Journal of Medicine* 299: 690–4.

Gitlin, M.J. and Gerner, R.H. (1986) 'The Dexamethasone Suppression Test and response to somatic treatment: a review', *Journal of Clinical Psychiatry* 47: 16–21.

Hamilton, M. (1986) *Assessment of Psychopathology* (Human Psychopharmacology Monographs, No. 1), Chichester: Wiley.

Helmchen, H. (1983) 'Ethical and practical problems in therapeutic research in psychiatry', in T. Helgason (ed.) *Methodology in Evaluation of Psychiatric Treatment*, Cambridge: Cambridge University Press, 251–64.

Hurst, J.W. (1984) 'Measuring the benefits and costs of medical care: the contribution of health status measurement', *Health Trends* 16: 16–19.

Johnson, A.L. (1983) 'Clinical trials in psychiatry', *Psychological Medicine* 13: 1–8.

Klerman, G.L., Coleman, J.H., and Purpura, R.P. (1986) 'The design and conduct of the Upjohn Cross-National Collaborative Panic Study', *Psychopharmacology Bulletin* 22: 59–64.

Lader, M.H., Lang, R.A., and Wilson, G.D. (1987) *Patterns of Improvement in Depressed In-patients*, Oxford: Oxford University Press.

Leff, J.P. and Wing, J.K. (1971) 'Trial of maintenance therapy in schizophrenia', *British Medical Journal* 3: 599–604.

Lewis, A.J. (1953) 'Health as a social concept', *British Journal of Sociology* 4: 109–24.

May, G.S., de Mets, D.L., Friedman, L.M., *et al.* (1981) 'The randomized clinical trial: bias in analysis, *Circulation* 64: 669–73.

Palmai, G., Blackwell, B., Maxwell, A.E., and Morgenstern, F. (1967) 'Patterns of salivary flow in depressive illness and during treatment', *British Journal of Psychiatry* 113: 1297–308.

Paris, J.A. (1833) *Pharmacologia* (eighth edition), London: Sherwood, Gilbert and Piper, p.50.

Paykel, E.S., Parker, R.R., Penrose, R.J.J., and Rassaby, E.R. (1979) 'Depressive classification and prediction of response to phenelzine, *British Journal of Psychiatry* 134: 572–81.

Rickels, K., Downing, R.W., and Winokur, A. (1978) 'Antianxiety drugs: clinical use in psychiatry' in L.L. Iversen, S.D. Iversen, and S.H. Snyder, (eds) *Handbook of Psychopharmacology, Volume 13*, New York: Plenum, 395–430.

Rosser, R. and Kind, P. (1978) 'A scale of valuations of states of illness: is there a social consensus? *International Journal of Epidemiology* 7: 347–58.

Sackett, D.L. (1980) 'The competing objectives of randomized trials', *New England Journal of Medicine* 303: 1059–60.

Schafer, A. (1982) 'The ethics of the randomized clinical trial', *New England Journal of Medicine* 307: 719–24.

Shagass, C. (1954) 'The sedation threshold: a method for estimating tension in psychiatric patients', *Electroencephalography and Clinical Neurophysiology* 6: 221–33.

Shepherd, M. (1959) 'Evaluation of drugs in the treatment of depression', *Canadian Psychiatric Association Journal* 4 (supplement): S120–8.

Spitzer, R.L., Endicott, J., and Robins, E. (1978) 'Research Diagnostic Criteria: rationale and reliability', *Archives of General Psychiatry* 35: 773–82.

Walker, S.R. and Asscher, A.W. (eds) (1987) *Medicines and Risk/Benefit Decisions*, Lancaster: MTP Press.

World Health Organization (1980) *International Classification of Diseases, 9th Revision, Clinical Modification: ICD*, Geneva: WHO.

21

Tranquillizer Use: Epidemiological and Sociological Aspects

Paul Williams and Jonathan Gabe

Although mood-altering drugs have been used for medicinal purposes throughout recorded history (Gabe and Williams 1986a), it is only recently that there has been a rapid development of a multiplicity of 'mood-altering' chemicals. This has in part resulted from the activities of the pharmaceutical industry, which, governed by market economics, sought to maximize profits (Rabin and Bush 1974). The bromides and chloral hydrate, which had replaced opium on the grounds that the latter was addictive (Berridge 1978), were themselves displaced in the 1930s by the barbiturates because they were considered 'safer'. By the 1950s the dependence-producing potential of barbiturates had also become clearly established, causing a great deal of concern (Hollister 1983). This encouraged the search for suitable non-barbiturate tranquillizers.

The first replacement was meprobamate, a drug which was received enthusiastically by physicians and much used in the late 1950s as an anti-anxiety agent until it too was found to cause dependence (Hollister 1983). The second was the benzodiazepine group of drugs which quickly made meprobamate obsolete, once it became clear that they were safer and more effective (Lader 1978). Chlordiazepoxide was the first benzodiazepine to be introduced in 1960, followed by diazepam in 1963. There are now eighteen generic benzodiazepine preparations available in Britain and their dominance of the field indicates that we are unquestionably living in the 'benzodiazepine era' (Hollister 1983: 13).

TRENDS IN PRESCRIBING

The large and regular increases in prescriptions for benzodiazepines and other tranquillizers that occurred during the late 1960s and early 1970s are well known. In 1960, some 28 million prescriptions for drugs classified as hypnotics or tranquillizers were dispensed at retail pharmacies in Great Britain: in 1974, the total was about 40 million, of which 25 million were for benzodiazepines. The peak in benzodiazepine prescribing occurred in 1979 (31 million prescriptions): the estimated figure for 1985 is 26 million, a decrease of about 16 per cent in six years (Taylor 1987). This pattern – an increase until the mid- or late-1970s, and a subsequent levelling off and decrease – has been found in many countries (Marks 1983a).

Comparison of three population surveys of the consumption of tranquillizers and other psychotropic drugs suggest that in England at least, there was no comparable increase at that time in the proportion of the population who reported consuming such drugs. Williams (1983a) suggested that this disparity (between prescribing and consuming) could be explained by a decrease in compliance and an increase in long-term drug use. This interpretation is supported by Marks' demonstration of substantial increases, over the same time period, in the extent to which benzodiazepines are prescribed on a 'repeat' basis (Marks 1983b).

Conversely, the prime factor in the subsequent decrease in tranquillizer prescribing is most likely to have been a reduction in new prescribing rather than discontinuation of treatment by long-term consumers. This suggests that there is a cohort of long-term benzodiazepine users (created during the 'phase of enthusiasm' in the mid-1960s and early 1970s) from which members will slowly be lost (a small proportion will discontinue treatment, others will die) and to which few new members will be recruited, since a reduction in new prescribing will inevitably lead to fewer people becoming long-term users (however 'long-term' is defined).

THE GROWTH OF CONCERN ABOUT MINOR TRANQUILLIZERS

When benzodiazepines were first introduced they were accepted enthusiastically by the medical profession as highly effective and safe drugs which did not create dependence and which had few other side effects (Owen and Tyrer 1983). This impression was reinforced a few years later by favourable reports of clinical practice (Svenson and Hamilton 1966).

In the early 1970s, concern started to be expressed by physicians and social scientists (e.g. Dunlop 1970; Jefferys 1973) about the extent of benzodiazepine prescribing. Social scientists talked of an 'overmedicated society' (Muller 1972) and suggested that benzodiazepines, by providing symptomatic relief, discouraged the search for a social solution to problems with social origins (Lennard et al. 1971). Moreover, those social scientists influenced by feminist theory argued that tranquillizer prescribing represented a means of social control, because it encouraged women, the major recipient of these drugs, to deny or ignore the social concomitants of their distress, thereby minimizing pressure for social change (Waldron 1977).

Physicians questioned whether the increase in tranquillizer prescribing reflected an increase in the number of people suffering from anxiety, or a too-ready recourse to a prescription (*Lancet* 1973a) by doctors who saw tranquillizers as a suitable way of modifying personal and interpersonal processes: this was thought likely to fuel demand for tranquillizers among patients (Trethowan 1975). Also questioned were the therapeutic (as opposed to the commercial) value of increasing the number of benzodiazepines available (Tyrer 1974), the cost of the drugs (Trethowan 1975), and the possibility that tranquillizers were no more effective than placebos for those suffering from minor mood changes (*Lancet* 1973b).

In the latter part of the 1970s the concern about prescribing levels abated, to be replaced at the start of the 1980s by a new concern: that of physical dependence on benzodiazepines. This possibility had been acknowledged as far back as 1961 for those suddenly withdrawn from high dosages of benzodiazepines (Hollister *et al.* 1961). Thereafter, the number of cases of dependence reported did not increase above a trickle and these generally referred to patients on high dosages (Tyrer 1980). Given the total number of benzodiazepines consumed, what impressed during this period was the rarity of benzodiazepine dependence: a view endorsed by Marks (1978) who concluded, after a comprehensive review of published case histories of dependence, that benzodiazepines had a negligible dependence risk if used in therapeutic doses.

Two years later, the picture started to change. The Committee on the Review of Medicines officially acknowledged for the first time a growing concern about physical dependence, even though it concluded that: 'on present available evidence the true addiction potential of benzodiazepines [is] low' (Committee on the Review of Medicines 1980: 910). Soon afterwards the evidence started to appear. Studies of relatively small numbers of people (usually about forty) agreeing to or requesting withdrawal from long-term benzodiazepine use at therapeutic dose found that a significant proportion developed a withdrawal syndrome (Petursson and Lader 1981; Tyrer *et al.* 1983), and that these symptoms could last a year or more (Ashton 1984). This was described as an 'epidemic in the making' (Lader 1981).

Current concern has not been limited to academics and clinicians. Recent studies of patients have demonstrated a marked awareness of the side effects of tranquillizers and, at best, an ambivalence about taking them (e.g. Gabe and Lipshitz-Phillips 1982, 1984). This kind of concern suggests that tranquillizer use has become a public issue.

Why has this happened now, when the prescribing of tranquillizers is actually declining? There are at least four reasons. *First* is the recent coverage of tranquillizer dependence in the media. Once discovered, this issue has featured regularly on television consumer programmes since at least 1981, in the up-market and popular press, and in women's magazines. Much of this coverage has been sensationalizing in tone.

Furthermore, the impression has frequently been given that everyone on tranquillizers is likely to be dependent on them and will automatically have 'terrible' withdrawal symptoms if they try and stop. Indeed, one recent television programme began with the statement that 'kicking the tranquillizer habit can be harder than coming off heroin'. As several commentators have remarked, this represents 'trial by media' (Lasagna 1980; Cohen 1983).

Second is the context of revived fears about *illegal* drug taking. The present climate in Britain is one of extreme concern if not outright panic over the use of illegal drugs (e.g. 'the greatest menace in peace time', Home Affairs Committee 1985). As the above quotation from a television programme illustrates, greater sensitivity to the deleterious effects of such drug taking is influencing responses to the use of tranquillizers.

Third, concern has also been fuelled by mental health campaigning bodies like MIND and RELEASE. These organizations have, with the help of one or two sympathetic academics, produced material on tranquillizer dependence for the general public (RELEASE 1982; MIND 1984), and have skilfully used and worked with the media in presenting their case.

Fourth, current concern has to be set against the backcloth of wider cultural changes. Over the last fifteen years or so there seems to have been a shift in attitudes away from a belief in the right to happiness and an unwillingness to tolerate 'normal' discomfort and malaise towards a more puritanical view of life based on abstinence, stoicism, and self-reliance (Hall 1983). The latter view has encouraged an attitude to drugs which Klerman (1971) has described as 'pharmacological calvinism'. Simply stated, this means 'if it makes you feel good it is wrong' (Blackwell 1977). The development of this 'anti-drug culture' (Gabe and Lipshitz-Phillips 1982) also coincides with increasing criticism of other forms of medical technology (Kennedy 1981) and the medical profession (Jefferys and Sachs 1983; Cartwright 1983), and an increasing enthusiasm for alternative medicines (Salmon 1985) and for self-help (Robinson 1978), at least among some social groups (Doyal 1983).

Not surprisingly, this concern about the danger of dependence is not shared to the same extent by all of those with an interest in tranquillizers. Some pharmaceutical companies, for example, have been fighting back by financing researchers who might provide ammunition to challenge the risks of benzodiazepine dependence. Other companies are developing alternatives to fill what they regard as a gap in the market (File 1987).

Also, some academics and clinicians have questioned the evidence about the extent of dependence (Rickels 1981), the adequacy of existing studies (Kraupl-Taylor 1984) and the availability of appropriate alternatives for chronic benzodiazepine users (Rickels *et al.* 1984). Even so, the future for benzodiazepines looks somewhat uncertain, given the level of current concern.

In Britain, this uncertainty is compounded by recent legislation concerning prescribing. As from 1 April 1985, the prescription under the NHS of seven categories of drug – including the benzodiazepines – has been limited in

331

range. That is, there is now a 'white list' of drugs which can be prescribed under the NHS and a 'black list' of drugs which cannot (although such drugs can still be prescribed privately).

The government's initial proposal was to limit the number of available benzodiazepines from eighteen to three, although, in the event, preparations of seven varieties were categorized as prescribable.

This legislation and the way in which it was introduced gives rise to a whole host of issues beyond the scope of this chapter (*British Medical Journal* 1984, 1985). However, from the point of view of tranquillizer use, there is some evidence that the regulations may have resulted in a sharp decline in NHS prescriptions. A recent press release from the DHSS (1987) claims that the NHS's financial outlay on benzodiazepines has been cut by £15.5m in a twelve-month period. Similarly, Taylor (1987) has asserted that the impact of the list has been to cut the NHS benzodiazepine drug bill by around 20 per cent in its first year of operation.

Even so, these figures only relate to prescriptions paid for under the NHS and not all prescriptions. No information is publicly available about trends in private prescribing, and it may well be that the fall in NHS prescriptions has been counterbalanced by a rise in private prescribing. There is certainly evidence that this happens in other countries. For example, in Italy, NHS prescriptions for benzodiazepines have decreased rapidly since their removal from the national formulary (Bellantuono *et al.* 1987), whereas sales have continued to increase (Williams *et al.* 1986). Thus, as Bellantuono *et al.* (1987) have observed, 'the exclusion of a drug or group of drugs from a national formulary, and their subsequent disappearance from official prescription audits, does not necessarily mean that the drugs will no longer be prescribed and (presumably) consumed'.

It is still too early to say what the long-term effect of the limited list will be on prescribing levels and on consumption patterns, especially among long-term users: close monitoring is essential.

LONG-TERM TRANQUILLIZER USE

The remainder of this chapter will be concerned with the long-term use of tranquillizers. Ideally, a prerequisite for research into such use is the development of a consensus about the interpretation of 'long-term'. One approach is to seek a common view as to 'how long is long'. Most researchers seem to regard the cut-off point as one year: using this criterion, the prevalence of long-term use in Britain is 1.5–3 per cent of the population (Rodrigo *et al.* 1988a).

An alternative, more realistic approach, is to regard the duration of use as a process rather than as a static criterion (Williams 1983b). Furthermore, more attention than is customary should be paid to distinguishing between intermittent and continuous use (Gabe and Thorogood 1986).

Clinical aspects of long-term use

Long-term users of tranquillizers report high levels of emotional distress. For example, half of the long-term users of anxiolytics studied in Mellinger *et al.*'s (1984) survey had high scores on a questionnaire measure of distress, as compared with 20 per cent of the non-users. They noted that 'the long-term users did not differ much from the other users in this respect', 45 per cent of whom were high scorers.

The study by Rodrigo *et al.* (1988a) is the first in which a standardized psychiatric assessment has been applied to long-term tranquillizer users in general practice. They found that twenty-four (38 per cent) of the sixty-four patients were rated as cases on the Standardised Psychiatric Interview (Goldberg *et al.* 1970). While in absolute terms this is a substantial level of psychiatric morbidity, it is not very different from that which would be found in an unselected series of general practice attenders (Marks *et al.* 1979). Rodrigo *et al.*'s study also found that three-quarters of the cases – i.e., just over a quarter of the long-term users – were classified under the rubric neurotic depression (ICD 300.4), and that none was assigned a diagnosis related to anxiety. This finding requires replication: if confirmed, it suggests that there exists a clearly-definable group of patients among whom a substantial proportion is suffering from unrecognized and untreated depression.

De novo prescription of benzodiazepines and other psychotropic drugs frequently occurs in response to physical rather than psychological disorder (Williams 1978). Similar findings apply to long-term users. For example, Murray and her colleagues (1982) interviewed twenty-two patients who had been prescribed psychotropic drugs continuously for six months or more. She found that 'chronic physical complaints were common in the sample (diverticulitis, arthritis, hypertension, migraine) and 13 people were long-term users of non-psychotropic prescribed drugs'. Furthermore, in a questionnaire of present and past long-term tranquillizer users (Murray 1981), only six out of 261 respondents scored as having no disability or physical symptoms on the Belloc scale (Belloc *et al.* 1971).

Mellinger *et al.* (1984) found that physical health distinguished between long-term users and other users more sharply than did any other factor. They noted that 'at least one-third of the long-term users reported four or more health problems – a rate twice that found among the other anxiolytic users and seven times that of the non users'. These differences persisted when age was controlled for, and much of the difference between the long-term users and the others was accounted for by cardiovascular disorders and arthritis.

The patients in Rodrigo *et al.*'s (1988a) study also reported substantial physical morbidity. For example, twenty-seven (42 per cent) had consulted their GP during the previous month for a physical illness (other than coughs, colds and influenza), and twenty-two (34 per cent) had attended medical or surgical out-patient clinics in the previous year.

Social factors in long-term use

There is general agreement that long-term tranquillizer users, as compared with all users, are older and predominantly women. These findings emerged from studies carried out in the late 1960s when barbiturates were still commonly used (Parish 1971). While the drugs may have changed in recent years, the relationship with age and sex has not (Cooperstock 1978, Mellinger *et al.* 1984, Rodrigo *et al.* 1988a).

The discussion here will focus on sex differences. Although most of the work in this area has been concerned with current, rather than with long-term, tranquillizer use, it can still throw light on the nature of long-term use.

One of the first social scientists to address this issue was the late Ruth Cooperstock (1971), who developed an explanatory model drawing on sex role theory. She hypothesized that women in western societies take more tranquillizers than men because (i) they are permitted greater freedom to explore their feelings than men, and are hence more likely to recognize emotional problems in themselves; (ii) they feel more able than men to bring their perceived emotional problems to the attention of a doctor; (iii) doctors – especially male doctors – expect women patients to be more expressive than men. They are therefore more likely to encourage such expressiveness among women patients and to prescribe tranquillizers.

Cooperstock's propositions were not tested empirically until the work of Mant *et al.* (1983) and Cafferata *et al.* (1983). Mant and her colleagues surveyed 1,300 adult patients attending fifteen randomly selected male general practitioners in Sydney, during a one-week period. They also collected information from these doctors on each of the patients in the sample.

They found clear support for a *consulting hypothesis* – i.e., that it is more socially acceptable for women than men to go to the doctor – and limited support for the *stereotyping hypothesis*, in that the doctors were much less likely to detect psychological ill-health among men. The findings did not support Cooperstock's *reporting hypothesis*, i.e., that it is more socially acceptable for women to admit to having symptoms, especially of emotional distress.

Cafferata and her colleagues (1983) broadened the debate by testing empirically not only the sex role theory but also *social support* and *social stress* theories. They conducted a secondary analysis of data on family circumstances and psychotropic drug use of adults in 11,000 households in the United States.

Evidence was found to support all three theories. For example, they reported that women in traditional families (in which the male is in paid work and the female fulfils the housewife role) were more likely than their spouses to be taking tranquillizers, suggesting that the traditional female role leads to more illness. They also found that women in non-intact families, and those caring for a spouse in poor health, were more likely to be using tranquillizers. This, they concluded, lent credence to social support and social stress theories, which suggest that women may be more sensitive than men to the effects of less supportive or more stressful family circumstances.

The views of long-term benzodiazepine users

The research on long-term use of benzodiazepines and other psychotropic drugs points to the importance of studying the point of view of the drug users themselves. While the term 'users' includes doctors as well as their patients (Cooperstock and Parnell 1982), relatively few studies have been concerned with doctors. For this reason, as well as constraints of space, we focus only on patients' views here.

It is only recently that researchers have begun to concern themselves, in a systematic way, with the views of the patients who use benzodiazepines and other tranquillizers on a long-term basis, and the impetus for such research has come primarily from social scientists rather than doctors. The methods used include postal surveys (Murray 1981), structured interviews and questionnaires (Rodrigo *et al.* 1988a), in-depth semi-structured interviews (Helman 1981; Gabe and Lipshitz-Phillips 1982, 1984; Gabe and Thorogood 1986) and group discussions (Cooperstock and Lennard 1979). Four issues arising out of this research will be discussed here: (i) long-term users' perceptions of the effects of the drugs; (ii) their views as to their continued need for their drugs; (iii) the way in which drug use is related to the availability of other resources for managing everyday life; and (iv) the meaning of long-term tranquillizer use.

Users' perceptions of the effects of tranquillizers. Do long-term users regard their drugs as helpful? It appears that, in a general sense, most do (Murray 1981, Rodrigo *et al.* 1988b). However, there is also evidence of considerable ambivalence: for example, 87 per cent of respondents in Murray's (1981) survey of women who were long-term psychotropic drug consumers agreed with the statement 'I don't like taking these tablets but I could not manage without them'. Furthermore, when Gabe and Thorogood (1986) asked women long-term users of benzodiazepines what they felt about taking the drugs, one-tenth of the sample emphasized the benefits, one-quarter the dangers, while the majority (about two-thirds) expressed mixed views. They also found that less ambivalence and fewer positive views were expressed by a sample of short-term users.

An important finding has been that when asked to specify the ways in which benzodiazepines and other tranquillizers are helpful, long-term users frequently mention social activities. For example, in Murray's (1981) questionnaire survey referred to above, travelling, shopping, mixing with people, and running the home were the four most frequently mentioned activities in this regard.

335

A similar finding emerged from Cooperstock and Lennard's (1979) series of group discussions with long-term benzodiazepine users. The women users in their study felt that taking the drug helped them to manage the strains they experienced in carrying out their traditional roles as wives, mothers, and homeworkers. Furthermore, over half of the long-term psychotropic drug users interviewed by Helman (1981) felt that withdrawal of the drugs would have a bad effect on their social relationships.

Users' views about their continued need for drugs. Fifty-eight per cent of the current long-term users surveyed by Murray (1981) said that they would find it 'very difficult' to manage without their drugs, and a further 33 per cent claimed that they would not be able to manage at all. A similar picture emerged from the long-term benzodiazepine consumers interviewed by Rodrigo *et al.* (1988b), most of whom were women. While only 17 per cent said that they could not 'do without', more than half (54 per cent) believed that they would need to take their drugs for 'years' or indefinitely.

An important aspect of the long-term use of prescribed drugs is the patients' perceptions of their doctor's attitude. Murray (1981) found a 'widespread belief in the general practitioner's acquiescence in continued drug taking' – 81 per cent of the respondents in her nationwide survey claimed that their doctors either wished them to continue or did not mind. Similarly, in Rodrigo *et al.*'s (1988b) study based in a two-doctor practice, thirty-three patients (52 per cent) had no idea as to their doctor's views, and a further twenty-four (38 per cent) believed that he encouraged their use. Fifty-two of the patients claimed that their GP had never suggested that they stop the drug. Conversely, the women interviewed by Gabe and Lipshitz-Phillips (1984), drawn from two practices with fourteen GPs, in general considered that their doctors were reluctant to prescribe benzodiazepines, and half of them said that their doctor had either restricted their supply or suggested that they cut down or stop taking the drug. A quarter of the users also believed that their doctors shared their doubts about benzodiazepines.

In Murray's (1981) and Rodrigo *et al.*'s (1988b) studies, users were asked to suggest alternative strategies that they would use if the drugs were not available. In both, the predominant strategy was the consumption of some alternative substance, other drugs, alcohol, and herbal remedies being the most frequently mentioned. Cigarette smoking was regarded as a resource by the women interviewed by Gabe and Thorogood (1986). In Rodrigo *et al.*'s study, 17 per cent of the patients interviewed could envisage no possible alternative to benzodiazepines and some expressed a fear of becoming mentally ill without their tablets.

The relationship between tranquillizer use and the availability of other resources. It is also important to consider how long-term users' tranquillizer use relates to the availability of other resources for the management of everyday life. As Gabe and Thorogood (1986) have argued, such resources are unequally distributed according to social group membership and can be variously experienced as enabling and/or constraining. In their study of working-class women, it was found that those who were long-term users of tranquillizers had access to fewer resources than other women in the study. Moreover, those resources that were available to them were rarely experienced in such a way as to enable them to manage their lives without recourse to tranquillizers.

Three resources in particular seemed to constrain the long-term users to maintain their pattern of drug use – paid work, children and partners, and leisure. Regarding paid work, Gabe and Thorogood found that the long-term users were not only markedly less likely to have a full-time job than other women, but that those who were so employed were more likely to express mixed feelings about their situation. It would thus seem that while the absence of paid work may deprive the long-term users of a resource which might make their lives easier, thereby reducing the need for tranquillizers, those users with access to this resource did not experience it in a sufficiently positive way to enable them to change the nature of their tranquillizer use.

The researchers also found that long-term use was related to being divorced and not having children living at home. Moreover, if these long-term users were living with partners and/or their children, they were less likely than the other women to find these kin supportive. It would thus appear that long-term users either lack access to potentially supportive social resources, or find that those that are available are unsupportive and a poor substitute for tranquillizers. In such circumstances, the existing pattern of drug use is likely to be maintained.

Gabe and Thorogood's study also revealed that long-term users were markedly more likely than other women to state either that they lacked all opportunities for leisure, or that they had few leisure options open to them. As this resource was only experienced as enabling and as a relaxant, these long-term users' limited access to it would seem to place them at a considerable disadvantage and further helps to explain why they continued to use tranquillizers to manage their daily lives.

Overall, then, it appears that three resources – paid work, children and partners, and leisure – had a particularly important influence upon the long-term drug users' behaviour. These women's access to and relationship with these resources combined with their views about tranquillizers to maintain their existing pattern of drug use.

The meaning of long-term use. Some of these various findings on users' perceptions and views can be integrated by using the concept of meaning, i.e., 'the interpretation a person gives to an object or event in his or her life' (Gabe and Williams 1986b). This approach has been taken by Helman (1981) and by Gabe and his colleagues (Gabe and Lipshitz-Phillips 1982, 1984;

337

Gabe and Thorogood 1986). Gabe has developed the concepts 'lifeline' and 'standby' to describe the meaning of benzodiazepines to consumers. Those who viewed their drugs as a lifeline felt them to be 'something which they needed to take regularly and depended on simply to keep going in the face of chronic, unresolved problems'. Others viewed their drugs as a standby, to be kept in reserve and used occasionally to meet some short-lived crisis, while a minority of their respondents characterized their drug-taking behaviour in terms of both these meanings.

Helman (1981) conducted in-depth interviews with fifty long-term (six months or more) benzodiazepine users. He found, on the basis of their beliefs, attitudes, and expectations concerning the drugs, that 'long-term users of psychotropics can be classified into three main groups – called "tonic", "food" and "fuel"'.

Patients classified as 'tonic' (about one-third of the sample) were those who expressed maximum control over the drug, its dosage, and when it was to be used, tending to use the drugs on an 'as required' (p.r.n.) basis rather than regularly. They placed the site of action of the drug on themselves rather than on their relationships, and tended to have more anti-drug views than the other groups. Patients classified as 'fuel' (some two-fifths of those interviewed) expressed a variable degree of control over their medication but nonetheless felt that the drug played an important and constant part in their daily lives. Its maximum effect was thought to be on their relationships with others: in some cases, the drug was seen as an essential constituent of the patients' relationships. Helman used the concept of 'fuel', since, as he observed, without the drug 'the patient would not disintegrate but would just not function in conformity with familial and social expectations'.

The third group of patients (about one-fifth of the sample), for whom benzodiazepines were conceptualized as a 'food', expressed least control over the drug, its ingestion, and over life generally. Helman noted that their psychological dependence was as much on the medical profession as on the drug. Furthermore, the drugs were seen by this group as acting both on the patient's emotional state and on social relationships: without it, both would disintegrate. Helman applied the concept of 'food' to these patients' drug use since, without it, they would not survive as an independent, sane person. There appears to be a parallel between Gabe's and Helman's categories. Helman's 'tonic' patients are similar to Gabe's 'standby' users, whereas his 'fuel' and 'food' patients are more like Gabe's 'lifeliners', being more dependent on their drugs.

CONCLUSION

It has long been recognized that the great majority of patients with a psychological problem are treated in primary medical care settings, rather than by specialists; the prescription of a psychotropic drug is one of the most commonly used methods of treatment for such problems in that setting (Shepherd *et al.* 1966).

While the previous chapter has dealt with the evaluation of psychotropic drugs in the context of the controlled clinical trial, this research strategy is, by its very nature, unable to throw light on the prescription and consumption of drugs in the real world. As we have demonstrated in this chapter, a purely medical approach is inadequate if a comprehensive understanding is to be obtained: indeed, it could be argued that a multi-disciplinary approach is mandatory rather than merely desirable (Gabe and Williams 1988).

Acknowledgement: The authors are supported by the Department of Health and Social Security.

REFERENCES

Ashton, H. (1984) 'Benzodiazepine withdrawal: an unfinished story', *British Medical Journal* 288: 1135–40.
Bellantuono, C., Fiorio, R., Williams, P., Martini, N. and Bozzini, L. (1987) 'Psychotropic drug monitoring in general practice in Italy: a two-year study', *Family Practice* 4: 41–9.
Belloc, N.B., Breslow, L., and Hochstim, J.R. (1971) 'Measurement of physical health in a general population survey', *American Journal of Epidemiology* 93: 328–36.
Berridge, V. (1978) 'Victorian opium eating: responses to opiate use in nineteenth century England', *Victorian Studies* 21: 437–61.
Blackwell, B. (1977) 'Medical, social and ethical issues in minor tranquilliser use', paper to the *World Congress in Mental Health*, Vancouver.
British Medical Journal (1984) 'Doctors, drugs and the DHSS: (editorial), *British Medical Journal* 289: 1397–8.
British Medical Journal (1985) 'Doctors, drugs and Government' (editorial), *British Medical Journal* 290: 880.
Cafferata, G.L., Kasper, J., and Bernstein, A. (1983) 'Family roles, structure and stressors in relation to sex differences in obtaining psychotropic drugs', *Journal of Health and Social behaviour* 24: 132–43.
Cartwright, A. (1983) 'Prescribing and the doctor-patient relationship', in D. Pendleton and J. Hasler (eds) *Doctor-Patient Communication*, London: Academic Press.
Cohen, S. (1983) 'Current attitudes about the benzodiazepines: trial by media', *Journal of Psychoactive Drugs* 15: 109–13.
Committee on the Review of Medicines (1980) 'Systematic review of the benzodiazepines', *British Medical Journal* 280: 910–12.
Cooperstock, R. (1971) 'Sex differences in the use of mood modifying drugs: an explanatory model', *Journal of Health and Social Behaviour* 12: 238–44.
Cooperstock, R. (1978) 'Sex differences in psychotropic drug use', *Social Science and Medicine* 12B: 179–86.
Cooperstock, R. and Lennard, H. (1979) 'Some social meanings of tranquilliser use', *Sociology of Health and Illness* 1: 331–47.

Cooperstock, R. and Parnell, P. (1982) 'Research on psychotropic drug use: a review of findings and methods', *Social Science and Medicine* 16: 1179–96.

Department of Health and Social Security (1987) 'Press release 87/127', 23 March.

Doyal, L. (1983) 'Women's health and the sexual division of labour', *Critical Social Policy* 7: 21–33.

Dunlop, D. (1970) 'The use and abuse of psychotropic drugs', *Proceedings of the Royal Society of Medicine* 63: 1279–82.

File, S. (1987) 'Beyond the benzodiazepines: the search for new anxiolytics', *Human Psychopharmacology* 2: 151–58.

Gabe, J. and Lipshitz-Phillips, S. (1982) 'Evil necessity? The meaning of benzodiazepine use for women patients from one general practice', *Sociology of Health and Illness* 4: 201–9.

Gabe, J. and Lipshitz-Phillips, S. (1984) 'Tranquillisers as social control?' *Sociological Review* 32: 524–46.

Gabe, J. and Thorogood, N. (1986) 'Prescribed drugs and the management of everyday life: the experiences of black and white working class women', *Sociological Review* 34: 737–72.

Gabe, J. and Williams, P. (1986a) 'Tranquilliser use: a historical perspective', in J. Gabe and P. Williams (eds) *Tranquillisers: Social, Psychological and Clinical Perspectives*, London: Tavistock.

Gabe, J. and Williams, P. (1986b) 'The meaning of tranquilliser use: introduction', in J. Gabe and P. Williams (eds) *Tranquillisers: Social, Psychological and Clinical Perspectives*, London: Tavistock.

Gabe, J. and Williams, P. (1988) 'A multidisciplinary approach to long-term tranquilliser use', unpublished paper, Institute of Psychiatry, London.

Goldberg, D., Cooper, B., Eastwood, M.R., Kedward, H.B., and Shepherd, M. (1970) 'A standardised psychiatric interview for use in community surveys', *Journal of Preventive and Social Medicine* 24: 18–23.

Hall, S. (1983) 'The great moving right show', in S. Hall and M. Jacques (eds) *The Politics of Thatcherism*, London: Lawrence & Wishart.

Helman, C. (1981) 'Tonic, fuel and food: social and symbolic aspects of the long-term use of psychotropic drugs', *Social Science and Medicine* 15B: 521–33.

Hollister, L. (1983) 'The pre-benzodiazepine era', *Journal of Psychoactive Drugs* 15: 9–13.

Hollister, L., Motzenbecker, F.P., and Degon, R.O. (1961) 'Withdrawal reactions from chlordiazepoxide (Librium)', *Psychopharmacologia* 2: 63–8.

Home Affairs Committee (1985) *Interim Report on Drug Misuse*, London: HMSO.

Jefferys, M. (1973) 'Medicine takers' *Journal of the Royal College of General Practitioners* 23 (supplement 2): 9–11.

Jefferys, M. and Sachs, H. (1983) *Rethinking General Practice*, London: Tavistock.

Kennedy, I. (1981) *The Unmasking of Modern Medicine*, London: Allen & Unwin.

Klerman, G. (1971) 'Drugs and social values', *International Journal of the Addictions* 5: 313–19.

Kraupl-Taylor, F. (1984) 'Benzodiazepines on trial', *British Medical Journal* 288: 1379.

Lader, M. (1978) 'Benzodiazepines: the opium of the masses?' *Neuroscience* 3: 159–65.

Lader, M. (1981) 'Epidemic in the making: benzodiazepine dependence', in G. Tognoni, C. Bellantuono, and M. Lader (eds) *The Epidemiological Impact of Psychotropic Drugs*, Amsterdam: Elsevier.

Lancet (1973a) 'Unreasonable profit' (editorial), *Lancet* i: 867.

Lancet (1973b) 'Benzodiazepines: use, overuse, misuse, abuse?' (editorial), *Lancet* i: 1101–2.

Lasagna, L. (1980)'The Halcion study: trial by media? *Lancet* i: 815–16.

Lennard, H.L., Epstein, L.J., Bernstein, A., and Ransom, D.C. (1971) *Mystification and Drug Misuse*, New York: Harper & Row.

Mant, A., Broom, D.H. and Duncan-Jones, P. (1983) 'The path to prescription: sex differences in psychotropic drug prescribing for general practice patients', *Social Psychiatry* 18: 185–92.

Marks, J. (1978) *The Benzodiazepines: Use, Overuse, Misuse and Abuse*, Lancaster: MTP Press.

Marks, J. (1983a) 'The benzodiazepines – for good or for evil?' *Neuropsychobiology* 10: 115–26.

Marks, J. (1983b) 'The benzodiazepines: an international perspective', *Journal of Psychoactive Drugs* 15: 137–49.

Marks, J., Goldberg, D., and Hillier, V.E. (1979) 'Determinants of the ability of general practitioners to detect psychiatric disorder', *Psychological Medicine* 9: 337–53.

Mellinger, G.D., Balter, M.B., and Uhlenhuth, E.H. (1984) 'Prevalence and correlates of long-term regular use of anxiolytics', *Journal of the American Medical Association* 251: 375–9.

MIND (1984) *Tranquillizers: Hard Facts, Hard Choices*, London, National Association for Mental Health.

Muller, C. (1972) 'The overmedicated society: forces in the marketplace for medical care', *Science* 176: 488–92.

Murray, J. (1981) 'Long-term psychotropic drug taking and the process of withdrawal', *Psychological Medicine* 11: 853–8.

Murray, J., Williams, P., and Clare, A.W. (1982) 'Health and social characteristics of long-term psychotropic drug takers', *Social Science and Medicine* 16: 1595–8.

Owen, R.T. and Tyrer, P. (1983) 'Benzodiazepine dependence: a review of the evidence', *Drugs* 25: 385–98.

Parish, P.A. (1971) 'The prescribing of psychotropic drugs in general practice', *Journal of the Royal College of General Practitioners* 21 (supplement 4): 1–77.

Petursson, H. and Lader, M. (1981) 'Benzodiazepine dependence', *British Journal of Addiction* 76: 133–45.

Rabin, D.L. and Bush, P.J. (1974) 'The use of medicines: historical trends and international comparisons', *International Journal of Health Services* 4: 61–87.

RELEASE (1982) *Trouble with Tranquillisers*, London: Release.

Rickels, K. (1981) 'Are benzodiazepines overused and abused?', *British Journal of Clinical Pharmacology* 11, (supplement 1): 71S–83S.

Rickels, K., Case, G.W., Winokur, A., and Svenson, C. (1984) 'Long-term benzodiazepine therapy: benefits and risks', *Psychopharmacology Bulletin* 20: 608–15.

Robinson, D. (1978) 'Self-help groups', *British Journal of Hospital Medicine*, September, 106–110.

Rodrigo, E., King, M., and Williams, P. (1988a) 'The health of long-term tranquilliser users', *British Medical Journal* 296: 603–6.

Rodrigo, E., King, M., and Williams, P. (1988b) 'Long-term tranquilliser use in a south London general practice', unpublished research report, Institute of Psychiatry.

Salmon, J.W. (1985) 'Introduction', in J.W. Salmon (ed.) *Alternative Medicines: Popular and Policy Perspectives*, London: Tavistock.

Shepherd, M., Cooper, B., Brown, A.C., and Kalton, G.W. (1966) *Psychiatric Illness in General Practice*, London: Oxford University Press.

Svenson, S.F. and Hamilton, R.G. (1966) 'A critique of over-emphasis of side effects with psychotropic drugs: an analysis of 18,000 chlordiazepoxide treated cases', *Current Therapeutic Research* 8: 455–64.

Taylor, D. (1987) 'Current usage of benzodiazepines in Britain', in H. Freeman and Y. Rue (eds) *The Benzodiazepines in Current Clinical Practice*, London: Royal Society of Medicine Services.

Trethowan, W.H. (1975) 'Pills for personal problems', *British Medical Journal* iii: 749–51.

Tyrer, P. (1974) 'The benzodiazepine bonanza', *Lancet* ii: 709–10.

Tyrer, P. (1980) 'Dependence on benzodiazepines', *British Journal of Psychiatry* 137: 576–7.

Tyrer, P., Owen, R., and Dawling, S. (1983) 'Gradual withdrawal of diazepam after long-term therapy', *Lancet* i: 1402–6.

Waldron, I. (1977) 'Increased prescribing of Valium, Librium and other drugs – an example of economic and social factors in the practice of medicine', *International Journal of Health Services* 7: 37–62.

Williams, P. (1978) 'Physical ill-health and psychotropic drug prescription: a review', *Psychological Medicine* 8: 683–93.

Williams, P. (1983a) 'Patterns of psychotropic drug use', *Social Science and Medicine* 17: 845–51.

Williams, P. (1983b) 'Factors influencing the duration of treatment with psychotropic drugs in general practice: a survival analysis approach', *Psychological Medicine* 13: 623–33.

Williams, P., Bellantuono, C., Fiorio, R., and Tansella, M. (1986) 'Psychotropic drug use in Italy: national trends and regional differences', *Psychological Medicine* 16: 841–50.

22

The Evaluation of Social Interventions

Roslyn Corney and Joanna Murray

Social interventions in the treatment of mental illness cover a broad spectrum of management techniques both of the individual's current symptoms and of the social circumstances with which they interplay. The focus of this chapter will be on social interventions directed at improving both the patient's symptoms and social functioning. We shall review studies of the effectiveness of various techniques employed primarily by trained social workers.

The crucial role of social factors in the causation of mental illness has been widely established and there exists a substantial literature documenting the positive associations between a number of socio-cultural factors (such as sex, socio-economic status and urban-rural location) and mental illness. The evidence has been reviewed by Dohrenwend and Dohrenwend (1969) and Dohrenwend (1975). The role of 'life events' and stress in the development of psychiatric morbidity has been investigated and discussed in a number of studies, although the theoretical difficulties in establishing the precise nature of the association remain to be resolved (Holmes and Rahe 1967; Brown and Birley 1968; Dohrenwend and Dohrenwend 1974; Paykel 1978). More recently there has been growing research activity in establishing the effects on illness of the presence or absence and the nature of personal relationships (Miller and Ingham 1976; Vaughn and Leff 1976; Brown and Harris 1978; Henderson *et al.* 1978).

In addition to the likely causative role in mental illness, social problems are found to exist with greater frequency in patients suffering from psychological disorders than in those unaffected. A higher degree of social impairment has been found in depressed patients than in normal subjects (Shepherd *et al.* 1966; Weissman and Paykel 1974; Brown and Harris 1978), and general practice patients with chronic neuroses have been shown to have a greater degree of social impairment than a matched group of non-psychiatric patients (Sylph *et al.* 1969; Cooper 1972). Although some of these problems may occur before the illness, the clinical symptoms themselves – such as irritability, anergia, and loss of libido – are likely to put extra strains on personal relationships and to have detrimental effects

343

upon work performance and social activities.

Social factors play a major part in the prognosis of mental illness, chronicity being associated with long-term social difficulties. In a follow-up study of general practice patients, Kedward (1969) found that those who had chronic social problems were less likely to have improved after three years than patients without chronic problems. 'Situational' factors noted in these chronic patients were severe marital disharmony, housing problems, long-term physical illness, and bereavement. Kedward commented that a great deal of suffering might have been alleviated by interventions aimed at improving the patients' social conditions.

Two longitudinal studies have found that patients' social circumstances are the most powerful predictors of illness outcome. Huxley and Goldberg (1975) found that material and objective conditions predicted outcome at six months in a study of fifty non-psychotic patients. Stress and lack of support in patients' marital, family, and social life were found to predict continued illness at twelve months follow-up in a group of one hundred general practice patients initially diagnosed as having neurotic disorders (Jenkins et al. 1981). Further evidence of the key role of social supports and family tensions in determining outcome is to be found in the work of Bullock et al. (1972) and Vaughn and Leff (1976). The pioneering studies of the latter authors and their colleagues have isolated aspects of family interaction which are associated with episodes of schizophrenic illness. High levels of 'expressed emotion' and frequent criticism of the patient were found in those families in which readmissions to hospital occurred most often.

Given the evidence on the role of social factors, interventions aimed at ameliorating social problems should be considered along with psychological and physical treatments. However, the time available to general practitioners and psychiatrists to attempt to effect change in a patient's social condition is strictly limited (Shepherd et al. 1966; Royal College of General Practitioners 1973). Lack of knowledge of social agencies and their resources also limits the doctor's ability to intervene in this way (Jeffreys 1965). The changing nature of modern medicine, with greater emphasis on pharmacological and technological interventions, has also led to a change in the relation between doctor and patient to the point where counsel and support have become a much reduced aspect of medical practice (British Medical Association 1986). The lack of opportunity to vent the personal problems and social difficulties which they perceive to be associated with their illnesses, has led increasing numbers of patients to look to non-medical sources of help (BMA 1986). Recognition of the change in the doctor-patient relationship is demonstrated by the growing involvement of counsellors, clinical psychologists, and social workers in the management of psychological problems. This chapter will concentrate on social interventions in hospital and general practice settings, presenting the findings of clinical trials on social work treatment in the management of mental illness and its outcome. Trials of more analytic psychotherapies will be excluded and behavioural methods are discussed by Falloon in the following chapter.

METHODS OF EVALUATION: THE CLINICAL TRIAL

Although subjective impressions of social work involvement with the mentally disturbed indicate that social workers can offer a great deal of support and counsel, it is important to evaluate their therapeutic role in the management of mental disorder. The established method for the evaluation of any form of treatment is the controlled clinical trial. This technique has been used to measure the efficacy of psychotropic drugs both in hospital settings and in general practice (MRC 1965; Wheatley 1972), but it has been used infrequently to evaluate social treatments of psychiatric patients. The very nature of the intervention leads to a number of difficulties in conducting such trials. First, there are the problems of defining the disorders and assessing outcome. In addition, there are ethical and practical problems: many clinical trials are difficult to carry out because of the ethical issues arising from the withholding of treatment from the control group of patients. Practical difficulties arise when patients refuse the treatment offered, move from the district, or fail to attend for the follow-up interviews.

In double-blind drug trials, placebos can be given when medication is being tested and arrangements can be made for the patients, physicians, and assessors to remain unaware of who is receiving the active drug. Thus, the observations made are not biased by the attitudes of either the research worker or the client, and the physician's management of the patients is unaffected. In contrast, when social or psychological treatment is being tested there are no suitable placebos to allow double-blind procedures to be employed. Studies have to be planned so that the assessors, at least, are unaware of the treatment received by the patients. Trials of social work present extra difficulties because the treatment given is very difficult to standardize. Unlike drugs, for which a fixed dose can be prescribed, the practitioners, the clients, the relationship built up between them, and the content of the interventions all vary considerably (Truax and Carkhuff 1967; Bergin 1971). It is, therefore, important to record in detail and to attempt to codify the social work interventions that have occurred and the type of help given.

It is also difficult to decide by which criteria improvement will be assessed. Social treatment may, for example, fail to improve clinical symptoms (Weissman and Paykel 1974), but may alleviate social problems. Thus, the criteria used in the assessments must take into account the social worker's aims and treatment, and not rely on biomedical outcome measures. As we have said, social disadvantage and dysfunction are major components of much psychological illness, and their amelioration should be seen as a successful outcome of social therapy.

CLINICAL TRIALS OF SOCIAL WORK WITH PSYCHIATRIC PATIENTS

There have been very few studies on the effectiveness of social work with psychiatric patients, no doubt because of the many difficulties involved. This paper will focus on seven studies which have taken place in either out-patient or general practice settings and have included patients suffering from depression, chronic neurosis, and schizophrenia.

In hospital settings

The first of these studies was conducted in the United States and investigated the effects of psychiatric social work and drug treatment in depressed female out-patients (Klerman *et al.* 1974; Weissman and Paykel 1974). On entry to the study, the women were first given amitriptyline for four to six weeks. Those who responded to the drug were then accepted for maintenance treatment. They were randomly assigned to eight months of either the same antidepressant or a placebo or no tablet at all, with or without psychiatric social work, using a 2 × 3 factorial design. Women referred to the psychiatric social worker were seen once or twice a week with a minimum of one hour a week devoted to individual 'psychotherapy'. Their therapy was not so much psychodynamic as supportive, emphasizing their present state and circumstances and orientated towards the patients' descriptive accounts of their own problems. The results indicated that the psychotherapy did not prevent the recurrence of clinical symptoms but that it did affect social adjustment in those who remained well. After eight months, psychotherapy significantly reduced friction and anxious rumination, improved overall adjustment, work performance, and communication. The drug amitriptyline, on the other hand, reduced the possibility of relapse but had no effect on social adjustment. The authors concluded that combined drug treatment and psychotherapy was the most beneficial in alleviating clinical symptoms and improving social adjustment.

Another study in which social work was directed at improving patients' subjectively selected social problems involved patients who had been admitted to hospital after a drug overdose (Gibbons *et al.* 1978). It included 539 patients, 200 of whom were referred to the control group for 'routine' services and the same number to an experimental service employing a social worker. One hundred and thirty-nine patients were not referred to either group, as patients were excluded if they had a formal psychiatric illness requiring immediate psychiatric treatment, or if they were considered to constitute an immediate suicide risk, or if they were already in treatment with a psychiatrist or social worker. Ninety per cent of the experimental group received social work help limited to three months duration in which the social workers concentrated on specific tasks which had been identified by the patient as most needing to be changed (Butler *et al.* 1978).

The two groups were checked on repeated admissions for self-poisoning

346

for a year after the index admission, and after four months a proportion completed the Beck self-rating depression inventory (Beck *et al.* 1961). There were no significant differences between the two groups in the repetition of self-poisoning or in scores on the Beck depression inventory. However, the patients differed in respect of their social scores and how they viewed the help given. This was measured by a semi-structured social questionnaire administered in hospital and repeated four months later. As in the study conducted by Weissman and Paykel (1974), the subjects receiving the social work service showed more improvement in their social scores than the control group. The patients in the experimental group also considered that they had received more help. One of the problems of this study was that the control group had more contact with the psychiatric services and also the social services department than the experimental group. This additional treatment might have had an effect on outcome, diminishing the difference between groups. Such problems are inherent in a study of this sort when it is impossible to restrict services given by other agencies or other departments.

The third study investigated outcome in 374 schizophrenics discharged from three Maryland state hospitals (Hogarty *et al.* 1974). Following discharge, patients were randomly assigned at clinic intake to 'major role therapy', defined as a combination of intensive social casework and vocational rehabilitation counselling. MRT was viewed as a problem-solving method designed to respond to the interpersonal, social, and rehabilitative needs of the study patients and their families. All patients were stabilized on chlorpromazine for two months and then randomly assigned identical-looking tablets of chlorpromazine or placebo. Relapse was defined as clinical deterioration of such magnitude that readmission to hospital was imminent. About 75 per cent of relapsed patients were actually readmitted.

At the end of the first year after discharge 68 per cent of placebo-treated patients and 31 per cent of drug-treated patients had relapsed. After two years, 80 per cent of the placebo group had relapsed in comparison with 48 per cent of the drug treated. 'Major role therapy' (MRT) had no effect on relapse rates in the first two years (46 per cent of the MRT group relapsed in comparison with 51 per cent of the non-MRT group in the first year) but did appear to lower relapse rates among those who survived in the community for six months after hospital discharge. Since the magnitude of the drug/placebo difference was the same for both sociotherapy (MRT) groups, the effects were judged to be additive rather than interactive.

In addition to relapse, patients were assessed at six, twelve, eighteen and twenty-four months on their personal and social adjustment and role performance. Among those patients who did not relapse, an interaction was found between drug treatment and MRT, suggesting that among drug-treated patients, those who received MRT adjusted better, and among placebo-treated patients those who did not receive MRT adjusted better. This effect was observed on the ratings made by the social worker, physician, the patients themselves, and a relative. As with the study on female out-patients, the investigators concluded that maximum restorative benefits require both maintenance phenothiazine and psychological treatment continued beyond a single year following discharge.

A combination of maintenance medication and sociotherapy was found again to be a most effective combination in the final hospital-based study. Leff and his colleagues (1982) developed a 'package' of social interventions to counteract the risk factors found in earlier studies (Vaughn and Leff 1976) to be associated with schizophrenic breakdown. Provoking agents included high levels of 'expressed emotion' from the patients' immediate relatives and excessive amounts of close contact between the two. The social interventions included an education programme for relatives on the aetiology, symptoms, course, and management of schizophrenia; relatives' groups to provide support; and individual family sessions in their own homes which included the patient. Twenty-four patients at high risk of relapse were selected for the study, with half of the families allocated to an experimental group to receive social therapy and the other half assigned to routine out-patient care. All were maintained on neuroleptic drugs. The social interventions had a significant effect in reducing relapse rates to 9 per cent in the experimental group compared with 50 per cent in the control group. Operationally defined therapeutic aims had been set for each experimental family, and these were achieved in 73 per cent of cases; none of the patients in this group of families relapsed. The authors concluded that the combination of interventions was necessary to maintain the patients' stability.

In general practice settings

The first study conducted in this area investigated ninety-two patients who were considered by their general practitioners to have chronic neurosis and who had had symptoms continually for over a year (Cooper *et al.* 1975; Shepherd *et al.* 1979). The patients were suffering from depression, anxiety and phobias; they were all over 18 and of both sexes. Ninety-seven controls from practices in the same neighbourhood were selected for comparison.

The two groups were assessed by means of standardized psychiatric and social interviews. Patients in the experimental group were then referred to a special service operating in the practice, which included a psychiatrist and a social worker, while the controls were referred back to the doctor for routine treatment. After one year both groups were interviewed again using the same standardized instruments. Details were also collected from the medical notes on the psychotropic drugs prescribed, and the general practitioner was asked how much care and supervision had been necessary for each patient.

The special service included therapeutic intervention from both the research psychiatrist and the social worker, who met regularly with the general practitioners involved. The social worker was involved in the management of approximately two-thirds of the patients, working alone with three-quarters of them and jointly with the psychiatrist for the remainder. Her main role was in helping the patient and their family to deal with their practical problems. In most cases, the social worker was the key worker with the psychiatrist's main role limited to a reassessment interview. Some of the patients refused her help, while others were not regarded as suitable for referral, either because they had markedly improved or because the treatment they were receiving from the doctor was considered adequate. Many did not want any more specific help and were referred back to the general practitioner with recommendations.

Both groups showed a reduction in psychiatric symptoms at follow-up, but the fall was more pronounced in the experimental group, 38 per cent of whom had been taken off psychotropic drugs compared with 25 per cent of the controls. In addition, continued medical care and supervision were deemed necessary for only 60 per cent of the experimental patients compared with 77 per cent of the controls. The experimental patients also achieved much more improvement in their social functioning compared with the controls. Measurement of social adjustment included items on housing, finance, work, marriage, children, and other relationships.

Clinical outcome proved to be unrelated to the social worker's activities, much of which were devoted to solving practical problems. Those who received short-term intervention were more likely to improve than those receiving episodic or continuous social work support. This result cannot be taken to indicate that short-term social work intervention is more effective than a longer-term variety since the social worker was permitted to discontinue treatment as soon as her patient improved. By definition, therefore, clients who did not respond or who actually deteriorated were more likely to remain in longer contact.

The second study in general practice concerns the application of social work among women aged between 18 and 45 years attending with depression (Corney 1984). Such women place a great demand on GPs and also represent a high proportion of the referrals to social workers operating in GP attachment schemes. In this investigation eighty women were referred from a health centre and a single-handed practice to the study. They were assessed using the same psychiatric and social interviews as in the previous study. They were classified as either 'acutely depressed', having had symptoms for three months or less, or 'acute on chronic', having had symptoms for a longer period but with intensification in the past three months. The women were then randomly allocated either to the experimental group, where they were referred to one of four attached social workers, or to the control group, with referral back to their doctor. After six months, they were reinterviewed using the same instruments, and their medical notes were examined for one year after referral.

Both the experimental and control groups were initially similar in respect of psychiatric and physical health and demographic features. When reassessed at six months, approximately two-thirds of both groups had recovered from their depression and were no longer receiving psychotropic drugs. There was little difference in outcome between experimental and control groups on clinical and social scores, number of visits to the doctor in the previous six months, or length of time on psychotropic medication. These findings indicate that the additional involvement of a social worker had not helped these women in general on either clinical or social measures. However, analysis of covariance indicated that one subgroup of patients had benefited from the increased help. These patients were assessed initially as having major marital or boyfriend problems and were suffering from 'acute on chronic' depression. With this particular group of women, 80 per cent had improved at follow-up in comparison with 31 per cent of the controls. This difference persisted one year after referral when the medical notes were examined.

As the results suggested that social work intervention was more beneficial to certain patients than others, the social worker's records were analysed, taking into account these different groups. Women who benefited most from the social worker's help were considered by the social workers to be more highly motivated to receive help than the other groups. They also had more social problems and received more practical help from the social worker, including housing and financial help, day nursery placements, and liaison with other agencies.

The final study was also carried out with depressed patients referred from general practice (Ross and Scott 1985), although the social worker used cognitive therapy as opposed to casework or practical help as his main technique. Patients considered by their GP to be depressed were first assessed by a psychiatrist using the Present State Examination (Wing 1982), the Montgomery-Asberg depression scale (1979) and the Beck Depression Inventory (1981). Those whose scores met the criteria for inclusion were then randomly allocated to individual cognitive therapy, group cognitive therapy, or a waiting list control group. Patients in all three groups also received practical social work help so that any differences emerging between the groups would be attributable to cognitive therapy. After three months, cognitive therapy was found to have a statistically significant beneficial effect upon depression compared with 'normal treatment', as assessed by the Montgomery-Asberg scale and the Beck Depression Inventory. Group and individual cognitive therapy were found to be equally effective. In addition, comparison with the scores of those who were on the waiting list provided further evidence of the beneficial influence of cognitive therapy. These treatment gains were maintained at twelve months follow-up.

CONCLUSIONS

Studies in hospital settings

The results of the four studies on the outcome of more severe depressions and schizophrenias suggest that social interventions alone do not prevent relapse or reduce clinical symptomatology. However, all four studies showed evidence of treatment gains in terms of social adjustment, and in the study by Leff *et al.* (1982), in preventing relapse. All indicate the need for a combined approach of drug treatment and socio- or psychotherapy. In the social treatment of schizophrenia, the work of Vaughn and Leff (1976) suggests a number of interventions with an emphasis on changes in the family. The patient might be encouraged to move into a hostel rather than try to adjust to living with hostile or overbearing relatives; or the family might be better educated on the nature of the illness and their own role in preventing relapse.

The application of 'major role therapy' (Hogarty *et al.* 1974) appears to be disappointing; more specific operational definitions of social intervention might have led to greater consistency in treatment and consequent outcomes.

Studies in general practice

In this setting studies suggest that patients with more long-standing depressions and neuroses can be helped more than those with acute symptoms by a social worker's involvement. In the latter case, patients are more likely to recover spontaneously without outside help. Early intervention may be harmful, the social worker interfering with the client's own abilities to cope, or affecting the support received from informal sources, such as friends and relatives.

Depressed women with a poor relationship with their spouse or boyfriend may benefit more than other depressed women from the help of the social worker. Many of the women in the second study (Corney 1984) had inadequate social contact and no one in whom to confide, so that they more readily accepted the emotional support offered by a social worker. These findings are closely related to the theoretical work on the value of social supports and close confidants in protecting individuals from the development of mental disorder and in affecting the prognosis of an existing episode (e.g. Miller and Ingham 1976).

Practical help in managing social difficulties appears to be of most benefit to those with long-standing neurotic illness. In the general practice setting the effectiveness of social work with depressed and anxious patients depends on the duration of symptoms, the support received from others (including the spouse), the patient's motivation to accept help and the coexistence of chronic social problems. A more structured form of treatment, such as the cognitive therapy exemplified in the third study (Ross and Scott 1985), may bring advantages over and above the practical help of social work.

351

As we noted at the outset, social factors have an undoubted influence on the development, course, and outcome of mental illness. The limited number of studies available indicate a varying degree of effectiveness of social intervention under different conditions. There are intrinsic difficulties in establishing the optimum use of sociotherapy, in particular its content. The research to date sheds some light on the characteristics of patients who might benefit most from social intervention but, with the exception of the study by Leff *et al.* (1982), there has been little success in producing suitable detailed operational goals for social treatment.

A number of questions remain to be answered through detailed experimental studies, particularly on the role of trained social workers with the mentally ill:

(i) Are any aspects of social work unique? Apart from their statutory duties and abilities to liaise with other professionals and agencies, do social workers provide more than the befriending and supportive role of a sensitive volunteer?

(ii) Which elements of the social worker's skills (e.g. practical knowledge, counselling) are of most benefit and to what type of patient? Future studies of social therapy should develop operational goals and detailed treatment plans against which the effectiveness of interventions can be measured.

The current levels of demand for social work time are very high and there is little prospect of increased resources. The value of social intervention in psychiatric care will need to be fully justified by carefully designed research in order to make the case for the deployment of social workers in this area.

Acknowledgement: The authors are supported by the Department of Health and Social Security.

REFERENCES

Beck, A. (1981) *Cognitive Theory in Depression*, Chichester: Wiley.

Beck, A.T., Ward, C.H., and Mendelson, M. (1961) 'An Inventory for measuring depression', *Archives of General Psychiatry* 4: 561–71.

Bergin, A.E. (1971) 'The evaluation of therapeutic outcomes', in A.E. Bergin and S.L. Garfield (eds) *Handbook of Psychotherapy and Behaviour Change: An Empirical Analysis*, New York: Wiley.

Brown, G.W. and Birley, J.L.T. (1968) 'Crises and life changes and the onset of schizophrenia' *Journal of Health and Social Behaviour* 9: 203–14.

Brown, G.W. and Harris, T. (1978) *Social Origins of Depression: A Study of Psychiatric Disorder in Women*, London: Tavistock.

Bullock, R.C., Siegel, R., Weissman, M., and Paykel, E.S. (1972) 'The weeping wife: marital relations of depressed women', *Journal of Marriage and the Family* 34: 488–95.

Butler, J., Bow, I. and Gibbons, J. (1978) 'Task centred casework with marital problems', *British Journal of Social Work* 8: 393–409.

British Medical Association (1986) *Alternative Therapy*, London: BMA.

Cooper, B. (1979) 'Clinical and social aspects of chronic neurosis', in P. Williams and A. Clare (eds) *Psychosocial Disorders in General Practice*, London: Academic Press.

Cooper, B., Harwin, B.G., Depla, C., and Shepherd, M. (1975), 'Mental health care in the community: an evaluative study', *Psychological Medicine*, 5: 372–80.

Corney, R.H., (1984) 'The effectiveness of attached social workers in the management of depressed female patients in general practice', *Psychological Medicine*, Monograph supplement no. 6: 47.

Dohrenwend, B.P. (1975) 'Social, cultural and social psychological factors in the genesis of mental disorders', *Journal of Health and Social Behaviour* 16: 365–92.

Dohrenwend, B.S. and Dohrenwend, B.P. (1969) *Social Status and Psychological Disorder*, New York: Wiley.

Dohrenwend, B.S. and Dohrenwend, B.P. (1974) *Stressful Life Events: Their Nature and Effects*, New York: Wiley.

Gibbons, J.S., Butler, J., Unwin, P., and Gibbons, J.L. (1978) 'Evaluation of a social work service for self-poisoning patients', *British Journal of Psychiatry* 133: 111–18.

Henderson, S., Duncan-Jones, P., McAuley, H., and Ritchie, K. (1978) 'The patient's primary group', *British Journal of Psychiatry* 132: 74–86.

Hogarty, G.E., Goldberg, S.C., and Schooler, N.R. (1974) 'Drug and social therapy in the aftercare of schizophrenic patients', *Archives of General Psychiatry* 31: 603–18.

Holmes, T.H., and Rahe, R.H. (1967) 'The social readjustment rating scale' *Journal of Psychosomatic Medicine* 11: 213–18.

Huxley, P. and Goldberg, D.P. (1975) 'Social versus clinical prediction in minor psychiatric disorders', *Psychological Medicine* 5: 96–100.

Jeffreys, M. (1965) *An Anatomy of Social Welfare Services*, London: Michael Joseph.

Jenkins, R., Mann, A.H., and Belsey, E. (1981) 'The background, design and use of a short interview to assess social stress and support in clinical settings', *Social Science and Medicine* 15E(3): 195–203.

Kedward, H. (1969) 'The outcome of neurotic illness in the community', *Social Psychiatry* 4: 1–4.

Klerman, G.L., Di Mascio, A., Weissman, M., Prusoff, B., and Paykel, E.S. (1974) 'Treatment of depression by drugs and psychotherapy', *American Journal of Psychiatry* 131: 186–91.

Leff, J., Knupers, L., Berkowitz, R., Eberlein, Vries, R., and Sturgeon, D. (1982) 'A controlled trial of social intervention in the families of schizophrenic patients', *British Journal of Psychiatry* 141: 121–34.

Medical Research Council (1965) *Clinical Trial of the Treatment of Depressive Illness*, Report by Clinical Psychiatry Committee.

Miller, P. McC. and Ingham, J.G. (1976) 'Friends, confidants and symptoms', *Social Psychiatry* 11: 51–8.

Montgomery, S.A. and Asberg, M. (1979) 'A new depression scale designed to be sensitive to change', *British Journal of Psychiatry* 134: 382–9.

Paykel, E.S. (1978) 'Contribution of life events to causation of psychiatric illness' *Psychological Medicine* 8: 245–53.

Ross, M. and Scott, M. (1985) 'An evaluation of the effectiveness of individual and group cognitive therapy in the treatment of depressed patients in an inner city health centre', *Journal of the Royal College of General Practitioners* 35: 239–42.

Royal College of General Practitioners (1973) *Present State and Future Needs of General Practice* (third edition) (Reports from General Practice, No. 16) London: RCGP.

Shepherd, M., Cooper, B., Brown, A.C., and Kalton, G.W. (1966) *Psychiatric Illness in General Practice* London: Oxford University Press.

Shepherd, M., Harwin, B.G., Depla, C., and Cairns, V. (1979) 'Social work and primary care of mental disorder', *Psychological Medicine* 9: 661–69.

Sylph, J.A., Kedward, H.B., and Eastwood, M.R. (1969) 'Chronic neurotic patients in general practice', *Journal of the Royal College of General Practitioners* 17: 162–70.

Truax, C. and Carkhuff, R.R. (1967) *Towards Effective Counselling and Psychotherapy*, Chicago: Aldine.

Vaughn, C.E. and Leff, J.P. (1976) 'The influence of family and social factors on the course of psychiatric illness: a comparison of schizophrenic and depressed neurotic patients', *British Journal of Psychiatry* 129: 125–37.

Weissman, M.M. (1971) 'The social role performance of depressed women: comparison with a normal group', *American Journal of Orthopsychiatry* 41: 391–405.

Weissman, M.M. and Paykel, E.S. (1974) *The Depressed Woman: A study of Social Relationships*, Chicago: University of Chicago Press.

Wheatley, D. (1972) 'Evaluation of psychotropic drugs in general practice', *Proceedings of the Royal Society of Medicine* 65: 317–20.

Wing, J.K. (1982) 'The use of the Present State Examination in general population survey', *Acta Psychiatrica Scandinavica* (supplement), 285: 230–40.

23

Behavioural Approaches in the Family Management of Schizophrenia

Ian Falloon

A RATIONALE FOR FAMILY MANAGEMENT OF SCHIZOPHRENIA

The detrimental effects of environmental stress upon the course and outcome of schizophrenia have been investigated in a series of studies of patients living in the community. Much of this work has emanated from the Social Psychiatry Unit of the Institute of Psychiatry and has focused upon two stress factors a) ambient stress, chiefly household tension, and b) stressful life events.

High levels of ambient stress in the household in which the patient resides after partial or full recovery from an episode of schizophrenia are associated with more frequent exacerbations of florid symptomatology (Brown, Birley and Wing 1972; Vaughn and Leff 1976; Vaughn et al. 1984). The more discrete stress of life events appears to trigger episodes of schizophrenia (Brown and Birley 1970; Leff et al. 1973) even when ambient tension is low (Leff and Vaughn 1980). Other stress factors, such as the work environment, have not been studied in a systematic fashion (Wing et al. 1964).

It is apparent that optimal regimens of neuroleptic drugs provide a significant but incomplete buffer against these stressors (Vaughn and Leff 1976; Birley and Brown 1970). An alternative psychosocial strategy would involve the provision of a low-stress environment such as that offered by the old-style asylum (Dunham and Weinberg 1960). However, such an environment, while reducing florid symptoms, tends to enhance deficit or negative symptoms and their associated social morbidity (Wing 1978).

Community care of schizophrenia places a considerable stress on family caregivers (Creer and Wing 1974). Furthermore, high levels of family burden are associated with high levels of 'expressed emotion', a marker of high ambient stress in a household (Brown, Birley and Wing 1972). Family members make specific complaints about their lack of understanding about the nature of schizophrenia and its optimal management and their need for specific guidelines rather than non-specific social support (Creer and Wing 1974; Vaughn 1977).

Thus, an effective programme for family-based management of schizophrenia must encompass the following goals:

1. Educate patients and families about the nature of schizophrenia and its drug and psychosocial treatments;
2. Provide methods for the efficient resolution of environmental stressors, both ambient and life event stress;
3. Minimize the social morbidity of the disorder for both patient and family members;
4. Provide specific strategies for dealing with persisting behavioural disturbance associated with unremitting symptoms.

In order to provide a clear framework we chose to use a problem-solving model as the basis for family management. This involves teaching families to convene regular (at least weekly) meetings to discuss specific problems or goals within a clearly defined structure that facilitates creative solutions, careful planning, and review. As well as providing a means for resolution of all forms of stress, this model enables the family to work towards social goals for all members, and to develop strategies for coping with a wide range of behavioural problems.

ESTABLISHING CLINICAL EFFICACY

Assessment of the effectiveness of a management approach that combines drug and psychosocial treatment in a flexible manner is an extremely difficult problem. We chose to compare the family management approach with a carefully constructed version of the patient-oriented case management approach that was currently provided in most clinics for the long-term care of schizophrenia. This patient-oriented management combined optimal neuroleptic drug therapy, rehabilitation counselling, problem-solving psychotherapy, crisis intervention, and practical assistance with problems such as finances and housing. Efforts were made to ensure that the patient-oriented management was of similar intensity, and conducted over a similar time span, by therapists with similar skill and enthusiasm to the family management. The main distinction was that one approach was clearly family-based and conducted in the family home, whereas the comparative approach was focused on the individual patient and was conducted predominantly in the out-patient clinic.

We were aware that psychotherapy and pharmacotherapy researchers would both criticize our study on the grounds that we could not tease out the crucial ingredients that might account for any differential effectiveness. Essentially, we planned a trial of two contrasting management approaches. However, we included a wide range of process measures so that we could explore several potential mediators of outcome.

A further consideration was that effective management of schizophrenia entailed not merely controlling the florid symptoms of the disorder but necessitated the restoration of unrestricted social and family functioning. For this reason the assessment of outcome included a battery of social and family measures to supplement measures of clinical morbidity.

PATIENT SELECTION

The selection of patients was made on the basis of a high risk of recurrent or persistent florid symptoms of schizophrenia in cases, owing to continued daily involvement in a stressful parental household. An age range of 18 to 45 years was imposed and non-English speaking families were excluded.

Patients entered the study on recovery (partial or full remission) from an episode diagnosed as definite schizophrenia (Classes S and P) on PSE/CATEGO criteria. (Coincidently all patients also met DSM-III criteria for schizophrenic disorder.)

A stressful household was determined after Camberwell Family Interviews had been completed on all adult household members. High ratings of critical or over-involved attitudes expressed towards the patient (Vaughn and Leff 1976b) or evidence of high levels of persisting household stress not associated specifically with the patient's behavioural disturbance were employed as criteria predictive of a poor clinical prognosis independent of the previous history of the disorder (which in first episode cases could not be applied).

Consecutive admissions to Los Angeles County Hospital were screened soon after admission. A few cases were excluded on the basis of a lack of response to in-patient treatment with stabilization of florid symptoms. While substance abuse was not an exclusionary criterion, it is probable that some cases were excluded because the drug use obscured the diagnosis.

The thirty-nine cases selected for the study after application of these criteria included twice as many males as females; 42 per cent Caucasian, 36 per cent Afro-American and 17 per cent Hispanic-American; 86 per cent had completed high school. Most families were in the lower socio-economic classes and lived in the more deprived areas of Los Angeles. More than one-third were single-parent households. All but thirty-nine households were rated high on the expressed emotion index ('high EE').

Most patients (81 per cent) showed evidence of nuclear schizophrenia on CATEGO; one-quarter were experiencing their first episode; the average duration of illness was four years, with three hospital admissions.

Random assignment to the management approaches occurred once patients had left hospital and were stabilized on out-patient neuroleptic medication. This assignment procedure produced two clearly matched groups. Three cases dropped out in the early stages of the study, but did not affect the matching of the two groups. Chi-squared analyses revealed no differences

357

approaching statistical significance on any of the clinical or demographic variables.

THE THERAPEUTIC TEAM

Each patient and family received therapeutic interventions from a team of mental health professionals. The same team provided both forms of management according to strict protocol instructions. The psychosocial treatment of each case was co-ordinated by a primary therapist, who remained constant throughout the twenty-four month study period. A psychiatrist, social worker, and clinical psychologist, who had all been trained in behaviour therapy methods and psychiatric assessment, were the three primary therapists. They were all experienced in out-patient management of schizophrenia. They received specific training in behavioural family management prior to starting work in the study and continued to meet for weekly supervision sessions throughout the study.

Three pharmacotherapists with a minimum of five years experience in neuroleptic drug treatment of schizophrenia provided the drug treatment of schizophrenia and conducted serial assessment of mental status. A research nurse with considerable experience in the management of schizophrenia collected blood samples, administered intramuscular drugs, assisted in crisis intervention, and conducted regular blood pressure and heart rate assessments.

Two rehabilitation counsellors facilitated entry into vocational, day care, and residential rehabilitation services.

Team work was limited somewhat by the need to keep the pharmacotherapists blind to the psychosocial management approach employed for each patient. However, regular discussions between all clinicians occurred on all matters of clinical importance.

THE MANAGEMENT APPROACHES

The primary aim of the study was to examine the benefit of a family-based approach to the community management of schizophrenia when compared with a patient-based approach of similar intensity. These contrasting psychosocial components were applied to patients who were receiving optimal pharmacotherapy, twenty-four crisis management and rehabilitation counselling and services. Because each of the contrasting psychosocial modalities was only one part of the entire management programme, it was crucial that every component was carefully operationalized and applied in a standardized manner.

Neuroleptic drugs were prescribed in a manner designed to maximize their benefits and minimize unwanted effects. Chlorpromazine was the drug of first choice, with cases requiring more potent prophylaxis receiving fluphenazine hydrochloride. Where intramuscular preparations proved necessary, owing to irregular tablet taking or poor absorption of oral preparations, fluphenazine decanoate was given. Two cases received other neuroleptics (haloperidol and thiothixene) due to intolerance of the recommended preparations.

Patients were randomly assigned after regular adherence to maintenance medication had been established. Checks on tablet-taking behaviour were conducted at each medication appointment through interviews with patients and relatives and by tablet counts. This information was supplemented by serial assays of the plasma levels of the drugs and of serum prolactin. Any evidence of erratic compliance was considered a clinical crisis and was addressed urgently by the primary therapists and pharmacotherapists. On occasions this necessitated home visits by the pharmacotherapists, project nurse, and primary therapists.

Levels of drugs were reviewed monthly and were adjusted according to clinical ratings. Increased evidence of florid symptoms of schizophrenia led to increased drugs, a decrease in florid symptoms or severe side effects led to decreased drug levels. Drug and prolactin levels in blood samples supplemented clinical assessments. Additional anti-parkinsonian, anti-depressant, anxiolytic, and sedative drugs were used sparingly when indicated. At all times the pharmacotherapists aimed to minimize the levels of drugs prescribed to minimize psychopathology.

Behavioural family management was based on behavioural family therapy with the addition of education about the nature and management of schizophrenia and the use of a range of behaviour therapy strategies to deal with specific problems.

Weekly sessions of one hour duration with all adult members of the household, including the index patient, were conducted in the home for three months, decreasing in frequency to fortnightly until nine months, after which monthly sessions were provided, often in a multi-family group in a convenient community setting.

The first two or three sessions were devoted to comprehensive education about the nature of schizophrenia and the rationale for combined drug and psychosocial interventions. The value of efficient family management of stress in promoting a good outcome for schizophrenia was emphasized along with the need to maximize the efficacy of neuroleptic drugs.

The core component of the therapy was training the family to convene regular discussions that employed a structured problem-solving approach to develop clearly defined plans to resolve problem issues affecting any member of the family. These included the achievement of personal goals as well as stressful events and situations. Where major deficits in interpersonal communication precluded effective problem-solving discussions, training in communication skills such as expressing specific positive or negative feelings, attentive listening, or making requests in a positive manner was implemented. Where specific problem issues such as parental conflict, aggressive behaviour, social skills deficits, persisting hallucinations, insomnia or depressive mood persisted in any family member, specific behaviour therapy strategies were employed within the problem solving framework. Details of this approach are available in a published manual (Falloon *et al*. 1984).

Patient-oriented management was based on a similar problem-oriented framework. It was of similar intensity and focus as the family-based approach, but directed primarily towards enhancing the community functioning of the index patient, while supporting his family in his care. Structured, goal-oriented sessions of one hour duration were conducted at the same frequency as the family sessions. Patients were educated about the nature of schizophrenia and the importance of drug and stress management in promoting adjustment. Specific behaviour therapy strategies, such as social skills training, anxiety management, or cognitive restructuring were employed where indicated.

Frequent contact was made with key family members to discuss treatment plans and to provide advice on patient care at home. These discussions were held in the absence of the patient in order to minimize problem-solving family discussions. Every effort was made to provide optimal community support.

Thus, the major differences between the two management approaches were a focus on enhancing family problem-solving efficiency; education of the entire family about schizophrenia and its management; home-based sessions; contrasted with a focus on solving the index patient's problems; education of the patient only; and clinic-based sessions. Identical drug therapy, crisis intervention, and rehabilitation services were provided to both management conditions.

STUDY DESIGN

Patients completed baseline assessments during a period of four to eight weeks of out-patient stabilization after an acute episode of schizophrenia. The final assessment included baseline measures of clinical, social, and family morbidity, as well as a series of family interaction measures. At the end of these assessments families were informed of their assignment and consent obtained to participate in the controlled study. The assignment to primary therapists was sequential with each therapist managing an equal number of cases in the two conditions. All index patients were scheduled to receive forty therapy sessions, twenty-four pharmacotherapy sessions, four vocational counselling sessions and four assessment sessions over twenty-four months. Additional sessions were scheduled when indicated according to clinical need.

ASSESSMENT PROCEDURES

Assessment of clinical, social, and family morbidity was conducted at baseline, nine and twenty-four months. Additional assessments of clinical morbidity were conducted monthly. Careful records were made of all contacts with medical and social agencies. Bi-weekly interviews with key family members were employed to assess family stress factors.

Clinical morbidity was assessed on several measures. These included:

a) *Clinical exacerbations:* The primary therapists assessed the mental status of each patient prior to therapy sessions using the Brief Psychiatric Rating Scale, BPRS (Overall and Goreham 1962) as a guideline. A time chart of all exacerbations of schizophrenia, affective disorders, anxiety disorders, emergent side effects, or other physical or mental disorders was maintained throughout the twenty-four months. Emergence of florid psychopathology that persisted for at least one week, or required a major management change was described as a 'major' exacerbation; less severe disturbance was described as a 'minor' exacerbation. These assessments were not standardized, not blind or independent although there was a high level of agreement among the three therapists concerning major exacerbations of schizophrenia.

b) *Community tenure:* All periods spent away from the family household were carefully recorded. These included hospital admissions, residential care and time spent in gaol. Decisions to admit patients to these institutions were made by personnel who were independent of the study.

c) *Target ratings of schizophrenia:* Two or three florid symptoms were selected that were most characteristic of the presentation of an acute episode of schizophrenia for each patient. These were rated monthly by blind assessors on a seven-point severity scale (1 = absent or trivial; 7 = severe). Inter-rater reliability was .95 (Pearson's product-moment coefficient).

d) *Brief Psychiatric Rating Scale, BPRS:* Blind ratings of the BPRS were made monthly. Four factors derived from this scale: assessed thought disorder, withdrawal ('negative' symptoms), hostile/suspiciousness, and depression/anxiety (Goldstein *et al.* 1978).

e) *Present State Examination, PSE:* At nought, nine, twenty-four months a blind assessment was made using the PSE to examine changes in the overall pattern of psychopathology.

f) *Hopkin's Symptom Checklist, HSCL:* The sixty-four item version of this self-report questionnaire was completed at nought, three and nine months to assess neurotic symptom patterns (Derogatis *et al.* 1974).

Social morbidity was assessed by therapists' observations, interviews with a key family member, and patients' self-reports. The measures included:

a) *Time spent in work and educational activity:* A careful record of all work and educational activity, both formal and informal, was made throughout the twenty-four months.

b) *Social Adjustment Scales, SAS-SR:* Patients completed a self-report

361

measure of social functioning at nought, three and nine months (Weissman *et al.* 1978).

c) *Social Behaviour Assessment Schedule, SBAS:* Social morbidity was measured in an interview by a blind assessor with the family member most involved with the patient's care on an abbreviated version of the SBAS (Platt *et al.* 1980). This concerned impairment in social role functioning as well as the relatives' satisfaction with levels of functioning during three months before the interview.

Family morbidity was measured in terms of the social and clinical adjustment of each family member, the distress associated with living with the index patient, the problem-solving functions of the family unit, and the efficiency of coping with life stresses.

a) *Hopkin's Symptom Checklist, HSCL:* Each family member completed the HSCL at nought and nine months to assess patterns of clinical morbidity in the family.

b) *SBAS: distress and burden scales:* Scales measuring the distress and burden key family members experienced as a result of the index patient's morbidity were used from the SBAS interview conducted by the blind assessor.

c) *Family problem-solving functions:* At nought, three and twenty-four months the family unit participated in two ten-minute discussions about current problem issues in the households. These discussions were audiotaped, transcribed, and rated for the communication and problem-solving skills that were observed (Doane and Falloon 1985).

d) *Family stress and coping:* From nought to twelve months fortnightly interviews were conducted with a key member of each family to ascertain all potentially stressful events and situations that had occurred, and the manner in which the family unit had coped with these circumstances. The independent interviewers transcribed details of the events and associated behavioural and cognitive responses, which were subsequently reviewed by a blind rater for a) threatening life events (Brown and Harris 1978); b) effectiveness of coping responses.

THE RESULTS

Clinical morbidity: The multiple measures indicated that family management was associated with less clinical morbidity during the twenty-four-month study period than the patient-oriented approach. There were fewer exacerbations of schizophrenia (thirty-six vs. fifty-four); in particular, fewer major exacerbations (seven vs. forty-one). These differences were less marked when episodes of depression and anxiety were considered, with seven major episodes of affective symptoms in family management and sixteen in patient-oriented management. However, this difference remains noteworthy, particularly when one considers that affective episodes were not recorded during periods when florid schizophrenia was evident, thereby reducing the opportunity for affective episodes in the patient-oriented condition.

On average, patient-oriented cases spent almost seven of the twenty-four months in a state of clinical instability sufficient to warrant active acute management. Family managed patients averaged a little more than one month in a similar state. As a consequence, patient-oriented cases averaged twenty-three days in hospital over the two years and family cases a mere four days. Over twenty-four months 83 per cent of family cases had not experienced a major episode of schizophrenia, whereas only 17 per cent of patient-oriented cases had escaped a major exacerbation.

These clinicians' observations were supported by blind standardized ratings. A repeated measures analysis of covariance over the twenty-four monthly target symptom ratings, with the baseline ratings as covariates, indicated a significant trend favouring family management ($F = 16.73$, df 1,32; $p < .0003$). An overall tendency for improvement with time was noted ($F = 1.96$, df 23,816; $p < .005$). The management group $\times$ time interaction was not significant. This meant that, although all patients tended to improve over the twenty-four months, the family management tended to expedite that trend. PSE interviews at twenty-four months showed no continued evidence of any psychiatric abnormality in half the family managed cases, and two-thirds were in remission from schizophrenic or paranoid disorders. In contrast, fourteen (83 per cent) patient-oriented cases showed schizophrenic or paranoid symptoms and only one of the eighteen cases was free of psychiatric disorder.

The BPRS ratings showed similar patterns over the twenty-four months. Of particular interest was the near-significant trend on the withdrawal factor that suggested that family management was associated with greater reductions in negative symptoms than the patient-oriented approach ($F = 3.32$; df 1,34; $p < .09$).

It was evident that family management was associated with clear clinical benefits over a carefully applied patient-oriented approach, which itself appeared associated with beneficial trends. These benefits involved fewer episodes of serious psychopathology, less need for hospital care, fewer negative symptoms, and a trend towards restoration of mental health. However, it was evident that schizophrenic symptoms did emerge from time to time in most patients receiving family management. These episodes did not escalate into major crises and were readily contained in an out-patient setting. The value of a community-based service, in close contact with family caregivers, providing a twenty-four-hour service should not be underestimated in the achievement of such benefits. Furthermore, it is not sufficient merely to target emergent episodes of schizophrenic symptoms in the management of this disorder. In family managed cases depression and anxiety were prominent and specific therapeutic skills were essential to deal effectively with these episodes.

It could be argued that the clinical benefits associated with family management may have been achieved through more effective neuroleptic drug treatment for those cases. Our careful records of the pharmacotherapy enabled a detailed analysis to be conducted (Moss *et al.* 1985). We were able to establish that prior to 29 per cent of episodes of schizophrenia compliance with the prescribed dosage of medication was less than 75 per cent. These levels of reduced compliance remained the same before major and minor episodes, and prior to episodes experienced in both management conditions. Therefore, it seems unlikely that reduced intake of drugs could explain either the differential outcome of the two forms of management, or whether minor episodes escalated into major exacerbations.

Because the aim of pharmacotherapy was to reduce levels of drugs continually until symptom exacerbation appeared imminent, it was possible that the differential outcome was caused by excessively lower doses prescribed to the patient-oriented cases. This was not evident. The mean daily dosage of family cases was 245 mg of chlorpromazine, or its equivalent, compared with 338 mg for patient-oriented cases. Examination of the pattern of drug ingestion levels over the first nine months by comparing linear regression lines of the monthly dosage for each case revealed a near-significant trend indicating that lower dosages were ingested by family than patient-oriented cases (Mann-Whitney $U = 219.5$; df; $p < .07$).

On the basis of these data there seems little evidence to suggest that the benefits of family management could be explained on the grounds of more effective pharmacotherapy. On the other hand, it could be suggested that family management may facilitiate prophylaxis with lower doses of neuroleptic drugs, with the attendant benefits of few side effects.

Social morbidity: Although the clinical outcome of disorders tends to dominate our thinking, restoration of social functioning is a more important criterion of successful medical intervention. Family management showed clear benefits in enhancing the quality of life for patients. Over the twenty-four months, family cases spent an average of 12.6 months engaged in some form of work or educational pursuit, compared to 7.2 months for individual cases.

The self-reported assessment of social adjustment, SAS, showed significant advantages for the family management on scales of social and leisure activity ($F = 7.53$; dfl, 35; $p < .01$) and family relationships ($F = 4.58$; df 1,35; $p < .04$), as well as on the aggregate score ($F = 4.58$; df 1,35; $p < .04$).

The blind interviewer ratings of key relatives provided the strongest support for family management benefits. No evidence of significant social impairment was found at twenty-four months in 41 per cent of family cases, compared to 6 per cent (i.e., one case) who received patient-oriented management. A repeated measures analysis of covariance, using baseline scores as covariates, was performed on the seven social performance scales.

Family management was superior on households tasks (p < .001), decision-making (p < .05), and the aggregate score (p < .02), and approached significance on leisure activities (p < .10).

The key family members' dissatisfaction with the patient's social performance showed greater difference between the conditions, with significant differences between the groups on five of the seven scales. This suggested that family participation may have led to a greater acceptance of suboptimal social functioning in the cases where disability persisted. Such changes in attitude, combined with more efficient problem-solving by the family unit, appeared to contribute to the more effective rehabilitation associated with the family-based approach (Doane and Falloon 1985).

FAMILY MORBIDITY

At the start of the study half the fifty-four parents who completed the Hopkins' Symptom Checklist, HSCL, scored within the abnormal range on at least one of the five factors: somatization, obsessive-compulsive, interpersonal sensitivity, depression, anxiety. After nine months the proportion of family-based parents with abnormal scores had dropped, whereas the trend was for parents of patient-oriented cases to show an increased proportion of abnormal scores. However, the data were skewed, with more morbidity reported by family-based patients at the initial assessment. The changes observed at nine months could have resulted from regression toward the mean.

The SBAS scales of family distress and burden suggested that family-based management was associated with greater benefits to family members than the patient-oriented approach (Falloon and Pederson 1985). Only one family (i.e., 6 per cent) who received family-based management reported moderate or severe burden at the twenty-four-month assessment. A repeated measures analysis of covariance, with baseline scores as covariates, showed a significant between-group effect (F = 14.96; df 2,33; p < .0005).

Standardized assessment of family problem-solving behaviour revealed increases in the number of constructive problem-solving statements after three months of family therapy (mean of twelve statements at baseline versus thirty-six at three months). Families in the patient-oriented condition showed no increases. A Scheffé test of pre-post difference in the number of problem solving statements was significant (α = .05; df 1,30; p < .01). Significant differences between the two treatment conditions were also noted on non-constructive statements of criticism (F = 5.25; df 1,30; p < .05) and intrusiveness (F = 5.24; df 1,30; p < .05). These latter measures are behavioural correlates of the expressed emotion indices (Miklowitz *et al.* 1984). However, the reduction in non-constructive statements associated with the family approach was less striking than the *increase* in critical and

365

intrusive remarks made by family members in the patient-oriented condition.

These laboratory ratings of family problem-solving were reflected in measures of the effectiveness with which families coped with everyday problems and life events that impinged on all household members during the first twelve months of the study. The family-oriented approach was associated with an enhancement in the effectiveness with which families coped with stresses, whereas no change was noted in the patient-oriented families. A repeated measures analysis of variance showed a significant difference between the two management conditions ($F = 26.5$; df 3,30; $p < .0001$). A fine-grained analysis revealed that although families in both conditions encountered a similar number of life events, the better coping skills of those who received behavioural family therapy appeared to prevent stress escalating into major life events. Only 4 per cent of events experienced by family-oriented households were rated major, compared with 22 per cent of those experience in patient-oriented households (Hardesty *et al.* 1985).

ECONOMIC FACTORS

A detailed assessment of the comparative costs of the two management approaches was conducted (Cardin *et al.* 1985). The direct treatment costs for the family-oriented approach averaged US$5,952 per patient (1980/81 costs) for the first year of the study. This compared with US$5,514 for the patient-oriented approach. Nearly one-third of the cost of family management comprised the cost of travel time to conduct home visits, which proved substantial in Los Angeles County. However, the indirect treatment costs, that included hospital and residential care, emergency evaluation, and rehabilitation programmes, were substantially less for the family condition ($523 versus $2,760). Total costs to the community, which included all treatment costs as well as social security benefits and law enforcement services, averaged $8,880 for family-oriented cases, and $10,908 for patient-oriented cases – a 19 per cent saving for the family approach.

CONSUMER SATISFACTION

An important consideration in the development of new services is the level of satisfaction of the consumers. This is often assessed by the number of cases who discontinue attending the service. Over the two-year programme two patients dropped out of family management; one left during the first month of treatment, the other refused to complete the family assessment procedures and was excluded on this basis. Two patient-oriented cases withdrew from the study. No patients or families refused to be considered for the study during the recruitment and stabilization phases of the study. Thus, an overall attrition rate of 10 per cent was achieved. This contrasted with very high attrition from the usual services for schizophrenia in Los Angeles County.

A questionnaire survey of the satisfaction of patients and family members with the service provided was conducted at nine and twenty-four months. This indicated that consumer satisfaction was high in both management conditions (Falloon 1985). At twenty-four months, 89 per cent of patients and 100 per cent of family members considered the family-oriented approach either 'good' or 'very good'; 94 per cent of patients and 88 per cent of family members expressed similar levels of satisfaction with patient-oriented management.

THERAPIST SATISFACTION

The importance of maintaining therapists' enthusiasm is crucial to the development of new therapeutic approaches. Throughout the study the primary therapists completed ratings of their enthusiasm for the two management approaches at six-month intervals. Although the enthusiasm for family management remained higher than that for the patient-oriented approach, there was some reduction in therapist enthusiasm for this approach during the second half of the four-year research project. During this period therapists were conducting follow-up sessions and the family cases were either functioning well, needing little active therapy, or struggling with problems that could not be resolved by any therapeutic intervention.

Of greater significance to the differential outcome of the two contrasting management approaches was a series of assessments of the therapists' attitudes towards specific patients and their families conducted at one, six and nine months. No significant differences were noted between the management conditions in the therapists' levels of attraction for the patients, or enthusiasm, effort, and support for the patients. Nor did therapists differ in their perceptions of patients' needs for services in addition to those provided by the study approaches. They did believe that the family-oriented approach provided significantly greater contact and support for the families, and that it was a more effective approach (Falloon 1985).

It may be concluded that the therapists were biased in favour of the family-oriented management. However, this bias did not appear to affect the patients' and family members' perceptions which appeared highly positive towards both approaches.

CONCLUSIONS

This study provided evidence that a psychological intervention that aimed to

367

reduce the impact of environmental stress on a person vulnerable to episodes of schizophrenia could add to the well-established benefits of long-term drug prophylaxis. A control group who received drug therapy alone was not considered feasible, because all drug therapy is supplemented by some psychosocial supportive interventions, albeit often merely to assist patients in coping with unwanted side effects and to maintain adherence to the drug regimen (Falloon 1984).

The patient-oriented comparison we employed was a clearly defined approach to provide continuous support to the patient and their family throughout the two-year study. Although this supportive approach did not appear to add to the clinical stabilizing effects of the drug therapy, there is little doubt that it provided benefits for many patients and their families in the overall management of their conditions. Only one-sixth of these patients and families were rated as experiencing no clinical, social, or family benefits over the two years. Mirror-image comparisons of the two years before and after entry to the study showed substantial reductions in the time spent in hospital during the study period.

Comprehensive crisis intervention that was available around the clock provided substantial support for patients and their families and probably contributed to the reduction in burden that many patient-oriented families reported, despite continued episodes of clinical instability.

Despite the apparent excellence of the community-based service provided in patient-oriented management, this approach did not appear to alter the course of the clinical morbidity of schizophrenia in a manner that would readily justify the extra costs involved. In contrast, the family-oriented approach appeared to provide substantial clinical, social, family and economic benefits. Similar benefits have been observed now in a series of studies that have compared family-based stress management methods with patient-based methods. There can be little doubt that these psychological interventions add to the prophylaxis of optimal drug therapy in a significant manner (Strachan 1986). The key question for future research is what are the clinical components of these interventions that are associated with these benefits.

It has been suggested that the benefits are achieved on the basis of improved adherence to drug therapy (Macmillan 1987). However, the clinical, social, and family morbidity associated with optimal pharmacotherapy for schizophrenia when adherence is assumed in trials of depot preparations is similar to that found in the patient-oriented management conditions (Falloon et al. 1978a, 1978b; Schooler et al. 1980; Hogarty et al. 1979). Although there was some evidence for inadequate adherence to drug regimens in this study, there was little evidence that this precipitated major exacerbations. Poor compliance with drugs appears to be a consequence of deteriorating cognitive function associated with florid episodes of schizophrenia, almost as often as it appears to precede such episodes.

However, it is extremely difficult to define the precise time that florid episodes begin. In clinic-based settings patients will avoid disclosing the earliest signs of cognitive dysfunction that presage a major exacerbation. A clear advantage of a family approach is the ability of family members to observe and report the earliest signs of behavioural disturbance and thereby alert the mental health team long before the patient may report symptoms. Furthermore, where patient and family have been alerted to links between environmental stressors and florid symptoms, they may begin looking for early signs after a stressful event, particularly where efforts to resolve the stress have proven unrewarding. The benefits of this collaboration between patient, family, and mental health professionals cannot be underestimated. But it is apparent that behavioural family therapy tended to facilitate its development. It is possible that this could have been achieved if the patient-oriented treatment sessions had also been conducted in the home.

One unexpected benefit of the family approach was the trend towards lower doses of medication (Moss *et al.* 1985). This may have contributed to the improved social functioning that was observed in this condition. Studies of low dosage pharmacotherapy have suggested that, despite a slightly higher frequency of minor exacerbation, improvements in social functioning, and a lower risk of side effects such as tardive dyskinesia, can be achieved (Kane 1983). If improved stability of florid symptoms can be promoted by combining low doses of neuroleptics with behavioural family interventions, this would seem to represent a major advance in the long-term management of schizophrenia. A multi-centred controlled trial is in progress to examine the interaction between behavioural family interventions and optimal, low (i.e., one-fifth the optimal dose), and targeted dose (i.e., drug given only when exacerbations begin to emerge) drug regimens. Two family approaches of differing intensity are compared: one similar to the method we have developed; the other a monthly family meeting that focuses on teaching families the practical skills of coping with the specific behavioural deficits that are associated with schizophrenia. The NIMH study should help advance our knowledge of the potential synergism between drug and psychosocial interventions.

It has been suggested that merely educating patients and their caregivers about schizophrenia and its management may enhance the clinical outcome. In a recently completed study Tarrier and Barrowclough and their colleagues (in press) demonstrated that education alone was insufficient to induce any major changes in the course of schizophrenia. However, a course that assisted families in resolving problems associated with the management of the disorder was effective in reducing clinical morbidity. However, benefits in terms of enhanced social functioning were not achieved by this essentially patient-focused approach.

The methodological difficulties of conducting research on multi-modal long-term management approaches are considerable. Despite this there is a substantial body of evidence that suggests that specific psychological interventions may enhance the outcome of schizophrenia and add to the benefits that can be achieved through drug therapy and psychosocial support. These methods are all effective in reducing the impact of environmental stress in the day-to-day lives of the patients. To date, lasting benefits and improvements in the quality of the lives of patients and caregivers have been limited to the behavioural family therapy method which has been shown to be highly cost-effective (Macmillan *et al.* 1987).

Several field trials of this method are being conducted in the US and Europe to examine its effectiveness in clinical settings. One such programme in Buckingham is examining the value of employing behavioural family management and low-dose neuroleptics to treat schizophrenia in its prodromal phase. Multi-disciplinary mental health teams have been integrated with primary care services in an effort to detect schizophrenia early in its development and to provide immediate intensive treatment. Early indications suggest new episodes of schizophrenia can be prevented by these interventions.

It would appear that the technology is now available that should enable persons who develop schizophrenia and their caregivers to enjoy lives relatively unrestricted by major clinical episodes or substantial functional disability. the introduction of such services is unlikely to prove costly, and may contribute to substantial savings in public expenditure, even in the initial phases of deployment. Continued research aimed at refining the components of drug and psychological interventions and the manner in which they are combined in the management of schizophrenia may prove as rewarding as the search for the causes of this disorder.

REFERENCES

Birley, J.L.T. and Brown, G.W. (1970) 'Crises and life changes preceding the onset or relapse of acute schizophrenia: clinical aspects', *British Journal of Psychiatry* 116: 327–33.

Brown, G.W., Birley, J.L.T., and Wing, J.K. (1972) 'Influence of family life on the course of schizophrenic disorders: a replication', *British Journal of Psychiatry* 121: 241–58.

Brown, G.W. and Harris, T.O. (1978) *Social Origins of Depression*, London: Tavistock.

Cardin, V.A., McGill, C.W., and Falloon, I.R.H. (1985) 'An economic analysis: costs, benefits and effectiveness', in I.R.H. Falloon (ed.) *Family Management of Schizophrenia*, Baltimore: Johns Hopkins University Press.

Creer, C. and Wing, J.K. (1974) *Schizophrenia at Home*, Surrey: National Schizophrenia Fellowship.

Derogatis, L.R., Lipman, R.S., Rickels, K., Uhlenhuth, E.H., and Cori, L. (1974) 'The Hopkins Symptom Checklist (HSCL)', in P. Pichot (ed.) *Modern Problems in Pharmacopsychiatry*, Basel: Karger.

Doane, J.A. and Falloon, I.R.H. (1985) 'Assessing change in family interaction: methodology and findings', in I.R.H. Falloon (ed.) *Family Management of Schizophrenia*, Baltimore: Johns Hopkins University Press.

Dunham, H.W. and Weinberg, S.K. (1960) *The Culture of the State Mental Hospital,* Detroit: Wayne State University Press.

Falloon, I.R.H. (1984) 'Developing and maintaining adherence to long-term drug-taking regimens: a behavioural analysis', *Schizophrenia Bulletin* 10: 412–17.

Falloon, I.R.H. (ed.) (1985) *Family Management of Schizophrenia: A Controlled Study of Clinical, Social, Family and Economic Benefits,* Baltimore: Johns Hopkins University Press.

Falloon, I.R.H., Boyd, J.L. and McGill, C.W. (1984) *Family Care of Schizophrenia,* New York: Guilford Publications.

Falloon, I.R.H. and Pederson, J. (1985) 'Family management in the prevention of morbidity of schizophrenia: The adjustment of the family unit', *British Journal of Psychiatry* 147: 156–63.

Falloon, I.R.H., Watt, D.C., and Shepherd, M. (1978a) 'A comparative controlled trial of pimozide and fluphenazine deconoate in the continuation therapy of schizophrenia', *Psychological Medicine* 8: 59–70.

Falloon, I.R.H., Watt, D.C., and Shepherd, M. (1978b) 'The social outcome of patients in a trial of long-term continuation therapy in schizophrenia: pimozide versus fluphenazine', *Psychological Medicine* 8: 265–74.

Goldstein, M.J., Rodnick, E.H., Evans, J.R., May, P.R., and Steinberg, M. (1978) 'Drug and family therapy in the aftercare treatment of acute schizophrenia', *Archives of General Psychiatry* 35: 1169–77.

Hardesty, J.P., Falloon, I.R.H., and Shirin, K. (1985) 'The impact of life events, stress and coping on the morbidity of schizophrenia', in I.R.H. Falloon (ed.) *Family Management of Schizophrenia: A Study of Clinical, Social, Family and Economic Benefits,* Baltimore: Johns Hopkins University Press.

Hogarty, G.E., Schooler, N.R., Ulrich, R.F. *et al.* (1979) 'Fluphenazine and social therapy in the aftercare of schizophrenic patients: Relapse analyses of a two-year controlled trial, *Archives of General Psychiatry* 36: 1283–94.

Kane, J.M. (1983) 'Low dose medication strategies in the maintenance treatment of schizophrenia', *Schizophrenia Bulletin* 9: 29–33.

Leff, J.P., Hirsch, S.R., Gaind, R., Rohde, P.D., and Stevens, B.C. (1973) 'Life-events and maintenance therapy in schizophrenic relapse', *British Journal of Psychiatry* 123: 659–60.

Leff, J. and Vaughn, C. (1980) 'The interaction of life events and relatives' expressed emotion in schizophrenia and depressive neurosis', *British Journal of Psychiatry* 136: 146–53.

Macmillan, J.F. (1987) 'Expressed emotion and relapse in first episodes of schizophrenia', *British Journal of Psychiatry* 151: 320–3.

Miklowitz, D., Goldstein, M.J., Falloon, I.R.H., and Doane, J.A. (1984) 'Interactional correlates of expressed emotion in the families of schizophrenics', *British Journal of Psychiatry* 144: 482–7.

Moss, H.B., MacDonald, N., Falloon, I.R.H., and Simpson, G.M. (1985) 'Biological factors affecting the outcome of schizophrenia', in I.R.H. Falloon (ed.) *Family Management of Schizophrenia: A Study of Clinical, Social, Family and Economic Benefits,* Baltimore: Johns Hopkins University Press.

Overall, J.E. and Gorham, D.R. (1962) 'The brief psychiatric rating scale', *Psychological Reports* 10: 799–812.

Platt, S., Weyman, A., Hirsch, S., and Hewett, S. (1980) 'The social behaviour assessment schedule (SBAS): rationale, contents, scoring and reliability of a new interview schedule', *Social Psychiatry* 15: 43–55.

Schooler, N.R., Levine, J., Severe, J.B. *et al.* (1980) 'Prevention of relapse in schizophrenia: an evaluation of fluphenazine decanoate', *Archives of General Psychiatry* 37: 16–24.

Strachan, A.M. (1986) 'Family intervention for the rehabilitation of schizophrenia: towards protection and coping', *Schizophrenia Bulletin* 12: 678–98.

Vaughn, C. (1977) 'Interaction characteristics in families of schizophrenic patients' in H. Katschnig (ed.) *Die andere Seite der Schizophrenie*, Vienna: Urban and Schwarzenberg.

Vaughn, E.E. and Leff, J.P. (1976a) 'The measurement of expressed emotion in the families of psychiatric patients', *British Journal of Social and Clinical Psychology* 15: 157–65.

Vaughn, C.E. and Leff, J.P. (1976b) 'The influence of family and social factors on the course of psychiatric illness: a comparison of schizophrenia and depressed neurotic patients', *British Journal of Psychiatry* 129: 125–37.

Vaughn, C.E., Snyder, K.S., Jones, S., Freeman, W.B., and Falloon, I.R.H. (1984) 'Family factors in schizophrenic relapse: a California replication of the British research on expressed emotion', *Archives of General Psychiatry* 41: 1169–77.

Weissman, M.M., Prusoff, B.A., Thompson, W.D., Harding, P.S., and Myers, J.K. (1978) 'Social adjustment by self-report in a community sample and in psychiatric outpatients', *Journal of Nervous and Mental Disease* 166: 317–26.

Wing, J.K. (1978) 'Social influences on the course of schizophrenia', in L.C. Wynne, R.L. Cromwell, and S. Matthysse (eds.) *The Nature of Schizophrenia*, New York: Wiley.

Wing, J.K., Bennett, D.H., and Denham, J. (1964) *The Industrial Rehabilitation of Long-Stay Schizophrenic Patients* (Medical Research Council Memo No. 42), London: HMSO.

Wing, J.K., Cooper, J.E., and Sartorius, N. (1974) *The Measurement and Classification of Psychiatric Symptoms*, London: Cambridge University Press.

Service Organization

24

Appraisal of Institutional Psychiatry

David Watt

A recent writer on the evaluation of psychiatric services observed that

> The evaluation of the psychiatric service of a community is a conceptually
> and technically difficult venture which calls for the exercise of a range of
> methods of epidemiological research and social enquiry . . . For the
> greater part of this enterprise, careful and comprehensive data collection
> is required. (Cawley 1983)

NATIONAL STATISTICS

National statistics clearly constitute 'comprehensive data collection' and are
typified in their most recent publication (DHSS 1980). This deals with
England only, a population of 46.4 million, and was the last of a series of
public productions from the National Mental Health Inquiry by which the
Ministry of Health collected information from all National Health Service
psychiatric hospitals on an individual patient basis. Returns were made for
each patient on admission and on discharge, or death, which recorded in standardized form comprehensive demographic information with some hospital
and social particulars. Diagnosis was the sole specifically clinical datum. This
information is arranged in the form of tables to show numbers of hospital
residents, admissions, discharges, and deaths which are divided according to
the type of hospital (psychiatric, general hospital unit, secure, and mental
handicap) and administrative Regions of the Health Service. They make a
separation of first admissions from readmissions because from readmission
tables the number of readmission events cannot be separated from the number
of persons involved, whereas for first admissions the number of events and
the number of persons is the same which, with knowledge of the size and
age-structure of the parent population, allows a calculation of the incidence
rate for mental disorder generally and for particular diagnoses. Variations in
incidence become manifest between Regions, and different types of service

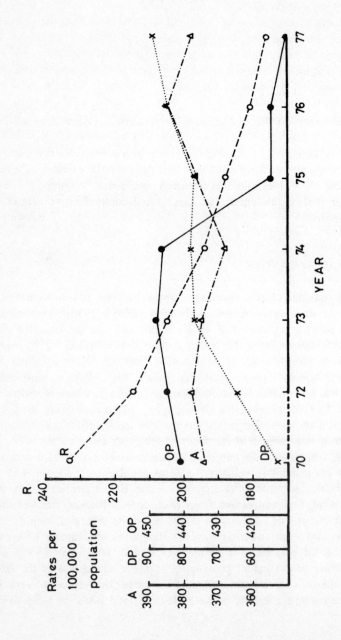

Figure 24.1 National statistics 1970–77 of psychiatric hospital residents (R, ○——○), day patients (DP, ×-----×), out-patients (OP, ●——●) and admissions (A, △-----△).

Source Adapted from HMSO, 1980, p. 8.

(e.g. psychiatric hospitals and general hospital units) can be compared in this respect. Mortality rates and duration of stay can be used in a comparison of outcome. Tables are broken down by sex and age, showing, among other effects, the increase of mental disorder with increasing age and its excess in females.

The understanding afforded by national statistics is considerably increased by the examination of figures for consecutive years. These bring to light trends which may occur in association with social changes (e.g. in the incidence of alcoholism or drug addiction) or the introduction of new treatments. However, it is the effect of policy change that arouses most interest. Figure 24.1 shows data for psychiatric in-patients, against those for out-patients and day-patients for the years 1970–77. This shows an increase in day hospital attenders coincident with a decrease in hospital residents on which the commentary observes that 'The overall picture which emerges is of a shift away from in-patient care towards more prolonged or intensive out-patient and day care – this is, of course, the intention under the new pattern of services.' This interpretation, however, leaves out of account the simultaneous decrease in new out-patient attenders which the table also discloses, suggesting the equally probable explanation that the increase in day-patients accommodates a transfer of those who would formerly have been out-patients. Clearly interpretation of the aerial view which national statistics afford must be guided by detailed knowledge of the terrain.

A JOINT SURVEY OF THREE PSYCHIATRIC HOSPITALS

A sharper focus is brought to bear in a regional survey of psychiatric hospital performance undertaken by Norris (1959) in a London population of 1.7 million, which comprised the defined catchment population of three hospitals, each with over 2,000 beds. Particulars of all admissions to these hospitals during the triennium 1947–9 were extracted from case notes and administrative records. A follow-up from administrative records showing outcome of all admissions in terms of mortality and readmission to hospital was maintained until the end of 1951.

Data are presented for these mental hospitals as representative of London as a whole. The three hospitals are compared in respect of first admission rates, divided by sex, diagnosis, and age, totalling forty-two items of comparison. These, as would be expected, show many similarities, for instance, that in all three hospitals the rate for schizophrenia in persons below the age of thirty is substantially higher for men than for women. Less likely to be anticipated is the fact that in half of the comparisons there is a significant (p < 0.01) difference between hospitals in first admission rates. This is striking in the case of psychoses of old age where the difference in the male rates per million of the general population for hospitals 2 and 3 are 376 and 1,370 respectively and the female rates for hospitals 1 and 3 are 521 and 1,798. Such differences draw attention to what the author has designated 'nosocomial influences'; in the comparison just cited, the fact that psychogeriatric patients were more freely admitted to hospital 3, as a matter of policy, than to the other two hospitals.

To reduce the numerous, overlapping, and disputed diagnoses by which the multifarious conditions and behaviours encountered in persons admitted to a mental hospital are labelled to a manageable, reliable, and comprehensible form, the author adopts a broad classification under the four headings: schizophrenia, manic depressive psychosis, mental disorder of old age, other psychiatric disorder. The 'old age' category covers first admissions diagnosed as pre-senile, senile, and cerebrovascular psychoses, and confusional states in subjects of at least sixty years of age. The last category includes toxic, alcoholic, and epileptic conditions, organic psychoses (other than cerebrovascular), neuroses, mental deficiency, disorders of behaviour, and character, and ill-defined conditions in those under 60 years of age. Separate chapters show data obtained from the survey which are tabulated separately for each of these four groupings and for their constituent diagnostic categories. First admission rates (based on the general population) give the numerical expectation at which particular diseases will occur in populations of known composition in terms of age, sex, and civil state. Outcome is similarly quantified for each category of disease in terms of discharge rates (by age, sex, and civil state) according to time since admission, mortality, duration of stay in hospital, frequency and duration of readmissions in the two years following discharge, and the proportion of patients remaining in hospital according to time since admission. Besides allowing a comparison in both expectation and outcome between the diagnostic categories adopted, these data, using information routinely and uniformly collected by hospitals and administrative bodies, provide a baseline for comparison between hospitals and between regions, and for the appraisal of varying types of service. The large numbers here (e.g. 2,279 schizophrenics of whom more than half were first admissions), the definition of catchment areas and their populations, the detailed local knowledge (e.g. of population structure, of diagnostic conventions; of preferential admission of specific diagnostic categories to particular hospitals), together with the author's combined medical, statistical, and epidemiological expertise, gave the findings of this survey and the authors' reservations particular authority and value for comparative purposes.

COMPARATIVE SURVEY AT SEPARATE PERIODS IN A SINGLE HOSPITAL

A different design is adopted in a study (Shepherd 1957) in which, instead of an interhospital comparison, a single hospital is compared at two periods of time (1931–3, 1945–7) between which social influences and the direction of policy changed considerably. A notable feature of this study was the considered choice of the hospital selected for study because of uncommon features in its situation favourable to precise definition and representativeness of the population served. The catchment area (about 400,000) was limited by the boundaries of an administrative county and had remained so for eighty years and was characterized by a fairly even balance of urban and rural character. The hospital had a central position within the catchment area for which the staff formed virtually the only source of psychiatric service. The choice of periods for study ensured that upheavals of the war years were avoided. The choice of the starting year of the study to coincide with the year of national census secured the most accurate denominator available for the calculation of rates. The maximum statutory bed provision during the periods of study was 600 (1.5 per 1,000, acute and long-stay) but occupation reached 800.

The aims of the study were to produce estimates of minimal incidence of illness, demand on hospital resources, outcome and variation of these features with time. Outcome was judged by duration of stay in hospital, readmissions, and mortality during the period of index admission and during a five-year follow-up period. For each triennium of the study first admission and readmission rates are given by sex, age, diagnosis, marital status, and legal status (voluntary or detained). Outcome is reported in the same categories in terms of discharge, transfer, continued residence or death in hospital, readmissions in the five years following discharge, and the time spent in and out of hospital during the five-year follow-up.

A substantially improved outcome is demonstrated for patients admitted during later triennium, in that less time was spent in hospital during the index admission and follow-up; continuous residence and mortality were reduced. At the same time, more frequent readmission during follow-up of patients admitted with a history of previous admission and greater numbers of female patients admitted in the later period adumbrated national trends prominent during subsequent decades, while the increased mean age of admissions was premonitory of the overwhelming surge in elderly psychiatric admissions, consequent upon the life-prolonging advances made in medicine, which have since required large administrative and policy adjustments.

The single hospital, relatively encapsulated population, and unitary psychiatric service studied here provide a reliable basis for estimating incidence and outcome. Detailed knowledge of social pressures on the service and the response in terms of policy make possible a firm quantitative

379

indication of the predominant influences, among which nosocomial factors are prominent, on indices of performance and outcome. The hospital had, for instance, 800 beds for a population of 500,000, which is sparse compared with the London hospitals in Norris's survey (1959), each of which had approximately the same catchment population as the Buckinghamshire hospital and around 2,000 beds. This discrepancy is reflected in overall first admission rates (per million per annum) which for the three London hospitals in 1949 were 791, 599 and 1,079 respectively (average 823) while for the Aylesbury hospital for 1931–3 and 1945–7 they were 434 and 395; that is, the average rate for the London hospitals was double that of the hospital in Buckinghamshire.

In the London and Buckinghamshire surveys performance and outcome of the institutional psychiatric service are evaluated entirely in terms of socio-demographic features of the general population, of the population admitted to hospital and the statistics of hospital events (admission, discharge, and death). These data sources have the advantages of being recorded routinely, precise, and suitable for statistical manipulation. They can be appraised in the perspective of national figures. Interpretation, however, which requires circumspection and illumination from local knowledge, is often tentative and inconclusive, demanding softer data to flesh out the skeletal framework such studies provide.

HOSPITAL EVALUATION USING CLINICAL AND BEHAVIOURAL OBSERVATIONS INCLUDING THE EFFECT ON FAMILY

In a prospective comparative evaluation of three hospitals, Brown and his colleagues (1966) extended their enquiry to include clinical progress and social functioning of patients. The hospitals surveyed had catchment populations ranging from 400,000 (hospital 3) to 650,000 (hospital 1) each with roughly 3,000 beds per million population. The areas they served were mainly: Hospital 1, the periphery of South London; Hospital 2, the compact industrial city of Nottingham and its surroundings; Hospital 3, a scattered rural area of Essex including three small towns and also a section of east London periphery. The feature of these hospitals most pertinent to the investigation, however, lay in the differing philosophy which informed and moulded the organization of their services: 1 emphasized an active rehabilitation programme within the hospital and aimed not to discharge patients before employment was available or, preferably, had been tried before departure; 2 had the poorest facilities both within the hospital and extramurally; 3 concentrated on early discharge of patients, mobilization of extramural services, and support for relatives undertaking care. The authors' purpose was to measure the effect of these differences in organization of service on the five-year outcome of schizophrenia.

For this purpose, during 1956, all patients admitted aged 15–59 whose address lay in the catchment area and where schizophrenia was exclusively diagnosed from hospital case records (independently by two psychiatrists applying prescribed criteria) formed a cohort for each of the three hospitals. Negligible numbers of patients from the catchment areas were found to have been admitted to other hospitals or to have been treated (in the case of hospital 3) without admission. Comparability of the three cohorts was checked in respect of socio-demographic data and no significant initial differences were apparent.

Information during follow-up, besides being provided from hospital, out-patient and after-care agencies, and employment records, was obtained by interview at home visit with the patient and separately with a relative. The interview was free in form but covered prescribed topics. To ensure uniformity the senior interviewer attended every tenth interview and the interviewers compared their procedures regularly. In this way clinical state, duration and competence in employment (including house-keeping and care of children), decline in occupational status, time unoccupied, leisure activity and recreation were assessed and given numerical value or ordinated.

Symptomatology which issued as decline or disruption in patients' social behaviour during a six-month period was recorded. Threats, violence, and destructiveness; slowness and withdrawal; inappropriate and embarrassing behaviour; moods and invalidism were recorded and each item rated minimal, moderate, or marked according to the degree of social disturbance each caused.

The restrictions and other disadvantages experienced by relatives were recorded and included limitation of employment, leisure, and social life; distress and ill-health; adverse effect on children; financial and accommodation difficulties. Both the patients' behaviour and the effect on relatives were quantified in terms of frequency, duration, and severity. The association of domestic living group (parents, wives, dependent children, supporting children) with outcome of patient's illness was assessed.

Table 24.1 shows how these indices of outcome were distributed in the three hospitals which are labelled 1. high standard hospital care; 2. community care; and 3. low standard hospital care, as a crude shorthand indication of their main difference in character. The distinction between hospital 2 (community care) and hospitals 1 and 3 is highlighted in the markedly shorter duration of admissions in hospital 2, the longer time spent in community care, the greater use of out-patient consultation, day hospital, and visits by mental welfare officers (MWO). There were no statistically significant differences between the three hospitals on the measures of outcome but certain tendencies appear; notably, the greater time spent employed in the community by patients in hospital 2, their higher proportion of disturbed behaviour, and the higher proportion of their children adversely affected. The trends are most prominent when the community care hospital

381

Table 24.1 Comparison of three hospitals, in terms of various criteria employed, during five-year follow-up

	Hospital 1: High hospital care	Hospital 2: Community care	Hospital 3: Low hospital care
Hospital criteria			
% time spent in hospital	30	20	31
% subjects readmitted	55	70	62
Community care criteria			
Average OP attendances per patient	1.4	2.1	1.1
% time in day hospital (final year)	0.3	14.0	–
MWO routine visits in final year	1.5	48.0	1.5
Duration under community care	8 times more in hospital 2 than in 1 and 3		
Patient criteria			
Employment			
% time employed for first admissions	62	60	47
% time employed for readmissions	31	20	26
% time in community unemployed for 1st admissions	9	28	26
% time in community unemployed for readmissions	20	48	28
Clinical			
% chronic course of illess (first and previous admissions combined)	41	41	40
Behavioural			
% disturbed behaviour for first admissions	65	63	66
% disturbed behaviour for readmissions	58	74	73
% danger to self or others for first admissions	25	39	19
% danger to self or others for readmissions	30	44	41
Effect on relatives			
% having three or more problems	18	41	28
% health affected	36	43	37
% children adversely affected	15	59	41
% relatives expressing welcoming attitude	86	63	74

Source: Brown *et al.* 1980.
MWO = mental welfare officer; OP = outpatient

(2) is compared with hospital 1 (high standard of in-patient care). An overall index of severe disability during the final six months of follow-up was constructed from the three most valid indices of outcome (hospitalization, severe disturbance, unemployment). By this meaure 35–45 per cent of first admissions and 59–66 per cent of readmissions suffered serious handicap in follow-up and there were no statistically significant differences between the hospitals.

In discussing their results, the authors refer to 'the reservations that must be attached to any conclusions drawn from the comparative data' and are restrained by a number of these reservations in expressing their own judgements. However, even allowing for their provisos, it can be firmly concluded that no superiority was demonstrated for community care over an accomplished high standard of hospital care as judged by the patients' clinical and social outcome, employment, the extent of disturbed or dangerous behaviour in the community, the adverse effects and disadvantages for relatives and children.

THE RELATION BETWEEN ENVIRONMENT AND INSTITUTIONALISM

In a subsequent study using the same three hospitals, the authors (Wing and Brown 1970) narrowed the field of examination, bringing into sharper focus the syndrome of 'institutionalism' which, although not confined to psychiatric hospitals, was first identified in these institutions, and has become a major charge in their blanket indictment. 'Institutionalism' appears in chronic schizophrenia as clusters of characteristic clinical features (Liddle 1987), comprising withdrawal, flatness of affect, poverty or incoherence of speech, coherent delusions, socially inappropriate behaviour, and hospital dependence. By the use of standardized scales these items were scored for a cohort of long-stay female schizophrenics at each of the three hospitals. Similarly, the social milieu of the hospitals was assessed in terms of patients' personal possessions, time spent unoccupied, occupation, contacts with the outside world, and restriction of spontaneous activity, to give indices of environmental poverty.

Over a period of four years a programme of improvement was undertaken at the hospitals. The measures of social milieu were repeated at the end of this time and all showed a substantial reduction of environmental poverty. Similarly, assessment of the clinical items characterizing institutionalism was repeated and showed an overall amelioration of this condition in a third of patients, which was most marked in hospital 3 which had originally shown the most severe degree of environmental poverty and of 'institutionalism' in patients.

A further refinement of the method used in this comparison of hospitals was the demonstration of associations between specific items of hospital

383

environmental poverty and particular features of institutionalism in patients. For instance, those patients who showed greatest increase in the proportion of time for which they were employed and decrease in time for which they were unoccupied showed greatest improvement in clinical features of institutionalism.

INTERNATIONAL COMPARISON OF HOSPITALS

It could not be assumed that the measures employed in the appraisal of hospitals in these studies would be applicable to all psychiatric hospitals in Britain and still less to those in other countries. In the case of indices derived from administrative records (e.g. duration of hospital stay), discrepancies in computing (e.g. through the method of recording patients' leave) will probably be discovered in preliminary scrutiny and taken into account. However, discrepancies in less standard, culture-bound features which are not routinely recorded (e.g. measures of hospital social milieu) are less likely to be readily evident. To test the feasibility of generalization Wing and Brown (1970) undertook a comparison of a British and an American hospital in respect of hospital environmental standards and the level of institutional syndrome in patients. The British hospital was number 2 in the study already described, a standard county mental hospital responsible for the care of all types of psychiatric illness, which had developed community care services to a degree exceptional at the time of this study. The American hospital was a relatively small unit (325 inmates) specializing in the care of long-stay patients with psychiatrically unqualified staff. Forty-five residents similar to the sample from the British hospital were selected for comparison. Assessments of social withdrawal, socially embarrassing behaviour, and patient attitude to discharge were made as had been done for the British hospital cohort, giving a measure of 'institutionalism'. Similarly, the measures of hospital social milieu that had been made in the comparison of British hospitals were applied in the American hospital. These two hospitals could thus be compared for significant features. The American hospital, for instance, adopted a more protective policy towards women patients which resulted in a notably higher average ward restrictiveness score for the American women (22.9) than for the British women (11.9) and there was a significant excess in average social withdrawal scores in the American (3.9) over British patients (2.3). The experience and results of this preliminary study enabled the authors to conclude that 'a full-scale comparative survey of the kind outlined here is feasible', provided that modifications are made to take account of sampling problems and socio-demographic differences and that 'under these conditions tentative hypothesis testing might be possible even using international comparisons'.

EVALUATION OF PSYCHIATRIC SERVICE AS CONTROLLED TRIAL

The appraisal of a psychiatric service involves comparison of the service to be evaluated with the measured outcome of an evaluated alternative. It shares its essential principle with that of the controlled trial; here two populations, identical in all respects except for the item to be evaluated, are compared as to the effect of the item for evaluation. Criteria for detecting and measuring the effect(s) of the item(s) for evaluation must be standardized and applied impartially to both populations. The widespread application and analysis of the controlled clinical trial during the last forty years has secured considerable refinement in the adaptations required in rigorously applying the principle in varying practical circumstances. Although the studies in the evaluation of institutional psychiatry examined here demonstrate the practical feasibility of the principle, application has been dilatory and little progress has been made. This is particularly true of 'community care' service which, as front-runner in the race to replace psychiatric hospitals, needs to know the direction in which it is heading and whether it can stand the pace or last the distance.

REFERENCES

Brown, G.W., Bone, M., Dalison, B., and Wing, J.K. (1966) *Schizophrenia and Social Care*, London: Oxford University Press.

Cawley, R.H. (1983) in M. Shepherd and O.L. Zangwill (eds) *Handbook of Psychiatry, Volume 1*, Cambridge: Cambridge University Press, 242.

Department of Health and Social Security (1980) *In-patient Statistics from the Mental Health Enquiry for England, 1977* (Statistical and research report series no. 23), London: HMSO.

Liddle, P.F. (1987) 'The symptoms of chronic schizophrenia: a re-examination of the positive-negative dichotomy', *British Journal of Psychiatry* 151: 145–51.

Norris, V. (1959) *Mental Illness in London*, London: Chapman and Hall.

Shepherd, M. (1957) *A Study of the Major Psychoses in an English County*, London: Chapman and Hall.

Wing, J.K. and Brown, G.W. (1970) *Institutionalism and Schizophrenia*, Cambridge: Cambridge University Press.

25

Evaluating Community Psychiatric Services

Michele Tansella

In the past twenty years there has been an increasing interest in the evaluation of health care delivery systems. This has been mainly due to the need for a more efficient utilization of resources in an era of steadily increasing costs. In mental health care a gradual move from hospital to community care, with substantial changes in the organization and use of mental health services, occurred in the same period, and this has also emphasized the importance of descriptive and evaluative studies.

In the report of a WHO symposium on *Trends in Psychiatric Care* it is stated: 'All participants accepted the need for evaluation of new services. It is no longer advisable to set up a new service alone. Its objectives must be stated and ways and means devised for assessing how far its aims are achieved' (WHO 1971: 14). The same point was made some fifteen years later by Professor John Wing, who underlined the importance of ensuring that 'planning and evaluation go hand in hand' (Wing 1986: 36) and pointed out the differences between policy makers and evaluators in their approach to the process of evaluation, as well as the utility of creative collaboration.

Similar statements on the importance of evaluating psychiatric services have often been made in the last two decades. In spite of this long history of suggestions and good advice for a wider evaluative approach to the delivery of mental health care, in recent years there has been much more planning and implementation than services evaluation. Moreover, there are no good reasons to be optimistic about creative collaboration between planners and researchers so far (Sartorius 1982; Kreitman 1984; Tansella 1985) and this possibility remains an interesting challenge for the future.

Several volumes on the evaluation of psychiatric services have appeared to date (Gruenberg 1966; Williams and Ozarin 1968; Wing and Hailey 1972; Wing and Häfner 1973; Feldman and Windle 1973; Struening and Guttentag 1975; Guttentag and Struening 1975; Coursey *et al.* 1977; EEC 1981; Wing 1982; Stahler and Tash 1982). However, the literature on evaluation research which goes beyond the descriptive stage is relatively scanty and the evidence on one particular aspect of evaluation, namely cost-benefit analysis, is inconclusive (Glass and Goldberg 1977; Frank 1981; McGuire and Weisbrod 1981; Weisbrod 1982; Wilkinson and Pelosi 1987).

In spite of recent progress on data gathering and processing and of the increasing availability of indicators of service use as well as standardized instruments for psychological and psychiatric assessment, there is still a long way to go to make the cycle of planning and evaluation of mental health care a productive one.

The aims of this chapter are, first, to focus on the aspects of evaluation which are particularly relevant for community psychiatric services and, second, to describe the first steps in the evaluation of the South-Verona Community Psychiatric Service (CPS), a new service set up in 1978 according to the provision of the Italian psychiatric reform.

DEFINITIONS

The title of this chapter contains two key concepts which need to be defined: evaluation and community psychiatric services. According to Sartorius (1983: 59): 'Evaluation at its best is a systematic way of learning from experience and using the lessons learned to improve both current and future action. At its worst, it is an activity used to justify the selection of a scapegoat for past failures.' Twenty years ago Suchman (1967) used the term 'evaluative research', stating that it is appropriate when scientific methods and techniques are used in making an evaluation. On the other hand, Roemer (1972) pointed out that, at its highest level, the evaluation of health services measures the extent to which the ultimate objective of a programme – an improvement in the health of the people serviced – has been attained. But, he observed, if this is the best type of evaluation to undertake, doubtless it is also the most difficult. One could argue that, of course, a clear outcome measure may be obtained only when the objectives to be achieved have been clearly identified and made explicit in advance, in the planning phase of the programme. In other words the evaluative process must start in the planning phase. Schulberg (1977) called the function of assessing the degree to which the objectives are being accomplished as the 'assessment of performance', to be differentiated from the 'assessment of adequacy' which refers to re-evaluating the validity of objectives and providing feedback, through the recycling of information, to systems change. The latter approach, which views programme outcomes from a more global perspective, has been referred to by Bachrach (1980, 1982) as 'impact evaluation'.

As may be seen from these definitions, the process of evaluating mental health services should be a timely, long-term, and complex process, and different approaches and strategies as well as various techniques need to be used. I will come back to this issue later.

As far as the terms 'community psychiatric services' and 'community care'

are concerned, I have discussed in a previous paper several definitions and their implications (Tansella 1986). It is worthwhile to recall here the risk that 'that over used word community' (Acheson 1985: 3) degenerates into a slogan and loses its actual meaning, becoming a generic expression to label different, not homogeneous functions and institutions. In this context, community care, as applied to mental health, is intended as:

A system of care devoted to a defined population and based on a comprehensive and integrated mental health service, which includes outpatient facilities, day and residential training centres, residential accommodation in hostels, sheltered workshops and inpatient units in general hospital and which ensures [with multidisciplinary team work], early diagnosis, prompt treatment, continuity of care, social support and a close liaison with other medical and social community services and, in particular, with general practitioners.   (Tansella 1986: 664)

HISTORICAL BACKGROUND

Historical perspectives in evaluating mental health care have been outlined by Cooper and Morgan (1973), by Sartorius and Harding (1984) as well as by Coursey (1977), who made particular reference to the American scene. It is sufficient to mention here that some evaluative-type activity took place as early as the mid-1800s in mental hospitals, in the form of tabulating admissions, discharges, and deaths. This record system, usually independent of individual case notes, 'monitored the demography and economy of a closed institution' (Sartorius and Harding 1984: 228). Afterwards hospital statistics became more patient-oriented and included information on diagnosis, treatment, and natural evolution of psychiatric disorders. The implementation of new extramural mental health services, often consisting of various independent agencies, together with the change of focus of treatment from the mental hospital to this more dispersed community-based system of care, demanded more sophisticated and integrated approaches in the description and evaluation of care provided. It became necessary, wherever possible for evaluation to be a continuing process rather than an isolated, occasional activity. Instruments for the assessments of specific conditions were developed (Sartorius and Harding 1984) while psychiatric case registers covering defined population areas proved to be, in many parts of the world, valuable and potent tools for monitoring and evaluating mental health services (Wing and Fryers 1976; Gibbons et al. 1984). The methodology derived from the work of social scientists and the availability of computers and of advanced databases recently made possible a wide range of other approaches, such as goal attainment, management by objectives, and systems analysis (Coursey 1977). However, until now evaluators have not gone very far along these new roads.

DESCRIPTIVE AND EVALUATIVE RESEARCH. FROM MONITORING SERVICE ACTIVITIES TO EVALUATING THEIR EFFICACY AND OUTCOME

Although 'it is never possible to be purely descriptive' (Wing 1972: 27), a distinction should be made between research which is mainly descriptive (the monitoring of services, which describes how many patients are in contact and what pattern of contacts they make over time) and that which goes beyond the descriptive stage to measure the extent to which the stated objectives have been attained. The former 'is an essential first step in an evaluation research, usually provides much important information regarding the operation of the service, and is frequently all that is required to answer the questions being posed' (Burvill 1978: 189). Indeed Wing *et al.* (1970: 3–4) some years ago stated that, if the need for services is defined in terms of reduction or containment of morbidity, evaluative studies may be elaborated in the form of six questions:

1. How many and what kinds of individuals are in contact with existing services?
2. What are their needs and those of their relatives?
3. Are the services at present provided meeting these needs effectively and economically?
4. How many others, not in touch with existing services, also have needs, and are they different from the needs of patients who do not see psychiatrists?
5. What new services, or modifications to existing services, are likely to cater for unmet needs?
6. When innovations are introduced, do they in fact meet these needs?

It is clear that only the first question may be answered by the use of descriptive statistics, particularly those provided by case registers. Other approaches and techniques, including surveys of the population not in touch with existing services as well as the planning and evaluation of *new* services, are required to answer the remaining questions.

EVALUATING COMPREHENSIVE, COMMUNITY-BASED PSYCHIATRIC SERVICES

The rationale for a shift from mental hospitals to a community-based system of care as well as the main critical views on this move and the distinctive features of 'alternative' community services have been reported elsewhere (Tansella and Zimmermann-Tansella 1988). It has been recently stated that several randomized controlled studies (Weisbrod *et al.* 1980; Fenton *et al.*

389

1982; Hoult *et al.* 1983; Cardin *et al.* 1985) show that 'care provided around the clock, seven days a week in the community has clinical, social and economic advantages over hospital care' (Wilkinson and Pelosi 1987: 140). A similar view was expressed by Tantam (1985), who, however, stated that 'the essential elements of the alternatives to hospital remain to be determined' (Tantam 1985: 3).

It is generally recognized that evaluation of community services is more difficult than the evaluation of a mental hospital. Examples of evaluative studies of comprehensive community services for patients from a defined catchment area are the evaluations of the 'Worthing Experiment' (Carse *et al.* 1958), of the Dutchess County Project in New York State (Hunt *et al.* 1961), of the Chichester service (Grad and Sainsbury 1966), of the Southwest Denver Program (Polak 1978), of the Madison experience (Stein and Test 1980), of the Swedish Nacka Project (Cullberg and Stefansson 1981; Cullberg *et al.* 1981), of the community service in Mannheim (Häfner and Klug 1982), of the Samsø project in Denmark (Munk-Jørgensen 1985) and the New South Wales (Australia) experience (Hoult 1983; Hoult *et al.* 1986). Classic studies are those conducted in England, in Camberwell (Wing and Hailey 1972; Wing 1982, 1986) and in Salford (Fryers and Wooff 1985). Other important studies are actually in progress, such as the Worcester Development Project (Tombs 1987). Studies on services for particular groups of patients, for example, the elderly or the mentally retarded have not been mentioned here.

Specific issues arising in the evaluation of comprehensive, community-based psychiatric services are:

1) The evaluation should become part of a longitudinal, long-term programme, 'with defined mechanisms to carry it out in an "integrated" manner (i.e., planning and implementing it together with service development)' (Sartorius and Harding 1984: 234).

2) Contacts with the psychiatric services, as well as data about type and amount of mental health care provided at the primary care level, particularly by GPs, have to be collected. Information about filters as well as about levels of the Goldberg and Huxley model (Goldberg and Huxley 1980) are essential for effective planning. It is well known that a *minor* increase in the permeability of the filter number 3 (general practice vs. psychiatric services) may well require a *substantial* increase in service provision at the specialist levels (Shepherd *et al.* 1966).

3) Information is needed on the socio-cultural context (characteristics of the area and of the resident population), and on the political and legal context (legislation regulating the delivery of mental health care, social assistance, provisions of pensions and subsidies, etc.).

4) Indicators need to be developed of the extent to which various agencies

and services providing care to the resident population are integrated. It may be expected that the same amount of resources may well have different outcomes in areas with well-integrated or unintegrated services, and this appears to be an interesting topic for future research.

STEPS IN THE EVALUATION OF THE SOUTH-VERONA COMMUNITY PSYCHIATRIC SERVICE (CPS)

The legal context

In the 1960s in Italy the existing gap between the principle and the practice of psychiatry began to be subjected to stringent criticism by professionals as well as by lay people. In those years rapid political, social, and cultural changes occurred, while the practice of psychiatry (which was taking place almost exclusively in old-fashioned, large mental hospitals) was still governed by statutes and regulations dating from 1904 and 1909 respectively. This contradictory situation provided a fertile background for the development of a movement for psychiatric reform which finally resulted in new psychiatric legislation, passed by the Italian parliament in 1978. The features of this movement and those of its final outcome (Law 180) have been described in detail elsewhere (De Plato and Minguzzi 1981; Tansella and Williams 1987).

The main proposal of the Italian reform was to develop comprehensive and integrated community services while blocking admissions to mental hospitals without inducing rapid and massive deinstitutionalization. For many years the pressure of policy and the call for action were allowed to overshadow the crucial need for evaluation, so there are now many community-based services, providing a high standard of care, but which do not produce quantitative data and have no evaluative studies in progress to support the quality of their practice. Although quantitative national and regional data have been analysed (Williams et al. 1986, 1987b; Tansella et al. 1987), the main issue remains whether or not the new pattern of psychiatric care delivery is effective where it is fully applied.

The South-Verona area and the psychiatric case register

South-Verona is a mainly urban area of 75,000 inhabitants in northern Italy where a Community Psychiatric Service (CPS) was set up in 1978, according to the principles of the Italian reform (Zimmermann-Tansella et al. 1985). Its care delivery is comprehensive and is based on staff intensive domiciliary visits, and on out-patient care and day care, designed to avoid hospitalization as much as possible (Jablensky and Henderson 1983; Burti et al. 1986). The style of intervention is psychosocial and special emphasis is given to integrating different interventions such as medication, family support, and social work. To ensure continuity of care all staff members (except for a group of hospital nurses) work both in hospital and in the community. The

Figure 25.1 Resident in-patients on 31 December 1976–83 in mental hospitals and private psychiatric hospitals

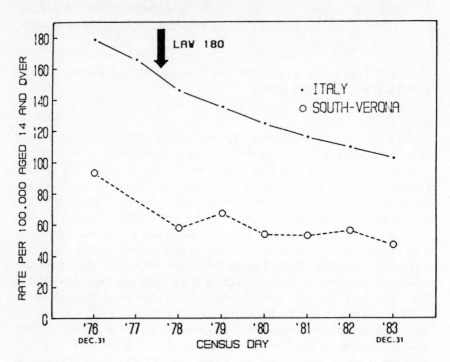

South-Verona CPS is run by the Institute of Psychiatry, University of Verona, which also provides training for undergraduate and post-graduate students (Burti and Mosher 1986). The area has been monitored since January 1979 by a Psychiatric Case Register (PCR) (Tansella *et al*. 1985) and by an epidemiological/evaluative research team.

Descriptive statistics

Figure 25.1 shows the trend in the rates for bed occupancy in mental hospitals and private psychiatric hospitals, in Italy (ISTAT, Roma) and in South-Verona (South-Verona PCR, unpublished annual reports) from December 1976 (more than one year before the psychiatric reform) to December 1983 (five years after).

It may be seen that South-Verona has lower rates than Italy (a gradual process of deinstitutionalization started before 1976) and that, after 1978, the decreasing trend in the in-patient population is more evident at the national than at the local level. In most recent years this decline is mainly due to death rather than discharge. Since the front doors of public mental hospitals have been closed since 1982, admissions are only possible to fifteen-bed

Figure 25.2 South-Verona. Build-up of 'new' long-stay patients (non-resident in mental hospitals, private psychiatric hospitals and general hospitals' psychiatric units for one year or more on triennial census days, but long-stay on subsequent annual census days)

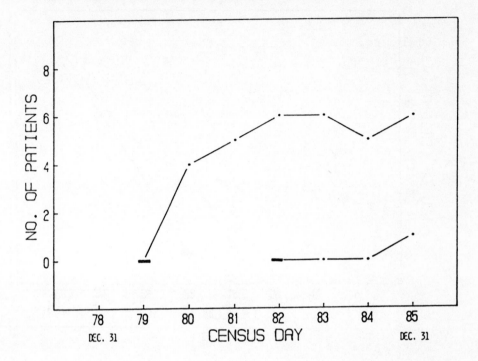

general hospital psychiatric units (with a length of stay that in most cases does not exceed two months – one such a unit is part of the South-Verona CPS) or to private psychiatric hospitals (where patients may remain a long time – there are two such hospitals in Verona and their total bed complement is 220). It is interesting to note that, under these circumstances, there was a negligible build-up of *new long-stay patients* in South-Verona.

The two curves in figure 25.2 indicate the number of people who have become long-stay since the two given starting dates and are still in hospital at the end of each subsequent year. This pattern, which is unusual as compared with international standards (Häfner and Klug 1982; Gibbons *et al.* 1984), is mainly due to the ban on new admissions (from 1978) and on all admissions (from 1982) to mental hospitals, the main places where long-stays are produced. It is also due to the change in psychiatric practice and to the development, since 1978, of an expanding community service. The South-Verona CPS is now taking care of most psychiatric patients who before the

Figure 25.3 South-Verona. Build-up of 'new' long-term patients (not in 'continuous care' in the community for one year or more on triennal census days, but long-term community patients on subsequent annual census days)

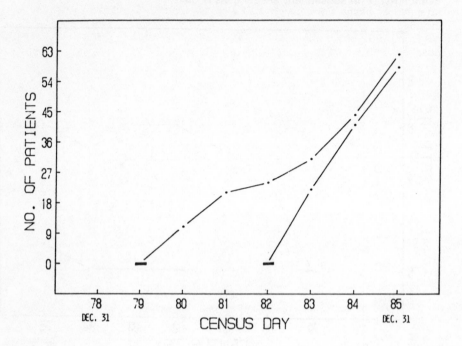

reform would have been admitted to the mental hospital, becoming long-stay. They receive intensive and continuous care in the community (out-patient care, including home visits and crisis intervention, and day care) and have spells of admission to hospital (the psychiatric unit in general hospital or private psychiatric hospitals) when necessary. In all settings but the private hospital they are under the care of the same team. The patients under continuous care (without a break between contacts of ninety-one days or more) for 365 days or longer may be defined as long-term patients. Figure 25.3 shows the build-up of 'new' long-term patients since 31 December 1980.

The curves show that the number in both cohorts are consistently rising. The clinical and social implications of the build-up of long-term patients *instead* of long-stay in-patients need to be considered. In fact, the outcome, in terms of service use, seems to be different in the two groups. In a follow-up study we showed that while 88 per cent of patients of the long-stay cohort were still long-stay after two years, only 45 per cent of the long-term patients remained long-term over the same period (Balestrieri *et al.* 1987). Further

Figure 25.4 South-Verona. Total number of days in hospital (long-stay in mental hospital included), total number of days in day hospital and centre (day care started in 1982) and all out-patient contacts (out-patient visits, home visits, attendances at the casualty departments, ward referrals, attendances at the Community Mental Health Centre). Drug addicts not included.
NB From 1982 onward admissions to neurological wards of general hospitals with psychiatric diagnosis, are also included

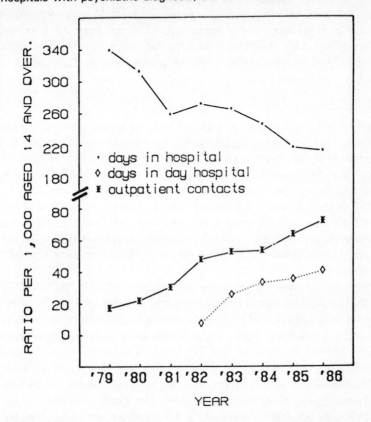

studies, using appropriate outcome measures, are necessary before concluding that long-term community care by the South-Verona CPS is inducing to a lesser extent dependence on the services and chronicity of their use, as compared with the old hospital-centred system of care.

One important aspect of the Italian model of community psychiatry is that hospital psychiatry is considered complementary to community care and not vice versa. The 1978 Italian reform prescribes that, as a rule, treatment would be made available to psychiatric patients in their own environment and that hospitalization, both voluntary and compulsory, would be regarded as an extraordinary intervention. We wanted to check if this is actually taking place in our area.

Several case-register studies showed that in South-Verona the great majority of patients (more than 70 per cent) are treated outside the hospital *only*, confirming the community orientation of our programme (see Burti *et al*. 1986; Tansella *et al*. 1987), and that compulsory admissions were much lower after the psychiatric reform (in 1979–86, mean number of 11 admissions/100,000 adult population per year) than before (in 1977, 55 admissions/100,000) (South-Verona PCR, unpublished annual reports).

Figure 25.4 confirms that, over the years, in South-Verona, out-patient care and day care are consistently increasing, while the extent of in-patient care is decreasing. This shows that, as expected, community care requires adequate time for implementation, even in places such as Italy where a radical policy has been adopted.

Monitoring patterns of care

The utilization of mental health services is a topic of special interest in areas where a major change in the organization of care provision has occurred. The South-Verona PCR has been used in several studies designed to describe patterns of care. For example, we studied high users and long-term users of the mental health services and showed that, after excluding long-stay in-patients and single consulters, 9.4 per cent of the patients seeking care in one year were high users and 12.1 per cent were long-term users. A log-linear analysis demonstrated a strong association between the pattern of service use and diagnosis, occupational status, and previous psychiatric contacts (Tansella *et al*. 1986a).

To study the relationship between the amount of care provided by specialist and by primary care services, the extent of patient contact for affective disorders at the extramural psychiatric service level (number of contacts) and its monthly fluctuations were compared with those at the in-patient level (number of admissions) and at the GP level (number of antidepressant prescriptions), in 1983 and 1984. Patients with a diagnosis of affective disorder accounted for about 20 per cent of the total number of patients contacting the specialized services in one year. The extent of patient contact was approximately ten times greater at the GP level (in one year about 150 antidepressant prescriptions per 1,000 adult inhabitants) than at the out-patient/community psychiatric service level. Similarly, the extent of patient contact at the latter level was approximately ten times greater than at the in-patient level. There was a clear correspondence between monthly fluctuations in the extent of care for affective disorders provided at the two community levels in 1984, but not in 1983 (Tansella *et al*. 1986b). The implications of these findings for service planning and evaluation have been discussed in the above quoted papers.

The study of seasonal variation in the expression of morbidity of several psychiatric disorders may be relevant not only to the investigation of the causes, but also to the organization, planning, and evaluation of psychiatric services. Seasonal variation in new episodes of affective disorders was investigated using the South-Verona PCR. Case-register data have considerable advantages over hospital admission statistics for this type of study, especially in case-register areas where community psychiatric care is well developed, as in South-Verona. We found evidence for a cyclical pattern in the occurrence of affective psychosis, but this was statistically significant only for the males; there was no cyclical variation in depressive neurosis (Williams *et al.* 1987a).

Monthly variation in the demand for extramural psychiatric care was also studied. Using harmonic analysis, a complex pattern of seasonal variation emerged, but the first harmonic (1 cycle/per year) was consistently the most important (in both sexes and in all diagnostic groups, except schizophrenic psychosis). The seasonal variation in extramural contacts could not be accounted for by variation in the number of patients in contact, but was found to be partly due to variation in the availability and supply of psychiatric care. After examining the amplitude of the cyclical fluctuation we concluded that it has trivial implications for service organization, thus supporting previous findings from the primary care setting (Balestrieri *et al.* 1987).

Descriptive surveys

In order to understand the decision to hospitalize at the first contact, rather than utilize the other services of a community-based system of care, forty-six consecutive patients who were admitted on first-contact with the South-Verona CPS were compared with all other in-patients over a two-year period with respect to socio-demographic characteristics, ICD-9 diagnosis and symptoms (on the PSE Syndrome Check List). Results suggested that first-contact hospitalized patients have significantly more neurotic depressive features than other in-patients and that alternatives to immediate admission were considered more often for patients with psychoses (except those with organic psychoses) than for those with depressive neurosis (Faccincani *et al.* 1987).

A survey of all sixty-one schizophrenia patients from the South-Verona area who contacted the psychiatric services in 1979 was conducted seven years later. Fifty-seven patients (93 per cent) were traced and all those still alive (N = 46) interviewed using PSE-9, DAS-2, PIRS, and other standardized instruments. The results are currently being analysed.

The risk of mortality over five to eight years for a total one-year prevalence cohort of schizophrenic patients, extracted by means of the South-Verona PCR, was assessed using three methods: case control with both non-psychotic patients and general population (matched for sex and age), indirect standardization using mortality tables, and indirect standardization with survival tables, according to the method described by Sturt (1983). All methods yielded an excess mortality: that is, around the two-fold increase described in other studies. Moreover, the findings do *not* support the view that excess mortality in South-Verona is linked to suicide, but to natural causes (Lesage *et al.* 1988).

It is well recognized that another index of the efficacy of a community service is its ability to help patients to maintain themselves in their community, without migration. Although the circumstances of migration, the quality of life, symptoms, and social disability of patients who migrate and those who do not need to be taken into account, the simple quantitative findings on migration are the first necessary step for evaluating this aspect of the practice of new services. Migration of the 1982 cohort of all South-Verona schizophrenic patients over a five-year period was compared to non-psychotic and general population control groups. The migration outside the catchment area was highest in the general population sample, but no significant difference was found between the groups. On the other hand, schizophrenic patients tended to migrate less than neurotics within South-Verona. These findings suggest that, following the application of the Italian psychiatric reform in South-Verona, schizophrenic patients do not drift from this small northern city of 270,000 into big cities. Moreover, except for mental hospital long-stay in-patients, the schizophrenic cohort shares the potential mobility of the general population (Lesage and Tansella 1988).

One of the limitations of the register method is related to the geographical mobility of the population outside the area covered by the case register. It is obvious that high mobility limits the value of longitudinal analyses conducted using register data. It is important, therefore, to have, from each register area, quantitative information on this demographic variable in order to evaluate the stability over time of the denominators of case-register analyses and to calculate the expected number of patients, among those in contact with the psychiatric services in one day and/or in one year, who may lose contact with the register simply because of migration and may therefore be excluded from any case-register follow-up.

For example, in the study quoted above, we showed that, over a five-year period (1982–86), 13.8 per cent of a South-Verona population sample moved outside the register area. The corresponding figures for the schizophrenic and the non-psychotic groups were 7.3 per cent and 11.8 per cent respectively (Lesage and Tansella 1988). If we use the highest figure and consider that one-day and one-year treated prevalence rates (mean values for the years 1982–86) in South-Verona were 257/100,000 and 1,184/100,000 respectively, we can assume that in a five-year case-register follow-up of cohorts of patients in contact with services in one day and in one year, the risk of being considered out of care due to migration out of the case-register area applies to 35 and 163 patients/100,000 residents respectively. In areas with higher geographical mobility and/or with higher treated prevalence rates this bias may have a substantially greater effect on longitudinal case-register analyses.

CONCLUSIONS

It was stated that 'The scope, extent and impact of community care are difficult to estimate. Official figures provide a starting point, but they may hide as much as they purport to disclose' (Wilkinson 1985: 1371). A number of properly designed studies, intensively conducted over a sufficiently long period of time, are therefore necessary. Case registers are invaluable tools for service use descriptions, and may well provide the sampling frame for *ad hoc* surveys and outcome evaluations. The work done until now in South-Verona shows that the Italian reform is effective and that our community-based system of care is able to cope with all the problems presented by the patients living in our area, without 'back up' from the psychiatric hospital, where only a small group of old long-stay in-patients (N = 18 on 31 December 1986) continues to reside. The efficacy of the system needs to be further evaluated and a cost-benefit analysis needs to be undertaken.

To conclude, I would like to refer to Pascal's dictum, recently quoted by Professor Michael Shepherd (1987), that words differently arranged have a different meaning and meanings differently arranged have a different effect. What is important in community care is not only the number and characteristics of various services, but the way in which they are actually arranged and integrated. Different arrangements of similar services may have a very different effect. The outcome due to the type of arrangement and collaboration among services in a particular area, in other words the outcome due to the existing *model of coordination and integration*, has been subjected to little assessment and evaluation until now. Reliable measures of process and outcome, as well as of the costs and benefits, need to be developed for this particular purpose. The effects due to the particular organization of psychiatric services which is operating in South-Verona and qualititative as well as quantitative aspects of the offered care deserve further studies.

Acknowledgements: This study has been supported by the Consiglio Nazionale della Richerche (CNR, Roma), Progetto Finalizzato Medicina Preventiva e Riabilitativa 1982–1987, Contract No. 86.01962.56, and by the Regione Veneto, Ricerca Sanitaria Finalizzata, Contract No. 134.03.86.

I am indebted to Dr M. Balestrieri and Mr R. Fianco, as well as to the staff of the South-Verona Psychiatric Case Register and especially to Mr G. Meneghelli, for their valuable help. Many thanks are also due to Dr D. De Salvia for the collection of national data reported in figure 25.1.

REFERENCES

Acheson, E.D. (1985) 'That over-used word community', *Health Trends* 17: 3.
Bachrach, L.L. (1980) 'Overview: model programs for chronic mental patients', *American Journal of Psychiatry* 137: 1023–31.

Bachrach, L.L. (1982) 'Assessment of outcomes in community support systems: results, problems, and limitations', *Schizophrenia Bulletin* 8: 39–61.

Balestrieri, M., Micciolo, R., and Tansella, M. (1987) 'Long-stay and long-term psychiatric patients in an area with a community-based system of care: a case-register follow-up study', *International Journal of Social Psychiatry*, 33, 251–62.

Balestrieri, M., Williams, P., Micciolo, R., and Tansella, M. (1987) 'Monthly variation in the pattern of extramural psychiatric care', *Social Psychiatry* 22: 160–6.

Burti, L. and Mosher, L.R. (1986) 'Training psychiatrists in the community: a report of the Italian experience', *American Journal of Psychiatry* 143: 1580–4.

Burti, L., Garzotto, N., Siciliani, O., Zimmermann-Tansella, Ch., and Tansella, M. (1986) 'South-Verona's psychiatric service: an integrated system of community care', *Hospital and Community Psychiatry* 37: 809–13.

Burvill, P.W. (1978) 'Evaluation of psychiatric services', *Australian and New Zealand Journal of Psychiatry* 12: 189–95.

Cardin, V.A., McGill, C.W., and Falloon, I.R.H. (1985) 'Economic analysis: costs, benefits and effectiveness', in I.R.H. Falloon, C.W. McGill and J.L. Boyd (eds) *Family Management of Schizophrenia. A Study of Clinical Social, Family, and Economic Benefits*, Baltimore: Johns Hopkins University Press.

Carse, J., Panton, N.E., and Watt, A. (1958) 'A district mental health service: the Worthing experiment', *Lancet* 1: 39–41.

Cooper, B. and Morgan, H.G. (1973) *Epidemiological Psychiatry*, Springfield: Thomas.

Coursey, R.D. (1977) 'Introduction: the need, history, definition, and limits of program evaluation', in R.D. Coursey, G.A. Specter, S.A. Murrell, and B. Hunt (eds) *Program Evaluation for Mental Health: Methods, Strategies, and Participants*, New York: Grune & Stratton.

Coursey, R.D., Specter, G.A., Murrell, S.A., and Hunt, B. (eds) (1977) *Program Evaluation for Mental Health: Methods, Strategies, and Participants*, New York: Grune & Stratton.

Cullberg, J. and Stefansson, C.G. (1981) *An Evaluation of the Nacka Project*, Stockholm: Spri Publications.

Cullberg, J., Stefansson, C.G., and Wennersten, E. (1981) 'Psychiatry in young low status dwelling areas', *Psychiatry and Social Science* 1: 117–23.

De Plato, G. and Minguzzi, G. (1981) 'A short history of psychiatric renewal in Italy', *Psychiatry and Social Science* 1: 71–7.

European Economic Community (1981) *Evaluation and Mental Health Care: Third European Seminar on Health Policy*, Brussels: Report EUR 7172.

Faccincani, C., Mignolli, G. and Munk-Jørgensen, P. (1987) 'Hospital admission as first contact with a community-based psychiatric service: a two-year study in South-Verona', *European Archives of Psychiatry and Neurological Sciences* 236: 247–50.

Feldman, S. and Windle, W. (1973) 'The N.I.M.H. approach to evaluating the community mental health centers program', *Health Services Report* 88: 174–99.

Fenton, F.R., Tessier, L., Contradiopoulos, A., Nguyen, H., and Struening, E.L. (1972) 'A comparative trial of home and hospital psychiatric treatment: financial costs', *Canadian Journal of Psychiatry* 27: 177–87.

Frank, R. (1981) 'Cost-benefit analysis in mental health services: a review of the literature', *Administration in Mental Health* 8: 161–76.

Fryers, T. and Wooff, K. (1985) 'Il controllo di servizi di salute mentale in una citta inglese', in M. Tansella (ed.) *L'Approccio Epidemiologico in Psichiatria*, Torino: Boringhieri.

Gibbons, J., Jennings, C., and Wing, J.K. (1984) *Psychiatric Care in Eight Register Areas*, copies obtainable from Southampton Case Register, Knowle Hospital, Fareham, PO17 5NA.

Glass, N.J. and Goldberg, D. (1977) 'Cost benefit analysis and the evaluation of psychiatric services', *Psychological Medicine* 7: 701–7.

Grad, J. and Sainsbury, P. (1966) 'Evaluating the community psychiatric service in Chichester: results', in E.M. Gruenberg (ed.) *Evaluating the Effectiveness of Mental Health Services*, New York: Milbank Memorial Fund.

Gruenberg, E.M. (ed.) (1966) *Evaluating the Effectiveness of Mental Health Services*, New York: Milbank Memorial Fund.

Guttentag, M. and Struening, E.P. (eds) (1975) *Handbook of Evaluation Research: Volume 2*, Beverley Hills: Sage.

Häfner, H. and Klug, J. (1982) 'The impact of an expanding community mental health service on patterns of bed usage: evaluation of a four-year period of implementation', *Psychological Medicine* 12, 177–90.

Hoult, J. (1986) 'Community care of the acutely mentally ill', *British Journal of Psychiatry* 149: 137–44.

Hoult, J., Reynolds, I., Charbonneau-Powis, M., Weekes, P., and Briggs, J. (1983) 'Psychiatric hospital versus community treatment: the results of a randomised trial', *Australian and New Zealand Journal of Medicine* 17: 160–7.

Hunt, R.C., Gruenberg, E.M., Hacken, E., and Huxley, M. (1961) 'A comprehensive hospital-community service in a state hospital', *American Journal of Psychiatry* 117: 817–21.

Istituto Centrale di Statistica (ISTAT) *Annuario Statistico Italiano*, 1979–1986 editions, Roma: ISTAT.

Jablensky, A. and Henderson, J. (1983) 'Report on a visit to the South-Verona community psychiatric service', WHO Assignment Report, Geneva and Copenhagen, WHO.

Kreitman, N. (1984) 'Operational research in a faltering economy', *Social Psychiatry* 19: 1–2.

Lesage, A.D. and Tansella, M. (1988) 'Migration of schizophrenic patients, non-psychotic patients and general population in a case register area', submitted for publication.

Lesage, A.D., Trapani, V., and Tansella, M. (1988) 'Excess mortality measured according to 3 methods: a study on a cohort of schizophrenic patients in the years following the Italian psychiatric reform', submitted for publication.

McGuire, T.G. and Weisbrod, B.A. (eds) (1981) *Economics and Mental Health*, Washington: US Government Printing Office.

Munk-Jørgensen, P. (1985) 'Cumulated need for psychiatric service as shown in a community psychiatric project', *Psychological Medicine* 15: 629–35.

Polak, P.R. (1978) 'A comprehensive system of alternatives to psychiatric hospitalization', in L.I. Stein and M.A. Test (eds) *Alternatives to Mental Hospital Treatment*, New York: Plenum Press.

Roemer, M.I. (1972) *Evaluation of Community Health Centres* (Public Health Papers, No. 48), Geneva: WHO.

Sartorius, N. (1982) 'Epidemiology and mental health policy', in M.O. Wagenfeld, P.V. Lemkan and B. Justice (eds) *Public Mental Health*, Beverly Hills: Sage.

Sartorius, N. and Harding, T.W. (1984) 'Issues in the evaluation of mental health care', in W.W. Holland (ed.) *Evaluation of Health Care*, Oxford: Oxford University Press.

Schulberg, H.C. (1977) 'Issues in the evaluation of community mental health programs', *Professional Psychology* 560–72.

Shepherd, M. (1987) 'Jean Starobinski', *Lancet* 6 April: 798.

Shepherd, M., Cooper, B., Brown, A.C., and Kalton, G.W. (1966) *Psychiatric Illness in General Practice*, London: Oxford University Press.

Stahler, G.J. and Tash, W.R. (eds) (1982) *Innovative Approaches in Mental Health Evaluation*, New York: Academic Press.

Stein, L.I. and Test, M.A. (1980) 'Alternative to mental hospital treatment: 1. Conceptual model, treatment program and clinical evaluation', *Archives of General Psychiatry* 37: 392–7.

Struening, E.L. and Guttentag, M. (1975) *Handbook of Evaluation Research*, California: Sage.

Sturt, E. (1983) 'Mortality in a cohort of long-term users of community psychiatric services', *Psychological Medicine* 13, 441–6.

Suchman, E.A. (1967) *Evaluation Research: Principles and Practice in Public Service and Social Action Programs*, New York: Russel Sage Foundation.

Tansella, M. (1985) 'Approccio epidemiologico e psichiatria italiana del dopo-riforma', in M. Tansella (ed.) *L'Approccio Epidemiologico in Psichiatria*, Torino: Boringhieri.

Tansella, M. (1986) 'Community psychiatry without mental hospitals: the Italian experience: a review', *Journal of the Royal Society of Medicine* 79: 664–9.

Tansella, M. and Williams, P. (1987) 'The Italian experience and its implications', *Psychological Medicine* 17: 283–9.

Tansella, M. and Zimmermann-Tansella, Ch. (1988) 'From mental hospitals to alter-native community services', in J.G. Howells (ed.) *Modern Perspectives in Clinical Psychiatry*, New York: Brunner-Mazel (in press).

Tansella, M., Faccincani, C., Mignolli, G., Balestrieri, M., and Zimmermann-Tansella, Ch. (1985) 'Il registro psichiatrico di Verona-Sud: epidemiologia per la valutazione dei nuovi servizi territoriali', in M. Tansella (ed.) *L'Approccio Epidemiologico in Psichiatria*, Torino: Boringhieri.

Tansella, M., Micciolo, R., Balestrieri, M., and Gavioli, I. (1986a) 'High and long-term users of the mental health services: a case-register study in Italy', *Social Psychiatry* 21: 96–103.

Tansella, M., Williams, P., Balestrieri, M., Bellantuono, C., and Martini, N. (1986b) 'The management of affective disorders in the community', *Journal of Affective Disorders* 11: 73–9.

Tansella, M., De Salvia, D., and Williams, P. (1987) 'The Italian psychiatric reform: some quantitative evidence', *Social Psychiatry* 22: 37–48.

Tantam, D. (1985) 'Alternatives to psychiatric hospitalisation', *British Journal of Psychiatry* 146: 1–4.

Tombs, D.A. (1987) personal communication.

Weisbrod, B.A. (1982) 'A guide to benefit-cost analysis, as seen through a controlled experiment in treating the mentally ill', *Journal of Health Political Policy Law* 7: 808–45.

Weisbrod, B.A., Test, M.A., and Stein, L.I. (1980) 'Alternative to mental hospital treatment: II Economic benefit-cost analysis', *Archives of General Psychiatry* 37: 400–5.

Wilkinson, G. (1985) 'Community care: planning mental health services', *British Medical Journal* 290: 1371–3.

Wilkinson, G. and Pelosi, A.J. (1987) 'The economics of mental health services', *British Medical Journal* 294: 139–40.

Williams, P., De Salvia, D., and Tansella, M. (1986) 'Suicide, psychiatric reform, and the provision of psychiatric services in Italy', *Social Psychiatry* 21: 89–95.

Williams, P., Balestrieri, M., and Tansella, M. (1987a) 'Seasonal variation in affective disorders: a case register study', *Journal of Affective Disorders* 12: 145–52.

Williams, P., De Salvia, D., and Tansella, M. (1987b) 'Suicide and the Italian psychiatric reform: an appraisal of two data collection systems', *European Archives of Psychiatry and Neurological Sciences* 236: 237–40.

Williams, R.D. and Ozarin, L.D. (eds) (1968) *Community Mental Health*, San Francisco: Jossey-Bass.

Wing, J.K. (1972) 'Principles of evaluation', in J.K. Wing and A.M. Hailey (eds) *Evaluating a Community Psychiatric Service*, London: Oxford University Press.

Wing, J.K. (ed.) (1982) 'Long-term community care experience in a London borough', *Psychological Medicine*, Monograph supplement no. 2.

Wing, J.K. (1986) 'The cycle of planning and evaluation', in G. Wilkinson and H. Freeman (eds) *The Provision of Mental Health Services in Britain: The Way Ahead*, London: Gaskell.

Wing, J.K. and Fryers, T. (1976) *Psychiatric Services in Camberwell and Salford, 1964–1974*, Manchester: University Department of Community Medicine.

Wing, J.K. and Häfner, H. (eds) (1973) *Roots of Evaluation*, London: Oxford University Press.

Wing, J.K. and Hailey, A.M. (1972) *Evaluating a Community Psychiatric Service: The Camberwell Register 1964–71*, London: Oxford University Press.

Wing, J.K., Wing, L., and Hailey, A. (1970) 'The use of case registers for evaluating and planning psychiatric services', in J.K. Wing and E.R. Bransby (eds) *Psychiatric Case Registers*, London: HMSO.

World Health Organization (1971) *Trends in Psychiatric Care: Day Hospitals and Units in General Hospitals*, Copenhagen: WHO Regional Office for Europe.

Zimmermann-Tansella, Ch., Burti, L., Faccincani, C., Garzotto, N., Siciliani, O., and Tansella, M. (1985) 'Bringing into action the psychiatric reform in South-Verona: a five year experience', in C. Perris and D. Kemali (eds) *Focus on the Italian Psychiatric Reform* (Supplement of *Acta Psychiatrica Scandinavica*, No. 316), 71: 71–86, Copenhagen: Munksgaard.

26

The Psychiatry of General Practice

Deborah Sharp and David Morrell

In Great Britain, health care is organized in a two-tier system. Primary care is provided by National Health Service general practitioners who are effectively responsible for most of the referrals into the second tier – the hospitals, where the service is provided by consultants in the different specialities. Ninety-eight per cent of the population is registered with a general practitioner; 60–70 per cent of whom consult at least once each year and only about 10 per cent will not consult at all in any three-year period. Thus, the general practitioner can be regarded as a personal physician who has access to the medical history and social background of his patients and who, by virtue of the continuity of care he provides, not only for the patient but often for the whole family, is in an unique position to monitor psychosocial disorder in the community.

It is commonly believed that between one-quarter and one-third of all illnesses treated by general practitioners comprise some form of psychological disorder (Goldberg and Blackwell 1970; Goldberg and Bridges 1987). On average each patient consults his or her general practitioner between three and four times a year. Thus, with an average list size of 2,000, most general practitioners will be confronted with a large amount of psychiatric morbidity.

Table 26.1 compares general practitioner consultation rates for diagnosed psychiatric disorders with those for out-patient and day-patient attendances and rates of admissions to psychiatric institutions. Despite the shortcomings of the data available for general practice from the Third National Morbidity Study (1986), mainly on account of problems in the classification of mental illness and inter-practice variation, it can be seen that consultations for psychiatric disorder in general practice outnumber psychiatric out-patient attendances by nearly 7:1.

In 1973 a WHO working party on psychiatry in general practice (WHO 1973) identified the general practitioner as playing a major role in mental health care. They argued that: 1) patients with psychosocial problems are high users of medical care and thus are well known to primary care physicians who may utilize this relationship for psychotherapeutic intervention;

404

Table 26.1 Comparative rates of attendance for different levels of psychiatric care (rates per 100,000 general population, all ages and sexes combined, in 1981)

	*General practitioner consultations**	*Out-patients attendances +*	*Day hospital attendances +*	*Psychiatric admissions +*
ICD-9 290–315 Mental Disorders	22,980	3,532	4,943	397

* Obtained from *Morbidity Statistics from General Practice* 1981–1982, Third National Study, RCGP, OPCS, DHSS.
+ Obtained from *Mental Health Enquiry for England*, 1981

2) patients with emotional disorders experience less stigma when treated by a primary care physician than by a psychiatrist; 3) physical and psychiatric complaints tend to co-occur and are often difficult to separate in diagnosis and treatment, which makes the non-psychiatrist, who is more able to treat the 'whole' person, the first choice as physician; 4) primary care physicians are best placed to provide long-term follow up and be available for successive episodes of illness.

IDENTIFICATION OF PSYCHIATRIC DISORDER IN GENERAL PRACTICE

The study of psychiatric disorder in general practice has received increasing interest in the last two decades (Clare and Lader 1982; Shepherd *et al.* 1986). The starting point for much of this work was the study by Shepherd and his colleagues at the Institute of Psychiatry over twenty years ago (Shepherd *et al.* 1966). They studied a one in eight sample of patients attending forty-six general practices in London for a period of one year. Of the 15,000 patients at risk, approximately 14 per cent consulted their doctor at least once for a condition diagnosed as entirely or largely psychiatric in nature. More than half of these conditions had been present for at least one year. However, less than one in twenty of these patients were known to have received specialist psychiatric care during the survey year. Doctors varied greatly in their estimates of psychiatric morbidity, reporting rates between 3.7 per cent and 65 per cent.

The arrival of psychiatric screening questionnaires linked to standardized psychiatric interviews has meant that it is now possible to make estimates of the prevalence of psychiatric illness in general practice that are independent of the varying abilities of general practitioners in making such assessments. The General Health Questionnaire (GHQ) (Goldberg 1972) has been used in

405

several studies which aimed to estimate the prevalence of psychiatric morbidity in general practice. This instrument is designed to identify non-psychotic psychiatric ill health in the community and was originally constructed to function as a first-stage screening tool in studies where the Clinical Interview Schedule (CIS) (Goldberg *et al.* 1970) was to be used to provide a standardized approach to confirming or denying the presence of psychiatric morbidity.

In order to try and quantify the disparity between the true prevalence of psychiatric morbidity in general practice and that identified by the general practitioner, Goldberg and Blackwell (1970) used the GHQ to screen for probable 'caseness' in 200 patients who were also assessed by psychiatrist, using the CIS. The 'conspicuous psychiatric morbidity', as assessed by the general practitioner and validated by the psychiatrist, was calculated to be 20 per cent and 'hidden psychiatric morbidity' accounted for one-third of all disturbed patients. They found that those patients with 'hidden psychiatric morbidity' were more likely to present their illness in somatic terms but that their illnesses were no less severe in terms of prognosis. Similar findings were reported by Skuse and Williams (1984) where the general practitioner regarded 24 per cent of a sample of consecutive attenders as 'psychiatric cases' and the true prevalence as assessed by the CIS was found to be 34 per cent.

The detection of psychiatric morbidity by primary care physicians has an important influence on the amount and type of disorder that is subsequently cared for in the mental health sector. Goldberg and Huxley (1980) have constructed a hierarchical model of levels and filters to describe the nature of psychiatric disorder in the community and how this is reflected in the organization of care (see figure 26.1). Level 1 refers to all psychological disorders in the community, a large proportion of which pass through filter 1 into level 2 when the patient decides to consult the general practitioner. However, a great deal of this psychological morbidity is not recognized by general practitioners, so these people do not pass through filter 2. Level 3 is therefore the 'conspicuous psychological morbidity' most of which will be treated by the general practitioner. A proportion will however be referred to the specialist mental health services, i.e., pass through filter 3 into level 4. An even smaller proportion will require admission to hospital, i.e., pass through filter 4 into level 5.

The large between-general practitioner variation in detecting psychiatric morbidity has already been mentioned. Filter 2, that separating the hidden and conspicuous psychiatric morbidity, allows about 60 per cent of morbidity through into level 3, and represents the doctor's ability to detect psychiatric disorder. Passage through this filter is affected by characteristics of both the patient and the doctor. Two particular aspects of the doctor's ability to detect these disorders are thought to be important. The first is bias – the tendency of a general practitioner to over- or under-identify psychiatric disorder. This

Figure 26.1 Goldberg and Huxley's model

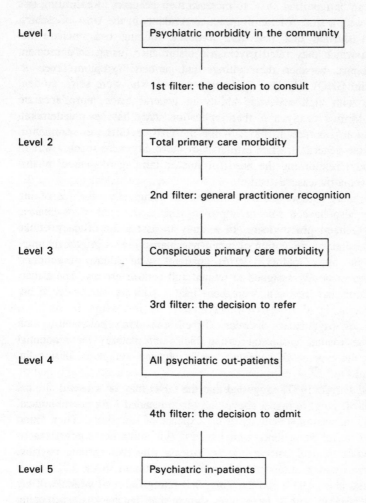

Level 1	Psychiatric morbidity in the community

1st filter: the decision to consult

Level 2	Total primary care morbidity

2nd filter: general practitioner recognition

Level 3	Conspicuous primary care morbidity

3rd filter: the decision to refer

Level 4	All psychiatric out-patients

4th filter: the decision to admit

Level 5	Psychiatric in-patients

Source: Goldberg and Huxley (1980).

is thought to be determined by factors such as personality, attitudes, training, and experience. The second is accuracy, which is the degree to which the general practitioner is correct in his assessment.

Marks *et al.* (1979) studied in detail some of the factors associated with general practitioners' ability to detect psychiatric morbidity. They suggested that the most important factor is the ability of the general practitioner to conduct a simple mental state examination in an empathic manner, together with an understanding of the association of psychiatric morbidity with social dysfunctioning. It appears that some aspects of the doctors' behaviour in the consultation can be modified so as to increase their accuracy. Replicating this British study with a study of family practice residents in the USA, Goldberg *et al.* (1980) showed that videotape feedback training can improve the accuracy with which they rated psychiatric disturbance (using an agreement coefficient, kappa, between their ratings and patients' symptom levels as reported on the GHQ). He also found that doctors who were self-confident and outgoing with high academic ability in general made more accurate assessments. More recently a further replication study has been undertaken in South London (Boardman 1987). While the GHQ results were similar in both studies, the general practice estimates of morbidity were much lower in this latest study, reinforcing the need for further training of general practitioners in psychiatric case detection.

The self-report questionnaires constructed originally for screening purposes may also have a role in improving the recognition of psychiatric morbidity by general practitioners. In a study to assess the efficacy of the GHQ in the secondary prevention of minor psychiatric illness in general practice (Johnstone and Goldberg 1976), patients with hidden psychiatric morbidity were randomly assigned to treated and control groups. The effects of case detection and treatment were beneficial – patients were more likely to get better quickly and have fewer symptoms at follow-up. In addition, identification of psychiatric disorder altered consulting behaviour, with patients in the treated group increasing their consultations for emotional complaints at the expense of consultations for physical symptoms during the follow-up year.

Wright and Perini (1987) suggested that the GHQ may be a useful clinical tool if the cut-off point is raised above that recommended for epidemiological research, i.e., increasing specificity at the expense of sensitivity. They found it particularly useful in patients with physical symptoms not conforming to any recognizable clinical pattern and in patients who had chronic physical illness or were frequent attenders. More recently, studies in the USA using the GHQ (Rand *et al.* 1987) and the Zung Self-rating Depression Scale (Zung and Magruder-Habib 1987) have also shown that feedback of screening results to general practitioners improves recognition of psychiatric morbidity.

It has been proposed that there are two types of clinical decision: the 'diagnostic decision' and the 'management decision' (Howie 1972). The relationship between diagnosis and treatment in psychiatry is not necessarily a strong one and this is particularly true in the general practice setting. Furthermore, while a psychiatric diagnosis may be only relatively infrequently recorded by a general practitioner, the record of the 'reason for visit', the prescribing of psychotropic drugs or the provision of psychotherapy suggest that recognition of 'distress' may be much more common but is not diagnosable in current terminology.

What are the characteristics of these patients with neurotic disorders, mainly anxiety and depression, that will enable a general practitioner to make a psychiatric diagnosis and is it necessary to make such a diagnosis before management can be considered? Indeed, does making a diagnosis really determine what is to be done and by whom?

As described by Eastwood elsewhere in this volume, many studies have found that psychiatric morbidity is often associated with physical complaints. It is widely believed by patients that doctors expect to hear about physical symptoms. In addition, it is still more socially acceptable to have a physical illness than a psychiatric one. Thus, depressed patients may well present a physical symptom to their general practitioner rather than their psychological symptoms. But this may also occur because a depressed patient is often more introspective than usual and will be more aware of their general bodily functions. Thus, a physical symptom which has been present for some time may appear worse in a period of emotional distress and thus will be presented as their main complaint to the doctor. On the other hand, depression may occur as a consequence of a physical illness or symptom and, while it is appropriate to offer the physical illness to the general practitioner, the onus is on the general practitioner to be aware of the likely psychological consequences of a serious or chronic physical illness. In addition, there appears to be a real association of physical illness with psychiatric illness. This was noted by Shepherd *et al.* (1966) and investigated further by Eastwood and Trevelyan (1972), and is discussed by Eastwood elsewhere in this volume.

Another group of patients in general practice who frequently suffer from psychological disorders are those who are subject to acute life events or chronic social stresses. Although there are individual and biological differences in the extent to which people are vulnerable to mental illness, many studies support the notion that adverse social circumstances are also aetiologically important (Cooper 1972). These social factors may, in addition, determine what sort of symptoms a patient develops and what 'treatment' he seeks. Social factors may also be relevant in the development or relapse of illnesses such as schizophrenia.

Stressful life events, often masquerading as an acute minor physical ailment or the exacerbation of a chronic symptom, are frequently the cause of depression in general practice patients (Cooper and Sylph 1973). Brown and Harris (1978), in a study of women in the community, found that working-class women were more prone to depression, in part due to an increased incidence of adverse life events.

Chronic social difficulties such as financial hardship, social isolation, and lower social class have also been shown to be associated with an increased prevalence of mental illness. When consultation rates are examined, those patients who consult their general practitioners and are found to have minor psychiatric morbidity more frequently tend to be women, often separated or divorced, of lower social class, who are unemployed with consequent housing and financial difficulties. The question as to whether women do actually experience more psychiatric ill health than men or whether they are just more likely to consult their general practitioner (Shepherd *et al.* 1966), and whether the general practitioner is more likely to detect psychiatric illness in women (Marks *et al.* 1979), has not been definitively answered. It would seem that women, especially if separated or divorced, with a family to bring up and without employment, are likely to be socially isolated and, thus lacking social support, are vulnerable to psychiatric illness (Henderson 1981). However, a recent study of a relatively homogeneous sample of British civil servants showed that there was no sex difference in the prevalence of minor psychiatric morbidity between these men and women of similar age, education, occupation, and social environment. The women did, however, report more somatic symptoms of psychogenic origin (Jenkins 1985). A survey of general practice attenders in Dundee (Ballinger *et al.* 1985; Hobbs *et al.* 1985) showed that psychiatric disturbance as assessed by GHQ score was more likely in men in association with ill health, unemployment, lower social class, poverty, being divorced or having a poor marital relationship, or having a wife who was ill or had a psychiatric history. Women were more likely to have a high GHQ score in the presence of poor personal relationships, having three or more children, low social class, and gynaecological symptoms. It is now generally accepted that depression and anxiety brought on by social stress are just as real and legitimate as those not so associated and as such merit attention and possibly treatment by general practitioners.

The conclusion from most of these studies is that a patient's 'life situation' is very likely to affect both their physical and their psychological functioning. A plethora of self-report questionnaires and interview schedules are now available to help the general practitioner assess social stresses – the Social Assessment Schedule (Clare and Cairns 1978), the Interview Schedule for Social Interaction (Henderson 1981) and the Social Support and Stress Interview (Jenkins *et al.* 1981) are all well validated instruments which could be used in the primary care setting to improve information gathering with a view to increasing the recognition of psychiatric disorder. Certain illnesses such as post-natal depression may be more specifically enquired for. The Edinburgh Postnatal Depression Scale (Cox *et al.* 1987) is a validated, ten-item self-report questionnaire which reliably predicts depression in post-partum women. Quick and simple to use, such questionnaires may help general practitioners, who are often short of time, in getting to the root of the problem more quickly.

DIAGNOSIS OF PSYCHIATRIC ILLNESS IN GENERAL PRACTICE

Psychiatric disorder, like most illness, behaves as a continuously distributed variable and a valid question from the general practitioner might therefore be 'how much of it is present?' In psychiatry there is an even more fundamental question – deciding what 'it', the disorder – actually is. The general practice setting further compounds the problem of psychiatric case definition – there is a high incidence of transient morbidity and the illness is often seen in its very early stages, before the full clinical picture has developed. For these reasons, in particular, the classifications of psychiatric disorder in current use are quite inappropriate for primary care, i.e., the Diagnostic and Statistical Manual of Mental Disorders, Third Edition (DSM-III), the International Classification of Disease, Ninth Edition (ICD-9), as well as the International Classification of Health Problems in Primary Care, Second Edition (ICHPPC-2). This latter system was in fact devised by and for general practitioners who recognized that the ICD did not provide satisfactory diagnostic labels for many of the problems seen in primary care.

For example, in ICD-9, the emotional disorders which occur at the level of primary care are classified not only in chapter V, 'Mental Illness', but also in chapter XVI, 'Symptoms, signs and ill defined conditions', and chapter XVIII, 'Supplementary classification of factors influencing health status and contact with health services' – known as the 'V' code. That there is an 'a priori' need to change from the ICD system, which is based on a mixture of symptomatology and aetiology, to a multi-axial system which would take into account a patient's personality and social status as well as symptom state was the conclusion of a study of outcome of neurotic illness in general practice (Mann *et al*. 1981). They found that apart from the initial severity of psychiatric morbidity, the quality of social life at the time of follow-up was the only other factor to predict psychiatric state after one year. A study of the classification of mental ill health in general practice was undertaken in order to underline the need for a new system of classification appropriate to primary care (Jenkins *et al*. 1985). They invited twenty-seven experienced general practitioners to watch videotaped real-life consultations and to record their diagnoses, using both ICD-9 and ICHPPC-2. They found a very high degree of inter-observer variation, with ICHPPC-2 performing no better than ICD-9.

When rates of diagnosis for general practice from the Third National Morbidity Survey are compared with in-patient statistics from the Mental Health Enquiry for England (1981/2), the rates for neuroses and psychoses are reversed. Thus it appears that not only are general practitioners seeing the majority of psychiatric morbidity in the population, but what they see, the psychoneuroses, is quite different from what the psychiatrist, who deals mainly with the psychoses, dementia, personality disorders, mental retardation, alcoholism, and drug addiction, sees. But at what point does a set of complaints become serious enough to be considered epidemiologically, sociologically, or clinically significant? The criterion of 'caseness' has been greatly enhanced by the availability of structured psychiatric interviews and diagnostic instruments such as the Present State Examination (PSE) (Wing *et al*. 1974) and the Research Diagnostic Criteria (RDC) (Spitzer *et al*. 1978).

However, there is evidence to suggest that such diagnostic criteria derived from and for patients seen in specialist psychiatric practice may incorporate threshold levels which are inappropriate for non-specialist settings.

There will of course always be a 'hard core' of patients who have a definable mental illness classifiable by any diagnostic schema and for whom medical treatment is of proven value. At the other end of the spectrum are those patients who do not really have a psychiatric illness as such at all, although they may well exhibit illness behaviour or be complaining of psychological symptoms. These patients either have too few symptoms for a formal 'syndrome' diagnosis to be made or their symptoms are transient and self-limiting, perhaps temporarily related to some external happening such as an 'anniversary'. Also in this group are patients whose symptoms are long standing, related to a 'life situation' and whose distress is understood by the doctor but not considered by either to require 'treatment'.

Patients with minor affective disorders, mainly depression with or without anxiety, form the largest group requiring treatment in primary care, although most of these cases would only be identified at the minimum threshold level on instruments such as the PSE.

Studies of diagnosis of psychiatric disorder in primary care have concentrated largely on depressive disorders. One by general practitioners in South West London (Sireling *et al.* 1985; Freeling *et al.* 1985) reported on three groups of depressed patients – those prescribed antidepressants, those given other treatment, and those missed by the general practitioner. The majority of patients qualified as psychiatric cases on the PSE Index of Definition, with those given other treatment most often failing to meet diagnostic criteria. The patients with unrecognized depression were less obviously depressed, more likely to have a concurrent physical illness, and their illness had lasted longer.

A review by Blacker and Clare (1987) addresses the issue in some detail. They conclude that the traditional notion that general practice depression is mild, self-limiting, and clinically unimportant is mistaken, and that, apart from the consequences of non-diagnosis for the patient, untreated patients also impose an increased burden on the primary care service.

MANAGEMENT OF PSYCHIATRIC DISORDER IN GENERAL PRACTICE

When faced with a patient in whom he identifies psychological symptoms, the general practitioner has a variety of treatment options open to him. The first decision to make may well be whether the patient requires any treatment at all. Sharing and understanding a transient situational disturbance or acknowledgement of a chronic life stress may be all that is required or the general practitioner may decide that he can treat the patient himself with drugs and/or some form of 'listening treatment'. This may be supplemented by simple guidance and advice, supportive non-directive counselling or psychotherapy. The doctor as the 'drug' is a concept developed by Michael Balint in the 1950s who adapted psychoanalytically based psychotherapy to meet the needs and realities of general practice (Balint 1957). Balint's views have wielded considerable influence, particularly among those doctors who have been able to attend training seminars based on his methods. These 'entail a limited, though considerable change in the doctor's personality' (Balint 1957). They have, however, also been criticized for not being appropriate in the primary care setting (Sowerby 1977; Madden 1979), particularly on the grounds of the time it requires both in the consultation and in supervision. An adaptation of the Balint technique to the 'six minute' consultation is the flash technique (Balint and Morrell 1973), whereby the doctor helps the patient develop insight into the meaning of his symptoms within the constraints of normal practice. Balint never intended to convert general practitioners into psychoanalysts, but all general practitioners should be able to provide supportive intervention for their patients when required. One of the most commonly employed treatments for psychiatric disorder in general practice is the prescription of a psychotropic drug. Trends in psychotropic drug prescription and factors which relate to the prescription and consumption of psychotropic drugs are described in the chapter by Williams and Gabe.

Attempts have also been made to identify the characteristics of general practitioners which might account for their prescribing behaviour. A study by Raynes (1979) aimed to test some of Howie's hypotheses on decision-making (Howie 1972). She compared the consultation process leading to the prescription of a psychotropic or an antibiotic and found that the focus of both patient and doctor on physical, social, and emotional issues was the commonest characteristic in consultations where a psychotropic was prescribed. To encourage an alternative approach to the treatment of minor affective disorder, patients selected by their general practitioners as suitable for anxiolytic medication were randomly divided into a drug group and a counselling group (Catalan et al. 1984). Similar improvements were found in both groups on measures of psychiatric symptoms and social functioning at follow-up one month and seven months later. This study has, in conjunction with the government restrictions on the prescribing of benzodiazepines, been instrumental in dissuading general practitioners from relying solely on pharmacotherapy in the treatment of minor affective disorders.

A second option open to the general practitioner is to involve other members of the 'multi-disciplinary primary health care team' in management – this may include social workers, counsellors, psychologists, or community psychiatric nurses.

These different professionals bring with them a variety of skills with which to approach the patient suffering from a psychiatric illness. Social workers and general practitioners have historically tended to work quite separately, although both are the responsibility of the same government department. The Seebohm Committee (1968) recommended greater liaison between the two professions and accordingly a social work attachment scheme was set up in South London and was the subject of several observational and experimental studies. Corney and Briscoe (1977) showed that general practitioners referred different patients to attached social workers when they became aware of the social workers' skill in dealing with social and emotional problems. Furthermore, it appears that clients referred to attached social workers, rather than an area team, present more emotional problems and spend more time with the social worker (Corney and Bowen 1980). Referral to social workers also seems to have beneficial effects in that patients with depression improve more when they have help from a social worker compared with only seeing their general practitioner (Cooper 1972; Corney 1981). The advantages and disadvantages of closer collaboration between general practitioner and social workers have been extensively reviewed (Clare and Corney 1982).

Recently, an increasing number of clinical psychologists have developed links with general practice and, instead of receiving referrals in the hospital, are beginning to see patients in the community and developing attachment schemes similar to those of social workers. The advantages of a primary-care-based clinical psychology service are reviewed by Johnston (1978) and include access to psychological help for patients who would not otherwise receive it owing to problems associated with travel, work, stigma, and the type of presenting complaint, such as agoraphobia. Increased communication between general practitioner and therapist, more flexible and relevant therapy, and seeing the patient in their own setting are also advantageous. Two studies (Ives 1979; Koch 1979) have reported that patients seeing a psychologist in the general practice make fewer visits to the surgery and are prescribed fewer psychotropic drugs in the months after treatment and that those changes are maintained one year later. About 27 per cent of psychology posts in England now include some involvement with general practice (Hall et al. 1986). The sorts of problems most often referred are phobias, anxiety states, panic attacks, habit disorders, and interpersonal, social, and marital problems. The methods used by psychologists are predominantly those of behaviour therapy, cognitive therapy (Teasdale et al. 1984), and supportive psychotherapy. There is currently some discussion about the types of assessment which have been used in determining the benefits of psychological treatment to patients (Trepka and Griffiths 1987). They suggest that rather than assessing the global effects of treatment, a more differentiated approach to evaluation is required to fully assess the effectiveness of clinical psychologists in primary care.

Some of these treatment options are equally well carried out with nurse therapists. A study by Marks (1985) showed that patients who had phobic or obsessive/compulsive symptoms and received behavioural psychotherapy from a community psychiatric nurse reported significantly greater benefit compared with patients who had routine treatment from a general practitioner. The patients seemed to prefer treatment in the primary care setting rather than in the hospital and the placing of nurse therapists in this setting may also save on health care resources. A study reporting a similar role for psychiatric nurses in the community found that neurotic patients who had been attending the psychiatric hospital were cared for equally well when nurses provided supportive home visits (Paykel *et al.* 1982). Social workers, psychologists, and community psychiatric nurses, despite having somewhat different backgrounds, all have certain therapeutic skills which make them the ideal people to treat the neurotic disorders so common in primary care, many of which respond to behaviour therapy (Gelder 1979).

Counsellors are not quite so specialized in their role. Their attachment to primary care teams is also on the increase and their value lies mainly in providing supportive 'psychotherapy' for those patients who are distressed by social, marital, and interpersonal problems. The effectiveness of some of these specialist mental health treatments in general practice is reviewed in a meta-analysis by Balestrieri *et al.* (1988). The third option open to the general practitioner is to refer the patient for a specialist psychiatric opinion. As was pointed out earlier, the number of new patients seen each year in psychiatric out-patient clinics represents somewhat less than 10 per cent of the total psychiatric morbidity recognized by general practitioners. Referred patients are not a random sample of the conspicuous psychiatric morbidity. Filter 3 (figure 26.1) is 'selectively permeable' to younger people, men, the more severely ill, and the psychotic.

Brook (1978) suggested four main motives behind general practitioners' referrals:

1) to obtain an expert opinion so that he can then continue treatment himself;
2) to arrange specialist treatment that he cannot provide himself;
3) to share the burden of a patient for whom little can be done;
4) to be relieved of the patient for a while.

An important move in the last few years has been the delivery of psychiatric care by psychiatrists consulting in general practices. A recent survey showed that one in five consultant psychiatrists now spend some time in general practice settings (Strathdee and Williams 1984). They describe three different models of working – the consultation model, the shifted out-patient model, and the liaison attachment team model. Although there are some logistic problems in getting both sides together, with increasing acceptance of the psychiatrist by the primary care team, the benefits of liaison psychiatry appear to outweigh the costs (Mitchell 1985; Tyrer 1986).

CONCLUSION

Much of the research on psychiatric disorders in the primary care setting has, over the last two decades, been carried out by psychiatrists rather than by general practitioners themselves. This is not surprising in that this has been a period in which investigative methods have been slowly evolving, resulting in a variety of questionnaires and scales which have been validated and are now accessible to those without specialist training who wish to work in this field. In addition, the enormous problems described in this chapter are concerned with effective labelling of psychiatric disorders and have deterred all but the most reckless or the very brave. Finally, the level of basic training in psychology and psychiatry which has characterized undergraduate medical training until recent years has not ensured the production of a cadre of general practitioners with the necessary interest or skills to develop research.

Hopefully, the situation is changing with improvements in medical education and with the closer communication between general practitioners and psychiatrists inherent in many of the experimental situations in which psychiatrists are now conducting clinical work in general practice. Imaginative training fellowships for general practitioners wishing to develop research skills in psychiatry, and introduced three years ago by the Mental Health Foundation, have pointed the way to developments in this field. They will hopefully be copied by the Department of Health whose financial concerns with mental illness must surely make them cognizant of the need for research in this field.

Much of the early work has been concerned with identifying and quantifying mental ill health in the community. There is now a growing need for the evaluation of the outcome of different modes of management and for what will undoubtedly be the most challenging task, the prevention of mental illness.

Acknowledgement: Deborah Sharp is supported by the Mental Health Foundation.

REFERENCES

American Psychiatric Association (1980) *Diagnostic and Statistical Manual of Mental Disorders*, third edition (DSM-III), Washington, DC: AMA.
Balestrieri, M., Williams, P. and Wilkinson, G. (1988) 'How effective is specialist mental health treatment in general practice?', *Psychological Medicine* (in press).
Balint, M. (1957) *The Doctor, his Patient and the Illness*, London: Pitman Medical.
Balint, E. and Norrell, J.S. (1973) *Six Minutes for the Patient: Interactions in General Practice Consultation*, London: Tavistock.

Ballinger, C.B., Smith, A.H.W. and Hobbs, P.R. (1985) 'Factors associated with psychiatric morbidity in women – a general practice survey', *Acta Psychiatrica Scandinavica* 71: 272–80.

Boardman, A.P. (1987) 'The General Health Questionnaire and the Detection of Emotional Disorder by General Practitioners: A replicated study', *British Journal of Psychiatry* 165: 373–81.

Blacker, C.V.R. and Clare, A.W. (1987) 'Depressive disorder in primary care', *British Journal of Psychiatry* 150: 737–51.

Brook, A. (1978) 'An aspect of community mental health – consultative work with general practice teams', *Health Trends*, 10: 37–9.

Brown, G.W. and Harris, T. (1978) *Social Origins of Depression: a Study of Psychiatric Disorder in Women*, London: Tavistock.

Catalan, J., Gath, D., Edmonds, G. and Ennis, J. (1984) 'The effects of non-prescribing of Anxiolytics in General Practice I. Controlled evaluation of psychiatric and social outcome', *British Journal of Psychiatry* 144: 593–602.

Clare, A.W. and Cairns, V.E. (1978) 'Design, development and use of a standardized interview to assess social maladjustment and dysfunction in community studies', *Psychological Medicine* 8: 589–605.

Clare, A.W. and Corney, R.H. (1982) *Social Work and Primary Health Care*, London: Academic Press.

Clare, A.W. and Lader, M. (eds) (1982) *Psychiatry and General Practice*, London: Academic Press.

Cooper, B. (1972) 'Clinical and social aspects of chronic neurosis', *Proceedings of Royal Society of Medicine* 65: 509–12.

Cooper, B. and Sylph, J. (1973) 'Life events and the onset of neurotic illness: an investigation in general practice', *Psychological Medicine* 3: 421–35.

Corney, R.H. (1981) 'Social work effectiveness in the management of depressed Women', *Psychological Medicine* 11: 417–23.

Corney, R.H. and Bowen, B.A. (1980) Referrals to social workers: a comparative study of a local authority intake team with a general practice attachment team. *Journal of the Royal College of General Practitioners* 30: 139–47.

Corney, R.H. and Briscoe, M.E. (1977) 'Social workers and their clients: a comparison between primary health care and local authority settings', *Journal of the Royal College of General Practitioners* 27: 295–301.

Cox, J.L., Holden, J.M. and Sagovsky, R. (1987) 'Detection of postnatal depression. Development of 10–item postnatal depression scale', *British Journal of Psychiatry* 150: 782–6.

Eastwood, M.R. and Trevelyan, M.H. (1972) 'Relationship between physical and psychiatric disorder', *Psychological Medicine* 2: 363–72.

Freeling, P., Rao, B.M., Paykel, E.S., Sireling, L.I. and Burton, R.H. (1985) 'Unrecognised depression in general practice', *British Medical Journal* 290: 1880–3.

Gelder, M.G. (1979) 'Behavioural treatment for psychiatric disorders in general practice: preliminary communication', *Journal of the Royal Society of Medicine* 72: 421–4.

Goldberg, D.P. (1972) *The Detection of Psychiatric Illness by Questionnaire*, (Maudsley Monograph No. 21), London: Oxford University Press.

Goldberg, D.P. and Blackwell, B. (1970) 'Psychiatric illness in general practice: a detailed study using a new method of case identification', *British Medical Journal* ii: 439–43.

Goldberg, D.P. and Bridges, K. (1987) 'Screening for psychiatric illness in general practice: the general practitioner versus the screening questionnaire', *Journal of the Royal College of General Practitioners* 37: 15–18.

Goldberg, D.P., Cooper, B., Eastwood, M.R., Kedward, H.B. and Shepherd, M. (1970) 'A standardised psychiatric interview for use in community surveys', *British Journal of Social and Preventative Medicine* 24: 18–23.

Goldberg, D.P. and Huxley, P. (1980) *Mental Illness in the Community: the Pathway to Psychiatric Care*, London: Tavistock.

Goldberg, D.P., Steele, J.J., Smith, C. and Spivey, L. (1980) 'Training family doctors to recognise psychiatric illness with increased accuracy', *Lancet* ii: 521–3.

Hall, J., Koch, H., Pilling, S. and Winter, K. (1986) 'Health Services information and clinical psychology', *Bulletin of British Psychological Society* 39: 126–30.

Henderson, S. (1981) 'Social relationships, adversity and neurosis: an analysis of prospective observations', *British Journal of Psychiatry* 138: 391–8.

Hobbs, P.R., Ballinger, C.B., McClure, A., Martin, B. and Greenwood, C. (1985) 'Factors associated with psychiatric morbidity in men – a general practice survey', *Acta Psychiatra Scandinavica* 71: 281–6.

Howie, J.G.R. (1972) 'Diagnosis – The Achilles Heel?' *Journal of the Royal College of General Practitioners* 22: 310–15.

Ives, G. (1979) 'Psychological treatment in general practice', *Journal of the Royal College of General Practitioners* 29: 343–51.

Jenkins, R. (1985) 'Sex differences in minor psychiatric morbidity: a survey of a homogeneous population', *Social Science and Medicine* 20: 887–9.

Jenkins, R., Mann, A.H. and Belsey, M. (1981) 'Design and use of a short interview to assess social stress and support in research and clinical settings', *Social Science and Medicine* 3: 195–203.

Jenkins, R., Smeeton, N., Marinker, M. and Shepherd, M. (1985) 'A study of the classification of mental ill health in general practice', *Psychological Medicine* 15: 403–9.

Johnston, M. (1978) 'The work of a clinical psychologist in primary care', *Journal of the Royal College of General Practitioners* 28: 661–7.

Johnstone, A. and Goldberg, D. (1976) 'Psychiatric screening in general practice: a controlled trial', *Lancet* i: 605–8.

Koch, H.C.H. (1979) 'Evaluation of behaviour therapy intervention in general practice', *Journal of the Royal College of General Practitioners* 29: 337–40.

Madden, T.A. (1979) 'The doctors, their patients and their care: Balint reassessed', *Psychological Medicine* 9: 5–8.

Mann, A.H., Jenkins, R. and Belsey, E. (1981) 'The twelve month outcome of patients with neurotic illness in general practice', *Psychological Medicine* 11: 535–50.

Marks, I. (1985) 'Controlled trial of psychiatric nurse therapists in primary care', *British Medical Journal* 290: 1181–4.

Marks, J.N., Goldberg, D.P. and Hillier, V.F. (1979) 'Determinants of the ability of general practitioners to detect psychiatric illness', *Psychological Medicine* 9: 337–53.

Mitchell, A.R.K. (1985) 'Psychiatrists in primary health care settings', *British Journal of Psychiatry* 147: 371–9.

Paykel, E.S., Mangen, S.P., Griffith, J.H. and Burns, T.P. (1982) 'Community psychiatric nursing for neurotic patients: a controlled trial', *British Journal of Psychiatry* 140: 573–81.

Rand, E.H., Badger, L.W. and Coggins, D.R. (1987) 'Recognition of mental disorders by family practice residents: the effect of GHQ feedback', paper given at 'Mental Disorder in General Health Care Settings: A Research Conference', Seattle, USA.

Raynes, N.V. (1979) 'Factors affecting the prescribing of psychotropic drugs in general practice consultations', *Psychological Medicine* 9: 671–9.

Royal College of General Practitioners, Office of Population Censuses and Surveys, Department of Health and Social Security (1986) *Morbidity Statistics from General Practice* (Third National Study 1981–2).

Shepherd, M., Cooper, B., Brown, A.C. and Kalton, G.W. (1986) *Psychiatric Illness in General Practice*, London: Oxford University Press.

Shepherd, M., Wilkinson, G. and Williams, P. (eds) (1986) *Mental Illness in a Primary Health Care Setting*, London: Tavistock.

Sireling, L.I., Paykel, E.S., Freeling, P., Rao, B.M. and Patel, S.P. (1985) 'Depression in general practice: case thresholds and diagnoses', *British Journal of Psychiatry* 147: 113–19.

Skuse, D. and Williams, P. (1984) 'Screening for psychiatric disorders in general practice', *Psychological Medicine* 14: 365–77.

Sowerby, P. (1977) 'The doctor, his patient and the illness: a reappraisal', *Journal of the Royal College of General Practitioners* 27: 583–9.

Spitzer, R.L., Endicott, J. and Robins, E. (1978) 'Research diagnostic criteria: rationale and reliability', *Archives of General Psychiatry* 35: 773–82.

Strathdee, G. and Williams, P. (1984) 'A survey of psychiatrists in primary care: the silent growth of a new service', *Journal of the Royal College of General Practitioners* 34: 615–18.

Teasdale, J.D., Fennell, M.J.V., Hibbert, G.A. and Amies, P.L. (1984) 'Cognitive therapy for major depressive disorder in primary care', *British Journal of Psychiatry* 144: 400–6.

Trepka, C. and Griffiths, T. (1987) 'Evaluation of psychological treatment in primary care', *Journal of the Royal College of General Practitioners* 37: 215–17.

Tyrer, P. (1986) 'What is the role of the psychiatrist in primary care?', *Journal of the Royal College of General Practitioners* 36: 373–5.

Wing, J.K., Cooper, J.E. and Sartorius, N. (1974) *The Measurement and Classification of Psychiatric Symptoms*, Cambridge: Cambridge University Press.

World Health Organization (1973) *Psychiatry and Primary Medical Care*, Copenhagen: WHO, Regional Office for Europe.

World Health Organization (1980) *International Classification of Diseases, 9th revision, Clinical Modification: ICD*, Geneva: WHO.

Wright, A.F. and Perini, A.F. (1987) 'Hidden psychiatric illness: use of the General Health Questionnaire in general practice', *Journal of the Royal College of General Practitioners* 37: 164–7.

Zung, W.W.K. and Magruder-Habib, K. (1987) 'Depressed patients in general medical care', paper given at 'Mental Disorder in General Health Care Settings: A Research Conference', Seattle, USA.

The Interface Between Primary and Secondary Psychiatric Care

Geraldine Strathdee and Michael King

In Britain there has long been a sharp division between the primary and secondary levels of medical care, with hospital out-patient clinics forming the main focus of interaction between the two. Inevitably, training and research have been similarly separated, resulting in two distinctive ideologies in the provision of patient care.

This chapter traces the nature of the interface between the two levels of service beginning with an historical perspective, subsequent developments in the last two to three decades, and finishing with a view of the future.

HISTORICAL PERSPECTIVE

Service

The strength of primary medicine in Britain is unique among western countries in that 98 per cent of the population are registered with a general practitioner from whom they receive all their primary medical care. Access to the secondary services is largely at the discretion of the general practitioner with little room for patient-initiated approaches to specialists. It is only in the past twenty years that it has been recognized that psychological disorders comprise a significant part of the workload of these primary care physicians (Shepherd et al. 1966).

As Goldberg and Huxley (1980) have demonstrated, the filter between those patients identified by the GP and those referred to secondary care is relatively impermeable in that only one in twenty are referred on to specialists. In the vast majority of cases this is to hospital out-patient clinics. Psychiatric out-patient departments arose from an uncritical replication of the general medical model. The function of this expedient development has never been officially defined and even attempts to delineate the referred patient population on an empirical basis have raised more questions than they have answered (Kessel 1963).

Little has been done to evaluate either the nature or quality of service delivered by the clinics from the perspective of either primary or secondary care. However, the two substantive studies in this area have shown deficiencies in the clinical and referral outcomes and considerable dissatisfaction among patients and doctors alike (Kaeser and Cooper 1971, Johnson 1973a, 1973b). In addition, a careful examination of communication patterns between primary and secondary care doctors revealed a significant lack of understanding of each other's needs (Williams and Wallace 1974). As both areas of enquiry have shown, the result for patients was a variable level of care in both short and long term. Thus, it would seem that a rigid hospital-based out-patient service precluded effective dialogue or consensus management between GP and specialist.

Training

The training relationship in psychiatry and primary care has likewise followed the traditional medical model. Very few psychiatric trainees have had any exposure to post-graduate general practice and those GP trainees on vocational training schemes which included a psychiatric placement received an almost exclusively hospital-based training. Both the appropriateness and adequacy of this training, often sited as it is in large mental hospitals for the severely mentally ill, has been questioned as an adequate preparation for dealing with the broad spectrum of psychosocial morbidity encountered in primary care (Lesser 1983).

For GPs established in practice the only in-service training available was either in Balint groups with a psychotherapeutic emphasis, in the occasional hospital-based study day which often focused on theoretical rather than practical management issues, or the infrequent clinical associate attachment. The only other training mechanism has been through scientific and educational journals.

Research

The foundations of psychiatric research in primary care were laid by Shepherd and his colleagues in the 1960s (Shepherd *et al.* 1966). These early studies have been described in the chapter by Sharp and Morrell. As they also noted, important fields of enquiry stemming from this work have included the development of questionnaires and interviews for the identification of psychiatric morbidity and social dysfunction, and the performance of the general practitioner as a case detector.

Considerable work has also been directed at the GPs themselves with regard to their attitudes to psychiatry, their training, their referral patterns, and their ability to recognize psychological disorder (Shepherd *et al.* 1966; Rawnsley *et al.* 1962; Gardiner *et al.* 1974).

THE INTERFACE OF THE 1980S

Service

The past decade has seen the development of a unique service innovation which is altering the whole nature of the interaction between psychiatry and primary care. In a survey reported from the General Practice Research Unit, it was established that a growing number of psychiatrists (almost one in five) in England and Wales had moved their out-patient service from their hospital bases and established liaison-consultation clinics in primary care (Strathdee and Williams 1984). This service was unique in the sense that it arose *de novo*, undirected by any official policy, that there were no monetary incentives, and that its proponents were largely rurally based, front-line, clinical psychiatrists.

In contrast to the traditional 'referred away' approach of hospital out-patient departments, these liaison-consultation clinics facilitated GP and specialist working together. Three integrated methods of working were described. First, there was the consultation method in which the psychiatrist undertook assessment of the patients with an agreed treatment plan being carried out by the referring GP. Second and more common, in the shifted out-patient model, the psychiatrist both assessed and treated the patient in a series of short-term therapeutic interventions, with the GP remaining involved and informed of the management. In the third pattern, which evolved in long-standing attachments, the psychiatrist, after developing working and training links with the primary care team, adopted a predominantly supervisory or consultative role.

The context of this innovative service has recently been identified (Strathdee 1987) and correlated with major changes in primary care, psychiatry, and the relationship between the two. Within general practice the old dissatisfactions with long waiting lists and unsatisfactory clinical outcome associated with hospital clinics (Morgan and Strathdee 1987) have been voiced yet again. Moreover, GPs had increasingly begun to question the role of out-patient clinics in all specialities. There had also been a growing criticism of the propensity of hospital specialists to assume long-term clinical responsibility and exclude the referrer from the therapeutic process (Todd 1984; Marsh 1982). In particular the proclivity of hospital clinics to create 'chronic careers' for patients has been decried. One critic has gone so far as to suggest that their *only* function was as training fodder for an ever-changing series of junior doctors (Todd 1984). Research in the 1980s into the communication process reflected similar findings (Pullen and Yellowlees 1985) to that of the 1970s (Williams and Wallace 1974) in that specialists and generalists continued to be unaware of each other's requirements.

The 1980s have seen an acceleration of changes in the structure and organization of primary care, which had begun some years earlier, and which were to have profound effects on its role within medicine. The rapid expansion of vocational training schemes and the growth of academic departments of general practice has improved the status of the discipline within the medical establishment. In addition, the majority of GPs now work in partnership with other doctors and increasingly are based in health centres, facilitating the development of multi-disciplinary teams which have included health visitors, practice nurses, practice managers, and occasionally social workers and psychologists (Jeffreys and Sachs 1983). To many GPs the logical extension of the primary care team is the involvement of specialists and, in addition to the psychiatric attachments already described, reports indicate that similar trends are occurring in obstetrics, paediatrics, dermatology, and ENT.

Psychiatry itself has also undergone radical reorientation in the impetus to establish a more community-based service. Hospital closures and the need to establish community initiatives have forced psychiatrists to break the 'short umbilical cord syndrome' and recognize that working in the community behoves them to learn new skills beyond the purely clinical (Sturt and Waters 1985). In particular, the importance of developing management, communication, and administrative expertise has been underlined by the Royal College of Psychiatrists (1984). The ability to recognize and mobilize resources is fundamental to this approach. Specialists have generally failed to take account of what in Great Britain can be seen as a unique resource – the strength of the primary care network. Jones (1982) has reminded psychiatrists to recognize the consequent opportunity cost of failing to take advantage of this resource. In countries without a primary infrastructure such as the USA it may seem logical to create a first contact mental health service in the form of community health centres, but in Great Britain it could be argued that the World Health Organization view that the GP must form the 'cornerstone' of community psychiatry should be upheld. A working party cited six reasons why the GP and not the psychiatrist should remain the doctor of first contact for patients with psychiatric disorder (WHO 1973). These included the frequent presentation of psychiatric disorder in physical terms, the close relationship between psychiatric and social problems, and the lesser stigma associated with the primary care setting.

Psychiatry has begun to address itself to two important issues, the first being how can it assist GPs in providing better care to the bulk of those with psychiatric disorder who remain within primary care. Secondly, how might it best interact with GPs in this era of community psychiatry. One suggested model is that of the hive system (Tyrer 1985) which has, at the centre of a well-defined catchment area, a hospital base co-ordinating peripherally sited sub-units of care such as day hospitals, day centres, and health centre outpatient clinics located in areas of greater psychiatric morbidity. Others have emphasized a more mobile team approach concentrating on personnel rather than buildings. Falloon (personal communication) in an English rural setting has established a core multi-disciplinary team which responds quickly to

423

referrals initially processed by community psychiatric nurses based in each general practice within a catchment area. In this system treatment takes place almost exclusively in the home setting thereby greatly reducing the need for in-patient care.

The hierarchical nature of the specialist-generalist relationship has come under increasing scrutiny. As in the changing face of doctor-patient relationships, the paternalistic model whereby the consultation is perceived as all-powerful is being replaced by a system whereby authority is based on expertise. This may be a difficult step for many GPs whose attitudes are a legacy from their training as junior doctors where consultants were regarded as omnipotent in carrying ultimate responsibility. Earlier commentators have pointed out that the optimal balance in this relationship can only effectively be achieved by an decrease in the power and authority of the specialist accompanied by a greater sharing in the burden of work and responsibility by all concerned (Horder 1986, Editorial 1978).

Training

More recently both the Royal College of Psychiatrists (Working Party report in progress) and the Royal College of General Practitioners (1980) have outlined the need for a reorientation in training to take account of the greater community emphasis in the provision of psychiatric care. There have been a number of innovations in this direction in the 1980s. First, GP trainees have been increasingly involved in the primary-care-based out-patient clinics already described. Among advantages cited are that they encounter psychiatrically ill patients in a setting akin to their future working environment and they acquire the practical skills of assessment and treatment adapted to the primary care setting. In addition, experience of the team approach common to community psychiatry will give them an understanding of how, in their future role as general practitioners, they might best liaise and communicate with the specialist services.

Second, for trainee psychiatrists, experience in liaison to general practice has introduced them to the need to develop more than purely clinical skills. It is envisaged that they will be able to identify and utilize resources not found in the hospital, as well as learn administrative, management, and communication skills essential for specialists working in the community. Working in a non-hospital setting may give the trainee a better understanding of the psychosocial components of psychiatric disorder and a recognition that psychiatric care involves much more than the period of hospital contact either as an in-patient or out-patient. More recently, a London teaching school has introduced a scheme whereby trainee psychiatrists work as general practitioners themselves for a limited period in order that they might gain a better understanding of the limitations and resources available within the primary care setting. This is in keeping with the General Medical Council's Education Committee's recommendation that all post-graduate education should include a mandatory six-month attachment in general practice (Turner 1987).

Third, established general practitioners have also reported substantial training benefits from close interaction with visiting specialists (Strathdee 1987). This has included increased theoretical knowledge about the nature of psychiatric disorders and treatments, as well as the mastery of practical skills of mental state assessment and management. These were acquired from face-to-face discussions and formal case presentations as well as directly from the joint management of patients.

Finally, psychiatric specialists gain a greater understanding of the limitations of time, interest, and skills of GPs and of the difficulties encountered in primary care psychiatry (Strathdee and Williams 1986). These include the assessment of earlier, less differentiated presentations of psychological disorder. Their GP colleagues often face patients whose behaviour and mental state seems clearly to separate them from the norm, but for whom, at the time of initial consultation, psychiatric diagnosis is unclear. Diagnosis is reached by a process of exploration by the doctor which inevitably leads to organization of the symptoms by the patient. Often this process only culminates on arrival at hospital when specialists, unaware of this resolution process, may be critical of GPs' diagnostic acumen, because of what is (by then) a classical clinical entity. While this is a problem in medicine or surgery, for example the vague abdominal pain referred by the GP which becomes an unquestionable appendicitis on arrival at casualty, it is even more compounded in psychiatry by the dimension of patient insight and the difficulties inherent for patients describing their own psychic phenomena. An example in psychiatry might be the 'disturbed' adolescent who isolates himself from peers, plays loud music, and loses interest in school work and his family. Even though the GP may feel that this patient is *qualitatively* distinct from other difficult adolescents, it may take some time for the patient himself to be able to divulge and discuss his bewildering array of psychotic experiences.

Research

Following on from the early work concentrating on the attitude and training attributes of GPs and their ability to recognize psychiatric disorders has been a generation of studies aimed at ways of improving identification and treatment skills (Goldberg *et al.* 1987).

Principal among these areas of development have been studies of depression among primary care populations, with a focus on recognition (Freeling *et al.* 1985; McDonald 1986; Blacker and Clare; 1987), intervention (Blackburn *et al.* 1981), Teasdale *et al.* 1984), and outcome (Blacker *et al.* 1987). The direction of work on minor psychiatric disorder has concentrated on treatment and outcome studies (Catalan *et al.* 1984: Corney 1984: Mann *et al.* 1981; Rodrigo *et al.* 1988, Johnstone and Shepley 1986), although the exact phenomenology of this syndrome remains rather vague. Other specific disorders which have received attention include problem drinking (Clements 1986: King 1986a; Wallace *et al.* 1987; Heather *et al.* 1987), eating disorders (Meadows *et al.* 1986; King 1987), and phobic disorders (Marks 1985).

Out of this research several training texts and manuals have been developed specifically to assist family doctors undertake psychological intervention in primary care (Williams 1984; France and Robson 1986).

In the 1980s research has expanded on the earlier evaluations of the service provided by psychiatric out-patient clinics. New impetus has come from the development of psychiatric clinics based in primary care. Conclusions from three studies have identified that moving the location of the clinics into the primary care setting results in an alteration of the spectrum of referrals to psychiatrists. This patient population more closely reflects the composition of patients with psychiatric morbidity in the community, i.e., more women, more chronically ill, and a wider representation of ethnic minorities (Tyrer 1984; Browning *et al.* 1987; Brown *et al.* 1988; Strathdee *et al.* 1988).

INTERFACE IN THE FUTURE

Services

One of the most crucial questions for the future structure of mental health services has been posed by the World Health Organization. In its First Contact Mental Health Care document (WHO 1983) it asks:

in what ways should mental health specialist services interact with primary health services? Should the model be one of supervision and of direction, or one of collaboration and working directly with families in the community? Are all members of the mental health team equally relevant to the work in primary care? . . . These questions raise issues of integration, teamwork, collaboration and co-ordination.

Within the development of community services in Great Britain the role of primary care within these parameters remains largely unexplored. To reiterate, we believe that the GP will continue to remain the point of first contact for the mentally disturbed in the community. He or she is involved in acute and emergency care, continuing care, and the follow-up of the chronically mentally ill discharged from hospital units. Although there has been little quantitative evaluation of this role, services need to be set up so as to maximize the potential of this important resource.

The development of medical services has historically proceeded in a largely ad hoc, unevaluated fashion. We would emphasize that the expansion of community psychiatry should be accompanied by systematic evaluation going beyond mere description of the process. Initiatives requiring this approach include the provision of crisis intervention teams; community psychiatric nurses based in primary care; the further expansion of general practice out-patient clinics; working links with community day hospitals and centres; and the co-ordination of the care of the long-term mentally ill. In addition, contacts between GPs and psychiatric units in district general hospitals, particularly the communication aspects and continuity of care, need to be evaluated. Only such a careful clinical and economic assessment will allow new services to respond to changing needs.

Much more emphasis needs to be placed on the importance of prevention. The Royal College of General Practitioners (1981) has already led the way with a thoughtful report on the possibilities for prevention of psychiatric morbidity in primary care. GPs and other members of the primary care team are particularly well placed to provide education on such areas as stress reduction, alcohol and drug use, eating habits, and the psychological health of mothers and babies. In particular, they have an important role in crisis pre-emption and would benefit from increased education on crisis prevention.

Training

It is uncertain what degree of extra work load new community services will place on GPs. Equally, it appears that with the move into the community the work of psychiatrists and other mental health workers will alter. The success of these changes will rest on innovative changes in training of all staff concerned.

Clear-cut lines of responsibility and a formalized support system need to be established. Psychiatrists need to become more responsive to the needs of GPs by being prepared to offer supervision and training for a whole range of psychotherapeutic interventions, such as elements of cognitive and behavioural therapies, marital and family therapy. There is fruitful ground for study of how these techniques can best be adapted to the primary care field. However, the success of this training can only come about given that psychiatrists themselves become more aware of the constraints of general practice. It would seem logical that this can be achieved only by continuing integration of vocational schemes for both trainee psychiatrists and GPs in the community setting itself.

In centres where the traditional hospital model continues, the training potential of existing contacts between the two specialities should be maximized. For example, information in the assessment letters of psychiatrists might serve a more practical function by paying more attention to management techniques and their rationale, and less to lengthy historical accounts and diagnostic debate. The educational potential of shared care cards such as exist in obstetrics has never been explored, nor has their role in improving continuity of care, particularly for the chronically mentally ill.

The need for established GPs to become more involved in post-graduate

427

education has been stressed in a recent government green paper 'Primary Health Care, An Agenda for Discussion' (DHSS 1986). Courses for these doctors should have an emphasis on the development of practical clinical skills. There is much scope for the development of a multi-disciplinary-based diploma course in psychosocial medicine on the same lines as for geriatric medicine and paediatrics. Already in England there are moves afoot to set up such a diploma (Higgs 1988).

Similar considerations must likewise apply to other professionals, such as social workers, community psychiatric nurses, psychologists, and counsellors. While the exact role of each group remains unclear they, too, will have to adapt to the new patterns of care both within their own work and in their relationship to the other disciplines.

Research

With the current economic constraints, patterns of research may change. At one level it could be argued that all practitioners should critically evaluate their services. This process of service audit is best undertaken by collaborative research between specialist and generalist. In the future therefore, it might be hoped that the current haphazard developments be replaced by a more planned approach which takes account of and adapts to joint efforts at evaluation.

At the other level there remain many areas where the possibilities for research are limitless. There has been a recent emphasis on the importance of establishing the natural history of psychiatric disorder. This can only be effectively delineated by studies which include the population at large rather than the narrow spectrum of disorders that present to hospital. Primary care, at least in the UK, represents an important community resource for this type of work. The importance of intervention and outcome studies has received increasing attention and it is a prerequisite for all such studies that we have a firm understanding of the natural history of the conditions in question. The work on intervention by GPs in the areas such as alcohol abuse (Heather *et al.* 1987) needs to be replicated and extended to other conditions with a psychiatric component.

It will be necessary to establish guidelines for collaborative management of psychiatric conditions, particularly the chronically ill. There are many models of integration between health professionals, staff of other agencies, and informal carers including the family, few of which have been systematically evaluated.

Little of the research into psychiatry in primary care has been undertaken by GPs themselves in contrast to areas such as family planning and medicine. Of course, it has been only in the last two decades that academic general practice has been widely established. Although the funding of primary care research remains problematical, the future is not so bleak. New developments in the primary care field, such as more universal use of age-sex and disease registers, computerization, together with recognition of the importance of research (Royal College of General Practitioners 1985) is likely to facilitate an expansion of research initiatives.

Economic appraisal of health care is a necessary component of all the above research considerations, but implicit in such an approach is a greater awareness and training in basic methods of economic evaluation. This is discussed elsewhere in this volume by Wilkinson and Pelosi.

The question of whether research leads or merely documents service developments has never been fully addressed. However, in the area of referral to specialists, research findings can inform clinical practice. It has been well established that the clinical reasons form only one part of the overall rationale for referral to psychiatrists. The other administrative and social reasons are seldom confronted in the standard out-patient consultation, resulting in the high level of dissatisfaction on the part of both consumers and doctors. Future research needs to establish if greater attention to these factors facilitates improved clinical outcome.

Finally, but of crucial importance for the direction of future research, is a consideration of how patients move in and out of treatment. Little attempt has been made to establish what influences movement of patients *back* into the community. Specialists need to accept that the time spent in contact with the hospital service represents only a small fraction of the total episode of illness. Goldberg and Huxley (1980) identified that the nature of the patient, his or her social environment, and the attitudes and training of the family doctor were the deciding factors in the referral of patients to psychiatric services. Although in their model little emphasis was placed on the nature of the service at each level, research has shown that there are considerable differences in the pattern of referral and outcome depending on whether the service is community or hospital-based (Grad and Sainsbury 1966, Brown *et al.* 1988). Moreover, as yet we know little about the effects of joint management by specialists and GPs.

The factors which determine the re-entry of patients back from hospital to out-patients to primary care and finally to the community, for even a single episode of illness, have not been identified. We would postulate that important among these might be the nature of the psychiatric and primary care services, the form and chronicity of the illness, treatment employed and patient compliance, social support, and the involvement of other community agencies. Delineation of the factors determining movement in either direction along this pathway might provide useful information for innovative changes in community services.

CONCLUSIONS

The specialist-generalist relationship forms the nidus of effective patient care.

429

Throughout the last three decades this interface has been subjected to increasing scrutiny with the result that the sharp division that characterized the early years is beginning to give way to closer collaboration. This has come about because of the growing strength of primary care as a speciality and new innovations in training in both specialities. Further impetus has arisen from the growing dissatisfaction with the traditional out-patient clinic, a new emphasis on evaluation which informs clinical practice and the increasing community orientation in psychiatry

In the future the interaction between psychiatrist and family doctor needs to be seen in the broader context, emphasizing that the interface between the two disciplines is only one component of the full circle of care. This will form a fruitful basis for future service, training and research initiatives.

Acknowledgement: The authors are supported by the Department of Health and Social Security.

REFERENCES

Blackburn, I.M., Bishops, S., Glen, A.I.M., Whalley, L.J. and Christie, J.E. (1981) 'The efficacy of cognitive therapy in depression: a treatment combination', *British Journal of Psychiatry* 139: 181–9.

Blacker, C.V.R., Clare, A.W. and Thomas, J. (1987) 'Depression in primary care', paper presented to 'Mental Disorders in General Health Care Settings', Seattle, USA.

Blacker, C.V.R. and Clare, A.W. (1987) 'Depressive disorder in primary care', *British Journal of Psychiatry* 150: 737–51.

Brown, R.M.A., Strathdee, G., Christie-Brown, J.R.W. and Robinson, P.H. (1988) 'A comparison of referrals to primary care and hospital outpatients clinics', *British Journal of Psychiatry*, in press.

Browning, S.M., Ford, M.F., Goddard, C.A. and Brown, A.C. (1987) 'A psychiatric clinic, in general practice: a description and comparison with an out-patient clinic', *Bulletin of the Royal College of Psychiatrists* 11, (4): 114–17.

Catalan, J., Gath, G., Edmonds, G., Bond, A., Mertin, P. and Ennis, J. (1984) 'Effects of non-prescribing of anxiolytics in general practice, 1. controlled evaluation of psychiatric and social outcome; 2. factors associated with outcome', *British Journal of Psychiatry*, 144: 593–610.

Clements, S. (1986) 'The identification of alcohol-related problems by general practitioners', *British Journal of Addiction* 81: 257–64.

Cooper, B., Harwin, B.G., Depla, G. and Shepherd, M. (1975) 'Mental health care in the community: an evaluative study', *Psychological Medicine* 5 (4): 372–80.

Corney, R.H. (1984) *The Effectiveness of Attached Social Workers in the Management of Depressed Female Patients in General Practice* (Monograph supplement 6) Cambridge: Cambridge University Press.

Department of Health and Social Security (1986) *Primary Health Care: An Agenda for Discussion*, London: HMSO.

Editorial (1978) 'General Practitioners and Psychiatrists – a new relationship', *Journal of the Royal College of General Practitioners* 28: 643–5.

France, R. and Robson, M. (1986) *Behaviour Therapy in Primary Care*, London: Croom Helm.

Freeling, P., Rao, B.M., Paykel, E.S., Sireling, L.I. and Burton, R.H. (1985) 'Unrecognised depression in general practice', *British Medical Journal* 290: 1880–82.

Gardiner, A., Petersen, J., and Hall, D. (1974) 'A survey of general practitioners' referrals to a psychiatric outpatient service', *British Journal of Psychiatry* 124: 536–41.

Goldberg, D.P., Bridges, K., Duncan-Jones, P. and Grayson, D. (1987) 'Dimensions of neurosis seen in primary care settings', *Psychological Medicine* 17: 461–70.

Goldberg, D. and Huxley, P. (1980) *Mental Illness in the Community: The Pathway to Psychiatric Care*, London: Tavistock.

Grad, J. and Sainsbury, P. (1966) 'Evaluating the community psychiatric service in Chichester: results', in E.M. Gruenberg (ed.) *Evaluating the Effectiveness of Mental Health Services*, New York: Milbank Memorial Fund.

Heather, N.M., Campion, P.D., Neville, R.G. and Maccabe, D. (1987) 'Evaluation of a controlled drinking minimal intervention for problem drinkers in general practice (the DRAMS scheme)', *Journal of the Royal College of General Practitioners* 37: 358–63.

Higgs, R., Strathdee, G., Corney, R. and Dammers, J. (1988) Personal communication.

Horder, J.P. (1986) 'The balance between primary and secondary care: a personal view', *Health Trends* 17: 64–8.

Jeffreys, M. and Sachs, H. (1983) *Rethinking General Practice*, London: Tavistock.

Johnson, D.A. (1973a) 'An analysis of out-patient services', *British Journal of Psychiatry* 122: 301–6.

Johnson, D.A. (1973b) 'A further study of psychiatric outpatient services in Manchester', *British Journal of Psychiatry* 123: 185–91.

Johnstone, A. and Shepley, M. (1986) 'The outcome of hidden neurotic illness treated in general practice', *Journal of the Royal College of General Practitioners* 36: 413–15.

Jones, K. (1982) 'Scull's dilemma', *British Journal of Psychiatry* 141: 221–6.

Journal of the Royal College of General Practitioners (1978) 'General practitioners and psychiatrists – a new relationship', editorial, *Journal of the Royal College of General Practitioners* 28: 643–5.

Kaeser, A.C. and Cooper, B. (1971) 'The psychiatric out-patient, the general practitioner and the out-patient clinic; an operational study: a review', *Psychological Medicine* 1: 312–25.

Kessel, N. (1963) 'Who ought to see a psychiatrist?' *Lancet* 1: 1092–5.

King, M. (1986) 'At risk drinking among general practice attenders: prevalence, characteristics and alcohol related problems', *British Journal of Psychiatry* 148: 533–50.

King, M. (1987) 'Eating disorders in general practice', *British Medical Journal* 293: 1412–14.

Lesser, A.L. (1983) 'Is training in psychiatry relevant for general practice?', *Journal of the Royal College of General Practitioners*, 39: 617–18.

Liaison Committee of the Royal College of Psychiatrists and the Royal College of General Practitioners (1980) 'Experience desirable for the general practice trainee occupying a senior house officer post in psychiatry', *Journal of the Royal College of General Practitioners* 30: 625–8.

MacDonald, A.J.D. (1986) 'Do general practitioners "miss" depression in elderly patients?', *British Medical Journal* 292: 1365–7.

Mann, A.H., Jenkins, R. and Belsey, E. (1981) 'The twelve month outcome of patients with neurotic illness in general practice', *Psychological Medicine* 11: 535–50.

Marks, I. (1985) 'Controlled trial of psychiatric nurse therapists in primary care', *British Medical Journal* 240: 1181–4.

Marsh, G.N. (1982) 'Are follow-up consultations in medical outpatient departments futile?', *British Medicine Journal* 284: 1176–7.

Meadows, G.N., Palmer, R.L., Newball, E.V.M. and Skentick, J.M.T. (1986) 'Eating attitudes and disorder in young women: a general practice based survey', *Psychological Medicine* 16: 351–7.

Morgan, D. and Strathdee, G. (1987) 'An ethnography of psychiatric referrals', unpublished research report.

Pullen, I. and Yellowlees, A.J. (1985) 'Is communication improving between general practitioners and psychiatrists?', *British Medical Journal* 290: 31–3.

Rawnsley, K., Loudon, J. and Miles, M. (1962) 'Factors influencing the reference of patients by general practitioners', *British Journal of Preventive and Social Medicine* 16: 174.

Rodrigo, E., King, M.B. and Williams, P. (1988) 'The health of long-term benzodiazepine consumers', *British Medical Journal*, in press.

Royal College of General Practitioners (1981) *Prevention of Psychiatric Disorders in General Practice* (Report of a Sub-Committee of the Royal College of General Practitioners' Working Party on Prevention).

Royal College of General Practitioners (1985) 'Quality of General Practice', *Policy Statement* 2: RCGPs.

Royal College of Psychiatrists (1984) 'Management Training', *Bulletin of the Royal College of Psychiatrists* 9: 84.

Royal College of Psychiatrists (1987) 'The front line of the health service'.

Shepherd, M., Cooper, B., Brown, A.C. and Kalton, G.W. (1966) *Psychiatric Illness in General Practice*, London: Oxford University Press.

Strathdee, G. (1987) 'Primary care – psychiatry interaction: a British perspective', *General Hospital Psychiatry* 9: 102–10.

Strathdee, G., King, M., Araya, R. and Lewis, S. (1988) 'The clinical and social status of patients referred to hospital and primary care outpatient clinics', unpublished research report.

Strathdee, G. and Williams, P. (1984) 'A survey of psychiatrists in primary care: the silent growth of a new service', *Journal of the Royal College of General Practitioners* 34: 615–18.

Strathdee, G. and Williams, P. (1986) 'Patterns of collaboration', in M. Shepherd, G. Wilkinson and P. Williams (eds) *Mental Illness in Primary Care Settings*, London: Tavistock.

Sturt, J. and Waters, H. (1985) 'Role of the psychiatrist in community-based mental health care', *Lancet* i: 507–8.

Teasdale, J.D., Fennell, M.J.V., Hibbert, G.A.R. and Amies, P.L. (1984) 'Cognitive therapy for major depressive disorder in primary care', *British Journal of Psychiatry* 144: 400–6.

Todd, J.W. (1984) 'Wasted resources: referral to hospital', *Lancet* 2: p. 1089.

Turner, T. (1987) 'GPs may soon train other specialists', *General Practitioner*, November 13: 4.

Tyrer, P. (1984) 'Psychiatric clinics in general practice: an extension of community care', *British Journal of Psychiatry* 145: 9–14.

Tyrer, P. (1985) 'The hive system: a model for a psychiatric service', *British Journal of Psychiatry* 146: 571–5.

Tyrer, P., Seivewright, N. and Wollerton, S. (1984) 'General practice psychiatric clinics: impact on psychiatric services', *British Journal of Psychiatry* 145: 15–19.

Wallace, P.G., Brennan, P.J. and Haines, A.P. (1987) 'Drinking patterns in general practice patients', *Journal of the Royal College of General Practitioners* 37: 354–7.

Williams, J.M.G. (1984) *The Psychological Treatment of Depression. A Guide to the Theory and Practice of Cognitive-Behaviour Therapy*, London: Croom Helm.

Williams, P. and Wallace, B.B. (1974) 'General practitioners and psychiatrists – do they communicate?' *British Medical Journal* 1: 505.

World Health Organization (1973) *Psychiatry and Primary Medical Care*, Copenhagen: WHO Regional Office for Europe.

World Health Organization (1983) *First Contact Mental Health Care* (report on a working group), Copenhagen: WHO Regional Office for Europe.

28

The Relationship Between Psychiatric Research and Public Policy

Leon Eisenberg

The relationship between psychiatric research and public policy embraces two separate but interrelated issues: how public policy for the support and regulation of research is, or should be, formulated, on the one hand; and the ways in which research findings are, or should be, utilized in formulating public policy, on the other. The two are obviously closely connected: the extent to which the public in a democratic society is persuaded that research can lead to more effective policy for the control of disease and the promotion of health will obviously influence the funds allocated to, and the latitude afforded for, health research. Drawing primarily on examples from the United States, I will first consider national policy for the support of research and then examine the extent to which research findings inform the debate on public policy.

POLICY GOVERNING RESEARCH SUPPORT

Although a National Institute of Health (NIH) was first created in 1930 (as successor to the Hygienic Laboratory established at the US Marine Hospital on Staten Island in 1887), its funding was quite modest. Not until the years following the Second World War did support for medical research in the federal budget begin to become substantial. The visible success of the war-time Office of Scientific Research and Development had persuaded the US Congress that investment in basic and applied research would lead to tangible results for public health. Between 1956, when federal appropriations for NIH were $98 million, and 1959, they tripled in response to a new health science coalition (Shannon 1987); by the late 1960s, funding passed the unprecedented $1 billion mark. Year after year, Senator Lester Hill and Representative John Fogarty, chairing the relevant Congressional committees, provided the leadership for an almost exponential increase in the commitment of public funds to health research; the Congress has authorized larger sums than successive Presidents have proposed in all but eight of the annual

434

budgets between 1933 and 1987 (Marshall 1987)!

Obviously such a rate of increase could not continue for long (or, as one wag proclaimed, half of the US population would soon be employed doing health research on the other half). The rate began to slow in the late 1960s and appropriations actually fell (in dollars corrected for inflation) during some budget years in the 1970s and again in the early 1980s. Allocations for health research and development from all sources in the US remained about level in constant dollars between 1975 and 1983 (Office of Program Planning and Evaluation 1986: 4). Fortunately, over the last five years, NIH funding has once again attained sustained growth amounting to 70 per cent in dollars appropriated and 28 per cent in real terms; it reached $6.2 billion for fiscal year 1987 (Wyngaarden 1987).

The National Institute of Mental Health (NIMH), a component of NIH from its founding in 1946 until it was split off in 1974 together with the National Institutes for Alcoholism and Alcohol Abuse (NIAAA) and for Drug Addiction (NIDA) to form a separate Alcohol, Drug Abuse and Mental Health Administration (ADAMHA), began more modestly and its research budget did not reach $100 million until 1966. Had the NIMH research budget kept pace with inflation or had it paralleled the growth at NIH during the 1970s and 1980s, it would have exceeded $300 million by 1983 (Institute of Medicine 1984); however, because of the lower priority assigned to mental health by the Congress, the actual allocation was $158 million, one-sixth of the amount awarded to the National Cancer Institute and one-quarter of that awarded to the National Heart, Lung and Blood Institute in that year.

I have thus far merely outlined the history of what has been a remarkable national commitment to the support of health research, unparalleled elsewhere, although it has not fully satisfied the scientific community and has at times proceeded by fits and starts. As the President's Biomedical Research Panel noted:

> The scientific enterprise needs stability and predictability. It does not require growth and expansion at the rate achieved in the 1950's and 1960's, but it cannot survive being turned on and off, nor will it succeed if held at a standstill without any opportunity for growth.
>
> (Murphy and Ebert 1976:3).

Concerns about stability, costs, and cost effectiveness in health research led Joseph Califano, the then Secretary of the Department of Health, Education and Welfare, to convene a National Conference on Health Research Principles in January of 1979 to help develop 'a multi-year research strategy to guide the allocation of limited government health research dollars' (Office of the Director, NIH 1979: 99). Many in the academic community were concerned that the conference was convened with a greater emphasis on 'limited government health research dollars' than on a 'multi-year research strategy'; yet it was clear that 'public funds . . . will be made available to us only insofar as we are able to make a persuasive case for their utility' (Eisenberg 1979: 97).

What are the grounds that justify government support of health research? Are there guidelines for the total amount that should be committed? And how should priorities be set for allocating monies to particular health problems within the total?

Justifying a national commitment to health research

To many in the academy, the justification for basic science is the pursuit of knowledge for its own sake. Although this intellectual position does not carry much cachet in political debates, it remains the case that science enriches human understanding; science is a way of knowing. In the words of Adam Smith, it 'introduces order into the chaos of jarring and discordant appearances . . . and [restores the imagination], when it surveys the grand revolutions of the universe, to that tone of tranquillity and composure, which is most agreeable in itself, and most suitable to its nature' (Smith 1790: 45). The gratification of man's aesthetic sensibilities is not often persuasive to the public as a rationale for expending tax funds; the body politic is much more likely to respond to the substantial practical benefits scientific discovery brings with it. As Francis Bacon put the matter in his Third Aphorism 'concerning the interpretation of nature and the kingdom of man' in the *Novum Organum*, 'Human knowledge and human power meet in one; for where the cause is not known the effect cannot be produced. Nature to be commanded must be obeyed' (Bacon 1620: 259).

Bacon's proposition that knowledge is power was borne out in the late Julius Comroe's (1976) analysis of the scientific patrimony of ideas which proved ultimately of great benefit to patient care; 41 per cent of the work essential for later clinical advance was not clinically oriented at the time it was undertaken (Comroe and Dripps 1976). Although the chemist von Baeyer synthesized barbituric acid as early as 1864, it was not until Fischer and von Mering produced barbital in 1903 that barbiturates were employed as sedatives. Even when scientists pursue health-related ends, the applicability of their findings may not be apparent. Michael Heidelberger and Walter Jacobs synthesized sulfanilamide in the laboratory in 1915; yet twenty years were to pass before sulfonamides were first used against infectious diseases; the concept that inhibiting the uptake of metabolites would produce bacteriostasis had not been conceived. In 1970, David Baltimore and Howard Temin independently found evidence for an enzyme in RNA viruses capable of constructing double-stranded DNA from single-stranded RNA templates. The discovery of reverse transcriptase was acknowledged as a scientific landmark by the award of a Nobel Prize five years later. That work was to provide the foundation for understanding the pathophysiology of the Acquired Immune Deficiency Syndrome, a disease not identified until 1981 (Centers for Disease Control 1981a, 1981b); its cause, the HIV retrovirus employing reverse transcriptase to integrate itself into the host cell genome, was not identified until 1983 (Barre-Sinoussi *et al.* 1983; Gallo *et al.* 1983). The pursuit of basic knowledge in the laboratory yielded a concept and a methodology essential for the understanding of an unprecedented epidemic (Eisenberg 1986a); it provides major insights into the evolutionary origins of genetic information (Varmus 1987).

The most common rationale for research support is its direct benefit for health. The goals of health research have been epitomized as: advancing the fundamental knowledge base; translating that knowledge into improved diagnostic, treatment, and preventive interventions in order to alleviate suffering, improve the quality of life, and enhance survival; providing the basis for regulatory actions to promote safety and health; and providing the basis for informed decision making on health policy (Institute of Medicine 1979: 11). The Presidential Panel Report heralded the promise of biomedical and behavioural science in these terms:

> Human beings have within reach the capacity to control or prevent human disease. Although this may seem an overly optimistic forecast, it is, in fact, a realistic, practical appraisal of the long term future . . . There do not appear to be any impenetrable, incomprehensible diseases.
>
> (Murphy and Ebert 1976: 2).

A decade later, it is not likely that the promise of biomedical science for creating a disease-free society would be stated in such self-confident terms. It is not that the capabilities of the scientific enterprise have diminished in the interim; indeed, they have increased. But so has our awareness of the complexity of disease virulence, the multiple determinants of host resistance and the ecologic consequences that follow technological fixes (Eisenberg 1986b). As this decade ends, we have reason to recall the words of Rene Dubos:

> There is no reason to doubt . . . the ability of the scientific method to solve each of the specific problems of disease by discovering causes and remedial procedures . . . But solving problems of disease is not the same thing as creating health . . . In the world of reality, places change and man also changes . . . Health and happiness cannot be absolute and permanent values . . . Biological success in all its manifestations is a measure of fitness, and fitness requires never-ending efforts of adaptation to the total environment, which is ever changing.   (Dubos 1959: 22–5)

The goal of interdisciplinary research in the health sciences must become a more complete understanding of the interactions between human populations and their salient physical, biological, and social environments.

The final – and least credible – argument for supporting research is a promise of reduction in health care costs. Advocates cite as a prototype the spectacular success of the WHO campaign against smallpox, which, by eliminating the virus, even removed the need for continuing vaccination costs. But that example has limited relevance. The biology of smallpox is unique: no animal reservoir, virtual life-long immunity after infection or vaccination, visible evidence of the immune state through scarification, transmissibility only while the vesicular eruption lasts, and no carrier state (Breman and Arita 1980). Other disease prevention measures are much less efficient and none has yet sufficed to eliminate the causal agent. Vaccinating those sixty-five and over against influenza costs an additional \$2,000 for each year of life gained, even though the vaccine is cheap and hospitalization for the complications of influenza dear, because the economic calculus takes into account the additional costs for medical care from other causes among those who survive (Office of Technology Assessment 1981).

None of this argues against research in disease prevention in order to diminish morbidity and mortality; to the contrary, prevention must be in the forefront of our endeavours (Eisenberg 1987a). But the claims for cost reduction are illusory. They are likely to discredit the research enterprise when it does not yield the vaunted benefits. As Gori and Richter (1979) and Russell (1986) have pointed out, prevention delays death but does not eliminate cumulative morbidity. Increased survivorship into later years inexorably foretells higher costs (unless one clings to the fantasy of eliminating all chronic diseases). Americans 65 and over, some 11 per cent of the population in 1980, 'consumed' 29 per cent of personal health care expenditures; by 2020, when they will constitute 26 per cent of the population, the figure for expenditures will rise to 40 per cent (Rice and Feldman 1983). Success in prolonging meaningful life is a cause for celebration, but it does not come cheap. To claim that health research will lower overall health costs is to issue an unredeemable promissory note.

How much is enough?

Are there guidelines governments might usefully employ to determine appropriate resource allocations for medical research? In the heady years of the 1950s and early 1960s in the United States, with the GNP increasing each year, little thought was given to the sustainable limits to expansion in the research enterprise. In the late 1970s and 1980s, at a time of budget deficits, a slow-down in growth of the GNP, and an unfavourable trade balance, the question of limits has become prominent in policy debates. In 1976, the President's Panel had stated:

In other fields of technological endeavor . . . it is customary to invest between 5 and 10 per cent of the total budget on research and development . . . At the present time the health industry as a whole invests a considerably smaller percentage in research . . . While 5 per cent would represent an abruptly large increase if committed overnight, it seems to us a rational percentage to head toward as a long-range goal.

(Murphy and Ebert 1976: A22)

In 1976, total health research and development costs were 3.6 per cent of total health costs; the estimate for 1985 was 3.1 per cent (Office of Program Planning and Evaluation 1986: 2).

US health care expenditures for 1987 can be expected to total more than $500 billion. If the Panel's recommendation for a 5 per cent set aside for health research had been in effect, that would have justified an allocation of some $25 billion. What are the actual figures likely to be be? Over the past decade, the NIH budget has provided from 35 per cent to 40 per cent of all national support for health research and development, with other federal sources providing 15 per cent to 20 per cent and industry about 30 per cent to 39 per cent (Office of Program Planning and Evaluation 1986: 4). *If* similar ratios obtain in 1987 (an uncertain assumption) with an NIH budget of $6.2 billion, total support will equal some $16 billion, about 3.2 per cent rather than 5 per cent of 'industry' costs. Moreover, what is listed under 'research and development' in the national total is likely to reflect expenditures for development far more than basic research.

The relative generosity of research funding in the US stands in stark contrast to the situation in the UK, which invests only 1.5 per cent of the NHS budget in medical research, according to Sir Walter Bodmer, Director of the Imperial Cancer Fund. The most recent commentary in *Nature* remarked bitterly:

For want of sufficient renewal over 15 years, the research community is aging. The depth and variety of its pattern of work, already constrained by the lack of funds, will be further restricted by the reorganizations now in the cards. There are good reasons to fear that the permanent loss of able people is potentially another undermining influence. The flight of able young people into fields other than science, made possible and even necessary by the British educational system, is a greater if more distant worry. Bankruptcy tomorrow is a threat. (*Nature*, editorial, 1987: 745)

From this side of the Atlantic, the state of affairs in the UK can only be described as appalling. Lacking detailed knowledge of the British scene, I have no insights to offer into the reason for the meanness of government policy toward scientific research. I am, however, acutely aware of the loss for us when British scientists are handcuffed. Science is an international enterprise; its fruits are shared by all. When its future is in jeopardy in any country, that must be a matter of concern to scientists and citizens everywhere.

439

Setting priorities within the research budget

Within the health research budget, how are priorities to be assigned for allocations to particular disease problems? A rationalist might argue that decisions should be based on a close analysis (a) of the scientific opportunity for discovery in a given area (the existence of exciting new concepts and the availability of reliable methods) and (b) of the health burden produced by the diseases under consideration. For example, a cogent argument can be made on both grounds for a much increased investment in research on Alzheimer's disease. Localization of the gene controlling the production of amyloid on chromosome 21 (Goldgaber *et al.* 1987; St George-Hyslop *et al.* 1987: Tanzi *et al.* 1987) in familial Alzheimer's disease offers a powerful weapon to dissect the molecular biology of the disease. Aggregate net social costs over their remaining lifetimes for all cases of Alzheimer's disease diagnosed in a single year have been estimated at some $30 billion (Hay and Ernst 1987). Further, a substantial increase in incidence and prevalence of Alzheimer's disease is inevitable because of the gains in longevity among those over 75, the most striking demographic phenomenon in our era.

The Board on Mental Health and Behavioral Medicine of the Institute of Medicine (1984) has argued that psychiatric research is grossly underfunded in relation both to progress in neuroscience and to the health burden produced by mental disorders. In 1980, mental disorders entailed direct health care costs of $20 billion (without taking into account their contributions to morbidity from cirrhosis, drunk driving accidents, chronic pain syndromes, etc.), exceeded in aggregate expense only by costs resulting from circulatory and digestive diseases. A five per cent set aside rule would have warranted $1 billion for ADAMHA research; the actual figure did not reach half that amount for all three institutes under its aegis until 1987. When indirect costs secondary to lost productivity, restricted activity, welfare transfer payments, and other social liabilities (i.e., losses from crime and the costs of law enforcement because of opiate addiction) are added, the overall fiscal impact of major mental disorders and addictive states was estimated by the Board to total $185 billion a year (Institute of Medicine 1984: 7). The Board called for annual expenditures of $300 million for NIMH and $100 million for each of the other two Institutes (in 1983 dollars). In 1987, ADAMHA research budgets, which I have converted into 1983 dollars by means of the NIH Biomedical Research and Development Price Index, were the equivalent in 1983 dollars of $198 million for NIMH, $107 million for NIDA and $57 million for NIAAA, not quite three-quarters of the total recommended four years earlier.

The fact is that the politics of the budgetary process reflect the power of constituencies extending well beyond the scientific establishment. The National Institute of Health became the National Institutes with the proliferation of disease-oriented Institutes at the insistence of patient groups and their lobbyists, the most recent being the splitting of the National Institute for

Arthritis, Diabetes, and Digestive and Kidney Disease into new Institutes for Arthritis and Musculoskeletal and Skin Disease and for Diabetes and Digestive and Kidney Diseases because of legislative lobbying for sports medicine (Booth 1987). The National Cancer Institute (NCI), founded in 1944, became the best endowed component of the entire complex with the passage of the National Cancer Act in 1971 for a 'war against cancer'. Although academic purists opposed each of the new Institutes in turn (at the same time that academics who foresaw greater funding for their own research lobbied for the change), it is probable that the overall research budget grew as rapidly as it did because more citizens had a tangible reason to support budgets targeted against diseases with a personal meaning for them.

THE USES OF RESEARCH IN THE FORMULATION OF PUBLIC POLICY

At a time when Thatcherism and Reaganism reign supreme in our two countries, laissez-faire has become the ideal public policy. Conservative politicians call for a return to Adam Smith's 'invisible hand' which ensures that individuals, motivated solely by self-interest, 'without intending it, without knowing it, advance the interests of the society, and afford means to the multiplication of the species' (Smith 1759: 304). In this view, the discipline of the market leads to self-regulating order; *sans* conscious plan, regulation, or enforcement, the market place co-ordinates the individual behaviours of the multitude of vendors and buyers for the common good. In the debate between those who believe that government to be best which governs least and those who opt for the planned use of the taxing and regulatory powers of the state, conviction rests on philosophical rather than empirical grounds. There are no 'controlled clinical trials' on such questions (think for a moment about the meaning of 'informed consent' for such trials!).

Whatever the virtues of the market for the exchange of material goods, 'the invisible hand' clearly does not suffice for the provision of services unaffordable to those in the greatest need of them. Psychiatric services for the chronically impaired stand as a compelling instance. Curiously enough, the most convinced advocates of laissez-faire are quite prepared to support laws to enforce monogamy, to ban abortion, or to uphold the sovereignty of private property. Moreover, every modern state since the time of Bismarck's Prussia transfers funds from those who work to those who are retired rather than leaving it to individuals to provide for their security in old age. Every western state, save the US, entitles its citizens to health care by insurance or a national system; the Thatcher government, though it is progressively depleting the NHS of resources, continues to profess allegiance to it.

Highlighting the follies which he supposed to result from interference with the marketplace, Adam Smith had this to say about planners:

The man of system . . . is apt to be very wise in his own conceit, and is often so enamoured with the supposed beauty of his own ideal plan of government, that he cannot suffer the smallest deviation from any part of it. He goes on to establish it completely and in all its parts, without any regard either to the great interests or to the strong prejudices which may oppose it: he seems to imagine that he can arrange the different members of a great society with as much ease as the hand arranges the different pieces upon a chess-board; he does not consider that the pieces on the chess board have no other principle of motion besides that which the hand imposes on them; but that, in the great chess-board of human society, every single piece has a principle of motion of its own, altogether different from that which the legislature might choose to impress upon it.

(Smith 1759: 380–1)

The notion that the 'man of system . . . wise in his own conceit' is able to establish his 'ideal plan of government . . . completely and in all its parts' corresponds as little with the reality of the planning process as does his free market with today's international market. Rudolf Klein (1972), in a fascinating essay, has contrasted the 'optimizing, rationalizing' model of the decision-making process with the 'satisficing' model. The latter is based on a course of action that is good enough: cautious, incremental, and based on compromises dictated by the conflicting claims of competing constituencies. In the case of the NHS, those constituencies include the DHSS and the Treasury, civil servants in the bureaucracy, physicians (themselves divided among competing speciality groups), regional health authorities and public opinion (or what is judged to be public opinion). Klein concluded his article with these words:

The problem for policy makers – and those who try to assess the outcome of the process – is to know whether the right balance has been struck between overestimating the frictional costs, and thus missing an opportunity for improvement, and underestimating the frictional costs, and thus creating a situation of opposition to evolving change. (Klein 1972: 420)

These prefatory remarks may help to clarify some of the reasons for the divergence between the views of the planning process held by government officials, on the one hand, and physicians and scientists, on the other. The political agenda is such that decisions must be made in the face of limited (and sometimes absent) data. The policy-maker wants answers now and is impatient with the scientist's reiteration of the need for more research. Moreover, politicians operate within a time frame set by the next election; yet the impact of policy changes (or failures to change) should be assessed over much longer periods. Scientists complain that research findings are ignored, that debates proceed without data, and that politicians are unwilling to submit proposals to empirical trial; i.e., comparing alternative policies in separate geographic areas. All too often, they feel that research findings are cited when they seem to support politically palatable alternatives and ignored when they don't (a phenomenon not unknown in medical debates).

Research findings are indeed often ignored, in part because they are themselves debatable, in part because larger political considerations come into play. An example may be informative. In 1965, as part of the War on Poverty, a national Head Start Program was established to provide pre-school education for economically disadvantaged children in order to improve their chances for successful performance when they enter elementary school. As programme costs mounted, the Westinghouse Learning Corporation (1969) was given a contract to evaluate effectiveness. Its report concluded that the increases in IQ for disadvantaged children observed early in the programme were not sustained after the children entered primary grades. The report diminished enthusiasm for the programme in the Nixon White House and reinforced efforts to reduce funding. Yet, despite the negative Westinghouse evaluation, funding has continued to grow in the years up to the present.

Head Start had, and continues to have, a large political constituency in local communities. Its emphasis on the children of the poor draws support even from those who oppose other welfare transfer payments. The Westinghouse study was heavily criticized because it lumped together data from programmes of very different quality and used IQ as the proxy for outcome rather than school progress. If its results were grist to the mill of Head Start opponents, they were roundly criticized as flawed by Head Start proponents. It was not until the 1970s and 1980s (Lazar *et al.* 1982; Berrueta-Clement *et al.* 1984) that longitudinal studies provided persuasive evidence of programme effectiveness: better school progress, fewer drop-outs, less delinquency, and an improved record of employment after high school. In the event, such research 'findings' as were available had little impact on a political process set in motion as part of a much larger national agenda.

Even when clinical and research data are solid, they may be unwelcome if they lead to social policy implications that contravene deeply held beliefs defined as 'moral'. Consider the prevalence of teenage pregnancy and of low birthweight infants, two strongly interconnected public health problems with high risk for maternal and neo-natal mortality and neuropsychiatric morbidity in both mothers and infants (Eisenberg 1987b). Among industrialized countries, the US has the highest teenage pregnancy, abortion, *and* birth rates because US teenagers have the lowest rate of contraceptive use (Jones *et al.* 1985). Although the percentage of unmarried adolescent women having had intercourse is higher by half in Sweden than in the US, pregnancy rates are only half as high because Sweden provides a compulsory sex education curriculum in its schools, closely linked to contraceptive clinic services. Evidence from US studies that school clinics lead to lower birth rates among secondary school students (Kenney 1986) and that they are associated with a *delay* in the age at which coitus is initiated (Zabin *et al*. 1986) has not deterred the Reagan Administration, and the 'moral majority' it speaks for, from opposing public health measures of demonstrated effectiveness.

Low birthweight is a major determinant of neo-natal mortality, total infant mortality and developmental retardation among the infants who survive (McCormick 1985). The Institute of Medicine (1985) has estimated that current rates of low birthweight in the US could be reduced by 15 per cent among whites and 12 per cent among blacks if all women began pre-natal care in the first trimester of pregnancy and continued to receive care through delivery. Yet, since 1978 the proportion of women in the US not receiving care until the third trimester or receiving no care at all has remained unchanged. What has been missing is a national commitment to abolishing the barriers to care. The problem persists, not because of a lack of knowledge, but because of a lack of social will. The issue is not further research, though much more remains to be done to improve on present performance, but the creation of a political coalition to press for universal access to the medical and social measures already available.

An impediment of a different kind arises when research yields strong, replicated, and important findings but the policy measures to change current practices are not readily implemented. Twenty years ago, Michael Shepherd and his colleagues demonstrated the crucial role of general practitioners in the provision of mental health care. They concluded that 'The cardinal require-ment for improvement of the mental health services in this country [the UK] is not a large expansion and proliferation of psychiatric agencies, but rather a strengthening of the family doctor in his therapeutic role' (Shepherd *et al*. 1966: 176). Goldberg *et al*. (1978) and Regier *et al*. (1978) obtained comparable data for the United States and came to similar conclusions. Moreover, there is solid evidence from a number of studies, of which those by Hankin *et al*. (1982) and Williams *et al*. (1986) are representative, that patients with mental disorder use general medical services at a dispropor-tionate rate. Yet, there has been little progress in upgrading psychiatric train-ing for family doctors and less in creating the conditions necessary in the US for changing practice patterns (i.e., providing adequate reimbursement for time spent in delivering mental health care). In his most recent commentary on the problem, Shepherd (1987) suggests that psychiatric protectionism may be an additional major obstruction.

What are the policy implications of these findings? Medical curricula are controlled locally rather than nationally; they are constructed by faculty committees on which psychiatrists have little representation. Proposals to increase funding for mental health services in primary care will be coldly received in a climate of cost control unless they include mechanisms to reduce payments in other sectors of the health service. As rational as that would be for improving primary care, it faces bitter opposition from procedure-based specialities whose incomes would fall. Nonetheless, I am persuaded that a more rational redistribution of health care funds is inevitable; that change, when it occurs, will provide a more powerful stimulus to needed curriculum reform than purely internal educational forces are able to muster (Eisenberg 1987c).

The failure of research to inform policy for the care of psychotic patients is clearly evident in the number of homeless mentally ill persons in the US, estimated in the hundreds of thousands. Massive release of formerly hospitalized patients followed upon policy decisions undertaken without systematic evaluation of the consequences. Wyatt and DeRenzo (1986) contrast the stringent demands established by the Food and Drug Administration before drugs are allowed on the market with the absence of any requirement for trials of efficacy and toxicity for social policy innovations. Thoughtful scholars had indeed warned against the danger of substituting good intention for evidence. Freedman had cautioned that a tradition in America of:

> veneration for change leads some to envision abandonment of all state hospitals immediately without thought to feasibility or consequences . . . [There is a danger that] in paying increased attention to the socially deviant and the neurotic in the community, the traditional responsibility of psychiatry for caring for the severely disturbed or psychotic will be minimized or abandoned. (Freedman 1967)

When short-term studies seemed to demonstrate the feasibility of caring for acutely psychotic patients in the community with psychotropic drugs *and* appropriate social support, the second part of the message (the costly part) was lost in the stampede to deinstitutionalization in hope of transferring costs from state to federal budgets. Moreover, no provision was made for care over the long run for patients whose disorders are chronic and marked by periodic exacerbations. The fate of the research by Pasamanick and his colleagues (1967) provides a distressing instance of the way in which good results can be transformed into tragedy when the long-term needs of patients are not met.

The study was designed to determine whether actively psychotic patients could be treated more effectively at home than in hospital. Patients eligible for entry into the trial were those diagnosed as schizophrenic, between 18 and 60 years of age, neither homicidal nor suicidal, resident within a defined geographic area, and with a family able and willing to provide supervision in the home. Note the age limitations, the exclusion of violent patients, and the requirement for a supportive family. Those eligible were randomized to conventional state hospital care or to home care on drug or placebo. The outcome was unequivocal. Those cared for at home with psychotropic drugs (but not placebos), visiting public health nurses, and psychiatric and social work back-up available as needed did better on all of the outcome measures than the hospital control cases. Even after an initial hospitalization averaging three months and remission of gross symptoms, the hospitalized patients were judged as treatment failures more often than were the home care patients at the termination of the study.

Despite its clear success, funding for the home care programme was not continued by state authorities after the NIMH supported research ended. What was the fate of the patients over the next five years? The investigators set out to determine the facts. To their distress, though not to their surprise, they found no significant differences between groups on any of the indicia of outcome; worst of all, the majority of patients, whatever their initial treatment assignment, showed evidence of major psychiatric and social impairment. They conclude bitterly:

> We must raise questions about the social implications of science, the expenditure of funds and personnel on research whose results are not utilized, and all the personal frustrations of investigators who must feel the tremendous anger of what are, fundamentally, wasted professional lives.
>
> (Davis *et al*. 1974: xii)

The situation is not quite so grim as it was when those words were written. Public policy is beginning to move toward a recognition of responsibility for chronic mental patients. There is great promise in the current joint effort by the Robert Wood Johnson Foundation and the US Department of Housing and Urban Development to establish model urban programmes for the care of chronic mental patients, with equal emphasis on the provision of social services and clinical care. The lesson still to be learned is that the effectiveness of the best designed model must be measured, not only when it is new and is under carefully chosen leadership, but also when it becomes the basis for routine and inevitably bureaucratized services. What is needed is the equivalent of post-marketing surveillance after the introduction of new drugs. Only by setting up a system sensitive to toxicity and ensuring the feedback and use of data obtained can we be confident that what works in a demonstration project in fact continues to perform as expected when it becomes the basis of routine care.

CONCLUSION

Public policy for the support of psychiatric research takes its primary justification from evidence that the results of research improve the health of the population. When discoveries come in the form of more effective new drugs and procedures, they are readily introduced into practice. When they come in the form of remedies which counter deeply held beliefs or are costly and manpower-intensive, they compete in the political arena with other social values.

Though I have limited this account to issues internal to the health policy sector, the fight for medical research and the application of its funding demand attention to broader questions of resource distribution. What is spent for 'defence' is not available for the improvement of health care. Advocates of public health must be prepared to challenge the disproportionate allocations of tax monies to military expenditures, themselves the greatest threat to the health of populations.

REFERENCES

Bacon, F. (1620) *Novum Organum*, in J.M. Robertson (ed.) (1905) *The Philosophical Works of Francis Bacon*, London: George Routledge and Sons, Ltd.

Barre-Sinoussi, F., Chermann, J.C., Rey, F., *et al.* (1983) 'Isolation of a T-lymphotrophic virus from a patient at risk for Acquired Immune Deficiency Syndrome', *Science* 220: 868–71.

Berrueta-Clement, J.R., Schweinhart, L.J., Barnett, W.S., *et al.* (1984) *Changed Lives: The Effects of the Perry Preschool Program on Youths Through Age 19*, Ypsilanti, Michigan: The High/Scope Press.

Booth, W. (1987) 'Arthritis Institute tackles sports', *Science* 237: 846–7.

Breman, J.G. and Arita, I. (1980) 'The confirmation and maintenance of smallpox eradication', *Science* 164: 262–70.

Centers for Disease Control (1981a) 'Pneumocystis pneumonia – Los Angeles', *Morbidity and Morality Weekly Report* 30: 250–2.

Centers for Disease Control (1981b) 'Kaposi's sarcoma and pneumocystis pneumonia among homosexual men – New York City and California', *Morbidity and Mortality Weekly Report* 30: 305–8.

Comroe, J.H. (1976) 'Lags between initial discovery and clinical application to cardiovascular and pulmonary surgery', in F.D. Murphy and R.H. Ebert, *Report of the President's Biomedical Research Panel*, Appendix B, 1–33.

Comroe, J.H. and Dripps, R.D. (1976) 'Scientific basis for the support of biomedical science', *Science* 192: 105–11.

Davis, A.E., Dinitz, S. and Pasamanick, B. 1974 *Schizophrenics in the New Custodial Community: Five Years After the Experiment*, Columbus, Ohio: Ohio State University Press.

Dubos, R. (1959) *Mirage of Health: Utopias, Progress and Biological Change*, New York: Harper and Brothers.

Eisenberg, L. (1979) 'The National Conference on Health Research Principles: bread and circuses or the great debate?' *Clinical Research* 27: 95–7.

Eisenberg, L. (1986a) 'The genesis of fear: AIDS and the public's response to science', *Law, Medicine and Health Care* 14: 243–9.

Eisenberg, L. (1986b) 'Human ecology and health: disease prevention and control', presented at a World Health Organization Meeting on Human Ecology and Health, Delphi, Greece, 30 September–3 October.

Eisenberg, L. (1987a) 'Preventing mental, neurological and psychosocial disorders', *World Health Forum* 8: 245–53.

Eisenberg, L. (1987b) 'Preventive pediatrics: the promise and the peril', *Pediatrics* 80: 415–22.

Eisenberg, L. (1987c) 'Science in medicine: too much or too little and too limited in scope:' presented at the Kaiser Family Foundation Conference on Biopsychosocial Medicine, Wickenburg, Arizona, 13 May 1987.

Freedman, A.M. (1967) 'Historical and political roots of the Community Mental Health Centers Act', *American Journal of Orthopsychiatry* 37: 487–94.

Gallo, R.C., Sarin, P.S., Gelmann, E.P., *et al.* (1983) 'Isolation of a human T-cell leukemia virus in Acquired Immune Deficiency Syndrome', *Science* 220: 865–7.

Goldberg, I.D., Babigian, H.M., Locke, B.A., *et al.* (1978) 'Role of non-psychiatrist physicians in the delivery of mental health services: implications from three studies', *Public Health Reports* 93: 240–5.

Goldgaber, D., Lerman, M.I., McBride, O.W., *et al.* (1987) 'Characterization and chromosomal localization of a cDNA encoding amyloid of Alzheimer's disease', *Science* 235: 877–80.

Gori, G.B. and Richter, B.J. (1979) 'Macroeconomics of disease prevention in the United States', *Science* 200: 1124–30.

Hankin, J.R., Steinwachs, D.M., Regier, D.A., *et al.* (1982) 'Use of general medical care by persons with mental disorders', *Archives of General Psychiatry* 39: 225–31.

Hay, J.W. and Ernst, R.L. (1987) 'The economic costs of Alzheimer's disease', *American Journal of Public Health* 77: 1169–75.

Institute of Medicine (1979) *DHEW's Research Planning Principles*, Washington, DC: National Academy of Sciences.

Institute of Medicine (1984) *Research on Mental Illness and Addictive Disorder: Progress and Prospects*, Washington, DC: National Academy Press.

Institute of Medicine (1985) *Preventing Low Birth Weight*, Washington, DC: National Academy Press.

Jones, E.F., Forrest, J.D., Goldman, N. *et al.* (1985) 'Teenage pregnancy in developed countries: determinants and policy implications', *Family Planning Perspectives* 17: 53–63.

Kenney, A.M. (1986) 'School-based clinics: a national conference', *Family Planning Perspectives* 18: 44–6.

Klein, R. (1972) 'NHS reorganization: the politics of the second best', *Lancet* ii: 418–20.

Lazar, I., Darlington, R., Murray, H., *et al.* (1982) *Lasting Effects of Early Education* (Monographs of the Society for Research in Child Development 47 (1–2, Serial No. 194).

McCormick, M.C. (1985) 'The contribution of low birth weight to infant mortality and childhood morbidity', *New England Journal of Medicine* 312: 82–90.

Marshall, E. (1987) 'OMB stalks the "burgeoning growth of biomedicine"', *Science* 237: 847–8.

Murphy, F.D. and Ebert, R.H. (1976) *Report of the President's Biomedical Research Panel*, Washington, DC: DHEW Publication No. (OS) 76–500.

Nature (1987) 'Formative turbulent months ahead', editorial in *Nature* 328: 745–6.

Office of the Director, NIH (1979) *DHEW Health Research Principles, Volume 1*, Washington, DC: DHEW(NIH).

Office of Program Planning and Evaluation (1986) *NIH Data Book*, Washington, DC: US Department of Health and Human Services.

Office of Technology Assessment (1981) *Cost Effectiveness of Influenza Vaccination*, Washington, DC: US Government Printing Office.

Pasamanick, B., Scarpitti, F. and Dinitz, S. (1967) *Schizophrenics in the Community: An Experimental Study in the Prevention of Hospitalization*, New York: Appleton-Century-Crofts.

Regier, D.A., Goldberg, I.D., and Taube, C.A. (1978) 'The de facto U.S. mental health services system: a public health perspective', *Archives of General Psychiatry* 35: 685–93.

Rice, D.P. and Feldman, J.J. (1983) 'Living longer in the United States: demographic changes and health needs of the elderly', *Milbank Memorial Fund Quarterly/Health and Society*, 61: 362–96.

Russell, L.B. (1986) *Is Prevention Better than Cure?* Washington, DC: The Brookings Institution.

St George-Hyslop, P.H., Tanzi, R.E., Polinsky, R.J., *et al.* (1987) 'The genetic defect causing familial Alzheimer's disease maps on chromosome 21', *Science* 235: 885–90.

Shannon, J.A. (1987) 'The National Institutes of Health: some critical years, 1955–1957', *Science* 237: 865–8.

Shepherd, M. (1957) 'An English view of American psychiatry', *American Journal of Psychiatry* 114: 417–20.

Shepherd, M. (1987) 'Mental illness and primary care', *American Journal of Public Health* 77: 12–13.

Shepherd, M. and Blackwell, B. (1968) 'Prophylactic lithium: another therapeutic myth', *Lancet* ii: 968–71.

Shepherd, M., Cooper, B., Brown, A.C. and Kalton, G.W. (1966) *Psychiatric Illness in General Practice*, London: Oxford University Press.

Smith, A. (1759) *The Theory of Moral Sentiments*, republished 1976, Indianapolis: Liberty Classics.

Smith, A. (1790) *The History of Astronomy*, reprinted (1980) in W.P.D. Wightman and J.C. Bryce (eds) *Essays on Philosophical Subjects*, Oxford: Clarendon Press.

Tanzi, R.E., Gusella, J.F., Watkins, P.C., *et al.* (1987) 'Amyloid beta-protein gene: cDNA, mRNA distribution, and genetic linkage near the Alzheimer locus', *Science* 235: 880–4.

Varmus, H. (1987) 'Reverse transcription', *Scientific American* 257: 56–64.

Westinghouse Learning Corporation (1969) *The Impact of Head Start: An Evaluation of Head Start on Children's Affective and Cognitive Development, (Volumes I and II)*, Athens, Ohio: Ohio University.

Williams, P., Tarnopolsky, A., Hand, D., and Shepherd, M. (1986) 'Minor psychiatric morbidity and general practice consultations: the West London Survey', *Psychological Medicine* (Monograph Supplement 9).

Wyatt, R.J. and DeRenzo, E.G. (1986) 'Scienceless to homeless', *Science* 234: 1309.

Wyngaarden, J.B. (1987) 'The National Institutes of Health in its Centennial year', *Science* 237: 869–74.

Zabin, L.S., Hirsch, M.B., Smith, E.A., *et al.* (1986) 'Evaluation of a pregnancy prevention program for urban teenagers', *Family Planning Perspectives* 18: 119–26.

Section Four

The International Perspective

Introduction

Social and epidemiological psychiatry are, by their very nature, not confined within national boundaries: the requirement for a global perspective is thus self-evident. This helps to orientate the international research community to prevalent and socially relevant problems; to enhance local research potential, particularly in developing countries; to generate and disseminate appropriate research methods and techniques; and to facilitate international collaboration (Sartorius 1980).

In appraising these issues, it is useful to consider the five headings which characterize the research component of the WHO mental health programme (Sartorius 1980): (i) the development of a common language; (ii) characteristics of mental and neurological disorders and of psychosocial problems of major public health importance; (iii) development and improvement of treatment methods; (iv) organization of mental health services – assessment and development of new models; and (v) psychosocial aspects of general health care and high risk group research.

As well as reflecting these topics, the papers included in this section are concerned with three levels – international, national, and local. These distinct but related levels apply not only to the nature of the enquiry but also to the organization and implementation of the research.

In the first paper, Assen Jablensky gives an overview of the WHO multi-centre studies of schizophrenia: these underline the heuristic importance of a global view. One of the most interesting results to emerge has been that, while the incidence of schizophrenia is relatively constant across cultures, the outcome is not, a finding which raises many important questions for further research.

While these WHO studies exemplify all three levels – international, national and local – the focus of the second paper in this section is national. Darrel Regier describes the psychiatric epidemiology research programme being undertaken at the National Institute of Mental Health (NIMH) in the USA. He draws particular attention to the Epidemiologic Catchment Area (ECA) Program, one of the largest and most ambitious studies of its kind. While a national programme of research is addressed to national priorities and many of the detailed findings are specially pertinent to the catchment areas involved, the experience gained and the broader implications of the findings are of international significance.

Both WHO and NIMH research activities have been directly influenced by Michael Shepherd's contributions. Moreover, his research unit at the Institute of Psychiatry in London has played an important role in training research workers from America, Asia, Europe, and the Third World, three of whom have written the third chapter in this section. Jair Mari, Biswajit Sen, and

453

Tai-Ann Cheng draw upon their experiences in studying psychiatric disorder in the community and in primary care settings in Brazil, India, and Taiwan respectively, and use them to make some observations on the problems which arise in the cross-cultural measurement of psychiatric morbidity.

The location of much of this research – the primary medical care setting – serves as a reminder that, as has been discussed previously, it has become widely accepted that the focus of the provision of mental health care should shift from specialist to general medical settings. This policy is endorsed by, among others, WHO (1973) and NIMH (1980): Michael Shepherd's work has played a seminal part in its formulation.

REFERENCES

National Institute of Mental Health (1980) *Mental Health Services in Primary Care Settings: Report of a Conference* Series DN: Health/Mental Health Research, DHHS publication no. (ADM)80-995), Washington, DC: US Government Printing Office.

Sartorius, N. (1980) 'The research component of the WHO mental health programme', *Psychological Medicine* 10: pp. 175–85.

World Health Organisation (1973) *Psychiatry and Primary Care*, Copenhagen: WHO Regional Office for Europe.

29

An Overview of the World Health Organization Multi-centre Studies of Schizophrenia

Assen Jablensky

Comparative psychiatry is to the study of the nature of mental disorders what comparative anatomy once was to the construction of a scientific taxonomy of the living organisms: a systematic search for the right building blocks of a nosology that could accommodate and reduce the outwardly bewildering variation of the phenomena of mental illness. While modern biological taxonomy is reaching beyond phenotypical variations and is now capable of classifying many living things on the basis of similarities in strings of DNA, psychiatry has yet to resolve the question whether its elementary units of observation, the psychopathological symptoms and syndromes, represent a universal code of abnormal mental life.

COMPARATIVE PSYCHIATRY: SOURCES AND BACKGROUND

With characteristic foresight, the need for comparative 'observation of mental disorders in different groups of people' was advocated more than eighty years ago by Kraepelin (1904), who suggested at least two ways in which cross-cultural studies could advance knowledge: by 'throwing light on the causes of mental disorders' and by providing 'means of determining the influence which the patient's personality exerts on the particular form his illness assumes'.

Kraepelin was himself wary of the methodological obstacles:

Reliable comparison is, of course, only possible if we are able to draw clear distinctions between identifiable illnesses, as well as between clinical states; moreover, our clinical concepts vary so widely that for the foreseeable future such comparison is possible only if the observations are made by one and the same observer.

His own explorations of psychoses in Java were one of the few attempts at the time to pursue the strategy of comparative research in a field which soon after became increasingly dominated by a psychoanalytically-oriented cultural anthropology. The latter was practically divorced from psychiatric epidemiology which in the 1920s and 1930s attained a level of sophistication marked by such milestones as Goldberger's discovery of the dietary aetiology of pellagra (Goldberger 1927), Brugger's census surveys (Brugger 1933), Faris and Dunham's studies on the social ecology of psychosis (Faris and Dunham 1938), and Strömgren's genetic epidemiological investigation of an entire insular population (Strömgren 1938).

However, the application of the epidemiological method remained restricted mainly to European and North American populations; it was not until the Taiwan studies (Rin and Lin 1962), the Mauritius survey (Murphy and Raman 1971), and the WHO International Pilot Study of Schizophrenia (WHO 1973), that comparative psychiatric epidemiology ventured into cultural settings different from the one in which its own concepts and methods originated.

At an early stage of WHO's involvement in cross-cultural mental health issues, the methodological problems facing psychiatric epidemiological research were reviewed by a WHO Expert Committee (WHO 1960) which, in a seminal report, pointed to: (a) the existence of 'individual factors in the causes and manifestations of many psychiatric diseases which . . . because they belong to the sphere of values, cannot be fully quantified'; (b) the 'essentially multifactorial' nature of the aetiology of mental disorders, complicated by the fact that 'in few branches of medicine are genetic, physiological and psychological factors as evenly distributed in the origin and distribution of disease as in psychiatry'; (c) the 'incongruities in the diagnostic appraisal in different countries and schools' and a 'tendency to use technical terms in different senses according to the theory favoured'; (d) the presence of 'considerable social and cultural differences in what is considered psychically abnormal in different surroundings, and the way such abnormality is treated'; and (e) the problem of 'infinite variations' in human character and behaviour deviations 'ranging from severe psychosis to mild personality disorders which many would not consider to be the concern of psychiatry'. The Committee concluded that 'these problems may make it difficult to advance the study of epidemiology of mental disorders as quickly and consistently as might be hoped'.

For all the thoroughness of its diagnosis of the problems, the Committee was overly guarded in its prognosis. The resolving of the difficulties barring the progress of comparative psychiatric research (and of mental health action consequent upon such research) became the chief objective of the mental health programme of WHO in the 1960s and 1970s. As an inter-governmental organization of a practically universal membership, WHO was in a unique position to set up a framework for cross-national mental health research which ensured access to: (a) populations representing a wide variation in socio-economic development, ecology, and culture; (b) individual experts and teams of investigators willing to apply their knowledge and skills to collaborative research.

One of the first steps resulted from the realization of the lack of a 'common language' in mental health research. In 1959 WHO requested Professor E. Stengel to review critically the field of psychiatric classification and to make recommendations about the future work of the Organization in this respect. In his comprehensive report, Stengel concluded that:

> The lack of a common classification of mental disorders has defeated attempts at comparing psychiatric observations and the results of treatments undertaken in various countries or even in various centres in the same countries . . . Diagnoses can rarely be verified objectively and the same, or similar conditions, are described under a confusing variety of names. This situation militates against the ready exchange of ideas and experiences, and hampers progress. (Stengel 1959)

THE WHO MENTAL HEALTH PROGRAMME

Stengel's findings provided a stepping-stone for the first major component of the WHO mental health programme: the so-called 'Programme A' which envisaged the development of common rules of usage of psychiatric concepts and terms; the standardization of methods and instruments; and the training of investigators in different parts of the world in using such a technology in a manner that is both congruent with their own culture and enabling them to generate comparable data. This was the prerequisite to the subsequent extension of the WHO programme into substantive areas such as:

(i) Research to explore the existence of culturally invariant reference points in mental morbidity, e.g. the occurrence of comparable forms of schizophrenia or depression and the applicability of diagnostic concepts in different cultures;

(ii) Investigation of the extent of culture-related variation in areas such as the phenomenology of mental disorders or their 'natural history';

(iii) The comparative incidence and disease expectancy of the major mental disorders in different populations;

(iv) Delineation of new syndromes or enrichment of the description of established clinical entities with data on their manifestation in different cultures;

(v) Identification of predictors of course and outcome and search for significant associated, and possibly causal, factors.

The WHO mental health programme has been consistent in pursuing the above objectives in spite of variable political winds and recurrent financial uncertainties. It should be noted that epidemiological and social psychiatry is only one of the several major areas of concern of the WHO mental health programme which includes, among other things, work on the psychosocial aspects of general health, service-orientated activities (including the designing and implementation of training programmes for mental health workers), research in alcohol- and drug-related problems, support to international legislative action concerning the control of psychoactive substances, studies on neurological disorders, and promotion of research in biological psychiatry. The mental health programme is an integral component of the WHO General Programme of Work which is renewed every six years (the seventh programme cycle ends in 1989) and contains three objectives in the area of protection and promotion of mental health: (i) psychosocial and behavioural factors in the promotion of health and human development; (ii) prevention and control of alcohol and drug abuse; and (iii) prevention and treatment of mental and neurological disorders.

WHO is a less monolithic body than most United Nations organizations; in fact, it consists of six regional organizations (Africa, the Americas, Eastern Mediterranean, Europe, South-East Asia, and the Western Pacific), each governed by a Regional Committee and managed by a Regional Office. The WHO Headquarters in Geneva is the strategic centre which is entrusted with global policy development and co-ordination (mandated by the World Health Assembly and the Executive Board) and with many of the research initiatives, especially those concerning global or inter-regional problems. In the past fifteen years, the ethos of WHO has been permeated by concerns about social issues, the predicament of the Third World, and the role of health in socio-economic development, a philosophy strongly espoused by its Director-General, Dr Halfdan Mahler. Since 1977, WHO has adopted a militant policy platform, epitomized in the idea of Health for All by the Year 2000, which (against all odds) is gradually acquiring the operational features of a structured and technically supported approach to health planning.

A glimpse of the background is indispensable for an understanding of the operation of the WHO mental health programme, because, in contrast to academic and research centres engaged in the pursuit of pure knowledge, the former is essentially a public health enterprise, in service of a constituency including over 165 member countries of extremely varied perception of needs and priorities. The *raison d'être* of epidemiological and social psychiatry within the WHO mental health programme has been expressed in a position paper entitled 'Social Dimensions of Mental Health' in the following terms:

There is a mass of neglected mental and neurological disorders, and associated social malfunctions, which specialized mental health services can never reach. Many of them can be managed by community health and other social sector workers, trained, supervised and supported by mental health professionals, in a primary health care setting. Although much improvement can be achieved if available knowledge were to be applied there are significant gaps in our understanding of mental and neurological functioning and disease. (WHO 1981)

It is precisely these 'significant gaps' that the research programme in epidemiological and social psychiatry set itself to cover, to the extent that is made possible by the opportunities provided by WHO's position *vis-à-vis* very different countries and cultures. The overall development of the research component of the WHO programme has been described by Sartorius (1980). What follows below is a summary of several activities, spanning over nearly two decades of research, and illustrating the way in which WHO has launched its 'attack on the lacunae in knowledge relating to the clinical epidemiology of mental disorders' (Shepherd 1983) with the example of schizophrenia, a condition of great public health importance and of inexhaustible scientific interest.

THE WHO MULTI-CENTRE STUDIES ON SCHIZOPHRENIA

The programme of collaborative clinical and epidemiological research into schizophrenia and related disorders, which began in the late 1960s, aimed to develop a methodology that would clear the way for reliable comparative investigations in different populations. It involved psychiatrists and other investigators in over twenty research centres in seventeen countries. The strategy of the programme was characterized by three principal features: (i) use of standardized instruments for case-finding, history-taking, and mental state assessment, translated into equivalent versions of the local languages of the study area population; (ii) data collection by highly qualified psychiatrists trained to use reliably the research instruments (the comparability of assessment was monitored through regular reliability exercises and tests); (iii) a two-tier diagnostic classification of the clinical data, including a clinical diagnosis made by the local team and a reference classification of the standardized mental state data, produced centrally at the study headquarters, using the CATEGO computer program (Wing *et al.* 1974); (iv) multiple assessments of the cases, with periodic follow-up examinations.

The schizophrenia programme included three major studies. The first (1969–77) was the International Pilot Study of Schizophrenia (IPSS) (WHO 1973–79), which involved nine centres in Africa, Asia, Europe, and North America, with a total of 1,202 patients aged 15–44. The patients were selected for presence of psychotic symptoms and for absence of gross organic brain pathology, chronicity, alcohol- or drug-dependence, sensory defects, and mental retardation. The majority of the patients (811) had a clinical diagnosis of schizophrenia; the remaining 391 were classified as affective disorders, reactive psychoses, neuroses, and personality disorders. Each

459

patient had a detailed standardized clinical examination at the point of inclusion into the study and full reassessments two years and five years later. The principal research instruments used in the IPSS were the Present State Examination (PSE) (Wing *et al.* 1974), a psychiatric history schedule, and a social description form.

The second WHO study aimed to explore the behavioural impairments and social disabilities in schizophrenic patients of recent onset. It included 520 patients in seven countries who were examined initially and also at one-year and two-year follow-up investigations. In addition to the PSE and a history schedule, two new instruments, the Psychological Impairments Rating Schedule (PIRS) and the WHO Disability Assessment Schedule (WHO-DAS), were developed for this study (Jablensky *et al.* 1980). The PIRS was designed to describe and quantify negative symptoms, such as deficits in social and communication skills, while the purpose of the WHO-DAS was to elicit and rate data on social role performance and the environmental factors influencing such performance.

The third study (1978–1984), bearing the title 'Determinants of Outcome of Severe Mental Disorders' (Sartorius *et al.* 1986; Jablensky *et al.* 1988), had a more complex design and included 1,379 patients assessed at twelve research centres in ten countries. The core of the project was an epidemiological case-finding and clinical study in which data were collected on the incidence of schizophrenic disorders in defined geographical areas in different cultures, the frequency of particular syndromes, the distribution of various patterns of course, and the dependence of incidence estimates on alternative schemes of diagnostic classification of the cases (a clinical ICD-9 diagnosis and a reference classification by the CATEGO computer program). The case-finding method involved an active search for people contacting any community facilities (medical services, social agencies, traditional or religious healers) for the first time in their lives because of symptoms that on screening could be considered psychotic. Each person with a suspected psychotic illness was given a full examination using standardized instruments (PSE, a psychiatric and personal history schedule, and a diagnostic and prognostic form). Follow-up re-examinations took place one year and two years after the initial evaluation. The series of incident cases collected in this manner were of particular interest from the point of view of psychiatric epidemiology because the great majority of them (over 85 per cent) had been identified within twelve months of the onset of the disorder, i.e., early enough to rule out any significant pathoplastic effects of treatment or of the social response to the symptoms. Apart from the standard clinical, social, and diagnostic assessment of all the cases, subgroups of the patients participated in special investigations. e.g. a study on the incidence of stressful life events prior to the acute onset of psychosis (Day *et al.* 1987), on the relationship between an index of expressed emotion in the family and the course of the disorder (Wig *et al.* 1987; Leff *et al.* 1987), on the perception of the patient's behaviour by the social environment, and on the rate of development of behavioural and social role dysfunctions.

CONTRIBUTIONS OF THE WHO STUDIES TO THE KNOWLEDGE BASE ON SCHIZOPHRENIA

The three studies referred to above have produced results which contribute to: (i) the completion of the spectrum of clinical manifestations of schizophrenia; (ii) the assessment of morbid risk; (iii) the establishment of outcome; (iv) the evaluation of the efficacy of treatment; and (v) the conceptual construction of the diagnosis and classification of the group of schizophrenic disorders – five categories which, according to Shepherd (1984), sum up the principal contributions of epidemiology to clinical psychiatry.

Spectrum of clinical manifestations

The major psychopathological syndromes defining the clinical entity of schizophrenia since its delimitation by Kraepelin (1896) and Bleuler (1911) were found to occur in all the populations and geographical areas covered by the WHO studies. Although the clinical picture of schizophrenia was shown to be highly variable (no single symptom being invariably present in every patient and in every setting), the overall profiles of psychopathology associated with a clinical diagnosis of schizophrenia were remarkably similar in the different cultures (figure 29.1).

Schizophrenic patients everywhere tended to have high PSE scores on lack of insight, suspiciousness, delusional mood, delusions or ideas of reference and persecution, flatness of affect, auditory hallucinations, and the delusion of being controlled by an external agency (table 29.1). Furthermore, there was a high degree of concordance between the clinical diagnosis made in the local research centre and the computer reference diagnosis made at the study headquarters (between 63 per cent and 95 per cent of the cases assessed in the different centres as schizophrenic were assigned to a CATEGO class selecting schizophrenic disorders on the basis of formalized classification rules). An average of 56 per cent of the patients with a clinical diagnosis of schizophrenia in the different centres also exhibited one or more of the 'first-rank' symptoms proposed by Schneider (1957) to serve as reliable demarcating features from other non-organic psychotic illnesses. The 'first-rank' symptoms defined a sub-population of schizophrenic patients characterized by generally elevated scores on 'positive' psychotic symptoms. These patients manifested an even greater similarity across the cultures than the total study population.

The spectrum of psychopathology of schizophrenia also includes variations in the presentation of the disorder in the different cultures. The principal

461

Figure 29.1 Profiles on 44 selected PSE items of 586 patients in developing countries and 746 patients in developed countries all meeting 'broad' diagnostic criteria for schizophrenia and related disorders

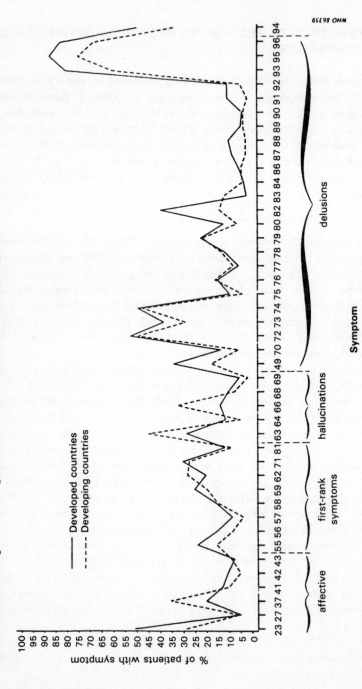

Source WHO Study on Determinants of Outcome of Severe Mental Disorders

Key to figure 29.1 *44 PSE symptoms used to construct psychopathology profiles of subgroups of patients*

AFFECT
23. Depressed mood
27. Morning depression (rating 2 only)
37. Early waking
41. Expansive mood
42. Ideomotor pressure
43. Grandiose ideas and actions

SUBJECTIVE THOUGHT
DISORDER
55. Thought insertion
56. Thought broadcast
57. Thought echo
58. Thought withdrawal
59. Thoughts being read
49. Delusional mood

HALLUCINATIONS
62. Voices in third person

63. Voices speaking to subject
64. Dissociative hallucinations
66. Visual hallucinations
68. Olfactory hallucinations
69. Delusion of smell
70. Other hallucinations

DELUSIONS
71. Control
72. Reference
73. Delusional misinterpretation
74. Persecution
75. Assistance
76. Grandiose abilities
77. Grandiose identity
78. Religious
79. Paranormal
80. Physical forces

81. Alien forces
82. Primary delusions
83. Subcultural
84. Morbid jealousy
86. Sexual
87. Fantastic
88. Guilt
89. Appearance
90. Depersonalization
91. Hypochondriacal
92. Catastrophe
93. Systematization of delusions
94. Evasiveness
95. Preoccupation with delusions or
    hallucinations
96. Acting out of delusions

Table 29.1 International Pilot Study of Schizophrenia (IPSS). Ten most frequently positive 'units of analysis' in patients with diagnosis of paranoid schizophrenia in Aarhus, Agra, Cali, Ibadan, London, Moscow, Prague, Taipei, and Washington

1) Lack of insight	55% (Was) – 100% (Agr, Mos)
2) Suspiciousness	67% (Pra) – 93% (Agr)
3) Delusions of persecution	60% (Cal) – 93% (Agr)
4) Delusions of reference	54% (Mos) – 73% (Agr)
5) Ideas of reference	46% (Aar) – 86% (Tai)
6) Uncooperativeness	28% (Lon) – 82% (Aar)
7) Inadequate description	32% (Lon) – 83% (Was)
8) Delusional mood	36% (Pra) – 75% (Cal)
9) Flatness of affect	41% (Iba) – 68% (Lon)
10) Auditory hallucinations	31% (Was) – 64% (Pra)

differences observed in the WHO studies were those between patients in the Third World and patients in the industrialized countries, and they are likely to reflect a pathoplastic effect of culture. For example, a significantly greater proportion of patients in the developing countries had an acute onset of the disorder, exhibited fewer affective symptoms (such as depression) in the initial phase of the disorder, and had higher scores on auditory and visual hallucinations. On the other hand, a higher percentage of the patients in the developed countries had Schneiderian 'first-rank' symptoms and systematized delusions. However, these were differences of degree rather than of kind, and the symptoms concerned did not cluster together in a way that would suggest separate culture-specific syndromes, different from the central schizophrenic syndrome which was present in all study areas.

Incidence and morbid risk

The WHO study on 'Determinants of Outcome of Severe Mental Disorders' was the first cross-cultural investigation in which the incidence of a major psychiatric disorder, such as schizophrenia, was assessed simultaneously in several different cultural settings, using a uniform methodology (a prospective monitoring of the first contacts with services over two years and an in-depth evaluation of each individual case including a special inquiry about the time and mode of onset of psychotic manifestations.). The incidence of schizophrenic illnesses diagnosed according to ICD-9 was found to be quite comparable in populations which are culturally distant from one another. It varied by no more than a factor of three between areas with high rates (such as the rural area of Raipur Rani near Chandigarh, India) and areas with low rates (such as the county of Aarhus, Denmark). Although the differences observed among those six centres which throughout the study maintained an effective coverage of all first contacts were statistically significant ($p < 0.05$), the size of these differences was not of an order that would suggest major

Figure 29.2 Annual incidence rates per hundred thousand population age 15–54 (both sexes); for the 'broad' and for the 'restrictive' definition of schizophrenia

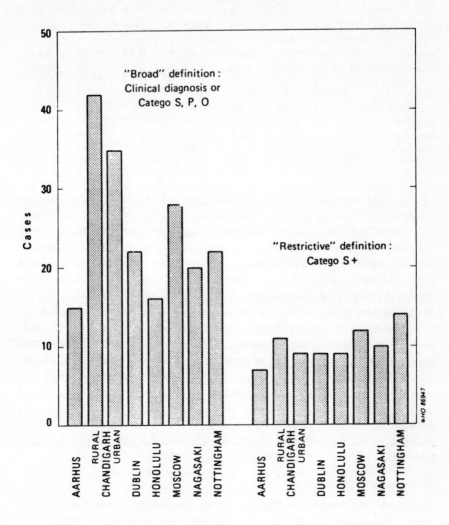

contrasts in the incidence of schizophrenia in different cultures (figure 29.2). Furthermore, a statistical comparison of the rates of the 'nuclear' schizophrenic syndrome (as defined by the CATEGO diagnostic class S+) failed to detect significant differences among the areas and resulted in a reduction of the inter-area variation of the incidence rates. This was contrary to the expectation that, as the mean rates of occurrence of a disease in several

Table 29.2 Morbid risk (percentage) for age 15–54 for a 'broad' and for a 'restrictive' case definition of schizophrenia

Centre	Clinical diagnosis or Catego S,P,O			Catego S+		
	M	F	M+F	M	F	M+F
Aarhus	0.66	0.49	0.52	0.33	0.20	0.27
Chandigarh (rural)	1.48	2.03	1.72	0.54	0.40	0.48
Chandigarh (urban)	1.04	1.21	1.10	0.22	0.42	0.30
Dublin	0.85	0.80	0.83	0.31	0.32	0.32
Honolulu	0.55	0.47	0.50	0.27	0.26	0.26
Moscow	1.08	1.17	1.13	0.39	0.54	0.47
Nagasaki	0.79	0.65	0.72	0.39	0.34	0.37
Nottingham	0.98	0.62	0.80	0.60	0.47	0.54

locations are lowered, the inter-area variation would increase as a result of a susceptibility of the low rates to random variation. The absence of this effect supported the tentative, potentially weighty conclusion that a 'core' schizophrenic syndrome occurs at a similar rate in very different populations.

Since different pathological processes may underlie the same phenotypical expression of a syndrome, it was essential to find supportive evidence, other than the pattern of psychopathology, that the schizophrenic illnesses observed in the different settings belong to the same genus of morbidity. Such evidence was provided by the highly characteristic and consistent age and sex distribution of onsets (a clustering of onsets in the age groups younger than 24 in males and a higher mean age at onset in females) which showed the same pattern in the different study areas. In the 'core' group of CATEGO S+ patients the age- and sex-related patterns of onset were even more sharply delineated than in the entire series of clinical schizophrenia. The age- and sex-specific incidence rates obtained in the WHO study made it possible to establish estimates of disease expectancy (morbid risk) which are shown in table 29.2.

Establishment of outcome

Against this background of important similarities in the incidence and presentation of schizophrenic illnesses in different parts of the world, there were also some striking differences, most pronounced in the longitudinal aspects of the disorder. In both the IPSS and the 'Determinants of Outcome' follow-up studies, there was a marked contrast between the symptomatological similarity of the initial picture of schizophrenia, both within and across the study areas, and the variation in course and outcome which was observed within a period of up to five years after the first examination. Schizophrenia presenting with reliably established symptoms that would meet the current operational criteria of the disorder did not exhibit a single pattern of course.

Figure 29.3 Distribution of 233 followed-up schizophrenic patients in developing countries and 295 followed-up schizophrenic patients in developed countries over 5 categories of 2-year overall outcome

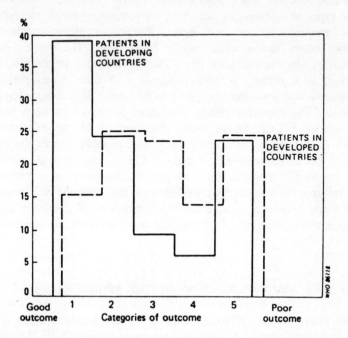

Source WHO International Pilot Study of Schizophrenia

In a proportion of the cases the initial psychotic episode was of a limited duration and resulted in a clinical and social recovery which remained stable throughout the follow-up. At the other extreme, there were cases of a similar initial symptom profile which, however, remained continuously ill and became severely incapacitated in the course of follow-up. There was also an intermediate group of patients with several psychotic attacks and interposed remissions of varying quality. This tripartite distribution of the temporal patterns of schizophrenic illnesses appeared in varying proportions in the different areas, the most marked differences being those between the series of patients in the developing countries and the series of patients in the developed countries. On most course and outcome dimensions (such as the cumulative percentage of the follow-up period during which psychotic symptoms were present, the quality of remissions, the degree of social impairment, and the overall pattern of course) the patients diagnosed as

467

schizophrenic in the developing countries scored significantly better than the patients in the developed countries (figure 29.3).

A number of statistical predictors of the course and outcome of schizophrenic illnesses were identified by stepwise multiple regression and log-linear types of analyses. In summary, the remitting type of schizophrenia was best predicted by an acute onset, absence of previous episode of psychiatric illness, and a stable family background. The chronic pattern represented usually the extension of an illness which had started insidiously in the past, in a socially withdrawn person with other manifestations of abnormal behaviour who was also likely to be single, divorced, or separated from spouse. The recurrent pattern was more frequent in females and the initial episodes of the illness were characterized by an admixture of schizophrenic, affective, and neurotic symptoms. Notably, neither the clinical ICD-9 subtypes of schizophrenia, nor the CATEGO classes predicted course and outcome as effectively as the fairly general characteristics of person and process referred to above. This underscores the difficulty of integrating within a single diagnostic schema the two dimensions of schizophrenia, one providing a symptomatological profile and the other describing course and outcome.

SIGNIFICANCE AND IMPLICATIONS OF THE FINDINGS

First and foremost, the WHO findings on schizophrenia provide a firm epidemiological foundation for further comparative research on the clinical, biological, and psychosocial aspects of a major mental disorder which, in spite of seven decades of research, remains the *Ding an sich* of psychiatry. By demonstrating that a characteristic profile of symptoms, and an age- and sex-related pattern in their occurrence, can be identified reliably in widely varying populations and cultural settings, these studies add significantly to the plausibility of a disease theory of schizophrenia. The tables of comparative age- and sex-specific incidence rates in different populations contain material of critical value to genetic epidemiology, while the standardized psychopathological and 'natural history' data provide ample opportunities for the testing of new clinical and diagnostic hypotheses. It is essential, therefore, that the unique WHO databases on schizophrenia, built up in the course of two decades, and containing over 3,000 patient records, be maintained in a manner that would make it accessible for secondary analysis.

Regardless of any future uses of the WHO data, certain research questions can be asked now, leading to conjectures about the nature of the disorder. For example, the similarity of the form in which the characteristic manifestations of schizophrenia appear in different cultures is a puzzling finding. Considering the variety of social norms, beliefs, attitudes, and stress coping techniques which exist in different cultures, the similarities in the subjective experience of schizophrenic symptoms reported by patients as distant from each other in background and culture as a Yoruba farmer in Nigeria and a Danish fisherman are striking. Why should they experience hallucinatory voices discussing their thoughts and actions precisely in the third person, or perceive their innermost feelings as being bared to others? Unless this observation is shown to be an artefact of the interviewing technique (which is unlikely), it can only suggest that certain basic forms of schizophrenic experience, i.e., the specific disorders of perception, thought, self-image, and ideation, have common pathophysiological mechanisms at a level of function which is relatively untouched by cultural learning. If this is the case, then at least some of the 'first rank' symptoms which index highly specific intra-psychic phenomena might serve as quasi-markers of those schizophrenic syndromes that merit a systematic investigation for underlying commonalties at a neurophysiological and biochemical level.

However, even if certain schizophrenic symptoms are shown to have a common pathophysiological basis in different cultures, the causation of the disorder need not be exclusively construed in 'biological' terms. The finding of similar incidence rates in different populations raises more questions than can be answered at present. Taking into account the genetic, constitutional, nutritional, and other biological differences among the populations studied, the ascertainment of similar incidence rates would hardly be expected. Schizophrenia appears to behave differently from other multifactorial diseases like diabetes or ischaemic heart disease, which show much greater variation in incidence both across and within populations. If schizophrenia is not a single disease of uniform aetiology and pathophysiology, but rather a 'final common pathway' for a variety of pathological processes and developmental anomalies – some with strong genetic contribution and some resulting primarily from environmental factors – then the relatively invariant rate of its occurrence could be the expression of a similarly distributed liability for a schizophrenic type of response to different causes rather than a reflection of a similar distribution of an identical primary cause. Analogies are provided by two other disorders which are known to be aetiologically heterogeneous and to occur with comparable rate of incidence in different populations: epilepsy and mental retardation. Both can be understood as a phenotypical expression of a liability anchored in the general structural and neuro-physiological organization of the brain which can be actuated by a variety of lesions, stresses, or developmental events.

In the instance of schizophrenia, there is also the possibility that some environmental contribution may be provided by psychosocial or cultural conditions modulating the probability of a 'schizophrenic' response to a genetic or developmental lesion. The WHO finding of a more favourable outcome of schizophrenia in the developing countries may be interpreted as an indication that in technologically less complex cultures schizophrenia is less likely to develop into a chronic, deteriorating condition than in societies imposing upon their members more complex, conflicting, and potentially disorienting cognitive requirements. This hypothesis is in need of further exploration, especially in societies which are more contrasting among each other than those already covered by the WHO research programme, e.g. in pre-literate cultures or hunter–gatherer groups in comparison with societies in transition to modernity and 'post-industrial' societies.

In a discussion of possible future strategies of schizophrenia research, Shepherd wrote:

> It is now clear that the design of a study aiming to elucidate the natural history of schizophrenia must take account of at least four factors: (1) the identification of all cases in a defined population during a fixed period of time; (2) the application of standardized diagnostic procedures with criteria of known reliability; (3) prospective follow-up procedures, preferably from the onset of first attachment for at least five years, with interim as well as end-point assessments and, preferably, uniform treatment regimes throughout the follow-up period; (4) standardized and independent clinical and social measures of outcome.   (Shepherd 1987)

The WHO programme on comparative cross-cultural research in schizophrenia has succeeded in meeting most of these methodological requirements. The real pay-off of the enterprise will be seen in the extent to which its results focus future investigations on those aspects of the disorder which point to its roots in basic and universal characteristics of human nature.

REFERENCES

Bleuler, E. (1911) *Dementia Praecox oder die Gruppe der Schizophrenien*, Leipzig, Wien: Deuticke.

Brugger, C. (1933) 'Psychiatrische Ergebnisse einer medizinischen, anthropologischen und soziologischen Bevölkerungsuntersuchung', *Zeitschrift für Neurologie und Psychiatrie* 146: 489–524.

Day, R., Nielsen, J.A., Korten, A., *et al.* (1987) 'Stressful life events preceding the acute onset of schizophrenia: a cross-national study from the World Health Organization', *Culture, Medicine and Psychiatry* 11: 123–205.

Faris, R.E.L. and Dunham, H.W. (1939) *Mental Disorders in Urban Areas*, Chicago: University of Chicago Press.

Goldberg, J. (1927) *DeLamar Lectures*, Baltimore: Williams & Wilkins.

Jablensky, A., Schwarz, R., and Tomov, T. (1980) 'WHO collaborative study on impairments and disabilities associated with schizophrenic disorders', *Acta Psychiatrica Scandinavica* 62 (supplement 285): 152–63.

Jablensky, A., Sartorius, N., Ernberg, G., *et al.* (1988) *Schizophrenia: Manifestations, Incidence and Course in Different Cultures: A World Health Organization Ten-Country Study* (Psychological Medicine Monograph), to be published.

Kraepelin, E. (1896) *Psychiatrie*, V Auflage, Leipzig: Barth.

Kraepelin, E. (1904) 'Comparative psychology', in S.R. Hirsch and M. Shepherd (eds) *Themes and Variations in European Psychiatry*, Bristol: Wright.

Leff, J., Wig, N.N., Ghosh, H., *et al.* (1987) 'Expressed emotion and schizophrenia in North India; III: Influence of relatives' expressed emotion on the course of schizophrenia in Chandigarh', *British Journal of Psychiatry* 151: 166–73.

Murphy, H.B.M. and Raman, A.C. (1971) 'The chronicity of schizophrenia in indigenous tropical peoples: results of a twelve-year follow-up survey in Mauritius', *British Journal of Psychiatry* 118: 489–97.

Rin, H. and Lin, T.Y. (1962) 'Mental illness among Formosan aborigines as compared with the Chinese in Taiwan', *Journal of Mental Science* 108: 134–46.

Sartorius, N. (1980) 'The research component of the WHO mental health programme', *Psychological Medicine* 10: 175–85.

Sartorius, N., Jablensky, A., Korten, A., *et al.* (1986) 'Early manifestations and first-contact incidence of schizophrenia in different cultures', *Psychological Medicine* 16: 909–28.

Schneider, K. (1957) 'Primäre und sekundäre Symptome bei der Schizophrenie', *Fortschrifte der Neurologie und Psychiatrie* 25: 487–90.

Shepherd, M. (1978) 'Epidemiology and clinical psychiatry', *British Journal of Psychiatry* 133: 289–98.

Shepherd, M. (1983) *The Psychosocial Matrix of Psychiatry: Collected Papers*, London, New York: Tavistock, 277.

Shepherd, M. (1984) 'The contribution of epidemiology to clinical psychiatry', *American Journal of Psychiatry* 141: 1574–5.

Shepherd, M. (1987) 'Formulation of new research strategies on schizophrenia', in H. Häfner, W.F. Gattaz and W. Janzarik (eds) *Search for the Causes of Schizophrenia*, Berlin, Heidelberg, New York, London, Paris, Tokyo: Springer, 29–38.

Stengel, E. (1959) 'Classification of mental disorders', *WHO Bulletin* 21: 601–3.

Strömgren, E. (1938) 'Beiträge zur psychiatrischen Erblehre, auf Grund von Untersuchungen an einer Inselbevolkerung', *Acta Psychiatrica et Neurologica*, supplement 19.

WHO (1960) *Epidemiology of Mental Disorders: Eighth Report of the Expert Committee of Mental Health* (Technical Report Series No. 185), Geneva: WHO.

WHO (1973) *Report of the International Pilot Study of Schizophrenia, Volume I*, Geneva: WHO.

WHO (1979) *Schizophrenia: An International Follow-Up Study*, Chichester: Wiley.

WHO (1981) *Social Dimensions of Mental Health*, Geneva: WHO.

Wig, N.N., Menon, D.K., Bedi, H., *et al.* (1987) 'Expressed emotion and schizophrenia in North India: I. Cross-cultural transfer of ratings of relatives' expressed emotion', *British Journal of Psychiatry* 151: 156–60.

Wing, J.K., Cooper, J.E., and Sartorius, N. (1974) *Measurement and Classification of Psychiatric Symptoms*, Cambridge: Cambridge University Press.

30

The NIMH Epidemiological Research Program: Past, Present, and Future

Darrel Regier

An overview will be provided of significant epidemiologic research conducted within the National Institute of Mental Health (NIMH). Admittedly selective in its emphasis, the paper will review a range of studies conducted since the initiation of the NIMH research programmes in 1949. Epidemiological research areas included are defined in textbooks as descriptive, analytic, or experimental studies (Morris 1964: Regier and Burke 1984) – areas which form the bases for much of clinical research in medicine (Feinstein 1985). The role of the NIMH in these studies is multifaceted and includes co-ordinating peer review of research applications, financial support judgements, 'state-of-the-art' analyses of scientific fields, stimulation of research fields to overcome barriers to further progress, administrative co-ordination and collaborative research in multi-centre studies, and the conduct of certain types of research – some of which cannot be accomplished by investigators outside a federal research setting.

NIMH was developed at the end of the Second World War during a period of widespread public concern about the extent of mental disorders in military recruits and in the general population. A basic laboratory research programme was established in the intramural programme under Seymour Kety and extramural research studies were supported for university-based investigators. Early intramural basic research studies included fundamental neuroscience work on brain physiology which led to a Nobel Prize for Julius Axelrod's work in identifying the metabolism of chemical neurotransmitters, their uptake at the presynaptic neurone, and the effect of psychoactive drugs in inhibiting such uptake (Axelrod 1970). A major advance in basic neuroscience techniques was accomplished by Sokoloff's Lasker Award winning development of the deoxyglucose method for determining brain metabolic activity – a method critical for the development of positron emission tomography (PET) scanning of the brain (Sokoloff et al. 1977). Among some of the earliest extramural research studies supported were descriptive epidemiological studies in Sterling County (Nova Scotia), mid-town Manhattan, and New Haven, Connecticut, to determine prevalence rates of mental disorders in the civilian population and their possible stress-related aetiology.

A major implicit objective of the Institute has been to integrate research findings about basic biological mechanisms with studies of clinical psychopathology and the behavioural expression of physiological mechanisms. Shepherd (1978) has described epidemiology as a useful integrating framework for bridging the gap which remains between basic and clinical research. Such a framework incorporates epidemiologically focused studies as an essential part of clinical research and a means of testing the strength of biological as well as psychosocial correlates of clinical disorders. This presentation uses the framework suggested by Shepherd to illustrate how epidemiological research has developed within the National Institute of Mental Health and how it has begun to bridge the gap between basic physiology and more descriptive clinical research. It will focus most specifically on the areas of affective disorders (depression), with illustrations of findings from a range of these studies, and will outline future opportunities now in the planning stage at the NIMH.

The basic framework of descriptive, experimental, and analytic epidemiological research will include selected examples of individual research studies in these areas and related developments in research methods. NIMH staff functions will also be emphasized in the previously described roles of carrying out research support judgements, 'state-of-the-art analyses' of scientific field opportunities and needs, collaborative research and co-ordination, and other direct participation of NIMH scientists in the conduct of research.

DESCRIPTIVE EPIDEMIOLOGY – COMMUNITY STUDIES

Shortly after the founding of the NIMH, there were three major community studies in the US and Canada that received NIMH support. These included the Stirling County (Leighton *et al.* 1963), Midtown-Manhattan (Srole *et al.* 1962), and Baltimore Morbidity (Commission on Chronic Illness 1957) studies. The first two studies used a range of case-identification methods which relied heavily on symptom scales to determine rates of mental disorder in the community whereas the Baltimore study relied on diagnoses by general medical physicians – diagnostic judgements were reviewed by psychiatrists in all three studies. Because of the absence of explicit research diagnostic criteria in these studies, it is difficult to interpret the prevalence rates of specific disorders. High symptom levels consistent with mental disorder diagnoses with 'significant impairment' were found at rates ranging from 10 per cent to 24 per cent of the population.

After these major community prevalence studies in the 1950s, additional smaller studies were conducted to disentangle the reasons for finding higher rates of severe psychiatric disorders in lower socio-economic classes (Dohrenwend and Dohrenwend 1969). There was continued reliance on dimensional scales, including a new one developed by the NIMH to identify rates of depressive symptomatology – the Center for Epidemiological Studies Depression (CES-D) Scale (Radloff and Locke 1986: Comstock and Helsing 1976). Additional studies were supported to examine the role of stress in the aetiology of mental disorders and a vigorous effort focused on stress related to major life events (Dohrenwend and Dohrenwend 1981).

In the mid-1970s, Weissman was able to conduct a community follow-up study by using the Schedule for Schizophrenia and Affective Disorders (SADS-L) (Endicott and Spitzer 1978) in a newly adapted lifetime form for use in community epidemiological surveys (Weissman and Myers 1978). The major significance of this NIMH-supported study was that it represented the first application of a structured diagnostic interview, based on the explicit Research Diagnostic Criteria (RDC) (Spitzer *et al.* 1978) ever performed in a community survey. The demonstration that such a survey could be carried out with non-psychiatrist interviewers was of major importance in paving the way for the later Epidemiological Catchment Area (ECA) studies in the US.

DESCRIPTIVE EPIDEMIOLOGY – SPECIALIZED TREATMENT SETTINGS

In addition to general population studies to determine prevalence rates of mental disorders and their correlation with domestic psychosocial stresses (in contrast to war-related stress), other descriptive studies focused on the correlates of disorders in treatment settings. A major study in this category was the Hollingshead and Redlich study of *Social Class and Mental Illness* in New Haven (Hollingshead and Redlich 1958). This landmark study graphically illustrated the higher rates of severe mental disorders and of institutionalization for those in lower social classes. Social concerns stimulated by this study included the inadequacy of community treatment for mental disorders which, in turn, helped launch the US Community Mental Health Centers legislation in the mid-1960s.

Two of the most significant and productive NIMH staff contributions to descriptive epidemiology were provided by Morton Kramer during his thirty-year tenure as Director of the NIMH Biometry Branch, a unit which later evolved into the Division of Biometry and Epidemiology and more recently reorganized with components in a Division of Clinical Research and a Division of Biometry and Applied Sciences. During his NIMH tenure, Dr Kramer, along with Drs Pollock and Taube, developed the NIMH National Reporting Program (Redick *et al.* 1983). This mental health statistical programme monitors psychiatric admissions and discharges, along with associated diagnoses, to in-patient and out-patient mental health facilities in the US. It has successfully traced variations in treated prevalence rates through the early 1950s period of increasing hospitalization for mental illness, and the period from the mid-1950s to the late 1970s covering deinstitutionalization and the expansion of community psychiatric services.

Kramer's second contribution was made possible by the availability of comparable mental health statistics from England and from the US National Reporting Program. Kramer noted that US mental hospitals were reporting rates of schizophrenia several times higher, and rates of affective disorder several times lower, than some facilities in the United Kingdom (Kramer 1961). This 'state-of-the art' analysis rapidly led to a US/UK study, supported by the NIMH, to determine the reason for these different treated prevalence rates. The findings of the study demonstrated that differences in observed treated prevalence rates for schizophrenia and affective disorders reflected differences in the application of relatively vague diagnostic criteria instead of any real differences in mental disorder rates (Kramer 1969: Cooper *et al.* 1972).

Under the auspice of the World Health Organization, the NIMH subsequently supported the International Pilot Study of Schizophrenia (IPSS) in nine countries to determine if any differences could be found in the characteristics of schizophrenia associated with widely varying cultures (WHO 1973). This landmark study also involved intramural and extramural NIMH scientific participation, including Wynn, Strauss, Carpenter, Kramer, and Bartko, and demonstrated the existence of a similar type of schizophrenic disorder in every culture studied (Sartorius *et al.* 1974). A longitudinal follow-up study of patients with schizophrenia was subsequently supported through WHO to assess the differential course of schizophrenia in different cultures and the 'determinants' of any differences in outcomes (Sartorius *et al.* 1986).

DESCRIPTIVE EPIDEMIOLOGY – PRIMARY CARE TREATMENT SETTINGS

Since large-scale community studies up to the mid-1970s were generally unable to assess prevalence rates of specific disorders, and specialized mental health treatment settings tended to include only the more seriously ill, prevalence studies in general medical practice settings offered several advantages. Such practices enable coverage of at least 70 per cent of the population in any one year who visit a general medical physician, they permit cross-sectional diagnoses based on a longitudinal relationship with a patient, and the general medical practitioner is a highly trained interviewer with the potential for making valid diagnostic assessments.

During the 1960s and 70s, there was a particular interest among NIMH investigators to follow a British tradition of examining prevalence rates of mental disorders in general medical practice settings. In England, these studies took on a more rigorous form under the direction of Michael Shepherd and the General Practice Research Unit (Shepherd *et al.* 1966). Stimulated in part by this interest, NIMH investigators Locke, Goldberg, and Rosen conducted a series of collaborative studies identifying rates of psychiatric disorder in primary care settings (Locke and Gardner 1969: Rosen *et al.* 1972). Goldberg, in particular, linked studies of prevalence with service use to determine the relative effect in decreasing use of general medical services when referrals to psychiatric specialists were made (Goldberg *et al.* 1970).

In the late 1970s, a Primary Care Research Section was established by Regier and Goldberg in the NIMH Division of Biometry and Epidemiology (Burns *et al.* 1979). This section was modelled in large part after the General Practice Research Unit of Shepherd and was developed to study systematically the prevalence rates of mental disorders (Goldberg *et al.* 1979: Goldberg *et al.* 1980; Hoeper *et al.* 1980), the level of service utilization by patients with these disorders (Hankin *et al.* 1982), the most appropriate division of responsibility between generalists and specialists in the care of these disorders (Regier *et al.* 1982), and the role of primary care physicians in caring for the chronic mentally ill (Regier *et al.* 1985). This research programme has continued with significant contributions from Burns, Burke, Kessler, Kamerow *et al.* (1986) and a wide range of investigators supported in extramural academic institutions.

DESCRIPTIVE EPIDEMIOLOGY – LINKAGE OF COMMUNITY, SPECIALIZED TREATMENT SETTING, PRIMARY CARE SETTING, AND SERVICE RESEARCH

The President's Commission on Mental Health

In the late 1970s, the President's Commission on Mental Health (1978) was established immediately after President Carter entered office. This Commission was a special concern of the First Lady, Rosalyn Carter, who personally guided its development. In the White House Executive Order establishing the Commission, the first priority given was to describe how the mentally ill were being served, determine the extent of underservice, and determine who was affected by such underservice (The White House 1977). An NIMH staff group of Regier, Goldberg, and Taube conducted a 'state-of-the-art' secondary analysis of prevalence data, and compared these data with service use or treated prevalence data obtained from the NIMH National Reporting Program and from the primary care sector research. The resulting synthesis of the most conservative estimate of prevalence, incidence, and service use rates in the US was published in the final report of the Commission and as a freestanding paper entitled, 'The *De Facto* U.S. Mental Health Services System'. The findings included an estimated 15 per cent annual prevalence of mental disorders with only 3 per cent (one-fifth of those affected) using specialist mental health services in one year (Regier *et al.* 1978). Of special

476

note was the estimate that 54 per cent of individuals with these disorders were seen exclusively in the primary care sector although the level of specific mental health services could not be determined.

Despite a considerable effort to document the data sources in support of prevalence and service use estimates, this undertaking highlighted the major gaps in our knowledge of prevalence rates of specific mental disorders and how these related to service utilization in general medical, specialized mental health, and other human service settings. The ADAMHA Administrator, at that time Dr Gerald Klerman, requested an agency-wide review of epidemiological, service system, and statistical reporting programmes (Regier and Rosenfeld 1979). Following this review, research programmes were announced in mental health service systems research and there was expansion of the Primary Care Research Section established in 1977. In addition, a framework for developing a clinical services research programme that would assess the effectiveness of primary care mental health services was conceptualized and developed by Burke.

A mental health economics research programme was established under Taube to address the health insurance and other financing issues affecting the delivery of mental health services (Taube et al. 1985). Finally, support was obtained to launch a new generation of psychiatric epidemiology studies that would use the new diagnostic criteria of DSM-III (American Psychiatric Association 1980) to identify prevalence rates, incidence rates, and service use rates that would more directly address a major need, identified by the President's Commission, to link epidemiology and services research findings.

The Epidemiological Catchment Area (ECA) study

Analyses for the President's Commission, reported on earlier, led the NIMH staff to conceptualize a comprehensive epidemiological and health services research study that would fill several of the major gaps identified. The Epidemiological Catchment Area (ECA) study was designed to start with a sample survey to determine the prevalence and incidence of mental disorder in a total (community and institutionalized) population. Individuals so identified would subsequently be followed longitudinally to determine their utilization of mental health services in all general medical, specialized mental health, or other human service facilities. Both prevalence and utilization data would then allow analysis of the population groups most affected by mental disorder and by an under-utilization of services (Regier et al. 1984).

Before any study could be conducted, it was necessary to develop a diagnostic instrument for use in a large enough population survey to obtain a sufficient number of subjects with low prevalence disorders, such as schizophrenia, to do meaningful analyses. The NIMH staff reviewed all available instruments and decided to develop a new one that was modelled on the St Louis, Renard Diagnostic Interview (Helzer et al. 1981) and would use the soon-to-be-published DSM-III criteria. Lee Robins was provided a

477

contract to develop the interview along with Robert Spitzer who received a separate contract to assure its coverage of the DSM-III criteria. The NIMH Diagnostic Interview Schedule (DIS) was the instrument developed for this study and it has subsequently been used in many additional national and international investigations (NIMH 1981: Robins *et al*. 1981). It is useful to note that several major diagnostic interviews now in active research use – the Present State Examination (PSE) (Wing *et al*. 1974), the SADS, the SADS-L, and the DIS – were all developed (or significantly refined) for specific NIMH-related collaborative research studies.

The ECA was a major collaborative study between the NIMH and academic investigators in five university sites including Yale, Johns Hopkins, Washington University – St Louis, Duke, and UCLA. The study would also never have been conducted without the active support of Mrs Carter who was called upon during the Office of Management and Budget (OMB) clearance process to certify that this study, and all of the sensitive data to be collected, were supported by the President's Commission recommendations.

Since the study design has been adequately described elsewhere (Eaton *et al*. 1984: Eaton and Kessler 1985), only a few of the major findings relating to affective disorders will be described. Data on the six-month prevalence (Myers *et al*. 1984: Blazer *et al*. 1985; Burnam *et al*. 1987), six-month service utilization (Shapiro *et al*. 1984; Hough *et al*. 1987), and life-time prevalence (Robins *et al*. 1984: Karno *et al*. 1987) have now been published for all five sites. One-month, six-month, and life-time prevalence rates, combined and standardized to the US population by age, sex, and race are also in press (Regier *et al*. 1988). The data to be presented here are drawn from the US standardized six-month prevalence data and service utilization analyses. They will be used to illustrate the linkage between community prevalence, specialized mental health treatment setting, primary care setting, and general service utilization studies.

ECA affective disorder results

In the first wave of interviews in the study, it was possible to determine that 19.1 per cent of the adult population could be identified as having at least one alcohol, drug abuse, or mental disorder. Affective disorders were found in 5.8 per cent of the population including 0.5 per cent with bipolar disorder, 3.0 per cent with major depressive episode, and 3.3 per cent with dysthymia. Overall, female rates (7.5 per cent) were found to be about twice those found for men (3.9 per cent) although rates for bipolar disorder were not significantly different by gender groups. Among age groups, the rates were highest in the 25–44 year age group with non-significant differences in the next highest age group of 45–64. When all other variables are controlled, there are no significant differences between white, or black, or Hispanic race/ethnicity groups or between socio-economic status groups. Significantly higher rates were found for separated/divorced and widowed persons in comparison with the married group.

Given the substantial number of people affected by depressive disorders, an immediate analytic issue was to determine the extent to which they receive some type of care in the mental health, general health, or other human service settings. Our analyses show that during a six-month period, slightly less than one in five (19 per cent) are seen by mental health specialists, three-quarters (74 per cent) are seen by general medical physicians, less than one in ten (9 per cent) are seen by other human service agencies (e.g. social service or clergy), and 21 per cent are not seen by any professional. Although there is significant overlap in service between mental health specialists and general medical physicians, 54 per cent of individuals with depressive disorders are seen exclusively by primary care physicians.

From a treatment perspective, a major issue is to determine the number identified as having a disorder and receiving treatment specifically for mental disorders in general medical and other human service settings. Despite the fact that three-quarters visit general medical physicians for some reason, only 17 per cent of individuals with these disorders receive some mental health treatment in these general medical settings. About 5 per cent receive mental health services in other human service settings. There is minimal overlap in services provided in general medical and other human service settings with the 19 per cent seen in specialized mental health settings. Fully 63 per cent receive no mental health treatment during a six-month time period. Individuals with major depression have the highest rate of treatment in specialized or general medical settings at 38 per cent, followed by 33 per cent with bipolar disorder and 24 per cent with dysthymia.

An additional question relates to the level of treatment intensity for individuals with these disorders. The average number of visits to any of the three service settings for all individuals, regardless of diagnosis, is three visits per person/six-months of which one in three is for a mental health reason. About one-half (48 per cent) of these visits are to mental health specialists, only 13 per cent are to general medical providers, and 38 per cent are to other human service professionals. For individuals with affective disorders, the average number of visits is three times as high (nine visits per six-months), of which five out of nine are for mental health reasons and slightly more than half (54 per cent) of these are to mental health specialists. If only the health sector is considered, 84 per cent of the mental health visits are to specialists.

A final question, which has yet to be addressed in a systematic way, is how effective are the mental health services provided in any of these treatment settings? The translation of research on treatment efficacy in controlled clinical trials, addressed in the next section, into treatment effectiveness in routine clinical practice is a major challenge in clinical medicine. The application of epidemiological methods to answer these questions is the field of clinical services research now under development at the NIMH (Regier and Burke 1984).

479

Conclusions from this analysis of depressive disorders include the following:

1. Affective disorders are widespread (about 6 per cent in six-months) and 80 per cent of affected persons are seen in professional settings in six-months where they could be screened, diagnosed, and treated.
2. The major location for early recognition and treatment is in the general medical sector where 74 per cent are seen in six-months.
3. Individuals with depression are heavy users of medical services, visiting for non-mental health reasons twice as frequently as the average and three times more frequently overall.
4. Of those with a depressive disorder who visited a general medical setting, only 23 per cent (17 per cent of the 74 per cent visiting) acknowledged receiving a mental health service in that setting. Overall about two-thirds of individuals with these disorders receive no mental health services.
5. In the absence of a robust method of primary prevention, the greatest potential for decreasing prevalence lies in the early identification and treatment of these disorders to reduce their duration and associated morbidity, and to prevent relapse. A new NIMH prevention programme, entitled the Depression Awareness, Recognition, and Treatment (D/ART) Program, has recently been launched. This programme is aimed at improving the recognition of affective disorders among the general public and general medical practitioners as well as increasing knowledge about the latest treatment advances.

EXPERIMENTAL EPIDEMIOLOGY – CONTROLLED CLINICAL TRIALS

The introduction of controlled clinical trials of psychotropic drugs received major support from the NIMH in the past twenty-five years. Clinical trials of phenothiazines (May 1968), antidepressants (Klerman and Cole 1965: Klein *et al.* 1980), and lithium (Baastrup *et al.* 1970; Prien *et al.*1973) have introduced prospective cohort intervention designs into the mainstream of psychiatric research. The same experimental epidemiology designs have more recently been applied to the study of psychosocial interventions for the treatment of depressive disorders (Elkin *et al.* 1985).

The need for methodological rigour in interpreting the results of controlled clinical trials was a recurrent theme for Shepherd (Blackwell and Shepherd 1968). Such an emphasis, although associated with considerable controversy in the case of lithium trials, ultimately contributed to clear methodological principles for clinical trials more generally (Grof *et al.* 1970; Medical Research Council Drug Trials Subcommittee 1981: Meinert 1986).

ANALYTIC EPIDEMIOLOGY – CASE CONTROL STUDIES

Collaborative depression studies

During the 1960s and early 1970s, NIMH staff developed a major interest in identifying biological and psychosocial correlates of affective disorders. The psychobiology of depression collaborative research studies, initiated by NIMH staff (Katz et al. 1979) and senior extramural research investigators, provided a major contribution to refining diagnostic criteria and developing standardized interviews. This study was responsible for development of the RDC and the SADS diagnostic interview. It also used a prospective cohort for examining multiple potential biological (Koslow et al. 1983) and psychosocial correlates of affective disorders. Longitudinal follow-up studies to examine naturalistic treatment of these disorders (Keller et al. 1986), clinical course, and familial aggregation (Klerman et al. 1985) have made significant contributions to this field.

Population genetic studies

Addressing the issue of schizophrenia from a more aetiological framework, Seymour Kety and David Rosenthal of NIMH and their Danish collaborators recognized an opportunity to separate environmental and genetic influences in the development of schizophrenia through the Danish Adoption Study. This classic case-control study identified higher rates of 'exposure' of adoptees with schizophrenia to a genetic history of schizophrenia in their biological relatives than was found in the genetic history of adoptees without the disorder (Kety and Rosenthal 1968).

It is ironic that one of the most significant studies to establish a biological predisposition to development of schizophrenia, was conducted by a biological psychiatrist (Kety) with no formal epidemiological training or disciplinary identification. The fact that an epidemiological research design was used to carry out such a study gives added credence to Shepherd's contention that epidemiology can serve the bridging function of integrating biological and clinical research.

Population and molecular genetic studies

Of all the epidemiological studies supported by the NIMH in the past forty years, none comes closer to the ideal of integrating basic and clinical research than the recent NIMH-supported study by Egeland et al. (1987). This study of affective disorders in an Amish population began as a population genetics epidemiological study and was supported for over a decade under the careful stewardship of the NIMH project officer Ben Locke. Despite several less-than-enthusiastic peer reviews of the study and modest priority scores, Locke facilitated expert technical assistance and exercised funding judgements to assure payment out of priority score order. He saw the excellent potential of this study and encouraged the linkage of molecular genetics experts with the population genetics originators of the study. The ultimate outcome of the study was identification of a specific gene fragment that was transmitted on chromosome 11 between three generations in one family, and was associated with transmission of bipolar affective disorder.

The linkage of clinicians, descriptive epidemiologists, population geneticists, and molecular genetics staff again supported Shepherd's contention that epidemiology can serve as the bridge between clinical and basic research. Future research studies should benefit from a greatly expanded thrust to develop other biological correlates which may in turn be studied for their naturally occurring rates in larger populations representative of the community and of the specific disorders.

RESEARCH METHODS

A distinguishing characteristic of epidemiology research, in contrast to clinical practice, is that such research focuses on a group as the unit of study rather than on individual patients. The ability to conduct studies in groups, large or small, is dependent upon a reliable case identification or diagnostic method which incorporates clinically relevant diagnostic criteria. The individual clinician may develop his or her own interviewing and physical examination procedure to apply to the group of patients in an individual practice. Although consistency in diagnosis may be relatively good for all patients in one clinician's practice, the US/UK study and others have shown the discrepancies that may be introduced in diagnoses involving large numbers of patients.

Since research studies require comparable diagnoses in all members of a group, there is considerable concern for development of good statistical reporting systems, clear diagnostic criteria, and the reliable application of these criteria. Statistical measures, such as Cohen's 'kappa' have been developed to assess reliability or the degree to which diagnostic agreement is obtained over that expected by chance alone. Increasingly explicit diagnostic criteria and structured diagnostic instruments, which facilitate consistent and thorough reviews of psychopathological symptoms, have become essential for advances in all clinical and epidemiological research.

Because of the centrality of diagnostic criteria and assessment instruments to the advancement of epidemiological research, NIMH staff have been actively involved in these activities since the beginning of the NIMH. Kramer was a key consultant to the committees developing ICD-8 and ICD-9 as well as the first and second editions of the American Psychiatric Association (APA) Diagnostic and Statistical Manuals (DSM-I and DSM-II). The NIMH also supported research studies that developed the Research Diagnostic Criteria (RDC) and then supported many of the subsequent diagnostic workgroups and field trials of DSM-III and DSM-IIIR – a set of diagnostic criteria that followed closely in the tradition of the RDC. NIMH staff have continued to serve as active participants in the evaluation of this major advance in psychiatric nosology (Regier 1987). With regard to diagnostic instruments, the previously described developments in the PSE, SADS, CES-D, and DIS instruments have all received substantial support from NIMH.

In 1978, the US Alcohol, Drug Abuse and Mental Health Administration (ADAMHA) Administrator, Gerald Klerman, and the World Health Organization (WHO) Mental Health Director, Norman Sartorius, initiated a joint programme to review diagnostic criteria on a world-wide basis (WHO/ADAMHA 1985). The formal co-operative agreement supporting this endeavour has advanced through the first two phases of multiple diagnostic workgroups (1979–82) and a major international conference (Copenhagen 1982) to the third phase focused on development of diagnostic instruments for use in epidemiological and clinical research studies. Field trials are now being conducted for several of these instruments including the Composite International Diagnostic Interview (CIDI), which combines elements of the DIS and PSE; the schedule for Clinical Assessment in Neuropsychiatry (SCAN), which is based on a tenth revision of the PSE; and the Personality Disorder Examination (PDE). All of these instruments are being constructed in conjunction with the new ICD-10 and DSM criteria developments. Although not covered under the co-operative agreement, ADAMHA staff are co-ordinating the North American field trial of the ICD-10 to assure a throrough review of these new international diagnostic criteria.

Within the US, NIMH has been involved in supporting Spitzer and Williams' development of the Structured Clinical Interview for DSM-III (SCID) through contracts and grants. This interview has been used in several international pharmacotherapy trials of anxiety disorders and in a multi-site NIMH collaborative study on treatment strategies for schizophrenia. A final diagnostic interview that has been under development by NIMH for the past several years is a Diagnostic Interview Schedule for Children (DISC) which will be used for future epidemiological studies of children and adolescents.

FUTURE DIRECTIONS

Epidemiological research studies supported by the NIMH have begun to bridge the gaps between clinical practice and research on basic mechanisms underlying psychopathology. Work on diagnostic criteria and assessment instruments required for epidemiological studies has greatly advanced the precision of clinical and research communication. It is now possible for clinicians around the world to specify both the explicit criteria used in describing a patient, and the operational application of those criteria in a diagnostic instrument. The potential for comparing more homogeneous patient populations in controlled clinical trials or in risk factor (biological or psychosocial

483

correlate) studies is greatly enhanced by these developments.

Of particular importance in future studies involving biological correlates, such as the Egeland *et al.* (1987) genetic studies, is the possibility of developing a reciprocal interaction between the initial descriptive diagnostic criteria and a more refined biologically-based diagnostic criterion which emerges from genetically similar subtypes of a disorder. In order to prevent spurious correlations, epidemiological studies will be necessary to assess the frequency of putative biological correlates of mental disorders in representative samples of individuals with those disorders. Past difficulties in replicating biological markers, such as Dexamethasone Suppression Test (DST) correlates with affective disorders, may be attributed in part to an insufficient attention to patient sampling.

We look forward to an increasingly synergistic relationship between clinical practice, clinical research, and basic research that will build on the existing scientific base briefly reviewed in this paper. Two new research programmes have just been launched within the NIMH including a 'National Plan for Research on Schizophrenia' and a programme directed toward 'Opportunities for NIMH Neuroscience Research – the Decade of the Brain'. Investments in these enterprises will clearly provide returns of higher quality if the epidemiological framework recommended by Shepherd finally enters the mainstream of psychiatric research. Such a framework will no longer confuse descriptive epidemiological studies, concerned only with mental disorder prevalence or incidence rates, with the whole of epidemiological research. Rather, such research will be seen as part of the research fabric that will eventually unlock us from our continuing ignorance of the basic mechanisms underlying some of humanity's most disabling disorders.

REFERENCES

American Psychiatric Association, Committee on Nomenclature and Statistics (1988) *Diagnostic and Statistical Manual of Mental Disorders*, third edition, Washington, DC: APA.

Axelrod, J. (1970) *Noradrenaline: Fate and Control of its Biosynthesis*, The Nobel Foundation.

Baastrup, P.C., Poulson, J.C., Schou, M., Thomsen, K. and Amdisen, A. (1970) 'Prophylactic lithium: double-blind discontinuation in manic-depressive and recurrent disorders', *Lancet* 2: 326–30.

Blackwell, B. and Shepherd, M. (1968) 'Prophylactic lithium: another therapeutic myth? An examination of the evidence to date', *Lancet*, i: 968–71.

Blazer, D., George, L.K., Landerman, R., Pennybacker, M., Melville, M.L., Woodbury, M., Manton, K.G., Jordan, K. and Locke, B.A. (1985) 'Psychiatric disorders: rural/urban comparison', *Archives of General Psychiatry* 42: 651–6.

Burnam, M.A., Hough, R.L., Escobar, J.I., Karno, M., Timbers, D.M., Telles, C.A. and Locke, B.Z. (1987) 'Six-month prevalence of specific psychiatric disorders among Mexican Americans and non-Hispanic whites in Los Angeles', *Archives of General Psychiatry* 44: (8): 687–94.

Burns, B.J., Regier, D.A., Goldberg, I.D. and Kessler, L.G. (1979) 'Future directions in primary care/mental health research', *International Journal of Mental Health* 8: 130–40.

Commission on Chronic Illness (1957) *Chronic Illness in the United States, IV: Chronic Illness in a Large city: The Baltimore Study*, Cambridge, Mass: Harvard University Press.

Comstock, G.W. and Helsing, K. (1976) 'Symptoms of depression in two communities', *Psychological Medicine* 6: 551–63.

Cooper, J.E., Kendell, R.E., Gurland, G.J., Sharpe, L., Copeland, J.R.M. and Simon, R. (1972) *Psychiatric Diagnosis in New York and London*, London: Oxford University Press.

Dohrenwend, B.P. and Dohrenwend, B.S. (1969) *Social Status and Psychological Disorder: A Causal Inquiry*, New York: Wiley.

Dohrenwend, B.S., And Dohrenwend, B.P. (1981) *Stressful Life Events and Their Contents*, New York: Prodist.

Eaton, W.W., Holzer, C.E., Von Korff, M., Anthony, J.C., Helzer, J.E., George, L., Burnam, M.A., Boyd, J.H., Kessler, L.G. and Locke, B.Z. (1984) 'The design of the Epidemiologic Catchment Area Surveys', *Archives of General Psychiatry* 41 (10): 942–8.

Eaton, W.W. and Kessler, L.G. (eds) (1985) *Epidemiologic Field Methods in Psychiatry: The NIMH Epidemiologic Catchment Area Program*, New York: Academic Press.

Egeland, J.A., Gerhard, D.S., Pauls, D.L., Sussex, J.N., Kidd, K.K., Allen, C.R., Hosterrer, A.M. and Housman, E.D. (1987) 'Bipolar affective disorders linked to DNA markers on chromosome 11', *Nature* 325: 783–7.

Elkin, I., Parloff, M.B., Hadley, S.W. and Autry, J.H. (1985) 'NIMH treatment of depression collaborative research program', *Archives of General Psychiatry* 42: 305–16.

Endicott, J. and Spitzer, R.L. (1978) 'A diagnostic interview: the schedule for affective disorders and schizophrenia', *Archives of General Psychiatry* 35: 837–44.

Feinstein, A. (1985) *Clinical Epidemiology: The Architecture of Clinical research*, Philadelphia: W.B. Saunders.

Goldberg, I.D., Krantz, G. and Locke, B.Z. (1970) 'Effect of a short-term outpatient psychiatric therapy benefit on the utilization of medical services in a prepaid group practice medical program', *Medical Care* 8: 419–28.

Goldberg, I.D., Regier, D.A., McInerny, T.K., Pless, I.B. and Roghmann, K.J. (1979) 'The role of the pediatrician in the delivery of mental health services to children', *Pediatrics* 63 (6): 898–909.

Goldberg, I.D., Regier, D.A. and Burns, B.J. (eds) (1980) *Use of Health and Mental Health Outpatient Services in Four Organized Health Care Settings*, National Institute of Mental Health, Series DN, No. 1, DHHS Publication No. (ADM) 80–859.

Graf, P., Schou, M., Angst, J., Baastrup, P.C. and Weis, P. (1970) 'Methodological problems of prophylactic trials in recurrent affective disorders', *British Journal of Psychiatry* 116: 599–619.

Hankin, J.R., Steinwachs, D.M., Regier, D.A., Burns, B.J., Goldberg, I.D. and Hoeper, E.W. (1982) 'Use of general medical care services by persons with mental disorders', *Archives of General Psychiatry* 39: 225–31.

Helzer, J.E., Robins, L.N., Croughan, J.L. and Weiner, A. (1981) 'Renard Diagnostic Interview', *Archives of General Psychiatry* 38: 393–8.

Hoeper, E.W., Nycz, G.R., Cleary, P.D., Regier, D.A. and Goldberg, I.D. (1980) 'Estimated prevalence of RDC mental disorder in primary medical care', *International Journal of Mental Health* 8 (2): 6–15.

Hollingshead, A.B. and Redlich, F.C. (1958) *Social Class and Mental Illness*, New York: Wiley.

Hough, R.L., Landsverk, J.A., Karno, M., Burnam, M.A., Timbers, D.M., Escobar, J.I. and Regier, D.A. (1987) 'Utilization of health and mental health services by Los Angeles Mexican Americans and non-Hispanic whites', *Archives of General Psychiatry* 44 (8): 702–9.

Kamerow, D.B., Pincus, H.A. and Macdonald, D.I. (1986) 'Alcohol abuse, other drug abuse, and mental disorders in medical practice: prevalence, costs, recognition and treatment', *Journal of the American Medical Association* 255 (15): 2054–7.

Karno, M., Hough, R.L., Burnam, M.A., Escobar, J.I., Timbers, D.M., Santana, F. and Boyd, J.H. (1987) 'Lifetime prevalence of specific psychiatric disorders among Mexican Americans and non-Hispanic whites in Los Angeles', *Archives of General Psychiatry* 44 (8): 695–701.

Katz, M.M., Secunda. S., Hirschfeld, R.M.A. and Koslow, S.H. (1979) 'NIMH Clinical Research Branch Collaborative Program on the Psychobiology of Depression', *Archives of General Psychiatry* 36: 765–71.

Keller, M.B., Lavori, P.W., Klerman, G.L., Andreasen, N.C., Endicott, J., Coryell, W., Fawcett, J., Rice, J.P. and Hirschfeld, R.M.A. (1986) 'Low levels and lack of predictors of somatotherapy and psychotherapy received by depressed patients', *Archives of General Psychiatry* 43: 458–66.

Kety, S.S., Rosenthal, D., Wender, P.H. and Schulsinger, F. (1968) 'The types and prevalence of mental illness in the biological and adoptive families of adopted schizophrenics', in D. Rosenthal, and S.S. Kety (eds) *Transmission of Schizophrenia*, London: Pergamon Press.

Klein, D., Gittelman, R., Quitkin, F. and Rifkin, A. (eds) (1980) *Diagnosis and Drug Treatment of Psychiatric Disorders in Adults and Children*, second edition, Baltimore: Williams and Wilkins.

Klerman, G.L. and Cole, J. (1965) 'Clinical pharmacology of imipramine and related antidepressant compounds', *Pharmacological Reviews* 17: 101–41.

Klerman, G.L., Lavori, P.W., Rice, J.., Reich, T., Endicott, J., Andreasen, N.C., Keller, M.B. and Hirschfeld, R.M.A. (1985) 'Birth-cohort trends in rates of major depressive disorder among relatives of patients with affective disorder', *Archives of General Psychiatry* 42 (7): 689–93.

Koslow, S.H., Maas, J.W., Bowden, C.L., Davis, J.M., Hanin, I. and Javaid, J. (1983) 'CSF and urinary biogenic amines and metabolites in depression and mania', *Archives of General Psychiatry* 40: 999–1010.

Kramer, M. (1961) 'Some problems for international research suggested by observations on differences in first admission rates to the mental hospitals of England and Wales and of the United States', *Proceedings of the Third World Congress of Psychiatry* 3: 153–60.

Kramer, M. (1969) 'Cross-national study of diagnosis of the mental disorders: origin of the problem', *American Journal of Psychiatry* 125: supplement I–II.

Leighton, D.C., Harding, J.S., Macklin, D.B., Macmillan, A.M. and Leighton, A.H. (1963) *The Character of Danger*, New York: Basic Books.

Locke, B.Z. and Gardner, E. (1969) 'Psychiatric disorders among the patients of general practitioners and internists', *Public Health Reports* 84: 167–73.

May, P.R.A. (1968) *Treatment of Schizophrenia: A Comparative Study of Five Treatment Methods*, New York: Science house, Inc.

Medical Research Council Drug Trials Subcommittee (1981) 'Continuation therapy with lithium and amitriptyline in unipolar depressive illness: a controlled trial', *Psychological Medicine* 11: 409–16.

Meinert, C.L. (1986) *Clinical Trials: Design, Conduct, and Analysis, Volume 8*, New York: Oxford University Press.

Morris, J.N. (1964) *Uses of Epidemiology*, Baltimore: Williams & Wilkins.

Myers, J.K., Weissman, M.M., Tischler, G.L., Holzer, C.E., Leaf, P.J., Orvaschel, H., Anthony, J.C., Boyd, J.H., Burke, J.D., Kramer, M. and Stoltzman, R. (1984) 'Six-month prevalence of psychiatric disorders in three communities', *Archives of General Psychiatry* 41 (10): 959–67.

National Institute of Mental Health (1981) *NIMH Diagnostic Interview Schedule: Version III*, Rockville, MD: NIMH mimeo.

Prien, R.F., Klett, C.J. and Caffey, E.M. (1973) 'Lithium carbonate and imipramine in prevention of affective episodes', *Archives of General Psychiatry* 29: 420–25.

The President's Commission on Mental health (1978) *Report to the President from the President's Commission on Mental Health* (Stock No. 040-000-00390-8, Volume 1), Washington, DC.

The President's Commission on Mental Health (1978) *Report to the President from the President's Commission on Mental Health*, (Stock No. 040-000-00390-8, Volume 2), Washington, DC.

Redick, R.W., Manderscheid, R.W., Witkin, M.J. and Rosenstein, M.H. (1983), National Institute of Mental health *A History of the US National Reporting Program for Mental Health Statistics, 1840–1983* (DHHS Pub. No. (ADM) 83–1296), Washington, DC: Superintendent of Documents, US Government Printing Office.

Radloff, L.S. and Locke, B.Z. (1986) 'The Community Mental Health Assessment Survey and the CES-D Scale', In M.M. Weissman *et al.* (eds) *Community Surveys of Psychiatric Disorders*, New Jersey: Rutgers University Press.

Regier, D.A., Goldberg, I.D. and Taube, C.A. (1978) 'The de facto US mental health services system', *Archives of General Psychiatry* 35: 685–93.

Regier, D.A. and Rosenfeld, A.H. (1979) *The Report of the ADAMHA Workgroup on Epidemiology, Health Systems Research, and Statistics/Data Systems*, KHHS/ADAMHA, mimeo.

Regier, D.A., Goldberg, I.D., Burns, B.J., Hankin, J.R., Hoeper, E.W. and Nycz, G.R. (1982) 'Specialist/generalist medical care services by persons with mental disorders', *Archives of General Psychiatry* 39: 219–24.

Regier, D.A. and Burke, J.D. (1984) 'Epidemiology', in H.I. Kaplan and B.J. Sadock (eds) *Comprehensive Textbook of Psychiatry*, fourth edition, Baltimore: Williams & Wilkins.

Regier, D.A., Myers, J.K., Kramer, M., Robins, L.N., Blazer, D.G., Hough, R.L., Eaton, W.W. and Locke, B.Z. (1984) 'The NIMH Epidemiological Catchment Area (ECA) program: historical context, major objectives, and study population characteristics', *Archives of General Psychiatry* 41: 934–41.

Regier, D.A., Burke, J.D., Manderscheid, R.W. and Burns, B.J. (1985) 'The chronically mentally ill in primary care', *Psychological Medicine* 15: 265–73.

Regier, D.A. (1987) 'Nosologic principles and diagnostic criteria (introduction and overview)', in G.L. Tischler (ed.) *Diagnosis and Classification in Psychiatry: A Critical Appraisal of DSM-III*, New York: Cambridge University Press.

Regier, D.L., Boyd, J.H., Burke, J.D., Rae, D.S., Myers, J.K., Kramer, M., Robins, L.N., George, L.K., Karno, M. and Locke, B.Z. (1988) 'One-month prevalence of mental disorders in the U.S. – based on five epidemiological catchment area sites', *Archives of General Psychiatry*, in press.

Robins, L.N., Helzer, J.E., Croughan, J. and Ratcliff, K.S. (1981) 'National Institute of Mental Health Diagnostic Interview Schedule: its history, characteristics, and validity', *Archives of General Psychiatry* 38: 381–9.

Robins, L.N., Helzer, J.E., Weissman, M.M., Orvaschel, H., Gruenberg, E., Burke, J.D. and Regier, D.A. (1984) 'Lifetime prevalence of specific psychiatric disorders in three sites', *Archives of General Psychiatry* 41 (10): 949–58.

Rosen, B.M., Locke, B.Z., Goldberg, I.D. and Babigian, H.M. (1972) 'Identification of emotional disturbance in patients seen in general medical clinics', *Hospital Community Psychiatry* 23: 364–70.

Sartorius, N., Jablensky, A., Korten, A., Ernberg, G., Anker, M., Cooper, J.E. and Day, R. (1986) 'Early manifestations and first-contact incidence of schizophrenia in different cultures: a preliminary report on the initial evaluation phase of the WHO Collaborative Study of Determinants of Outcome of Severe Mental Disorders', *Psychological Medicine* 16: 909–28.

Sartorius, N., Shapiro, R. and Jablensky, A. (1974) 'The international pilot study of schizophrenia', *Schizophrenia Bulletin* 1 (experimental issue no. 11) : 21–34.

Shapiro, S., German, P.S., Skinner, E.A., Von Korff, M., Turner, R.W., Klein, L.E., Teitelbaum, M.L., Kramer, M., Burke, J.D. and Burns, B.J. (1987) 'An experiment to change detection and management of mental morbidity in primary care', *Medical Care* 25 (4): 327–39.

Shapiro, S., Skinner, E.A., Kessler, L.G., von Korff, M., German, P.S., Tischler, G.L., Leaf, P.J., Benham, L., Cottler, L. and Regier, D.A. (1984) 'Utilization of health and mental health services', *Archives of General Psychiatry* 41 (10): 971–8.

Shepherd, M. (1978) 'Epidemiology and clinical psychiatry', *Journal of Psychiatry* 133: 289–98.

Shepherd, M., Cooper, B., Brown, A.C. and Kalton, G.W. (1966) *Psychiatric Illness in General Practice*, London: Oxford University Press.

Sokoloff, L., Reivich, M., Kennedy, C., Des Rosiers, M.H., Patlak, C.S., Pettigrew, K.D., Sakurada, O. and Shinohara, M. (1977) 'The [^{14}C]Deoxyglucose method for the measurement of local cerebral glucose utilization: theory, procedure, and normal values in the conscious and anesthetized albino rat^1', *Journal of neurochemistry* 28: 897–916.

Spitzer, R.L., Endicott, J. and Robins, E. (1978) 'Research diagnostic criteria: rationale and reliability', *Archives of General Psychiatry* 35: 773–83.

Srole, L. (1962) *Mental Health in the Metropolis: The Midtown Manhattan Study*, New York: McGraw-Hill.

Taube, C.A., Thompson, J.W., Burns, B.J., Widem, P. and Prevost, C. (1985) 'Prospective payment and psychiatric discharges from general hospitals with and without psychiatric units', *Hospital and Community Psychiatry* 36 (7): 754–60.

Weissman, M. and Myers, J.K. (1978) 'Affective disorders in a U.S. urban community: the use of research diagnostic criteria in an epidemiological survey', *Archives of General Psychiatry* 35: 1304–11.

The White House (1977) 'Executive Order No. 11973 – President's Commission of Mental Health', Office of the White House Press Secretary.

Wing, J.H., Cooper, J.E. and Sartorius, N. (1974) *The Description and Classification of Psychiatric Symptoms: An Instruction Manual for the PSE and CATEGO system*, London: Cambridge University Press.

WHO/ADAMHA (1985) *Mental Disorders, Alcohol – Drug-Related Problems*, New York: Elsevier.

World Health Organization (1973) *The International Pilot Study of Schizophrenia, Volume I*, Geneva: WHO.

31

Case Definition and Case Identification in Cross-cultural Perspective

Jair Mari, Biswajit Sen, and Tai-Ann Cheng

While psychopathology may imply that there is an inner core of suffering shared by human beings, unanswered questions remain about whether concepts and definitions of psychiatric disturbance developed in western societies can equally be applied to other cultures or whether there are culturally specific psychiatric entities which do not fit into a global classification.

The concept of culture itself can be used in different senses. Operationally, culture can be equated with a nation. This involves two basic assumptions: first, that each nation contains distinctive cultural features and, second, that the possible ethnic differences within a nation are less prominent than those between two nations under scrutiny. Culture can also be used in the traditional anthropological tribal sense and as an ethnic concept in reference to the pluralistic multi-cultural groups within a nation (Murphy 1982).

A variety of standardized psychiatric interviews have been developed in the last two decades, and a number of such instruments have been applied in several nations and to different ethnic groups (the assumptions which have been made about the development of such instruments were described by Wing *et al.* 1981). This article will focus on the methodology adopted in the development of such instruments by highlighting the limitations and achievements of their use in Brazil, India, and Taiwan.

CULTURAL BACKGROUND

Brazil

Brazil has a population of approximately 140 million inhabitants, the spoken language throughout the country is Portuguese (except for some tribal groups accounting for less than 0.5 per cent of the population), and illiteracy is around 30 per cent. Although the 'official' religion of the majority of the population is Roman Catholic, the folk religions 'Umbanda' and 'Kardecismo' are widespread and have a strong influence. These two religions have places of worship, *centros espiritas*, where ill people can be advised and where 'bad spirits' can be expelled; as these *centros* are very accessible (no bureaucracy, queueing, or appointments), families with psychiatrically disturbed members resort to them. There is approximately one of these *centros* per 20,000 inhabitants (Mari 1983).

Neither religion makes a distinction between body and mind. The ceremonies of Umbanda are related to the worship of black ancestors, Indian ancestors, and Catholic saints. In the last century, the slaves used to mask their *Orishas* (literally master of the head; god or goddess) with Catholic saints because they were not free to celebrate their original African rituals. The Umbanda religion is regarded as 'low spiritism' and is deeply rooted in the community. 'Disease' (*Encosto*) is said to be caused by 'spirits without light' (Exus and Qiumbas) wandering around and possessing people. Treatment of such 'disease' consists in exorcising the 'spirit without light'.

Kardecismo is a philosophico-religious system based on the Hindu idea of Karma. There is a belief in the idea of reincarnation and in communication between the dead and the living. It is regarded as 'high spiritism', probably due to the strong influence of the white middle class in this religion. Disease (Karmica disease) is thought to be caused because the spirit has committed faults in a previous life, and is seen as a kind of test which the patient must face. The treatment is based on the development of the spirit.

Although there is no 'official' integration between the 'formal' and 'informal' care systems in Brazil, it is well known that psychiatrists rarely discourage patients from participating in spiritist cults and, in many cases, psychiatrists make referrals and co-operate with them. For instance, Brody gives an interesting account of the way doctors and spiritists work together in 'The Hospital Espirita Pedro de Alcantara' in Rio de Janeiro (Brody 1973: 429–31). This hospital combines spiritist sessions and traditional psychiatric treatments, and patients referred to these sessions are required to be functioning reasonably well by the spiritual leader (*chefe do terreiro*) before attendance. For instance, treatment is not given to those who are hypertensive, receiving insulin, agitated, or very depressed.

Brody randomly selected twenty first admissions from a psychiatric hospital in Rio de Janeiro to investigate how many sought a *centro espirita* and the reasons for doing so: fourteen patients turned out to have attended religious ceremonies at least once, largely because either the patient or a relative believed that spirits were causing the psychiatric condition. Richeport (1984) interviewed 220 families living in a *favela*, in the outskirts of Natal, to compare the pattern of use of 'formal' and 'informal' systems of care in this population. The majority of people had consulted both health professionals and 'spiritists' for problems such as physical symptoms, depression, difficulties arising from unemployment, marital tensions, dealing with retarded children, and alcoholism.

India

India has a population of about 800 million, speaking more than a score of languages and several hundred dialects. The rate of illiteracy is 65 per cent. Approximately 80 per cent of the population are Hindu, believing in the concept of rebirth and explaining human suffering in terms of expiation of accumulated sins in the former and present incarnations (the doctrine of Karma). Between 12 per cent and 14 per cent of the population are Muslim, the rest being Christians, Sikhs, Jains, Buddhists, Parsees, and 'animists', i.e., tribes like Santals, Mundas, etc. While cultural differences undoubtedly exist between these groups, it is believed that 'idioms of distress' are broadly similar across them, varying more with the extent of formal education and degree of westernization than religious affiliation per se. No significant differences in the prevalence of mental illness have been found between important religious groups. However, the prevalence of mental illness among the tribes is known to be fairly low (Nandi et al. 1980).

Belief in the evil influences of the spirit world controlled by people with supernatural powers and malefic intent is deeply rooted in India, including, for example, many of the urban elite. There is a corresponding belief in faith healers (ojhas or mantarwadis) who are believed to possess powers to counteract these evil influences, which may give rise to, among other manifestations, mental illness. Even a decade ago it would have been rare for a psychiatrist in the rural areas to see a patient who had not previously visited a faith healer. This picture is now slowly changing, but it is expected that the influence of faith healers will continue to remain substantial.

Taiwan

Taiwan (R.O.C.) has a population of about nineteen million distributed between villages, towns, and cities, each with approximately one-third of the total inhabitants. The main ethnic group is the Chinese who migrated to Taiwan from mainland China and constitute over 98 per cent of the total population. The rest are Malayo-Polynesian aborigines. Eighty per cent of the Chinese are early immigrants whose mother tongues were the southern Fukien and the Hakka dialects. The 20 per cent late immigrants speak a variety of dialects. Mandarin is the official common language which can be well understood by most people under 50 years of age. The proportion of illiteracy was around 8 per cent in 1986 (Ministry of the Interior 1987). The majority of people in Taiwan believe in Chinese folk religion (65 per cent), and the rest have various religious beliefs including Buddhism (15 per cent), Taoism (7 per cent), and Christianity (5 per cent).

Rapid modernization over the past two to three decades has made Taiwan into a newly industrialized country with a commodity-export-oriented economic policy. Although considerable difference in family size has been found across urban-rural communities in recent years, the strong traditional parent-child kinship, emphasizing filial piety (Hsu 1971), still dominates the

491

family relationship in Taiwan. The divorce rate is rather low, being 5.5 per 1,000 currently married population in 1986 (Ministry of the Interior 1987).

The traditional Chinese medical concept mainly emphasizes both a correspondence between macrocosm and microcosm, as well as a harmony between 'yin' and 'yang' of body and environment. 'Yang' signifies not only the apparent, active, excited, external, upward, forward, aggressive, volatile, hard, bright, hot, but also the abstract and functional. In contrast, 'yin' signifies not only the passive, inhibited, unclear, inward, downward, retrogressive, cold, dark, soft, submissive, but also the material and concrete (Lin 1981). Disharmony would bring about either an excessive or an insufficiency of the *jin-Chi* (vital energy) and thus cause illness.

Although this medical concept explicitly includes only physical illness, it implicitly uses physical terms to describe somatic manifestations arising from emotional distress (Tseng 1975; Kleinman 1982). Hence, while psychotics often seek help first from a folk therapist, people with minor psychiatric morbidity largely look for help from both Chinese and western medicine in Taiwan. There, they always report, their somatic discomfort and their psychosocial distress is often neglected. Very few of them would consult mental health professionals and the general practitioner seldom refers them to the psychiatrists.

DEVELOPING INSTRUMENTS FOR CROSS-CULTURAL STUDIES

There are five major aims of cross-cultural research: a) to compare rates of psychiatric morbidity; b) to develop culturally sensitive instruments; c) to investigate the aetiology of psychopathology; d) to study changes in the pattern of psychopathology over time; and e) to investigate the relationship between psychiatric disturbance and cultural determinants. The contrasting perspective between the two leading aims is one of the main problems of developing psychiatric research instruments for cross-cultural comparison: these should be able to identify symptoms and syndromes which represent the same phenomena in different cultural settings and simultaneously be sensitive to cultural variations.

Flaherty (1987) has pointed to five major mutually exclusive dimensions of equivalence to be considered when developing a psychiatric research instrument for cross-cultural application: *Content Equivalence* – each item of the measuring instrument should have a content relevant to each culture under study; *Semantic Equivalence* – each item of the measuring instrument should have the same meaning for each language; *Technical Equivalence* – the act of measuring should be unaffected by the cultural differences; *Criterion Equivalence* – the interpretation of the results of a measure should remain the same when compared against a norm in each culture; and *Conceptual Equivalence* – responses to the measuring instrument should indicate the measurement of the same theoretical construct across cultures. The first three items are mainly related to the structure of the language being used while the last two refer to the psychiatric taxonomy.

There are basically three methods of case identification using standardized research instruments: clinical evaluation by means of a psychiatric interview, the use of screening questionnaires, and the combination of both in a two-way design. The definition of a case will, of course, depend on the purpose of the study, i.e., a case for what (Copeland 1981)? A number of these instruments have now been applied in Brazil, India, and Taiwan.

Brazil

The Present State Examination (PSE) (Wing *et al.* 1974) has been translated into Portuguese by Caetano and Gentil Filho (1983), and Gentil Filho *et al.* (1986) have raised the problems they have had in the translation of the PSE and its use in some training sessions at the psychiatric unit of the University of Sao Paulo. From a semantic point of view, some original English or German words in the glossary would not have the same meaning in Portuguese vocabulary. It was difficult to translate terms such as 'thought broadcast', '*mitgehen*', and idiomatic expressions such as 'knight's move'. From a conceptual point of view, the definition of '*deliroide*' largely applied by Brazilian psychiatrists had no equivalence in the PSE original version. Moreover, they raised difficulties in detecting specific syndromes such as alcoholism, organic brain disorders, endogenous panic anxiety, affective atypical disorders, mental handicap, and atypical non-paranoid states, though the reasons have not been clearly specified.

Caetano (1986) applied the PSE to an in-patient sample in Cambridge (n = 152), from which he selected forty-one cases presenting either a panic disorder or a generalized anxiety disorder according to DSM-III, to carry out a comparison of symptom profiles with an out-patient clinic Brazilian sample. According to the original version, depersonalization can only be rated if lasting for some hours. However, he noticed that patients in both samples would frequently manifest this state over shorter periods of time. Thus, in the Brazilian version, depersonalization has been rated, even when transient, providing there is an important clinical degree of intensity and/or high frequency.

These two studies provide a list of a number of questions which have been misunderstood by Brazilian patients, probably because of the number of those with few years of schooling and/or illiteracy. The validity of the Portuguese version was not checked by back-translation but appears to be good and both authors have emphasized the feasibility of using the PSE in Brazil provided a proper training period is undertaken to acquaint users with the instrument.

The aim of the study conducted by Mari (1987) was to assess the prevalence of psychiatric morbidity in three primary medical care clinics in the city of Sao Paulo and to develop research instruments to be applied in

493

this setting. A time-sample of consecutive attenders were asked to complete two screening questionnaires, the Self Report Questionnaire (SRQ) (Harding *et al.* 1980), and the General Health Questionnaire (GHQ) (Goldberg 1972), and a subsample of the attenders were selected for a psychiatric interview, the Clinical Interview Schedule (CIS) (Goldberg *et al.* 1970).

For the pilot study, the GHQ-30 was translated into Portuguese, back-translated by workers unfamiliar with the original version, and the back-translation checked by a British psychiatrist. Minor adjustments were made to the original translation, so as to keep the original meaning while trying to conform as closely as possible with Brazilian concepts and idioms. However, the GHQ-30 presented several difficulties in the pilot study: the questionnaire was too long and it became apparent that some of the questions were being misunderstood by the subjects. For example, 'concentration' was occasionally understood to mean preparation to contact 'holy spirits' and this was probably due to the strong influence of the folk religions in Brazil (Mari and Williams 1984). So, for the main study it was decided to use a shorter version of the GHQ, the GHQ-12, while rephrasing some of the questions which were poorly understood by the respondents in the pilot study.

A Portuguese version of the SRQ was made available in a previous WHO collaborative study carried out by Harding *et al.* (1980, 1983), and the two screening questionnaires (GHQ-12 and SRQ-20) were found to be equally valid for the detection of minor psychiatric morbidity in the primary medical care setting in the city of Sao Paulo (Mari and Williams 1985, 1986).

The Clinical Interview Schedule is a semi-structured interview developed to study psychiatric morbidity in general practice and community settings. The translation and back-translation of the CIS into Portuguese has been carried out in the same manner as described for the GHQ without major problems (the glossary was, however, used in the original language). A reliability study of the Portuguese version of the CIS was conducted with two other psychiatrists (Mari *et al.* 1986) and there was only one out of twenty-two items where there was no agreement between the investigators: euphoria (ICC via ANOVA = 0.02, n.s.). The item 'histrionic' showed the lowest agreement (weighted Kappa = + 0.48) in the study conducted by Goldberg *et al.* (1970) and similar findings were reported in the Brazilian assessment and in the pilot study conducted by Campillo-Serrano *et al.* (1981) in Mexico with fifteen interviews. The low agreement found in euphoria was, however, specific to the Brazilian study.

It is plausible to suppose that constant cross-cultural low agreements would point to problems in the way symptoms are defined or interpreted while specific low reliability agreements might indicate transcultural differences in the use of the instrument (or simply be related to observer bias: examples in the literature can be found in Shepherd *et al.* 1968 and Leff 1974).

A few culture-specific screening instruments of psychiatric disorders have been developed and tested in Brazil, without direct reference to foreign scales. Almeida-Filho (1981) developed a 35-item screening questionnaire to identify psychiatric disturbance in children, the Infant Psychiatric Morbidity Questionnaire (QMPI), and Santana (1978) designed a 44-item questionnaire for the detection of psychiatric disorders in adult populations, the Adult Psychiatric Morbidity Questionnaire (QMPA). Both instruments combined questions from well-known screening questionnaires with those derived from the socio-cultural Brazilian context and they showed good validity when tested by means of unstructured psychiatric interviews.

India

The GHQ, SRQ, PSE, and CIS have also been used in India (Harding *et al.* 1983; Bagadia *et al.* 1985; Sen 1987). For the PSE, translation into Hindi and back-translation was carried out, checking the 'semantic equivalence of the items'. Some concepts (e.g. anxiety) proved difficult to translate 'when significant cultural variations in the perception and intrapsychic phenomena existed' (Harding *et al.* 1983). However, in general, the PSE has been found to be acceptable for use in different regions of India with high inter-rater reliability (Verghese *et al.* 1985). The GHQ-60 and GHQ-12 have also been translated into several Indian languages without difficulty and with satisfactory validity indices. Translation and back-translation of the CIS in Bengali have also been carried out without major problems, with more attention being paid to conceptual than semantic equivalence (Sen *et al.* 1987). The use of these instruments in India and Brazilian cultural contexts has also been discussed in Sen and Mari (1986).

Kapur *et al.* (1974a, 1974b) developed the Indian Psychiatric Interview Schedule (IPIS) and the Indian Psychiatric Survey Schedule (IPSS) as a culture-specific (or emic) instrument for detecting mental illness in India because they felt that phenomena like those of spirit possession, preoccupation with symptoms of sexual inadequacy, and the frequency of vague somatic symptoms of psychological origin are not paid sufficient attention in the standardized interview schedules developed in the west (Carstairs and Kapur 1976). The IPSS 'is an instrument designed to investigate the presence or absence of 125 psychiatric symptoms, with special emphasis on those commonly encountered in a Indian setting . . . [it] enquires about symptoms only; no attempt has been made to combine the symptoms into psychiatric syndromes!' The IPSS and the IPIS have been used both in community and primary care settings in India (Carstairs and Kapur 1976, Gautam *et al.* 1980, Mehta *et al.* 1985, Shamasunder *et al.* 1986), but there is no evidence that the cases detected by the instruments differ either qualitatively or quantitatively (i.e., in terms of prevalence) from those detected by other standardized instruments e.g. PSE and CIS.

Taiwan

Over the past two decades, a few psychiatric interview schedules have been translated into Chinese and used in Taiwan. The Chinese version PSE was used in the IPSS (WHO 1973), and the Chinese version DIS was also applied in an epidemiological study in Taiwan (Hwu *et al*. 1986). Although the inter-rater reliability of the PSE in the IPSS was reported to be acceptable, there has been no report about its cross-cultural comparability. Furthermore, the PSE has been criticized as being primarily constructed for the study of psychotic patients (Dohrenwend *et al*. 1978; Williams *et al*. 1980). In a large-scale epidemiological study, the agreement between diagnoses made by the DIS and psychiatrists was found to be rather unsatisfactory (Folstein *et al*. 1985). The authors concluded that the DIS is better regarded as a screening instrument. If this view is taken, then the over-lengthy DIS is obviously not feasible for community study.

Since there was no valid, reliable, and cross-culturally comparable case-finding instrument for use in community studies of minor psychiatric morbidity in Taiwan, a pilot study was conducted to construct such an instrument (Cheng 1985). Based on a presumption that certain symptom expressions might be common to many cultures, an experimental screening questionnaire – the Chinese Health Questionnaire (CHQ) – was designed by the inclusion of the translated GHQ-30 items, as well as thirty specially designed, culturally relevant items. The resulting 'hybrid' was then tested in a two-stage survey of a representative community sample (n = 150) in Taiwan. The second-stage psychiatric interview was conducted by one of the authors (Cheng), using a Chinese version of the CIS.

The Chinese CIS was derived from a two-stage translation of the English version. Two inter-rater reliability studies were conducted. The first was between two British and one Chinese senior psychiatrists on an English-speaking community sample in London (Cheng *et al*. 1983), and the second between two Chinese psychiatrists on a community sample in Taiwan (Chong and Cheng 1985). Reliability coefficients derived from these two studies were found to be satisfactory. It is believed that the only way to tackle the problem of cross-cultural comparability of any case-finding instrument is to modify the different language version of an instrument based on extensive field experience obtained from that particular culture. This task was carried out in the pilot study and a main community study of minor psychiatric morbidity in Taiwan (Cheng 1987).

The Chinese CIS was found to be feasible for use in the community study of minor psychiatric morbidity in Taiwan. Its first part, concerning physical health, was found to be especially useful in making a good initial contact and establishing rapport. Thus, the following parts covering psychological phenomena became far less sensitive to the respondents. The semi-structured form of the CIS was found to allow for effective and more free elicitation of the respondent's unpleasant emotions. The wording and sequence of the questions were found to be acceptable to the respondents. Many of the CIS questions were found to be culturally relevant to the Chinese in Taiwan.

However, modification was still needed, particularly for items concerning emotional distress, and extra questions were added. Any psycholinguistic equivalent expressed by the Chinese respondents to any of the questions of the CIS was taken to substitute the original. A similar exercise was also performed in the Ugandan survey (Orley and Wing 1979). The operational definition of a few items was also modified in order to fit the characteristic of the Chinese culture. These modifications, which were based on field experience, were believed to have contributed to the resolution of psycholinguistic problems and the cross-cultural comparability of the CIS.

Since it has been suggested that the optimal method in the development of a screening tool would be to apply a discriminant function technique to find the best set of items with the highest classification power (Hand 1979), this method was used on the CHQ data. A classical linear discriminant analysis with stepwise variable selection method and a prior probability equal to group size was applied to 150 community respondents divided into case (n = 38) and non-case (n = 112) groups. Twelve of the items of the CHQ had an overall classification power of 98 per cent: these became the new CHQ-12, a valid screening tool for use in community studies in Taiwan (Cheng and Williams 1986). It is interesting to note that half the CHQ-12 items came from the GHQ-30 and the remaining six items were newly designed. The former were items about anxiety, depression, and sleep disturbance, while the latter could be grouped into two categories – 'somatic symptoms and somatic concern' and 'family and interpersonal difficulties' which were in accordance with the conceptual construct for the thirty new items.

The validity of the CHQ-12 has been further assessed in the main community study (n = 1023) and the classification power was found to be highly satisfactory (88.6 per cent) (Cheng 1988). Further analyses concerning the misclassification and the factorial structure of the CHQ-12 are being undertaken.

IS THERE A CASE FOR THE CULTURE-BOUND SYNDROME?

In Brazil, the evidence that psychiatric patients often resort to spiritist centres probably led some investigators, mainly in the third and fourth decades of this century, to speculate whether these religious practices are related to the onset of psychiatric disorders and/or whether they might be associated with specific psychiatric conditions reflecting this strong cultural influence. The first attempt to link religious experience and a psychiatric disorder was conducted by Roxo (1918) who described a syndrome named *Delirio Espirita Episodico* (Spiritist Episodic Delusion). This syndrome was said to appear in 'an atypical form of psychopathic personality', with repeated short-term hallucinatory states following the emotional shock experienced in spiritist sessions, and Roxo compared this psychotic phenomenon with that of the

497

French *boufee delirante*. This might be a transmitted state (contagious) being more frequent among black people due to the influence of African religion heritages and their suggestibility. The idea that ceremonies could trigger acute psychiatric states in people who are not mentally ill before attending the rituals was also raised by Ribeiro and Campos (1931), though they emphasized the role of predisposition.

Stainbrook (1952) studied 200 patients admitted to psychiatric hospitals in Salvador, Bahia, with an already existing diagnosis of schizophrenia and reported that female low-class patients were acting out being possessed by an African god or goddess. However, Brody (1973) studied 254 first admissions to three psychiatric hospitals in the city of Rio de Janeiro by means of two questionnaires, one socio-cultural and the other designed to describe psychopathology. The latter, entitled the Initial Interview Inventory, was derived from the Mental Status Schedule (Spitzer and Endicott 1966) by including 'primitive and folkloric references couched in general terms'. He noted that patients would frequently mention magical, spiritual or cult beliefs during the interview but there was no difference between those who attended African spiritist sessions (they comprised 22 per cent of his sample) and the others. Indeed, the Afro-spiritist attenders did not differ from other patients regarding psychotic phenomena: the majority of lower-class men and both lower- and middle-class women did not make reference to religious beliefs in their deluded thinking. According to Brody, 'in only rare instances were the spiritist or cult-related experiences woven into a delusional system. They were most typically offered by patients in order to explain their depression, weakness, confusion or anxiety' (Brody 1973).

During the last three decades, a number of cultural-specific phenomena have been described in Indian literature. Wig (1960) first used the term *'Dhat* syndrome' which typically occurs in a young adult male who presents with a primary complaint of loss of semen either by 'frequent nocturnal emissions' or by 'semen passing in urine'. Singh (1985) studied fifty consecutive patients with male potency disorders attending the psychiatric out-patient department of a teaching hospital and found a primary complaint of *'Dhat'* in thirty one of them. The majority of these patients, Singh states, were suffering from depressive states. However, almost a third of them could not be given a psychiatric diagnosis. Similar clinical manifestations were reported as Bangladeshi syndrome in Bangladesh (Clyne 1964), Prameha disease in Sri Lanka (Obeyesekere 1976), and *'shen-kuei'* syndrome in Taiwan (Wen and Wang 1981). Wen and Wang found that patients consulting a urologist with this as the chief complaint (n = 23) have psychiatric symptoms similar to neurotic out-patients and can be fitted into contemporary psychiatric diagnostic nosology as anxiety neurosis, depression, and hypochondriacal neurosis.

Teja *et al.* (1970) analysed fifteen cases of 'spirit possession' and reclassified all of them in three categories, viz. hysteria (7), schizophrenia (6), and mania (2).

Dutta *et al.* (1982) reported a Koro epidemic – formerly thought to occur exclusively among people from Malaysia, the southern part of China (Rin 1965, Yap 1965) – in the state of Assam in the north-eastern part of India. Nandi *et al.* (1983) reported a similar epidemic from the district of Murshidabad in the state of West Bengal adjoining Assam. Nandi chose to describe the syndrome as an acute anxiety reaction centred around a culturally elaborated fear of the loss of a valued organ, i.e. penis or breast. Nandi *et al.* (1987) described another culturally-specific epidemic, colloquially known in West Bengal as *Jhin-Jhini* (literally meaning 'the tingling disease') which also was thought by him to be a variant of an acute anxiety reaction or panic attack in which tingling and numbness beginning in the legs and spreading throughout the body, along with an overwhelming fear of death, were the main features.

Somatization has repeatedly been described by some researchers as a culture-specific manifestation of neurosis among certain ethnic groups (Dube 1970; Tseng 1975; Lin 1982). However, the rates of somatic symptoms reported by these researchers were no higher than those found in a number of western surveys among depressive patients (Woodruff *et al.* 1967; Mathew *et al.* 1981). The rates of somatic symptoms and somatic concern found in community surveys carried out in London (Jenkins 1985) and Taiwan, using similar case-finding instruments, were very similar. It is argued that this notion of somatization might better be explained by psycholinguistic expression and illness behaviour of the Chinese (Cheng 1988).

The answer to the question of whether there is a case for culture-bound syndromes in non-western countries can be obtained from the fact that epidemiological studies in some of these countries, whether hospital or community, have not found it necessary to postulate the existence of culture-specific entities to classify psychiatric disorder. For instance, the majority of clinicians in India are now of the opinion that the so-called culture-bound syndromes can almost always be re-classified under internationally accepted diagnostic categories and, among Brazilian psychiatrists, such a need seems to have never been mentioned, at least in the clinical realm. Although Lin (1982) emphasized the existence of certain culture-specific neurotic syndromes (such as somatization and *shin-jin-shui-jo*) in the Chinese, Cheng (1987) has argued that they are laymen's terms referring to a mixture of neurotic symptoms in minor psychiatric morbidity.

As Varma (1986) has pointed out, the attention of psychiatric research workers has now shifted from culture-bound syndromes to 'universal' illness, e.g. schizophrenia, depression, and neuroses. According to him, transcultural differences in psychiatric phenomena should now 'be considered with regard to incidence, types, manifestations, natural history, course, outcome and treatment of mental illness' instead of culture-specific diagnostic entities.

CONCLUSIONS AND RECOMMENDATIONS

Cross-cultural research can be divided into two main streams: the *universalist*, which would be more inclined in emphasize the similarities, and the *specificist*, which would tend to show possible differences among the groups compared. As an example of such debate, Singer (1975), when reviewing the literature on depression, concluded that it was not clear whether depressive illness in primitive and other non-western cultures presented outstanding features. This was previously predicted by Yap (1965) who stated that some specific disorders reported in the literature could be regarded as pathoplastic variants of disorders commonly recognized by western psychiatrists. German (1972) further argued that socio-cultural influences on psychopathology are likely to be less prominent as development progresses in non-western cultures. On the other hand, researchers like Kleinman (1987) have heavily criticized this view. Taking the case of depression he pointed out that, if a narrow concept of depression is applied, cross-cultural studies would find solely what is 'universal', missing out aspects which would be striking examples of the influence of culture on depression. The cultural influence on depression, as he has repeatedly mentioned, determines help-seeking, course, and treatment response of the 'disease'.

It is now widely accepted that an integration of culture-general (etic) and culture-specific (emic) approaches are essential for cross-cultural comparisons. For instance, Beiser and Fleming (1986) compared the pattern of psychiatric disorders among south-east Asian refugees with those of Vancouver residents stratified by sex, age and marital status. The authors applied a questionnaire combining questions derived from well-known instruments such as the DIS and the SRQ-24 with emic items extracted from the Vietnamese Depression Scale. The statistical analysis was performed with a principal component factor technique followed by varimax rotation on the mental health items from each of the two survey samples. The factor analysis produced four mental health dimensions (panic, depression, somatization, and well-being) and they found a high correlation across each pair of similar appearing factors. These results suggest that Asians and Caucasians experience depressive symptoms and express them in similar ways though doubt remains on the possible selective migration bias.

The development of the CHQ-12 is another example of attempting to integrate both etic and emic approaches. The production of a 'hybrid' screening instrument might well imply a difference between 'disease phenomenon' and 'illness expression'. Since there was no difference on symptom manifestations between the British and Chinese neurotics on the CIS interview, the 'emic' items in the CHQ-12 would better be regarded as culture-specific expressions of 'etic' symptoms. Here two questions would then be raised:

(a) Will the validity of a screening tool be lowered without the inclusion of emic items?

(b) Will the study of psychopathology be hampered when the case-finding instrument consists only of a self-administered questionnaire?

It is too early to give an affirmative answer to the first question and further investigations are still needed. Although the answer to the second question might be positive, it can reasonably be neglected when a two-stage case-finding strategy is applied.

Cross-cultural psychopharmacology is a promising field for research in cross-cultural psychiatry. The number of cross-ethnic studies is still limited but there is some evidence that Hispanics, for instance, would respond differently to anti-depressant medication (they may need lower doses and display more side-effects with the same dose of medication when compared with other ethnic groups). A research design comparing treatment responses between homogeneous ethnic groups might elucidate whether possible ethnic differences are variants of the same underlying disorder, i.e., a pathoplastic manifestation, or whether they are related to culturally-bound distinct entities.

According to Beiser et al. (1976), 'comparative studies using standardized instruments are going to continue despite their recognized faults, but it is unlikely to satisfy the anthropologist.' In addition, Murphy (1982) stated that 'comparative psychiatry must lean to the etic rather than to the emic position, since with the emic no comparisons are usually possible.' None the less, it might be more appropriate to establish a practical way to combine anthropological and epidemiological methods in the planning and design of new cross-cultural research strategies. For instance, further cross-cultural comparative studies with the integration of both emic and etic approaches by applying the state of the art of these apparent contrasting techniques might be pursued.

Acknowledgements: We are grateful to Mr Jonathan Gabe from the General Practice Research Unit and Dr Naomar Almeida Filho from the Federal University of Bahia for commenting on earlier versions of this paper. J.J. Mari was funded by the Brazilian Research Council (Conselho Nacional de Pesquisa CNPq, II-C) in the Department of Psychiatry of Escola Paulista de Medicina. His contribution to this chapter was written during leave funded by the British Council and the State of Sao Paulo Research Council (Fundacao de Amparo a Pesquisa do Estado de Sao Paulo – FAPESP). Biswajit Sen was supported by a grant from the Strømme Foundation, Norway, while the work by T.A. Cheng was funded by the National Science Council, Taiwan (ROC) (NSC 72–74–0301–H114–01).

REFERENCES

Almeida-Filho, N. (1981) 'Development and assessment of the QMPI: a Brazilian children's behaviour questionnaire for completion by parents, *Social Psychiatry* 16: 205–11.

Bagadia, V. N., Ayyar, K.S., Lakdawala, P.D., Susainathan, U., and Pradhan, P.V. (1985) 'Value of the General Health Questionnaire in detecting psychiatric morbidity in a general hospital out-patient population, *Indian Journal of Psychiatry* 27 (4): 293–6.

Beiser, M., Benfari, R.C., Collomb, H., and Ravel, J.C. (1976) 'Measuring psychoneurotic behaviour in cross-cultural surveys', *The Journal of Nervous and Mental Disease* 163: 10–23

Beiser, M. and Fleming, J.A.E. (1986) 'Measuring psychiatric disorder among Southeast Asian refugees', *Psychological Medicine* 16: 627–39.

Brody, E. (1973) *The Lost Ones: Social Forces and Mental Illness in Rio de Janeiro*, New York: International University Press.

Caetano, D. (1986) 'Experiencia com o Present State Examination (PSE) em pacientes ingleses e brasileiros', *Revista da Associacao Brasileira de Psiquiatria*, supplement, 8: 34–43.

Caetano, R. and Gentil-Filho, V. (1983) *P.S.E. – Exame do Estado Psiquico*, Sao Paulo.

Campillo-Serrano, C., Caraveo-Anduaga, J., Mora, M.E.M., and Lanz, P.M. (1981) 'Confiabilidad entre clinicos utilisando la "Entrevista Estandarizada" de Goldberg en una version mexicana', *Acta Psiquiatrica Psicologica de America Latina* 27: 44–53.

Carstairs, G.M. and Kapur, R.L. (1976) *The Great Universe of Kota*, London: Hogarth Press.

Cheng, T.A. (1985) 'A pilot study of mental disorders in Taiwan', *Psychological Medicine* 15: 195–203.

Cheng, T.A. (1987) *A Community Study of Minor Mental Disorders in Taiwan*, unpublished PhD thesis: University of London.

Cheng, T.A. (1988) 'A community study of minor psychiatric morbidity in Taiwan', in preparation.

Cheng, T.A. (1988) 'Symptomatology of minor psychiatric morbidity: a crosscultural comparison between British and Chinese community cases', in preparation.

Cheng, T.A. and Williams, P. (1986) 'The design and development of a screening questionnaire (CHQ) for use in community studies of mental disorders in Taiwan', *Psychological Medicine* 16: 415–22.

Cheng, T.A., Williams, P., and Clare, A.W. (1983) 'Reliability study of the Clinical Interview Schedule (CIS) between the British and Chinese psychiatrists', *Bulletin of the Chinese Society of Neurology and Psychiatry* 9: 54–5.

Chong, M.Y. and Cheng, T.A. (1985) 'Reliability study of the Clinical Interview Schedule (CIS): the use of community sample', *Bulletin of the Chinese Society of Neurology and Psychiatry* 11: 27–34.

Clyne, M.B. (1964) 'Indian patients', *Practitioner* 193: 195–9.

Copeland, J. (1981) 'What is a case? A case for what?', in J.K. Wing, P. Bebbington, and L.N. Robins (eds) *What is a Case? The Problem of Definition in Psychiatric Community Surveys*, London: Grant McIntyre.

Dohrenwend, B.P., Yager, T.J., Egri, F. and Mendelson, F.S. (1978) 'The Psychiatric Status Schedule as a measure of dimensions of psychopathology in the general population', *Archives of General Psychiatry* 35: 731–7.

Dube, K.C. (1970) 'A study of prevalence and biosocial variables in mental illness in rural and urban community in Uttar Pradesh, India', *Acta Psychiatrica Scandinavica* 46, 327–59.

Dutta, D., Phookan, H.R., and DAS, P.O. (1982) 'The Koro epidemic in lower Assam', *Indian Journal of Psychiatry* 24: 370–5.

Flaherty, J.A. (1987) 'Appropriate and inappropriate methodologies for Hispanic mental health', in M. Gaviria and J.D. Arana (eds) *Health and Behaviour: Research Agenda for Hispanics – Research Monograph 1* Chicago: The University of Illinois.

Folstein, M., Romanoski, A.J., Nestadt, G., Chahal, R., Merchant, A., Shapiro, S., Kramer, M., Anthony, J., Gruenberg, E.M., and McHugh, P.R. (1985) 'Brief report on the clinical reappraisal of the Diagnostic Interview Schedule carried out at the Johns Hopkins site of the Epidemiological Catchment Area Program of the NIMH', *Psychological Medicine* 15: 809–14.

Gautam, S., Kapur, R.L., and Shamasundar, C. (1980) 'Psychiatric morbidity and referral in general practice – a survey of general practitioners in Bangalore city', *Indian Journal of Psychiatry* 22: 295–7.

Gentil-Filho, V., Guerra-Andrade, L.H.S., and Lotufo-Neto, F. (1986) 'PSE: traducao, treinamento e limitacoes ao seu uso no Brasil', *Revista da Associacao Brasileira de Psiquiatria* supplement 8, 30–33.

German, G.A. (1972) 'Aspects of clinical psychiatry in Sub-Saharan Africa', *British Journal of Psychiatry* 121: 461–79.

Goldberg, D.P. (1972) *The Detection of Psychiatric Illness by Questionnaire* (Maudsley Monograph no. 21), London: Oxford University Press.

Goldberg, D.P., Cooper, B., Eastwood, M.R., Kedward, H.B., and Shepherd, M. (1970) 'A standardized psychiatric interview for use in community surveys', *British Journal of Preventive and Social Medicine* 24: 18–23.

Hand, D.J. (1979) *Improving questionnaires for detecting psychiatric morbidity*, unpublished paper, Institute of Psychiatry.

Harding, T.W., Arango, M.V., Baltazar, J., Climent, C.E., Ibrahim, H.H.A., Ignacio, L.L., Murthy, R.S., and Wig, N.N. (1980) 'Mental disorders in primary health care: a study of their frequency and diagnosis in four developing countries', *Psychological Medicine* 10: 231–41.

Harding, T.W., Climent, C.E., Diop, M., Giel, R., Ibrahim, H.H.A., Murthy, R.S., Suleiman, M.A., and Wig, N.N. (1983) 'The WHO collaborative study on strategies for extending mental health care: II: the development of new research methods', *American Journal of Psychiatry* 140: 1474–80.

Hsu, F.L.K. (1971) 'Psychosocial homeostasis and Jen: concepts for advancing psychological anthropology', *American Anthropologist* 73: 23–44.

Hwu, H.G., Yeh, E.K., and Chang, L.Y. (1986) 'Chinese diagnostic interview schedule: I: agreement with psychiatrist's diagnosis', *Acta Psychiatrica Scandinavica* 73: 225–33.

Jenkins, R. (1985) *Sex Differences in Minor Psychiatric Morbidity: Psychological Medicine* (Monograph Supplement 7), Cambridge: Cambridge University Press.

Kapur, R.L., Kapur, M., and Carstairs, G.M. (1974a) 'Indian Psychiatric Survey Schedule: IPSS', *Social Psychiatry* 9: 71–9.

Kapur, R.L., Kapur, M., and Carstairs, G.M. (1974b) 'Indian Psychiatric Survey Schedule: IPSS', *Social Psychiatry* 9: 61–70.

Kleinman, A.M. (1977) 'Depression, somatization and the "New cross-cultural psychiatry"', *Social Science & Medicine* 11: 3–10.

Kleinman, A. (1982) 'Neurasthenia and depression: a study of somatisation and culture in China', *Culture, Medicine, and Psychiatry* 6: 117–89.

503

Kleinman, A. (1987) 'Anthropology and psychiatry: the role of culture in cross-cultural research on illness', *British Journal of Psychiatry* 151: 447–54.

Leff, J. (1974) 'Transcultural influences on psychiatrists' rating of verbally expressed emotion', *British Journal of Psychiatry* 125: 336–40.

Lin, K.M. (1981) 'Traditional Chinese medical beliefs and their relevance for mental illness and psychiatry', in A. Kleinman and T.Y. Lin (eds) *Normal and Abnormal Behaviour in Chinese Culture*, Dordrecht, Boston, London: Reidel, pp. 95–111.

Lin, T.Y. (1982) 'Culture and psychiatry: a Chinese perspective', *Australian and New Zealand Journal of Psychiatry* 16: 235–45.

Mari, J.J. (1983) 'Psychiatric care in Brazil', in S. Brown (ed.) *Psychiatry in Developing Countries*, London: Gaskell Books.

Mari, J.J. (1987) 'Minor psychiatric morbidity in three primary medical care clinics in the city of Sao Paulo: issues on the mental health of the urban poor', *Social Psychiatry*, 22: 129–138.

Mari, J.J. and Williams, P. (1984) 'Minor psychiatric disorder in primary care in Brazil: a pilot study', *Psychological Medicine* 14: 223–7.

Mari, J.J. and Williams, P. (1985) 'A comparison of the validity of two psychiatric screening questionnaires (GHQ-12 and SRQ-20) in Brazil, using Relative Operating Characteristics (ROC) analysis', *Psychological Medicine* 15: 651–9.

Mari, J.J. and Williams, P. (1986) 'A validity of a psychiatric screening questionnaire (SRQ-20) in primary care in the city of Sao Paulo', *British Journal of Psychiatry* 148: 23–6.

Mari, J.J., Blay, S.L., and Iacoponi, E. (1986) 'Um estudo de confiabilidade da versao brasileira da Clinical Interview Schedule', *Boletim de la Oficina Sanitaria Panamericana* 100 (1): 77–83.

Matthew, R.J., Weinman, M.L., and Mirabi, M. (1981) 'Physical symptoms of depression', *British Journal of Psychiatry* 139: 293–6.

Mehta, P., Joseph, A., and Verghese, A. (1985) 'An epidemiologic study of psychiatric disorders in a rural community in Tamilnadu', *Indian Journal of Psychiatry* 27 (2): 153–8.

Ministry of the Interior (1987) *Taiwan-Fukien Demographic Fact Book*, Taipei.

Murphy, H.B.M. (1982) *Comparative Psychiatry: The International and Intercultural Distribution of Mental Illness*, Berlin: Springer-Verlag.

Nandi, D.N., Mukherjee, S.P., Boral, G.C., Banerjee, G., Ghosh, A., Sarkar, S., and Ajmany, S. (1980) 'Socio-economic status and mental morbidity in certain tribes and castes in India: a cross-cultural study', *British Journal of Psychiatry* 136: 73–85.

Nandi, D.N., Banerjee, G., Saha, H., and Boral, G.C. (1983) 'Epidemic Koro in West Bengal, India', *The International Journal of Social Psychiatry* 83: 265–8.

Nandi, D.N., Saha, H., Banerjee, G., Mukherjee, A., Sarkar, S., Bhattacharya, A., Boral, G.C. (1987) 'An epidemic of "Jhin-Jhini" – a strange contagious disorder – in a village in West Bengal', paper read at the third annual conference of the *Indian Association for Social Psychiatry* in Hyderabad in March 1987.

Obeyesekere, G. (1976) 'The impact of Ayurvedic ideas on the culture and the individual in Sri Lanka', in C. Leslie (ed.) *Asian Medical Systems: A Comparative Study*, Berkeley: University of California Press, 201–26.

Orley, J. and Wing, J.K. (1979) 'Psychiatric disorder in two African villages', *Archives of General Psychiatry* 36: 513–20.

Ribeiro, L. and Campos, M. (1931) *O Espiritismo no Brasil*, Sao Paulo: Companhia Editora Nacional.

Richeport, M. (1984) 'Strategies and outcomes of introducing a mental health plan in Brazil', *Social Science and Medicine* 19: 261–71.

Rin, H. (1965) 'A study of the aetiology of koro in respect of the Chinese concept of illness', *International Journal of Social Psychiatry* 11: 7–13.

Roxo, H.B.B. (1918) 'Delirio Espirita Episodico', in L. Guanabara (ed.) (1946) *Manual de Psiquiatria*, Rio de Janeiro: Livraria Guanabara.

Santana, V. (1978) *Estudo Epidemiologico das Doencas Mentais em um Bairro de Salvador*, M.Sc. thesis, Federal University of Bahia, Salvador.

Sen, B. (1987) 'Psychiatric phenomena in primary health care: their extent and nature', *Indian Journal of Psychiatry* 29 (1): 33–40.

Sen, B. and Mari, J.J. (1986) 'Psychiatric research instruments in the transcultural setting: experiences in India and Brazil', *Social Science & Medicine* 23 (3): 277–81.

Sen, B., Wilkinson, G., and Mari, J.J. (1987) 'Psychiatric morbidity in primary health care: a two-stage screening procedure for developing countries – choice of instruments and cost-effectiveness', *British Journal of Psychiatry* 151: 33–8.

Shamasundar, C., Murthy, K., Prakash, O., Prabhakar, N., and Subba, K.D.K. (1986) 'Psychiatric morbidity in a general practice in an Indian city', *British Medical Journal* 292: 1713–15.

Shepherd, M., Brooke, E.M., and Cooper, J.E. (1968) 'An experimental approach to psychiatric diagnosis', *Acta Psychiatrica Scandinavica*, supplementum 201: 13–26.

Singer, K. (1975) 'Depressive disorders from a transcultural perspective', *Social Science & Medicine* 9: 289–301.

Singh, G. (1985) 'Dhat syndrome revisited', *Indian Journal of Psychiatry* 27 (2): 119–22.

Spitzer, R.L. and Endicott, J. (1966) *Mental Status Schedule*, New York: Department of Psychiatry, Columbia University.

Stainbrook, E. (1952) 'Some characteristics of the schizophrenic behavior in Bahian society', *American Journal of Psychiatry* 109: 330–5.

Teja, J.S., Khanna, S., and Subramanyam, J.B. (1970) '"Possession states" in Indian patients', *Indian Journal of Psychiatry* 12: 71–87.

Tseng, W.S. (1975) 'The nature of somatic complaints among psychiatric patients: the Chinese case', *Comprehensive Psychiatry* 16: 237–45.

Varma, V.K. (1986) 'Cultural psychodynamics and mental illness', *Indian Journal of Psychiatry* 28 (10): 13–34.

Verghese, A., Dube, K.C., Menon, J.J., Menon, M.S., Rajkumar, S., Richard, S., Richard, J., Sethi, B.B., Trivedi, J.K., and Wig, N.N. (1985) 'Factors associated with the course and outcome of schizophrenia: a multi-centred follow up study; Part I: objectives and methodology', *Indian Journal of Psychiatry* 27 (3): 201–6.

Wen, J.K. and Wang, C.L. (1981) 'Shen-K'uei Syndrome: a culture-specific sexual neurosis in Taiwan', in A. Kleinman and T.Y. Lin (eds) *Normal and Abnormal Behaviour in Chinese Culture*, Dordrecht, Boston, London: Reidel, pp. 357–69.

Wig, N.N. (1960) 'Problems of mental health in India', *Journal of Clinical Society*, Medical College, Lucknow, 17: 48–56.

Williams, P., Tarnopolsky, A., and Hand, D.J. (1980) 'Case-definition and case-identification in psychiatric epidemiology: review and reassessment', *Psychological Medicine* 10: 101–14.

Wing, J.K., Cooper, J.E., and Sartorius, N. (1974) *The Measurement and Classification of Psychiatric Symptoms*, Cambridge: Cambridge University Press.

Wing, J.K., Bebbington, R., and Robin, L.N. (1981) (eds) *What is a Case? The Problem of Definition in Psychiatric Community Surveys*, London: Grant McIntyre.

Woodruff, R.A., Murphy, G.E., and Herjanic, M. (1967) 'The natural history of affective disorders; 1: symptoms of 72 patients at the time of index hospital admission', *Journal of Psychiatric Research* 5: 255–63.

World Health Organization (1973) *Report of the International Pilot Study of Schizophrenia, volume 1*, Geneva: WHO.

Yap, P.M. (1965) 'Koro – a culture-bound depersonalisation syndrome', *British Journal of Psychiatry* 111: 43–50.

Yap, P.M. (1965) 'Phenomenology of affective disorder in Chinese and other cultures', in A. Rueck and R. Porter (eds) *Transcultural Psychiatry*, Boston: Little, Brown, & Co.

Section Five

The Scientific Approach to Epidemiological and Social Psychiatry: The Contribution of Michael Shepherd

32

The Contribution of Michael Shepherd

Kenneth Rawnsley

In 1943 John Ryle vacated the Regius Chair of Physic at Cambridge to become the first Professor of Social Medicine in the University of Oxford. Many of his colleagues reacted much as one imagines did those of John Elliotson who, in the early nineteenth century, resigned his position as Professor of Medicine in the University of London to take up Mesmerism. Ryle's standing, however, as a teacher and clinician of the highest calibre, compelled attention to this 'new' subject and focused interest especially on the epidemiology of non-infective disorders. Among those sensitized was Michael Shepherd, then a young medical student in Oxford.

Writing some 35 years later about the training of psychiatrists for research, Shepherd used Ryle's perspective to point the way ahead. After commenting on the agonizing reappraisal within medicine of the pre-eminence of biotechnology and the increasing awareness even among the arch representatives of that approach of the importance of social factors, he says:

> At the core of Ryle's position was his defence of the clinician as an observer, a naturalist with an essentially holistic view of man in disease, for whom scrupulous clinical inquiry is as much a scientific procedure as any other measure of research. Here may be found a key to the dilemma of clinical research in psychiatry. A determined attack on the lacunae in knowledge relating to the clinical epidemiology of mental disorders would help bridge the gap between clinical and basic research casting clinicians in a more substantial role than that of medically qualified entrepreneurs or laboratory ancillaries.　　　　　　　　　　　　　　(Shepherd 1981a)

In the early 1950s, during his apprenticeship to psychiatry at the Maudsley Hospital, Shepherd's interest in the social aspects of mental illness was stimulated and nurtured by the commanding presence of Professor Aubrey Lewis, his illustrious mentor. Lewis combined a rare clinical expertise with a profound interest in many of the sciences cognate to psychiatry, not least those in the social and epidemiological sphere (Shepherd 1980).

Psychiatry in Britain during the first half of the 1950s was beginning to tingle. The new psychotropic drugs had not yet entered the arena but a few pioneers were setting in train the 'open door' policies in mental hospitals which would revolutionize practice. Others were exploring new ways of helping patients with disordered characters and were raising the curtain on the 'therapeutic community' movement. Psychotherapy was breaking new ground, for example in the use of 'group' approaches. Lysergic acid diethylamide was to be the key to the understanding of the chemistry of endogenous psychoses.

Lewis filled the Maudsley with a rich and varied assortment of senior psychiatrists representing the many facets of this diverse and rapidly growing branch of medicine. The young post-graduate doctors were often hard put to it to find their bearings in this bewildering broth and many responded to the siren call from some dogmatic safe haven, be it psychoanalytic or organic in timbre.

In the midst of this clamour, Shepherd was quietly getting on with some epidemiological spade-work in a study of the pattern of major psychoses hospitalized in the county of Buckinghamshire during two periods 1931–3 and 1945–7. This material was to form the basis of his DM thesis and was published as a Maudsley Monograph (Shepherd 1957). Basically, it was an exercise in counting declared cases from a defined catchment area. The use of the results to illuminate the impact of changing styles of patient management and of specific treatments will be mentioned later in this paper.

At about the same time he was collecting material of a very different stamp, culled from his own clinical practice and from that of colleagues, which was to form the basis of an important contribution to the literature on morbid jealousy (Shepherd 1961). The subtitle of the paper is significant, 'Some clinical and social aspects of a psychiatric symptom'. His analysis of the complex interweaving of these two inseparable elements in the disorder provide a pointer to the development of his theoretical thinking in clinical epidemiology.

Not that he distanced himself or retired from the intellectual market-place of the Maudsley. His approach was that of the acutely interested sceptic, possessed of a zealous, burning curiosity, endlessly questing, requiring evidence of validity beyond mere assertion, scraping down to the bedrock of truth through the detritus of speculation.

Studies of the frequency of mental disorders based on counting cases entering psychiatric hospitals had been pursued for over a century but the limitations of these materials weighed increasingly with epidemiologists. The undeclared, submerged part of the clinical iceberg became an object of study in a number of large-scale population surveys in many parts of the world, though the theoretical and practical problems of defining boundaries between the ice and the surrounding water were manifold.

Moving beyond his studies of mental hospital populations, Shepherd very

510

shrewdly chose a middle ground which, to a degree, avoided the formidable problems of method attending case definition in straight general population sample surveys. In Britain, most people are registered with a general practitioner in the National Health Service and the majority of the population actually consult their doctors at least once in the course of a year. Here, then, was a laboratory in which psychiatric morbidity could be studied from a variety of angles and with a very practical flavour to the findings. The small beginnings of this work were given a fine boost in 1958 through a grant from the Nuffield Foundation, allowing the establishment of a research unit which still exists, though funded from other sources. The work of the first few years was collated and published in book form in 1966. In his foreword to the volume Aubrey Lewis neatly summarizes the intention and the product:

> The study has been conducted with a close regard to the many problems of method involved. It was exploratory in design, as the nature of the problem required; a survey of this kind helps to provide the baseline from which future controlled studies may be carried out and hypotheses tested. It is not surprising that the present findings pose as many questions as they answer. The authors do not pretend otherwise; they are content to have been employed, in Locke's words, 'in clearing the ground a little, and removing some of the rubbish that lies in the way of knowledge'.
>
> (Shepherd et al. 1966)

This characteristically low-key summing up of achievement by Lewis should not deflect attention from the substantive results of this large-scale work. The pooled inception rate for a period of one year was fifty-two per 1,000 which placed psychiatric illness among the commoner causes of consultation in general practice. The distribution by diagnosis was sharply different from that found in hospital patients, neuroses and psychophysiological disorders predominating.

One finding of great interest was that, during the survey year, of the identified psychiatric cases only one in twenty had been under specialist care. It was noted that the treatment of minor psychiatric disorders in general practice is often haphazard and inadequate. Despite this, practitioners regarded the management of these conditions as an integral part of their work but wished for better training to deal more effectively with them. An important conclusion follows:

> Administrative and medical logic alike therefore suggest that the . . . cardinal requirement for improvement of the mental health services . . . in this country is not a large expansion and proliferation of . . . psychiatric agencies, but rather a strengthening of the family . . . doctor in his therapeutic role. (Shepherd et al. 1966)

From the small beginnings of this epidemiological work in the field of primary care an enduring framework of operations had been rapidly created. A base was firmly established at the Institute of Psychiatry of the University of London situated at the Maudsley Hospital. Very fundamental questions were being asked about psychiatric morbidity and ways in which answers might be obtained were being carefully explored. Resources were building up, and among these the most important of all was the recruitment of a cadre of investigators which, over the years, was to include individuals of the highest calibre, many of whom went on to occupy senior academic posts in Britain and abroad.

A *tour d'horizon* was provided in 1979 by two of these collaborators in a book entitled *Psychosocial Disorders in General Practice* (Williams and Clare 1979). Many of the papers brought together in that volume had been written by members of the Shepherd Unit and provide some notion of the wide field of endeavour which had been cultivated during the previous two decades. The evolution of standard reproducible measures of psychiatric morbidity and of social adjustment are a basic feature of the whole undertaking and certain of the instruments devised are now used throughout the world.

In the primary care laboratory, grounded upon the trust and good will developing between participating GPs and researchers, together with sound and acceptable methodology, new and important questions were now addressed. What is the link between onset of neurotic illness and life events? How frequently are psychotropic drugs prescribed in general practice and what are the consequences of this? What is the optimum division of labour between the GP and the psychiatrist? What is the most effective and appropriate pattern of working relationship between doctors and para-medical workers in the extramural setting?

Population surveys in many parts of the world, using representative samples, had revealed a large pool of psychiatric morbidity of which only a fraction was ever brought to medical attention. Workers from the General Practice Unit were able to throw some light on the factors which influenced decisions to consult a general practitioner, through secondary analysis of data originally assembled by Unit colleagues to study the possible effects of aircraft noise on mental health. This West London material was drawn from the largest general population psychiatric survey mounted to date in Britain. It revealed that about one-fifth of GP consultations could be attributed to minor psychiatric morbidity and that the presence of such morbidity doubles the probability of consulting. Health-related factors appeared to exert more influence on decisions to consult than did socio-demographic variables (Williams *et al.* 1986).

Introducing a recent conference on 'Mental Illness in Primary Care Settings' held at the Institute of Psychiatry, the Chief Medical Officer for England and Wales made the comment,

Within the structure of the National Health Service, the medical responsibility for the care of these [psychiatric] patients falls principally on the
general practitioner. Much of what we know about the nature and extent
of their disorders derives from the work of Michael Shepherd and his
colleagues in the distinguished General Practice Research Unit.

(Acheson 1986)

In 1964 a World Health Organization Scientific Group on Mental Health
Research called for (a) development of a Classification of Mental Disorders
internationally acceptable and capable of uniform application and (b) development of standardized procedures for case-finding and for the assessment of
severity of illness.

This was followed in 1965 by a WHO seminar held in London on 'Standardization of Psychiatric Diagnosis, Classification and Mental Health
Statistics' in which Shepherd played a leading role. An experimental
approach to the problem of observer variation in diagnosis was applied by
the use of written case vignettes and also by the exhibition of video recordings of samples of psychiatric interviews. The fact that the expert doctors
present differed in their diagnoses is perhaps not surprising to anyone
familiar with the cut and thrust of psychiatric case conferences but a dissection of the basis of these differences, succinctly presented in the conclusions
to the Report, pointed to future hopes of refinement.

The factors which lead to disagreements and difficulties of . . .
communication can be regarded as deriving from three principal . . .
sources. These comprise, first, variations at the level of observation and
perception by the clinician; secondly, variations . . . in the inferences
drawn from such observation; and, thirdly, variation in the nosological
schemata employed by the individual clinicians. These sources of variation
are open to investigation. (Shepherd et al. 1968)

The WHO chariot of fire thus launched was set to roll for a decade ahead
pursuing four linked programmes of enquiry. It was hoped that these
programmes would, first, illuminate the ninth revision of ICD due in 1975;
second, test the applicability of definition and criteria agreed for a particular
disease in different countries of contrasting cultures and differing schools of
psychiatry: the International Pilot Study of Schizophrenia (WHO 1979) was
the vehicle for this endeavour. The other two programmes were to result in
comprehensive epidemiological study of geographically defined populations
and also in the education of research scientists to embark on work of this
nature through training courses and workshops, to which Shepherd made a
particular contribution (Shepherd 1982a).

The products of all this labour were indeed fed into the revision process
which culminated in Section 5 of ICD-9. They also contributed to the

513

updating of the remarkable glossary of diagnostic terms published in 1974 which owed much in its original form to Sir Aubrey Lewis. This set of definition/descriptions of the categories in Section 5 was a major landmark in the attempt to bring some measure of uniformity to the usage of diagnostic categories, vital for comparative epidemiology.

Paradoxically, the evolution of a successful and reliable classification applicable to the variety of psychiatric problems common in Shepherd's field of primary care has proved elusive to date (Shepherd 1987). The ICD itself has serious limitations in this arena and this led in 1979 to the development of the special International Classification of Health Problems in Primary Care (ICHPPC) (Froom 1976; WONCA 1979). An experimental examination of the reliability of this system by Shepherd and colleagues (Jenkins et al. 1985) revealed a high level of observer variation – a disappointing lacuna which awaits further research.

One of the uses of epidemiology is in deepening knowledge of the clinical progress and outcome of particular categories of illness and the work of Shepherd's General Practice Unit in the field of neurosis has already been mentioned. Working with other colleagues, he turned his attention in 1980 to a follow-up study of a group of schizophrenics studied earlier by him for another purpose (Watt et al. 1983). They comprised a cohort of patients from the county of Buckinghamshire, being all the individuals from that area fulfilling strict clinical criteria admitted to the local psychiatric hospital over a twenty-month period in 1973–4. A very careful follow-up investigation after five years revealed a good outcome in about half the patients. Females fared significantly better than did males.

The hallmarks of this study were the rigorous clinical definition of the cohort; its representative character within the defined catchment population; the thoroughness of the follow-up and the conclusion that in the evaluation of treatment, knowledge of the expected outcome from a representative sample of cases must form an important backdrop.

These patients had originally been investigated in a comparative controlled drug trial of pimozide versus fluphenazine decanoate (Falloon et al. 1978a, 1978b). Shepherd always emphasized the epidemiological nature of drug trials.

> the comparative trial is essentially an epidemiological procedure and reflects the outlook of the statistician, who inevitably tends to think less as a physician and more as a metaphysician, specializing therefore in the description of the types of proof which are appropriate to various types of statement.　　　　　　　　　　　　　　　　　　　(Shepherd 1959)

He regarded such trials as of fundamental importance in the evaluation and refinement of treatment, provided they were intelligently constructed and properly applied (Shepherd 1970).

In the field of childhood psychiatric disorders Shepherd used an epidemiological approach to address certain questions: how is deviant behaviour in childhood to be conceptualized, identified, and measured? What is the relationship between deviant behaviour and morbidity? What are the influences which determine whether particular 'cases' come within the ambit of services? What are the benefits, if any, of referral to the specialist? (Shepherd *et al.* 1971).

Epidemiological studies of many common ailments in medicine have shown that for every case attending medical services there are many more untreated in the community. The findings of the child study in Buckinghamshire, based upon a random sample of over 6,000 children aged 5–15, were no exception to this rule. Attempts made to discover factors leading to specialist referral pointed the finger at characteristics of parents rather than at the children themselves:

> Thus, the mothers of children attending child-guidance tended to . . . be more anxious, depressed and . . . easily upset by stress. Still more significantly, they were less able to manage their children's . . . disturbances of behaviour and accept them as temporary . . . difficulties; at the same time they were more liable to discuss their problems with and seek advice from other people. (Shepherd 1971)

This conclusion was based on a critical comparison of fifty children attending child-guidance clinics in the county and fifty children with similar levels of disturbance not so attending.

Naturally enough, the question arose as to how these two groups of children fared over time; in effect an evaluation of the therapeutic influence of clinic contact. Two years after the initial appraisal there was found to be no significant difference in the progress of the two groups. In both about two-thirds of the children manifested evidence of improvement.

The importance of this essay into the realm of childhood disorders lies, first, in the clear exposition of the criteria employed for measuring 'deviance' and in the explicit correlation of deviance with functional disturbance; second, in the scrutiny of factors which appear to bring a particular child to the specialist service; third, in the assessment of the results of specialist intervention in terms of outcome after two years. The study follows good epidemiologic precepts in the unambiguous definition of numerators and denominators and in the utilization of findings to illuminate questions concerning the effectiveness and efficiency of services.

A further contribution to child psychiatry was the publication, following a pioneering exercise, of the first tri-axial system of classification of mental disorders of childhood by the World Health Organization (Rutter *et al.* 1975).

In the scientific study of drugs, clinical and experimental approaches spring to mind as the traditional methods. In compiling what was, in fact, the first textbook of clinical psychopharmacology Shepherd and his colleagues also inserted the epidemiological approach as a third methodology (Shepherd *et al.* 1968). The social angle on psychotropic drug use was discussed in more detail in a later monograph (Shepherd 1981b).

Reference is made in that book to a retrospective study which Shepherd mounted drawing on material from the survey of mental hospital patients in Buckinghamshire already mentioned (Shepherd 1957) when the movement of patients over a four-year period from 1954–57 was scrutinized. 1954 was the year prior to the introduction of the new psychotropic drugs and by 1957 they were in common use:

> The results of a study of this type, depend on detailed . . . statistical analysis and they showed that very little change . . . had occurred during this period. The major movement of the hospital population, defined in terms of a higher discharge . . . rate and shorter hospital stay, had in fact taken place ten . . . years earlier and was attributable partly to the somatic treatments of the day but much more to the setting up of an . . . unusually progressive mental health service in the area.   (Shepherd 1981c)

Similar findings were reported from Norway by Ødegaard who commented:

> in hospitals with a favourable situation the psychotropic . . . drugs brought little or no improvement or even a decrease in . . . the rate of discharges. In hospitals with a low pre-drug discharge rate, on the other hand, the improvement was considerable.   (Ødegaard 1964)

In his Maudsley Bequest lecture (1978) Shepherd set out very clearly the wide-ranging importance of epidemiology, not only as a discipline in its own right but as the fundamental basis of clinical psychiatry. The transmission of mental disorder in populations and indeed in families by the process of psychic contagion affecting vulnerable individuals exemplifies the lay concept of 'epidemic'. However, the epidemiologist may contribute to a deeper understanding of the phenomena of illness:

> We now know from epidemiological inquiries that psychiatric illness in the community is composed largely of minor affective disorders. From a clinical standpoint it is apparent that this large pool of affective illnesses not only extends the spectrum of the concept of such disorders but also bears pointedly on the aetiology of these illnesses and on the sterility of much work on their classification based on hospital cases.
> (Shepherd 1978)

Shepherd had many dealings with the British Medical Research Council and in the course of these was able occasionally to bring psychiatry into play as a facilitator of research in other medical fields. An example arises in the large-scale MRC trial in the screening and prophylaxis of mild to moderate hypertension. Concern had been expressed about the possible adverse effects of discovering hypertension in subjects and in 'labelling' them. Shepherd was consulted and promoted a trial carried out by Dr A.H. Mann which showed not only that the labelling was innocuous but that it led to an improvement in the emotional state of certain subjects (Mann 1984).

Michael Shepherd is known as an outstanding clinician, a man to whom colleagues will confidently refer difficult and problematic cases for second opinion. As a practising doctor, he brings to bear not only his profound knowledge of psychiatric theory but also those vaguer skills and propensities which inform the clinical art. His attitude, however, to the future of psychiatry is crystal clear: that, for survival, it must rest ever more firmly upon scientific foundations. This view is manifest insistently in his personal teaching, in his professional writings, and in his discussions both public and private.

It has found trenchant expression many a time in a merciless commentary on all unsubstantiated vapourings, whether these spring from psychoanalysis or from the purveyors of psychotropic drugs. He has, on occasion, an arrestingly mordant style of delivery, whether spoken or written, honed to perfection over the years, which is a scourge to the woolly-minded or the pretentious. Like Sherlock Holmes, a character whose name he recently linked in terms of styles of thought with that of Sigmund Freud (Shepherd 1985), he has a disconcerting ability to materialize from the shadows and to deliver a decisive body-blow, but one springing from a sounder basis than the strange inductions of the legendary detective.

It led him to establish in 1969 what has become a prestigious international journal *Psychological Medicine*, subtitled 'A journal for research in psychiatry and the allied sciences' and which he continues to edit. Describing the setting up of this publication in the course of his Presidential address to the Section of Psychiatry of the Royal Society of Medicine, he remarks:

Our initial task was to tackle three questions – namely the . . . colour of the dust-jacket, an agreement on objectives, and a . . . title. The first was easily resolved: since nothing in psychiatry is black or white, grey was evidently the colour . . . of choice. With regard to objectives, we had thought . . . originally of aiming at the education of professors in psychiatry but their halo of omniscience appeared to be . . . impenetrable, so we settled for the goal of indispensability . . . by determining to concentrate on original, high-quality work across the wide spectrum of both psychiatry and its allied disciplines. In so doing we were virtually compelled to resurrect Winslow's title [Forbes Winslow's *Journal of Psychological Medicine and Mental Pathology*, the first British journal to be concerned exclusively with mental illness, which had appeared in 1848]. (Shepherd 1986b)

517

The arrangement of the five volumes of his monumental *Handbook of Psychiatry* is significant (Shepherd 1982b). The middle three volumes, devoted to the clinical manifestations of psychiatric illness, are sandwiched between volume 1 on 'General Psychopathology' and volume 5 on 'The Scientific Foundations of Psychiatry'. Furthermore, Shepherd reveals his catholic approach to the proper limits of science in relation to psychiatry; in the introduction of volume 1, he implicitly supports Karl Jaspers:

> Inveighing against the futility of 'endlessness', the attempt to establish absolute knowledge through the application of any one scientific discipline, he [Jaspers] urges the psychiatrist to 'acquire some of the view-points and methods that belong to the world of the Humanities and Social Studies . . . since the methods of almost all the Arts and Sciences converge on psychopathology' (Jaspers 1963). With this ambiguous phrase Jaspers indicates the complex nature of a discipline which, in his view, extended the notion of scientific enquiry as it is usually understood.
>
> (Shepherd 1982b)

This chapter has concerned itself principally with Shepherd's epidemiological and social psychiatric interests and it is for his contributions in this domain that he is best known. It has led to high professional recognition in the presentation of the Donald Reid Medal for Epidemiology in 1982 and the Lapousse Award of the American Public Health Association in 1983. He has laboured steadily in a number of other psychiatric vineyards producing intellectual wine of superb vintage but amazing in its diversity.

What is perhaps less well recognized, however, is that he has also made indirect contributions to other scientific disciplines. One example is statistics. Three of the statisticians appointed to Shepherd's General Practice Research Unit when they were young became, in time, full professors of statistics and leaders in their own fields. While indicating Shepherd's skill in selecting able people, it also underlines his recognition of the growing importance of quantitative methods in psychiatric research and of the need for close collaborative work. Further instances may be cited in his co-directorship of a psychopharmacological research group with Professor Heinz Schild of University College, London; also in his involvement with, and influence upon, professional historians manifest in the volumes, *Anatomy of Madness, Essays in the History of Psychiatry* (Bynum *et al.* 1985).

Shepherd described the career, contributions, and legacies of Sir Aubrey, his great mentor, in the Adolf Meyer Lecture and in the ninth Aubrey Lewis Lecture, later combining these papers within a single cover (Shepherd 1986a). He quotes Lewis on Edward Mapother, the first Professor of Psychiatry at the Maudsley, and observes that Lewis might have been writing a self-description. To carry the argument on to the third generation and adding a few more sentences from Lewis's encomium (Lewis 1969) the pen portrait would supply a fine likeness for the subject of this Festschrift:

> He was intensely distrustful of anything that seemed to him humbug, and he disliked sentimentality almost as much. Anything that savoured of professional commercialism was likewise anathema. His own integrity was beyond question in small matters as well as large ones. He insisted on strict, at times austere, standards of clinical probity. His intellect was sharp and shrewd, with a touch of legal inquisition, and at its best when examining a complex issue or – in a very different way – making the case for some Maudsley need. His wit served as an astringent partner to his zest for controversy . . .. Fundamentally the temper of his mind was partisan, in the good sense; he was not serene and detached, but eager, pertinacious, argumentative, scathing in criticism and powerful in reasoned support. With all his enjoyment of swordplay and iconoclasm, he remained hopeful and positive, by no means a cynic.

Michael Shepherd will, hopefully, remain with us for years to come, continuing to persuade, cajole, nay demand, that while practising our art we base it increasingly and relentlessly on scientific research findings, thereby ensuring the future viability of our subject and the better care of our patients.

REFERENCES

Acheson, E.D. (1986) 'Introduction', in M. Shepherd, G. Wilkinson and P. Williams (eds) *Mental Illness in Primary Care Settings*, London: Tavistock.

Bynum, W.F., Porter, R., and Shepherd, M. (eds) (1985) *The Anatomy of Madness, Essays in the History of Psychiatry*, two volumes, London: Tavistock.

Falloon, I., Watt, D.C., and Shepherd, M. (1978a) 'A comparative controlled trial of pimozide and fluphenazine decanoate in the continuation therapy of schizophrenia', *Psychological Medicine* 8: 59–70.

Falloon, I., Watt, D.C., and Shepherd, M. (1978b) 'The social outcome of patients in a trial of long-term continuation therapy in schizophrenia: pimozide vs fluphenazine', *Psychological Medicine* 8: 265–74.

Froom, J. (1976) 'The international classification of health problems in primary care', *Medical Care* 14: 450–4.

Jaspers, K. (1963) *General Psychopathology*, seventh edition, translated by J. Hoenig and M. Hamilton, Manchester: Manchester University Press.

Jenkins, R., Smeeton, N., Marinker, M., and Shepherd, M. (1985) 'A study of the classification of mental ill-health in general practice', *Psychological Medicine* 15: 403–9.

Lewis, A. (1969) 'Edward Mapother and the making of the Maudsley Hospital', *British Journal of Psychiatry*, 115: 1349–66.

Mann, A.H. (1984) *Hypertension: Psychological Aspects and Diagnostic Impact in a Clinical Trial* (Psychological Medicine Monograph Supplement No. 5) Cambridge: Cambridge University Press.

Ødegaard, Ø. (1964) 'Pattern of discharge from Norwegian psychiatric hospitals before and after the introduction of the psychotropic drugs', *American Journal of Psychiatry* 120: 772–8.

Rutter, M., Shaffer, D., and Shepherd, M. (1975) *A Multi-axial Classification of Child Psychiatric Disorders*, Geneva: WHO.

Shepherd, M. (1957) *A Study of the Major Psychoses in an English County* (Maudsley Monograph Series No. 3) London: Chapman and Hall.

Shepherd, M. (1959) 'Evaluation of drugs in the treatment of depression', *Canadian Psychiatric Association Journal* Supplement 4: S120.

Shepherd, M. (1961) 'Morbid jealousy: some clinical and social aspects of a psychiatric symptom', *Journal of Mental Science* 107: 687–753.

Shepherd, M. (1970) 'A critical review of clinical drug trials', *Excerpta Medica International Congress Series No. 239 Depression in the 1970s. Proceedings of a Symposium.* New York.

Shepherd, M. (1971) 'Childhood behaviour, mental health and medical services', in G. McLachlan (ed.) *Problems and Progress in Medical Care*, Oxford: Nuffield Provincial Hospitals Trust, Oxford University Press.

Shepherd, M. (1978) 'Epidemiology and clinical psychiatry', *British Journal of Psychiatry* 133: 289–98.

Shepherd, M. (1980) 'From social medicine to social psychiatry: the achievement of Sir Aubrey Lewis', *Psychological Medicine* 10: 211–18.

Shepherd, M. (1981a) 'Psychiatric research in medical perspective', *British Medical Journal* 282: 961–3.

Shepherd, M. (1981b) *Psychotropic Drugs in Psychiatry*, New York: Jason Aronson.

Shepherd, M. (1981c) 'The epidemiological impact of psychotropic medication', in G. Tognoni, C. Bellantuono, and M. Lader (eds) *Epidemiological Impact of Psychotropic Drugs*, Elsevier/North-Holland Biomedical Press.

Shepherd, M. (1982a) 'The application of the epidemiological method in psychiatry', in T.A. Baasher, J.E. Cooper, H. Davidian, A. Jablensky, N. Sartorius, and E. Strömgren (eds) *Acta Psychiatrica Scandinavica*, Supplement 296, volume 65, Copenhagen: Munksgaard.

Shepherd, M. (1982b) *Handbook of Psychiatry Volume 1: General Psychopathology*, Cambridge: Cambridge University Press

Shepherd, M. (1983) *The Psychosocial Matrix of Psychiatry: Collected Papers*, London: Tavistock.

Shepherd, M. (1985) *Sherlock Holmes and the Case of Dr Freud*, London: Tavistock.

Shepherd, M. (1986a) *A Representative Psychiatrist: the Career, Contributions and Legacies of Sir Aubrey Lewis* (Psychological Medicine Monograph Supplement 10) Cambridge: Cambridge University Press.

Shepherd, M. (1986b) 'Psychological medicine redivivus: concept and communication', *Journal of the Royal Society of Medicine* 79: 639–45.

Shepherd, M. (1987) 'Classification of mental disorders', *Practitioner* 231: 985.

Shepherd, M., Brooke, E.M., Cooper, J.E., and Lin, T. (1968) *An Experimental Approach to Psychiatric Diagnosis*, Acta Psychiatrica Scandinavica Supplement 201, Copenhagen: Munksgaard.

Shepherd, M., Cooper, B., Brown, A.C., and Kalton, G.W. (1966) *Psychiatric Illness in General Practice*, (1981) Second edition (additional material jointly with A.W. Clare), London: Oxford University Press.

Shepherd, M., Lader, M.H., and Rodnight, R. (1968) *Clinical Psychopharmacology*, London: English Universities Press.

Shepherd, M., Oppenheim, A.N., and Mitchell, S. (1971) *Childhood Behaviour and Mental Health*, London: University Press.

Watt, D.C., Katz, K., and Shepherd, M. (1983) 'The natural history of schizophrenia: a 5-year prospective follow-up of a representative sample of
schizophrenics by means of a standardised clinical and social assessment',
Psychological Medicine 13: 663–70.

Williams, P. and Clare, A. (1979) *Psychosocial Disorders in General Practice*,
London: Academic Press.

Williams, P. Tarnopolsky, A., Hand, D., and Shepherd, M. (1986) *Minor Psychiatric
Morbidity and General Practice Consultations: the West London Survey*
(Psychological Medicine Monograph Supplement 9), Cambridge: Cambridge
University Press.

WONCA (World Organization of National Colleges, Academies and Academic
Associations of General Practitioners/Family Physicians) *International Classifica-
tion of Health Problems in Primary Care* (1979 Revision) (ICHPPC-2), Oxford:
Oxford University Press.

World Health Organization (1979) *Schizophrenia: An International Follow-up Study*,
Chichester: Wiley.

Name Index

Subject Index